Programming with Microsoft®

Visual Basic® 6.0

ENHANCED EDITION

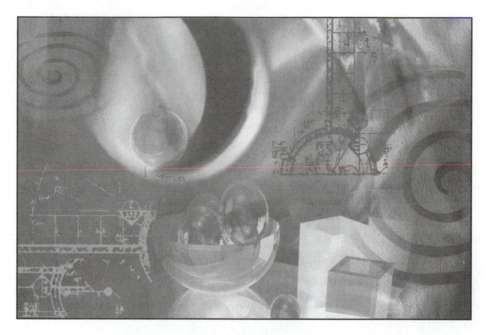

Diane Zak
College of DuPage

**COURSE
TECHNOLOGY**

THOMSON LEARNING

Australia • Canada • Mexico • Singapore • Spain • United Kingdom • United States

COURSE TECHNOLOGY
™
THOMSON LEARNING

Programming with Microsoft® Visual Basic® 6.0, Enhanced Edition
by Diane Zak

Contributing Author:
Anne Nelson

Senior Product Manager:
Jennifer Muroff

Managing Editor:
Jennifer Locke

Senior Acquisitions Editor:
Christine Guivernau

Development Editors:
Amanda Brodkin,
Mary-Terese Cozzola,
Kim Crowley

Editorial Assistant:
Janet Aras

Production Editors:
Aimee Poirier, Jean Bermingham

Cover Designer:
Betsy Young

Compositor:
GEX Publishing Services

Manufacturing Coordinator:
Alexander Schall

Disclaimer
Course Technology reserves the right to revise this publication and make changes from time to time in its content without notice.

Microsoft, Visual Basic, Visual Studio.NET, and Windows are registered trademarks of the Microsoft Corporation.

ISBN 0-619-06204-5

Preface

Welcome to the Enhanced Edition of *Programming with Microsoft Visual Basic 6.0*. This updated version provides a preview of the Microsoft Visual Studio.NET programming environment and the Microsoft Visual Basic.NET programming language. Two new tutorials, Tutorials 11 and 12, introduce you to the newest features and updates to the software by exploring Beta 1 from Microsoft. To ease your transition to Visual Basic.NET, Course Technology gives you an advance glimpse of the next generation of this powerful programming tool before the final version of the software is released. Within these new lessons, you will plan and create your own interactive Windows applications, as well as explore the power of Visual Basic.NET on the World Wide Web.

Programming with Microsoft Visual Basic 6.0, Enhanced Edition is designed for a beginning programming course. This book uses Visual Basic 6.0 for Windows 95 or 98, an object-oriented/event-driven language, to teach programming concepts. This book capitalizes on the energy and enthusiasm students naturally have for Windows-based applications and clearly teaches students how to take full advantage of Visual Basic's power. It assumes students have learned basic Windows skills and file management.

Organization and Coverage

Programming with Microsoft Visual Basic 6.0, Enhanced Edition contains an Overview and 12 tutorials that present hands-on instruction. In these tutorials, students with no previous programming experience learn how to plan and create their own interactive Windows applications. Using this book, students will be able to do more advanced tasks sooner than they would using other introductory texts; a perusal of the table of contents affirms this. By the end of the book, students will have learned how to write If...Then...Else, Select Case, Do...While, Do...Until, and For...Next statements, as well as how to create and manipulate sequential access files, random access files, and arrays. Students will also learn how to create executable files and how to include multiple forms in a project. GUI design skills are emphasized, and advanced skills such as accessing information in a database, creating and printing reports, referencing objects, and using OLE are taught. The text also introduces students to OOP terminology.

Approach

Programming with Microsoft Visual Basic 6.0, Enhanced Edition distinguishes itself from other Windows textbooks because of its unique two-pronged approach. First, it motivates students by demonstrating why they need to learn the concepts and skills. This book teaches programming concepts using a task-driven, rather than a command-driven, approach. By working through the tutorials—which are each motivated by a realistic case—students learn how to use programming applications they are likely to encounter in the workplace. This is much more effective than memorizing a list of commands out of context. Second, the content, organization, and pedagogy of this book exploit the Windows environment. The material presented in the tutorials capitalizes on Visual Basic's power to perform complex programming tasks earlier and more easily than was possible under DOS.

Features

Programming with Microsoft Visual Basic 6.0, Enhanced Edition is an exceptional textbook because it also includes the following features:

- **"Read This Before You Begin" Sections** These sections are consistent with Course Technology's unequaled commitment to helping instructors introduce technology into the classroom. Technical considerations and assumptions about hardware, software, and default settings are listed in one place to help instructors save time and eliminate unnecessary aggravation.

- **Tutorial Cases** Each tutorial begins with a programming-related problem that students could reasonably expect to encounter in business, followed by a demonstration of an application that could be used to solve the problem. Showing the students the completed application before they learn how to create it is motivational and instructionally sound. By allowing the students to see the type of application they will be able to create after completing the tutorial, the students will be more motivated to learn because they can see how the programming concepts they are about to learn can be used and, therefore, why the concepts are important.

- **Lessons** Each tutorial is divided into three lessons—A, B, and C. Lesson A introduces the programming concepts that will be used in the completed application. In Lessons B and C, the student creates the application required to solve the problem specified in the Tutorial Case. (Tutorials 11 and 12 use two lessons instead of three.)

- **Step-by-Step Methodology** The unique Course Technology methodology keeps students on track. They click or press keys always within the context of solving the problem posed in the Tutorial Case. The text constantly guides students, letting them know where they are in the process of solving the problem. The numerous illustrations include labels that direct students' attention to what they should look at on the screen.

- **Help?** paragraphs anticipate the problems students are likely to encounter and help them resolve these problems on their own. This feature facilitates independent learning and frees the instructor to focus on substantive conceptual issues rather than on common procedural errors.

- **Tips** provide additional information about a procedure—for example, an alternative method of performing the procedure. They also relate the OOP terminology learned in the Overview to applications created in Visual Basic.

- **GUI Design Tips** contain guidelines and recommendations for designing applications that follow Windows standards, as outlined in *The Windows Interface Guidelines for Software Design*, published by Microsoft Press.

- **Summaries** Following each lesson is a Summary, which recaps the programming concepts, commands, and controls covered in the lesson.

- **Questions and Exercises** Each lesson concludes with meaningful, conceptual Questions that test students' understanding of what they learned in the lesson. The Questions are followed by Exercises, which provide students with additional practice of the skills and concepts they learned in the lesson.

- **Discovery Exercises** Unlike DOS, the Windows environment allows students to learn by exploring and discovering what they can do. The Discovery Exercises are designated by the word "Discovery" in the margin. They encourage students to challenge and independently develop their own programming skills while exploring the capabilities of Visual Basic.

- **Debugging Techniques and Exercises** One of the most important programming skills a student can learn is the ability to correct problems in an existing application. The Debugging Techniques and Exercises at the end of each tutorial introduce various bug-detecting techniques and then provide an opportunity for students to apply the techniques to detect and correct errors in an existing application.

Resources for Instructors

- **Instructor's Manual**   The Instructor's Manual has been written by the author and has been quality assurance tested. It is available in printed form and through the Course Technology Faculty Online Companion on the World Wide Web. (Call your customer service representative for the URL and your password.) The Instructor's Manual contains the following items:
  - Additional coverage of Visual Basic concepts such as Sorting and Binary Search.
  - Cases that can be assigned as semester projects.
  - Answers to all of the questions and solutions to all of the exercises. Suggested solutions are also included for Discovery Exercises.
  - Teaching Suggestions, which contain an outline of the lesson and additional information to cover during the lecture.
  - Technical Notes, which include troubleshooting tips as well as information on how to customize the students' screens to closely emulate the screen shots in the book.

- **ExamView®**   This textbook is accompanied by ExamView, a powerful testing software package that allows instructors to create and administer printed, computer (LAN-based), and Internet exams. ExamView includes hundreds of questions that correspond to the topics covered in this text, enabling students to generate detailed study guides that include page references for further review. The computer-based and Internet testing components allow students to take exams at their computers, and also save the instructor time by grading each exam automatically.

- **PowerPoint Presentations**   This book comes with Microsoft PowerPoint slides for each tutorial. These are included as a teaching aid for classroom presentation, to make available to students on the network for chapter review, or to be printed for classroom distribution. Instructors can add their own slides for additional topics they introduce to the class.

- **Solutions Files**   Solution Files contain every file students are asked to create or modify in the tutorials, Exercises, and Debugging Techniques and Exercises.

- **Student Files**   Student Files, containing all of the data that students will use for the tutorials, Exercises, and Debugging Techniques and Exercises, are provided through Course Technology's Online Companion, as well as on disk. A Help file includes technical tips for lab management. See the inside front cover of this book and the "Read This Before You Begin" page before the Overview for more information on Student Files.

- **Distance Learning**   Course Technology is proud to present online courses in WebCT and Blackboard, as well as at MyCourse.com, Course Technology's own course enhancement tool, to provide the most complete and dynamic learning experience possible. When you add online content to one of your courses, you're adding a lot: self tests, links, glossaries, and, most of all, a gateway to the twenty-first century's most important information resource. We hope you will make the most of your course, both online and offline. For more information on how to bring distance learning to your course, contact your local Course Technology sales representative.

Acknowledgments

I would like to thank all of the people who helped to make this book a reality, especially Kim Crowley, M.T. Cozzola, Amanda Brodkin (Development Editors), Jennifer Muroff (Senior Product Manager), and the very, very organized Jean Bermingham and Aimee Poirier (Production Editors).

Thanks also to Kristen Duerr, Publisher; John Bosco, Quality Assurance Manager and Nicole Ashton, Quality Assurance Engineer. I am grateful to the many reviewers who provided invaluable comments on the first edition of this book, in particular: Jon E. Juarez, Dona Ana Branch Community College; Ronald Burgher, Metropolitan Community College; Mary Amundson-Miller, Greenville Technical College; and Dave Cooper, New River Community College.

Finally, I dedicate this book to my father, Henry.

Diane Zak

Brief Contents

PREFACE iii

READ THIS BEFORE YOU BEGIN xxi

overview

AN OVERVIEW OF VISUAL BASIC *VB 1*

tutorial 1

AN INTRODUCTION TO VISUAL BASIC *VB 15*

tutorial 2

DESIGNING APPLICATIONS *VB 89*

tutorial 3

USING VARIABLES AND CONSTANTS *VB 161*

tutorial 4

THE SELECTION STRUCTURE *VB 237*

tutorial 5

THE REPETITION STRUCTURE *VB 337*

tutorial 6

SEQUENTIAL ACCESS FILES, MENUS, AND REPORTS *VB 413*

tutorial 7

DIALOG BOXES AND ERROR TRAPPING *VB 517*

tutorial 8

RANDOM ACCESS FILES *VB 577*

tutorial 9

DATABASE ACCESS *VB 645*

tutorial 10

VARIABLE ARRAYS *VB 717*

tutorial 11

WHAT'S NEW WITH VISUAL BASIC.NET? *VB 801*

tutorial 12

MORE ON VISUAL BASIC.NET AND THE INTERNET *VB 843*

appendix a

CREATING A WEB PAGE WITH VISUAL BASIC *VB 883*

appendix b

VISUAL BASIC'S DRAG-AND-DROP FEATURE *VB 892*

appendix c

USING THE CLIPBOARD, DDE, AND OLE *VB 897*

appendix d

CREATING YOUR OWN ACTIVEX CONTROL *VB 920*

index *VB 925*

Contents

PREFACE iii

READ THIS BEFORE YOU BEGIN xxi

AN OVERVIEW OF VISUAL BASIC *VB 1*

A History and a Demonstration *VB 1*

  A Brief Description of Visual Basic *VB 1*

  A Brief History of Programming Languages *VB 2*

    Machine Languages *VB 2*

    Assembly Languages *VB 2*

    High-Level Languages *VB 3*

    Procedure-Oriented High-Level Languages *VB 3*

    The Introduction of Windows *VB 4*

    Object-Oriented/Event-Driven High-Level Languages *VB 5*

  OOP Terminology *VB 5*

  A Visual Basic Demonstration *VB 7*

  Using the Tutorials Effectively *VB 10*

  Questions *VB 11*

tutorial 1

AN INTRODUCTION TO VISUAL BASIC *VB 15*

case ▶ Creating a Copyright Screen *VB 15*

  Previewing the Copyright Screen *VB 16*

  Lesson A: Creating a New Project *VB 17*

  Starting Visual Basic *VB 17*

  The Visual Basic Startup Screen *VB 19*

    The Main Window *VB 19*

    The Form Window *VB 19*

    The Toolbox Window *VB 20*

    The Project Explorer Window *VB 21*

    The Properties Window *VB 23*

    Setting the Caption Property *VB 25*

    Setting an Object's Name Property *VB 26*

    Setting the BackColor Property *VB 28*

  Setting the Project's Name Property *VB 28*

  Saving a Visual Basic Project *VB 29*

  Starting and Ending a Visual Basic Project *VB 30*

  Opening a New Project *VB 31*

  Opening an Existing Project *VB 31*

  Exiting Visual Basic *VB 32*

  Summary *VB 32*

  Questions *VB 34*

  Exercises *VB 37*

Lesson B: Working with Controls *VB 39*
  Getting Help in Visual Basic *VB 39*
    Using the F1 Key *VB 42*
  Adding a Control to a Form *VB 43*
  Sizing, Moving, and Deleting a Control *VB 44*
  Adding Label Controls to the Copyright Screen *VB 44*
  Setting the Properties of a Label Control *VB 45*
  Setting the Left and Top Properties *VB 46*
  Changing the Property for More than One Control at a Time *VB 47*
  Saving Files Under a Different Name *VB 48*
  Summary *VB 50*
  Questions *VB 51*
  Exercises *VB 52*
Lesson C: Writing Code *VB 57*
  Adding an Image Control to the Form *VB 57*
  Adding a Command Button to the Form *VB 59*
  Writing Visual Basic Code *VB 60*
  Setting the BorderStyle Property *VB 64*
  Adding a Frame Control to a Form *VB 65*
  Hiding and Displaying Controls *VB 68*
  The Options Dialog Box *VB 72*
  Adding a Scroller Control to the Form *VB 73*
  Changing the Code Window Display *VB 76*
  Printing a Visual Basic Application *VB 77*
  Making an Executable (.exe) File *VB 78*
  Summary *VB 80*
  Questions *VB 81*
  Exercises *VB 83*
  Debugging *VB 87*

t u t o r i a l   2

DESIGNING APPLICATIONS *VB 89*

case ▶ Creating an Order Screen *VB 89*
  Solving the Problem Using a Procedure-Oriented Approach *VB 90*
  Solving the Problem Using an Object-Oriented/Event-Driven (OOED) Approach *VB 93*
Lesson A: Planning an OOED Application in Visual Basic *VB 96*
  Creating an OOED Application *VB 96*
  Planning an OOED Application *VB 97*
    Identifying the Application's Tasks *VB 97*
    Identifying the Objects *VB 99*
    Identifying the Events *VB 100*
    Drawing a Sketch of the User Interface *VB 102*
  Summary *VB 104*
  Questions *VB 105*
  Exercises *VB 107*
Lesson B: Building the User Interface *VB 109*
  Preparing to Create the User Interface *VB 109*
    Including Graphics in the User Interface *VB 111*

Including Different Fonts in the User Interface VB 111
Including Color in the User Interface VB 112
The BackStyle Property VB 113
The BorderStyle and Appearance Properties VB 114
Setting the Text Property VB 115
Adding a Text Box Control to the Form VB 115
Controlling the Focus with the TabIndex Property VB 118
Locking the Controls on a Form VB 119
Assigning Access Keys VB 120
Summary VB 124
Questions VB 125
Exercises VB 127
Lesson C: Coding, Testing, Debugging, and Documenting
the Application VB 129
Coding the Application VB 129
Coding the Print Order Button VB 131
Assigning a Value to a Property During Run Time VB 131
Using the PrintForm Method VB 133
Using the SetFocus Method VB 134
Internally Documenting the Program Code VB 134
Coding the Clear Screen Button VB 135
Writing Visual Basic Equations VB 138
Coding the Calculate Order Button VB 139
The Val Function VB 143
Using the Format Function VB 144
The MinButton, MaxButton, ControlBox, and BorderStyle
Properties VB 146
Testing and Debugging the Application VB 148
Assembling the Documentation VB 149
Summary VB 149
Questions VB 150
Exercises VB 151
Debugging VB 159

t u t o r i a l 3

USING VARIABLES AND CONSTANTS VB 161

case ▶ Revising the Skate-Away Sales Application VB 161
Previewing the Completed Application VB 162
Lesson A: Creating Variables and Constants VB 164
Using Variables to Store Information VB 164
Data Types VB 164
Naming Variables VB 167
Declaring a Variable VB 168
Storing Data in a Variable VB 169
The Scope of a Variable VB 170
The Option Explicit Statement VB 171
Creating a Local Variable VB 173
Creating a Form-Level Variable VB 176

Creating a Global Variable *VB 179*
   Adding a Code Module to a Project *VB 180*
Removing and Adding a File *VB 182*
Symbolic Constants *VB 183*
Summary *VB 186*
Questions *VB 186*
Exercises *VB 188*
Lesson B: Modifying the Skate-Away Sales Application *VB 190*
Storing Information Using Local and Form-Level Variables *VB 190*
Modifying the Calculate Order Button's Code *VB 192*
Concatenating Strings *VB 198*
The InputBox Function *VB 201*
The Newline Character *VB 204*
The Object Browser *VB 204*
Making a Command Button the Default Button *VB 207*
Summary *VB 208*
Questions *VB 208*
Exercises *VB 210*
Lesson C: Improving the Appearance of the Skate-Away Sales
Application *VB 214*
Using a Dialog Box *VB 214*
Adding an Existing Form to the Application *VB 215*
   Specifying the Startup Form *VB 215*
Loading and Displaying a Form *VB 216*
Adding a Code Module to a Project *VB 218*
   Making a Form Resemble a Standard Windows Dialog Box *VB 219*
Adding the Copyright Form to the Project *VB 221*
   Using a Timer Control *VB 223*
   Removing a Coded Control from the Form *VB 223*
   Changing the Appearance of the Mouse Pointer *VB 224*
Summary *VB 225*
Questions *VB 226*
Exercises *VB 228*
Debugging *VB 234*

t u t o r i a l   4

THE SELECTION STRUCTURE *VB 237*

case ▶ Creating a Math Application *VB 237*

Previewing the Completed Application *VB 238*
Lesson A: The If... Then... Else and Select Case Statements *VB 241*
The Selection Structure *VB 241*
Writing Pseudocode for the Selection Structure *VB 242*
Using a Flowchart *VB 243*
Coding the Selection Structure in Visual Basic *VB 245*
   Relational Operators *VB 245*
Example 1 *VB 247*
Example 2 *VB 248*
Logical Operators *VB 250*
   Examples of the And and the Or Operators *VB 252*

Example 3 *VB 253*

Example 4 *VB 255*

The UCase Function *VB 256*

Nested Selection Structures *VB 257*

Example 5 *VB 259*

The Case Form of the Selection Structure *VB 261*

The Select Case Statement *VB 262*

Example 1 *VB 265*

Using To and Is in an Expressionlist *VB 266*

    Example 2 *VB 266*

    Example 3 *VB 269*

Summary *VB 270*

Questions *VB 271*

Exercises *VB 275*

Lesson B: More Visual Basic Controls *VB 280*

  The Math Application *VB 280*

  Using Visual Basic's Icons *VB 282*

  Adding an Option Button Control to the Form *VB 282*

    Grouping Option Button Controls *VB 283*

  Adding a Check Box Control to the Form *VB 287*

  Drawing a Control in a Frame *VB 289*

    Locking the Controls and Setting the TabIndex Property *VB 290*

  Coding the Level 1 and Level 2 Option Buttons *VB 292*

  Creating a User-Defined Sub Procedure *VB 294*

  The Call Statement *VB 296*

  Coding the Addition and Subtraction Option Buttons *VB 298*

  Creating a Default Option Button *VB 299*

    Modifying the RandomNumbers User-Defined Sub Procedure *VB 300*

  Summary *VB 302*

  Questions *VB 303*

  Exercises *VB 305*

Lesson C: Completing the Math Application *VB 307*

  Static Variables *VB 307*

  Coding the Verify Answer Button *VB 308*

    The LoadPicture Function *VB 312*

    The MsgBox Function *VB 313*

    The SelStart and SelLength Properties *VB 319*

    The Len Function *VB 320*

  The GotFocus Event *VB 321*

  Coding the Display Summary Information Check Box *VB 321*

  Summary *VB 323*

  Questions *VB 324*

  Exercises *VB 325*

  Debugging *VB 334*

t u t o r i a l   5

THE REPETITION STRUCTURE *VB 337*

case ▶ Creating a Grade Calculation Application *VB 337*

Previewing the Completed Application *VB 338*

Lesson A: The Repetition Structure (Looping) *VB 339*

The Repetition Structure *VB 339*

The For Next (Automatic Counter) Loop *VB 340*

Example 1 *VB 342*

Example 2 *VB 343*

The Do While and the Do Until Loops *VB 344*

Flowchart and Pseudocode for the Do While and the Do Until Loops *VB 346*

Do While Example *VB 348*

Do Until Example *VB 349*

Another Example of the Do While Loop *VB 352*

Counters and Accumulators *VB 354*

Summary *VB 362*

Questions *VB 363*

Exercises *VB 366*

Lesson B: Using Control Arrays *VB 371*

The Grade Application *VB 371*

Creating a Control Array While Adding Controls to the Form *VB 374*

Making Existing Controls into a Control Array *VB 377*

The Enabled Property *VB 379*

Viewing the Code Window for a Control Array *VB 380*

Coding the Check Box Array *VB 382*

Coding a Control's Array's GotFocus Event *VB 384*

Summary *VB 385*

Questions *VB 386*

Exercises *VB 388*

Lesson C: Completing the Grade Application *VB 391*

Coding the Display Grade Command Button *VB 391*

The Change Event *VB 395*

Centering the Contents of a Label Control *VB 399*

Using the MsgBox Function to Communicate with the User *VB 399*

The Unload Event *VB 401*

Summary *VB 404*

Questions *VB 404*

Exercises *VB 405*

Debugging *VB 410*

t u t o r i a l   6

SEQUENTIAL ACCESS FILES, MENUS, AND REPORTS
VB 413

case ▶ The PAO Application *VB 413*

Previewing the Completed Applications *VB 414*

Lesson A: Sequential Access Data Files and Reports *VB 417*

Creating the PAO Application *VB 417*

Creating a List Box *VB 418*

The AddItem Method *VB 420*

The Sorted Property *VB 422*
The ListIndex Property *VB 422*
Data Files *VB 423*
Sequential Access Data Files *VB 425*
Coding the Enter Information Command Button *VB 426*
Opening a Data File *VB 426*
Writing to a Sequential Access File *VB 429*
Closing a Sequential Access File *VB 430*
Coding the Display Totals Button *VB 431*
The EOF Function *VB 434*
Reading a Record from a Sequential Access File *VB 435*
Updating the Appropriate Label Control *VB 435*
The Print Method *VB 438*
Changing the Type and Size of the Printer Font *VB 441*
Justifying and Aligning the Numbers in a Column *VB 445*
Completing the PAO Application *VB 449*
Modifying the Print Report Button's Click Event Procedure *VB 450*
Summary *VB 452*
Questions *VB 453*
Exercises *VB 457*
Lesson B: Menus *VB 466*
Creating the Text Editor *VB 466*
The MultiLine Property and the ScrollBars Property *VB 467*
Sizing a Control Along With the Form *VB 467*
Adding a Menu Control to the Form *VB 468*
Creating a Separator Bar *VB 473*
Creating the Edit Menu *VB 474*
Coding Menu Items *VB 476*
The Clipboard Object *VB 477*
The SetText, GetText( ), and Clear Methods *VB 477*
The SelText Property *VB 478*
Coding the Edit Menu *VB 478*
Coding the Edit Menu's Copy Command *VB 480*
Coding the Edit Menu's Cut Command *VB 481*
Coding the Edit Menu's Paste Command *VB 481*
Summary *VB 482*
Questions *VB 484*
Exercises *VB 487*
Lesson C: String Manipulation *VB 491*
Visual Basic's String Manipulation Functions *VB 491*
The Left and Right Functions *VB 491*
The Mid Function *VB 494*
The Instr Function *VB 496*
Coding the Edit Menu's Find Command *VB 497*
Coding the Edit Menu's Find Next Command *VB 501*
Summary *VB 505*
Questions *VB 505*
Exercises *VB 507*
Debugging *VB 514*

t u t o r i a l 7

DIALOG BOXES AND ERROR TRAPPING *VB 517*

case ▶ Completing the Text Editor Application *VB 517*

Previewing the Completed Application *VB 518*

Lesson A: Dialog Boxes *VB 520*

The Common Dialog Control *VB 520*

Displaying an Open Dialog Box *VB 522*

The Filter Property *VB 524*

The Filename Property *VB 526*

Displaying a Save As Dialog Box *VB 526*

Displaying a Print Dialog Box *VB 528*

The Flags Property *VB 529*

Displaying a Font Dialog Box *VB 531*

Displaying a Color Dialog Box *VB 533*

Summary *VB 535*

Questions *VB 536*

Exercises *VB 537*

Lesson B: Coding the Text Editor's File Menu *VB 539*

Opening the Text Editor Application *VB 539*

Coding the Text Editor Application *VB 540*

Coding the File Menu's Save As Command *VB 541*

The Print # Statement *VB 543*

Setting the CancelError Property *VB 545*

The On Error Statement and the Error-Handling Routine *VB 546*

Coding the File Menu's New Command *VB 548*

Summary *VB 552*

Questions *VB 553*

Exercises *VB 555*

Lesson C: Completing the Text Editor Application *VB 557*

Coding the File Menu's Save Command *VB 557*

Coding the File Menu's Print Command *VB 559*

Coding the File Menu's Open Command *VB 560*

The Input and LOF Functions *VB 562*

Coding the Form's Unload Event *VB 563*

Summary *VB 567*

Questions *VB 567*

Exercises *VB 568*

Debugging *VB 572*

t u t o r i a l 8

RANDOM ACCESS FILES *VB 577*

case ▶ The Cole's Playhouse Application *VB 577*

Previewing the Application *VB 578*

Lesson A: Random Access Files *VB 580*

Random Access Files Versus Sequential Access Files *VB 580*

Sequential Access Versus Random Access File Storage *VB 581*

The Type Statement *VB 584*

Coding the Code Module *VB 586*

Creating and Opening a Random Access File *VB 587*

Coding the Form's Load Event Procedure VB 587
Closing a Random Access File VB 588
Writing Records to a Random Access File VB 588
Coding the Enter Item Button VB 589
Initializing a Random Access File VB 592
Reading Records from a Random Access File VB 594
Coding the Display Item Button VB 594
Summary VB 596
Questions VB 598
Exercises VB 601
Lesson B: The Cole's Playhouse Application VB 604
The Cole's Playhouse Application VB 604
Coding the Cole's Playhouse Application VB 608
Coding the File Menu's New Command VB 609
Passing Information to a Sub Procedure VB 610
Using Visual Basic's Color Constants VB 611
Creating a User-Defined Procedure that Receives Data VB 612
Coding the File Menu's Open Command VB 616
Summary VB 620
Questions VB 621
Exercises VB 623
Lesson C: Completing the Cole's Playhouse Application VB 627
Coding the lblSeat Control Array VB 627
Referencing a Control in Another Form VB 628
Coding the Enter Ticket Button VB 630
The Trim Function VB 633
Coding the Cancel Ticket Button VB 634
Coding the Return to Main Button VB 635
Summary VB 636
Questions VB 637
Exercises VB 638
Debugging VB 642

tutorial 9

DATABASE ACCESS VB 645

case ▶ Modifying the Cole's Playhouse Application VB 645
Previewing the Modified Cole's Playhouse Application VB 646
Lesson A: Using Visual Data Manager VB 648
Database Concepts and Terminology VB 648
Designing the Cole's Playhouse Database VB 649
Using Visual Data Manager to Create the Cole Database VB 652
Creating an Index VB 658
Including Data Validation Rules in a Table VB 659
Opening an Existing Database VB 661
Summary VB 666
Questions VB 666
Exercises VB 668
Lesson B: Using the ADO Data Control VB 672
Microsoft's UDA Approach to Accessing Data VB 672
The Cole's Playhouse Application VB 672

Using the ADO Data Control *VB 673*
Binding Controls to an ADO Data Control *VB 678*
Using the SQL Select Command *VB 679*
Summary *VB 683*
Questions *VB 683*
Exercises *VB 685*
Lesson C: Writing Code to Add, Delete, and Update Records *VB 689*
The Cole's Playhouse Application *VB 689*
The Recordset and Field Objects *VB 689*
The ADO Data Control's Refresh Method *VB 691*
Completing the Cole's Playhouse Application *VB 691*
Coding the lblSeat Array's Click Event *VB 694*
Coding the Return to Main Button *VB 697*
Coding the Enter Ticket Button *VB 698*
Coding the Cancel Ticket Button *VB 700*
Summary *VB 702*
Questions *VB 703*
Exercises *VB 705*
Debugging *VB 713*

tutorial 10

VARIABLE ARRAYS *VB 717*

case ▶ Creating A Payroll Application *VB 717*
Previewing the Completed Application *VB 718*
Lesson A: Storing Data in a Variable Array *VB 720*
Variable Arrays *VB 720*
Advantages of Variable Arrays *VB 721*
Creating a One-dimensional Variable Array *VB 722*
Storing Data in a One-dimensional Variable Array *VB 723*
The President Application *VB 724*
Coding the President Application *VB 724*
The Form's Load Event Procedure *VB 725*
The Display Name Button *VB 725*
The Display Number Button *VB 728*
The Test Score Application *VB 730*
The Average Score Button *VB 732*
The Highest Score Button *VB 733*
The Update Scores Button *VB 735*
The Classroom Application *VB 738*
Summary *VB 744*
Questions *VB 744*
Exercises *VB 750*
Lesson B: The DataGrid Control and Object Variables *VB 756*
The Colfax Industries Payroll Application *VB 756*
The DataGrid Control *VB 758*
Improving the Appearance of the DataGrid Control's Data *VB 761*
Coding the DataGrid Control *VB 768*
Creating an Object Variable *VB 770*
Rounding Numbers *VB 772*

Summary *VB 773*
Questions *VB 773*
Exercises *VB 776*
Lesson C: Completing the Colfax Payroll Application *VB 783*
Storing the Federal Withholding Tax Tables in Two Two-dimensional
Arrays *VB 783*
Creating a Function Procedure to Calculate the FWT *VB 787*
Invoking a Function Procedure *VB 791*
Summary *VB 792*
Questions *VB 793*
Exercises *VB 793*
Debugging *VB 794*

t u t o r i a l 11
WHAT'S NEW WITH VISUAL BASIC.NET?   *VB 801*

case ▶ Creating a Visual Basic.NET Windows Forms Calendar Screen Application *VB 801*
Previewing the Calendar Screen *VB 802*
Lesson A: Working with Visual Studio.NET *VB 804*
The Visual Studio.NET Environment VB 804
Identify the Components of Visual Studio.NET and the new IDE *VB 806*
Modify Your Profile in the Visual Studio.NET IDE VB 806
Customizing the New Visual Studio.NET IDE *VB 808*
Using Solution Explorer *VB 810*
Working with Dynamic Help *VB 811*
Using the Task List *VB 812*
The Command Window *VB 813*
Summary *VB 814*
Questions *VB 815*
Exercises *VB 816*
Lesson B: Creating a Windows Forms Application Using Visual
Basic.NET *VB 819*
Starting Visual Basic.NET *VB 819*
Using Windows Forms *VB 821*
Viewing Code in Windows Forms *VB 821*
Differences Between Visual Basic.NET Windows Forms and Visual Basic
6.0 Forms *VB 822*
Setting Appearance Properties *VB 822*
Adding a Label Control to the Windows Forms Calendar Application
VB 823
Adding Picture, Text, and Frame Controls *VB 824*
Adding ActiveX Calendar, Date, and Time Controls *VB 826*
Adding a Button Control and Code *VB 827*
Visual Basic 6.0 and Visual Basic.NET: Differences in Coding *VB 828*
Completing the Code for the Button *VB 829*
Variable Declarations in Visual Basic.NET *VB 829*
Passing Parameters in Visual Basic.NET *VB 830*
Adding a Link Label to the Windows Forms Calendar Application *VB 831*
Adding a Menu and Menu Items *VB 832*
Printing Windows Forms Application Code *VB 836*

Saving and Exiting a Windows Forms Application *VB 836*
Summary *VB 837*
Questions *VB 838*
Exercises *VB 839*

tutorial 12

MORE ON VISUAL BASIC.NET AND THE INTERNET *VB 843*

case ▶ Creating a Visual Basic.NET Web Forms Application *VB 843*
Previewing the Web Forms Application *VB 844*
Lesson A: The New Web Forms Environment *VB 846*
Creating a New Web Forms Page *VB 846*
Adding HTML Text to the Web Forms Page *VB 848*
Setting HTML Text Attributes *VB 850*
Creating Web Forms HTML Server Controls *VB 851*
Creating Web Forms Server Controls *VB 852*
Web Forms Controls *VB 853*
Adding Web Forms Server Controls to Your Project *VB 855*
Creating an Event Handler *VB 857*
Running the Web Forms Application *VB 857*
Saving and Exiting the Web Forms Application *VB 858*
Summary *VB 859*
Questions *VB 860*
Exercises *VB 861*
Lesson B: Completing Your Web Forms Application Project *VB 863*
The Pets Online Web Application Data Project *VB 863*
Learning More About Web Application Projects *VB 863*
Technical Requirements for Your Web Applications Project *VB 863*
The Visual Studio.NET Cache *VB 864*
Files Created with Web Applications *VB 864*
Creating the PetProj Web Application Project *VB 864*
Creating a Data-Access Component *VB 866*
Binding the DataGrid *VB 869*
Adding a Details Panel to Your Web Forms Application *VB 874*
Deploying the Web Forms Application Project *VB 877*
Summary *VB 879*
Questions *VB 880*
Exercises *VB 881*

appendix a

CREATING A WEB PAGE WITH VISUAL BASIC *VB 883*

appendix b

VISUAL BASIC'S DRAG-AND-DROP FEATURE *VB 892*

appendix c

USING THE CLIPBOARD, DDE, AND OLE *VB 897*

appendix d

CREATING YOUR OWN ACTIVEX CONTROL *VB 920*

index *VB 925*

Read This Before You Begin, Part 1

To the Student

Student Disks

To complete the tutorials, Exercises, and Debugging Techniques and Exercises in this book, you need Student Disks. Your instructor will either provide you with Student Disks or ask you to make your own.

If you are told to make your own Student Disks, you will need 6 blank, formatted high-density disks. You will need to copy a set of folders from a file server or standalone computer onto your disks. Your instructor will tell you which computer, drive letter, and folders contain the files you need. The following table shows you which folders go on each of your disks, so that you will have enough disk space to complete all the tutorials, Exercises, and Debugging Techniques and Exercises:

Student Disk	Write this on the disk label	Put these folders on the disk
1	Overview, Tutorials 1–3	*Overview* *Tut01* *Tut02* *Tut03*
2	Tutorials 4–6	*Tut04* *Tut05* *Tut06*
3	Tutorials 7–8	*Tut07* *Tut08*
4	Tutorial 9	*Tut09*
5	Tutorial 10	*Tut10*
6	Appendices A, B, C, & D	*AppendA* *AppendB* *AppendC* *AppendD*

When you begin each tutorial, be sure you are using the correct Student Disk. For more information on Student Disk files ask your instructor or technical support person for assistance.

Using Your Own Computer

If you are going to work through this book using your own computer, you will need:
- **Computer System** Microsoft Visual Basic 6.0 Professional Edition, Working Model, or Enterprise Edition for Windows 95 must be installed on your computer. This book assumes a complete installation of Microsoft Visual Basic 6.0, excluding Microsoft Visual SourceSafe 6.0, and including Graphics. It also assumes that you have access to the Visual Basic documentation contained in the MSDN Library.

    Microsoft Visual Basic 6.0 for Windows 95, Working Model is provided with each copy of this book. The following system requirements apply.
  - Personal computer with a 486 or higher processor
  - Microsoft Windows 95 or later, or Windows NT version 4.0 or later
  - 16 MB of RAM for Windows 95 or later
  - 24 MB of RAM for Windows NT
  - VGA or higher-resolution monitor (Super VGA recommended)
  - Microsoft Mouse or compatible pointing device

- Hard Disk Requirements:
  - 52 MB for typical installation
  - 65 MB for maximum installation
- CD-ROM drive

The Working Model has all the functionality of the commercial version of Visual Basic, excluding the ability to make executable files and the ability to create Web pages and ActiveX controls (Appendices A and D). The Working Model also does not include the MSDN Library. Be sure to read the Help file on the CD for information on which sections of the book cannot be completed using the Working Model.

- **Student Disks** Ask your instructor or lab manager for details on how to get Student Disks. You will not be able to complete the tutorials or exercises in this book using your own computer until you have Student Disks. The student files may also be obtained electronically through the Internet.

Visit Our World Wide Web Site

Additional materials designed especially for you are available on the World Wide Web. Go to **www.course.com.**

Installing Visual Basic 6.0 and setting up your environment:

To install Visual Basic 6.0 and set up your environment so that your screens match the figures shown in the book, do the following:

1 When installing Visual Basic 6.0, use the Custom button in the Microsoft Visual Basic 6.0 Setup dialog box to include the Graphics files in the installation. When installing the MSDN Library, install the VB Documentation. If you want to use the MSDN Library without having to put the MSDN CD in the CD-ROM drive, then also install the Full Text Search index.

2 Click Tools on the Visual Basic menu bar, and then click Options. When the Options dialog box appears, click the Editor tab, and then click the Default to Full Module View check box to deselect it. Click the Advanced tab in the Options dialog box, then click the SDI Development Environment check box to select it, and then click the OK button.

3 Size the Visual Basic Toolbox so that the tools appear in two columns, rather than three columns.

4 Double-click the My Computer icon on the Windows 95 desktop.

Click View on the menu bar, and then click Options. Click the View tab, then click the Hide MS-DOS file extensions for file types that are registered check box to deselect it, and then click the OK button.

To the Instructor

To complete the tutorials in this book, your students must use a set of student files. These files are included in the Instructor's Resource Kit. They may also be obtained electronically through the Internet. Follow the instructions in the Help file to copy the student files to your server or standalone computer. You can view the Help file using a text editor such as WordPad or Notepad.

Once the files are copied, you can make Student Disks for the students yourself, or tell students where to find the files so they can make their own Student Disks. Make sure the files get copied correctly onto the Student Disks by following the instructions in the Student Disks section on the previous page, which will ensure that students have enough disk space to complete all the tutorials, Exercises, and Debugging Techniques and Exercises.

Course Technology Student Files

You are granted a license to copy the Student Files to any computer or computer network used by students who have purchased this book.

Read This Before You Begin, Part 2

Special Instructions For Working with Visual Basic.NET in Tutorials 11 and 12

To the Student

Data Files

Visual Basic.NET has more technical requirements than its predecessor, Visual Basic 6.0, therefore, you will need to make some changes to your file structure when working with Tutorials 11 and 12. To complete the tutorials and the exercises at the end of the tutorials, you need data files. In Tutorials 1 through 10, you used the data files that were provided on the Student Disks. In Tutorials 11 and 12, you will access files from and save files to folders stored on your computer's hard drive or a workstation shared drive. For Tutorial 11, you will use the Tut11 folder, and for Tutorial 12, you will use the Tut12 folder.

Using Your Own Computer

If you are going to complete these tutorials using your own computer, you will need:

- **Computer System** The prerelease version of Microsoft Visual Studio.NET must be installed on your computer. The prerelease Beta 1 version of Visual Studio.NET is available to the public. You must also be running Microsoft Internet Information Server (IIS) version 4.0 or higher and Microsoft Access 2000. See the "Setting Up Your Computer" section.
- Personal computer with a 486 or higher processor
- Microsoft Windows 98, 2000, or NT
- 128 MB of RAM
- 256-color monitor
- Hard drive: 3 GB for installation
- CD-ROM drive
- Mouse or other pointing device
- **Data files** Ask your instructor or lab manager for details on how to get the data files. You may need to create Tut11 and Tut12 folders on your computer and copy the data files to these folders. You will not be able to complete the tutorials or exercises without the data files. The files also may be obtained electronically through the Internet. Go to **www.course.com**, click Student Downloads, and search for the title of this book.

Setting Up Your Computer

Tutorials 11 and 12 require that your computer be set up as a server, which means you must have IIS running.

If you are running Windows 98:

1   Locate the Windows\System\Inetsrv folder on your computer's hard drive.
2   Open the Inetsrv folder and double-click the pws.exe file to start Internet Information Server.

If you are running Windows NT or Windows 2000:

1   Locate the Winnt\Systems32\Inetsrv folder on your computer's hard drive.

2   Open the Inetsrv folder and double-click the pws.exe file to start IIS. If the pws.exe file is not on your workstation, then IIS might not be installed on your computer.

3   To install IIS from the operating system disk that came with your computer, run the operating system disk setup.

4   Choose Install Add-on Components from the Start Page menu to activate the Windows Components Wizard.

5   To add the IIS component, check the corresponding check box.

6   Click the Details button and verify that the subcomponents of IIS are also checked. These files are required by IIS, however, they should only be installed at the time you install IIS.

7   Click OK and Next. The Windows Components Wizard will now configure your hardware and install the software. This may take a few minutes.

8   When the installation is successful and complete, click Finish to exit the wizard.

9   Restart your computer. If IIS does not begin running at startup or is not displayed on the right side of the taskbar on your Windows desktop, review the steps above to start IIS.

After you have started IIS, right-click the IIS icon on the taskbar. A menu is displayed that allows you to start and shut down the IIS service and change configurations from the Properties window. Verify that the service is started. You must also check the configuration settings. To do so, select Properties from the shortcut menu and open the IIS Main page. On the Main page, verify that Web publishing is on. To turn on Web publishing, click the Start button. Your home page should be displayed as a URL address when Web publishing is on. Your home directory will also be displayed and may be changed as necessary on the Main properties page.

To install Visual Studio.NET, simply insert the Beta 1 compact disk into your disk drive and follow the installation instructions. Accept the default setting suggestions.

To the Instructor

To complete Tutorials 11 and 12, your students must use a set of data files. These files are included in the Instructor's Resource Kit or may be obtained through the Internet by going to **www.course.com**. Follow the instructions in the Help file to copy the data files to your server or standalone computer. You can view the Help file using a text editor such as WordPad or Notepad.

Once the files are copied, you can distribute them to students on floppy disks or through a shared drive. Make sure that students set up the Tut11 and Tut12 folders and that these folders contain the appropriate files.

Course Technology Data Files

You are granted a license to copy the data files to any computer or computer network used by students who have purchased this book.

This overview contains basic definitions and background information, including:

- A brief description of Visual Basic
- A brief history of programming languages
- An introduction to the terminology used in object-oriented programming languages
- A Visual Basic demonstration
- Information on using the tutorials effectively

An Overview of Visual Basic:

A History and a Demonstration

A Brief Description of Visual Basic

Although computers appear to be amazingly intelligent machines, they cannot yet think on their own. Computers still rely on human beings to give them directions. These directions are called **programs**, and the people who write the programs are called **programmers**.

Just as human beings communicate with each other through the use of languages such as English, Spanish, Hindi, or Chinese, programmers use a variety of special languages, called **programming languages**, to communicate with the computer. Some popular programming languages are COBOL (Common Business Oriented Language), Pascal, C, BASIC (Beginner's All-Purpose Symbolic Instruction Code), and Visual Basic. As its name implies, Visual Basic is more visually oriented than most other programming languages. In fact, you might think of Visual Basic as a sort of sign language. Visual Basic represents a new way to write computer programs.

A Brief History of Programming Languages

It is difficult to appreciate the Visual Basic language, and to understand its impact on the future of programming, without looking back at the programming languages that preceded it. In the next sections, you will take a quick look at the forerunners to Visual Basic.

Machine Languages

Within a computer, all data is represented by microscopic electronic switches that can be either off or on. The off switch is designated by a 0, and the on switch is designated by a 1. Because computers can understand only these on and off switches, the first programmers had to write the program instructions using nothing but combinations of 0s and 1s. Instructions written in 0s and 1s are called **machine language** or **machine code**. The machine languages (each type of machine has its own language) represent the only way to communicate directly with the computer. Figure 1 shows a program written in a machine language.

```
0100
001101   100000   001101   110001
00101    10001    10000
01110
111001
111001   001   11000   001
11000
0011100
100010   00110
```

Figure 1: Machine language

As you can imagine, programming in machine language is very tedious and error-prone; it also requires highly trained programmers.

Assembly Languages

Slightly more advanced programming languages are called **assembly languages**. Figure 2 shows a program written in an assembly language.

```
main proc pay
     mov ax, dseg
     mov ax, 0b00h
     add ax, dx
     mov al, bl
     mul bl, ax
     mov bl, 04h
```

Figure 2: Assembly language

The assembly languages simplify the programmer's job by allowing the programmer to use mnemonics in place of the 0s and 1s in the program. **Mnemonics** are memory aids—in this case, alphabetic abbreviations for instructions. For example, most assembly languages use the mnemonic ADD to represent an add operation and the mnemonic MUL to represent a multiply operation. Programs written in an assembly language require an **assembler,** which is also a program, to convert the assembly instructions into machine code—the 0s and 1s the computer can understand. Although it is much easier to write programs in assembly language than in machine language, programming in assembly language still is tedious and requires highly trained programmers.

High-Level Languages

High-level languages, which allow the programmer to use instructions that more closely resemble the English language, represent the next advance in programming languages. High-level languages require either an interpreter or a compiler to convert the English-like instructions into the 0s and 1s the computer can understand. Like assemblers, both interpreters and compilers are separate programs. An **interpreter** translates the high-level instructions into machine code, line by line, as the program is running; a **compiler** translates the entire program into machine code before running the program. Like their predecessors, most high-level languages are procedure-oriented.

Procedure-Oriented High-Level Languages

In **procedure-oriented high-level languages,** the emphasis of a program is on *how* to accomplish a task. The programmer must instruct the computer every step of the way, from the start of the task to its completion. The programmer determines and controls the order in which the computer should process the instructions. COBOL, BASIC, Pascal, and C are popular procedure-oriented languages.

Figure 3 shows a program written in BASIC. Notice how closely the instructions resemble the English language. Even if you do not know the BASIC language, it is easy to see that the program shown in Figure 3 tells the computer, step by step, *how* to compute and print an employee's net pay.

```
input "Enter Name";names$
input "Enter Hours";hours
input "Enter Rate";rate
gross = hours * rate
fwt = .2 * gross
socsec = .07 * gross
state = .06 * gross
net = gross - fwt - socsec - state
print names$, net
end
```

Figure 3: BASIC—a procedure-oriented high-level language

In all procedure-oriented programs, the order of the instructions is extremely important. For example, in the program shown in Figure 3, you could not put the instruction to print the net pay before the instruction to calculate the net pay and expect the computer to print the correct results. When writing programs in a procedure-oriented language, the programmer must determine not only the proper instructions to give the computer, but the correct sequence of those instructions as well.

Procedure-oriented high-level languages are a vast improvement over machine languages and assembly languages. Many of the high-level languages do not require a great amount of technical expertise; you do not need to be a professional programmer to write a program using these languages.

The Introduction of Windows

As you know, Windows software provides an easy-to-use **graphical user interface**, referred to as a **GUI**, with which a user can interact. This GUI is common to all applications written for the Windows environment. It is this standard interface that makes Windows applications so popular: once you learn one Windows application, it is very easy to learn another.

Although the standard interface found in all Windows applications makes the user's life much easier, it complicates the programmer's life a great deal. In the beginning, writing programs for the Windows environment was extremely tedious. Programmers found themselves spending countless hours writing instructions to create the buttons, scroll bars, dialog boxes, and menus needed in all Windows applications. Because the programmer has no control over which button the user will click in a Windows application, or which scroll bar the user will employ, the first Windows programmers had to write instructions that could handle any combination of actions the user might take. Tasks that used to take a few lines of program code now needed pages. Because programming Windows applications required a great amount of expertise, it appeared that the beginning of the Windows environment meant the end of the do-it-yourself, nonprofessional programmer. But then a new category of high-level languages emerged—the object-oriented/event-driven programming languages.

Object-Oriented/Event-Driven High-Level Languages

The object-oriented/event-driven high-level languages simplified the task of programming applications for Windows. In **object-oriented/event-driven languages**, the emphasis of a program is on the *objects* included in the user interface (such as scroll bars and buttons) and the *events* (such as scrolling and clicking) that occur when those objects are used.

Visual Basic is an object-oriented/event-driven programming language that is easy enough for a nonprogrammer to use, yet sophisticated enough to be used by professional programmers. (C++ and Smalltalk are also object-oriented/event-driven programming languages.) With Visual Basic it takes just a few clicks of the mouse to include standard Windows objects such as buttons, list boxes, scroll bars, and icons in your Windows application. Once the objects are created, the programmer then concentrates on writing the specific instructions telling each object how to respond when clicked, double-clicked, scrolled, and so on. For example, Figure 4 shows the Visual Basic instructions that direct an object to end the application when the user clicks the object. (In this case the object is an Exit button.)

```
Private Sub cmdExit_Click ()
    End
End Sub
```

Figure 4: Visual Basic—an object-oriented/event-driven language

Before running a sample object-oriented/event-driven application, you will learn about the terminology used by object-oriented programmers.

OOP Terminology

Although you may have either heard or read that object-oriented languages are difficult to learn, don't be intimidated. Admittedly, creating object-oriented programs does take practice, but most of the concepts upon which object-oriented programming is based are concepts with which you are already familiar. Much of the fear of object-oriented programming stems from the terminology used when discussing it. Many of the terms are unfamiliar because they are not typically used in everyday conversations. This section will help to familiarize you with the terms used in discussions about object-oriented programming. Don't be concerned if you don't understand everything right away; you will see further explanations and examples of these terms throughout this book.

When discussing object-oriented programs, you will hear programmers use the terms OOP (pronounced like *loop*) and OOD (pronounced like *mood*). **OOP** is an acronym for object-oriented programming and simply means that you are using an object-oriented language to create a program that contains one or more objects. OOD, on the other hand, is an acronym for object-oriented design. Like top-down design, which is used to plan procedure-oriented programs, **OOD** is also a design methodology, but it is used to plan object-oriented programs. Unlike top-down design, which breaks up a problem into one or more tasks, OOD divides a problem into one or more objects.

An **object** is anything that can be seen or touched. You deal with objects every day. This book, for example, is an object, and so is your car. The advantage of using an object-oriented language is that it allows the programmer to use familiar objects, such as a book and a car, to solve problems. You can use a book, for example, to learn C++; you can use a car to get to school.

Every object has attributes and behaviors. **Attributes**, also called **data** or **properties**, are characteristics that describe the object. For example, when you tell someone that your car is a red Pontiac Firebird, you are describing the car (an object) in terms of some of its attributes—in this case, its color, manufacturer, and model type. Your car also has many other attributes, such as a steering wheel, tires, an engine, and so on. An object's **behaviors**, on the other hand, are the operations (actions) that the object can either perform or have performed on it. Your car, for example, can accelerate and brake; it can also be steered and have its oil changed.

You will also hear the term *class* in OOP discussions. A **class** is simply a pattern or blueprint for creating an object. A class contains all of the attributes and behaviors that describe the object. The object that you create from a class is referred to as an **instance** of the class. Notice that a class is not an object; an instance of a class, however, *is* an object. The blueprint that the manufacturer used to create your car is a class; your car, as well as any other car that is made from that blueprint, is an instance of the class—an object. Here is another analogy that may help to differentiate between a class and an instance of a class: think of a class as being similar to a cookie-cutter, and an instance of a class (an object) as being similar to a cookie that is made using the cookie-cutter.

Human beings typically don't use the word "encapsulation" in everyday conversations. *Encapsulation* is a derivative of the word *encapsulate*, which means "to enclose in a capsule." **Encapsulation** in the context of OOP refers to the combining of an object's attributes and behaviors into one package—a class. The manufacturer of your car, for example, encapsulated the car's attributes (color, manufacturer, model type, steering wheel, tires, engine, and so on) and behaviors (accelerate, brake, steer, tune-up, and so on) into one package—a blueprint of your car.

Another OOP term that is not used much in everyday conversations is *abstraction*. **Abstraction** refers to hiding the internal details of an object from the user, which helps prevent the user from making inadvertent changes to the object. Car manufacturers, for example, hide much of a car's internal details—engine, spark plugs, and so on—under the hood. Also hidden from the driver is how the transmission takes rotary motion from the engine and converts it to forward motion of the wheels. Attributes and behaviors that are not **hidden** are said to be **exposed** to the user. For example, a car's steering wheel, gas pedal, and brake pedal are exposed to the driver. The idea behind abstraction is to expose to the user only those attributes and behaviors that are necessary to use the object, and to hide everything else.

Another OOP term, **inheritance**, refers to the fact that you can create one class from another class. The new class, called the **derived class**, inherits the attributes and behaviors of the original class, called the **base class**. For example, your car's manufacturer might create a blueprint of a 1999 Firebird from a blueprint of a 1998 Firebird. The 1999 blueprint (the derived class) would inherit all of the attributes and behaviors of the 1998 blueprint (the base class), but it could be modified to fit the new design for the 1999 Firebird. For example, the blueprint for a 1999 Firebird may contain an additional option—for instance, a passenger-side air bag—that may not be included in the 1998 blueprint. Figure 5 uses the car example to illustrate most of the OOP terms discussed in this section.

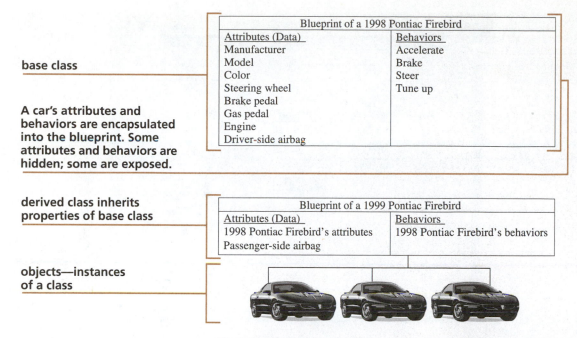

base class

A car's attributes and behaviors are encapsulated into the blueprint. Some attributes and behaviors are hidden; some are exposed.

Blueprint of a 1998 Pontiac Firebird	
Attributes (Data)	Behaviors
Manufacturer	Accelerate
Model	Brake
Color	Steer
Steering wheel	Tune up
Brake pedal	
Gas pedal	
Engine	
Driver-side airbag	

derived class inherits properties of base class

Blueprint of a 1999 Pontiac Firebird	
Attributes (Data)	Behaviors
1998 Pontiac Firebird's attributes	1998 Pontiac Firebird's behaviors
Passenger-side airbag	

objects—instances of a class

Figure 5: Illustration of OOP terms

In the next section you will run a Visual Basic application that will give you a quick look at some of the objects you will learn how to create in the following tutorials.

A Visual Basic Demonstration

The Visual Basic application you are about to run will show you only some of the objects you will learn how to create in the tutorials. For now, it is not important for you to understand how these objects were created or why the objects perform the way they do. Those questions will be answered in the tutorials.

To run the Visual Basic application:

1 If necessary, start Windows, then place your Student Disk in the appropriate disk drive. Click the **Start** button on the taskbar, and then click **Run** on the Start menu. The Run dialog box opens. Click the **Browse** button in the Run dialog box. The Browse dialog box opens. You want to run the Month (Month.exe) file, which is located in the Overview folder on your Student Disk.

2 Click the **Look in** list arrow, then click the disk drive containing your Student Disk. Click the **Overview** folder, and then click the **Open** button to open the Overview folder. Click **Month** (Month.exe) in the list of filenames, and then click the **Open** button. The Browse dialog box closes and the Run dialog box appears again. The Run box should display either A:\Overview\Month.exe or B:\Overview\Month.exe. Click the **OK** button. After a few moments, Visual Basic displays the application shown in Figure 6.

menu

text box

list box

option buttons

label controls

command button

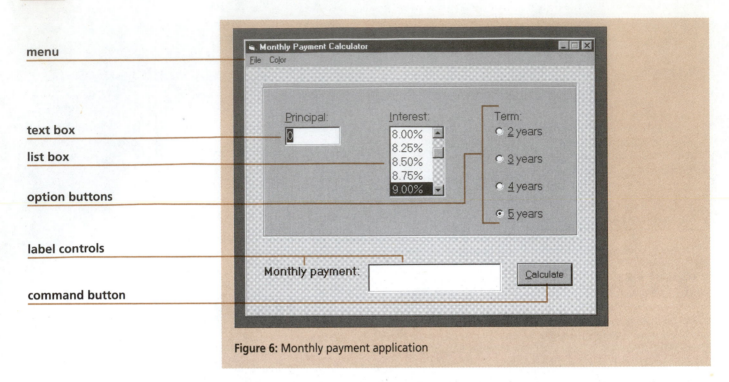

Figure 6: Monthly payment application

Figure 6 identifies some of the different objects appearing in the application's interface. Notice that the interface contains a text box, a list box, a command button, option buttons, label controls, and a menu. You can use this application to calculate the monthly payment for a car loan. For example, what would your monthly payment be if you wanted to borrow $30,000 at 8% interest for five years?

To compute the monthly car payment:

1 Type **30000** in the Principal text box, and then click **8.00%** in the Interest list box. Notice that Visual Basic highlights the 8.00% entry in the list box.

2 The option button corresponding to the five-year term is already selected, so you just need to click the **Calculate** button to compute the monthly payment. Visual Basic computes and displays the monthly payment, as shown in Figure 7.

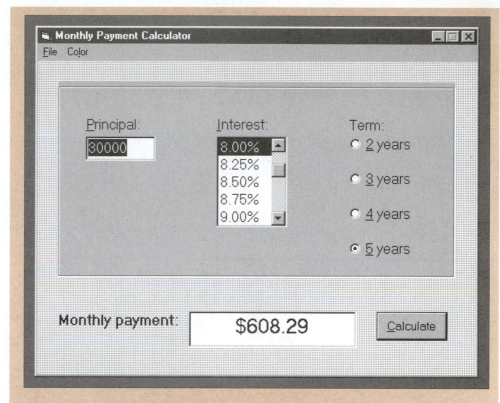

Figure 7: Computed monthly payment

Now determine what your monthly payment would be if you wanted to borrow $10,000 at 7.25% interest for four years.

3 Type **10000** in the Principal text box. Notice that the 10000 replaces the previously highlighted 30000.

4 Scroll the Interest list box until the 7.25% rate is visible, and then click **7.25%**.

5 Click the **4 years** option button. Notice that Visual Basic deselects the five-year option button as it selects the four-year option button.

6 Click the **Calculate** button to compute the monthly payment. Visual Basic computes and displays the monthly payment of $240.62.

Notice that the application's menu bar has two menus: File and Color. View the options on both menus.

To view the options on the Color and File menus:

1 Click **Color**. The Color menu opens and displays two options: Background and Information Box.

You use the Background option to change the background color of the application's interface.

2 Click **Background**. The Color dialog box opens. Click a color of your choice, and then click the **OK** button. The application's background changes accordingly.

If you don't like the current color, you can use the Background option on the Color menu to select a different color. Now see what the Information Box option on the Color menu does.

3 Click **Color**, and then click **Information Box**. The Color dialog box opens. Click a color of your choice, and then click the **OK** button. The color of the information box changes accordingly. (The information box is the box in which you enter the principal, interest, and term information.)

If you don't like the current color, you can use the Information Box option on the Color menu to select a different color. Now view the options on the File menu.

4 Click **File**. The File menu opens and shows two options: Print and Exit.

You use the Print option to print the monthly payment screen. (If you chose a dark color for the background and/or the information box, you should change the dark color to a light color before printing; otherwise, your printout may be unreadable.)

5 If your computer is connected to a printer, click **Print**. The monthly payment screen prints on the printer.

You use the Exit option on the File menu to end the demonstration application.

6 Click **File**, and then click **Exit**. The demonstration is now finished.

In the tutorials you will learn how to create Visual Basic applications that you can run directly from Windows, just as you did in the demonstration.

As you can see, programming languages have come a long way since the first machine languages. This brief history and demonstration should give you a better appreciation for the Visual Basic programming language.

Using the Tutorials Effectively

The tutorials in this book will help you learn about Microsoft Visual Basic Version 6.0. They are designed to be used at your computer. Begin by reading the text that explains the concepts. Then when you come to the numbered steps, follow the steps on your computer. Read each step carefully and completely before you try it.

As you work, compare your screen with the figures to verify your results. Don't worry if your screen display differs slightly from the figures. The important parts of the screen display are labeled in each figure. Just be sure you have these parts on your screen.

Don't worry about making mistakes; that's part of the learning process. Help? notes identify common problems and explain how to get back on track. You should complete the steps in the Help? notes only if you are having the problem described. Tip notes provide additional information about a procedure—for example, an alternative method of performing the procedure.

Each tutorial is divided into three lessons. You might want to take a break between lessons. Following each lesson is a Summary section that lists the important elements of the lesson. After the Summary section are multiple-choice questions and exercises designed to review and reinforce that lesson's concepts. You should complete all of the end-of-lesson questions and exercises before going on to the next lesson. You can't learn Visual Basic without a lot of practice, and future tutorials assume that you have mastered the information found in the previous tutorials. Some of the end-of-lesson exercises are Discovery exercises, which allow you to both "discover" the solutions to problems on your own and experiment with material that is not covered in the tutorial.

At the end of each tutorial you will find a Debugging section. In programming, the term **debugging** refers to the process of finding and fixing the errors in a program. Each Debugging section includes debugging tips, as well as exercises designed to let you practice debugging applications.

Throughout the book you will find GUI (Graphical User Interface) boxes. These boxes contain guidelines and recommendations for designing applications. You should follow these guidelines and recommendations so that your applications follow the Windows standard.

Before you begin the tutorials, you should know how to use Microsoft Windows 95. This book assumes you have learned basic Windows-navigation and file-management skills from Course Technology's *New Perspectives on Microsoft Windows 95 Brief* or an *equivalent* book.

QUESTIONS

1. The set of directions given to a computer is called _____ .
   a. computerese
   b. commands
   c. instructions
   d. a program
   e. rules

2. Instructions written in 0s and 1s are called _____ .
   a. assembly language
   b. booleans
   c. computerese
   d. machine code
   e. mnemonics

3. _____ languages allow the programmer to use mnemonics, which are alphabetic abbreviations for instructions.
   a. Assembly
   b. High-level
   c. Machine
   d. Object
   e. Procedure

4. _____ languages allow the programmer to use instructions that more closely resemble the English language.
   a. Assembly
   b. High-level
   c. Machine
   d. Object
   e. Procedure

5. A(n) _____ translates high-level instructions into machine code, line by line, as the program is running.
   a. assembler
   b. compiler
   c. interpreter
   d. program
   e. translator

6. A(n) _____ translates the entire high-level program into machine code before running the program.
   a. assembler
   b. compiler
   c. interpreter
   d. program
   e. translator

7. A(n) _____ converts assembly instructions into machine code.
   a. assembler
   b. compiler
   c. interpreter
   d. program
   e. translator

8. Visual Basic is a(n) _____ language.
   a. assembler
   b. mnemonic
   c. object-oriented/event-driven
   d. procedure-oriented

9. In procedure-oriented languages, the emphasis of a program is on how to accomplish a task.
   a. True
   b. False

10. In object-oriented languages, the emphasis of a program is on the objects included in the user interface and the events that occur on those objects.
    a. True
    b. False

11. A(n) _____ is a pattern or blueprint.
    a. attribute
    b. behavior
    c. class
    d. instance
    e. object

12. Which of the following is not an attribute that can be used to describe a human being?
    a. brown eyes
    b. female
    c. red hair
    d. talk
    e. thin

13. The object that you create from a class is called a(n) _____ .
    a. abstraction
    b. attribute
    c. instance
    d. procedure
    e. subclass

14. In the context of OOP, the combining of an object's attributes and behaviors into one package is called _____ .
    a. abstraction
    b. combining
    c. encapsulation
    d. exposition
    e. inheritance

15. In the context of OOP, the hiding of the internal details of an object from the user is called _____ .
   a. abstraction
   b. combining
   c. encapsulation
   d. exposition
   e. inheritance

16. Alcon Toys manufacturers several versions of a basic doll. Assume that the basic doll is called Model A and the versions are called Models B, C, and D. In the context of OOP, the Model A doll is called the _____ class; the other dolls are called the _____ class.
   a. base, derived
   b. base, inherited
   c. derived, base
   d. exposed, hidden
   e. inherited, derived

17. In the context of OOP, _____ refers to the fact that you can create one class from another class.
   a. abstraction
   b. combining
   c. encapsulation
   d. exposition
   e. inheritance

18. Use Figure 8 to answer the following questions

Figure 8

   a. What are the attributes (data or properties) associated with a dog class?
   b. What are the behaviors associated with a dog class?
   c. How many instances (objects) of the dog class are shown in Figure 8?

An Introduction to Visual Basic

Creating a Copyright Screen

case ▶ Interlocking Software Company, a small firm specializing in custom programs, hires you as a programmer trainee. In that capacity, you will learn to write Windows applications using the Visual Basic language, an object-oriented/event-driven programming language.

On your second day of work, Chris Statton, the senior programmer at Interlocking Software, assigns you your first task: create a copyright screen. The copyright screen will serve as a splash screen for each custom application created by Interlocking Software. A **splash screen** is the first image that appears when an application is run; it is used to introduce the application and to hold the user's attention while the application is being read into the computer's memory. The copyright screen you will create will identify the application's author and copyright year and will include the Interlocking Software Company logo. Although this first task is small, the copyright screen will give you an opportunity to learn the fundamentals of Visual Basic without having to worry about the design issues and programming concepts necessary for larger applications.

Previewing the Copyright Screen

Before starting the first lesson, you will preview a completed copyright screen that was created using Visual Basic.

To preview the completed copyright screen:

1 If necessary, start Windows, then place your Student Disk in the appropriate disk drive. Click the **Start** button on the taskbar. The Start menu opens. Click **Run** on the Start menu. The Run dialog box opens. Click the **Browse** button in the Run dialog box. The Browse dialog box opens. You want to run the Copy (Copy.exe) file, which is located in the Tut01 folder on your Student Disk.

2 If necessary, click the **Look in** list arrow, and then click the drive containing your Student Disk. Click the **Tut01** folder, and then click the **Open** button to open the Tut01 folder. Click **copy** (copy.exe) in the list of filenames. (Depending on how Windows 95 is set up on your computer, you may see the .exe extension on the filename. If you do, click the copy.exe filename.) Click the **Open** button. The Browse dialog box closes and the Run dialog box appears again. The Run box should display either A:\Tut01\copy.exe or B:\Tut01\copy.exe. Click the **OK** button. A copyright screen appears.

3 Click the **Interlocking Software logo**. The author's name and the copyright year appear, as shown in Figure 1-1.

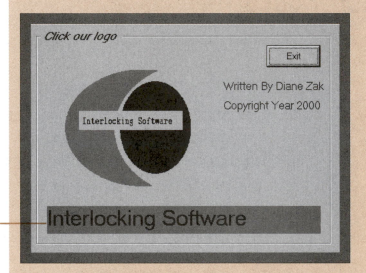

ActiveX control

Figure 1-1: Copyright screen

In lesson C you will learn how to display a special control, called an ActiveX control, in an interface. The ActiveX control that you will use will scroll the Interlocking Software company name across the bottom of the interface.

4 Click the **Exit** button. The application ends.

Now you will create your own copyright screen.

Tutorial 1 is designed to get you comfortable with the Visual Basic environment. You will also learn about the Visual Basic language. Remember, each tutorial contains three lessons and a Debugging section. You should complete a lesson in full and do the end-of-lesson questions and exercises before moving on to the next lesson.

LESSON A

objectives

In this lesson you will learn how to:

- Start and exit Visual Basic
- Identify the components of the Visual Basic display
- Set the properties of an object
- Create, save, run, and stop a Visual Basic application
- Open both a new project and an existing project

tip

If you are using Visual Basic at home or at work, be sure to read page xvi, which explains how to set your Visual Basic environment so that your screens match the figures shown in the book.

tip

You use the New tab in the New Project dialog box to open a new project, the Existing tab to open an existing project, and the Recent tab to open a project that was opened recently.

Creating a New Project

Starting Visual Basic

Before you can begin creating your copyright screen, you must start Visual Basic.

To start Visual Basic:

1 If necessary, start Windows, then place your Student Disk in the appropriate disk drive. Click the **Start** button on the Windows 95 taskbar. The Start menu appears. Point to **Programs** on the Start menu. The Programs menu appears to the right of the Start menu. Point to **Microsoft Visual Basic 6.0** on the Programs menu. (If Microsoft Visual Basic does not appear on the Programs menu, then point to Microsoft Visual Studio 6.0 on the Programs menu.) Click **Microsoft Visual Basic 6.0**. The Visual Basic copyright screen appears momentarily, and then the New Project dialog box appears as shown in Figure 1-2.

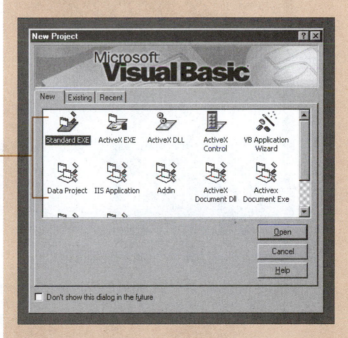

your options may differ

Figure 1-2: New Project dialog box

2 If necessary, click **Standard EXE** on the New tab, then click the **Open** button to open a new project. The Visual Basic startup screen appears.

3 Hide the Windows 95 taskbar. (If you don't know how to hide the Windows 95 taskbar, read the HELP? statement below.)

HELP? To hide the Windows 95 taskbar, click the Start button, point to Settings, and then click Taskbar to display the Taskbar Properties window. On the Taskbar Options tab, click the Auto hide check box. A check mark appears in the check box. Click the OK button to remove the Taskbar Properties window. The taskbar is now hidden from view; only a thin line appears in its place at the bottom of the screen. (Depending on how you have Windows 95 set up, your taskbar could be at the top, right, left, or bottom edge of the screen. The thin line will appear in the location of the taskbar. This book assumes that the taskbar is located at the bottom of the screen.) To display the hidden taskbar temporarily, move the mouse pointer to a location below the thin line at the bottom of the screen. To hide the taskbar again, move the mouse pointer back to a location above the thin line at the bottom of the screen.

The Visual Basic startup screen is shown in Figure 1-3. Your screen might not look identical to Figure 1-3, but it should have all the parts labeled in the figure.

Project Explorer window

main window (your menu titles and toolbar buttons may differ)

Toolbox window (your toolbox may contain other tools)

Form window

Properties window

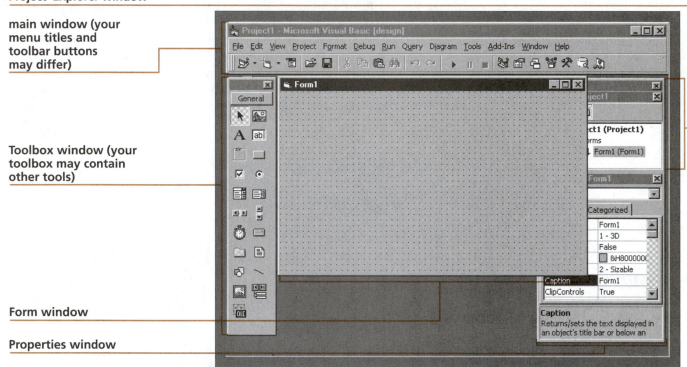

Figure 1-3: Visual Basic startup screen

HELP? Be sure that you followed the installation instructions shown on page xvi. If the Toolbox window is not displayed on the screen, click View on the menu bar, then click Toolbox. Your Toolbox window may include other tools. If the Properties window is not displayed on the screen, click View, and then click Properties Window. If the Project Explorer window is not displayed, click View, and then click Project Explorer.

HELP? Don't be concerned if your toolbox shows three columns of tools, rather than two columns. If you want your screen to match the figures in the book, simply place the mouse pointer on the toolbox's right border until it becomes a double arrow ←→, then drag the border to the left until the tools display in two columns.

The Visual Basic Startup Screen

As Figure 1-3 shows, the Visual Basic startup screen contains five separate windows: the Visual Basic main window, the Toolbox window, the Form window, the Properties window, and the Project Explorer window. You can't see all of the Properties window and the Project Explorer window right now because the Form window overlaps them. You will learn how to display those windows in a little while. For now, take a closer look at Visual Basic's main window, Form window, and Toolbox window.

The Main Window

The Visual Basic main window, at the top of the screen, contains the title bar, the menu bar, and the Standard toolbar. Figure 1-4 shows these parts of the Visual Basic display.

title bar
menu bar
Standard toolbar

Figure 1-4: Visual Basic main window

HELP? If the Standard toolbar is not displayed on the screen, click View on the menu bar, point to Toolbars, and then click Standard. Depending on your version of Visual Basic, your menu titles and toolbar buttons may differ from those shown in Figure 1-4.

The title bar indicates that Microsoft Visual Basic is currently working in **design time,** which means it is waiting for you to design your application. The title bar also shows that the name of the current application is Project1. Below the Visual Basic title bar is the menu bar. The **menu bar** displays the commands you will use to build your application. Buttons on the **Standard toolbar,** located below the menu bar, provide quick access to the most commonly used menu commands.

The Form Window

A Visual Basic Form window, one of many objects you can create in Visual Basic, appears in the center of the screen, as shown in Figure 1-5.

default caption

title bar

Minimize button

Maximize button

Close button

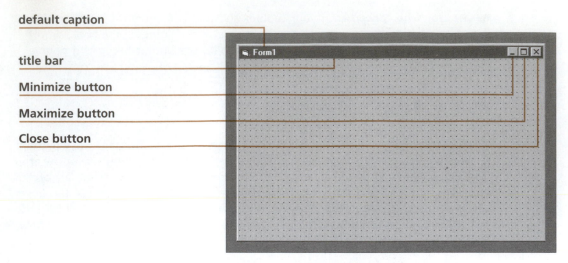

Figure 1-5: Visual Basic Form window

In the context of OOP, the Form window is an instance of Visual Basic's form class. Recall that a class is simply a pattern or blueprint for creating an instance of the class—an object.

A Visual Basic **Form window** is a window in which you design the user interface for your application. As you might recall, a **user interface** is what you see and interact with when running a Windows application. Notice that the Form window (or form) already contains its own title bar, as well as Minimize 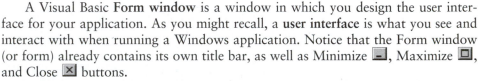, Maximize , and Close buttons.

Visual Basic assigns the default caption, Form1, to the first form. This caption appears in the form's title bar.

In these tutorials, you will learn how to customize a form by attaching other objects, such as buttons, boxes, and scroll bars, to the form. (Notice that a form is an object that can contain other objects.) During design time, Visual Basic displays dots in the form to assist you in aligning these objects. The dots are not visible when you run the application.

The Toolbox Window

In the context of OOP, each tool in the toolbox is a class—a pattern from which one or more objects, called controls, are created. Visual Basic encapsulates (combines) the object's attributes and behaviors in the tool. Some of the attributes and behaviors are hidden, while others are exposed.

On the left of the screen is the Toolbox window. The **toolbox** contains the set of tools you use when designing a Visual Basic application. These tools allow you to place objects (also called **controls**) such as buttons, boxes, and scroll bars on the form. Figure 1-6 describes the purpose of each of the basic tools. (Your toolbox may include other tools.)

Tool	Control	Purpose
☑	Check box	Displays a box that is either checked or unchecked
▦	Combo box	Combines and displays a text box with a list box
▭	Command button	Performs a command when clicked
▦	Data	Displays information from a database
▢	Directory list box	Displays a list of directories from which the user can select
▭	Drive list box	Displays a list of drives from which the user can select
▤	File list box	Displays a list of filenames from which the user can select
▦	Frame	Provides a visual and functional container for controls
◀▶	Horizontal scroll bar	Displays a horizontal scroll bar containing a range of values
▣	Image	Displays a picture; simpler version of the Picture box control
A	Label	Displays text that the user cannot change
◣	Line	Draws lines on a form
▤	List box	Displays a list of choices from which a user can select
▦	OLE	Allows object linking and embedding
⦿	Option button	Displays a button that can be either on or off
▦	Picture box	Displays a picture
▧	Pointer	Allows you to move and size forms and controls
◯	Shape	Draws a circle, ellipse, square, or rectangle on a form
abl	Text box	Accepts or displays text that the user can change
⏱	Timer	Displays a clock that performs events at specified time intervals
▦	Vertical scroll bar	Displays a vertical scroll bar containing a range of values

Figure 1-6: List of tools in the toolbox

> **tip**
>
> If you have trouble distin-
> guishing the tools in the
> toolbox, you can display
> the tool's name by resting
> the mouse pointer on the
> tool.

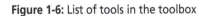

Take a look at the Project Explorer window next.

The Project Explorer Window

An application (project) can contain many files. The **Project Explorer window** (often just called the **Project window**) displays a hierarchical list of the projects included in the application you are creating currently, as well as all of the items contained in each project. Display the Project window to see the names of the files included in this application.

To display the Project window:

1 Position the mouse pointer on the **Project Explorer** button ⬕ on the Standard toolbar. After a few seconds a **tooltip**, which contains the button's name, appears; in this case, the tooltip says Project Explorer. If you have trouble distinguishing the icons in the toolbar buttons, you can always display a button's name by resting the mouse pointer on a button. Click the **Project Explorer** button ⬕ on the toolbar. The Project window displays with its title bar highlighted, indicating that it is the currently selected window. (The Properties window, which is typically attached to the Project window, may also appear.) See Figure 1-7.

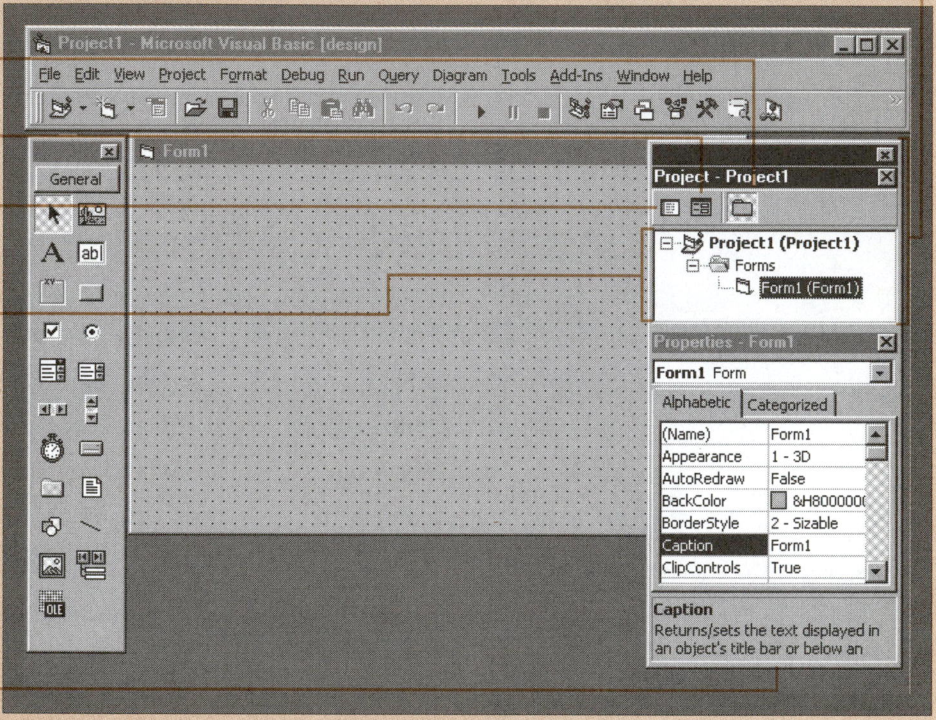

Project Explorer window

Toggle Folders button

View Object button

View Code button

List window

The Properties window may also appear

Figure 1-7: Project Explorer window displayed in the interface

HELP? If the Project Explorer's List window does not show the Forms folder, click the Toggle Folders button ▭ in the Project Explorer window.

Whenever you run Visual Basic and open a new project, Visual Basic automatically creates a default project named Project1. The name appears in both the Project window's title bar and its List window, which lists all of the loaded projects and the items included in each project. The default project contains the Form1 file, which is the default filename for the form appearing on the screen. If you don't change the name of the form when you save it, this is the name Visual Basic will use to save the form. (A Visual Basic project can contain many different files, as you will see in future tutorials.)

Notice that the Project window also contains three buttons: View Code, View Object, and Toggle Folders. The **View Code button** displays the program instructions, called code, associated with the selected file. The **View Object button** displays the object that is associated with the selected file. You can use this button, for example, to view the various forms included in a project or to display a form you closed unintentionally. The **Toggle Folders button** controls the display of the folders in the List window. The default is that the folders, as well as the items contained within the folders, display, as shown in Figure 1-7. If you click the Toggle Folders button, only the items contained within the folders, not the folders themselves, will display in the List window. View how this looks.

To change the display of the folders and items in the Project Explorer's List window:

1   Click the **Toggle Folders** button in the Project window. See Figure 1-8.

Minus box

Figure 1-8: Project Explorer's List window with Toggle Folders button toggled off

Clicking the Minus box that is located to the left of the Project1 icon will hide the display of the files contained in the project.

Visual Basic's Project Explorer window operates similarly to the Windows Explorer window in that the Plus box next to an item indicates that the item contains information that is not displayed currently, and the Minus box indicates that you are viewing all of the item's information.

2   Click the **Minus** box that is located to the left of the Project1 icon in the Project Explorer window. The Minus box changes to a Plus box, and Visual Basic hides the name of the file (Form1) contained in the Project1 project.

3   Click the **Plus** box, then click the **Project Explorer** button on the Standard toolbar. The Plus box changes to a Minus box, and Visual Basic displays the name of the file (Form1) contained in the Project1 project.

So far you have learned about four of the five Visual Basic windows: the main window, the Form window, the Toolbox window, and the Project Explorer window. The Properties window is next.

The Properties Window

Each object in Visual Basic has a set of characteristics, called **properties**, associated with it. These properties, listed in the **Properties window**, control the object's appearance and behavior.

tip

• • • • • • • • • • • • • • • •

The Properties window lists only the properties that can be set at design time; it does not list the properties that can be set only at run time, through code. To view a complete listing of an object's properties, display the object's Help screen. You will learn how to display an object's Help screen in Lesson B.

Visual Basic assigns a default setting to the properties of each object, but you can use the Properties window to change a setting from its default value. (You can also change a property's value through code, as you will see in Lesson C.) In order to use the Properties window to change the value in an object's property, you first must select the object. For example, to change one of the form's properties, you first must select the form.

To display the form's Properties window:

1   Click the **form** to select it, then click the **Properties Window** button 🗐 on the Standard toolbar. See Figure 1-9.

the Project Explorer window may also display

Properties window title bar

Object box

Properties list

Settings box

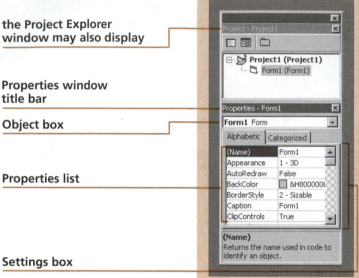

Figure 1-9: Properties window listing the form's properties

As indicated in Figure 1-9, the Properties window includes an Object box and a Properties list. The **Object box**, located immediately below the Properties window's title bar, displays the name and type of the selected object—in this case, Form1 Form. You can use the Object box to select an object in the user interface. You must select an object before you can either display or change the value of its properties. (You'll learn more about the Object box in Lesson B.)

The **Properties list**, which can be displayed either alphabetically or by category, has two columns. The left column displays all the properties associated with the selected object (in this case, the form). The right column, called the **Settings box**, displays the current value, or setting, of each of those properties. For example, the current value of the Name property is Form1. Notice that Visual Basic displays, below the Properties list, a brief description of the selected property.

To view the properties in the Properties window:

1   Click the **down scroll arrow** in the Properties window's vertical scroll bar to scroll through the entire Properties list. As you scroll, notice the various properties associated with a form.

You can also use the ↓ and ↑ keys on your keyboard, as well as the Home, End, Page Down, and Page Up keys to scroll the Properties window, but you first must make the Properties window the active window.

2 Drag the scroll box to the top of the vertical scroll bar to display the beginning of the Properties list once again.

Notice that the currently selected property in the Properties list is highlighted. In this case, the currently selected property is the Name property; the value of the Name property is Form1.

HELP? If the Name property is not highlighted, click (Name) in the Properties list.

You can change the setting for many of the listed properties simply by typing a new value in the property's Settings box. Some properties, however, have predefined settings. If a property has predefined settings, either a list arrow or an ellipsis (...) will appear in the Settings box when the property is selected. When you click the list arrow, either a list or a color palette appears containing the valid predefined settings for that property; you then select the setting you want from that list or color palette. Clicking the ellipsis in the Settings box displays a dialog box in which you select the settings for the property. You will get a chance to practice with both the list arrow and ellipsis as you change various properties throughout this lesson. You will begin by changing the Caption property.

Setting the Caption Property

Programmers who create applications for the Windows environment need to be aware of the conventions used in Windows applications. One such convention is that the name of the application usually appears in the application window's title bar. Notice, for example, that "Project1 - Microsoft Visual Basic [design]" appears in the title bar of Visual Basic's window. Because the form on the screen will become your application's window when the application is run, its title bar should display an appropriate name.

In Visual Basic the **Caption property** controls the text displayed in the form's title bar. The Caption property is also displayed on the application's button on the taskbar when the application is running.

Visual Basic automatically assigns the default caption Form1 to the first form in a project. A better, more descriptive caption would be "Interlocking Software Company"—the name of the company responsible for the copyright screen application.

To set the Caption property for the selected form:

1 Click **Caption** in the Properties list.

Notice that the Settings box does not contain either a list arrow or an ellipsis, which means this property does not have any predefined settings.

2 Type **Interlocking Software Company** and press the **Enter** key. The new caption appears in the Settings box to the right of the Caption property; it also appears in the form's title bar.

Notice that you do not have to erase the old caption before entering the new caption. You need simply to select the appropriate property and then type the new value; the new value replaces the old value for the selected property.

You will change the form's Name property next.

Setting an Object's Name Property

Visual Basic automatically assigns a default name to every object it creates. For example, the default name for the first form in a project is Form1, the default name for the second form in a project is Form2, and so on. Because a project can contain many forms, it is a good practice to give each one a more meaningful name; this will help you keep track of the various forms in the application.

An object's name must begin with a letter and it must contain only letters, numbers, and the underscore character. You cannot use punctuation characters or spaces in an object's name, and the name cannot exceed 40 characters. One popular naming convention is to have the first three characters in the name represent the object's type (form, scroll bar, and so on), and the remainder of the name represent the object's purpose. For example, a more descriptive name for this form would be frmCopyright. The "frm" identifies the object as a form, and the "Copyright" reminds you of the form's purpose. Figure 1-10 contains a list of the three characters usually associated with the form and the basic tools (controls) in the toolbox. (The pointer tool is not really a control; it simply provides a way to move and resize forms and controls.)

tip

During design time, you can't have two forms with the same name in the same project.

tip

If an object's name contains more than one word, you can capitalize the first character in each word to make the name easier to read; for example, use txtFirstName rather than txtFirstname.

Object	ID	Object	ID
Check Box	chk	Label	lbl
Combo Box	cbo	Line	lin
Command Button	cmd	List Box	lst
Data	dat	OLE	ole
Directory List Box	dir	Option Button	opt
Drive List Box	drv	Picture Box	pic
File List Box	fil	Shape	shp
Form	frm	Text Box	txt
Frame	fra	Timer	tmr
Horizontal Scroll Bar	hsb	Vertical Scroll Bar	vsb
Image	img		

Figure 1-10: Objects and their three-character IDs for the Name property

You assign a new name to an object by setting the object's **Name property**. Although you can type the entire name in uppercase letters, lowercase letters, or a combination of uppercase and lowercase letters, it is a common practice to type the three-character ID in lowercase and capitalize just the first letter in the part of the name that identifies the purpose. For example, you will capitalize only the "C" in "frmCopyright."

To set the Name property for the Form1 form, which is the currently selected object:

1 Click (**Name**) in the Properties list to select that property. The Name property is now highlighted.

Notice that the Name property does not have any predefined settings as its Settings box does not contain a list arrow or an ellipsis. That means that you can simply type the new name into the Settings box.

2 Type **frmCopyright** and press the **Enter** key. (Remember, you can't use spaces in the name.) The new name, frmCopyright, is displayed in both the Properties and Project windows, as shown in Figure 1-11.

form filename

form object's name

form object's name

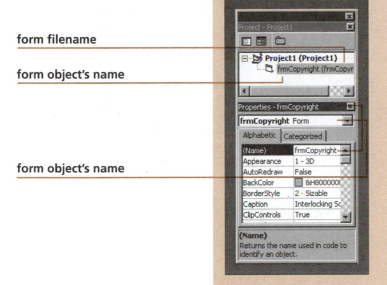

Figure 1-11: Name changes shown in Project window and in Properties window

Notice that the Project Explorer window now shows frmCopyright (frmCopyright) in its list. (You may need to scroll the Project Explorer window to see all of the frmCopyright filename.) The first frmCopyright listed in the Project Explorer window is the form object's name; this is the name the programmer will use when referring to the form in code. The frmCopyright within the parentheses, on the other hand, is the name of the file on disk that contains the form. By default, Visual Basic assumes that you will want to use the form object's name as the form's filename when you save the form. If you prefer, you can change the filename when you save the form. You will learn how to change the filename when saving a form later in this lesson.

It can be very easy to confuse the Name property with the Caption property. Recall that the form's Caption property controls the text displayed in the form's title bar, as well as the text displayed on the application's taskbar button when the application is running. The Name property, however, assigns a name to an object. When writing Visual Basic instructions (called code), you use an object's name, not its caption, to refer to the object. In other words, the name is used by the programmer, whereas the caption is read by the user.

Programmers typically give meaningful names to the form, the project, and to any controls that will be either coded or referred to in code. Controls that are not coded and are not referred to in code are not given meaningful names; programmers leave the names of these controls at their default values.

Next you will make the copyright screen more interesting by adding some color to it.

Setting the BackColor Property

The **BackColor property** controls the background color of an object. Unlike the Caption and Name properties, the BackColor property has predefined settings.

To change the background color of an object:
1 As the Object box in the Properties window shows, the form is the currently selected object, so you just need to click **BackColor** in the Properties list. Notice the list arrow in the Settings box.
2 Click the **Settings box** list arrow, then click the **Palette** tab. A color palette displays.
3 If you have a color monitor, click a **light blue square**. The background color of the form changes to a light blue. If you do not have a color monitor, click the **Settings box** list arrow to close the color palette.

Before saving the work you have done so far, you will give the project a more meaningful name.

Setting the Project's Name Property

In addition to setting the properties of the objects included in an application, the Properties window also allows you to assign a more meaningful name to the project itself. In this case, you will change the name of the project from its default name, Project1, to Copyright, which is a more meaningful name for the project. In order to change the project's Name property, you first must select the project in the Project window.

To change the project's name:
1 If necessary, display the Project Explorer window, then click **Project1** (**Project1**) in the Project window. The Properties window shows that the project has one property only, the Name property.
2 Click (**Name**) in the Properties list, type **Copyright** and then press the **Enter** key. Copyright appears in the Properties window, Project - Copyright appears in the Project window's title bar, and Copyright (Copyright) appears in the Project window's list of filenames.
You will now learn how to save the work you have done so far.

Saving a Visual Basic Project

It is a good practice to save the current project every 10 or 15 minutes so you won't lose a lot of work if the computer loses power. When you save a project for the first time, Visual Basic asks you for a name for the form file and a name for the project file. The project file will contain the names of the files appearing in the Project window, along with their location on the disk.

The easiest way to save the form and the project is to click the Save Project button on the Standard toolbar.

To save a Visual Basic project:

1 Click the **Save Project** button 🖫 on the Standard toolbar. The Save File As dialog box opens.

The dialog box prompts you for the name of the form file first; you can tell that by looking in the Save as type list box.

Notice that the name appearing in the File name text box is the name you assigned to the form with the Name property, but with a .frm extension. You can keep the name that Visual Basic offers in the File name text box or, if you prefer, you can change the name. In this case, to keep the files you create in these tutorials grouped together in a meaningful way, you will save this form file as laCopy. The "laCopy" indicates that the Copyright application was created or saved in Lesson A.

2 Type **laCopy** in the File name text box. (Be sure to use the lowercase "l" and not the number one.) Visual Basic will automatically append a .frm extension when it saves this file. The ".frm" extension indicates that the file is a form.

You want to save the form file in the Tut01 folder on your Student Disk.

3 If necessary, click the **Save in** list arrow, and then click the drive containing your Student Disk. Click the **Tut01** folder, and then click the **Open** button to open the Tut01 folder. The Tut01 folder opens, as shown in Figure 1-12.

current folder

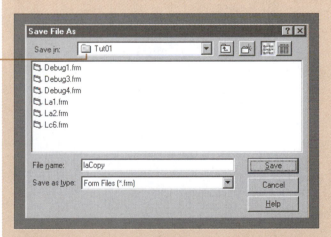

Figure 1-12: Save File As dialog box

4 Click the **Save** button to save the laCopy form file. Visual Basic saves the laCopy form file in the Tut01 folder on your Student Disk.

HELP? If this is the second or subsequent time you are practicing this lesson, Visual Basic will display a dialog box that asks if you want to replace the existing file. Click the Yes button.

Now that the form is saved, Visual Basic displays the Save Project As dialog box, which prompts you for the project name. The Save in list box shows Tut01 as the open folder. The File name text box shows that the current project will be saved as Copyright.vbp. Here again, to keep the files grouped together in a meaningful way, you will name the project file laCopy also. Visual Basic automatically appends the .vbp extension when it saves a project file. The ".vbp" stands for "Visual Basic project." (It is not necessary for the project file to have the same name as the form file, as you will see in later tutorials.)

5 Type **laCopy** in the File name text box and click the **Save** button to save the project. Visual Basic saves the laCopy project file in the Tut01 folder on your Student Disk.

HELP? If this is the second or subsequent time you are practicing this lesson, Visual Basic will display a dialog box that asks if you want to replace the existing file. Click the Yes button.

6 Display the Project Explorer window. If necessary, use the horizontal scroll bar, located at the bottom of the Project window, to scroll the Project window until both filenames are visible. Notice the changes in the Project window displayed in Figure 1-13.

name of the project file on your Student Disk

project object's name

form object's name

name of the form file on your Student Disk

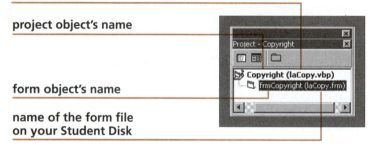

Figure 1-13: Project Explorer window

tip

It is a good practice to save the project before running it.

The Project window shows that the project object's name is Copyright and the form object's name is frmCopyright. The Copyright project and the frmCopyright form are saved on your Student Disk in the laCopy.vbp and laCopy.frm files, respectively.

Now that the form and the project are saved, you can run the project to see what you have accomplished so far.

Starting and Ending a Visual Basic Project

The only way you can tell if your application works is by starting (running) it. When you run the application, Visual Basic displays the user interface you created.

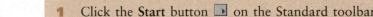

To start (run), then end, the copyright screen application:

1 Click the **Start** button on the Standard toolbar. Visual Basic enters run time, as shown in Visual Basic's title bar, and the user interface appears.

2 Click the **End** button ▪ on the toolbar to end the application. Visual Basic leaves run time and returns to design time, as Visual Basic's title bar now indicates.

Before finishing Lesson A, you will learn how to begin a new project and how to open an existing project. Both of these skills will help you complete the end-of-lesson exercises.

Opening a New Project

When you are finished with one project and want to begin another project, you can simply click File, then click New Project. You can open a new project while a previous project is on the screen. When you open the new project, Visual Basic closes the previous project. Try opening a new project now.

To open a new project:

1 Click **File**, and then click **New Project**. The New Project dialog box appears. If necessary, click **Standard EXE** in the dialog box, then click the **OK** button. Visual Basic closes the current project before opening a new project.

Now you will open a project that was saved previously.

Opening an Existing Project

If you want to continue working on an existing project, you simply click the Open Project button on the Standard toolbar and then tell Visual Basic which project you want to open. Open the existing laCopy project and change the form's BackColor property to a light gray.

To open an existing project:

1 Click the **Open Project** button on the Standard toolbar. The Open Project dialog box, which contains two tabs (Existing and Recent), displays. You can use the Existing tab to display a list of existing projects. The Recent tab displays a list of recently opened projects.

HELP? If you were working on a project before choosing the Open Project option and you did not save that form and/or project, Visual Basic will display a dialog box asking if you want to save the current files before opening another project.

You want to open the laCopy project file, which is located in the Tut01 folder on your Student Disk. In this case, because the laCopy project file was opened recently, you can use either the Recent tab or the Existing tab to open the file. You will use the Existing tab.

 tip

You can also start an application by pressing the F5 key or by using the Start command on the Run menu.

tip

You can also end an application by using the End command on the Run menu.

 tip

If you did not save the current project first, Visual Basic displays a dialog box asking if you want to save the current form and/or project before a new project is opened.

tip

You can also open an existing project by using the Open Project command on the File menu, or by pressing Ctrl+O.

2 If necessary, click the **Existing** tab, then open the Tut01 folder on your Student Disk. Click **laCopy** (laCopy.vbp) in the list of project file names, then click the **Open** button to open the Copyright project.

3 Click the **form** to select it, and then set the form's BackColor property to a light gray.

HELP? If the form does not appear on the screen, click frmCopyright (laCopy.frm) in the Project window, and then click the Project window's View Object button.

4 Click the **Save Project** button 🖬 to save the application.

Although the application is not completed, it's time for a break. You will complete the copyright screen in the remaining two lessons.

Exiting Visual Basic

As in most Windows applications, you exit an application using either the Close button or the Exit command on the File menu.

To exit Visual Basic:

1 Click the **Close** button ☒ on the Visual Basic title bar, and then redisplay the Windows 95 taskbar.

HELP? To redisplay the Windows 95 taskbar, move the mouse pointer to the thin line at the bottom of the screen until the taskbar appears. Click the Start button, point to Settings, then click Taskbar. Click the Auto hide check box on the Taskbar Options tab. No check mark should appear in the Auto hide check box. Click the OK button.

Now you can either take a break or complete the end-of-lesson questions and exercises.

S U M M A R Y

To start Visual Basic:

■ Start Windows 95 and place your Student Disk in the appropriate disk drive.

■ Click the Start button on the Windows 95 taskbar. The Start menu appears.

■ Point to Programs in the Start menu, then point to Microsoft Visual Basic 6.0 in the Programs menu. (If Microsoft Visual Basic does not appear on the Programs menu, then point to Microsoft Visual Studio 6.0 on the Programs menu.)

■ Click Microsoft Visual Basic 6.0. The New Project dialog box appears. If necessary, click Standard EXE on the New tab, then click the Open button. The Visual Basic startup screen appears.

■ If you prefer, you can hide the Windows 95 taskbar to show more of the Visual Basic screen.

To display the Standard toolbar:

■ Click View, point to Toolbars, then click Standard.

To display the toolbox:

■ Click View, then click Toolbox.

To display the Project window:

■ Click the Project Explorer button ▨ on the Standard toolbar. You can also click View, then click Project Explorer, or press Ctrl+R.

To display the Properties window:

■ Click the Properties Window button ▧ on the Standard toolbar. You can also press the F4 key, or click View, and then click Properties Window.

To set the value of a property:

■ Select the object whose property you want to set.
■ Display the Properties window.
■ Select the property whose value you want to set.

If a list arrow appears in the Settings box:

■ Click the list arrow in the Settings box, then click the desired value in either the list or the palette.

If an ellipsis (...) appears in the Settings box:

■ Click the ellipsis, then enter the appropriate information in the dialog box.

If the Settings box does not display either a list arrow or an ellipsis:

■ Enter the new value into the Settings box.

To control the text appearing in the form's title bar, and on the application's button on the Windows 95 taskbar when the application is running:

■ Set the form's Caption property.

To give a more meaningful name to an object:

■ Set the object's Name property.

To change the background color of an object:

■ Set the object's BackColor property.

To save a new Visual Basic project:

■ Click the Save Project button ▤ on the Standard toolbar. Enter a filename for the form in the File name text box, then select the appropriate drive and folder, and then click the Save button to save the form file. Enter a filename for the project in the File name text box, then click the Save button to save the project file.

or

■ Click File, then click Save *<filename>* As. Enter a filename for the form in the File name text box, then select the appropriate drive and folder, and then click the Save button to save the form file. Click File, then click Save Project As. Enter a filename for the project in the File name text box, then click the Save button to save the project file.

To run a Visual Basic application:

■ Click the Start button ▶ on the Standard toolbar. You can also press the F5 key, or click Run, then click Start.

To stop running a Visual Basic application:

■ Click the End button ■ on the Standard toolbar. You can also click Run, then click End.
or
■ Click the form's Close button ⊠. (You may not be able to use ⊠ to end an application that stops because of an error.)

To open a new project:

■ Click File, then click New Project; or press Ctrl+N. (If you were working on a project before choosing the New Project option and you did not save that form and/or project, Visual Basic will display a dialog box asking if you want to save the current files before opening another project.) When the New Project dialog box appears, click Standard EXE, then click the OK button.

To open an existing project:

■ Click the Open Project button 🗁 on the Standard toolbar. You can also press Ctrl+O; or click File, then click Open Project. Select the appropriate drive and folder. Click the project name in the list of files, then click the Open button to open the project. (If you were working on a project before choosing the Open Project option and you did not save that form and/or project, Visual Basic will display a dialog box asking if you want to save the current files before opening another project.)

To exit Visual Basic:

■ Click the Close button ⊠ on the Visual Basic title bar. You can also click File, then click Exit; or press Alt+Q.

Q U E S T I O N S

1. You design your user interface in a _____ .
   a. design bar
   b. form
   c. menu bar
   d. Properties window
   e. toolbar

2. The tools you use when designing your application are found in the _____ .
   a. design bar
   b. toolbox
   c. toolbar
   d. user interface
   e. user screen

3. In which window do you set the characteristics that control an object's appearance and behavior?
   a. Main
   b. Form
   c. Project Explorer
   d. Properties
   e. Toolbox

4. When you save a form, which of the following extensions does Visual Basic add to the filename you enter?
   a. .ffr
   b. .ffl
   c. .for
   d. .form
   e. .frm

5. When you save a project, which of the following extensions does Visual Basic add to the filename you enter?
   a. .frm
   b. .prg
   c. .prj
   d. .pro
   e. .vbp

6. The _____ property controls the background color of an object.
   a. BackColor
   b. BackGround
   c. BelowColor
   d. Color
   e. FormColor

7. The _____ property controls the text appearing in the form's title bar.
   a. Caption
   b. Name
   c. Text
   d. Title
   e. Window

8. The _____ property controls the text that appears on the application's button on the Windows 95 taskbar when the application is running.
   a. Application
   b. Button
   c. Caption
   d. Name
   e. Text

9. You give an object a more meaningful name by setting the object's _____ property.
   a. Application
   b. Caption
   c. Form
   d. Name
   e. Text

10. When coding an application, you use the _____ property to refer to an object.
    a. Application
    b. Caption
    c. Form
    d. Name
    e. Text

11. Refer to Figure 1-14. Identify the location of the following Visual Basic components by writing the appropriate letter on the line to the left of the component.

    ___ Form window　　___ Properties list
    ___ Main window　　___ Properties window
    ___ Menu bar　　　___ Settings box
    ___ Object box　　　___ Toolbar
    ___ Project window　___ Toolbox window

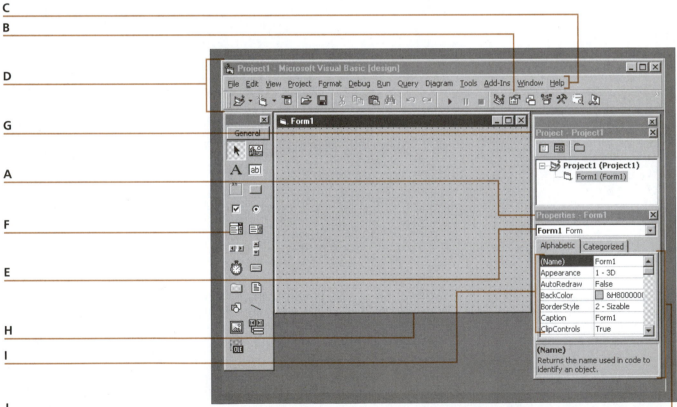

Figure 1-14: Visual Basic startup screen

12. Explain the difference between a form's Caption property and a form's Name property.

13. Explain how to open a new project.

14. Explain how to open an existing project.

15. Explain how to display the Project window and the Properties window.

E X E R C I S E S

1. In this exercise, you will change the properties of an existing form.
   a. If necessary, start Visual Basic. Your Student Disk should be in the appropriate disk drive.
   b. Open the La1 (La1.vbp)(Lesson A, Exercise 1) project, which is located in the Tut01 folder on your Student Disk. (Notice that the form contains some text. You will learn how to include text in a form in Lesson B.)
   c. Change the project's name to Charity, then set the following properties for the form:

Caption:	Charities Unlimited
BackColor:	Dark blue
Name:	frmCharity

   d. Run the application, then stop the application.
   e. Click File, then click Print. When the Print dialog box opens, click the Form As Text check box to select it, then click the Code check box to deselect it, and then click the OK button. The Form As Text option will print the properties of the form. You do not need to save this application.

2. In this exercise, you will change the properties of an existing form.
   a. If necessary, start Visual Basic. Your Student Disk should be in the appropriate disk drive.
   b. Open the La2 (La2.vbp)(Lesson A, Exercise 2) project, which is located in the Tut01 folder on your Student Disk. (Notice that the form contains a picture. You will learn how to include a picture in a form in Lesson C.)
   c. The form's title bar should say Photos Inc. (Be sure to type the period.) Set the appropriate property.
   d. Give the form a more meaningful name. Call it frmPhotos. Name the project Photos.
   e. Change the form's background color to red.
   f. Run the application. (You do not need to save the application.) Then stop the application.
   g. Click File, then click Print. When the Print dialog box opens, click the Form As Text check box to select it, then click the Code check box to deselect it, and then click the OK button. The Form As Text option will print the properties of the form. You do not need to save this application.

3. As you learned in Lesson A, some properties have predefined settings and some do not. You can tell if a property has predefined settings by first selecting the property in the Properties list, and then looking in the Settings box next to the selected property. Use the following key to complete Exercise 3.

   A This property has no predefined settings.

   B This property has predefined settings. The list arrow in the Settings box will display either a list of the valid choices or a palette.

   C This property has predefined settings. The ellipsis in the Settings box will display a dialog box.

   Below are the names of 10 properties for a form. If necessary, start Visual Basic and open a new project. Select each of the 10 properties, one at a time, in the Properties list. On the line to the left of the property, write A, B, or C, according to the key given above.

   ___ Caption   ___ ForeColor
   ___ Enabled   ___ Icon
   ___ FillColor   ___ Left
   ___ FillStyle   ___ Name
   ___ Font   ___ Picture

Exercises 4 and 5 are Discovery Exercises, which allow you both to "discover" the solutions to problems on your own and to experiment with material that is not covered in the tutorial.

discovery ▶ 4. In Lesson A you learned about Visual Basic's Standard toolbar. Visual Basic also has three other toolbars: Debug, Edit, and Form Editor.

   a. Open a new Visual Basic project, if necessary. Click View on the menu bar, point to Toolbars, and then click Debug to select this toolbar. What buttons are available on the Debug toolbar? Close the Debug toolbar.

   b. Click View on the menu bar, point to Toolbars, then click Edit to select this toolbar. What buttons are available on the Edit toolbar? Close the Edit toolbar.

   c. Click View on the menu bar, point to Toolbars, then click Form Editor to select this toolbar. What buttons are available on the Form Editor toolbar? Close the Form Editor toolbar.

   d. Click View on the menu bar, point to Toolbars, then click Customize. What tabs are on the Customize dialog box? What does each tab allow you to do? Close the Customize dialog box.

discovery ▶ 5. Recall that the bottom portion of the Properties window contains a brief description of the selected property. You will use the Properties window to research four properties of a form.

   a. Open a new Visual Basic project, if necessary. Click the form to select it, then display the Properties window.

   b. On a piece of paper, write down the description that appears in the bottom portion of the Properties window for each of the following four properties: BorderStyle, Icon, MaxButton, and WindowState. Also write down the three values of the WindowState property.

In this lesson you will learn how to:

- Access Visual Basic Help
- Add a label control to a form
- Move and size a control
- Delete a control from a form
- Select multiple controls
- Save files under a different name

Working with Controls

Getting Help in Visual Basic

You will begin this lesson by spending some time looking at Visual Basic's on-line Help system. If you encounter any problems during the tutorials or if you have any questions, you will then be able to get help on your own.

To start this lesson:

1   Start Visual Basic, if necessary, and make sure your Student Disk is in the appropriate disk drive. Use the Open Project button ⏏ on the Standard toolbar to open the **laCopy** (laCopy.vbp) project that you created in Lesson A. Recall that the file is located in the Tut01 folder on your Student Disk.

2   Click the **form** to select it.

HELP? If the form does not appear on the screen, click frmCopyright (laCopy.frm) in the Project window, and then click the Project window's View Object button.

You can access Visual Basic Help by using either the F1 key or the Help menu. You can practice with both of these methods right now, beginning with the Help menu.

tip

MSDN stands for Microsoft Development Network. The MSDN Library contains more than a gigabyte of technical programming information, including sample code, documentation, technical articles, the Microsoft Developer Knowledge Base, and anything else you might need to develop solutions that implement Microsoft technology. Depending on how the MSDN Library was installed on your system, you may need to have the MSDN CD available in the CD drive to access the Help screens.

To access Help through the Help menu:

1   Click **Help** on the menu bar. The Help menu opens.

Notice that the Help menu contains the following options: Contents, Index, Search, Technical Support, Microsoft on the Web, and About Microsoft Visual Basic. You can use either the Contents, Index, or Search options to display the MSDN Library Visual Studio 6.0 window, which allows you to select and display Help screens for many Microsoft products, such as Visual Basic, Visual C++, and Visual J++. The Help menu's Technical Support option displays information on how you can obtain technical support from Microsoft. You can use this option if you can't find the answers you need in the MSDN library. You use the Help menu's Microsoft on the Web option to display a menu that contains Internet sites where you can find additional information about Microsoft and its products. The Help menu's About Microsoft Visual Basic option displays a dialog box that shows the Visual Basic version number and a copyright notice. The dialog box also contains a System Info button that you can use to display information about your computer system.

2   Click **Index** on the Help menu. The MSDN Library Visual Studio 6.0 window appears as shown in Figure 1-15.

Active Subset list box

tabbed dialog box

Selection pane

Display pane

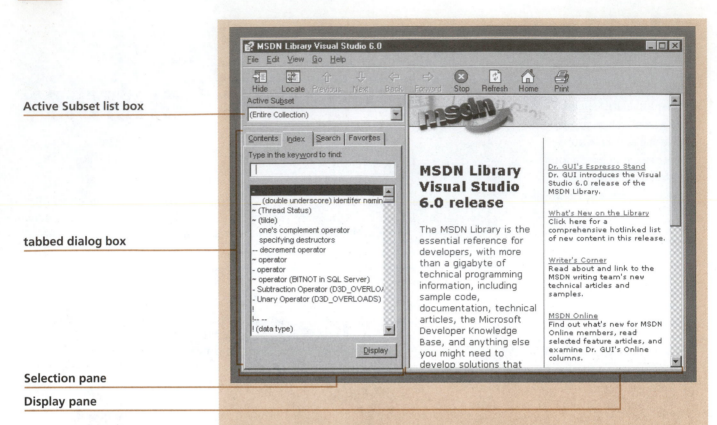

Figure 1-15: Index tab in MSDN Library Visual Studio 6.0 window

As Figure 1-15 indicates, the MSDN Library Visual Studio 6.0 window is divided into two panes: the Selection pane and the Display pane. You use the Selection pane to select the topic whose Help screen you want to display; the Help screen will be displayed in the Display pane.

You will notice that the Selection pane contains the Active Subset list box, as well as a dialog box that has four tabs labeled Contents, Index, Search, and Favorites. You will learn how to use the Index tab and the Active Subset list box in this lesson. You will get an opportunity to practice with the Contents, Search, and Favorites tabs in Discovery Exercise 4 at the end of this lesson.

The Index tab, which is currently displayed, contains an alphabetical list of keywords, similar to the index in a book. The Index tab allows you to search the MSDN library, or a portion of the library, for information on specific topics. You use the Active Subset list box to control how much of the MSDN library you want to search; the default is that the entire collection of library information will be searched.

3   Scroll the list of keywords that appears on the Index tab. Because Entire Collection is selected in the Active Subset list box, almost all of the keywords are darkened, which means that they are all part of the active subset.

   HELP? If Entire Collection is not selected in the Active Subset list box, click the Active Subset list box arrow, then scroll the list box, if necessary, and click Entire Collection in the list.

If you are looking for a Help screen on Visual Basic's Caption property, you can perform a more efficient search by changing the active subset from Entire Collection to Visual Basic Documentation.

4 Click the **Active Subset** list box arrow, then scroll the list box and click **Visual Basic Documentation**.

5 Scroll the list of keywords. You will notice that some of the keywords now appear dimmed (grayed-out); this is because they are not a part of the Visual Basic documentation.

To access Help on a particular topic, you can either type a topic (or just the first few letters of the topic) in the Type in the keyword to find text box at the top of the Index tab or select one of the topics from the list of keywords. Use the Index tab to display the Caption property's Help screen.

6 Click the **Type in the keyword to find** text box to place the insertion point in the text box, and then type **caption p** in the text box. The selection bar in the list box moves to the keywords, Caption property. Click the **Display** button. The Topics Found dialog box opens and shows a list of Help screens pertaining to the Caption property.

7 Scroll the list, if necessary, then click the first **Caption Property Visual Basic Reference** entry in the list, and then click the **Display** button. The Help screen for the Caption property opens, as shown in Figure 1-16.

HELP? If a dialog box asking you to insert the MSDN CD-ROM disc appears, it means that not all of the Help files were installed on your computer system. If you have access to the MSDN CD-ROM disc, you can insert it in the CD-ROM drive, and then click the OK button. If you do not have access to the MSDN CD-ROM disc, simply click the Cancel button; you will not be able to display the Caption property's Help screen.

tip

If you click the Index tab's Display button when a dimmed keyword is selected, a dialog box that contains the following message will appear: *Selection does not appear in current subset. Please create or choose a different subset.*

Hide button

Active Subset list box

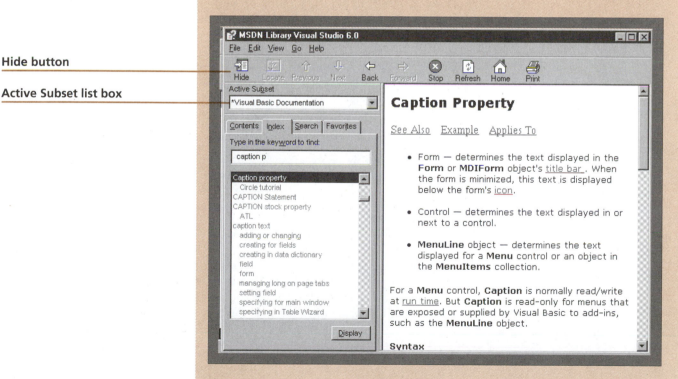

Figure 1-16: Help screen for the Caption property

You can hide the Selection pane so that you can see more of the Help screen in the Display pane.

8 Click the **Hide** button ⬜ in the MSDN window's toolbar to hide the Selection pane, then click the MSDN window's **Maximize** button ⬜ to display more of the Caption property's Help screen. Notice that the Hide button ⬜ becomes a Show button ⬜.

To redisplay the Selection pane, simply click the Restore button, and then click the Show button.

9 Click the **Restore** button ⬜, and then click the **Show** button ⬜.

You can also print the contents of a Help screen.

10 If your computer is connected to a printer, click the **Print** button ⬜, and then click the **OK** button.

11 Click the MSDN Library window's **Close** button ⬜ to close the window.

In addition to using the commands on the Help menu, you can also access Visual Basic Help by pressing the F1 key.

Using the F1 Key

The F1 key provides you with context-sensitive help. That means a Help screen will be displayed for whatever is currently selected. In many instances, using the F1 key is a faster way of getting help. You can use the F1 key, for example, to display the Help screen for the Caption property, but you first must select that property in the Properties window.

To use the F1 key to display the Help screen for the Caption property:

1 Display the Properties window, if necessary, then click **Caption** in the Properties list. If you were able to display the Help screen shown earlier in Figure 1-16, then press the **F1** key. The Caption property's Help screen, shown earlier in Figure 1-16, appears on the screen.

Important Note: In future steps you will not be instructed specifically to display the Properties window to locate a property; instead, you will be told simply to click the property. If you do not see the Properties window, you will need to display it.

2 Close the MSDN Library window.

In summary, you use the F1 key to obtain context-sensitive help. You can use the Help menu to obtain help on specific topics. Be sure to refer to Help if you have any questions or problems while you are working in Visual Basic.

Now you will add some objects to the current form.

Adding a Control to a Form

The tools in the toolbox allow you to add objects, called **controls**, to a form. The terms "object" and "control" are often used interchangeably in Visual Basic. Technically, however, a control refers to an object placed on a form. Although the form itself is an object, it is not a control. (The tutorials in this book use "object" to refer both to a form and a control; "control" refers only to the objects placed on the form—not the form itself.)

The first tool you will use is the Label tool—the large letter A in the toolbox. The **Label tool** creates a label control that you can use to display text you don't want the user to modify. In other words, while your application is running, Visual Basic will not allow the user to make any changes to the contents of a label control. In this application, you do not want the user to modify the information on the copyright screen, so a label control is the correct control to use.

To create a default-size label control in the center of the form:

1 Double-click the **Label** tool **A** in the toolbox. A default-size label control appears in the center of the form, with the default caption Label1. Click **Caption** in the Properties list. See Figure 1-17.

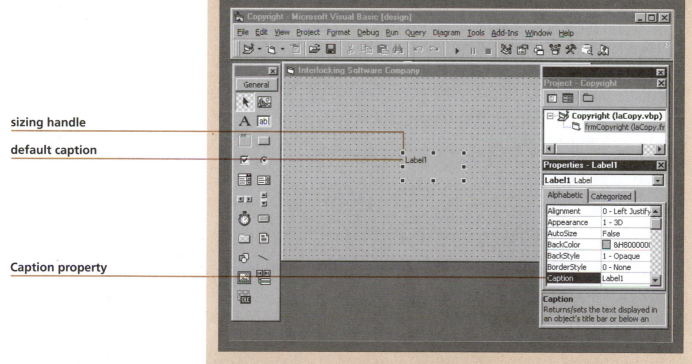

sizing handle

default caption

Caption property

Figure 1-17: Default-size label control added to form

HELP? If a label control does not appear in the center of the form, make sure the form is selected, then double-click the Label tool again. If a different control appears, press the Delete key to remove the incorrect control, then repeat Step 1.

tip

You can also size a control by selecting it, then pressing and holding down the Shift key as you press either the ↑, ↓, →, or ← key on your keyboard. You can move a control by pressing and holding down the Ctrl key as you press either the ↑, ↓, →, or ← key.

Notice that a label control's caption—in this case, Label1—appears inside the control. Visual Basic also assigns Label1 as the default setting of this control's Name property. You can verify that, if you want, by scrolling the Properties window until you see the Name property in the Properties list.

In order to use Visual Basic efficiently, you must know how to size, move, and delete the controls you've placed on the form. You will learn these three skills next.

Sizing, Moving, and Deleting a Control

You size, move, and delete a Visual Basic control in the same manner as you do in any Windows application. First, you must select the control that you want to size, move, or delete. You select a control by clicking it; when a control is selected, sizing handles appear around it. For example, notice the sizing handles around the Label1 control in Figure 1-17, indicating that the control is selected. Practice sizing, moving, and deleting the Label1 control.

tip

In order to delete a control, the control must be selected in the form and the Form window must be the active window. In other words, you can't delete a control if the main, Properties, Project Explorer, or toolbox title bar is highlighted. To avoid any problems with deleting controls, make it a practice to click the control in the form before you press the Delete key.

To size, move, and then delete the Label1 control, which is currently selected:

1   Place the mouse pointer on the label control's lower-right sizing handle until the mouse pointer becomes a double arrow, then drag the sizing handle until the object is a little larger than the default size. (You don't need to worry about the exact size.) When the control is the desired size, release the mouse button.

Now move the Label1 control.

2   To move the Label1 control, position the mouse pointer anywhere on the Label1 control, except on a sizing handle. Drag the Label1 control to the upper-left corner of the screen, then release the mouse button. (Don't worry about the exact location.)

Next, delete the Label1 control.

3   The Label1 control should still be selected; press the **Delete** key to delete the control.

Now that you know how to add, size, move, and delete controls, you can continue building the copyright screen.

Adding Label Controls to the Copyright Screen

The copyright screen application requires two label controls: one for the name of the application's author and the other for the copyright year.

tip

You can also add a control to the form by clicking the appropriate tool in the toolbox, then placing the mouse pointer on the form until it becomes a crosshair +, and then dragging until the control is the desired size.

To add two label controls to the copyright screen:

1   Double-click the **Label** tool [A] in the toolbox. The Label1 control appears in the center of the form.

2   Drag the Label1 control to the upper-left corner of the screen. (Don't worry about the exact location.)

3   Double-click the **Label** tool [A] in the toolbox again. The Label2 control appears in the center of the form.

4   Drag the Label2 control to a location immediately below the Label1 control.

Now that the controls are on the form, the next step is setting their properties.

Setting the Properties of a Label Control

The first property you will set is the Name property. Recall that programmers typically give meaningful names to the form, the project, and to any controls that will be either coded or referred to in code. In this case the two label controls you added to the form will be referred to in code, so you should change their default names (Label1 and Label2) to more meaningful names. Following the naming convention discussed earlier, you will assign the name lblAuthor to the first label control and the name lblYear to the second label control. The "lbl" identifies the objects as label controls, and "Author" and "Year" indicate each control's purpose in the form.

The three-character IDs associated with the form and the basic tools (controls) in the toolbox are listed in Figure 1-10.

To set the Name property for the two label controls:

1 Click the **Label1** control in the form to select it. Sizing handles appear around the control. If necessary, display the Properties window. Both the Properties window's title bar and its Object box show that the Label1 control is the currently selected object.

2 Click (**Name**) in the Properties list, then type **lblAuthor** and press the **Enter** key to enter a new name for this control. lblAuthor appears as the value of the Name property in the Properties list; it also appears in the Properties window's title bar and in its Object box.

3 Select the **Label2** control, and then set its Name property to **lblYear**.

Like forms, label controls also have a Caption property, which controls the text that appears inside the label control. The lblAuthor control's caption is currently Label1; the lblYear control's caption is currently Label2. In this application you want the words "Written By" and your name to appear in the lblAuthor control, and the words "Copyright Year" and the year 2000 to appear in the lblYear control, so you will need to set both controls' Caption properties accordingly.

To set the Caption property for the two label controls:

1 The lblYear control is currently selected, so just click **Caption** in the Properties list, then type **Copyright Year 2000** and press the **Enter** key. The new caption appears in the lblYear control.

Because the caption is longer than the width of the control, some of the information wraps around to the next line. You can use the sizing handles to size the label control until the entire caption appears on one line, or you can change the label control's AutoSize property. The **AutoSize property** does just what its name implies: it automatically sizes the control to fit its current contents. You will set the AutoSize property.

2 Click **AutoSize** in the Properties list. A list arrow appears in the Settings box. Recall that the list arrow means this property has predefined settings.

3 Click the **Settings box** list arrow to see the valid settings for the AutoSize property. A list appears.

As the list indicates, Visual Basic allows you to set the AutoSize property to either True or False. Many of the other properties shown in the Properties list also have only these two settings. (These settings are called **Boolean** values, named after the English mathematician George Boole.) The True setting turns the property on; the False setting turns the property off. To tell Visual Basic to size the selected control automatically, you will set the control's AutoSize property to True.

4 Click **True** in the list. The lblYear control stretches automatically to fit the contents of the Caption property.

5 Select the **lblAuthor** label control and set its AutoSize property to **True**.

6 Click **Caption** in the Properties list to select the Caption property for the lblAuthor control.

7 Type **Written By** and press the **spacebar**, then type your name and press the **Enter** key.

Now specify the placement of these two label controls on the form.

Setting the Left and Top Properties

Recall that you can drag a control to any position on the form. So that your screen agrees with the figures in the book, however, you will sometimes be given the value of each control's **Left property** and **Top property**. These two properties control the position of the upper-left corner of the object. You will use the Left and Top properties to move the lblYear control to its proper position on the form. This time, instead of selecting the control by clicking it on the form, you will use the Properties window's Object box to select the control.

To select a control using the Properties window's Object box, and then set the control's Left property and its Top property:

1 Display the Properties window, if necessary, then click the **Object box** list arrow, located immediately below the Properties window's title bar, to display its list. The list shows both the name and the type of the form and the two controls included on the form.

2 Click **lblYear Label** in the list to select that label control. The lblYear control is now selected, as the sizing handles around that control indicate.

3 Click **Left** in the Properties list to select that property.

The location of an object in a form is measured in twips from the edges of the form. A **twip** is 1/1440 of an inch. If you set the Left property to 1440, Visual Basic positions the control one inch from the left edge of the form. (Actual physical distances on the screen vary according to the size of the monitor.) Position the lblYear control 4200 twips (almost three inches) from the left edge of the form.

4 Type **4200** as the Left property and press the **Enter** key. Visual Basic moves the lblYear control accordingly.

Now position the lblYear control 1440 twips (1") from the top of the form.

5 Click **Top** in the Properties list, type **1440** and then press the **Enter** key. Visual Basic positions the lblYear control accordingly.

Next, you will set the lblAuthor control's Left and Top properties.

6 Select the lblAuthor control, then set its Top property to **1000** and its Left property to **4200**.

The final modification you will make to these label controls is to set their Font property. As you will see in the next section, you can set the Font property for both controls at the same time.

Changing the Property for More Than One Control at a Time

You can change the appearance of many of the objects in your user interface by changing the object's Font property. The **Font property** allows you to change the type of font used to display the text in the object, as well as the style and size of the font. A **font** is the general shape of the characters in the text. Courier and MS Sans Serif are examples of font types; regular, bold, and italic are examples of font styles. The size of a font is measured in points, with 1 **point** equaling 1/72 of an inch; 8, 10, and 18 are examples of font sizes.

One reason for changing a font is to bring attention to a specific part of the screen. In the copyright application, for example, you can make the text in the two label controls more noticeable by increasing the size of the font Visual Basic uses. You can change the size for both controls at the same time by clicking one control and then pressing and holding down the Control key as you click the other control in the form. (You must hold down the Control key as you click the control in the form; you can't hold down the Control key and click the control's name in the Properties window's Object box.) You can use the Control-click method to select as many controls as you want. You cancel the selection by clicking on the form or on any unselected control in the form.

tip

You can also select a group of controls on the form by placing the mouse pointer ⬧ slightly above and to the left of the first control you want to select, then pressing the left mouse button and dragging. A dotted rectangle will appear as you drag. When all of the controls you want to select are within the dotted rectangle, release the mouse button. Visual Basic will select all of the controls surrounded by the dotted rectangle.

To select both label controls, then set their Font property:

1 The lblAuthor control should still be selected. Verify that by looking in the Properties window or by looking for sizing handles around the control in the form. (If the lblAuthor control is not selected, then click the control in the form.)

2 Press and hold down the **Ctrl** key as you click the **lblYear control**. Both label controls are now selected, as the sizing handles indicate. See Figure 1-18.

both label controls are selected

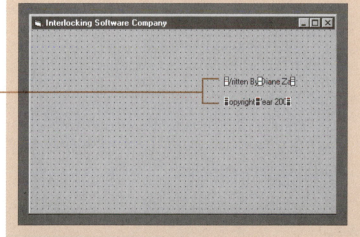

Figure 1-18: Both label controls selected

Notice that the sizing handles on the lblYear control are a solid color, whereas the sizing handles on the lblAuthor control are not; the lblAuthor control's sizing handles are white with a colored border. When you select more than one control, the last control you select will have solid-color sizing handles; the other selected controls will have white sizing handles with a colored border. In Lesson B's Discovery Exercise 5, you will learn the significance of the solid-color sizing handles.

3 If necessary, display the Properties window, and then click **Font** in the Properties list. The ellipsis, which appears in the Settings box, indicates that this property has predefined settings. When you click the ellipsis, a dialog box will appear. You will need to enter the appropriate information in the dialog box.

4 Click the ... (ellipsis) button in the Settings box to display the dialog box. The Font dialog box shown in Figure 1-19 opens.

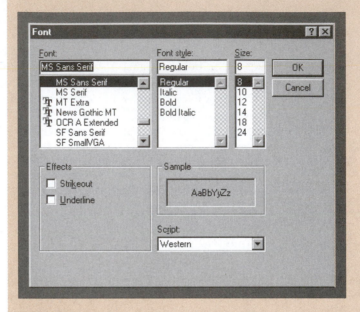

Figure 1-19: Font dialog box

The default font is typically the regular style of the MS Sans Serif font. The default font size is 8 points, or 1/9 of an inch. (Recall that one point is 1/72 of an inch.) To make the text in the two label controls more noticeable, you will increase the font size to 12 points, or 1/6 of an inch.

5 Click **12** in the Size list box to increase the font size to 12 points, then click the **OK** button. The text in the two label controls displays in the new font size.

6 Click the **form** to deselect the label controls.

HELP? If your name extends beyond the right border of the form, you can either make the form larger by dragging its right border, or you can drag the label controls to the left until your full name appears on the form. You can also use a smaller font for the label controls.

Saving Files Under a Different Name

Before ending Lesson B, you will save what you have completed so far and then run the application to see how it looks. Usually you save the form and the project using their original names. In this case, however, you will give the form and the project different names. By saving the form and the project under different names, you can repeat this lesson as often as you want because the original files from Lesson A will still be on your Student Disk. One very important note: when saving forms and projects, you always save the form first, then save the project.

To save the form and the project under a different name:

1 If necessary, click the **form** to select it. Click **File**, and then click **Save laCopy.frm As** to save the form under a new name. The Save File As dialog box opens with the current name of the form (either laCopy or laCopy.frm), displayed in the File name text box. The open folder is Tut01.

2 Change the filename to **lbCopy** (or lbCopy.frm), then click the **Save** button to save the form under the new name. A copy of the frmCopyright form is now saved as lbCopy.frm on your Student Disk.

> **HELP?** If this is the second or subsequent time you are practicing this lesson, Visual Basic will display a dialog box that asks if you want to replace the existing file. Click the Yes button.

3 Display the Project window.

Notice that Visual Basic updates the Project window to reflect the new name of the form file, lbCopy.frm. That's why you must give the form a new name before giving the project a new name; when you save the project, Visual Basic saves the information that is currently listed in the Project window. (Notice that the name of the form object within the .frm file, however, is still frmCopyright.) You can now save the project under a new name.

4 Click **File**, and then click **Save Project As** to save the project under a new name. The Save Project As dialog box appears with the current name of the project (either laCopy or laCopy.vbp) showing in the File name text box. The open folder is Tut01.

5 Change the filename to **lbCopy** (or lbCopy.vbp), and then click the **Save** button to save the project under the new name. A copy of the project is now saved as lbCopy.vbp on your Student Disk. Now that the files are saved, you can run the project.

> **HELP?** If this is the second or subsequent time you are practicing this lesson, Visual Basic will display a dialog box that asks if you want to replace the existing file. Click the Yes button.

6 Click the **Start** button on the Standard toolbar. The copyright screen appears as shown in Figure 1-20. (Recall that the copyright screen will display your name instead of Diane Zak.)

your name will appear here

two label controls

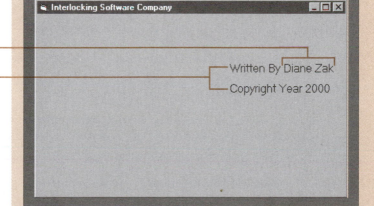

Figure 1-20: Current status of the Copyright screen

7 Click the **End** button ■ on the Standard toolbar to stop the application.

Now you can either exit Visual Basic and take a break, or complete the end-of-lesson questions and exercises. (If necessary, remember to redisplay the Windows 95 taskbar.) In Lesson C you will complete the copyright screen.

S U M M A R Y

To access the Visual Basic Help screens:

■ Click Help on the menu bar, then click either the Contents, Index, or Search commands to display the MSDN Library Visual Studio 6.0 window. Select Visual Basic Documentation in the Active Subset list box. Use the MSDN Library's Contents tab to search the library for information on general topics. Use the Index tab to search for information on specific topics. Use the Search tab to search for words or phrases that may be contained in the library's Help screens. Use the Favorites tab to maintain a list of frequently used Help screens.
or
■ Click the object, window, property, and so on for which you want to display a Help screen, then press the F1 key. The F1 key provides you with context-sensitive help, which means that it will display a Help screen for whatever is currently selected.

To add a control to a form:

■ In the toolbox, double-click the tool representing the control you want to add to the form. Move and/or size the control as necessary.

To select an object:

■ Click the object. Sizing handles will appear around the object.
or
■ Display the Properties window, click the Object box list arrow, then click the name of the object in the list. Sizing handles will appear around the object.

To size an object:

■ Select the object you want to size. Then position the mouse pointer on one of the sizing handles and drag until the object is the desired size.

To move an object:

■ Position the mouse pointer on the object you want to move, being careful not to position the pointer on any of the sizing handles. Then drag the object to its new location.

To delete a control:

■ Select the control you want to delete, then press the Delete key. Be sure to select the proper control in the form. In order to delete a control, the Form window must be the active window.

To select multiple controls:

■ Click the first control you want to select in the form.
■ Press and hold down the Control (Ctrl) key as you click the other controls you want to select. You must select the controls directly on the form, not their names in the Properties window's Object box.

To cancel the selection of one of the selected controls:

■ Press and hold down the Ctrl key as you click the control.

To cancel the selection of all of the selected controls:

■ Click the form or any unselected control in the form.

To control the position of an object's left edge:

■ Set the object's Left property.

To control the position of an object's top edge:

■ Set the object's Top property.

To automatically size a label control to fit its current contents:

■ Set the label control's AutoSize property to True.

To control the type, style, and size of the font used to display text in an object:

■ Set the object's Font property.

To save the open form and project using a different name:

■ Click File, then click Save *<filename>* As to save the form. Enter the new name for the form in the File name text box, select the appropriate drive and folder in the Save in list box, and then click the Save button. If a file with that name already exists on the disk, Visual Basic will display a dialog box asking if you want to replace the existing file. If you want to replace the form file on the disk with the current form, click the Yes button; otherwise, click the No button.

■ Click File, then click Save Project As to save the project. Enter the new name for the project in the File name text box, select the appropriate drive and folder in the Save in list box, and then click the Save button. If a file with that name already exists on the disk, Visual Basic will display a dialog box asking if you want to replace the existing file. If you want to replace the project file on the disk with the current project, click the Yes button; otherwise, click the No button.

QUESTIONS

1. You can open a context-sensitive Help window by selecting an object and pressing the _____ key.
    a. F1
    b. F2
    c. F3
    d. F4
    e. F5

2. The _____ tool creates a control in which you display text that you don't want the user to change.
    a. Caption
    b. Command
    c. Control
    d. Label
    e. Text

3. The location of an object in a form is measured in _____ from the edges of the form.
    a. characters
    b. inches
    c. points
    d. twips
    e. twups

4. The size of a font is measured in _____ .
    a. characters
    b. inches
    c. points
    d. twips
    e. twups

5. Which of the following properties tells a label control to adjust automatically to the size of its caption?
    a. AutoAdjust
    b. AutoCaption
    c. AutoControl
    d. AutoLblSize
    e. AutoSize

6. In order to delete a control on a form, the _____ window must be the active window, which means that its title bar must be highlighted.
    a. Form
    b. main
    c. Project
    d. Properties
    e. Toolbox

7. Explain how to a) select more than one control at a time, b) deselect one of the selected controls, and c) deselect all of the selected controls.

8. Explain how to size, move, and delete a control on a form.

9. Explain how to save an existing form file and an existing project file under a different name.

E X E R C I S E S

1. In this exercise, you will add a label control to a form. You will also change the properties of the form and its controls.
    a. If necessary, start Visual Basic and open a new project. Your Student Disk should be in the appropriate disk drive.
    b. Save the form and the project as lb1Done in the Tut01 folder on your Student Disk. Remember to save the form *before* saving the project.
    c. Change the project's name to IMA , then set the following properties for the form:
       Caption: IMA
       BackColor: White
       Name: frmIMA
    d. Add a label control to the form. The label control will not be coded or referred to in code, so you will not need to change its name from the default value (Label1). Set the following properties for the label control:
       Caption: International Mechanics Association
       Left: 800 twips
       Font: 12 points, bold
       AutoSize: True
       Top: 1000 twips

e. Save and run the application. Then stop the application.

f. Click File, then click Print. When the Print dialog box opens, click the Form As Text check box to select it, click the Code check box to deselect it, and then click the OK button. The Form As Text option will print the properties of the form.

2. In this exercise, you will add label controls to a form. You will also change the properties of the form and its controls.

a. If necessary, start Visual Basic and open a new project. Your Student Disk should be in the appropriate disk drive.

b. Save the form and the project as lb2Done in the Tut01 folder on your Student Disk. Remember to save the form *before* saving the project.

c. The form's title bar should say Jefferson Cleaning Inc. (include the period). Set the appropriate property.

d. Give the form a more meaningful name. Call it frmJefferson. Name the project Cleaners.

e. Change the form's background color to a light blue.

f. Add two label controls to the form. The size of both label controls should adjust automatically to their contents, so you will need to set the appropriate property. (The label controls will not be coded or referred to in code, so you will not need to change their names from the default values.)

g. The Label1 control should say Welcome To. The Label2 control should say Jefferson Cleaning Inc. (with the period).

h. Set the font size for both controls to 24 points, and set their font to Arial.

i. Drag both label controls to the center of the form, with the Label1 control first and the Label2 control below it.

j. Set the BackColor for both label controls to white. Set the ForeColor to red.

k. Save and run the application. Then stop the application.

l. Print only the Form Image and the Form As Text. The Form Image option will print the form and the Form As Text option will print the properties of the form.

3. In this exercise, you will create the user interface shown in Figure 1-21.

a. If necessary, start Visual Basic and open a new project. Your Student Disk should be in the appropriate disk drive.

b. Save the form and the project as lb3Done in the Tut01 folder on your Student Disk. Remember to save the form *before* saving the project.

c. Create the user interface shown in Figure 1-21. You can use any name for the form, as long as it is meaningful and follows the naming convention you learned in this tutorial. You can also use any font type, style, and size for the label controls. You can also choose any color for the form and the label controls in the form.

two label controls

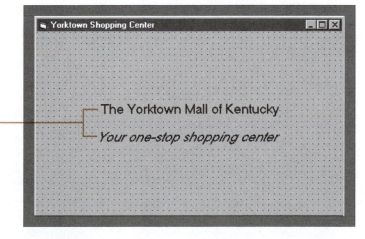

Figure 1-21

d. Name the project Yorktown. Save and run the application. Then stop the application.

e. Print only the Form Image and the Form As Text. The Form Image option will print the form, and the Form As Text option will print the properties of the form.

Exercises 4 and 5 are Discovery Exercises, which allow you both to "discover" the solutions to problems on your own and to experiment with material that is not covered in the tutorial.

discovery ▶

4. In this exercise, you will practice with the Contents, Search, and Favorites tabs in the MSDN Library Visual Studio 6.0 window. **Important Note:** You can complete this exercise only if the MSDN library is installed on your hard drive, or if you have access to the MSDN CD-ROM disc.

   a. Open a new project. First you will practice with the Contents tab. Click Help on Visual Basic's menu bar, then click Contents. You use the Contents tab to display a list of general topics for which Help is available.

   b. If necessary, select Visual Basic Documentation in the Active Subset list box. Click the Plus box next to MSDN Library Visual Studio 6.0, then click the Plus box next to Visual Basic Documentation, and then click Visual Basic Start Page. The appropriate Help screen appears in the Display pane, as shown in Figure 1-22.

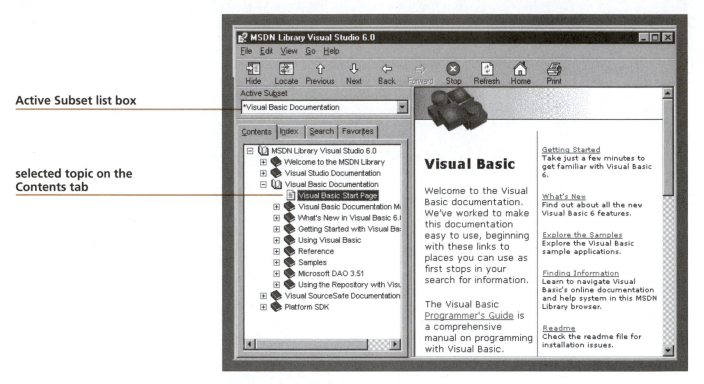

Active Subset list box

selected topic on the Contents tab

Figure 1-22: Visual Basic Start Page Help screen

   c. Close the MSDN Library's window.

   d. Now practice with the Search tab. Click Help on Visual Basic's menu bar, then click Search. You use the Search tab to search for words or phrases that may be contained in the library's Help screens. Type *msdn library* in the Type in the word(s) to search for text box, then click the List Topics button. A list of Help screens that contain either *msdn*, *library*, or *msdn library* displays in the Select topic list box.

   e. Select MSDN Library Help in the Select topic list box, then click the Display button. The MSDN Library Help screen appears in the Display pane, as shown in Figure 1-23.

search words

**selected topic on
the Search tab**

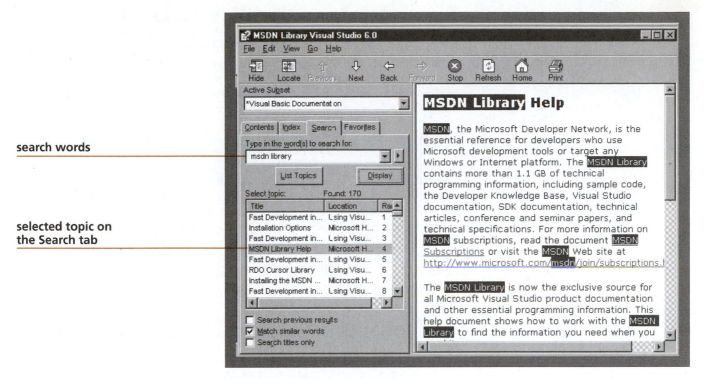

Figure 1-23: MSDN Library Help screen

f. Notice that one or more of the words for which you were searching appear highlighted in the Help screen. Use the MSDN Library Help screen to learn how to display Help screens that contain only the phrase *msdn library*. (*Hint*: Use the Finding Information with Full-Text Search link located on the MSDN Library Help screen.) On a piece of paper, record what you discovered. When you are finished, close the MSDN Library window.

g. Now experiment with the Favorites tab. You can use the Favorites tab to maintain a list of Help screens to which you refer frequently. Write a summary explaining how to use the Favorites tab. (*Hint*: Use the Creating a List of Favorite Topics link located on the MSDN Library Help screen.)

h. Submit your answers to steps f and g.

discovery ▶ 5. In this exercise you will learn about the Align and Make Same Size commands on Visual Basic's Format menu. (If the controls are locked in the form, you will not be able to use the Align and Make Same Size commands on the Format menu; you will need to unlock the controls first. You will learn how to lock and unlock controls in Tutorial 2's Lesson B.)

a. Use Visual Basic's Help menu to display a Help screen on the Format Menu, then display and read the Help screens on the Format menu's Align and Make Same Size commands. **Important Note:** You can complete this step only if the MSDN library is installed on your hard drive, or if you have access to the MSDN CD-ROM disc.

b. Open a new project, if necessary. Place three label controls on the form. Drag one of the label controls to the upper-left corner of the form, drag another to the center of the form, and drag the remaining label control to the lower-right corner of the form.

c. Click one of the label controls, then press and hold down the Ctrl key as you click the remaining two label controls.

Recall from the tutorial that when you select more than one object, the sizing handles for the last object selected appear in a solid color. The sizing handles on the last label control you selected should be a solid color; the sizing handles on the other two label controls should be white with a colored border. The Format menu's Align and Make Same Size commands use the control with the solid-color sizing handles as the reference control when aligning and sizing the selected controls. First practice with the Format menu's Align command. The Format menu's Align command aligns selected objects with each other using the last selected object, the one with the solid-color handles, as the reference. Align the three label controls by their left-most edges.

d. Click Format, point to Align, and then click Lefts. Visual Basic aligns the left border of the first two controls you selected with the left border of the last control you selected.

The Format menu's Make Same Size command makes the selected objects the same height, width, or both height and width. Here again, the size is determined by the last object you select—the object with the solid-color sizing handles.

e. If the label controls on the form are the same size, use their sizing handles to size them differently. Select the three label controls. Click Format, point to Make Same Size, and then click Both. Visual Basic changes the height and width of the first two controls you selected to match the height and width of the last control you selected. Click the form to deselect the label controls.

This exercise was for practice only. You do not need to save this form or project.

- Add an image control, a command button, and a frame control to the form
- Add an ActiveX control to both the toolbox and the form
- Enter code in a Code window
- Explore the Options dialog box
- Print the form, the properties of the objects in the form, and the code
- Make an executable file

Writing Code

Adding an Image Control to the Form

According to the copyright screen you previewed at the beginning of this tutorial, you need to include the Interlocking Software Company logo in your application. You can use either the Image tool or the Picture box tool to add a picture (or icon) to a form. One advantage of the Image tool over the Picture box is that the Image tool requires less of the computer's memory. You will use the Image tool to create an image control for the copyright screen.

To add an image control to the form:

1   Start Visual Basic, if necessary, and make sure your Student Disk is in the appropriate disk drive.

2   Use the Open Project button on the Standard toolbar to open the lbCopy project that you created in Lesson B. Recall that the project file is in the Tut01 folder on your Student Disk. Display the form.

   HELP? You display the form by clicking its name in the Project window, and then clicking the Project window's View Object button.

You will now save the form and the project under a different name so that both the lbCopy form file and the lbCopy project file remain intact. This approach will allow you to practice Lesson C as often as you like.

3   Use both the Save lbCopy.frm As and the Save Project As commands on the File menu to save the form and the project, respectively, as lcCopy. (Recall from Lesson B that you must save the form before you save the project.)

   HELP? If the Save <*filename*)> As command is dimmed in the File menu, either click the form or click the form's name in the Project Explorer window.

   HELP? If this is the second or subsequent time you are practicing this lesson, Visual Basic will display a dialog box that asks if you want to replace the existing file. Click the Yes button.

4   Position the mouse pointer on the **Image** tool 🖾 in the toolbox. After a few seconds a tooltip, which contains the tool's name, appears; in this case the tooltip says Image. If you have trouble distinguishing the tools in the toolbox, you can always display the tool's name by resting the mouse pointer on the tool to display the tooltip.

5   Double-click the **Image** tool 🖾 in the toolbox. An empty rectangular box with sizing handles appears in the center of the form. This is the image control into which you will place the company's logo.

   You place (or load) a picture into an image control by setting the control's **Picture property**.

tip

You can also use either the Open Project command on the File menu or Crtl + O to open an existing project.

6   Click **Picture** in the Properties list, then click the ... (ellipses) button in the Settings box. The Load Picture dialog box appears.

7   Open the Tut01 folder on your Student Disk. A list of filenames appears.

8   Click **Inter** (Inter.bmp) in the list, and then click the **Open** button. The Interlocking Software logo appears in the image control.

You will now give the image control a more meaningful name, and then position the control appropriately in the form. You are giving the image control a more meaningful name because the control will be coded.

tip

The image control shown in Figure 1-24 is an instance of the Visual Basic image class.

To give the image control a more meaningful name, and then position the control in the form:

1   Set the image control's Name property to **imgLogo**. (The "img" identifies the object as an image control.)

2   Set the image control's Left property to **240** and its Top property to **360**. (Recall that you are given the values for the Left and Top properties in order for your screen to match the figure in the book. Instead of setting the Left and Top properties, you could simply drag the control to its proper location.)

3   Click the **imgLogo** control in the form to select it, and then drag the image control's right border to match Figure 1-24.

drag the right border to this position

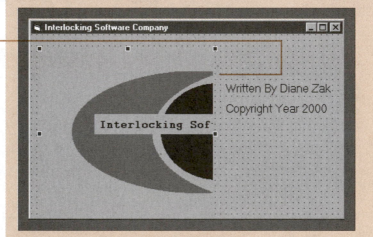

Figure 1-24: Copyright screen with image control added

Notice that the picture in the image control did not shrink along with the control itself. If you want the picture to be sized with the image control, you need to set the control's **Stretch property** to True. Do that now.

4   Set the image control's Stretch property to **True**. The picture in the image control shrinks to fit the current size of the control.

5   Click the **Save Project** button 🖫 to save the form and the project under their current names, lcCopy.

Next you will add an Exit button to the copyright screen.

Adding a Command Button to the Form

Every Windows application should give the user a way to exit the program. Most Windows applications provide either an Exit option on a File menu or an Exit button. As you saw earlier, the copyright application uses an Exit button. You create the Exit button by using the CommandButton tool.

In Windows applications, command buttons perform an immediate action when clicked. The OK and Cancel buttons are examples of command buttons found in many applications. In the copyright screen, the Exit command button will end the application when the button is clicked by the user.

tip

▶ Recall that the copyright screen will serve as a splash screen for each custom application created by Interlocking Software. Splash screens do not typically contain an Exit button; rather, they use a Timer control to remove the splash screen from the screen. You will learn how to include a Timer control in a splash screen in Tutorial 3. For this tutorial, you will use an Exit button.

tip

▶ The command button control shown in Figure 1-25 is an instance of the Visual Basic command button class.

To add a command button control to the form:

1 Double-click the **CommandButton** tool 🔲 in the toolbox. A default-size button appears in the center of the form. The default name and caption of this control is Command1.

You will now set the Name, Caption, and Font properties for this control. You will also move the command button to the top right corner of the screen. Remember that you can position a control on the form either by dragging it or by setting its Left and Top properties.

2 Set the command button's Name property to **cmdExit**. The "cmd" identifies the control as a command button. The "Exit" identifies the purpose of this control.

3 Set the command button's Caption property to **Exit**.

4 Click **Font** in the Properties list. Set the font size to **10** points.

5 Drag the command button to the upper right corner of the form, as shown in Figure 1-25.

command button ─────────────────

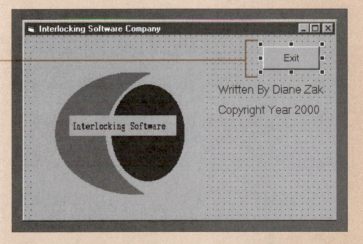

Figure 1-25: Copyright screen with command button

Although the Exit button appears on the screen and its properties are set, you're not done with this control yet, as you'll see in the next section.

Writing Visual Basic Code

Think about the Windows environment for a moment. Did you ever wonder why the OK and Cancel buttons respond the way they do when you click them, or how the Exit option on the File menu knows to close the application? The answer to these questions is very simple: a programmer gave the buttons and menu option explicit instructions on how to respond to the actions of the user. Those actions—such as clicking, double-clicking, and scrolling—are called **events**. The Visual Basic instructions, or **code**, that tells an object how to respond to an event is called an **event procedure**.

At this point, the Exit button in the copyright screen does not know what it is supposed to do; you must tell it what to do by writing an event procedure for it. You write the event procedure in the object's Code window, which is a window you have not yet seen. Each object has its own set of Code windows—one window for each of the events the object can recognize. You open a Code window by double-clicking the object.

You will now open the Code window for the Exit button. Inside the Code window, you will enter instructions that tell the button to end the application when the button is clicked by the user.

To open the Exit button's Code window:

1 Double-click the **Exit** command button on the form. The button's Code window opens.

The event procedure that appears when you open an object's Code window is typically the most commonly used procedure for that object. As Figure 1-26 shows, the most commonly used procedure for a command button is the Click event procedure.

Object box

input area

current event procedure

Procedure box

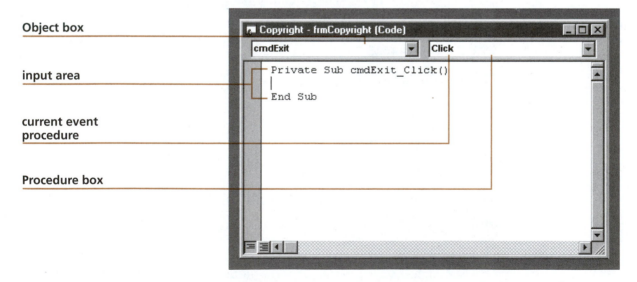

Figure 1-26: Open Code window for the Exit command button

The Visual Basic Code window contains an Object box, a Procedure box, and an input area. The **Object box** performs the same function as the Object box in the Properties window; both allow you to choose either the form or one of the controls on the form. You can also use the Object box to verify the name of a control while you are writing instructions in the Code window.

The **Procedure box** in the Code window lists the event procedures to which the selected object is capable of responding. The Procedure box shows that the current event procedure—the event procedure shown in the input area of the Code window—is Click. You can see what other event procedures an object can recognize by clicking the Procedure box's list arrow. Check out what other event procedures a command button can recognize.

To display the event procedures in the Procedure box:

1   Click the **Procedure box** list arrow located in the Code window. A list of event procedures appears. See Figure 1-27.

tip

If you want to verify which is the Object box and which is the Procedure box, simply rest the mouse pointer on one of the list arrows until a tooltip appears.

Figure 1-27: List of event procedures that a command button can recognize

The scroll bars on the list box indicate that not all of the event procedures are currently displayed. You would need to scroll down the list box to see the remaining event procedures. To change to another event procedure, simply click the one you want in the list.

2   Click **GotFocus** in the Procedure list box. Notice that both the `Private Sub` statement and the Procedure box now show that the GotFocus event procedure is the current one. See Figure 1-28.

current event procedure

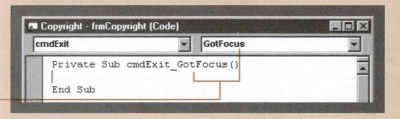

Figure 1-28: Command button's GotFocus event procedure

Because you need to enter the instruction to end the application in the Click event, you will switch back to that procedure.

3   Click the **Procedure box** list arrow to open the list of event procedures. Scroll the list, if necessary, and then click **Click**. The Click event procedure appears. See Figure 1-29.

keywords

control name

current event

Figure 1-29: Click event procedure for the Exit button

You will notice that the input area of the Code window already contains some Visual Basic code (instructions). To help you follow the rules of its language, called **syntax**, Visual Basic provides you with a **code template** for every event procedure. The code template begins with the two keywords: `Private Sub`. A **keyword** is a word that has a special meaning in a programming language. The **Private** keyword tells Visual Basic that the event procedure can be used only within the form in which it is defined; it can't be used by any other form in the application. The **Sub** keyword is an abbreviation of the term **subprocedure**, which, in programming terminology, refers to a block of code that performs a specific task. Following the `Sub` keyword is the name of the control (cmdExit), an underscore (_), the name of the current event (Click), and parentheses. The code template ends with the keywords `End Sub`. You must enter your Visual Basic instructions between the `Private Sub` and `End Sub` lines. The instructions in the Code window tell the object (cmdExit) how to respond to the current event (Click).

If you are using a color monitor, notice that the keywords `Private Sub` and `End Sub` appear in a different color from both the object's name and the word `Click`. Visual Basic displays keywords in a different color to help you quickly identify these elements in the Code window. In this case, the color coding helps you easily locate the beginning and end of the event procedure. Now enter the instruction that will tell the Exit button to end the application when clicked by the user.

The insertion point located in the input area of the Code window means that Visual Basic is waiting for you to type something in the window. In this case you want to instruct the Exit button to end the application whenever the button is clicked. For this you will use the **End statement**, which has a very specific meaning in Visual Basic; it tells Visual Basic to terminate the current application. You'll indent the code in the Code window to make the instructions easier to read.

tip

In Tutorials 1 through 4, you will use the `End` statement to end the simple applications that you create. However, beginning in Tutorial 5, you will use the `Unload` statement, rather than the `End` statement. The `Unload` statement is typically used in applications that contain multiple forms and those that require specific tasks to be performed before the application ends.

To enter the code into the open Code window for the Click event procedure, then save and run the application:

1 Press the **Tab** key to indent the line, type **end** in the Code window, and then press the **Enter** key. See Figure 1-30.

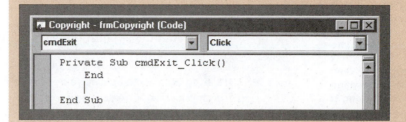

Figure 1-30: End statement entered in the Exit button's Click event procedure

When the user clicks the Exit button, Visual Basic reads and processes the instructions entered in the Click event procedure's Code window. It is probably no surprise to you that Visual Basic processes the instructions, one after another, in the order in which the instructions are entered in the Code window. In programming, this is referred to as **sequential processing** or as the **sequence structure**. (You will learn about two other programming structures, selection and repetition, in future tutorials.) You're finished with the Code window, so you can close it.

2 Click the Code window's **Close** button ☒ to close the Code window.

3 Click the **Save Project** button 🖫 to save the form and the project.

Now that the files are saved, you can run the project to see if it is working correctly.

4 Click the **Start** button ▶ on the Standard toolbar. The copyright screen appears. See Figure 1-31.

tip

It is a good practice to save both the form and project before running an application.

Minimize button

Maximize button

Close button

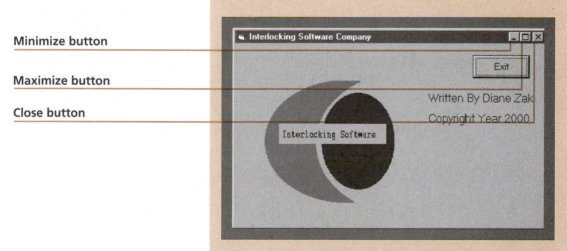

Figure 1-31: Copyright screen with Minimize, Maximize, and Close buttons

Notice that the copyright form's title bar contains a Minimize button ▭, a Maximize button ▭, and a Close button ☒. Recall that the copyright screen will be used as a splash screen for the custom applications created by Interlocking Software. As a general rule, the user is not typically allowed to change the size of a splash screen, nor is the user allowed to use the Close button to close a splash screen. You can fix this problem by changing the form's BorderStyle property, which you will do in the next section. First, however, see if the Exit button ends the application when it is clicked.

5   Click the **Exit** button.

> **HELP?** If an error message appears on the screen, click the OK button, then stop the application. Correct the error in the open Code window, then close the Code window. Save and run the application, then try clicking the Exit button again.

Now learn how to use the BorderStyle property.

Setting the BorderStyle Property

The **BorderStyle property** determines the border style of an object. The default BorderStyle for a form is 2-Sizable, which means that the form can be minimized, maximized, or closed while the application is running; the user can also drag the form's borders to change the form's size during run time. If you want to prevent the user both from sizing the user interface and from exiting using the Close button, as you do when creating a splash screen, you can reset the form's BorderStyle property to 0-None. Changing the BorderStyle property to 0-None removes the form's border, its title bar, and its Minimize, Maximize, and Close buttons.

To change the form's BorderStyle property, then save and run the project:

1   Click the **form's title bar** to select the form. Click **BorderStyle** in the Properties list. Set the BorderStyle property to **0-None**.

2   Click the **Save Project** button ▦, and then click the **Start** button ▶. Notice that the 0-None BorderStyle setting removes the form's border, its title bar, and its border elements (Minimize, Maximize, and Close buttons) when you run the application. In the next section, you can make this interface more professional-looking by adding a frame control to the form.

3   Click the **Exit** button to end the application. Visual Basic returns to the design screen.

Now add a frame control to the form.

Adding a Frame Control to a Form

You use the Frame tool to draw a frame control. A frame control serves as a container for other controls. You can use a frame control to visually separate related controls from other controls on the form. In the copyright form, you will use the frame control to visually separate the controls from the form itself.

When you place controls inside a frame, Visual Basic treats the controls and the frame as one unit; moving the frame also moves all of the controls inside the frame, and deleting the frame also deletes all of the controls contained inside it.

You label a frame control by setting its Caption property. Labeling a frame control is optional.

You will now add a frame control to the copyright form, then place the form's existing controls in the frame.

To add a frame control to the form, then place the existing controls in the frame:

1   Click the form to select it, then double-click the **Frame** tool 🔲 in the toolbox. The Frame1 control appears on the form. (This control will not be coded or referred to in code, so you do not need to change its name from the default value, Frame1.)

2   Set the Frame1 control's Caption property to **Click our logo** and press the **Enter** key. Set its Font style to **Bold**.

3   Click the **form** to select it. Drag the form's bottom border and its right border until the form is approximately the size shown in Figure 1-32. Also drag the Frame1 control to the lower-right corner of the form, as shown in the figure.

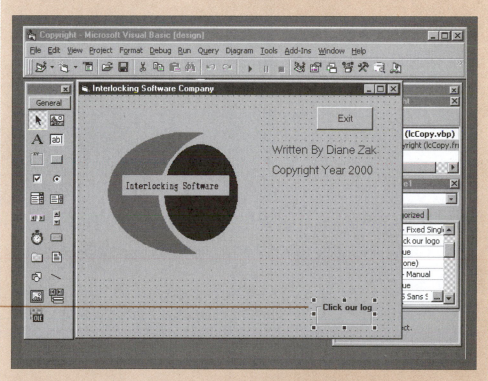

frame control

Figure 1-32: Screen showing resized form and location of frame control

The objects you add to a form belong to the form itself. Therefore, if you want to put the copyright form's existing controls into the Frame1 control, you will need to detach the existing controls from the form first. In Windows terminology, you will cut the controls from the form; that process will place the controls on the clipboard. You will then select the frame control, and then paste the controls from the clipboard into the frame control. Keep in mind that you can't just *drag* existing controls into a frame control; you must cut them from the form first, then paste them into the frame control.

Before cutting controls from the form, you should always save the form. Then, if something goes wrong with the cut operation, you can simply reopen the project.

4   Click the **Save Project** button ▣ to save the application.

5   Click the **imgLogo** image control to select it, then press and hold down the **Ctrl** key as you click the **lblAuthor**, **lblYear**, and **cmdExit** controls. Sizing handles appear around the four controls.

6   Click **Edit** on the menu bar, and then click **Cut** to cut the selected controls from the form. Visual Basic removes the selected controls from the form and places them on the clipboard. Only the frame control remains in the form.

7   Move and size the Frame1 control as shown in Figure 1-33.

tip

You can also use Ctrl + x to cut the selected controls from the form. Then, after selecting the frame control, you can use Ctrl + v to paste the controls into the frame.

frame control —————

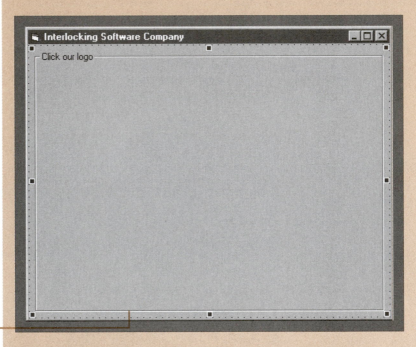

Figure 1-33: Screen showing correct location and size of Frame1 control

8   The Frame1 control should still be selected. Click **Edit** on the menu bar, and then click **Paste** to paste the controls from the clipboard into the frame.

9   Place the mouse pointer ▷ on one of the selected controls, then drag the controls further into the frame control, as shown in Figure 1-34.

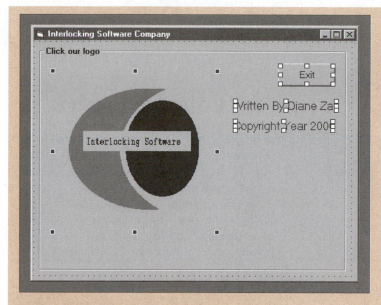

Figure 1-34: Controls positioned in the frame control

HELP? If you inadvertently deselected the controls, simply click one of the controls, then press and hold down the Ctrl key as you click the other controls.

10 Click the **Frame1** control to select it, and then click **Font** in the Properties list. Set the Frame1 control's Font style to **Bold Italic** and set its Font size to **12**.

11 Save and **run** the application. The copyright screen appears as shown in Figure 1-35.

Figure 1-35: Copyright screen showing controls within the frame

12 Click the **Exit** button to end the application.

In the next section you will learn how to hide and display the controls in an interface. In the current application, you will hide the lblAuthor and lblYear controls when the copyright screen first appears; then, when the user clicks the imgLogo image control, you will display both label controls.

Hiding and Displaying Controls

An object's **Visible property** determines whether an object is visible or hidden at run time. The property has two predefined settings: the Boolean values True and False. If the property is set to True, the object appears during run time; if the property is set to False, the object is hidden from view during run time.

In this application, you will hide the lblAuthor and lblYear label controls when the copyright screen first appears; you will display both label controls when the user clicks the imgLogo image control. You can hide the label controls when the interface first appears by setting their Visible property to False in the Properties window.

> **To hide the label controls when the interface first appears:**
>
> **1** Select both the **lblAuthor** label control and the **lblYear** label control. Click **Visible** in the Properties list. Set the Visible property to **False**.
>
> **2** **Save** and **run** the application. Notice that neither label control appears in the interface.
>
> **3** Click the **Exit** button to end the application.

Recall that the application should display both label controls when the user clicks the imgLogo image control. You can display the label controls by setting their Visible property to True. When programming in an object-oriented/event-driven language such as Visual Basic, you must determine not only the proper instructions to get the objects to perform the way you want, but also *where* in the application to enter those instructions. In other words, you must specify at what point in the application you want those instructions processed. You must decide on the object that should perform the instructions and also on which of the object's event procedures the instructions should be performed. In this case you want the label controls to appear when the user clicks the imgLogo image control, so you will need to enter the instructions that set their Visible property in the image control's Click event procedure. Before doing so, however, you will display a Help screen on the Visible property.

> **To display the Visible property's Help screen:**
>
> **1** Click the **lblAuthor** control, then click **Visible** in the Properties list.
>
> **2** If the MSDN library is installed on your computer, or if you have access to the MSDN CD-ROM disc, then press the **F1** key. The Visible property's Help screen appears in the MSDN Library window. Click the **Hide** button ⊞ in the toolbar, then maximize the window. See Figure 1-36.

Syntax section

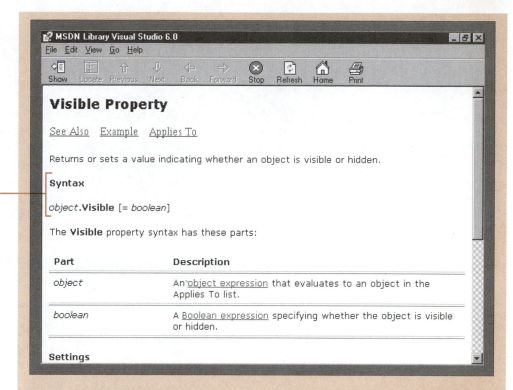

Figure 1-36: Visible property's maximized Help screen

The Visible property stores a value that indicates whether an object is visible or hidden. Notice the syntax section of the Help window. In programming terminology, the word **syntax** refers to the rules of the programming language. The Visible property's syntax section, for example, shows *object*.**Visible** [= *boolean*]. In the syntax, items appearing in square brackets ([ ]) are optional parts of the instruction. Words in bold, however, are required. Items in *italics* indicate where the programmer must supply information pertaining to the current application. In the Visible property's syntax, *object* is the name of the object that you want to either hide or display, and *boolean* is either the Boolean value True or the Boolean value False. Recall that if the property is set to True, the object appears during run time; if the property is set to False, the object is hidden from view during run time. You will learn more about how to read and apply Visual Basic's syntax in future tutorials. For now, just notice how the instructions you will type into the image control's Click event follow the Visible property's syntax.

3 Scroll the Help screen and read its contents. When you are finished, click the **Restore** button 🔲, then click the **Show** button 🔲, and then close the MSDN Library window.

You will now code the imgLogo control's Click event so that it displays both label controls when the image control is clicked.

To code the image control's Click event:

1 Double-click the **imgLogo** control to open its Code window. The image control's Click event procedure appears.

The Visual Basic instruction you will use to display the lblAuthor control is `lblAuthor.Visible = True`; the instruction to display the lblYear control is `lblYear.Visible = True`. These two instructions are referred to as assignment statements because they assign a value to the property of an object. (You will learn more about assignment statements in Tutorial 2.) Notice that you can set the value of a property through code.

2 Press the **Tab** key. Type **lblauthor** and then type a . (period). A listing of the lblAuthor control's properties and methods appears, as shown in Figure 1-37. (A method is a predefined procedure. You will learn about methods in Tutorial 2.)

items appear in alphabetical order

scroll bar

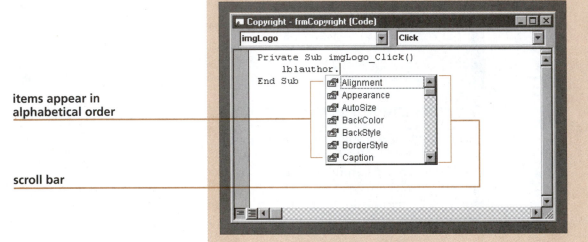

Figure 1-37: Listing of the lblAuthor control's properties and methods

HELP? If the listing does not appear, click Tools on the menu bar, then click Options. Click the Editor tab's Auto List Members check box to select it, and then click the OK button. Delete the . (period) that appears after lblauthor in the Code window, and then type the . (period) again.

When entering a Visual Basic instruction in a Code window, you can either type the complete instruction yourself—in this case, you could type `lblAuthor.Visible = True`—or you can use the property and method listing to assist you in entering the instruction.

Notice that the properties and methods shown in the list are in alphabetical order. Also notice that the list contains a scroll bar.

3 Scroll the list until you see the Visible property, and then click **Visible** in the list.

HELP? If you inadvertently closed the list, delete the . (period) that appears after lblauthor in the Code window, then type the . (period) again.

4 Press the **Tab** key. Notice that the Tab key enters the Visible property at the current location of the insertion point in the Code window.

5 Type = (an equals sign). A listing of the valid settings for the Visible property appears—in this case, False and True appear.

6 Click **True** in the list, and then press the **Tab** key to enter True in the Code window.

7 Press the **Enter** key both to enter the instruction and to move the insertion point to the next line in the Code window.

Notice that Visual Basic keeps the indentation for the next line. If you want to remove the indentation, you simply press the Backspace key. In this case, however, you want to keep the indentation. Now enter the lblYear.Visible = True instruction.

8 Type **lblyear** and a . (period). The listing of properties and methods for the lblYear control appears.

9 This time, instead of scrolling the list until you locate the Visible property, type the letter v. (Don't type the period, just the letter v.) When you type the letter v, Visual Basic highlights, automatically, the first property in the list that begins with the letter v—in this case, Visual Basic highlights the Visible property in the list.

10 Press the **Tab** key to enter the Visible property in the Code window, and then type = (an equals sign). When the listing of valid settings for the Visible property appears, type **t** and press the **Tab** key. (When you type the letter t, Visual Basic highlights the True entry in the list. The Tab key then enters True in the Code window.)

11 Press the **Enter** key both to enter the instruction in the Code window and to move the insertion point to the next line. The completed Code window is shown in Figure 1-38.

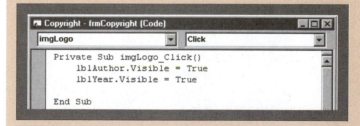

Figure 1-38: Completed Code window for the imgLogo control's Click event

12 Close the Code window, and then **save** and **run** the application. When the copyright screen appears, both label controls are hidden. Click the **Interlocking Software logo** (the image control). The author's name and copyright year appear on the screen.

> **HELP?** If an error message appears on the screen, click the OK button, then stop the application. Correct the error in the open code window, then repeat step 12.
>
> **13** Click the **Exit** button to end the application.

In the remaining tutorials, when you are told to enter an instruction in a Code window, you will always be shown the complete instruction to enter. You can enter the instruction either by typing it yourself or by using the listings that appear at various times in the Code window. If you prefer to enter the instructions yourself, you can use the Options option on the Tools menu to tell Visual Basic not to display the listings.

The Options Dialog Box

The Options option on the Tools menu displays the Options dialog box. You use the Options dialog box to specify the characteristics of your Visual Basic programming environment. View some of these options now.

> To open the Options dialog box:
>
> **1** Click **Tools** on the menu bar, then click **Options**. The Options dialog box appears. The first tab in the dialog box is the Editor tab, as shown in Figure 1-39.

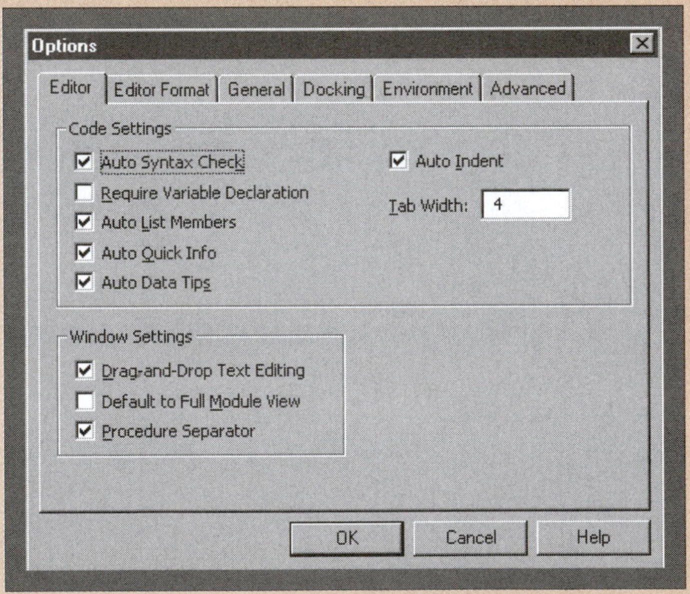

Figure 1-39: Editor tab in the Options dialog box

HELP? Don't be concerned if you have different options selected on your Editor tab.

2   If the MSDN library is installed on your computer, or if you have access to the MSDN CD-ROM disc, then click the **Help** button on the Editor tab to display the Editor Tab (Options Dialog Box) Help screen. Read the Help screen to learn about the various settings available on the Editor tab. Specifically, notice that the Auto List Members setting controls whether Visual Basic displays a listing of information that could be used to logically complete a statement at the location of the insertion point. You would deselect this option if you wanted to stop the display of this listing.

3   Close the MSDN Library window.

Now view the settings on the Editor Format tab.

4   Click the **Editor Format** tab. If the MSDN library is installed on your computer, or if you have access to the MSDN CD-ROM disc, then click the **Help** button on the Editor Format tab to display the Editor Format Tab (Options Dialog Box) Help screen. Read the Help screen to learn about the various settings available on the Editor Format tab. Notice that you can use the settings on this tab to change the color, font type, and font size of the code displayed in the Code window.

5   Close the MSDN Library window, then close the Options dialog box.

The final modification you will make to the copyright screen is to add a Scroller control to the interface.

Adding a Scroller Control to the Form

Before Visual Basic 5.0, all Visual Basic controls had to be created using other programming languages, such as C or C++. Visual Basic 5.0, and now Visual Basic 6.0, however, allow you to use Visual Basic to create your own controls. The controls you create, referred to as ActiveX controls because they are based on Microsoft's ActiveX technology, can be used in any program that supports ActiveX. For example, you can include an ActiveX control in a Visual Basic application, in a Microsoft Word document, in a Microsoft Excel spreadsheet, or in a Microsoft Access database. You can also include an ActiveX control in a Web page on either the Internet or your company's intranet.

In this lesson you will use an ActiveX control named Scroller that will allow you to scroll the Interlocking Software company's name across the bottom of the interface. (You will learn how to use Visual Basic to create your own ActiveX control in the Creating Your Own ActiveX Control appendix.) Before you can place a control on a form, the tool that creates the control must be available in Visual Basic's toolbox.

To add a tool to Visual Basic's toolbox:

1   Click **Project** on the menu bar, then click **Add User Control**. See Figure 1-40.

Figure 1-40: Add User Control dialog box

2   Click the **Existing** tab. If necessary, open the Tut01 folder on your Student Disk. Click **Scroller** (Scroller.ctl) in the list of filenames, then click the **Open** button. The Scroller tool appears in Visual Basic's toolbox. Place the mouse pointer on the Scroller control in the toolbox. See Figure 1-41.

tooltip appears when you point to the Scroller control

Figure 1-41: The Scroller tool shown in the toolbox

Because you want the scroller control to be a part of the frame control, rather than a part of the form itself, you will use another method of placing a control in the interface. Instead of double-clicking the tool in the toolbox, which will attach the control to the form, you will click the tool in the toolbox, place the mouse pointer inside the frame control, then drag until the scroller control is the desired size.

3   Click the **Scroller** tool in the toolbox. The tool appears indented in the tool-box. When you move the mouse pointer onto the frame control, it becomes a crosshair $+$. Position the crosshair $+$ as shown in Figure 1-42.

position crosshair here

Figure 1-42: Position of crosshair within the frame control

4   Drag the mouse down and to the right. When the scroller control is about the same size shown in Figure 1-43, release the mouse button.

tip

The Scroller control shown in Figure 1-43 is an instance of the Scroller class.

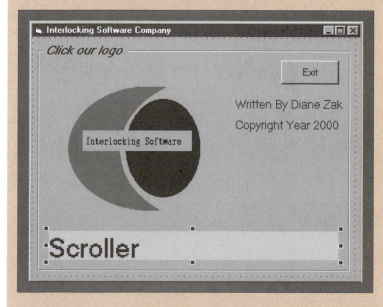

Figure 1-43: Scroller control drawn in the frame control

5   If necessary, display the Properties window. Notice that the name Visual Basic assigns to the first scroller control added to an interface is Scroller1.

6   Click the **Save Project** button 🖫 to save the application.

You will now set two of the scroller control's properties, Caption and BackColor. The Caption property controls the text that scrolls across the control; you will change this property to Interlocking Software. The BackColor property controls the background color of the control; you will change the BackColor property to red.

To set the scroller control's Caption and BackColor properties:

1   Click the **Scroller1** control to select it. Set the control's Caption property to **Interlocking Software**, then set its BackColor property to **red**.

2   **Save** and **run** the application. The name of the company, Interlocking Software, scrolls across the scroller control. Click the **Interlocking Software logo**. The author's name and copyright year appear in the interface. Click the **Exit** button to end the application. Visual Basic returns to the design screen.

tip

You can change the speed at which the text in the scroller control is scrolling by changing the control's Interval property.

Your first application is finally complete. Notice that, using Visual Basic, you can create an impressive application with just one form, a few controls, and a few lines of code. In the next section you will learn how you can display a listing of an application's code.

Changing the Code Window Display

Recall that when you double-click an object, its Code window opens and displays the most commonly used event procedure for that object. For example, when you open a command button's Code window, its Click event procedure appears because that is the most common event performed on a command button. Also recall that you can use either the Code window's Object box or its Procedure box to switch to another Code window. It is sometimes helpful to see all of the application's code in a single listing. You will learn how to do that now.

To view an application's code as a single listing:

1   Double-click the **Exit** button to open its Code window. The Exit button's Click event procedure appears.

2   In the lower-left corner of the Code window, you will find two buttons, the Procedure View button ▣ and the Full Module View button ▦. Place the mouse pointer on the ▣ button, which is currently indented. The Procedure View tooltip appears.

When the Procedure View button ▣ is selected, each procedure appears in its own Code window.

3   Place the mouse pointer on the ▦ button in the Code window. The Full Module View tooltip appears.

When the Full Module View button ▦ is selected, the application's code appears as a single listing. View that now.

4   Click the **Full Module View** button ▤ in the Code window, then maximize the Code window. The application's code appears as shown in Figure 1-44.

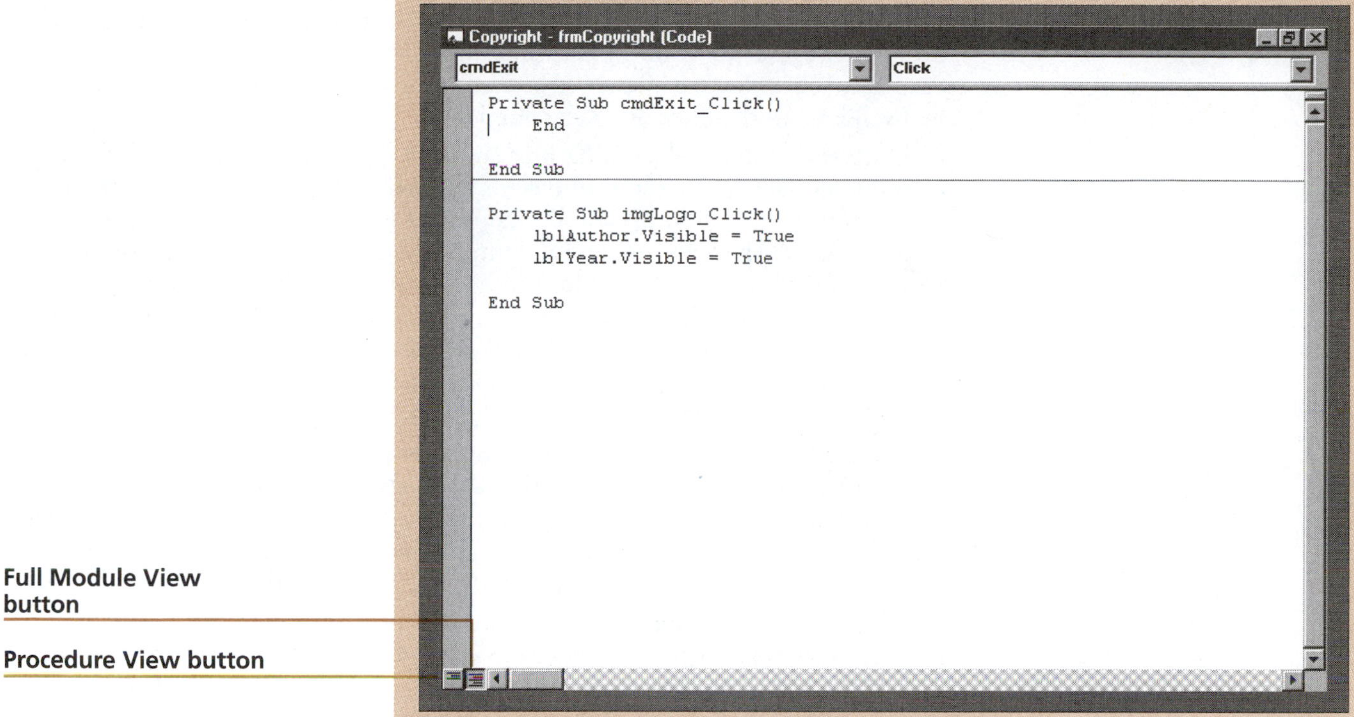

Full Module View
button

Procedure View button

Figure 1-44: Code shown in the full module view

HELP? Don't be concerned if your listing includes extra blank lines or a line that says `Option Explicit`. If you'd like, you can use the Delete key on your keyboard to delete any extra blank lines.

5   Click the **Procedure View** button ▤ in the Code window to return to that view, then close the Code window.

Before ending this lesson you will learn how to print the application and how to make the application into an executable (.exe) file that can be run directly from Windows, like the applications you previously ran in the Overview and at the beginning of this tutorial.

Printing a Visual Basic Application

You should always print a copy of the form, the properties of the application's objects, and the code you wrote. This information, called **documentation**, will help you understand and maintain the application in the future.

To print the documentation for the current application:

1   Click **File** on the menu bar, then click **Print**. The Print - lcCopy.vbp dialog box appears.

The Print What section contains three check boxes: Form Image, Code, and Form As Text. When you select the Form Image check box, Visual Basic prints a copy of the form. When you select the Code check box, Visual Basic prints the application's code. When the Form As Text check box is selected, Visual Basic prints the properties of the application's objects. You can select one or more of the Print What check boxes. Notice that the Code check box is selected, automatically, when the Print dialog box appears.

The Range section of the dialog box contains three option buttons: Selection, Current Module, and Current Project. Only one option button can be selected at a time. The Selection option allows you to print only the selected text in a Code window. The Selection option button is dimmed currently because there is no text selected in a Code window. The Current Module option prints what is selected in the Print What section for the current form. The Current Project option prints what is selected in the Print What section for the entire project; you would select this option, for example, when printing the form, properties, and/or code for a project that contains more than one form.

You will print a copy of the copyright form, as well as the application's properties and its code. The copyright application contains only one form, so you will not need to select a different option in the Range section; the Current Module selection is the appropriate one to use. You will, however, need to select the Form Image and Form As Text check boxes in the Print What section.

2   The Code check box is already selected, so you need simply to click both the **Form Image** check box and the **Form As Text** check box. Check marks should appear next to each of the three selections in the Print What section.

3   If your computer is connected to a printer, click the **OK** button to begin printing; otherwise, click the **Cancel** button. If you clicked the OK button, Visual Basic prints the form, the application's properties, and the application's code.

HELP? If the labels in the printout do not appear the same as on the screen, you may need to select a different font for the labels. Select the labels in the interface, then use the Font property to change the font; try the Arial font.

The final task in this lesson is to make the copyright screen into an executable (.exe) file that can be run directly from Windows. (Recall that the Monthly Payment application in the Overview, and the copyright screen you previewed in this tutorial, were run directly from Windows.)

Making an Executable (.exe) File

In the Overview you learned that high-level languages require either an interpreter or a compiler to convert the English-like instructions into machine code—the 0s and 1s the computer can understand. Recall that both interpreters and compilers are separate programs. An interpreter translates the high-level instructions into machine code, line by line, as the program is executing. A compiler, on the other hand, translates the entire program into machine code before executing the program.

Visual Basic 6.0 uses both an interpreter and a compiler. When you enter an instruction in a Code window, Visual Basic's interpreter checks the instruction for both syntax and spelling errors. If the interpreter encounters an error, it highlights the error in the Code window. If the interpreter does not find any errors in the code, Visual Basic's compiler partially compiles the code. As a result of this, when you run your application, there is only a brief delay before your application begins. If the compiler finds an error in the code, it highlights the error in the Code window. You can then fix the error and continue compiling without having to start over.

You can use the File menu's Make *<projectname.exe>* command to save the compiled code in a separate file that can then be run outside of Visual Basic, on any computer system that is running Microsoft Windows. (The .exe extension on the filename stands for "executable.") Whenever you want to run your application, you simply tell the computer to run the .exe file, which contains the machine code version of your application.

If you are distributing your application to a user, you will need to give the user a copy of the .exe file and a copy of the Visual Basic run time file (msvbvm60.dll). The msvbvm60.dll file, which is located in the Windows\System folder, comes with Visual Basic, and Microsoft allows you to distribute the file with your applications without violating any licensing agreement. Depending on your application, you may also need to give the user additional files, such as data files, custom control (.ocx) files, and other .dll files. It is strongly suggested that you use Visual Basic's Package and Deployment Wizard, which comes with Visual Basic, to create the distribution disks for your application's users.

To make an executable (.exe) file and then run it from Windows:

1 Use the form's title bar to drag the form to the center of the screen. (In Tutorial 3 you will learn how to use code to center a form on a screen.) Click **File**, then click **Make lcCopy.exe**. The Make Project dialog box appears with lcCopy.exe entered in the File name text box. If necessary, open the Tut01 folder on your Student Disk.

2 Click the **OK** button. Visual Basic's compiler translates your application into machine code, which it saves in the lcCopy.exe file on your Student Disk.

   HELP? If this is the second or subsequent time you are practicing this lesson, Visual Basic will display a dialog box that asks if you want to replace the existing file. Click the Yes button.

You will now save the project and exit Visual Basic before running the lcCopy.exe file from Windows.

3 Click the **Save Project** button ▣ to save the project

4 Exit Visual Basic.

5 Click the **Start** button on the Windows 95 taskbar, then click **Run**. Click the **Browse** button in the Run dialog box, then open the Tut01 folder on your Student Disk. Click **lcCopy** (lcCopy.exe) in the list of filenames, then click the **Open** button. When the Run dialog box appears again, click the **OK** button. The copyright screen appears.

6 Click the **Interlocking Software logo**. The author's name and copyright year appear in the interface.

7 Click the **Exit** button to end the application.

Now you can either exit Visual Basic and take a break, complete the end-of-lesson questions and exercises, or continue to the Debugging section. The Debugging section may contain information that will help you to complete the end-of-lesson exercises. (If necessary, remember to redisplay the Windows 95 taskbar.)

S U M M A R Y

To open an object's Code window:

■   Double-click the object whose Code window you want to open.

To close an object's Code window:

■   Click the Code window's Close button ☒.

To print the form image, the properties of the objects, and the code:

■   Click File, then click Print.
■   Select the Form Image check box to print the form. Select the Form As Text check box to print the properties of the objects. Select the Code check box to print the contents of the Code windows.
■   Click the OK button to start printing.

To specify the range to print:

■   Click File, then click Print.
■   Select the Selection option to print only the text selected in a Code window. If no text is selected in a Code window, the Selection option button will be dimmed.
■   Select the Current Module option to print the form, properties, and/or code for the current form.
■   Select the Current Project option to print the form, properties, and/or code for the entire project.

To make an executable (.exe) file:

■   Click File, then click Make <*projectname*.exe>. The Make Project dialog box opens.
■   If necessary, enter a filename and select the appropriate disk drive and folder.
■   Click the OK button.

To display a picture in an image control:

■   Set the image control's Picture property. You may also need to set the image control's Stretch property.

To add a user control's tool to Visual Basic's toolbox:

■   Click Project on the menu bar, then click Add User Control.

To place an existing control inside a frame:

■   Cut the existing control from the form, then select the frame, and then paste the control inside the frame.

To draw a control on either a form or a frame control:

■   Click (do not double-click) the appropriate tool in the toolbox. Position the crosshair + on the form or inside the frame, then drag until the control is the desired size.

To specify the characteristics of your Visual Basic programming environment:

■   Use the Options option on the Tools menu.

To change the display of code in the Code window:

■ Open any Code window. In the lower-left corner of the Code window, you will find two buttons: Procedure View ▦ and Full Module View ▤. When the Procedure View button ▦ is selected, each procedure appears in its own Code window. When the Full Module View button ▤ is selected, the application's code appears as a single listing.

To hide/display an object:

■ To hide an object, set the object's Visible property to False.
■ To display an object, set its Visible property to True.

To prevent a user from sizing, minimizing, maximizing, and closing a form:

■ Set the form's BorderStyle property to 0-None.

To allow the user to end a running application:

■ One way of allowing the user to end a running application is to include the End statement in the Click event procedure of a command button.

Q U E S T I O N S

1. You display a picture in an image control by setting the control's _____ property.
    a. ControlImage
    b. Icon
    c. Image
    d. Load
    e. Picture

2. The _____ instruction tells Visual Basic to end an application.
    a. Done
    b. End
    c. Finish
    d. Stop
    e. Timer

3. Printing the _____ will print the properties of the application's objects.
    a. Code
    b. Form As Text
    c. Form Image
    d. Properties
    e. Text

4. You tell an object what you want it to do by entering instructions in the object's _____ window.
    a. Code
    b. Form
    c. Instruction
    d. Main
    e. Text

5. Actions such as clicking, double-clicking, and scrolling are called _____ .
    a. episodes
    b. events
    c. happenings
    d. procedures

6. The Visual Basic instructions that tell an object how to respond to an event are called _____.
   a. action procedures
   b. code procedures
   c. event procedures
   d. object procedures
   e. text procedures

7. The rules of a programming language are called its _____.
   a. code
   b. events procedures
   c. guidelines
   d. regulations
   e. syntax

8. A(n) _____ is a word that has a special meaning in a programming language.
   a. code word
   b. command
   c. event
   d. key
   e. keyword

9. To prevent the user from sizing, closing, maximizing, and minimizing a form, set the form's _____ property to 0-None.
   a. BorderStyle
   b. ButtonStyle
   c. ElementStyle
   d. TitleBar
   e. TitleStyle

10. To print the code selected currently in a Code window, select the _____ option in the Print dialog box's Range section.
    a. Current Module
    b. Current Project
    c. Entry
    d. Selected
    e. Selection

11. To print the current form's image, select the _____ option in the Print dialog box's Range section.
    a. Current Module
    b. Current Project
    c. Entry
    d. Selected
    e. Selection

12. To print the properties of the objects in the current form, select the _____ check box in the Print dialog box's Print What section.
    a. Code
    b. Form
    c. Form As Text
    d. Form Image
    e. Picture

13. Explain how to place an existing control into a frame.

14. Explain how to draw a control on either a form or inside a frame.

15. Differentiate between the Code window's Procedure View button and its Full Module View button.

16. Explain how to open an object's Code window.

17. Write a one-sentence definition of an event procedure.

18. Explain the purpose of the Code window's Object box and its Procedure box.

19. Write a one-sentence definition of syntax.

20. Explain the purpose of the Make *<projectname*.exe> command. Why would you want to use it?

E X E R C I S E S

1. In this exercise, you will add a label control, a command button, and an image control to a form. You will also change the properties of the form and its objects. You will also code two event procedures.

   a. If necessary, start Visual Basic and open a new project. Your Student Disk should be in the appropriate disk drive.

   b. Name the project Shelter. Save the form and the project as lc1Done in the Tut01 folder on your Student Disk. Remember to save the form *before* saving the project.

   c. Set the following properties for the form:

Caption:	Peoria Animal Shelter
BackColor:	white
Name:	frmAnimal

   d. Add a label control to the form. Set the following properties for the label control:

Caption:	Welcome to the Peoria Animal Shelter
Name:	lblTitle
Visible:	False
Font:	12 points, bold
AutoSize:	True

   e. Drag the lblTitle control to the top, center of the form.

   f. Add an image control to the form. Set the following properties for the image control:

Name:	imgLogo
Picture:	Set the Picture property to the logo (logo.bmp) file, which is located in the Tut01 folder on your Student Disk
Stretch:	True

   g. Drag the image control to the center of the form. Make the image control larger than its current size.

   h. Add a frame control to the form. Change the following properties of the frame control:

Caption:	Click the logo
Font:	12 points

   i. Cut the label control and the image control from the form. Size the frame control so that it fills almost the entire form. Select the frame, then paste the label and image controls from the clipboard into the frame. Position the controls within the frame. Resize the form if necessary.

   j. Draw a command button in the frame. Drag the command button to the lower-right corner of the frame.

k. Set the following properties for the command button:

Name: cmdExit
Caption: Exit
Font: 12 points

l. Open the command button's Click event procedure. Enter the End instruction, then close the Code window.

m. Code the imgLogo control so that it displays the lblTitle control when the image control is clicked.

n. Save and run the application. Click the image control, then use the Exit button to end the application.

o. Make an executable file for the project. Name the executable file lclDone, and save it in the Tut01 folder.

p. Print the form, properties, and code.

Exercises 2 through 10 are Discovery Exercises, which allow you to both "discover" the solutions to problems on your own and experiment with material that is not covered in the tutorial.

discovery ▶   2.   In this exercise, you will design your own user interface.

a. If necessary, start Visual Basic and open a new project. Your Student Disk should be in the appropriate disk drive.

b. Save the form and the project as lc2Done in the Tut01 folder on your Student Disk.

c. Design your own user interface according to the following specifications:

1) Be sure to include an Exit button that will end the application.

2) Use label controls, image controls, and frame controls.

3) You can either set the image control(s) Picture property to the Interlocking picture you used in the tutorial, or you can use one of Visual Basic's icons. The Visual Basic icons are typically located in the Program Files\Microsoft Visual Studio\Common\Graphics\Icons folder on either the local hard drive or on the network drive. (Verify the location of the icon files with your instructor.)

4) Be sure to name the objects and the project appropriately.

5) Experiment with color and font types, styles, and sizes.

d. Add the Scroller tool to the toolbox, and then place a scroller control on the interface. Change the Caption property appropriately.

e. Save and run the application.

f. Make an executable file for the application, then print the form, properties, and code.

discovery ▶   3.   In this exercise, you will experiment with image controls and command buttons.

a. If necessary, start Visual Basic and open a new project. Your Student Disk should be in the appropriate disk drive.

b. Save the form and the project as lc3Done in the Tut01 folder on your Student Disk. Remember to save the form *before* saving the project.

c. Add an image control and three command buttons to a form. The captions for the three command buttons should be On, Off, and Exit.

d. Name the project, the form, and the four controls appropriately.

e. Set the image control's Picture property to the Interlocking picture you used in the tutorial.

f. Make the image control smaller than its current size. The picture should size along with the control.

g. In the Exit button, enter the command to end the application.

h. In the On button's Click event procedure, include an instruction to display the image control. In the Off button's Click event procedure, include an instruction to hide the image control.

i. Save and run the application. Use the Off button to hide the image control, then use the On button to display the image control. Lastly, use the Exit button to end the application. If necessary, correct any errors and repeat this step again.

j. Print the properties and the code.

discovery ▶ 4. In this exercise you will experiment with Visual Basic's Package and Deployment Wizard. **Important Note:** You must have saved and compiled the project before you can run this wizard.

a. Copy the lc1Done files, which you created in Lesson C's Exercise 1, to the hard drive.

b. Click the Start button, point to Programs, point to Microsoft Visual Basic 6.0, point to Microsoft Visual Basic 6.0 Tools, then click Package and Deployment Wizard. The Package and Deployment Wizard dialog box appears.

c. If your computer system contains the MSDN library, or if you have access to the MSDN CD-ROM disc, then use the Help button in the Package and Deployment Wizard dialog box to learn how to use the Wizard.

d. Make a distributable Standard Setup Package for the lc1Done project. You will need to use five disks. Be sure to use blank, formatted disks for your distribution disks; do not use your Student Disks.

e. After making the setup disks, try to locate a computer that does not have Visual Basic 6.0 installed on it, then run the setup.exe file and follow the directions on the screen. (If you can't find a computer that does not have Visual Basic 6.0 installed on it, then try to locate one that does not contain the lc1Done project.)

f. Submit the setup disks.

discovery ▶ 5. In this exercise you will learn how to set the attributes for an executable file.

a. If necessary, start Visual Basic. Open the lcCopy project that you created in Tutorial 1's Lesson C. Click File on the menu bar, then click Make lcCopy.exe. When the Make Project dialog box appears, click the Options button. When the Copyright - Project Properties dialog box appears, click the Make tab.

b. If your computer system contains the MSDN library, or if you have access to the MSDN CD-ROM disc, then use the Help button to research the options on the Make tab.

c. Change the minor version number to 1. Type Interlocking Software as the company name. Change the application's title to Interlocking.

d. Click the OK button to remove the Copyright - Project Properties dialog box, then click the OK button to make the .exe file. When the prompt asking if you want to replace the existing lcCopy.exe file appears, click the Yes button.

e. Save the lcCopy project.

f. Use either the My Computer icon or Windows Explorer to open the Tut01 folder on your Student Disk. Right-click the lcCopy.exe file, then click Properties on the popup menu. When the lcCopy.exe Properties dialog box appears, click the Version tab to view the information you entered when creating this .exe file. Click the Cancel button to remove the dialog box.

discovery ▶ 6. In this exercise you will learn how to step through the code in your application. Doing so will help you understand how Visual Basic processes your application's code. Programmers also find it useful to step through the code when they are debugging an application, as you will discover in Tutorial 9's Debugging section.

a. If necessary, start Visual Basic. Open the Lc6 project, which is located in the Tut01 folder on your Student Disk.

b. Click Debug, then click Step Into. Notice that the Step Into command runs the copyright application.

c. Click the Interlocking Software logo. Visual Basic opens the imgLogo control's Click event procedure and highlights the `Private Sub imgLogo_Click( )` instruction—the first instruction processed by Visual Basic. To continue stepping through the code, you can either click Debug, then click Step Into, or you can press the F8 key on your keyboard.

d. Press the F8 key. Visual Basic highlights the next instruction in the Code window—the `lblAuthor.Visible = True` instruction.

e. Press the F8 key again. Visual Basic highlights the `lblYear.Visible = True` instruction.

f. Press the F8 key again. Visual Basic highlights the `End Sub` instruction.

g. Press the F8 key again, then close the Code window. The copyright screen appears.

h. Click the Exit button. (You may need to drag the Project or Properties window to a different location in order to see the Exit button.) Visual Basic opens the cmdExit control's Click event procedure and highlights the `Private Sub cmdExit_Click( )` instruction.

i. Press the F8 key twice. Visual Basic highlights the `End` statement, which ends the application. Close the Code window.

discovery ▶ 7. In this exercise you will learn about the line continuation character, which is a space, followed by the _ (underscore) and the Enter key. When a line of code is very long, you can make the code more readable by using the line continuation character to break the long line into short lines.

a. If necessary, start Visual Basic and open a new project. Add a label control and a command button to the form.

b. Set the label control's AutoSize property to True.

c. Open the command button's Click event procedure. In the procedure you will enter the instruction `Label1.Caption = "Hello, how are you?"`. Although this line of code will fit easily on one line, you will use the line continuation character to break it into two lines. The line continuation character tells Visual Basic that the next line in the Code window is a part of the current line.

d. Press the Tab key, then type `label1.caption=` and press the spacebar. Type the _ (underscore) and then press the Enter key. The insertion point moves to the next line in the Code window.

e. Type "Hello, how are you?" and press the Enter key.

f. Close the Code window, then run the application. Click the command button. The message appears in the label control.

g. Stop the application. You do not need to save this application.

discovery ▶ 8. In this exercise you will use Visual Basic's Application Wizard to create a splash screen and an About box.

a. Start Visual Basic. Click File, then click New Project. Click VB Application Wizard in the New Project dialog box, then click the OK button.

b. Use the Wizard to create a splash screen and an About box.

c. Name the files appropriately, then save the files in the Tut01 folder on your Student Disk.

discovery ▶ 9. In this exercise, you will learn how to create a tooltip for a control.

a. Start Visual Basic, if necessary. Open the lcCopy project that you created in Lesson C. The project is located in the Tut01 folder on your Student Disk.

b. Select the Exit command button. Set the command button's ToolTipText property to "Ends the application" (don't type the quotation marks).

c. Save and run the application. Place the mouse pointer on the Exit command button. The "Ends the application" tooltip appears. Click the Exit button to end the application.

discovery ▶ 10. In this exercise, you will learn how to display a picture (graphic) in a command button.

a. Start Visual Basic, if necessary. Open the lcCopy project that you created in Lesson C. The project is located in the Tut01 folder on your Student Disk.

b. Select the Exit command button.

c. A command button's Style property controls whether a command button can display a picture (graphic). The Style property has two settings: 0 – Standard and 1 – Graphical. When the Style property is set at its default of 0 – Standard, a command button can display only the value in its Caption property. By setting the Style property to 1 – Graphical, the command button can display a graphic in addition to the value in its Caption property. Change the Exit button's Style property to 1 – Graphical.

d. As you do with an image control, you place a picture in a command button by setting the command button's Picture property. Set the Exit button's Picture property to the anidoor.gif file, which is located in the Tut01 folder on your Student Disk. If you want to display the Exit caption along with the image, use the sizing handles to increase the height of the command button so that the caption appears below the image. (If necessary, drag the two label controls down slightly.) To display the image only, simply remove the caption from the Caption property.

e. Save and run the application. Click the Interlocking Software logo, then click the Exit button to end the application.

f. If your computer system contains the MSDN library, or if you have access to the MSDN CD-ROM disc, click the command button's DownPicture property, and then press F1 to display the property's Help screen. What is the purpose of this property? Set the Exit button's DownPicture property to the anihand.gif file, which is located in the Tut01 folder on your Student Disk.

g. Save and run the application. Click the Exit button to end the application.

DEBUGGING

Technique

The simplest technique a programmer uses for debugging an application is to print the application's properties (Form As Text) and code. In the printout of the properties, the programmer looks for a property that is set incorrectly. In the code printout, the programmer looks for an instruction that is either in the wrong object's Code window or in the wrong event procedure.

At the end of each tutorial you will find a Debugging Section. In programming, the term "debugging" refers to the process of finding the errors in a program. Each Debugging Section will include debugging techniques, from the simple to the more complex, as well as exercises designed to let you practice debugging applications.

Tutorial 1's Debugging Section contains four debugging exercises. In each exercise you will open and then run an application that is not working correctly. Your task is to find and correct the errors in the application—in other words, to debug the application—using this tutorial's debugging technique.

Exercises

1. Open the Debug1 project, which is located in the Tut01 folder on your Student Disk.
   a. Notice two problems. 1) The form's title bar does not say Glamour-Us (the name of the beauty salon). 2) The label control does not display all of its contents on one line.
   b. Display the Print dialog box and select the Form As Text option to print the properties of the objects in the user interface.
   c. Use the Form As Text printout to locate the errors.
   d. Correct the errors, then run the application to make sure it works correctly.
   e. Stop the application, then display the Print dialog box and select the Form As Text option.
   f. Circle your corrections on the Form As Text printout from step e. (You do not need to save this application.)

discovery ▶

2. In this Debugging exercise you will learn how to remove unnecessary code from your application.
   a. If necessary, start Visual Basic and open a new project.
   b. Add a command button to the form. Change its Caption property to Exit.
   c. Enter the **End** statement in the Exit button's Click event procedure.
   d. Run the application, then click the Exit button to be sure it ends the application.
   e. Now change the Exit button's Name property to cmdExit.
   f. Run the application, then click the Exit button. Notice that the button does not end the application as it did in step d.

g. Stop the application, then open the Exit button's Click event procedure. Notice that it does not contain the End statement that you entered in step c. Enter the End statement again.

h. Print the application's code. Notice that the code printout contains both the Command1_Click and the cmdExit_Click event procedures.

When you change the name of a control that already contains code, or when you delete a control that contains code, Visual Basic no longer associates the code with the control. Because the code is not associated with any control on the form, Visual Basic places the code in the General Declarations section of the form. The Command1_Click event procedure that you see at the top of the code printout is stored in that section.

i. Use the Code window's Object box to open the General Declarations section of the form. Click the Code window's Procedure list arrow to display a list of procedures included in the application. Notice that Command1_Click, which is the event that you coded in step c, appears in the list.

To remove this excess code from the application, you need simply to select Command1_Click in the list and delete its code.

j. Click Command1_Click in the list. Highlight all of the instructions in the Code window, including the `Private Sub` and `End Sub` instructions, then press the Delete key.

k. Run the application, then click the Exit button to end the application. Print the code. You do not need to save this application.

3. Open the Debug3 project, which is located in the Tut01 folder on your Student Disk.

a. Run the application, then click the Display button. Visual Basic displays the "Object required" error message.

b. Click the Debug button in the error message box. Visual Basic highlights the `lblMesage.Caption = "OK"` instruction in the Display button's Click event procedure. The "Object required" error message tells you that Visual Basic does not recognize the name of an object referred to in the highlighted instruction—in this case, Visual Basic does not recognize the name lblMesage.

At this point, you can print the Form As Text and Code to find the problem, or you can click the Code window's Object list arrow to display a list of the objects included in the application.

c. Click the Code window's Object list arrow to display the list. Notice that the name of the label control is lblMessage, not lblMesage.

d. Click the Object list arrow to close the list. Correct the highlighted instruction, then click the Continue button ▶. OK appears in the label control on the form.

e. Click the Exit button to end the application, then print the code.

f. Circle your correction on the Code printout from step e. You do not need to save this application.

4. Open the Debug4 project, which is located in the Tut01 folder on your Student Disk.

a. Display the Print dialog box. Print only the Form As Text and the Code.

b. Run the application.

c. Click the command button. Notice two problems. 1) The command button should say Exit. 2) The command button does not work (it should end the application when clicked by the user).

d. Stop the application, then use both the Form As Text and Code printouts to locate the errors.

e. Correct the errors, then run the application to make sure it works correctly. (Be sure to remove any unnecessary code.)

f. Display the Print dialog box. Print only the Form as Text and the Code.

g. Circle your corrections on the Form As Text and Code printouts from step f. (You do not need to save this application.)

Designing Applications

Creating an Order Screen

case ▶ During your second week at Interlocking Software, you and Chris Statton, the senior programmer, meet with the sales manager of Skate-Away Sales. The sales manager, Jacques Cousard, tells you that his company sells skateboards by phone. The skateboards are priced at $100 each and are available in two colors—yellow and blue. He further explains that Skate-Away Sales employs 20 salespeople to answer the phones. The salespeople record each order on a form that contains the customer's name, address, and the number of blue and yellow skateboards ordered. They then calculate the total number of skateboards ordered and the total price of the skateboards, including a 5% sales tax.

Mr. Cousard feels that having the salespeople manually perform the necessary calculations is much too time-consuming and prone to errors. Also, the company now wants to send confirmation notices to the customers, and the handwritten form the salespeople currently complete is too informal to send. Mr. Cousard wants Interlocking to create a computerized application that will solve the problems of the current order-taking system.

Solving the Problem Using a Procedure-Oriented Approach

As you learned in the Overview, procedure-oriented languages preceded OOED (object-oriented/event-driven) languages. Recall that in procedure-oriented languages, the emphasis of a program is on *how* to accomplish a task. The programmer must instruct the computer every step of the way, from the start of the task to the completion of the task. The procedure-oriented approach to problem solving requires a programmer to think in a step-by-step, top-to-bottom fashion. Planning tools such as flowcharts and pseudocode make this approach easier. A **flowchart** uses standardized symbols to show the steps needed to solve a problem. **Pseudocode** uses English-like phrases to represent the required steps. Some programmers prefer to use flowcharts, while others prefer pseudocode; it's really a matter of personal preference. (You will learn more about pseudocode in this tutorial, and about flowcharts in Tutorial 4, as these planning tools are also useful in object-oriented/event-driven programming.) Take a look at a procedure-oriented approach to solving Skate-Away's problem. Figure 2-1 shows the solution written in pseudocode.

1. Get customer name, street address, city, state, zip, number of blue skateboards, number of yellow skateboards

2. Calculate total skateboards = number of blue skateboards + number of yellow skateboards

3. Calculate total price = total skateboards * $100 * 105%

4. Print customer name, street address, city, state, zip, number of blue skateboards, number of yellow skateboards, total skateboards, total price

5. End

Figure 2-1: Pseudocode for the procedure-oriented solution

You will notice that the pseudocode indicates the sequence of steps the computer must take to process an order. Using the pseudocode as a guide, the programmer then translates the solution into a language that the computer can understand. Figure 2-2 shows the pseudocode translated into Microsoft's QuickBASIC language. QuickBASIC, a procedure-oriented language, is a predecessor of Visual Basic.

```
Ans$ = "Y"
While Ans$ = "Y" or Ans$ = "y"
        Input "Enter the customer's name", Names$
        Input "Enter the street address:", Address$
        Input "Enter the city:", City$
        Input "Enter the state:", State$
        Input "Enter the zip code:", Zip$
        Input "Enter the number of blue skateboards:", Blue
        Input "Enter the number of yellow skateboards:", Yellow
        Totboards = Blue + Yellow
        Totprice = Totboards * 100 * 1.05
        Print "Customer name:", Names$
        Print "Address:", Address$
        Print "City:", City$
        Print "State:", State$
        Print "Zip:", Zip$
        Print "Blue skateboards:", Blue
        Print "Yellow skateboards:", Yellow
        Print "Total skateboards:", Totboards
        Print "Total price: $", Totprice
        Input "Do you want to enter another order? Enter Y if you
        do, or N if you don't.", Ans$
Wend
End
```

Figure 2-2: Procedure-oriented solution written in QuickBASIC

You will now enter an order using this procedure-oriented application.

To use the procedure-oriented application to enter an order:

1   If necessary, start Windows, then place your Student Disk in the appropriate drive.

2   Use the Run command on the Start menu to run the **Procedur** (Procedur.exe) file, which is located in the Tut02 folder on your Student Disk. A prompt requesting the customer's name appears on the screen.

Assume that Sport Warehouse wants to place an order for 10 blue skateboards and 20 yellow skateboards.

3   Type **Sport Warehouse** and press the **Enter** key. A prompt requesting the street address appears on the screen.

4   Type **123 Main** and press the **Enter** key, then type **Glendale** for the city and press the **Enter** key, then type **IL** for the state and press the **Enter** key, and then type **60134** for the zip code and press the **Enter** key. The program now prompts you to enter the number of blue skateboards ordered.

5   Type **10** as the number of blue skateboards ordered, then press the **Enter** key. A prompt requesting the number of yellow skateboards ordered appears next.

6   Type **20** as the number of yellow skateboards ordered, then press the **Enter** key. The program computes and displays the total skateboards ordered (30) and the total price of the order ($3,150.00). (Recall that skateboards are $100 each and there is a 5% sales tax.) See Figure 2-3.

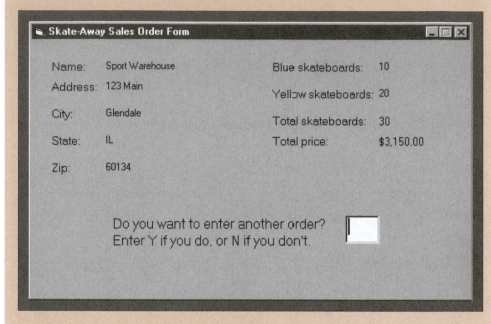

Figure 2-3: Results of procedure-oriented program

Notice that the screen also contains a prompt that asks if you want to enter another order. If you do, you simply type the letter "Y" (for "yes"); otherwise, you type the letter "N" (for "No").

7   Type **n** and press the **Enter** key to end the program.

Although Skate-Away Sales could use this procedure-oriented program to record its phone orders, the program has one very important limitation that is inherent in all procedure-oriented programs: the user has little, if any, control over the processing of the program. Recall, for example, that you could not control the sequence in which the order information was entered. What if the customer wants to order the yellow skateboards before the blue skateboards? Also recall that you couldn't change the information once you entered it. What if the customer changes his or her mind about how many blue skateboards to order? And, last, recall that you had no control over when the program calculated the total order and the total price. What if the customer wants to know the total price of the blue skateboards before placing the yellow skateboard order?

Now look at the object-oriented/event-driven approach to programming.

Solving the Problem Using an Object-Oriented/Event-Driven (OOED) Approach

As you learned in the Overview, in object-oriented/event-driven languages, the emphasis of a program is on the *objects* included in the user interface (such as scroll bars or buttons) and the *events* that occur on those objects (such as scrolling or clicking). Unlike the procedure-oriented approach to problem solving, the OOED approach does not view the solution as a step-by-step, top-to-bottom process; instead, the OOED programmer's goal is to give the user as much control over the program as possible.

When using the OOED approach to problem solving, the programmer begins by identifying the tasks the application needs to perform. Then the programmer decides on the appropriate objects to which those tasks will be assigned, and on the event(s) necessary to trigger those objects to perform their assigned task(s). For example, in Tutorial 1, the copyright screen had to provide the user with a way to end the application. Recall that you assigned that task to the Exit command button. The event that triggered the Exit button to perform its assigned task was the Click event. In this book, you will use a TOE (Task, Object, Event) chart to assist you in planning your object-oriented/event-driven programs.

Before we discuss planning OOED applications further, you will run an OOED application designed to solve Skate-Away's problem. The OOED application, which is written using Visual Basic, contains a new control, a text box. You use a **text box** to provide areas in the form where the user can enter information.

To run the OOED application:

1   Use the Run command on the Start menu to run the **OOED** (OOED.exe) file, which is located in the Tut02 folder on your Student Disk. The order screen shown in Figure 2-4 appears.

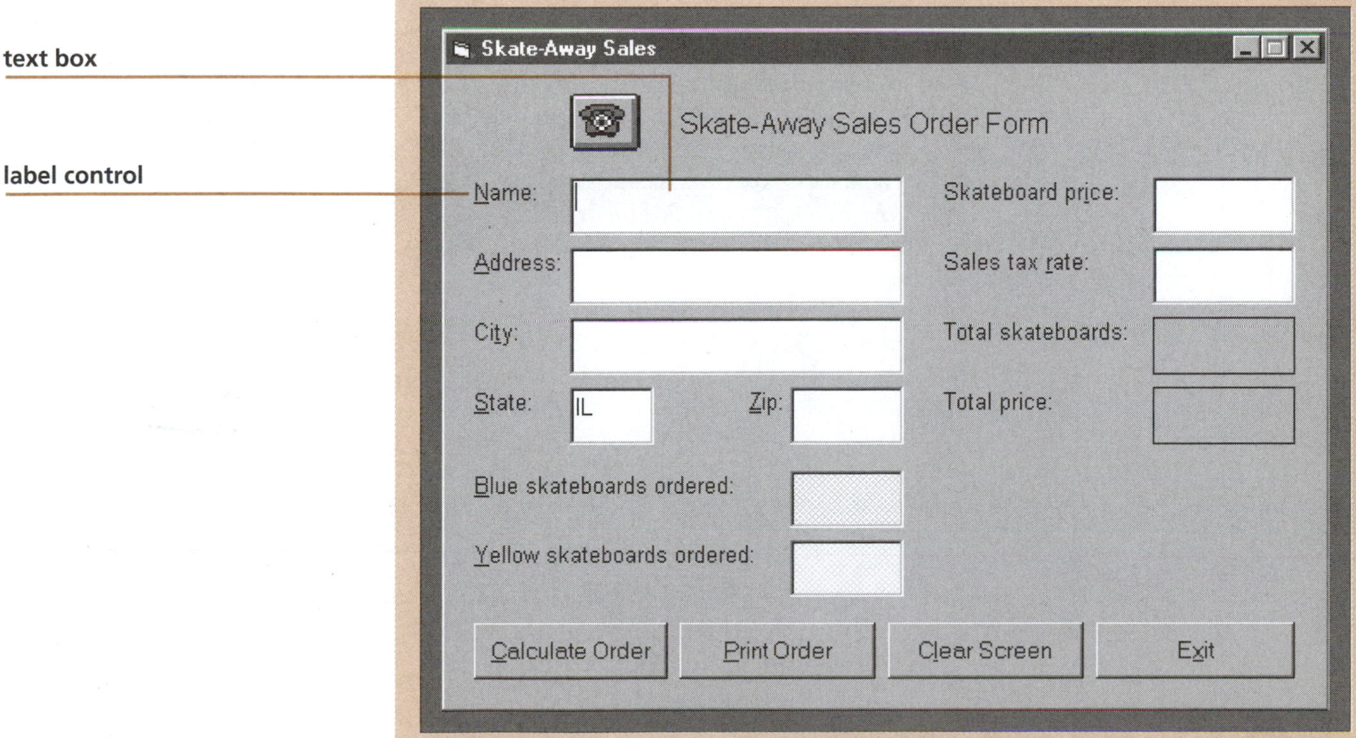

text box

label control

Figure 2-4: Order screen created by the OOED application

You will notice that Visual Basic displays an insertion point in the first text box. The label control to the left of the text box identifies the information the user should enter—in this case, the customer's name. Enter Sport Warehouse's information.

tip

You can also click inside a text box to place the insertion point in the text box.

To enter the order information using the OOED application:

1   Type **Sport Warehouse** as the customer's name, then press the **Tab** key twice. The insertion point appears in the City text box.

2   Type **Glendale** as the city, then press **Shift + Tab** (press and hold down the Shift key as you press the Tab key) to move the insertion point to the Address text box.

Notice that the OOED application allows you to enter the order information in any order.

3   Type **123 Main** as the address, then press the **Tab** key twice. Because most of Skate-Away's customers reside in Illinois, the OOED application already contains IL in the State box.

4   Press the **Tab** key, then type **60134** as the zip code, and then press the **Tab** key. The insertion point appears in the Blue skateboards text box.

5   Type **10** as the number of blue skateboards ordered and press the **Tab** key twice. Type **100** as the skateboard price and press the **Tab** key, then type **.05** as the sales tax rate and press the **Tab** key. Click the **Calculate Order** button. The Calculate Order button calculates the total skateboards (10) and the total price ($1,050.00). Notice that the OOED application allows you to tell the customer how much the blue skateboards will cost before the yellow skateboard order is placed.

6   Click the **Yellow skateboards ordered** text box, type **20**, then click the **Calculate Order** button. The application recalculates the total skateboards (30) and the total price ($3,150.00).

Now assume that Sport Warehouse wants to change its order to 20 blue skateboards.

7   Click to the **immediate left** of the **10** in the **Blue skateboards ordered** text box, press the **Delete** key to remove the 1, then type **2**. The number of blue skateboards ordered should now say 20. Click the **Calculate Order** button. The application recalculates the total skateboards ordered (40) and the total price ($4,200.00). See Figure 2-5.

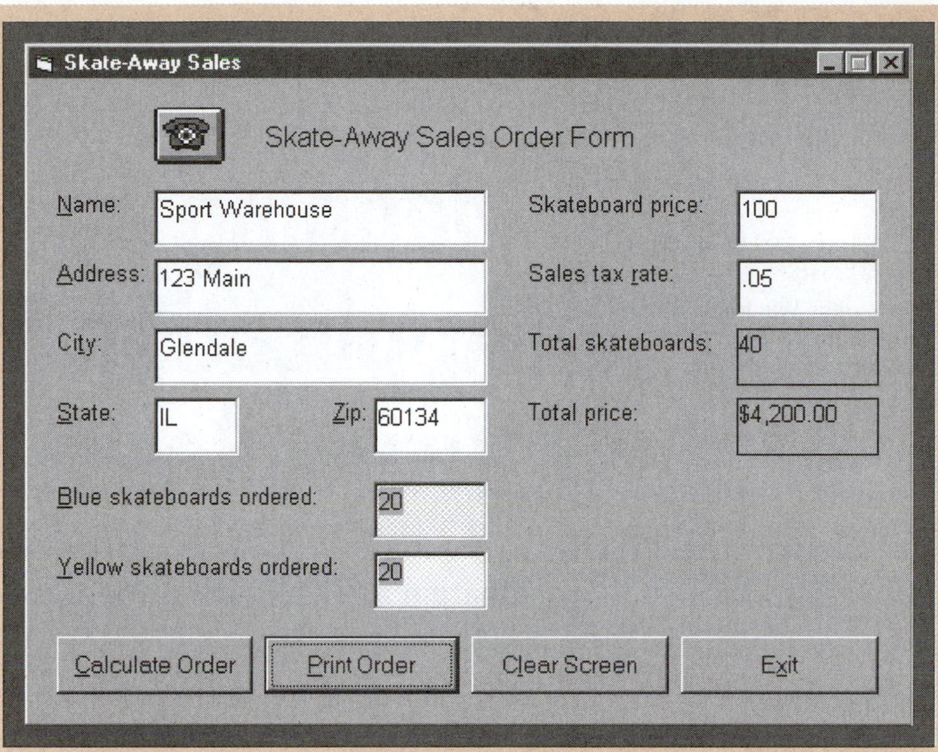

Figure 2-5: Completed order using the OOED program

8 If your computer is connected to a printer, click the **Print Order** button. The confirmation notice prints on the printer.

Notice that each command button's caption, as well as most of the label controls, has an underlined letter, which is called an access key. An **access key** allows the user to select a control using the Alt key in combination with a letter. For example, when the salesperson is finished with an order, he or she can clear the screen either by clicking the Clear Screen button or by pressing the Alt key along with the letter l—the Clear Screen button's access key.

9 Press **Alt + l** (the letter "l") to clear the screen for the next order. The previous customer's information (except the state, skateboard price, and sales tax rate) disappears, and the insertion point is placed in the Name text box.

   HELP? Pressing Alt + l means to press and hold down the Alt key as you type the letter l. Be sure to press the letter l, and not the number 1.

   You will learn more about access keys in Lesson B.

10 Press **Alt + x** (or click the Exit button) to end the application.

Unlike the procedure-oriented program, the OOED application gives users a great deal of control over the program. Users can enter information in any order, change what they entered at any time, and calculate a subtotal whenever they like.

In Lesson A, you will learn how a Visual Basic programmer plans an OOED application. Then, in Lessons B and C, you will create the OOED application that you just viewed.

LESSON A
objectives

In this lesson you will learn how to:

- Plan an OOED application in Visual Basic
- Complete a TOE (Task, Object, Event) chart
- Follow the Windows standards regarding the layout and labeling of controls

Planning an OOED Application in Visual Basic

Creating an OOED Application

The process a programmer follows when creating an OOED application is similar to the process an architect follows when building a home. Both processes are shown in Figure 2-6.

An architect's process	A programmer's process
1. Plan the home (blueprint)	1. Plan the application (TOE chart)
2. Build the frame	2. Build the user interface
3. Complete the home	3. Code the application
4. Inspect the home and fix any problems	4. Test and debug the application
5. Assemble the documentation	5. Assemble the documentation

Figure 2-6: Processes used by an architect and a programmer

As Figure 2-6 shows, both the architect and the programmer first create a plan (blueprint) for the project. After the plan is approved by the customer, the architect builds the home's frame; likewise, the programmer builds the user interface, which is the application's frame. Once the frame is built, the architect completes the home by adding the electrical wiring, walls, and so on. Similarly, the programmer completes the application by adding the necessary code (instructions) to the user interface. When the home is complete, the architect makes a final inspection and corrects any problems before the customer moves in. Likewise, the completed application is tested by the programmer, and any problems, called **bugs**, are fixed before the application is given to the user. The final step in both processes is to assemble the project's documentation (paperwork), which is then given to the customer/user.

You will learn how to plan an OOED application in this lesson. The remaining four steps of the process are covered in Lessons B and C.

Planning an OOED Application

As any architect will tell you, the most important aspect of a home is not its beauty; rather, it is how closely the home matches the buyer's wants and needs. For example, a large dining room may be appropriate for someone who frequently entertains. For someone who does not, it may be a waste of space. The same is true for an OOED application. In order for an application to meet the user's needs, therefore, it is essential for the programmer to plan the application jointly with the user. It can't be stressed enough that the only way to guarantee the success of an application is to actively involve the user in the planning phase. Planning an OOED application in Visual Basic requires the following four steps:

1. Identify the tasks the application needs to perform.
2. Identify the objects to which you will assign those tasks.
3. Identify the events required to trigger an object into performing its assigned tasks.
4. Draw a sketch of the user interface.

You can use a TOE (Task, Object, Event) chart to plan your Visual Basic applications. The TOE chart lists the application's tasks, objects, and events. You will complete a TOE chart for the Skate-Away Sales application. Begin by identifying the tasks.

Identifying the Application's Tasks

Realizing that it is essential to involve the user when planning the application, you meet with the sales manager of Skate-Away Sales, Mr. Cousard, to determine his requirements. You ask Mr. Cousard to bring the form the salespeople currently use to record the orders. Viewing the current forms and procedures will help you gain a better understanding of the application. You can also use the current form as a guide when designing the user interface. The Skate-Away Sales company's current order-taking form is shown in Figure 2-7.

Figure 2-7: Current order-taking form used by Skate-Away Sales

When identifying the tasks an application needs to perform, it is helpful to ask the following questions:

- What information, if any, will the user need to enter into the user interface?
- What information, if any, will the application need to calculate?
- What information, if any, will the application need to display on the screen and/or print on the printer?
- How will the user end the application?
- Will previous information need to be cleared from the screen before new information is entered?

The answers to these questions will help you identify the application's major tasks. Answer each question for the Skate-Away Sales application.

What information, if any, will the user need to enter into the user interface? In the Skate-Away Sales application, the salesperson (the user) must enter the customer's name, street address, city, state, zip code, skateboard price, sales tax rate, and the number of blue and yellow skateboards ordered.

What information, if any, will the application need to calculate? The Skate-Away Sales application needs to calculate the total number of skateboards ordered and the total price of the order.

What information, if any, will the application need to display on the screen and/or print on the printer? (Notice that "display" refers to the screen; "print" refers to the printer.) The application must display the order information entered by the user, as well as the total number of skateboards ordered and the total price of the order. Also recall that the sales manager wants the application to print a confirmation notice.

How will the user end the application? In Tutorial 1, you learned that all applications should give the user a way to exit the program. The Skate-Away Sales application needs to provide a way to end the application.

Will previous information need to be cleared from the screen before new information is entered? After Skate-Away's salesperson enters and prints an order, he or she will need to clear the previous order's information from the screen before the next order is entered.

Figure 2-8 shows the Skate-Away Sales application's tasks listed in a TOE chart. Unlike procedure-oriented planning, OOED planning does not require the TOE chart tasks to be in any particular order. In this case, they are listed in the order in which they were identified in this lesson.

Task	Object	Event

Get the following order information from the user:
    Customer's name
    Street address
    City
    State
    Zip code
    Price of a skateboard
    Sales tax rate
    Number of blue skateboards ordered
    Number of yellow skateboards ordered		

Calculate the total skateboards ordered and the total price		

Display the following information:
    Customer's name
    Street address
    City
    State
    Zip code
    Price of a skateboard
    Sales tax rate
    Number of blue skateboards ordered
    Number of yellow skateboards ordered
    Total skateboards ordered
    Total price		

Print a confirmation notice		
End the application		
Clear the screen for the next order		

Figure 2-8: Tasks entered in TOE chart

Identifying the Objects

After completing the Task column of the TOE chart, you then assign each task to an object in the user interface. For this application, the only objects you will use, besides the form itself, are the command button, the label control, and the text box. As you learned in Tutorial 1, you use a label control to display information that you don't want the user to change while your application is running, and you use a command button to perform an action immediately after it is clicked by the user. As you saw in the OOED application you ran earlier, you use a text box to give the user an area in which to enter data. Now assign each of the tasks in the TOE chart to an object.

The first task listed in Figure 2-8 is to get the order information from the user. For each order, the salesperson will need to enter the customer's name, address, city, state, and zip code, as well as the skateboard price, sales tax rate, and the number of blue and yellow skateboards ordered. Because you need to provide the salesperson with areas in which to enter that information, you will assign the first task to nine text boxes—one for each item of information. The names of the text boxes will be txtName, txtAddress, txtCity, txtState, txtZip, txtPrice, txtRate, txtBlue, and txtYellow. The "txt" prefix indicates that these objects are text boxes.

The second task listed in the TOE chart is to calculate the total skateboards ordered and the total price. So that the salesperson can calculate these amounts at any time, you will assign the task to a command button that will be named cmdCalc. As you learned in Tutorial 1, the "cmd" prefix indicates that the object is a command button.

The third task listed in the TOE chart is to display the order information, the total skateboards ordered, and the total price. The order information will be displayed automatically when the user enters that information in the nine text boxes. The total skateboards ordered and the total price, however, are not entered by the user; those amounts are calculated by the cmdCalc button. Because the user should not be allowed to change either amount, you will have the cmdCalc button display the total skateboards ordered and the total price in two label controls, which you will name lblTboards and lblTprice. Recall from Tutorial 1 that the "lbl" prefix indicates that a control is a label control, and that label controls do not allow the user to change their contents when the application is running. Notice that the task of displaying the total skateboards ordered involves two objects: cmdCalc and lblTboards; the task of displaying the total price also involves two objects: cmdCalc and lblTprice.

The last three tasks listed in the TOE chart are "Print a confirmation notice," "End the application," and "Clear the screen for the next order." You will assign these tasks to command buttons so that the user has control over when the tasks are performed. You will call the command buttons cmdPrint, cmdExit, and cmdClear. Figure 2-9 shows the TOE chart with the Task and Object columns completed.

Task	Object	Event
Get the following order information from the user:		
Customer's name	txtName	
Street address	txtAddress	
City	txtCity	
State	txtState	
Zip code	txtZip	
Price of a skateboard	txtPrice	
Sales tax rate	txtRate	
Number of blue skateboards ordered	txtBlue	
Number of yellow skateboards ordered	txtYellow	
Calculate the total skateboards ordered and the total price	cmdCalc	
Display the following information:		
Customer's name	txtName	
Street address	txtAddress	
City	txtCity	
State	txtState	
Zip code	txtZip	
Price of a skateboard	txtPrice	
Sales tax rate	txtRate	
Number of blue skateboards ordered	txtBlue	
Number of yellow skateboards ordered	txtYellow	
Total skateboards ordered	cmdCalc, lblTboards	
Total price	cmdCalc, lblTprice	
Print a confirmation notice	cmdPrint	
End the application	cmdExit	
Clear the screen for the next order	cmdClear	

Figure 2-9: Tasks and objects entered in TOE chart

After defining the application's tasks and assigning those tasks to objects in the user interface, you must then determine which objects will need an event (such as clicking or double-clicking) to occur for the object to do its assigned task. Look at the tasks and the objects listed in Figure 2-9's TOE chart.

Identifying the Events

The nine text boxes listed in the TOE chart in Figure 2-9 are assigned the task of getting and displaying the order information. Text boxes accept and display information automatically, so no special event is necessary for them to do their assigned task.

The two label controls listed in the TOE chart are assigned the task of displaying the total number of skateboards ordered and the total price of the order. Label controls automatically display their contents so, here again, no special event needs to occur. (Recall that the label controls will get their values from the cmdCalc button.)

The remaining objects listed in the TOE chart are the four command buttons: cmdCalc, cmdClear, cmdExit, cmdPrint. In this application you will have the command buttons perform their assigned tasks when they are clicked by the user. Figure 2-10 shows the TOE chart with the tasks, objects, and events necessary for the Skate-Away Sales application.

Task	Object	Event
Get the following order information from the user:		
Customer's name	txtName	None
Street address	txtAddress	None
City	txtCity	None
State	txtState	None
Zip code	txtZip	None
Price of a skateboard	txtPrice	None
Sales tax rate	txtRate	None
Number of blue skateboards ordered	txtBlue	None
Number of yellow skateboards ordered	txtYellow	None
Calculate the total skateboards ordered and the total price	cmdCalc	Click
Display the following information:		
Customer's name	txtName	None
Street address	txtAddress	None
City	txtCity	None
State	txtState	None
Zip code	txtZip	None
Price of a skateboard	txtPrice	None
Sales tax rate	txtRate	None
Number of blue skateboards ordered	txtBlue	None
Number of yellow skateboards ordered	txtYellow	None
Total skateboards ordered	cmdCalc, lblTboards	Click, None
Total price	cmdCalc, lblTprice	Click, None
Print a confirmation notice	cmdPrint	Click
End the application	cmdExit	Click
Clear the screen for the next order	cmdClear	Click

Figure 2-10: Completed TOE chart ordered by task

If the application you are creating is small, as is the Skate-Away Sales application, you can use the TOE chart in its current form to help you write the code. When the application you are creating is large, however, it is helpful to rearrange the TOE chart so that it is ordered by object instead of by task. To do so, you simply list all of your objects in the Object column, being sure to list each object only once. Then list the tasks you have assigned to each object in the Task column and the event in the Event column. Figure 2-11 shows the rearranged TOE chart, ordered by object rather than by task.

Task	Object	Event
1. Calculate the total skateboards ordered and the total price 2. Display the total skateboards ordered and the total price in the lblTboards and lblTprice objects	cmdCalc	Click
Clear the screen for the next order	cmdClear	Click
End the application	cmdExit	Click
Print a confirmation notice	cmdPrint	Click
Display the total skateboards ordered (from cmdCalc)	lblTboards	None
Display the total price (from cmdCalc)	lblTprice	None
Get and display the order information	txtName, txtAddress, txtCity, txtState, txtZip, txtPrice, txtRate, txtBlue, txtYellow	None

Figure 2-11: Completed TOE chart ordered by object

After completing the TOE chart, the next step is to draw a rough sketch of the user interface.

Drawing a Sketch of the User Interface

Although the TOE chart lists the objects you need to include in the application's user interface, it does not tell you *where* to place those objects in the interface. While the design of an interface is open to creativity, there are some guidelines to which you should adhere so that your application is consistent with the Windows standards. This consistency will make your application easier to both learn and use because the user interface will have a familiar look to it.

In Western countries, you should organize the user interface so that the information flows either vertically or horizontally, with the most important information always located in the upper-left corner of the screen. In a vertical arrangement the information flows from top to bottom; the essential information is located in the first column of the screen, while secondary information is placed in subsequent columns. In a horizontal arrangement, on the other hand, the information flows from left to right; the essential information is placed in the first row of the screen, with secondary information placed in subsequent rows. You can use either white space or a frame to group related controls together.

If command buttons appear in the interface, they should be either centered along the bottom of the screen or stacked in either the upper-right or lower-right corner. Limit to six the number of command buttons in the interface, and place the most commonly used button first—either on the left when the buttons are centered along the bottom of the screen, or on the top when the buttons are stacked in either the upper-right or lower-right corner.

Figures 2-12 and 2-13 show two different sketches of the Skate-Away Sales interface. In Figure 2-12, the information is arranged vertically; white space is used to group the related controls together and the command buttons are centered along the bottom of the screen. In Figure 2-13, the information is arranged horizontally; a frame is used to group the related controls together and the command buttons are stacked in the upper-right corner of the screen.

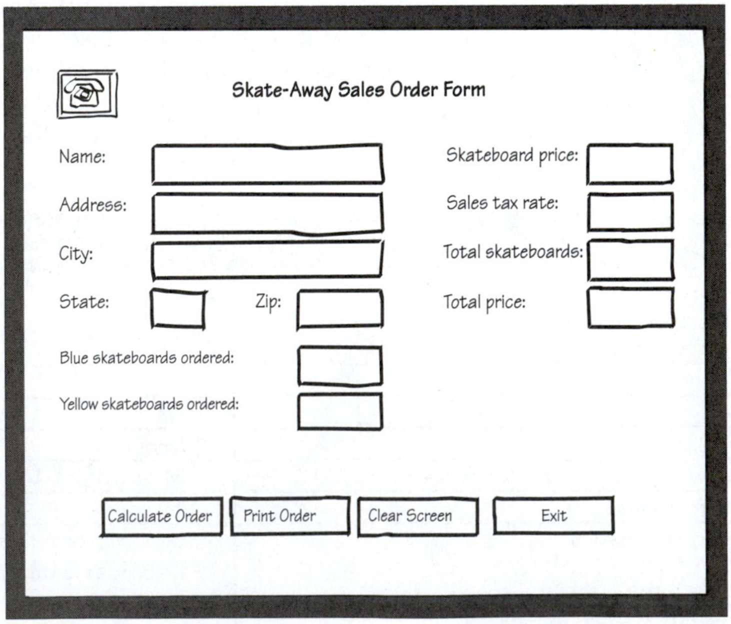

Figure 2-12: Vertical arrangement of the Skate-Away Sales application

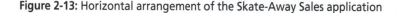

Skate-Away Sales Order Form

Name: Address: Calculate Order

City: State: Zip: Print Order

Blue skateboards ordered: Yellow skateboards ordered: Clear Screen

Exit

Skateboard price: Sales tax rate: Total skateboards: Total price:

Figure 2-13: Horizontal arrangement of the Skate-Away Sales application

Notice that each control in the user interface is labeled so the user knows the control's purpose. Identifying labels should be left-aligned and positioned either above or to the left of the control, except in the case of command buttons. As you learned in Tutorial 1, a command button's label, called its **caption**, appears *inside* the button. Identifying labels, including captions, should be from one to three words only, and each should appear on one line. Labels and captions should be meaningful. Captions, for example, should tell the user what action the command button will perform when the button is clicked.

Except for the captions inside the command buttons, notice that each control's identifying label ends with a colon (:). The colon distinguishes the label from other text in the user interface. The Windows standard is to use **sentence capitalization** for labels, which means you should capitalize only the first word and any words that are customarily capitalized. For command button captions, however, the Windows standard is to use book title capitalization. When using **book title capitalization**, you capitalize the first letter in each word, except for articles, conjunctions, and prepositions that do not occur at either the beginning or the end of the caption.

When laying out the controls in the user interface, try to minimize the number of different margins so that the user can more easily scan the information; you can do so by aligning the labels and controls wherever possible, as shown in both Figures 2-12 and 2-13.

In this section you learned some basic guidelines to follow when sketching a GUI (Graphical User Interface). You will learn more GUI guidelines as you progress through this book. For now, however, you have completed the first of the five steps involved in creating an application: plan the application. Recall that the planning step requires you to:

1. Identify the tasks the application needs to perform.
2. Identify the objects to which you will assign those tasks.

3. Identify the events required to trigger an object into performing its assigned tasks.
4. Draw a sketch of the user interface.

In Lesson B you will use the sketch shown in Figure 2-12 to build the interface for the Skate-Away Sales application. Recall that building the user interface is the second of the five steps involved in creating an OOED application. In Lesson C, you will complete the third (code the application), fourth (test and debug the application), and fifth (assemble the documentation) steps. For now, however, you can either take a break or complete the end-of-lesson questions and exercises.

Design Tips

Layout and Organization of Your Interface
- Organize the user interface so that the information flows either vertically or horizontally, with the most important information always located in the upper-left corner of the screen.
- Group related controls together using either white space or a frame.
- Either center the command buttons along the bottom of the screen or stack them in either the upper-right or lower-right corner. Use no more than six command buttons on a screen. Place the most commonly used command button first (either on the left or on the top).
- Use meaningful captions in command buttons. Place the caption on one line and use from one to three words only. Use book title capitalization for command button captions.
- Label each control in the user interface. The label should be from one to three words only, and entered on one line. Align each label on the left, and position each either above or to the left of the control. Follow the label with a colon (:) and use sentence capitalization. (Remember that the captions in command buttons have different guidelines.)
- Align the labels and controls in the user interface in order to minimize the number of different margins.

S U M M A R Y

To create an OOED application:

- Follow these five steps:
    1 Plan the application.
    2 Build the user interface.
    3 Code the application.
    4 Test and debug the application.
    5 Assemble the documentation.

To plan an OOED application in Visual Basic:

- Follow these four steps:
    1 Identify the tasks the application needs to perform.
    2 Identify the objects to which you will assign those tasks.
    3 Identify the events required to trigger an object into performing its assigned tasks.
    4 Draw a sketch of the user interface.

To assist you in identifying the tasks an application needs to perform, ask the following questions:

- What information, if any, will the user need to enter?
- What information, if any, will the application need to calculate?

- What information, if any, will the application need to display or print?
- How will the user end the application?
- Will prior information need to be cleared from the screen before new information is entered?

Q U E S T I O N S

1. You use a _____ control to display information you don't want the user to change.
   a. command button
   b. form
   c. label
   d. text box
   e. user

2. You use a _____ control to accept or display information you will allow the user to change.
   a. changeable
   b. command button
   c. form
   d. label
   e. text box

3. You use a _____ control to perform an immediate action when it is clicked by the user.
   a. command button
   b. form
   c. label
   d. text box

4. You can use a _____ chart to plan your OOED applications.
   a. EOT
   b. ETO
   c. OET
   d. OTE
   e. TOE

5. When designing a user interface, you should organize the information _____ .
   a. either horizontally or vertically
   b. horizontally only
   c. vertically only

6. When designing a user interface, the most important information should be placed in the _____ of the screen.
   a. center
   b. lower-left corner
   c. lower-right corner
   d. upper-left corner
   e. upper-right corner

7. You can use _____ to group related controls together in an interface.
   a. a frame
   b. a label control
   c. a text box
   d. white space
   e. either a or d

8. Command buttons in an interface should be _____.
   a. centered along the bottom of the screen
   b. stacked in either the upper-left or lower-left corner of the screen
   c. stacked in either the upper-right or lower-right corner of the screen
   d. either a or b
   e. either a or c

9. Use no more than _____ command buttons on a screen.
   a. five
   b. four
   c. seven
   d. six
   e. two

10. If more than one command button is used in an interface, the most commonly used command button should be placed _____.
    a. first
    b. in the middle
    c. last
    d. either a or c

11. Which of the following statements is false?
    a. A command button's caption should appear on one line.
    b. A command button's caption should be from one to three words only.
    c. A command button's caption should be entered using book title capitalization.
    d. A command button's caption should end with a colon (:).

12. The labels for controls (other than command buttons) should be entered using

    _____.
    a. book title capitalization
    b. sentence capitalization
    c. either a or b

13. Which of the following statements is false?
    a. Labels for controls (other than command buttons) should be aligned on the left.
    b. Labels for controls (other than command buttons) should be positioned either above or to the left of the control.
    c. Labels for controls (other than command buttons) should be entered using book title capitalization.
    d. Labels for controls (other than command buttons) should end with a colon (:).

14. Use _____ for labels, which means you capitalize only the first word and any words that are customarily capitalized.
    a. book title capitalization
    b. sentence capitalization

15. Use _____ for command button captions, which means you capitalize the first letter in each word, except for articles, conjunctions, and prepositions that do not occur at either the beginning or the end of the caption.
    a. book title capitalization
    b. sentence capitalization

16. Listed below are the four steps you should follow when planning an OOED application. Put them in the proper order by placing a number (1 to 4) on the line to the left of the step.
    _____ Identify the objects to which you will assign those tasks.
    _____ Draw a sketch of the user interface.
    _____ Identify the tasks the application needs to perform.
    _____ Identify the events required to trigger an object into performing its assigned tasks.

17. Listed below are the five steps you should follow when creating an OOED application. Put them in the proper order by placing a number (1 to 5) on the line to the left of the step.

    _____ Test and debug the application.

    _____ Build the user interface.

    _____ Code the application.

    _____ Assemble the documentation.

    _____ Plan the application.

E X E R C I S E S

The following list summarizes the GUI design guidelines you have learned so far. You can use this list to verify that the interfaces you create in the following exercises adhere to the GUI standards outlined in the book.

- Information should flow either vertically or horizontally, with the most important information always located in the upper-left corner of the screen.

- Related controls should be grouped together using either white space or a frame.

- Command buttons should either be centered along the bottom of the screen or stacked in either the upper-right or lower-right corner.

- Use no more than six command buttons on a screen.

- The most commonly used command button should be placed first.

- Command button captions should:
    - be meaningful
    - be from one to three words
    - appear on one line
    - be entered using book title capitalization

- Use labels to identify the controls in the interface.

- Identifying labels should:
    - be from one to three words
    - appear on one line
    - be aligned by their left borders
    - be positioned either above or to the left of the control that they identify
    - end with a colon (:)
    - be entered using sentence capitalization

- Align labels and controls to minimize the number of different margins.

---

1. In this exercise, you will prepare a TOE chart and create two sketches of the application's user interface. (Refer to the list at the beginning of the Exercises section.)

   Scenario: Sarah Brimley is the accountant at Paper Products. The salespeople at Paper Products are paid a commission, which is a percentage of the sales they make. The current commission rate is 10%. (In other words, if you have sales totaling $2,000, your commission is $200.) Sarah wants you to create an application that will compute the commission after she enters the salesperson's name, territory number, and sales. She also wants to print this information.

   a. Prepare a TOE chart ordered by task.

b. Rearrange the TOE chart created in step a so that it is ordered by object.

c. Draw two sketches of the user interface—one using a horizontal arrangement and the other using a vertical arrangement.

2. In this exercise, you will prepare a TOE chart and create two sketches of the application's user interface. (Refer to the list at the beginning of the Exercises section.)

Scenario: RM Sales divides its sales territory into four regions: North, South, East, and West. Robert Gonzales, the sales manager, wants an application in which he can enter the current year's sales for each region and the projected increase (expressed as a percentage) in sales for each region. He then wants the application to compute the following year's projected sales for each region. (For example, if Robert enters 10000 as the current sales for the South region, and then enters a 10% projected increase, the application should display 11000 as next year's projected sales.) He also wants to print a report showing the four current year's sales, the four projected sales percentages, and the four projected sales amounts.

a. Prepare a TOE chart ordered by task.

b. Rearrange the TOE chart created in step a so that it is ordered by object.

c. Draw two sketches of the user interface—one using a horizontal arrangement and the other using a vertical arrangement.

3. In this exercise, you will modify an existing application's user interface so that the interface follows the GUI design tips covered in Tutorial 2's Lesson A. (Refer to the list at the beginning of the Exercises section.)

a. Open the La3 (La3.vbp) project, which is located in the Tut02 folder on your Student Disk.

b. Save the form and the project as La3Done in the Tut02 folder on your Student Disk.

c. Lay out and organize the interface so it follows all of the GUI design tips specified in Lesson A. (Refer to the *Layout and Organization of Your Interface* GUI design tips at the end of Lesson A.)

d. Save and run the application, then click the Print Time Report button to print the interface. (The Print Time Report button contains the code to print the interface. If the labels in the printout do not appear the same as on the screen, you may need to select a different font for the labels. Exit the application, select the labels, then use the Font property to change the Font; try the Arial font.)

e. Click the Exit button to end the application. (The Exit button contains the code to end the application.)

f. Submit the printout from step d.

In this lesson you will learn how to:

- Build the user interface using your TOE chart and sketch
- Follow the Windows standards regarding the use of graphics, color, and fonts
- Apply the BackStyle, BorderStyle, and Appearance properties
- Add a text box control to a form
- Use the TabIndex property to control the focus
- Lock the controls on the form
- Assign access keys to the controls

Building the User Interface

Preparing to Create the User Interface

In Lesson A you completed the first of the five steps involved in creating an OOED application (plan the application). You are now ready to tackle the second step (build the user interface). You use the TOE chart and sketch you created in the planning step as guides when building the interface, which involves placing the appropriate controls on the form and setting the applicable properties of those controls. Recall that a property controls the appearance and behavior of the objects included in the interface, such as the object's font, size, and so on. Some programmers create the entire interface before setting the properties of each object; other programmers change the properties of each object as it is added to the form. Either way will work, so it's really just a matter of preference.

To save you time, your Student Disk contains a partially completed application for Skate-Away Sales. When you open the application, you will notice that most of the user interface has been created and most of the properties have been set. One control, however, is missing from the form: a text box control. You'll add the missing control later in this lesson. First open the project and save it under a different name so that the original files remain intact in case you want to practice this lesson again.

tip

Another way to make a form the active window is to click its name in the Project window, then click the Project window's View Object button.

To open the partially completed project, then save the files under a new name:

1 Start Visual Basic, if necessary, and make sure your Student Disk is in the appropriate drive.

2 Open the **T2case** (T2case.vbp) file, which is located in the Tut02 folder on your Student Disk. Click the **form's title bar** to make it the active window.

3 Use the **Save T2CASE.FRM As** option on the File menu to save the form as **lbOrder**, then use the Save Project As option on the File menu to save the project as **lbOrder**.

Figure 2-14 identifies the controls already included in the application. (You won't see the names of the controls on your screen. The names are included in Figure 2-14 for your reference only.)

frmOrder

cmdExit

cmdPrint

cmdCalc

cmdClear

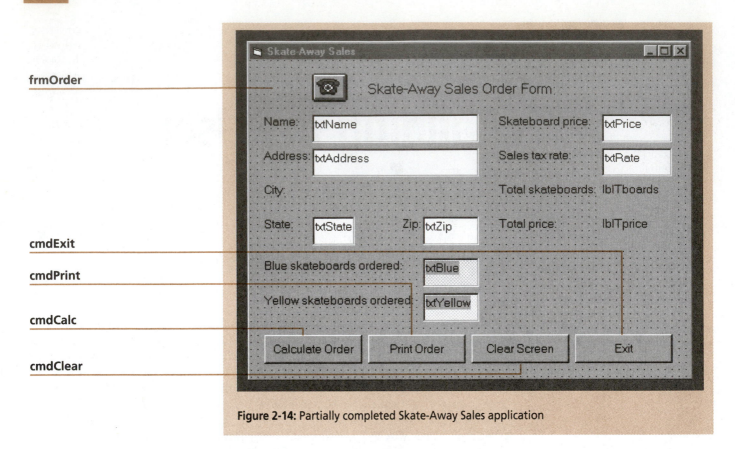

Figure 2-14: Partially completed Skate-Away Sales application

Notice that Figure 2-14 shows only the names of those controls whose names were changed from their default values. Only the form and objects that will contain code or objects that will be referred to in code need to have their names changed to more meaningful ones.

The user interface shown in Figure 2-14 resembles the sketch shown in Lesson A's Figure 2-12. Recall that that sketch was created using the guidelines you learned in Lesson A. For example, the information is arranged vertically, with the most important information located in the upper-left corner of the screen. The command buttons are centered along the bottom of the screen, with the most commonly used button positioned first. The command buttons contain meaningful captions, which are entered using book title capitalization. Each caption appears on one line, and no caption exceeds the three-word limit. The labels identifying the controls other than the command buttons are left-aligned and positioned to the left of their respective controls; each uses sentence capitalization and each ends with a colon.

Notice that the labels and controls are aligned wherever possible to minimize the number of different margins appearing in the user interface. You can use the dots that Visual Basic displays on the form during design time to help you align the various controls in the interface. When positioning the controls, be sure to maintain a consistent margin from the edge of the window; two or three dots is recommended. As illustrated in Figure 2-14, related controls are typically placed on succeeding dots. For example, notice that the top of the txtAddress control is placed on the horizontal line of dots found immediately below the txtName control. Also notice that the left edge of the Print Order command button is placed on the vertical line of dots found to the immediate right of the Calculate Order command button. (Controls that are not part of any logical grouping may be positioned from two to four dots away from other controls.)

Always size the command buttons in the interface relative to each other. When the command buttons are centered on the bottom of the screen, as they are in this interface, all the buttons should be the same height; their widths, however, may vary if necessary. If the command buttons are stacked in either the upper-right or lower-right corner of the screen, on the other hand, all the buttons should be the same height and the same width.

When building the user interface, keep in mind that you want to create a screen that no one notices. Snazzy interfaces may get "oohs" and "aahs" during their initial use, but they become tiresome after a while. The most important point to remember is that the interface should not distract the user from doing his or her work. Unfortunately, it's difficult for many application developers to refrain from using the many different colors, fonts, and graphics available in Visual Basic; actually, using these elements isn't the problem—overusing them is. So that you don't overload your user interfaces with too much color, too many fonts, and too many graphics, the next three sections will give you some guidelines to follow regarding these elements. Consider the graphics first.

Placing and Sizing Design Elements

- Maintain a consistent margin of two or three dots from the edge of the window.
- Position related controls on succeeding dots. Controls that are not part of any logical grouping may be positioned from two to four dots away from other controls.
- Command buttons in the user interface should be sized relative to each other. If the command buttons are centered on the bottom of the screen, then each button should be the same height; their widths, however, may vary. If the command buttons are stacked in either the upper-right or lower-right corner of the screen, then each should be the same height and the same width.
- Try to create a user interface that no one notices.

Including Graphics in the User Interface

The human eye is attracted to pictures before text, so include a graphic only if it is necessary to do so. You can use a graphic, for example, to either emphasize or clarify a portion of the screen. You can also use a graphic for aesthetic purposes, as long as the graphic is small and as long as it is placed in a location that does not distract the user. The small graphic in the Skate-Away Sales interface, for example, is included for aesthetics only. The graphic is purposely located in the upper-left corner of the interface, which is where you want the user's eye to be drawn first anyway. The graphic adds a personal touch to the Skate-Away Sales order form without being distracting to the user.

In the next section you will learn some guidelines pertaining to the use of different fonts in the interface.

Including Different Fonts in the User Interface

As you learned in Tutorial 1, you can change the type of font used to display the text in an object, as well as the style and size of the font. Recall that Courier and MS Sans Serif are examples of font types; regular, bold, and italic are examples of font styles; and 8, 10, and 18 points are examples of font sizes. The default font

GUI
Design Tips

Adding Graphics

- The human eye is attracted to pictures before text, so include a graphic only if it is necessary to do so. If the graphic is used solely for aesthetics, use a small graphic and place it in a location that will not distract the user.

used for interface elements in Windows is MS Sans Serif 8-point. A point, you may remember, is 1/72 of an inch; so each character in an 8-point font is 1/9 of an inch. You can use either 8, 10, or 12 point fonts for the elements in the user interface, but be sure to limit the number of font sizes used to either one or two. The Skate-Away Sales application uses two font sizes: 10 point and 12 point. The heading at the top of the interface is in 12 point; all of the other labels and captions are in 10 point.

Some fonts are serif, and some are sans serif. A **serif** is a light cross stroke that appears at the top or bottom of a character. The characters in a serif font have the light strokes, whereas the characters in a sans serif font do not. ("Sans" is a French word meaning "without.") Books use serif fonts because those fonts are easier to read on the printed page. Sans serif fonts, on the other hand, are easier to read on the screen, so use a sans serif font for the text in the user interface. You should use only one font type for all of the text in the interface. Avoid using italics and underlining because both make text difficult to read. The Skate-Away Sales interface uses the default MS Sans Serif font.

Selecting Appropriate Font Style and Size

- Use 8, 10, or 12 point fonts for the elements in the user interface.
- Limit the number of font sizes used to either one or two.
- Use a sans serif font for the text in the interface.
- Use only one font type for all of the text in the interface.
- Avoid using italics and underlining because both make text difficult to read.

In addition to overusing graphics and fonts, many application developers make the mistake of using either too much color or too many different colors in the user interface. In the next section you will learn some guidelines pertaining to the use of color.

Including Color in the User Interface

Just as the human eye is attracted to graphics before text, it is also attracted to color before black and white, so use color sparingly. It is a good practice to build the interface using black, white, and gray first, then add color only if you have a good reason to do so. Keep the following four points in mind when deciding whether to include color in the interface:

1. Some users will be working on monochrome monitors.
2. Many people have some form of either color-blindness or color confusion, so they will have trouble distinguishing colors.
3. Color is very subjective; what's a pretty color to you may be hideous to someone else.
4. A color may have a different meaning in a different culture.

It is usually best to follow the Windows standard of using black text on either a white, off-white, or light gray background. The Skate-Away Sales interface, for example, displays black text on a light gray background. If you want to add some color to the interface, you can also use black text on either a pale blue or a pale yellow background. Because dark text on a light background is the easiest to read, never use a dark color for the background or a light color for the text; a dark background is hard on the eyes, and light-colored text can appear blurry.

If you are going to include color in the interface, limit the number of colors to three, not including white, black, and gray. Be sure that the colors you choose complement each other.

Although color can be used to identify an important element in the interface, you should never use it as the only means of identification. In the Skate-Away Sales application, for example, the colors blue and yellow help the salesperson quickly identify where to enter the order for blue skateboards and where to enter the order for yellow skateboards. Notice, however, that color is not the only means of identifying those areas in the interface; the labels to the left of the controls also tell the user where to enter the orders for blue and yellow skateboards.

Selecting Appropriate Colors

- The human eye is attracted to color before black and white. Build the interface using black, white, and gray first, then add color only if you have a good reason to do so.
- Use either white, off-white, or light gray for an application's background, and black for the text. You can also use black text on either a pale blue or a pale yellow background. Dark text on a light background is the easiest to read.
- Never use a dark color for the background or a light color for the text; a dark background is hard on the eyes, and light-colored text can appear blurry.
- Limit the number of colors to three, not including white, black, and gray. The colors you choose should complement each other.
- Never use color as the only means of identification for an element in the user interface.

Now complete the user interface for the Skate-Away Sales application. First see what the interface looks like with a white background instead of a gray one.

Another way to display the Properties window for the form is to right-click an empty area of the form, then select Properties from the popup menu. You can also click the Properties Window button on the Standard toolbar.

To change the background color of the interface:

1   Click the **form's title bar** to select the form. Press the **F4** key to display the Properties window, then set the form's BackColor property to **white**. The form's background color changes to white.

   HELP? To change the BackColor property, click BackColor in the Properties window, then click the Settings list arrow. Click the Palette tab, then click the desired color square.

Notice that the background color of the label controls, however, is still gray. You can fix this problem in two ways. You can either set each label control's BackColor property to white, just as you did for the form, or you can set each label control's BackStyle property to 0-Transparent. For reasons you will learn in the next section, setting the BackStyle property is the preferred way.

The BackStyle Property

Recall from Tutorial 1 that the BackColor property determines an object's background color. The default background color for forms and label controls is gray. Because each form and each label control can have its own BackColor setting, changing the background color of the form does not change the background color of the label controls on that form. You can match the color of a label control to the background color of the form by setting the label control's BackStyle property.

A label control's **BackStyle property** determines whether the label is transparent or opaque. The default setting is 1-Opaque, which means that the color value stored in the control's BackColor property fills the control and obscures any color behind it—in this case, the gray in the label controls obscures the white background of the form. When a control's BackStyle property is set to 0-Transparent,

Visual Basic ignores the setting in the control's BackColor property; instead, Visual Basic allows you to see through the control. In most cases it is more efficient to change the BackStyle property of the label controls, instead of their BackColor property; then, if you want to experiment with the background color of the form, you won't have to change the BackColor property of the label controls each time to match the form. Observe how this works by changing the BackStyle property for the label controls to 0-Transparent.

To change the BackStyle property:

1 Select all of the gray label controls except the lblTboards and lblTprice controls. (There are 12 label controls, not counting the lblTboards and lblTprice controls.) Selection handles appear around each selected control.

 HELP? Recall from Tutorial 1 that to select more than one control, you click the first control, then Ctrl-click the other controls.

2 Display the Properties window, then set the BackStyle property of the selected controls to **0-Transparent**. (Remember to press the **Enter** key after selecting the 0-Transparent setting.) You can now see the form's white background through the label controls.

3 Click the **form** to deselect the selected label controls. (Be sure to click the form, and not one of the selected controls on the form.)

Suppose you decide that the user interface looked better with a gray background.

4 Display the Properties window, then set the BackColor property of the form to a **light gray**.

5 Click the **form** to select it.

Notice that you can still see the form's background color, which is now gray, through the 12 label controls.

Before you set the BackStyle property for the lblTboards and lblTprice controls, you will change their BorderStyle property and their Appearance property.

The BorderStyle and Appearance Properties

As you learned in Tutorial 1, the BorderStyle property determines the style of the object's border. The **BorderStyle property** for a label control can be either 0-None, which is the default, or 1-Fixed Single. The 1-Fixed Single setting surrounds the label control with a thin line, so it looks similar in appearance to a text box. A control's **Appearance property**, on the other hand, determines if the control appears flat (0-Flat) or three-dimensional (1-3D) on the screen. Although the default setting of a label control's Appearance property is 1-3D, you will not see the three-dimensional effect unless you set the label control's BorderStyle property to 1-Fixed Single. You will change the BorderStyle property of the lblTboards and lblTprice controls to 1-Fixed Single, so that the label controls will have a border. You will then change their Appearance property to 0-Flat because, in Windows applications, controls that contain data that the user is not allowed to edit do not typically appear three-dimensional. The last change you will make to the lblTboards and lblTprice controls is to change their BackStyle property to 0-Transparent.

To change the properties of the lblTboards and lblTprice controls:

1 Select the **lblTboards** and **lblTprice** controls.

   HELP? Refer back to Figure 2-14 for the location of these two controls.

2 Display the Properties window. Set the selected controls' BorderStyle property to **1-Fixed Single**, then click the **form** to deselect the controls. Notice that both label controls appear three-dimensional.

3 Now select the **lblTboards** and **lblTprice** controls again and set their Appearance property to **0-Flat**, then set their BackStyle property to **0-Transparent**.

4 Click the **form** to deselect the controls. The two label controls appear as flat boxes on the screen.

Now continue building the interface.

Setting the Text Property

Recall that most of Skate-Away's customers are in Illinois. Instead of having the salesperson enter IL in the txtState control for each order, it would be more efficient to have IL appear, automatically, in the state text box when the application is run. If the user needs to change the state entry while the application is running, he or she can simply click the State text box, then delete the current entry and retype the new one. You can display IL in the txtState control by setting that control's Text property to IL. Do that now.

To set the txtState control's Text property:

1 Click the **txtState** control, then display the Properties window. Click **Text** in the Properties list, then type **IL** and press the **Enter** key.

2 Click the **form** to select it. IL appears in the txtState control.

Notice that the text box control in which the user enters the city is missing from the interface. You will add that control next.

Adding a Text Box Control to the Form

A **text box control** provides an area in the form where the user can enter data. Add the missing text box control to the form and then set its properties.

To add the text box control to the form, set its properties, and then save and run the application:

1 Double-click the **Text Box** tool ▥ in the toolbox. A default-sized text box control appears in the middle of the form.

The Text1 text you see inside the text box is the current setting of this control's Text property. The **Text property** for a text box is similar to the Caption property for a label control; both properties manage the text shown inside their respective controls. Because you don't want the Text1 text to appear when the application is run, you will delete the contents of this control's Text property.

2   Display the Properties window. Double-click **Text** in the Properties list. Visual Basic highlights the Text1 text in the Settings box, as shown in Figure 2-15.

double-click here to
highlight Text1 text

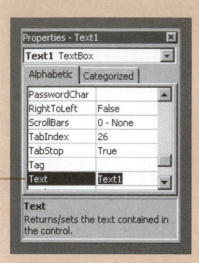

Figure 2-15: Text property highlighted in Settings box

HELP? If the Text1 text is not highlighted in the Settings box, double-click the Text property again until the Text1 text is highlighted. You can also drag in the Settings box to highlight the Text1 text.

3   Press the **Delete** key, then press the **Enter** key to remove the highlighted text. The text box is now empty.

4   Set the following two properties for this text box control:

Name: **txtCity** ("txt" stands for text box)
Font: **10** points

HELP? Recall that the Name property is listed first on the Alphabetic tab in the Properties window; it's listed in the Misc category on the Categorized tab.

5   Drag the **txtCity** control to a location immediately below the txtAddress control, then drag the txtCity control's right border until the control is as wide as the txtAddress control. The correct location and size are shown in Figure 2-16.

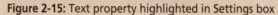

tip

Be sure to use either the Delete key or the Backspace key to delete the highlighted text in the Properties window. Do not use the Spacebar to delete the highlighted text. Pressing the Spacebar does not clear the property's contents; rather, it replaces the highlighted text with a space.

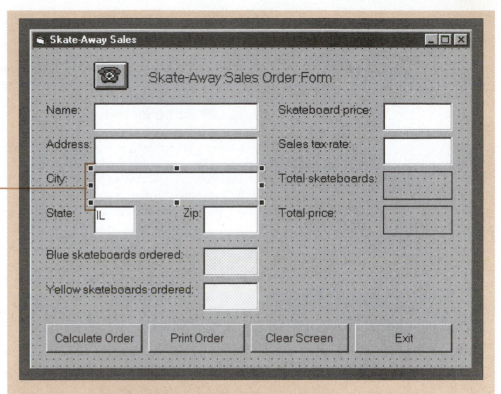

correct size and placement of the txtCity control

Figure 2-16: Correct size and placement of the txtCity control

Now save and run the project to see if it is working correctly.

6 **Save** and **run** the project. An insertion point appears in the txtName control.

The insertion point indicates that this text box is the active control. In Windows terminology, the txtName control has the **focus**, which means that the control is ready to receive input from you. Try this next.

7 Type **Sport Warehouse** as the customer name. Notice that a text box displays the information it receives from you. The information is recorded in the text box's Text property. In this case, for example, the information is recorded in the Text property of the txtName control.

In Windows applications, you can move the focus from one control to another by pressing the Tab key.

8 Press the **Tab** key to move the focus to the txtAddress control, then type **123 Main**.

The city entry is next.

9 Press the **Tab** key to move the focus to the txtCity control. Notice that the focus skips the txtCity control and moves to the txtState control.

Stop the application and think about why this happened. The End statement has already been entered in the Exit button's Click event procedure.

10 Click the **Exit** button to end the application. The application ends, and Visual Basic returns to the design screen.

tip

The easiest way to save a project using its current name is to click the Save Project button on the Standard toolbar. The Save Project button will save any file in the project that has been changed since the last time it was saved.

Controlling the Focus with the TabIndex Property

The **TabIndex property** determines the order in which a control receives the focus when the user is using the Tab key to tab through the application. Not all controls have a TabIndex property; Menu, Timer, CommonDialog, Data, Image, Line, and Shape controls do not. When you add a control that has a TabIndex property to a form, Visual Basic sets the control's TabIndex property to a number representing the order in which that control was added to the form. Keep in mind that when assigning these numbers Visual Basic starts counting at 0 (zero). In other words, the TabIndex property for the first control added to a form is 0 (zero), the TabIndex property for the second control is 1, and so on. Visual Basic uses the TabIndex property to determine the Tab order for the controls. To get a better idea of how this works, check the TabIndex property for the txtAddress, txtState, and txtCity controls.

To view the TabIndex property:

1   Click the **txtAddress** control, then click **TabIndex** in the Properties list. Notice that Visual Basic set the TabIndex property to 13. A TabIndex property of 13 means that this was the fourteenth control added to the form.

Now look at the TabIndex property for the txtState control.

HELP? If the TabIndex property is not 13, you might have selected the Address: label control instead of the txtAddress text box. Click the txtAddress text box, then repeat Step 1.

2   Click the **Object box** list arrow, which is located below the Properties window's title bar, then click **txtState** in the list. Notice that the txtState control's TabIndex property is set to 14. A control with a TabIndex of 14 will receive the focus immediately after the control with a TabIndex of 13. In this case, for example, the txtState control will receive the focus immediately after the txtAddress control.

Now look at the TabIndex property for the txtCity control, which was the last control added to the form.

3   Use the Properties window's Object box to select the **txtCity** control. Notice that the txtCity control's TabIndex property is set to 26, which means that it was the 27th control added to the form.

To tell Visual Basic that you want the txtCity control to receive the focus immediately after the txtAddress control, you need to change the TabIndex property of the txtCity control to 14, which is one number greater than the TabIndex of the txtAddress control (13). Figure 2-17 shows the current TabIndex values for the txtAddress, txtCity, and txtState controls and what their TabIndex values should be.

Control Name	Current TabIndex Value	New TabIndex Value
txtAddress	13	13
txtCity	26	14
txtState	14	15

Figure 2-17: TabIndex values

The only TabIndex value you will need to change is the one for the txtCity control. Changing the txtCity control's TabIndex property to 14 will cause Visual Basic to renumber the controls on the form, beginning with the control that originally had a TabIndex of 14. For example, the TabIndex of the txtState control, which was originally 14, will be assigned a TabIndex of 15. The control that had a TabIndex of 15 will be assigned a TabIndex of 16, and so on. After you change the TabIndex for the txtCity control, you will verify the renumbering by selecting the txtState control and looking at its TabIndex value.

To change the txtCity control's TabIndex property, then save and run the project:

1 The TabIndex property for the txtCity control should already be selected in the Properties window, so just type **14** and press the **Enter** key.

Verify that the txtState control's TabIndex property is now 15.

2 Use the Properties window's Object box to select the **txtState** control. The value of its TabIndex property should be 15.

3 **Save** and **run** the project.

4 Type **Sport Warehouse** as the customer name, then press the **Tab** key to move the focus to the txtAddress control.

5 Type **123 Main** as the address, then press the **Tab** key. Notice that the focus now moves to the txtCity control.

You can check the focus order of the remaining controls by simply pressing the Tab key.

6 Press the **Tab** key. The focus moves from the txtCity control to the txtState control, which is correct.

7 Press the **Tab** key, slowly, ten times. The focus correctly moves to the following controls: txtZip, txtBlue, txtYellow, txtPrice, txtRate, cmdCalc, cmdPrint, cmdClear, cmdExit, and finally back to the txtName control.

In Windows applications, the Tab key moves the focus forward, and the Shift+Tab key combination moves the focus backward. Try the Shift + Tab key combination.

8 Press **Shift + Tab**. The focus moves to the Exit button, as indicated by its highlighted border and the dotted rectangle around its caption.

9 Because the Exit button has the focus, you can simply press the **Enter** key to end the application. The application ends and Visual Basic returns to the design screen.

Now that all of the controls are on the user interface, you can lock them in place.

Locking the Controls on a Form

Once you have placed all of the controls in the desired locations on the form, it is a good idea to lock the controls in their current positions so you don't inadvertently move them. Once the controls are locked, you will not be able to move them until you unlock them; you can, however, delete them.

tip

....

▶ You can also move a locked control by selecting it in the form, and then pressing and holding down the Ctrl key as you press the up, down, right, or left arrow key on the keyboard.

To lock the controls on the form:

1 Right-click an empty area of the form, then click **Lock Controls** on the popup menu.

2 Try dragging one of the controls to a different location on the form. You won't be able to.

If you need to change the location of a control after you've locked the controls in place, you will need to select the Lock Controls command again. The Lock Controls command is a toggle command. Selecting it once activates it, and selecting it again deactivates it.

The user interface is almost complete. The final task is to assign access keys to the controls.

Assigning Access Keys

An access key allows the user to select an object using the Alt key in combination with a letter or number. For example, you can use Alt + F to open Visual Basic's File menu because the letter "F" is the File menu's access key. Access keys are not case sensitive—in other words, you can open Visual Basic's File menu by pressing either Alt + F or Alt + f.

You should assign access keys to each of the essential elements in the interface for the following three reasons. First, access keys allow a user to work with the application even if the mouse becomes inoperative. Second, access keys allow users who are fast typists to keep their hands on the keyboard. Third, and most important, access keys allow people with disabilities, which may prevent them from working with a mouse, to use the application.

You can assign an access key to any control that has a Caption property. You assign the access key by including an ampersand (&) in the control's caption. The ampersand is entered to the immediate left of the character you want to designate as the access key.

Each access key appearing in the interface must be unique. The first choice for an access key is the first letter of the caption, unless another letter provides a more meaningful association. For example, the letter X is typically the access key for an Exit button because the letter X provides a more meaningful association than does the letter E. If you can't use the first letter (perhaps because it is already used as the access key for another control) and no other letter provides a more meaningful association, then use a distinctive consonant in the caption. The last choices for an access key are a vowel or a number in the caption.

In the Skate-Away Sales application, you will assign an access key to each of the four command buttons. Then, instead of clicking the command button, the user can simply press the Alt key along with its access key.

To assign an access key to each of the four command buttons:

1 Select the **Calculate Order** button in the user interface. Display the Properties window. The Caption property should be selected in the Properties list.

HELP? If the Caption property is not selected in the Properties list, then click Caption in the Properties list.

You'll use the letter C as the access key for the Calculate Order button.

2 Place the mouse pointer in the Caption property's Settings box. The mouse pointer becomes an I-bar I.

3 Place I to the left of the C in Calculate, then click at that location. The insertion point appears before the word Calculate.

4 Type & (ampersand), then press the **Enter** key. The Caption property should now say &Calculate Order. (You may not be able to read the entire Caption in the Settings box.)

Now assign the letter "P" as the access key for the Print Order button.

5 Use the Properties window's Object box to select the **cmdPrint** control, then change its Caption property to **&Print Order**.

Next, you'll assign an access key to the Clear Screen button. In this interface, you can't use the letter "C" for the access key because that is the access key for the Calculate Order button; remember, access keys must be unique. Assign the letter "L" as the access key for the Clear Screen control.

6 Use the Properties window's Object box to select the **cmdClear** control, then change its Caption property to **C&lear Screen**.

In Windows applications, the letter "X" is customarily the access key for an Exit button.

7 Use the Properties window's Object box to select the **cmdExit** control, then change its Caption property to **E&xit**.

8 Click the **form** to select it.

The caption inside each of the command buttons should now have an underlined letter, which is that button's access key. But you are not finished assigning access keys yet. Recall that you should give users a way to access all of the important elements of the interface without using the mouse; that includes the text boxes in which the order information must be entered. But, you may be thinking, you can't assign an access key to a text box because text box controls do not have a Caption property. The answer to this dilemma is to assign an access key to the label control that identifies the text box—in this case, to the label control that appears to the left of each text box. Do that next.

To assign access keys to the label controls that identify the text boxes in the interface:

1 Display the Properties window. Use the Object box to select the **Label2** control. Sizing handles appear around the Name: label in the user interface. Change the Label2 control's Caption to **&Name:**.

2 Use Figure 2-18 to assign access keys to the other label controls.

Control Name	Caption	Access Key
Label3	Address:	A
Label4	City:	T
Label5	State:	S
Label6	Zip:	Z
Label7	Blue skateboards ordered:	B
Label8	Yellow skateboards ordered:	Y
Label9	Skateboard price:	I
Label10	Sales tax rate:	R

Figure 2-18: Access keys for label controls

(You will not assign access keys to the Total skateboards: and Total price: label controls because the controls to their immediate right are label controls, not text boxes. Recall that users cannot access label controls.)

In addition to assigning an access key to the label control that identifies the text box, you must also set the label control's TabIndex property so that its value is one number less than the TabIndex value of its corresponding text box. (In other words, the text box's TabIndex value should be one number greater than the label control's TabIndex value.) Since label controls cannot receive the focus, pressing the label control's access key will automatically send the focus to the next control in the tab order sequence—in other words, to the text box. For example, if the Name: label control has a TabIndex of 5 and its corresponding text box (txtName) has a TabIndex of 6, pressing Alt + N will move the focus to the txtName text box. You will now adjust the TabIndex values appropriately.

To set the TabIndex values, then save and run the application:

1   Use the information shown in Figure 2-19 to set the TabIndex values of the controls.

Control Name	Caption for Label Controls	TabIndex Value
Label2	Name:	0
txtName		1
Label3	Address:	2
txtAddress		3
Label4	City:	4
txtCity		5
Label5	State:	6
txtState		7
Label6	Zip:	8
txtZip		9
Label7	Blue skateboards ordered:	10
txtBlue		11
Label8	Yellow skateboards ordered:	12
txtYellow		13
Label9	Skateboard price:	14
txtPrice		15
Label10	Sales tax rate:	16
txtRate		17
cmdCalc		18
cmdPrint		19
cmdClear		20
cmdExit		21

Figure 2-19: TabIndex values for controls

2 **Save** and **run** the application.

3 Press **Alt + b** to move the focus to the txtBlue control. Type **10** for the number of blue skateboards ordered.

4 Press **Alt + s** to move the focus to the txtState control. Press the **Delete** key on your keyboard twice to remove the IL, then type **CA**.

5 Press **Alt + x** to access the Exit button. The application ends, and Visual Basic returns to the design screen.

GUI Design Tips

Rules for Assigning Access Keys

- When assigning an access key to a control, use the first letter of the caption, unless another letter provides a more meaningful association. If you can't use the first letter and no other letter provides a more meaningful association, then use a distinctive consonant in the caption. Lastly, use a vowel or a number in the caption.

- Access keys must be unique.

- To give users keyboard access to text boxes, assign an access key to the text box control's identifying label. Set the TabIndex property of the label control so that its value is one number less than the value in the TabIndex property of the corresponding text box. (In other words, the TabIndex value of the text box should be one number greater than the TabIndex value of its identifying label control.)

You have now finished two of the five steps involved in creating an OOED application: planning the application and building the user interface. You will complete the remaining three steps in Lesson C. For now, you can either take a break or complete the end-of-lesson questions and exercises.

SUMMARY

To set the tab order:

■   Set each control's TabIndex property to a number that represents the order in which you want that control to receive the focus. Remember to begin with 0 (zero).

To lock/unlock the controls on the form:

■   Right-click an empty area of the form, then select Lock Controls on the popup menu. If the controls are locked, the Lock Controls button will appear indented. To unlock the controls, simply select the Lock Controls command again. You can also lock/unlock controls by using the Lock Controls command on the Format menu, or the Lock Controls toggle button on the Form Editor toolbar.

To assign an access key to a control:

■   In the control's Caption property, type an ampersand (&) to the immediate left of the letter or number you want to designate as the access key. (The ampersand in a label control's Caption property designates an access key only if the label control's UseMnemonic property is set to True, which is the default for that property.)

To give users keyboard access to a text box:

■   Assign an access key to the text box control's identifying label control. Set the label control's TabIndex property so that its value is one number less than its corresponding text box's TabIndex value.

To access a control that has an access key:

■   Press and hold down the Alt key as you press the control's access key.

To control the border around a label control:

■   Set the label control's BorderStyle property to 1-Fixed Single if you want a border; otherwise, set the control's BorderStyle property to 0-None, which is the default.

To see through a label control:

■   Set the label control's BackStyle property to 0-Transparent. The default is 1-Opaque.

To view a control as either flat or three-dimensional:

■   Set the control's Appearance property to either 0-Flat or 1-3D; 1-3D is the default.

Q U E S T I O N S

1. The _____ property determines the order in which a control receives the focus when the user is tabbing.
   a. OrderTab
   b. SetOrder
   c. TabIndex
   d. TabOrder
   e. TabStop

2. When placing controls on a form, you should maintain a consistent margin of _____ dots from the edge of the window.
   a. one or two
   b. two or three
   c. two to five
   d. three to ten
   e. ten to twenty

3. If the command buttons are centered on the bottom of the screen, then each button should be _____ .
   a. the same height
   b. the same width
   c. the same height and the same width

4. If the command buttons are stacked in either the upper-right or the lower-right corner of the screen, then each button should be _____ .
   a. the same height
   b. the same width
   c. the same height and the same width

5. The human eye is attracted to _____ .
   a. black and white before color
   b. color before black and white
   c. graphics before text
   d. text before graphics
   e. both b and c

6. When building an interface, always use _____ .
   a. dark text on a dark background
   b. dark text on a light background
   c. light text on a dark background
   d. light text on a light background
   e. either b or c

7. Use either _____ fonts for the elements in the user interface.
   a. 6, 8, or 10 point
   b. 8, 10, or 12 point
   c. 10, 12, or 14 point
   d. 12, 14, or 16 point

8. Limit the number of font sizes used in an interface to _____ .
   a. one or two
   b. two or three
   c. three or four

9. Use a _____ font for the text in the user interface.
   a. sans serif
   b. serif

10. Limit the number of font types used in an interface to _____ .
   a. one
   b. two
   c. three
   d. four

11. You can lock the controls on a form by _____ .
   a. clicking the Lock Controls Toggle button on the Form Editor toolbar
   b. using the Lock Controls command on the Format menu
   c. right-clicking an empty area of the form, then selecting Lock Controls on the popup menu
   d. all of the above

12. If you want to put a border around a label control, set the label control's _____ property to 1-Fixed Single.
   a. Appearance
   b. BackStyle
   c. Border
   d. BorderStyle
   e. Caption

13. If you want a label control to appear flat on the screen, set the label control's _____ property to 0-Flat.
   a. Appearance
   b. BackStyle
   c. Border
   d. BorderStyle
   e. Caption

14. If you want to see through a label control, set the label control's _____ property to 0-Transparent.
   a. Appearance
   b. BackStyle
   c. Border
   d. BorderStyle
   e. Caption

15. You use the _____ character to assign an access key to a control.
   a. &
   b. *
   c. @
   d. $
   e. ^

16. You can assign an access key to any control that has a(n) _____ property.
   a. Access
   b. Caption
   c. Key
   d. KeyAccess
   e. Text

17. Explain the procedure for choosing a control's access key.

18. Explain how you give users keyboard access to a text box.

E X E R C I S E S

1. In this exercise, you will finish building a user interface.
    a. Open the Lb1 (Lb1.vbp) project, which is located in the Tut02 folder on your Student Disk.
    b. Finish building the user interface shown in Figure 2-20 by adding a text box named txtName. Change the txtName control's font size to 10 points. Be sure to assign access keys to the text boxes and command buttons. Also adjust the TabIndex values appropriately. Change the text box's font to Arial.

add this text box

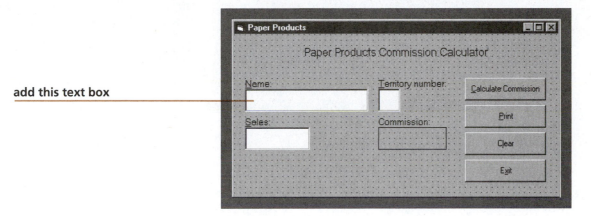

Figure 2-20

    c. Lock the controls on the form.
    d. Change the background color of the form to pale yellow.
    e. Change the BackStyle property of the six label controls to 0-Transparent. Change the lblComm control's BorderStyle property to 1-Fixed Single. Change its Appearance property to 0-Flat.
    f. Save the form and the project as lb1Done in the Tut02 folder on your Student Disk.
    g. Run the application. The Print button and the Exit button have already been coded for you. (You will code both the Calculate Commission and the Clear buttons in Lesson C, Exercise 1. You will learn how to code a Print button in Lesson C.)
    h. Click the Print button to print the form on the printer. (If the labels in the printout do not appear the same as on the screen, you may need to select a different font for the labels. Return to the design screen. Select the labels, then use the Font property to change the font.)
    i. Click the Exit button to end the application.
2. In this exercise, you will finish building a user interface.
    a. Open the Lb2 (or Lb2.vpb) project, which is located in the Tut02 folder on your Student Disk.
    b. Finish building the user interface shown in Figure 2-21 by adding a text box named txtNsales. Change the txtNsales control's font size to 10 points. Be sure to adjust the TabIndex values appropriately. The user will enter the North region's sales and increase percentage before entering the South region's sales and increase percentage. Change the text box's font to Arial.

place txtNsales control here

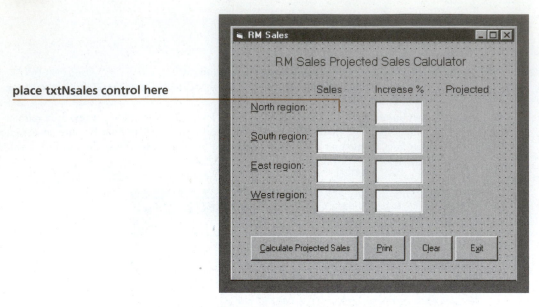

Figure 2-21

c. Lock the controls on the form.

d. Change the background color of the form to pale blue.

e. Change the BackStyle, BorderStyle, and Appearance properties of the label controls appropriately.

f. Save the form and the project as lb2Done in the Tut02 folder on your Student Disk.

g. Run the application. The Print button and the Exit button have already been coded for you. (You will code both the Calculate Projected Sales and the Clear buttons in Lesson C, Exercise 2. You will learn how to code a Print button in Lesson C.)

h. Click the Print button to print the form on the printer. (If the labels in the printout do not appear the same as on the screen, you may need to select a different font for the labels. Return to the design screen. Select the labels, then use the Font property to change the font.)

i. Click the Exit button to end the application.

3. In this exercise, you will modify the application that you saved in Lesson A's Exercise 3.

a. If you completed Lesson A's Exercise 3, then open the la3Done project, which is located in the Tut02 folder on your Student Disk.

b. Save the form and the project as lb3Done.

c. Lock the controls on the form.

d. Set the BackStyle and Appearance properties of the lblWeekEnd and lblWeekDay controls appropriately.

e. Assign access keys to the important elements of the interface.

f. Set each control's TabIndex property appropriately.

g. Save and run the application, then click the Print Time Report button to print the interface. (The Print Time Report button contains the code to print the interface. If the labels in the printout do not appear the same as on the screen, you may need to select a different font for the labels. Exit the application, select the labels, then use the Font property to change the Font; try the Arial font.)

h. Submit the printout from step g.

LESSON C
objectives

In this lesson you will learn how to:

- Use the TOE chart to code the application
- Use pseudocode to plan an object's code
- Use the SetFocus and PrintForm methods
- Write an assignment statement
- Include internal documentation in the code
- Write Visual Basic equations
- Use the Val and Format functions
- Set the MinButton, MaxButton, and ControlBox properties

Coding, Testing, Debugging, and Documenting the Application

Coding the Application

After planning the application and building the user interface, you can then write the Visual Basic instructions to tell the objects in the interface how to respond to events. The instructions are called **code**, and the process of writing the instructions is called **coding**. You will need to write code for each object that has an event listed in the third column of the TOE chart you created in Lesson A. For your reference while coding, the TOE chart is shown in Figure 2-22.

Task	Object	Event
1. Calculate the total skateboards ordered and the total price 2. Display the total skateboards ordered and the total price in the lblTboards and lblTprice objects	cmdCalc	Click
Clear the screen for the next order	cmdClear	Click
End the application	cmdExit	Click
Print a confirmation notice	cmdPrint	Click
Display the total skateboards ordered (from cmdCalc)	lblTboards	None
Display the total price (from cmdCalc)	lblTprice	None
Get and display the order information	txtName, txtAddress, txtCity, txtState, txtZip, txtPrice, txtRate, txtBlue, txtYellow	None

Figure 2-22: Completed TOE chart ordered by object

According to the TOE chart, you will need to write code for the four command buttons, as they are the only objects with an event listed in the third column of the chart. The Exit button has already been coded for you, so you need to write the code for only the Print Order, Clear Screen, and Calculate Order buttons. First, however, open the lbOrder project that you created in Lesson B.

To open the lbOrder project, then save the form and the project under a different name:

1   Start Visual Basic, if necessary, and make sure your Student Disk is in the appropriate drive.

2   Open the **lbOrder** (lbOrder.vbp) project, which is located in the Tut02 folder on your Student Disk.

3   Click the **form's title bar** to select the form. Use the File menu's Save lbOrder.frm As option to save the form as **lcOrder**, then use the File menu's Save Project As option to save the project as **lcOrder**.

Figure 2-23 identifies the controls included in the user interface. (You won't see the names of the controls on your screen. The names are included in Figure 2-23 for your reference only.)

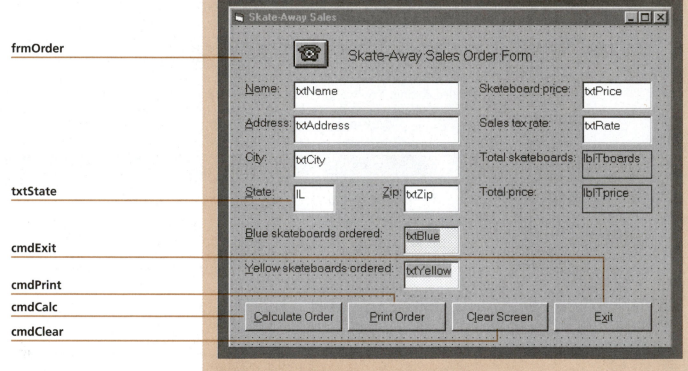

Figure 2-23: Skate-Away Sales user interface

Recall that the controls are locked on the form. Also recall that only the form and controls that will be either coded or referred to in code need to have their names changed to more meaningful ones. You'll code the Print Order button first.

Coding the Print Order Button

According to the TOE chart, the Print Order button is assigned the task of print-ing the confirmation notice, which is basically the form itself, but without the command buttons showing. The Print Order button, therefore, must first hide the command buttons, then print the confirmation notice, and then redisplay the com-mand buttons. Last, the Print Order button should send the focus to the Clear Screen button; after printing an order, the salesperson will typically need to clear the screen for the next order. Sending the focus to the Clear Screen button will allow the user to select that button by pressing the Enter key. (Remember, not everyone can, or wants to, use a mouse.) Figure 2-24 lists what you want the Print Order button to do.

Print Order button

1. Hide the 4 command buttons
2. Print the form
3. Display the 4 command buttons
4. Send the focus to the Clear Screen button

Figure 2-24: Steps for the Print Order button

Notice that the list shown in Figure 2-24 is composed of short statements in English. The statements represent the steps the Print Order button needs to follow in order to print the confirmation notice. In programming terms, the list of steps shown in Figure 2-24 is called pseudocode. **Pseudocode** is a tool programmers use to help them plan the steps that an object needs to take in order to perform its assigned task. Even though the word *pseudocode* might be unfamiliar to you, you've already written pseudocode without even realizing it. Think about the last time you gave directions to someone. You wrote each direction down on paper, in your own words; your directions were a form of pseudocode.

The programmer uses the pseudocode as a guide when coding the application. For example, you will use the pseudocode shown in Figure 2-24 to write the appro-priate Visual Basic instructions for the Print Order button. The first step in that pseudocode is to hide the four command buttons. In Tutorial 1 you learned that you hide a control by setting its Visible property to False. You also learned that you can use an assignment statement to set the value of a property during run time.

Assigning a Value to a Property During Run Time

You can use an **assignment statement**, which is simply a Visual Basic instruction, to assign a value to the property of an object while the application is running. In this case you want to assign the False value to the Visible property of each of the four command buttons when the Print Order button is clicked. Assigning the False value to the Visible property will hide the command buttons. Then, after the form is printed, you want to assign the True value to the Visible property of each of the command buttons. Assigning the True value to the Visible property will display the buttons on the form.

As you learned in Tutorial 1, an assignment statement that assigns a value to the property of an object must follow this syntax: *[form.]object.property = value*. *Form* is the name of the form in which the object is located, *object* is the name of the object, and *property* is the name of the property to which you want the value assigned. Recall that items appearing in square brackets ([ ]) in an instruction's syntax are optional parts of the instruction, and items in *italics* indicate where the programmer must supply information pertaining to the current application. According to the syntax of an assignment statement, the name of the form is optional; if the object is in the current form, you can omit the form name and simply use the syntax: *object.property = value*. Notice that you use a period to separate the form's name, if used, from the object's name, and the object's name from the property name. You follow the *[form.]object.property* information with an equal sign (=) and the value you want to assign to the object's property. For example, the assignment statement to change the Calculate Order button's Visible property to False, which will hide the button from view, could be written as either `frmOrder.cmdCalc.Visible = False`, or simply as `cmdCalc.Visible = False`. Because the Calculate Order button is in the current form, both versions of the assignment statement will work correctly.

When Visual Basic sees an assignment statement in a Code window, Visual Basic assigns the value on the right side of the equal sign to the object and property appearing on the left side of the equal sign. For example, the `cmdCalc.Visible = False` assignment statement tells Visual Basic to assign the Boolean value of False to the Visible property of the cmdCalc control. You will now enter the code to tell the Print Order button to hide the four command buttons before printing the form.

To begin coding the Print Order command button:

1   Open the Print Order button's Code window. The Click event procedure for the cmdPrint control appears.

    HELP? Recall that you open an object's Code window by double-clicking the object.

2   Press the **Tab** key, then type **cmdcalc.visible = false** and press the **Enter** key. Visual Basic changes the instruction to cmdCalc.Visible = False. (Notice the capitalization.)

When entering code, you can type the names of commands, objects, and properties in lowercase letters. When you move to the next line, Visual Basic will automatically change your code to reflect the proper capitalization of those elements. This provides a quick way of verifying that you entered an object's name and property correctly, and that you entered the code using the correct syntax; if the capitalization does not change, then Visual Basic does not recognize the object, command, or property.

3   Type **cmdprint.visible = false** and press the **Enter** key.

4   Type **cmdclear.visible = false** and press the **Enter** key.

5   Type **cmdexit.visible = false** and press the **Enter** key.

These four assignment statements will hide the four command buttons. Now enter the instructions that will print the form and redisplay the command buttons.

Using the PrintForm Method

You can use Visual Basic's PrintForm method to print the form. A **method** is a predefined Visual Basic procedure. The syntax of the PrintForm method is [*form.*]**PrintForm** where *form* is the name of the form you want to print and PrintForm is the name of the method. Recall that items appearing in bold in an instruction's syntax are required—in this case, the method's name, PrintForm, is required. The name of the form, on the other hand, is optional; if specified, however, notice that you use a period to separate the form's name from the name of the method. If you omit the form's name from the instruction, Visual Basic prints the current form only—in this case, for example, the instruction frmOrder.PrintForm will print the current form, and so will the instruction PrintForm.

To finish coding the Print Order button, then save and run the application:

1 The Code window showing the cmdPrint control's Click event procedure should still be open. Type **printform** and press the **Enter** key.

After the form is printed, you need to display the four command buttons for the user. To do that you must enter four additional assignment statements into the Code window. These assignment statements will set the Visible property of the four command buttons to True. Instead of typing the four additional statements, you will copy the existing assignment statements to the clipboard, and then paste them into the Code window, below the PrintForm instruction. Then, in each of the copied statements, you can simply change the False to True.

2 Position the I-bar I at the beginning of the first assignment statement in the Code window. Press and hold down the left mouse button and drag until all four assignment statements are highlighted, then release the mouse button. See Figure 2-25.

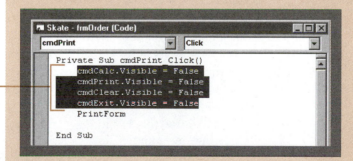

drag to highlight these four assignment statements

Figure 2-25: Four assignment statements highlighted in the Print Order button's Code window

3 Press **Ctrl + c** to copy the assignment statements to the clipboard.

4 Position I in the empty line below the PrintForm instruction (immediately below the P), then click at that location. The insertion point appears at that location.

5 Press **Ctrl + v** to paste the four assignment statements into the Code window, then press the **Enter** key.

6 In the four assignment statements you just copied, change the False to True. (You can look ahead to Figure 2-26 to see the end result.)

Methods and events constitute an object's behaviors. An event is a behavior that can be performed on an object—for example, a command button object can be clicked. A method is a behavior that an object can perform—for example, a form object can print itself.

The period between *form* and PrintForm is called the dot member selection operator. It tells Visual Basic that the method is a member of the form class.

You can also use the Copy option on the Edit menu to copy the statements to the clipboard, and the Paste option on the Edit menu to paste the statements into the Code window.

The last step in the Print Order button's pseudocode is to send the focus to the Clear Screen button. You can use Visual Basic's SetFocus method to do so.

Using the SetFocus Method

The SetFocus method allows you to move the focus to a specified control or form while the application is running. The syntax of the SetFocus method is *object*.**SetFocus**, where *object* is the name of the object in which you want the focus and **SetFocus** is the name of the method.

To enter the SetFocus method in the Print Order button's Click event:

1   The cmdPrint control's Click event procedure should still be open. Position the I-bar I in the blank line below the `cmdExit.Visible = True` instruction, immediately below the c, then click at that location. Type **cmdclear.setfocus** and press the **Enter** key. (You can look ahead to Figure 2-26 to see the end result.)

Internally Documenting the Program Code

It's a good practice to leave yourself some comments as reminders in the Code window; programmers refer to this as **internal documentation**. Visual Basic provides an easy way to document a program internally. You simply place an apostrophe (') before the statement you want Visual Basic to treat as a comment. Visual Basic ignores everything after the apostrophe on that line. Add some comments to the Print Order button's Code window.

To document the code in the Print Order button, then save and run the application:

1   Position the I-bar I at the end of the first line in the Code window (the line with the `Private Sub` instruction), then click at that location. The insertion point appears at that location.

2   Press the **Enter** key to insert a new line. Press the **Tab** key, then type **'hide command buttons before printing the form**. Don't type the period, but be sure to type the apostrophe (').

3   Position I after the `PrintForm` instruction, then click at that location. Notice that the internal documentation changes to a different color when you move the insertion point to another line. Recall from Tutorial 1 that Visual Basic displays keywords and key symbols in a different color to help you quickly identify these elements in the Code window. In this case, the color coding helps you easily locate the internal documentation.

4   Press the **Enter** key to insert a blank line below the `PrintForm` instruction. Type **'display command buttons after the form is printed**. Don't type the period, but be sure to type the apostrophe ('). Figure 2-26 shows the completed Code window for the Print Order button's Click event.

```
Skate - frmOrder (Code)                                    _ □ ×
cmdPrint                    ▼   Click                       ▼
Private Sub cmdPrint_Click()
     'hide command buttons before printing the form
     cmdCalc.Visible = False
     cmdPrint.Visible = False
     cmdClear.Visible = False
     cmdExit.Visible = False
     PrintForm
     'display command buttons after the form is printed
     cmdCalc.Visible = True
     cmdPrint.Visible = True
     cmdClear.Visible = True
     cmdExit.Visible = True
     cmdClear.SetFocus

End Sub
```

Figure 2-26: The completed Code window for the Print Order button's Click event

HELP? You may need to size the Code window in order to see all of the instructions.

5   Compare your code with the code shown in Figure 2-26 and make any necessary corrections, then close the Code window.

It is a good programming practice to write the code for one object at a time and then test and debug that object's code before coding the next object. This way, if something is wrong with the program, you know exactly where to look for the error.

6   **Save** and **run** the application.

7   If your computer is connected to a printer, click the **Print Order** button to print the confirmation notice.

HELP? If an error message appears in a dialog box, close the dialog box, then stop the application, if necessary. Open the Print Order button's Code window and compare your code with Figure 2-26. Make the necessary corrections, then repeat Steps 6 and 7.

HELP? If the labels in the printout do not appear the same as on the screen, you may need to select a different font for the labels. Return to the design screen and select all of the labels, then use the Font property to change the font; try the Arial font.

Following the instructions you entered in the Print Order button's Code window, Visual Basic hides the command buttons, prints the form, redisplays the command buttons, and sends the focus to the Clear Screen button. You can tell that the Clear Screen button has the focus because the button has a darkened border and a dotted rectangle around its caption.

8   Click the **Exit** button to end the application. Visual Basic returns to the design screen.

Code the Clear Screen button next.

Coding the Clear Screen Button

According to the TOE chart, the Clear Screen button is assigned the task of clearing the screen for the next order. Here again, you can use assignment statements to accomplish this task. To clear the prior customer information from the screen, you will need to remove the contents of seven of the nine text boxes. The two text boxes whose contents you won't need to remove are the txtPrice and txtRate controls; after the user enters the price and tax rate for the first order, the user should not have to enter that information again. You will also need to remove the entries recorded in the Caption property of two of the label controls, lblTboards and lblTprice. After the screen is cleared, the Clear Screen button should place the focus in the txtName control so that the user will be ready to enter the next order. Figure 2-27 lists the steps—the pseudocode—you want the Clear Screen button to follow.

Clear Screen button

1. Clear the Text property of the Text box controls (except txtPrice and txtRate)
2. Clear the Caption property of the Label controls (lblTboards and lblTprice)
3. Send the focus to the txtName control

Figure 2-27: Pseudocode for the Clear Screen button

You are assigning IL to the txtState control in case the user changed the state when he or she entered an order. Remember that most, but not all, of Skate-Away's customers are in Illinois.

You will use an assignment statement to assign the string "IL" to the txtState control, and a zero-length string to the remaining eight controls. A **string** is a group of characters enclosed in quotation marks. For example, the word "Jones" is considered a string. Likewise, "45" is a string, but 45 is not; 45 is a number. "Jones" is a string with a length of five because there are five characters between the quotation marks, and "45" is a string with a length of two because there are two characters between the quotation marks. Following this logic, a **zero-length string** is a set of quotation marks with nothing between them, like this: "". You will assign a zero-length string, also called an **empty string**, to the Text property of each of the text boxes (except the state, price, and sales tax rate text boxes) and to the Caption property of the two label controls, lblTboards and lblTprice. Assigning the zero-length string to the Text property and to the Caption property will clear the prior customer's information from the controls.

Recall that the syntax of an assignment statement is *[form.]object.property = value.* In this case, you don't need the form name in the assignment statements because the controls are in the current form.

To code the Clear Screen button:

1 Open the Clear Screen button's Code window. The cmdClear control's Click event procedure appears.

First, include some documentation in the Code window.

2 Press the **Tab** key, then type **'clear the screen for the next order** and press the **Enter** key. Be sure to type the apostrophe (').

Recall that the names of the text boxes are txtName, txtAddress, txtCity, txtState, txtZip, txtBlue, and txtYellow.

3 Type **txtname.text = ""** and press the **Enter** key. (Don't type any spaces between the quotation marks.)

4 Copy the txtName.Text = "" assignment statement to the clipboard, then paste the assignment statement into the Code window six times, between the original assignment statement and the End Sub instruction. Change the names of the controls in the assignment statement, as well as the value assigned to the txtState control, to match Figure 2-28.

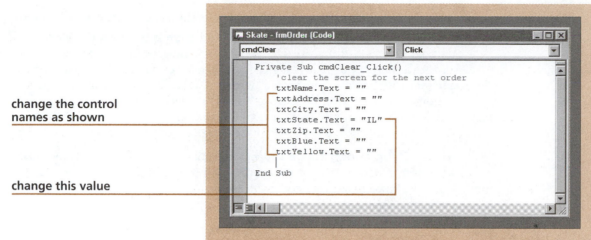

**change the control
names as shown**

change this value

Figure 2-28: Assignment statements entered in the Clear Screen button's Code window

HELP? To copy the `txtName.Text = ""` statement to the clipboard, high-light the statement, then press Ctrl + c. To paste the `txtName.Text = ""` statement into the Code window, first click at the location where you want to begin pasting, then press Ctrl + v.

The two label controls are next.

5 Position the insertion point in the blank line immediately below the last assignment statement, as shown in Figure 2-28.

6 Type **lbltboards.caption = ""** and press the **Enter** key, then type **lbltprice. caption = ""** and press the **Enter** key. (Don't enter any spaces between the "".)

According to the pseudocode, you should set the focus to the txtName control next.

7 Type **txtname.setfocus** and press the **Enter** key. The completed Code window is shown in Figure 2-29.

tip
• • • • • • • • • • • • • • • •

You also can use the `txtName = ""` instruction to clear the Text property of the txtName control, and the `lblTboards = ""` instruction to clear the Caption property of the lblTboards control; this is because every control has a default property. When you do not specify a property after a control's name in an instruction, Visual Basic uses the control's default property when processing the instruction. The default property for a text box is the Text property, and the default property for a label control is the Caption property. It is highly recommended that you always specify a property after a control's name in an instruction; doing so will make your programs more readable and self-documenting.

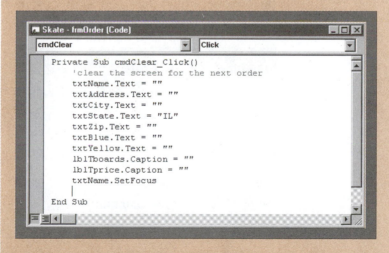

Figure 2-29: The completed Code window for the Clear Screen button's Click event

8   Close the Clear Screen button's Code window, then **save** and **run** the application.

9   To test the application, enter your name and address information (including the city, state, and zip), then enter **10** for the number of blue skateboards and **10** for the number of yellow skateboards. Enter **100** for the skateboard price and **.05** for the sales tax rate. Click the **Clear Screen** button. The prior customer's information disappears from the screen, and the focus is in the txtName control. Notice that the text in the txtState control returns to IL, the txtPrice control still contains 100, and the txtRate control still contains .05.

HELP? If an error message appears in a dialog box, close the dialog box, then stop the application, if necessary. Open the Clear Screen button's Code window and compare your code with Figure 2-29. Make the necessary corrections, then repeat Steps 8 and 9.

10 Click the **Exit** button to end the application. Visual Basic returns to the design screen.

The Calculate Order button is the only object that still needs to be coded. Before you can code that button, however, you will need to learn how to write mathematical equations in Visual Basic.

Writing Visual Basic Equations

Most applications require the computer to perform some calculations. You instruct the computer to perform a calculation by writing an arithmetic equation in an object's Code window. The mathematical operators you can use in your arithmetic equations, along with their precedence numbers, are listed in Figure 2-30. The precedence numbers represent the order in which Visual Basic performs the mathematical operations in an equation. You can, however, use parentheses to override the order of precedence. Operations within parentheses are always performed before operations outside of parentheses.

Operator	Operation	Precedence Number
^	exponentiation (raises a number to a power)	1
–	negation	2
*, /	multiplication and division	3
\	integer division	4
Mod	modulus arithmetic	5
+, –	addition and subtraction	6

Important Note: You can use parentheses to override the order of precedence. Operations within parentheses are always performed before operations outside parentheses.

Figure 2-30: Mathematical operators and their order of precedence

When you create an arithmetic equation, keep in mind that Visual Basic follows the same order of precedence as you do when solving equations; that is, operations with a precedence number of 1 are done before operations with a precedence number of 2, and so on. If the equation contains more than one operator having the same priority, those operators are evaluated from left to right. For example, in the equation 3+9/3*5, the division (/) would be done first, then the multiplication (*), and then the addition (+). In other words, Visual Basic would first divide 9 by 3, then multiply by 5, and then add 3. The equation evaluates to 18. You can use parentheses to change the order in which the operators will be evaluated. For example, the equation (3+9)/3*5 (notice the parentheses around the 3+9) evaluates to 20, not 18. That's because the parentheses tell Visual Basic to add 3 + 9 first, then divide by 3, and then multiply by 5.

Two of the mathematical operators listed in Figure 2-30 might be less familiar to you; these are the integer division operator (\) and the modulus arithmetic operator (Mod). The integer division operator (\), like the standard division operator (/), is used to divide two numbers. Unlike the standard division operator, however, the integer division operator returns an integer (whole number) result. For example, the expression 211\4 results in 52, whereas the expression 211/4 results in 52.75. The modulus arithmetic operator is also used to divide two numbers, but it results in the remainder of the division. For example, 211 Mod 4 equals 3 (the remainder of 211 divided by 4). One use for the modulus operator is to determine if a year is a leap year—one that has 366 days, rather than 365 days. As you may know, if a year is a leap year, then its year number is evenly divisible by the number 4—in other words, if you divide the year number by 4 and the remainder is 0 (zero), then the year is a leap year. You can determine if the year 2000 is a leap year by using the expression 2000 Mod 4. This expression would evaluate to 0 (the remainder of 2000 divided by 4), so the year 2000 is a leap year. Similarly, you can determine if the year 2001 is a leap year by using the expression 2001 Mod 4. This expression would evaluate to 1 (the remainder of 2001 divided by 4), so the year 2001 is not a leap year.

When entering equations in Visual Basic, you do not enter the dollar sign ($) or the percent sign (%). If you want to enter a percentage, you must convert the percentage to its decimal equivalent—for example, you would need to convert 5% to .05.

In addition to the mathematical operators, Visual Basic also allows you to use relational operators and logical operators in your equations. You will learn about those two types of operators in Tutorial 4. For now, you will need to know only the mathematical operators in order to code the Calculate Order button in the Skate-Away Sales application.

Coding the Calculate Order Button

According to your TOE chart for this application, the Calculate Order button is responsible for calculating both the total number of skateboards ordered and the total price of the order, as well as displaying those amounts in the two label controls. The instructions to accomplish the Calculate Order button's tasks must be placed in the button's Click event procedure. The Calculate Order button's pseudocode, which lists the steps the button will need to take in order to accomplish its tasks, is shown in Figure 2-31.

Calculate Order button

1. Calculate total skateboards = blue skateboards + yellow skateboards
2. Calculate total price =
   total skateboards * skateboard price * (1 + sales tax rate)
3. Display total skateboards and total price in lblTboards and lblTprice label controls
4. Send the focus to the Print Order button

Figure 2-31: Pseudocode for the Calculate Order button

The first step listed in the pseudocode shown in Figure 2-31 is to calculate the total number of skateboards. To do this, the Calculate Order button will need to add the number of blue skateboards to the number of yellow skateboards. Recall that the number of blue skateboards is recorded in the txtBlue control's Text property as the user enters that information. Likewise, the number of yellow skateboards is recorded in the txtYellow control's Text property. Recall from your TOE chart that the total number of skateboards should be displayed in the lblTboards control. You can use an assignment statement to add the two Text properties together and then assign the sum to the Caption property of the lblTboards control. This is illustrated in Figure 2-32.

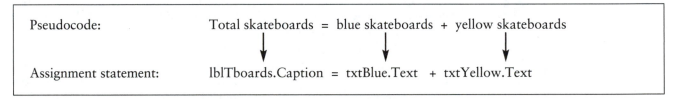

Pseudocode: Total skateboards = blue skateboards + yellow skateboards

Assignment statement: lblTboards.Caption = txtBlue.Text + txtYellow.Text

Figure 2-32: Illustration of the total skateboards calculation

The next step shown in the pseudocode is to compute the total price of the order. To do this, the application needs to multiply the total number of skateboards by the skateboard price ($100); it then must add a 5% sales tax to that amount. The total number of skateboards is recorded in the lblTboards control, the price is entered in the txtPrice control, and the sales tax rate is entered in the txtRate control. Recall from your TOE chart that the total price should be displayed in the lblTprice control. The total price equation is illustrated in Figure 2-33.

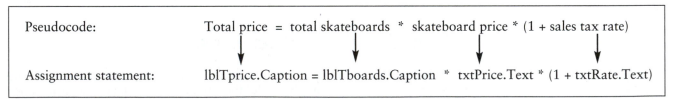

Pseudocode: Total price = total skateboards * skateboard price * (1 + sales tax rate)

Assignment statement: lblTprice.Caption = lblTboards.Caption * txtPrice.Text * (1 + txtRate.Text)

Figure 2-33: Illustration of the total price calculation

The last step in the Calculate Order button's pseudocode is to set the focus to the Print Order command button; after calculating an order, the salesperson will typically print the confirmation notice. Open the Calculate Order button's Code window and write the necessary code.

To code the Calculate Order button:

1 Open the Calculate Order button's Code window. The current event procedure is Click, which is the event you want.

2 Maximize the Code window. Press the **Tab** key, then type **'calculate total number of skateboards** and press the **Enter** key.

3 Type **lbltboards.caption = txtblue.text + txtyellow.text** and press the **Enter** key.

4 Type **'calculate total price** and press the **Enter** key.

5 Type **lbltprice.caption = lbltboards.caption * txtprice.text * (1 + txtrate.text)** and press the **Enter** key.

6 Type **cmdprint.setfocus** and press the **Enter** key. See Figure 2-34.

the code in the Code window was compressed so that you could read the entire line

```
Skate - frmOrder (Code)                                    _ □ ×
cmdCalc                          ▼    Click                        ▼
Private Sub cmdCalc_Click()
    'calculate total number of skateboards
    lblTboards.Caption = txtBlue.Text + txtYellow.Text
    'calculate total price
    lblTprice.Caption = lblTboards.Caption * txtPrice.Text * (1 + txtRate.Text)
    cmdPrint.SetFocus

End Sub
```

Figure 2-34: The Calculate Order button's Click event

7 Compare your code with the code shown in Figure 2-34. Make any needed corrections before continuing to the next step. (The code in Figure 2-34 was compressed so that you could read the entire line. You may not be able to see the entire equation that calculates the total price without scrolling the Code window.)

8 Close the Calculate Order button's Code window, then **save** and **run** the application.

9 Press the **Tab** key five times to move the focus to the txtBlue control, type 5 as the number of blue skateboards ordered, then press the **Tab** key. Type **10** as the number of yellow skateboards ordered, then press the **Tab** key. Type **100** as the skateboard price and press the **Tab** key. Type **.05** as the sales tax rate, then click the **Calculate Order** button. The Calculate Order button calculates, incorrectly, the total skateboards and the total price, then moves the focus to the Print Order button, as shown in Figure 2-35.

HELP? If an error message appears in a dialog box, close the dialog box, then stop the application, if necessary. Open the Calculate Order button's Code window and compare your code with Figure 2-34. Make the necessary corrections, then repeat steps 8 and 9.

tip

You can compress your code by using the Options option on the Tools menu. When the Options dialog box appears, select the Editor Format tab, then change the font size to either 8 or 9.

these figures are incorrect

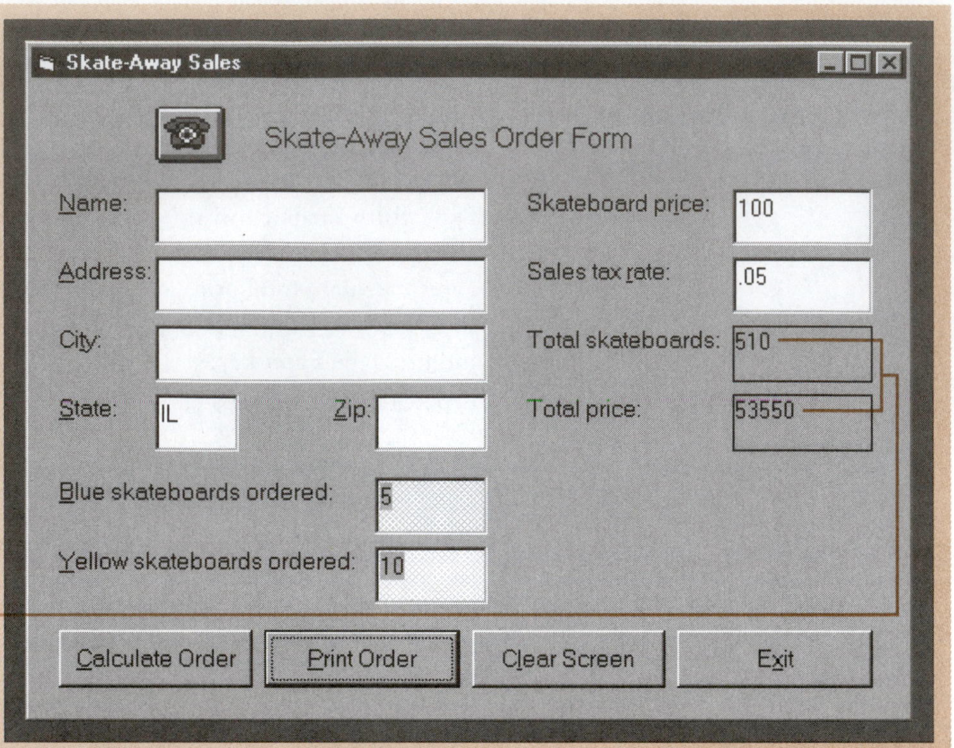

Figure 2-35: Screen showing incorrect figures calculated by the Calculate Order button

Notice that the application shows 510 as the total number of skateboards. Instead of mathematically adding the two order quantities together, which should have resulted in a total of 15, Visual Basic appended the second order quantity to the end of the first order quantity, giving 510. When the total skateboards figure is incorrect, it follows that the total price figure will also be incorrect, as the total skateboards figure is used in the total price equation. Exit the application and think about what went wrong.

10 Click the **Exit** button to end the application. Visual Basic returns to the design screen.

The `lblTboards.Caption = txtBlue.Text + txtYellow.Text` equation you entered in the Calculate Order button's Code window is supposed to calculate the total skateboards, but the equation is not working correctly. Instead of the plus sign (+) adding the blue skateboard quantity to the yellow skateboard quantity, the plus sign appends the latter quantity to the end of the first one. This occurs because the plus sign in Visual Basic performs two roles: it adds numbers together and it concatenates (links together) strings. You will learn about string concatenation in Tutorial 3. (Recall that strings are groups of characters enclosed in quotation marks.)

In Visual Basic, values in both the Caption and Text properties of objects are treated as strings, not numbers, even though you don't see the quotation marks. Adding strings together will not give you the same result as adding numbers together. As you saw in the Skate-Away Sales application, adding the string "5" to the string "10" results in the string "510," whereas adding the number 5 to the number 10 results in the number 15. To fix this problem, you need to tell Visual Basic to treat the entries in the Text property of both the txtBlue and txtYellow controls as numbers, not as strings. For this, you need to use the Val function.

The Val Function

Like a method, a **function** is a predefined procedure that performs a specific task. Unlike a method, however, a function results in a value. For example, the **Val function**, which tells Visual Basic to treat a character string as a numeric value, results in a number. The syntax of the Val function is **Val**(*string*), where *string* is the character string you want treated as a number. Because Visual Basic must be able to interpret the *string* as a numeric value, the *string* cannot include a letter or a special character, such as the dollar sign, the comma, or the percent sign (%); it can, however, include the period. When Visual Basic encounters an invalid character in the Val function's *string*, Visual Basic stops converting the *string* to a number at that point. Figure 2-36 shows some examples of how the Val function would interpret various *strings*.

This Val function:	Would be converted to:
Val("456")	456
Val("24,500")	24
Val("123X")	123
Val("$56.88")	0
Val("Abc")	0
Val("")	0
Val("25%")	25

Figure 2-36: Examples of the Val function

Notice that the Val function converts the "$56.88", the "Abc", and the "" (empty string) to the number 0.

To fix the assignment statement entered in the Calculate Order button's Code window, you will use the Val function to tell Visual Basic to treat the Text property of both the txtBlue and txtYellow controls as numbers instead of strings.

To include the Val function in the Calculate Order button's Code window, then print the confirmation notice:

1. Open the Calculate Order button's Code window, then maximize the Code window. The cmdCalc control's Click event procedure fills the screen.
2. Change the `lblTboards.Caption = txtBlue.Text + txtYellow.Text` assignment statement to **lblTboards.Caption = val(txtBlue.Text) + val(txtYellow.Text)**. Be sure to watch the placement of the parentheses.
3. Also change the `lblTprice.Caption = lblTboards.Caption * txtPrice.Text * (1 + txtRate.Text)` to **lblTprice.Caption = val(lblTboards.Caption) * val(txtPrice.Text) * (1 + val(txtRate.Text))**. See Figure 2-37. Be sure to watch the placement of the parentheses; notice that there are two parentheses at the end of the equation. (The code in Figure 2-37 was compressed so that you could read more of each instruction. On your screen, you may need to scroll the Code window to see the instructions in their entirety.)

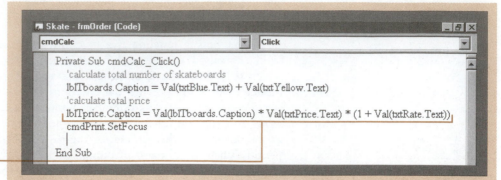

the code in the Code window was compressed and the font was changed so that you could read the entire line

Figure 2-37: The Calculate Order button's Code window showing Val function

tip

If you are thinking that the instructions are getting a bit unwieldy, you are correct. In Tutorial 3 you will learn how to write more compact assignment statements.

4 Close the Code window, then **save** and **run** the project.

5 Click the **txtBlue** control, type 5 as the number of blue skateboards ordered, then press the **Tab** key. Type 10 as the number of yellow skateboards ordered, 100 as the skateboard price, and .05 as the sales tax rate. Click the **Calculate Order** button. The application correctly calculates the total skateboards (15) and the total price (1575), then sends the focus to the Print Order button.

HELP? If an error message appears in a dialog box, close the dialog box, then stop the application, if necessary. Open the Calculate Order button's Code window and compare your code with Figure 2-37. Make the necessary corrections, then repeat Steps 4 and 5.

6 If your computer is connected to a printer, then press the **Enter** key to select the Print Order button. The confirmation notice prints on the printer, and the cmdClear button receives the focus.

7 If you printed the confirmation notice, then the Clear Screen button has the focus, so you can simply press the **Enter** key to clear the screen. If you did not print the confirmation notice because your computer was not connected to a printer, then click the **Clear Screen** button to clear the screen.

The information is cleared from the screen, and the focus moves to the txtName control.

8 Click the **Exit** button. Visual Basic returns to the design screen.

Another change you will make to this application is to display a dollar sign ($) and a comma in the lblTprice control.

Using the Format Function

You can use the **Format function** to improve the appearance of the numbers in your application. The syntax of the Format function is: **Format**(*expression, format*). *Expression* specifies the number, date, time, or string whose appearance you want to format. *Format* is either the name of a predefined Visual Basic format or, if you want more control over the appearance of the expression, a string containing special symbols that tell Visual Basic how you want the expression displayed. (You can display the Help window for the Format function to learn more about these special symbols.) In this case, you will use one of Visual Basic's predefined formats, some of which are explained in Figure 2-38.

Format Name	Description
Currency	Displays a number with a dollar sign and two decimal places; if appropriate, displays a number with a thousand separator; negative numbers are enclosed in parentheses
Fixed	Displays a number with at least one digit to the left and two digits to the right of the decimal point
Standard	Displays a number with at least one digit to the left and two digits to the right of the decimal point; if appropriate, displays a number with a thousand separator
Percent	Multiplies a number by 100 and displays the number with a percent sign (%); displays two digits to the right of the decimal point

Figure 2-38: Some of Visual Basic's predefined formats

Because you want a dollar sign and a comma to display in the lblTprice control, you will use the "Currency" format in the Format function. You will enter the Format function in the Calculate Order button's Code window.

tip

You could have added the Format function in the equation that calculates the total price, but then the equation would be so long that it would be hard to understand.

To enter the Format function in the Calculate Order button's Code window:

1 Open the Calculate Order button's Code window. The Code window displays the cmdCalc Click event procedure.

2 Click at the beginning of the cmdPrint.SetFocus instruction and press the **Enter** key to insert a blank line above that instruction. Press ↑ on your keyboard. If necessary, position the insertion point immediately above the c in the cmdPrint.SetFocus instruction.

3 Enter the additional line of code shown in Figure 2-39.

enter this line of code

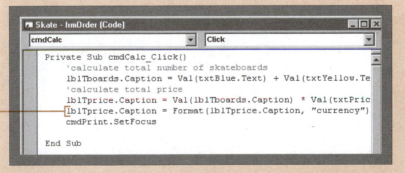

Figure 2-39: Format function entered in the Calculate Order button's Click event

4 Close the Code window, then **save** and **run** the application.

5 Enter the following order:
Sport Warehouse, 123 Main, Glendale, IL, 60134, 100 blue skateboards, 150 yellow skateboards.

6 Enter 100 as the skateboard price and .05 as the sales tax rate.

7 Click the **Calculate Order** button. The application calculates the total skateboards and total price, as shown in Figure 2-40.

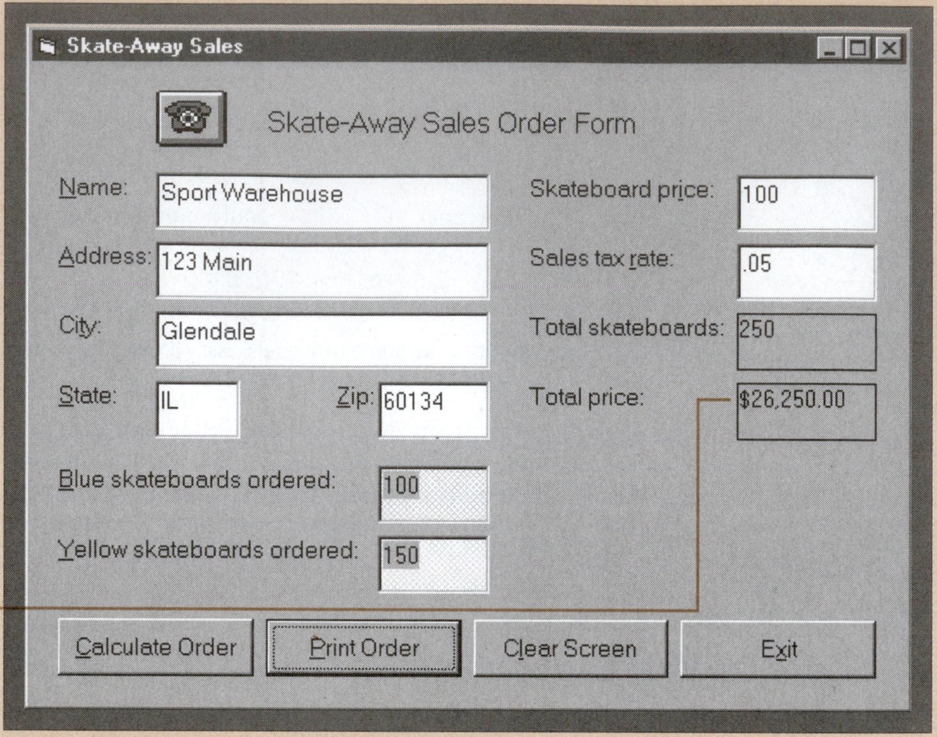

total price appears with a $ and two decimal places

Figure 2-40: Total price displayed using the Format function

8 Click the order form's **Maximize** button ⬜. Notice that the objects in the interface are no longer centered within the form's borders. Click the **Restore** button ⬛ to restore the form to its normal size.

9 Make the form smaller by using the mouse to drag one or more of the form's borders. Notice that if you make the form smaller than its normal size, some of the objects will not be visible to the user.

Stop the application so you can learn ways to handle this sizing dilemma.

10 Click the **Exit** button. Visual Basic returns to the design screen.

You can control which border elements (Minimize, Maximize, and Close buttons) appear in a form's title bar, as well as whether the form is sizable, by setting the MinButton, MaxButton, ControlBox, and BorderStyle properties, respectively.

The MinButton, MaxButton, ControlBox, and BorderStyle Properties

You learned about the BorderStyle property in Tutorial 1. Recall that the BorderStyle property determines the border style of an object. As you may remember, the default BorderStyle for a form is 2-Sizable, which means that the form can be minimized, maximized, or closed while the application is running; the user can also drag the form's borders to change the form's size during run time. In Tutorial 1's copyright

screen application, recall that you changed the form's BorderStyle property to
0-None because you wanted to prevent the user from minimizing, maximizing,
and sizing the copyright screen and from exiting using the Close button. Changing
the BorderStyle to 0-None removes the border, the title bar, and the border elements from the form.

Unlike the interface you created in Tutorial 1, the order form interface that
you created in Tutorial 2 is not a splash screen. When an interface is not a splash
screen, the user should always be allowed both to close the application using the
form's Close button and to minimize the application using the form's Minimize
button. It is up to you, however, to decide whether the user can maximize the
form during run time, and whether he or she can change the size of the form by
dragging its borders.

To prevent the user from sizing a form using its borders, simply change the form's
BorderStyle property to 1-Fixed Single. You can control whether the Minimize,
Maximize, and Close buttons appear in a form's title bar by setting the form's
MinButton, MaxButton, and ControlBox properties, respectively. The valid settings for the MinButton, MaxButton, and ControlBox properties are the Boolean values True and False. In the order form application, you will not allow the user to size
the form using either its borders or the Maximize button. You will, however, allow the
user to use both the Minimize and the Close buttons.

To prevent the user from sizing the form using its borders and the Maximize button, and to display both the Minimize and Close buttons:

1 Click the **form's** title bar to select the form, then change the form's
BorderStyle property to **1-Fixed Single**.

2 **Run** the application.

Notice that the 1-Fixed Single setting displays the Close button ☒ in the form's
title bar; however, it does not display either the Minimize ▬ or Maximize ▢
buttons. When you set a form's BorderStyle property to 1-Fixed Single, Visual
Basic sets both the MinButton and MaxButton properties to False, so neither
button displays in the title bar. You can display the Minimize button ▬ by setting the form's MinButton property to True. You will do that next.

3 Click the **Exit** button. Visual Basic returns to the design screen. Select the
form, then set the form's MinButton property to **True**.

4 **Save** and **run** the application. Notice that the form now contains a
Minimize button ▬, a grayed-out (disabled) Maximize button ▢, and a
Close button ☒.

5 Try dragging one of the form's borders in order to change the size of the
form. You will not be able to change the size of the form using either border.

6 Click the **Exit** button. Visual Basic returns to the design screen.

You have now completed the first three of the five steps involved in creating
an OOED application: planning the application, building the user interface, and
coding the application. The fourth step is to test and debug the application. You
will do that next.

Testing and Debugging the Application

You test an application by running it and entering some sample data. You should use both valid and invalid test data. **Valid data** is data that the application is expecting—for example, the Skate-Away Sales application is expecting the user to enter a numeric value as the skateboard price. **Invalid data**, on the other hand, is data that the application is not expecting. In this application, for example, the application is not expecting the user to enter a letter for the number of either blue or yellow skateboards ordered. You should test the application as thoroughly as possible; you don't want to give the user an application that ends abruptly because invalid data was entered. (You will learn more about handling invalid data in later tutorials.)

Debugging refers to the process of locating errors in the program. Program errors can be either syntax errors or logic errors. When you enter an instruction incorrectly—for example, typing `Edn` instead of `End`—you create a syntax error. Visual Basic can detect syntax errors for you, as you will learn in Tutorial 3. (Because you typically test each object's code before coding another object, as you did in this lesson, the syntax errors will already have been corrected by the time you get to testing and debugging the entire application.)

An example of a much more difficult type of error to find, and one that Visual Basic cannot find for you, is a logic error. When you enter an instruction that won't give you the results for which you are looking, you create a logic error. The instruction `lblAverage.Caption = Val(txtNum1.Text) + Val(txtNum2.Text) / 2`, which is supposed to calculate the average of two numbers, is an example of a logic error. Although the instruction is syntactically correct, it is logically incorrect. The instruction to calculate the average of two numbers, written correctly, should be `lblAverage.Caption =(Val(txtNum1.Text) + Val(txtNum2.Text)) / 2`; because division has a higher precedence number than does addition, you must place parentheses around the `Val(txtNum1.Text) + Val(txtNum2.Text)`.

To test and debug the current application with both valid and invalid data:

1 **Run** the application, then test the application by clicking the **Calculate Order** button without entering any data. The application displays 0 for the total number of skateboards, and $0.00 for the total price.

2 Try entering a letter (any letter) for the number of blue skateboards ordered and a letter for the number of yellow skateboards ordered. Enter **100** for the skateboard price and .05 for the sales tax rate. Click the **Calculate Order** button. The application displays 0 for the total number of skateboards, and $0.00 for the total price. (Recall that the Val function converts letters to the number 0.)

3 Click the **Clear Screen** button. Enter **10** as the number of blue skateboards ordered, and **10** as the number of yellow skateboards ordered. Now highlight the **100** in the txtPrice control, then type the letters **xyz**. Click the **Calculate Order** button. The application displays 20 as the total number of skateboards ordered, and $0.00 as the total price.

4 Click the **Clear Screen** button, then enter an order that is correct. Click the **Calculate Order** button.

5 Click the **Clear Screen** button, then practice with other entries to see how the application responds.

6 When you are finished, click the **Exit** button to end the application.

After you've tested the application to verify that it is working correctly, you can move to the last step involved in creating an OOED application, which is to assemble the documentation.

Assembling the Documentation

Assembling the documentation refers to placing your planning tools and a printout of the application in a safe place, so you can refer to them if you need to change the application in the future. Your planning tools include the TOE chart, sketch of the user interface, and either the flowcharts or pseudocode. The printout of the application includes the form image, form as text, and code.

To print the Form Image, Form as Text, and Code:

1 Click **File** on the menu bar, then click **Print.**

2 Click **Form Image**, then click **Form As Text**. Checkmarks should appear next to each of the three Print What selections. Click the **OK** button to begin printing.

You have now completed the five steps involved in creating an application:
1. Planning the application.
2. Building the user interface.
3. Coding the application.
4. Testing and debugging the application.
5. Assembling the documentation.

You can either take a break, complete the end-of-lesson questions and exercises, or read and complete the Debugging section and exercises. The Debugging section may contain information that will help you complete the end-of-lesson exercises.

S U M M A R Y

To move the focus to an object while the program is running:

■ Use the SetFocus method. Its syntax is [*form.*]*object*.**SetFocus**.

To print a form:

■ Use the PrintForm method. Its syntax is [*form.*]**PrintForm**.

To assign a value to the property of an object:

■ Use an assignment statement. Its syntax is [*form.*]*object.property* = *value*.

To document Visual Basic code with comments:

■ Begin the comment with an apostrophe (').

To clear an object's Caption/Text property:

■ Use an assignment statement to assign a zero-length string (""), also called an empty string, to the object's Caption/Text property.

To tell Visual Basic to treat a character string as a numeric value:

■ Use the Val function. Its syntax is **Val**(*string*).

To improve the appearance of numbers in the user interface:

■ Use the Format function. Its syntax is **Format** (*expression, format*).

To control the border style of an object, and whether the Minimize, Maximize, and Close buttons appear on the title bar:

■ Set the form's BorderStyle, MinButton, MaxButton, and ControlBox properties.

QUESTIONS

1. The _____ method prints a form.
   a. Form
   b. FormPrint
   c. Print
   d. Printer
   e. PrintForm

2. Which of the following is a valid assignment statement?
   a. txtName.Caption = 'Jones'
   b. txtName.Caption = "Jones"
   c. txtName.Text = 'Jones'
   d. txtName.Text = "Jones"
   e. None of the above is valid

3. Which of the following is a valid assignment statement?
   a. lblName.Caption = Jones
   b. txtName.Caption = "Jones"
   c. txtName.Caption = 'Jones'
   d. cmdExit.Visible = "Yes"
   e. None of the above is valid

4. Which of the following assignment statements will not calculate correctly?
   a. txtTotal.Text = Val(txtSales1.Text) + Val(txtSales2.Text)
   b. txtTotal.Text = Val(lblSales1.Caption) + Val(lblSales2.Caption)
   c. txtTotal.Text = Val(txtRed.Text) * 2
   d. txtTotal.Text = Val(lblBlue.Caption) * 1.1
   e. All of the above are correct

5. When a form's BorderStyle property is set to 1-Fixed Single, which buttons will appear in the form's title bar during run time?
   a. Close
   b. Maximize
   c. Minimize
   d. All of the above

6. Which property controls whether the Close button appears in the form's title bar during run time?
    a. BoxControl
    b. Close
    c. Control
    d. ControlBox

7. You use the _____ function to display dollar signs and commas in numbers.
    a. Focus
    b. Format
    c. PrintForm
    d. SetFocus
    e. Val

8. The _____ function tells Visual Basic to treat a string as a numeric value.
    a. Focus
    b. Format
    c. PrintForm
    d. SetFocus
    e. Val

9. Listed below are the five steps you should follow when creating an OOED application. Put them in the proper order by placing a number (1 to 5) on the line to the left of the step.
    _____ Assemble the documentation.
    _____ Plan the application.
    _____ Code the application.
    _____ Build the user interface.
    _____ Test and debug the application.

10. The instruction `txtTotal.Text = Val(txtNum.Text) / 2`, which should multiply the contents of the txtNum text box by 2 and assign the result to the txtTotal text box, is an example of _____ .
    a. a logic error
    b. a syntax error
    c. a correct instruction

11. The instruction PrintFrm is an example of _____ .
    a. a logic error
    b. a syntax error
    c. a correct instruction

E X E R C I S E S

NOTE: In Exercises 4 through 19 you will perform the five steps involved in creating an OOED application. Recall that those five steps are:

1. Plan the application. (Prepare a TOE chart, ordered by object, and draw a sketch of the user interface.)
2. Build the user interface. (To help you remember the names of the controls as you are coding, print the Form Image and write the names next to each object.)
3. Code the application. (Be sure to write pseudocode for each of the objects that will be coded.)
4. Test and debug the application. (Use the sample data provided in each of the exercises.)
5. Assemble the documentation. (TOE chart, sketch, printout of the form, form as text, and code)

The following list summarizes the GUI design guidelines you have learned so far. You can use this list to verify that the interfaces you create in the following exercises adhere to the GUI standards outlined in the book.

- Information should flow either vertically or horizontally, with the most important information always located in the upper-left corner of the screen.

- Maintain a consistent margin of two or three dots from the edge of the window.

- Related controls should be grouped together using either white space or a frame.

- Position related controls on succeeding dots.

- Command buttons should either be centered along the bottom of the screen or stacked in either the upper-right or lower-right corner.

- If the command buttons are centered along the bottom of the screen, then each button should be the same height; their widths, however, may vary.

- If the command buttons are stacked in either the upper-right or lower-right corner of the screen, then each button should be the same height and the same width.

- Use no more than six command buttons on a screen.

- The most commonly used command button should be placed first.

- Command button captions should:
  - be meaningful
  - be from one to three words
  - appear on one line
  - be entered using book title capitalization

- Use labels to identify the controls in the interface.

- Identifying labels should:
  - be from one to three words
  - appear on one line
  - be aligned by their left borders
  - be positioned either above or to the left of the control that they identify
  - end with a colon (:)
  - be entered using sentence capitalization
  - have their BackStyle property set to 0-Transparent
  - have their BorderStyle property set to 0-None

- Labels that display program output (for example, the results of calculations):
  - should have their BorderStyle set to 1-Fixed Single
  - should have their Appearance property set to 0-Flat
  - can have their BackStyle property set to either 0-Transparent or 1-Opaque

- Align labels and controls to minimize the number of different margins.

- If you use a graphic in the interface, use a small one and place it in a location that will not distract the user.

- Use no more than two different font sizes, which should be 8, 10, or 12 points.

- Use only one font type, which should be a sans serif font, in the interface.

- Avoid using italics and underlining.

- Use either white, off-white, light gray, pale blue, or pale yellow for an application's background, and black for the text.

- Use color sparingly and don't use it as the only means of identification for an element in the interface.

- Set each control's TabIndex property to a number that represents the order in which you want that control to receive the focus (begin with 0).

- A text box's TabIndex value should be one more than the TabIndex value of its identifying label.

- Lock the controls in place on the form.

- Assign a unique access key to each essential element of the interface (text boxes, command buttons, and so on).

- Document the program internally.

- Use the Val function on Text and Caption properties.

- Set the form's BorderStyle, MinButton, MaxButton, and ControlBox properties appropriately:

  - Splash screens should not have a Minimize, Maximize, or Close button, and their borders should not be sizable.

  - Forms other than splash screens should always have a Minimize button and a Close button, but you can choose to disable the Maximize button.

  - Forms other than splash screens typically have a BorderStyle property setting of either 1-Fixed Single or 2-Sizable.

- Test the application with both valid and invalid data (test the application without entering any data; also test it by entering letters where numbers are expected).

tip

The exercises on this page require you to print the interface. If the labels in the printouts do not appear the same as on the screen, you may need to select a different font for the labels. Select the labels in the interface, then use the Font property to change the font; try the Arial font.

1. In this exercise you will complete the application that you saved in Lesson B's Exercise 1.

    a. If you completed Lesson B's Exercise 1, then open the lb1Done project, which is located in the Tut02 folder on your Student Disk.
    b. Save the form and the project as lc1Done.
    c. Change the form's BorderStyle property to 1-Fixed Single. Change the form's MinButton property so that the Minimize button appears in the form's title bar.
    d. Code the Calculate Commission button appropriately. Recall that the commission rate is 10%. Be sure to use the Val function.
    e. Use the Format function to display the commission with a dollar sign.
    f. Code the Clear button appropriately.
    g. Code the Print button so that it prints the interface without the command buttons showing.
    h. Save and run the application. Be sure to test the application with both valid and invalid data. Use the following information for the valid data:
        Name: Enter your name
        Territory number: 10
        Sales: 2500
    i. After entering the valid data, click the Calculate Commission button, then print the interface with the valid data showing.
    j. Stop the application, then print the code.
    k. Submit the printout from step i and the code from step j.

2. In this exercise you will complete the application that you saved in Lesson B's Exercise 2.
    a. If you completed Lesson B's Exercise 2, then open the lb2Done project, which is located in the Tut02 folder on your Student Disk.

The exercises on this page require you to print the interface. If the labels in the printouts do not appear the same as on the screen, you may need to select a different font for the labels. Select the labels in the interface, then use the Font property to change the font; try the Arial font.

b. Save the form and the project as lc2Done.

c. Change the form's MaxButton property so that the Maximize button is disabled.

d. Code the Calculate Projected Sales button appropriately. Be sure to use the Val function.

e. Use the Format function to display the projected sales using the Standard format.

f. Code the Clear button appropriately.

g. Code the Print button so that it prints the interface without the command buttons showing.

h. Save and run the application. Be sure to test the application with both valid and invalid data. Use the following information for the valid data:

North sales and percentage:	25000, .05
South sales and percentage:	30000, .07
East sales and percentage:	10000, .04
West sales and percentage:	15000, .11

i. After entering the valid data, click the Calculate Projected Sales button, then print the interface with the valid data showing.

j. Stop the application, then print the code.

k. Submit the printout from step i and the code from step j.

3. In this exercise you will complete the application that you saved in Lesson B's Exercise 3.

a. If you completed Lesson B's Exercise 3, then open the lb3Done project, which is located in the Tut02 folder on your Student Disk.

b. Save the form and the project as lc3Done.

c. Set the appropriate properties that will allow the user to size the form by dragging its borders, but will not allow the user to maximize the form.

d. Code the Calculate button appropriately. Be sure to use the Val function.

e. Code the Print Time Report button so that it prints the interface without the command buttons showing.

f. Save and run the application. Be sure to test the application with both valid and invalid data. Use the following information for the valid data:

Monday hours:	7
Tuesday hours:	8
Wednesday hours:	6
Thursday hours:	5
Friday hours:	4
Saturday hours:	2
Sunday hours:	0

g. After entering the valid data, click the Calculate button, then print the interface with the valid data showing.

h. Stop the application, then print the code.

i. Submit the printout from step h and the code from step i.

4. Scenario: Recall that 1440 twips is equal to one inch. Create an application that allows you to enter the number of twips, convert the twips to inches, and print the user interface.

a. Perform the five steps involved in creating an OOED application. (See the Note and list at the beginning of the Exercises section.)

b. Save the form and the project as lc4Done in the Tut02 folder on your Student Disk.

c. Test the application two times, with the following data. Print the application with the test data showing. Twips: 2880   Twips: abc

d. Assemble the documentation (TOE chart, pseudocode, 2 printouts of the form from step c, Form as Text, and Code).

e. Make an executable file. Name it lc4Done.exe.

5. Scenario: John Lee wants an application in which he can enter the following three pieces of information: his cash balance at the beginning of the month, the amount of money he earned during the month, and the amount of money he spent during the month. He wants the application to compute his ending balance, then print all of the information.

tip

. . . .

The exercises on this page require you to print the interface. If the labels in the printouts do not appear the same as on the screen, you may need to select a different font for the labels. Select the labels in the interface, then use the Font property to change the font; try the Arial font.

a. Perform the five steps involved in creating an OOED application. (See the Note and list at the beginning of the Exercises section.)

b. Save the form and the project as lc5Done in the Tut02 folder on your Student Disk.

c. Test the application twice using the following data. Print the application with the test data showing.

   Beginning cash balance: 5000   Earnings: 2500   Expenses: 3000
   Beginning cash balance: xyz   Earnings: xyz   Expenses: xyz

d. Assemble the documentation (TOE chart, pseudocode, 2 printouts of the form from step c, Form as Text, and Code).

6. Scenario: Lana Jones wants an application that will compute and print the average of any three numbers she enters.

a. Perform the five steps involved in creating an OOED application. (See the Note and list at the beginning of the Exercises section.)

b. Save the form and the project as lc6Done in the Tut02 folder on your Student Disk.

c. Test the application twice using the following data. Print the application with the test data showing.

   First Number: 27   Second Number: 9   Third Number: 18
   First Number: A   Second Number: B   Third Number: C

d. Assemble the documentation (TOE chart, pseudocode, 2 printouts of the form from step c, Form as Text, and Code).

7. Scenario: Martha Arito, manager of Bookworms Inc., needs an inventory application. Martha will enter the title of a book, the number of paperback versions of the book currently in inventory, the number of hardcover versions of the book currently in inventory, the cost of the paperback version, and the cost of the hardcover version. Martha wants the application to compute the value of the paperback versions of the book, the value of hardcover versions of the book, the total number of paperback and hardcover versions, and the total value of the paperback and hardcover versions. Martha will need to print this information.

a. Perform the five steps involved in creating an OOED application. (See the Note and list at the beginning of the Exercises section.)

b. Save the form and the project as lc7Done in the Tut02 folder on your Student Disk.

c. Test the application twice using the following data. Print the application with the test data showing.

   Book Title: An Intro to Visual Basic
   Paperback versions: 100   Paperback cost: 40
   Hardcover versions: 50   Hardcover cost: 75

   Book Title: Advanced Visual Basic
   Paperback versions: A   Paperback cost: B
   Hardcover versions: C   Hardcover cost: D

d. Assemble the documentation (TOE chart, pseudocode, 2 printouts of the form from step c, Form as Text, and Code).

8. Scenario: Jackets Unlimited is having a 25% off sale on all its merchandise. The store manager asks you to create an application that requires the clerk simply to enter the original price of a jacket. The application should then compute and print both the discount and the new price.

a. Perform the five steps involved in creating an OOED application. (See the Note and list at the beginning of the Exercises section.)

b. Save the form and the project as lc8Done in the Tut02 folder on your Student Disk.

c. Test the application twice using the following data. Print the application with the test data showing.

   Jacket's original price: 50
   Jacket's original price: ***

d. Assemble the documentation (TOE chart, pseudocode, 2 printouts of the form from step c, Form as Text, and Code).

The exercises on this page require you to print the interface. If the labels in the printouts do not appear the same as on the screen, you may need to select a different font for the labels. Select the labels in the interface, then use the Font property to change the font; try the Arial font.

9. Scenario: Typing Salon charges $.10 per typed envelope and $.25 per typed page. The company accountant wants an application to help her prepare bills. She will enter the customer's name, the number of typed envelopes, and the number of typed pages. The application should compute and print the total bill.

   a. Perform the five steps involved in creating an OOED application. (See the Note and list at the beginning of the Exercises section.)

   b. Save the form and the project as lc9Done in the Tut02 folder on your Student Disk.

   c. Test the application twice using the following data. Print the application with the test data showing.

      Customer's name: Alice Wong
      Number of typed envelopes: 250   Number of typed pages: 200

      Customer's name: Alice Wong
      Number of typed envelopes: $4   Number of typed pages: AB

   d. Assemble the documentation (TOE chart, pseudocode, 2 printouts of the form from step c, Form as Text, and Code).

10. Scenario: Management USA, a small training center, plans to run two full-day seminars on December 1. The seminars are called "How to Be an Effective Manager" and "How to Run a Small Business." Each seminar costs $200. Registration for the seminars will be done by phone. When a company calls to register its employees, the phone representative will ask for the following information: the company's name, address (including city, state, and zip), the number of employees registering for the "How to Be an Effective Manager" seminar, and the number of employees registering for the "How to Run a Small Business" seminar. Claire Jenkowski, the owner of Management USA, wants the application to calculate the total number of employees the company is registering and the total cost. Ms. Jenkowski also wants to print the company information.

    a. Perform the five steps involved in creating an OOED application. (See the Note and list at the beginning of the Exercises section.)

    b. Save the form and the project as lc10Done in the Tut02 folder on your Student Disk.

    c. Test the application twice using the following data. Print the application with the test data showing.

       Company Name: ABC Company
       Address: 345 Main St.
       City, State, Zip: Glen, TX 70122
       "How to Be an Effective Manager" registrants: 10
       "How to Run a Small Business" registrants: 5

       Company Name: 1
       Address: 2
       City, State, Zip: 3
       "How to Be an Effective Manager" registrants: A
       "How to Run a Small Business" registrants: B

    d. Assemble the documentation (TOE chart, pseudocode, 2 printouts of the form from step c, Form as Text, and Code).

11. Scenario: Suman Gadhari, the payroll clerk at Sun Projects, wants an application that will compute net pay for each of the company's employees. Suman will enter the employee's name, hours worked, and rate of pay. For this application, you do not have to worry about overtime, as this company does not allow anyone to work more than 40 hours. Suman wants the application to compute the gross pay, the federal withholding tax (FWT), the social security tax (FICA), the state income tax, and the net pay. Suman also wants to print the payroll information on the printer. Use the following information when computing the three taxes:

    FWT: 20% of gross pay
    FICA: 8% of gross pay
    state income tax : 2% of gross pay

tip

• • • • • • • • • • • • • • • • •

The exercises on this page require you to print the interface. If the labels in the printouts do not appear the same as on the screen, you may need to select a different font for the labels. Select the labels in the interface, then use the Font property to change the font; try the Arial font.

a. Perform the five steps involved in creating an OOED application. (See the Note and list at the beginning of the Exercises section.)

b. Save the form and the project as lc11Done in the Tut02 folder on your Student Disk.

c. Test the application twice using the following data. Print the application with the test data showing.

> Employee's name: Susan Reha
>
> Hours worked: 40
>
> Rate of pay: 12
>
> Employee's name: Susan Reha
>
> Hours worked: X
>
> Rate of pay: Y

d. Assemble the documentation (TOE chart, pseudocode, 2 printouts of the form from step c, Form as Text, and Code).

e. Make an executable (.EXE) file. Name it lc11Done.exe.

Exercises 12 through 19 are Discovery Exercises, which allow you to "discover" the solutions to problems on your own. Discovery Exercises may include topics that are not covered in the tutorial.

discovery ▶

12. In this exercise you will research the TabStop property.

a. Open the lcOrder (lcOrder.vbp) project that you created in Lesson C. The project is located in the Tut02 folder on your Student Disk.

b. Save the form and the project as lc12Done in the Tut02 folder on your Student Disk.

c. Use the Microsoft Visual Basic Help Topics command on the Help menu to display the TabStop property's Help window.

d. What is the purpose of the TabStop property? How can you use the TabStop property to make the current application easier for the user to use?

discovery ▶

13. Scenario: Colfax Industries needs an application that allows the shipping clerk to enter the quantity of an item in inventory and how many of the item can be packed in a box for shipping. When the shipping clerk clicks a command button, the application should compute and display the number of full boxes that can be packed and how many of the item are left over. Include a Print button in the interface.

a. Perform the five steps involved in creating an OOED application. (See the Note and list at the beginning of the Exercises section.)

b. Save the form and the project as lc13Done in the Tut02 folder on your Student Disk.

c. Test the application using the following data, then print the application with the test data showing. Colfax has 45 skateboards in inventory. If six skateboards can fit into a box for shipping, how many full boxes could the company ship, and how many skateboards will remain in inventory?

d. Assemble the documentation (TOE chart, pseudocode, printout of the form from step c, Form as Text, and Code).

discovery ▶

14. Scenario: Perry Brown needs an application that will allow him to enter the length of four sides of a polygon. When he clicks a command button, the application should compute and display the perimeter of the polygon. Include a Print button in the interface.

a. Perform the five steps involved in creating an OOED application. (See the Note and list at the beginning of the Exercises section.)

b. Save the form and the project as lc14Done in the Tut02 folder on your Student Disk.

c. Test the application using the following data, then print the application with the test data showing. Each day Perry rides his bike around a park that has side lengths of 1/2 mile, 1 mile, 1/2 mile, and 1 mile. How far does Perry ride his bike each day?

d. Assemble the documentation (TOE chart, pseudocode, printout of the form from step c, Form as Text, and Code).

discovery ▶

15. Scenario: Builders Inc. needs an application that will allow their salesclerks to enter both the diameter of a circle and the price of railing material per foot. When the clerk clicks a command button, the application should compute and display the circumference of the circle and the total price of the railing material. (Use 3.14 as the value of pi.)

a. Perform the five steps involved in creating an OOED application. (See the Note and list at the beginning of the Exercises section.)

b. Save the form and the project as lc15Done in the Tut02 folder on your Student Disk.

c. Test the application using the following data, then print the application with the test data showing. Jack Jones, one of Builders Inc.'s customers, is building a railing around a circular deck having a diameter of 36 feet. The railing material costs $2 per foot. What is the circumference of the deck and the total price of the railing material?

d. Assemble the documentation (TOE chart, pseudocode, printout of the form from step c, Form as Text, and Code).

discovery ▶

tip

▶ The exercises on this page require you to print the interface. If the labels in the printouts do not appear the same as on the screen, you may need to select a different font for the labels. Select the labels in the interface, then use the Font property to change the font; try the Arial font.

16. Scenario: Temp Employers wants an application that will allow their employees to enter the number of hours worked. When the employee clicks a command button, the application will compute and display the number of weeks (assume a 40-hour week), days (assume an 8-hour day), and hours worked. For example, if the user enters the number 70, the application will display 1 week, 3 days, and 6 hours.

a. Perform the five steps involved in creating an OOED application. (See the Note and list at the beginning of the Exercises section.)

b. Save the form and the project as lc16Done in the Tut02 folder on your Student Disk.

c. Test the application three times using the following data, then print the application with each of the test data showing.
   1) Hours worked: 88
   2) Hours worked: 111
   3) Hours worked: 12

d. Assemble the documentation (TOE chart, pseudocode, 3 printouts of the form from step c, Form as Text, and Code).

discovery ▶

17. Scenario: Tile Limited wants an application that will allow their salesclerks to enter the length and width, in feet, of a rectangle, and the price of a square foot of tile. When the clerk clicks a command button, the application will compute and display the area of the rectangle and the total price of the tile.

a. Perform the five steps involved in creating an OOED application. (See the Note and list at the beginning of the Exercises section.)

b. Save the form and the project as lc17Done in the Tut02 folder on your Student Disk.

c. Test the application using the following data, then print the application with the test data showing. Susan Caper, one of Tile Limited's customers, is tiling a floor in her home. The floor is 12 feet long and 14 feet wide. The price of a square foot of tile is $1.59. What is the area of the floor and how much will the tile cost?

d. Assemble the documentation (TOE chart, pseudocode, printout of the form from step c, Form as Text, and Code).

discovery ▶

18. Scenario: Willow Pools wants an application that will allow their salespeople to enter the length, width, and height of a rectangle. When the salesperson clicks a command button, the application will compute and display the volume of the rectangle.

a. Perform the five steps involved in creating an OOED application. (See the Note and list at the beginning of the Exercises section.)

b. Save the form and the project as lc18Done in the Tut02 folder on your Student Disk.

c. Test the application using the following data, then print the application with the test data showing. The swimming pool at a health club is 100 feet long, 30 feet wide, and 4 feet deep. How many cubic feet of water will the pool contain?

d. Assemble the documentation (TOE chart, pseudocode, printout of the form from step c, Form as Text, and Code).

discovery ▶

19. Scenario: Quick Loans wants an application that will allow their clerks to enter the amount of a loan, the interest rate, and the term of the loan (in years). When the clerk clicks a command button, the application should compute and display the total amount of interest and the total amount to be repaid. Use the Pmt function. (*Hint:* Use the Help menu to display the Pmt function's Help window.) Include a Print button in the interface.

a. Perform the five steps involved in creating an OOED application. (See the Note and list at the beginning of the Exercises section.)

b. Save the form and the project as lc19Done in the Tut02 folder on your Student Disk.

c. Test the application using the following data, then print the application with the test data showing. You visit Quick Loans because you want to borrow $9000 in order to buy a new car. The loan is for three years at an annual interest rate of 12%. How much will you pay in interest over the three years, and what is the total amount you will repay?

d. Assemble the documentation (TOE chart, pseudocode, printout of the form from step c, Form as Text, and Code).

D E B U G G I N G

Technique

As you saw in this tutorial, you may not get the expected results when a calculation includes either the Text property or the Caption property of a control; that's because both properties are treated as strings, not as numbers. Recall that you should use the Val function in equations to tell Visual Basic to treat the Text property and the Caption property as numbers instead of strings. Observe what happens when you don't use the Val function in the equations.

Exercises

To test an application without the Val function included:

1   Open the **Debug** (Debug.vbp) project, which is located in the Tut02 folder on your Student Disk. The application allows you to enter a number; it then doubles the number and displays the result in the lblAnswer control.

2   Open the Double Number button's Code window and view the code. Notice that the equation does not contain the Val function.

3   Close the Code window. **Run** the application.

Now see what happens if the user forgets to enter a number.

4   Click the **Double Number** button without entering any data.

Visual Basic displays a dialog box informing you of an error in the application. The error is "Run-time error '13': Type mismatch." A "Type mismatch" error means that Visual Basic has encountered something that it wasn't expecting in an instruction—for example, a string where a number is required or a number where a string is needed. In this case, Visual Basic expected to find a number in the txtNum control's Text property, but it found the empty string there instead.

Notice the four buttons that appear in the dialog box: Continue (which is currently dimmed), End, Debug, and Help. You will have a lot more practice with this dialog box as you progress through this book.

5   Click the **Debug** button. The cmdDouble control's Click event procedure appears in the Code window. Notice that Visual Basic highlights the instruction that is causing the error. See Figure 2-41.

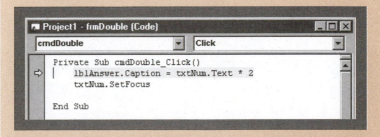

Figure 2-41

6   Close the Code window, then click the **End** button ■ on the toolbar to end the application.

Now observe what happens if the user enters a letter in the txtNum control.

7   **Run,** the application. Type **a** in the txtNum control, then click the **Double Number** button.

The "Type mismatch" error occurs again because Visual Basic found a string, instead of a number, in the txtNum control's Text property.

8   Click the **End** button in the dialog box to remove the dialog box and end the application.

You can prevent the "Type mismatch" error by including the Val function in the Double Number button's equation. Do that now and see how the application will handle both an empty txtNum control and a txtNum control that contains a letter.

To test the application with the Val function included:

1   Open the Double Number button's Code window, then include the Val function in the equation. The equation should now say
`lblAnswer.Caption = Val(txtNum.Text) * 2.`

2   Close the Code window, then **run** the application. Click the **Double Number** button without entering any data. A 0 (zero) appears in the lblAnswer control; that's because Visual Basic converts the empty string in the txtNum control's Text property to zero, and zero times two is zero.

3   Type **a** in the txtNum control, then click the **Double Number** button. A 0 (zero) appears in the lblAnswer control; that's because Visual Basic converts the letter in the txtNum control's Text property to zero, and zero times two is zero.

4   Click the **Exit** button to end the application.

As this debugging exercise shows, the Val function can prevent an application from ending in an error when the user enters invalid data.

Using Variables and Constants

Revising the Skate-Away Sales Application

case ▶ In Tutorial 2 you created an order screen for Skate-Away Sales. In order to complete the application, you just need to add the Interlocking Software copyright screen to the project. Before doing so, however, Mr. Cousard, the manager of Skate-Away Sales, calls to tell you that he wants to make a modification to the application. He now wants to include a message on each confirmation notice. The message should say "Thank you for your order. The sales tax was", followed by the sales tax amount and the name of the salesperson who recorded the order. You will need to modify the application's code to accommodate this change. Preview the completed application.

Previewing the Completed Application

To preview the completed application:

1 If necessary, start Windows, then place your Student Disk in the appropriate disk drive.

2 Use the Run command on the Start menu to run the **Skate** (Skate.exe) file, which is located in the Tut03 folder on your Student Disk. A copyright screen similar to the one that you created in Tutorial 1 appears first. The copyright form contains a Timer control that removes the form from the screen. After a few seconds, a dialog box that requests the salesperson's name appears as shown in Figure 3-1.

a dialog box contains a Close button only

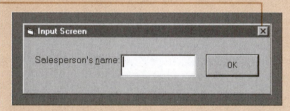

Figure 3-1: The dialog box that requests the salesperson's name

You will learn how to use a Timer control, as well as how to create a dialog box, in Lesson C.

3 Type your name in the Salesperson's name text box and press the **Enter** key. An order screen similar to the one that you created in Tutorial 2 appears.

4 Enter the following customer information: **Skaters Inc., 34 Plum Drive, Chicago, IL, 60654.**

5 Click the **Skateboard price** text box, then type **100** and press the **Tab** key. Type **.05** for the sales tax rate.

6 Click the **Blue skateboards ordered** text box, then type **25** as the number of blue skateboards ordered.

Although the Calculate Order button does not have the focus, you can still select it by pressing the Enter key; that's because the Calculate Order button is the default command button in the user interface. You will learn how to assign a default button in Lesson B.

7 Press the **Enter** key to calculate the order. The application calculates the order as shown in Figure 3-2.

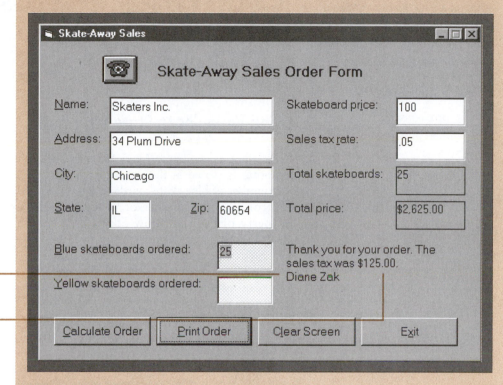

your name will
appear here

sales tax is
calculated and
appears here

Figure 3-2: Completed order screen

Notice that a message, which contains the amount of sales tax and the salesperson's name (your name), appears in the confirmation notice. The application uses string concatenation, which you will learn about in Lesson B, to display the message.

8 Click the **Exit** button to end the application.

In Lesson A you will learn how to store information, temporarily, in memory locations inside the computer. You will modify the Skate-Away Sales application in Lessons B and C.

In this lesson you will learn how to:

- Create a local, form-level, and global variable
- Assign a data type to a variable
- Control the scope of a variable
- Use the Option Explicit statement
- Add and remove a file from a project
- Create a symbolic constant

Creating Variables and Constants

Using Variables to Store Information

Recall that in the Skate-Away Sales application, all the skateboard information is temporarily stored in the properties of various controls on the form. For example, the number of blue skateboards ordered is stored in the Text property of the txtBlue control, and the number of yellow skateboards ordered is stored in the Text property of the txtYellow control. Also recall that the assignment statement `lblTboards.Caption = Val(txtBlue.Text) + Val(txtYellow.Text)`, which calculates the total skateboards ordered, adds the value stored in the txtBlue control's Text property to the value stored in the txtYellow control's Text property, and then assigns that sum to the Caption property of the lblTboards control. The total price equation, `lblTprice.Caption = Val(lblTboards.Caption) * Val(txtPrice.Text) * (1 + Val(txtRate.Text))`, calculates the total price of the order and assigns the result to the lblTprice control.

Besides storing data in the properties of controls, a programmer can also store data, temporarily, in memory locations inside the computer. These memory locations are called **variables** because the contents of the locations can change as the program is running. It may be helpful to picture a variable as a tiny box inside the computer. You can enter and store data in the box, but you can't actually see the box.

One use for a variable is to hold information that is not stored in a control on the user interface. For example, if the Skate-Away Sales application did not require you to display the total number of skateboards ordered, you could eliminate the lblTboards control from the form and store that information in a variable instead. You would then use the value stored in the variable, instead of the value stored in the Caption property of the lblTboards control, to compute the total price of the order.

You can also assign the properties of controls to variables. For example, you can assign the Text property of a text box to a variable; doing so allows you to control the preciseness of the numbers used in calculations, as you will see in the next section. It also makes your code more efficient because data stored in a variable can be processed 10 to 20 times faster than data stored in the property of an object.

Data Types

Each variable (each tiny box in memory) must be assigned a data type by the programmer. The data type determines the type of data the variable (memory location) can store. Figure 3-3 describes the basic data types used in Visual Basic.

Type	Stores	Memory required	Range of values
Byte	Binary numbers	1 byte	0 to 255
Boolean	Logical values	2 bytes	True or False
Currency	Numbers with up to 15 digits to the left of the decimal and 4 digits to the right of the decimal	8 bytes	+/- 9E14
Date	Date and time information	8 bytes	January 1, 100 to December 31, 9999
Double	Floating-point numbers	8 bytes	+/- 5E-324 to 1.8E308
Integer	Integers	2 bytes	-32,768 to 32,767
Long	Integers	4 bytes	+/- 2 billion
Object	Any object reference	4 bytes	N/A
Single	Floating-point numbers	4 bytes	+/- 1E-45 to 3E38
String	Text information	Fixed-length: 1 byte per character Variable-length: 10 bytes + 1 byte per character	Fixed-length: 1 to 65,400 Variable-length: 0 to 2 billion
Variant	Any of the other data types	With numbers: 16 bytes With characters: 22 bytes + 1 byte per character	With numbers: Same as Double With characters: Same range as for variable-length string

Figure 3-3: Basic data types in Visual Basic

Notice that Figure 3-3 shows the range of values that each data type can store and the amount of memory required to do so. For instance, variables assigned either the Integer or the Long data type can store **integers**, which are whole numbers—numbers without any decimal places. The differences between the two data types are in the range of numbers each type can store and the amount of memory each type needs to store the numbers. The memory requirement of a data type is an important consideration when coding an application; if you want to optimize an application's code, and thereby conserve system resources, you should use variables with smaller memory requirements wherever possible. For example, although a Long type variable can store numbers in the Integer type range of −32768 to 32767, the Long data type takes twice as much memory to do so. Therefore, it would be more efficient to store a person's age in an Integer variable. You would need to use a Long variable, however, to store the population of a large city.

Figure 3-3 also shows that both the Single type variable and the Double type variable can store a floating-point number. A **floating-point number** is a number that is expressed as a multiple of some power of 10. In Visual Basic, floating-point numbers are written in E (exponential) notation, which is similar to scientific notation. For example, the number 3,200,000 written in E (exponential) notation is

3.2E6; written in scientific notation it is 3.2×10^{6}. Notice that exponential notation simply replaces "$\times 10^{6}$" with the letter E followed by the power number—in this case, 6.

Another way of viewing the 3.2E6 is that the positive number after the E indicates how many places to the right to move the decimal point. In this case, E6 says to move the decimal point six places to the right; so 3.2E6 becomes 3,200,000. Moving the decimal point six places to the right is the same as multiplying the number by 10 to the sixth power.

Floating-point numbers can also have a negative number after the E. For example, 3.2E–6 means 3.2 divided by 10 to the sixth power, or .0000032. The negative number after the E tells you how many places to the left to move the decimal point. In this case, E–6 means to move the decimal point six places to the left.

Floating-point numbers, which can be stored in either a Single type variable or a Double type variable, are used to represent both extremely small and extremely large numbers. The differences between the Single type and the Double type are in the range of numbers each type can store and the amount of memory each type needs to store the numbers. Although the Double type can store numbers in the Single type's range, the Double type takes twice as much memory to do so.

The Currency data type listed in Figure 3-3 stores numbers with a fixed decimal point. Unlike floating-point numbers, fixed-point numbers are not expressed as a multiple of some power of 10. For example, the number 32000 expressed in the Single data type is 3.2E4, but that same number expressed in the Currency data type is simply 32000. Calculations involving fixed-point numbers are not subject to the small rounding errors that may occur when floating-point numbers are used. In most cases, these small rounding errors create no problems in the application. One exception, however, is when the application contains complex equations dealing with money, where you need accuracy to the penny. In those cases, the Currency data type is the best type to use.

Also listed in Figure 3-3 is the String data type, which can store from one to approximately two billion characters. A string, you may remember from Tutorial 2, is a group of characters enclosed in quotation marks. "Desk" and "AB345" are two examples of strings.

You use the Boolean data type to store the Boolean values True and False. You use the Date data type to store date and time information. The Object data type is used to store object references, and the Byte data type is used to store binary numbers.

The last data type listed in Figure 3-3 is Variant. If you don't assign a specific data type to a variable, Visual Basic assigns the Variant type to it. Unlike other variables, a Variant variable can store many different types of data, and it also can freely change the type of stored data while the program is running. For example, you can store the number 40 in a Variant variable at the beginning of the program and then, later on in the program, store the string "John Smith" in that same variable. Although the Variant data type is the most flexible, in many cases it is less efficient than the other data types. At times it uses more memory than necessary to store a value and, because the application has to determine which type of data is stored currently in the variable, your application will run more slowly.

Assigning an appropriate data type to the variables in a program will make the application run more efficiently. Here are some guidelines to follow when assigning the data type:

■ Assign the Integer or Long data type when you are sure that a variable will always contain whole numbers—numbers without decimal places. Which type you choose, Integer or Long, will depend on the size of the numbers you expect to store in the variable.

■ Assign the Single, Double, or Currency data type when you need to store numbers with a decimal fraction. Here again, which type you choose will depend on the size of the numbers you expect to store in the variable and whether the variable will hold large money values.

■ Assign the String data type if the variable will always contain a string.

■ Assign the Boolean data type if the variable will always contain Boolean values (True and False).

■ Assign the Date data type if the variable will need to store date and time information.

■ Assign the Object data type if the variable will contain a reference to an object.

■ Assign the Variant data type if your variable needs to be flexible about the type of data it will store and if you are not concerned with speed and the amount of memory used.

In addition to assigning a data type to the variables used in an application, the programmer must also assign a name to each variable. (You will learn *how* to assign both the data type and name later in this lesson.)

Naming Variables

You should use a descriptive name for each variable; the name should help you remember both the data type and purpose of the variable. One popular naming convention is to have the first three characters in the name represent the data type, and the remainder of the name represent the variable's purpose. Figure 3-4 lists the three characters typically associated with the Visual Basic data types.

Type	ID
Byte	byt
Boolean	bln
Currency	cur
Date (Time)	dtm
Double	dbl
Integer	int
Long	lng
Object	obj
Single	sng
String	str
Variant	vnt

Figure 3-4: Data types and their three-character IDs

It is a common practice to type the three-character ID in lowercase and capitalize the first letter in the part of the name that identifies the purpose. For example, a good name for a variable that contains sales amounts is curSales. Although S could also be used as the name for that variable, notice that it is not as descriptive as the name curSales. In the latter case, the name reminds you that the variable is a Currency variable that stores sales amounts.

In addition to being descriptive, the name that a programmer assigns to a variable must follow several specific rules. These rules are listed in Figure 3-5, along with examples of valid and invalid variable names.

Rules for naming variables
1. The name must begin with a letter.
2. The name must contain only letters, numbers, and the underscore. No punctuation characters or spaces are allowed in the name.
3. The name cannot be more than 255 characters long.
4. The name cannot be a reserved word, such as Print, because reserved words have special meaning in Visual Basic.

Valid variable names:	Invalid variable names:	
cur94Sales	94SalesCur	(the name must begin with a letter)
intRegionWest	intRegion West	(the name cannot contain a space)
lngEastPop	lngEast.Pop	(the name cannot contain punctuation)
blnPrint	Print	(the name cannot be a reserved word)

Figure 3-5: Rules for variable names along with examples of valid and invalid names

In the next section you will learn how to declare (create) a variable in Visual Basic.

Declaring a Variable

You use either the **Dim statement** or the **Public statement** to create, or declare, a variable. (Dim comes from the word "dimension.") Which statement you use will depend on whether you want to create a local, form-level, or global variable. You will learn about local, form-level, and global variables later in this lesson.

Declaring a variable tells Visual Basic to create the variable in memory—in other words, to set aside a tiny section of the computer's internal memory. The basic syntax of both the Dim statement and the Public statement is identical, with the exception of the keywords Dim and Public—in other words, the Dim statement's syntax is **Dim** *variablename* [**As** *datatype*] and the Public statement's syntax is **Public** *variablename* [**As** *datatype*]. Notice that both statements allow you to assign the name and the data type to the variable you are creating. Although the "**As** *datatype*" part of both statements is optional, as indicated by the brackets in the syntax, you should always assign a specific data type to each variable. If you don't assign a data type, Visual Basic assigns the Variant type, which may not be the most efficient data type. Figure 3-6 shows examples of the Dim and Public statements used to declare (create) variables.

tip

A variable is considered an object in Visual Basic and is an instance of the class specified in the *datatype* information. The `Dim intHours as Integer` statement, for example, creates an object named intHours; intHours is an instance of the Integer class.

Statement	Explanation
Dim intHours as Integer	Creates an Integer variable named intHours
Dim sngDiscount as Single	Creates a Single variable named sngDiscount
Dim curPrice as Currency	Creates a Currency variable named curPrice
Public strFname as String	Creates a String variable named strFname

Figure 3-6: Examples of both Dim and Public statements

When you declare a variable using one of the numeric data types, Visual Basic automatically stores the number 0 (zero) in the variable. This is referred to as **initializing** the variable—in other words, giving the variable a beginning value. For example, the statement `Dim curSales as Currency` creates a Currency variable named curSales, which Visual Basic initializes to 0. Visual Basic initializes String and Variant variables by assigning a zero-length string to them. (Recall from Tutorial 2 that a zero-length string is called an empty string.) You can use an assignment statement to store other data in the variable, as you will see in the next section.

Storing Data in a Variable

An assignment statement is one way of storing data in a variable. In Tutorial 2 you learned that the format of an assignment statement that assigns a value to an object's property is [*form.*]*object.property* = *value*. Similarly, the format of an assignment statement that stores a value in a variable is *variablename* = *value*. The two instructions, `curSales = 500` and `strName = "Mary"`, are examples of assignment statements that assign values to variables. The `curSales = 500` assignment statement, for example, stores the number 500 in a currency variable named curSales. The `strName = "Mary"` assignment statement stores the string "Mary" (without the quotes) in the strName variable. The number 500 and the string "Mary" are called literal constants. A **literal constant** is simply an item of data whose value does not change while the program is running; 500 is a numeric literal constant, and "Mary" is a string literal constant. Notice that you store literal constants in variables. Also notice that string literal constants are enclosed in quotation marks, but numeric literal constants and variable names are not. The quotation marks differentiate a string from both a number and a variable name. In other words, 500 is a number, but "500" is a string; "Mary" is a string, but Mary (without the quotes) would be interpreted by Visual Basic as the name of a variable.

It's easy to confuse literal constants with symbolic constants, which are also available in Visual Basic. **Symbolic constants** are memory locations whose contents cannot be changed while the program is running. To avoid confusing the two types of constants, simply remember that a literal constant is an item of data, whereas a symbolic constant is a memory location that stores an item of data. Unlike variables, which are memory locations whose contents *can* change while the program is running, the contents of a symbolic constant *cannot* change. You will learn more about symbolic constants at the end of this lesson.

It's important to remember that, like an object's property, a variable can store only one item of data at any one time. When you use an assignment statement to assign another item to the variable, the new data replaces the existing data. For example, assume that the Click event procedure for a command button contains the following three lines of code:

```
Dim curSales as Currency
curSales = 500
curSales = curSales * 2
```

When you run the application and click the command button, the three lines of code are processed as follows:

- The Dim statement creates the curSales variable in memory. Here again, you may want to picture the curSales variable as a tiny box inside the computer. Because the curSales variable is a numeric variable, Visual Basic initializes it to 0—in other words, Visual Basic places the number 0 inside the box.
- The `curSales = 500` assignment statement removes the zero from the curSales variable and stores the number 500 there instead. The variable (box) now contains the number 500 only.
- The `curSales = curSales * 2` assignment statement first multiplies the contents of the curSales variable (500) by the number 2, giving 1000. The assignment statement then removes the number 500 from the curSales variable and stores the number 1000 there instead. Notice that Visual Basic performs the calculation appearing on the right side of the equal sign before assigning the result to the variable whose name appears on the left side.

As you can see, after data is stored in a variable, you can use the data in calculations, just as you can with the data stored in the properties of controls. When you refer to a variable's name, the computer uses the value stored inside the variable.

You now know how to use the Dim and Public statements to declare a variable. Recall that the statements allow you to assign both a name and data type to the variable you are creating. You also know how to use an assignment statement to store data inside a variable. There's just one more thing about variables that you need to learn: in addition to a name and a data type, every variable also has a scope.

The Scope of a Variable

A variable's **scope** indicates which procedures in the application can use the variable. The scope, which can be either global, form-level, or local, is determined by *where* you declare the variable—in other words, where you enter either the Dim or Public statement. You can declare a variable in three places:

- an object's event procedure
- a form's General Declarations section
- a code module's General Declarations section

(You have not yet seen the General Declarations section of either a form or a code module; you will see both in this lesson.)

You use the Dim statement, which you learned earlier, to declare a variable in an object's event procedure. When you declare a variable in an event procedure, only that event procedure can use the variable. For example, if you enter the `Dim curSales as Currency` statement in a command button's Click event procedure, only that command button's Click event procedure can use the curSales variable. A variable declared in an event procedure is called a **local variable** because its use is limited to only the procedure in which it is declared. No other procedures in the application are allowed to use the variable. Actually, no other procedure in the application will even know that the variable exists. When the event procedure ends, Visual Basic removes the local variable from the computer's memory. Most of the variables in your applications will be local variables.

You also use the Dim statement to declare a variable in a form's General Declarations section. When you declare a variable in the General Declarations section of a form, all procedures in that form, including the procedures of the controls contained on the form, can use the variable. For example, if you enter the `Dim curSales as Currency` statement in the form's General Declarations section, every procedure in the form can use the curSales variable. A variable declared in a form's General Declarations section is called a **form-level variable**. Form-level variables remain in memory until the application ends.

You use the Public statement to declare a variable in the General Declarations section of a code module. If you declare a variable in a code module's General Declarations section, all procedures in every form and control included in the application can use the variable. Variables declared in a code module's General Declarations section are called **global variables**. Global variables, which are used in applications containing multiple forms, remain in memory until the application ends.

To recap, you use the Dim statement to declare both local and form-level variables. When creating a local variable, you enter the Dim statement in the event procedure of an object; only the procedure in which the local variable is declared can use the variable. When creating a form-level variable, on the other hand, you enter the Dim statement in the form's General Declarations section; all of the procedures in that form, including the procedures of its controls, can use the form-level variable. Last, when creating a global variable, you enter the Public statement in the General Declarations section of a code module; every procedure in the application can use the global variable.

The difference between local, form-level, and global variables is best illustrated with a few examples. On your Student Disk are two project files that contain examples designed to help clarify the concept of scope. Before looking at those examples, however, you will need to learn about the `Option Explicit` statement.

The Option Explicit Statement

In the previous sections you learned that it is important to declare the variables used in an application; by doing so you have control over their data type. Unfortunately, in Visual Basic you can create variables "on the fly," which means that if your code contains the name of an undeclared variable—a variable that does not appear in either a Dim or a Public statement—Visual Basic creates one for you and assigns the Variant data type to it. Recall that the Variant type is many times not the most efficient data type. Because it is so easy to forget to declare a variable—and so easy to misspell a variable's name while coding, thereby inadvertently creating an undeclared variable—Visual Basic provides a way that will prevent you from using undeclared variables in your code. You simply enter the `Option Explicit` statement in the form's General Declarations section. Then if your code contains the name of an undeclared variable, Visual Basic informs you of the error.

tip

You can use the Static statement to create a local variable that retains its value when the procedure ends. You will learn more about the Static statement in Lesson A's Discovery Exercise 20.

tip

In some instances you may want to create a variable in a code module that can be used by the code module only. In those cases you would use the Private statement, instead of the Public statement, to declare the variable in the General Declarations section of the code module.

tip

If the application includes a code module or more than one form, the Option Explicit statement must be entered in the code module's General Declarations section and in each form's General Declarations section.

tip

▶ To have Visual Basic enter the `Option Explicit` statement automatically in every new form and module, click Tools, then click Options. Click the Require Variable Declaration option, which is located on the Editor tab, to select that option.

In the next set of steps, you will open the first application designed to help illustrate the concept of scope. You will then enter the `Option Explicit` statement in the form's General Declarations section. The `Option Explicit` statement will prevent you from using an undeclared variable in the code.

To enter the `Option Explicit` statement in an application:

1 Start Visual Basic, if necessary, then place your Student Disk in the appropriate disk drive. Open the **Scope1** (Scope1.vbp) file, which is located in the Tut03 folder on your Student Disk.

2 Click the **form's title bar** to select the form. Save the form as **laScope1**, then save the project as **laScope1**. Figure 3-7 identifies the controls already included in the application.

cmd2Comm
cmdDisplay

lblSales
lblCommission
cmd5Comm

cmdExit

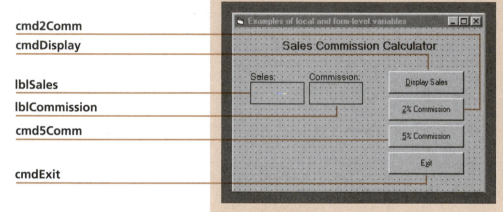

Figure 3-7: The laScope1 user interface

3 Double-click the **Exit** button to open its Code window. The cmdExit control's Click event procedure appears.

Notice that the Exit button already contains the `End` statement. Before coding the other command buttons, you will enter the `Option Explicit` statement in the form's General Declarations section. Recall that the `Option Explicit` statement tells Visual Basic to warn you if your code contains the name of an undeclared variable—a variable that does not appear in either a Dim or Public statement.

4 Click the **Object** list arrow, then click **(General)**, which is at the top of the list. The form's General Declarations section appears in the Code window. Type **option explicit** and press the **Enter** key. See Figure 3-8.

tip

▶ Each form has its own General Declarations section.

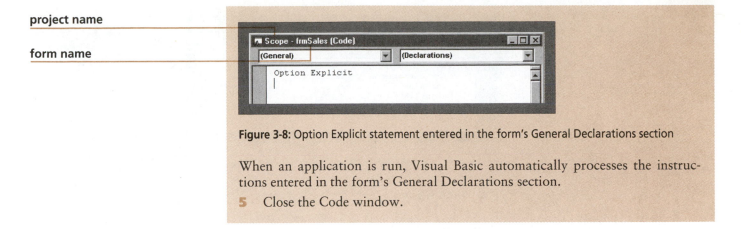

project name

form name

Figure 3-8: Option Explicit statement entered in the form's General Declarations section

When an application is run, Visual Basic automatically processes the instructions entered in the form's General Declarations section.

5 Close the Code window.

The current application will give you an opportunity to experiment with local and form-level variables only. Global variables will be shown in another application, which you will open later in this lesson. Begin by creating a local variable.

Creating a Local Variable

Recall that local variables are declared with the Dim statement in the event procedure of an object. In this case, you will create a local Currency variable, named curSales, in the Click event procedure of the Display Sales button. It is customary to enter the Dim statements at the beginning of the event procedure, immediately below the Private Sub instruction.

To experiment with a local variable:

1 Double-click the **Display Sales** button. The cmdDisplay control's Click event procedure appears in the Code window. Press the **Tab** key, type **dim curSales as currency** and press the **Enter** key. When the application is run, this statement will create and initialize (to zero) a local Currency variable named curSales.

You can now use an assignment statement to store data in the local curSales variable.

2 Type **cursales = 500** and press the **Enter** key. When the application is run, this instruction will assign the number 500 to the local curSales variable; in other words, it will store the literal constant 500 in the memory location named curSales.

Next, use an assignment statement to display the contents of the curSales variable in the lblSales control on the form.

3 Type **lblsales.caption = cursales** and press the **Enter** key. This assignment statement tells Visual Basic to assign the contents of the curSales variable to the Caption property of the lblSales control. See Figure 3-9.

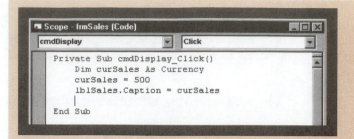

Figure 3-9: Code entered in Display Sales button's Click event procedure

You can now run the application and test the Display Sales button.

4   Close the Code window, then **save** and **run** the application.

First Visual Basic processes the `Option Explicit` statement found in the form's General Declarations section. Recall that instructions in the form's General Declarations section are processed automatically when the application is run.

5   Click the **Display Sales** button.

Following the instructions entered in the button's Click event procedure, Visual Basic first creates and initializes a local variable named curSales. Visual Basic then assigns the literal constant 500 to the curSales variable, and then displays the contents of the curSales variable (500) in the lblSales control. When the Click event procedure ends, which occurs when Visual Basic processes the `End Sub` statement in the procedure's Code window, the local curSales variable is removed from the computer's memory.

6   Click the **Exit** button to end the application. Visual Basic returns to the design screen.

As this example shows, a local variable can be used by the event procedure in which it is declared. Now see if another event procedure can use the local variable. You can do that by coding the 2% Commission button. The 2% Commission button should calculate a 2% commission on the sales entered in the curSales variable and then display the result in the lblCommission control.

To code the 2% Commission button:

1   Open the 2% Commission button's Code window. The cmd2Comm control's Click event procedure appears.

2   Press the **Tab** key, type **lblcommission.caption = cursales * .02** and press the **Enter** key. This instruction tells Visual Basic to multiply the contents of the curSales variable by .02 (the decimal equivalent of 2%) and then assign the result to the Caption property of the lblCommission control.

HELP? Recall from Tutorial 2 that, in Visual Basic, you must convert percentages in an equation to their decimal equivalents.

3   Close the Code window, then **save** and **run** the application. Click the **Display Sales** button, then click the **2% Commission** button. Visual Basic displays the warning message shown in Figure 3-10.

Figure 3-10: Warning message caused by an undeclared (undefined) variable

4   Click the **OK** button to remove the "Variable not defined" message from the screen. Visual Basic highlights the name of the undefined variable, curSales, in the Code window. (An undefined variable is the same as an undeclared variable.) Notice that the undefined variable is in the cmd2Comm control's Click event procedure. See Figure 3-11.

undefined variable

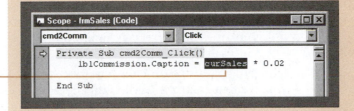

Figure 3-11: Undefined variable highlighted in the Code window

5   Close the Code window, then click the **End** button ⬛ on the toolbar. The application ends and Visual Basic returns to the design screen.

Recall that the `Option Explicit` statement, which you entered in the form's General Declarations section, tells Visual Basic to display a warning message if your code contains the name of an undeclared variable. In this case the undeclared variable is the curSales variable appearing in the cmd2Comm control's Click event procedure. At this point you may be thinking "But I did declare the curSales variable." Recall, however, that you declared the curSales variable in the cmdDisplay control's Click event procedure; only the cmdDisplay control's Click event procedure can use that variable. The cmd2Comm control's Click event procedure doesn't know about the curSales variable, so it treats it as an undefined variable. In other words, we have just shown that a local variable can be used only by the event procedure in which it is declared.

Now observe what happens if you declare the same variable in two event procedures. Specifically, you will declare a curSales variable in the cmdDisplay control's Click event procedure and a curSales variable in the cmd2Comm control's Click event procedure. The `Dim curSales as Currency` statement is already in the cmdDisplay control's Click event procedure, so you just need to enter the same statement in the cmd2Comm control's Click event procedure.

To declare a curSales variable in the cmd2Comm control's Click event procedure, then save and run the application:

1 Open the 2% Commission button's Code window. The cmd2Comm control's Click event procedure appears.

2 Press the **Enter** key to insert a blank line below the `Private Sub` instruction.

3 In the blank line below the `Private Sub` instruction, press the **Tab** key, type **dim curSales as currency** and then close the Code window.

4 **Save** and **run** the application, then click the **Display Sales** button. The contents of the cmdDisplay control's local curSales variable (500) appears in the lblSales control.

When the Click event procedure ends, the cmdDisplay control's curSales variable is removed from memory. You can confirm that by clicking the 2% Commission button, whose Click event procedure contains the `Dim curSales as Currency` instruction and the `lblCommission.Caption = curSales * .02` instruction.

5 Click the **2% Commission** button. A zero appears in the lblCommission control. The correct commission, however, should be 10 (2% of the $500 sales).

The zero appears because the `Dim curSales as Currency` instruction in the cmd2Comm control's Click event procedure creates and initializes (to zero) its own local curSales variable. The `lblCommission.Caption = curSales * .02` instruction multiplies the contents of the cmd2Comm control's local curSales variable (0) by .02, giving zero, and then assigns the zero to the Caption property of the lblCommission control. When the cmd2Comm control's Click event procedure ends, its local curSales variable is removed from the computer's memory.

6 Click the **Exit** button to end the application. Visual Basic returns to the design screen.

As this example shows, when you use the same name to declare a variable in more than one event procedure, each procedure creates its own local variable. Although the variables have the same name, each refers to a different location (box) in memory.

But what if you want both command buttons to use the same curSales variable? In that case you will need to declare the variable in the form's General Declarations section.

Creating a Form-Level Variable

Recall that variables declared in the form's General Declarations section are called form-level variables. Form-level variables can be used by every procedure in the form, and they remain in memory until the application ends. Observe what happens when you declare the curSales variable as a form-level variable.

tip
. . . .

▶ Recall that each form has its own General Declarations section.

To declare the curSales variable as a form-level variable:

1   Open the form's General Declarations section. All form-level variables must be declared in this section of the form.

    HELP? To open the General Declarations section, open any Code window, then click the Object list arrow and select (General), which is at the top of the list.

2   In the blank line immediately below the `Option Explicit` statement, type **dim curSales as currency** and press the **Enter** key.

You will need to remove the `Dim curSales as Currency` statement from both the cmdDisplay and cmd2Comm controls' Click event procedures, as those Dim statements tell Visual Basic to create two local curSales variables.

3   Use the Code window's Object list box to open the cmd2Comm control's Click event procedure. Remove only the `Dim curSales as Currency` statement from the Code window.

4   Use the Code window's Object list box to open the cmdDisplay control's Click event procedure. Remove only the `Dim curSales as Currency` statement from the Code window.

5   Close the Code window, then **save** and **run** the application.

Visual Basic processes both the `Option Explicit` and the `Dim curSales as Currency` statements, which are in the form's General Declarations section. The Dim statement creates and initializes a form-level variable named curSales. Observe what happens when you click the Display Sales button.

6   Click the **Display Sales** button. Visual Basic processes the instructions in the button's Click event procedure. The `curSales = 500` instruction stores the number 500 in the form-level curSales variable. The `lblSales.Caption = curSales` instruction displays the contents of the form-level curSales variable (500) in the lblSales control.

Now see what happens when you click the 2% Commission button.

7   Click the **2% Commission** button. Visual Basic processes the instructions in the button's Click event procedure. The `lblCommission.Caption = curSales * .02` instruction multiplies the contents of the form-level curSales variable (500) by .02, giving 10. The instruction then displays the result (10) in the lblCommission control.

8   Click the **Exit** button to end the application. Visual Basic removes the form-level curSales variable from the computer's memory and then returns to the design screen.

As this example shows, when you declare a form-level variable, every procedure in the form can use the variable.

In this next example, you will see what happens when you declare a variable both as a form-level variable and as a local variable. The `Dim curSales as Currency` statement is already entered in the form's General Declarations section, so you will simply enter the same instruction in the 5% Commission button's Click event procedure.

To see what happens when you declare a variable both as a form-level variable and as a local variable:

1 Open the Code window for the 5% Commission button's Click event.

2 Press the **Tab** key, then type **dim curSales as currency** and press the **Enter** key.

The cmd5Comm control should calculate a 5% commission on the sales.

3 Type **lblcommission.caption = cursales * .05** and press the **Enter** key.

4 Close the Code window, then **save** and **run** the application.

Recall that when the application is run, the `Dim curSales as Currency` instruction in the form's General Declarations section instructs Visual Basic to create and initialize a form-level variable named curSales. The form-level curSales variable remains in memory until the application ends.

5 Click the **Display Sales** button. The `curSales = 500` instruction stores the number 500 in the form-level curSales variable. The `lblSales.Caption = curSales` instruction displays the contents of the form-level curSales variable (500) in the lblSales control.

6 Click the **2% Commission** button. The `lblCommission.Caption = curSales * .02` instruction multiplies the contents of the form-level curSales variable (500) by .02, giving 10. The instruction then displays the result (10) in the lblCommission control.

7 Click the **5% Commission** button. A zero appears in the lblCommission control. The zero appears because the `Dim curSales as Currency` instruction in the cmd5Comm control's Click event procedure creates and initializes (to zero) a local variable named curSales. The local curSales variable is different from the form-level curSales variable. The next instruction in the cmd5Comm control's Click event procedure, `lblCommission.Caption = curSales * .05`, multiplies the contents of the local curSales variable (0) by .05, giving 0. The instruction then displays the result (0) in the lblCommission control. When the Click event procedure ends, Visual Basic removes the local curSales variable from the computer's memory. The form-level curSales variable, however, remains in memory, as you will see in the next step.

8 Click the **2% Commission** button. The number 10, which is the form-level curSales variable multiplied by .02, appears in the lblCommission control.

9 Click the **Exit** button to end the application. Visual Basic removes the form-level curSales variable from the computer's memory and then returns to the design screen.

As this example shows, if you use the same name to declare both a form-level variable and a local variable, the event procedure in which the local variable is declared will use its local variable instead of the form-level variable.

The next example you will view deals with global variables.

Creating a Global Variable

You have probably seen computer programs where the first screen prompts the user to enter his or her name. The name is then used to create personalized messages that are displayed to the user during the program. That type of application typically uses two or more forms: one form simply requests the user to enter his or her name; the remaining forms constitute the applications's user interface. The application you will open in this section will work similarly. It will use one form to request the user's name, then display the name, along with a message, on a second form. When you open the application and look at the code, don't be concerned if you do not understand all of the instructions; you will be learning those instructions in Lessons B and C. For now, just pay attention to *how* and *where* you must declare a variable that will be used by procedures in more than one form.

To open the project that contains an example of a global variable, then save the project under a different name:

1 Open the **Scope2** (Scope2.vbp) project, which is located in the Tut03 folder on your Student Disk. The Project window shows that this application contains two forms, frmName and frmWelcome. (You may need to open the Form folder to view the form names.) The frmName (Name Screen) form appears, currently, on the screen.

2 Click the **Name Screen form's title bar** to select the form. Save the Name Screen form as **laName**.

3 Click **frmWelcome (Welcom.frm)** in the Project window, then click the Project window's **View Object** button ▣. The Welcome Screen form appears on the screen. Save the Welcome Screen form as **laWelcom**.

4 Save the project as **laScope2**.

5 Click **frmName (laName.frm)** in the Project window, then click the Project window's **View Object** button ▣. The frmName form appears on the screen.

The Name Screen form contains a text box (txtName) in which the user enters his or her name. The form also contains an OK command button (cmdOK). Look at the code in the OK command button.

6 Open the Code window for the OK button's Click event procedure. See Figure 3-12.

form name

assigns Text property to
strName variable

displays frmWelcome
form

removes frmName
form

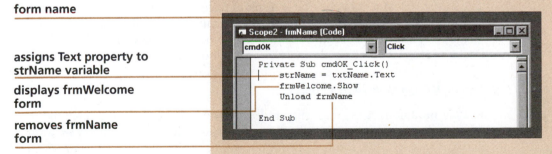

```
Scope2 - frmName [Code]
cmdOK                          Click

    Private Sub cmdOK_Click()
        strName = txtName.Text
        frmWelcome.Show
        Unload frmName

    End Sub
```

Figure 3-12: The OK button's Click event procedure

Don't be concerned that you don't recognize a couple of the instructions; you will learn them in Lesson C.

Basically, the code for the OK button assigns the Text property of the txtName text box to a variable named strName. The code then displays (shows) the frmWelcome form on the screen and removes (unloads) the frmName form from the screen and from memory.

7 Close the Code window, then close the frmName form. The frmWelcome form appears on the screen.

The frmWelcome form contains a label control (lblWelcome) that will display a message to the user. The form also contains an image control, as well as a command button that will end the application. Look at the code in the frmWelcome form's Load event procedure.

8 Double-click the **frmWelcome form** to open its Load event procedure, then maximize the Code window. See Figure 3-13.

form name

string concatenation operator

displays the user's name

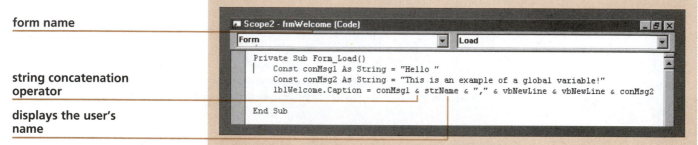

Figure 3-13: The frmWelcome form's Load event procedure

The Load event's code uses string concatenation (linking) to display a message, along with the contents of the strName variable, in the lblWelcome control on the frmWelcome form. You will learn how to concatenate strings in Lesson B.

9 Close the Code window, then close the frmWelcome form.

When this application is run, the frmName form, which requests the user's name, will appear on the screen first. When the user enters his or her name and clicks the OK button, the OK button's Click event procedure will store the user's name in the strName variable. The Click event procedure will then both display the frmWelcome form on the screen and remove the frmName form from the screen. The frmWelcome form's Load event procedure will use the strName variable in the welcome message that it displays to the user. In order for both forms to use the strName variable, the variable's scope must be global; that means that you will need to use the Public statement to declare the strName variable in the General Declarations section of a code module. You will do that in the next section.

An application can contain more than one module, but that is rare.

Adding a Code Module to a Project

A **code module** is a separate file, added to your application, that contains only code; it does not contain any forms or controls. All variables that you want to make available to all forms in the application should be declared in the General Declarations section of a code module. In this application, for example, you will declare the strName variable in a code module's General Declarations section so that both the frmName and frmWelcome forms can use the variable.

tip

You can remove a file from a project by clicking the file's name in the Project window, then using the Remove <*filename*> command on the Project menu.

To add a code module to the current project:

1   Click **Project** on the menu bar, then click **Add Module**. The Add Module dialog box appears. Click **Module** on the New tab if necessary, then click the **Open** button. Visual Basic adds the Module1 file name to the Project window, and the General Declarations section of the Module1 module appears on the screen.

If an application contains more than one form and/or module, you must enter the `Option Explicit` statement in each form's General Declarations section and in each module's General Declarations section.

2   Type **option explicit** and press the **Enter** key.

    HELP? If the Require Variable Declaration option is selected in the Editor tab in the Tools menu's Options dialog box, the `Option Explicit` statement may already be entered in the code module's General Declarations section.

You can now enter the Public statement that will declare a global variable named strName.

3   Type **public strName as string** and press the **Enter** key. See Figure 3-14.

statement declares a global variable

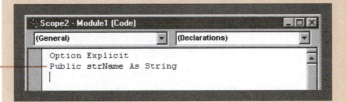

Figure 3-14: Option Explicit and Public statements entered in the code module

Now save the code module under a more descriptive name.

4   Use the Save Module1 As command on the File menu to save the code module as **laModule**, then close the code module's Code window. As the Project window now shows, the code module is saved as laModule.bas. (The .bas extension stands for "Basic.")

Whenever you make a change to the information in the Project window, you must be sure to save the project so that the change is saved.

5   Click the **Save Project** button 🖫 to save the project under its current name.

Now run the application.

6   **Run** the application. When the frmName form appears, type your first name, then press the **Enter** key. The frmWelcome form appears with your name included in the welcome message.

7   Click the **Exit** button to end the application. Visual Basic removes the global strName variable from memory, then returns to the design screen.

Lastly, confirm that the current application will not run properly if you declare the strName variable either as a form-level variable or as a local variable. You can do so by removing the laModule.bas file from the project, and then experiment by placing a `Dim strName as String` statement in an object's event procedure and in the form's General Declarations section.

Removing and Adding a File

To remove a file from a project, you first select the file's name in the Project window, then use the Remove *<filename>* command on the Project menu.

tip

....
▶ The Remove *<filename>* command removes the file from the project only; it does not remove the file from the disk.

To remove the laModule.bas file from the current project, then experiment by entering the Dim instruction in different locations:

1   Click Module1 (laModule.bas) in the Project window. Click **Project** on the menu bar, then click **Remove laModule.bas.** Visual Basic removes the laModule.bas file from the Project window.

   HELP? If you inadvertently removed the wrong file, use the Add File command on the Project menu to add the file to the project.

Remember, whenever you make a change to the information in the Project window, you must save the project.

2   Click the **Save Project** button 🖫 to save the project under its current name.

First see what happens if you declare the strName variable as a local variable.

3   View the frmName form. Open the OK button's Click event procedure, then press the **Enter** key to insert a blank line below the `Private Sub` instruction. Type **dim strName as string** in the new blank line. Close the Code window, then **run**, but don't save, the application. When the screen prompts you for your name, type your name and press the **Enter** key. When the "Variable not defined" warning message appears, click the **OK** button.

Notice that the frmWelcome form's Load event procedure does not recognize the local strName variable that you declared in the frmName form.

4   Close the Code window, then click the **End** button ◾ on the toolbar to end the application.

This example shows that the application will not work if the strName variable is declared as a local variable. Next observe what happens if you declare the strName variable as a form-level variable.

5   Open the OK button's Click event procedure and remove the `Dim strName As String` instruction.

6   Open the frmName form's General Declarations section, then type **dim strName as string** immediately below the `Option Explicit` statement. Close the Code window, then **run**, but don't save, the application. When the screen prompts you for your name, type your name and press the **Enter** key. When the "Variable not defined" warning message appears, click the **OK** button. Notice that the frmWelcome form does not recognize the form-level strName variable that you declared in the frmName form's General Declarations section.

7   Close the Code window, then click the **End** button ◾ on the toolbar to stop the application.

This example shows that the application will not work if the strName variable is declared as a form-level variable.

8   Open the frmName form's General Declarations section and remove the `Dim strName As String` instruction, then close the Code window.

Now add the laModule.bas file, which you created earlier, to the project.

Now review what you have learned about local, form-level, and global variables:

- Local variables are declared in an event procedure, and they can be used only by the event procedure in which they are declared. You use the Dim statement to declare local variables.

- If a variable with the same name is declared in more than one event procedure, each event procedure creates and uses its own variable with that name.

- Form-level variables are declared in a form's General Declarations section, and they can be used by every event procedure in that form. You use the Dim statement to declare form-level variables. Each form has its own General Declarations section.

- If a variable with the same name is declared as a local variable and as a form-level variable, the event procedure declaring the local variable uses the local variable. All other procedures use the form-level variable.

- Global variables are declared in the General Declarations section of a code module, and every procedure in every form in the application can use the variable. You use the Public statement to declare global variables.

- If a variable with the same name is declared as a local, form-level, and global variable, the event procedure declaring the local variable uses the local variable; all other procedures in that form use the form-level variable. Procedures that are not affected by local or form-level variables use the global variable.

Next you will learn how to create a symbolic constant.

Symbolic Constants

Recall that Visual Basic has two types of constants, literal and symbolic. A literal constant is a specific value (such as 3) that does not change while a program is running. A **symbolic constant**, on the other hand, is a memory location whose *contents* cannot change while the program is running. Like variables, symbolic constants can be local, form-level, or global. Local constants are declared in an object's event procedure, form-level constants are declared in a form's General Declarations section, and global constants are declared in the General Declarations section of a code module.

You create a symbolic constant with Visual Basic's Const statement, whose syntax is [**Public**] **Const** *constname* [**As** *datatype*] = *expression*. In the syntax, *constname* is the name of the symbolic constant and *expression* is the value you want assigned to the symbolic constant. The rules for naming a symbolic constant are the same as for variables, except you precede the symbolic constant's name with the three letters "con", which is short for "constant." Beginning the constant's name with "con" allows you to distinguish the symbolic constants from variables. The *expression* can be a literal constant or another symbolic constant; it can also contain arithmetic and logical operators. The *expression*, however, cannot contain variables or functions (such as Val).

Notice that both "**Public**" and "**As** *datatype*" are optional parts of the syntax. You use the Public keyword when declaring a global constant in the General Declarations section of a code module. You use the **As** *datatype* clause to assign a data type to the symbolic constant. If you do not assign a data type, Visual Basic assigns the type that it feels is the most appropriate, which may not be the most efficient type. For example, if you create a symbolic constant for the number 45.6 and you don't assign a data type, Visual Basic assigns the Double data type to it, even though a Single data type is more efficient. Figure 3-15 shows some examples of the Const statement.

Const Statement	
Const conPi as Single = 3.141593	Creates a Single symbolic constant named conPi and assigns the literal constant 3.141593 to it.
Const conMsg as String = "Welcome!"	Creates a String symbolic constant named conMsg and assigns the literal constant "Welcome!" to it.
Const conPrice as Currency = 25	Creates a Currency symbolic constant named conPrice and assigns the literal constant 25 to it.
Public Const conMaxAge as Integer = 65	Creates a global Integer symbolic constant named conMaxAge and assigns the literal constant 65 to it.

Figure 3-15: Examples of the Const statement

Symbolic constants make your program more self-documenting and, therefore, easier to modify because they allow you to use meaningful words in place of values that are less clear. The symbolic constant conPi, for example, is much more meaningful than 3.141593, the numeric value of pi (rounded to six decimal places). Once you create the symbolic constant, you can then use the constant's name, instead of its value, in the code. Unlike variables, symbolic constants can't be inadvertently changed while your program is running.

The formula for the area of a circle, $A = \pi r^2$, points out the differences among literal constants, symbolic constants, and variables. Converted into Visual Basic code, the formula is: `sngArea = conPi * sngRadius ^ 2`. SngArea and sngRadius are Single variables, conPi is a symbolic constant, and 2 is a literal constant. The ^ symbol is the exponentiation operator that tells Visual Basic to raise the variable sngRadius to the second power. You will create a symbolic constant for pi in the next application.

To open the project in which you will create a symbolic constant:

1 Open the **Symcon** (Symcon.vbp) project, which is located in the Tut03 folder on your Student Disk. The frmArea form appears on the screen.

The frmArea user interface contains a text box (txtRadius), a label control (lblArea), and two command buttons (cmdCalc and cmdExit). The user can enter the radius of a circle in the txtRadius control, then click the Calculate the Area button to calculate and display the area of the circle. The Exit button will end the application.

2 Double-click the **Calculate the Area** button. The cmdCalc control's Click event appears.

3 Enter the Const statement and the assignment statement that calculates the area. Both statements are shown in Figure 3-16.

enter these statements

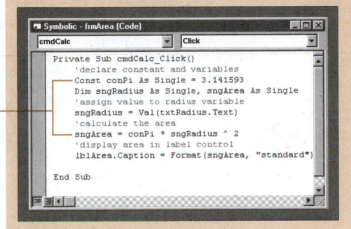

```
Symbolic - frmArea (Code)

cmdCalc                              Click

Private Sub cmdCalc_Click()
    'declare constant and variables
    Const conPi As Single = 3.141593
    Dim sngRadius As Single, sngArea As Single
    'assign value to radius variable
    sngRadius = Val(txtRadius.Text)
    'calculate the area
    sngArea = conPi * sngRadius ^ 2
    'display area in label control
    lblArea.Caption = Format(sngArea, "standard")

End Sub
```

Figure 3-16: The Calculate the Area button's Click event procedure

The `Const conPi as Single = 3.141593` statement creates the symbolic constant in memory, and assigns the 3.141593 value to it. The `sngArea = conPi * sngRadius ^ 2` statement calculates the area of the circle.

4 Close the Code window. **Run**, but don't save, the application. Type **5** as the radius, then click the **Calculate the Area** button. Visual Basic displays 78.54 as the area of the circle.

5 Click the **Exit** button to end the application.

You have now completed Lesson A. You will use local, form-level, and global variables in the Skate-Away Sales application, which you will modify in Lessons B and C. You can either take a break or complete the end-of-lesson questions and exercises. (When you exit Visual Basic, or when you open another project, you do not need to save the modified symcon application.)

S U M M A R Y

To tell Visual Basic to check for undeclared variables:

■ Enter the `Option Explicit` statement in the General Declarations section of every form and module in the application.

■ To have Visual Basic enter the `Option Explicit` statement automatically in every new form and module, click Tools on the menu bar, then click Options. Select the Require Variable Declaration option, which is located on the Editor tab in the Options dialog box.

To create a variable:

■ See naming rules in Figure 3-4 and 3-5 and data types listed in Figure 3-3.

■ To create a local variable, enter the Dim statement in the event procedure of an object. Its syntax is **Dim** *variablename* [**As** *datatype*].

■ To create a form-level variable, enter the Dim statement in a form's General Declarations section. Its syntax is **Dim** *variablename* [**As** *datatype*].

■ To create a global variable, enter the Public statement in a code module's General Declarations section. Its syntax is **Public** *variablename* [**As** *datatype*].

To use an assignment statement to assign data to a variable:

■ Use the syntax *variablename* = *value*.

To create a symbolic constant:

■ Use the Const statement. Its syntax is [**Public**] **Const** *constname* [**As** *datatype*] = *expression*.

■ The rules for naming constants are the same as for variables, except you precede the constant's name with the three letters "con", which is short for "constant."

■ Use the Const statement to declare local and form-level constants in an object's event procedure and form's General Declarations section, respectively.

■ Use the Public Const statement to declare a global constant in the General Declarations section of a code module.

To add a file to a project:

■ Use the Add File command on the Project menu.

To remove a file from a project:

■ Click the file's name in the Project window, then use the Remove *<filename>* command on the Project menu.

Q U E S T I O N S

1. _____ are memory locations in which you store information, temporarily.
   a. Boxes
   b. Forms
   c. Labels
   d. Variables
   e. Variances

2. Which of the following are valid variable names?
   a. cur94Income
   b. curIncome

    c. curInc_94

    d. curIncomeTax

    e. All of the above

3. Which of the following is the correct data type to use for a variable that will always contain whole numbers in the range 0 to 20,000?

    a. Currency

    b. Integer

    c. Long

    d. Single

    e. Variant

4. Which of the following is the only data type that can store numbers and strings?

    a. Currency

    b. Integer

    c. Long

    d. Single

    e. Variant

5. A variable known only to the procedure in which it is declared is called a(n) _____ variable.

    a. Event

    b. Form-level

    c. Local

    d. Procedure

    e. Protected

6. A data item whose value doesn't change while the program is running is called a _____ .

    a. literal constant

    b. literal variable

    c. symbolic constant

    d. symbolic variable

    e. variable

7. A memory location whose value can change while the program is running is called a _____ .

    a. literal constant

    b. literal variable

    c. symbolic constant

    d. symbolic variable

    e. variable

8. A memory location whose value cannot be changed while the program is running is called a _____ .

    a. literal constant

    b. literal variable

    c. symbolic constant

    d. symbolic variable

    e. variable

9. If you don't provide a *datatype* on the Dim or Public statement, Visual Basic creates a(n) _____ variable.

    a. Currency

    b. Integer

    c. String

    d. Variant

    e. None of the above

10. Data stored in a variable can be processed 10 to 20 times faster than data stored in the property of an object.
    a. True
    b. False

E X E R C I S E S

1. Assume your application needs to store an item's name and its price. On a piece of paper, write the appropriate Dim statements to create the necessary variables.

2. Assume your application needs to store the name of an item in inventory and its height and weight. The height may have decimal places; the weight will be whole numbers only. On a piece of paper, write the appropriate Dim statements to create the necessary variables.

3. Assume your application needs to store the name of an inventory item, the number of units in stock at the beginning of the current month, the number of units purchased during the current month, the number of units sold during the current month, and the number of units in stock at the end of the current month. (The number of units is always a whole number that will never be larger than 10000.) On a piece of paper, write the appropriate Dim statements to create the necessary variables.

4. Assume your application needs to store the name and the population of a city. (The population will never be more than 75000.) On a piece of paper, write the appropriate Dim statements to create the necessary variables.

5. Assume your application needs to store the part number of an item and its cost. (An example of a part number for this application is A103.) On a piece of paper, write the appropriate Dim statements to create the necessary variables.

6. Assume your application needs to store a person's name. On a piece of paper, write the appropriate Public statement to create the necessary global variable.

7. Assume your application needs to store a person's age. On a piece of paper, write the appropriate Public statement to create the necessary global variable.

8. On a piece of paper, write an assignment statement that assigns Miami to an existing variable named strCity.

9. On a piece of paper, write an assignment statement that assigns the part number AB103 to an existing variable named strPartno.

10. On a piece of paper, write the assignment statements that will assign the word Desk to an existing variable named strName, the number 40 to an existing variable named intInstock, and the number 20 to an existing variable named intOnorder.

11. On a piece of paper, write an assignment statement that will add the contents of the curReg1sales variable to the contents of the curReg2sales variable, then assign that sum to an existing variable named curTotalsales.

12. On a piece of paper, write an assignment statement that will multiply the contents of the curSalary variable by the number 1.5, then assign that result to the curSalary variable.

13. Assume a form contains two command buttons: cmdSalary and cmdBonus. Both buttons' Click event procedures need to use the strEmpName variable. On a piece of paper, write the appropriate statement to declare the strEmpName variable. Also write down where you will need to enter the statement and whether the variable is a local, form-level, or global variable.

14. Assume a form contains two command buttons: cmdWest and cmdSouth. The Click event procedure for the cmdWest button needs to use a variable named curWestsales. The Click event procedure for the cmdSouth button needs to use a variable named curSouthsales.

Both buttons' Click event procedures need to use the curCompany variable. On a piece of paper, write the appropriate statements to declare the curWestsales variable, the curSouthsales variable, and the curCompany variable. Also write down where you will need to enter each statement and whether each variable is a local, form-level, or global variable.

15. Assume an application contains two forms: frmName and frmDisplay. Both forms need to use a variable named strEmployee. On a piece of paper, write the appropriate statement to declare the strEmployee variable. Also write down where you will need to enter the statement and whether the variable is a local, form-level, or global variable.

16. Assume an application contains two forms: frmRate and frmTax. The frmRate form's Load event procedure needs to use a variable named strState. The Click event procedure for the cmdDisplay control, which is on the frmRate form, also needs to use the strState variable. The Click event procedure for the cmdCalc control, which is on the frmTax form, needs to use a variable named curStateTax. Both the cmdDisplay and cmdCalc controls' Click event procedures need to use a variable named sngStateRate. (Remember that the cmdDisplay control is on the frmRate form and the cmdCalc control is on the frmTax form.) On a piece of paper, write the appropriate statements to declare the strState, curStateTax, sngStateRate variables. Also write down where you will need to enter each statement and whether each variable is a local, form-level, or global variable.

17. On a piece of paper, write the statement to declare a local constant named conTaxRate whose value is .05.

18. Assume two procedures in a form need to use a constant named conAge whose value is 21. On a piece of paper, write the statement to declare the constant. Also write down where you will need to enter the statement and whether the constant is a local, form-level, or global constant.

19. Assume two procedures in two forms need to use a constant named conMessage whose value is "Welcome!". On a piece of paper, write the statement to declare the constant. Also write down where you will need to enter the statement and whether the constant is a local, form-level, or global constant.

Exercise 20 is a Discovery Exercise. Discovery Exercises, which may include topics that are not covered in the tutorial, allow you to "discover" the solutions to problems on your own.

discovery ▶

20. In this exercise you will see the effect of declaring a Static variable.
   a. Open the Static (Static.vbp) project, which is located in the Tut03 folder on your Student Disk. The project is supposed to count the number of times you press the Count button, but it is not working correctly.
   b. Run, but don't save, the project. Click the Count button. The message tells you that you have pressed the Count button 1 time, which is correct.
   c. Click the Count button again. Notice that the message still says that you have pressed the Count button 1 time; it should say that you have pressed the button 2 times.
   d. Click the Count button several more times. Notice that the number of times remains at 1.
   e. Click the Exit button to end the application.
   f. Open the Count button's Code window to view its Click event procedure. The procedure first declares a local variable named intCounter. It then adds 1 to the intCounter variable, and then displays the variable's value in the lblCounter control on the form.
   g. Change the `Dim intCounter as Integer` instruction to `Static intCounter as Integer`, then close the Code window.
   h. Run, but don't save, the application.
   i. Click the Count button several times. The message now tells you that you have pressed the Count button 1 time, 2 times, 3 times, and so on.
   j. Click the Exit button to end the application.
   k. Use the Help menu to display the Static statement's Help window. Then write a one-paragraph summary explaining the difference between using the Dim statement to declare a local variable and using the Static statement to declare a local variable. (You do not need to save the modified static application.)

In this lesson you will learn how to:

■ Use local and form-level variables in an application

■ Concatenate strings

■ Use the InputBox function

■ Find information in the Object Browser

■ Include the vbNewLine constant in code

■ Set the default button for a form

Modifying the Skate-Away Sales Application

Storing Information Using Local and Form-Level Variables

Recall that Mr. Cousard, the manager of Skate-Away Sales, called to tell you that the company now wants to include a message on each confirmation notice. The message should say "Thank you for your order. The sales tax was," followed by the sales tax amount and the name of the salesperson who recorded the order. You will need to modify the application's code to accommodate this change.

When making modifications to existing code, you should review the application's documentation and revise the necessary documents. In this case, you will need to revise the TOE chart and the pseudocode for the Calculate Order button, which is responsible for making the application's calculations. The revised TOE chart for the Skate-Away Sales application is shown in Figure 3-17. You will see the revised pseudocode for the Calculate Order button later in this lesson.

Task	Object	Event
1. Calculate the total skateboards ordered and the total price 2. Display the total skateboards ordered and the total price in the lblTboards and lblTprice objects 3. Calculate the sales tax 4. Display the message, the sales tax, and the salesperson's name in the lblMsg object	cmdCalc	Click
Clear the screen for the next order	cmdClear	Click
End the application	cmdExit	Click
Print a confirmation notice	cmdPrint	Click
Display the total skateboards ordered (from cmdCalc)	lblTboards	None
Display the total price (from cmdCalc)	lblTprice	None
Get and display the order information	txtName, txtAddress, txtCity, txtState, txtZip, txtPrice, txtRate, txtBlue, txtYellow	None
Get the salesperson's name	frmOrder	Load
Display the message, the sales tax, and the salesperson's name (from cmdCalc)	lblMsg	None

new tasks → (tasks 3 and 4)

new tasks → (Get the salesperson's name / Display the message...)

Figure 3-17: Revised TOE chart for the Skate-Away Sales application

If you compare the revised TOE chart with the original TOE chart shown in Tutorial 2's Figure 2-11, you will notice that the cmdCalc control now has two more tasks. It must calculate the sales tax and also display the message, sales tax, and salesperson's name in the lblMsg control. Two additional objects and events are also included in the revised TOE chart. The frmOrder form's Load event is responsible for getting the salesperson's name when the application is run. The lblMsg control will display the message, sales tax, and salesperson's name. According to the revised TOE chart, you will need to change the code in the cmdCalc control's Click event procedure, and you will also need to code the form's Load event procedure. The lblMsg control, which shows None in the event procedure, does not need to be coded; the control will get its value from the cmdCalc control.

Before you can begin modifying the code, you will need to open the Skate-Away Sales application.

To open the Skate-Away Sales application, then save the files under a new name:

1 Start Visual Basic, if necessary, and make sure your Student Disk is in the appropriate disk drive.

2 Open the **T3Case** (T3Case.vbp) project, which is located in the Tut03 folder on your Student Disk.

3 Save the form and the project as **lbOrder**.

Figure 3-18 identifies the controls already included in the application. (You won't see the names of the controls on your screen, except for the lblMsg control's name. The names are included in Figure 3-18 for your reference only.)

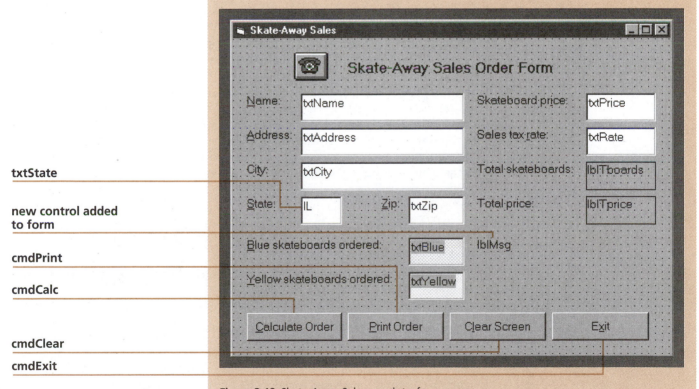

Figure 3-18: Skate-Away Sales user interface

> You will notice that one minor modification was made to the user interface that you created in Tutorial 2. Specifically, the interface now contains a label control named lblMsg. You will use that control to display the "Thank you" message that contains both the sales tax amount and the name of the salesperson. The lblMsg control's font size is set to 10 points to match the other controls in the interface, and its BackStyle property is set to 0-Transparent.
>
> **4** Click the **lblMsg** control, then display the Properties window and delete the contents of its Caption property.
>
> > **HELP?** To delete the contents of the Caption property, double-click Caption in the Properties list. Visual Basic highlights the contents of the Caption property in the Settings box. Press the Delete key to delete the highlighted caption, then press the Enter key.
>
> **5** Click the **form's title bar** to make the form the active window.

Besides the minor modification to the user interface, one additional line of code was included in the Clear Screen button's Click event procedure. The Click event now contains an instruction that will remove the "Thank you" message from the lblMsg control when the user clicks the Clear Screen button.

Now begin modifying the Skate-Away Sales application so that it prints the sales tax amount on the order.

Modifying the Calculate Order Button's Code

Currently, the Calculate Order button calculates the sales tax in the total price equation. Recall that the total price equation from Tutorial 2 is lblTprice.Caption= Val(lblTboards.Caption)*Val(txtPrice.Text)*(1+ Val(txtRate.Text)). Because Skate-Away Sales now wants the sales tax amount to print on the order, in the Calculate Order button's code you will need to include a separate equation for the sales tax. In this lesson, you will remove the Calculate Order button's code, which you entered in Tutorial 2, and then recode the button's Click event procedure—this time, however, you will use variables instead of control properties in the equations. As you learned in Lesson A, when an application uses variables, you should enter the Option Explicit statement in the form's General Declarations section. Adding that statement to the application prevents you from inadvertently using an undeclared variable in the code.

> To enter the Option Explicit statement in the form's General Declarations section:
>
> **1** Open the form's General Declarations section, then type **option explicit** and press the **Enter** key.

Recall that before making changes to existing code, you should review the application's documentation and revise the necessary documents. You've already seen the revised TOE chart for the Skate-Away Sales application in Figure 3-17. Figure 3-19 shows the revised pseudocode for the Calculate Order button.

> **Calculate Order button**
> 1. Declare variables
> 2. Assign values to variables
> 3. Calculate total skateboards = blue skateboards + yellow skateboards
> 4. Calculate subtotal = total skateboards * skateboard price
> 5. Calculate sales tax = subtotal * sales tax rate
> 6. Calculate total price = subtotal + sales tax
> 7. Display total skateboards and total price in lblTboards and lblTprice label controls
> 8. Display the "Thank you" message, sales tax, and salesperson's name in the lblMsg control
> 9. Send the focus to the Print Order button

Figure 3-19: Revised pseudocode for the Calculate Order button

If you compare the revised pseudocode with the original pseudocode shown in Tutorial 2's Figure 2-31, you will notice that the Calculate Order button will now make two additional calculations: a subtotal and the sales tax. The subtotal is computed by multiplying the total skateboards by the skateboard price. The sales tax is computed by multiplying the subtotal by the sales tax rate. The button will also display the "Thank you" message, the sales tax, and the salesperson's name in the lblMsg control.

First review, then remove, the code contained in the Calculate Order button's Click event procedure.

To review the code in the Calculate Order button's Click event procedure:
1   Open the cmdCalc control's Click event procedure, then maximize the Code window. The Click event procedure fills the screen.

tip

You are using Single (4 bytes of memory) rather than Currency (8 bytes of memory) variables for the price, subtotal, sales tax, and total price because these variables will not need to store large money values. Also, the equations that will use these variables are not complex, so rounding errors will not be a problem. Recall that it is best to use a smaller data type whenever possible.

The equations that calculate the total skateboards and the total price use the following six properties: txtBlue.Text, txtYellow.Text, lblTboards.Caption, txtPrice.Text, txtRate.Text, and lblTprice.Caption. The Val function in the equations is necessary because the Caption and Text properties of controls are treated as strings, not numbers. As you learned in Tutorial 2, the Val function returns the numeric equivalent of a string. What you didn't learn in Tutorial 2, however, is that the Val function returns a Double data type number. Therefore, the total skateboard equation first converts the contents of both the txtBlue.Text and txtYellow.Text properties to Double type numbers, then adds the Double numbers together and assigns the sum to the lblTboards control. Because a customer can order only a whole number of blue and yellow skateboards and, based on past sales, the number of skateboards ordered is typically under 1000 for each color, it would be more efficient to store the blue and yellow skateboard information in Integer variables. An Integer variable, you may remember, can store whole numbers between −32,768 and 32,767. As you learned in Lesson A, it is always more efficient to use a smaller data type wherever possible. By assigning the Text and Caption properties to variables, you can control the data type of the numbers used in the equations. In this case you will assign the Text and Caption properties of the controls to two Integer variables (intBlue and intYellow), and two Single variables (sngPrice and sngRate).

You will assign the result of the total skateboard equation to an Integer variable (intTboards), and assign the result of the total price equation to a Single variable (sngTprice). Additionally, you will store the subtotal and the sales tax in two Single variables (sngSubtotal and sngStax). Figure 3-20 lists the variables and what you will assign to each.

Variable:	Assign:
intBlue	Value of txtBlue.Text
intYellow	Value of txtYellow.Text
intTboards	Sum of intBlue + intYellow
sngPrice	Value of txtPrice.Text
sngRate	Value of txtRate.Text
sngSubtotal	Product of intTboards * sngPrice
sngStax	Product of sngSubtotal * sngRate
sngTprice	Sum of sngSubtotal + sngSTax

Figure 3-20: List of variables and what you will assign to each

Now remove the existing code from the Code window.

To remove the code in the calculate order button's Click event procedure:

1   Highlight all of the instructions between the Private Sub and the End Sub instructions, as shown in Figure 3-21. Be sure that you don't highlight the Private Sub and End Sub instructions.

highlight only these instructions

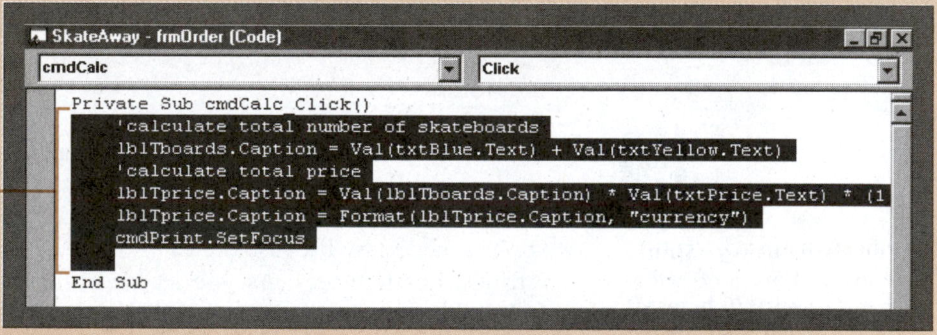

```
SkateAway - frmOrder (Code)                                    _ □ ×
cmdCalc                           ▼     Click                          ▼

Private Sub cmdCalc_Click()
      'calculate total number of skateboards
      lblTboards.Caption = Val(txtBlue.Text) + Val(txtYellow.Text)
      'calculate total price
      lblTprice.Caption = Val(lblTboards.Caption) * Val(txtPrice.Text) * (1
      lblTprice.Caption = Format(lblTprice.Caption, "currency")
      cmdPrint.SetFocus

End Sub
```

Figure 3-21: Instructions highlighted in the Calculate Order button's Code window.

2   Press the **Delete** key to remove the selected code.

HELP? If you inadvertently deleted the Private Sub and End Sub instructions, click the Object list arrow, then click cmdCalc in the list.

The first step listed in the pseudocode shown in Figure 3-19 is to declare the variables. Because only the Calculate Order button's Click event procedure will need to use the eight variables listed in Figure 3-20, you will declare all eight variables as local variables.

To begin coding the Calculate Order button's Click event procedure:

1   Enter the three `Dim` statements shown in Figure 3-22.

**enter these
instructions**

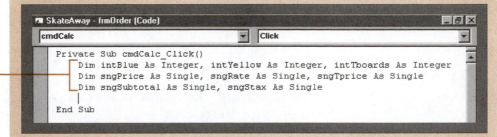

```
SkateAway - frmOrder (Code)
cmdCalc                                    Click
    Private Sub cmdCalc_Click()
        Dim intBlue As Integer, intYellow As Integer, intTboards As Integer
        Dim sngPrice As Single, sngRate As Single, sngTprice As Single
        Dim sngSubtotal As Single, sngStax As Single

    End Sub
```

Figure 3-22: Dim statements entered in the Code window

Notice that you can declare more than one variable in a `Dim` statement, but you must be sure to specify each variable's data type. If you leave a data type off a variable's declaration, Visual Basic assigns the Variant data type to the variable.

The next step in the pseudocode is to assign values to the variables. The intBlue, intYellow, sngPrice, and sngRate variables will get their values from the txtBlue, txtYellow, txtPrice, and txtRate text boxes. The remaining variables will get their values from the equations that calculate the total skateboards, subtotal, sales tax, and total price.

2   Enter the one line of documentation and the four assignment statements shown in Figure 3-23.

enter these instructions

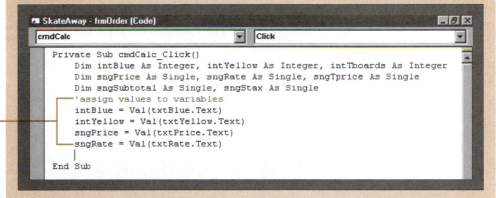

```
SkateAway - frmOrder (Code)
cmdCalc                                    Click
    Private Sub cmdCalc_Click()
        Dim intBlue As Integer, intYellow As Integer, intTboards As Integer
        Dim sngPrice As Single, sngRate As Single, sngTprice As Single
        Dim sngSubtotal As Single, sngStax As Single
        'assign values to variables
        intBlue = Val(txtBlue.Text)
        intYellow = Val(txtYellow.Text)
        sngPrice = Val(txtPrice.Text)
        sngRate = Val(txtRate.Text)

    End Sub
```

Figure 3-23: Documentation and assignment statements in Code window

tip
• • • • • • • • • • • • • • •

In the `Dim` statement, type the variable names using the exact capitalization you want. Then, any time you want to refer to the variables in the code, you can enter their names using any case and Visual Basic will adjust the name to match the case used in the Dim statement.

The `intBlue = Val(txtBlue.Text)` and `intYellow = Val(txtYellow.Text)` statements first convert the contents of the txtBlue and txtYellow text boxes to Double type numbers. The statements then store the numbers, as integers, in the intBlue and intYellow variables, respectively. Notice that Visual Basic changes the Double type numbers to integers before storing them in the Integer variables. Similarly, the `sngPrice = Val(txtPrice.Text)` and `sngRate = Val(txtRate.Text)` statements first convert the values in the Text properties of the txtPrice and txtRate controls to Double type numbers. These statements then store the numbers in the sngPrice and sngRate variables, respectively. The numbers in both the sngPrice and sngRate variables are stored as a Single data type.

The next step in the pseudocode is to calculate the total number of skateboards by adding the number of blue skateboards to the number of yellow skateboards. When entering the equation, you will use the variables instead of the control properties that you used in Tutorial 2's equation. In other words, you will enter `intTboards = intBlue + intYellow`, instead of `lblTboards.Caption = Val(txtBlue.Text) + Val(txtYellow.Text)`. Notice how, in addition to making your application run more efficiently and allowing you to control the preciseness of the numbers used in the calculations, variables also make the lines of code much shorter and easier to understand.

3   Type **'perform calculations** and press the **Enter** key, then type **inttboards = intblue + intyellow** and press the **Enter** key.

The next steps in the pseudocode are to calculate the subtotal, sales tax, and total price. You calculate the subtotal by multiplying the number of skateboards ordered, which is stored in the intTboards variable, by the skateboard price, which is stored in the sngPrice variable.

4   Type **sngsubtotal = inttboards * sngprice** and press the **Enter** key.

You calculate the sales tax by multiplying the subtotal, which is stored in the sngSubtotal variable, by the sales tax rate, which is stored in the sngRate variable.

5   Type **sngstax = sngsubtotal * sngrate** and press the **Enter** key.

To calculate the total price, you simply add the sales tax to the subtotal. The subtotal is stored in the sngSubtotal variable, and the sales tax is stored in the sngStax variable.

6   Type **sngtprice = sngsubtotal + sngstax** and press the **Enter** key.

The next step in the pseudocode is to display the total skateboards and the total price, formatted as currency, in the appropriate label controls on the form. As you did in Tutorial 2, you will use the Format function to format the total price as currency, which will display a dollar sign ($) and two decimal places.

7   Type **'display variable values in controls** and press the **Enter** key.

8   Type **lbltboards.caption = inttboards** and press the **Enter** key, then type **lbltprice.caption = format(sngtprice, "currency")** and press the **Enter** key.

The next step in the pseudocode is to display the "Thank you" message, sales tax, and salesperson's name in the lblMsg control. For now, just display the sales tax so you can verify that the sales tax equation is working correctly. You'll use the Format function to display the sales tax in the currency format—in other words, with a dollar sign and two decimal places.

9 Type **lblmsg.caption = format(sngstax, "currency")** and press the **Enter** key.

The last step in the pseudocode is to send the focus to the Print Order button. You can use the SetFocus method to do so.

10 Type **cmdprint.setfocus** and press the **Enter** key.

11 Compare your code to the code shown in Figure 3-24. Make any necessary corrections before continuing.

```
SkateAway - frmOrder (Code)
cmdCalc                                    Click
Private Sub cmdCalc_Click()
    Dim intBlue As Integer, intYellow As Integer, intTboards As Integer
    Dim sngPrice As Single, sngRate As Single, sngTprice As Single
    Dim sngSubtotal As Single, sngStax As Single
    'assign values to variables
    intBlue = Val(txtBlue.Text)
    intYellow = Val(txtYellow.Text)
    sngPrice = Val(txtPrice.Text)
    sngRate = Val(txtRate.Text)
    'perform calculations
    intTboards = intBlue + intYellow
    sngSubtotal = intTboards * sngPrice
    sngStax = sngSubtotal * sngRate
    sngTprice = sngSubtotal + sngStax
    'display variable values in controls
    lblTboards.Caption = intTboards
    lblTprice.Caption = Format(sngTprice, "currency")
    lblMsg.Caption = Format(sngStax, "currency")
    cmdPrint.SetFocus
    |
End Sub
```

Figure 3-24: Calculate Order button's Click event procedure

Now save and run the application to test the code you've entered so far.

To test the code in the Calculate Order button's Click event:

1 Close the Code window, then **save** and **run** the application. Enter the following order:

| blue skateboards ordered | 10 | skateboard price | 100 |
| yellow skateboards ordered | 10 | sales tax rate | .05 |

2 Click the **Calculate Order** button. Visual Basic displays the total number of skateboards ordered in the lblTboards control, the total price in the lblTprice control, and the sales tax in the lblMsg control, then sends the focus to the Print Order button, as shown in Figure 3-25.

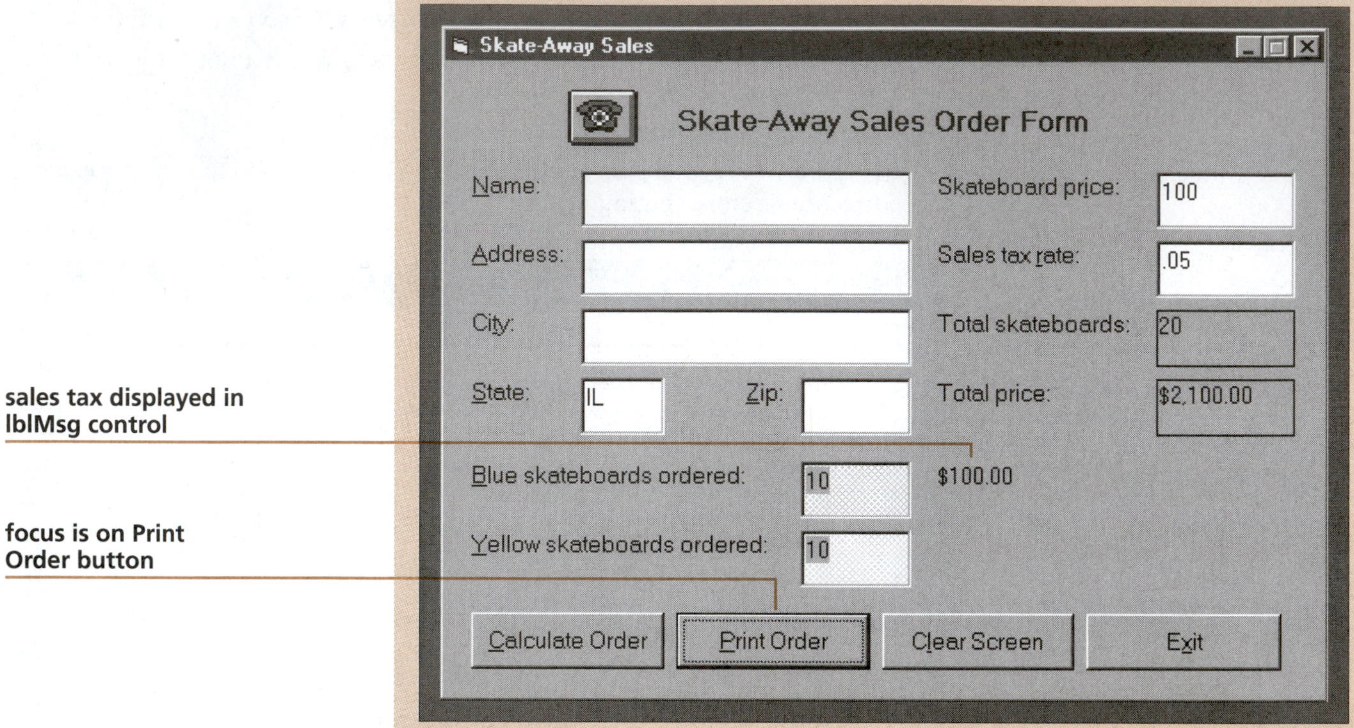

sales tax displayed in
lblMsg control

**focus is on Print
Order button**

Figure 3-25: Order screen showing sales tax

3 Click the **Exit** button. Visual Basic returns to the design screen.

In addition to displaying the sales tax, the lblMsg control must also display the message "Thank you for your order. Your sales tax was" and the name of the salesperson. To accomplish that task, you will need to learn how to concatenate (link together) strings.

Concatenating Strings

Connecting (or linking) strings together is called **concatenating**. In Visual Basic, you concatenate strings with the **concatenation operator**—the ampersand (&). Figure 3-26 shows some examples of string concatenation. Notice that you can also concatenate a number with a string. In those cases, Visual Basic treats the number as if it were a string.

Assume you have the following variables:		
Variables	**Data Type**	**Contents**
strFname	String	Sue
strLname	String	Chen
intAge	Integer	21
Using the above variables:		
This concatenated string:		**Would result in:**
strFname & strLname		SueChen
strFname & " " & strLname		Sue Chen
strLname & ", " & strFname		Chen, Sue
"She is " & intAge & "!"		She is 21!

Figure 3-26: Examples of string concatenation

When concatenating strings, you must be sure to include a space before and after the concatenation operator—the ampersand (&). If you do not enter a space before and after the ampersand, Visual Basic will not recognize the ampersand as the concatenation operator.

You will use the concatenation operator to link the string "Thank you for your order. The sales tax was" to the sales tax stored in the sngStax variable, and then concatenate the sales tax to a period, which will mark the end of the sentence. Using the examples shown in Figure 3-26 as a guide, the correct syntax for the lblMsg control's assignment statement would be `lblMsg.Caption = "Thank you for your order. The sales tax was " & Format(sngStax, "currency") & "."`. However, to make that assignment statement shorter and easier to understand, you will first create a symbolic constant for the "Thank you" message, and then use that symbolic constant, instead of the long message, in the assignment statement.

You may be wondering why we are using a symbolic constant for the message instead of a variable, which would work just as well. Unlike the number of blue and yellow skateboards ordered, the "Thank you" message will never change as the program is running. Assigning the message to a constant reminds us of that fact in the future.

To create a symbolic constant, then concatenate that symbolic constant to the sales tax variable:

1 Open the Calculate Order button's Click event procedure.

2 Maximize the Code window, then insert a blank line below the **Private Sub** statement. If necessary, press the **Tab** key to indent the line. Type **const conMsg as string = "Thank you for your order. The sales tax was "** in the blank line. Be sure to include a space between the last letter s and the last quotation mark. You are including the space so that a space prints between the message and the sales tax amount. (You can look ahead to Figure 3-27 to see the end result.)

You can now concatenate the conMsg symbolic constant, the sngStax variable, and a period to end the sentence.

3   Change the `lblMsg.Caption = Format(sngStax, "currency")` assignment statement as shown in Figure 3-27.

enter this
statement

include a
space here

add this to the original
assignment statement

add this to the original
assignment statement

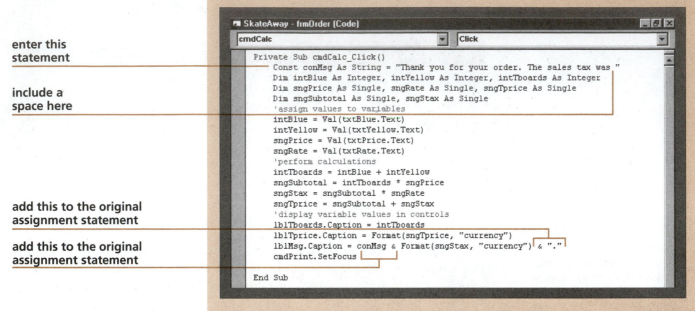

```
SkateAway - frmOrder (Code)                                    _ □ ×
cmdCalc                          ▼    Click                             ▼

Private Sub cmdCalc_Click()
    Const conMsg As String = "Thank you for your order. The sales tax was "
    Dim intBlue As Integer, intYellow As Integer, intTboards As Integer
    Dim sngPrice As Single, sngRate As Single, sngTprice As Single
    Dim sngSubtotal As Single, sngStax As Single
    'assign values to variables
    intBlue = Val(txtBlue.Text)
    intYellow = Val(txtYellow.Text)
    sngPrice = Val(txtPrice.Text)
    sngRate = Val(txtRate.Text)
    'perform calculations
    intTboards = intBlue + intYellow
    sngSubtotal = intTboards * sngPrice
    sngStax = sngSubtotal * sngRate
    sngTprice = sngSubtotal + sngStax
    'display variable values in controls
    lblTboards.Caption = intTboards
    lblTprice.Caption = Format(sngTprice, "currency")
    lblMsg.Caption = conMsg & Format(sngStax, "currency") & "."
    cmdPrint.SetFocus

End Sub
```

Figure 3-27: Const statement and modified assignment statement entered in the Code window

Now save and run the application to test the code you've entered so far.

4   Close the Code window, then **save** and **run** the application. Enter the following order:

blue skateboards ordered	10	skateboard price	100
yellow skateboards ordered	10	sales tax rate	.05

5   Click the **Calculate Order** button. Visual Basic displays the total number of skateboards ordered, the total price, and the message, including the sales tax, as shown in Figure 3-28.

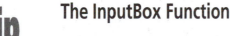

message and sales tax displayed in lblMsg control

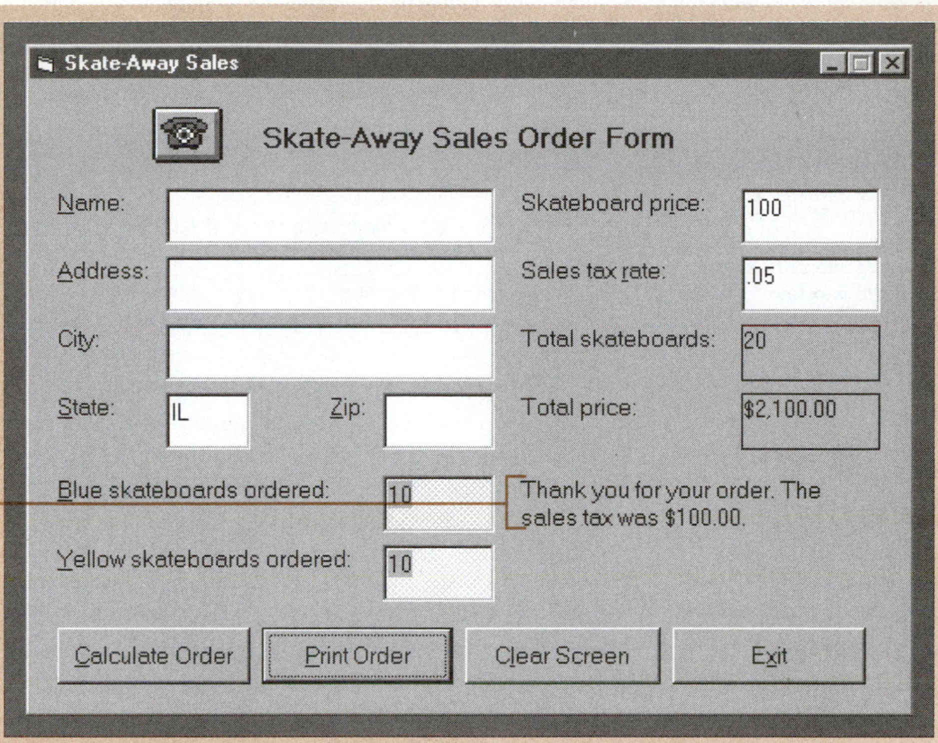

Figure 3-28: Order screen showing message and sales tax.

6 Click the **Exit** button. Visual Basic returns to the design screen.

Now that you have the message and the sales tax displaying correctly in the lblMsg control, you just need to get the salesperson's name and then concatenate it to the end of the message. Recall from the revised TOE chart shown in Figure 3-17, the form's Load event procedure is responsible for getting the salesperson's name. You can use Visual Basic's InputBox function to prompt the user for his or her name at the beginning of the application. You can then concatenate the salesperson's name to the message displayed in the lblMsg control.

The InputBox Function

The InputBox function displays one of Visual Basic's predefined dialog boxes. The dialog box contains a message, along with an OK button, a Cancel button, and an input area in which the user can enter information. The message that you display in the dialog box should prompt the user to enter the appropriate information in the input area of the dialog box. The user will then need to click either the OK button or the Cancel button in order to continue the application.

The syntax of the InputBox function is **InputBox**(*prompt, title*), where *prompt* is the message you want displayed inside the dialog box, and *title* is the text you want displayed in the dialog box's title bar. Both the *prompt* and *title* must be enclosed in quotation marks. Use sentence capitalization for the *prompt*, but book title capitalization for the *title*. (You learned about both sentence and book title capitalization in Tutorial 2's Lesson A.) If you omit the *prompt*, no message appears inside the dialog box. If you omit the *title*, the application's name appears in the title bar. Figure 3-29 shows some examples of the InputBox function used in assignment statements.

tip

You can also assign the prompt and/or the title to either a variable or a constant. When using a variable or a constant in the InputBox function, you don't need the quotation marks.

You can also include other information in the InputBox function. If you want to learn more about the InputBox function, use the Help menu to search for its Help window.

GUI
Design Tips

InputBox Function's Prompt and Title Capitalization

• In the InputBox function, use sentence capitalization for the *prompt*, and book title capitalization for the *title*.

Examples of the InputBox function

strName = InputBox("Enter your name:")

strCity = InputBox("Enter the capital:", "Capital Screen")

intAge = Val(InputBox("How old are you?", "Age"))

Note: Be sure to use the Val function when assigning the user's response to a numeric variable.

Figure 3-29: Examples of the InputBox function in assignment statements

Recall that a function is a predefined procedure that returns a value. In the case of the InputBox function, the value returned to the application is the value entered by the user in response to the prompt. In this application, you will use the InputBox function to prompt the salesperson to enter his or her name when he or she runs the application. You will store the user's response in a String variable named strSperson.

Now that you know that the InputBox function will require a variable in which to store the user's response, you must decide where to declare the variable. In other words, should the strSperson variable be a local, form-level, or global variable? When deciding, consider the fact that the form's Load event, which is responsible for getting the name, needs to use the variable; and so does the Calculate Order button's Click event procedure, which is responsible for concatenating the name to the message that displays in the lblMsg control. Recall from Lesson A that when two procedures in the *same* form need to use the *same* variable, you declare the variable as a form-level variable by entering the Dim statement in the form's General Declarations section.

To continue coding the Skate-Away Sales application, then save and run the application:

1 Open the form's General Declarations section.

First declare the strSperson String variable as a form-level variable.

2 Press ↓ on your keyboard to position the insertion point below the Option Explicit statement, then type **dim strSperson as string** and press the **Enter** key.

Now you will enter the InputBox function in the form's Load event procedure, so the function will be processed as soon as the salesperson runs the application. You'll use "Enter the salesperson's name:" as the *prompt*, and "Salesperson's Name" as the *title*. You will create constants for both the *title* and *prompt*.

3 Open the form's Load event procedure, then press the **Tab** key. Type **const conPrompt as string = "Enter the salesperson's name"** and press the **Enter** key, then type **const conTitle as string = "Salesperson's Name"** and press the **Enter** key.

4 Type **strsperson = inputbox(conprompt, contitle)** and press the **Enter** key.

The InputBox function will prompt the user to enter his or her name, and then store the response in the form-level strSperson variable. Recall that form-level variables remain in memory until the application ends.

You can now open the Calculate Order button's Click event procedure and concatenate the strSperson variable to the message assigned to the lblMsg control.

5   Open the Calculate Order button's Click event procedure, then maximize the Code window. Modify the message assigned to the lblMsg control as shown in Figure 3-30.

add this to the assignment statement

```
SkateAway - frmOrder (Code)                                    _ | 8 | X

cmdCalc                          ▼      Click                          ▼

    Private Sub cmdCalc_Click()
        Const conMsg As String = "Thank you for your order. The sales tax was "
        Dim intBlue As Integer, intYellow As Integer, intTboards As Integer
        Dim sngPrice As Single, sngRate As Single, sngTprice As Single
        Dim sngSubtotal As Single, sngStax As Single
        'assign values to variables
        intBlue = Val(txtBlue.Text)
        intYellow = Val(txtYellow.Text)
        sngPrice = Val(txtPrice.Text)
        sngRate = Val(txtRate.Text)
        'perform calculations
        intTboards = intBlue + intYellow
        sngSubtotal = intTboards * sngPrice
        sngStax = sngSubtotal * sngRate
        sngTprice = sngSubtotal + sngStax
        'display variable values in controls
        lblTboards.Caption = intTboards
        lblTprice.Caption = Format(sngTprice, "currency")
        lblMsg.Caption = conMsg & Format(sngStax, "currency") & "." & strSperson
        cmdPrint.SetFocus

    End Sub
```

Figure 3-30: Modified message assigned to lblMsg control

Next save and run the application to test the code you've entered so far.

6   Close the Code window, then **save** and **run** the application. The dialog box created by the InputBox function appears. See Figure 3-31.

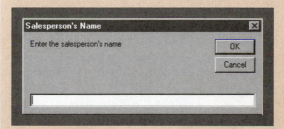

```
Salesperson's Name                                    X

Enter the salesperson's name                        ┌─────┐
                                                    │ OK  │
                                                    └─────┘
                                                    ┌──────┐
                                                    │Cancel│
                                                    └──────┘

┌────────────────────────────────────────────────────────┐
│                                                          │
└────────────────────────────────────────────────────────┘
```

Figure 3-31: Dialog box created by the InputBox function

7   Type your name in the input area of the dialog box, then click the **OK** button. The order screen appears.

8   Click the **Calculate Order** button. Your name now appears in the message.

In looking at the message, you decide that the name appears too close to the sales tax message. At this point you could modify the assignment statement in the cmdCalc control's Click event procedure so that it concatenates a period followed by two spaces (". "), instead of just a period ("."), as it does now. Or, you could display the salesperson's name on the next line. You decide to place the name on a separate line. You can use the newline character, which you will learn about in the next section, to do so.

9   Click the **Exit** button to end the application.

The Newline Character

The **newline character**, which is Chr(13) & Chr(10), instructs Visual Basic to issue a carriage return followed by a line feed. The combination of the carriage return followed by a line feed will advance the insertion point to the next line in the lblMsg control. Whenever you want Visual Basic to start a new line, you simply type the newline character at that location in your code. In this case, for example, you want Visual Basic to advance to a new line after displaying the sales tax message—in other words, before displaying the salesperson's name.

You could include the newline character in the instruction that assigns, to the lblMsg control, the "Thank you" message, sales tax, and salesperson's name. For example, you could change the instruction to lblMsg.Caption = conMsg & Format(sngStax, "currency") & "." & Chr(13) & Chr(10) & strSperson. The disadvantage of using Chr(13) & Chr(10) in your code is that it forces you and the next programmer looking at your code to remember that this combination of the Chr function displays a new line. A better way of displaying a new line is to use one of Visual Basic's intrinsic constants in your code. An **intrinsic constant** is a constant that is built into Visual Basic itself; you don't need to create the constant on your own because Visual Basic has already done that for you. You can use Visual Basic's Object Browser to view Visual Basic's intrinsic constants.

The Object Browser

The Object Browser is a dialog box that provides information about the various objects available to your application. The information includes properties, methods, events, and constants. You can open the Object Browser dialog box by clicking the Object Browser button on the Standard toolbar.

To use the Object Browser dialog box to search for an intrinsic constant, then copy and paste the constant into the Code window:

1 Click the **Object Browser** button 🔲 on the Standard toolbar. The Object Browser dialog box appears as shown in Figure 3-32. (Your Object Browser may display a Search Results list, as shown in Figure 3-33.)

Search text box

Copy to Clipboard button

Help button

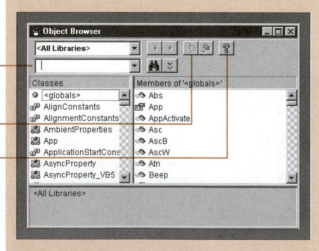

Figure 3-32: Object Browser dialog box

The insertion point is located in the Search text box. Search for the constant that represents the newline character.

2 Type **newline** in the Search text box, then press the **Enter** key. See Figure 3-33.

Search Results list

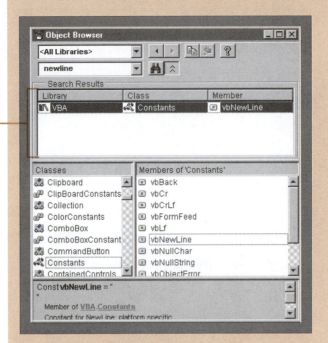

You can use the Help button, which is located at the top of the Object Browser dialog box, to view a Help window on the selected item.

Figure 3-33: Newline constant shown in the Object Browser dialog box

As the Search Results list in the dialog box shows, the name of the constant that represents the newline character is vbNewLine. VbNewLine is a member of the VBA (Visual Basic for Applications) Library's Constants class. To include the constant in your code, you can either type it into a Code window, or you can copy it from the Object Browser to the clipboard, then paste it into the Code window. You will use the copy–and–paste method.

3 Click the **Copy to Clipboard** button , which is located at the top of the Object Browser, then close the Object Browser.

4 Open the Calculate Order button's Click event, then maximize the Code window.

5 Position the insertion point immediately after the "." in the `lblMsg.Caption = conMsg & Format(sngStax, "currency") & "." & strSperson` instruction, then press the **spacebar** to insert a space after the closing quotation mark.

6 Type **&** and press the **spacebar**, then press **Ctrl + v** to paste the vbNewLine constant into the instruction. Make sure that a space follows the vbNewLine constant, as shown in Figure 3-34.

You can also use the Paste command on Visual Basic's Edit menu to paste the vbNewLine constant into the Code window. First, however, you will need to press the Alt key to display Visual Basic's menu.

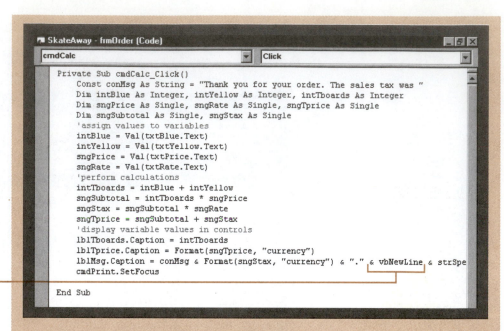

add this to the
assignment statement

Figure 3-34: vbNewLine constant shown in Code window

7 Close the Code window, then **save** and **run** the application. The dialog box created by the InputBox function appears.

Notice that the OK button in the dialog box has a darkened border, even though it does not have the focus; the text box has the focus, as indicated by the position of the insertion point. In Windows terminology, a command button that has a darkened border when it doesn't have the focus is called the default button. You can select a default button by pressing the Enter key at any time. In this case the user can select the OK button without taking his or her hands off the keyboard after typing the name. Try this.

8 Type your name in the InputBox function's dialog box. Then, instead of clicking the OK button, simply press the **Enter** key. The order screen appears.

9 Click the **Calculate Order** button. Your name now appears on a separate line in the lblMsg control.

10 Click the **Exit** button to end the application. Visual Basic returns to the design screen.

In this next section, you will learn how to create a default command button for the frmOrder form.

Making a Command Button the Default Button

As you already know from using Windows applications, you can choose a command button by pressing the Enter key when the button has the focus. If you make a command button the **default button**, however, you can select it by pressing the Enter key even when the button does not have the focus. An interface's default button should be the button that represents the user's most likely action, except in cases where that action is both destructive and irreversible—for example, a command button that deletes information should not be designated as the default button. If you assign a default button in an interface, it is typically the first command button, which means that it is on the left when the buttons are centered along the bottom of the screen, and on the top when the buttons are stacked in either the upper-right or lower-right corner.

In the Skate-Away Sales interface, the command button that represents the user's most likely action is the Calculate Order button. Because that button's action is neither destructive nor irreversible, it is a safe choice for a default button. Assigning the Calculate Order button as the default command button will allow the user to calculate the order at any time by simply pressing the Enter key.

A command button's Default property determines which command button is the default button. When you create a command button, its Default property is initially set to False, which means that it is not the default button. If you want a command button to be the default button, you must set its Default property to True. Because only one command button on a form can be the default button, setting a command button's Default property to True sets the Default property of every other command button in the form to False. Make the Calculate Order button the default button for the order screen.

To make the Calculate Order button the default button, then save and run the application:

1 Click the **Calculate Order** button to select it, then set the button's Default property to **True**.

2 **Save** and **run** the application. When prompted for the salesperson's name, type your name and press the **Enter** key. When the order screen appears, press the **Enter** key to calculate the order. The order calculates and the message appears.

Now use the Exit button's access key to end the application.

3 Press **Alt + x** to select the Exit button. The application ends and Visual Basic returns to the design screen.

You have now completed Lesson B. In Lesson C you will learn ways to make the Skate-Away Sales application more professional-looking. For now, you can either take a break or complete the end-of-lesson questions and exercises.

SUMMARY

To concatenate strings:

■ Use the concatenation operator—the ampersand (&). Be sure to put a space before and after the ampersand.

To display a dialog box containing a prompt, an input area, an OK button, and a Cancel button:

■ Use the InputBox function. Its syntax is **InputBox**(*prompt*, *title*). Both *prompt* and *title* must be enclosed in quotation marks unless they are either a variable or a constant. Use sentence capitalization for the *prompt*, and book title capitalization for the *title*.

To make a command button the default button:

■ Set its Default property to True. Only one of the command buttons on a form can be the default button.

To tell Visual Basic to advance to the next line:

■ Use the vbNewLine constant. Its value is Chr(13) & Chr(10).

To view information (properties, methods, events, constants) about the various objects available to an application:

■ Use the Object Browser dialog box. To open the Object Browser, either click the Object Browser 📖 button in the Standard toolbar, or use the Object Browser command on the View menu, or press the F2 key.

QUESTIONS

1. The InputBox function displays a dialog box containing which of the following?
   a. Cancel button
   b. input area
   c. OK button
   d. prompt
   e. all of the above

2. Which of the following is the concatenation operator?
   a. @
   b. #
   c. $
   d. &
   e. *

3. Assume the strReg1 variable contains the string "North" and the strReg2 variable contains the string "West". Which of the following will display the string "NorthWest" (one word) in the lblRegion control?
   a. lblRegion.Caption = strReg1 & strReg2
   b. lblRegion.Caption = "strReg1" & "strReg2"
   c. lblRegion.Caption = strReg1 $ strReg2
   d. lblRegion.Caption = strReg1 # strReg2
   e. lblRegion.Caption = strReg1 @ strReg2

4. Assume the strCity variable contains the string "Boston" and the strState variable contains the string "MA". Which of the following will display the string "Boston, MA" (the city, a comma, a space, and the state) in the lblAddress control?
   a. lblAddress.Caption = strCity #, & strState
   b. lblAddress.Caption = "strCity" & ", " & "strState"
   c. lblAddress.Caption = strCity $ ", " $ strState
   d. lblAddress.Caption = strCity & ", " & strState
   e. lblAddress.Caption = "strCity," & "strState"

5. Which of the following constants tells Visual Basic to advance to the next line?
   a. Advance
   b. NewLine
   c. vbAdvance
   d. vbNewLine
   e. None of the above

6. If you want to give the user the ability to select a specific command button when the button does not have the focus, set the command button's _____ property to True.
   a. Command
   b. Default
   c. Enter
   d. Focus
   e. SetFocus

7. You can use the _____ dialog box to view the constants available to your application.
   a. Constant Browser
   b. Constant Finder
   c. Find Constant
   d. Object Browser
   e. Object Finder

8. Which of the following will prompt the user for a number, then correctly assign the user's response to the sngNum variable?
   a. InputBox("Enter a number:", "Number") = sngNum
   b. sngNum = Chr(InputBox("Enter a number:", "Number"))
   c. sngNum = InputBox("Enter a number:", "Number")
   d. sngNum = Val(InputBox("Enter a number:", "Number"))

9. Which of the following will prompt the user for a city, then correctly assign the user's response to the strCity variable?
   a. InputBox("Enter the city:", "City") = strCity
   b. strCity = Chr(InputBox("Enter the city:", "City"))
   c. strCity = InputBox("Enter the city:", "City")
   d. strCity = Val(InputBox("Enter the city:", "City"))

E X E R C I S E S

NOTE: In the following exercises, be sure to enter the `Option Explicit` statement in the appropriate location. Also be sure to use variables.

1. In this exercise, you will modify the code in an existing application.

Scenario: The existing application calculates the commission earned on a salesperson's sales. The commission rate is 10%.

a. Open the Lb1 (Lb1.vbp) project, which is located in the Tut03 folder on your Student Disk.

b. Save the form and the project as lb1Done in the Tut03 folder on your Student Disk.

c. Make the Calculate Commission button the default button.

d. Review the code in the Calculate Commission button's Click event procedure. Then recode the button's Click event procedure so that it uses variables, instead of control properties, in the equation that calculates the commission.

e. Save and run the application.

f. Enter Mary Smith as the name, 3405 as the territory number, and 7500 as the sales.

g. Click the Calculate Commission button, then click the Print button, which has already been coded for you, to print the form on the printer.

h. Click the Exit button, which has already been coded for you, to end the application.

i. Print the code.

j. Submit the printout from step g and the code from step i.

2. In this exercise, you will use variables to code an application.

Scenario: Your math instructor has asked you to create an application that will calculate the square root of a number.

a. Open the Lb2 (Lb2.vbp) project, which is located in the Tut03 folder on your Student Disk.

b. Save the form and the project as lb2Done in the Tut03 folder on your Student Disk.

c. Make the Square Root button the default button.

d. Code the Square Root button so that it calculates and displays the square root of a whole number. Be sure to assign the numeric equivalent of the txtNumber.Text property to an Integer variable. Assign the square root to a Single variable. You can use Visual Basic's Sqr function to calculate the square root. Its syntax is **Sqr**(*number*).

e. Save and run the application.

f. Enter the number 144, then click the Square Root button. Click the Print button, which has already been coded for you, to print the form on the printer.

g. Click the Exit button, which has already been coded for you, to end the application.

h. Print the code.

i. Submit the printout from step f and the code from step h.

3. In this exercise, you will use variables to code an application.

Scenario: Mingo Sales needs an application in which they can enter the sales made in three states. The application should calculate the total sales and the commission.

a. Open the Lb3 (Lb3.vbp) project, which is located in the Tut03 folder on your Student Disk.

b. Save the form and the project as lb3Done in the Tut03 folder on your Student Disk.

c. Make the Commission button the default button.

d. Code the Exit button so that it ends the application when it is clicked.

e. Code the Clear Screen button so that it clears the screen when it is clicked. Send the focus to the New York sales text box.

f. Code the Print button so that it prints the form when it is clicked. Send the focus to the Clear Screen button.

g. Use the pseudocode shown in Figure 3-35 to code the Commission button. Format the total sales and the commission to standard.

Commission button
1. Declare variables for the 3 state sales, the total sales, and the commission
2. Assign values to variables
3. Calculate total sales = New York sales + Maine sales + Florida sales
4. Calculate commission = total sales * 5%
5. Display total sales and commission in lblTsales and lblComm
6. Send the focus to the Print button

Figure 3-35: Pseudocode for the Commission button

h. Save and run the application. Enter the following information:

New York sales:	15000
Maine sales:	25000
Florida sales:	10500

i. Click the Commission button, then click the Print button to print the form with the test data showing, then click the Clear Screen button.

j. Click the Exit button to end the application.

k. Print the code.

l. Modify the code in the Commission button so that it uses the InputBox function to ask the user for the commission rate. (Use the InputBox function in the Commission button's Click event.) Store the commission rate in a variable and use the variable in the equation that calculates the commission.

m. Save and run the application. Enter the following information:

New York sales:	26000
Maine sales:	34000
Florida sales:	17000

n. Click the Commission button. Enter .1 (the decimal equivalent of 10%) as the commission rate, then click the OK button. Click the Print button to print the form with the test data showing.

o. Click the Exit button to end the application.

p. Print the code.

q. Submit the printouts from steps i and n, and the printed code from steps k and p.

4. In this exercise, you will use variables, constants, and string concatenation to code the application.

Scenario: IMY Industries needs an application that their personnel clerks can use to calculate the new hourly pay, given the current hourly pay for each of three job codes and the raise percentage (entered as a decimal). They also want to display the message "Raise percentage: XX" on the screen. The XX in the message should be replaced by the actual raise percentage, formatted to percent.

a. Open the Lb4 (Lb4.vbp) project, which is located in the Tut03 folder on your Student Disk.

b. Save the form and the project as lb4Done in the Tut03 folder on your Student Disk.

c. Use the Properties window to verify that the New Hourly Pay button is the default button.

d. Code the Exit button so that it ends the application when it is clicked.

e. Code the Print button so that it prints the form when it is clicked. Send the focus to the Job Code 1 text box.

f. Use the InputBox function to prompt the personnel clerk to enter the raise percentage at the beginning of the application; in other words, when he or she runs the application. The raise percentage will be used to calculate the new hourly pay for each job code. (You may want to refer to this tutorial's Debugging section for hints on using the InputBox function.)

g. Use the pseudocode shown in Figure 3-36 to code the New Hourly Pay button. Assign the "Raise percentage: " message to a constant. Format the new hourly pay to standard. Format the raise rate (in the message) to percent.

New Hourly Pay button

1. Declare variables and constant
2. Assign values to variables
3. Calculate new hourly pay = current hourly pay * raise rate + current hourly pay
4. Display new hourly pay in appropriate label control
5. Display message and raise rate in lblMsg control
6. Send the focus to the Print button

Figure 3-36: Pseudocode for the New Hourly Pay button

h. Save and run the application. Enter the following information. (Enter the raise percentage when prompted by the InputBox function. Enter the current hourly pay for each job code in the appropriate text boxes.)

    Raise percentage (in decimal form):   .05
    Job Code 1's current hourly pay: 5
    Job Code 2's current hourly pay: 6.50
    Job Code 3's current hourly pay: 8.75

i. Calculate the new hourly pay, then print the form with the test data showing.

j. Click the Exit button to end the application.

k. Print the code.

l. Modify the application's code so that it asks the personnel clerk to enter the raise for each job code separately. Remove the InputBox function from the form's Load event. Replace it with three InputBox functions in the New Hourly Pay button's Click event.

m. Change the message so that each rate appears on a separate line in the label control as follows:

    Job Code 1: XX%
    Job Code 2: XX%
    Job Code 3: XX%

Assign each message to a constant.

n. Format the current hourly pay and the new hourly pay to standard.

o. Save the form and the project as lb4Done2 in the Tut03 folder on your Student Disk, then run the application. Enter the following information:

    Job Code 1's current hourly pay: 5
    Job Code 2's current hourly pay: 6.50
    Job Code 3's current hourly pay: 8.75

p. Click the New Hourly Pay button, then enter the following information:

    Job Code 1 raise percentage: .03   (the decimal equivalent of 3%)
    Job Code 2 raise percentage: .05   (the decimal equivalent of 5%)
    Job Code 3 raise percentage: .045   (the decimal equivalent of 4.5%)

q. Print the form with the test data showing, then click the Exit button to end the application.

r. Print the code.

s. Submit the printouts from steps i and q, and the code from steps k and r.

Use the following information to answer questions 5–7.

Variable/Constant Name	Contents
strCity	Madison
strState	WI
strZip	53711
conMessage	The capital of

5. On a piece of paper, write an assignment statement that will display the string "Madison, WI" in the lblAddress control. Be sure to use the information shown above.

6. On a piece of paper, write an assignment statement that will display the string "The capital of WI is Madison." in the lblAddress control. Be sure to use the information shown above.

7. On a piece of paper, write an assignment statement that will display the string "My zip code is 53711." in the lblAddress control. Be sure to use the information shown above.

Exercises 8 and 9 are Discovery Exercises, which allow you to both "discover" the solutions to problems on your own and to experiment with material that is not covered in the tutorial.

discovery ▶

8. In this exercise you will learn about the Cancel property of a command button.
   a. Open the Lb8 (Lb8.vbp) project, which is located in the Tut03 folder on your Student Disk.
   b. Use the Help menu to research the Cancel property of a command button.
   c. Set the Undo Clear button's Cancel property to True.
   d. Run, but don't save, the application.
   e. Type your first name in the text box, then press the Enter key. Notice that the Enter key selects the Clear button, which is the default button in the interface. The Clear button removes the entry from the text box.
   f. Now assume that you want to undo what the Clear button did in step e; in other words, you want to place your name back in the text box. Because the Undo Clear button's Cancel property is set to True, you can select that button simply by pressing the Esc key. Press the Esc key. Your name appears in the text box.
   g. Stop the application. You do not need to save this application.

discovery ▶

9. In this exercise you will practice using the Object Browser.
   a. Use the Object Browser to find the name of the intrinsic constant that can be used to change the mouse pointer to an hourglass.
   b. Use the Object Browser to find the name of the intrinsic constant that can be used to change a form's BorderStyle property to fixed-single.
   c. Submit the names of the two constants.

LESSON C
objectives

In this lesson you will learn how to:

- Add a form to a project
- Distinguish between a modal and a modeless form
- Create a dialog box
- Define the startup form
- Add a module to a project
- Use a global variable in an application
- Center a form on the screen
- Use the Load and Unload statements
- Use the Show and Hide methods
- Use a Timer control
- Remove a coded control from a form
- Change the appearance of the mouse pointer

Improving the Appearance of the Skate-Away Sales Application

Using a Dialog Box

Although the InputBox function is a quick and easy way to create a dialog box, it has some limitations—for example, you can't control its appearance. Also, the user can enter only one item of data at a time; so if you wanted the user to enter both the salesperson's name and the date, you would need to use two InputBox functions. Instead of using the InputBox function, you can use a form to create more professional-looking dialog boxes that can request as much input as necessary. In this lesson you will replace the InputBox function's dialog box with a form that will resemble a dialog box. To save you time, the form that will act as a dialog box is already on your Student Disk. First open the Skate-Away Sales application that you modified in Lesson B.

To continue coding the Skate-Away Sales application:

1. Start Visual Basic, if necessary, and make sure your Student Disk is in the appropriate disk drive.

2. Open the **lbOrder** (lbOrder.vbp) file, which is located in the Tut03 folder on your Student Disk.

3. Save the form and the project as **lcOrder**.

First remove the InputBox function from the form's Load event procedure.

4. Open the form's Load event procedure. Highlight the three instructions between the `Private Sub` and `End Sub` instructions, then press the **Delete** key. Visual Basic removes the three instructions from the Code window.

5. Close the Code window.

Now add the input screen to the current application.

Adding an Existing Form to the Application

You use the Add Form command on the Project menu to add an existing form to a project. In this case, you will add the t3input form file to the application.

To add the t3input form file to the project:

1 Click **Project** on the menu bar, click **Add Form**, and then click the **Existing** tab in the Add Form dialog box. Click **T3Input** (T3Input.frm) in the list of file-names, then click the **Open** button.

2 Display the Project window, if necessary. Notice that Visual Basic adds the frmInput (T3Input.frm) name to the Project window.

3 Click **frmInput (T3Input.frm)** in the Project window, then click the Project window's **View Object** button. The frmInput form appears on the screen.

Recall that when you make a change to the Project window, you must save the project.

4 Save the **T3Input** form as **lcInput** in the Tut03 folder on your Student Disk, then click the **Save Project** button 🖫 on the toolbar.

The frmInput form is sized to resemble a dialog box. The form contains a text box (txtSperson) in which the salesperson enters his or her name, and an OK button (cmdOK) that will remove the dialog box (form) from the screen. The OK button's Default property is set to True, which makes the OK button the default button on the frmInput form.

5 Open the frmInput form's General Declarations section.

6 Type **option explicit** in the frmInput form's General Declarations section, press the **Enter** key, and then close the Code window.

When a project includes more than one form, you must tell Visual Basic which of the forms you want automatically displayed when the application is run. You do that by specifying the startup form.

Specifying the Startup Form

When a multiform project is run, Visual Basic automatically loads and displays only one of the forms contained in the project; that form, called the **startup form**, can be any one of the forms in the project. You use the *<Project Name>* Properties command on the Project menu to specify which form you want Visual Basic to use as the startup form. In this case you want the frmInput form to be the startup form.

To specify the startup form:

1 Click **Project** on the menu bar, then click **SkateAway Properties**. When the SkateAway - Project Properties dialog box opens, click the **Startup Object** list arrow on the General tab, then click **frmInput** in the list, and then click the **OK** button.

When you run this multiform application, Visual Basic will automatically load and display the frmInput form on the screen. You can then use the Show method, which you will learn about in the next section, to both load and display the frmOrder form.

2 **Save** and **run** the application. The frmInput form appears on the screen.

Don't be concerned if the frmInput form does not appear centered on the screen. You will learn how to center the form later in this lesson. You will also learn the Windows standards for dialog boxes.

3 Click the **End** button ■ on the toolbar to end the application. Visual Basic returns to the design screen.

In the next section you will learn how to load, unload, show, and hide forms.

Loading and Displaying a Form

Visual Basic has two statements and two methods that control the loading and displaying, respectively, of forms. The two statements are Load and Unload, and the two methods are Show and Hide. The **Load statement** brings a form into memory, but it does not display the form on the screen. The **Unload statement**, on the other hand, removes a form from memory and from the screen. The syntax of the Load statement is **Load** *object*, and the syntax of the Unload statement is **Unload** *object*.

When you want to remove a form from the screen, but leave it in memory, you use the **Hide method** to do so. The syntax of the Hide method is *object*.**Hide**. Conversely, when you want to display a form on the screen, you use the **Show method** to do so. If the form is not already loaded, the Show method loads it before displaying it. The syntax of the Show method is *object*.**Show** [*style*]. *Style* is an integer, either 0 or 1, that determines if the form is modal or modeless. If *style* is either omitted or 0, the form is modeless; if *style* is 1, the form is modal. A **modeless form** is a form that does not require the user to take any action before the focus can switch to another form or dialog box, or before subsequent code is executed. The MSDN Library window is an example of a modeless form. A **modal form**, on the other hand, is a form that requires the user to take some action before the focus can switch to another form or dialog box, or before any subsequent code can be executed. When the form is modal, no input from the keyboard or mouse can occur in the application until the current form is either hidden or unloaded. Although other forms in your application are disabled when a modal form is displayed, other applications are not; you can still access these other applications either using Alt-Tab or clicking the application's button on the Windows 95 taskbar. The Open Project dialog box in Visual Basic is an example of a modal form.

tip

Don't confuse the Load statement with the form's Load event. The Load statement brings a form into memory, whereas the Load event occurs when the form is loaded into memory.

tip

To help clarify the concept of modal and modeless, complete Lesson C's Exercise 1.

Figure 3-37 recaps the Load and Unload statements and the Show and Hide methods. Notice that the statement name always comes before the object name, but the method name always comes after.

Instruction:	Used To:	Syntax:
Load statement	Bring a form into memory.	**Load** *object*
Unload statement	Remove a form from memory.	**Unload** *object*
Show method	Display a form on the screen; if the form is not already loaded, the Show method loads it before displaying it.	*object*.**Show** [*style*]
Hide method	Hides a form from view, but leaves it in memory.	*object*.**Hide**

Figure 3-37: Recap of Load, Unload, Show, and Hide methods

Now that you know how to load, unload, hide, and show forms, you can continue coding the Skate-Away Sales application. You will code the frmInput form first.

tip

⯈ To prevent the interface from flickering, momentarily, when switching between forms, always show the next form before you either hide or unload the current form.

To begin coding the frmInput form:

1   Double-click the **OK** button to open its Click event procedure.

When the user enters the salesperson's name and clicks the OK button, you want to assign the txtSperson control's Text property to the strSperson variable, then both load and display the frmOrder form. (Recall that the form-level strSperson variable is declared in the frmOrder form's General Declarations section.) Last, you want to unload the frmInput form, as the frmInput form is no longer necessary.

2   Press the **Tab** key, then type **strsperson = txtsperson.text** and press the **Enter** key.

3   Type **frmorder.show** and press the **Enter** key to both load and display the frmOrder form. Recall that the Show method will load an unloaded form before displaying it on the screen.

4   Type **unload frminput** and press the **Enter** key to unload the frmInput form.

5   Close the Code window, then **save** and **run** the application.

6   When prompted for the salesperson's name, type your name and press the **Enter** key. Visual Basic displays the "Variable not defined" warning message.

7   Click the **OK** button to remove the warning message from the screen. Visual Basic highlights the problem variable in the Code window.

According to the Code window, the cmdOK control's Click event procedure, which is located in the frmInput form, does not recognize the strSperson variable. Stop the application and consider the problem.

8   Close the Code window, then click the **End** button ◼ on the toolbar to end the application. Visual Basic returns to the design screen.

In Lesson B you declared the strSperson variable as a form-level variable in the General Declarations section of the frmOrder form. Recall that in Lesson B the strSperson variable was used by the frmOrder form's Load event procedure and the cmdCalc control's Click event procedure. Because both procedures were in the same form, you declared the strSperson variable as a form-level variable. Now that you've changed the application, however, a form-level variable will no longer work.

In the current application, the frmInput form's Load event procedure gets the salesperson's name, so the frmInput form needs to use the strSperson variable. The cmdCalc control on the frmOrder form, however, also needs to use that variable in order to include the name in the message displayed in the lblMsg control. As you learned in Lesson A, when two procedures in *different* forms need to use the *same* variable, you declare the variable as a global variable by entering the Public statement in the General Declarations section of a code module. In the next section, you will add a code module to the current application and declare a global variable in its General Declarations section.

Adding a Code Module to a Project

As you learned in Lesson A, a code module is a separate file, added to your application, that contains only code; it does not contain any forms or controls. All variables that you want to make available to all forms in the application must be declared in the General Declarations section of a code module. In this application, you will declare the strSperson variable in a code module's General Declarations section so that both the frmInput and frmOrder forms can use the variable.

tip

You can remove a file from a project by clicking the file's name in the Project window, then using the Remove <*filename*> command on the Project menu.

To add a code module to the current project, then continue coding the application:

1 Click **Project** on the menu bar, then click **Add Module**. When the Add Module dialog box appears, click **Module** on the New tab if necessary, then click the **Open** button. Visual Basic adds the Module1 file to the Project window, and the General Declarations section of the Module1 module appears.

2 Enter the two instructions shown in Figure 3-38.

declares a global
variable

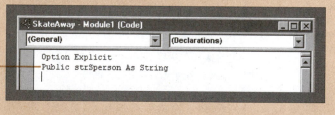

Figure 3-38: Instructions entered in the code module's General Declarations section

3 Save the Module1 code module as **lcModule**, then click the **Save Project** button on the toolbar to save the project.

4 Close the code module's Code window.

5 Scroll the Project window, if necessary, until the lcModule filename is visible in the window. The Project window shows that the code module is saved as lcModule.bas. (The .bas extension stands for "Basic.")

Before saving and running the application, you must first remove the Dim statement that declares the form-level variable in the frmOrder form's General Declarations section.

To remove the form-level variable declaration, then save and run the application:

1 Click **frmOrder (lcOrder.frm)** in the Project window, then click the **View Object** button in the Project window. Open the frmOrder form's General Declarations section.

2 Highlight the `Dim strSperson as String` instruction, then press the **Delete** key to remove the instruction from the Code window.

3 Close the Code window.

Now save and run the application.

4 **Save** and **run** the application. When the frmInput form appears, type your name, then press the **Enter** key. The frmOrder form appears. Press the **Enter** key to select the Calculate Order button.

Your name appears in the message in the lblMsg control.

5 Click the **Exit** button to end the application. Visual Basic returns to the design screen.

Now work on improving the appearance of the frmInput form so that it resembles a standard Windows dialog box.

Making a Form Resemble a Standard Windows Dialog Box

A standard Windows dialog box is centered on the screen, is not resizable, and contains only a Close button in its title bar; the Minimize and Maximize buttons do not appear in the title bar of a standard dialog box. In the Skate-Away Sales application, you will need to center the frmInput form on the screen, make it nonresizable, and remove its Minimize and Maximize buttons so that the form resembles a standard dialog box. First, make the form nonresizable and remove its Minimize and Maximize buttons.

You can remove a form's Minimize and Maximize buttons, as well as make the form nonresizable, by changing the form's BorderStyle property to 3-Fixed Dialog.

To remove a form's Minimize and Maximize buttons and make the form nonresizable:

1 Click the **Input Screen's title bar** to select the frmInput form, then set the frmInput form's BorderStyle property to **3-Fixed Dialog**.

Now make sure that the frmInput form is centered when it appears on the screen. To center a form, you will need to set both its Top and Left properties. What you set them to is based on both the height and width of the screen and the height and width of the form itself. The height and width of both the screen and the form is measured in twips. A twip, you may remember from Tutorial 1, is 1/1440 of an inch.

Suppose, for example, that the screen's height is 7000 twips and the form's height is 3900 twips. To center the form vertically, you simply subtract the form's height from the screen's height, then divide the remainder by 2; the result will give you the value for the form's Top property. In this example, for instance, you subtract 3900 from 7000, giving 3100. You then divide the 3100 by 2, giving 1550. Setting the form's Top property to 1550 twips will center the form vertically on the screen.

To center the form horizontally, you subtract the form's width from the screen's width, then divide the remainder by 2; the result will give you the value for the form's Left property. Suppose, for example, that the screen's width is 9000 twips and the form's width is 6500 twips. To calculate the value of the form's Left property, you subtract 6500 from 9000, then divide the remainder (2500) by 2. The result in this case is 1250. Setting the form's Left property to 1250 will center the form horizontally on the screen. Figure 3-39 shows an illustration of centering a form on the screen.

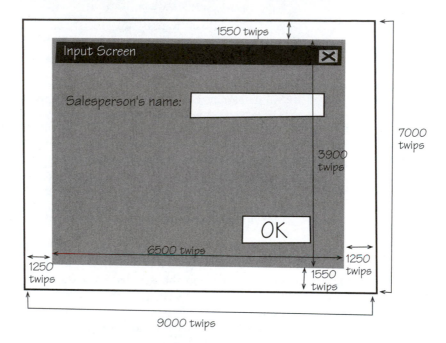

Figure 3-39: Illustration of a centered form

In Visual Basic the screen is considered an object; it is called the **Screen object**. You refer to the Screen object by using the keyword **Screen**. Therefore, the formula to center a form vertically on the screen is written as `formname.Top=(Screen.Height—formname.Height)/2`, where *formname* is the name of the form you want to center. The formula to center a form horizontally on the screen is written as `formname.Left=(Screen.Width—formname.Width)/2`. Notice that you do not need to know the actual height and width of the screen; the Height and Width properties of the Screen object contain the appropriate dimensions.

Because you want the frmInput form centered as soon as it appears on the screen, you will need to place the formulas in the form's Load event procedure.

To center a form when it first appears on the screen:

1   Open the frmInput form's Load event procedure, then enter the three instructions shown in Figure 3-40.

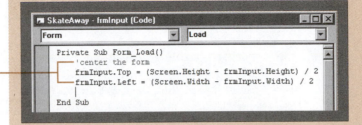

enter these instructions

```
SkateAway - frmInput (Code)
Form                          Load

Private Sub Form_Load()
    'center the form
    frmInput.Top = (Screen.Height - frmInput.Height) / 2
    frmInput.Left = (Screen.Width - frmInput.Width) / 2

End Sub
```

Figure 3-40: Instructions to center the form

HELP?   Remember that division has a higher precedence number than does subtraction, so you need to place parentheses around the subtraction part of the formula in order to change the order of precedence.

You will also center the frmOrder form.

2   Highlight the three instructions between the `Private Sub` and `End Sub` instructions in the frmInput form's Load event, then copy the three instructions to the clipboard. Close the Code window.

3   Open the frmOrder form's Load event procedure, then paste the three instructions between the `Private Sub` and `End Sub` instructions.

4   In the frmOrder form's Load event, change the four occurrences of frmInput to frmOrder. The instructions should now read `frmOrder.Top = (Screen.Height - frmOrder.Height)/2` and `frmOrder.Left = (Screen.Width - frmOrder.Width)/2`.

5   Close the Code window, then **save** and **run** the project. The frmInput form appears centered on the screen. Press the **Enter** key. The frmOrder form appears centered on the screen.

6   Click the **Exit** button. Visual Basic returns to the design screen.

Next, you will add, to the project, a copyright screen that is similar to the one you created in Tutorial 1.

Adding the Copyright Form to the Project

Recall that you use the Add Form command on the Project menu to add a form to an open project. In this case, you will add a copyright screen similar to the one that you created in Tutorial 1 to the current project. The copyright screen, which is named copy, is located in the Tut03 folder on your Student Disk.

To add the copy form file to the current project:

1   Click **Project** on the menu bar, then click **Add Form**. Click the **Existing** tab, then click **copy** (copy.frm) in the list of filenames, and then click the **Open** button.

◢ **GUI**
Design Tips

Dialog Box Standards

• The standard Windows dialog box is centered on the screen, is not resizable, and contains only a Close button on its title bar.

2   Click **frmCopyright (copy.frm)** in the Project window, then click the Project window's **View Object** button ▣. The frmCopyright form appears on the screen.

3   Save the copy form file as **lcCopy** in the Tut03 folder on your Student Disk.

Recall that when you run a multiform project, Visual Basic loads, automatically, only one form—the startup form. Change the startup form to the frmCopyright form.

4   Click **Project** on the menu bar, then click **SkateAway Properties**. Click the **Startup Object** list arrow on the General tab, then click **frmCopyright** in the list, and then click the **OK** button.

5   Click the **Save Project** ▣ button on the toolbar to save the project.

Now code the frmCopyright form so that it loads and displays both the frmInput and frmOrder forms. You'll load both forms in the frmCopyright form's Load event procedure, then display them when the user clicks the Exit button. Displaying the frmCopyright form will give the users something to look at while the other forms are being loaded. (Complex forms take time to load.)

To code the frmCopyright form:

1   Change the Caption of the lblAuthor control to say "Written By" (without the quotes), followed by your name.

2   Open the copyright screen form's Load event procedure. Press the **Tab** key, then enter the two instructions that will center the frmCopyright form on the screen.

Recall that you use the Load statement when you want to bring a form into memory without displaying it.

3   In the line below the centering instructions, type **load frminput** and press the **Enter** key, and then type **load frmorder** and press the **Enter** key.

Now have the Exit button show the frmInput form and unload the frmCopyright form.

4   Open the cmdExit control's Click event procedure. Highlight the **End** statement, then press the **Delete** key to remove the statement from the Code window.

5   Press the **Tab** key, if necessary, then type **frminput.show** and press the **Enter** key, and then type **unload frmcopyright** and press the **Enter** key.

6   Close the Code window, then **save** and **run** the application.

7   When the copyright screen appears, click the **Exit** button. When the input screen appears, press the **Enter** key. When the order screen appears, click the **Exit** button.

Most introductory screens wait a set period of time and then close on their own, without any user intervention. You can have the copyright form first load both the frmInput and frmOrder forms, then show the frmInput form, and then unload itself on its own by using a Timer control.

A millisecond is 1/1000 of a second. In other words, there are 1000 milliseconds in a second.

Using a Timer Control

You can use a Timer control to process code at regular time intervals. You simply need to set the control's Interval property to the length of the time interval, in milliseconds, and enter the code you want processed into the control's Timer event. The **Timer event** tells Visual Basic what to do after each time interval has elapsed. Add a Timer control to the current application.

To add a Timer control to the copyright form:

1   Click the **copyright form's title bar** to select the frmCopyright form.

2   Use the **Lock Controls** command on the Format menu to unlock the controls on the form.

3   Double-click the **Timer** tool in the toolbox. A Timer control, a stop watch, appears on the form. Drag the Timer control to the upper-left corner of the form. (The Timer control will not appear in the interface when the application is run, so it really doesn't matter where you place it in the design screen.)

You will now have the Timer control unload the frmCopyright form after eight seconds—in other words, after 8000 milliseconds.

4   Display the Properties window, then set the Timer control's Name property to **tmrCopy**. Set its Interval property to 8000.

5   Click the copyright form's **title bar** to select the frmCopyright form. Use the **Lock Controls** command on the Format menu to lock the controls on the form.

Next you will move the code from the Exit button's Click event to the Timer control's Timer event.

6   Open the cmdExit control's Click event procedure. The instructions in the Click event show the frmInput form and unload the frmCopyright form.

7   Highlight the `frmInput.Show` and `Unload frmCopyright` instructions.

When moving important code from one Code window to another, it is oftentimes safer to copy the data to the clipboard, then paste the code in its proper place, and then go back and remove the code from its original location.

8   Press **Ctrl + c** to copy the instructions to the clipboard. Open the tmrCopy control's Timer event, then press **Ctrl + v** to paste the instructions into the Code window. The `frmInput.Show` and `Unload frmCopyright` instructions are now in the tmrCopy control's Timer event.

9   Close the Code window.

In the next section you will learn the proper way of removing a coded control—in this case, the Exit button—from a form.

You can also use the Edit menu to copy and paste instructions.

Removing a Coded Control from the Form

If a control does not contain any code, you can remove the control from the form by selecting the control and pressing the Delete key. If a control contains code, however, you should delete the code that you entered in its Code window(s) before deleting the control from the form; otherwise, Visual Basic retains the unnecessary code in your application, even though the control is gone.

To remove the Exit button from the frmCopyright form:

1   Open the Exit button's Click event procedure.

The only procedure coded for the cmdExit control is the Click event procedure, so that is the only code you will need to delete before removing the control from the form. If other procedures were coded, you would also need to delete their code before deleting the control.

2   Highlight all of the instructions in the Code window, including the Private Sub and the End Sub instructions, then press the **Delete** key to delete the instructions in the Code window. Visual Basic removes the cmdExit control's Code window from the screen. The form's General Declarations section appears.

3   Close the Code window. The Exit button should still be selected, so just press the **Delete** key to remove the control from the form. Visual Basic removes the Exit button from the form.

In the next step you will save and run the application. While the application is running, pay particular attention to the mouse pointer that appears when the copyright screen is showing.

4   **Save** and **run** the application.

Recall that the copyright screen is on the screen for eight seconds, which in computer time is a long time. It is a Windows standard that when a process will take a long period of time, the interface should display an hourglass. You can change the appearance of the mouse pointer by setting the form's MousePointer property.

5   Click the **End** button ■ to end the application.

Changing the Appearance of the Mouse Pointer

The **MousePointer property** controls the type of mouse pointer Visual Basic displays when the mouse is over an object during run time. It is a Windows standard that when a process will take a long period of time, the mouse pointer should appear in the interface as either an hourglass 🛇 or an arrow and an hourglass 🜪. Both the 🛇 and 🜪 mouse pointers tell the user that the application is processing some information and that nothing will happen on the screen for a while. The difference between the pointers is that the 🛇 pointer indicates that the mouse pointer is temporarily inactive in the current application, whereas the 🜪 pointer indicates that the mouse pointer can still be used in the current application. In the Skate-Away Sales application, you want the user to know that he or she can use the mouse pointer to click the Interlocking Software logo, which appears in the copyright form, while the other forms are loading. The correct mouse pointer to use in this case is 🜪.

To change the frmCopyright form's mouse pointer:

1   Click the **copyright form's title bar** to select the frmCopyright form.

2   Set the frmCopyright form's MousePointer property to **13-Arrow and Hourglass**.

3   **Save** and **run** the application. When you place the mouse pointer on the copyright screen, notice that the mouse pointer changes to 🜪.

GUI Design Tips

Changing the Mouse Pointer

- It is a Windows standard that when a process will take a long period of time, the mouse pointer should appear in the interface as either an hourglass ⌛ or an arrow and an hourglass ⌛.

4. Click the **Interlocking Software logo**. The author and copyright information appear on the screen.
5. When the input screen appears, type your name and press the **Enter** key. When the order screen appears, enter an order, then press the **Enter** key to select the Calculate Order button.
6. If your computer is connected to a printer, click the **Print Order** button.
7. Click the **Clear Screen** button, then press **Alt + x** to select the Exit button.

The Skate-Away Sales application is finally complete. You can take a break, complete the end-of-lesson questions and exercises, or read and complete the Debugging Section, which may contain information that will help you when completing the exercises.

S U M M A R Y

To add an existing form to a project:

- Use the Add Form command on the Project menu.

To specify the startup form:

- Use the <*Project Name*> Properties command on the Project menu. When the <*Project Name*> Project Properties dialog box appears, click the Startup Object list arrow on the General tab, then click the name of the startup form in the list.

To bring a form into memory, but not display it on the screen:

- Use the Load statement. Its syntax is **Load** *object*.

To remove a form from both memory and the screen:

- Use the Unload statement. Its syntax is **Unload** *object*.

To display a form on the screen:

- Use the Show method. Its syntax is *object*.**Show** [*style*]. If the form is not already loaded, the Show method loads it before displaying it.
- If style is either omitted or 0, the form is modeless. If style is 1, the form is modal.

To add a code module to a project:

- Use the Add Module command on the Project menu.

To center a form on the screen:

- Enter the following two lines of code in the form's Load event procedure:
  formname.Top = (Screen.Height - *formname*.Height) /2
  formname.Left = (Screen.Width - *formname*.Width) /2

To have the form resemble a standard dialog box:

- Change the form's BorderStyle property to 3-Fixed Dialog.
- Center the form on the screen.

To have Visual Basic perform code at specified intervals of time:

■ Include a Timer control on the form. Set the Timer control's Interval property to the number of milliseconds for each interval. Code the Timer control's Timer event.

To change the appearance of the mouse pointer while an application is running:

■ Set the form's MousePointer property.

To remove a coded control from the form:

■ Select the control you want to remove from the form.
■ Delete the code from the control's Code window(s), including the Private Sub and End Sub instructions.
■ Press the Delete key to remove the control from the form.

To verify that a deleted control's code was removed from the application:

■ Open the form's General Declarations section and click the Procedure list arrow. If the name of the deleted control appears in the list, click the control's name in the list, then highlight the instructions in its Code window (including the `Private Sub` and `End Sub` instructions), and then press the Delete key.

Q U E S T I O N S

1. You use the _____ command on the Project menu to add an existing form to a project.
   a. Add
   b. Add Module
   c. Add Form
   d. Create

2. When you run a multiform project, Visual Basic automatically loads and displays _____ .
   a. all of the forms in the application
   b. the first form created
   c. the first form saved
   d. the initial form
   e. the startup form

3. The _____ brings a form into memory, but it does not display the form on the screen.
   a. Display statement
   b. Load method
   c. Load statement
   d. Show method
   e. Show statement

4. The _____ removes a form from memory and from the screen.
   a. Erase method
   b. Hide method
   c. Remove statement
   d. Unload method
   e. Unload statement

5. You use the _____ to display a form on the screen.
   a. Display statement
   b. Load method
   c. Load statement
   d. Show method
   e. Show statement

6. If a form is not already loaded into memory, the _____ loads it before displaying it.
   a. Display statement
   b. Load method
   c. Load statement
   d. Show method
   e. Show statement

7. The _____ removes a form from the screen, but leaves it in memory.
   a. Erase method
   b. Hide method
   c. Remove statement
   d. Unload method
   e. Unload statement

8. A _____ is a form that does not require the user to take any action before the focus can switch to another form or dialog box, or before subsequent code is executed.
   a. modal form
   b. modeless form

9. A _____ is a form that requires the user to take some action before the focus can switch to another form or dialog box, or before any subsequent code can be executed.
   a. modal form
   b. modeless form

10. When a form is _____ , you can still access other applications either by using Alt-Tab or by clicking the application's button on the Windows 95 taskbar.
    a. modal
    b. modeless
    c. either modal or modeless

11. When two procedures in *different* forms need to use the *same* variable, you declare the variable as a _____ variable.
    a. form-level
    b. global
    c. local

12. You center a form by setting its _____ and _____ properties.
    a. Height
    b. Left
    c. Size
    d. Top
    e. Width

13. To make a form resemble a standard dialog box, change its _____ property to 3-Fixed Dialog.
    a. Border
    b. BorderSize
    c. BorderStyle
    d. Dialog
    e. Style

14. You can use a(n) _____ control to execute code at regular intervals.
a. Clock
b. Interval
c. Time
d. Timer

15. A form's _____ property controls the appearance of the mouse pointer while the application is running.
a. Button
b. Mouse
c. MouseButton
d. MousePointer
e. MouseStyle

E X E R C I S E S

NOTE: The following list reviews the GUI design and programming guidelines you have learned so far. You can use this list to verify that the applications you create in the following exercises adhere to the standards outlined in the book.

- Information should flow either vertically or horizontally, with the most important information always located in the upper-left corner of the screen.
- Maintain a consistent margin of two or three dots from the edge of the window.
- Related controls should be grouped together using either white space or a frame.
- Position related controls on succeeding dots.
- Command buttons should either be centered along the bottom of the screen or stacked in either the upper-right or lower-right corner.
- If the command buttons are centered along the bottom of the screen, then each button should be the same height; their widths, however, may vary.
- If the command buttons are stacked in either the upper-right or lower-right corner of the screen, then each button should be the same height and the same width.
- Use no more than six command buttons on a screen.
- The most commonly used command button should be placed first.
- Command button captions should:
  - be meaningful
  - be from one to three words
  - appear on one line
  - be entered using book title capitalization
- Use labels to identify the controls in the interface.

- Identifying labels should:
  - be from one to three words
  - appear on one line
  - be aligned by their left borders
  - be positioned either above or to the left of the control that they identify
  - end with a colon (:)
  - be entered using sentence capitalization
  - have their BackStyle property set to 0-Transparent
  - have their BorderStyle property set to 0-None
- Labels that display program output (for example, the results of calculations):
  - should have their BorderStyle set to 1-Fixed Single
  - should have their Appearance property set to 0-Flat
  - can have their BackStyle property set to either 0-Transparent or 1-Opaque
- Align labels and controls to minimize the number of different margins.
- If you use a graphic in the interface, use a small one and place it in a location that will not distract the user.
- Use no more than two different font sizes, which should be 8, 10, or 12 points.
- Use only one font type, which should be a sans serif font, in the interface.
- Avoid using italics and underlining.
- Use either white, off-white, light gray, pale blue, or pale yellow for an application's background, and black for the text.
- Use color sparingly and don't use it as the only means of identification for an element in the interface.
- Set each control's TabIndex property to a number that represents the order in which you want that control to receive the focus (begin with 0).
- A text box's TabIndex value should be one more than the TabIndex value of its identifying label.
- Lock the controls in place on the form.
- Assign a unique access key to each essential element of the interface (text boxes, command buttons, and so on).
- Document the program internally.
- Enter the Option Explicit statement in the General Declaration section of every form and module.
- Use variables to control the preciseness of numbers in the interface.
- Use the Val function on Text and Caption properties, and when assigning the result of the InputBox function to a numeric variable.
- Set the form's BorderStyle, MinButton, MaxButton, and ControlBox properties appropriately:
  - Splash screens should not have a Minimize, Maximize, or Close button, and their borders should not be sizable.
  - Forms that are acting as dialog boxes should have a BorderStyle property of 3-Fixed Dialog.
  - Forms other than splash screens and dialog boxes should always have a Minimize button and a Close button, but you can choose to disable the Maximize button.
  - Forms other than splash screens and dialog boxes typically have a BorderStyle property setting of either 1-Fixed Single or 2-Sizable.

> ■ Test the application with both valid and invalid data (test the application without entering any data; also test it by entering letters where numbers are expected).
>
> ■ In the InputBox function, use sentence capitalization for the *prompt*, and book title capitalization for the *title*.
>
> ■ Center a form by including the appropriate formulas in the form's Load event.
>
> ■ Display an hourglass or an arrow and an hourglass if a procedure will take a long period of time.
>
> ■ Remove excess code from the application.

1. In this exercise you will practice with both a modal and a modeless form.
    a. Click File, then click Open Project to view the Open Project dialog box. Try clicking other areas of the screen. Were you able to move the focus out of the Open Project dialog box? Does that mean the Open Project dialog box is modal or modeless?
    b. Close the Open Project dialog box.
    c. Click Help, then click Contents. When the MSDN Library Visual Studio 6.0 window appears, try clicking other areas of the screen. Were you able to move the focus out of the MSDN Library Visual Studio 6.0 window? Does that mean that the MSDN Library Visual Studio 6.0 window is modal or modeless?
    d. Close the MSDN Library Visual Studio 6.0 window.
    e. On a piece of paper, answer the questions posed in steps a and c.

2. In this exercise, you will use two forms and string concatenation.

    Scenario: RM Sales wants an application that will allow the user to enter the name of a salesperson. The salesperson's name will then be displayed in a label control that is located on another form, along with the following message "The award goes to ". For example, if the user enters Anu Patel, the message will say "The award goes to Anu Patel." (without the quotes, but with the period after the name).

    a. Open the Lc2 (Lc2.vbp) project, which is located in the Tut03 folder on your Student Disk.
    b. Read the Note at the beginning of the Exercises section.
    c. Save the form and the project as lc2Done.
    d. Add the T3Input (T3Input.frm) file to the project, which is located in the Tut03 folder on your Student Disk, then save the T3Input form file as lc2Input.
    e. Add a code module to the form, then save the code module as lc2Mod.
    f. Save the project using its current name (lc2Done).
    g. Have the application display the frmInput form, which requests the salesperson's name, first. The frmInput form should be a standard dialog box. Change the appropriate property. The frmInput form's OK button should assign the salesperson's name to a global variable, then display the frmAward form and unload the frmInput form.
    h. Code the frmAward form's Load event procedure so that it displays the message and the salesperson's name. Assign the message to a constant.
    i. Save and run the application. Enter your name as the salesperson's name. Print the frmAward form with the test data showing, then exit the application.
    j. Print the code for the entire project. (Click Current Project in the Range section of the Print dialog box.)
    k. Submit the printouts and code from steps i and j.

3. In this exercise you will create a dialog box and add a form to it.

Scenario: RM Sales wants an application that allows the clerk to enter the current sales for four sales regions and the projected sales percentages for those regions. They want the application to calculate the projected sales.

   a. Read the Note at the beginning of the Exercises section.

   b. Open a new project, if necessary. Name the form frmRate. Name the project Sales, then save the form and the project as lc3Done.

   c. Design the frmRate form so that it allows the user to enter the decimal equivalent of four percentage rates: the North region's rate, the South region's rate, the East region's rate, and the West region's rate. Include an OK button on the form. The form should resemble a standard dialog box.

   d. Add the Lc3 (Lc3.frm) file, which is located in the Tut03 folder on your Student Disk, to the project. Save the form as lc3Sales.

   e. Add a code module to the form, then save the code module as lc3Mod.

   f. Have the application display the frmRate form first. The rates entered on the frmRate form will need to be used by the Projected Sales button, which is on the frmRMSales form. The Projected Sales button should display the rates, formatted to percent, in the appropriate label controls on the frmRMSales form. It should also calculate and display the projected sales, formatted to standard, in the appropriate label controls on the frmRMSales form.

   g. The Projected Sales button should send the focus to the Print button. The Print button should send the focus to the North region's text box.

   h. Save and run the application. First enter the four rates in the frmRate form. When the frmRMSales form appears, enter the four sales. Calculate the projected sales, then print the form with the test data showing. Use the following rates and sales:

	Rates	Sales
North region:	.10	25000
South region:	.25	50000
East region:	.15	124000
West region:	.20	111000

   i. Click the Exit button to end the application. Print the frmRate form's Form Image. Also print the code for the entire project. (Click Current Project in the Range section of the Print dialog box.)

   j. Submit the printouts and code from steps h and i.

4. In this exercise you will create a dialog box and a form.

Scenario: The math teacher at the local high school has asked you to create an application that will display the square and square root of a number.

   a. Read the Note at the beginning of the Exercises section. Although the design of the application is up to you, you must use two forms in the application. One of the forms should prompt the student for his or her name; that form should resemble a standard dialog box. You also must display the name on the main form when the main form is first run. The main form should include a Square/Square Root button, a Print button, and an Exit button. Use the InputBox function in the Square/Square Root button to prompt the user for the number. The application should display both the square and square root of the number. (*Hint*: You can use Visual Basic Sqr function, whose syntax is **Sqr**(*number*), to calculate the square root.)

   b. The Print button should send the focus to the Square/Square Root button.

   c. Save the main form and the project as lc4Done. Save the dialog box form as lc4Name. Save the code module as lc4Mod.

    d. Follow the five steps involved in creating an application:
1) Plan the application. (Prepare a TOE chart, ordered by object, and draw a sketch of the user interface.)
2) Build the user interface.
3) Code the application. (Be sure to write pseudocode for each of the objects that will be coded.)
4) Test and debug the application. (Use the sample data provided in the exercise.)
5) Assemble the documentation.

    e. Save and run the application. Enter your name, then print the application twice, using the following test data: 144 and 9.

    f. Print the code for the entire project, and also print the Form Image for both forms. (Click Current Project in the Range section of the Print dialog box.)

    g. Submit the TOE chart, sketch, pseudocode, printouts, and code from steps e and f.

5. In this exercise you will design and create an application on your own.

Scenario: Your friend Joe accumulates a lot of pennies in a jar, which he empties every month when he goes to the bank. As a favor, you decide to create an application that allows him to enter the number of pennies, and then calculates the number of dollars, quarters, dimes, nickels, and pennies he will receive when he trades the pennies in at the bank. (*Hint*: Review the mathematical operators listed in Figure 2-30 in Tutorial 2.)

    a. Read the Note at the beginning of the Exercises section. Although the design of the application is up to you, you must include a Print button that will print the user interface, and an Exit button that will end the application.

    b. Save the form and the project as lc5Done.

    c. Follow the five steps involved in creating an application:
1) Plan the application. (Prepare a TOE chart, ordered by object, and draw a sketch of the user interface.)
2) Build the user interface.
3) Code the application.
4) Test and debug the application. (Use the sample data provided in the exercise.)
5) Assemble the documentation.

    d. Save and run the application. Print the application twice, using the following test data: 2311 pennies and 7333 pennies.

    e. Print the application's code.

    f. Submit the TOE chart, sketch, pseudocode, printouts, and code from steps d and e.

6. In this exercise you will design and create an application on your own.

Scenario: The principal of Hinsbrook School would like you to create an application that will help her students, who are in grades 1 through 6, learn how to make change. The application should allow the student to enter the amount the customer owes and the amount of money the customer paid. The application should calculate the amount of change, as well as how many dollars, quarters, dimes, nickels, and pennies to return to the customer. For now, you do not have to worry about the situation where the price is greater than what the customer pays. You can always assume that the customer paid either the exact amount or more than the exact amount. (*Hints*: Review the mathematical operators listed in Figure 2-30 in Tutorial 2. Or, you can also display the Help window on the Int function.)

    a. Read the Note at the beginning of the Exercises section. Although the design of the application is up to you, you must Include a Calculate Change button, which uses the InputBox function to prompt the user for the amount due and the amount paid. The Calculate Change button will display the amount due, amount paid, change, number of dollars, number of quarters, number of dimes, number of nickels, and number of pennies. Format the amount due, amount paid, and change to currency. You must also include a Print button that will print the user interface, a Clear button that will clear the user interface, and an Exit button that will end the application.

b. The Print button should send the focus to the Clear Screen button. The Clear Screen button should send the focus to the Calculate Change button.

c. Save the form and the project as lc6Done.

d. Follow the five steps involved in creating an application:

1) Plan the application. (Prepare a TOE chart, ordered by object, and draw a sketch of the user interface.)

2) Build the user interface.

3) Code the application.

4) Test and debug the application. (Use the sample data provided in the exercise.)

5) Assemble the documentation.

e. Save and run the application. Print the application three times, using the following test data:

> 75.33 as the amount due and 80.00 as the amount paid
>
> 39.67 as the amount due and 50.00 as the amount paid
>
> 45.55 as the amount due and 45.55 as the amount paid

f. Print the application's code.

g. Submit the TOE chart, sketch, pseudocode, printouts, and code from steps e and f.

Exercises 7 through 9 are Discovery Exercises. Discovery Exercises, which may include topics that are not covered in the tutorial, allow you to "discover" the solutions to problems on your own.

discovery ▶

7. In this exercise, you will discover the difference between setting a form's BorderStyle property to 3-Fixed Dialog, and setting the form's MinButton and MaxButton properties to False.

a. Open a new project. Set the form's BorderStyle property to 3-Fixed Dialog. Run, but don't save the project. Notice the border. End the project.

b. Set the form's BorderStyle property back to its default, 2-Sizable. Set the form's MinButton property to False and set its MaxButton property to False. Run, but don't save the project. Notice the border. End the project.

c. Although the borders in step a and step b look similar, they do not react to the user in the same way. Explain the difference between setting a form's BorderStyle property to 3-Fixed Dialog and setting it to 2-Sizable, with both the MinButton and MaxButton properties set to False. You may find it helpful to display the Help windows for the BorderStyle, MinButton, and Maxbutton properties.

discovery ▶

8. In this exercise, you will discover the difference between the Val function and Visual Basic's type conversion functions.

a. Open the lc8 (lc8.vbp) project, which is located in the Tut03 folder on your Student Disk.

b. Use the Help menu to research the Data Type Conversion functions.

c. Open the Display button's Click event procedure. Maximize the Code window. The instructions in the Code window will allow you to see how the Val function and some of the data type conversion functions handle various values.

d. Highlight all of the code in the Code window. Press the Alt key to display the menu. Click File on the menu bar, then click Print. Notice that the Selection option button is selected in the Range section of the Print dialog box. Click the OK button.

e. Close the Code window, then run, but don't save, the project.

f. Click the Display button. The interface shows the original value, how the Val function converts the original value, and how one of the data type conversion functions converts the original value. (Refer to the code printout to see which conversion function was used.)

g. Click the Exit button to stop the application.

h. Use this application to discover how the Val function and the CCur function handle the empty string.

i. Use this application to discover how the Val function and the CSng function handle a letter.

j. Submit your answers to steps h and i.

discovery ▶

9. In this exercise, you will discover the difference between setting a form's MousePointer property to 11-Hourglass and 13-Arrow and Hourglass.

a. Open the lc9 (lc9.vbp) project, which is located in the Tut03 folder on your Student Disk. The project contains two forms: frmCopyright and frmMain. Use the Project window to view the frmCopyright (lc9a.frm) form.

b. Display the Properties window for the frmCopyright form. You will notice that the MousePointer property is set to 13-Arrow and Hourglass.

c. Run the application, then place the mouse pointer on the copyright form. The ⬚ pointer appears. Recall that the ⬚ pointer indicates to the user that the mouse pointer is active in the current form. To see if that is, in fact, the case, click the Next button. The application processes the instructions in the cmdNext control's Click event procedure. That procedure contains the `frmMain.Show` instruction, which displays the frmMain form, and the `Unload frmCopyright` instruction, which removes the frmCopyright form from both the screen and memory. When the main form appears, click the Exit button. Visual Basic returns to design mode.

d. Assume that you do not want to allow the user to remove the copyright screen so quickly. In other words, you want to be sure that the copyright information displays for at least five seconds before the user can remove it from the screen. You can do so by first disabling the cmdNext control. When you disable a command button, it does not respond to the user. In other words, if the user clicks a disabled command button, Visual Basic does not process the instructions in the button's Click event. View the frmCopyright form, then change the cmdNext control's Enabled property to False.

e. Next, you will change the form's mouse pointer to an hourglass to indicate that the mouse pointer is inactive. Change the copyright form's MousePointer property to 11-Hourglass. (Be sure to change the form's MousePointer property, and not the frame control's MousePointer property.)

f. Lastly, you will open the timer control's Timer event and enter the instructions to both enable the Next command button and to change the copyright form's mouse pointer back to the default. Both instructions will be processed after five seconds have elapsed. (The timer control's Interval property has already been set to 5000.) Open the timer control's Timer event, then press the Tab key. Type `cmdNext.Enabled = True` and press the Enter key, then type `frmCopyright.MousePointer = vbDefault` and press the Enter key.

g. Close the Code window. Run the application, then place the mouse pointer on the copyright form. The ⬚ pointer appears and the Next command button is dimmed, which indicates that it is not available to the user at this time. Try clicking the dimmed Next command button. You will notice that clicking the dimmed command button does not invoke its Click event. After five seconds the Next command button is enabled and the mouse pointer is changed to the default arrow.

h. Click the Next button. When the main form appears, click the Exit button. Visual Basic returns to the design screen. You do not need to save the application.

D E B U G G I N G

Technique   **A.** One of the most common errors made in writing code is mistyping the name of a variable. When you don't keep a variable's name consistent throughout the code, you create a bug in the program. You can have Visual Basic help you find this type of bug by entering the Option Explicit statement in the General Declarations section of the form. Then, if you use the name of a variable that has not been previously declared, Visual Basic will inform you of the error when you run the application.

B.   If your application uses the InputBox function, remember that the user can:

- enter a valid response, then click the OK button
- enter an invalid response, then click the OK button
- click the OK button without entering a response
- click the Cancel button

You should test your application to see how it handles the various InputBox responses.

C.   Remember that the Val function converts a string expression into a numeric value. Because Visual Basic must be able to interpret the string expression as a numeric value, the expression cannot include a letter or a special character, such as the dollar sign, comma, or the percent sign (%); it can, however, include a period. When Visual Basic encounters an invalid character in the Val function's string expression, Visual Basic stops converting the string expression to a number at that point.

Following are three debugging exercises that will allow you to practice your debugging skills.

Exercises

1.   In this exercise, you will debug an application. Use the information in the debugging techniques section to help you.

   a. Start Visual Basic and open the **T3db1** (T3db1.vbp) project, which is located in the Tut03 folder on your Student disk. **Run,** but don't save, the project.

   b. Click the **Calculate Average** button, type **300** as the first number and press the **Enter** key, then type **100** as the second number and press the **Enter** key. The average of both numbers (200) should appear in the lblAnswer control. Notice that the application is not working correctly. Click the **Exit** button to end the application.

   c. Print the code.

   d. To help you find some of the errors in the code, type the `Option Explicit` statement in the form's General Declarations section. (*Note*: The `Option Explicit` statement will not find all the errors.)

   e. **Run,** but don't save, the application. Click the **Calculate Average** button, then correct the errors.

   f. After all of the errors are corrected, test the application with the following data:

   First number: 300
   Second number: 100

   The average should be 200.

   g. When the application is working correctly, print the code. You do not need to save the corrected application.

2.   In this exercise, you will debug an application. Use the information in the debugging techniques section to help you.

   a. Start Visual Basic and open the **T3db2** (T3db2.vbp) project, which is located in the Tut03 folder on your Student disk. **Run,** but don't save, the project.

   b. Click the **Compute Sum** button, then click the **OK** button without entering a number. Click the **Debug** button. Notice the line of code that does not work correctly when you click the OK button without entering anything in the input area of the dialog box. Click the **End** button ■ to end the application. Close the Code window.

   c. **Run,** but don't save, the application. Click the **Compute Sum** button, then click the **Cancel** button. Click the **Debug** button. Notice the line of code that does not work correctly when you click the Cancel button. Click the **End** button ■ to end the application. Close the Code window.

   d. Use the Help menu to display the InputBox function's Help window. Read the Help window, then close it.

   e. Use the Val function to correct the problem line(s) of code so that the application will not result in an error message when the user either clicks the OK button without entering any data or clicks the Cancel button.

f. **Run**, but don't save, the application. Click the **Compute Sum** button, then click the **Cancel** button when prompted for the first number. Also click the **Cancel** button when prompted for the second number. The application should not result in an error message. Click the **Compute Sum** button again. This time click the **OK** button when prompted for both the first and second numbers. The application should not result in an error message.

g. When the application is working correctly, print the code. You do not need to save the corrected application.

3. In this exercise, you will debug an application. Use the information in the debugging techniques section to help you.

a. Start Visual Basic and open the **T3db3** (T3db3.vbp) project, which is located in the Tut03 folder on your Student Disk.

b. **Run**, but don't save, the project. Type **10000** as the sales, then click the **Compute Commission** button. The application calculates, correctly, a 5% commission ($500.00) on the sales. Click the **Compute Commission** button again. This time the Compute Commission button displays, incorrectly, $0.00 as the commission. Click the **Exit** button to end the application.

c. Open the Compute Commission button's Click event. Change curComm = Val(txtSales.Text) * 0.05 to **curComm = Val(Format(txtSales.Text, "fixed"))** * **0.05**, then close the Code window. **Run**, but don't save, the project. Type 10000 as the sales, then click the **Compute Commission** button. The application calculates, correctly, a 5% commission ($500.00) on the sales. Click the **Compute Commission** button again. The Compute Commission button displays, correctly, $500.00 as the commission. Click the **Exit** button to end the application.

d. Reread this tutorial's Debugging Technique section. Based on what you discovered in steps b and c, why did the Compute Commission button calculate the commission incorrectly in step b?

e. Submit your answer to step d.

The Selection Structure

Creating a Math Application

case ▶ On Monday you meet with Susan Chen, the principal of a local primary school. Ms. Chen needs an application that the first and second grade students can use to practice both adding and subtracting numbers. The application should display the addition or subtraction problem on the screen, then allow the student to enter the answer, and then verify that the answer is correct. If the student's answer is not correct, the application should give him or her as many chances as necessary to answer the problem correctly.

The problems displayed for the first grade students should use numbers from 1 through 10 only; the problems for the second grade students should use numbers from 10 through 100. Because the first and second grade students have not learned about negative numbers yet, the subtraction problems should never ask them to subtract a larger number from a smaller one.

Ms. Chen also wants the application to keep track of how many correct and incorrect responses the student makes; this information will help her assess the student's math ability. Because she doesn't want any additional pressure placed on the student while he or she is using the application, Ms. Chen wants to be able to control the display of this information.

Previewing the Completed Application

You'll begin by previewing the completed Math application.

To preview the completed application:

1 If necessary, start Windows, then place your Student Disk in the appropriate disk drive.

2 Use the Run command on the Start menu to run the **Math** (Math.exe) file, which is located in the Tut04 folder on your Student Disk. The Math application's user interface appears on the screen. See Figure 4-1.

your numbers may differ

enter the answer here

check box

option buttons

frame

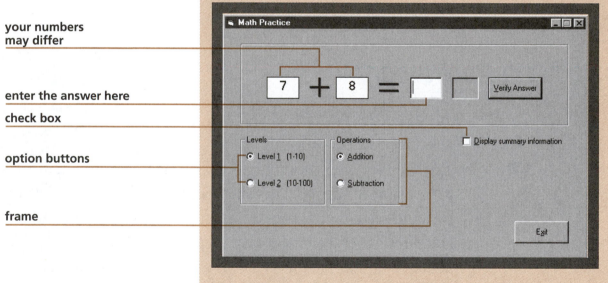

Figure 4-1: Math application's user interface

Don't worry if the numbers on your screen do not match the ones in the figure. This application uses the Randomize statement and the Rnd and Int functions to display random numbers in the two label controls. You will learn how to use the Randomize statement and the Rnd and Int functions in Lesson B.

The Math application contains two new controls—option buttons and a check box. You will learn about these controls in Lesson B.

3   Type the correct answer to the addition problem appearing in the interface, then press the **Enter** key. (The Verify Answer button is the default command button.)

4   Click the **Display summary information** check box to select it. A check mark appears inside the check box, and a frame control, which displays the number of correct and incorrect responses, appears below the check box. See Figure 4-2.

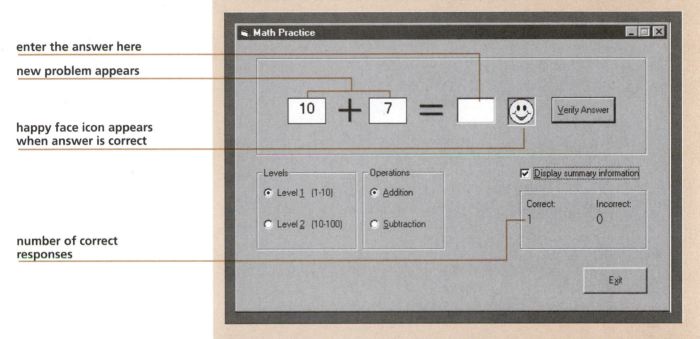

enter the answer here

new problem appears

happy face icon appears when answer is correct

number of correct responses

Figure 4-2: Interface showing that a correct response was made to the previous problem

When you answer the problem correctly, a happy face icon appears in the image control located to the left of the Verify Answer button. The number 1 appears as the number of correct responses, and a new problem appears in the interface.

5   Click the **Subtraction** option button. A black dot appears in the center of the Subtraction option button, which indicates that the option button is selected. The math problem changes to one involving subtraction.

6   Click inside the text box in which you enter the answer. Type an incorrect answer to the subtraction problem appearing on the screen, then press the **Enter** key. The application removes the happy face from the image control and displays a dialog box that says "Try again."

7   Press the **Enter** key to remove the dialog box. The application highlights the incorrect answer in the text box and gives you another chance to enter a correct response. The interface shows that you have made one correct response and one incorrect response.

8 Type the correct answer to the subtraction problem, then press the **Enter** key. The happy face icon reappears, and the number of correct responses now says 2. The application displays a new math problem in the interface.

9 Click the **Display summary information** check box to deselect it. Visual Basic removes the check mark from the check box, and hides the frame control that contains the summary information.

10 Click the **Exit** button. The application ends.

Before you can begin coding the Math application, you will need to learn about the selection structure. You will learn that structure in Lesson A. In Lesson B you will complete the Math application's interface as you learn how to use two new controls: option buttons and check boxes. You will begin coding the application in Lesson B, and complete the application in Lesson C.

In this lesson you will learn how to:

- Write pseudocode for the selection structure
- Create a flowchart to help you plan an application's code
- Write an If...Then...Else statement
- Write code that uses relational operators and logical operators
- Use the UCase function
- Write a nested selection structure
- Write the Select Case statement
- Include the To and Is keywords in a Select Case statement

The If...Then...Else and Select Case Statements

The Selection Structure

The applications you created in the previous three tutorials used the sequence programming structure only, where each of the program instructions was processed, one after another, in the order in which they appeared in the Code window. In many applications, however, the next instruction to be processed will depend on the result of a decision or a comparison that the program must make. For example, a payroll program might need to decide if an employee worked overtime. Assuming a 40-hour workweek, the program can make that determination by comparing the number of hours the employee worked with the number 40. Based on the result of that comparison, the program will then select either an instruction that computes regular pay or an instruction that computes overtime pay.

You use the **selection structure**, also called the **decision structure**, when you want a program to make a decision or comparison and then, based on the result of that decision or comparison, to select one of two paths. You can think of the selection structure as being a fork in the road. The selection structure, you might recall, is one of the three programming structures. The other two are sequence, which was covered in the previous tutorials, and repetition, which will be covered in Tutorial 5. You will need to use the selection structure to complete the Math application.

Each day you probably make hundreds of decisions, some so minor that you might not even realize you've made them. For example, every morning you have to decide if you are hungry and, if you are, what you are going to eat. Figure 4-3 shows other decisions you might have to make today.

Example 1	Example 2
If *it's raining* then	If *you have a test tomorrow* then
wear a rain coat	study tonight
bring an umbrella	Otherwise
	watch a movie

Figure 4-3: Decisions you might need to make today

In the examples shown in Figure 4-3, the portion in *italics*, called the **condition**, specifies the decision you are making and is phrased so that it results in either a true (yes) or a false (no) answer only. For example, either it's raining (true/yes) or it's not raining (false/no); either you have a test tomorrow (true/yes) or you don't have a test tomorrow (false/no).

If the condition is true, you perform a specific set of tasks. If the condition is false, however, you might or might not need to perform a different set of tasks. For instance, look at the first example shown in Figure 4-3. If it's raining (a true condition), then you will wear a raincoat and bring an umbrella. Notice, however, that you don't have anything in particular to do if it's not raining (a false condition). Compare this to the second example shown in Figure 4-3. If you have a test tomorrow (a true condition), then you will study tonight. If you don't have a test tomorrow (a false condition), however, then you will watch a movie.

Writing Pseudocode for the Selection Structure

Like you, the computer can also evaluate a condition and then select the appropriate tasks to perform based on that evaluation. The programmer must be sure to phrase the condition so that it results in either a true or a false answer only. The programmer must also specify the tasks to be performed when the condition is true and, if necessary, the tasks to be performed when the condition is false. Programmers refer to this as the **selection structure** (or the **decision structure**). Figure 4-4 shows two examples of the selection structure written in pseudocode.

Selection with a true path only	Selection with both true and false paths
If *the part number is "AB203"* then	If *sales > 1500* then
Assign "Desk" as the item name	Calculate commission = .02 * sales
Assign 56.60 as the item price	Else
End If	Calculate commission = .01 * sales
Display the part number in the lblPartno control	End If
	Display the commission in the lblComm control

Figure 4-4: Two examples of the If...Then...Else selection structure written in pseudocode

Although pseudocode is not standardized—every programmer has his or her own version—you will find some similarities among the various versions. For example, many programmers begin the selection structure with the word `If` and end the structure with the two words `End If`. The reason for the similarity in pseudocode is quite simple: the pseudocode written by many programmers greatly resembles the programming language they are using to code the program. Because many programming languages require the keywords `If` and `End If` in the selection structure code, those words generally appear in the programmer's pseudocode.

In the examples shown in Figure 4-4, the *italicized* portion of the instruction indicates the condition to be evaluated. Notice that each condition results in either a true or a false answer only. Either the part number is "AB203" or it isn't. Either the sales are greater than the number 1500, or they aren't.

When the condition is true, the set of instructions following the `Then` is selected for processing. The instructions following `Then` are referred to as the true path—the path you follow when the condition is true. The true path ends when you come to the `Else` or, if there is no `Else`, when you come to the end of the selection structure (the `End If`). After the true path instructions are processed, the instruction following the `End If` is processed. In the examples shown in Figure 4-4, the "Display" instructions would be processed after the true instructions.

The instructions selected for processing when the condition is false—the false path—depend on whether the selection structure contains an `Else`. When there is no `Else`, as in the first example shown in Figure 4-4, the instruction following the `End If` is processed when the condition is false. In the first example, for instance, the "Display the part number in the lblPartno control" is processed when the part number is not "AB203." In cases where the selection structure contains an `Else`, as in the second example shown in Figure 4-4, the set of instructions between the `Else` and the `End If` are processed first and then the instruction after the `End If` is processed. In the second example, the "Calculate commission = .01 * sales" is processed first, then the "Display the commission in the lblComm control" is processed.

In the next section you will learn how to show the selection structure in a flowchart.

Using a Flowchart

Besides using pseudocode, programmers also use flowcharts to help them plan each object's code. Unlike pseudocode, which consists of English-like statements, a flowchart uses standardized symbols to show the steps an object needs to take in order to accomplish its tasks. Figure 4-5 shows Figure 4-4's examples in flowchart form.

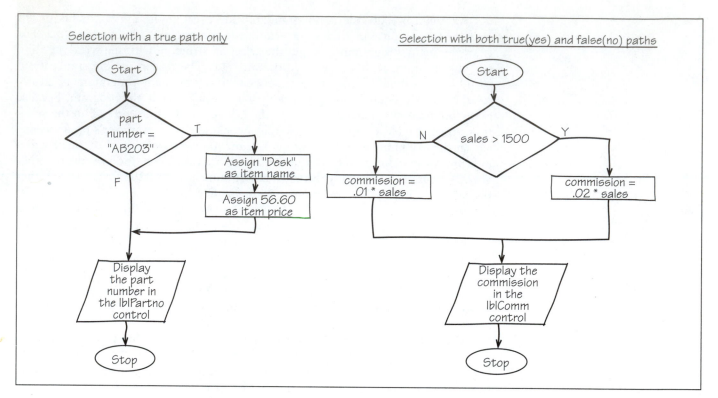

Figure 4-5: Two examples of the If...Then...Else selection structure drawn in flowchart form

You will notice that the flowcharts contain four different symbols—an oval, a rectangle, a parallelogram, and a diamond. The symbols are connected together with lines, called **flowlines**. The oval symbol is called the **start/stop symbol**. The start oval indicates the beginning of the flowchart, and the stop oval indicates the end of the flowchart. Between the start and the stop ovals are two rectangles, called **process symbols**. You use the process symbol to represent tasks such as declaring variables, assigning values to variables and to the properties of controls, and for calculations. In the first example, both rectangles represent assignment tasks. In the second example, both rectangles represent calculations.

The parallelogram is called the **input/output symbol**; it is used to represent input tasks, such as getting information from the user, and output tasks, such as displaying information. In both flowchart examples, the parallelograms represent output tasks.

The diamond in a flowchart is called the **selection/repetition symbol** because it is used to represent both selection and repetition. In Figure 4-5's flowcharts, the diamonds represent the selection structure. (You will learn how to use the diamond for repetition in Tutorial 5.) Notice that inside each diamond is a question that has a true (yes) or false (no) answer only. Each diamond also has one flowline entering the symbol and two flowlines leaving the symbol. The two flowlines leading out of the diamond should be marked so that anyone reading the flowchart can distinguish the true path from the false path. You can mark the flowlines either with a "T" and an "F" (for true and false) or a "Y" and an "N" (for yes and no).

To translate the flowchart into Visual Basic code, you simply start at the top of the flowchart and write the code for each symbol as you follow the flowlines down to the bottom of the flowchart. Some symbols in a flowchart may require more than one line of code. The only symbol that is not coded is the start oval. In the next section you will learn how to code the selection structure in Visual Basic.

Coding the Selection Structure in Visual Basic

You use the **If...Then...Else statement** to code the selection structure in Visual Basic. The syntax of the If...Then...Else statement is shown in Figure 4-6.

If *condition* **Then**

    [*instructions when the condition is true*]

[**Else**

    [*instructions when the condition is false*]]

End If

Figure 4-6: Syntax of If...Then...Else statement

In the syntax, the items in square brackets ([ ]) are optional. For example, the Else portion of the syntax, referred to as the Else clause, is optional; you don't need to include an Else clause in an If...Then...Else statement. Words in **bold**, however, are essential components of the If...Then...Else statement. The words If, Then, and End If, for instance, must be included in the statement. (The word Else must be included only if the statement uses the Else clause.) Items in *italics* indicate where the programmer must supply information pertaining to the current application. For instance, the programmer must supply the *condition* to be evaluated. The *condition* can contain variables, constants, properties, functions, mathematical operators, relational operators, and logical operators. You already know about variables, constants, properties, functions, and the mathematical operators. You will now learn about the relational operators and the logical operators.

Relational Operators

Figure 4-7 lists the relational operators you can use in the If...Then...Else statement's *condition*.

Relational Operator	Meaning
=	Equal to
>	Greater than
>=	Greater than or equal to
<	Less than
<=	Less than or equal to
<>	Not equal to

Figure 4-7: Relational operators

Unlike the mathematical operators, the relational operators do not have an order of precedence. If an expression contains more than one relational operator, Visual Basic evaluates the relational operators from left to right in the expression. Keep in mind, however, that relational operators are evaluated after any mathematical operators in the expression. In other words, in the expression 5 – 2 > 1 + 2, the two mathematical operators (–, +) will be evaluated before the relational operator (>). The result of the expression is False, as shown in Figure 4-8.

Original Expression: 5 - 2 > 1 + 2

Evaluation steps:	Result:
5 - 2 is evaluated first	3 > 1 + 2
1 + 2 is evaluated second	3 > 3
3 > 3 is evaluated last	False

Figure 4-8: Evaluation steps for an expression containing mathematical and relational operators

All expressions containing a relational operator will result in either a True or False answer only. To illustrate this, your Student Disk contains a partially completed project, named "If." You will use this project to practice various If...Then...Else statements that contain relational operators in the *condition*.

To open the If project:

1 Start Visual Basic, if necessary, and open the **If** (If.vbp) project, which is located in the Tut04 folder on your Student Disk. Save the form and the project as **laIf**. Click the **form's title bar** to select the form. The frmIf form appears on the screen. See Figure 4-9.

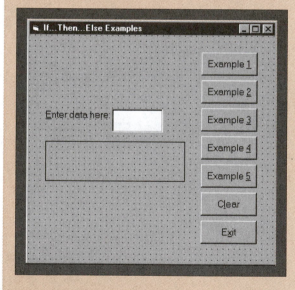

Figure 4-9: frmIf form

Some of the command buttons have been coded for you. For example, the Exit button contains the `End` instruction, which will end the application. The Clear button contains the following three instructions: `lblMsg.Caption = ""`, `txtData.Text = ""`, and `txtData.SetFocus`. These instructions clear the contents of the label control and the text box, then place the focus in the text box. You will now code the Click event procedure for the Example 1 command button.

Example 1

Assume you are creating a checkbook application. You will enter the amount of a transaction as a number in the text box on the screen. If the number entered in the text box is less than 0, you want to display the string "Withdrawal" in the label control. Figure 4-10 shows the flowchart, pseudocode, and Visual Basic code to accomplish this.

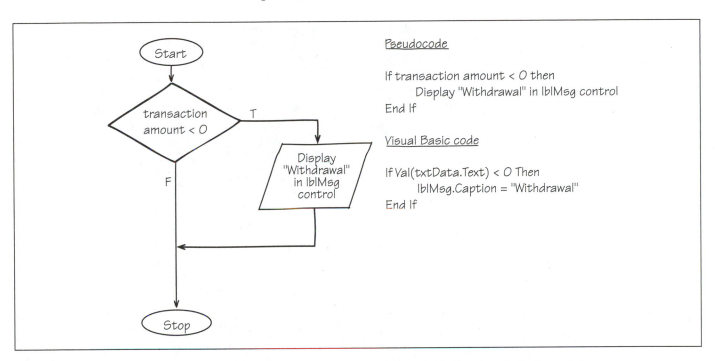

Figure 4-10: Flowchart, pseudocode, and Visual Basic code for Example 1

The Val(txtData.Text) < 0 condition tells Visual Basic to compare the contents of the txtData control's Text property, converted to a number, with the number 0. If the condition evaluates to True, which means the number entered is less than 0, then the string "Withdrawal" will appear in the label control. If the condition evaluates to False, which means the number entered is not less than 0 (in other words, it's greater than or equal to 0), nothing will appear in the label control.

To code the Example 1 button:

1 Open the **Example 1** button's Click event procedure.

2 Press the **Tab** key, then type **if val(txtdata.text) < 0 then** and press the **Enter** key. Be sure to type the number 0, and not the letter O.

Now enter the true path instructions. Programmers usually indent these instructions for easier readability.

3 Press the **Tab** key, then type **lblmsg.caption = "Withdrawal"** and press the **Enter** key.

4 Press the **Backspace** key to cancel the indentation, then type **end if** and press the **Enter** key. Compare your instructions with Figure 4-11.

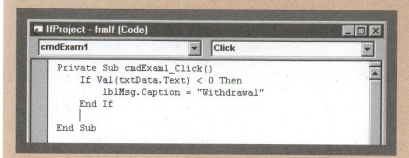

```
IfProject - frmIf (Code)
cmdExam1                        Click

Private Sub cmdExam1_Click()
    If Val(txtData.Text) < 0 Then
        lblMsg.Caption = "Withdrawal"
    End If

End Sub
```

Figure 4-11: Code window for Example 1 button

5 Close the Code window, then **save** and **run** the application.

6 Type **-25** (be sure to type the minus sign) in the text box, then click the **Example 1** button to process the instructions in the Click event procedure. The string "Withdrawal" appears in the label control, then the Click event procedure ends. In this case, because the number entered in the text box is less than zero, Visual Basic processes the true path instruction before processing the instruction following the End If—in this case, the End Sub instruction.

7 Click the **Clear** button to clear the contents of the text box and the label control.

8 Type **500** in the text box, then click the **Example 1** button. This time nothing appears in the label control. Notice that when the number in the text box is not less than zero—a false condition—the instruction in the true path is not processed. Instead, Visual Basic processes the instruction following the End If—in this case, the End Sub instruction.

9 Click the **Exit** button. Visual Basic returns to the design screen.

Example 2

This time you will display the string "Withdrawal" when the number entered in the text box is less than zero and the string "Deposit" when the number is greater than or equal to zero. Figure 4-12 shows the flowchart, the pseudocode, and the Visual Basic code to accomplish this.

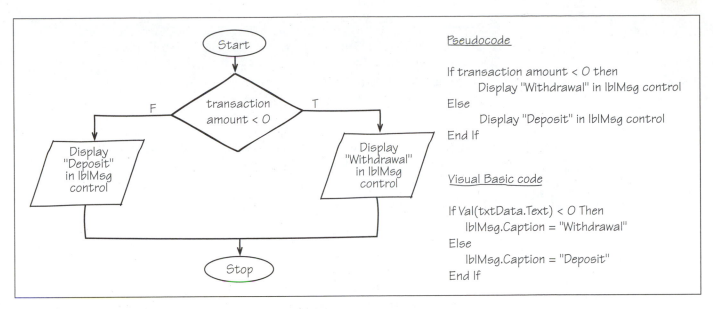

Figure 4-12: Flowchart, pseudocode, and Visual Basic code for Example 2

To save you time, the Visual Basic instructions have already been entered in the Example 2 button's Click event procedure.

To view the instructions in the Example 2 button's Click event procedure:

1 Open the **Example 2** button's Click event procedure. See Figure 4-13.

Else must be entered on its own line

```
IfProject - frmIf (Code)                              _ □ ×
cmdExam2                    ▼    Click                ▼
Private Sub cmdExam2_Click()
    If Val(txtData.Text) < 0 Then
        lblMsg.Caption = "Withdrawal"
    Else
        lblMsg.Caption = "Deposit"
    End If

End Sub
```

Figure 4-13: Code window for Example 2 button

When using the Else clause, notice that the `Else` must be entered on its own line.

2 Close the Code window, then **run** the application.

3 Type **–15** (be sure to type the minus sign) in the text box, then click the **Example 2** button. "Withdrawal" appears in the label control, then the Click event procedure ends.

> **4** Click the **Clear** button, type 5 in the text box, then click the **Example 2** button. This time, "Deposit" appears in the label control, then the Click event procedure ends.
>
> **5** Click the **Exit** button. Visual Basic returns to the design screen.

Recall that you can also use logical operators to form the If...Then...Else statement's *condition*. Visual Basic has six logical operators—the most commonly used ones are Not, And, and Or.

Logical Operators

You can use the logical operators to combine several conditions into one compound condition. Figure 4-14 shows the three most commonly used logical operators, their meaning, and their order of precedence.

If you want to see information about the other logical operators, use the Help menu to search for a Help window on logical operators.

Logical Operator	Meaning	Precedence
Not	Reverses the value of the condition; True becomes False, False becomes True	1
And	All conditions connected by the And operator must be true for the compound condition to be true	2
Or	Only one of the conditions connected by the Or operator needs to be true for the compound condition to be true	3

Figure 4-14: Logical operators

The tables shown in Figure 4-15, called **truth tables**, summarize how Visual Basic evaluates the logical operators in an expression.

Truth Table for the Not Operator

Value of *condition*	Value of Not *condition*
True	False
False	True

Truth Table for the And Operator

Value of *condition1*	Value of *condition2*	Value of *condition1* And *condition2*
True	True	True
True	False	False
False	True	False
False	False	False

Truth Table for the Or Operator

Value of *condition1*	Value of *condition2*	Value of *condition1* Or *condition2*
True	True	True
True	False	True
False	True	True
False	False	False

Figure 4-15: Truth tables for the Not, And, and Or logical operators

tip

If you use the And operator to combine two conditions, Visual Basic does not evaluate the second condition if the first condition is False. Because both conditions combined with the And operator need to be True for the compound condition to be True, there is no need to evaluate the second condition if the first condition is False. If, on the other hand, you use the Or operator to combine two conditions, Visual Basic does not evaluate the second condition if the first condition is True. Because only one of the conditions combined with the Or operator needs to be True for the compound condition to be True, there is no need to evaluate the second condition if the first condition is True.

As Figure 4-15 indicates, the Not operator reverses the truth value of the *condition*. If the value of the *condition* is True, then the value of Not *condition* is False. Likewise, if the value of the *condition* is False, then the value of Not *condition* is True. As you can see, the Not operator can be confusing, so it is best to avoid using it if possible. In Tutorial 6, which covers sequential files, you will see a useful purpose for the Not operator. For now you don't need to worry about the Not operator; just be aware that it exists.

Now look at the truth tables for the And and Or logical operators. Notice that when you use the And operator to combine two conditions, *condition1* And *condition2*, the resulting compound condition is True only when both conditions are True. If either condition is False or if both conditions are False, then the compound condition is False. Compare that to the Or operator. When you combine conditions using the Or operator, *condition1* Or *condition2*, notice that the compound condition is False only when both conditions are False. If either condition is True or if both conditions are True, then the compound condition is True. Two examples might help to clarify the difference between the And and the Or operators.

Examples of the And and the Or Operators

Assume that you want to pay a bonus to the salespeople in Virginia whose sales total more than $10,000. To receive a bonus, the salesperson must live in the state of Virginia and he or she must sell more than $10,000 in product. Assuming the application uses the two variables, strState and curSales, you can phrase *condition1* as `strState = "Virginia"` and *condition2* as `curSales > 10000`. Now the question is "Should you use the And operator or the Or operator to combine both conditions into one compound condition?" To answer this question, you will need to look at the truth tables, shown in Figure 4-15, for the And and the Or operators.

To receive a bonus, remember that both *condition1* (`strState = "Virginia"`) and *condition2* (`curSales > 10000`) must be true at the same time. If either condition is false, or if both conditions are false, then the compound condition should be false, and the salesperson should not receive a bonus. According to the truth tables, both the And and the Or operators will evaluate the compound condition as True when both conditions are true. Only the And operator, however, will evaluate the compound condition as False when either one or both of the conditions is false. The Or operator, you will notice, evaluates the compound condition as False only when *both* conditions are false. Therefore, the correct compound condition to use here is `strState = "Virginia" And curSales > 10000`.

Now assume that you want to send a letter to all customers living in Virginia and all customers living in Texas. Assuming the application uses the variable strState, you can phrase *condition1* as `strState = "Virginia"` and *condition2* as `strState = "Texas"`. Now which operator do you use—And or Or?

At first it might appear that the And operator is the correct one to use. That's probably because the example says to send the letter to "all customers living in Virginia and all customers living in Texas." In our everyday conversations, you'll find that we sometimes use the word "and" when what we really mean is "or." Although both words do not mean the same thing, using "and" instead of "or" generally doesn't cause a problem because we are able to infer what another person means. Computers, however, cannot infer anything; they simply process the directions you give them, word for word. In this case, you actually want to send a letter to all customers living either in Virginia or in Texas, so you will need to use the Or operator. The Or operator is the only operator that will evaluate the compound condition as True if either one of the conditions is true. The correct compound condition to use here is `strState = "Virginia" Or strState = "Texas"`.

Like expressions containing relational operators, expressions containing logical operators always result in either a True or False answer. The logical operators have an order of precedence as follows: the Not operator is evaluated first, then the And operator, and then the Or operator. Logical operators are evaluated after any mathematical operators or relational operators in the expression. In other words, in the expression, 12 > 0 And 12 < 10 * 2, the mathematical operator (*) is evaluated first, followed by the two relational operators (>, <), followed by the logical operator (And). The expression evaluates to True, as shown in Figure 4-16.

Original Expression: 12 > 0 And 12 < 10 * 2

Evaluation steps:	Result:
10 * 2 is evaluated first	12 > 0 And 12 < 20
12 > 0 is evaluated second	True And 12 < 20
12 < 20 is evaluated third	True And True
True And True is evaluated last	True

Figure 4-16: Evaluation steps for an expression containing mathematical, relational, and logical operators

The Example 3 button in the current application will enable you to observe how the logical operators work.

Example 3

Assume you want the Example 3 button to display the string "In-range" when the number entered in the text box is greater than or equal to 1500, but less than 3000. If the number does not fall in that range, then you want to display the string "Out-of-range". Figure 4-17 shows the flowchart, the pseudocode, and the Visual Basic code to accomplish this.

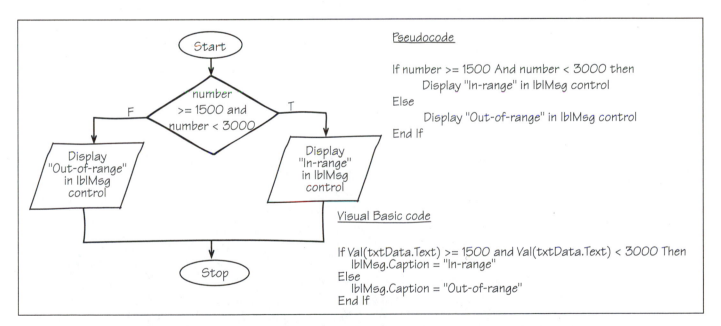

Figure 4-17: Flowchart, pseudocode, and Visual Basic code for Example 3

The necessary Visual Basic instructions have already been entered into the Example 3 button's Code window.

To view Example 3's code, then run the application:

1 Open the **Example 3** button's Click event, then maximize the Code window. The Click event procedure appears as shown in Figure 4-18.

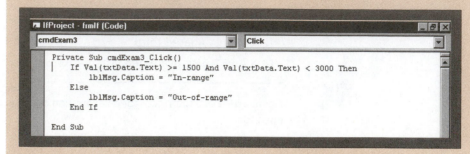

```
IfProject - frmIf (Code)                                          _ 8 X
cmdExam3                        ▼    Click                        ▼

Private Sub cmdExam3_Click()
    If Val(txtData.Text) >= 1500 And Val(txtData.Text) < 3000 Then
        lblMsg.Caption = "In-range"
    Else
        lblMsg.Caption = "Out-of-range"
    End If

End Sub
```

Figure 4-18: Code window for Example 3 button

2 Close the Code window, then **run** the application.

3 Type **2500** in the text box, then click the **Example 3** button. The string "In-range" appears in the label control because the number 2500 satisfies both of the conditions listed in the compound condition—it is greater than or equal to 1500 and it is less than 3000.

4 Click the **Clear** button, type **6500** in the text box, then click the **Example 3** button. The string "Out-of-range" appears in the label control because the number 6500 does not satisfy both of the conditions listed in the compound condition. Although 6500 is greater than or equal to 1500, it is not less than 3000.

5 Click the **Exit** button. Visual Basic returns to the design screen.

Now you'll modify Example 3's code to see what happens when you use the Or operator, instead of the And operator, in the If...Then...Else statement.

To modify the Example 3 button's code, then run the application:

1 Open the **Example 3** button's Click event. Change the And in the If statement's *condition* to an **Or**. The If statement should now say `If Val(txtData.Text)>=1500 Or Val(txtData.Text)<3000 Then`.

2 Close the Code window, then **run** the application.

3 Type **2500** in the text box, then click the **Example 3** button. The string "In-range" appears in the label control because the number 2500 satisfies both conditions listed in the compound condition.

4 Click the **Clear** button, type **6500** in the text box, then click the **Example 3** button. The string "In-range" appears in the label control because the number 6500 satisfies one of the conditions listed in the compound condition—specifically, the number 6500 is greater than or equal to the number 1500. Remember, when you use the Or operator, only one of the conditions needs to be true for the compound condition to be true.

5 Click the **Clear** button, type **3** in the text box, then click the **Example 3** button. The string "In-range" appears in the label control because the number 3 satisfies one of the conditions listed in the compound condition—specifically, the number 3 is less than the number 3000.

6 Click the **Exit** button. Visual Basic returns to the design screen.

By changing the And to an Or, the *condition* `Val(txtData.Text)>=1500 Or Val(txtData.Text)<3000`, will always evaluate as True; it will never evaluate as False because all numbers lie within this range.

7 Open the **Example 3** button's Click event, then change the Or back to an **And** in the If statement's *condition*.

8 Close the Code window, then **save** the application.

Next you'll learn how to include a string comparison in an If...Then...Else statement.

Example 4

Assume you want the Example 4 button to display the word "Pass" if the text box contains the letter P and the word "Fail" if the text box contains anything else. The Visual Basic instructions that would accomplish this have already been entered in the Example 4 button's Click event procedure, as shown in Figure 4-19. (You can open the Code window and view the code, if you want.)

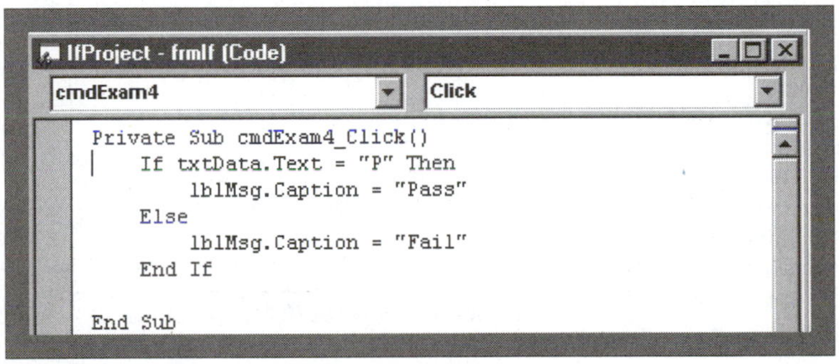

```
IfProject - frmIf (Code)                                    _ □ ✕

cmdExam4                    ▼      Click                     ▼

Private Sub cmdExam4_Click()
    If txtData.Text = "P" Then
            lblMsg.Caption = "Pass"
    Else
            lblMsg.Caption = "Fail"
    End If

End Sub
```

Figure 4-19: Code window for Example 4 button

To test the Example 4 button:

1 **Run** the application, type **P** (be sure to use an uppercase letter P) in the text box, and then click the **Example 4** button. The string "Pass" appears in the label control.

Next you'll enter a letter other than the letter P.

2 Click the **Clear** button, type **K** in the text box, then click the **Example 4** button. The string "Fail" appears in the label control.

Now enter a lowercase letter p.

3 Click the **Clear** button, type **p** (be sure to type a lowercase letter p) in the text box, then click the **Example 4** button.

Although one might expect the word "Pass" to appear, the word "Fail" appears instead. Stop the application at this point and consider why this happened.

4 Click the **Exit** button. Visual Basic returns to the design screen.

The UCase Function

As is true in many programming languages, string comparisons in Visual Basic are case sensitive. That means that the uppercase version of a letter is not the same as its lowercase counterpart. So, although a human recognizes "P" and "p" as being the same letter, a computer does not; to a computer, a "P" is different from a "p." As you saw in Example 4, a problem occurs when you need to include a string, entered by the user, in a comparison. The problem occurs because you can't control the case in which the user enters the string.

One way of handling the string comparison problem is to include the UCase (uppercase) function, whose syntax is **UCase**(*string*), in your string comparisons. As you learned in Tutorial 2, all functions return a value. The UCase function, for example, returns the uppercase equivalent of the *string*. Figure 4-20 shows some examples of the UCase function.

> **tip**
>
> The UCase function does not actually change the *string* to uppercase. For example, `UCase(txtData.Text)` simply returns the uppercase equivalent of the txtData control's Text property; it does not change the control's Text property to uppercase. To change the Text property to uppercase, you would need to use the `txtData.Text = UCase(txtData.Text)` assignment statement.

UCase function:	Meaning:
If UCase(txtData.Text) = "YES" Then	Compares the uppercase version of the string entered in the text box to the string "YES"
If UCase(txtData.Text) > UCase(strItem)	Compares the uppercase version of the string entered in the text box to the uppercase version of the string contained in the strItem variable.
If "RENO" = UCase(lblCity.Caption)	Compares the string "RENO" to the uppercase version of the string contained in the label control.
txtName.Text = UCase(strEmpName)	Assigns the uppercase version of the string contained in the strEmpName variable to the Text property of the text box.

Figure 4-20: Examples of the UCase function

In the Example 4 button's Click event, you will need to change the `If` statement's *condition* from `txtData.Text = "P"` to `UCase(txtData.Text) = "P"`. Then when Visual Basic processes the If statement, the UCase function will return the uppercase equivalent of the string entered in the text box. Visual Basic will then compare the uppercase version of the string to the uppercase letter P. If both are equal, Visual Basic will process the true path instructions; otherwise, it will process the false path instructions. By including the UCase function in the instruction, the user will be able to enter the letter P in any case and have the "Pass" message appear.

When using the UCase function, be sure that everything you are comparing is in uppercase. In other words, UCase(txtData.Text) = "p" is incorrect because it tells Visual Basic to compare the uppercase version of a string with the lowercase letter p; this condition would always evaluate as False.

tip

Visual Basic also has an LCase function that temporarily converts a string to lowercase. In order to produce the same results in Example 4, you could use the LCase function as follows: LCase(txtData.Text) = "p".

be sure to include the parentheses

To modify the If instruction in Example 4's Click event procedure:

1 Open the **Example 4** button's Click event. Enter the UCase function as shown in Figure 4-21.

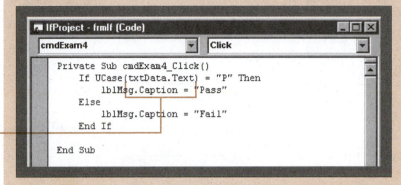

```
IfProject - frmIf (Code)
cmdExam4                          Click

Private Sub cmdExam4_Click()
    If UCase(txtData.Text) = "P" Then
        lblMsg.Caption = "Pass"
    Else
        lblMsg.Caption = "Fail"
    End If

End Sub
```

Figure 4-21: UCase function in Example 4's Click event

2 Close the Code window, then **save** and **run** the application.

3 Type **p** in the text box, then click the **Example 4** button. This time "Pass" appears in the label control.

4 Click the **Exit** button. Visual Basic returns to the design screen.

Selection structures can also be nested, which means you can place one selection structure inside another selection structure.

Nested Selection Structures

A nested selection structure is one in which either the true path or the false path includes yet another selection structure. Figures 4-22 and 4-23 show examples of writing a nested selection structure both in pseudocode and in a flowchart. Figure 4-22 shows the nested selection structure in the true path; Figure 4-23 shows the nested selection structure in the false path. (The lines connecting the If, Else, and End If in the pseudocode are not necessary. They are included in the figures to help you see which clauses match up with each other.)

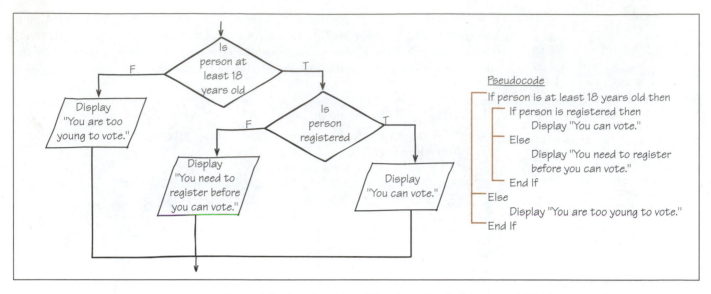

Figure 4-22: Pseudocode and flowchart showing the nested If in the true path

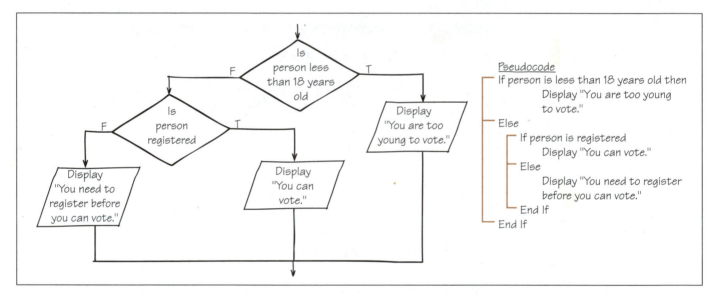

Figure 4-23: Pseudocode and flowchart showing the nested If in the false path

You will notice that Figure 4-22 shows the nested If statement as the first instruction in the true path, whereas Figure 4-23 shows the nested If statement as the first instruction in the false path. When writing a nested selection structure, keep in mind that any of the statements within either the true or false path of one If statement may, in turn, be another If statement. In other words, the nested If statement will not always be the first instruction in either the true or false path.

Figure 4-24 shows two ways of writing the syntax of the nested selection structure in Visual Basic—with the nested If statement in the true path and with the nested If statement in the false path.

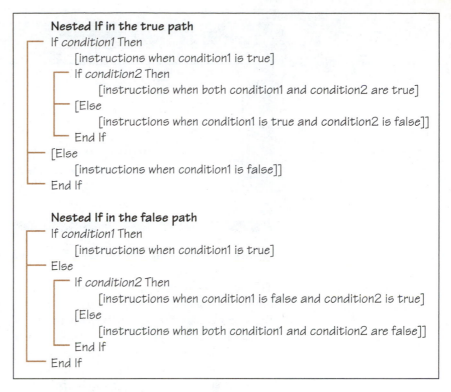

Figure 4-24: Syntax of Visual Basic's nested selection structure

Notice that each If...Then...Else statement is matched with an `End If`, which marks the end of that If...Then...Else statement. The Example 5 button in the current application uses a nested selection structure with the nested If in the false path. Observe how the code in the Example 5 button's Click event works.

Example 5

The Example 5 button's Click event procedure contains a nested selection structure with the nested If in the false path. You can use the Example 5 button to determine if a person is eligible to vote, and then display an appropriate message.

To open the Example 5 button's Code window, and then test the code:

1 Open the **Example 5** button's Click event, then maximize the Code window. See Figure 4-25.

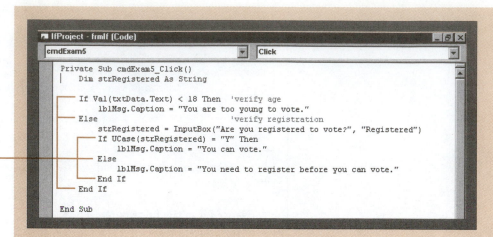

nested If statement

```
IfProject - frmIf (Code)                                          _ | 5 | x
cmdExam5                        ▼    Click                              ▼

Private Sub cmdExam5_Click()
    Dim strRegistered As String

    If Val(txtData.Text) < 18 Then   'verify age
        lblMsg.Caption = "You are too young to vote."
    Else                              'verify registration
        strRegistered = InputBox("Are you registered to vote?", "Registered")
        If UCase(strRegistered) = "Y" Then
            lblMsg.Caption = "You can vote."
        Else
            lblMsg.Caption = "You need to register before you can vote."
        End If
    End If

End Sub
```

Figure 4-25: Code window for Example 5 showing nested If in the false path

The nested selection structure first compares the contents of the text box to the number 18. If the number entered in the text box is less than 18, then Visual Basic processes the instruction in the true path (the `lblMsg.Caption = "You are too young to vote."` instruction); otherwise, it processes the instructions in the false path. Notice that the false path contains an assignment statement that uses the InputBox function to ask the user if he or she is registered to vote, and then stores the response in the strRegistered variable. The false path also contains another If...Then...Else statement. This If...Then...Else statement compares the uppercase version of the user's response, stored in the strRegistered variable, to the letter "Y." If the strRegistered variable contains either "Y" or "y," then Visual Basic processes the instruction in the nested If statement's true path (the `lblMsg.Caption = "You can vote."` instruction); otherwise, it processes the instruction in the false path (the `lblMsg.Caption = "You need to register before you can vote."` instruction).

2 Close the Code window, then **run** the application.

First you will enter the number 17 in the text box. A person who is 17 years old is too young to vote.

3 Type **17** in the text box, then click the **Example 5** button. The "You are too young to vote." message appears in the label control.

Now you will enter the number 21. A person who is 21 years old can vote, but only if he or she is registered.

4 Click the **Clear** button, type **21** in the text box, then click the **Example 5** button. The InputBox function displays a dialog box containing the "Are you registered to vote?" prompt.

5 Type **y** and press the **Enter** key. The "You can vote." message appears in the label control.

Now you'll try answering "n" to the "Are you registered to vote?" prompt.

6 Click the **Example 5** button. Type **n** in answer to the "Are you registered to vote?" prompt and press the **Enter** key. The "You need to register before you can vote." message appears in the label control.

7 Click the **Exit** button to end the application. Visual Basic returns to the design screen.

In summary, the If...Then...Else statement first evaluates the condition specified in the If clause. Based on that evaluation, the statement then selects and processes the instructions in one of two paths—either the true path (the Then) or the false path (the Else).

In many applications, however, you might have more than two paths from which a selection structure must choose. When a selection structure has several paths from which to choose, it is most times simpler and clearer to use the Case form of the selection structure instead of the nested If form.

The Case Form of the Selection Structure

Suppose, for example, that your application needs to display a message based on a letter grade that the user enters in a text box. The letter grades and their corresponding messages are as follows:

Letter Grade	Message
A	Excellent
B	Above Average
C	Average
D, F	Below Average
I	Incomplete
W	Withdrawal
Other	Incorrect Grade

You could use a nested If...Then...Else statement to code this selection structure. However, when a selection structure has several paths from which to choose, it is usually clearer to use the Case form of the selection structure. The Case form is sometimes referred to as an **extended selection structure**. Figure 4-26 shows the flowchart and the pseudocode for the Case selection structure that would display a message based on the grade contained in a text box named txtInput.

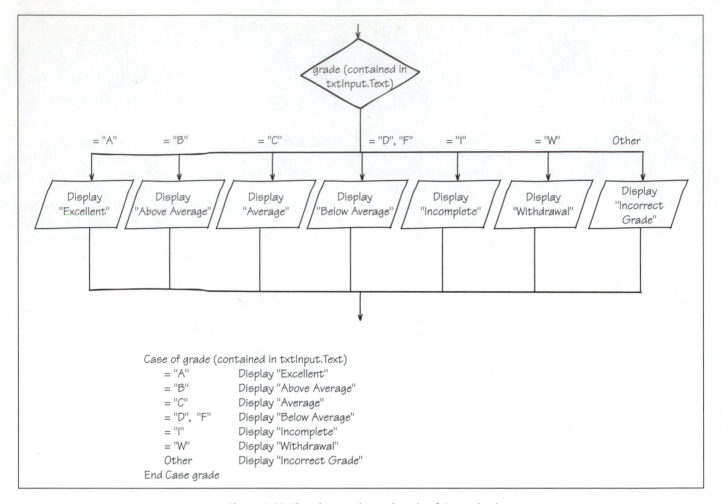

Figure 4-26: Flowchart and pseudocode of Case selection structure

Notice that the flowchart symbol for the Case selection structure is the same as the flowchart symbol for the If...Then...Else selection structure—a diamond. Unlike the If...Then...Else diamond, however, the Case diamond does not contain a condition requiring a true/false (yes/no) answer. Instead, the Case diamond contains an expression—in this case, grade—whose value will control which path is chosen.

Like the If...Then...Else diamond, the Case diamond has one flowline leading into the symbol. Unlike the If...Then...Else diamond, however, the Case diamond has many flowlines leading out of the symbol. Each flowline represents a possible path for the selection structure. The flowlines must be marked appropriately, indicating which value(s) are necessary for each path to be chosen. In Visual Basic, you use the Select Case statement to code the Case selection structure.

The Select Case Statement

You use Visual Basic's **Select Case statement** to code the Case selection structure. Figure 4-27 shows the syntax of the Select Case statement. It also shows the Select Case statement that will display a message based on the grade entered in the txtInput text box.

Select Case Syntax	Example
Select Case *testexpression*	Select Case UCase (txtInput.Text)
[**Case** *expressionlist1*	Case "A"
[instructions for the first Case]]	lblMsg.Caption = "Excellent"
[**Case** *expressionlist2*	Case "B"
[instructions for the second Case]]	lblMsg.Caption = "Above Average"
[**Case** *expressionlistn*	Case "C"
[instructions for the nth Case]]	lblMsg.Caption = "Average"
[**Case Else**	Case "D", "F"
[instructions for when the *testexpression* does not match any of the *expressionlists*]]	lblMsg.Caption = "BelowAverage"
	Case "I"
End Select	lblMsg.Caption = "Incomplete"
	Case "W"
	lblMsg.Caption = "Withdrawal"
	Case Else
	lblMsg.Caption = "Incorrect Grade"
	End Select

Figure 4-27: The syntax and an example of the Case selection structure

The Select Case statement begins with the Select Case clause and ends with the two words `End Select`. Between the Select Case clause and the `End Select` are the individual Case clauses. Each Case clause represents a different path that the selection structure can follow. You can have as many Case clauses as necessary in a Select Case statement. If the Select Case statement includes a Case Else clause, the Case Else clause must be the last clause in the statement.

Notice that the Select Case clause must include a *testexpression*. The *testexpression* can be any numeric or string expression, which means it can contain a combination of variables, constants, functions, operators, and properties. In the example shown in Figure 4-27, the *testexpression* is UCase(txtInput.Text).

Each of the individual Case clauses, except the `Case Else`, must contain an *expressionlist*, which can include one or more numeric or string expressions. You include more than one expression in an *expressionlist* by simply separating each expression with a comma, as in `Case "D", "F"`. The data type of the expressions must be compatible with the data type of the *testexpression*. In other words, if the *testexpression* is numeric, the expressions must be numeric. Likewise, if the *testexpression* is a string, the expressions must be strings. In the example shown in Figure 4-27, the *testexpression* (txtInput.Text) is a string, and so are the expressions—"A", "B", "C", "D", "F", "I", "W"—as the surrounding quotation marks indicate. (Recall from Tutorial 2 that the value in the Text property of a control is treated as a string, not as a number.)

When processing the Select Case statement, Visual Basic first compares the value of the *testexpression* with the values listed in *expressionlist1*. If a match is found, Visual Basic processes the instructions for the first Case and then skips to the instruction following the `End Select`. If a match is not found in *expressionlist1*, Visual Basic skips to the second Case clause, where it compares the *testexpression* with the values listed in *expressionlist2*. If a match is found, Visual Basic processes the instructions for the second Case clause and then skips to the instruction following the `End Select`. If a match is not found, Visual Basic skips to the third Case clause and so on. If the *testexpression* does not match any of the values listed in any of the *expressionlists*, Visual Basic then processes the instructions listed in the `Case Else` clause or, if there is no `Case Else` clause, it processes the instruction following the `End Select`. Keep in mind that if the *testexpression* matches a value in more than one Case clause, only the instructions in the first match are processed.

The SelCase project on your Student Disk contains three examples of the Select Case statement.

To view the examples in the SelCase project:

1 Open the **SelCase** (SelCase.vbp) project, which is located in the Tut04 folder on your Student Disk. Click the **form's title bar** to select the form. The frmSelCase form appears on the screen, as shown in Figure 4-28.

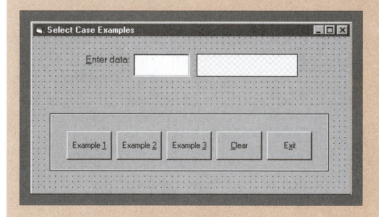

Figure 4-28: frmSelCase form

Each of the command buttons has been coded for you. You'll look at the code in the Example 1 button's Click event procedure first.

Example 1

Example 1 uses the Select Case statement to display a message based on the grade entered in the txtInput text box. (The flowchart and pseudocode for this example are shown in Figure 4-26.)

To view the code for Example 1, then test the Example 1 button:

1   Open the **Example 1** button's Click event, then maximize the Code window. See Figure 4-29.

returns the uppercase equivalent of the txtInput control's Text property

```
SelCaseProj - frmSelCase (Code)

cmdExam1                        Click

    Private Sub cmdExam1_Click()
        Select Case UCase(txtInput.Text)
            Case "A"
                lblMessage.Caption = "Excellent"
            Case "B"
                lblMessage.Caption = "Above Average"
            Case "C"
                lblMessage.Caption = "Average"
            Case "D", "F"
                lblMessage.Caption = "Below Average"
            Case "I"
                lblMessage.Caption = "Incomplete"
            Case "W"
                lblMessage.Caption = "Withdrawal"
            Case Else
                lblMessage.Caption = "Incorrect Grade"
        End Select
    End Sub
```

Figure 4-29: Code window for Example 1 button

Notice that the code uses the UCase function to return the uppercase equivalent of the txtInput control's Text property, and then compares the return value with the uppercase letter grades. By doing so, the user can enter the grade in either uppercase or lowercase.

2   Close the Code window, then **run** the application. Type **c** in the Enter data text box, then click the **Example 1** button. Visual Basic processes the instructions in the button's Click event procedure. "Average" appears in the label control.

So how does the Example 1 button work? (You may find it helpful to refer back to Figure 4-29 as you read the following explanation.) First, Visual Basic temporarily converts the contents of the txtInput control's Text property ("c") to uppercase, giving "C". It then compares the value of the *testexpression* ("C") with the value listed in the first Case's *expressionlist* ("A"). Because "C" does not match "A", Visual Basic skips to the second Case clause where it compares "C" with that Case's *expressionlist* ("B"). Because "C" does not match "B", Visual Basic skips to the third Case clause where it compares "C" with that Case's *expressionlist* ("C"). Here there is a match, so Visual Basic processes the `lblMessage.Caption = "Average"` instruction, which displays the string "Average" in the label control. Visual Basic then skips the remaining instructions in the Select Case statement and processes the instruction after the `End Select`—in this example, the `End Sub` instruction.

Now see what happens if you enter an incorrect grade in the text box.

3 Click the **Clear** button to clear the label control and the text box, type **t** in the text box, then click the **Example 1** button. Because the value in the text box does not match any of the values listed in any of the Case clauses, the `Case Else` instruction is processed and the string "Incorrect Grade" appears in the label control. Visual Basic then processes the instruction following the `End Select`—the `End Sub` instruction.

4 Click the **Exit** button to end the application. Visual Basic returns to the design screen.

In the next two examples, you will learn how to specify a range of values in an *expressionlist*—such as the values 1 through 4, and values greater than 10. You will also learn how to use numbers, instead of strings, in the *testexpression* and in the *expressionlists*.

Using To and Is in an Expressionlist

You can use either the keyword **To** or the keyword **Is** to specify a range of values in an *expressionlist*. The specified values can be either numeric or strings. You will use the keyword **To** in Example 2 and the keyword **Is** in Example 3.

Example 2

XYZ Corporation offers programming seminars to a variety of companies. The price per person depends on the number of people the company registers, as shown in the following chart.

Number of registrants	Charge
1 – 4	$ 100 per person
5 – 10	$ 80 per person
More than 10	$ 60 per person

Figure 4-30 shows the flowchart and the pseudocode for this example.

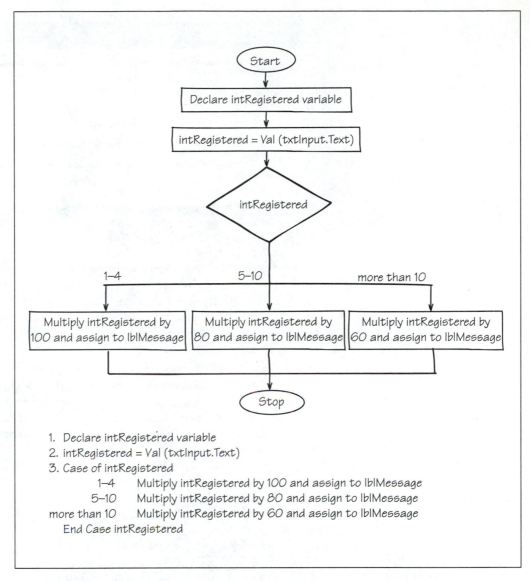

Figure 4-30: Example 2's flowchart and pseudocode

To view the code for Example 2, then test the Example 2 button:

1   Open the **Example 2** button's Click event, then maximize the Code window. See Figure 4-31.

```
SelCaseProj - frmSelCase (Code)                                    _ 5 X

cmdExam2                         ▼    Click                           ▼

Private Sub cmdExam2_Click()
    Dim intRegistered As Integer
    intRegistered = Val(txtInput.Text)
    Select Case intRegistered
        Case 1 To 4
            lblMessage.Caption = Format(intRegistered * 100, "Currency")
        Case 5 To 10
            lblMessage.Caption = Format(intRegistered * 80, "Currency")
        Case Else
            lblMessage.Caption = Format(intRegistered * 60, "Currency")
    End Select

End Sub
```

Figure 4-31: Code window for Example 2 button

The code first declares an Integer variable named intRegistered. It then uses the Val function to assign the numeric equivalent of the txtInput control's Text property to the intRegistered variable. The intRegistered variable, instead of the txtInput control's Text property, is then used as the *testexpression* in the Select Case clause. Because the intRegistered variable contains a number, the values listed in each *expressionlist* must be numeric.

According to the XYZ Corporation's chart, the charge for one to four registrants is $100 each. You could, therefore, write the first Case clause as Case 1, 2, 3, 4. A more convenient way of writing that range of numbers, however, is to use the keyword To, but you must follow this syntax: *smallest value in the range* **To** *largest value in the range*. The expression 1 To 4 in the first Case clause, for example, specifies the range of numbers from 1 to 4, inclusive. The expression 5 To 10 in the second Case clause specifies the range of numbers from 5 to 10, inclusive. When you use the keyword To, the value preceding the To must always be smaller than the value after the To. In other words, 10 To 5 is not a correct expression. In Example 2, the Case Else clause will be processed when the number of registrants is greater than 10. (It will also be processed when the number of registrants is less than 1, as you will see in Step 5.)

2 Close the Code window, then **run** the application.

Assume a company registers seven people.

3 Type 7 in the text box, then click the **Example 2** button. $560.00, which is 7 times the $80 charge for 5 to 10 registrants, appears in the label control. That's because the number 7 matches a number in the range specified in the Case 5 To 10 clause.

4 Click the **Clear** button. On your own, verify that 3 registrants will cost $300.00—3 times the $100 charge for 1 to 4 registrants. Also verify that 15 registrants will cost $900.00—15 times the $60 charge for more than 10 registrants. (The charge for the 15 registrants will be calculated by the Case Else clause.)

Always keep in mind that users will, at times, make mistakes when entering data. For example, the user might accidentally enter a negative number.

5 Click the **Clear** button, type **–3** (be sure to type the minus sign) in the text box, then click the **Example 2** button. The negative number, ($180.00), appears in the label control. The parentheses indicate a negative currency value.

Because the –3 did not fall into either the 1 To 4 range or the 5 To 10 range, Visual Basic processed the lblMessage.Caption = Format(intRegistered * 60, "Currency") instruction in the Case Else clause, which multiplied the –3 times the $60 charge. It would be better if the application displayed a message alerting the user that an input error was made. You will learn how to display such a message in Example 3.

6 Click the **Exit** button to end the application. Visual Basic returns to the design screen.

Example 3

Example 3 is the same as Example 2, except that it requires the application to display an error message if the user enters an incorrect number of registrants. An incorrect number would include 0 (zero), a negative number, or a letter.

Number of registrants	Charge
1 – 4	$ 100 per person
5 – 10	$ 80 per person
More than 10	$ 60 per person
0, negative number, letter	"Incorrect Data"

Most of the code for Example 3 will be similar to the code for Example 2. Example 3, however, will include one additional Case clause, and its Case Else clause will be different.

To view the code for Example 3, then test the Example 3 button:

1 Open the **Example 3** button's Click event, then maximize the Code window. See Figure 4-32.

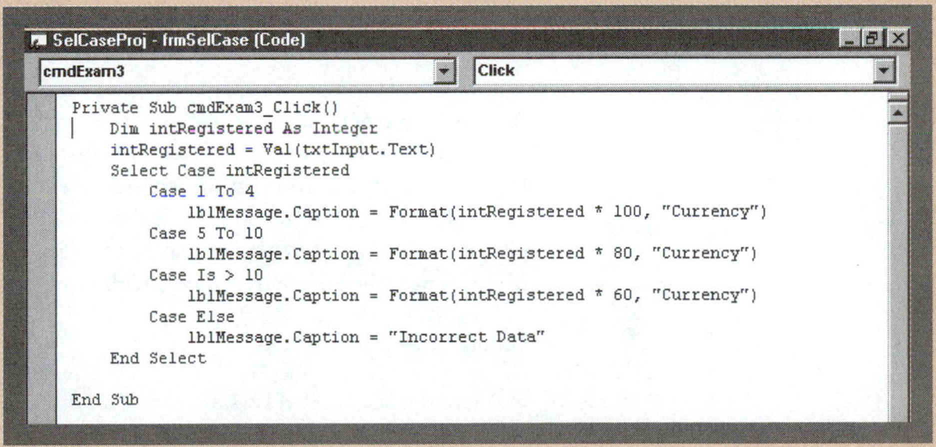

```
SelCaseProj - frmSelCase (Code)
cmdExam3                                    Click

Private Sub cmdExam3_Click()
    Dim intRegistered As Integer
    intRegistered = Val(txtInput.Text)
    Select Case intRegistered
        Case 1 To 4
            lblMessage.Caption = Format(intRegistered * 100, "Currency")
        Case 5 To 10
            lblMessage.Caption = Format(intRegistered * 80, "Currency")
        Case Is > 10
            lblMessage.Caption = Format(intRegistered * 60, "Currency")
        Case Else
            lblMessage.Caption = "Incorrect Data"
    End Select

End Sub
```

Figure 4-32: Code window for Example 3 button

tip

If you forget to type the Is in the expression, Visual Basic types it in for you. In other words, if you enter Case > 10, Visual Basic changes the clause to Case Is > 10. Because intRegistered is declared as an Integer variable, you can also write the clause as Case Is >= 11.

tip

You also could have written Example 3's Select Case statement with Case Is <= 0 as the first Case, Case 1 To 4 as the second Case, Case 5 To 10 as the third Case, and then let the Case Else clause handle the numbers greater than 10. The difference between both Select Case statements is the position of the error checking clause—the clause that catches the input errors. Unless you expect the user to enter mostly incorrect values, you can save computer time by putting the error checking at the end of the Case structure, as shown in Example 3, instead of at the beginning of the structure.

Notice the third Case clause, Case Is > 10, which was not included in Example 2's code. In addition to the keyword To, you can also use the keyword Is to specify a range of values. You use the Is keyword in combination with the relational operators, like this: **Is** relational operator *value*. Recall that the relational operators are =, <, <=, >, >=, and < >. The expression Is > 10, for example, specifies all numbers greater than the number 10.

Notice that, in this example, the Case Else clause is used to display an "Incorrect Data" message when the user enters something that is not included in any of the Case clauses—namely, a zero, a negative number, or a letter. (When using the Val function, you may remember, the numeric equivalent of a letter is zero.)

2 Close the Code window, then **run** the application.

Now enter a negative number.

3 Type –3 in the text box, then click the **Example 3** button. "Incorrect Data" appears in the label control.

4 Click the **Clear** button.

5 On your own, verify that the Example 3 button will display the "Incorrect Data" message when the user enters a letter.

6 Click the **Exit** button to end the application. You can now exit Visual Basic or open another project. You do not need to save the SelCase project.

You have now completed Lesson A. You can either take a break or complete the end-of-lesson questions and exercises.

S U M M A R Y

To evaluate an expression containing mathematical, relational, and logical operators:

■ Evaluate the mathematical operators first, then evaluate the relational operators, and then evaluate the logical operators.

To create a flowchart:

■ Use the start/stop oval to mark the beginning and the end of the flowchart.
■ Use the input/output parallelogram to represent steps that get data from the user and steps that display or print information.
■ Use the process rectangle to represent steps that declare variables, assign values to variables or properties, and for calculations.
■ Use the selection/repetition diamond to represent both selection and repetition.
■ Connect the flowchart symbols with flowlines

To code a selection structure:

■ Use the If...Then...Else statement. Its syntax is:
   If *condition* **Then**
      [*instructions when condition is true*]
   [**Else**
      [*instructions when condition is false*]]
   End If

To code a nested selection structure:

■ Use the nested If...Then...Else statement. Its syntax is shown in Figure 4-24.

To return the uppercase equivalent of a string:

■ Use the UCase function. The syntax is **UCase**(*string*).

To return the lowercase equivalent of a string:

■ Use the LCase function. The syntax is **LCase**(*string*).

To code a Case (an extended selection) structure:

■ Use the Select Case statement. Its syntax is shown in Figure 4-27.

To specify a range of values in a Case clause's expressionlist:

■ Use the keyword **To** in the following syntax: *smallest value in the range* **To** *largest value in the range*. Examples: `Case 1 To 4, Case "A" To "C"`
■ Use the keyword **Is** in the following syntax: **Is** *relational operator* *value*. Examples: `Case Is > 10, Case Is <= "JONES"`

Q U E S T I O N S

1. Which of the following is a valid condition for an If...Then...Else statement?
    a. Val(txtAge.Text > 65)
    b. Val(lblPrice.Caption) > 0 and < 10
    c. curSales > 500 and < 800
    d. curCost > 100 And curCost <= 1000
    e. UCase(strState) = "Alaska" and UCase(strState) = "Hawaii"

2. You can use the _____ function to return the uppercase equivalent of a string.
    a. Caseupper
    b. CaseU
    c. LCase
    d. UCase
    e. Upper

3. Assume you want to compare the string contained in the Text property of the txtName control with the name Bob. Which of the following conditions should you use in the If...Then...Else statement? (Be sure the condition will handle Bob, BOB, bob, and so on.)
   a. txtName.Text = "BOB"
   b. txtName.Text = UCase("BOB")
   c. txtName.Text = UCase("Bob")
   d. UCase(txtName.Text) = "Bob"
   e. UCase(txtName.Text) = "BOB"

4. Which of the following will change the contents of the txtName text box to uppercase?
   a. txtName.Text = UCase(txtName.Text)
   b. txtName.Text = TXTNAME.TEXT
   c. txtName.Text = "TXTNAME.TEXT"
   d. UCase(txtName.Text) = txtName.Text
   e. Upper(txtName.Text) = "txtName.Text"

5. The three logical operators are listed below. Indicate their order of precedence by placing a number (1, 2, or 3) on the line to the left of the operator.

   _____ And   _____ Not   _____ Or

6. An expression can contain mathematical, relational, and logical operators. Indicate the order of precedence for the three types of operators by placing a number (1, 2, or 3) on the line to the left.

   _____ Mathematical _____ Logical _____ Relational

7. Evaluate the following expression: 3 > 6 And 7 > 4
   a. True   b. False

8. Evaluate the following expression: 4 > 6 Or 10 < 2 * 6
   a. True   b. False

9. Evaluate the following expression: 7 >= 3 + 4 Or 6 < 4 And 2 < 5
   a. True   b. False

Use the following information to answer questions 10–16:
   X=5, Y=3, Z=2, A=True, B=False.

10. Evaluate the following expression: X – Y = Z
    a. True   b. False

11. Evaluate the following expression: X * Z > X * Y And A
    a. True   b. False

12. Evaluate the following expression: X * Z < X * Y Or A
    a. True   b. False

13. Evaluate the following expression: A And B
    a. True   b. False

14. Evaluate the following expression: A Or B
    a. True   b. False

15. Evaluate the following expression: X * Y > Y ^ Z
    a. True   b. False

16. Evaluate the following expression: X * Y > Y ^ Z And A Or B
    a. True   b. False

Use the following selection structure to answer questions 17–19.

```
If intNumber <= 100 Then
    intNumber = intNumber * 2
Else
    If intNumber > 500 Then
        intNumber = intNumber * 3
    End If
End If
```

17. Assume the intNumber variable contains the number 90. What value will be in the intNumber variable after the above selection structure is processed?
    a. 0
    b. 90
    c. 180
    d. 270
    e. null

18. Assume the intNumber variable contains the number 1000. What value will be in the intNumber variable after the above selection structure is processed?
    a. 0
    b. 1000
    c. 2000
    d. 3000
    e. null

19. Assume the intNumber variable contains the number 200. What value will be in the intNumber variable after the above selection structure is processed?
    a. 0
    b. 200
    c. 400
    d. 600
    e. null

20. Which of the following flowchart symbols represents the If...Then...Else selection structure?
    a. diamond
    b. hexagon
    c. oval
    d. parallelogram
    e. rectangle

21. Which of the following flowchart symbols represents the Case selection structure?
    a. diamond
    b. hexagon
    c. oval
    d. parallelogram
    e. rectangle

22. If the *testexpression* used in the Select Case clause is the numeric variable curSales, which two of the following Case clauses are valid?
    a. Case 2, 4, 6, 8
    b. Case "1" To "3"
    c. Case Is < "6"
    d. Case Is >= 8
    e. Case 4.5 Through 8.5

23. Assume the application uses a string variable named strState. If the *testexpression* used in the Select Case clause is UCase(strState), which three of the following Case clauses are valid?
    a. Case "TEXAS"
    b. Case "ALABAMA" And "ARKANSAS"
    c. Case Is > "Illinois"
    d. Case "COLORADO", "CALIFORNIA"
    e. Case "ALABAMA" To "ARKANSAS"

24. The _____ symbol is used in a flowchart to represent a calculation task.
    a. input
    b. output
    c. process
    d. start
    e. stop

25. The _____ symbol is used in a flowchart to represent a step that gets information from the user.
    a. input/output
    b. process
    c. selection/repetition
    d. start
    e. stop

26. The process symbol in a flowchart is the _____ .
    a. diamond
    b. oval
    c. parallelogram
    d. rectangle
    e. square

27. The input/output symbol in a flowchart is the _____ .
    a. diamond
    b. oval
    c. parallelogram
    d. rectangle
    e. square

28. The selection/repetition symbol in a flowchart is the _____ .
    a. diamond
    b. oval
    c. parallelogram
    d. rectangle
    e. square

29. Use the Help menu to search for a Help window on the Select Case statement. Print the Help window. How would you write an *expressionlist* that would match strings falling between the word "nuts" and the word "soup"?

E X E R C I S E S

1. Draw the flowchart that corresponds to the following Visual Basic code.
   ```
   If Hours > 40 Then
           Display "Overtime"
   Else
           Display "Regular"
   End If
   ```

2. Draw the flowchart that corresponds to the following Visual Basic code:
   ```
   Select Case curSales
        Case Is >= 10000
             Commission = .1 * curSales
        Case Is >= 5000
             Commission = .05 * curSales
        Case Else
             Commission = 0
   End Select
   ```

3. Draw the flowchart that corresponds to the following Visual Basic code:
   ```
   Select Case sngHours
        Case Is > 40
             Display "Overtime"
        Case Else
             Display "Regular"
   End Select
   ```

4. Write the Visual Basic code that corresponds to the flowchart shown in Figure 4-33.

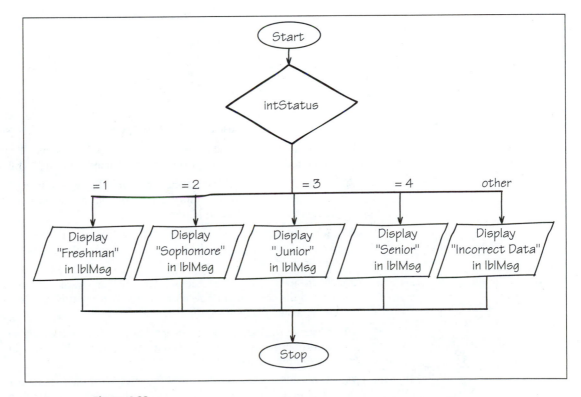

Figure 4-33

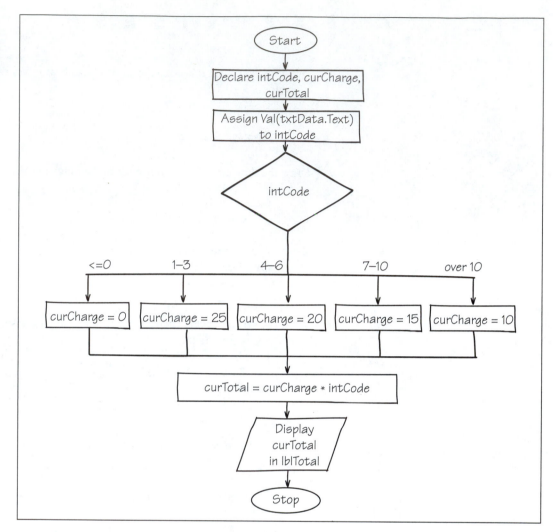

Figure 4-34

5. Write the Visual Basic code that corresponds to the flowchart shown in Figure 4-34.

6. Write an If...Then...Else statement that will display the string "Pontiac" in the lblType control if the txtCar control's Text property contains the string "Grand Am" (in any case).

7. Write an If...Then...Else statement that will display the string "Entry error" in the lblMsg control if the intUnits variable contains a number that is less than 0; otherwise, display the string "Valid Number".

8. Write an If...Then...Else statement that will display the string "Reorder" in the lblMsg control if the curPrice variable contains a number that is less than 10; otherwise, display the string "OK".

9. Write an If...Then...Else statement that will assign the number 10 to the curBonus variable if the curSales variable contains a number that is less than or equal to $250; otherwise, assign the number 15.

10. Write an If...Then...Else statement that will display the number 25 in the lblShipping control if the strState variable contains the string "Hawaii" (in any case); otherwise, display the number 50.

11. Assume you want to calculate a 3% sales tax if the strState variable contains the string "Colorado" (in any case); otherwise, you want to calculate a 4% sales tax. You can calculate the sales tax by multiplying the tax rate by the contents of the curSales variable. Display the sales tax in the lblStax control. Draw the flowchart, then write the Visual Basic code. Use the If...Then...Else selection structure.

12. Assume you want to calculate an employee's gross pay. Employees working more than 40 hours should receive overtime pay (time and one-half) for the hours over 40. Use the variables sngHours, sngRate, sngGross. Display the contents of the sngGross variable in the lblGross control. Write the pseudocode, then write the Visual Basic code. Use the If...Then...Else selection structure.

13. Display the string "Dog" in the lblType control if the strAnimal variable contains the letter "D" (in any case); otherwise, display the string "Cat". Draw the flowchart, then write the Visual Basic code. Use the If...Then...Else selection structure.

14. Assume you want to calculate a 10% discount on desks sold to customers in Colorado. Use the variables strItem, strState, and curSales. Format the discount to Standard and display it in the lblDisc control. (You don't know the case of either the strItem or the strState variables. In other words, the contents of those two variables can be in uppercase, lowercase, or a combination of uppercase and lowercase letters.) Write the pseudocode, then write the Visual Basic code. Use the If...Then...Else selection structure.

15. Assume you want to calculate a 10% discount on sales made to customers in California and in Texas. You can use the variables strState and curSales. Format the discount to Standard and display it in the lblDisc control. (You don't know the case of the strState variable. In other words, the contents of the variable can be in uppercase, lowercase, or a combination of uppercase and lowercase letters.) Write the Visual Basic code. Use the Case selection structure.

16. Display the string "Valid Entry" in the lblEntry control if the user enters either the number 1 or the number 2 in the txtEntry text box; otherwise, display the string "Entry Error". Use the Case selection structure.

17. Assume you want to calculate a 2% price increase on all red shirts, but a 1% price increase on all other items. In addition to calculating the price increase, also calculate the new price. You can use the variables strColor, strItem, sngOrigPrice, sngIncrease, and sngNewPrice. Format the original price to Standard and display it in the lblOrig control. Format the price increase to Standard and display it in the lblIncrease control. Format the new price to Currency and display it in the lblNew control. (You don't know the case of either the strColor variable or the strItem variable. In other words, the contents of those variables can be in uppercase, lowercase, or a combination of uppercase and lowercase letters.) Write the Visual Basic code. Use the If...Then...Else selection structure.

18. Display the string "Dog" in the lblAnimal control if the intAnimal variable contains the number 1. Display the string "Cat" if the intAnimal variable contains the number 2. Display the string "Bird" if the intAnimal variable contains anything other than the number 1 or the number 2. Write the Visual Basic code. Use the Case selection structure.

19. Assume you offer programming seminars to companies. Your price per person depends on the number of people the company registers. (For example, if the company registers 7 people, then the total amount owed by the company is $560.)

Number of registrants	Charge
1 – 4	$ 100 per person
5 – 10	$ 80 per person
11 or more	$ 60 per person
less than 1	$ 0 per person

The number of people registered is stored in the Text property of the txtReg control. Calculate the total amount owed by the company. Store the amount in the curTotalDue variable. Write the Visual Basic code. Use the Case selection structure.

20. An application needs to display a shipping charge based on the state entered in the txtState control. Use the Case selection structure to display the shipping charge in the lblShip control. Use the chart below. (The state could be typed by the user in either uppercase or lowercase.) Assign the text box contents to the strState variable.

State entered in txtState control	Shipping charge
Hawaii	$25.00
Oregon	$30.00
California	$32.50

(Any other state should result in an "Incorrect State" message.)
a. Write the pseudocode. Use the Case selection structure.
b. Write the Visual Basic code.

21. The price of a concert ticket depends on the seat location entered in a text box named txtSeat. Display the price in the lblPrice control. Use the chart below. (The seat location could be entered by the user in either uppercase or lowercase.) Assign the text box contents to the strSeat variable.

Seat location	Concert ticket price
Box	$75.00
Pavilion	$30.00
Lawn	$21.00

(Any other seat location should result in an "Incorrect Seat Location" message.)
a. Write the Visual Basic code. Use the If...Then...Else selection structure.
b. Write the Visual Basic code. Use the Case selection structure.

22. In most companies the amount of vacation you receive depends on the number of years you've been with the company. The number of years is entered in a text box named txtYears. Store the numeric equivalent of the years in an Integer variable named intYears. Display the weeks of vacation in the lblWeeks control. Use the following chart:

Years with the company	Weeks of vacation
0	0
1 to 5	1
6 to 10	2
11 and over	3

a. Write the Visual Basic code. Use the If...Then...Else selection structure.
b. Write the Visual Basic code. Use the Case selection structure.

23. XYZ Corporation pays its salespeople a commission based on the amount of their sales. The sales amount is entered in a text box named txtSales. Store the numeric equivalent of the sales amount in a Currency variable named curSales. Use the following chart to calculate and display the commission.

Sales	Commission rate
$10,000.01 and over	10.0%
$5,000.01 – $10,000	7.5%
$1.00 – $5,000	5.0%
less than $1.00	Data Error

  a. Write the Visual Basic code. Use the If...Then...Else selection structure.

  b. Write the Visual Basic code. Use the Case selection structure.

24. Assume you want to calculate a 10% discount on sales made to customers in California and in Texas, a 7% discount on sales made to customers in Oregon and New Mexico, and a 6% discount on sales made to customers in all other states. The state is entered in the strState variable, and the sales amount is entered in the curSales variable. Format the discount to Standard and display it in the lblDisc control. (You don't know the case of the strState variable. In other words, the contents of the variable might be in uppercase, lowercase, or a combination of uppercase and lowercase letters.)

  a. Write the Visual Basic code. Use the If...Then...Else selection structure.

  b. Write the Visual Basic code. Use the Case selection structure.

25. Recall that string comparisons in Visual Basic are case sensitive, which means that a "P" is different from a "p." In Lesson A you learned how to use the UCase function (and the LCase function) to handle the string comparison problem. Recall that the Example 4 button's Click event procedure (in the laIf project) contains the following code:

```
If UCase(txtData.Text) = "P" Then
        lblMsg.Caption = "Pass"
Else
        lblMsg.Caption = "Fail"
End If
```

Not all languages have a UCase function or an LCase function. Just for practice, assume that Visual Basic does not have either function. Without using either the UCase function or the LCase function, rewrite the If statement's condition so that it displays the "Pass" message when the user enters the letter "P" in either lowercase or uppercase.

In this lesson you will learn how to:

- Include Visual Basic icons in an interface
- Add option buttons and a check box to a form
- Use GUI design standards for a frame control, option buttons, and check boxes
- Draw a control on the form and in a frame
- Use the Randomize statement, and the Rnd and Int functions
- Create a user-defined sub procedure
- Execute the Call statement
- Create a default option button

More Visual Basic Controls

The Math Application

Recall that Susan Chen, the principal of a local primary school, wants an application that the first and second grade students can use to practice both adding and subtracting numbers. The application should display the addition or subtraction problem on the screen, then allow the student to enter the answer, and then verify that the answer is correct. If the student's answer is not correct, the application should give him or her as many chances as necessary to answer the problem correctly.

The problems displayed for the first grade students should use numbers from one through 10 only; the problems for the second grade students should use numbers from 10 through 100. Because the first and second grade students have not learned about negative numbers yet, the subtraction problems should never ask them to subtract a larger number from a smaller one.

Ms. Chen also wants the application to keep track of how many correct and incorrect responses the student makes; this information will help her assess the student's math ability. Recall that Ms. Chen wants to be able to control the display of this information. The sketch of the user interface is shown in Figure 4-35.

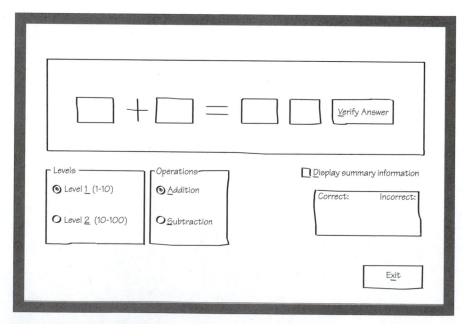

Figure 4-35: Sketch of the Math application's user interface

The math application's interface will contain one text box, four option buttons, one check box, three image controls, four frame controls, and various label controls. To save you time, your Student Disk contains a partially completed Math application. When you open the application, you will notice that most of the user interface has already been created and the properties of the existing objects have been set. You will finish creating the user interface in this lesson.

To open the partially completed application:

1 Start Visual Basic, if necessary, and open the **T4case** (T4case.vbp) project, which is located in the Tut04 folder on your Student Disk.

2 Save the form and the project as **lbMath**.

3 Click the **form's title bar** to select the frmMath form. Figure 4-36 identifies the controls already included in the application. (To see the lblCorrect and lblIncorrect controls, you will need to click inside the fraInfo frame control. The fraInfo frame control was given a more meaningful name because it will be referred to in code. "fra" is the three-character ID for a frame control.)

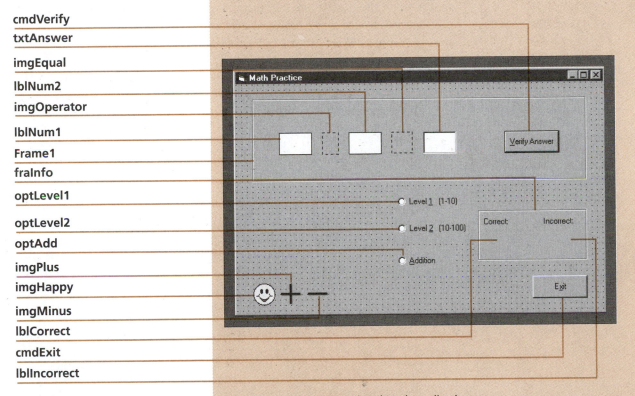

cmdVerify
txtAnswer
imgEqual
lblNum2
imgOperator
lblNum1
Frame1
fraInfo
optLevel1
optLevel2
optAdd
imgPlus
imgHappy
imgMinus
lblCorrect
cmdExit
lblIncorrect

Figure 4-36: Partially completed Math application

The Verify Answer button is the default command button. For now, don't worry about the three image controls at the bottom of the form. You will learn what they are for later in this lesson.

Before adding the missing controls to the user interface, you will set the Picture property of the imgEqual control. (Although the imgEqual control will not be either coded or used in code, it was given a name to make it easier to refer to in this lesson.)

Using Visual Basic's Icons

Visual Basic comes with a collection of over 500 icons. You will find the icons in the Icons folder, which is typically located in the Program Files\Microsoft Visual Studio\Common\Graphics folder on either the local hard drive or on the network drive. In this application, you will display the equal sign icon in the imgEqual control.

To display the equal sign icon in the imgEqual control:

1 Click the **imgEqual** control to select it. (Refer to Figure 4-36 for the location of the imgEqual control.) Sizing handles appear around the control.

2 Look in the Properties window's Object box to verify that the imgEqual control is selected.

3 If necessary, click **Picture** in the Properties list. Click the ... button in the Settings box. The Load Picture dialog box appears.

4 The main Visual Basic folder—usually named Vb98—should be open. Click the Look in list arrow, then click the Microsoft Visual Studio folder. Open the Common folder, then open the Graphics folder, and then open the Icons folder.

The various Visual Basic icons are grouped by category. The icon you will use is located in the Misc (miscellaneous) folder.

5 Click the **Misc** folder, then click the **Open** button to open the Misc folder. Visual Basic displays each icon, as well as its filename, in the filename list box. Scroll the list box until you locate the Misc22 icon—an equal sign. Click **Misc22** (Misc22.ico) in the list box, then click the **Open** button. An equal sign appears in the imgEqual control.

tip

Be sure to refer to the installation instructions on the Read This Before You Begin page. Depending on your version of Visual Basic, the Graphics folder may be located elsewhere.

The three image controls at the bottom of the interface also contain Visual Basic icons. The files for all three icons are in the Misc folder. The plus sign's file name is Misc18, the minus sign is Misc19, and the happy face is Face03. When you run the application in the next section, you will notice that the three icons do not appear in the interface; that's because their Visible property is set to False.

Now you can begin adding the missing controls. You'll start with the Subtraction option button.

Adding an Option Button Control to the Form

The Option Button tool draws an option button control. When option button controls are grouped together, only one of the buttons in the group can be selected at any one time. The **option button control** is the control to use in situations where you want to limit the user to only one of two or more related and mutually exclusive choices. In the Math application, for example, you want to limit the mathematical operation to either addition or subtraction, and you want to limit the user's level to either Level 1 or Level 2.

The minimum number of option buttons in a user interface is two because the only way to deselect an option button is to select another option button. The recommended maximum number of option buttons in an interface is seven. (If you have more than seven choices from which the user can choose, you should consider using a list box control, which you will learn about in Tutorial 6.) You

should always label each option button so that the user knows its purpose. You enter the label using sentence capitalization in the option button's Caption property. You should also assign an access key to each button.

GUI

Design Tips

Option Button Standards

- Use option buttons when you want to limit the user to one of two or more related and mutually exclusive choices.

- The minimum number of option buttons in an interface is two, and the recommended maximum is seven.

- The label in the option button's Caption property should be entered using sentence capitalization.

- Assign a unique access key to each option button.

tip

The option button controls that appear on the Math form are instances of the option button class.

To add an option button to the form:

1   Double-click the **Option button** tool 🔘 in the toolbox. An option button control appears on the form.

2   Set the option button's Name property to **optSub**, then set its Caption property to **&Subtraction**. "opt" is the three-character ID for an option button control.

3   Drag the Subtraction button to a location immediately below the Addition button.

4   **Save** and **run** the application.

You select an option button by clicking it; you can click either its circle or its caption.

5   Click the **Addition** button. A black dot appears inside the circle. The black dot indicates that the option button is selected.

6   Click the **Subtraction** button. Visual Basic selects the Subtraction button as it deselects the Addition button.

7   Click the **Level 1** button. Visual Basic selects the Level 1 button as it deselects the Subtraction button.

Notice a problem with the way the option buttons are working: selecting the Level 1 button deselects the Subtraction button. That means the user will not be able to choose the level and the mathematical operation at the same time. You actually want Visual Basic to treat the Addition and Subtraction buttons as a separate group, independent of the Level 1 and Level 2 buttons. You create a separate group of option buttons by placing the buttons in a frame, which you learned about in Tutorial 1.

8   Click the **Exit** button, which contains the End statement, to end the application. Visual Basic returns to the design screen.

Grouping Option Button Controls

Recall from Tutorial 1 that the purpose of a frame control is to be a container for other controls. When you place controls inside a frame, the controls and the frame are treated as one unit. You must use a frame control if you want more than one group of options buttons on a form. In this application, for example, you will group the Addition and Subtraction option buttons in one frame control, and the Level 1 and Level 2 option buttons in another frame control.

GUI

Design Tips

Frame Control Standards

- You can use a frame control to visually separate controls from one another. You must use a frame control to create separate groups of option buttons.

- Use sentence capitalization for the optional label, which is entered in the frame control's Caption property.

To add a frame control to the form:

1   Click the form to select it. Double-click the **Frame** tool 🔳 in the toolbox. The Frame2 control appears on the form.

2   Set the Frame2 control's Caption property to **Levels**.

You will now position the frame control and also make it larger.

3   Size and drag the frame control as shown in Figure 4-37. If you want to match the figure exactly, you can set the frame control's Height property to 1575, its Left property to 360, its Top property to 2400, and its Width property to 1935.

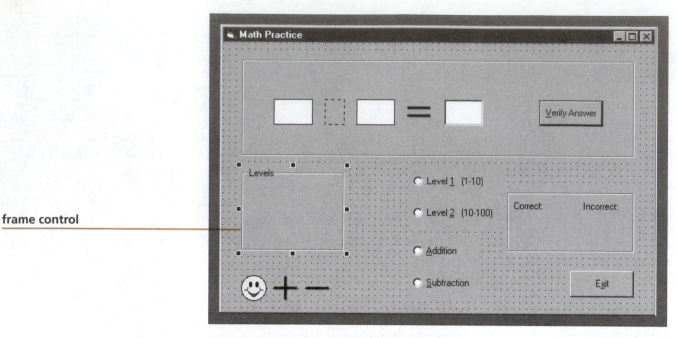

frame control

Figure 4-37: Frame control added to the form

The objects you add to a form belong to the form itself. Therefore, if you want to put the existing option buttons in a frame, you will need to detach the option buttons from the form first. In Windows terminology, you will cut the buttons from the form. That process will place the option buttons on the clipboard. You can then paste the option buttons from the clipboard into the frame control. Keep in mind that you can't just *drag* existing controls into a frame control. You must cut them from the form first, then paste them into the frame control.

tip

You can also use Ctrl + X to cut the selected controls from the form. Then, after selecting the frame control, you can use Ctrl + V to paste the controls into the frame.

To cut both the Level 1 and Level 2 option buttons from the form, then paste them into the Levels frame:

1 Click the **Level 1** button to select it, then press and hold down the **Ctrl** key as you click the **Level 2** button. Sizing handles appear around both option buttons.

Now cut the selected controls from the form, then paste them into the Levels frame.

2 Click **Edit** on the menu bar, then click **Cut** to cut the selected option buttons from the form. Visual Basic removes the two buttons from the form and places them on the clipboard.

Before you can paste the buttons into the frame control, you must first select the frame control.

3 Click the **Levels** frame to select it. Sizing handles appear around the frame control. Now click **Edit** on the menu bar, then click **Paste** to paste the option buttons into the selected frame.

4 Place the mouse pointer on one of the selected option buttons. With the mouse pointer on one of the selected option buttons, drag the option buttons further into the frame control, as shown in Figure 4-38.

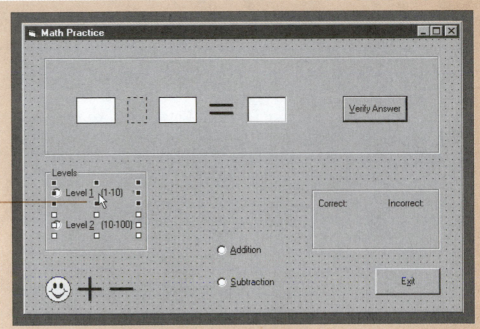

Figure 4-38: Option buttons positioned in the frame control

HELP? If you inadvertently deselected the option buttons, simply click one of the buttons and then press and hold down the Ctrl key as you click the other button.

5 Click the **form** to deselect the option buttons.

6 **Save** and **run** the application.

7 Click the **Addition** button to select it, then click the **Level 1** button to select it. Notice that selecting the Level 1 button does not deselect the Addition button.

8 On your own, try clicking the other option buttons. You should notice that when you select the Subtraction button, the Addition button is deselected; when you select the Addition button, the Subtraction button is deselected. The Addition and Subtraction buttons, however, have no effect on the Level buttons. Also notice that selecting one of the buttons in the Levels frame deselects the other button in the Levels frame, but it has no effect on the Addition and Subtraction buttons.

9 Click the **Exit** button. Visual Basic returns to the design screen.

Although you don't need to put the Addition and Subtraction option buttons in their own frame for the buttons to work, you will do so anyway. The frame will improve the appearance of the user interface by visually separating the option buttons from the other controls on the form.

To group the Addition and Subtraction option buttons in a frame control:

1 Click the **form's title bar** to select the form. Double-click the **Frame tool** in the toolbox. The Frame3 control appears on the form.

2 Set the Frame3 control's Caption property to **Operations**.

---

drag buttons into the frame

---

tip
....
▶ After selecting an option button in a group, you can then use either the ↑ or ↓ key on your keyboard to select another button in the group.

3   Set the frame control's Height property to 1575, its Left property to 2700, its Top property to 2400, and its Width property to 1575.

4   Select the **Addition** and **Subtraction** option buttons. Sizing handles appear around both buttons. Use Visual Basic's Edit menu to cut the selected buttons from the form. Click the **Operations** frame to select it, then use Visual Basic's Edit menu to paste the option buttons into the Operations frame.

5   With the mouse pointer on one of the selected option buttons, drag the option buttons further inside the frame.

6   Click the **form** to deselect the option buttons.

When you use a frame to group controls, Visual Basic treats the frame and the controls inside the frame as one unit. When you move or delete a frame control, Visual Basic moves or deletes the frame and the controls contained inside it.

7   Place the mouse pointer on the Frame3 control's caption (Operations), then drag the frame to match Figure 4-39. Notice that the controls inside the frame move along with the frame.

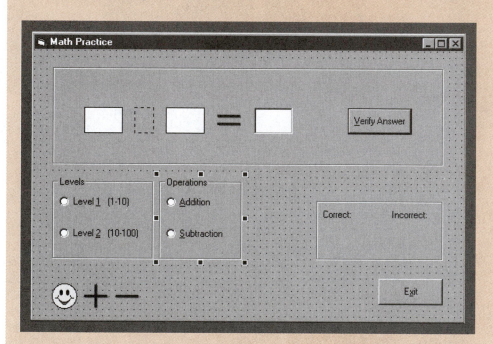

Figure 4-39: Location of both frame controls in the interface

8   **Save** and **run** the application.

9   On your own, try clicking each of the option buttons to make sure they are still working correctly, then click the **Exit** button. Visual Basic returns to the design screen.

The next control you will add to the interface is the missing check box control.

GUI
Design Tips

Check Box Standards

- Use check boxes to allow the user to select any number of choices from a group of one or more independent and nonexclusive choices.

- Enter the check box control's caption using sentence capitalization.

- Assign a unique access key to each check box.

Adding a Check Box Control to the Form

Check boxes work like option buttons in that they are either selected or deselected only; but that is where the similarity ends. You use option buttons when you want to limit the user to only one choice from a group of related and mutually exclusive choices. You use **check boxes**, on the other hand, to allow the user to select any number of choices from a group of one or more independent and nonexclusive choices. Unlike option buttons, where only one button in a group can be selected at any one time, any number of check boxes on a form can be selected at the same time.

You should always label each check box so that the user knows its purpose. You enter the label using sentence capitalization in the check box's Caption property. Be sure to assign an access key to each check box.

Besides double-clicking a tool in the toolbox, you can also draw a control on the user interface by first clicking the tool in the toolbox, then moving the mouse pointer onto the interface, and then dragging the mouse pointer until the control is the size you want. You will use this click and drag method to draw a check box on the form.

To draw a control on the form:

1 Click the **form's title bar** to select the form, then click (don't double-click) the **Check box** tool ☑. When you move the mouse pointer onto the form, it becomes a crosshair +.

2 Place the crosshair + as shown in Figure 4-40.

place the crosshair here

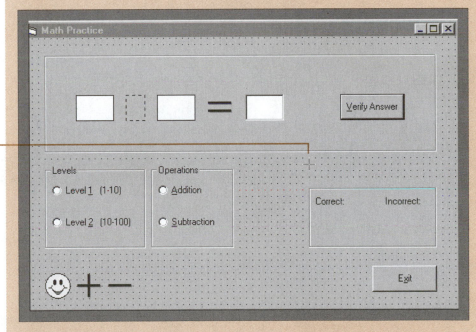

Figure 4-40: Placement of crosshair

3 Drag the mouse down and to the right. When the check box control is about the same size shown in Figure 4-41, release the mouse button.

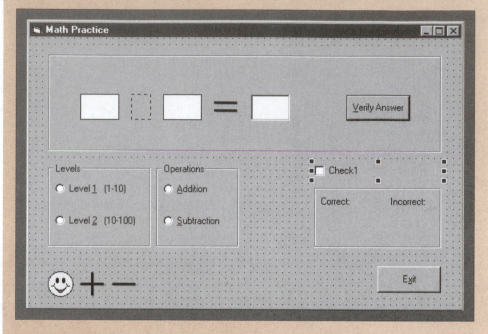

Figure 4-41: Check box control drawn on the form

HELP? If your check box is too small or too large, use its sizing handles to resize it. You can also use the Shift key along with one of the arrow keys on your keyboard.

4 Set the check box control's Name property to **chkDisplay**, then set its Caption property to **&Display summary information**. "chk" is the three-character ID for a check box control.

5 Click the **form** to select it, then **save** and **run** the application.

You select a check box by clicking it. You can click either the square or the caption.

6 Click the **Display summary information** check box to select it. A check mark appears inside the check box. The check mark indicates that the check box is selected.

7 Click the **Display summary information** check box to deselect it. Visual Basic removes the check mark from the check box.

8 Click the **Exit** button. Visual Basic returns to the design screen.

The last control you will add to the interface is the image control that will display the happy face icon when the student enters the correct answer to the mathematical problem. That control should be placed inside the frame control at the top of the form.

Drawing a Control in a Frame

As you learned earlier in this lesson, in order to place *existing* controls inside a frame, you need to cut the controls from the form, then select the frame, and then paste the controls into the frame. If the control is not already on the form, however, you can use the click and drag method to draw the control right inside the frame.

To draw a control inside a frame:

1 Click the **form's title bar** to select the form, then click the **Image tool** 🖾 in the toolbox. When you move the mouse pointer onto the form or into the frame, it becomes a crosshair +.

2 Position the crosshair + in the frame at the top of the form, then draw the image control to match Figure 4-42.

image control

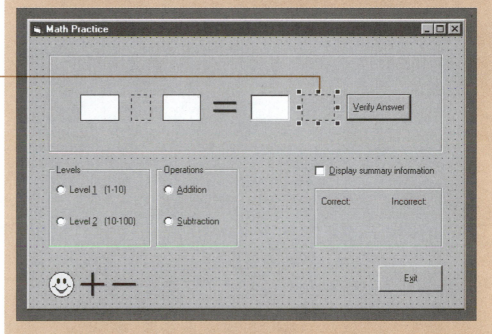

Figure 4-42: Image control drawn in the frame

3 Set the image control's Name property to **imgIcon**.

You will now put a border around the image control. As you learned in Tutorial 1, the BorderStyle property determines the border style of an object.

4 Set the imgIcon control's BorderStyle property to **1-Fixed Single**.

You have now completed the user interface, so you can lock the controls in place, then set each control's TabIndex property appropriately.

Locking the Controls and Setting the TabIndex Property

When you have completed a user interface, you should lock the controls in place, then set each control's TabIndex property appropriately. In this application, the first control to receive the focus should be the txtAnswer text box, so you will set its TabIndex property to 0. When the user presses the Tab key, the focus should move from the txtAnswer text box to the Verify Answer command button, then to the Levels option buttons, the Operations option buttons, the Display summary information check box, and lastly to the Exit button.

To lock the controls, then set each control's TabIndex property:

1 Right-click the **form**, then click **Lock Controls** on the popup menu.

2 Set the TabIndex property of the controls as follows:

txtAnswer	0	optAdd	4
cmdVerify	1	optSub	5
optLevel1	2	chkDisplay	6
optLevel2	3	cmdExit	7

3 **Save** and **run** the application.

4 Press the **Tab** key. The focus moves from the txtAnswer text box to the Verify Answer button. Notice the dotted rectangle around the button's caption.

5 Press the **Tab** key, slowly, five times. The focus moves to the Level 1 option button, the Addition option button, the Display summary information check box, the Exit command button, and back to the txtAnswer text box.

Notice that the Tab key does not move the focus to either the Level 2 or the Subtraction option buttons. In Windows applications, only one option button in a group of option buttons receives the focus. When one of the option buttons in the group has the focus, the user can select the other option buttons in the group by pressing either the ↓ or the ↑ keys on the keyboard.

6 The focus should be in the txtAnswer text box. Press the **Tab** key two times to move the focus to the Level 1 option button, then press the ↓ key on your keyboard. The Level 2 option button is now selected. Press the ↑ key on your keyboard; the Level 1 option is now selected. Press the **Tab** key two times to move the focus to the Display summary information check box. You can use the spacebar to select and deselect a check box when it has the focus. Press the **Spacebar** to select the check box, then press the **Spacebar** again to deselect it.

7 Click the **Exit** button to end the application. Visual Basic returns to the design screen.

You can now begin coding the application. The TOE chart for the Math application is shown in Figure 4-43.

Task	Object	Event
Display/hide number of correct and incorrect responses	chkDisplay	Click
End the application	cmdExit	Click
1. Calculate the correct answer to the math problem 2. Compare the correct answer to the user's answer 3. Display/remove a happy face icon 4. Add 1 to the number of either correct or incorrect responses 5. If the user's answer is incorrect, then prompt the user to "Try again"; otherwise display a new math problem 6. Display the number of correct and incorrect responses in the lblCorrect and lblIncorrect controls, respectively	cmdVerify	Click
Display the equal sign	imgEqual	None
Display the happy face icon	imgIcon	None
Display either the plus sign or the minus sign	imgOperator	None
Display the number of correct responses	lblCorrect	None
Display the number of incorrect responses	lblIncorrect	None
Display a random number	lblNum1	None
Display a random number	lblNum2	None
1. Display two random numbers in the lblNum1 and lblNum2 controls 2. Display the plus sign in the imgOperator control	optAdd	Click
Display two random numbers from 1 to 10 in the lblNum1 and lblNum2 controls	optLevel1	Click
Display two random numbers from 10 to 100 in the lblNum1 and lblNum2 controls	optLevel2	Click
1. Display two random numbers in the lblNum1 and lblNum2 controls 2. Display the minus sign in the imgOperator control	optSub	Click
Get and display the user's answer	txtAnswer	None

Figure 4-43: TOE chart for the Math application

To save you time, the `Option Explicit` statement has already been entered in the form's General Declarations section, and the code to center the frmMath form on the screen has already been entered in the form's Load event procedure. You will begin by coding the Level 1 and Level 2 option buttons.

Coding the Level 1 and Level 2 Option Buttons

According to the TOE chart, the Level 1 and Level 2 buttons are responsible for displaying two random numbers—one in the lblNum1 control and the other in the lblNum2 control. In Visual Basic, you use both the Randomize statement and the Rnd function to generate random numbers. The **Randomize statement** initializes Visual Basic's random-number generator, and the **Rnd function** generates the random number. The Rnd function produces decimal numbers within the 0 to 1 range, including 0 but not including 1. For example, the instruction `lblNum1.Caption = Rnd` would display, in the lblNum1 control, a decimal number that is greater than or equal to 0, but less than 1.

You can use the following formula to generate random decimal numbers in a range other than 0 to 1: $(upperbound - lowerbound + 1) * Rnd + lowerbound$. In the formula, *lowerbound* is the lowest number in the range, and *upperbound* is the highest number in the range. For example, to produce decimal numbers from 1 through $10.99\overline{9}$, you would use the formula `(10 - 1 + 1) * Rnd + 1`.

If you want to generate a range of integers, as you do in the Math application, you need to include the Int function (Int stands for Integer) in the random number formula, like this: Int(($upperbound - lowerbound + 1$) * Rnd + *lowerbound*). The **Int function**, whose syntax is **Int**(*number*), returns the integer portion of a number. Figure 4-44 shows some examples of formulas that generate random numbers.

This formula:	Generates these numbers:
(10 − 1 + 1) * Rnd + 1	decimal numbers from 1 through $10.99\overline{9}$
(25 − 5 + 1) * Rnd + 5	decimal numbers from 5 through $25.99\overline{9}$
Int((10 − 1 + 1) * Rnd + 1)	integers from 1 through 10
Int((25 − 5 + 1) * Rnd + 5)	integers from 5 through 25
Int((100 − 10 + 1) * Rnd + 10)	integers from 10 through 100

Figure 4-44: Examples of formulas that generate random numbers

In the Math application, you will need to generate two random numbers for each math problem. If the user selects the Level 1 option button, both numbers should be in the range of 1 through 10; otherwise the numbers should be in the 10 through 100 range. You will store the random numbers in two Integer variables named intNum1 and intNum2. According to the TOE chart, the random numbers will be used by the Level 1 and Level 2 option buttons, the Addition and Subtraction option buttons, and the Verify Answer command button. Because more than one procedure in the form will need to use the variables, you will declare the variables in the form's General Declarations section—in other words, you will make them form-level variables.

To declare the intNum1 and intNum2 variables as form-level variables:

1 Double-click the **form** to open its Code window. The code to center the form is already entered in the form's Load event procedure. Use the Code window's Object box to open the form's General Declarations section.

The `Option Explicit` statement is already in the form's General Declarations section.

2 Position the insertion point below the `Option Explicit` statement, then type **dim intNum1 as integer, intNum2 as integer** and press the **Enter** key.

The flowchart for the Level 1 and Level 2 option buttons is shown in Figure 4-45.

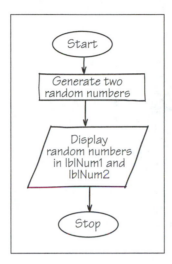

Figure 4-45: Flowchart for the Level 1 and Level 2 option buttons

As the flowchart indicates, the Level 1 and Level 2 controls must generate and display two random numbers in the appropriate label controls on the form. The code for both controls' Click event procedures is almost identical, as shown in Figure 4-46.

Level 1 button's code	Level 2 button's code
Randomize	Randomize
intNum1 = Int((10 − 1 + 1) * Rnd + 1)	intNum1 = Int((100 − 10 + 1) * Rnd + 10)
intNum2 = Int((10 − 1 + 1) * Rnd + 1)	intNum2 = Int((100 − 10 + 1) * Rnd + 10)
lblNum1.Caption = intNum1	lblNum1.Caption = intNum1
lblNum2.Caption = intNum2	lblNum2.Caption = intNum2

Figure 4-46: Code for the Level 1 and Level 2 buttons' Click event procedures

Notice that the only difference in the code for both procedures is in the random number formulas. The Level 1 button's formulas use a *lowerbound* value of 1 and an *upperbound* value of 10 to generate integers from 1 through 10. The

Level 2 button's formulas, on the other hand, use a *lowerbound* value of 10 and an *upperbound* value of 100 to generate integers from 10 through 100. Although you could enter the code shown in Figure 4-46 in both Click event procedures, that would be inefficient because several lines of code would be duplicated. A better approach is to place the code that generates and displays the random numbers in a user-defined sub procedure and then have the Level 1 and Level 2 option buttons invoke (call) the sub procedure as needed. You will name the sub procedure that generates and displays the random numbers, RandomNumbers. Figure 4-47 shows the revised flowchart for the Level 1 and Level 2 option buttons. The revised flowchart reflects the fact that the buttons will call the RandomNumbers user-defined sub procedure.

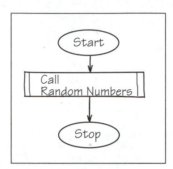

Figure 4-47: Revised flowchart for the Level 1 and Level 2 option buttons

Notice the symbol—a rectangle with side borders—used to represent a call to a sub procedure. The symbol is called the **sub procedure box**. You will now create the RandomNumbers user-defined sub procedure, which will both generate and display the random numbers.

Creating a User-Defined Sub Procedure

You are already familiar with procedures. Clicking a command button, for example, causes an event procedure to be processed, provided you have added the appropriate code. A **user-defined sub procedure**, often just called a **user-defined procedure**, is a collection of code that can be invoked from one or more places in your program. When the code, or a portion of the code, for two or more objects is almost identical, it is more efficient to enter the code once, in a user-defined procedure, instead of duplicating the code in each event procedure.

The user-defined procedure you will create for the Math application will initialize the random number generator first. Next, it will determine which of the level option buttons—either Level 1 or Level 2—is selected, and then generate and display the appropriate random numbers in the lblNum1 and lblNum2 controls in the interface.

To create a user-defined sub procedure, you simply open any Code window, then click Tools on the menu bar, and then click Add Procedure on the Tools menu. The rules for naming a user-defined procedure are the same as those for naming variables and constants. You will name the user-defined procedure RandomNumbers.

To create the RandomNumbers procedure:

1   A Code window is already open, so you can simply click **Tools** on the menu bar, then click **Add Procedure**. The Add Procedure dialog box appears. See Figure 4-48.

Figure 4-48: Add Procedure dialog box

2   Type **RandomNumbers** in the Name text box.

You want to create a sub procedure, so leave the Sub option button selected in the Type box. The user-defined procedure will be used only by the form in which it is created, so you will make its scope Private.

3   Click the **Private** option button in the Scope box, then click the **OK** button. The Add Procedure dialog box closes, and the Code window for the RandomNumbers procedure appears. See Figure 4-49.

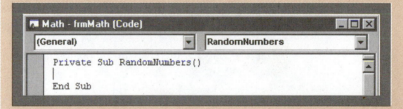

Figure 4-49: RandomNumbers procedure Code window

tip

You can learn more about passing information to a procedure in Lesson C's Discovery Exercises 11 and 12.

A user-defined procedure can receive variables or constants, called **arguments**, that you send (pass) to it; the arguments, if any, are listed inside the parentheses following the procedure's name. You pass arguments when you want the procedure to process them in some way. For example, you might create a procedure that sorts a list of numbers. The arguments you pass would be the numbers themselves; the procedure would then sort, and perhaps display, those numbers. (You will learn how to pass arguments in Tutorial 8.) The RandomNumbers procedure does not receive any variables or constants, so you will not need to list any information inside the parentheses.

The first task the RandomNumbers procedure will perform will be to initialize the random number generator. Recall that you use the Randomize statement to do so.

4   Press the **Tab** key, then type **randomize** and press the **Enter** key.

The procedure now needs to generate and display the random numbers. The range of random numbers depends on which of the level option buttons—either Level 1 or Level 2—is selected. If the Level 1 button is selected, then the application should generate random numbers from 1 through 10; otherwise, it should generate numbers from 10 through 100. You will use the selection structure, which you learned about in Lesson A, to determine which of the level option buttons is selected before generating the random numbers. You can tell if an option button is selected by looking at its Value property. When an option button is selected, its Value property contains the Boolean value True; otherwise, it contains the Boolean value False. After generating the random numbers, you will display them in the lblNum1 and lblNum2 controls.

5   Enter the additional code shown in Figure 4-50.

**Add these
9 lines of code**

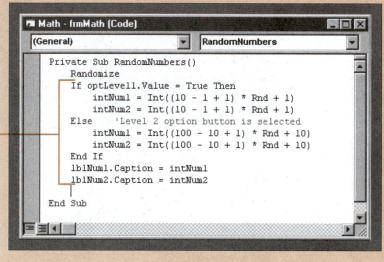

Figure 4-50: Code entered in the RandomNumbers procedure

You invoke a user-defined procedure with Visual Basic's Call statement.

The Call Statement

You use Visual Basic's Call statement, whose syntax is **Call** *name* [(*argumentlist*)], to invoke a user-defined sub procedure. The brackets in the syntax indicate that the *argumentlist* is optional and, if included, must be enclosed in parentheses. If you have no information to pass to the sub procedure that you are calling, as is the case in the Math application, you do not need to enter anything inside the parentheses.

The Level 1 and Level 2 option buttons should call the RandomNumbers procedure when each is clicked by the user. You will therefore enter the Call statement in each button's Click event procedure.

To enter the Call statement in the Level 1 and Level 2 buttons' Click event procedures:

1 Use the Code window's Object box to open the optLevel1 control's Click event procedure, which is the most common event for an option button. Press the **Tab** key, then type **call randomnumbers** and press the **Enter** key.

When the Call statement is processed, the program will leave the option button's Click event procedure, temporarily, in order to process the instructions in the RandomNumbers procedure. When the RandomNumbers procedure ends, the program will return to the option button's Click event procedure, to the line below the Call statement. In this application, the line below the Call statement will be the End Sub instruction, which will end the option button's Click event procedure. Figure 4-51 illustrates this concept.

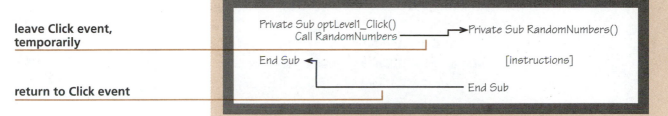

leave Click event, temporarily

return to Click event

Figure 4-51: Illustration of the Call statement

Now copy the Call instruction to the Level 2 button's Click event procedure.

2 Select the Call RandomNumbers instruction in the open Code window. Click **Edit**, then click **Copy**. Use the Code window's Object box to open the optLevel2 control's Click event procedure. Click **Edit**, then click **Paste**. (You may then need to position the insertion point at the beginning of the Call instruction and press the Tab key to indent the instruction.)

3 Close the Code window, then **save** and **run** the application.

4 Click the **Level 1** button. The program leaves the Level 1 button's Click event procedure, temporarily, in order to process the instructions in the RandomNumbers procedure. The RandomNumbers procedure generates and displays, in the label controls, two numbers between 1 and 10, inclusive. When the RandomNumbers procedure ends, the program returns to the Level 1 button's Click event procedure to process its End Sub instruction, which ends the Click event.

5 Click the **Level 2** button. The program leaves the Level 2 button's Click event procedure, temporarily, in order to process the instructions in the RandomNumbers procedure. The RandomNumbers procedure generates and displays, in the label controls, two numbers between 10 and 100, inclusive. When the RandomNumbers procedure ends, the program returns to the Level 2 button's Click event procedure to process its End Sub instruction, which ends the Click event.

6 Click the **Exit** button. Visual Basic returns to the design screen.

Next, code the Addition and Subtraction option buttons.

Coding the Addition and Subtraction Option Buttons

According to the TOE chart shown in Figure 4-43, the Addition and Subtraction option buttons should display two random numbers in the label controls, as well as display the appropriate operator, either a plus or a minus sign, in the imgOperator control. You can have the Addition and Subtraction buttons call the RandomNumbers procedure to display the random numbers. When the RandomNumbers procedure ends, each option button can then display the appropriate operator.

The Addition and Subtraction option buttons should perform their assigned tasks when they are clicked by the user, so you will need to code their Click event procedures.

To code the Click event procedures for the Addition and Subtraction option buttons:

1 Open the **Addition** button's Click event procedure.

First have the Addition button call the RandomNumbers procedure.

2 Press the **Tab** key, then type **call randomnumbers** and press the **Enter** key.

The Addition button must also display the plus sign icon in the imgOperator control. You can do this by assigning the Picture property of the imgPlus control, which is located at the bottom of the form, to the Picture property of the imgOperator control. In other words, you can use the assignment statement `imgOperator.Picture = imgPlus.Picture`.

3 Type **imgoperator.picture = imgplus.picture** and press the **Enter** key.

Now copy the Addition button's code to the Subtraction button's Click event procedure.

4 Select both the `Call RandomNumbers` and `imgOperator.Picture = imgPlus.Picture` instructions. Click **Edit** on the menu bar, then click **Copy** to copy the instructions to the clipboard. Use the Code window's Object box to open the Click event procedure for the optSub control. Click **Edit** on the menu bar, then click **Paste** to paste the instructions into the optSub control's Code window.

You want the Subtraction button to display the minus sign, which is stored in the imgMinus control at the bottom of the form.

5 Change imgPlus in the optSub Code window to **imgMinus**.

6 Close the Code window, then **save** and **run** the application.

Notice that none of the option buttons are selected in the interface. It is customary in Windows applications to have an option button selected in each group when the interface first appears. You'll learn how to select an option button, automatically, in the next section.

7 Click the **Addition** option button. The program leaves the Addition button's Click event procedure, temporarily, in order to process the instructions in the RandomNumbers procedure. The RandomNumbers procedure generates and displays the random numbers. When the RandomNumbers procedure ends, the program returns to the Addition button's Click event procedure to process the `imgOperator.Picture = imgPlus.Picture` instruction, which displays the plus sign in the imgOperator control, and the `End Sub` instruction, which ends the Click event.

8 Click the **Subtraction** option button. The program leaves the Subtraction button's Click event procedure, temporarily, in order to process the instructions in the RandomNumbers procedure. The RandomNumbers procedure generates and displays the random numbers. When the RandomNumbers procedure ends, the program returns to the Subtraction button's Click event procedure to process the imgOperator.Picture = imgMinus.Picture instruction, which displays the minus sign in the imgOperator control, and the End Sub instruction, which ends the Click event.

9 Click the **Exit** button. Visual Basic returns to the design screen.

In the next section you will learn how to have an option button selected, automatically, when the interface first appears on the screen.

Creating a Default Option Button

It is customary in Windows applications to have an option button already selected when the interface first appears. The selected button is called the **default option button**. If an interface contains more than one group of option buttons, you should select a default button in each group. In the Math application, for example, you will make the Level 1 button the default button in the Levels group, and the Addition button the default button in the Operations group.

You make an option button the default button by assigning the Boolean value True to the button's Value property; assigning True to the Value property selects the option button and also triggers its Click event. Because you want the Level 1 and Addition option buttons selected when the user interface first appears on the screen, you will need to place the appropriate assignment statements in the form's Load event procedure. Recall that instructions in the form's Load event procedure are processed when the application is run and the form is loaded into memory.

GUI
Design Tips

Default Option Button

- A default button should be selected in each group of option buttons.

Setting an option button's Value property to True in the Properties window does not trigger the option button's Click event procedure. To trigger the Click event, you must set the Value property from code.

To make the Level 1 and Addition option buttons the default buttons in their respective groups:

1 Open the form's Load event procedure.

2 Position the insertion point below the two instructions that center the form. If necessary, press the **Tab** key to indent the instruction. Type **optlevel1.value = true** and press the **Enter** key, then type **optadd.value = true** and press the **Enter** key.

These two instructions will select the Level 1 and Addition option buttons in the interface, and also trigger their Click event procedures.

3 Close the Code window, then **save** and **run** the application.

Notice that the application selects, automatically, the Level 1 and Addition option buttons. The first math problem appears in the interface.

4 Click the **Level 2** option button. Random numbers in the range of 10 through 100 appear in the label controls.

5 Click the **Subtraction** option button. A subtraction problem appears in the interface.

If you continue to select option buttons, you will notice that sometimes the number in the lblNum2 control is greater than the number in the lblNum1 control. For the addition problems, it doesn't make any difference if the second number is greater than the first number. For the subtraction problems, however, it does make a difference; recall that Ms. Chen does not want any subtraction problems that result in negative numbers. You will fix this problem in the next section.

6 Click the **Exit** button to end the application.

Modifying the RandomNumbers User-Defined Sub Procedure

If the Subtraction button is selected, you always want the number in the lblNum2 control to be less than or equal to the number in the lblNum1 control—in other words, the second number should never be greater than the first number. You can use a selection structure to accomplish this. You will place the selection structure in the RandomNumbers procedure.

To modify the RandomNumbers procedure:

1 Open the form's General Declarations section. Click the **Procedure** list arrow, then click **RandomNumbers** in the list. The RandomNumbers procedure appears.

2 Maximize the Code window, then enter the additional code shown in Figure 4-52. Be sure to enter the Dim statement, the selection structure, and the internal documentation.

enter this line of code

enter these 5 lines of code

enter this documentation

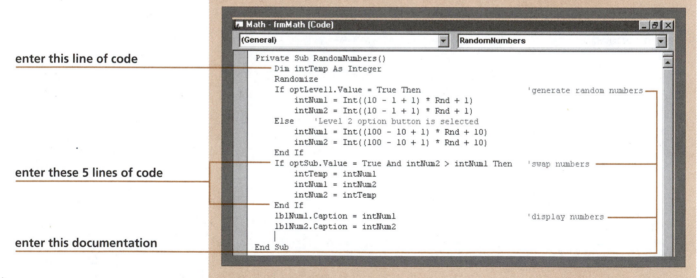

```
Math - frmMath (Code)                                            _ □ ×
(General)                              ▼   RandomNumbers                ▼
Private Sub RandomNumbers()
    Dim intTemp As Integer
    Randomize
    If optLevel1.Value = True Then                'generate random numbers
        intNum1 = Int((10 - 1 + 1) * Rnd + 1)
        intNum2 = Int((10 - 1 + 1) * Rnd + 1)
    Else     'Level 2 option button is selected
        intNum1 = Int((100 - 10 + 1) * Rnd + 10)
        intNum2 = Int((100 - 10 + 1) * Rnd + 10)
    End If
    If optSub.Value = True And intNum2 > intNum1 Then   'swap numbers
        intTemp = intNum1
        intNum1 = intNum2
        intNum2 = intTemp
    End If
    lblNum1.Caption = intNum1                     'display numbers
    lblNum2.Caption = intNum2
    |
End Sub
```

Figure 4-52: Modified RandomNumbers procedure

The modified code creates an Integer variable named intTemp (short for "temporary"). The If statement contains two conditions that are combined with the And logical operator. The first condition, `optSub.Value = True`, checks to see if the Subtraction button is selected. The second condition, `intNum2 > intNum1`, checks to see if the second number is greater than the first number. Recall that when you combine conditions using the And operator, both conditions must be true for the entire condition to be true. In this case, the Subtraction button must be selected *and* the second number must be greater than the first number in order for the entire condition to be true. If the entire condition is true, you simply interchange (swap) the numbers in the intNum1 and intNum2 variables.

The three instructions that accomplish the swap are `intTemp = intNum1`, `intNum1 = intNum2`, and `intNum2 = intTemp`. First, the `intTemp = intNum1` instruction assigns the value in the intNum1 variable to the intTemp variable. Next, the `intNum1 = intNum2` instruction assigns the value in the intNum2 variable to the intNum1 variable. Lastly, the `intNum2 = intTemp` instruction assigns the value in the intTemp variable to the intNum2 variable. The intTemp variable is necessary to store the contents of the intNum1 variable temporarily so that the swap can be made. If you did not store the intNum1 value in the intTemp variable, the intNum2 value would write over the value in the intNum1 variable and the value in the intNum1 variable would be lost. Figure 4-53 illustrates the concept of "swapping."

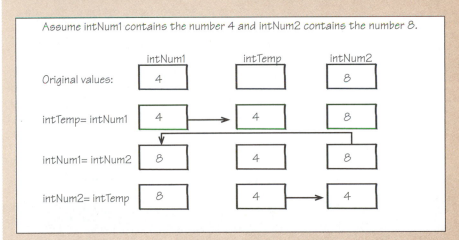

Figure 4-53: Illustration of "swapping" concept

3 Close the Code window, then **save** and **run** the application.

4 Try clicking each of the option buttons. Notice that when the Subtraction button is selected, the number in lblNum2 is never greater than the number in lblNum1.

5 Click the **Exit** button to end the application.

You have now completed Lesson B. You can either take a break or complete the end-of-lesson questions and exercises. You will complete the Math application in Lesson C.

S U M M A R Y

To limit the user to only one of several related and mutually exclusive choices:

- Use the option button tool

To allow the user to select any number of choices from a group of independent and nonexclusive choices:

- Use the check box tool

To create separate groups of option buttons, or to visually separate areas of the form:

- Use the frame tool

To place an existing control into a frame:

- Cut the existing control from the form, then select the frame, and then paste the control into the frame.

To draw a control on a form or in a frame:

- Click (do not double-click) the appropriate tool in the toolbox. Position the crosshair + on the form or inside the frame, then drag until the control is the desired size.

To generate random numbers:

- First use the Randomize statement to initialize the random number generator. You can then use the Rnd function to generate random decimal numbers between zero and 1, including 0 but not including 1. To generate decimal numbers within a specific range, use the formula (*upperbound* − *lowerbound* + 1) * **Rnd** + *lowerbound*. To generate integers within a specific range, use the formula **Int**((*upperbound* − *lowerbound* + 1) * **Rnd** + *lowerbound*).

To return the integer portion of a number:

- Use the Int function. (Int stands for Integer.) Its syntax is **Int**(*number*).

To create a collection of code that can be invoked from one or more places in your program:

- Create a user-defined sub procedure. First open any Code window, then click Tools in Visual Basic's menu bar, then click Add Procedure. Give the procedure a name, type, and scope. The rules for naming a user-defined procedure are the same as those for naming variables and constants.

To invoke a user-defined sub procedure:

- Use the Call statement. Its syntax is **Call** *name* [(*argumentlist*)].

To swap the values contained in two variables:

- Assign the value in the first variable to a temporary variable, then assign the value in the second variable to the first variable, and then assign the value in the temporary variable to the second variable.

QUESTIONS

1. Which of the following controls allows the user to select only one choice?
   a. check box
   b. command button
   c. label
   d. option button
   e. shape

2. Which of the following controls allows the user to select none, one, or more choices?
   a. check box
   b. command button
   c. label
   d. option button
   e. shape

3. If you want to create separate groups of option buttons, you will need to place each group in its own _____ control.
   a. check box
   b. circle
   c. container
   d. frame
   e. shape

4. Assume the form contains three option buttons. (The buttons are not in a frame control.) How many option buttons can be on at any one time?
   a. one
   b. two
   c. three
   d. four
   e. five

5. Assume the form contains two frame controls. Each frame control contains three option buttons. How many option buttons can be on at any time?
   a. one
   b. two
   c. three
   d. four
   e. five

6. Assume the form contains three check boxes. (The check boxes are not in a frame control.) How many check boxes can be on at any one time?
   a. one
   b. two
   c. three
   d. four
   e. five

7. Assume the form contains two frame controls. Each frame control contains two check boxes. How many check boxes can be on at any time?
   a. one
   b. two
   c. three
   d. four
   e. five

8. Assume the form contains two frame controls. One frame control contains two option buttons; the other frame control contains three check boxes. What is the total number of option buttons and check boxes that can be on at any one time?
   a. one
   b. two
   c. three
   d. four
   e. five

9. Which one of the following statements initializes Visual Basic's random number generator?
   a. Generate
   b. Initialize
   c. Randomize
   d. RandomNumb
   e. Rnd

10. The `lblNumber.Caption = Rnd` instruction will display random numbers _____.
    a. between 0 and 1, including 0 and 1
    b. between 0 and 1, including 0 but not including 1
    c. between 0 and 1, including 1 but not including 0
    d. greater than 0 but less than 1
    e. less than 0 and greater than 1

11. Which of the following will generate random decimal numbers from 5 through 30.99$\overline{9}$?
    a. (5 − 30 + 1) * Rnd + 30
    b. (30 − 5 + 1) * Rnd + 5
    c. (30 + 5 − 1) * Rnd + 1
    d. (30 + 5 − 1) * Rnd + 5
    e. (30 − 5 − 1) * Rnd + 30

12. Which of the following will generate random integers from 1 through 25?
    a. Int((1 − 25 + 1) * Rnd + 25)
    b. Int((25 − 1 + 1)) * Rnd + 1
    c. Int((25 + 1 − 1) * Rnd + 25)
    d. Int((25 + 1 − 1)) * Rnd + 25
    e. Int((25 − 1 + 1) * Rnd + 1)

13. You use the _____ statement to invoke a user-defined sub procedure.
    a. Call
    b. DoProcedure
    c. Get
    d. Invoke
    e. ProcedureCall

14. Which of the following instructions will select the optInsured option button and trigger its Click event procedure?
    a. optInsured.Button = on
    b. optInsured.Button = true
    c. optInsured.Status = on
    d. optInsured.Value = on
    e. optInsured.Value = true

15. Assume the form contains a command button named cmdExit. How could you place this control in a frame?

16. How do you draw a control in a frame?

17. Explain how to swap the values contained in two variables named curPrice1 and curPrice2.

EXERCISES

1. In this exercise you will use the If...Then...Else structure.

   Scenario: Woodland School wants an application that the students can use to study the capitals of five states. After selecting a state and its corresponding capital, the user will click the Check Answer command button to verify that the capital he or she chose is correct. If the capital is correct, display the word "Correct" in the label control; otherwise, display the word "Incorrect."

   a. Open the lb1 project, which is located in the Tut04 folder on your Student Disk.
   b. Save the form and the project as lb1Done.
   c. Center the form on the screen.
   d. Make the Check Answer button the default command button. Make the California and Denver buttons the default option buttons in their respective groups.
   e. Code the Exit control so that it ends the application.
   f. Code the Print control so that it prints the form with the command buttons showing.
   g. Declare two form-level variables named strCapital and strChoice.
   h. Use the flowcharts shown in Figure 4-54 to code the state and capital option buttons and the Check Answer command button's Click event procedures.

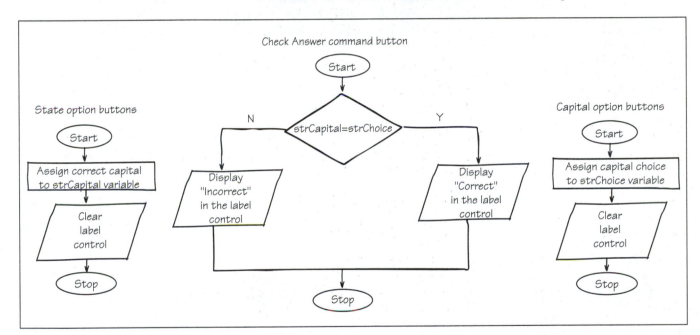

Figure 4-54

   i. Save and run the application.
   j. Test the application by selecting Illinois from the State group and Salem from the Capital group. Click the Check Answer button, then click the Print button.
   k. Test the application again by selecting Wisconsin from the State group and Madison from the Capital group. Click the Check Answer button, then click the Print button.
   l. Click the Exit button to end the application.
   m. Print the application's code.
   n. Submit the printouts from steps j and k, and the code from step m.

2. In this exercise you will open an application that contains check boxes and a frame control. You will use the If...Then...Else structure to code the application.

Scenario: Willow Health Club needs an application that they can use to calculate each member's monthly dues. The basic fee is $80. After the user selects the additional charges, if any, the user will click the Calculate Total button to calculate and display the total additional charge and the total due. The total due is calculated by adding the basic fee to the total additional charge. The individual additional charges are as follows: Tennis, $30 per month; Golf, $25 per month; Racquetball, $20 per month.

a. Open the Lb2 project, which is located in the Tut04 folder on your Student Disk.

b. Save the form and the project as lb2Done in the Tut04 folder on your Student Disk.

c. Make the Calculate Total button the default command button.

d. Center the form on the screen.

e. Draw the flowcharts or write the pseudocode for the application, then code the application.

f. Save and run the application.

g. Test the application by selecting Golf. Click the Calculate Total button, then click the Print button.

h. Test the application again by deselecting Golf, then selecting Tennis and Racquetball. Click the Calculate Total button, then click the Print button.

i. Exit the application, then print the application's code.

j. Submit the printouts from steps g and h, and the code from step i.

LESSON C
objectives

In this lesson you will learn how to:

- Create a static variable
- Use the LoadPicture, MsgBox, and Len functions
- Set the SelStart and SelLength properties
- Code the GotFocus event

Completing the Math Application

Static Variables

To complete the math application, you still need to code the Verify Answer button and the chkDisplay check box. Before doing so, however, you will learn about static variables. A **static variable** is a local variable that retains its value when a procedure ends.

To learn about static variables:

1. Start Visual Basic, if necessary, then open the **Static** (Static.vbp) project, which is located in the Tut04 folder on your Student Disk.

2. **Run,** but don't save, the project.

The static application should count the number of times you press the Count button, but it is not working correctly, as you will see in the next step.

3. Click the **Count** button. The message tells you that you have pressed the Count button one time, which is correct. Now click the **Count** button several more times. Notice that the message still says that you pressed the Count button one time, which is incorrect.

4. Click the **Exit** button to end the application.

5. Open the Count button's Click event procedure. See Figure 4-55.

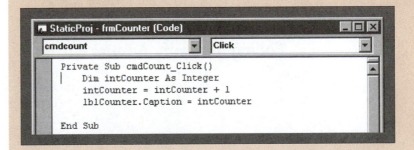

Figure 4-55: Code entered in the Count button's Click event procedure

Each time you click the Count button, the Dim statement in the button's Click event procedure declares and initializes a local variable named intCounter. The procedure then adds 1 to the intCounter variable, whose value it displays in the lblCounter control on the form. When Visual Basic processes the End Sub statement, the intCounter variable is removed from the computer's memory.

In order for this application to work correctly, you need the intCounter variable to remain in memory until the application ends. The way to accomplish this is to declare the local variable as a static variable. When you declare a variable as a static variable, Visual Basic does not remove the variable from memory when the procedure in which it is declared ends; instead, the variable and its value remain in memory until the application ends. You declare a static variable by using the keyword Static, instead of the keyword Dim.

6 Change the `Dim intCounter as Integer` instruction to **Static intCounter as Integer**, then close the Code window.

7 **Run** the application.

8 Click the **Count** button.

The Count button's Click event procedure declares and initializes a static variable named intCounter. It then adds 1 to the intCounter variable and displays a 1 in the lblCounter control on the form. When the End Sub instruction is processed, the Click event procedure ends, but the intCounter variable is not removed from the computer's memory; it remains in memory with its current value, 1.

9 Click the **Count** button again.

This time the Count button's Click event procedure does not declare and initialize the intCounter variable; rather, it simply adds 1 to the existing intCounter variable, giving 2, and displays a 2 in the lblCounter control on the form. When the End Sub instruction is processed, the intCounter variable remains in memory with its current value of 2.

10 Click the **Count** button several times. The message now tells you that you pressed the Count button 3 times, 4 times, 5 times, and so on.

11 Click the **Exit** button to end the application.

Now that you know how to use a static variable, you can finish coding the Math application.

Coding the Verify Answer Button

To complete the Math application, you still need to code the Verify Answer button and the Display summary information check box. You will code the Verify Answer button first.

tip

Although you could also use the Dim statement to declare the intCounter variable as a form-level variable, which will maintain the variable and its value until the application ends, that is not the preferred way. The intCounter variable is not needed by more than one procedure in the form, so it should not be declared as a form-level variable.

To finish coding the Math application:

1   Open the **lbMath** (lblMath.vbp) project that you created in Lesson B. The project is located in the Tut04 folder on your Student Disk. (You do not need to save the static application.)

2   Save the form and the project as **lcMath**.

3   Click the **form's title bar** to select the frmMath form.

According to the TOE chart, shown earlier in Figure 4-43, the Verify Answer button has the following tasks:

- Calculate the correct answer to the math problem.
- Compare the correct answer to the user's answer.
- Display/remove a happy face icon.
- Add 1 to the number of either correct or incorrect responses.
- If the user's answer is incorrect, then prompt the user to "Try again"; otherwise, display a new math problem.
- Display the number of correct and incorrect responses in the lblCorrect and lblIncorrect controls, respectively.

The Click event procedure will use the four local variables shown in Figure 4-56.

Variable's Name	Data Type	Use to store:
intUserAnswer	Integer	the user's answer to the math problem
intCorrectAnswer	Integer	the correct answer to the math problem
intNumCorrrect	Integer	the number of correct responses made by the user
intNumIncorrect	Integer	the number of incorrect responses made by the user

Figure 4-56: Four variables used by the Verify Answer button's Click event procedure

The flowchart for the Verify Answer button's Click event procedure is shown in Figure 4-57.

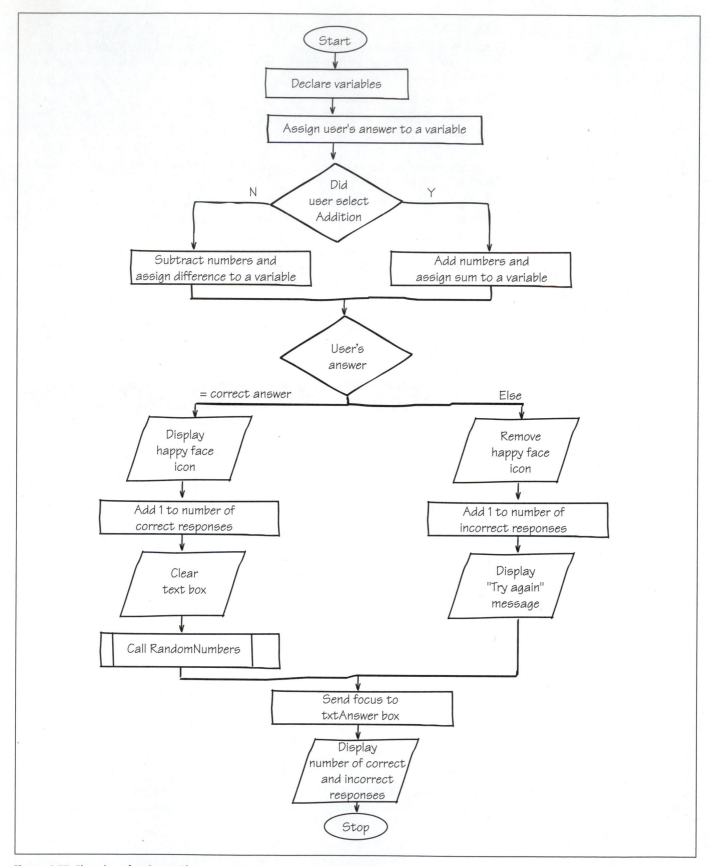

Figure 4-57: Flowchart for the Verify Answer button's Click event procedure

Each time the Verify Answer button is clicked, you want its Click event procedure to declare and initialize the intUserAnswer and intCorrectAnswer variables; you will declare those two variables with the Dim statement. You do not, however, want the Click event procedure to declare and initialize the intNumCorrect and intNumIncorrect variables each time the Verify Answer button is clicked; instead, you want the value of these variables to remain in memory until the application ends. Therefore, you will need to declare the intNumCorrect and intNumIncorrect variables as static variables.

To code the Verify Answer button's Click event procedure:

1   Open the **Verify Answer** button's Click event, then maximize the Code window. Enter the Dim and Static statements shown in Figure 4-58.

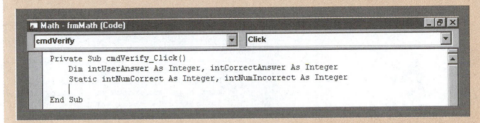

Figure 4-58: Dim and Static statements entered in the Verify Answer button's Click event procedure

Next you will assign the user's response, which he or she entered in the txtAnswer control, to the intUserAnswer variable.

2   Type **intuseranswer = val(txtanswer.text)** and press the **Enter** key.

You now need to determine which of the option buttons in the Operations frame is selected—the Addition button or the Subtraction button—in order to calculate the correct answer to the math problem appearing in the interface. You can determine if an option button is selected by looking at its Value property. If an option button is selected, then its Value property contains the Boolean value True; otherwise, its Value property contains the Boolean value False. You can use either the If...Then...Else selection structure or the Case selection structure to determine which option button is selected. You will use the If...Then...Else structure.

3   Enter the selection structure shown in Figure 4-59.

enter the selection structure

```
Math - frmMath (Code)                                          _ |8|X
cmdVerify                        ▼   Click                             ▼
    Private Sub cmdVerify_Click()
        Dim intUserAnswer As Integer, intCorrectAnswer As Integer
        Static intNumCorrect As Integer, intNumIncorrect As Integer
        intUserAnswer = Val(txtAnswer.Text)
        If optAdd.Value = True Then
            intCorrectAnswer = intNum1 + intNum2
        Else
            intCorrectAnswer = intNum1 - intNum2
        End If
    |
    End Sub
```

Figure 4-59: Selection structure entered in the Verify Answer button's Click event procedure

The next step is to determine if the user entered the correct answer. You can use either the If...Then...Else selection structure or the Case selection structure to do so. Just for practice, this time you will use the Case selection structure.

The first possibility is that the user entered the correct answer—in other words, the value in the intUserAnswer variable is equal to the value in the intCorrectAnswer variable. According to the flowchart, when the user enters the correct answer, you should assign the happy face icon, which is located at the bottom of the form, to the imgIcon control. You then need to add 1 to the number of correct responses, which is stored in the intNumCorrect variable. Lastly, you need to clear the txtAnswer text box so the user can enter the answer to the next problem, then display a new problem for the user.

4 Enter the additional code shown in Figure 4-60, then position the insertion point as shown in the figure.

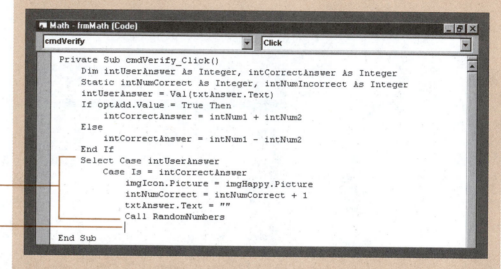

enter this code

position insertion
point here

```
Math - frmMath (Code)

cmdVerify                              Click

Private Sub cmdVerify_Click()
    Dim intUserAnswer As Integer, intCorrectAnswer As Integer
    Static intNumCorrect As Integer, intNumIncorrect As Integer
    intUserAnswer = Val(txtAnswer.Text)
    If optAdd.Value = True Then
        intCorrectAnswer = intNum1 + intNum2
    Else
        intCorrectAnswer = intNum1 - intNum2
    End If
    Select Case intUserAnswer
        Case Is = intCorrectAnswer
            imgIcon.Picture = imgHappy.Picture
            intNumCorrect = intNumCorrect + 1
            txtAnswer.Text = ""
            Call RandomNumbers
            |
End Sub
```

Figure 4-60: Current status of the Verify Answer button's Click event procedure

You can now code the Case Else part of the structure.

5 With the insertion point positioned as shown in Figure 4-60, press the **Backspace** key, then type **case else** and press the **Enter** key.

If the user's answer is incorrect, then you want to remove the happy face icon from the imgIcon control, add the number 1 to the number of incorrect responses, and display a "Try again" message. You can use Visual Basic's LoadPicture function to remove the happy face icon, and Visual Basic's MsgBox function to display the "Try again" message.

The LoadPicture Function

You can use the **LoadPicture function** to display a graphic in a form, picture box control, or image control; you can also use it to clear a graphic from those objects. The syntax of the LoadPicture function is **LoadPicture**([*stringexpression*]), where *stringexpression* represents the location and name of a graphics file; the *stringexpression* should be enclosed in quotation marks. For example, assume that the misc01.ico graphics file is located in the Program Files\Microsoft Visual Studio\ Common\Graphics\Icons\Misc folder on the local hard drive. You would use the following instruction to display the icon in the imgIcon control: `imgIcon.Picture = LoadPicture ("c:\Program Files\Microsoft Visual Studio\Common\Graphics\Icons\Misc\Misc01.ico").`

If you omit the *stringexpression* from the LoadPicture function, the function clears the existing picture from the image control. In this application, for example, you can use the `imgIcon.Picture = LoadPicture()` instruction to remove the happy face icon from the imgIcon image control.

To continue coding the Verify Answer button:

1   Press the **Tab** key, then type **imgicon.picture = loadpicture**() and press the **Enter** key.

Now add the number 1 to the number of incorrect responses. Recall that the number of incorrect responses is stored in the intNumIncorrect variable.

2   Type **intnumincorrect = intnumincorrect + 1** and press the **Enter** key.

Recall that the application should allow the student to answer the problem as many times as necessary. You can use Visual Basic's MsgBox function to prompt the user to answer the problem again. At this point you will close the Code window; you will return to complete the Verify Answer button's Click event procedure after learning about the MsgBox function.

3   Close the Code window.

The MsgBox Function

The **MsgBox function** displays one of Visual Basic's predefined dialog boxes. The dialog box contains a message, one or more command buttons, and an optional icon. After displaying the dialog box, the MsgBox function waits for the user to choose a button. It then returns a value that indicates which button the user chose. To learn more about the MsgBox function, you will view its Help screen, the top portion of which is shown in Figure 4-61.

Syntax

MsgBox Function

<u>See Also</u>   <u>Examples</u>   <u>Specifics</u>

Displays a message in a dialog box, waits for the user to click a button, and returns an **Integer** indicating which button the user clicked.

Syntax

MsgBox(*prompt*[, *buttons*] [, *title*] [, *helpfile*, *context*])

The **MsgBox** function syntax has these <u>named arguments</u>:

Part	Description
prompt	Required. <u>String expression</u> displayed as the message in the dialog box. The maximum length of ***prompt*** is approximately 1024 characters, depending on the width of the characters used. If ***prompt*** consists of more than one line, you can separate the lines using a carriage return character (**Chr**(13)), a linefeed character (**Chr**(10)), or carriage return – linefeed character combination (**Chr**(13) & **Chr**(10)) between each line.
buttons	Optional. <u>Numeric expression</u> that is the sum of values specifying the number and type of buttons to display, the icon style to use, the identity of the default button, and the modality of the message box. If omitted, the default value for ***buttons*** is 0.
title	Optional. String expression displayed in the title bar of the dialog box. If you omit ***title***, the application name is placed in the title bar.
helpfile	Optional. String expression that identifies the Help file to use to provide context-sensitive Help for the dialog box. If ***helpfile*** is provided, ***context*** must also be provided.
context	Optional. Numeric expression that is the Help context number assigned to the appropriate Help topic by the Help author. If ***context*** is provided, ***helpfile*** must also be provided.

Figure 4-61: MsgBox function's Help screen

The syntax of the MsgBox function is **MsgBox**(*prompt*[, *buttons*][, *title*] [, *helpfile*, *context*]). *Prompt* is the message you want displayed in the dialog box; the message should be enclosed in quotation marks and entered using sentence capitalization. *Buttons* is an optional numeric expression that represents the sum of values specifying the number and type of buttons to display, the icon style to use, the identity of the default button, and the dialog box's modality. If you omit the *buttons* argument, the dialog box contains an OK button only. *Title* is a string expression displayed in the title bar of the dialog box. It is customary in Windows applications to display the application's name in the title bar; if you omit the *title* argument in the MsgBox function, the application's name appears, automatically, in the title bar. If you want to use a different string expression for the title argument, be sure to enter the string expression using book title capitalization. You use the optional *helpfile* and *context* arguments to provide context-sensitive help for the dialog box. Take a closer look at the valid settings for the *buttons* argument, which are shown in Figure 4-62.

Constant	Value	Description
vbOKOnly	0	Display **OK** button only.
vbOKCancel	1	Display **OK** and **Cancel** buttons.
vbAbortRetryIgnore	2	Display **Abort**, **Retry**, and **Ignore** buttons.
vbYesNoCancel	3	Display **Yes**, **No**, and **Cancel** buttons.
vbYesNo	4	Display **Yes** and **No** buttons.
vbRetryCancel	5	Display **Retry** and **Cancel** buttons.
vbCritical	16	Display **Critical Message** icon.
vbQuestion	32	Display **Warning Query** icon.
vbExclamation	48	Display **Warning Message** icon.
vbInformation	64	Display **Information Message** icon.
vbDefaultButton1	0	First button is default.
vbDefaultButton2	256	Second button is default.
vbDefaultButton3	512	Third button is default.
vbDefaultButton4	768	Fourth button is default.
vbApplicationModal	0	Application modal; the user must respond to the message box before continuing work in the current application.
vbSystemModal	4096	System modal; all applications are suspended until the user responds to the message box.

Group 1 → (vbOKOnly through vbRetryCancel)
Group 2 → (vbCritical through vbInformation)
Group 3 → (vbDefaultButton1 through vbDefaultButton4)
Group 4 → (vbApplicationModal, vbSystemModal)

Figure 4-62: MsgBox function's Help screen showing four groups of settings for the button's argument

tip

Below the vbSystemModal constant in the MsgBox function's Help screen, you will find four additional constants that can be included in the *buttons* argument: vbMsgBoxHelp Button, vbMsgBoxSetFore ground, vbMsgBoxRight, and vbMsgBoxRtl Reading. The use of these constants are beyond the scope of this book.

Notice that each argument setting has a constant and a numeric value associated with it. When entering the *buttons* argument in the MsgBox function, you can use either the setting's value or its constant. Using the constant makes the program more self-documenting, so it is the preferred way of entering the *buttons* argument.

The settings for the *buttons* argument are split into four groups. The first group controls the number and types of buttons displayed in the dialog box. The vbOKOnly setting, for example, displays one button, the OK button. The vbYesNoCancel setting, on the other hand, displays three buttons—Yes, No, and Cancel.

The second group of settings controls the style of the icon displayed in the dialog box. The vbCritical setting, for example, displays the Critical Message icon ⊗, which alerts the user to a serious problem that requires intervention or correction before the application can continue. You would use the Critical Message icon in a dialog box that alerts the user that the disk in the disk drive is write-protected.

The vbQuestion setting displays the Warning Query icon ⍰; you would use this icon in a Windows 3.1 dialog box that contains a message phrased as a question. To avoid confusion, the Warning Query icon is not used, typically, in a Windows 95 application because the question mark icon in Windows 95 is the Help icon.

The vbExclamation setting displays the Warning Message icon ⚠. You use the Warning Message icon to alert the user that he or she must first make a decision and then enter a response before the application can continue. The message to the user can be phrased as a question—for example, "Do you want to continue?"

The vbInformation setting displays the Information Message icon ⓘ, which you use in a dialog box whose purpose is to display information only. The dialog box should display the OK button only; it should not offer the user any choices. The user acknowledges the informational message by clicking the OK button. This is the proper icon to use for the "Try again" message in the Math application.

The third group of settings for the *buttons* argument identifies the default button, which is the button that is chosen automatically when the user presses the Enter key. The default button should be the one that represents the user's most likely action, as long as that action is not destructive.

The fourth group controls the dialog box's modality, which can be either application modal or system modal. **Application modal**, the default modality, means that the user must respond to the message in the dialog box before he or she can continue working in the current application; however, the user can still access other applications either using Alt-Tab or clicking the application button on the Windows 95 taskbar. When a dialog box is **system modal**, on the other hand, all applications are suspended until the user responds to the message.

The *buttons* argument is the sum of one of the numbers from each group. The default value for the *buttons* argument is 0 (vbOKOnly + vbDefaultButton1 + vbApplicationModal), which means that the dialog box will display an OK button only; it will not contain an icon. The OK button will be the default button and the dialog box will be application modal. Now say that you want the dialog box to display Yes and No buttons along with the Warning Message icon. Additionally, you want the No button to be the default button, and you want the dialog box to be application modal. To display a dialog box matching that description, you would enter, as the *buttons* argument, either the expression `vbYesNo + vbExclamation + vbDefaultButton2 + vbApplicationModal`, or the number 308 (4 + 48 + 256 + 0). To make your programs more self-documenting, it is a good practice to enter the expression that contains the constants instead of the numeric value.

Now here's one for you to try. Say that you want the Abort, Retry, and Ignore buttons, with the Critical Message icon, the second button as the default, and the dialog box to be system modal. What expression would you enter as the *buttons* argument? You should enter `vbAbortRetryIgnore + vbCritical + vbDefaultButton2 + vbSystemModal`. (The numeric value you could enter would be 4370, which is 2 + 16 + 256 + 4096.)

GUI Design Tips

MsgBox Function Standards

- Enter the dialog box message using sentence capitalization.
- Display the application's name in the dialog box's title bar. The title bar text should be entered using book title capitalization.
- Display the Critical Message icon ☒ when you want to alert the user of a serious problem that must be corrected before the application can continue.
- Display the Warning Query icon ☒ in a Windows 3.1 dialog box whose message is phrased as a question; don't use the Warning Query icon in a Windows 95 application.
- Display the Warning Message icon ⚠ in a dialog box when you want to alert the user that he or she must first make a decision and then enter a response before the application can continue; you can phrase the message as a question.
- Display the Information Message icon ⓘ in a dialog box that displays an informational message along with an OK button only. The dialog box should not offer any choices to the user.
- The default button in the dialog box should be the one that represents the user's most likely action, as long as that action is not destructive.

The dialog box produced by the MsgBox function remains on the screen until the user selects one of its buttons, at which time the MsgBox function returns a value that represents which button was selected. Figure 4-63 shows the values that correspond to the various buttons.

Return Values

Constant	Value	Description
vbOK	1	OK
vbCancel	2	Cancel
vbAbort	3	Abort
vbRetry	4	Retry
vbIgnore	5	Ignore
vbYes	6	Yes
vbNo	7	No

Figure 4-63: MsgBox function's Help screen showing values returned by the MsgBox function

The Help screen lists the constants and numeric values returned by the MsgBox function. The information returned by the MsgBox function indicates which button the user selected in the dialog box. For example, if the Yes button was selected, the MsgBox function returns the integer 6, which can be referred to as vbYes.

In this application the MsgBox function should display a dialog box that contains a "Try again" message, an OK button, and an Information Message icon, as well as the words "Math Application" in its title bar. The dialog box should be application modal and the first button, which is the only button in the dialog box, should be the default. The correct MsgBox function is `MsgBox("Try again.", vbOKOnly + vbInformation + vbDefaultButton1 + vbApplicationModal, "Math Application")`. To shorten the instruction, which will make it easier to read in the future, you will assign the *buttons* argument, `vbOKOnly + vbInformation + vbDefaultButton1 + vbApplicationModal`, to a constant named conBtns. ("Btns" is short for "buttons.") You will then use the constant instead of the long expression in the MsgBox function—in other words, you will enter the MsgBox function as `MsgBox("Try again.", conBtns, "Math Application")`.

Because the MsgBox function returns a value—an integer that represents which button was selected—you will need to declare a variable in which to store the value. You will declare an Integer variable named intRetVal (for "Returned Value") for this purpose.

To continue coding the Verify Answer button's Click event procedure:

1 Open the Verify Answer button's Click event procedure. Maximize the Code window, then enter the code shown in Figure 4-64. Be sure to declare the intRetVal variable, and enter both the Const statement and the MsgBox function.

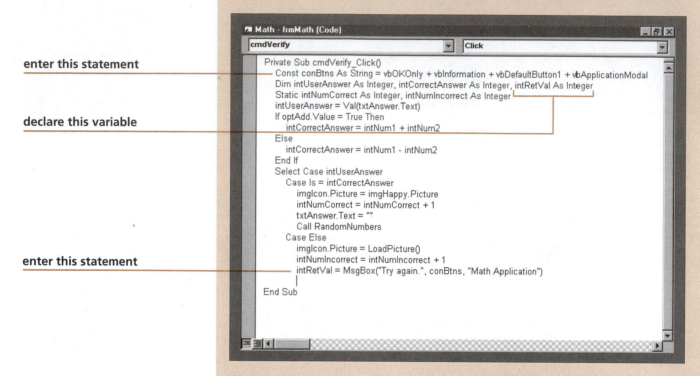

enter this statement

declare this variable

enter this statement

```
Math - frmMath (Code)
cmdVerify                                          Click
    Private Sub cmdVerify_Click()
        Const conBtns As String = vbOKOnly + vbInformation + vbDefaultButton1 + vbApplicationModal
        Dim intUserAnswer As Integer, intCorrectAnswer As Integer, intRetVal As Integer
        Static intNumCorrect As Integer, intNumIncorrect As Integer
        intUserAnswer = Val(txtAnswer.Text)
        If optAdd.Value = True Then
            intCorrectAnswer = intNum1 + intNum2
        Else
            intCorrectAnswer = intNum1 - intNum2
        End If
        Select Case intUserAnswer
            Case Is = intCorrectAnswer
                imgIcon.Picture = imgHappy.Picture
                intNumCorrect = intNumCorrect + 1
                txtAnswer.Text = ""
                Call RandomNumbers
            Case Else
                imgIcon.Picture = LoadPicture()
                intNumIncorrect = intNumIncorrect + 1
                intRetVal = MsgBox("Try again.", conBtns, "Math Application")
    End Sub
```

Figure 4-64: Current status of the Verify Answer button's Click event procedure

You can now end the Select Case statement, then send the focus to the txtAnswer control, and then display the number of correct and incorrect responses in the lblCorrect and lblIncorrect controls, respectively.

2 Enter the additional code shown in Figure 4-65.

enter this code

```
        Case Else
            imgIcon.Picture = LoadPicture()
            intNumIncorrect = intNumIncorrect + 1
            intRetVal = MsgBox("Try again.", conBtns, "Math Application")
        End Select
        txtAnswer.SetFocus
        lblCorrect.Caption = intNumCorrect
        lblIncorrect.Caption = intNumIncorrect
    End Sub
```

Figure 4-65: Additional code entered in the Verify Answer button's Click event procedure

3 Close the Code window, then **save** and **run** the application.

4   Enter a correct answer to the math problem that appears in the interface, then press the **Enter** key. (Recall that the Verify Answer button is the default command button in the interface.) The application displays the happy face icon in the imgIcon control. It also displays the number 1 in the lblCorrect control, clears the txtAnswer text box, and displays a new math problem.

5   Enter an incorrect answer to the math problem appearing in the interface, then press the **Enter** key. The application removes the happy face icon from the imgIcon control, then the MsgBox function displays the dialog box shown in Figure 4-66.

Figure 4-66: MsgBox function's dialog box

6   Press the **Enter** key to remove the dialog box from the screen. The application displays the number 1 in the lblIncorrect control and places the focus in the txtAnswer text box.

Notice that the user will need to press the Backspace key to remove the text in the txtAnswer control before entering another answer. When the focus is sent to a text box that contains text, it is customary in Windows applications to highlight the existing text. By doing so, the new text entered by the user replaces, automatically, the highlighted, or selected, text. You can use Visual Basic's SelStart and SelLength properties to highlight the existing text in a text box.

7   Click the **Exit** button to end the application. Visual Basic returns to the design screen.

The SelStart and SelLength Properties

You will need to use both the SelStart and the SelLength properties to highlight (select) the text in the txtAnswer text box. The **SelStart property** tells Visual Basic where in the text box to position the insertion point—in other words, where to start the text selection; the **SelLength property** tells Visual Basic how many characters to select.

The syntax of the SelStart property is *object*.**SelStart** [= *index*]. *Object* is the name of the control in which the characters are to be selected, and *index* is a number that indicates the position of the insertion point. The first position in the control is position 0, the second is position 1, and so on. The instruction, `txtAnswer.SelStart = 0`, for example, will place the insertion point in position 0—the first position in the text box.

After positioning the insertion point in its proper place, you can use the SelLength property to select (highlight) the text in the control. The syntax of the SelLength property is *object*.**SelLength** [= *number*], where *object* is the name of the control in which the text is to be selected and *number* indicates the number of characters to select. The `txtAnswer.SelLength = 5` instruction, for example, will select five characters, beginning with the character to the immediate right of the insertion point.

But how do you select all of the text in a text box when you don't know precisely how many characters it contains? In those cases, you can use the Len function to determine the number of characters for you.

The Len Function

You can use the Len (short for "length") function to determine the number of characters contained in a text box. The syntax of the Len function is **Len**(*string*). The `Len(txtAnswer.Text)` instruction, for example, returns the number of characters contained in the Text property of the txtAnswer control—in other words, if the txtAnswer control contains two characters, the function returns the number 2. To select the number of characters contained in the txtAnswer text box, you would use the instruction, `txtAnswer.SelLength=Len(txtAnswer.Text)`.

To continue coding the Verify Answer button's Click event procedure:

1 Open the Verify Answer button's Code window to view its Click event procedure, then maximize the Code window. Enter the two instructions shown in Figure 4-67.

enter these two instructions

```
Math - frmMath [Code]                                          _ |8|X
cmdVerify                          ▼    Click                            ▼
    Private Sub cmdVerify_Click()
        Const conBtns As String = vbOKOnly + vbInformation + vbDefaultButton1 + vbApplicationModal
        Dim intUserAnswer As Integer, intCorrectAnswer As Integer, intRetVal As Integer
        Static intNumCorrect As Integer, intNumIncorrect As Integer
        intUserAnswer = Val(txtAnswer.Text)
        If optAdd.Value = True Then
            intCorrectAnswer = intNum1 + intNum2
        Else
            intCorrectAnswer = intNum1 - intNum2
        End If
        Select Case intUserAnswer
            Case Is = intCorrectAnswer
                imgIcon.Picture = imgHappy.Picture
                intNumCorrect = intNumCorrect + 1
                txtAnswer.Text = ""
                Call RandomNumbers
            Case Else
                imgIcon.Picture = LoadPicture()
                intNumIncorrect = intNumIncorrect + 1
                intRetVal = MsgBox("Try again.", conBtns, "Math Application")
                txtAnswer.SelStart = 0
                txtAnswer.SelLength = Len(txtAnswer.Text)
        End Select
        txtAnswer.SetFocus
        lblCorrect.Caption = intNumCorrect
        lblIncorrect.Caption = intNumIncorrect
    End Sub
```

Figure 4-67: Values assigned to the SelStart and SelLength properties

2 Close the Code window, then **save** and **run** the application.

3 Enter an incorrect response to the math problem appearing in the interface, then press the **Enter** key. When the "Try again." message appears, press the **Enter** key to remove the dialog box.

The application places the focus in the txtAnswer control. This time, however, the existing text is highlighted.

4   Enter a correct response to the math problem appearing in the interface, then press the **Enter** key.

Notice that you did not need to remove the existing text before entering the new text; the new text replaces the highlighted text in the txtAnswer control.

5   Enter an incorrect response to the math problem, but this time don't press the Enter key. Instead, press the **Tab** key to send the focus to the Verify Answer button, then press the **Tab** key five more times to send the focus back to the txtAnswer text box.

Notice that the existing text is not highlighted when the user uses the Tab key to send the focus to the txtAnswer text box. As mentioned earlier, it is customary in Windows applications to highlight the existing text when a text box receives the focus. You can fix this problem by entering, in the txtAnswer control's GotFocus event, the same SelStart and SelLength instructions that you entered in the Verify Answer button's Click event.

6   Click the **Exit** button to end the application.

The GotFocus Event

As its name implies, the **GotFocus event** occurs when an object receives the focus, either by user action, such as tabbing to or clicking the object, or by changing the focus in code using the SetFocus method.

GUI
Design Tips

Highlighting Existing Text

• It is customary in Windows applications to highlight, or select, the existing text in a text box when the text box receives the focus.

To code the txtAnswer control's GotFocus event:

1   Open the txtAnswer control's Code window. The txtAnswer control's Change event appears. Click the **Procedure** list arrow, then click **GotFocus** in the list. The txtAnswer control's GotFocus event procedure appears.

2   Press the **Tab** key. Type **txtanswer.selstart = 0** and press the **Enter** key, then type **txtanswer.sellength = len(txtanswer.text)** and press the **Enter** key.

3   Close the Code window, then **save** and **run** the application.

4   Enter an incorrect response to the math problem. Press the **Tab** key to send the focus to the Verify Answer button, then press **Shift + Tab** to send the focus back to the txtAnswer text box. Because you entered the SelStart and SelLength instructions in the txtAnswer control's GotFocus event, the existing text is highlighted when the text box receives the focus.

5   Click the **Exit** button to end the application.

The next control you will code is the Display summary information check box.

Coding the Display Summary Information Check Box

When the interface first appears, the Display summary information check box should be unchecked (not selected) and the fraInfo frame control should not be visible in the user interface. When the user selects the Display summary information check box, the application should display the fraInfo frame control. When the user deselects the Display summary information check box, the application should hide the fraInfo frame control.

Recall that option buttons also have a Value property. If an option button is selected, however, its Value property contains the Boolean value True; otherwise, its Value property contains the Boolean value False.

To code the Display summary information check box:

1 Click the **Display summary information** check box, then click **Value** in the Properties list.

The Value property indicates the status of the check box. If the check box is selected (checked), then its Value property contains the number 1. If the check box is not selected (unchecked), which is the default, then its Value property contains the number 0. The Value property of the Display summary information check box is 0; that means that the Display summary information check box will be unchecked when the interface first appears.

2 Use the Object box, located in the Properties window, to select the **fraInfo** frame control. Sizing handles appear around the frame. Set the fraInfo control's Visible property to **False** so that the frame control will not be visible when the interface first appears.

3 Click the **form** to select it, then double-click the **Display summary information** check box to open its Code window. The Click event procedure, which is the most common event for a check box, opens.

Each time the check box is clicked, its Click event must first determine if the user is either selecting (checking) the check box or deselecting (unchecking) it. If the user is checking the check box, then the Click event should display the fraInfo frame; otherwise, which means the user is unchecking the check box, the Click event should hide the fraInfo frame. You can determine if a check box is either unchecked or checked by comparing its Value property with 0 and 1, respectively. Because it is difficult to remember that 0 means unchecked and 1 means checked, you will use the Object Browser dialog box, which you learned about in Tutorial 3, to search for the constants pertaining to a check box.

4 Click the **Object Browser** button on the toolbar. In the Object Browser dialog box, type **checkbox** in the Search text box and press the **Enter** key. Click **VBRUN CheckBoxConstant** in the Search Results list.

The 'Members of CheckBoxConstants' list shows three constants associated with a check box: vbChecked, vbGrayed, and vbUnchecked. You will use the vbChecked constant in the check box's Click event procedure.

5 Close the Object Browser window, then enter the code shown in Figure 4-68.

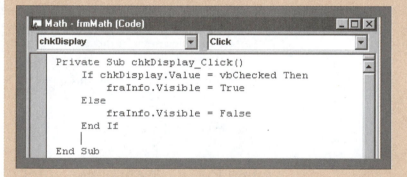

```
Private Sub chkDisplay_Click()
    If chkDisplay.Value = vbChecked Then
        fraInfo.Visible = True
    Else
        fraInfo.Visible = False
    End If

End Sub
```

Figure 4-68: Code entered in the Display summary information box's Click event procedure

6 Close the Code window, then **save** and **run** the application.

When the interface appears, notice that the Display summary information check box is unchecked and the fraInfo control is not visible.

You can also select and deselect a check box by pressing the Spacebar when the check box has the focus.

7 Click the **Display summary information** check box to select it. (You can click either the square or the Caption.) The check box's Click event procedure displays the fraInfo frame control.

8 Click the **Display summary information** check box to deselect it. The check box's Click event procedure hides the fraInfo frame control.

9 Click the **Exit** button to end the application.

You have now completed Lesson C. You can take a break or complete the end-of-lesson questions and exercises, or read and complete the Debugging section, which may contain information that will help you when completing the exercises.

SUMMARY

To determine if a check box is checked (selected) or unchecked (not selected):

■ Look at the check box's Value property. If the Value property contains the number 1, then the check box is checked. If the Value property contains the number 0, then the check box is not checked. You can use the constants vbChecked and vbUnchecked in code.

To determine if an option button is selected or unselected:

■ Look at the option button's Value property. If the Value property contains the Boolean value True, then the option button is selected. If the Value property contains the Boolean value False, then the option button is not selected.

To retain a local variable's value when the procedure ends:

■ Declare a static variable in the object's event procedure. Its syntax is **Static** *variablename* [As *datatype*].

To display a graphic in a form, picture box, or image; or to clear a graphic from these objects:

■ Use the LoadPicture function. Its syntax is **LoadPicture**([*stringexpression*]), where *stringexpression* represents the location and name of a graphics file; the *stringexpression* should be enclosed in quotation marks. If you omit the stringexpression, the LoadPicture function clears the graphic from the object.

To display one of Visual Basic's predefined dialog boxes:

■ Use the MsgBox function. Its syntax is **MsgBox**(*prompt*[, *buttons*][, *title*][, *helpfile*, *context*]). The dialog box contains a message, one or more command buttons, and an optional icon. After displaying the dialog box, the MsgBox function waits for the user to choose a button. It then returns a value that indicates which button the user chose.

To select the existing text in a text box:

■ Use the SelStart and SelLength properties, and the Len function. Set the SelStart property to 0, then set the SelLength property to the length (Len) of the text in the text box.

To process code when an object receives the focus:

■ Enter the code in the object's GotFocus event

QUESTIONS

1. If a check box is checked, its Value property is set to _____ .
   a. 0 (zero)
   b. 1 (One)
   c. vbChecked
   d. both a and c
   e. both b and c

2. If an option button is not selected, its Value property is set to _____ .
   a. 0 (zero)
   b. 1 (One)
   c. False
   d. True
   e. Yes

3. A _____ is a local variable that retains its value when a procedure ends.
   a. consistent variable
   b. constant variable
   c. static variable
   d. stationary variable
   e. term variable

4. Which of the following instructions will clear the contents of the imgCalc image control?
   a. Clear.imgCalc
   b. imgCalc.Clear
   c. imgCalc.Picture = LoadPicture
   d. imgCalc.Picture = LoadPicture(Clear)
   e. imgCalc.Picture = LoadPicture()

5. The MsgBox function displays a dialog box that contains _____ .
   a. a message
   b. one or more command buttons
   c. an optional icon
   d. all of the above

6. The MsgBox function's *buttons* argument controls _____ .
   a. the number and types of buttons displayed in the dialog box
   b. the style of the optional icon displayed in the dialog box
   c. the default button
   d. the dialog box's modality
   e. all of the above

7. You use the _____ icon in the MsgBox function's dialog box to alert the user to a serious problem that requires intervention or correction before the application can continue.
   a. Critical Message ⊠
   b. Warning Message ⚠
   c. Information Message ⓘ

8. You use the _____ icon in the MsgBox function's dialog box to alert the user that he or she must first make a decision and then enter a response before the application can continue.
   a. Critical Message ⊠
   b. Warning Message ⚠
   c. Information Message ⓘ

9. You use the _____ icon in the MsgBox function's dialog box when the message in the dialog box is for informational purposes only.
   a. Critical Message ⊗
   b. Warning Message ⚠
   c. Information Message ⓘ

10. When a dialog box is _____ , the user can still access other applications by either using Alt + Tab or clicking the application button on the Windows 95 taskbar.
   a. application modal
   b. consistent modal
   c. system modal
   d. user modal

11. When a dialog box is _____ , the user cannot access other applications until he or she responds to the message in the dialog box.
   a. application modal
   b. consistent modal
   c. system modal
   d. user modal

12. Which of the following instructions will position the insertion point at the beginning of a text box named txtName?
   a. txtName.SelBegin = 0
   b. txtName.SelBegin = 1
   c. txtName.SelLength = 0
   d. txtName.SelStart = 0
   e. txtName.SelStart = 1

13. Assume that the insertion point is positioned at the beginning of the txtName text box. Which of the following instructions will select the contents of the txtName text box?
   a. txtName.SelAll = txtName.Text
   b. txtName.SelAll = Len(txtName.Text)
   c. txtName.SelLen = Length(txtName.Text)
   d. txtName.SelLength = txtName.Text
   e. txtName.SelLength = Len(txtName.Text)

14. To select the existing text when a text box receives the focus, enter the appropriate code in the text box's _____ event.
   a. Focus
   b. GotFocus
   c. ReceiveFocus
   d. Select
   e. SelectFocus

E X E R C I S E S

NOTE: The following list shows the GUI design and programming guidelines you have learned so far. You can use this list to verify that the applications you create in the following exercises adhere to the standards outlined in the book.

- Information should flow either vertically or horizontally, with the most important information always located in the upper-left corner of the screen.

- Maintain a consistent margin of two or three dots from the edge of the window.

- Related controls should be grouped together using either white space or a frame.

- Position related controls on succeeding dots.

- Command buttons should either be centered along the bottom of the screen or stacked in either the upper-right or lower-right corner.

- If the command buttons are centered along the bottom of the screen, then each button should be the same height; their widths, however, may vary.

- If the command buttons are stacked in either the upper-right or lower-right corner of the screen, then each button should be the same height and the same width.

- Use no more than six command buttons on a screen.

- The most commonly used command button should be placed first.

- Command button captions should:
  - be meaningful
  - be from one to three words
  - appear on one line
  - be entered using book title capitalization

- Use labels to identify the controls in the interface.

- Identifying labels should:
  - be from one to three words
  - appear on one line
  - be aligned by their left borders
  - be positioned either above or to the left of the control that they identify
  - end with a colon (:)
  - be entered using sentence capitalization
  - have their BackStyle property set to 0-Transparent
  - have their BorderStyle property set to 0-None

- Labels that display program output (for example, the results of calculations):
  - should have their BorderStyle set to 1-Fixed Single
  - should have their Appearance property set to 0-Flat
  - can have their BackStyle property set to either 0-Transparent or 1-Opaque

- Align labels and controls to minimize the number of different margins.

- If you use a graphic in the interface, use a small one and place it in a location that will not distract the user.

- Use no more than two different font sizes, which should be 8, 10, or 12 points.

- Use only one font type, which should be a sans serif font, in the interface.

- Avoid using italics and underlining.

- Use either white, off-white, light gray, pale blue, or pale yellow for an application's background, and black for the text.

- Use color sparingly and don't use it as the only means of identification for an element in the interface.

- Set each control's TabIndex property to a number that represents the order in which you want that control to receive the focus (begin with 0).

- A text box's TabIndex value should be one more than the TabIndex value of its identifying label.

- Lock the controls in place on the form.

- Assign a unique access key to each essential element of the interface (text boxes, command buttons, and so on).

- Document the program internally.

- Enter the Option Explicit statement in the General Declaration section of every form and module.

- Use variables to control the preciseness of numbers in the interface.

- Use the Val function on Text and Caption properties, and when assigning the result of the InputBox function to a numeric variable.

- Set the form's BorderStyle, MinButton, MaxButton, and ControlBox properties appropriately:

  - Splash screens should not have a Minimize, Maximize, or Close button, and their borders should not be sizable.

  - Forms that are acting as dialog boxes should have a BorderStyle property of 3-Fixed Dialog.

  - Forms other than splash screens and dialog boxes should always have a Minimize button and a Close button, but you can choose to disable the Maximize button.

  - Forms other than splash screens and dialog boxes typically have a BorderStyle property setting of either 1-Fixed Single or 2-Sizable.

- Test the application with both valid and invalid data (test the application without entering any data; also test it by entering letters where numbers are expected).

- In the InputBox function, use sentence capitalization for the *prompt*, and book title capitalization for the *title*.

- Center a form by including the appropriate formulas in the form's Load event.

- Display an hourglass or an arrow and an hourglass if a procedure will take a long period of time.

- Remove excess code from the application.

- Option buttons:

  - use a minimum of two and a maximum of seven in an interface
  - use sentence capitalization for the caption
  - use a frame control to create separate groups of option buttons
  - select a default button in each group

- Use sentence capitalization for a frame control's caption.

- Use sentence capitalization for a check box's caption.

- MsgBox functions:

  - use sentence capitalization for the message
  - display the application's name in the title bar, using book title capitalization
  - display the appropriate icon
  - The default button should be one that represents the user's most likely action, as long as that action is not destructive.

- Use the SelStart and SelLength properties, as well as the Len function, to highlight (select) the existing text when a text box receives the focus.

1. In this exercise you will use the Randomize statement, the Rnd function, and the Int function.

   Scenario: Jacques Cousard has been playing the lotto for four years and has yet to win any money. He wants an application that will select the six lotto numbers for him. Each lotto number can range from 1 to 54 only. (An example of six lotto numbers would be: 4, 8, 35, 15, 20, 3.)

   a. Create a user interface that will display the six lotto numbers. (Read the Note at the beginning of the Exercises section.) Place each lotto number in a separate label control. In the user interface, be sure to include a Print button, which will print the interface without the command buttons showing, and an Exit button.

   b. Save the form and the project as lc1Done in the Tut04 folder on your Student Disk.

   c. Run the application. Display the six lotto numbers, then click the Print button. (For now, do not worry if the lotto numbers are not unique. You will learn how to display unique numbers in Tutorial 10, which covers arrays.) Display another six lotto numbers, then click the Print button.

   d. Click the Exit button to end the application, then print the application's code.

   e. Submit the two printouts from step c and the code from step d.

2. In this exercise you will practice with the Case selection structure.

   Scenario: Expand the Math application to include multiplication and division.

   a. Open the lcMath application that you created in Lesson C.

   b. Save the form and the project as lc2Done in the Tut04 folder on your Student Disk.

   c. Add two image controls to the interface. Position the image controls at the bottom of the form. Name the image controls imgMultiply and imgDivide. Set the Picture property of the imgMultiply control to display the misc20 icon (a multiplication sign), then set the Picture property of the imgDivide control to display the misc21 icon (a division sign). Recall that the icon files are typically located in the Program Files\Microsoft Visual Studio\Common\Graphics\Icons folder, which is located on either the local hard drive or the network drive.

   d. Change the application's variables from Integer to Single. Be sure to change the variables' names appropriately.

   e. Add two option buttons to the Operations frame. Name the option buttons optMultiply and optDivide. Set the optMultiply button's Caption property to Multiplication. Set the optDivide button's Caption property to Division. The new option buttons should call the RandomNumbers user-defined sub procedure, then display the appropriate icon in the imgOperator control.

   f. Open the Verify Answer button's Click event procedure. Currently, the Code window contains an If...Then...Else statement that determines which of the Operations buttons—either Addition or Subtraction—is selected, then calculates the correct answer to the math problem. Change the If...Then...Else statement to a Select Case...End Select statement that determines which of the Operations buttons—either Addition, Subtraction, Multiplication, or Division—is selected, then calculates the correct answer to the math problem. *Hint:* The *testexpression* in a Select Case statement can be a Boolean value.

   g. Open the RandomNumbers procedure. If the user selects the Division option button, then swap the first and second numbers when the second number is greater than the first number.

   h. Save and run the application. Test the application to be sure that it is working correctly, then print the application's code.

   i. Submit the code from step h.

3. In this exercise you will practice with option buttons, check boxes, a frame control, and the MsgBox function.

   Scenario: Ferris Seminars runs computer seminars. The owner of Ferris Seminars wants an application that the registration clerks can use to calculate the registration fee for each customer. Many of Ferris Seminars' customers are companies that register more than one person for a seminar. The registration clerk will need to enter the number registered for the seminar, then select either the Seminar 1 option button or the Seminar 2 option button. If a company is entitled to a 10% discount, the clerk will need to click the 10% discount check box. After the selections are made, the clerk will click the Calculate Total Due command button to calculate the total registration fee. Seminar 1 is $100 per person, and Seminar 2 is $120 per person.

a. Open the lc3 (lc3.vbp) project, which is located in the Tut04 folder on your Student Disk. (Read the Note at the beginning of the Exercises section.)

b. Save the form and the project as lc3Done in the Tut04 folder on your Student Disk.

c. Be sure to center the form on the screen, code the Exit button, and code the Print button. The Print button should print the interface without the command buttons and its surrounding frame showing. (Remember that the frame and its controls are treated as one unit.)

d. Draw the flowcharts or write the pseudocode for the option buttons, the check box, and the Calculate Total Due command button. Use your flowcharts or pseudocode to code the application. Use the MsgBox function to display an appropriate message if the user enters a negative number.

e. Save and run the application.

f. To test the application, enter 3 as the number registered, then select the Seminar 2 button. Click the Calculate Total Due button, then click the Print button.

g. Test the application again by entering 5 in the text box. Select the Seminar 1 button and the 10% discount check box. Click the Calculate Total Due button, then click the Print button.

h. Test the application again by entering a −4 as the number registered, then click the Calculate Total Due button. Remove the MsgBox function's dialog box.

i. Exit the application, then print the application's code.

j. Submit the printouts from steps f and g, and the code from step i.

4. In this application you will practice with the If...Then...Else, Select Case...End Select, and MsgBox function.

Scenario: Jacob Heaters Inc. wants an application that the clerks can use to calculate the total amount due on an order. The clerk will need to enter the number of units ordered. The application should calculate the total amount due by multiplying the number of units by the price per unit. The price per unit depends on how many units are ordered, as follows:

Number of units	Price per unit
1 – 4	$ 10
5 – 10	9
11 and over	7

a. Create an appropriate user interface. (Read the Note at the beginning of the Exercises section.) Be sure to include a Print button, which will print the interface without any command buttons showing, and an Exit button. Also be sure to center the form on the screen.

b. Save the form and the project as lc4Done in the Tut04 folder on your Student Disk.

c. Code the application using the If...Then...Else statement. Use the MsgBox function to display an appropriate message if the user enters a 0 or a negative number as the number of units.

d. Save and run the application.

e. To test the application, enter 10 as the number of units ordered, then calculate the total amount due, and then print the interface.

f. Test the application again by entering 15 as the number of units ordered. Calculate the total amount due, then print the interface.

g. Test the application again by entering −2 as the number of units ordered. Remove the MsgBox function's dialog box.

h. Click the Exit button to end the application, then print the application's code.

i. Change the If...Then...Else statement that calculates the price per unit to a Select Case...End Select statement.

j. Save and run the application. To test the application, enter 6 as the number of units ordered, then calculate the total amount due, and then print the interface.

k. Test the application again by entering 11 as the number of units ordered. Calculate the total amount due, then print the interface.

l. Test the application again by entering −4 as the number of units ordered. Remove the MsgBox function's dialog box.

m. Click the Exit button to end the application, then print the application's code.

n. Submit the printouts from steps e, f, j, and k. Also submit the code from steps h and m.

5. In this exercise you will practice with the Select Case...End Select statement and the MsgBox function.

Scenario: Flowers Forever wants an application that the clerks can use to calculate each salesperson's annual bonus. The clerk will need to enter the sales. The application should calculate the bonus based on the amount of sales, as follows:

Amount of sales	Bonus
0 – 3000.99 $ 0	
3001 – 5000.99	50
5001 – 9999.99	100
10000 and over	250

a. Create an appropriate user interface. (Read the Note at the beginning of the Exercises section.) Be sure to include a Print button, which will print the interface without any command buttons showing, and an Exit button. Also be sure to center the form on the screen.

b. Save the form and the project as lc5Done in the Tut04 folder on your Student Disk.

c. Code the application using the Select Case statement. Use the MsgBox function to display an appropriate message if the user enters a negative sales amount.

d. Save and run the application.

e. To test the application, enter −90 as the sales, then calculate the bonus. Remove the MsgBox function's dialog box.

f. Test the application again by entering 3001 as the sales. Calculate the bonus, then print the interface.

g. Test the application again by entering 9000 as the sales. Calculate the bonus, then print the interface.

h. Test the application again by entering 20500 as the sales. Calculate the bonus, then print the interface.

i. Click the Exit button to end the application, then print the application's code.

j. Submit the printouts from steps f, g, and h. Also submit the code from step i.

Exercises 6 through 12 are Discovery Exercises, which allow you to both "discover" the solutions to problems on your own and to experiment with material that is not covered in the tutorial.

discovery ▶

6. In this exercise you will practice with the Select Case...End Select statement, string data, and the MsgBox function.

Scenario: Western Veterinarians wants an application that their receptionist can use to look up the doctor's fee for performing a specific medical procedure. The receptionist will need to enter a two-letter code that represents the procedure. The application should then display the doctor's fee. The two-letter codes are as follows:

Code	Procedure	Fee
TC	Teeth Cleaning	$50
RV	Rabies Vaccination	15
OS	Other Shots	5
HW	Heartworm Test	15
FC	Fecal Check	5
OV	Office Visit	15
Other Codes		Invalid Entry (use the MsgBox function.)

a. Create an appropriate user interface. (Read the Note at the beginning of the Exercises section.) Be sure to include a Print button, which will print the user interface without the command buttons showing, and an Exit button.

b. Save the form and the project as lc6Done in the Tut04 folder on your Student Disk.

c. Plan the application's code using either a flowchart or pseudocode, then code the application using the Select Case...End Select statement.

d. Save and run the application.

e. Test the application by entering RR. Remove the MsgBox function's dialog box.

f. Test the application again by entering TC. Display the fee, then print the interface.

g. Test the application again by entering OS. Display the fee, then print interface.

h. Exit the application, then print the application's code.

i. Submit the printouts from steps f and g, and the code from step h.

discovery ▶ 7. In this exercise you will practice with the selection structure and the MsgBox function.

Scenario: Marine Packing Company wants an application that the order department can use to calculate the price of an order. The order clerks will need to enter the number of units ordered, and whether the customer is a retailer or a wholesaler. The application should calculate the total due. The price per unit depends on both the customer type (wholesaler or retailer) and the number of units ordered, as follows:

Wholesaler:		Retailer:	
Number of units	Price per unit	Number of units	Price per unit
1 – 4	$ 10	1 – 3	$ 15
5 and over	9	4 – 8	14
		9 and over	12

a. Create an appropriate user interface. (Read the Note at the beginning of the Exercises section.) Be sure to include a Print button, which will print the user interface without the command buttons showing, and an Exit button.

b. Save the form and the project as lc7Done in the Tut04 folder on your Student Disk.

c. Plan the application's code using either a flowchart or pseudocode, then code the application. Use the MsgBox function to display an appropriate message when the user enters invalid data.

d. Save and run the application.

e. Test the application by calculating the total due for a retailer that orders 10 units. Print the interface.

f. Test the application by calculating the total due for a retailer that orders 2 units. Print the interface.

g. Test the application again by calculating the total due for a wholesaler that orders 10 units. Print the interface.

h. Test the application again by calculating the total due for a wholesaler ordering 2 units. Print the interface.

i. Test the application again by calculating the total due for a wholesaler ordering −4 units. Remove the MsgBox function's dialog box.

j. Exit the application, then print the application's code.

k. Submit the printouts from steps e, f, g, and h and the code from step j.

discovery ▶ 8. In this exercise, you will learn more about the SetFocus method.

a. Open a new project, if necessary. Add a check box and a text box to the form. Remove the Text1 from the text box's Text property.

b. Enter the `Check1.Value = vbChecked` instruction in the form's Load event. This instruction will select the Check1 check box and trigger its Click event when the form is loaded.

c. Enter the `Text1.SetFocus` instruction in the check box's Click event procedure. When the check box's Click event is triggered, it will send the focus to the Text1 text box.

d. Run, but don't save, the application. Visual Basic displays the error dialog box on the screen. Click the Debug button. Notice that the `Text1.SetFocus` instruction is causing the error.

e. Stop the application, then close the Code window.

f. Use the Help menu to display the SetFocus method's Help window. Use the information in the Help window to fix the application.

g. Run, but don't save, the application. No error message should appear. The check box should be selected and the text box should have the focus.

h. Stop the application. Print the application's code, which you will need to submit. You do not need to save this application.

discovery ▶ 9. In this exercise you will practice entering formulas.

Scenario: Your brother is currently taking a geometry class. He would like you to create an application that he can use to verify his calculations. Specifically, he wants the application to calculate the area of a square, rectangle, parallelogram, circle, and triangle.

a. Create an appropriate interface. (Read the Note at the beginning of the Exercises section.)

b. Save the form and the project as lc9Done in the Tut04 folder on your Student Disk.

c. Save and run the application. Test the application with the following data: square side measurement of 4, rectangle length of 5 and width of 3, parallelogram base of 3 and height of 4, circle radius of 2, triangle base of 4 and height of 3.

d. Write the answers to the calculations on a piece of paper.

e. Exit the application, then print the form and the application's code.

f. Submit the answers from step d and the printout and code from step e.

discovery ▶ 10. In this exercise you will discover the difference between using the Int function and the Fix function.

a. If you have access to the MSDN Library, then use the Help menu to view the Help screens on the Int and Fix functions.

b. Open a new project. Place one command button on the form. Enter the following code in the command button's Click event procedure:

```
Print "Original", "Int", "Fix"
Print 7.4, Int(7.4), Fix(7.4)
Print 7.5, Int(7.5), Fix(7.5)
Print 7.6, Int(7.6), Fix(7.6)
Print -7.4, Int(-7.4), Fix(-7.4)
Print -7.5, Int(-7.5), Fix(-7.5)
Print -7.6, Int(-7.6), Fix(-7.6)
```

c. Close the Code window, then run, but don't save, the application.

d. Click the command button. After viewing the information on the screen, submit your answer to the following question: What is the difference between using the Int function and using the Fix function? Stop the application. You do not need to save this application.

discovery ▶ 11. In this exercise, you will pass information to a user-defined sub procedure.

a. Open the lc11 (lc11.vbp) file, which is located in the Tut04 folder on your Student Disk. The application is similar to the Math application you completed in the tutorial, except it displays addition problems only. If the Level 1 option button is selected, the numbers in the problem will be in the range of 1 through 10. If the Level 2 option button is selected, the numbers will be in the range of 10 through 100.

b. Save the form and project as lc11Done, then print the existing code.

Both Level option buttons will need to call a sub procedure named RandomNumbers and pass it their respective *lowerbound* and *upperbound* information. The Level 1 button, for example, will use the `Call RandomNumbers(1, 10)` statement to invoke the RandomNumbers procedure, passing it a *lowerbound* value of 1 and an *upperbound* value of 10. The RandomNumbers procedure will use this information to generate and display integers in the range of 1 through 10. The Level 2 button, on the other hand, will use the `Call RandomNumbers(10, 100)` statement to invoke the procedure and pass it a *lowerbound* value of 10 and an *upperbound* value of 100. The RandomNumbers procedure will use this information to generate and display integers in the range of 10 through 100.

c. Enter the `Call RandomNumbers(1, 10)` statement in the Level 1 button's Click event. Enter the `Call RandomNumbers(10, 100)` statement in the Level 2 button's Click event.

The user-defined procedure you will create for the current application will initialize the random number generator first. The procedure will then use the *lowerbound* and *upperbound* information, passed to it by either the Level 1 or Level 2 option button, to generate and display the random numbers in the lblNum1 and lblNum2 controls in the interface.

d. Create a form-level sub procedure named RandomNumbers.

e. Change the `Private Sub RandomNumbers()` statement to `Private Sub RandomNumbers(intMin as Integer, intMax as Integer)`.

f. Use the following pseudocode to code the RandomNumbers procedure:
    Initialize the random number generator
    Generate the first random number and assign it to the lblNum1 control
    Generate the second random number and assign it to the lblNum2 control

g. Open the Verify Answer button's Click event. Enter the appropriate Call statement(s) to call the RandomNumbers procedure to display a new math problem.

h. Save and run the application. When the program is working correctly, print the code.

discovery ▶

12. In this exercise, you will create a user-defined sub procedure in a code module. The user-defined procedure will center a form. You will also learn about the Form object.

Scenario: In addition to the Screen object, which you learned about in Tutorial 3, Visual Basic also has a Form object. The Form object refers to the form itself. You can use the Form object to pass a form from one procedure to another.

In this exercise, you will create a user-defined procedure, called CenterForm, that will center a form. Because the CenterForm procedure will need to be used by any number of forms in a project, you will create it as a global (public) procedure. You declare a global procedure by entering the Public statement in the General Declarations section of a code module. (Recall from Tutorial 3 that this is also the way you declare global variables.)

a. Open a new project, if necessary. Add a new module to the project. Use the Tools menu to add a sub procedure to the project. Call the sub procedure CenterForm, and make its scope Public.

b. To pass a form to the CenterForm procedure, change the `Public Sub CenterForm()` statement to `Public Sub CenterForm(FormName as Form)`. The `FormName as Form` argument tells the CenterForm procedure that it will be receiving a form, and to accept the form as FormName.

c. Enter the following two instructions in the CenterForm prcedure. These instructions tell the CenterForm procedure to center the form that is passed to it.
```
FormName.Left = (Screen.Width — FormName.Width) / 2
FormName.Top = (Screen.Height — FormName.Height) / 2
```

d. Save the module as Procs (short for "Procedures") in the Tut04 folder on your Student Disk. You do not need to save the form or the project. You should create one module that will store all of your global procedures and variables. You can then include the module in each of your projects. By doing so, the project will have access to these global procedures and variables; you won't have to retype them.

e. Use the File menu to remove the current project. You do not need to save the current project or form.

f. Open the lc12 (lc12.vbp) project, which is located in the Tut04 folder on your Student Disk.

g. Save the form and the project as lc12Done in the Tut04 folder on your Student Disk.

h. Run the application. Notice that the form is not centered on the screen.

i. Exit the application.

j. Use the Project menu to add the Procs.bas module file to the project.

k. If you have access to the MSDN Library, then use the Help menu to display a Help screen on the Me keyword. Read the Help screen, then close the MSDN Library window.

l. Open the frmSales form's Load event. Enter the `Call CenterForm(Me)` instruction, then close the Code window.

m. Save and run the project. The CenterForm procedure centers the form on the screen. Exit the application, then print the application's code.

D E B U G G I N G

Technique

Use Visual Basic's Print method to verify the contents of the variables in the application. The syntax of the Print method that prints information on a form is **Print** [*outputlist*]. Notice that the *outputlist* part of the instruction is optional, as indicated by the brackets; if you omit the *outputlist*, the Print method prints a blank line. You can also include other information in the Print method. To learn more about the Print method, use the Help menu to search for its Help window.

Exercises

1. Open the Debug1 (Debug1.vbp) project, which is located in the Tut04 folder on your Student Disk.

a. Print the code, then **run**, but don't save, the application. This application calculates the total cost of the tapes, records, and CDs ordered by a customer.

b. Enter 5 as the number of tapes, enter 5 as the number of records, enter 5 as the number of CDs, then click the **Calculate Total Price** button. (Be sure to enter all three numbers.) The application calculates and displays the total price of the order ($149.35). Notice that the application does not display the individual totals for the tapes, records, and CDs.

c. Click the **Exit** button to end the application. You will now use the Print method to print the contents of the curTotTape, curTotRecord, and curTotCD variables on the form. The sum of these three variables should equal the total price of the order.

d. Open the Calculate Total Price button's Code window, then maximize the Code window. In the blank line immediately above the End Sub instruction, type **print curtottape, curtotrecord, curtotcd** and press the **Enter** key. Notice that you can include more than one item on a Print instruction. You can separate each item with either a comma (,) or a semicolon (;). Using the comma to separate the items allows you to take advantage of Visual Basic's preset tabs. The comma tells Visual Basic to tab to the next print zone before printing; each print zone is 14 columns wide. If you use a semicolon to separate one item from another, the second item prints immediately after the first item. (When printing positive numbers, Visual Basic prints the number with both a leading and a trailing space. When printing negative numbers, Visual Basic prints the number with a negative sign on the left and a trailing space on the right.)

e. Close the Code window, then **run**, but don't save, the application.

f. Enter 5 as the number of tapes, enter 5 as the number of records, enter 5 as the number of CDs, then click the **Calculate Total Price** button. The total price ($149.35) appears in the label control. The contents of the curTotTape variable ($49.95), the curTotRecord variable ($39.95), and the curTotCD variable ($59.45) appear in the upper-left corner of the form. If you add those three amounts together, you will get $149.35, which appears correctly as the total price. Click the **Exit** button to end the application, then print the code.

g. You can now exit Visual Basic or open another project. You do not need to save the Debug1 project.

2. Open the Debug2 (Debug2.vbp) project, which is located in the Tut04 folder on your Student Disk.

a. Print the code. Notice that the Wholesale option button assigns 10 (the wholesale price per unit) to the curPrice variable, and the Retail option button assigns 15 (the retail price per unit) to the curPrice variable.

b. **Run**, but don't save, the application. Notice that the Wholesale button is already selected. As you learned in Tutorial 4, it is customary in Windows applications to have a default option button selected when the application first appears. In this application, the Value property was set to True in the Properties window.

c. Type **10** as the quantity ordered, then click the **Calculate** button. Notice that the application calculates the total due as 0, which is not correct. Click the **Retail** button, then click the **Calculate** button. This time the application calculates the total due correctly. Click the **Wholesale** button, then click the **Calculate** button. The application calculates the total due correctly.

d. Find and correct the problem with the application, then print the code. (*Hint:* Use the Print method to print the contents of the curPrice variable. Enter the Print method in the Calculate button's Click event procedure.)

e. Explain the difference between setting an option button's Value property to True in the Properties window and setting its Value property to True in code.

The Repetition Structure

Creating a Grade Calculation Application

case ▶ Next Monday is Career Day at your alma mater. Professor Carver, one of your computer programming instructors, has asked you to be a guest speaker in his Introduction to Programming class. You gladly accept this speaking engagement and begin planning your presentation. You decide to show the students how to create an application that will calculate their grade in Professor Carver's class.

Previewing the Completed Application

First, preview the completed grade application.

To preview the completed application:

1 If necessary, start Windows, then place your Student Disk in the appropriate disk drive.

2 Use the Run command on the Start menu to run the **Grade** (Grade.exe) file, which is located in the Tut05 folder on your Student Disk. The Grade application's user interface appears on the screen.

3 Type your name in the Name text box. Click the **Project 1** check box, then type 9 in the Project 1 text box.

4 Click the **Midterm** check box, then type 45 in the Midterm text box.

5 Click the **Display Grade** button. A grade of A appears in the Grade label control. See Figure 5-1.

your name will appear
here

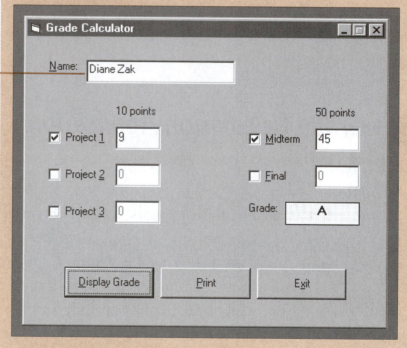

Figure 5-1: Grade application showing grade

6 Click the **Exit** button, then click the **Yes** button to end the application.

The grade application uses the repetition structure, a counter, an accumulator, and control arrays. You will learn about the repetition structure, as well as counters and accumulators, in Lesson A. Control arrays are covered in Lesson B, where you will begin coding the application. You will complete the application in Lesson C.

LESSON A
objectives

In this lesson you will learn how to:

■ Create the For Next, Do While, and Do Until repetition structures

■ Move a control across the screen

■ Initialize and update counters and accumulators

The Repetition Structure (Looping)

The Repetition Structure

As you may remember from Tutorial 1, the three structures used in programs are sequence, selection, and repetition. The programs you created in Tutorials 1 through 3 used the sequence programming structure only, where each of the program instructions was processed, one after another, in the order in which they appeared in the program. In Tutorial 4, you learned how to include both the sequence and selection structures in a program. Recall that the selection structure allows the program to make a decision and then select the appropriate action to take based on the result of that decision. In addition to the sequence and selection structures, most programs also use the repetition structure.

Like the sequence and selection structures, you are already familiar with the repetition structure. Figure 5-2 shows examples of repetition structures that you may have encountered today. Example 1's instructions are similar to those found on a shampoo bottle. Example 2's instructions, which indicate how to make a glass of chocolate milk, are similar to those found on a can of chocolate syrup.

Example 1	Example 2
repeat two times	pour 8 ounces of milk into a glass
apply shampoo to wet hair	pour 2 teaspoons of chocolate syrup into the glass
lather	repeat until milk and syrup are mixed thoroughly
rinse	stir

Figure 5-2: Examples of the repetition structure

You will notice that both examples direct the user to repeat one or more instructions either a specified number of times or until a specified condition is met. The repetition structure shown in Example 1, for instance, directs the user to repeat the "apply shampoo to wet hair," "lather," and "rinse" instructions two times. In Example 2, the repetition structure directs the user to repeat the "stir" instruction until the milk and syrup are mixed thoroughly.

Programmers use the **repetition structure**, also called **looping** or **iteration**, to tell the computer to repeat one or more program instructions either a specified number of times or until some condition, referred to as the *loop condition*, is met. The three forms of the repetition structure are For Next, Do While, and Do Until. First learn about the For Next loop.

The For Next (Automatic Counter) Loop

The **For Next loop**, also called an **automatic counter loop**, repeats a block of statements a specified number of times. You use Visual Basic's **For...Next statement** to code the automatic counter loop. Figure 5-3 shows both the syntax and an example of the `For...Next` statement. The example repeats the Print method three times. (You learned about the Print Method in Tutorial 4's Debugging section).

Syntax	Example
For *counter* = *startvalue* To *endvalue* [**Step** *stepvalue*]	For intCount = 1 to 3 Step 1
[*instructions*]	Print intCount
Next *counter*	Next intCount

Figure 5-3: Syntax and an example of the For...Next statement

Notice that the syntax begins with the `For` statement and ends with the `Next` statement. Between those two statements, you enter the instructions you want the loop to repeat. In the syntax, *counter* is the name of a numeric variable, which is a variable that can store a number. Visual Basic uses the numeric variable to keep track of the number of times the loop instructions are processed. The name of the numeric variable in Figure 5-3's example is intCount.

The *startvalue*, *endvalue*, and *stepvalue* items control how many times to process the loop instructions. The *startvalue* tells the loop where to begin, the *endvalue* tells the loop when to stop, and the *stepvalue* tells the loop how much to add to (or subtract from) the *counter* each time the loop is processed. If you omit the *stepvalue*, Visual Basic uses a *stepvalue* of positive 1. In Figure 5-3's example, the *startvalue* is 1, the *endvalue* is 3, and the *stepvalue* is 1. Those values tell the loop to start counting at 1 and, counting by 1's, stop at 3—in other words, count 1, 2, and then 3.

Startvalue, *endvalue*, and *stepvalue* must be numeric and they can be either positive or negative, integer or non-integer. If *stepvalue* is positive, then *startvalue* must be less than or equal to *endvalue* for the loop instructions to be processed. In other words, the instruction `For intCount = 1 To 3 Step 1` is correct, but the instruction `For intCount = 3 To 1 Step 1` is not correct because you can't count from 3 (the *startvalue*) to 1 (the *endvalue*) by adding increments of 1 (the *stepvalue*). If, on the other hand, *stepvalue* is negative, then *startvalue* must be greater than or equal to *endvalue* for the loop instructions to be processed. For example, the instruction `For intCount = 3 To 1 Step −1` is correct, but the instruction `For intCount = 1 To 3 Step −1` is not correct because you can't count from 1 to 3 by subtracting increments of 1. The For Next loop performs the following three tasks:

1. The loop initializes the *counter* (the numeric variable) to the *startvalue*. This is done only once, at the beginning of the loop.

2. If the *stepvalue* is positive, the loop checks if the value in the *counter* is greater than the *endvalue*. (Or, if the *stepvalue* is negative, the loop checks if the value in the *counter* is less than the *endvalue*.) If it is, the loop stops; if it's not, the instructions within the loop are processed and the next task, task 3, is performed.

3. The loop adds the *stepvalue* to the *counter*. It then repeats tasks 2 and 3 until the *counter* is greater than (or less than, if the *stepvalue* is negative) the *endvalue*.

On your Student Disk is a project that contains two examples of the For Next loop. Before opening the project, however, you will look at the flowchart and the pseudocode for the For Next loop structure that will print the numbers 1 through 3 on the form. Both are shown in Figure 5-4.

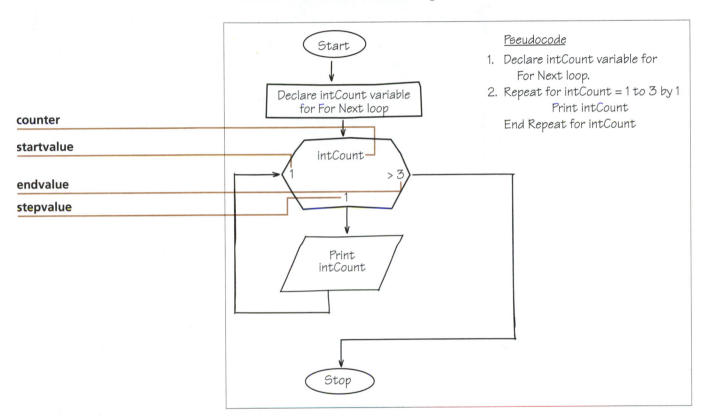

Figure 5-4: Flowchart and pseudocode for the For Next (automatic counter) loop

The For Next loop is represented in a flowchart by a hexagon—a six-sided symbol. Four values are recorded inside the hexagon: the name of the *counter*, the *startvalue*, the *stepvalue*, and the *endvalue*. Notice that the *endvalue* is preceded by a > (greater-than sign). That's to remind you that the loop will stop when the value in the *counter* is greater than the *endvalue*. (If the *stepvalue* is negative, however, a < (less-than sign) should precede the *endvalue*, as that loop will stop when the value in the *counter* is less than the *endvalue*.) Now open the project that contains the examples of the For Next loop.

To open the project that contains the For Next loop examples:

1. Start Visual Basic, if necessary, and open the **For** (For.vbp) project, which is located in the Tut05 folder on your Student Disk. Click the **form's title bar** to select the frmFor form. The frmFor form appears on the screen, as shown in Figure 5-5.

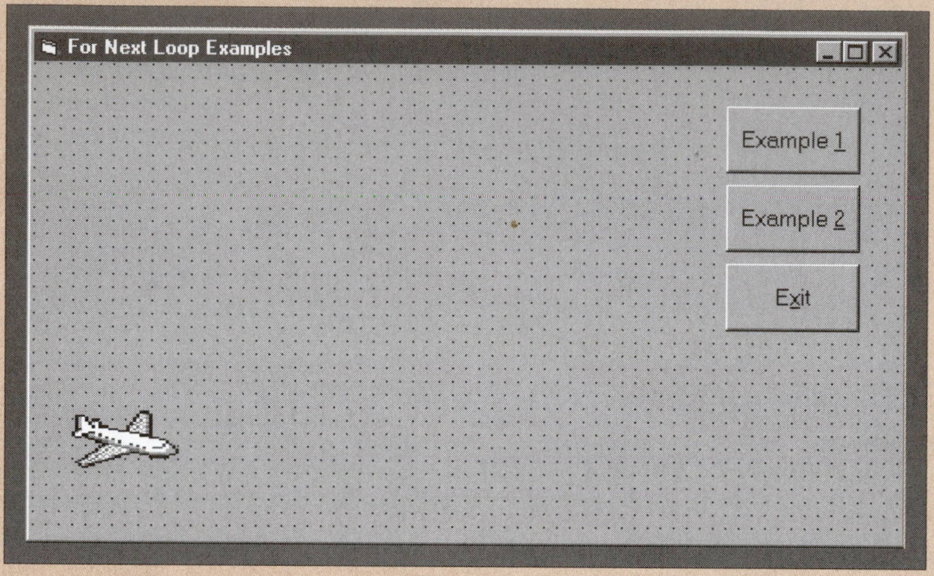
For Next Loop Examples
Example 1
Example 2
Exit

Figure 5-5: frmFor interface

Each of the command buttons has been coded for you. First, you will look at the code in the Example 1 button's Click event procedure.

Example 1

The Example 1 button's Click event procedure contains the code that will display the numbers 1 through 3 on the form.

To view the Example 1 button's code, then test the Example 1 button:

1. Open the Example 1 button's Click event procedure. See Figure 5-6.

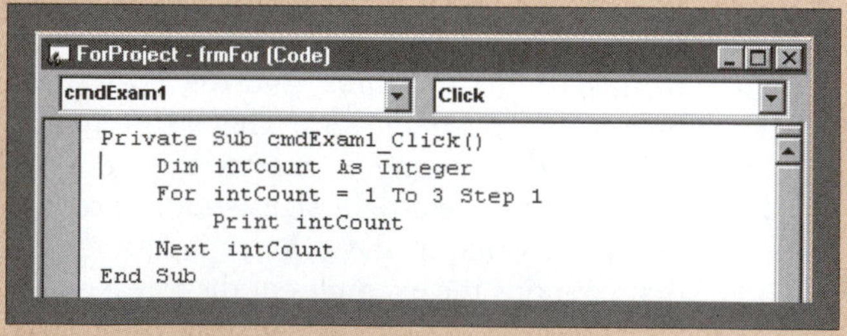
ForProject - frmFor (Code)
cmdExam1
Click
Private Sub cmdExam1_Click()
Dim intCount As Integer
For intCount = 1 To 3 Step 1
Print intCount
Next intCount
End Sub

Figure 5-6: Example 1 button's Click event procedure

The code first declares a numeric variable, intCount, which will be used as the *counter* in the `For...Next` statement. Because the *counter* will contain only whole numbers, the intCount variable is declared as an Integer variable. The `For...Next` statement then instructs Visual Basic to print the contents of the intCount variable on the form, three times.

2   Close the Code window, then **run** the application.

3   Click the **Example 1** button. Visual Basic processes the `For...Next` statement as shown in Figure 5-7, and the numbers 1, 2, and 3 appear in the upper-left corner of the form.

---

1. Loop initializes the *counter*, intCount, to 1 (*startvalue*).

2. Loop checks if value in intCount is greater than 3 (*endvalue*). It's not.

3. Visual Basic prints 1 (contents of intCount) on the form.

4. Loop adds 1 (*stepvalue*) to intCount, giving 2.

5. Loop checks if value in intCount is greater than 3 (*endvalue*). It's not.

6. Visual Basic prints 2 (contents of intCount) on the form.

7. Loop adds 1 (*stepvalue*) to intCount, giving 3.

8. Loop checks if value in intCount is greater than 3 (*endvalue*). It's not.

9. Visual Basic prints 3 (contents of intCount) on the form.

10. Loop adds 1 (*stepvalue*) to intCount, giving 4.

11. Loop checks if value in intCount is greater than 3 (*endvalue*). It is.

12. Loop stops.

13. End Sub statement ends the Click event procedure.

Figure 5-7: Processing steps for Example 1's For...Next statement

4   Click the **Exit** button to end the application. Visual Basic returns to the design screen.

In Example 2, you will use a For Next loop to move an object across the screen.

Example 2

You can move an object across the screen by setting its Left property within a For Next loop, as you will see when you open the Example 2 button's Click event procedure.

To view the Example 2 button's code, then test the Example 2 button:

1   Open the Example 2 button's Click event procedure. See Figure 5-8.

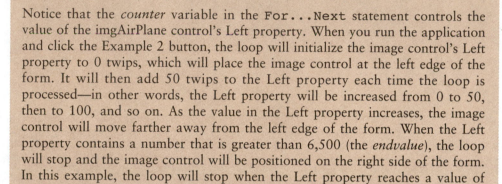

Figure 5-8: Example 2 button's Click event procedure

Recall that the Left property
is measured in twips from
the left edge of the form.

Notice that the *counter* variable in the For...Next statement controls the value of the imgAirPlane control's Left property. When you run the application and click the Example 2 button, the loop will initialize the image control's Left property to 0 twips, which will place the image control at the left edge of the form. It will then add 50 twips to the Left property each time the loop is processed—in other words, the Left property will be increased from 0 to 50, then to 100, and so on. As the value in the Left property increases, the image control will move farther away from the left edge of the form. When the Left property contains a number that is greater than 6,500 (the *endvalue*), the loop will stop and the image control will be positioned on the right side of the form. In this example, the loop will stop when the Left property reaches a value of 6,550, which is 50—the *stepvalue*—more than the *endvalue* of 6,500.

2 Close the Code window, then **run** the application.

3 Click the **Example 2** button. The airplane icon moves from the left edge of the form to the right edge of the form.

4 Click the **Example 2** button again. The airplane icon again moves from left to right across the form.

5 Click the **Exit** button to end the application. Visual Basic returns to the design screen.

Recall that the three forms of the repetition structure (loops) are: For Next, Do While, and Do Until. You can use any loop to repeat a set of instructions a specified number of times, although the For Next loop is usually used in those situations because it requires less coding. When you don't know precisely how many times the loop instructions should be repeated, which is the case in many applications, then you must use either the Do While loop or the Do Until loop.

The Do While and the Do Until Loops

The **Do While loop** repeats a block of instructions *while* a condition is true, whereas the **Do Until loop** repeats a block of instructions *until* a condition becomes true. You can use Visual Basic's **Do While...Loop statement** to code the Do While loop, and Visual Basic's **Do...Loop Until statement** to code the Do Until loop. Figure 5-9 shows the syntax for each loop. It also gives an example of how you could use either loop to display the numbers 1 through 3 on the form.

Do While Loop	Do Until Loop
Syntax:	**Syntax:**
Do While *condition*	**Do**
[loop instructions]	*[loop instructions]*
Loop	**Loop Until** *condition*
Example:	**Example:**
Dim intCount as Integer	Dim intCount as Integer
intCount = 1	intCount = 1
Do While intCount < = 3	Do
Print intCount	Print intCount
intCount = intCount + 1	intCount = intCount + 1
Loop	Loop Until intCount > 3

Figure 5-9: Syntax and examples of the Do While and the Do Until loops

The Do While loop begins with the `Do While` statement and ends with the `Loop` statement. The Do Until loop, on the other hand, begins with the `Do` statement and ends with the `Loop Until` statement. Between each loop's beginning and ending statements, you enter the instructions you want the loop to repeat.

Both loops require a *condition*, which is located at the top of the Do While loop and at the bottom of the Do Until loop. The *condition* can contain variables, constants, properties, functions, mathematical operators, relational operators, and logical operators. Like the *condition* used in the If...Then...Else statement, which you learned about in Tutorial 4, the loop *condition* must also evaluate to either True or False. The *condition* determines if the loop instructions will be processed. In the Do While loop, the loop instructions are processed only if the *condition* evaluates to True; if the *condition* evaluates to False, the loop instructions are not processed. In the Do Until loop, the loop instructions are processed only if the *condition* evaluates to False; if the *condition* evaluates to True, the loop instructions are not processed.

Programmers call the Do While loop a **pretest loop** because the loop evaluates (tests) the *condition* before processing any of the instructions within the loop. Depending on the *condition*, the instructions in a Do While loop may not be processed at all. For example, if the *condition* evaluates initially to false, Visual Basic skips the instructions within the loop; processing then continues with the instruction immediately following the end of the loop.

Programmers call the Do Until loop a **posttest loop** because the loop evaluates (tests) the *condition* after processing the instructions within the loop. The Do Until loop always processes the loop instructions at least once.

Take a closer look at the two examples shown in Figure 5-9. Begin with the example of the Do While loop, which will display the numbers 1 through 3 on the form. The example first declares and initializes, to 1, an Integer variable named intCount. The `Do While` statement then evaluates the *condition*, `intCount <= 3`, to determine if the instructions within the loop should be processed. If intCount contains a

tip

The For Next loop is also a pretest loop.

number that is less than or equal to 3, the loop instructions, which display the value of intCount on the form and also add 1 to intCount, are processed. Then the Loop statement, which marks the end of the loop, sends the program back to the beginning of the loop (the Do While statement), where the *condition* is tested again. If the value in intCount is still less than or equal to 3, the loop instructions are processed again, and so on.

If intCount does not contain a number that is less than or equal to 3 (in other words, if intCount is greater than 3), the loop stops—that is, the instructions within the loop are not processed. Processing then continues with the instruction following the Loop statement.

To summarize, the Do While loop repeats the loop instructions as long as the *condition* evaluates to True. When the *condition* evaluates to False, the Do While loop stops. Next, look at the Do Until example, which also displays the numbers 1 through 3 on the form.

The Do Until example first declares and initializes, to 1, an Integer variable named intCount. The Do statement, which simply marks the beginning of the loop, is processed next. Visual Basic then processes the loop instructions, which display the value of intCount on the form and also add 1 to intCount. The Loop Until statement then evaluates the *condition*, intCount > 3, to determine if the loop instructions should be processed again. Notice that the *condition* is not evaluated until after the loop instructions are processed the first time. If intCount contains a number that is greater than 3, the loop stops; processing then continues with the instruction following the Loop Until statement. If intCount contains a number that is not greater than 3 (in other words, if it's less than or equal to 3), the loop instructions are processed again.

To summarize, the Do Until loop repeats the loop instructions as long as the *condition* evaluates to False. When the *condition* evaluates to True, the Do Until loop stops. Now look at the flowchart and pseudocode for both loops.

Flowchart and Pseudocode for the Do While and the Do Until Loops

The flowcharts for the Do While and the Do Until loops that display the numbers 1 through 3 on the form are shown in Figure 5-10; the pseudocode is shown in Figure 5-11.

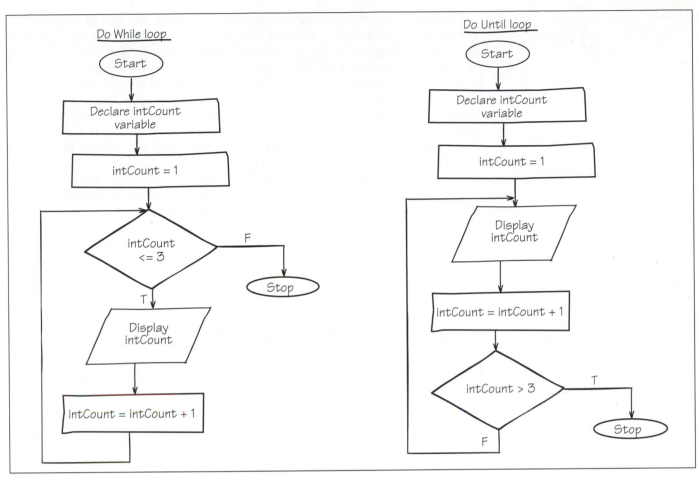

Figure 5-10: Flowchart for the Do While and the Do Until loops

Recall that the oval in the flowchart is the start/stop symbol, the rectangle is the process symbol, the parallelogram is the input/output symbol, and the diamond is the selection/repetition symbol.

Pseudocode for the Do While loop	Pseudocode for the Do Until loop
1. Declare intCount variable	1. Declare intCount variable
2. Assign 1 to intCount variable	2. Assign 1 to intCount variable
3. Repeat while intCount <= 3	3. Repeat
Display intCount	Display intCount
Add 1 to intCount	Add 1 to intCount
End Repeat while intCount <= 3	End Repeat until intCount > 3

Figure 5-11: Pseudocode for the Do While and the Do Until loops

You will notice that both loops are represented in a flowchart by a diamond. As with the selection structure diamond, which you learned about in Tutorial 4, the repetition structure diamond contains a question that has a True or False answer only. The question represents the *loop condition* that the repetition structure must evaluate.

Like the selection diamond, the repetition diamond has one flowline leading into the diamond and two flowlines leading out of the diamond. In Figure 5-10, the two flowlines leaving the diamond are marked with a "T" (for True) and an "F" (for False). In the Do While loop's flowchart, the flowline marked with a "T" leads to the body of the loop—the instructions to process when the *loop condition* evaluates to True. The flowline marked with an "F" (for False) leads to the instructions to process when the loop ends, which is when the *loop condition* evaluates to False. In the Do Until loop's flowchart, the situation is reversed: the flowline marked with an "F" leads to the body of the loop and the flowline marked with a "T" leads to the instructions to process when the loop ends.

In the Do While loop's flowchart, you will notice that the flowline leading into the repetition diamond, as well as the symbols and flowlines within the True path, form a circle or loop. In the Do Until loop's flowchart, on the other hand, the loop is formed by all of the symbols and flowlines in the False path. It is this loop, or circle, that distinguishes the repetition structure from the selection structure in a flowchart.

On your Student Disk is a project that contains the code for the flowcharts and pseudocode shown in Figures 5-10 and 5-11.

To view the examples of the Do While and Do Until loops:

1   Open the **DoLoops** (DoLoops.vbp) project, which is located in the Tut05 folder on your Student Disk. The interface contains three command buttons: Do While, Do Until, and Exit.

The command buttons have already been coded for you. The Exit button will end the application, and the Do While and Do Until buttons will each display the numbers 1 through 3 on the form. You will look at the code in the Do While button first.

Do While Example

The Do While command button uses the `Do While...Loop` statement to display the numbers 1 through 3 on the form.

To look at the code, then test the Do While button:

1   Open the Do While button's Click event procedure. See Figure 5-12.

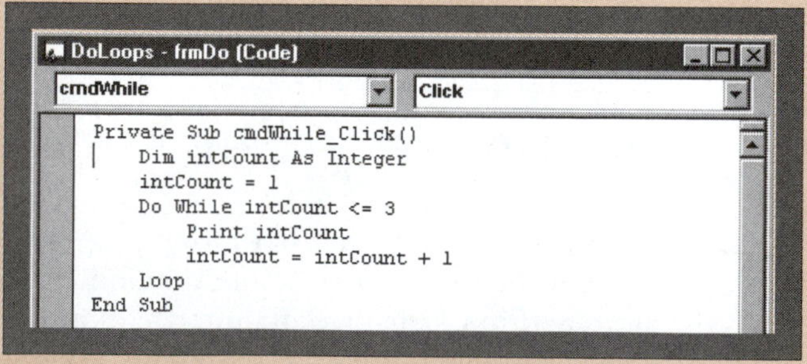

```
DoLoops - frmDo (Code)
cmdWhile                          Click

Private Sub cmdWhile_Click()
    Dim intCount As Integer
    intCount = 1
    Do While intCount <= 3
        Print intCount
        intCount = intCount + 1
    Loop
End Sub
```

Figure 5-12: Do While button's Click event procedure

2 Close the Code window, then **run** the application. Click the **Do While** button. Visual Basic processes the instructions as shown in Figure 5-13, and the numbers 1, 2, and 3 appear in the upper-left corner of the form.

1. intCount variable is declared as an integer.

2. intCount variable is assigned the number 1.

3. Do While statement checks if the value in intCount is less than or equal to 3. It is.

4. Visual Basic prints 1 (the contents of intCount) on the form.

5. Visual Basic adds 1 to intCount, giving 2.

6. Loop statement sends the program to the beginning of the loop (the Do While statement).

7. Do While statement checks if the value in intCount is less than or equal to 3. It is.

8. Visual Basic prints 2 (the contents of intCount) on the form.

9. Visual Basic adds 1 to intCount, giving 3.

10. Loop statement sends the program to the beginning of the loop (the Do While statement).

11. Do While statement checks if the value in intCount is less than or equal to 3. It is.

12. Visual Basic prints 3 (the contents of intCount) on the form.

13. Visual Basic adds 1 to intCount, giving 4.

14. Loop statement sends the program to the beginning of the loop (the Do While statement).

15. Do While statement checks if the value in intCount is less than or equal to 3. It's not.

16. Loop stops.

17. End Sub statement ends the Click event procedure.

Figure 5-13: Processing steps for Do While button

3 Click the **Exit** button to end the application. Visual Basic returns to the design screen.

Next, look at the code in the Do Until button's Click event procedure.

Do Until Example

The Do Until command button uses the `Do...Loop Until` statement to display the numbers 1 through 3 on the form.

To look at the code in the Do Until button's Click event procedure, then test the button:

1   Open the Do Until button's Click event procedure. See Figure 5-14.

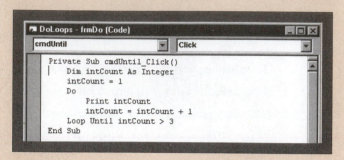

```
DoLoops - frmDo (Code)                            _ □ ×
cmdUntil                    ▼    Click                    ▼
Private Sub cmdUntil_Click()
    Dim intCount As Integer
    intCount = 1
    Do
        Print intCount
        intCount = intCount + 1
    Loop Until intCount > 3
End Sub
```

Figure 5-14: Do Until button's Click event procedure

2   Close the Code window, then **run** the application. Click the **Do Until** button. Visual Basic processes the instructions as shown in Figure 5-15, and the numbers 1, 2, and 3 appear in the upper-left corner of the form.

---

1. intCount variable is declared as an integer.

2. intCount variable is assigned the number 1.

3. Do statement marks the beginning of the loop.

4. Visual Basic prints 1 (the contents of intCount) on the form.

5. Visual Basic adds 1 to intCount, giving 2.

6. Loop Until statement checks if the value in intCount is greater than 3. It's not.

7. Loop Until statement sends the program to the beginning of the loop (the Do statement).

8. Visual Basic prints 2 (the contents of intCount) on the form.

9. Visual Basic adds 1 to intCount, giving 3.

10. Loop Until statement checks if the value in intCount is greater than 3. It's not.

11. Loop Until statement sends the program to the beginning of the loop (the Do statement).

12. Visual Basic prints 3 (the contents of intCount) on the form.

13. Visual Basic adds 1 to intCount, giving 4.

14. Loop Until statement checks if the value in intCount is greater than 3. It is.

15. Loop stops.

16. End Sub statement ends the Click event procedure.

Figure 5-15: Processing steps for the Do Until button

3   Click the **Exit** button to end the application. Visual Basic returns to the design screen.

Although it appears that the Do While loop and Do Until loop work identically—in this case, both loops displayed the numbers 1 through 3 on the form—that will not always be the case. In other words, the two loops are not always interchangeable. The difference between the Do While (pretest) loop and the Do Until (posttest) loop will be more apparent in the next set of steps.

To see the difference between the Do While and the Do Until loops:

1   Open the Do While button's Click event procedure.

2   Change the `intCount = 1` instruction to **intCount = 10**.

By setting the initial value of intCount to 10, the loop's *condition* (`intCount <= 3`) will evaluate to False, so Visual Basic will skip the loop instructions. See if that is, in fact, what happens.

3   Close the Code window, then **run** the application. Click the **Do While** button. As expected, the numbers 1 through 3 do not appear in the upper-left corner of the form. Because the Do While loop's *condition* (`intCount <= 3`) evaluated to False, the instructions within the loop were not processed. Figure 5-16 shows how Visual Basic processed the Do While command button's code.

---

1. intCount variable is declared as an integer.

2. intCount variable is assigned the number 10.

3. Do While statement checks if the value in intCount is less than or equal to 3. It's not.

4. Loop stops.

5. End Sub statement ends the Click event procedure.

Figure 5-16: Processing steps for the modified code in the Do While button

4   Click the **Exit** button. Visual Basic returns to the design screen.

Now make the same change to the Do Until button.

5   Open the Do Until button's Click event procedure. Change the `intCount = 1` instruction to **intCount = 10**.

See how the Do Until loop handles this change.

6   Close the Code window, then **run** the application. Click the **Do Until** button. This time the number 10 appears in the upper-left corner of the form. Because the Do Until loop instructions are processed before the *condition* (`intCount > 3`) is tested, the value in intCount, 10, appears on the form. Figure 5-17 shows how Visual Basic processed the Do Until command button's code.

1. intCount variable is declared as an integer.

2. intCount variable is assigned the number 10.

3. Do statement marks the beginning of the loop.

4. Visual Basic prints 10 (the contents of intCount) on the form.

5. Visual Basic adds 1 to intCount, giving 11.

6. Loop Until statement checks if the value in intCount is greater than 3. It is.

7. Loop stops.

8. End Sub statement ends the Click event procedure.

Figure 5-17: Processing steps for the modified code in the Do Until button

As this example shows, it is possible for the Do While and the Do Until loops to give different results. When deciding which loop to use, keep in mind that the Do Until loop will always process the loop instructions at least once, whereas the Do While loop might not process the instructions at all.

7   Click the **Exit** button. Visual Basic returns to the design screen.

You will now look at another example that uses the Do While loop.

Another Example of the Do While Loop

In this next example you will see how the Do While loop can be used to play a game that races two rocket ships against each other. The game program will include the three control structures: sequence, selection, and repetition.

To look at the rocket ship game:

1   Open the **Rocket** (Rocket.vbp) project, which is located in the Tut05 folder on your Student Disk. You do not need to save the DoLoops project.

2   Maximize the form. The user interface appears, as shown in Figure 5-18.

The Start Race and Exit command buttons have already been coded for you. Look at the code in the Start Race button.

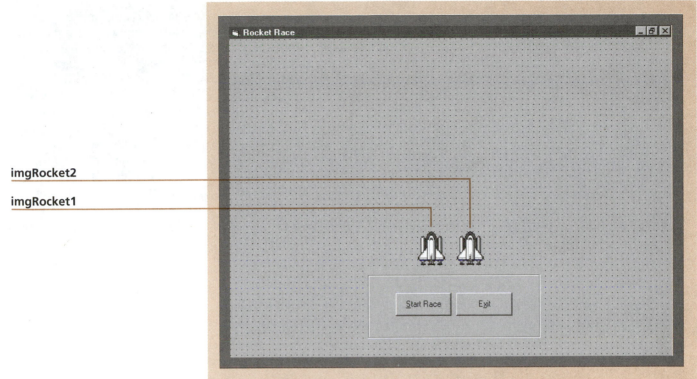

imgRocket2

imgRocket1

Figure 5-18: frmRocket user interface

3   Open the Start Race button's Click event procedure, then maximize the Code window. The maximized Code window appears as shown in Figure 5-19.

tip

. . . .

▶ You learned about the Randomize statement and the Rnd function in Tutorial 4.

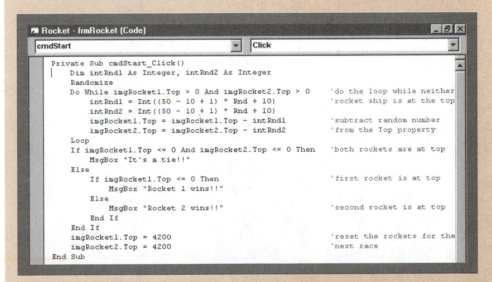

```
Private Sub cmdStart_Click()
    Dim intRnd1 As Integer, intRnd2 As Integer
    Randomize
    Do While imgRocket1.Top > 0 And imgRocket2.Top > 0      'do the loop while neither
        intRnd1 = Int((50 - 10 + 1) * Rnd + 10)             'rocket ship is at the top
        intRnd2 = Int((50 - 10 + 1) * Rnd + 10)
        imgRocket1.Top = imgRocket1.Top - intRnd1           'subtract random number
        imgRocket2.Top = imgRocket2.Top - intRnd2           'from the Top property
    Loop
    If imgRocket1.Top <= 0 And imgRocket2.Top <= 0 Then     'both rockets are at top
        MsgBox "It's a tie!!"
    Else
        If imgRocket1.Top <= 0 Then                         'first rocket is at top
            MsgBox "Rocket 1 wins!!"
        Else
            MsgBox "Rocket 2 wins!!"                        'second rocket is at top
        End If
    End If
    imgRocket1.Top = 4200                                   'reset the rockets for the
    imgRocket2.Top = 4200                                   'next race
End Sub
```

Figure 5-19: Start Race button's Click event procedure

The Click event procedure first declares two Integer variables, intRnd1 and intRnd2, then uses the Randomize statement to initialize Visual Basic's random number generator. The instructions within the Do While loop generate two random numbers, which are stored in the intRnd1 and intRnd2 variables. The loop instructions then subtract the contents of the intRnd1 and intRnd2 variables from the Top property of the imgRocket1 and imgRocket2 controls, respectively. Visual Basic will process the Do While instructions as long as the Top property of both image controls is greater than zero, which indicates that neither control has reached the top of the form. (When a control is at the top of the form, its Top property has a value of 0.) The Do While loop will stop when the Top property of one, or both, of the image controls contains a value that is less than or equal to zero, which indicates that the control is at the top of the form. When the Do While loop stops, the selection structure that follows the loop uses the Top property to determine which control is at the top of the form. If the Top property of both image controls contains a value that is less than or equal to zero, then the application displays the "It's a tie!!" message. If, however, the Top property of only one of the controls is less than or equal to zero, the application displays the appropriate message—either "Rocket 1 wins!!" or "Rocket 2 wins!!". The code then resets the Top property of the image controls for the next race.

4   Close the Code window, then restore the form to its standard size. **Run** the application, then click the **Start Race** button. A message box appears on the screen; the message box will either say "It's a tie!!", "Rocket 1 wins!!", or "Rocket 2 wins!!".

5   Press the **Enter** key to remove the dialog box. The application resets each rocket to its original location, ready for the next race.

6   Click the **Exit** button to end the application.

Now that you know how to use the For Next, Do While, and Do Until repetition structures, you can learn about counters and accumulators. You will often find either a counter or an accumulator, or both, within a repetition structure. Counters are used to answer the question "How many?"—for example, "How many salespeople live in Virginia?" Accumulators, on the other hand, are used to answer the question "How much?"—for example, "How much did the salespeople sell this quarter?"

Counters and Accumulators

Counters and accumulators are used within a repetition structure to calculate subtotals, totals, and averages. A **counter** is a numeric variable used for counting something—such as the number of employees paid in a week. An **accumulator** is a numeric variable used for accumulating (adding together) something—such as the total dollar amount of a week's payroll.

Two tasks are associated with counters and accumulators: initializing and updating. **Initializing** means to assign a beginning value to the counter or accumulator. Although that beginning value is usually zero, counters and accumulators can be initialized to any number.

Updating, also called **incrementing**, means adding a number to the value stored in the counter or the accumulator. A counter is always incremented by a constant value, whereas an accumulator is incremented by a value that varies. The assignment statement that updates a counter or an accumulator is placed within the repetition structure.

On your Student Disk is a project that contains examples of a counter and an accumulator. Both examples will show you how to use a counter and an accumulator to calculate the average of the sales amounts that are entered by the user. One example uses the Do While loop; the other uses the Do Until loop. Before opening the project, look at the flowcharts, shown in Figure 5-20, for each of the examples.

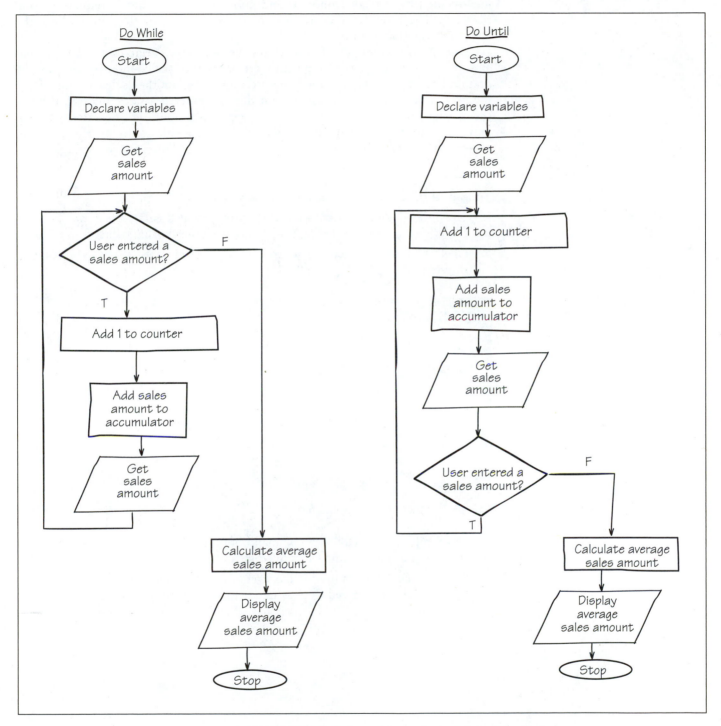

Figure 5-20: Flowcharts for counter and accumulator examples

The Do While loop first declares the necessary variables, then gets a sales amount from the user. The loop then checks to see if the user entered a sales amount. If the user did not enter a sales amount, the loop stops and the average sales amount is calculated and displayed. If, on the other hand, the user did enter a sales amount, the counter is incremented by one, the accumulator is incremented by the sales amount, and another sales amount is requested from the user. The program then returns to the beginning of the loop, where the *condition* is tested again.

The Do Until loop also first declares the necessary variables and gets a sales amount from the user. The loop then increments both the counter by one and the accumulator by the sales amount before requesting another sales amount from the user. The loop then checks to see if the user entered a sales amount; if he or she did not, the loop stops and the average sales amount is calculated and displayed. If, on the other hand, the user did enter a sales amount, the program returns to the beginning of the loop and processes the loop instructions again.

To look at the counter and accumulator examples:

1 Open the **CtrAccum** (CtrAccum.vbp) project, which is located in the Tut05 folder on your Student Disk. (You do not need to save the Rocket files.)

2 Click the **form** to select it. The frmCtrAccum form appears on the screen as shown in Figure 5-21.

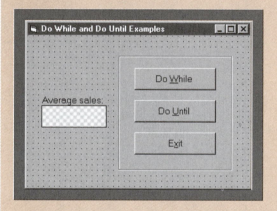

Figure 5-21: frmCtrAccum user interface

The Do While and the Do Until command buttons have already been coded for you. Look at the code for the Do While button first.

3 Open the Do While button's Click event procedure, then maximize the Code window. The maximized Code window appears, as shown in Figure 5-22.

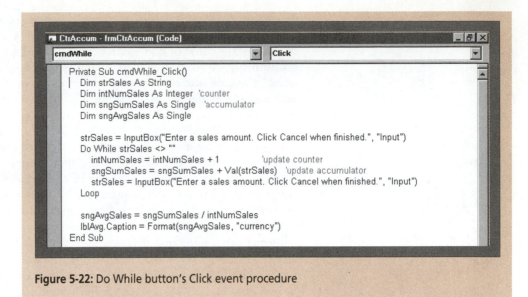

```
CtrAccum - frmCtrAccum (Code)                                    _ | & | x
cmdWhile                    ▼    Click                               ▼

Private Sub cmdWhile_Click()
  Dim strSales As String
  Dim intNumSales As Integer   'counter
  Dim sngSumSales As Single    'accumulator
  Dim sngAvgSales As Single

  strSales = InputBox("Enter a sales amount. Click Cancel when finished.", "Input")
  Do While strSales <> ""
      intNumSales = intNumSales + 1            'update counter
      sngSumSales = sngSumSales + Val(strSales)   'update accumulator
      strSales = InputBox("Enter a sales amount. Click Cancel when finished.", "Input")
  Loop

  sngAvgSales = sngSumSales / intNumSales
  lblAvg.Caption = Format(sngAvgSales, "currency")
End Sub
```

Figure 5-22: Do While button's Click event procedure

The code begins by declaring four variables; strSales, intNumSales, sngSumSales, and sngAvgSales. The strSales variable will store the sales amounts entered by the user. The intNumSales variable is the counter variable that will count the number of sales amounts entered by the user. The sngSumSales variable is the accumulator variable that will store the total of the sales amounts entered by the user. The remaining variable, sngAvgSales, will store the average sales amount.

Recall that counters and accumulators must be initialized, or given a beginning value. Because the `Dim` statement automatically assigns a zero to Integer and Single variables when the variables are created, you do not need to enter any additional code to initialize the intNumSales counter or the sngSumSales accumulator—in other words, the `Dim` statement initializes the variables for you. If you want to initialize a counter or an accumulator to a value other than zero, however, you would need to include the appropriate assignment statement in your code. For example, to initialize the intNumSales counter to 1, you would need to include the `intNumSales = 1` assignment statement in your code. The statements that initialize counters and accumulators to a value other than zero are entered after any `Dim` statements in the Code window. In this application, you want both the counter and the accumulator initialized to zero, so no assignment statements are necessary.

After the variables are declared, the InputBox function, which you learned about in Tutorial 3, displays a dialog box that prompts the user either to enter a sales amount or to click the Cancel button when he or she has no more sales amounts to enter. When the user enters a sales amount and selects the OK button, the function stores the sales amount in the strSales variable. However, when the user fails to enter a sales amount before selecting the OK button, or when he or she selects the dialog box's Cancel button, the function stores a zero-length string ("") in the strSales variable.

The `Do While` statement then evaluates the *condition*, `strSales <>""`, to determine if the loop instructions should be processed. If the strSales variable does not contain a zero-length string, which means that the user entered a sales amount, the loop instructions are processed; otherwise—meaning the user either did not enter a sales amount or selected the Cancel button—the loop instructions are not

tip

Recall that the InputBox function's dialog box contains an input area, as well as OK and Cancel buttons.

processed. Now take a closer look at the instructions within the loop.

The `intNumSales = intNumSales + 1` instruction updates the counter by a constant value of one. Notice that the counter variable, intNumSales, appears on both sides of the assignment statement. The statement tells Visual Basic to add one to the contents of the intNumSales variable, then place the result back in the intNumSales variable. intNumSales will be incremented by one each time the loop is processed.

The `sngSumSales = sngSumSales + Val(strSales)` instruction updates the accumulator. Notice that the accumulator variable, sngSumSales, also appears on both sides of the assignment statement. The statement tells Visual Basic to add the numeric equivalent of the strSales variable to the contents of the sngSumSales variable, then place the result back in the sngSumSales variable. sngSumSales will be incremented by a sales amount, which will vary, each time the loop is processed.

After the counter and the accumulator are updated, the Inputbox function is used again to ask the user for another sales amount. Notice that the `strSales = InputBox ("Enter a sales amount. Click Cancel when finished.", "Input")` instruction appears twice in the code—before the Do While loop and within the Do While loop. You may be wondering why you need to repeat the same instruction. Recall that the `Loop` statement sends the program to the top of the loop—to the `Do While` statement. Because the first Inputbox instruction is located before the `Do While` statement, the program will never return to that instruction once the loop begins. (It may help to refer to the flowchart shown in Figure 5-20.) In other words, the `strSales = InputBox ("Enter a sales amount. Click Cancel when finished.", "Input")` instruction located above the loop gets only the first sales amount from the user. The `strSales = InputBox ("Enter a sales amount. Click Cancel when finished.", "Input")` instruction located within the loop gets each of the remaining sales amounts, if any, from the user.

After the user enters another sales amount, the `Loop` statement sends the program to the `Do While` statement where the *condition* is tested again. If the *condition* evaluates to True, the loop instructions are processed again. If the *condition* evaluates to False, the loop stops and the instruction after the `Loop` statement is processed. That statement calculates the average sales amount by dividing the contents of the accumulator variable (sngSumSales) by the contents of the counter variable (intNumSales). The result is assigned to the sngAvgSales variable. The next instruction displays the average sales amount, formatted as currency, in the lblAvg control.

To test the Do While button:

1   Close the Code window, then **run** the application.

Recall that the Do While button will calculate the average of the sales amounts that are entered by the user.

2   Click the **Do While** button, type 3000 in the dialog box and press the **Enter** key. The loop instructions add 1 to the intNumSales variable, giving 1, and also add 3000 to the sngSumSales variable, giving 3000. The user is then prompted for another sales amount.

3   Type **4000** in the dialog box and press the **Enter** key. The loop instructions add 1 to the intNumSales variable, giving 2, and also add 4000 to the sngSumSales variable, giving 7000.

tip

You should always test your application with both correct and incorrect data. Incorrect data is data that the application is not expecting.

Now stop the loop. Recall that you stop the loop by clicking the Cancel button.

4 Click the **Cancel** button in the dialog box. The loop stops and the average sales amount, $3,500.00, is calculated and displayed in the lblAvg control. The Click event procedure then ends.

See what happens if the user clicks the Do While button and then selects the Cancel button without entering any sales amounts.

5 Click the **Do While** button, then click the **Cancel** button. A dialog box containing the "Run-time error '6': Overflow" error message appears on the screen, as shown in Figure 5-23.

Figure 5-23: Dialog box showing Overflow error message

6 Click the **Debug** button to remove the dialog box, then maximize the Code window. Visual Basic highlights the `sngAvgSales = sngSumSales / intNumSales` instruction in the Code window.

When you click the Cancel button immediately after clicking the Do While button, the loop instructions are never processed. That means that the intNumSales variable is not updated from its initial value of zero. Because division by zero is not allowed, Visual Basic displays an error message when it attempts to process the `sngAvgSales = sngSumSales / intNumSales` assignment statement. You can verify the contents of the intNumSales variable by placing the mouse pointer I over intNumSales in the assignment statement. Do that now.

7 Place the mouse pointer I over intNumSales as shown in Figure 5-24.

```
CtrAccum - frmCtrAccum (Code)                                    _ □ ×
cmdWhile                    ▼      Click                         ▼
    Private Sub cmdWhile_Click()
        Dim strSales As String
        Dim intNumSales As Integer    'counter
        Dim sngSumSales As Single     'accumulator
        Dim sngAvgSales As Single

        strSales = InputBox("Enter a sales amount. Click Cancel when finished.
        Do While strSales <> ""
            intNumSales = intNumSales + 1              'update counter
            sngSumSales = sngSumSales + Val(strSales)  'update accumulator
            strSales = InputBox("Enter a sales amount. Click Cancel when finis
        Loop

⇨  |     sngAvgSales = sngSumSales / intNumSales
            lblAvg.Caption = Format(sngA intNumSales = 0 urrency")
    End Sub
```

current value of
intNumSales

Figure 5-24: Current value of intNumSales variable

8 Close the Code window, then click the **End** button ▪. Visual Basic returns to the design screen.

You can use a selection structure to determine if the program will encounter the division by zero problem, and then take the appropriate action to avoid displaying the Overflow error message. Before calculating the average sales amount, the selection structure will first determine if the value in intNumSales is greater than zero. If it is, the selection structure will calculate and display the average sales amount; otherwise, the selection structure will display a "No sales" message in the lblAvg control.

9 Open the Do While button's Click event procedure. Maximize the Code window and enter the comment and selection structure shown in Figure 5-25.

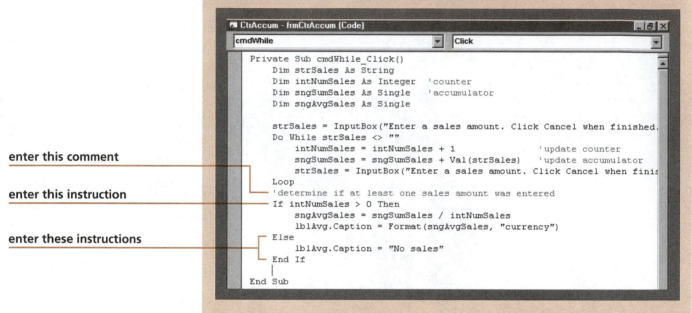

enter this comment

enter this instruction

enter these instructions

```
CtrAccum - frmCtrAccum (Code)                                    _ | 8 | X
cmdWhile                          ▼     Click                              ▼
Private Sub cmdWhile_Click()
    Dim strSales As String
    Dim intNumSales As Integer    'counter
    Dim sngSumSales As Single     'accumulator
    Dim sngAvgSales As Single

    strSales = InputBox("Enter a sales amount. Click Cancel when finished.
    Do While strSales <> ""
        intNumSales = intNumSales + 1                    'update counter
        sngSumSales = sngSumSales + Val(strSales)    'update accumulator
        strSales = InputBox("Enter a sales amount. Click Cancel when finis
    Loop
    'determine if at least one sales amount was entered
    If intNumSales > 0 Then
        sngAvgSales = sngSumSales / intNumSales
        lblAvg.Caption = Format(sngAvgSales, "currency")
    Else
        lblAvg.Caption = "No sales"
    End If

End Sub
```

Figure 5-25: Selection structure entered in the Do While button's Click event procedure

10 Close the Code window, then **run** the application. Click the **Do While** button, then click the **Cancel** button. This time an error does not occur; rather, the "No sales" message appears in the lblAvg control.

11 Click the **Exit** button to end the application. Visual Basic returns to the design screen.

Now look at the same example written with the Do Until loop.

To view the code in the Do Until button:

1 Open the Do Until button's Click event procedure, then maximize the Code window. The maximized Code window appears, as shown in Figure 5-26.

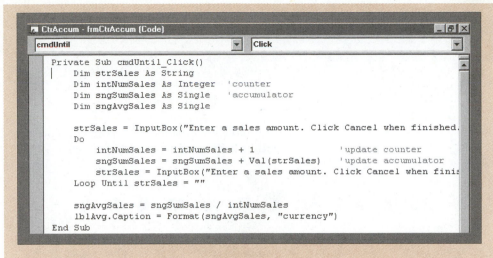

Figure 5-26: Do Until button's Click event procedure

Notice that the condition, `strSales = ""`, appears at the bottom of the Do Until loop.

2   Close the Code window, then **run** the application.

Now enter two sales amounts.

3   Click the **Do Until** button, then type **3000** in the dialog box and press the **Enter** key. The loop instructions add 1 to intNumSales, giving 1, and add 3000 to sngSumSales, giving 3000. The user is then prompted to enter another sales amount.

4   Type **4000** in the dialog box and press the **Enter** key. The loop instructions add 1 to intNumSales, giving 2, and add 4000 to sngSumSales, giving 7000. The user is then prompted to enter another sales amount.

Now stop the Do Until loop by clicking the Cancel button.

5   Click the **Cancel** button. The loop stops and the average sales amount, $3,500.00, is calculated and displayed in the lblAvg control.

As you did with the Do While loop, see what happens if the user clicks the Do Until button and then clicks the Cancel button without entering any sales amounts.

6   Click the **Do Until** button, then click the **Cancel** button. The loop instructions add 1 to intNumSales and add 0 (zero), the numeric equivalent of a zero-length string, to sngSumSales. (Recall that when the user selects the Cancel button, the InputBox function stores a zero-length string in the strSales variable.) A dialog box requesting another sales amount appears.

Because the Do Until loop's *condition* (`strSales = ""`) is not tested until after the second sales amount is entered, you will need to click the Cancel button again to stop the loop.

7   Click the **Cancel** button. The loop stops and $0.00 appears in the lblAvg control. The $0.00 is the result of dividing the contents of sngSumSales (0) by the contents of intNumSales (1).

Because you can never be sure what a user might do, it is usually safer to use the Do While loop instead of the Do Until loop. Use the Do Until loop only in situations where you know that the loop definitely can and will be processed at least once.

8 Click the **Exit** button to end the application. Visual Basic returns to the design screen.

9 Click **File** on the menu bar, then click **New Project**. When you are asked if you want to save the CtrAccum files, click the **No** button. You can now open a Standard EXE project.

You have now completed Lesson A. You can either take a break or complete the end-of-lesson questions and exercises.

S U M M A R Y

To code the For Next (automatic counter) loop:

■ Use the `For...Next` statement. The syntax is:
   For *counter* = *startvalue* **To** *endvalue* [**Step** *stepvalue*]

   [*instructions*]

   Next *counter*

■ The loop performs the following three tasks:
   1. The loop initializes the *counter* (the numeric variable) to the *startvalue*. This is done only once, at the beginning of the loop.
   2. If the *stepvalue* is positive (negative), the loop checks if the value in the *counter* is greater (less) than the *endvalue*. If it is, the loop stops; if it's not, the instructions within the loop are processed.
   3. The loop adds the *stepvalue* to the *counter*. It then repeats steps 2 and 3 until the *counter* is greater than the endvalue (or, if the *stepvalue* is negative, until the *counter* is less than the *endvalue*).

To move a control across the screen (from left to right or from right to left):

■ Use a For Next loop to set the control's Left property.

To code the Do While loop:

■ Use the `Do While...Loop` statement. Its syntax is:
   Do While *condition*

   [*loop instructions*]

   Loop

To code the Do Until loop:

■ Use the `Do...Loop Until` statement. Its syntax is:
   Do

   [*loop instructions*]

   Loop Until *condition*

To use a counter:

■ Initialize the counter, if necessary.
■ Use an assignment statement, within a repetition structure, to update the counter. You update a counter by incrementing (or decrementing) its value by a constant amount.

To use an accumulator:

■ Initialize the accumulator, if necessary.
■ Use an assignment statement, within a repetition structure, to update the accumulator. You update an accumulator by incrementing (or decrementing) its value by an amount that varies.

Q U E S T I O N S

1. Which of the following flowchart symbols represents the For Next loop?
   a. diamond
   b. hexagon
   c. oval
   d. parallelogram
   e. rectangle

2. Assuming intCount is a numeric variable, how many times will the Print intCount instruction be processed?

   ```
   For intCount = 1 to 6
           Print intCount
   Next intCount
   ```
   a. 0
   b. 1
   c. 5
   d. 6
   e. 7

3. What is the value of intCount when the loop in question 2 stops?
   a. 1
   b. 5
   c. 6
   d. 7
   e. 8

4. Assuming intCount is a numeric variable, how many times will the Print intCount instruction be processed?

   ```
   For intCount = 4 to 10 Step 2
           Print intCount
   Next intCount
   ```
   a. 0
   b. 3
   c. 4
   d. 5
   e. 12

5. What is the value of intCount when the loop in question 4 stops?
   a. 4
   b. 6
   c. 10
   d. 11
   e. 12

6. When the *stepvalue* in a For Next loop is positive, the instructions within the loop are processed only when the *counter* is _____ the *endvalue*.
   a. equal to
   b. greater than
   c. greater than or equal to
   d. less than
   e. less than or equal to

7. When the *stepvalue* in a For Next loop is negative, the instructions within the loop are processed only when the *counter* is _____ the *endvalue*.
   a. equal to
   b. greater than
   c. greater than or equal to
   d. less than
   e. less than or equal to

8. Which of the following is a valid `For` instruction?
   a. `For intTemp = 1.5 To 5 Step .5`
   b. `For intTemp = 5 To 1 Step .25`
   c. `For intTemp = 1 To 3 Step −1`
   d. `For intTemp = 3 To 1`
   e. `For intTemp = 1 To 10`

9. The For Next loop performs three tasks, as shown below. Put these tasks in their proper order by placing the numbers 1 through 3 on the line to the left of the task.

   _____ Adds the *stepvalue* to the *counter*.

   _____ Initializes the *counter* to the *startvalue*.

   _____ Checks if the value in the *counter* is greater (less) than the *endvalue*.

10. If you omit the *stepvalue* in a `For…Next` statement, Visual Basic uses a *stepvalue* of _____ .
    a. 0
    b. 1
    c. −1
    d. It results in an error message

11. The three forms of the repetition structure are:
    a. Do For
    b. Do Until
    c. Do While
    d. For Now
    e. For Next

12. You can use the _____ loop(s) when you don't know how many times the loop instructions should be processed.
    a. Do Until
    b. Do While
    c. For Next
    d. a or b
    e. a, b, or c

13. You can use the _____ loop(s) when you know precisely how many times the loop instructions should be processed.
    a. Do Until
    b. Do While
    c. For Next
    d. a or b
    e. a, b, or c

14. Programmers call the _____ loop a pretest loop because the condition is tested at the beginning of the loop.
    a. Do Until
    b. Do While
    c. For Next
    d. a and c
    e. b and c

15. Programmers call the _____ loop a posttest loop because the condition is tested at the end of the loop.
    a. Do Until
    b. Do While
    c. For Next
    d. a and c
    e. b and c

16. The _____ loop repeats the loop instructions as long as the condition is true. Once the condition becomes false, this loop stops.
    a. Do Until
    b. Do While

17. The _____ loop repeats the loop instructions as long as the condition is false. Once the condition becomes true, this loop stops.
    a. Do Until
    b. Do While

18. The _____ loop processes the loop instructions at least once, whereas the _____ loop instructions might not be processed at all.
    a. Do Until, Do While
    b. Do While, Do Until

19. A(n) _____ is a numeric variable used for counting something.
    a. accumulator
    b. adder
    c. constant
    d. counter
    e. integer

20. A(n) _____ is a numeric variable used for accumulating something.
    a. accumulator
    b. adder
    c. constant
    d. counter
    e. integer

21. Counters and accumulators must be _____ and _____.
    a. added
    b. counted
    c. initialized
    d. printed
    e. updated

22. A(n) _____ is always incremented by a constant amount, whereas a(n) _____ is incremented by an amount that varies.
    a. accumulator, counter
    b. counter, accumulator

23. Which of the following will correctly update the counter variable named intNumber?
    a. `intNumber = 0`
    b. `intNumber = 1`
    c. `intNumber = intNumber + intNumber`
    d. `intNumber = intNumber + curSales`
    e. `intNumber = intNumber + 1`

24. Which of the following will correctly update the accumulator variable named curTotal?
    a. `curTotal = 0`
    b. `curTotal = 1`
    c. `curTotal = curTotal + curTotal`
    d. `curTotal = curTotal + curSales`
    e. `curTotal = curTotal + 1`

25. Counters and accumulators are automatically initialized to zero by _____ .
    a. an assignment statement
    b. the `Dim` statement
    c. the `Initialize` statement
    d. the `Update` statement

E X E R C I S E S

1. If you have access to the MSDN Library, then search for a Help screen on the `For Next` statement and a Help screen on the `Do Loop` statement. Print both Help screens. Can you nest For Next loops? Can you nest Do loops?

2. Write the Visual Basic code that corresponds to the flowchart shown in Figure 5-27.

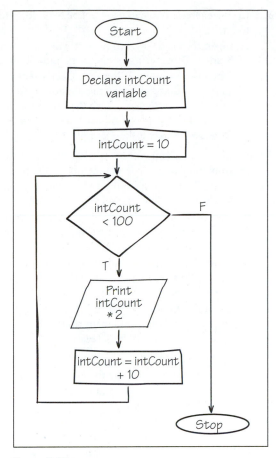

Figure 5-27

3. Draw the flowchart that corresponds to the following Visual Basic code.

    ```
    For intNumber = 1 To 10 Step 1

       Print "Hello"

    Next intNumber
    ```

4. In this exercise you will use the For Next loop to print numbers on the form.
    a. Open a new project. Add one command button to the form. In the command button's Click event procedure, enter a For Next loop that will print the numbers 0 through 117, in increments of 9, on the form. Use the Print method, which you learned about in Tutorial 4's Debugging section. Use intTemp as the numeric variable in the For Next loop. What value will intTemp have when the loop stops?
    b. Run, but don't save, the project. Click the command button to test your code. Mark down the value the intTemp variable has when the loop stops, then exit the application.
    c. Print the code. On the printout, mark the value intTemp has when the loop stops.

5. In this exercise, you will use the For Next loop to calculate and display the square of the even numbers from 2 to 12. Use the For Next loop and the Print method (which you learned about in Tutorial 4's Debugging section) to display the squares on the form.
    a. Open a new project. Add one command button to the form. Code the command button's Click event procedure appropriately.
    b. Run, but don't save, the project. Click the Command1 button to test your code. Mark down the squares of the even numbers from 2 through 12, then exit the application.
    c. Print the code. On the printout, mark the squares of the even numbers from 2 through 12.

6. In this exercise you will use the For Next loop to move an image control from right to left.

   a. Open the For (For.vbp) project, which is located in the Tut05 folder on your Student Disk, then save the form and the project as la6Done in the Tut05 folder.

   b. Open the Example 2 button's Click event procedure. Add another `For Next` statement that will move the image control from right to left. (Enter the additional `For Next` statement above the End Sub statement. Use 6500 as the *startvalue*, use −50 as the *stepvalue*, and use 0 as the *endvalue*.)

   c. Save, run, and test the Example 2 button. Then print the code.

7. In this exercise you will use the For Next loop to move an image control from top to bottom and diagonally from the upper-left corner to the lower-right corner of the form.

   a. Open the For (For.vbp) project, which is located in the Tut05 folder on your Student Disk. Save the form and the project as la7Done in the Tut05 folder.

   b. Add two command buttons to the form. Name one of the command buttons cmdExam3 and change its Caption to Example <u>3</u>. Name the other command button cmdExam4 and change its Caption to Example <u>4</u>.

   c. Open the Example 3 button's Click event procedure. In the Click event procedure, enter a `For Next` statement that will move the image control from the top of the screen to the bottom of the screen.

   d. Open the Example 4 button's Click event procedure. In the Click event procedure, enter a `For Next` statement that will move the image control diagonally from the upper-left corner of the screen to the lower-right corner of the screen.

   e. Save, run, and test the Example 3 and Example 4 command buttons. Print the code.

8. In this exercise you will use the For Next loop to print the first 10 Fibonacci numbers.

   a. Create a user interface that contains two command buttons. Name one of the command buttons cmdDisplay and change its Caption to <u>D</u>isplay Fibonacci Numbers. Name the other command button cmdExit and change its Caption to E<u>x</u>it.

   b. Save the form and the project as la8Done in the Tut05 folder on your Student Disk.

   c. Open the cmdDisplay control's Code window. In the Click event procedure, enter a `For Next` statement that will print the first 10 Fibonacci numbers (1, 1, 2, 3, 5, 8, 13, 21, 34, 55) on the form. (*Hint:* Notice that, beginning with the third number in the series, each Fibonacci number is the sum of the prior two numbers. In other words, 2 is the sum of 1 plus 1, 3 is the sum of 1 plus 2, 5 is the sum of 2 plus 3, and so on.)

   d. Code the cmdExit control's Click event procedure so that it will end the application.

   e. Save and run the application. Click the Display Fibonacci Numbers button, then click the Exit button.

   f. Print the code.

9. In this exercise you will use the Do While loop to display the word Hello on the form 10 times.

   a. Open a new project. Place a command button on the form. Code the command button's Click event procedure so that it prints the word Hello on the form 10 times. The partial code is shown below; you will need to complete the code.

```
Dim intCount as Integer
intCount = 1
Do _____
    Print "Hello"
    intCount = intCount + 1
Loop
```

   b. Run, but don't save, the application. Click the command button. Stop the application and print the code.

10. In this exercise you will use the Do Until loop to display the word Hello on the form 10 times.

    a. Open a new project. Place a command button on the form. Code the command button's Click event procedure so that it prints the word Hello on the form 10 times. The partial code is shown below; you will need to complete the code.

```
Dim intTemp as Integer

intTemp = 1

Do

    Print "Hello"

    intTemp = intTemp + 1

Loop _____
```

    b. Run, but don't save, the application. Click the command button. Stop the application and print the code.

11. Write a `Do While` statement that tells Visual Basic to stop the loop when the value in the curSales variable is equal to zero.

12. Write a `Loop Until` statement that tells Visual Basic to stop the loop when the value in the curSales variable is equal to zero.

13. Write a `Do While` statement that tells Visual Basic to stop the loop when the user enters the word "Done" (in either uppercase or lowercase letters) in the strName variable.

14. Write a `Loop Until` statement that tells Visual Basic to stop the loop when the user enters the word "Done" (in either uppercase or lowercase letters) in the strName variable.

15. What will print on the form when the following code is processed?

```
Dim intTemp as Integer

Do While intTemp < 5

    Print intTemp

    intTemp = intTemp + 1

Loop
```

16. What will print on the form when the following code is processed?

```
Dim intTemp as Integer

Do

    Print intTemp

    intTemp = intTemp + 1

Loop Until intTemp > 5
```

17. An instruction is missing from the following code. What is the missing instruction and where does it belong in the code?

```
Dim intNum as Integer

intNum = 1

Do While intNum < 5

    Print intNum

Loop
```

18. An instruction is missing from the following code. What is the missing instruction and where does it belong in the code?

```
Dim intNum as Integer

intNum = 10

Do

    Print intNum

Loop Until intNum = 0
```

19. The following code should print the commission (curSales * .1) for each sales amount that is entered. The code is not working properly because an instruction is missing. What is the missing instruction and where does it belong in the code?

```
Dim curSales as Currency
curSales = Val(Inputbox("Enter a sales amount"))
Do While curSales > 0
   Print curSales * .1
Loop
```

20. The following code should print the commission (curSales * .1) for each sales amount that is entered. The code is not working properly. What is wrong with the code and how will you fix it?

```
Dim curSales as Currency
curSales = Val(Inputbox("Enter a sales amount"))
Do
   curSales = Val(Inputbox("Enter a sales amount"))
   Print curSales * .1
Loop Until curSales <= 0
```

21. Write an assignment statement that updates a counter variable, named intNumStudents, by 1.

22. Write an assignment statement that updates a counter variable, named intQuantity, by 5.

23. Write an assignment statement that updates an accumulator variable, named curTotal, by the value in the curSales variable.

24. Write an assignment statement that updates an accumulator variable, named sngTotal, by the value in the sngGross variable.

25. Write an assignment statement that initializes a counter variable, named intEmployees, to 1.

26. Look at the following two assignment statements. Which will correctly update a counter, and which will correctly update an accumulator? How do you know which one updates a counter and which one updates an accumulator?

```
intTotal = intTotal + 1
sngTotal = sngTotal + sngSales
```

27. What will print when the following code is processed?

```
Dim intTotEmp as Integer
Do While intTotEmp <= 5
   Print intTotEmp
   intTotEmp = intTotEmp + 2
Loop
```

28. What will print when the following code is processed?

```
Dim intTotEmp as Integer
   intTotEmp = 1
Do
   Print intTotEmp
   intTotEmp = intTotEmp + 2
Loop Until intTotEmp >= 3
```

LESSON B
objectives

In this lesson you will learn how to:

- Create a control array
- Set the Enabled property
- Code a control array's Click and GotFocus events

Using Control Arrays

The Grade Application

Recall that your task in this tutorial is to create an application that Professor Carver's students can use to calculate their grade during the semester. A student must complete three projects, worth 10 points each, and a midterm and final, worth 50 points each. If the student accumulates 90% of the points, a grade of A is assigned; 80% is a B; 70% is a C; 60% is a D; and below 60% is an F. The sketch of the user interface for the grade application is shown in Figure 5-28.

Name: [_____]

    10 points   50 points

☐ Project 1 [0]   ☐ Midterm [0]

☐ Project 2 [0]   ☐ Final [0]

☐ Project 3 [0]   Grade: [_____]

[Display Grade]   [Print]   [Exit]

Figure 5-28: Sketch of user interface for grade application

The grade application will contain various label controls, check boxes, text boxes, and command buttons. To determine the grade, the student needs simply to click the appropriate check boxes, then enter the scores in the corresponding text boxes, and then click the Display Grade button. The Display Grade button will display the letter grade based on the work that has been completed so far.

To save you time, your Student Disk contains a partially completed grade application. When you open the application you will notice that most of the user interface has already been created and most of the properties of the existing objects have been set. You will finish creating the user interface in this lesson. You will also begin coding the application.

To open the partially completed application:

1 Start Visual Basic, if necessary. Open the **T5Case** (T5Case.vbp) project, which is located in the Tut05 folder on your Student Disk.

2 Save the form and the project as **lbGrade**, then click the **form** to select it. See Figure 5-29.

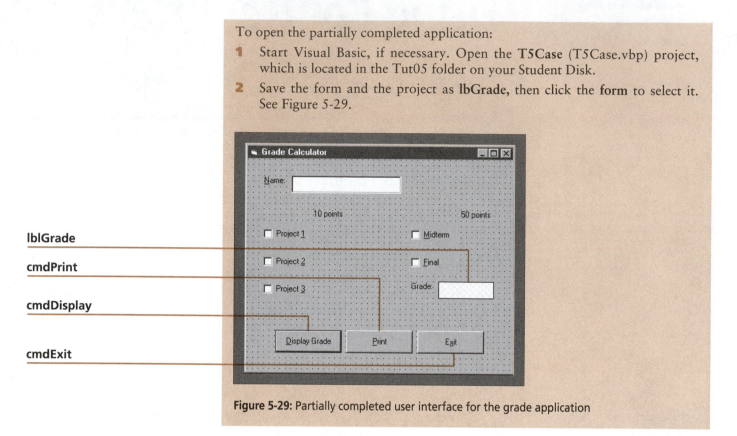

Figure 5-29: Partially completed user interface for the grade application

Notice that the user interface is not complete; you still need to add the five text boxes. Before doing so, however, you will view the application's TOE chart, which is shown in Figure 5-30.

Task	Object	Event

1. If the user selects a check box, then
 	
   a. enable the corresponding text box
 	
   b. send the focus to the corresponding text box
 	
2. If the user deselects a check box, then
 	
   a. enter a zero in the corresponding text box
 	
   b. disable the corresponding text box
	chkDone array	Click

1. For each selected check box,
 	
   a. add the score found in its associated text box to the total earned points accumulator
 	
   b. if the check box is for a project, then add 10 to the total possible points accumulator; otherwise, add 50
 	
2. Calculate the ratio by dividing the value in the total earned points accumulator by the value in the total possible points accumulator
 	
3. Display the appropriate letter grade, based on the ratio, in the lblGrade control
	cmdDisplay	Click

End the application	cmdExit, frmGrade	Click, Unload
Print the interface	cmdPrint	Click
Display the letter grade (from cmdDisplay)	lblGrade	None
Get and display the project and test scores	txtScore array	None

Figure 5-30: TOE chart for the grade application

You will code the chkDone array's Click event procedure in this lesson. You will code the cmdDisplay control's Click event and the form's Unload event in Lesson C. You will not need to code either the Exit or the Print button because both controls have been coded for you; the Exit button's Click event contains the `End` instruction, and the Print button's Click event contains the `PrintForm` instruction. (You will, however, modify the code in the Exit button in Lesson C.) Also, the `Option Explicit` statement has been entered in the form's General Declarations section. In addition, the Display Grade button's Default property is set to True, which means that the button is the default command button on the form.

First you will add the five text boxes to the interface. While doing so, you will make the text boxes into a control array.

Creating a Control Array While Adding Controls to the Form

Many times an application will contain a group of controls, of the same type, that perform essentially the same task. In the grade application, for example, each of the five text boxes will get and display the score a student earned on either a project or a test. Instead of giving each of the related controls a different name, which can be difficult to remember, Visual Basic allows you to assign the same name to each of them. When you give the same name to more than one control, you create a **control array**—a group of controls of the same type that have the same name and share the same set of event procedures. All of the controls in an array must be of the same type—in other words, they must all be text boxes, or label controls, or check boxes, and so on.

Visual Basic assigns a unique number, called an **index**, to each of the controls in an array. It might help to picture a control array as a group of mailboxes on a street. The name of the array is the name of the street, and the index is the address on each mailbox. The index reflects the control's position in the array, just as the address reflects a mailbox's position on a street. The first control (mailbox) in an array has an index (address) of 0, the second control has an index of 1, and so on. You refer to each control in an array by the array's name (street name) and the control's index (address). The index is specified in a set of parentheses immediately following the name. For example, the first control in an array named txtScore is referred to as txtScore(0), the second control is txtScore(1), and so on. The name of the array is stored in each control's Name property; the index is stored in each control's Index property.

If the controls to be included in an array are not already on the form, you can use the copy and paste method to create the control array; you will use this method to create the txtScore control array, which will consist of five text boxes. Before you can use the copy and paste method, you need to add the first array control—in this case, a text box—to the form and then set its properties.

tip

You can also have an array of variables, which you will learn about in Tutorial 9.

tip

If the interface contains a group of related controls, you can save system resources by assigning the controls to a control array. If you want to create a new control at run time, that control must be a member of a control array.

To add the first text box to the form, then use copy and paste to create the txtScore control array:

1 Double-click the **TextBox** tool 🔲 in the toolbox, then drag the text box until it is positioned to the right of the Project 1 check box, and immediately below the "10 points" label. (If you want to match the figures in this book exactly, you can set the text box's Left property to 1440 and its Top property to 1440.)

2 Set the text box's Text property to the number 0, then set its Font size to 10, its Height property to 375, and its Width property to 735.

3 Scroll the Properties list, if necessary, until the Name property is visible.

Notice that the default name of the first text box is Text1.

4 Scroll the Properties list, if necessary, until the Index property is visible. Notice that the Index property is empty. When the Index property is empty, it means that the control is not a member of an array.

You will set the Name property of this text box to txtScore; this will become the name of the control array when the array is created.

5 Click (**Name**) in the Properties list, then type **txtScore** and press the **Enter** key.

Now that the text box is on the form and its properties are set, you can use the copy and paste method to create the control array. First, copy the text box to the clipboard.

6 Click the **txtScore** control to return to the form. Click **Edit** on the menu bar, then click **Copy** to copy the text box to the clipboard. Click the **form** to select it. Visual Basic highlights the form's title bar. Click **Edit**, then click **Paste** to paste a copy of the text box on the form. Visual Basic displays the message dialog box shown in Figure 5-31.

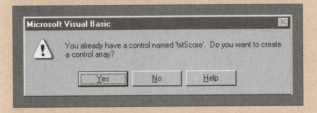

Figure 5-31: Message dialog box

HELP? If Copy is dimmed on the Edit menu, then repeat step 6. This time be sure to click the txtScore control in the form before opening the Edit menu.

The dialog box warns you that the form already contains a control named txtScore, and it asks if you want to create a control array.

7 Click the **Yes** button to create the control array. Another text box appears in the upper-left corner of the form.

8 Click **Index** in the Properties list. See Figure 5-32.

new text box

Index property

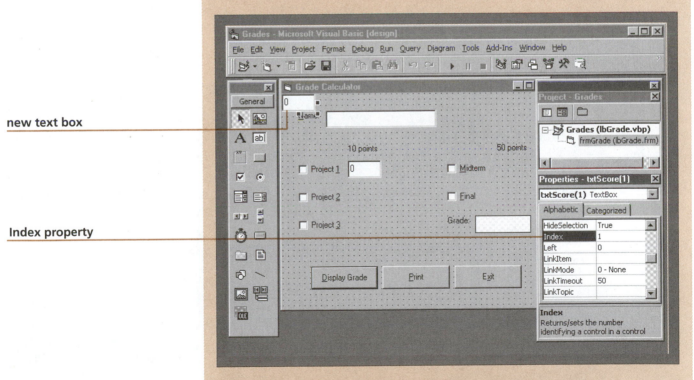

Figure 5-32: Interface showing Properties window and new text box copied to upper-left corner

HELP? If a copy of the text box does not appear on the form, repeat steps 6 through 8. This time, be sure to click the txtScore control in the form before copying the text box to the clipboard.

The Properties window shows the number 1 in this control's Index property.

9   Scroll the Properties list until the Name property is visible.

The Properties window shows txtScore (the name of the control array) in this control's Name property. txtScore(1)—the full reference to this control—appears in the Object box. Visual Basic also copies the font size, as well as the text, height, and width property values from the original text box to the new text box. (You can scroll the Properties list to verify that, if you want.)

10   Drag the **txtScore(1)** control until it is positioned to the immediate right of the Project 2 check box.

Now see what changes Visual Basic made to the properties of the first text box you added to the form.

11   Click the **first text box**, then scroll the Properties list until the Name property is visible. The Name property says txtScore, as it did before.

12   Scroll the Properties list until the Index property is visible. Notice that the Index property now contains a zero, and the Object box now shows that the full name of the control is txtScore(0). Both the zero in the Index property and the (0) after the name in the Object box indicate that the control is the first control in an array.

The text box is still on the clipboard, so you just need to paste it onto the form three more times.

13   Click the **form** to select it. Use the Edit menu to paste three more text boxes onto the form. Position each text box to the right of its corresponding check box as shown in Figure 5-33. (Be sure to position the txtScore(2) control next to the Project3 check box, the txtScore(3) control next to the Midterm check box, and the txtScore(4) control next to the Final check box.)

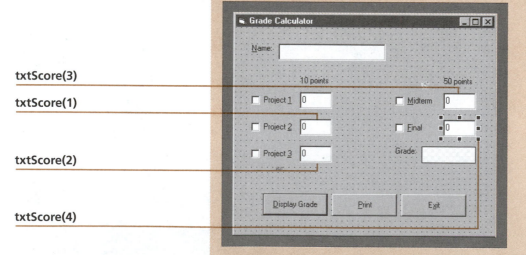

Figure 5-33: Correct position of text boxes in the user interface

Now verify that the controls were named correctly.

14 Click the **Object box** list arrow in the Properties window. The names of the five text boxes in the txtScore array should appear as shown in Figure 5-34.

5 text box names

Figure 5-34: Open Object box showing the names of the five text boxes in the txtScore array

You have now finished creating the txtScore text box array.

15 Click the **Object box** list arrow to close the Object box, then click the **form** to select it.

tip

If the Object box does not contain the correct names for the text box controls, then close the Object box and rename the controls whose names are either missing or incorrect.

You can also make existing controls into a control array.

Making Existing Controls into a Control Array

According to the TOE chart shown earlier in Figure 5-30, each of the five check boxes has the same responsibilities. For example, each check box should send the focus to a text box in the txtScore array when the check box is selected by the user. Each check box should also assign a zero to the text box when the check box is deselected by the user. Because each check box has the same responsibilities, you will make them into a control array named chkDone. You make existing controls into a control array simply by giving them the same name—in other words, by setting their Name property to the same value.

To make the check boxes into a control array named chkDone:

1 Click the **Project 1** check box to select that control. Scroll the Properties list, if necessary, until the Name property is visible.

Notice that the default name of the first check box is Check1.

2 Scroll the Properties list, if necessary, until the Index property is visible. Notice that the Index property is empty. Remember that when the Index property is empty, it means that the control is not a member of an array.

3 Click (**Name**) in the Properties list, type **chkDone**, and press the **Enter** key. chkDone appears both in the Name property and in the Object box, and the Index property is still empty. Be sure to verify, in the Properties window, that you have typed chkDone correctly.

4 Click the **Project 2** check box to select it. The Name property should be selected in the Properties list, so you just need to type **chkDone** and press the **Enter** key. When Visual Basic displays the dialog box that asks if you want to create a control array, click the **Yes** button. chkDone appears in the Name property, 1 appears in the Index property, and chkDone(1) appears in the Object box. This control is the second control in the chkDone array.

HELP? If the dialog box does not appear, repeat step 4. Be careful to type chkDone correctly. The Name property for this control must match the Name property of the first check box.

Now name the remaining three check boxes.

5 Click the **Project 3** check box, then type **chkDone** in the Name property and press the **Enter** key. Look in the Properties window to verify that chkDone appears in the Name property, 2 appears in the Index property, and chkDone(2) appears in the Object box. chkDone(2) indicates that this is the third control in the array.

6 Click the **Midterm** check box, then type **chkDone** in the Name property and press the **Enter** key. Look in the Properties window to verify that chkDone appears in the Name property, 3 appears in the Index property, and chkDone(3) appears in the Object box. The chkDone(3) control is the fourth control in the array.

7 Click the **Final** check box, then type **chkDone** in the Name property and press the **Enter** key. Look in the Properties window to verify that chkDone appears in the Name property, 4 appears in the Index property, and chkDone(4) appears in the Object box. This control is the fifth control in the chkDone array.

8 Click the **form** to select it.

Now that you have completed the user interface, you can lock the controls and set their TabIndex properties appropriately.

tip

You can also use the Lock Controls command on the Format menu.

To lock the controls, then set their TabIndex values:

1 Right-click the **form**, then click **Lock Controls** on the pop-up menu.

2 Set each object's TabIndex property according to Figure 5-35.

Control	TabIndex	Control	TabIndex
Label1 (Name:)	0	chkDone(3)	8
txtName	1	txtScore(3)	9
chkDone(0)	2	chkDone(4)	10
txtScore(0)	3	txtScore(4)	11
chkDone(1)	4	cmdDisplay	12
txtScore(1)	5	cmdPrint	13
chkDone(2)	6	cmdExit	14
txtScore(2)	7		

Figure 5-35: TabIndex values

3   **Save** and **run** the application. Press the **Tab** key several times, until the focus returns to the Name text box. Notice that the focus goes from the Name text box to the first check box, then to the first text box, then to the second check box, the second text box, and so on. When the focus is in the fifth text box, it then moves to each of the command buttons before returning to the Name text box.

In this application, you will not allow the user to tab into the project and test text boxes, or to enter information into those text boxes, unless the text box's corresponding check box is selected. In order to accomplish that, you will need to set each text box's Enabled property; you will do that in the next section.

4   Click the **Exit** button to end the application.

The Enabled Property

The **Enabled property** determines whether an object can respond to user-generated events, such as tabbing to the control or entering information into the control. You can set the Enabled property to the Boolean values of either True or False. When the Enabled property is set to its default value, True, the object can respond to a user-generated event. Setting the object's Enabled property to False prevents the object from responding to the user.

It is customary in Windows applications to disable objects that don't apply to the current state of the application. In this application, for example, you don't want to allow the user to either tab into the Project, Midterm, and Final text boxes, or enter information into those text boxes, until the user selects the corresponding check box, which indicates that the project or test has been completed. Therefore, you will have the project and test text boxes disabled when the interface first appears on the screen.

GUI
Design Tips
Enabling and Disabling Controls

• It is customary in Windows applications to disable objects that don't apply to the current state of the application.

To disable the Project, Midterm, and Final text boxes when the interface first appears:

1 Select the five txtScore text boxes, then set the Enabled property to **False**.

2 **Save** and **run** the application. Notice that the 0s in the txtScore text boxes appear dimmed. In a Windows application, when the contents of a control appear dimmed, it indicates to the user that the control is not currently available for use.

3 Press the **Tab** key several times, until the focus returns to the Name text box. Notice that the focus moves from the Name text box to each of the check boxes, then to the command buttons, and then back to the Name text box. The Project, Midterm, and Final text boxes do not receive the focus.

4 Try to click inside the **Midterm** text box. Because the text box's Enabled property is set to False, the text box cannot receive the focus; therefore, the user cannot enter anything in the text box.

5 Click the **Exit** button to end the application.

You will enable the Project, Midterm, and Final text boxes when the user clicks the text box's corresponding check box. Before coding the check box array's Click event procedure, you will look at the code window for a control array.

Viewing the Code Window for a Control Array

The controls in an array not only share the same name, they also share the same event procedures. That means that the code you enter in an array's Code window applies to all of the controls in the array. In other words, when you code one of the controls in an array, you're actually coding all of the controls in the array. The Code window associated with a control array differs slightly from the Code windows you've seen so far—specifically, the Code window includes an additional item of information. Because the controls in an array share the same event procedures, you can open their Code window by double-clicking any one of the controls in the array.

To open the check box array's Code window:

1 Double-click **one of the check boxes**. The Code window opens as shown in Figure 5-36.

argument

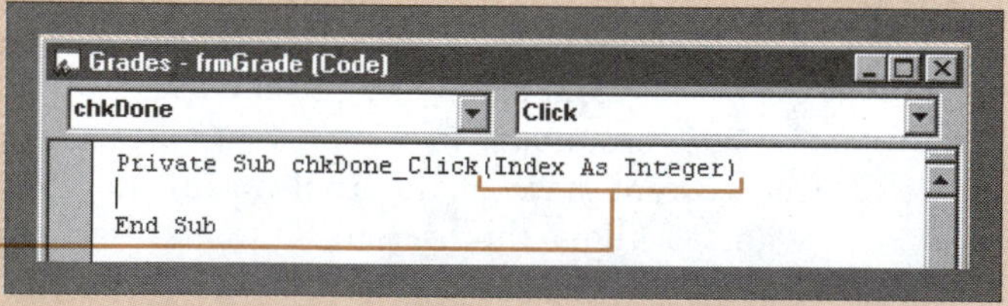

Figure 5-36: Click event procedure for the chkDone control array

In the Code windows you've seen so far, an empty set of parentheses followed the name of the event procedure. If a Code window belongs to a control array, however, `Index as Integer` will appear inside the parentheses. Items inside the parentheses are called **arguments**; they are used by Visual Basic to pass information to the event procedures. The information passed to the event procedures of control arrays is

tip

You learned about the Print method in Tutorial 4's debugging section. The syntax of the Print method that prints information on a form is **Print** [*outputlist*].

tip

It is easy to confuse the Index property with the Index argument. The Index property stores a number that identifies each control in a control array; each control in an array has a value in its Index property. You can think of the Index property value as being the address of the control in the array. The Index argument is not a property; rather, it is a variable created by Visual Basic. The Index argument stores a number that represents the address of the control that is receiving the event.

the value in the Index property of the control that is receiving the event. In this case, for example, if the user clicks the first check box, Visual Basic records the first check box's Index property value—0—in the Index argument. If the user clicks the second check box, Visual Basic records the second check box's Index property value—1—in the Index argument, and so on. You can prove this by entering a `Print Index` instruction, temporarily, in the Click event's Code window; when you click a check box, this instruction will print the value of the Index argument on the form.

To enter the `Print Index` instruction in the Click event procedure, then save, run, and test the application:

1 The Code window for the chkDone array's Click event should still be open. Type **print index** in the open Code window, then press the **Enter** key.

Recall that the code in the Code window applies to each of the controls in the array. In other words, Visual Basic will process the `Print Index` instruction when any one of the check boxes is clicked.

2 Close the Code window, then **save** and **run** the application.

See what Visual Basic assigns to the Index argument when you click the first check box.

3 Click the **Project 1** check box. Visual Basic prints a 0, the first check box's index, in the upper-left corner of the form.

4 On your own, click each of the remaining four check boxes to select them. Visual Basic will print the numbers 1, 2, 3, and 4 when you click the second, third, fourth, and fifth check boxes, respectively.

5 On your own, click each of the five check boxes to deselect them. Visual Basic prints the corresponding index—either 0, 1, 2, 3, or 4—on the form.

Now that you know what values Visual Basic records in the Index argument when the Click event occurs, you can stop the application, open the chkDone array's Code window, and delete the `Print Index` instruction.

6 Click the **Exit** button to stop the application. Open the chkDone control array's Click event procedure. Delete the `Print Index` instruction from the Code window, then close the Code window.

You can now begin coding the application. Begin with the chkDone control array's Click event procedure.

Coding the Check Box Array

The pseudocode for the check box array's Click event is shown in Figure 5-37.

If the check box is selected then

    enable the corresponding text box

    send the focus to the corresponding text box

Else

    assign 0 to the corresponding text box

    disable the corresponding text box

End If

Figure 5-37: Pseudocode for the check box array's Click event

As you learned in Tutorial 4, you click a check box to select it, and you also click a check box to deselect it. According to the pseudocode, if the user selects a check box, then the chkDone array's Click event should perform two tasks; it should perform two different tasks if the user deselects a check box. As you learned in Tutorial 4, when a check box is selected, its Value property contains the number 1; otherwise, it contains the number 0. Recall that, because it is difficult to remember that 0 means unchecked and 1 means checked, you should use the constants vbUnchecked and vbChecked, rather than the numbers 0 and 1, in your code. In this application, you will use an If...Then...Else selection structure to determine if the check box is selected. The `If...Then...Else` statement will compare the check box's Value property to the constant vbChecked.

If chkDone was the name of a check box that was not a member of a control array, the `If` statement to determine if the check box is selected would be written as `If chkDone.Value = vbChecked Then`. In this application, however, because chkDone is the name of a control array, the `If` statement to determine if the check box is selected is written as `If chkDone(Index).Value = vbChecked Then`. Notice how you use the event procedure's Index argument to determine if the current check box—the one that was just clicked—is selected.

tip

Recall that Visual Basic records, in the Index argument, the index of the control receiving the event—in this case, the index of the check box that the user clicked.

To code the chkDone array's Click event, then save and run the application:

1 Open the chkDone control array's Click event procedure. Press the **Tab** key, then type **if chkdone(index).value = vbchecked then** and press the **Enter** key.

If the user clicks a check box to select it, the Click event should enable the corresponding text box, then send the focus to that text box. In other words, the first check box should enable the first text box, then send the focus to the first text box; the second check box should enable the second text box, then send the focus to the second text box, and so on. Figure 5-38 shows the relationship between the check boxes and the text boxes.

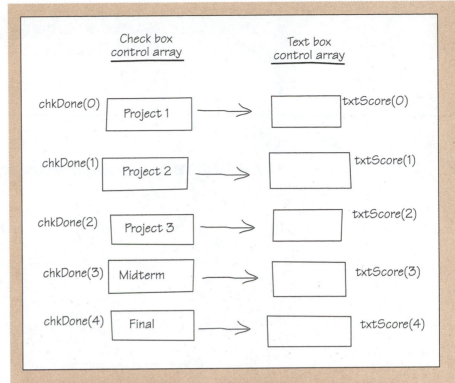

Figure 5-38: Relationship of controls in the chkDone and txtScore arrays

Notice that each check box has the same index as its corresponding text box, which is the text box located to its right. The first check box in the chkDone array and the first text box in the txtScore array, for example, both have an index of 0. Likewise, the second check box and its corresponding text box both have an index of 1. The same relationship is true for the remaining check boxes and text boxes contained in the two arrays. Arrays whose controls are related by their position in the arrays—in other words, by their index—are called **parallel arrays**.

You can use the `txtScore(Index).Enabled = True` instruction to enable the appropriate text box. When the user clicks a check box, this instruction tells Visual Basic to enable the text box that has the same index as the check box. If the user clicks the first check box, for example, the Index argument in the chkDone array's Click event procedure will contain a zero and Visual Basic will enable the txtScore(0) control, which is the first text box in the txtScore array.

2 Press the **Tab** key. Type **txtscore(index).enabled = true** and press the **Enter** key.

You can use the SetFocus method, along with the Click event procedure's Index argument, to send the focus to the check box's corresponding text box.

3 Type **txtscore(index).setfocus** and press the **Enter** key.

If the user clicks the check box to deselect it, then the Click event should assign the number 0 to the corresponding text box, then disable the text box.

4 Enter the additional code shown in Figure 5-39.

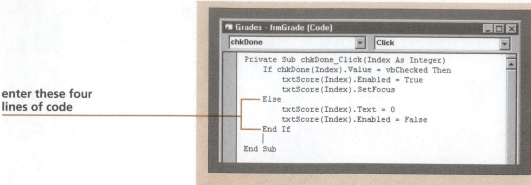

enter these four lines of code

Figure 5-39: Else branch shown in the Code window

5 Close the Code window, then **save** and **run** the application.

6 Click the **Project 1** check box. The Click event enables the first text box, then sends the focus to that text box. Notice that the user will need to delete the zero from the text box before entering the score. It would be more efficient for the user if the application automatically highlighted the zero in the text box; then, when the user entered the score, the score would replace the highlighted text. You will make this modification in the next section.

7 Press the **Delete** key, then click the **Project 1** check box to deselect it. The check box array's Click event assigns a zero to the corresponding text box, then disables the text box.

8 Click the **Exit** button to end the application.

In the next section you will have Visual Basic highlight the existing text when a text box in the txtScore control array receives the focus.

Coding a Control Array's GotFocus Event

As you learned in Tutorial 4, when the focus is sent to a text box that contains text, it is customary in Windows applications to highlight the existing text. By doing so, the new text entered by the user automatically replaces the highlighted text. Recall that you use the SelStart and SelLength properties, as well as the Len function, to highlight, or select, the existing text. The SelStart property tells Visual Basic where in the text box to position the insertion point—in other words, where to start the text selection. The SelLength property tells Visual Basic how many characters to select. You use the Len (short for "length") function to determine the number of characters contained in the text box.

In this application, you will have Visual Basic highlight the existing text when a text box in the txtScore control array receives the focus. In order to do that, you will need to place the appropriate code in the txtScore array's GotFocus event. Recall from Tutorial 4 that the GotFocus event occurs when an object receives the focus, either by user action, such as tabbing to or clicking the object, or by changing the focus in code using the SetFocus method.

GUI
Design Tips

Highlighting Existing Text

• It is customary in Windows applications to highlight, or select, the existing text in a text box when the text box receives the focus.

To code the txtScore array's GotFocus event:

1 Double-click **one of the text boxes** in the txtScore array. The Change event appears.

2 Use the Procedure box to open the txtScore array's GotFocus event, then enter the code shown in Figure 5-40.

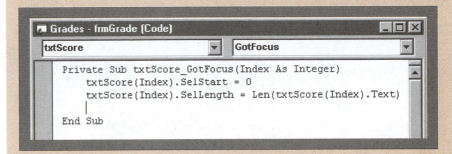

```
Grades - frmGrade (Code)                          _ □ ×

txtScore                    ▼    GotFocus                    ▼

Private Sub txtScore_GotFocus(Index As Integer)
    txtScore(Index).SelStart = 0
    txtScore(Index).SelLength = Len(txtScore(Index).Text)
    |
End Sub
```

Figure 5-40: Code entered in txtScore array's GotFocus event

3 Close the Code window, then **save** and **run** the application.

4 Click the **Project 1** check box. The check box's Click event enables its corresponding text box, then sends the focus to that text box. The text box's GotFocus event highlights the existing text in the text box.

5 Type **8** as the first project score and press the **Tab** key. The 8 replaces the highlighted text in the text box, and the focus moves to the Project 2 check box.

6 Press **Shift+Tab** to move the focus back to the Project 1 text box. The txtScore array's GotFocus event highlights the existing text in the text box.

7 Click the **Exit** button to end the application. Visual Basic returns to the design screen.

You have now completed Lesson B. You can either take a break or complete the questions and exercises at the end of the lesson. In Lesson C you will finish coding the application.

S U M M A R Y

To create a control array when the controls are already on the form:

■ Enter the same name in the Name property for each of the controls to be included in the array. When you are asked if you want to create a control array, click the Yes button.

To create a control array as you are entering the controls on the form:

■ Add the first control to the form and set its properties. Click Edit, then click Copy to copy the control to the clipboard. Click Edit, then click Paste to paste a copy of the control on the form. When you are asked if you want to create a control array, click the Yes button. Continue pasting copies of the control until the entire array is created.

To process code when an object receives the focus:

■ Place the code in the object's GotFocus event.

To control whether an object can or cannot respond to user-generated events:

■ If you want an object to respond to user-generated events, set the object's Enabled property to True (default). If you want to prevent an object from responding to user-generated events, set the object's Enabled property to False.

QUESTIONS

1. When you give the same name to more than one control, you create a _____ .
   a. control array
   b. control group
   c. group
   d. name array
   e. name group

2. Visual Basic assigns a unique number, called a(n) _____ , to each of the controls in an array.
   a. address
   b. control number
   c. control value
   d. index
   e. value

3. Which of the following is the name of a control in an array?
   a. txtName.1
   b. txtName-1
   c. txtName[1]
   d. txtName_1
   e. txtName(1)

4. The index of the fourth control in an array is _____ .
   a. 3
   b. 4
   c. 5

5. Items appearing within the parentheses after an event procedure's name are called _____ .
   a. arguments
   b. controls
   c. indexes
   d. properties
   e. values

6. Arrays that have corresponding elements are called _____ arrays.
   a. associated
   b. coordinated
   c. matching
   d. parallel
   e. same

7. To select the existing text when a text box receives the focus, place the appropriate code in the text box's _____ event.
   a. Focus
   b. GotFocus
   c. ReceiveFocus
   d. Select
   e. SelectFocus

8. To prevent an object from responding to user-generated events, set the object's _____ property to False.
   a. Enabled
   b. Focus
   c. Prevent
   d. Response
   e. Select

9. Assume that an application contains four option buttons named optChoice(0), optChoice(1), optChoice(2), and optChoice(3). When the user clicks the optChoice(2) button, Visual Basic stores _____ in the control array's Index argument.
   a. optChoice
   b. optChoice(2)
   c. 2

10. Assume the user interface contains four option buttons. Explain how to make these option buttons into a control array named optChoice. What values will be contained in each of the button's Index properties?

11. Assume you want to create a control array named chkChoice that contains three check boxes. The check boxes are not, as yet, on the form. Explain how to create the array at the same time as you add the controls to the form. What values will be contained in each of the check box's Index properties?

E X E R C I S E S

1. In this exercise you will create and code a control array.
    a. Open the lb1 (lb1.vbp) project, which is located in the Tut05 folder on your Student Disk. See Figure 5-41.

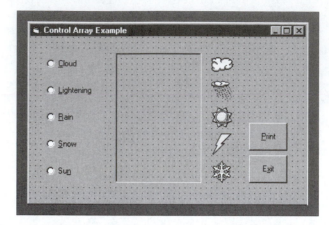

Figure 5-41

    b. Save the form and the project as lb1Done in the Tut05 folder on your Student Disk.
    c. Make the option buttons into a control array named optElement. Make the image controls into a control array named imgElement. (*Hint:* Make both control arrays parallel.)
    d. Have the form's Load event select the first option button when the interface first appears on the screen.
    e. Center the form on the screen.
    f. Code the option button array so that it displays, in the imgPicture control, the corresponding image from the imgElement array.
    g. Make the imgElement controls invisible when the interface first appears on the screen.
    h. Code the Print and Exit buttons appropriately.
    i. Save and run the project. Click each of the option buttons to make sure they are working correctly.
    j. Stop the application, then print the code.

2. In this exercise, you will use the For Next and Do While repetition structures, as well as control arrays.
    a. Open the lb2 (lb2.vbp) project, which is located in the Tut05 folder on your Student Disk. The interface contains three label controls and three command buttons.
    b. Save the form and the project as lb2Done in the Tut05 folder on your Student Disk.
    c. Make the label controls into a control array named lblColor.
    d. Center the form on the screen.
    e. Code the Exit button so that it ends the application.
    f. Code the cmdBlue button so that it assigns the intrinsic constant vbBlue to the BackColor property of each of the controls in the lblColor array. Use the For Next loop.
    g. Code the cmdYellow button so that it assigns the intrinsic constant vbYellow to the BackColor property of each of the controls in the lblColor array. Use the Do While loop.

h. Save and run the project. Click the Blue button. The background color of the label controls should be blue. Click the Yellow button. The background color of the label controls should be yellow.

i. Click the Exit button, then print the code.

3. In this exercise, you will use the selection structure and control arrays.

a. Open the lb3 (lb3.vbp) project, which is located in the Tut05 folder on your Student Disk. The interface contains three image controls, one label control, and one command button.

b. Save the form and the project as lb3Done in the Tut05 folder on your Student Disk.

c. Make the image controls into a control array name imgFace.

d. Code the image control array so that it displays the word "Sad" (without the quotes) when the first face is clicked, the word "Neutral" when the second face is clicked, and the word "Happy" when the third face is clicked. Display the appropriate word in the lblWord control.

e. Save, run, and test the project.

f. Click the Exit button, then print the code.

Exercises 4 through 6 are Discovery Exercises, which allow you both to "discover" the solutions to problems on your own and to experiment with material that is not covered in the tutorial.

discovery ▶

4. In this exercise, you will use the selection structure and control arrays.

a. Before creating the project, use Windows to run the Face (Face.exe) file, which is located in the Tut05 folder on your Student Disk. When you run the project, you will notice that four faces appear, one at a time, in the interface; then the four faces disappear, one at a time. Click the Exit button to end the application.

b. Open the lb4 (lb4.vbp) project, which is located in the Tut05 folder on your Student Disk. The interface contains four image controls, two timer controls, and one command button. The four image controls belong to a control array named imgFace. The Visible property of the image controls is set to False.

c. Save the form and the project as lb4Done in the Tut05 folder on your Student Disk.

d. The Interval property for both timer controls is set to 500 milliseconds (1/2 of a second). Verify that the tmrFace1 control's Enabled property is set to True, and that the tmrFace2 control's Enabled property is set to False.

e. Code the tmrFace1 control's Timer event so that it displays one of the four faces every 500 milliseconds. In other words, when the application is run, the first face should appear after 500 milliseconds have elapsed. After another 500 milliseconds have elapsed, the second face should appear, and so on. When the four faces appear in the interface, the tmrFace1 control's Timer event should disable the tmrFace1 timer and enable the tmrFace2 timer.

f. Code the tmrFace2 control's Timer event so that it hides one of the four faces every 500 milliseconds. Begin by hiding the last face and end by hiding the first face. When the four faces are hidden, the tmrFace2 control's Timer event should disable the tmrFace2 timer and enable the tmrFace1 timer.

g. Save and run the project. The four faces should appear, one at a time, in the interface, and then disappear, one at a time. This process should continue until you click the Exit button.

h. Click the Exit button, then print the code.

discovery ▶

5. In this exercise you will learn about horizontal and vertical scroll bars, which you can use to get numeric input from the user.

a. If necessary, start Visual Basic and open a new project.

b. Place one label control on the form.

c. Save the form and the project as lb5Done in the Tut05 folder on your Student Disk.

d. If you have access to the MSDN Library, then display the Help screen for the HScrollBar (horizontal scroll bar) and VScrollBar (vertical scroll bar) controls. Research the Min, Max, Value, SmallChange, and LargeChange properties. Also research the Scroll event and the Change event.

e. Place a horizontal scroll bar control on the form. Position the scroll bar immediately below the label control.

f. The scroll bar should display a number in the range of 0 through 50 in the label control. When the user clicks a scroll arrow, the label control should display numbers in increments of 1. When the user clicks the scroll bar, on the other hand, the label control should display numbers in increments of 10. When the user drags the scroll box, the number in the label control should adjust accordingly. Set the appropriate properties and code the appropriate events.

g. Save and run the application, then test the scroll bar to be sure it is working correctly.

h. Stop the application. Print the form as text and the code.

discovery ▶ 6. In this exercise you will learn about the slider control, which you can use to get numeric input from the user.

a. Start Visual Basic and open a new project, if necessary. Click Project on the menu bar, then click Components. Click Microsoft Windows Common Controls 6.0 in the list of available controls, then click the OK button. (You may need to size Visual Basic's Toolbox to see all of the new controls added to it.)

b. Place one label control and one slider control on the form. Position the slider control immediately below the label control.

c. Save the form and the project as lb6Done in the Tut05 folder on your Student Disk.

d. If you have access to the MSDN Library, then display a Help screen on the slider control.

e. The slider control should allow the user to enter numbers from 1 to 20 in the label control. Set the appropriate properties and code the appropriate events.

f. Save and run the project to make sure the slider control is working correctly.

g. Stop the application. Print the form as text and the code.

LESSON C
objectives

In this lesson you will learn how to:
- Code the Change event
- Align the contents of a label control
- Communicate with the user using the MsgBox function
- Code a form's Unload event

Completing the Grade Application

Coding the Display Grade Command Button

The grade application is almost complete; you just need to code the Display Grade button's Click event procedure and the form's Unload event procedure. Begin with the Display Grade button's Click event procedure, whose pseudocode is shown in Figure 5-42.

1. Declare variables

2. Repeat for each check box

   If the check box is selected then

       add the text box score to the earned points accumulator

       Case of check box's Index property

           = 0, 1, 2   add 10 to the possible points accumulator

           Other   add 50 to the possible points accumulator

       End Case check box's Index property

   End If

   End Repeat for each check box

3. Calculate ratio by dividing the earned points accumulator by the possible points accumulator

4. Case of ratio

       > = .9   Display "A" in label control

       > = .8   Display "B" in label control

       > = .7   Display "C" in label control

       > = .6   Display "D" in label control

       Other   Display "F" in label control

   End Case ratio

Figure 5-42: Pseudocode for the Display Grade button's Click event procedure

The Display Grade button's Click event procedure will use four local variables: intEarned, intPossible, sngRatio, and intCount. Two of the variables, both Integer variables, will be accumulators. The intEarned variable will accumulate the total points earned by the student, and the intPossible variable will accumulate the total possible points based on which check boxes are selected. sngRatio, a Single variable, will store the ratio found by dividing the number of points earned by the number of points possible—in other words, dividing the value in the intEarned variable by the value in the intPossible variable. intCount, an Integer variable, will serve as the *counter* variable for a For Next loop.

To begin coding the Display Grade button:

1   Start Visual Basic, if necessary, then open the **lbGrade** (lbGrade.vbp) project, which is located in the Tut05 folder on your Student Disk.

2   Save the form and the project as **lcGrade** in the Tut05 folder on your Student Disk.

3   Open the Display Grade button's Click event procedure. Press the **Tab** key, then type **dim intEarned as integer, intPossible as integer** and press the **Enter** key.

4   Type **dim sngRatio as single, intCount as integer** and press the **Enter** key.

For each selected check box, you want to add the score entered in the corresponding text box to the intEarned variable, and add either 10 or 50 points to the intPossible variable. Whether you add 10 or 50 points to the intPossible variable depends on which check box is selected. Project check boxes are each worth 10 points; the midterm and final check boxes are each worth 50 points.

To code the Display Grade button's Click event procedure, you will need to use both a repetition structure and a selection structure to determine which of the five check boxes, if any, is selected, then update the intEarned variable appropriately. You will then use a selection structure to determine how many points to add to the intPossible variable, 10 or 50.

Figure 5-43 shows two ways of writing the code to determine which check boxes, if any, are selected, then update the intEarned and intPossible variables appropriately. The two examples show the code written with a For Next loop and a Do While loop. Either loop will work; however, when a programmer knows precisely how many times the loop instructions are to be processed, he or she will typically use the For Next loop.

Recall that the check boxes in the chkDone array have indexes of 0 through 4, which explains why the intCount loop begins at 0 and ends at 4.

The examples shown in Figure 5-43 use the Case selection structure to determine the number of points to add to the intPossible variable. You could have used an If...Then...Else selection structure instead.

Display Grade button's code using a For Next loop

```
For intCount = 0 to 4
    If chkDone(intCount).Value = vbChecked then
        intEarned = intEarned + Val(txtScore(intCount).Text)
        Select Case intCount
            Case 0 To 2
                intPossible = intPossible + 10
            Case Else
                intPossible = intPossible + 50
        End Select
    End If
Next intCount
```

Display Grade button's code using a Do While loop

```
Do While intCount < = 4
    If chkDone(intCount).Value = vbChecked then
        intEarned = intEarned + Val(txtScore(intCount).Text)
        Select Case intCount
            Case 0 To 2
                intPossible = intPossible + 10
            Case Else
                intPossible = intPossible + 50
        End Select
    End If
    intCount = intCount + 1
Loop
```

Figure 5-43: Display Grade button's code using a For Next loop and a Do While loop

5 Maximize the Code window, then enter the additional code shown in Figure 5-44.

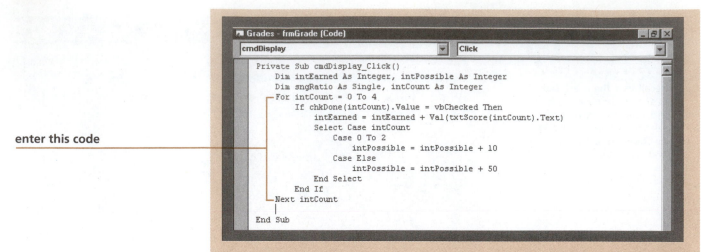

Figure 5-44: Current status of Display Grade button's Click event procedure

After accumulating the number of points earned and the number of points possible in the intEarned and intPossible variables, respectively, you will then divide the value in the intEarned variable by the value in the intPossible variable, and assign the result to the sngRatio variable. You will then use a Case structure to determine if the student should receive a grade of A, B, C, D, or F. The appropriate grade is determined by the value in the sngRatio variable. If the sngRatio variable contains a value that is .9 or above, which means that the student has earned at least 90% of the possible points, then he or she should receive an A.

6   Enter the additional code shown in Figure 5-45.

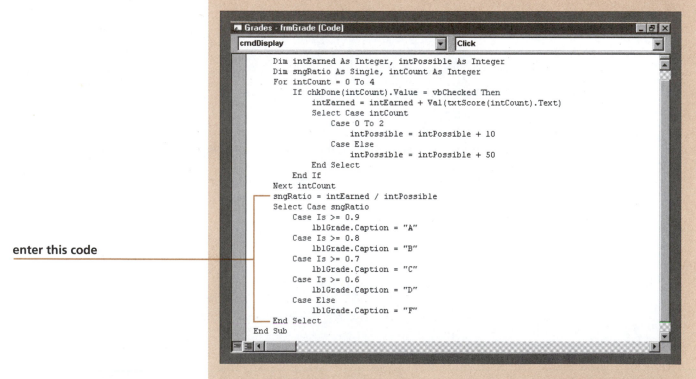

Figure 5-45: Calculation and Case structure in Display Grade button's Click event procedure

7   Close the Code window, then **save** and **run** the application.

8   Click the **Project 1** check box, then type **6** and press the **Enter** key to select the Display Grade button, which is the default command button on the form. A grade of D appears in the lblGrade control.

9   Press the **Tab** key. The Project 2 check box now has the focus, as indicated by the dotted rectangle around its caption.

Another way to select a check box is to press the Spacebar on your keyboard when the check box has the focus. Try that now.

10 Press the **Spacebar** on your keyboard. The Spacebar selects the Project 2 check box and moves the focus to the corresponding text box. Type **10** and press the **Enter** key. A grade of B appears in the lblGrade control.

11 Click the **Project 2** check box to deselect it. The check box's Click event procedure changes the score in the corresponding text box to a zero. Notice that the B grade, however, still appears, incorrectly, in the lblGrade control. You will correct this problem in the next section. Click the **Display Grade** button. The grade in the lblGrade control changes to a D.

12 Change the Project 1 grade from 6 to **10**. Here again, although the score in the text box was changed, notice that the D grade still appears, incorrectly, in the lblGrade control. You will correct this problem in the next section. Click the **Display Grade** button. The grade in the lblGrade control changes to an A.

13 Click the **Exit** button to end the application.

In the next section you will learn how to have Visual Basic clear the contents of the lblGrade control when the contents of a text box change.

The Change Event

A text box's Change event occurs when the contents of the text box are changed. This can happen as a result of either the user entering data into the text box, or the program code changing the contents of the text box's Text property. In this application, you will code the txtScore array's Change event so that it clears the lblGrade control when either the user or the check box's Click event procedure changes the existing score in a text box.

To code the txtScore array's Change event:

1   Open the txtScore array's GotFocus event procedure.

2   Use the Code window's Procedure box to open the txtScore array's Change event.

3   Press the **Tab** key, then type **lblgrade.caption = " "** and press the **Enter** key. (Be sure to enter this code in the txtScore array's Change event.)

4   Close the Code window, then **save** and **run** the application.

5   Click the **Midterm** check box to select it, then type **50** and press the **Enter** key. A grade of A appears in the lblGrade control.

6 Change the midterm grade from 50 to **40**. Changing the contents of the text box from 50 to 40 invokes the text box's Change event, which clears the contents of the lblGrade control. Click the **Display Grade** button. A grade of B appears in the lblGrade control.

7 Click the **Midterm** check box to deselect it. Recall that the check box array's Click event procedure contains the `txtScore(Index).Text = 0` instruction; that instruction changes the contents of the text box from 40 to 0 (zero), thereby invoking the text box's Change event.

Now see what happens when the user clicks the Display Grade button without clicking any of the check boxes.

8 Click the **Display Grade** button. A dialog box containing the "Run-time error '6': Overflow" error message appears.

9 Click the **Debug** button in the dialog box. The Display Grade button's Click event procedure appears as shown in Figure 5-46. Notice that Visual Basic highlights the instruction that is causing the problem—the `sngRatio = intEarned / intPossible` instruction.

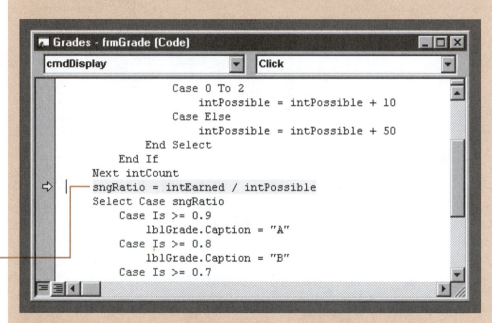

this instruction is causing error

Figure 5-46: Problem instruction highlighted in the Display Grade button's Click event procedure

10 Position I on intPossible in the `sngRatio=intEarned/intPossible` instruction.

Notice that the intPossible variable contains a zero. Recall that, unless a check box is selected, the intPossible variable is not updated from its initial value of zero. (You may want to review the code in the Display Grade button's Click event procedure to verify that.) Because division by zero is not allowed, Visual Basic displays an error message. You can stop the application at this point.

11 Click the **End** button ■ to stop the application, then close the Code window.

Like the txtScore text boxes, the Display Grade button also does not apply until a check box is selected. You will therefore disable the Display Grade command button when the interface first appears, then enable it when the user selects a check box.

To enable and disable the Display Grade button:

1   Click the **Display Grade** button, then set the button's Enabled property to **False**.

The Display Grade button will remain disabled until the user selects a check box. When the user selects a check box, the check box array's Click event will need to enable the Display Grade button by setting the button's Enabled property to True.

2   Open the chkDone array's Click event procedure. Maximize the Code window, then enter the `cmdDisplay.Enabled = True` statement as shown in Figure 5-47.

enter this instruction

```
 Grades - frmGrade (Code)                                                    _ ☐ ✕
chkDone                              ▼   Click                                   ▼
Private Sub chkDone_Click(Index As Integer)
    If chkDone(Index).Value = vbChecked Then
        cmdDisplay.Enabled = True
        txtScore(Index).Enabled = True
        txtScore(Index).SetFocus
    Else
        txtScore(Index).Text = 0
        txtScore(Index).Enabled = False
    End If

End Sub
```

Figure 5-47: Current status of the chkDone array's Click event procedure

This instruction will enable the Display Grade button when the user selects a check box.

When the user deselects a check box, the check box array's Click event will need to determine if any of the check boxes are selected. If no check boxes are selected, then the Click event will disable the Display Grade button.

3   Enter the additional code and documentation shown in Figure 5-48.

enter these variable declarations

enter these ten instructions

enter this documentation

```
 Grades - frmGrade (Code)                                                    _ ☐ ✕
chkDone                              ▼   Click                                   ▼
Private Sub chkDone_Click(Index As Integer)
    Dim intCount As Integer, strChecked As String
    If chkDone(Index).Value = vbChecked Then       'if check box is selected
        cmdDisplay.Enabled = True
        txtScore(Index).Enabled = True
        txtScore(Index).SetFocus
    Else                                           'if check box is deselected
        txtScore(Index).Text = 0
        txtScore(Index).Enabled = False
        strChecked = "N"        'assume that no check boxes are selected
        Do While intCount <= 4 And strChecked = "N"    'determine if any check box
            If chkDone(intCount).Value = vbChecked Then 'is selected
                strChecked = "Y"
            End If
            intCount = intCount + 1
        Loop
        If strChecked = "N" Then                    'if no check box is
            cmdDisplay.Enabled = False              'selected, disable the
        End If                                      'Display Grade button
    End If

End Sub
```

Figure 5-48: Additional code and documentation in the chkDone array's Click event procedure

The additional code declares an Integer variable named intCount and a String variable named strChecked. The intCount variable serves as a counter for the Do While loop. As the loop is processed, the intCount variable will take on values of 0 through 4; these values correspond to the indexes of the five controls in the chkDone array. The intCount variable allows the loop to look at each check box in the array to determine if the check box is selected.

The strChecked variable is used to keep track of whether a check box in the array is selected. Before the Do While loop begins, the strChecked variable is assigned the literal constant "N" (for *No*) to indicate that no check boxes are selected. The selection structure within the Do While loop compares each check box's Value property to the intrinsic constant vbChecked. If a check box is selected, the literal constant "Y" (for *Yes*) is assigned to the strChecked variable to indicate that a check box is selected.

You will notice that the Do While loop will process its instructions as long as the intCount variable contains a value that is less than or equal to 4 and the strChecked variable equals "N". The Do While loop will stop either when intCount is greater than 4, which means that there are no more check boxes to test, or when strChecked contains a value other than "N", which means that a check box is selected.

When the loop has completed its processing, the selection structure below the loop compares the contents of the strChecked variable to the literal constant "N". If the strChecked variable contains an "N", then no check boxes are selected, so the Display Grade button is disabled; otherwise, the chkDone array's Click event ends, leaving the Display Grade button enabled.

4   Close the Code window, then **save** and **run** the application. Notice that the Display Grade button appears dimmed, which indicates that it is disabled.

5   Click the **Display Grade** button. The button will not respond until you select a check box.

6   Click the **Project 1** check box. The Display Grade button darkens to indicate that it is now enabled. Type **9** as the number of points earned on the first project. Press the **Tab** key until the Midterm check box has the focus, then press the **Spacebar** to select the check box. Type **40** as the number of points earned on the midterm, then press the **Enter** key to select the Display Grade button. A grade of B appears in the lblGrade control.

7   Click the **Midterm** check box to deselect it, then click the **Display Grade** button. A grade of A appears in the lblGrade control.

8   Click the **Project 1** check box to deselect it. Notice that the Display Grade button now appears dimmed. Because none of the check boxes are currently selected, the check box array's Click event procedure disables the Display Grade button.

9   Click the **Exit** button to end the application.

You can improve the appearance of the user interface by centering the grade in the lblGrade control.

Centering the Contents of a Label Control

The caption in a label control aligns, automatically, on the left side of the control. You can change the alignment to either center- or right-aligned by setting the label control's Alignment property.

> To center the lblGrade control's caption, then save and run the application:
>
> **1** Click the **lblGrade** control, then set the label control's Alignment property to **2-Center**.
>
> **2** **Save** and **run** the application. Type your name in the Name text box. Enter scores for the three projects, the midterm, and the final. Click the **Display Grade** button. Visual Basic centers the appropriate grade in the label control.
>
> **3** If your computer is connected to a printer, click the **Print** button to print the application, then click the **Exit** button to end the application. Visual Basic returns to the design screen.

In order to complete the grade application, you will need to change the code in the Exit button's Click event procedure, and also code the form's Unload event. In the form's Unload event you will use the MsgBox function to display a dialog box that allows the application to communicate with the user.

Using the MsgBox Function to Communicate with the User

In Tutorial 4 you learned that the MsgBox function displays one of Visual Basic's predefined dialog boxes. The dialog box contains a message, one or more command buttons, and an icon. The syntax of the MsgBox function, you may remember, is **MsgBox**(*prompt*[, *buttons*][, *title*][, *helpfile, context*]). *Prompt* is the message you want displayed in the dialog box. *Buttons* is an expression that represents the number and type of buttons to display, the icon style to use, the identity of the default button, and the dialog box's modality. *Title* is a string expression, typically the application's name, displayed in the title bar of the dialog box. You use the optional *helpfile* and *context* arguments to provide context-sensitive help for the dialog box.

Recall that, after displaying the dialog box, the MsgBox function waits for the user to choose one of the buttons. The function then returns a value that indicates which button the user chose. If the Yes button is selected, for example, the MsgBox function returns the intrinsic constant vbYes.

When the user clicks the grade application's Exit button, you will use the MsgBox function to ask the user to verify that he or she wants to exit. The function's dialog box will be application modal and will include Yes and No buttons, as well as the Warning Message icon , which alerts the user that he or she must first make a decision and then enter a response before the application can continue.

As you learned in Tutorial 4, one of the buttons in the MsgBox function's dialog box is the default button—the button that is selected when the user presses the Enter key. In Windows applications, the default button in a dialog box is typically the button that represents the user's most likely action, as long as that action is not destructive. In this case, the most likely action is that the user does want to quit the application, so the Yes button should be the default button. If the user selects the Yes button in error, he or she will simply need to reenter the five scores, which does not involve a lot of work. (If the user were to lose much more data by exiting in error, you should make the No button the default button.)

The correct MsgBox function to use in this application is `MsgBox("Do you want to exit?", vbYesNo + vbExclamation + vbDefaultButton1 + vbApplicationModal, "Grade Application")`. As you did in Tutorial 4, you will shorten the instruction by assigning the *buttons* argument, `vbYesNo + vbExclamation + vbDefaultButton1 + vbApplicationModal`, to a constant named conBtns. ("Btns" is short for "buttons.") You will then use the constant, instead of the long expression, in the MsgBox function. You will assign the user's response to an Integer variable named intUserResponse.

tip

Recall that each setting for the *buttons* argument has a constant and a numeric value associated with it. To make your code more self-documenting, always use the constant.

To modify the code in the Exit button:

1 Open the Exit button's Click event procedure, then maximize the Code window.

2 Insert a blank line between the `Private Sub` statement and the `End` statement.

3 In the blank line below the `Private Sub` statement, press the **Tab** key, if necessary, then type
const conBtns as integer = vbyesno + vbexclamation + vbdefaultbutton1 + vbapplicationmodal and press the **Enter** key.

4 Now enter the `Dim` statement and the assignment statement shown in Figure 5-49. Also compare the code that you entered with the code in the figure.

enter these two instructions

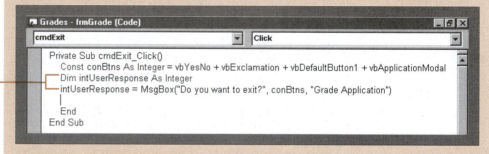

Figure 5-49: Current status of the Exit button's Click event procedure

If the user chooses the Yes button, then the application should end; otherwise, the user should be returned to the application.

5 Enter the additional code shown in Figure 5-50.

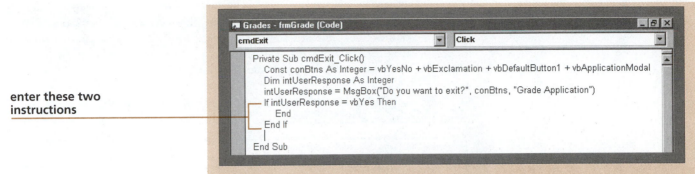

enter these two instructions

Figure 5-50: Selection structure entered in the Exit button's Click event procedure

6 Close the Code window, then **save** and **run** the application.

7 Click the **Exit** button. When the MsgBox function's dialog box appears, click the **No** button. Visual Basic returns to the application.

8 Click the **Exit** button. This time when the dialog box appears, press the **Enter** key to choose the Yes button. Visual Basic ends the application and returns to the design screen.

Recall that the user can also exit an application by using the Close button ☒. See how the application responds when this method of exiting is used.

9 **Run** the application, then click the **Close** button ☒ on the application's title bar. The application ends without displaying the "Do you want to exit?" message.

Notice that the application does not display the MsgBox function's dialog box; rather, the application simply ends. That's because the Exit button's Click event is triggered only when you click the Exit button; it is not triggered when the user clicks the Close button ☒. To fix this problem, you will move the Exit button's code to the form's Unload event, which you will learn about in the next section. You will then enter Visual Basic's `Unload` statement in the Exit button's Click event. First learn about the Unload event.

The Unload Event

tip

You can also use the Unload event to specify other instructions that should be processed when the form is unloaded—for example, instructions that save data to a file. You will learn about files in Tutorials 6, 7, and 8.

The **Unload event**, which occurs when a form is about to be removed from the screen, is triggered when you use the Close button ☒ to close the form; it is also triggered when you use the `Unload` statement in code. If you want to verify that the user wants to exit the application, you should place the appropriate code in the form's Unload event.

In the grade application, most of the code that verifies that the user wants to exit is already entered in the Exit button's Click event procedure; you will move the code to the form's Unload event procedure. You are moving the Exit button's instructions to the form's Unload event so that the instructions will be processed when the user closes the form with the Close button ☒.

To move the Exit button's code to the form's Unload event:

1 Open the Exit button's Click event procedure, then maximize the Code window.

2 Select the six statements between the `Private Sub` and `End Sub` instructions. Press **Ctrl+x** to move the highlighted instructions to the clipboard.

3 Use the Code window's Object box to open the form's Code window. The form's Load event appears. Use the Code window's Procedure box to open the form's Unload event. Press **Ctrl+v** to paste the instructions into the form's Unload event, then position the insertion point as shown in Figure 5-51.

position insertion point here

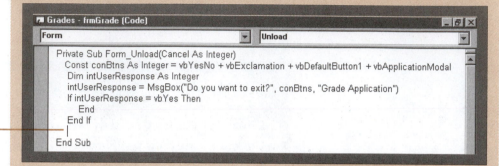

Figure 5-51: Instructions moved from the Exit button's Click event to the form's Unload event

Notice the `Cancel As Integer` between the parentheses following the procedure's name. When you close a form, Visual Basic passes the number 0 to the Unload event's Cancel argument. If the Unload event does not contain an instruction that changes the value in the Cancel argument, Visual Basic removes the form from the screen and from memory. Setting the Cancel argument to any nonzero value stops Visual Basic from removing the form. In this application, if the user selects the Yes button in the MsgBox function's dialog box, then you will allow the form to be removed from the screen and from memory. If the user selects the No button, on the other hand, you will set the Cancel argument to the number 1, which tells Visual Basic that you do not want to remove the form.

4 Modify the selection structure in the Unload event procedure as shown in Figure 5-52. Also enter the documentation shown in the figure.

modify the selection structure as shown

enter this documentation

```
Grades - frmGrade (Code)
Form                          Unload

Private Sub Form_Unload(Cancel As Integer)
    Const conBtns As Integer = vbYesNo + vbExclamation + vbDefaultButton1 + vbApplicationModal
    Dim intUserResponse As Integer
    intUserResponse = MsgBox("Do you want to exit?", conBtns, "Grade Application")
    If intUserResponse = vbNo Then      'user does not want to quit the application
        Cancel = 1                      'prevent form from being unloaded
    End If

End Sub
```

Figure 5-52: Modified selection structure in the Unload event procedure

Notice that you do not need to use the **End** statement in the Unload event. If you do not set the Unload event's Cancel argument to a value other than the number 0, Visual Basic will automatically end the application when the Unload event occurs.

In the grade application, the Exit button also needs to display the MsgBox function's dialog box, and then either allow the form to be removed or return the user to the application. For the Exit button to work appropriately, you need simply to enter the Unload statement in the button's Click event. Recall that the Unload statement triggers the form's Unload event.

To enter the Unload statement in the Exit button's Click event procedure, then save and run the application:

1   Use the Code window's Object box to open the cmdExit control's Click event. Enter the code shown in Figure 5-53.

```
Grades - frmGrade (Code)                                          _ 8 x

cmdExit                              ▼    Click                        ▼

    Private Sub cmdExit_Click()
        Unload frmGrade
        |
    End Sub
```

Figure 5-53: Unload statement entered in the Exit button's Click event

2   Close the Code window, then **save** and **run** the application.

First see what happens when the user closes the form using the Close button ☒.

3   Click the **Close** button ☒ on the application's title bar to end the application. This time the MsgBox function's dialog box appears. Click the **No** button. Visual Basic returns to the grade application.

4   Click the **Close** button ☒ on the application's title bar to end the application. This time when the dialog box appears, click the **Yes** button. Visual Basic ends the application and returns to the design screen.

Now see how the application responds when the user clicks the Exit button.

5   **Run** the application again. Click the **Exit** button, then click the **No** button in the dialog box. Visual Basic returns to the grade application. Click the **Exit** button again, then click the **Yes** button. Visual Basic ends the application and returns to the design screen.

You have now completed Lesson C. You can take a break, complete the questions and exercises at the end of the lesson, or read and complete the Debugging Section. The Debugging Section may contain information that will help you with problems you might encounter when doing the exercises at the end of the lesson.

SUMMARY

To process code when the contents of a control have changed:

■   Place the code in the control's Change event.

To align the contents of a label control:

■   Set the label control's Alignment property to either 0-Left, 1-Right, or 2-Center.

To display a dialog box that enables the application to communicate with the user:

■   Use the MsgBox function.

To process code before a form is removed from the screen:

■   Enter the code in the form's Unload event. The Unload event is triggered when you use the Close button ⊠ to close the form; it is also triggered when Visual Basic encounters the `Unload` statement in code.

QUESTIONS

1.   You can use the _____ function to display a dialog box that enables the application to communicate with the user.
     a. Communicate
     b. DialogBox
     c. Message
     d. MsgBox
     e. UserMsg

2.   The _____ event is triggered when you use the Close button ⊠ or the `Unload` statement in code.
     a. FormUnload
     b. FormRemove
     c. Remove
     d. RemoveForm
     e. Unload

3.   The _____ event occurs when the contents of a control are modified.
     a. Change
     b. ControlChange
     c. Edited
     d. Modified
     e. SelChange

4.   You can align the contents of a label control by setting the control's _____ property.
     a. Align
     b. Alignment
     c. Change
     d. Center
     e. LabelAlign

5. Assume the application contains a control array named txtSales. The txtSales array contains three text boxes. Which of the following loops will accumulate the contents of each text box in the array?

   a. `For intX = 2 To 0 Step −1`
   `    sngTotal = sngTotal + Val(txtSales(intX).Text)`
   `Next intX`

   b. `For intX = 3 To 1 Step −1`
   `    sngTotal = sngTotal + Val(txtSales(intX).Text)`
   `Next intX`

   c. `For intX = 1 To 3 Step 1`
   `    sngTotal = sngTotal + Val(txtSales(intX).Text)`
   `Next intX`

   d. `For intX = 0 To 2 Step 1`
   `    sngTotal(intX) = sngTotal(intX) + Val(txtSales.Text)`
   `Next intX`

6. In question 5, what will be the value of intX when the loop stops?
   a. −1
   b. 0
   c. 1
   d. 2
   e. 3

E X E R C I S E S

Note: The following list shows the GUI design and programming guidelines you have learned so far. You can use this list to verify that the applications you create in the following exercises adhere to the standards outlined in the book.

- Information should flow either vertically or horizontally, with the most important information always located in the upper-left corner of the screen.
- Maintain a consistent margin of two or three dots from the edge of the window.
- Related controls should be grouped together using either white space or a frame.
- Position related controls on succeeding dots.
- Command buttons should either be centered along the bottom of the screen or stacked in either the upper-right or lower-right corner.
- If the command buttons are centered along the bottom of the screen, then each button should be the same height; their widths, however, may vary.
- If the command buttons are stacked in either the upper-right or lower-right corner of the screen, then each button should be the same height and the same width.
- Use no more than six command buttons on a screen.
- The most commonly used command button should be placed first.
- Command button captions should:
  - be meaningful
  - be from one to three words
  - appear on one line
  - be entered using book title capitalization

- Use labels to identify the controls in the interface.
- Identifying labels should:
  - be from one to three words
  - appear on one line
  - be aligned by their left borders
  - be positioned either above or to the left of the control that they identify
  - end with a colon (:)
  - be entered using sentence capitalization
  - have their BackStyle property set to 0-Transparent
  - have their BorderStyle property set to 0-None
- Labels that display program output (for example, the results of calculations):
  - should have their BorderStyle set to 1-Fixed Single
  - should have their Appearance property set to 0-Flat
  - can have their BackStyle property set to either 0-Transparent or 1-Opaque
- Align labels and controls to minimize the number of different margins.
- If you use a graphic in the interface, use a small one and place it in a location that will not distract the user.
- Use no more than two different font sizes, which should be 8, 10, or 12 points.
- Use only one font type, which should be a sans serif font, in the interface.
- Avoid using italics and underlining.
- Use either white, off-white, light gray, pale blue, or pale yellow for an application's background, and black for the text.
- Use color sparingly and don't use it as the only means of identification for an element in the interface.
- Set each control's TabIndex property to a number that represents the order in which you want that control to receive the focus (begin with 0).
- A text box's TabIndex value should be one more than the TabIndex value of its identifying label.
- Lock the controls in place on the form.
- Assign a unique access key to each essential element of the interface (text boxes, command buttons, and so on).
- Document the program internally.
- Enter the Option Explicit statement in the General Declaration section of every form and module.
- Use variables to control the preciseness of numbers in the interface.
- Use the Val function on Text and Caption properties, and when assigning the result of the InputBox function to a numeric variable.
- Set the form's BorderStyle, MinButton, MaxButton, and ControlBox properties appropriately:
  - Splash screens should not have a Minimize, Maximize, or Close button, and their borders should not be sizable.
  - Forms that are acting as dialog boxes should have a BorderStyle property of 3-Fixed Dialog.

- Forms other than splash screens and dialog boxes should always have a Minimize button and a Close button, but you can choose to disable the Maximize button.
- Forms other than splash screens and dialog boxes typically have a BorderStyle property setting of either 1-Fixed Single or 2-Sizable.

■ Test the application with both valid and invalid data (test the application without entering any data; also test it by entering letters where numbers are expected).

■ In the InputBox function, use sentence capitalization for the *prompt*, and book title capitalization for the *title*.

■ Center the form on the screen by including the appropriate formulas in the form's Load event.

■ Display an hourglass or an arrow and an hourglass if a procedure will take a long period of time.

■ Remove excess code from the application.

■ Option buttons:
  - Use a minimum of two and a maximum of seven in an interface.
  - Use sentence capitalization for the caption.
  - Use a frame control to create separate groups of option buttons.
  - Select a default button in each group.

■ Use sentence capitalization for a frame control's caption.

■ Use sentence capitalization for a check box's caption.

■ MsgBox function:
  - Use sentence capitalization for the message.
  - Display the application's name in the title bar, using book title capitalization.
  - Display the appropriate icon.
  - Default button should be one that represents the user's most likely action, as long as that action is not destructive.

■ Use the SelStart and SelLength properties, as well as the Len function, to highlight (select) the existing text when a text box receives the focus.

■ Disable objects that don't apply to the current state of the application.

1. In this exercise you will create a control array. You will then code the application using the For Next and Do While loops.

    Scenario: Colfax Industries wants an application that they can use to sum the sales made in four regions: North, South, East, and West.

    a. Open the lc1 (lc1.vbp) project, which is located in the Tut05 folder on your Student Disk. Save the form and the project as lc1Done in the Tut05 folder on your Student Disk.
    b. Make the text boxes into a control array named txtRegion.
    c. Center the form on the screen. Also, center the contents of the lblTotal control.
    d. Code the Exit button so that it unloads the form. Code the form's Unload event so that it asks the user if he or she wants to exit.
    e. Code the Print button so that it prints the form, without the frame and its controls showing.
    f. Code the txtRegion array so that the existing text is highlighted when a text box receives the focus.
    g. Code the txtRegion array so that it clears the lblTotal control when a change is made to the contents of a text box.

h. Use the For Next loop to code the Add button. The Add button should add the four sales amounts together, and display the sum in the lblTotal control.

i. Save and run the application. Test the application by entering the following four sales amounts: 1000, 2000, 3000, 4000. Click the Add button, then click the Print button. Click the Exit button to end the application.

j. Print the code.

k. Change the Add button's code so that it uses the Do While loop instead of the For Next loop.

l. Save and run the application. Test the application by entering the following four sales amounts: 5000, 10000, 15000, 20000. Click the Add button, then click the Print button. Click the Exit button to end the application.

m. Print the code.

n. Submit the printouts from steps i and l. Also submit the code from steps j and m.

2. In this exercise, you will create two parallel control arrays.

Scenario: Your niece needs an application that she can use to practice for a test on state capitals.

a. Open the lc2 (lc2.vbp) project, which is located in the Tut05 folder on your Student Disk. Save the form and the project as lc2Done in the Tut05 folder on your Student Disk.

b. Make the State option buttons into a control array named optState. Make the Capital option buttons into a control array named optCapital. (*Hint:* Make the arrays parallel.)

c. Have the application select the first option button in the optState array and the first option button in the optCapital array when the form first appears on the screen.

d. Center the form on the screen. Also, center the contents of the lblAnswer control.

e. Code the Exit button so that it unloads the form. Code the form's Unload event so that it asks the user if he or she wants to exit.

f. Code the Print button so that it prints the form on the printer.

g. Code the application so that the lblAnswer control is cleared when either a state or a capital option button is clicked.

h. To use the application, the user just needs to click both a state and a capital option button, then click the Verify button to verify that the capital is correct. Code the Verify command button so that it displays "Correct" in the lblAnswer control when the user selects the correct capital; otherwise, display "Incorrect".

i. Save and run the application. Test the application by clicking Illinois, then clicking Denver. Click the Verify button, then click the Print button.

j. Test the application again by clicking California, then clicking Sacramento. Click the Verify button, then click the Print button. Click the Exit button to end the application.

k. Print the code.

l. Submit the printouts from steps i and j, and the code from step k.

3. In this exercise, you will use the repetition structure.

Scenario: RM Sales wants an application that the sales manager can use to calculate a salesperson's bonus.

a. Open the lc3 (lc3.vbp) project, which is located in the Tut05 folder on your Student Disk. Save the form and the project as lc3Done in the Tut05 folder on your Student Disk.

b. Center the form on the screen.

c. Code the Calculate button so that it allows the user to enter as many sales amounts as needed by the user. (*Hint:* Use the InputBox function.) When the user has completed entering a salesperson's sales amounts, the Calculate button should display the total sales in the lblTotal control. It should also display a 10% bonus in the lblBonus control.

d. Code the Exit button so that it unloads the form. Code the form's Unload event so that it asks the user if he or she wants to exit.

e. Save and run the application. Test the application by entering your name into the Name text box. Then enter the following six sales amounts: 60000, 45000, 35000, 20000, 10000, 67000. Click the Print button, then click the Exit button.

f. Print the code. Submit the printout from step e and the code from step f.

4. In this exercise, you will use the repetition structure.

Scenario: Premium Paper wants an application that will allow it to enter the company's income and expense amounts. The number of income and expense amounts may vary each time the application is run. (For example, the user may enter five income amounts and three expense amounts, or 20 income amounts and 30 expense amounts.) The application will calculate and display the total income, the total expense, and the company's profit (or loss). (*Hint:* Use the InputBox function to get the income and expense amounts. Recall that you learned about the InputBox function in Tutorial 3.)

a. Create an appropriate interface. Include a Print button that will print the interface with the command buttons showing. Be sure to read the Note at the beginning of the Exercises section.

b. Save the form and the project as lc4Done in the Tut05 folder on your Student Disk.

c. Code the application appropriately.

d. Save and run the project. Test the project twice, using the below data. Be sure to print the interface after calculating the profit (loss).

First test: Income amounts: 5000, 6000, 35000, 78000
              Expense amounts: 1000, 2000, 600
Second test: Income amounts: 8000, 2000
              Expense amounts: 12000

e. When the program is working correctly, print the code. Submit the printouts from step d and the code from step e.

Exercises 5 and 6 are Discovery Exercises, which allow you to both "discover" the solutions to problems on your own and experiment with material that is not covered in the tutorial.

discovery ▶

5. In this exercise, you will align the contents of a text box.

a. Open the lc5 (lc5.vbp) project, which is located in the Tut05 folder on your Student Disk. Save the form and the project as lc5Done in the Tut05 folder on your Student Disk.

b. Set the lblTotal label control's Alignment property to 1-Right Justify.

c. Like label controls, text boxes also have an Alignment property. Display a Help window on the Alignment property of a text box. If you read the Help screen, you will notice that a text box's Alignment property is ignored unless the text box's MultiLine property is set to True.

d. Set the txtFirst and txtSecond control's MultiLine property to True, and set their Alignment property to 1-Right Justify.

e. Save and run the application. Type the number 5 in the first text box, then type the number 9 in the second text box. Click the Calculate button. The number 14 appears in the lblTotal control. Notice that the contents of the text boxes align with the contents of the label control. Click the Exit button.

f. Now observe what happens when the user inadvertently presses the Enter key after typing a number. Run the application again. Type the number 2 in the first text box and press the Enter key. Notice that the number 2 no longer appears in the text box. Type the number 4 in the first text box and press the Tab key, then type the number 8 in the second text box. Click the Calculate button. The number 32 appears in the lblTotal control. To discover why this happened, click the txtFirst control. Although it appears that the txtFirst control contains only the number 4, by pressing the ↑ and ↓ keys on your keyboard, you will notice that the text box actually contains two numbers: 2 and 4. When you set a text box's MultiLine property to True, it tells Visual Basic to allow the text box to accept more than one line of text. When you pressed the Enter key after typing the number 2, Visual Basic stored the number 2 in the control's Text property, and then advanced the cursor to the next line in the text box. Click the Exit button.

g. Explain why the Calculate button displayed a total of 32. How was this total calculated?

h. Read this tutorial's Debugging Technique. Code each text box's KeyPress event so that it prevents the text box from accepting the Enter key.

i. Save and run the application. Enter the number 2 in the txtFirst text box and press the Enter key. You should still see the number 2 in the text box. Enter the number 7 in the txtSecond text box, then click the Calculate button. The number 9 should appear in the lblTotal control. Click the Exit button.

j. Print the code.

discovery ▶ 6.   In this exercise, you will use three parallel control arrays to create a Tic-Tac-Toe game.

Scenario: After studying for a big test, you and your friend like to relax by playing a few games of Tic-Tac-Toe. In this exercise, you will finish creating a Tic-Tac-Toe game that you and your friend can play.

a. Open the TicTacTo (TicTacTo.vbp) project, which is located in the Tut05 folder on your Student Disk. The interface contains option buttons, frame controls, label controls, and command buttons. The form's General Declarations section contains the `Option Explicit` statement, and the form's Load event contains the instructions to center the form. The Exit button contains the `Unload` statement.

b. Save the form and the project as lc6Done in the Tut05 folder on your Student Disk. Create three parallel control arrays named optX, optO, and lblXO. The optX control array should contain the nine X option buttons. The optO control array should contain the nine O option buttons. The lblXO control array should contain the nine label controls.

c. Center the contents of the label controls.

d. The BorderStyle property of the label controls was set to 1-Fixed Single to help you identify the label controls in the user interface. You can improve the appearance of the interface by removing the border on the label controls. Set the label controls' BorderStyle property to 0-None.

e. When the user clicks an option button, the appropriate letter (X or O) should appear in the corresponding label control, and the opponent's corresponding option button should be disabled.

f. Use the MsgBox function to display a message to the user indicating who won the game, either the Xs or the Os. You do not need to display a message if there is no winner. In order to win the game, you must have three Xs or Os placed either vertically, horizontally, or diagonally.

g. Code the Clear button so that it clears the Tic-Tac-Toe board for a new game.

h. When the application is working correctly, print the code.

DEBUGGING

Technique   Users will, at times, make mistakes when entering data. For example, a user may enter a letter when a number is expected. In previous applications, you used the Val function to tell Visual Basic to treat a string as a number. In this Debugging section you will learn how to use the KeyPress event to prevent a user from entering anything other than a number in a text box.

The KeyPress event occurs when the user presses and releases a key that is a member of the ANSI (American National Standards Institute) character set. The ANSI character set contains 256 characters. The first 128 characters (0–127) correspond to the letters and symbols on a standard U.S. keyboard. For example, the ANSI characters 48 through 57 correspond to the numbers 0 through 9, respectively. The ANSI character 8 corresponds to the Backspace key. The remaining 128 characters (128–255) in the ANSI character set represent special characters, such as letters in international alphabets, accents, currency symbols, and fractions. To view the ANSI character set, use the Help menu to search for the topic "Character Sets."

Exercises

1. In the following Debugging exercise, you will use the KeyPress event, as well as the ANSI characters, to prevent the user from entering anything other than a number into a text box.

To prevent a user from entering a letter into a text box:

1 Open the **lcGrade** (lcGrade.vbp) project that you created in the tutorial's Lesson C. The file is located in the Tut05 folder on your Student Disk. **Save** the form and the project as Debug1 in the Tut05 folder on your Student Disk. **Run** the project.

2 Click the **Project 1** check box, type the letter **a** into the text box, then press the **Enter** key.

Because you used the Val function in the equation that calculates the grade, the application does not end in an error. The application does, however, display a grade of F, which can be misleading. It would be better if the user were prevented from entering anything other than a number into the text box.

3 Click the **Exit** button, then click the **Yes** button to end the application.

4 Open the txtScore array's Code window. Use the Procedure box to open the txtScore array's KeyPress event, then maximize the Code window. See Figure 5-54.

stores index of text box receiving event

stores the ANSI character that corresponds to the key pressed by user

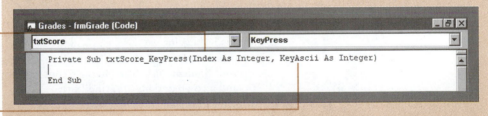

Figure 5-54: txtScore control array's KeyPress event

Notice that the KeyPress event has two arguments: `Index as Integer` and `KeyAscii as Integer`. As you learned in Lesson B, the Index argument stores the index of the text box that is receiving the event. The KeyAscii argument stores the ANSI character that corresponds to the key pressed by the user. In this case you want to tell the KeyPress event to allow the user to press only the numbers 0 through 9, and the Backspace key. (The user may need to use the Backspace key to edit the contents of the text box.) Recall that the numbers 0 through 9 on the keyboard are represented in the ANSI character set by the characters 48 through 57, respectively. Also recall that the Backspace key is represented by the ANSI character 8.

To make the code more self-documenting, you will create constants for these ANSI characters.

5 Press the **Tab** key, then type **const conZero as integer = 48, conNine as integer = 57** and press the **Enter** key.

6 Type **const conBackspace as integer = 8** and press the **Enter** key.

7 Type **if (keyascii < conzero or keyascii > connine) and keyascii < > conbackspace then** and press the **Enter** key.

If the user presses an invalid key (a key other than the Backspace and the numbers 0 through 9), then you want the KeyPress event to cancel the key. You cancel the key by assigning the ANSI character 0 (zero) to the KeyAscii argument.

8 Press the **Tab** key, then type **keyascii = 0** and press the **Enter** key. (Be sure you type the number 0, and not the letter O.)

9 Press the Backspace key to cancel the indentation, then type **end if** and press the **Enter** key. See Figure 5-55.

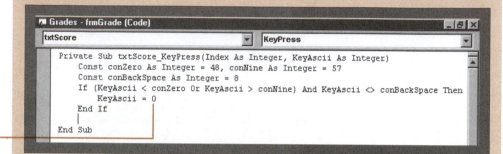

cancels key pressed by user

```
Grades - frmGrade (Code)                                            _ | 8 | x

txtScore                          ▼      KeyPress                           ▼

Private Sub txtScore_KeyPress(Index As Integer, KeyAscii As Integer)
    Const conZero As Integer = 48, conNine As Integer = 57
    Const conBackSpace As Integer = 8
    If (KeyAscii < conZero Or KeyAscii > conNine) And KeyAscii <> conBackSpace Then
        KeyAscii = 0
    End If

End Sub
```

Figure 5-55: Completed KeyPress event

10 Close the Code window, then **save** and **run** the application.

11 Click the **Project 1** check box. Try entering a letter into the text box; the text box will not allow you to do so. Enter a number, then use the Backspace key to remove the number. Notice that you can enter a number and also use the Backspace key.

12 Click the **Exit** button, then click the **Yes** button to end the application.

2. In this Debugging exercise, you will need to find and correct the bug(s).
   a. Open the Debug2 (Debug2.vbp) project, which is located in the Tut05 folder on your Student Disk. The interface contains two text boxes (txtFirst and txtSecond) and a command button (cmdExit).
   b. Print the existing code.
   c. If the user presses the Enter key when the txtFirst text box has the focus, the txtFirst control's KeyPress event should move the focus to the txtSecond control. If the user presses the Enter key when the txtSecond text box has the focus, the txtSecond control's KeyPress event should move the focus to the cmdExit control. Run the project. Test the application to see if it is working properly, then stop the application and correct any errors.
   d. When the application is working correctly, print the code. You do not need to save the application.

Sequential Access Files, Menus, and Reports

The PAO Application

case ▶ During July and August of each year, the Political Awareness Organization (PAO) sends a questionnaire to the voters in their district. The questionnaire asks the voter to provide his or her name, political party (Democrat, Republican, Independent), and age group (18–35, 36–50, 51–65, Over 65). From the returned questionnaires, the organization's secretary tabulates the number of Democrats, Republicans, and Independents in each of the four age groups—a time-consuming and tedious job. The secretary then sends a report summarizing the data to the organization's members and to various political offices in the district. The organization's president has asked for your help in simplifying this process.

In this tutorial you will create two applications for the PAO. One of the applications will tabulate the questionnaire data and print the summary report. The other can be used to write a cover letter to send along with the summary report. As you've done in previous tutorials, you will preview the applications before creating them.

Previewing the Completed Applications

The first application you will preview is the one that will tabulate the questionnaire data and print the report.

To preview the completed applications:

1   If necessary, start Windows, then place your Student Disk in the appropriate disk drive.

2   Use the Run command on the Start menu to run the **Pao** (Pao.exe) file, which is located in the Tut06 folder on your Student Disk. The PAO application's user interface appears on the screen. See Figure 6-1.

list boxes

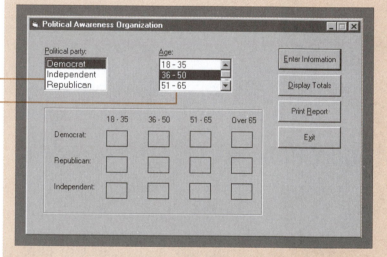

Figure 6-1: PAO application's user interface

This application contains a new control, a list box, which you will learn about in Lesson A. The organization's secretary will use the two list box controls to enter the respondent's political party and age group. Observe how the application works by simulating the entry of two records.

3   Click **Republican** in the Political party list box, then click **18 - 35** in the Age list box.

When the user clicks the Enter Information button, the party and age information will be saved in a sequential access file on your Student Disk. You will learn about sequential access data files in Lessons A and C.

4   Click the **Enter Information** button to write the respondent's information to the data file. (Because this preview application is for demonstration purposes only, it is not coded to actually write the respondent's information to the data file. The application you will create in Lesson A, however, will allow you to write information to a file.)

5   Click **Independent** in the Political party list box. Scroll the Age list box, then click **Over 65** in the list. Click the **Enter Information** button to write the respondent's information to the data file.

When the organization wants to tabulate the responses, the secretary needs simply to click the Display Totals button.

6   Click the **Display Totals** button. The application counts and displays the total number of Democrats, Republicans, and Independents in each of the four age groups, as shown in Figure 6-2.

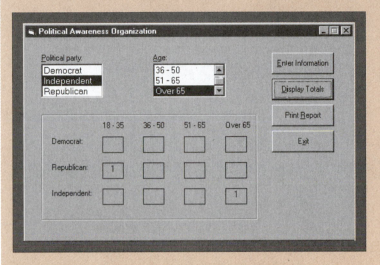

Figure 6-2: PAO application showing tabulated data

tip

• • • • • • • • • • • • • • •

Because this preview application is for demonstration only, it is coded so that it always displays the tabulated data shown in Figure 6-2. The application you will create in Lesson A will allow you to enter and tabulate other data.

7   If your computer is connected to a printer, click the **Print Report** button to print the PAO report. Figure 6-3 shows the printed report.

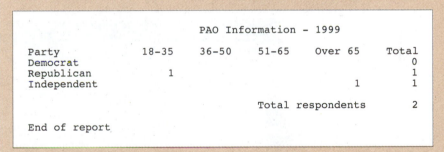

```
                       PAO Information - 1999
Party              18-35    36-50    51-65    Over 65    Total
Democrat                                                    0
Republican           1                                      1
Independent                                        1        1

                            Total respondents           2

End of report
```

Figure 6-3: Printed PAO report

8   Click the **Exit** button to end the application.

You will learn how to create this application in Lesson A. In Lessons B and C you will learn how to create a text editor that the organization's secretary can use to type a letter. Take a look at this text editor now.

To preview the text editor application:

1   Use the Run command on the Start menu to run the **Edit** (Edit.exe) file, which is located in the Tut06 folder on your Student Disk. The text editor's user interface appears on the screen. See Figure 6-4.

Figure 6-4: Text editor's user interface

2   Type **Text example editor** and press the **Enter** key.

3   Select the word **example** in the line that you just typed. Click **Edit** on the text editor menu bar, then click **Cut**. Visual Basic removes the word "example" from the typed line, and places it on the Clipboard.

4   Position the I-bar I at the end of the typed line, immediately after the word "editor," then click at that location. The insertion point appears after the word "editor."

5   Press the **Spacebar** on your keyboard to insert a blank space. Click **Edit** on the text editor menu bar, then click **Paste**. Visual Basic pastes the word "example" at the end of the typed line as shown in Figure 6-5.

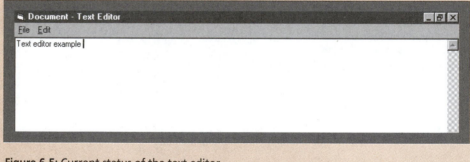

Figure 6-5: Current status of the text editor

6   Click **File**, then click **Exit** to end the application.

In Lesson A you will learn about list boxes and sequential access data files as you code the first PAO application. You will learn about menus and string manipulation functions in Lessons B and C as you code the text editor application.

In this lesson you will learn how to:

- Add a list box control to the form
- Add items to a list box with the AddItem method
- Set the Sorted and the ListIndex properties
- Create, open, and close a sequential access data file
- Write records to and read records from a sequential access data file
- Right-align information in a column
- Align numbers by decimal point
- Use a printer spacing chart
- Print a report

Sequential Access Data Files and Reports

Creating the PAO Application

Recall that each year the Political Awareness Organization (PAO) sends a questionnaire to the voters in their district. The questionnaire asks the voter to provide his or her name, political party, and age group. A sample questionnaire is shown in Figure 6-6.

PAO Questionnaire
Circle your political party affiliation:
Democrat   Republican   Independent
Print your full name: _____
Please circle your age group: 18-35   36-50   51-65   Over 65
Thank you for taking the time to complete this questionnaire.

Figure 6-6: Sample PAO questionnaire

When the questionnaires are returned, the organization's secretary tabulates the number of Democrats, Republicans, and Independents in each of the four age groups shown on the questionnaire, and then creates and prints a summary report. The president of the PAO wants you to create an application that will do this time-consuming task for the organization's secretary.

On your Student Disk is a partially completed application for the PAO organization.

To open the partially completed application:

1 Start Visual Basic, if necessary, and open the **t6Case** (t6Case.vbp) project, which is located in the Tut06 folder on your Student Disk. The `Option Explicit` statement has already been entered into the General Declarations section of the form.

2 Save the form and the project as **laPao**. Click the **form's title bar** to select the frmPao form. The partially completed interface is shown in Figure 6-7.

cmdEnter

list box

cmdDisplay

cmdPrint

lblDem control array

lblRep control array

lblInd control array

frame control

cmdExit

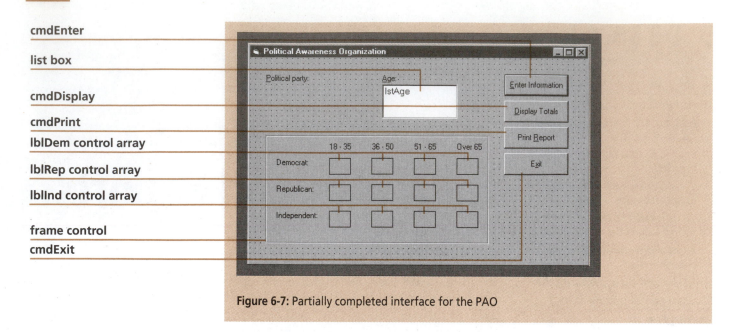

Figure 6-7: Partially completed interface for the PAO

The frame control contains three parallel control arrays—lblDem, lblRep, and lblInd—and each control array consists of four label controls. The Enter Information button is the default button on the form.

Notice that the interface contains a new control, a list box named lstAge. To complete the interface, you will need to add another list box to the form.

Creating a List Box

tip

....

▶ You can also create list boxes that allow the user to select more than one item in the list. You will learn how to create multi-selection list boxes in Lesson A's Discovery Exercise 11.

Using the completed questionnaires, the organization's secretary will enter two items of information about each respondent into the interface: his or her political party and age group. The secretary will use two list boxes to record this information from the respondents. Like option buttons, which you learned about in Tutorial 4, a **list box control** also can be used to display a set of choices from which the user can select only one. Unlike option buttons, however, a list box does not require you to display all of the choices on the screen at the same time. You can make a list box any size you want, and if you have more items than will fit into the list box, Visual Basic will automatically supply scroll bars on the box, which you can use to view the complete list of items. So if you have many possible choices, you can save space on the form by using a list box instead of option buttons.

The Windows standard is to display, in the list box, a minimum of three selections and a maximum of eight selections at a time. If you have only two options to offer the user, you should use option buttons instead of a list box.

To add a list box control to the form, then lock the controls and set the TabIndex property:

1 Double-click the **ListBox tool** 📧 in the toolbox. The List1 list box appears in the center of the form.

   HELP? If your control says Combo1, you inadvertently selected the ComboBox tool instead of the ListBox tool. Press the Delete key to remove the combo box from the form, then repeat Step 1.

The **lstAge** and **lstParty** controls are instances of the list box class.

2 Set the list box control's Name property to **lstParty**. Be sure to type the letter l and not the number 1. ("lst" is the three-character ID for the list box control.)

3 Set the list box control's Font size to **10** and its Width property to **1455**.

4 Drag the list box to the location shown in Figure 6-8, then size the list box as shown in the figure.

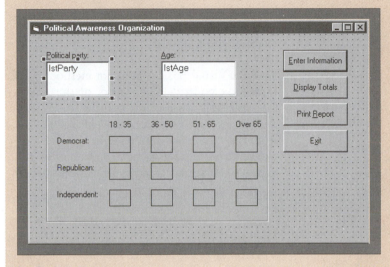

Figure 6-8: Correct location and size of the lstParty list box in the form

Don't be concerned that the list box's Name property, lstParty, appears inside the list box; the name won't appear when you run the application.

Now that the user interface is complete, you can lock the controls on the form.

5 Right-click the **form,** then select **Lock Controls** from the shortcut menu to lock the controls on the form.

Recall from Tutorial 2 that you should give keyboard access to the essential elements of the interface. In this interface, for example, you should give keyboard access to the four command buttons, which has already been done, and to the two list boxes. As with a text box, you give keyboard access to a list box by assigning an access key to the label control that identifies the list box. You must then set the label control's TabIndex value to a number that is one less than the list box's TabIndex value. In other words, if the "Political party:" label has a TabIndex of 0, as it does in this interface, then its corresponding list box (lstParty) should have a TabIndex value of 1. Likewise, if the "Age:" label has a TabIndex of 2, then its corresponding list box (lstAge) should have a TabIndex of 3. Figure 6-9 shows both the current and the new TabIndex values of the four controls.

GUI
Design Tips

List Box Standards

- List boxes should contain a minimum of three selections.
- Display a minimum of three selections and a maximum of eight selections at a time.
- Use a label control to provide keyboard access to the list box. Set the label control's TabIndex property to a value that is one less than the list box's TabIndex value.

Control	Current TabIndex Value	New TabIndex Value
Label1 (Political party:)	0	0
lstParty	27	1
Label2 (Age:)	1	2
lstAge	2	3

Figure 6-9: Current and new TabIndex values

In this case, you will simply need to set the TabIndex property of the lstParty list box to 1; Visual Basic will then renumber the TabIndex values of the Label2 and lstAge controls appropriately.

6   Click the **lstParty** list box, then set its TabIndex property to **1**.

Next you will use the AddItem method to specify what items you want displayed in each list box.

The AddItem Method

You use Visual Basic's **AddItem method** to specify the items you want displayed in a list box control. The syntax of the AddItem method is *object*.**AddItem** *item*. *Object* is the name of the control to which you want the item added, **AddItem** is the name of the method, and *item* is the expression you want displayed in the control. The expression can be either numeric or string. However, if you want to display a string in the list box, you must surround the string with quotation marks. Figure 6-10 shows some examples of using the AddItem method to display items in a list box.

The AddItem method also allows you to specify the position within the object where the new item is placed. To learn more about the AddItem method, view its Help window.

Example	Result
`lstAnimal.AddItem "Dog"`	Displays the string "Dog" in the lstAnimal list box
`lstAge.AddItem 35`	Displays the number 35 in the lstAge list box

`For sngCount = 0 to 5 step .5`
`    lstRate.AddItem sngCount`
`Next sngCount`
	Displays the numbers from 0 through 5, in increments of .5, in the lstRate list box

Figure 6-10: Examples of using the AddItem method

The lstParty list box should offer the user the following three selections: Republican, Democrat, Independent. That means you will need to enter three AddItem instructions—one for each of the selections. Because you want the lstParty list box to display its values when the form first appears on the screen, you will define the list box items in the form's Load event procedure. The Load event occurs when an application is run and the form is loaded into the computer's memory. Visual Basic automatically executes the instructions contained in the Load event procedure's Code window when the Load event occurs.

To enter the AddItem instructions for the lstParty list box:

1   Open the form's Load event, which already contains the AddItem instructions for the lstAge list box.

2   Enter the additional AddItem instructions shown in Figure 6-11.

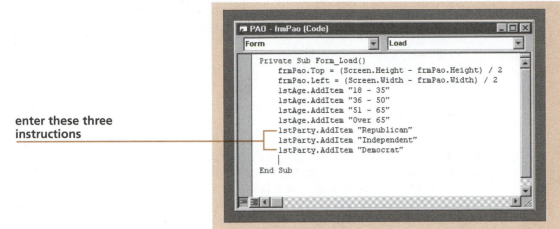

enter these three instructions

Figure 6-11: Additional AddItem instructions entered in the form's Load event procedure

When you run this application and the form is loaded into the computer's memory, Visual Basic will fill both list boxes with the values entered in the Load event procedure's Code window.

3 Close the Code window, then **save** and **run** the application. Visual Basic displays the form on the screen, as shown in Figure 6-12.

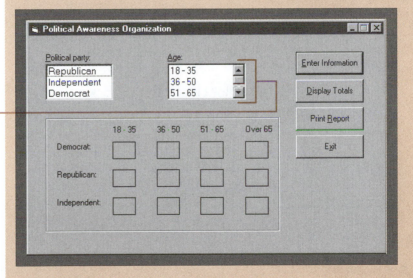

scroll bar, indicating more than three choices

Figure 6-12: List boxes displayed in form

4 Click **Republican** in the Political party list box.

When you select an item in a list box, Visual Basic stores the item in the list box's Text property. In this case, "Republican" is stored in the lstParty control's Text property.

Because the Age list box is too small to display its four items at the same time, Visual Basic supplies scroll bars on the list box. You can use those scroll bars to scroll through the various choices.

5 Scroll the Age list box until the Over 65 option appears, then click **Over 65** to select it. Visual Basic stores the string "Over 65" in the lstAge control's Text property.

6 Click the **Exit** button, which already contains the `Unload frmPao` statement. The application ends and Visual Basic returns to the design screen.

In the next section you will learn how to put list box items in alphabetical order. Arranging information in alphabetical, numerical, or chronological order is called **sorting**.

The Sorted Property

In Windows applications, list box items are either arranged by use, with the most used entries appearing first in the list, or the items are arranged (sorted) in ascending order alphabetically, numerically, or chronologically. To arrange the list box items by use, you simply enter the AddItem instructions in the order in which you want the items to appear in the list. To arrange the items in ascending order, you can either add the items to the list box in the correct order or you can set the list box's Sorted property to True. Setting the list box's Sorted property to True automatically sorts the items as they are added to the list box. Use the Sorted property to sort the items in the lstParty list box.

> To sort the items in the Political party list box:
> 1   Click the **lstParty** list box. Set the list box's Sorted property to **True**. Now Visual Basic will sort the items alphabetically as they are added to the list box.

It is customary in Windows applications to have one of the items in a list box selected when the interface appears. You can use a list box's ListIndex property to select this item. (See the *Default Item Selected in a List Box* GUI Design Tip regarding multi-selection list boxes.)

The ListIndex Property

Similar to the TabIndex property, which keeps track of the various objects in a form, the **ListIndex property** keeps track of the various items in a list box. The first item in a list box has a ListIndex of 0 (zero), the second item has a ListIndex of 1, and so on. When the user selects an item in a list box, Visual Basic records that item's index in the ListIndex property. For example, if the user selects the first item in the list box, the ListIndex property contains the number 0. You can use the ListIndex property to have the application, rather than the user, select an item in a list box. The `lstParty.ListIndex = 0` instruction, for instance, selects the first item in the lstParty list box.

When using a list box in an interface, it is customary to have a default item selected in the list when the application first appears. The default item should be either the most used selection or the first selection in the list. In this application, because most of the voters in the district are Democrats in the 36 to 50 age group, you will have Visual Basic select "Democrat" in the Political party list box and "36 - 50" in the Age list box. Because you want the list box items selected when the form first appears on the screen, you will need to set the ListIndex property in the form's Load event procedure.

To select a default item in each list box:

1   Open the form's Load event procedure.

When the application is run, "Democrat" will be the first item in the Political party list box, so its ListIndex value will be 0. (Recall that the lstParty control's Sorted property is set to True.) "36 - 50" will be the second item in the Age list box, so its ListIndex value will be 1.

2   Enter the two instructions shown in Figure 6-13.

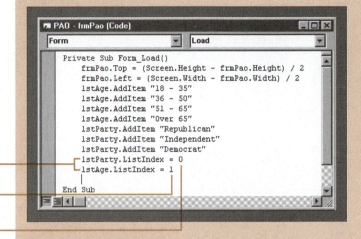

enter these two instructions

selects second item in the list box

selects first item in the list box

Figure 6-13: ListIndex instructions entered in the form's Load event procedure

3   Close the Code window, then **save** and **run** the application. Visual Basic displays the form on the screen.

Notice that the items in the Political party list box are in alphabetical order. Also notice that Visual Basic automatically selects the first item (Democrat) in the Political party list box, and the second item (36 - 50) in the Age list box.

4   Click the **Exit** button to end the application. Visual Basic returns to the design screen.

GUI
Design Tips

Default Item Selected in a List Box

• If a list box allows the user to make only one selection at a time, then a default item should be selected in the list box when the interface first appears. The default item should be either the most used selection or the first selection in the list. However, if a list box allows more than one selection at a time, you do not select a default item. You will learn about multiselection list boxes in Lesson A's Discovery Exercise 11.

Before you can continue coding the application, you will need to learn about data files. The information pertaining to each respondent will be saved in a data file.

Data Files

In previous tutorials you saved the form and the project in separate files on your Student Disk. Those files, called **program files**, contain the instructions that both create the user interface and tell the objects how to respond to events. Although the form and the project were saved, recall that the data entered into the user interface—for example, the student's scores in Tutorial 5's grade application—was not saved. That means you will need to enter the data (the student's scores) each time the grade application is run. So that the PAO's secretary will not have to enter the party and age information every time he or she runs the program, you will save that information in a file, called a **data file**, on your Student Disk.

The information in a data file is organized into fields and records. A **field**, also called a **data element**, is a single item of information about a person, place, or thing—for example, a Social Security number, a city, or a price. A **record** is a group of related fields that contain all of the necessary data about a specific person, place, or thing. For example, the college you are attending maintains a student record on you. Your student record might contain the following fields: your Social Security number, name, address, phone number, credits earned, grades earned, grade point average, and so on. The place where you are employed also maintains a record on you. Your employee record might contain your Social Security number, name, address, phone number, starting date, salary or hourly wage, and so on. A collection of related records is called a **data file**. The collection of records for each of the students in your class forms the class data file; the collection of employee records forms the employee data file. Figure 6-14 illustrates the concept of a field, a record, and a data file.

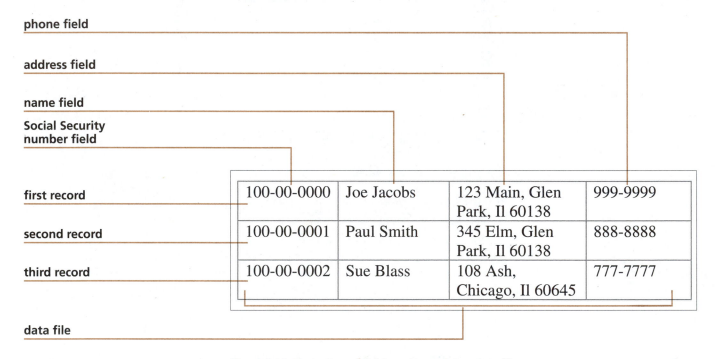

Figure 6-14: Illustration of fields and records in a data file

In the PAO only two elements of data are important—the respondent's political party and his or her age group. Together, those two fields form each respondent's record. The collection of respondents' records forms the PAO data file.

Visual Basic has three types of data files: sequential, random, and binary. The data file type refers to how the data is accessed. For example, the data in a sequential access file is always accessed sequentially—in other words, in consecutive order. The data in a random access file, on the other hand, can be accessed either in consecutive order or in random order. The data in a binary access file can be accessed by its byte location in the file. You will learn about sequential access files in this tutorial and random access files in Tutorial 8. Although full coverage of binary access files is beyond the scope of this book, you can learn how to open, save to, and read from a binary access file in Appendix C.

Sequential Access Data Files

Sequential access files are similar to cassette tapes in that each record in the file, like each song on a cassette tape, is both stored and retrieved in consecutive order (sequentially). Sequential access files have the advantage of being very easy to create. The drawback of this file type is the same drawback encountered with cassette tapes: the records in a sequential access file, like the songs on a cassette tape, can be processed only in the order in which they are stored. In other words, if you want to listen to the third song on a cassette tape, you must play (or fast-forward through) the first two songs. Likewise, if you want to read the third record in a sequential access file, you must first read the two records that precede it. Sequential access files work best when you want to process either a small file, like the one needed by the PAO, or a file consisting only of text, such as a file created with a typical text editor.

In this lesson you will learn how to create, open, and close a sequential access file, as well as write records to and read records from a sequential access file. The TOE chart for the PAO application is shown in Figure 6-15.

Task	Object	Event
Get the respondent's political party	lstParty	Click
Get the respondent's age group	lstAge	Click
Write the respondent's party and age group to a sequential access file	cmdEnter	Click
1. Read the data from the sequential access file 2. Count the number of Democrats, Republicans, and Independents in each of the age groups 3. Display the results in the appropriate label controls in the lblDem, lblRep, and lblInd arrays	cmdDisplay	Click
End the application	cmdExit	Click
Print report	cmdPrint	Click
Display the number of Democrats, Republicans, and Independents in each of the age groups (from cmdDisplay)	lblDem array lblRep array lblInd array	None

Figure 6-15: TOE chart for the PAO application

The PAO secretary will use the lstParty and lstAge controls to enter the respondent's party and age group information, respectively. After entering a respondent's information, the secretary will use the Enter Information button to write the information to the sequential file, and use the Display Totals button to tabulate the responses and display the results. To print the report, the secretary needs simply to click the Print Report button. The Exit button will end the application.

You will need to code only three of the four command buttons shown in Figure 6-15 because the Exit button already contains the `Unload frmPao` statement. In this application, you don't need to code either of the list box's Click event procedures; when you click an item in a list box, Visual Basic assigns the item to the list box's Text property automatically. You will begin by coding the Enter Information button, which is responsible for saving each respondent's political party and age group in a sequential file on your Student Disk.

Coding the Enter Information Command Button

For each returned questionnaire, recall that the organization's secretary will use the lstParty and lstAge controls to enter the respondent's political party and age group, respectively. After entering a respondent's data into the user interface, the secretary will then click the Enter Information button to write the record to a data file. The pseudocode and flowchart for the Enter Information button are shown in Figure 6-16.

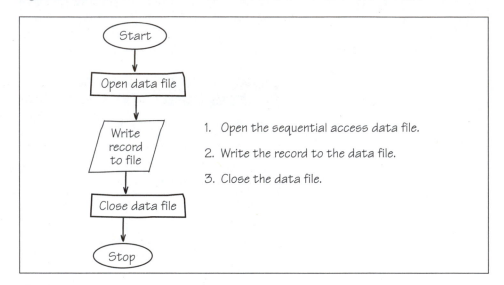

Figure 6-16: Flowchart and pseudocode for the Enter Information button

The first step is to open the sequential access data file. You must open a data file before you can use it.

Opening a Data File

You open a data file with Visual Basic's **Open statement**. Its syntax is **Open** *pathname* **For** *mode* **As #** *filenumber*. *Pathname* is the name of the file you want to open; it should include the drive letter and path, and it must be enclosed in quotation marks. For sequential access files, *mode* can be Input, Output, or Append. You open a sequential access file for **Input** when you want to read its contents; if a file opened for Input does not exist, Visual Basic displays an error message when it attempts to open the file. You open the file for **Output** when you want to create a new sequential access file and then write data to it; if the file already exists, Visual Basic erases its contents before writing the new information. You open a file for **Append** when you want to add data to the end of an existing sequential access file; if the file does not already exist, Visual Basic creates it before adding the data to it. Figure 6-17 recaps the three modes used with sequential access files.

Open statement mode	Use to:
Append	Add data to an existing sequential access data file. The file is created if it does not already exist.
Input	Read data from an existing sequential access data file. If the file does not exist, Visual Basic displays an error message when it attempts to open the file.
Output	Create a new sequential access data file and write data to it. If the file already exists, its contents are erased before the new data is written.

Figure 6-17: Summary of Open statement modes for sequential access files

Filenumber is a number that you assign to the file; it must be an integer between 1 and 511, inclusive. When the Open statement is processed, Visual Basic associates the *filenumber* with the file. You use the *filenumber* to refer to the file in other statements. The *filenumber* will be associated with the file as long as the file is open. Figure 6-18 shows examples of the Open statement.

Open statement	Result
Open "a:\tut06\Test.dat" for Append as #1	Opens a sequential access data file for append
Open "a:\tut06\Employee.dat" for Input as #1	Opens a sequential access data file for input
Open strFileName for Output as #2	Opens a sequential access data file, whose name is stored in the strFileName variable, for output

Figure 6-18: Examples of the Open statement for sequential access files

Visual Basic uses a **record pointer** to keep track of the next record to either read or write in a data file. When you open a file for Input, Visual Basic positions the record pointer at the beginning of the file, immediately before the first record. When you open a file for Output, Visual Basic also positions the record pointer at the beginning of the file, but recall that the file is empty. (As you may remember, opening a file for Output tells Visual Basic to create a new, empty file or erase the contents of an existing file.) When you open a file for Append, Visual Basic positions the record pointer immediately after the last record in the file. Figure 6-19 illustrates the positioning of the record pointer when files are opened for Input, Output, and Append.

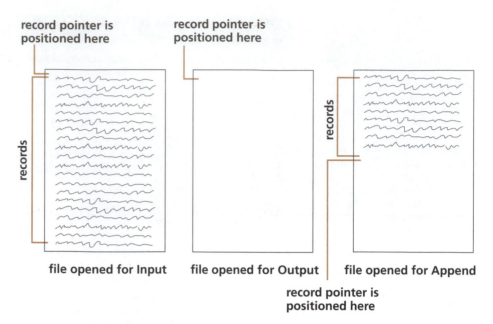

record pointer is
positioned here

record pointer is
positioned here

records

records

file opened for Input   file opened for Output   file opened for Append

record pointer is
positioned here

Figure 6-19: Position of the record pointer when files are opened for Input, Output, and
Append

Because the organization's secretary will be adding new records to the file as
the questionnaires are returned, you will need to open the PAO file for Append;
new records will then be added automatically to the end of the data file. You will
name the data file Pao.dat and assign file number 1 to it. A .dat extension is commonly used in a filename to indicate that the file is a data file.

To enter the Open statement:

1   Open the Enter Information button's Click event procedure, then press the
Tab key.

2   Type one of the following Open statements into the Code window. Which
statement you type will depend on the location of your Student Disk. Be
sure to type the backslash (\), not the front slash (/), in the appropriate
places.

open "a:\tut06\pao.dat" for append as #1

open "b:\tut06\pao.dat" for append as #1

3   Press the **Enter** key.

tip

Recall that when you open
a file for Append, Visual
Basic creates the file if it
does not already exist.

When the application is run and the user clicks the Enter Information button,
the Open statement will open the sequential data file named pao.dat. If the
pao.dat file does not exist, the Open statement will create the data file before
opening it.

The next step shown in Figure 6-16 is to write the respondent's record to the
data file—in other words, to enter the record in the file. Recall that a respondent's
record consists of his or her political party and age group.

Writing to a Sequential Access File

You use Visual Basic's **Write # statement** to write a record to a sequential access file. The syntax of the Write # statement is **Write #** *filenumber,* [*outputlist*]. *Filenumber* is the number used in the Open statement to open the sequential access file, and *outputlist* is one or more numeric or string expressions, separated by commas. Figure 6-20 shows examples of the Write # statement.

Write # statement	Result
Write #1, txtCity.Text	Writes the Text property of the txtCity control to the sequential access data file opened as file #1.
Write #2, strCity, curSales	Writes the contents of both the strCity and curSales variables to the sequential access data file opened as file #2.
Write #1, lstParty.Text, lstAge.ListIndex	Writes the contents of the lstParty control's Text property and the contents of the lstAge control's ListIndex property to the sequential access data file opened as file #1.
Write #1,	Writes a blank line to the sequential access data file opened as #1.

Figure 6-20 Examples of the Write # statement for sequential access files

In this application you want to write the respondent's party (which is entered in the lstParty list box) and his or her age group (which is entered in the lstAge list box) to the data file. One method of doing so is to write each list box's Text property to the file; recall that when the user selects an item in a list box, Visual Basic stores the item in its Text property. Therefore, you could use the `Write #1, lstParty.Text, lstAge.Text` statement to write the respondent's record to the data file. If the user selects Democrat from the Political party list box and 36 - 50 from the Age list box, for example, the Write # statement would write `"Democrat","36 - 50"` to the data file.

You can also enter the respondent's information by writing each list box's ListIndex property, rather than its Text property, to the data file. Recall that the ListIndex property stores the index of the currently selected list box item. In other words, you could also use the `Write #1, lstParty.ListIndex, lstAge.ListIndex` statement to write the respondent's record to the data file. If the user selects Democrat from the Political party list box and 36 - 50 from the Age list box, for example, the Write # statement would write `0,1` to the data file. An advantage of writing the ListIndex property, rather than the Text property, is that it results in a smaller data file because fewer characters need to be stored for each record. In this case, instead of storing two strings (`"Democrat","36 - 50"`), the data file would store two numbers (`0,1`). The disadvantage of recording the ListIndex property in the file is that if the contents of the list box change, the value recorded in the file may no longer refer to the correct item in the list. For example, if you were to add a new party as the first item in the Political party list box, the 0 ListIndex value previously recorded in the Pao.dat file would not refer to Democrat; rather it would refer, incorrectly, to the new party.

In this application, you will not be adding any new items to either the Political party or the Age list boxes. So that you can observe the difference between recording the Text property and recording the ListIndex property, you will write the lstParty control's Text property and the lstAge control's ListIndex property to the sequential data file.

To add the Write # statement to the open Code window:

1   The cmdEnter control's Click event procedure should still be open. Type **write #1, lstparty.text, lstage.listindex** and press the **Enter** key. This statement will write the lstParty control's Text property and the lstAge control's ListIndex property to the pao.dat file on your Student Disk.

When you are finished with a data file, you should close it.

tip

If you have already completed this lesson and are now practicing it again, you should use Windows to delete the pao.dat file from your Student Disk before running the PAO application; otherwise, the records will be added to the existing pao.dat file.

Closing a Sequential Access File

You use Visual Basic's **Close statement** to close a data file. Its syntax is **Close [# *filenumber*]**, where *filenumber* is the number used in the Open statement to open the file. A Close statement with no *filenumber* closes all open files. When a file is closed, its *filenumber* is disassociated from the file. The *filenumber* can then be used by another file. In this case you want to close the pao.dat file, which was opened as #1.

To complete the Enter Information button's code, then save and run the application:

1   Maximize the Code window, then enter the Close statement and the documentation shown in Figure 6-21.

enter this
documentation

enter this statement

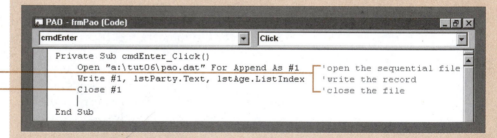

```
PAO - frmPao (Code)

cmdEnter                              Click

    Private Sub cmdEnter_Click()
        Open "a:\tut06\pao.dat" For Append As #1    'open the sequential file
        Write #1, lstParty.Text, lstAge.ListIndex   'write the record
        Close #1                                     'close the file

    End Sub
```

Figure 6-21: Enter Information button's Click event procedure

2   Compare your code with the code shown in Figure 6-21. Make any necessary corrections before continuing to the next step.

3   Close the Code window.

You will now test the Enter Information button by entering the data from three completed questionnaires.

4   **Save** and **run** the application.

The first questionnaire is from a Republican in the 18 - 35 age group.

5   Click **Republican** in the Political party list box, then click **18 - 35** in the Age list box. Click the **Enter Information** button. Because the pao.dat file

tip

Because you opened the pao.dat file for Append, Visual Basic writes the second record after the first record in the file.

doesn't yet exist, Visual Basic creates the pao.dat file on your Student Disk. Visual Basic writes the record to the file, then closes the file before the cmdEnter Click event procedure ends.

The second questionnaire is from a Democrat in the 36 - 50 age group.

6 Click **Democrat** in the Political party list box, then click **36 - 50** in the Age list box. Click the **Enter Information** button. Visual Basic opens the existing pao.dat file on your Student Disk, writes the second record to the file, and closes the file. The cmdEnter Click event procedure then ends.

The third questionnaire is from an Independent in the Over 65 age group.

7 Click **Independent** in the Political party list box, then click **Over 65** in the Age list box. Click the **Enter Information** button. Visual Basic opens the existing Pao.dat file on your Student Disk, writes the third record to the file, and closes the file. The cmdEnter Click event procedure then ends.

8 Click the **Exit** button. Visual Basic returns to the design screen.

You can use a basic word processor or text editor to verify that the records were written to the data file. For example, you can use WordPad, the word processor that comes with Windows 95, to view the contents of a data file. You can also make changes to the data file while you are using a word processor, but you must be careful not to add any unnecessary characters—for example, don't leave any blank lines in the file by pressing the Enter key unnecessarily—or Visual Basic will have trouble reading the file. You also must be careful not to remove any needed punctuation. The pao.dat file, shown in WordPad, would look similar to Figure 6-22.

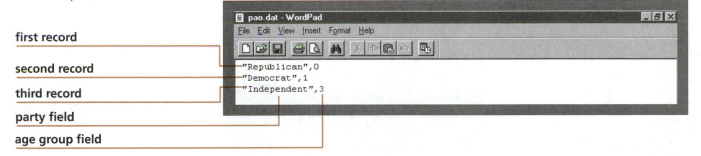

first record
second record
third record
party field
age group field

Figure 6-22: Pao.dat file shown in WordPad

Each line in the data file represents a record and each record is composed of two fields: the respondent's party and his or her age group. The two fields are separated by a comma. The party field is a string expression, as indicated by the surrounding quotation marks, and the age group field is numeric. When you write a record to a sequential access file, Visual Basic automatically supplies the quotation marks around the string data and separates the data in each field by commas.

Next you will code the Display Totals button.

Coding the Display Totals Button

The pseudocode and flowchart for the Display Totals button's Click event procedure are shown in Figure 6-23. Before coding the Display Totals button, study the logic shown in this figure.

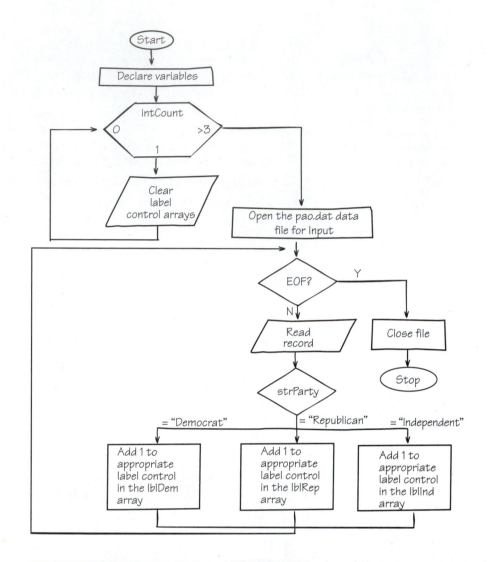

Pseudocode for the Display Totals button

1. Declare variables.
2. Repeat for intCount = 0 to 3
      Clear label control arrays
   End Repeat for
3. Open the pao.dat sequential access data file for Input
4. Repeat while not EOF
      Read a record from the file
      Case of strParty
         = "Democrat" add 1 to appropriate label control in the lblDem array
         = "Republican" add 1 to appropriate label control in the lblRep array
         = "Independent" add 1 to appropriate label control in the lblInd array
      End Case
   End Repeat while
5. Close the data file.

Figure 6-23: Flowchart and pseudocode for the Display Totals button's Click event procedure

The Click event procedure begins by declaring the necessary variables. It then uses a For Next (automatic counter) loop to clear the contents of the three label control arrays on the form. (You can look ahead to Figure 6-24 for the location of these control arrays.) After clearing the label controls, the Click event opens the pao.dat sequential access data file for Input, then uses a loop to read each record, one at a time. Recall that each record consists of the respondent's party and his or her age group. As each record is read, a Case structure compares the Political party entry with "Democrat", "Republican", and "Independent". If the respondent is a Democrat, the appropriate label control in the lblDem control array is updated. If the respondent is a Republican, the appropriate label control in the lblRep control array is updated. Lastly, if the respondent is an Independent, the appropriate label control in the lblInd control array is updated. Notice that the loop will stop when there are no more records to read, a point referred to by programmers as "EOF" ("end of file"). When the loop stops, the pao.dat data file is closed.

To begin coding the Display Totals button:

1 Open the Display Totals button's Click event procedure.

The cmdDisplay Click event procedure will need three local variables: strParty, intAge, and intCount. The intCount variable will be used by the For Next loop. The strParty and intAge variables will be used by the Input # statement to read a record from the data file. You will learn about the Input # statement later in this lesson.

2 Maximize the Code window. Press the **Tab** key, then type **dim strParty as string, intAge as integer, intCount as integer** and press the **Enter** key.

Next you will clear the contents of the three label control arrays in the interface. The label controls and their names are shown in Figure 6-24.

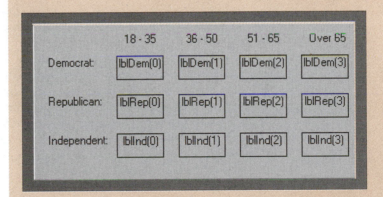

Figure 6-24: Label controls and their names

Notice that the three control arrays are named lblDem, lblRep, and lblInd. Also notice that the four label controls in each control array have indexes of 0, 1, 2, and 3. You can use a For Next (automatic counter) loop to clear the contents of the label controls in each control array. The For Next loop's *startvalue* will be 0, its *endvalue* will be 3, and its *stepvalue* will be 1.

3 Type the For Next loop shown in Figure 6-25.

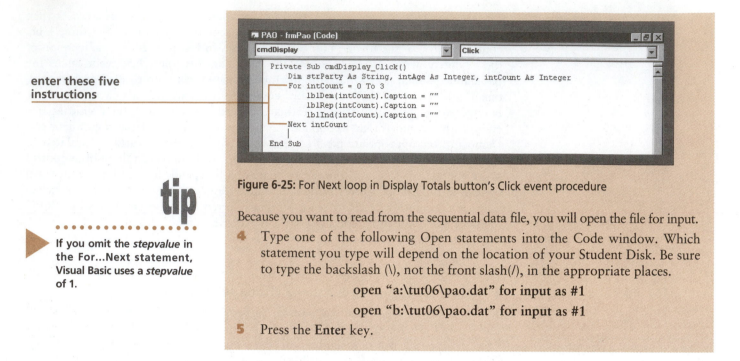

enter these five instructions

Figure 6-25: For Next loop in Display Totals button's Click event procedure

Because you want to read from the sequential data file, you will open the file for input.

4   Type one of the following Open statements into the Code window. Which statement you type will depend on the location of your Student Disk. Be sure to type the backslash (\), not the front slash(/), in the appropriate places.

open "a:\tut06\pao.dat" for input as #1

open "b:\tut06\pao.dat" for input as #1

5   Press the **Enter** key.

The next step is to enter a Do While loop that tells Visual Basic to stop processing the loop instructions when the end of the file is reached.

The EOF Function

Recall that Visual Basic uses a record pointer to keep track of the next record to either read or write in a data file. When you first open a sequential access file for Input, Visual Basic sets the record pointer to the first record in the file. Each time you read a record, the record pointer moves to the next record in the file. (Recall that sequential access files are read sequentially—one record after another in the order in which they were written to the file.) You can use the **EOF function**, which stands for "end of file," along with the Not logical operator to determine if the record pointer is at the end of the file. The syntax of the EOF function is **EOF**(*filenumber*), where *filenumber* is the number of the file used in the Open statement. When the record pointer is at the end of the file, the EOF function returns the Boolean value True; otherwise, the function returns the Boolean value False. The instruction, `Do While Not EOF(1)`, tells Visual Basic to repeat the loop instructions while it is not the end of the file. When the end of the file is reached, the loop stops.

To continue coding the Display Totals button:

1   The cmdDisplay control's Click event procedure should still be open. Type **do while not eof(1)** and press the **Enter** key. When the application is run, this instruction will tell Visual Basic to look in the pao.dat file, which was opened as file number 1, to see if the record pointer is at the end of the file.

tip

If you omit the *stepvalue* in the For...Next statement, Visual Basic uses a *stepvalue* of 1.

tip

Recall from Tutorial 4 that the Not operator reverses the truth value of a *condition*.

According to the pseudocode and flowchart, you now need to read a record from the open pao.dat file.

Reading a Record from a Sequential Access File

You use Visual Basic's **Input # statement** to read a record from a sequential access file. The syntax of the Input # statement is **Input #** *filenumber, variablelist*, where *filenumber* is the number used in the Open statement to open the sequential file and *variablelist* is one or more numeric or string variables, separated by commas. Because each variable in the *variablelist* is associated with a field in the record, the number of variables listed in the Input # statement must be the same as the number of fields in the record, and the order of the variables in the *variablelist* must correspond to the order of the fields in the record. In this case, for example, because each record in the pao.dat file contains two fields—a party and an age group—the Input # statement's *variablelist* must contain two variables, strParty and intAge. The strParty variable must be listed first in the *variablelist* because the respondent's party is the first field in his or her record. When Visual Basic reads a record from the file, the value in each field is stored in the corresponding variable listed in the *variablelist*. Figure 6-26 illustrates the relationship between the *variablelist* and the fields in a record.

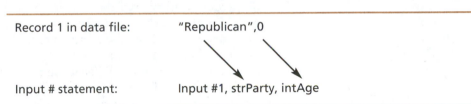

Figure 6-26: Relationship between the Input # statement's *variablelist* and the fields in a record

Now add the Input # statement, which will read a record from the file, to the open Code window.

> **To continue coding the Display Totals button:**
> 1 The cmdDisplay control's Click event procedure should still be open. Press the **Tab** key to indent the loop instructions, then type **input #1, strparty, intage** and press the **Enter** key.

The next step in the pseudocode and flowchart is to use a Case selection structure to update the appropriate label control in one of the three control arrays.

Updating the Appropriate Label Control

For each respondent's record, you will need to add one to the appropriate label control in the interface. In order to understand how the application will determine the appropriate label control to update, you will need to look closely both at the names of the label controls in the interface and at the indexes of the items in the Age list box. The label controls and their names, as well as the indexes of the Age list box items, are shown in Figure 6-27.

index is 0

index is 1

index is 2

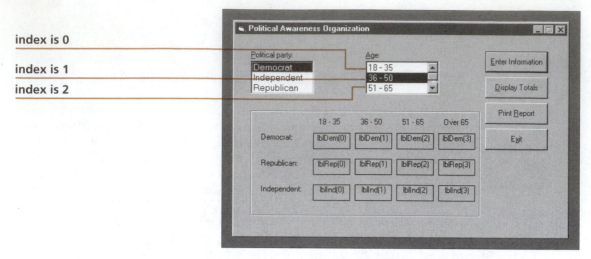

Figure 6-27: Label controls' names and Age list box indexes

Notice that each row of label controls belongs to a control array, and each control array is associated with a political party. The four label controls in the first row belong to the lblDem control array, the four in the second row belong to the lblRep control array, and the four in the third row belong to the lblInd control array. You can use the respondent's party, which is stored in the strParty variable, to determine the row of label controls to update—in other words, to determine the appropriate control array to update. For example, if the respondent is a Democrat, then you would update the lblDem control array.

Also notice in Figure 6-27 that all of the label controls in the first column have an index of 0, the controls in the second column have an index of 1, the controls in the third column have an index of 2, and the controls in the fourth column have an index of 3. The PAO interface was designed so that the indexes of the label controls (0, 1, 2, and 3) in each of the three control arrays (lblDem, lblRep, and lblInd) correspond directly to the indexes of the items listed in the Age list box. For example, the index of the first item (18 - 35) in the Age list box is 0, and so are the indexes of the three label controls that correspond to this age group. Likewise, the index of the second item (36 - 50) in the Age list box is 1, and so are the indexes of its corresponding label controls.

Recall that, in addition to writing the lstParty control's Text property (which stores the respondent's party), the Write # statement in the Enter Information button's Click event writes the lstAge control's ListIndex property (which stores the index of the selected item) to the pao.dat sequential data file. When the Input # statement in the Display Totals button reads the respondent's record from the file, it stores the party in the strParty variable and the index in the intAge variable. Similar to the way you use the strParty variable to determine the proper array to update, you can use the intAge variable to determine the appropriate label control to update in the array. The statement lblDem(intAge).Caption = Val(lblDem(intAge).Caption) + 1, for example, will update the lblDem(0) control if the intAge variable contains the number 0; it will update the lblDem(1) control if intAge contains the number 1, and so on.

In summary, you can use the strParty variable to determine which row of label controls to update, and the intAge variable to determine which column.

According to the pseudocode and flowchart, you will use a Case selection structure, along with the strParty variable, to determine which row to update. Do that now.

tip

In the Pao application, notice that you are using the labels in the control arrays as counters. Recall from Tutorial 3, however, that Visual Basic can process information faster if that information is contained in a variable rather than in the property of a control. In Tutorial 9's Lesson A you will learn about variable arrays, which you can use to make the Pao application more efficient. You will rewrite the Pao application, using variable arrays, in Exercise 21 in Tutorial 9's Lesson A.

To complete the Display Totals button's Click event, then save and run the application:

1 The Display Totals button's Click event should still be open. Type **select case strparty** and press the **Enter** key.

One possibility is that the strParty variable contains "Democrat."

2 Press the **Tab** key to indent the Case structure, then type **case "Democrat"** and press the **Enter** key.

If the strParty variable contains "Democrat," then the application should update one of the four label controls in the lblDem control array. Which of the four label controls to update depends on the value in the intAge variable.

3 Press the **Tab** key, then type **lbldem(intage).caption = val(lbldem(intage).caption) + 1** and press the **Enter** key.

This instruction tells Visual Basic to update the label control whose index matches the number in the intAge variable.

If the respondent is not a Democrat, he or she could be either a Republican or an Independent.

4 Complete the Case structure and the Do While loop as shown in Figure 6-28. Also enter the Close #1 statement to close the pao.dat file, and the documentation.

enter these seven lines of code and the documentation

```
PAO - frmPao (Code)
cmdDisplay                          Click

Private Sub cmdDisplay_Click()
    Dim strParty As String, intAge As Integer, intCount As Integer
    For intCount = 0 To 3                        'clear the label controls
        lblDem(intCount).Caption = ""
        lblRep(intCount).Caption = ""
        lblInd(intCount).Caption = ""
    Next intCount
    Open "a:\tut06\pao.dat" For Input As #1      'open the sequential file
    Do While Not EOF(1)
        Input #1, strParty, intAge               'read a record
        Select Case strParty                     'update appropriate label control
            Case "Democrat"
                lblDem(intAge).Caption = Val(lblDem(intAge).Caption) + 1
            Case "Republican"
                lblRep(intAge).Caption = Val(lblRep(intAge).Caption) + 1
            Case "Independent"
                lblInd(intAge).Caption = Val(lblInd(intAge).Caption) + 1
        End Select
    Loop
    Close #1                                      'close the file

End Sub
```

Figure 6-28: Completed Display Totals button's Click event procedure

5 Close the Code window, then **save** and **run** the application.

6 Click the **Display Totals** button. The interface appears as shown in Figure 6-29. (Recall that you wrote three records to the pao.dat file when you tested the Enter Information button.)

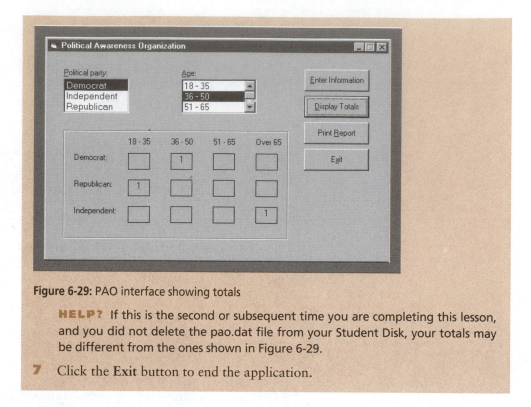

Figure 6-29: PAO interface showing totals

HELP? If this is the second or subsequent time you are completing this lesson, and you did not delete the pao.dat file from your Student Disk, your totals may be different from the ones shown in Figure 6-29.

7 Click the **Exit** button to end the application.

The last event you need to code in the PAO application is the Print Report button's Click event, which will print a report showing the number of Democrats, Republicans, and Independents in the four age groups, as well as the total number of respondents. Before you can code the event, however, you will need to learn about Visual Basic's Print method.

The Print Method

You can use Visual Basic's Print method, which you first learned about in Tutorial 4's Debugging section, to print the PAO report. Recall that the syntax of the Print method to print information on a form is **Print** [*outputlist*]. The syntax of the Print method to print information on the printer, however, is **Printer.Print** [*outputlist*], where **Printer** is a keyword that refers to the Printer object, and *outputlist* is the expression or list of expressions you want to print. If *outputlist* is omitted, Visual Basic prints a blank line.

Visual Basic provides two characters—a comma and a semicolon—that you can use to align the output listed in the Print method's *outputlist*. These characters are referred to as **separators** because you use them to separate the items in the *outputlist*. The comma separator allows you to take advantage of Visual Basic's preset tabs. The comma tells Visual Basic to tab to the next print zone before printing the next character of data. In Visual Basic, a new print zone begins after every 14 print positions. In other words, the first print zone contains print positions one through 14, the second print zone contains print positions 15 through 28, and so on. The semicolon separator, on the other hand, tells Visual Basic to move to the next print position before printing the next character. Figure 6-30 shows some examples of using the comma and semicolon separators in the Print method.

tip

The number of print zones and the number of characters that print in each print zone, as well as the exact location of the preset tabs, are dependent on both the type and size of the printer font.

	Print zone 1	Print zone 2	Print zone 3	Print zone 4	Print zone 5
Examples using the comma separator					
Printer.Print "Visual", "Basic"	Visual	Basic			
Printer.Print "First Name", "Last Name",	First Name	Last Name	City	State	Zip
Printer.Print "City", "State", "Zip"					
Printer.Print -10, 20, 5 * 3	-10	20	15		
Examples using the semicolon separator					
Printer.Print "A"; "B"; "C"	ABC				
Printer.Print "Visual ";	Visual Basic				
Printer.Print "Basic"					
Printer.Print 1; -2; 3	1 -2 3				

Figure 6-30: Examples of the comma and semicolon separators used in the Print method

tip

Visual Basic prints a leading space rather than a plus (+) sign to indicate that the number is positive.

tip

Notice that you can include a calculation in the Print method's *outputlist*.

tip

You can also use the spacebar, rather than the semicolon, when entering the items in the Print method's *outputlist*. For example, you could enter the `Printer.Print "A"; "B"; "C"` statement as `Printer.Print "A" "B" "C"`. When you move the insertion point to a different line in the Code window, Visual Basic will replace the space that separates each item with a semicolon.

First study the examples that use the comma separator. As Figure 6-30 indicates, the `Printer.Print "Visual", "Basic"` instruction will print the string "Visual" in the first print zone, then tab to the second print zone before printing the string "Basic." Visual Basic will then advance the printer to the next line in the printout.

The `Printer.Print "First Name", "Last Name",` instruction, on the other hand, tells Visual Basic to print the string "First Name" in the first print zone, then tab to the second print zone and print the string "Last Name". The comma at the end of the instruction tells Visual Basic to tab to the next print zone—in this case, the third print zone—rather than advance to the next print line. Because of this, the next Print instruction—`Printer.Print "City", "State", "Zip"`—will print "City" in the third print zone, "State" in the fourth print zone, and "Zip" in the fifth print zone in the current print line. After printing "Zip", Visual Basic will advance the printer to the next print line.

Visual Basic prints numbers slightly differently than it prints strings. When you print a string—for example, the word "Hello"—Visual Basic prints only the characters included within the quotation marks; in this example, Visual Basic will print the letters H, e, l, l, and o. The manner in which Visual Basic prints a number, however, depends on whether the number is positive or negative. Visual Basic prints positive numbers with both a leading and a trailing space. A leading space is a space that appears before the first digit in the number, and a trailing space is a space that appears after the last digit in the number. Visual Basic prints negative numbers, on the other hand, with a leading minus (-) sign and a trailing space. To observe this, look closely at the `Printer.Print -10, 20, 5 * 3` instruction and its output shown in Figure 6-30. The instruction prints -10 and a trailing space in the first four positions of print zone 1. It then prints a leading space, the number 20, and a trailing space in the first four positions of print zone 2. In the third print zone it prints a leading space, the number 15 (the result of multiplying the number 5 by the number 3), and a trailing space. Visual Basic then advances the printer to the next print line.

Now study the examples that use the semicolon separator. The `Printer.Print "A"; "B"; "C"` instruction shown in Figure 6-30 prints ABC in the first three positions of print zone 1. Notice that each letter immediately follows the prior letter. This is because, unlike the comma separator, which tells Visual Basic to advance to the next print zone, the semicolon separator tells Visual Basic to advance one print position before printing the next character. After printing the letter C, Visual Basic will advance the printer to the next print line.

Also shown in Figure 6-30 is the `Printer.Print "Visual";` instruction, which will print "Visual " (notice the space after the letter l) in the first seven positions in print zone 1. The semicolon at the end of the instruction tells Visual Basic

Spc stands for "space."

If you omit *number* in the Tab function—in other words, if you use Tab()— Visual Basic positions the insertion point at the beginning of the next print zone.

You can use both the Spc and Tab functions in the same statement.

to advance the printer to the next print position—in this case, to print position eight—in the current print line. Because of this, the `Printer.Print "Basic"` instruction will print "Basic" immediately after "Visual ".

The `Printer.Print 1; -2; 3` instruction shown in Figure 6-30 prints a leading space, the number 1, and a trailing space in print positions one through three. It then prints a leading minus sign, the number 2, and a trailing space in print positions four through six, followed by a leading space, the number 3, and a trailing space in positions seven through nine. Visual Basic then advances the printer to the next print line.

In addition to the comma and semicolon separators, Visual Basic provides two functions—Spc and Tab—that give you greater control than do the separators over the output's appearance. The syntax of the Spc function is **Spc**(*number*), where *number* represents the number of spaces to insert before displaying or printing the next item in the *outputlist*. The syntax of the Tab function is similar; it is **Tab**(*number*). In the Tab function, however, *number* represents the column number, or print position, to which you want Visual Basic to tab before printing the next item. Figure 6-31 shows some examples of the Spc and Tab functions.

										Print positions									
Examples using the Spc function	1	2	3	4	5	6	7	8	9	10	11	12	13	14	15	16	17	18
Dim intX as Integer, intY as Integer																		
intX = -2																		
intY = 80																		
Printer.Print "Answer"; Spc(2); intX →	A	n	s	w	e	r			-	2								
Printer.Print "Answer"; Spc(2); intY →	A	n	s	w	e	r				8	0							
Printer.Print Spc(2); "First"; Spc(4); "Last" →			F	i	r	s	t					L	a	s	t			
Examples using the Tab function																		
Printer.Print Tab(10); intX; Tab(15); intY →										-	2					8	0	
Printer.Print Tab(5); "First"; Tab(15); "Last" →					F	i	r	s	t						L	a	s	t

Figure 6-31: Examples of Spc and Tab functions used in the Print method

Study the three examples that use the Spc function. As Figure 6-31 indicates, the `Printer.Print "Answer"; Spc(2); intX` instruction prints the string "Answer" in print positions one through six. It then prints a space in print positions seven and eight, followed by the contents of the intX variable—a negative 2—in print positions nine, 10, and 11. (Recall that Visual Basic prints a trailing space after negative numbers.) Visual Basic will then advance the printer to the next print line. Notice that you use the semicolon separator, and not the comma separator, between the Spc function and the next item you want to print.

The `Printer.Print "Answer"; Spc(2); intY` instruction also prints the string "Answer" in print positions one through six, followed by a space in print positions seven and eight. When printing the contents of intY—the positive number 80—Visual Basic prints a leading space in print position nine, the number 80 in print positions 10 and 11, and a trailing space in print position 12. (Recall that positive numbers are printed with both a leading and a trailing space.) Visual Basic will then advance the printer to the next print line.

The `Printer.Print Spc(2); "First"; Spc(4); "Last"` instruction prints a space in print positions one and two, the string "First" in print positions three through seven, a space in print positions eight through 11, and the string "Last" in print positions 12 through 15. Visual Basic will then advance the printer to the next print line.

Now study the two examples that use the Tab function. The `Printer.Print Tab(10); intX; Tab(15); intY` instruction tells Visual

Basic to tab to column (print position) 10 before it prints the contents of the intX variable—a negative 2. After printing –2 and a trailing space in print positions 10 through 12, the instruction tells Visual Basic to tab to print position 15 before printing the contents of intY—a positive 80. When printing the number 80, Visual Basic prints a leading space in position 15, the number 80 in positions 16 and 17, and a trailing space in position 18. Visual Basic will then advance the printer to the next print line. Notice that you use the semicolon separator, and not the comma separator, between the Tab function and the next item in the *outputlist*.

The last instruction shown in Figure 6-31 is `Printer.Print Tab(5);` `"First"; Tab(15); "Last"`. This instruction tells Visual Basic to print the string "First" beginning in print position 5, then print the string "Last" beginning in print position 15, and then advance the printer to the next print line.

The number of print zones and the number of characters that print in each zone, as well as the exact location of the preset tabs, are dependent on both the type and size of the printer font. In the next section you will learn how to change both the type and size of the font used to print information.

Changing the Type and Size of the Printer Font

Some fonts are proportionally-spaced, while others are fixed-spaced, often referred to as monospaced. **Fixed-spaced** or **monospaced fonts** use the same amount of space to print each character, whereas **proportionally-spaced fonts** use varying amounts of space to print characters. For example, with a fixed-spaced font, such as Courier New, the wide letter W and the narrow letter l will occupy the same amount of print space. However, with a proportionally-spaced font, such as MS Sans Serif, the letter W will occupy more print space than will the letter l. Open a project that will allow you to observe the difference between fixed-spaced and proportionally-spaced fonts.

To open the project that will allow you to observe the difference between fixed-spaced and proportionally-spaced fonts:

1 Open the **print** (print.vbp) project, which is located in the Tut06 folder on your Student Disk. The interface contains both a Print and an Exit command button.

2 Save the form and the project as **laPrint** in the Tut06 folder on your Student Disk.

3 Open the Print command button's Click event, then maximize the Code window. The partially-completed code is shown in Figure 6-32.

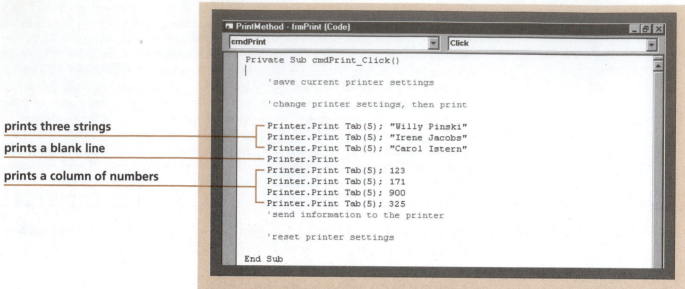

prints three strings

prints a blank line

prints a column of numbers

```
PrintMethod - frmPrint (Code)
cmdPrint                              Click

Private Sub cmdPrint_Click()

        'save current printer settings

        'change printer settings, then print

        Printer.Print Tab(5); "Willy Pinski"
        Printer.Print Tab(5); "Irene Jacobs"
        Printer.Print Tab(5); "Carol Istern"
        Printer.Print
        Printer.Print Tab(5); 123
        Printer.Print Tab(5); 171
        Printer.Print Tab(5); 900
        Printer.Print Tab(5); 325
        'send information to the printer

        'reset printer settings

End Sub
```

Figure 6-32: Partially-completed code for the Print button's Click event procedure

The first three Print statements will print their respective string beginning in print position 5 in the first three lines of the printout. Notice that each string contains the same number of characters. After printing the strings, the `Printer.Print` statement will print a blank line. The remaining Print statements will print a column of numbers beginning in print position 5 in the printout.

Visual Basic stores the name and size of the printer font in the Printer object's Font and FontSize properties, respectively. You should save the values stored in those properties before making any changes to them. By doing so, you can return the printer to its default settings after printing the output. You can save the property values simply by assigning the values to variables.

After saving the current Font and FontSize settings, the Print button's Click event will change the Font property to MS Sans Serif—a proportionally-spaced font—and the FontSize property to 10. The Click event will then print the strings and numbers, after which it will reset the Printer object's Font and FontSize properties to their original values.

To save the name and size of the printer font, then change the name and size, and then reset the name and size to their default values:

1 In the blank line below the `Private Sub cmdPrint_Click()` line, press the **Tab** key to indent the line, then type **dim strFont as string, sngSize as single**. You will use these variables to save the name and size of the Printer object's font.

2 In the blank line below the `'save current printer settings` comment, press the **Tab** key, if necessary, to indent the line. Type **strfont = printer.font** and press the Enter key, then type **sngsize = printer.fontsize**.

Now change the Font property to MS Sans Serif and the FontSize property to 10.

3 In the blank line below the `'change printer settings, then print` comment, press the **Tab** key, if necessary, to indent the line. Type **printer.font = "ms sans serif"** and press the **Enter** key, then type **printer.fontsize = 10**.

After printing, you should return the printer's font type and size to their original settings.

4   In the blank line below the `'reset printer settings` comment, press the **Tab** key, if necessary, to indent the line. Type **printer.font = strfont** and press the **Enter** key, then type **printer.fontsize = sngsize**.

The Print method does not send the output to the printer immediately; rather, it sends the output to the **print buffer**, which is an area in memory that temporarily holds the output to be printed. You will need to use the Printer object's EndDoc method to signal the print buffer that the end of the document has been reached, so the buffer should send the information to the printer. Upon receiving the information from the buffer, the printer will print the page and then eject the paper. Enter the EndDoc method in the current procedure.

5   In the blank line below the `'send information to the printer` comment, type **printer.enddoc** and press the Enter key. Figure 6-33 shows the current status of the Print button's Click event.

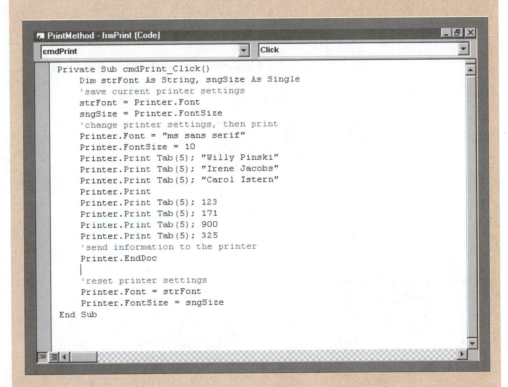

```
PrintMethod - frmPrint (Code)

cmdPrint                              Click

Private Sub cmdPrint_Click()
    Dim strFont As String, sngSize As Single
    'save current printer settings
    strFont = Printer.Font
    sngSize = Printer.FontSize
    'change printer settings, then print
    Printer.Font = "ms sans serif"
    Printer.FontSize = 10
    Printer.Print Tab(5); "Willy Pinski"
    Printer.Print Tab(5); "Irene Jacobs"
    Printer.Print Tab(5); "Carol Istern"
    Printer.Print
    Printer.Print Tab(5); 123
    Printer.Print Tab(5); 171
    Printer.Print Tab(5); 900
    Printer.Print Tab(5); 325
    'send information to the printer
    Printer.EndDoc

    'reset printer settings
    Printer.Font = strFont
    Printer.FontSize = sngSize
End Sub
```

Figure 6-33: Current status of the Print button's Click event procedure

6   Close the Code window, then **save** and **run** the application. If your computer is connected to a printer, click the **Print** button. Figure 6-34 shows the printed output using the proportionally-spaced MS Sans Serif font.

each string prints in a different amount of space

Willy Pinski
Irene Jacobs
Carol Istern

123
171
900
325

Figure 6-34: Printed output using the proportionally-spaced MS Sans Serif font

Although each of the three strings shown in Figure 6-34 contains the same number of characters, you will notice that the amount of space required to print each string varies. This is because characters in a proportionally-spaced font such as MS Sans Serif occupy different amounts of space. For example, notice that it takes the same amount of space to print the two letters Ir (in "Irene Jacobs") as it does to print the letter W (in "Willy Pinski"). Unlike letters, each number in the MS Sans Serif font occupies the same amount of space.

7 Click the **Exit** button to return to the design screen.

Now observe how changing the font type from a proportionally-spaced font (MS Sans Serif) to a fixed-spaced font (Courier New) affects the appearance of the printout.

To change the font type to a fixed-spaced font:

1 Open the Print button's Click event procedure. Change the `Printer.Font = "ms sans serif"` statement to **Printer.Font = "courier new"**.

2 Close the Code window, then **save** and **run** the application. If your computer is connected to a printer, click the **Print** button. Figure 6-35 shows the printed output using the fixed-spaced Courier New font.

each string prints in the same amount of space

Willy Pinski
Irene Jacobs
Carol Istern

123
171
900
325

Figure 6-35: Printed output using the fixed-spaced Courier New font

Notice that the Courier New font uses the same amount of space to print each of the three strings shown in Figure 6-35. This is because each character in a fixed-spaced font occupies an identical amount of space. In other words, in a fixed-spaced font, it takes the same space to print the letter W as it does to print the letter I. Like the proportionally-spaced MS Sans Serif font, the fixed-spaced Courier New font also uses the same amount of space to print each number.

3 Click the **Exit** button to return to the design screen.

When printing or displaying a column of numbers, it is a common practice to right-justify the numbers in the column and to align the numbers by their decimal point. Doing so makes the numbers easier to read and makes the printout look more professional. You will learn how to right-justify and align numbers in the next section.

Justifying and Aligning the Numbers in a Column

tip

You can also align whole numbers by their decimal point. Recall that whole numbers have an implicit decimal point after their last digit.

Although the comma and semicolon separators, as well as the Spc and Tab functions, give you a great deal of control over the appearance of the printed output, they have two very important limitations when it comes to printing numeric output. First, neither provide a way to right-justify the numbers in a column when those numbers are of various lengths; second, neither allows you to align a column of numbers by decimal points. To both right-justify and align the numbers in a column, you will need to use the Format function, which you learned about in Tutorial 2, along with the RSet statement. You use the Format function to ensure that each number in the column has the same number of digits to the right of the decimal point, and you use the RSet statement to right-align the numbers within the column. Because each number has the same number of digits to the right of the decimal point, aligning each number on the right will, in effect, align each by their decimal point.

As you may remember, the syntax of the Format function is **Format**(*expression*, *format*), where *expression* specifies the number, date, time, or string whose appearance you want to format. In the syntax, *format* is either the name of a predefined Visual Basic format or, if you want more control over the appearance of the *expression*, a string containing special symbols that tell Visual Basic how you want the *expression* displayed. Recall that Currency, Fixed, Standard, and Percent are the names of some of Visual Basic's predefined formats.

tip

You will find a description of the Currency, Fixed, Standard, and Percent formats in Figure 2-38 of Tutorial 2.

The syntax of the RSet (which stands for "right set") statement is **RSet** *stringvariable* = *string*, where *stringvariable* is the name of a fixed-length String variable and *string* is the expression you want right-aligned. A **fixed-length String variable** is one whose maximum length is defined (fixed) when the variable is created. You declare a fixed-length String variable by including an asterisk (*), along with the maximum number of characters the variable will store, in the statement that creates the variable. For example, whereas the `Dim strName as String` statement declares a String variable named strName that can store a maximum of two billion characters, the `Dim strName as String * 10` statement declares a String variable named strName that can store a maximum of 10 characters.

After creating the fixed-length String variable, you use the RSet statement to right-align a string within the String variable. For example, the `RSet strName = "Joe"` statement will right-align the string "Joe" within a fixed-length String variable named strName. Assuming that the strName variable has a maximum length of 10 characters, the `RSet strName = "Joe"` statement tells Visual Basic to assign seven spaces followed by the letters J, o, and e to the strName variable. Notice that the RSet statement fills any unused characters in the String variable with spaces. Figure 6-36 shows some examples of the RSet statement.

GUI
Design Tips

Numbers should be aligned by decimal points on the right side of a column.

Example	Contents of strItem (ƀ denotes a blank space)
`RSet strItem = "A"`	ƀƀƀƀƀƀƀƀƀA
`RSet strItem = "Dog"`	ƀƀƀƀƀƀƀDog
`RSet strItem = Format (12.5, "fixed")`	ƀƀƀƀƀ12.50
`RSet strItem = Format (1.35, "fixed")`	ƀƀƀƀƀƀ1.35
`RSet strItem = Format (106, "fixed")`	ƀƀƀƀ106.00
Note: Assume that the fixed-length strItem variable was declared with the following statement: `Dim strItem as String * 10`	

Figure 6-36: Examples of the RSet statement

tip

As you may remember, the "fixed" format displays a number with at least one digit to the left and two digits to the right of the decimal point. If the number has less than two digits to the right of the decimal point—for example, 12.5 and 106—the "fixed" format displays a zero in place of the missing digits.

As Figure 6-36 shows, the `RSet strItem = "A"` statement right-aligns the letter A in the 10-character strItem variable by assigning nine blank spaces and the letter A to the variable. The `RSet strItem = "Dog"` statement right-aligns the word Dog by assigning seven blank spaces and the letters D, o, and g to the strItem variable. When processing the `RSet strItem = Format(12.5, "fixed")` statement shown in Figure 6-36, Visual Basic first formats the 12.5 to the "fixed" format, giving 12.50; the instruction then assigns five blank spaces and the number 12.50 to the strItem variable. Visual Basic processes the `RSet strItem = Format(1.35, "fixed")` statement by formatting the 1.35 to the "fixed" format and then assigning the resulting value, 1.35, preceded by six spaces to the strItem variable. When processing the last example shown in Figure 6-36, Visual Basic assigns four spaces and the number 106.00, which is the number 106 formatted to "fixed", to the strItem variable. As Figure 6-36 shows, you can right-justify the numbers in a column, as well as align the numbers by their decimal point, simply by using the Format function within the RSet statement.

Open a project that will allow you to observe how you can use the Format function and the RSet statement to align the information in a column.

To observe how the Format function and the RSet statement align the information in a column:

1   Open the **align** (align.vbp) project, which is located in the Tut06 folder on your Student Disk. The interface contains three command buttons: Print without RSet, Print with RSet, and Exit. Save the form and the project as **laAlign** in the Tut06 folder on your Student Disk.

2   Open the Print without RSet command button's Click event, then maximize the Code window. See Figure 6-37.

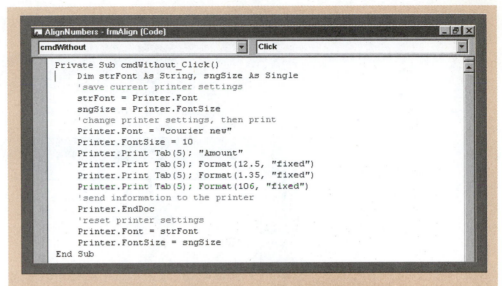

Figure 6-37: Print without RSet command button's Click event procedure

You will notice that the code contains the Format function, but it does not contain the RSet statement. Observe how the numbers print when only the Format function is used.

3   Close the Code window, then **run** the application. If your computer is connected to a printer, click the **Print without RSet** command button. Figure 6-38 shows the printed output.

```
Amount
12.50
1.35
106.00
```

Figure 6-38: Output printed by the Print without RSet command button

Notice that the numbers in the column do not line up appropriately. To align the numbers by their decimal point, you will need to use the RSet statement in addition to the Format function. You will also right-align the string "Amount", which appears at the top of the column.

4   Click the **Exit** button to return to the design screen.

5   Open the Print with RSet command button's Click event procedure, then maximize the Code window.

To use the RSet statement, you need first to declare a fixed-length String variable. You will name the String variable strPS (for "print string") and set its maximum size to 10 characters.

6   In the blank line below the `'declare a fixed-length String variable` comment, press the **Tab** key, if necessary, to indent the line, then type **dim strPS as string * 10**.

To right-align the string "Amount", which appears at the top of the column, you need simply to use the RSet statement to assign the string to the strPS variable.

7   In the blank line below the `'use RSet statement and Format function to align, then print` comment, press the **Tab** key, if necessary, to indent the line, then type **rset strps = "Amount"** and press the **Enter** key.

Now use the Print method to Tab to print position 5 before printing the contents of the strPS variable.

8   Type **printer.print tab(5); strps** and press the **Enter** key.

To complete the code, you just need to align and then print the three numbers 12.5, 1.35, and 106.

9   Enter the additional code shown in Figure 6-39.

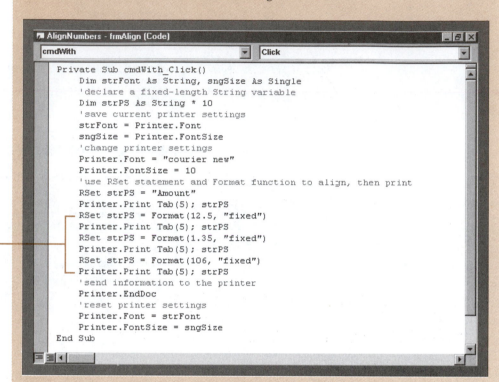

enter these six statements

```
AlignNumbers - frmAlign [Code]                          _ |8| X
cmdWith                        ▼    Click                         ▼
   Private Sub cmdWith_Click()
       Dim strFont As String, sngSize As Single
       'declare a fixed-length String variable
       Dim strPS As String * 10
       'save current printer settings
       strFont = Printer.Font
       sngSize = Printer.FontSize
       'change printer settings
       Printer.Font = "courier new"
       Printer.FontSize = 10
       'use RSet statement and Format function to align, then print
       RSet strPS = "Amount"
       Printer.Print Tab(5); strPS
       RSet strPS = Format(12.5, "fixed")
       Printer.Print Tab(5); strPS
       RSet strPS = Format(1.35, "fixed")
       Printer.Print Tab(5); strPS
       RSet strPS = Format(106, "fixed")
       Printer.Print Tab(5); strPS
       'send information to the printer
       Printer.EndDoc
       'reset printer settings
       Printer.Font = strFont
       Printer.FontSize = sngSize
   End Sub
```

Figure 6-39: Completed Click event for the Print with RSet command button

10   Close the Code window, then **save** and **run** the application. If your computer is connected to a printer, click the **Print with RSet** command button. The printed output is shown in Figure 6-40.

```
Amount
 12.50
  1.35
106.00
```

Figure 6-40: Output printed by the Print with RSet command button

Notice that the string "Amount", as well as the numbers, appear on the right side of the column. Also, the numbers are now aligned by their decimal point.

11   Click the **Exit** button to return to the design screen.

Now that you know how to use the Print and EndDoc methods and the RSet statement, you can complete the PAO application.

Completing the PAO Application

The last event you need to view in the PAO application is the Print Report button's Click event procedure. Recall that the Print Report button's task is to print a report showing the total number of Democrats, Republicans, and Independents in each of four age groups, as well as the total number of respondents. Similar to the way you plan the layout of an interface before you build the interface, you should also plan the layout of a report before you create the report. Many programmers use a printer spacing chart when designing the report. Figure 6-41 shows a printer spacing chart for the PAO report.

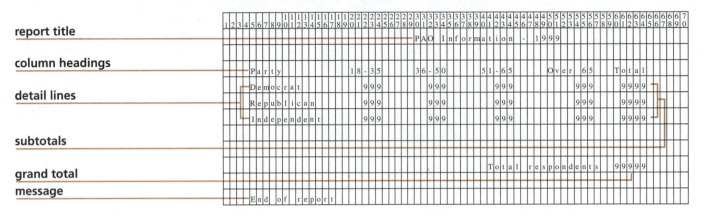

Figure 6-41: Printer spacing chart used to plan the PAO report

As Figure 6-41 indicates, the PAO report contains a report title, column headings, detail lines, subtotals, and a grand total. The **report title** describes the contents of the report. In this case, the report title indicates that this report contains the PAO information for the year 1999. The **column headings** in the report identify the information listed in each column in the report. The **detail lines** show the information used to calculate the subtotals and grand total. You will notice that 999 appears in each detail line in the report. The 999 indicates that the report will display numbers in that location, and that the numbers will contain a maximum of three digits. You use a series of Xs rather than 9s to indicate that a report will display a string. The number of Xs depends on the maximum number of characters to be displayed. For example, you would use 10 Xs (XXXXXXXXXX) in a column to indicate that the column will display a string that can contain a maximum of 10 characters.

You will notice that the PAO report includes three subtotals that show the total number of respondents in each political party, and a grand total showing the total number of respondents. **Grand totals**, which are calculated by adding together the various subtotals in the report, typically appear after the detail lines in a report. Here again, the subtotals and grand total will be numeric, so a series of 9s are used to indicate such.

It is a good programming practice to print an "End of report" (or similar) message as the last line in the report. In the PAO report, you will print the message "End of report" to indicate that the report has been printed in its entirety.

In the next section, you will observe how the printer spacing chart shown in Figure 6-41 was used to code the Print Report button.

Modifying the Print Report Button's Click Event Procedure

The code to print the PAO report has already been entered in the Print Report button's Click event. You will just need to make one modification to the code in that procedure. Open the Code window and view the code.

To view, modify, and test the code in the Print Report button's Click event:

1 Open the **laPao** (laPao.vbp) project, which is located in the Tut06 folder on your Student Disk.

2 Open the Print Report button's Click event, then maximize the Code window. Highlight the `Exit Sub 'you will remove this line in Lesson A` statement that appears at the top of the procedure, then press the **Delete** key to remove the statement from the procedure. Figure 6-42 shows the code contained in the Click event procedure.

```
Private Sub cmdPrint_Click()

    Dim intX As Integer, intDem As Integer, intRep As Integer
    Dim intInd As Integer, intTotal As Integer
    Dim strFont As String, sngSize As Single
    Dim strPS1 As String * 3, strPS2 As String * 3, strPS3 As String * 3
    Dim strPS4 As String * 3, strPS5 As String * 4

    'accumulate totals
    For intX = 0 To 3
        intDem = intDem + Val(lblDem(intX).Caption)
        intRep = intRep + Val(lblRep(intX).Caption)
        intInd = intInd + Val(lblInd(intX).Caption)
    Next intX
    intTotal = intDem + intRep + intInd

    strFont = Printer.Font            'save current printer settings
    sngSize = Printer.FontSize
    Printer.Font = "courier new"      'change printer settings
    Printer.FontSize = 10             'print title and headings
    Printer.Print Tab(30); "PAO Information - 1999"
    Printer.Print
    Printer.Print Tab(5); "Party"; Tab(20); "18-35"; Tab(30); "36-50"; _
                  Tab(40); "51-65"; Tab(50); "Over 65"; Tab(60); "Total"
    'align democrat numbers and print
    RSet strPS1 = Format(lblDem(0).Caption, "general number")
    RSet strPS2 = Format(lblDem(1).Caption, "general number")
    RSet strPS3 = Format(lblDem(2).Caption, "general number")
    RSet strPS4 = Format(lblDem(3).Caption, "general number")
    RSet strPS5 = Format(intDem, "general number")
    Printer.Print Tab(5); "Democrat"; Tab(22); strPS1; Tab(32); strPS2; _
                  Tab(42); strPS3; Tab(54); strPS4; Tab(61); strPS5
    'align republican numbers and print
    RSet strPS1 = Format(lblRep(0).Caption, "general number")
    RSet strPS2 = Format(lblRep(1).Caption, "general number")
    RSet strPS3 = Format(lblRep(2).Caption, "general number")
    RSet strPS4 = Format(lblRep(3).Caption, "general number")
    RSet strPS5 = Format(intRep, "general number")
    Printer.Print Tab(5); "Republican"; Tab(22); strPS1; Tab(32); strPS2; _
                  Tab(42); strPS3; Tab(54); strPS4; Tab(61); strPS5
    'align independent numbers and print
    RSet strPS1 = Format(lblInd(0).Caption, "general number")
    RSet strPS2 = Format(lblInd(1).Caption, "general number")
    RSet strPS3 = Format(lblInd(2).Caption, "general number")
    RSet strPS4 = Format(lblInd(3).Caption, "general number")
    RSet strPS5 = Format(intInd, "general number")
    Printer.Print Tab(5); "Independent"; Tab(22); strPS1; Tab(32); strPS2; _
                  Tab(42); strPS3; Tab(54); strPS4; Tab(61); strPS5
    Printer.Print                               'print two blank lines
    Printer.Print
    'print grand total
    RSet strPS5 = Format(intTotal, "general number")
    Printer.Print Tab(41); "Total respondents"; Tab(61); strPS5
    Printer.Print                     'print a blank line
    Printer.Print Tab(5); "End of report"     'print message
    Printer.EndDoc                            'send report to printer
    Printer.Font = strFont
    Printer.FontSize = sngSize
End Sub
```

Figure 6-42: Print Report button's Click event procedure

The Click event procedure begins by declaring 12 variables. The intX, intDem, intRep, and intInd variables are used in the For Next loop that calculates the political party subtotals. The intTotal variable is used to store the grand total—in this case, the total number of respondents. The strFont and sngSize are used to store the current printer settings. The five fixed-length String variables (strPS1, strPS2, strPS3, strPS4, and strPS5) are used to right-align the report's numeric output.

After declaring the variables, the procedure then calculates the subtotals and the grand total, after which it prints the report. Look closely at how the instructions that print the report follow the layout shown in the printer spacing chart. For example, according to the printer spacing chart shown in Figure 6-41, the "PAO Information – 1999" report title should begin in print position 30 of the report. You will notice that the `Printer.Print Tab(30); "PAO Information - 1999"` instruction uses the Tab function to tab to the appropriate print position before printing the report title.

The next instruction in the Code window (`Printer.Print`) will print the blank line that appears between the report title and the column headings in the printer spacing chart. Notice that the instruction that prints the column headings uses the Tab function to begin each heading in the print position specified in the printer spacing chart. For example, the instruction tells Visual Basic to tab to print position 5 before printing the heading "Party", and then tab to print position 20 before printing the heading "18-35".

After printing the headings, the code uses the RSet statement and the Format function to right-align, in the fixed-length String variables, the contents of the label control arrays. Recall that the label control arrays in the interface display the total number of Democrats, Republicans, and Independents in each of the four age groups. You will notice that the Format function uses the predefined "general number" format to format the numbers. Unlike the Currency, Standard, Fixed, and Percent formats you learned about in Tutorial 2, the "general number" format does not display integers (whole numbers) with a decimal point and two decimal places, so it is the perfect format to use in the PAO report, which prints integers only.

You will notice that the Print method instructions that print the detail lines also follow the printer spacing chart. For example, the Tab function will tab to print position 5 before printing "Democrat", then tab to print position 22 before printing the contents of the strPS1 variable, then tab to print position 32 before printing the contents of the strPS2 variable, and so on.

Following the printer spacing chart, the code prints two blank lines below the last detail line, then the grand total line, a blank line, and the "End of report" message line. The last two statements in the Code window reset the printer's Font and FontSize properties to their original values. Run the application and test the Print Report button.

To test the Print Report button:

1 Close the Code window, then **save** and **run** the application. First click the **Display Totals** button to display the total number of Democrats, Republicans, and Independents in each of the four age groups.

2 If your computer is connected to a printer, click the **Print Report** button to print the report. Figure 6-43 shows the printed report.

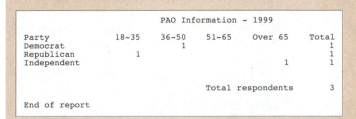

Figure 6-43: Printed PAO report

3 Click the **Exit** button to return to the design screen.

You have now completed the PAO application and Lesson A. You can either take a break or complete the end-of-lesson questions and exercises.

SUMMARY

To add a list box to the form:

- Use the ListBox tool ▣.
- Use the AddItem method to specify the items you want to display in the list box. The syntax of the AddItem method is *object*.**AddItem** *item*. Enter the AddItem instructions in the appropriate event procedure, which is usually the form's Load event procedure.
- Use the ListIndex property to refer to the location of an item in a list box.
- Use the Sorted property to arrange the items in ascending order.
- Use the Text property to refer to the item selected in a list box.

To execute instructions automatically when a form is loaded into memory:

- Enter the instructions in the form's Load event procedure.

To open a sequential access data file:

- Use the Open statement. Its syntax is **Open** *pathname* **For** *mode* **As #** *filenumber*.
- *Pathname* is the name of the file, including the drive letter and path, and must be enclosed in quotation marks, unless it's stored in a variable.
- *Mode* can be Input, Output, or Append. Use Input mode to open the file for reading. Use Output mode to create a new file and write information to it. Use Append mode to add records to an existing file.
- *Filenumber* is an integer expression with a value between 1 and 511, inclusive.

To write a record to an open sequential access file:

- Use the Write # statement. Its syntax is **Write #** *filenumber, [outputlist]*.
- *Filenumber* is the number used in the Open statement to open the sequential access file. *Outputlist* is one or more numeric or string variables separated by a comma.

To close a file:

- Use the Close statement. Its syntax is **Close** [# *filenumber*].
- *Filenumber* is the number used in the Open statement to open the file. A Close statement with no *filenumber* closes all open files.

To read a record from an open sequential access file:

- Use the Input # statement. Its syntax is **Input #** *filenumber, variablelist*.
- *Filenumber* is the number used in the Open statement to open the sequential access file. *Variablelist* is one or more numeric or string variables, separated by commas. Each variable in the list is associated with a field in the record.

To test for the end of the file:

- Use the EOF function. Its syntax is **EOF**(*filenumber*). *Filenumber* is the number of the file used in the Open statement.

To print information:

■ Use the Print method, whose syntax is **Printer.Print** [*outputlist*]. If *outputlist* is omitted, Visual Basic prints a blank line.

■ You can use the comma and semicolon separators, as well as the Spc and Tab functions, in the *outputlist*. The syntax of the Spc function is **Spc**(*number*). The syntax of the Tab function is **Tab**(*number*).

■ Use the Printer object's EndDoc method to send information from the print buffer to the printer. The syntax of the EndDoc method is **Printer.EndDoc**.

To align a column of numbers by their decimal point on the right side of the column:

■ Use the Format function and the RSet statement. The syntax of the Format function is **Format**(*expression*, *format*). The syntax of the RSet statement is **RSet** *stringvariable* = *string*, where *stringvariable* is the name of a fixed-length String variable and *string* is the expression you want right-aligned. You declare a fixed-length String variable by including an asterisk (*), along with the maximum number of characters the variable will store, in the statement that creates the variable.

Q U E S T I O N S

1. You use this method to define the items in a list box control.
    a. AddItem
    b. Addlist
    c. ItemAdd
    d. ItemDefine
    e. ListAdd

2. The Windows standard for list boxes is to show a minimum of _____ selections, and a maximum of _____ selections, at a time.
    a. three, eight
    b. three, seven
    c. two, eight
    d. two, seven
    e. two, six

3. When you select an item in a list box, Visual Basic stores the item in the list box's _____ property.
    a. AddItem
    b. Caption
    c. Item
    d. ListIndex
    e. Text

4. Sorting means arranging information in _____ order.
    a. alphabetical
    b. chronological
    c. numerical
    d. all of the above

5. To sort the list box items, set the list box's _____ property to True.
a. Alignment
b. Alphabetical
c. Arrangement
d. Sorted
e. Text

6. The _____ property stores the index of the currently selected list box item.
a. Caption
b. Index
c. List
d. ListIndex
e. ListNum

7. This event occurs when an application is run.
a. Copy_Form
b. Form_Run
c. Load
d. Run
e. Run_Form

8. Which of the following will add the word DESK to a list box named lstOffice?
a. AddItem.lstOffice DESK
b. AddItem.lstOffice "DESK"
c. ItemAdd.lstOffice "DESK"
d. lstOffice.AddItem "DESK"
e. lstOffice.ItemAdd DESK

9. Which of the following will display 1999 in a list box named lstYear?
a. AddItem.lstYear 1999
b. AddItem.lstYear 1999
c. ItemAdd.lstYear 1999
d. lstYear.AddItem 1999
e. lstYear.ItemAdd 1999

10. The second item in a list box has a ListIndex of _____ .
a. 1
b. 2
c. 3

11. This assignment statement will select the first item in a list box named lstTerm.
a. lstTerm.ItemList = 0
b. lstTerm.ListIndex = 0
c. lstTerm.ListIndex = 1
d. lstTerm.ListItem = 1
e. lstTerm.ListNum = 0

12. A _____ , also called a data element, is a single item of information about a person, place, or thing.
a. data file
b. field
c. program file
d. record

13. A group of related data elements that contain all of the data about a specific person, place, or thing is called a _____ .
a. data file
b. field
c. program file
d. record

14. A collection of related records is called a _____ .
   a. data file
   b. field
   c. program file
   d. record collection

15. You open a sequential file for _____ when you want to read its contents.
   a. Append
   b. Input
   c. Output
   d. Read
   e. Sequential

16. You open a sequential file for _____ when you want to create a new file and write information to it.
   a. Append
   b. Input
   c. Output
   d. Read
   e. Sequential

17. You open a sequential file for _____ when you want to add information to an existing file.
   a. Append
   b. Input
   c. Output
   d. Read
   e. Sequential

18. Which of the following is a valid Open statement?
   a. Open a:\data.dat for sequential as #1
   b. Open a:\data.dat for "append" as #1
   c. Open "a:\data.dat" for append as #1
   d. Open "a:\data.dat" for append
   e. Open "a:\data.dat" for sequential as #1

19. Which of the following is a valid Write statement?
   a. Write #1, strLname, strFname
   b. Write, strLname, strFname to #1
   c. Write to #1, strLname, strFname
   d. Write, #1, strLname, strFname
   e. Write strLname, strFname, to #1

20. Which of the following will close a file opened as file number #3?
   a. Close filenumber 3
   b. Close #3 file
   c. Close file #3
   d. Close #3
   e. Close file 3

21. Which of the following will correctly update a counter named intTotal?
   a. intTotal = intTotal + intAge
   b. intTotal = intTotal + 1
   c. intTotal + intAge = intTotal
   d. intTotal + 1 = intTotal
   e. intTotal = 1

22. Which two of the following will stop the loop when the record pointer is at the end of the file opened as #1?
   a. Do While EOF(1)
   b. Do Until EOF(1)
   c. Do While Not EOF(1)
   d. Do Until Not EOF(1)

23. The "EOF" in the EOF function stands for _____ .
    a. each open file
    b. end of file
    c. end of function
    d. every open file

24. Which of the following is a correct Input statement?
    a. Input #1, strName, curSalary
    b. Input strName, curSalary as #1
    c. Input into #1, strName, curSalary
    d. Input strName, curSalary into #1

25. Explain how you give keyboard access to a list box.

26. Which of the following instructions will print the word "January" in the first print zone, the word "February" in the second print zone, and then advance the printer to the next print line?
    a. Printer.Print "January", "February"
    b. Printer.Print "January"; "February"
    c. Printer.Print "January", "February",
    d. Printer.Print "January", "February";

27. Which of the following instructions will print the number 5 in the second print zone, and then advance the printer to the next print zone?
    a. Printer.Print 5
    b. Printer.Print 5,
    c. Printer.Print , 5;
    d. Printer.Print , 5,
    e. Printer.Print ; 5,

28. Which of the following is a false statement?
    a. Visual Basic prints positive numbers with both a leading and a trailing space.
    b. Visual Basic prints negative numbers with a leading minus sign (-) and a trailing space.
    c. Visual Basic prints strings with a trailing space.
    d. The semicolon tells Visual Basic to advance to the next print position before printing the next item.
    e. The comma tells Visual Basic to advance to the next print zone before printing the next item.

29. Which of the following will print the word "Item", five spaces, and the word "Price" on the same line?
    a. Printer.Print "Item"; Spc(5); "Price"
    b. Printer.Print "Item"; Spc(5);
       Printer.Print "Price"
    c. Printer.Print "Item";
       Printer.Print Spc(5);
       Printer.Print "Price"
    d. All of the above

30. Which of the following will print the word "Item" beginning in column 13, and the word "Price" beginning in column 25?
    a. Printer.Print "Item"; Tab(13); "Price"; Tab(25)
    b. Printer.Print Tab(13); "Item"; Spc(25); "Price"
    c. Printer.Print Tab(13); "Item"; Tab(25); "Price"
    d. Printer.Print Col(13); "Item"; Col(25); "Price"

31. Which of the following statements declares a fixed-length String variable named strName that can contain a maximum of 20 characters?
    a. Dim strName * 20 as String
    b. Dim strName(20) as String
    c. Dim strName as String (20)
    d. Dim strName as String & 20
    e. Dim strName as String * 20

32. Which of the following will right-align the contents of the intNum variable in the strNumber variable? (The strNumber variable is a 10-character fixed-length String variable.)
    a. Format strNumber = Right(intNum)
    b. RSet strNumber = Format(intNum, "general number")
    c. Right strNumber = Format(intNum, "fixed")
    d. RSet intNum = Format(strNumber, "general number")
    e. Right Format strNumber = intNum

33. You use the _____ method to send information from the print buffer to the printer.
    a. Done
    b. DocEnd
    c. End
    d. EndDoc
    e. PrintDoc

E X E R C I S E S

1. In this exercise you will use a list box and the Case selection structure.

    Scenario: At work you typically call five people. Rather than having to look up each person's telephone extension in the company's directory, create an application that will display the extension when you click the person's name in a list box. Use the following names and extensions:

Smith, Joe	3388
Jones, Mary	3356
Adkari, Joel	2487
Lin, Sue	1111
Li, Vicky	2222

    a. Open the la1 (la1.vbp) project, which is located in the Tut06 folder on your Student Disk.
    b. Save the form and the project as la1DoneA in the Tut06 folder on your Student Disk.
    c. Set the list box's Sorted property to True.
    d. Code the form's Load event so that it fills the list box with the names shown above, then selects the first name in the list.
    e. Code the list box's Click event so that it uses the Case selection structure to display the correct extension when a name is clicked in the list box. Use the list box's Text property as the Case statement's *testexpression*.
    f. Save and run the application. Test the application by selecting Sue Lin's entry in the list box. Print the form with the test data showing.
    g. Stop the application and print the code.
    h. Save the form and the project as la1DoneB in the Tut06 folder on your Student Disk.

     i. Change the Case statement in the list box's Click event so that it uses the list box's ListIndex property, rather than its Text property, as the Case statement's *testexpression*.

     j. Save and run the application. Test the application by selecting Joe Smith's entry in the list box. Print the form with the test data showing.

     k. Stop the application and print the code.

     l. Submit the printouts from steps f and j, and the code from steps g and k.

2. In this exercise you will open, write, print, and close a sequential access file.

   Scenario: Consolidated Advertising, a new advertising firm, sends mail-order catalogs to businesses in many U.S. cities. They want an application that will record and print the various cities and their corresponding zip codes. Use the following information:

Darien	60561
Hinsdale	60544
Glen Ellyn	60137
Downers Grove	60135
Burr Ridge	60136

   a. Open the la2 (la2.vbp) project, which is located in the Tut06 folder on your Student Disk.

   b. Save the form and the project as la2Done in the Tut06 folder on your Student Disk.

   c. Code the Write Record button so that it writes the city and its zip code to a sequential access file named la2.dat in the Tut06 folder on your Student Disk.

   d. Code the Print Records button so that it prints a report showing the city and zip code. Print the city in the first column of the report and the zip code in the second column. Include an appropriate report title and column headings. Also include the total number of records at the end of the report, along with the "End of report" message.

   e. Save and run the application. Test the application by entering the cities and zip codes shown above, then printing the report. Stop the application.

   f. Print the code. Submit the report and the code.

3. In this exercise you will open, read, write, close, and print a sequential file.

   Scenario: Boggs Inc. wants an application that will allow the user to enter the inventory number, quantity, and price of each item in inventory. The application should allow the user to record this information in a sequential access file named la3.dat in the Tut06 folder on your Student Disk. In addition, the application should allow the user to print a report showing the inventory number, quantity, and price of each inventory item, as well as the average price. (*Hint*: To calculate the average price, multiply each item's quantity by its price; add these amounts together, then divide that sum by the total quantity of all the items in inventory.)

   a. Create an appropriate interface. (Refer to the list of GUI design and programming guidelines at the beginning of Lesson C's Exercises section.)

   b. Save the form and the project as la3Done in the Tut06 folder on your Student Disk.

   c. Code the application appropriately, then save and run the application. Test the application by entering and saving the following records:

Inventory Number	Quantity	Item Price
ABC12	100	10.50
XYZ35	50	15.99
KLK25	150	20.00

   d. Print the report.

   e. Stop the application, then run the application again. Enter and save the following records, which should be added to the records already in the file.

Inventory Number	Quantity	Item Price
WER10	110	5.53
JAN24	20	4.56

   f. Print the report.

   g. Stop the application, then print the code.

   h. Submit the printouts from steps d and f, and the code from step g.

4. In this exercise you will use a list box.

    Scenario: Mary Kaye wants an application that will allow her to calculate, display, and print the area of a rectangle, a circle, or a triangle. (Use 3.14 as the value of pi.)

    a. Create an appropriate interface. (Refer to the list of GUI design and programming guidelines at the beginning of Lesson C's Exercises section.) Display the Circle, Rectangle, and Triangle choices in a list box.
    b. Save the form and the project as la4Done in the Tut06 folder on your Student Disk.
    c. Code the application appropriately.
    d. Save and run the application. Test the application by displaying the area of a rectangle that has a length of 9 inches and a width of 8 inches. Then display the area of a circle that has a radius of 10 inches. Lastly, display the area of a triangle that has a base of 15 inches and a height of 5 inches.
    e. Stop the application, then print the code. Indicate the answers to step d on the printout.

5. In this exercise you will modify an existing application.

    a. Open the laPao (laPao.vbp) project, which you completed in Lesson A. The file is located in the Tut06 folder on your Student Disk.
    b. Save the form and the project as la5Done in the Tut06 folder on your Student Disk.
    c. Change the name of the data file used in the application from pao.dat to la5.dat. The data file's name appears in the Enter Information and Display Totals buttons' Click event.
    d. Save and run the application, then enter the following two records:
        Democrat   36-50
        Republican   51-65
    e. Click the Display Totals button. The interface shows that the la5.dat file contains the records for one Democrat in the 36-50 age group and one Republican in the 51-65 age group.
    f. Now enter the following record:
        Republican   51-65
        Although the la5.dat file now contains the records for two Republicans in the 51-65 age group, you will notice that the interface still shows that the total number of Republicans in that age group is one. This is because the totals displayed in the interface are not updated until the user clicks the Display Totals button. In other words, the totals do not reflect the addition of new records until the Display Totals button is clicked. To ensure that the interface always displays the correct totals, you should have the Enter Information button remove the totals from the label controls when a new record is added to the file. By removing the totals, the user will be forced to click the Display Totals button, which will then update the totals appropriately.
    g. Code the Enter Information button's Click event so that it removes the totals from the label control arrays when a new record is added to the file.
    h. Save and run the application. Click the Display Totals button. Now add the following record to the data file:
        Democrat   36-50
        The Enter Information button should clear the prior totals from the label control arrays.
    i. Click the Display Totals button, then exit the application.
    j. To print the report, recall that the user will need to click the Display Totals button before clicking the Print Report button. Modify the application so that the Print Report button is disabled until the Display Totals button is clicked. Also modify the application so that the Enter Information button disables the Print Report.
    k. Save and run the application. The Print Report button should be disabled. Click the Display Totals button. The Print Report button should be enabled. Enter the following record:
        Democrat   Over 65
        When you click the Enter Information button, the Print Report button should be disabled. Click the Display Totals button. The Print Report button should be enabled.
    l. Print the application's code.

6. In this exercise you will modify an existing application.

   a. Open the laPao (laPao.vbp) project, which you completed in Lesson A. The file is located in the Tut06 folder on your Student Disk.

   b. Save the form and the project as la6Done in the Tut06 folder on your Student Disk.

   c. Change the name of the data file used in the application from pao.dat to la6.dat. The data file's name appears in the Enter Information and Display Totals buttons' Click event.

   d. In addition to recording the political party and age group in the data file, the PAO would like to record the respondent's name. Make the appropriate modifications to the interface.

   e. Modify the Enter Information button's Click event so that it writes the respondent's name, political party, and age group to the la6.dat file.

   f. Modify the Input # statement in the Display Totals button's Click event to reflect the fact that each record in the file now contains three fields rather than two fields.

   g. Code the Print Report button's Click event so that it prints a report showing the respondent's name, age group, and party. Use an appropriate report title and column headings. At the end of the report, print the total number of records in the file and an "End of report" message.

   h. Save and run the application. To test the application, enter the following records:

Jean Rowe	Democrat	18-35
Pat Smith	Democrat	18-35
Carol Key	Republican	36-50
Paul Utes	Independent	Over 65
Sabrina Elm	Republican	18-35

   i. Click the Print Report button.

   j. Stop the application, then print the code. Submit the printout from step i and the code from step j.

7. In this exercise you will modify the la1Done project, which you created in Exercise 1, so that it loads information from a sequential access file into a list box.

Scenario: In Lesson A's Exercise 1, you created an application that displayed a telephone extension when you clicked a person's name in a list box. In that application you entered five AddItem instructions in the form's Load event procedure—one AddItem instruction for each of the five names. In this exercise, you will remove the five AddItem instructions from the form's Load event and replace them with code that reads the names from a sequential access file. The names shown in Exercise 1 have already been entered into a sequential access file (la7.ori) for you.

   a. Open the la1DoneA (la1DoneA.vbp) project that you created in Lesson A's Exercise 1.

   b. Save the form and the project as la7done in the Tut06 folder on your Student Disk.

   c. Use Windows to copy the la7.ori file, which is located in the Tut06 folder on your Student Disk, to la7.dat. Place the la7.dat file in the Tut06 folder on your Student Disk.

   d. Remove the five AddItem instructions from the form's Load event.

   e. Code the form's Load event so that it reads the five names from the la7.dat file. As each name is read, the name should be entered into the list box.

   f. Save and run the application. Test the application by selecting Vicky Li's entry in the list box. Click the Print button to print the interface.

   g. Exit the application. Print the code.

   h. Submit the printout from step f and the code from step g.

Exercises 8 through 14 are Discovery Exercises, which allow you to both "discover" the solutions to problems on your own and experiment with material that is not covered in the tutorial.

discovery ▶

8. In this exercise you will search a sequential access file for a zip code, then display the corresponding city. You will learn about the LostFocus event and the Enabled property.

Scenario: Dr. Jonas, a dentist, has many patients under the age of 10. To encourage these patients to brush their teeth regularly, she mails them monthly reminder cards. Dr. Jonas wants an application that her receptionist can use to record the names, addresses, and birthdays of the patients who are under the age of 10. To make the information easier for the receptionist to enter, the application should display the appropriate city when the receptionist enters the zip code. The zip codes and cities have already been entered into a sequential access file (la8Zip.ori) for you.

a. Open the la8 (la8.vbp) project, which is located in the Tut06 folder on your Student Disk.

b. Save the form and the project as la8Done in the Tut06 folder on your Student Disk.

c. Use Windows to copy the la8Zip.ori file, which is located in the Tut06 folder on your Student Disk, to la8Zip.dat. Put the la8Zip.dat file in the Tut06 folder on your Student Disk. Use WordPad to print the la8Zip.dat file.

d. If you have access to the MSDN Library, then search for the LostFocus event's Help screen. Notice that the LostFocus event occurs when an object loses the focus. Also display the Help screen on the Enabled property.

e. Code the txtZip control's LostFocus event so that it searches the la8Zip.dat file for the zip code entered in the txtZip control, then displays the corresponding city in the lblCity control. If the zip code entered by the user is not in the file, use the MsgBox function to display an appropriate message to the user.

f. Code the Record Patient button so that it writes the patient's name, address, city, zip code, and birthday to a sequential access file named la8.dat. Don't allow a record with an incorrect zip code (one that's not in the file) to be written to the la8.dat data file.

g. Code the Print Report button so that it prints a report showing the patient's name and birthday.

h. Code the form's Unload event so that it asks the user if he or she wants to leave the application.

i. Save and run the application. Test the application by entering the following patient information: Sally Bramas, 123 Main Street, 60145, 3/9/95. Click the Record Patient button. (Northlake should appear in the lblCity control.) Print the report. Also, test the application by entering an incorrect zip code.

j. Exit the application. Print the code.

k. Submit the code from step j and the printouts from steps c and i.

discovery ▶

9. In this exercise you will use a list box and an image control array.

Scenario: Create an application that displays an icon when the user makes a selection in a list box. The application should also print the form.

a. Open the la9 (la9.vbp) project, which is located in the Tut06 folder on your Student Disk.

b. Save the form and the project as la9Done in the Tut06 folder on your Student Disk.

c. Set the list box's Font property to 12 points. Set its Sorted property to True.

d. Code the form's Load event so that it fills the list box with the following data: Cloud, Rain, Snow, Sun, Lightning. When the interface appears on the screen, the first item in the list box should be selected.

e. Code the Exit button so that it unloads the form.

f. Code the Print button so that it prints the form when clicked.

g. Code the list box's Click event so that it displays, in the imgElement control, the correct icon from the imgIcons control array. (*Hint*: When the list box is sorted, notice that the indexes of the list box items correspond to the indexes of the icons in the imgIcons array.)

h. Save and run the application. Test the application by selecting Snow in the list box. The appropriate icon should appear in the imgElement control. Click the Print button.

i. Exit the application. Print the code.

j. Submit the printout from step h and the code from step i.

discovery ▶

10. In this exercise you will learn about the Kill statement and the Dir function. You will use both to modify the laPao project that you created in Lesson A.

Scenario: Recall from Lesson A that you can't open a file for Input unless the file exists. If you try to open a file that doesn't exist, Visual Basic displays an error message. Currently, the laPao project's Display Totals button, which opens the pao.dat file for Input, will result in an error if the data file does not exist in the Tut06 folder on your Student Disk. You can use the Dir function to verify that the file exists before you try opening it. You will modify the laPao project accordingly.

You will also make another modification to the laPao project. At the beginning of each year, the PAO secretary needs to erase the contents of the data file so he or she can begin entering the data for the new year. You will add a command button to the laPao project's interface that allows the secretary to do that. You will use the Kill statement in the command button's code.

a. Open the laPao (laPao.vbp) project that you created in Lesson A. The laPao project is located in the Tut06 folder on your Student Disk.

b. Save the form and the project as la10Done in the Tut06 folder on your Student Disk.

c. If you have access to the MSDN Library, then display the Dir function's Help screen. Notice what the function returns when the file does not exist.

d. Open the Display Totals button's code window. Use the Dir function to verify that the pao.dat file exists. If it doesn't, display a message for the user, then return the user to the application.

e. If you have access to the MSDN Library, then display the Kill statement's Help screen.

f. Add a command button to the form. Set its Name property to cmdNew, then set its caption to New File. Position the New File button above the Exit button.

g. Code the New File button so that it prompts the user to verify that he or she wants to erase the current file. Erase the current file from the disk only if the user wants to do so.

h. Save and run the application.

i. Click the Display Totals button to display the report. No error message should appear because the pao.dat file does exist on the disk.

j. Use the New File button to erase the pao.dat file from the disk.

k. Click the Display Totals button to display the report. An error message should appear because the pao.dat file does not exist on the disk. After removing the error message, the user should be returned to the application.

l. Exit the application, then print the code for the Display Totals and New File buttons only. (*Hint*: Open the Display Totals button's Click event procedure, then select all of the code. Click File on the menu bar, then click Print. Both the Selection option button and the Code check box should be selected. Click the OK button. Repeat the same procedure for the New File button's Click event procedure.)

m. Submit the code from step l.

discovery ▶

11. In this exercise you will create a multiselection list box. You will use three new list box properties: MultiSelect, Selected, and List.

Scenario: The list box control has a MultiSelect property that determines whether a user can make multiple selections in a list box control, and how the multiple selections can be made. When you create a list box control, Visual Basic also creates a List property array and a Selected property array.

a. If you have access to the MSDN Library, then research the list box's MultiSelect property.

b. Explain the difference between the three settings of the MultiSelect property.

c. Open a new project. Add a command button and a list box to the form. Set the list box's Sorted property to True. Leave the list box's MultiSelect property at its default value 0-None.

d. Save the form and the project as la11Done in the Tut06 folder on your Student Disk.

e. Code the form's Load event so that it fills the list box with the following five names: Ahmad, Jim, Debbie, Jeanne, Bill.

f. Code the command button so that it prints the selected item on the form. In other words, if the user clicks Debbie in the list box, and then clicks the command button, the name Debbie will print on the form.

g. Save and run the application. To test the application, click Debbie in the list box, then click the command button. The name Debbie should print on the form.

h. Exit the application and print the code.

i. If you have access to the MSDN Library, then research the list box control's Selected property and its List property. (Both properties are property arrays.)

j. Explain the purpose of a list box control's Selected and List properties.

k. Change the list box's MultiSelect property to 1-Simple. Change the code in the command button so that it prints the selected items on the form. In other words, if the user clicks Ahmad and Jeanne in the list box, the names Ahmad and Jeanne should print on the form.

l. Save and run the application. To test the application, click Ahmad, Debbie, and Jeanne to select the items in the list box. Click Debbie to deselect that item. Click the command button. The names Ahmad and Jeanne should print on the form.

m. Exit the application.

n. Change the list box's MultiSelect property to 2-Extended.

o. Save and run the application. To test the application, click Ahmad in the list box to select that item, then use Shift+Click to select Jim in the list box. All of the names should be highlighted in the list box. Use Ctrl+Click to deselect Debbie and Bill in the list. Use Ctrl+Click to select Bill in the list box. Click the command button. The names Ahmad, Bill, Jeanne, and Jim should print on the form.

p. Exit the application and print the code.

q. Submit the written explanations from steps b and j, and the code from steps h and p.

discovery  12. In this exercise you will move items from one list box to another. You will use one new list box control method (RemoveItem) and three new properties (MultiSelect, List, and Selected).

Scenario: ABC Corporation maintains two sequential access files. One of the files stores the active employees and the other stores the inactive employees. At the end of each year, the corporation's Personnel department reviews the names in the active file. Employees who are no longer active are removed from the active file and are added to the inactive file. Employees who are reactivated are removed from the inactive file and added to the active file. Employees who the personnel clerk knows will never be reactivated are removed permanently from the inactive file. ABC Corporation wants an application that they can use to handle this process for the personnel clerk.

a. Use Windows to make a copy of the la12act.ori and la12inac.ori files, which are located in the Tut06 folder on your Student Disk. Name the copied files la12act.dat and la12inac.dat, respectively, and place them in the Tut06 folder on your Student Disk. Remember that you can always recopy the .ori files if your .dat files get ruined while you are doing this exercise.

b. Use WordPad to print the la12act.dat and la12inac.dat files. Mark the printout "Step b."

c. Open the la12 (la12.vbp) project, which is located in the Tut06 folder on your Student Disk. If you have access to the MSDN Library, then research the list box control's RemoveItem method, and its MultiSelect, Selected, and List properties. (*Hint*: The Selected and List properties are property arrays.)

d. Set both list box controls' Sorted property to True. Set both list box controls' MultiSelect property to 1-Simple.

e. Save the form and the project as la12Done in the Tut06 folder on your Student Disk.

f. Code the form's Load event so that it adds the contents of the la12act.dat file to the lstActive list box, and adds the contents of the la12inac.dat file to the lstInactive list box.

g. Code the Send to Inactive button's Click event procedure so that it removes the selected items from the lstActive list box and adds them to the lstInactive list box.

h. Code the Reactive button's Click event procedure so that it removes the selected items from the lstInactive list box and adds them to the lstActive list box.

i. Save and run the application. Test the application to see if it is working correctly. Correct any errors before continuing to the next step.

j. Code the form's Unload event procedure so that it writes the contents of the lstActive control to the la12act.dat file before ending the program, and writes the contents of the lstInactive control to the la12inac.dat file. The la12act.dat file should contain only active employees, and the la12inac.dat file should contain only inactive employees.

k. Save and run the application. To test the application, place Tom Willard and Jerry Krisen in the inactive list. Exit the application, then run the application again. The two names should appear in the lstInactive list box, and not in the lstActive list box. Exit the application.

l. Use WordPad to print the la12act.dat and la12inac.dat files. Mark the printouts "Step l."

m. Run the application again. Place Tom Willard back on the active list. Exit the application, then run the application again. Tom Willard's name should appear in the lstActive list box, and not in the lstInactive list box. Exit the application.

n. Use WordPad to print the la12act.dat and la12inac.dat files. Mark the printouts "Step n."

o. Code the Remove button's Click event procedure so that the personnel clerk can remove, permanently, the selected items from the lstInactive list box.

p. Save and run the application. To test the application, remove Jerry Krisen and Scotty Jones from the inactive list. Exit the application, then run the application again. The names Jerry Krisen and Scotty Jones should not appear in either list box. Exit the application.

q. Use WordPad to print the la12act.dat and la12inac.dat files. Mark the printouts "Step q."

r. Print the code.

s. Submit the printouts from steps b, l, n, and q, and the code from step r.

discovery ▶ 13. In this exercise you will print a multiplication table report.

Scenario: Your niece is in second grade and is studying multiplication. You would like to create a program that will print a multiplication table. Your niece will need simply to enter the number for which the multiplication table should be printed. The application should print a multiplication table similar to the one shown in Figure 6-44. The first column of the table will always contain the numbers 1 through 9. The number in the third column, however, will be the number entered by the user. For example, if the user enters the number 5, the number 5, rather than the number 1, will appear in the third column of the table.

```
Multiplication Table

1      X      1      =      1
2      X      1      =      2
3      X      1      =      3
4      X      1      =      4
5      X      1      =      5
6      X      1      =      6
7      X      1      =      7
8      X      1      =      8
9      X      1      =      9
```

Figure 6-44

a. Create a printer spacing chart for the multiplication table.

b. Open a new project, if necessary. Create an applicable interface. Refer to the Note that appears before the Exercise section in Lesson C.

c. Save the form and the project as la13Done in the Tut06 folder on your Student Disk.

d. Use the printer spacing chart to code the application.

e. Save and run the application. Print the multiplication table for the number 5, then print it for the number 9.

f. When the application is working correctly, print the code. Submit the printouts from step e and the code from step f.

discovery ▶ 14. In this exercise, you will create a user-defined format that you can use to display numbers.

a. Open a new project. Add a Print command button and an Exit command button to the form. Save the form and the project as la14Done in the Tut06 folder on your Student Disk.

b. If you have access to the MSDN Library, then display the Help screen for the Format function. Click See Also, then display the User-Defined Numeric Formats (Format Function) Help screen. Print the Help screen.

c. Create a numeric format that you can use to print integers with a comma separator. Use the numeric format in the Print button to print the following three columns of integers with a comma separator. Align the integers by the decimal point. (Recall that there is an implicit decimal point at the end of an integer.)

564	777	909
4500	888	9
4	59	34556

d. Save and run the application. Click the Print button, then click the Exit button.

e. When the application is working correctly, print the code. Submit the printout from step d and the code from step e.

LESSON B

o b j e c t i v e s

In this lesson you will learn how to:

- Set a text box control's MultiLine and ScrollBars properties
- Code the Resize event
- Set the ScaleHeight and ScaleWidth properties
- Add a menu control to the form
- Access the Clipboard object using the Clear, GetText(), and SetText methods
- Use the SelText property to determine the selected text

Menus

Creating the Text Editor

In this lesson you will create a simple text editor that the PAO's secretary can use to type a cover letter for the PAO report, which is sent to the organization's members and to various political offices in the district. The sketch of the user interface is shown in Figure 6-45.

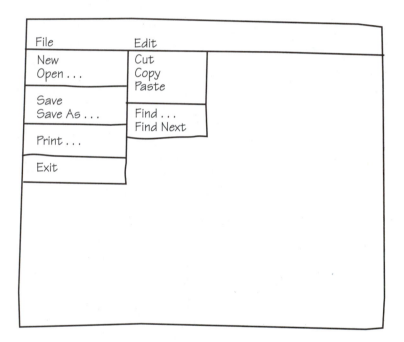

Figure 6-45: Sketch of the text editor's interface

Your Student Disk contains a partially completed text editor application. Open that application now.

To open the partially completed text editor:

1 Start Visual Basic, if necessary, then open the **t6Edit** (t6Edit.vbp) project, which is located in the Tut06 folder on your Student Disk.

The text editor's interface contains one text box named txtEdit. Notice that Document - Text Editor appears as the caption in the form's title bar.

2 Set the form's WindowState property to **2-Maximized**. When the WindowState property is set to 2-Maximized, Visual Basic maximizes the form when the application is run.

3 Save the form and the project as **lbEdit** in the Tut06 folder on your Student Disk.

The txtEdit text box will need to both accept and display multiple lines of text entered by the user. To accomplish this, you will need to set the text box control's MultiLine and ScrollBars properties.

The MultiLine Property and the ScrollBars Property

The **MultiLine property** controls how many lines can appear in a text box. When the property is set at its default value of False, only one line of text can be entered in the text box. When the MultiLine property is set to True, on the other hand, the text box can both accept and display more than one line of text. Visual Basic automatically wraps the text in a multiline box if the text extends beyond the size of the box.

The **ScrollBars property** specifies whether a text box has no scroll bars (the default), horizontal scroll bars, vertical scroll bars, or both horizontal and vertical scroll bars. The scroll bars allow the user to scroll the text box in order to view all of the text. In this application, you will place a vertical scroll bar on the text box so that the user can scroll the text from top to bottom.

To set the MultiLine and ScrollBars properties:

1 Click the **txtEdit control**. Set the txtEdit control's MultiLine property to **True**, then set its ScrollBars property to **2-Vertical**.

2 Click the **form** to select it. A scroll bar now appears along the right border of the txtEdit control.

In the next section you will learn how to change the size of a control when the size of the form changes. In this application, you will want the text box to size along with the form.

Sizing a Control Along with the Form

In previous tutorials, you have had experience with an object's Height and Width properties. Those properties measure the size of a control from the center of one border to the center of the opposite border. The properties measure the size of a form, however, from the outer edge of one border to the outer edge of the opposite border (including the title bar). A form also has a ScaleHeight property and a ScaleWidth property. The ScaleHeight and ScaleWidth properties measure the interior of the form—the area between the form's borders.

In order to size the txtEdit control so that it fits the interior of the form, you need simply to assign the form's ScaleHeight property to the txtEdit control's Height property, and assign the form's ScaleWidth property to the txtEdit control's Width property. Assigning the value in the form's ScaleHeight property to the text box's Height property tells Visual Basic to size the text box so that it fits within the form's top and bottom borders. Likewise, assigning the value in the form's ScaleWidth property to the text box's Width property tells Visual Basic to size the text box so that it fits within the form's left and right borders. You will place both assignment statements in the form's Resize event so that the statements are processed whenever the size of the form changes. A form's **Resize event** occurs when the form is first displayed on the screen; it also occurs when the user changes the size of the form either by minimizing, maximizing, or restoring it, or by using the form's borders to resize it.

To size the text box along with the form:

1   Open the form's Resize event. Enter the code shown in Figure 6-46.

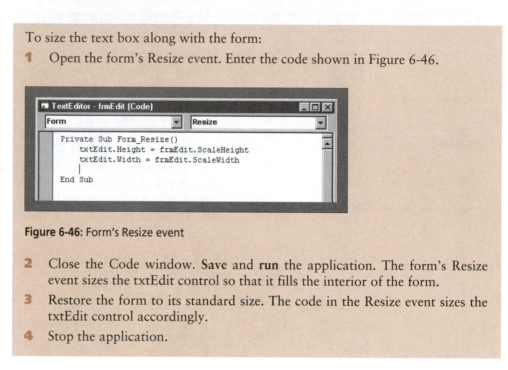

Figure 6-46: Form's Resize event

2   Close the Code window. **Save** and **run** the application. The form's Resize event sizes the txtEdit control so that it fills the interior of the form.

3   Restore the form to its standard size. The code in the Resize event sizes the txtEdit control accordingly.

4   Stop the application.

In addition to a text box, the text editor's user interface will also contain a menu control.

Adding a Menu Control to the Form

In Visual Basic, you create a menu in the **Menu Editor**. The menus you create can contain the following elements: menu titles, menu items, submenu titles, and submenu items. Figure 6-47 identifies the location of these elements in a menu.

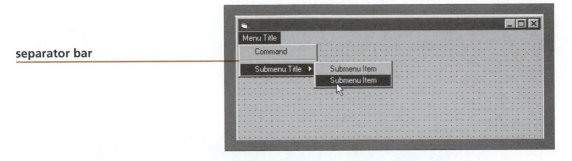

separator bar

Figure 6-47: Menu elements in a menu

As Figure 6-47 shows, menu titles appear on the menu bar at the top of the form. When you click a menu title, its corresponding menu opens and displays a list of options, called menu items. These menu items can be commands (such as Open or Exit), separator bars, or submenu titles. As in all Windows applications, clicking a command on a menu executes the command, and clicking a submenu opens an additional menu of options. The purpose of a separator bar is to group related menu items together.

Although you can create up to four levels of submenus, it's best to use only one level in your application. Too many layers of submenus can be confusing. Create a menu for the text editor application.

tip

You can also open the Menu Editor by clicking Tools, then clicking Menu Editor, or by pressing Ctrl+E.

To display the Menu Editor window:

1 Click the **Menu Editor** button 🔲 on the toolbar. The Menu Editor appears on the screen. See Figure 6-48.

    HELP? If the Menu Editor button is dimmed, click the form to select it, then repeat Step 1. Either the form or one of its controls must be selected in order to open the Menu Editor.

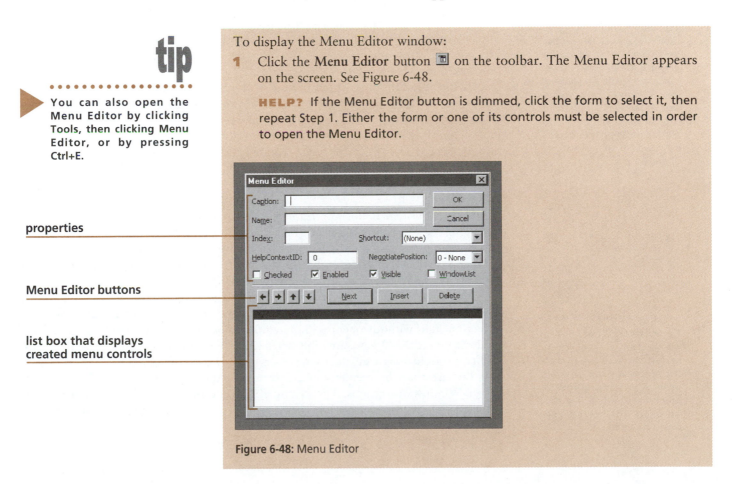

properties

Menu Editor buttons

list box that displays created menu controls

Figure 6-48: Menu Editor

The top portion of the Menu Editor contains the properties associated with menu controls. At the bottom of the Menu Editor is a list box that displays the menu controls as you are creating them. Visual Basic treats each entry in the list box as a separate menu control, so each entry can have its own properties and its own Visual Basic code.

Immediately above the list box are seven buttons. Figure 6-49 explains the purpose of each button.

Button	Purpose
Left arrow and right arrow	Change the indentation level of a menu control
Up arrow and down arrow	Move a menu control to another location in the list box
Next	Create a new menu control or move the highlight to the next menu control in the list
Insert	Insert a new menu control above the highlighted menu control
Delete	Delete the highlighted menu control

Figure 6-49: The Menu Editor buttons

You must complete the Caption property and the Name property for each menu control in the list box. The Caption property controls the text appearing on the menu control, and the Name property gives the menu control a name to which you can refer when writing Visual Basic code.

Menu title captions, which appear in the title bar, should be one word only, with the first letter capitalized. Each menu title should have a unique access key. Menu item captions, on the other hand, can be from one to three words. Use book title capitalization for the menu item captions, and assign each menu item a unique access key. If a menu item requires additional information from the user, the Windows standard is to place an ellipsis (...) at the end of its caption. The ellipsis alerts the user that the command will require more information before it can be processed.

If a menu item is not applicable to the current state of the application—for example, the Cut command on an Edit menu is not applicable until the user makes a selection in the document—you can disable the item either by setting its Enabled property to False in code or by deselecting the Enabled property in the Menu Editor. A disabled menu item appears dimmed when the menu is open.

The Menu Editor also allows you to assign shortcut keys to menu items. **Shortcut keys**, which are displayed to the right of the menu items, allow you to select an item without opening the menu. For example, in Windows applications you can select the Open command when the File menu is closed by pressing Ctrl + O. You should assign shortcut keys to commonly used menu items.

Be sure that the menus you create follow the standard conventions used in other Windows programs. For example, the File menu is always the first menu title on the menu bar. The File menu typically contains commands for opening, saving, and printing files, as well as exiting the application. The text editor's File menu will contain six commands: New, Open, Save, Save As, Print, and Exit.

tip

You learned about access keys in Tutorial 2. A menu title's access key allows the user to open the menu by pressing the Alt key in combination with the access key. A menu item's access key, however, allows the user to select the item simply by pressing the access key when the menu is open.

tip

The difference between a menu item's access key and its shortcut key is that the access key can be used only when the menu is open; the shortcut key can be used only when the menu is closed.

In addition to the File menu, the text editor will also include an Edit menu. The Edit menu will have five commands: Cut, Copy, Paste, Find, and Find Next. You will begin by creating the File menu. As is customary in Windows applications, the letter "F" will be the File menu's access key. To stipulate this, you type an ampersand before the letter in the menu caption that you want designated as an access key.

GUI Design Tips

Designing Menus

- Menu titles, which appear on the menu bar, should be one word, with the first letter capitalized. Each menu title should have a unique access key.

- Menu items, which appear on a menu, can be from one to three words. Use book title capitalization and assign a unique access key to each item. Assign shortcut keys to commonly used menu items.

- If a menu item requires additional information from the user, place an ellipsis (...) after the item's Caption.

- Follow the Windows standards for the placement of menu titles and items. For example, the File menu is always the first menu title, and it typically contains the New, Open, Save, Save As, Print, and Exit commands. The Edit menu is typically the second menu title, and it typically contains Cut, Copy, and Paste commands.

- Disable (dim) menu items that are not applicable to the current state of the application.

To begin creating the text editor's menu:

1 The Menu Editor should still be open. Type **&File** in the Caption text box, then press the **Tab** key. &File appears in the Caption text box and in the list box, and the insertion point is now located in the Name text box.

2 Type **mnuFile** in the Name text box, but don't press the Enter key yet. "mnu" is the three-character ID for a menu control.

To enter the next menu control, you can either click the Next button or, because the Next button is the default button in the Menu Editor, you can press the Enter key.

3 Press the **Enter** key to select the Next button. The highlight moves down one line in the Menu Editor list box.

You want New to be the first item on the File menu. The New command will remove the existing document from the screen and allow the user to create a new one. The letter N is the standard access key for the New option.

4 Type **&New** in the Caption text box, press the **Tab** key, then type **mnuFileNew** in the Name text box. The mnuFileNew name will help you remember that New is a menu item on the File menu. &New appears as a menu control in the Menu Editor list box.

See what the menu looks like so far.

5 Click the **OK** button both to save the menu information and to close the Menu Editor. Visual Basic displays the menu in the form.

Notice that both File and New appear, incorrectly, as menu titles on the menu bar. You actually want File to be the menu title, and New to be a menu item on the File menu.

You control the placement of menu titles, menu items, and submenu items by indenting the entries in the Menu Editor list box. As you just saw, entries appearing flush left in the Menu Editor list box are displayed as menu titles on the menu bar. If you want a control to be an item on a menu, you must indent the entry once in the Menu Editor list box. Entries indented even further in the Menu Editor list box become submenu items. Figure 6-50 illustrates the placement of menu titles, menu items, and submenu items in the Menu Editor list box.

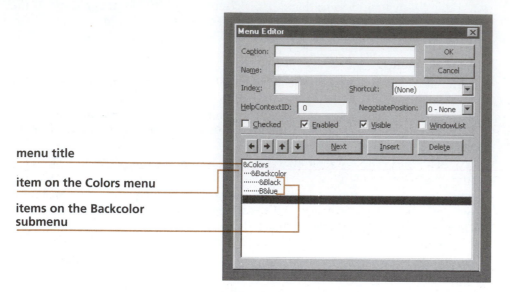

menu title

item on the Colors menu

items on the Backcolor
submenu

Figure 6-50: Menu elements in the Menu Editor list box

You can now open the Menu Editor and designate New as an item on the File menu.

To continue creating the text editor's menu:

1 Click the **Menu Editor** button 🔲 on the toolbar. The Menu Editor opens.

Click **&New** in the list box, then click the **right arrow** button above the list box to indent &New. Four dots (....) appear before &New in the list box. Visual Basic will now display New as an item on the File menu, instead of as a separate menu title on the menu bar.

Now assign a shortcut key to the New command.

2 Click the **Shortcut** list arrow in the Menu Editor. A list of shortcut keys appears.

The standard shortcut key for the New command is Ctrl+N.

3 Scroll the list until Ctrl+N appears, then click **Ctrl+N** in the list. Ctrl+N appears in the Shortcut list box and to the right of the ....&New item in the Menu Editor list box.

Next you will include an Open command on the File menu. Because the Open command will need the user to enter the name of the file to open, you will place an ellipsis after its Caption. Recall that the ellipsis indicates that the command will require the user to enter some additional information before the command can be processed.

4 Click the **Next** button, then use the following information to enter the Open command.

Caption: &Open...
Name: mnuFileOpen
Shortcut: Ctrl+O

You also need to include the Save and Save As commands on the File menu. Because both commands will perform a task that is entirely different from the tasks performed by the New and Open commands, you will use a horizontal line, called a **separator bar**, to separate the two groups of menu items.

Creating a Separator Bar

Using a separator bar to divide menu items into logical groups is another Windows convention. In Visual Basic, you create a separator bar by placing one hyphen (-) in the Caption text box of a menu control. (You must also give the separator bar a name.) Add a separator bar to this menu and then complete the File menu.

To enter a separator bar in the File menu:

1   If necessary, click **&Open...** in the Menu Editor list box. Click the **Next** button to enter a new menu control below the &Open item. Visual Basic assumes that this new entry will be another menu item, so it indents the entry for you.

2   Type - (a hyphen) in the Caption text box, then press the **Tab** key. Recall that you must complete the Name box for each menu control. Type **Hyphen1** in the Name text box. Be sure you don't include a space between Hyphen and 1. When the application is run, the File menu will display a separator bar below the Open command.

3   Press the **Enter** key to add a new menu control. The highlight moves down one line in the Menu Editor list box.

4   Use Figure 6-51 to finish creating the File menu. The names of the menu controls are shown next to each item in the figure.

mnuFileSave

mnuFileSaveAs

Hyphen2

mnuFilePrint

Hyphen3

mnuFileExit

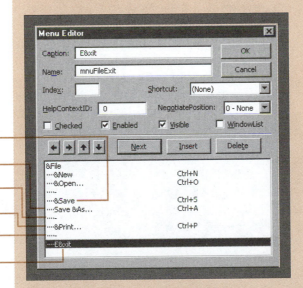

Figure 6-51 Completed File menu for the text editor application

HELP? If you need to delete a menu control, simply select the control in the list box and then click the Delete button.

5   When you have finished creating the File menu, click the **OK** button both to save the menu information and to close the Menu Editor.

6   Click the **Save Project** button 🖫 on the toolbar to save the form and the project.

7   Click **File** on the form's menu bar to open the File menu. The open File menu appears as shown in Figure 6-52.

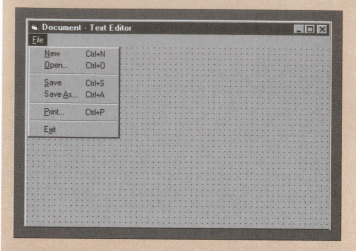

Figure 6-52 Open File menu

8   Click **File** on the form's menu bar to close the menu. The File menu closes.

You still need to add the Edit menu to the application.

Creating the Edit Menu

In Windows applications the Edit menu is typically the second menu listed on the menu bar. Five commands found on the Edit menu are Cut, Copy, Paste, Find, and Find Next. Cut is listed first, followed by Copy, Paste, a separator bar, Find, and Find Next. The standard access keys for these commands are the letters T, C, P, F, and N, respectively; the standard shortcut keys are Ctrl+X, Ctrl+C, Ctrl+V, Ctrl+F, and F3, respectively. You will include these five commands in the text editor's Edit menu.

To add the Edit menu to the application:

1   Click the **Menu Editor** button 🖻 on the toolbar. Use Figure 6-53 to add the Edit menu to the application. The names of the menu controls are shown next to each item in the figure.

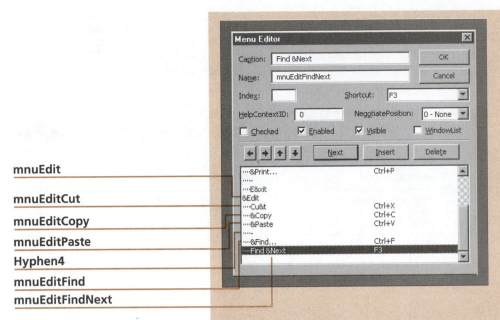

mnuEdit

mnuEditCut

mnuEditCopy

mnuEditPaste

Hyphen4

mnuEditFind

mnuEditFindNext

Figure 6-53 Completed Edit menu for the text editor application

2 When you have finished creating the Edit menu, click the **OK** button both to save the menu information and to close the Menu Editor.

3 Click the **Save Project** button 🖫 on the toolbar to save the form and the project.

4 Click **Edit** on the form's menu bar to open the Edit menu. The Edit menu appears as shown in Figure 6-54.

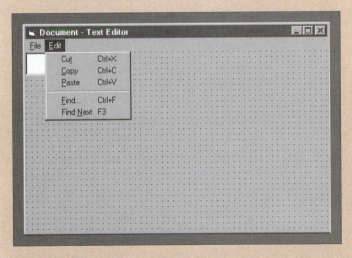

Figure 6-54: Open Edit menu

5 Click **Edit** on the form's menu bar to close the Edit menu.

Now that you've created the menu, you can begin coding the application.

Coding Menu Items

The TOE chart for the text editor application is shown in Figure 6-55. Notice that you will need to code the Click event for each of the menu items and for the mnuEdit menu title.

Task	Object	Event
Accept and display text entered by the user	txtEdit	None
Open a new document	mnuFileNew	Click
Open an existing document	mnuFileOpen	Click
Save the document using its current name	mnuFileSave	Click
Save the document using a new name	mnuFileSaveAs	Click
Print the document	mnuFilePrint	Click
Exit the application	mnuFileExit	Click
Enable/disable the Cut, Copy, and Paste commands	mnuEdit	Click
Remove selected text from the txtEdit control and place it on the clipboard	mnuEditCut	Click
Copy the text selected in the txtEdit control to the clipboard	mnuEditCopy	Click
Paste the text from the clipboard into the txtEdit control	mnuEditPaste	Click
1. Ask the user for the search string 2. Search the txtEdit control for the first occurrence of the search string	mnuEditFind	Click
Search for subsequent occurrences of the search string	mnuEditFindNext	Click

Figure 6-55 TOE chart for the text editor application

You will begin by coding the File menu's Exit option. When the user clicks this option, the application should use the Unload statement to unload the form.

To code the Exit option, then save and run the application:

1 Click **File** on the form's menu bar to open the File menu. (Be sure to open the form's File menu, not Visual Basic's File menu.)

You open a menu item's Code window by clicking the menu item, not double-clicking as you do with other controls.

2 Click **Exit** to open the mnuFileExit control's Code window. The Code window opens and displays the Click event procedure, which is the only event procedure a menu control recognizes.

> Recall that you unload a form with the Unload statement.
>
> **3** Press the **Tab** key, type **unload frmedit** and press the **Enter** key.
>
> As you learned in Tutorial 5, the Unload statement triggers the form's Unload event, which removes the form from memory and from the screen.
>
> See if the Exit command works correctly.
>
> **4** Close the Code window. **Save** and **run** the application. Click **File** to open the File menu, then click **Exit** to end the application. Visual Basic unloads the frmEdit form and returns to the design screen.

You will code the remainder of the File menu in Tutorial 7. In this tutorial, you will code only the Edit menu. Before you can begin coding the Edit menu, you need to learn about the Clipboard object.

The Clipboard Object

In addition to the Screen object that you learned about in Tutorial 3, Visual Basic also has a **Clipboard object**, which provides access to the Windows clipboard. The Clipboard object allows you to include cut, copy, and paste features in your application. In order to use the Clipboard object in the text editor application, you will need to learn three methods of the Clipboard object, as well as one new text box property. The three methods of the Clipboard object are SetText, GetText( ), and Clear. The new text box property is SelText. Begin with the three methods.

The SetText, GetText( ), and Clear Methods

In the Clear method's syntax, object can be a list box, combo box (which you will learn about in Tutorial 9), or the Clipboard object. Therefore, in addition to using the Clear method to clear the contents of the Clipboard object, you can also use the Clear method to remove the contents of a list box or a combo box.

You use the **SetText method** to send text to the clipboard. The syntax of the SetText method is **Clipboard.SetText** *data*, where *data* is the text you want placed on the clipboard. When you want to retrieve text from the clipboard, you use the **GetText( ) method** to do so. The syntax of the GetText( ) method is **Clipboard.GetText( )**. If no text is on the clipboard, the GetText( ) method returns a zero-length string (""). You use the **Clear method**, with the syntax *object*.**Clear**, to clear the contents of the clipboard. Figure 6-56 recaps these methods.

Method	Purpose
SetText	Places text on the clipboard
GetText( )	Retrieves text from the clipboard
Clear	Clears the clipboard

Figure 6-56: Recap of SetText, GetText( ), and Clear methods

A zero-length string is often referred to as an empty string.

In addition to the three methods of the Clipboard object, you will also need to use a text box control's SelText property when coding the Edit menu.

The SelText Property

When a user selects text in a text box, Visual Basic records the selected text in the text box's **SelText property**. For example, if the user selects the word "and" in a text box, Visual Basic records "and" in the text box's SelText property. If no text is selected in the text box, the SelText property contains a zero-length string (""). Figure 6-57 shows examples of how to use the methods of the Clipboard object, as well as the SelText property of a text box.

Instruction	Result
Clipboard.SetText "Have a nice day"	Places the string "Have a nice day" on the clipboard
Clipboard.SetText txtEdit.Text	Places a copy of the txtEdit control's contents on the clipboard
Clipboard.SetText txtEdit.SelText	Places a copy of the text currently selected in the txtEdit control on the clipboard
txtEdit.Text = Clipboard.GetText( )	Retrieves the text from the clipboard and places a copy of it in the txtEdit control; the text replaces the entire contents of the text box
txtEdit.SelText = Clipboard.GetText( )	Retrieves the text from the clipboard and places a copy of it in the txtEdit control; the text replaces the selected text in the txtEdit control
txtEdit.SelText = ""	Removes the selected text from the txtEdit control
Clipboard.Clear	Clears the contents of the clipboard

Figure 6-57: Examples of the Clipboard object's SetText, GetText( ), and Clear methods and the text box's SelText property

You can now begin coding the Edit menu.

Coding the Edit Menu

tip

Not every menu title's Click event will need to be coded. You only code a menu title's Click event when you need to set the properties of its commands, and the proper setting is based on some condition that must be evaluated during run time.

In Windows applications, recall that the Edit menu's Cut and Copy commands are not available until the user selects either some text or a graphic in the document, and the Paste command is not available until something, either text or graphics, is placed on the clipboard. You can enable and disable the Cut, Copy, and Paste commands at the appropriate times by coding the Edit menu title's Click event procedure.

When the user clicks Edit on the text editor's menu bar, the menu title's Click event will verify that the user selected some text in the document. If no text is selected in the document, then the Click event will disable the Cut and Copy commands; otherwise—which means that some text is selected in the document—the Click event will enable the Cut and Copy commands. The Click event will also check if any text resides currently on the clipboard. If the clipboard does not contain any text, then the Edit menu's Click event will disable the Paste command; otherwise, it will enable the Paste command.

The text editor will not contain any graphics, so you do not need to check if any are selected in the txtEdit control, or if any reside on the clipboard. To learn more about sending and retrieving graphics to and from the clipboard, search Help for information on the GetData and SetData methods.

To code the Edit menu title, then save and run the application:

1   Click **Edit** on the form's menu bar. The Edit menu opens. Notice that clicking a menu title does not open the menu title's Code window.

To code a menu title's Click event, you need simply to open any Code window, then use the Object box to open the menu title's Code window.

2   Click **Cut**. The mnuEditCut command's Click event procedure appears. Use the Object box to open the mnuEdit Code window. The mnuEdit Click event procedure appears.

First you will use a selection structure, along with the txtEdit control's SelText property, to determine if any text is selected in the document. (Recall that the SelText property contains a zero-length string if no text is currently selected.) If the user did not select any text, then you will disable the Cut and Copy commands; otherwise, you will enable the Cut and Copy commands.

3   Maximize the Code window, then enter the code and documentation shown in Figure 6-58.

be sure you are entering the code in the mnuEdit control's Click event

enter these lines of code and documentation

```
TextEditor - frmEdit (Code)
mnuEdit                                          Click

Private Sub mnuEdit_Click()
    If txtEdit.SelText = "" Then        'if no text is selected
        mnuEditCut.Enabled = False
        mnuEditCopy.Enabled = False
    Else                                'if some text is selected
        mnuEditCut.Enabled = True
        mnuEditCopy.Enabled = True
    End If

End Sub
```

Figure 6-58: Selection structure that enables and disables the Cut and Copy commands

You can also use a text box's SelLength property to determine if any text is selected in the text box. The SelLength property contains a 0 (zero) when no text is selected.

Now you will use the GetText( ) method to determine if any text exists currently on the clipboard. If the clipboard does not contain any text, then you will disable the Paste command; otherwise, you will enable it.

4   Complete the mnuEdit control's Click event by entering the code and documentation shown in Figure 6-59.

enter these lines of code and documentation

```
TextEditor - frmEdit (Code)
mnuEdit                                          Click

Private Sub mnuEdit_Click()
    If txtEdit.SelText = "" Then        'if no text is selected
        mnuEditCut.Enabled = False
        mnuEditCopy.Enabled = False
    Else                                'if some text is selected
        mnuEditCut.Enabled = True
        mnuEditCopy.Enabled = True
    End If
    If Clipboard.GetText() = "" Then    'if no text is on the clipboard
        mnuEditPaste.Enabled = False
    Else                                'if some text is on the clipboard
        mnuEditPaste.Enabled = True
    End If

End Sub
```

Figure 6-59: Additional selection structure that enables and disables the Paste command

5   Close the Code window, then **save** and **run** the application.

6   Type **Visual Basic** in the Text Editor window, then click **Edit** on the menu bar. Notice that the Cut and Copy commands are dimmed, which indicates that they are not available at the present time. The Paste command may or may not be dimmed; it depends on whether you have cut or copied any text to the clipboard prior to running the application.

7   Click **Edit** on the menu bar to close the Edit menu.

8   Select the word "Visual" in the text box, then click **Edit** on the menu bar. Notice that the Cut and Copy commands are no longer dimmed, which indicates that they are now available.

9   Click **Edit** on the menu bar to close the Edit menu.

10 Click **File**, then click **Exit**. Visual Basic returns to the design screen.

Next you will code the Edit menu's Copy command.

Coding the Edit Menu's Copy Command

When the user clicks Copy on the Edit menu, its Click event should clear the clipboard of its current contents, then place a copy of the selected text on the clipboard.

To code the Copy command:

1   Click **Edit** on the form's menu bar, then click **Copy**. The mnuEditCopy control's Click event procedure appears.

2   Maximize the Code window, then enter the code and documentation shown in Figure 6-60.

be sure you are entering the code in the mnuEditCopy control's Click event

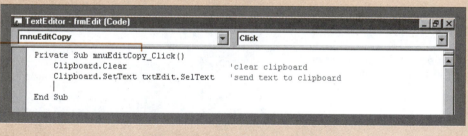

Figure 6-60: Copy command's Click event procedure

The `Clipboard.Clear` instruction will clear the contents of the clipboard. The `Clipboard.SetText txtEdit.SelText` instruction will send a copy of the text selected in the txtEdit control to the clipboard.

Next code the Cut command.

Coding the Edit Menu's Cut Command

When the user selects the Cut command, its Click event procedure should clear the clipboard; here again, you can use the Clipboard object's Clear method to do so. After clearing the clipboard, the Cut command's Click event should place the selected text on the clipboard, then remove the selected text from its location in the document. As you did in the Copy command's code, you can use the Clipboard object's SetText method and the txtEdit control's SelText property to place the selected text on the clipboard. After the text is on the clipboard, you can use the txtEdit.SelText = "" to replace the selected text in the txtEdit control with a zero-length string.

To code the Cut command:

1 The mnuEditCopy control's Code window should be open. Use the Object box to open the mnuEditCut control's Click event procedure, then enter the code and documentation shown in Figure 6-61.

be sure you are entering the code in the mnuEditCut control's Click event

enter these lines of code and documentation

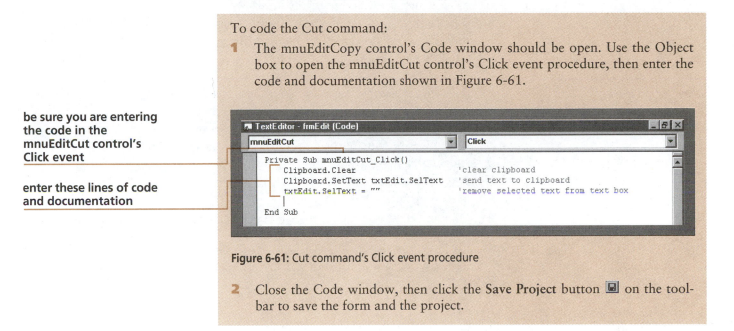

```
TextEditor - frmEdit (Code)
mnuEditCut                                  Click
    Private Sub mnuEditCut_Click()
        Clipboard.Clear                     'clear clipboard
        Clipboard.SetText txtEdit.SelText   'send text to clipboard
        txtEdit.SelText = ""                'remove selected text from text box

    End Sub
```

Figure 6-61: Cut command's Click event procedure

2 Close the Code window, then click the **Save Project** button 🖫 on the toolbar to save the form and the project.

You will code the Paste command next.

Coding the Edit Menu's Paste Command

The Paste command needs to retrieve the text from the clipboard and place it in the Text Editor document window beginning at the current location of the insertion point. The instruction txtEdit.SelText = Clipboard.GetText() will accomplish this task. If no text is currently selected in the text box, this instruction will paste the retrieved text at the current location of the insertion point. If some text is currently selected in the document window, this instruction will replace the selected text with the retrieved text.

To code the Paste command, then save and run the application:

1 Click **Edit** on the **form's** menu bar, then click **Paste**. The mnuEditPaste control's Click event procedure appears.

2 Maximize the Code window, then enter the code and documentation shown in Figure 6-62.

be sure you are entering
the code in the
mnuEditPaste control's
Click event

Figure 6-62 Paste command's Click event procedure

3 Close the Code window, then **save** and **run** the application.

4 Type **Visual Basic** and press the **Enter** key.

5 Select the word **Visual** in the Text Editor document window. Click **Edit**, then click **Cut**. Visual Basic removes the word Visual from the document window and places it on the clipboard.

6 Click in the line below the word Basic in the document window. Click **Edit**, then click **Paste**. Visual Basic pastes the word "Visual" at that location in the document.

7 Select the word **Basic** in the document. Click **Edit**, then click **Copy**. Visual Basic places a copy of the word "Basic" on the clipboard.

8 Click after the word Visual in the Text Editor document window. Click **Edit**, then click **Paste**. Visual Basic pastes the word "Basic" at that location in the document.

9 On your own, enter some text in the document window, then practice cutting, copying, and pasting.

10 When you are finished practicing with the Cut, Copy, and Paste commands, click **File**, then click **Exit** to end the application. Visual Basic returns to the design screen.

You have now finished Lesson B. You can either take a break or complete the end-of-lesson questions and exercises. You will code the Edit menu's Find and Find Next commands in Lesson C. Then, you will code the remainder of the File menu in Tutorial 7.

S U M M A R Y

To adjust the size of a control when the size of the form changes:

■ In the form's Resize event, assign the form's ScaleHeight property to the control's Height property, and assign the form's ScaleWidth property to the control's Width property.

To determine the measurements of the interior of an object, which is the part of the object that lies within the borders:

■ Use the ScaleHeight and ScaleWidth properties.

To allow a text box to accept and display more than one line of text:

■   Set the text box control's MultiLine property to True.

To control whether a text box contains scroll bars:

■   Set the text box control's ScrollBars property to either 0-None (the default), 1-Horizontal, 2-Vertical, or 3-Both.

■   For a text box to display scroll bars, you must set the MultiLine property to True.

To create a menu control:

■   Click the Menu Editor button ▣ on the toolbar. You can also click Tools, then click Menu Editor; you can also press Ctrl+E.

■   Complete the Caption property and the Name property for each menu control. Complete other properties as necessary. Click the OK button to close the Menu Editor.

To create a separator bar in a menu:

■   Type - (a hyphen) in the Caption property of the menu control. Also type a name in the Name property of the menu control.

To assign a shortcut key to a menu control:

■   Open the Menu Editor, then click the appropriate menu control in the list box. Click the Shortcut list arrow, then click the desired shortcut key in the list.

To assign an access key to a menu control:

■   Open the Menu Editor, then click the appropriate menu control in the list box. In the Caption property of the control, type an ampersand (&) to the immediate left of the letter you want to designate as the access key.

To open the Code window for a menu control:

■   If the menu control is a menu title, open any Code window, then use the Code window's Object box to open the menu title's Code window.

■   If the menu control is a menu item, click the menu item on the menu to open its Code window.

To enable/disable menu controls:

■   To enable a menu control, set its Enabled property to True. To disable a menu control, set its Enabled property to False.

To access the Windows clipboard:

■   Use the Clipboard object.

■   Use the Clear method to clear the contents of the Clipboard object. The syntax of the Clear method is *object*.**Clear**, where *object* can be a list box, combo box, or the Clipboard object.

■   Use the SetText method to place text on the Clipboard object. The syntax of the SetText method is **Clipboard.SetText** *data*, where data is the text you want to put on the Clipboard object.

■ Use the GetText( ) method to retrieve text from the clipboard. The syntax of the GetText method is **Clipboard.GetText( )**. If no text is on the clipboard, this method returns a zero-length string ("").

To determine the text selected in a text box:

■ Use the SelText property. If no text is selected in the text box, the SelText property contains a zero-length string ("").

Q U E S T I O N S

1. The _____ event occurs when a form is first displayed on the screen, and when the user changes the size of the form.
   a. Caption
   b. Change
   c. FormSize
   d. Resize
   e. Size

2. To change the width of a control when the width of the form changes, assign the form's _____ property to the control's _____ property.
   a. Change, Size
   b. Resize, Size
   c. ScaleWidth, Width
   d. Size, Resize
   e. Width, ScaleWidth

3. To change the size of a control when the size of the form changes, place the appropriate instructions in the _____ event.
   a. control's Resize
   b. control's Size
   c. form's Resize
   d. form's Size
   e. form's SizeForm

4. The _____ properties measure the size of a control from the center of one border to the center of the opposite border.
   a. Height
   b. ScaleHeight
   c. ScaleWidth
   d. Width

5. The _____ properties measure the interior of an object, which is the part of the object that lies between the borders.
   a. Height
   b. ScaleHeight
   c. ScaleWidth
   d. Width

6. You must complete two of these properties for each menu control.
   a. Caption
   b. Menu
   c. Name
   d. Shortcut
   e. Text

7. Which of the following is the only event to which a menu control can react?
   a. Change
   b. Click
   c. Double-click
   d. Load
   e. Show

8. Entries that are flush left in the list box of the Menu Editor will appear as
   _____ .
   a. menu items
   b. menu titles
   c. submenu items
   d. submenu titles

9. The horizontal line in a menu is called a(n) _____ .
   a. dashed line
   b. hyphen line
   c. item separator
   d. menu bar
   e. separator bar

10. You create the horizontal line in a menu by typing a(n) _____ in the Caption property of a menu control.
    a. asterisk
    b. ampersand
    c. hyphen
    d. underscore

11. The underlined letter in a menu title, menu item, submenu title, or submenu item is called a(n) _____ key.
    a. access
    b. dash
    c. menu
    d. open
    e. shortcut

12. A(n) _____ key allows you to access a menu item without opening the menu.
    a. access
    b. dash
    c. menu item
    d. open
    e. shortcut

13. You create an access key for a control by entering a(n) _____ to the immediate left of the appropriate character in the Caption property.
    a. ampersand (&)
    b. asterisk (*)
    c. dash (–)
    d. plus sign (+)
    e. underscore (_)

14. Which of the following is NOT true about menus?
    a. Menu titles appear on the menu bar.
    b. Menu titles should be one word only.
    c. Each menu title should have a unique access key.
    d. You can code a menu title's event procedure.
    e. If a menu title requires additional information from the user, follow the menu title's name with an ellipsis (...).

15. Which of the following is NOT true about menus?

    a. Menu items, which can be from one to three words, should be entered using sentence capitalization.

    b. You should disable menu items that are not applicable to the current state of the application.

    c. You should use a separator bar to separate groups of related menu items.

    d. You should assign a unique access key to each menu item.

    e. You should assign shortcut keys to commonly used menu items.

16. Which of the following instructions will remove the contents of the Clipboard object?

    a. Clipboard.Clear

    b. Clipboard.Erase

    c. Clipboard.Null

    d. Clipboard.Remove

17. Which of the following instructions will place the word "Hello" on the Clipboard object?

    a. Clipboard.Get ("Hello")

    b. Clipboard.GetText ("Hello")

    c. Clipboard.Set "Hello"

    d. Clipboard.SetText "Hello"

    e. Clipboard.Text "Hello"

18. Which of the following instructions will display the contents of the Clipboard object in a label control named lblMsg?

    a. lblMsg.Caption = Clipboard.Get( )

    b. lblMsg.Caption = Clipboard.GetText( )

    c. lblMsg.Caption = Clipboard.Set

    d. lblMsg.Caption = Clipboard.SetText

    e. lblMsg.Caption = Clipboard.Text

19. When you select text in a text box, Visual Basic records the selected text in the text box's _____ property.

    a. Selected

    b. SelText

    c. SetText

    d. Text

    e. TextSel

20. If the Clipboard object does not contain any text, the _____ method returns a zero-length string.

    a. GetText( )

    b. SelText( )

    c. SetText( )

    d. TextGet( )

    e. TextSel( )

21. You enable/disable a menu control by setting its _____ property.

    a. Change

    b. Disabled

    c. Enabled

    d. Use

22. When set to True, the _____ property allows a text box to accept and display more than one line of code.

    a. DisplayMultiple

    b. MultiLine

    c. MultiText

    d. Text

23. This property controls the type of scroll bars displayed on a text box.
   a. Bars
   b. Scroll
   c. ScrollBars
   d. VerticalBars

24. For a text box to display scroll bars, this property must be set to True.
   a. Bars
   b. MultiLine
   c. MultiText
   d. Scroll
   e. ScrollBars

E X E R C I S E S

1. In this exercise you will create and code a menu.

Scenario: Mr. Barrows, an elementary school teacher, wants an application that he can use to calculate and display a student's grade. Mr. Barrows will enter the student's name and his or her scores on two projects, as well as the scores on the midterm and final. The projects are worth 50 points each, and the midterm and final are worth 100 points each. Mr. Barrows also wants to be able to print the interface.

   a. Create an appropriate user interface. (Refer to the list of GUI design and programming guidelines at the beginning of Lesson C's Exercises section.) Use a command button to calculate and display the grade. Use a File menu that contains Print and Exit commands. Be sure to include a separator bar. Also be sure to assign access keys to the menu and its options. Assign the appropriate shortcut key to the Print option.

   b. Save the form and the project as lb1Done in the Tut06 folder on your Student Disk.

   c. Code the command button's Click event procedure so that it sums the project and test scores and then assigns the appropriate grade according to the following chart.

Total Points	Grade
270 – 300	A
240 – 269	B
210 – 239	C
180 – 209	D
Less than 180	F

   d. Code the Print command so that it prints the form. Code the Exit command so that it unloads the form.

   e. Save and run the application. Test the application by entering the following data: Jill Strait, 50, 45, 75, 80. Calculate and display the grade, then open the File menu and click Print.

   f. Use the File menu's Exit option to exit the application.

   g. Print the code. Submit the printout from step e and the code from step g.

2. In this exercise you will create and code a menu.

Scenario: Venus Motors, a car dealer, wants an application that the salespeople can use to calculate price quotes. The salesperson will need to enter the customer's name, the value of any trade-in, the car model, and the package type. The application should calculate the price before sales tax, the sales tax, and the total price including the sales tax.

   a. Open the lb2 (lb2.vbp) project, which is located in the Tut06 folder on your Student Disk. Notice that the car model option buttons belong to the optModel control array, and the package option buttons belong to the optPkg control array.

   b. Save the form and the project as lb2Done in the Tut06 folder on your Student Disk.

c. Code the car model option button array so that it displays the appropriate base price in the lblBase control. The base prices are as follows:

Car Model	Base Price
Star XL	10500
Comet JS	21000
Orbit J10	15500

d. Code the package option button array so that it displays the appropriate package price in the lblPkg control. The Standard package costs $2000, and the Deluxe package costs $3000.

e. Add a File menu to the application. The File menu should contain a Clear option, a Print option, and an Exit option. Include a separator bar between each option. Assign access keys to the menu title and to the Clear and Print options.

f. The Print option should have two submenu options, With Logo and No Logo. Code the With Logo option so that it prints the form with the imgLogo control showing. Code the No Logo option so that it prints the form without the imgLogo control showing. (Recall that you hide/display a control by setting its Visible property.)

g. Code the Clear option so that it removes the data from the Name and Trade-in Text boxes. It should also remove the data from the Subtotal, Sales tax, and Total price label controls.

h. Code the Exit option so that it unloads the form.

i. Add a Compute menu to the application. The Compute menu should contain a Rate – 5% option and a Rate – 7% option. Assign access keys to the menu title and its options.

j. Code the Rate – 5% option so that it calculates and displays the subtotal, the sales tax, and the total price. To calculate the subtotal, add the base price to the package price, then subtract the trade-in value. Display the subtotal in the lblSub control. To calculate the sales tax, multiply the subtotal by .05. Display the sales tax in the lblTax control. To calculate the total price, add the subtotal to the sales tax. Display the total price in the lblTotal control.

k. Code the Rate – 7% option so that it calculates and displays the subtotal, the sales tax, and the total price. Use the same calculations shown in step j above, except use a 7% sales tax rate.

l. Code the txtTrade control's Change event so that it clears the Subtotal, Sales tax, and Total price label controls when a change is made to the Trade-in value.

m. Code the Click event of both the optModel and optPkg control arrays so that each clears the Subtotal, Sales tax, and Total price label controls when the user selects a different car model or package.

n. Refer to the list at the beginning of Lesson C's Exercises section to verify that the application follows the GUI design and programming standards. Save and run the application. Test the application as follows:

1) Enter Darlene Zimmer as the name and 2000 as the trade-in value. Click Comet JS and Deluxe.

2) Open the Compute menu and click Rate – 7%.

3) Open the File menu and point to Print, then click No Logo.

4) Open the File menu and click Clear.

5) Enter Dana Chou as the name and 1500 as the trade-in value. Click Orbit J10 and Standard.

6) Open the Compute menu and click Rate – 5%.

7) Open the File menu and point to Print, then click With Logo.

8) Open the File menu and click Exit.

o. Print the code.

p. Submit the printouts from steps n(3) and n(7), and the code from step o.

Exercises 3 and 4 are Discovery Exercises, which allow you to both "discover" the solutions to problems on your own and experiment with material that is not covered in the tutorial.

discovery ▶ 3. In this exercise you will use a menu control's Checked property.

Scenario: In Windows applications, a check mark in a menu control indicates that the menu item is active. For example, in Microsoft Word's Window menu, a check mark indicates which of several open documents is currently displayed on the screen. You will use a check mark in this exercise to control which of two label and image controls are displayed in the interface.

a. Open the lb3 (lb3.vbp) project, which is located in the Tut06 folder on your Student Disk. The interface contains two label controls (lblRocket and lblBike) and two image controls (imgRocket and imgBike).

b. Save the form and the project as lb3Adone in the Tut06 folder on your Student Disk.

c. Set both the lblBike and imgBike controls' Visible property to False.

d. Drag the lblBike control directly on top of the lblRocket control, and then drag the imgBike control directly on top of the imgRocket control.

e. You will use this application to switch between the two different headings and two different icons included in the interface. Add a Display menu to the application. The Display menu should have two options, Rocket and Bicycle. Assign access keys to the menu and its options. Assign Ctrl+R as the shortcut key for the Rocket option and Ctrl+B as the shortcut key for the Bicycle option.

f. If you have access to the MSDN Library, then use the Help menu to research the menu control's Checked property. Open the Menu Editor and select the Rocket option's Checked check box. (You are checking the Rocket option in the Display menu because only the Rocket label and its icon will appear in the form when the application is run. Recall that you set the Visible property of both the Bicycle label and its icon to False.)

g. Code the Rocket and Bicycle menu commands appropriately. The Rocket command should display the lblRocket and imgRocket controls, and hide the lblBike and imgBike controls. When the lblRocket and imgRocket controls are displayed in the interface, the Rocket command should be checked in the Display menu. Similarly, the Bicycle command should display the lblBike and imgBike controls, and hide the lblRocket and imgRocket controls. When the lblBike and imgBike controls are displayed in the interface, the Bicycle command should be checked in the Display menu.

h. Save and run the application. The Rocket Company heading and the rocket logo should appear in the interface.

i. Open the Display menu. The Rocket option should be checked; the Bicycle option should be unchecked. Click Bicycle in the menu. The Bicycle Company heading and the bicycle logo should appear.

j. Open the Display menu again. The Bicycle option should be checked. The Rocket option should be unchecked. Click Rocket in the menu. The Rocket Company heading and rocket logo should appear.

k. Exit the application and print the code.

In the Display menu example that you just completed, only one of the menu items could be selected at a time—selecting one menu item deselected the other. In the next example, you will allow some, none, or all of the menu items to be selected.

l. Drag the lblBike and imgBike controls away from the lblRocket and imgRocket controls so that you can see all four controls on the form.

m. Set the lblRocket and imgRocket controls' Visible property to False. (Recall that both the lblBike and imgBike controls' Visible properties are already set to False.)

n. Open the Menu Editor and deselect the Rocket option's Checked check box.

o. Modify the code in the Rocket option's Click event so that it displays the Rocket label and Rocket icon when the Rocket option is selected, and hides the Rocket label and icon when the Rocket option is deselected.

p. Modify the code in the Bicycle option's Click event so that it displays the Bicycle label and Bicycle icon when the Bicycle option is selected, and hides the Bicycle label and icon when the Bicycle option is deselected.

q. Save the form and the project as lb3Bdone in the Tut06 folder on your Student Disk.

r. Run the application. No labels or icons should appear in the interface. Open the Display menu. No option should be checked in the menu.

s. Practice selecting and deselecting the Bicycle and Rocket options. When you select an option, its corresponding label and icon should appear on the form. When you deselect an option, its corresponding label and icon should be hidden.

t. Exit the application and print the code.

u. Submit the code from steps k and t.

discovery ▶ 4. In this exercise you will create a sub procedure and use the Call statement. You must have completed Lesson B's Exercise 2 in order to do Discovery Exercise 4.

a. Open the lb2Done (lb2done.vbp) project, which is located in the Tut06 folder on your Student Disk.

b. Save the form and the project as lb4Done in the Tut06 folder on your Student Disk. In steps l and m of Lesson B's Exercise 2, you coded the txtTrade control's Change event, as well as the optModel and optPkg control arrays' Click events, so that each clears the Subtotal, Sales tax, and Total price label controls when a change is made to the trade-in, car model, and package information. Instead of duplicating the code in each of these procedures, you can create a sub procedure that contains the code and then call the sub procedure from each of the events.

c. Create a sub procedure that will clear the Subtotal, Sales tax, and Total price label controls, then call the procedure from the txtTrade control's Change event, and from both the optModel and optPkg control arrays' Click events. Also call it from the File menu's Clear option.

d. Save and run the application. Test the application to be sure it is working properly, then exit the application.

e. Print the application's code.

String Manipulation

Visual Basic's String Manipulation Functions

In many applications, your code will need to manipulate (process) string data. For example, the code may need to verify that an inventory part number begins with a specific letter; or the code may need to determine if the last three characters in the part number are valid. You may also need to locate a string contained within another string. Visual Basic provides a set of functions that makes string manipulation an easy task. In this lesson you will learn how to use four of Visual Basic's string manipulation functions: Left, Right, Mid, and Instr. You will use the Instr function in the code for the text editor application's Find and Find Next commands.

The Left and Right Functions

As you learned in Tutorial 2, functions always return a value. The Left and Right string functions, for example, return one or more characters from a string. Figure 6-63 shows the syntax and the purpose of both functions, as well as some examples of each.

Syntax	Purpose
Left(*string*, *length*)	Returns the leftmost *length* number of characters of the *string*
Right(*string*, *length*)	Returns the rightmost *length* number of characters of the *string*

Examples:

Assume that the strProgName variable contains "Visual Basic."

Function	Resulting String
Left("January", 3)	Jan
Right("January", 2)	ry
Left(strProgName, 6)	Visual
Right(strProgName, 5)	Basic

Figure 6-63: Syntax and examples of the Left and Right functions

In the first two examples, the Left and Right functions are used to return one or more characters from the *string* "January". In the first example, the Left function returns the leftmost three characters in the *string*—Jan. In the second example, the Right function returns the rightmost two characters in the *string*—ry.

In the last two examples shown in Figure 6-63, a string variable is used as the *string*. When the *string* is a string variable, the Left and Right functions use the contents of the variable, not the variable name itself. In other words, the leftmost six characters in the string contained in the strProgName variable are "Visual"; the rightmost five characters in the string are "Basic".

Your Student Disk contains an application that uses the Left and Right functions.

To view the application that contains examples of the Left and Right functions:

1 Start Visual Basic, if necessary, and open the **LftRgt** (LftRgt.vbp) project, which is located in the Tut06 folder on your Student Disk. Click the **form** to select it. The interface is shown in Figure 6-64.

txtCode
lblSize
imgDesign

imgEarth
imgSnow
imgSun

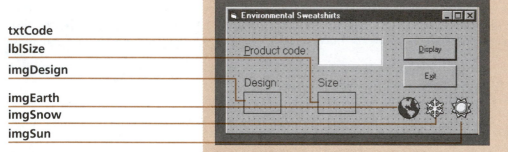

Figure 6-64: User interface for the LftRgt application

The Environmental Sweatshirts application will display a sweatshirt's design and its size based on the product code entered in the txtCode control. The product code consists of five characters. The first three characters—which can be 100, 200, or 300—indicate the type of design. The last two characters—which can be XS, SM, MD, LG, or XL—indicate the size. Design 100 is a picture of the earth, Design 200 is a picture of a snowflake, and Design 300 is a picture of the sun. XS stands for "extra small," SM for "small," MD for "medium," LG for "large," and XL for "extra large." View the code in the Display button's Click event procedure.

To view the Display button's code, then run the application:

1 Open the Display button's Click event procedure, then maximize the Code window. See Figure 6-65.

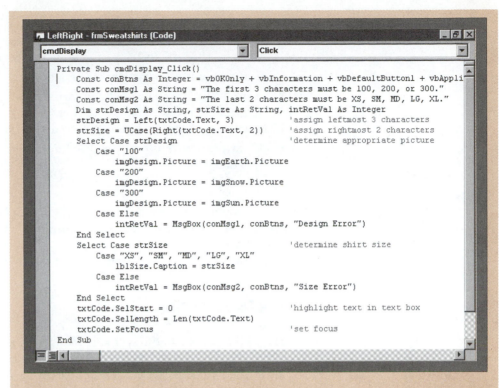

Figure 6-65: Display button's Click event procedure

The procedure begins by declaring three constants and three variables. The `strDesign = Left(txtCode.Text, 3)` instruction assigns the product code's leftmost three characters to the strDesign variable. The `strSize = UCase(Right(txtCode.Text, 2))` instruction assigns the product code's rightmost two characters to the strSize variable. Two Case structures are then used to assign the appropriate picture and caption to the imgDesign and lblSize controls, respectively. Before the procedure ends, the code highlights the existing text in the txtCode control and sends the focus to that control.

2   Close the code window, then **run** the application. Notice that the earth, snowflake, and sun icons do not appear on the form during design time; that's because their Visible properties are set to False.

First enter a correct product code.

3   Type **200sm** in the Product code text box and press the **Enter** key to select the Display button, which is the default button on the form. The Display button's Click event assigns the leftmost three characters (200) to the strDesign variable, and assigns the rightmost two characters (sm), in upper-case, to the strSize variable. The two Case structures then display the appropriate picture (the snowflake icon) and caption (SM) in the imgDesign and lblSize controls, respectively.

Now enter a product code that has an incorrect design type. As you enter the product code, you will notice that the application removes the contents of the imgDesign and lblSize controls; that's because the txtCode control's Change event contains the `imgDesign.Picture = LoadPicture()` and `lblSize.Caption = ""` instructions.

tip

As you learned in Tutorial 4, LoadPicture() clears the existing picture from a control.

4 Type **500xs** in the Product code text box and press the **Enter** key. The MsgBox function's dialog box displays the message "The first 3 characters must be 100, 200, or 300." Click the **OK** button to remove the dialog box.

Now enter a product code that has an incorrect size.

5 Type **100ss** and press the **Enter** key. The MsgBox function's dialog box displays the message "The last 2 characters must be XS, SM, MD, LG, XL." Click the **OK** button to remove the dialog box.

6 Click the **Exit** button to end the application. Visual Basic returns to the design screen.

As you just learned, the Left and Right functions allow you to access the characters in a string, beginning from either the first character or the last character. The Mid function, which you will learn about in the next section, allows you to access the characters in a string, beginning with any of the characters in the string.

The Mid Function

The Mid function, whose syntax is Mid(*string*, *start*[, *length*]), returns *length* number of characters from a *string*, beginning with the *start* character. Figure 6-66 shows the syntax, purpose, and examples of the Mid function.

Syntax	Purpose
Mid(*string*, *start* [, *length*])	Returns *length* number of characters of the *string* beginning at position *start*. If *length* is omitted, the function returns all characters from the *start* position through the end of the *string*.

Examples:

Assume that the strProgName variable contains "Visual Basic."

Function	Resulting String
Mid("January", 2, 1)	a
Mid("January", 4, 2)	ua
Mid(strProgName, 8, 1)	B
Mid(strProgName, 8)	Basic

Figure 6-66: Syntax and examples of the Mid function

In the first two examples, the Mid function is used to return one or more characters from the *string* "January". The first example, Mid("January", 2, 1), returns one character, beginning with the second character, in the *string*—the letter "a." In the second example, the Mid function returns two characters, beginning with the fourth character, in the *string*—the letters "ua."

In the last two examples shown in Figure 6-66, the strProgName variable is used as the *string*. As the Mid(strProgName, 8, 1) example shows, the one character, beginning with the eighth character in the string contained in the strProgName variable, is the letter B. Notice that the Mid(strProgName, 8) instruction returns the word "Basic"; because the *length* is omitted from the instruction, Visual Basic returns all of the characters from the *start* position (8) through the end of the *string*.

Your Student Disk contains an application that uses the Mid function.

To view the application that contains an example of the Mid function:

1   Open the **Mid** (Mid.vbp) project, which is located in the Tut06 folder on your Student Disk. If Visual Basic asks if you want to save the LftRgt files, click the No button.

2   Click the **form's title bar** to select the form. The interface is shown in Figure 6-67.

txtCode

lblStatus

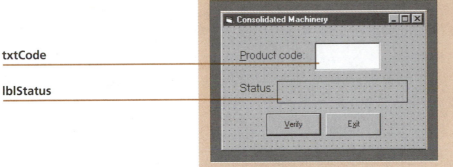

Figure 6-67: User interface for the Mid application

All products at Consolidated Machinery have either the letter A or the letter C as the third character in the product code. When the user enters the product code in the txtCode control and clicks the Verify button, the application will display the message "The product code is valid." if the third character in the code is either an A or a C (entered in any case); otherwise, it will display the message "The product code is not valid." View the code in the Verify button's Click event procedure.

To view the Verify button's code, and then run the application:

1   Open the Verify button's Click event procedure, then maximize the Code window. See Figure 6-68.

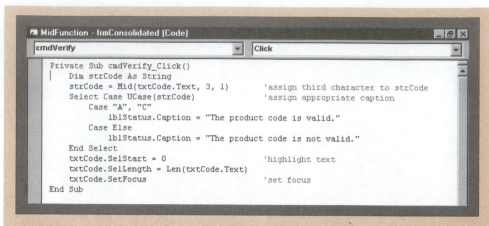

Figure 6-68: Verify button's Click event procedure

The procedure begins by declaring a string variable named strCode. The `strCode = Mid(txtCode.Text, 3, 1)` instruction assigns the one character, beginning with the third character in the txtCode control, to the strCode variable. A Case structure is then used to assign the appropriate message to the lblStatus control. Before the procedure ends, the code highlights the existing text in the txtCode control and sends the focus to that control.

2   Close the code window, then **run** the application.

First enter an incorrect product code.

3   Type **xyz5** in the Product code text box and press the **Enter** key to select the Verify button, which is the default button on the form. The message "The product code is not valid." appears in the Status label control.

Now enter a correct product code. As you enter the product code, you will notice that the message in the Status label control will disappear; that's because the txtCode control's Change event contains the `lblStatus.Caption = ""` instruction.

4   Type **abc5** in the Product code text box and press the **Enter** key. The message "The product code is valid." appears in the Status label control.

5   Click the **Exit** button to end the application. Visual Basic returns to the design screen.

In the next section you will learn how to use the Instr function to determine if a specific string is contained within another string. You will use the Instr function in the text editor application's Find and Find Next commands.

The Instr Function

You can use the Instr function to search a string to determine if it contains another string. For example, you can use the Instr function to determine if the string "nice" appears in the string "Have a nice day". The syntax of the Instr function is **Instr**(*start*, *string1*, *string2*[, *compare*]), where *start* is a numeric expression that sets the starting position for the search—in other words, the character at which the search will begin. *String1* is the string expression being searched, and *string2* is the string expression being sought. In the example, "Have a nice day" is *string1* and "nice" is *string2*.

In the syntax, *compare* is either the number 0 or the number 1. If *compare* is set to its default value of 0, Visual Basic performs a case-sensitive search; otherwise, it performs a case-insensitive search. For example, if *string2* is the word "nice" (entered in lowercase) and *compare* is set to 0, Visual Basic searches *string1* for the word "nice" entered in lowercase only. If *compare* is set to 1, on the other hand, Visual Basic searches *string1* for the word "nice" entered in either lowercase, or uppercase, or a combination of both cases.

If *string2* is not contained within *string1*, then the Instr function returns the number 0. If *string2* is contained within *string1*, then the Instr function returns the starting position of *string2*. Figure 6-69 shows the syntax and some examples of the Instr function.

Function	Result (starting position of *string2* within *string1*)
Instr(1, "Have a nice day", "nice", 0)	8
Instr(1, "Have a nice day", "NICE", 0)	0
Instr(1, "Have a nice day", "NICE", 1)	8
Instr(9, "This is an Instr function example", "instr")	0
Instr(9, "This is an Instr function example", "instr", 1)	12

Figure 6-69: Syntax and examples of the Instr function

You will need to use the Instr function to complete the text editor's Edit menu. You will code the Edit menu's Find command first.

To open the text editor application:

1   Open the **lbEdit** (lbEdit.vbp) project that you created in Lesson B. The project is located in the Tut06 folder on your Student Disk. If Visual Basic asks if you want to save the Mid files, click the No button.

2   Click the **form**, then save the form and the project as **lcEdit**.

Coding the Edit Menu's Find Command

The Edit menu's Find command will allow the user to locate a specific string within the text box. The pseudocode and flowchart for the Find command's Click event are shown in Figure 6-70.

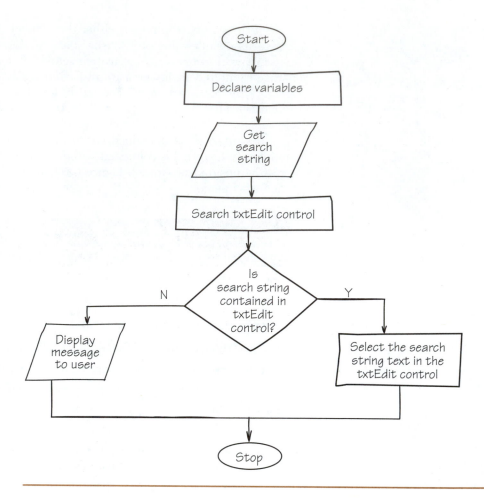

1. Declare the variables.

2. Get the search string from the user.

3. Search the txtEdit control for the search string.

4. If the search string is not found in the txtEdit control then

        display a message to the user

  Else

        select the search string text in the txtEdit control

  End If

Figure 6-70: Flowchart and pseudocode for the Edit menu's Find command

According to Figure 6-70, the first step is to declare the necessary variables. The Find command's Click event procedure will use a form-level variable named strSearchFor and a local variable named intFoundPos. The strSearchFor variable will store the search string—the string the user wants to find. You will declare strSearchFor as a form-level variable because it will also need to be used by the Find Next command's Click event procedure. The intFoundPos variable will store either the number 0, if the search string is not found in the txtEdit control, or it will store the starting position of the search string if the search string is found in the txtEdit control.

To begin coding the Find command's Click event:

1 Open the form's General Declarations section. Type **option explicit** and press the **Enter** key, then type **dim strSearchFor as string** and press the **Enter** key.

2 Use the Code window's Object box to open the mnuEditFind control's Click event procedure. Press the **Tab** key, then type **dim intFoundPos as integer** and press the **Enter** key.

After declaring the necessary variables, the Click event procedure will prompt the user for the search string—the string the user wants to find. You can use the InputBox function, which you learned about in Tutorial 3, to display a dialog box that contains a prompt and an input area in which the user can enter the search string. You will assign the user's response to the form-level strSearchFor variable.

3 Type **strsearchfor = inputbox("Find what?", "Find")** and press the **Enter** key.

You can now use the Instr function to search the txtEdit control for the string stored in the strSearchFor variable. You will perform a case-insensitive search, beginning with the first character in the txtEdit control. You will assign the result of the Instr function to the local intFoundPos variable. (Recall that the Instr function returns a number—either a 0 if the search string is not found, or the starting position of the search string if it is found.)

4 Maximize the Code window, then type **intfoundpos = instr(1, txtedit.text, strsearchfor, 1)** and press the **Enter** key.

If the intFoundPos variable contains the number 0, then the Instr function did not find the search string in the txtEdit text box, so you should display an appropriate message to the user. You can use the MsgBox function, which you learned about in both Tutorials 4 and 5, to display the message in a dialog box.

5 Enter the additional instructions shown in Figure 6-71, then position the insertion point as shown in the figure.

the line continuation character (a space followed by an underscore)

enter these seven lines of code

position insertion point here

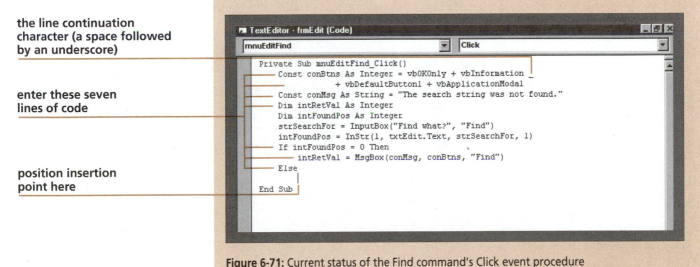

Figure 6-71: Current status of the Find command's Click event procedure

If the intFoundPos variable does not contain the number 0, then the Instr function found the search string in the txtEdit text box. The Instr function, remember, returns the starting position of *string2* (the strSearchFor variable) within *string1* (the txtEdit control's Text property). You can use the number stored in the intFoundPos variable, along with the SelStart and SelLength properties, to highlight the text found in the txtEdit control.

As you learned in Tutorial 4, the SelStart property tells Visual Basic where in the text box to position the insertion point—in other words, where to start the text selection. The first position in the text box, you may remember, is position 0. The SelLength property, on the other hand, tells Visual Basic the number of characters to select. Recall that the SelLength property begins the selection with the character to the immediate right of the insertion point. Therefore, in order to highlight all of the characters in a text box, beginning with the first character, you must set the SelStart property to 0. Likewise, if you want to highlight a group of characters beginning with the fifth character, you must set the SelStart property to 4. Notice that, when selecting text, the SelStart value must always be 1 less than the position of the first character you want to select. Figure 6-72 illustrates this concept.

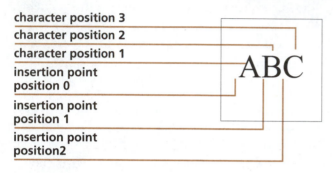

character position 3
character position 2
character position 1
insertion point position 0
insertion point position 1
insertion point position2

Figure 6-72: Illustration of insertion point positions and character positions

In the text editor application, recall that the intFoundPos variable contains a number that represents the position of the first character you want to select. In order to begin the selection with that character, you will need to position the insertion point to its immediate left. You can do so by subtracting 1 from the contents of the intFoundPos variable. After positioning the insertion point, you can use the SelLength property to tell Visual Basic to highlight the remaining characters that correspond to the search string.

To complete the Find command's Click event procedure, then save and run the application:

1   Enter the additional instructions and documentation shown in Figure 6-73. Also compare your code with the code shown in the figure. Correct any errors before continuing to the next step.

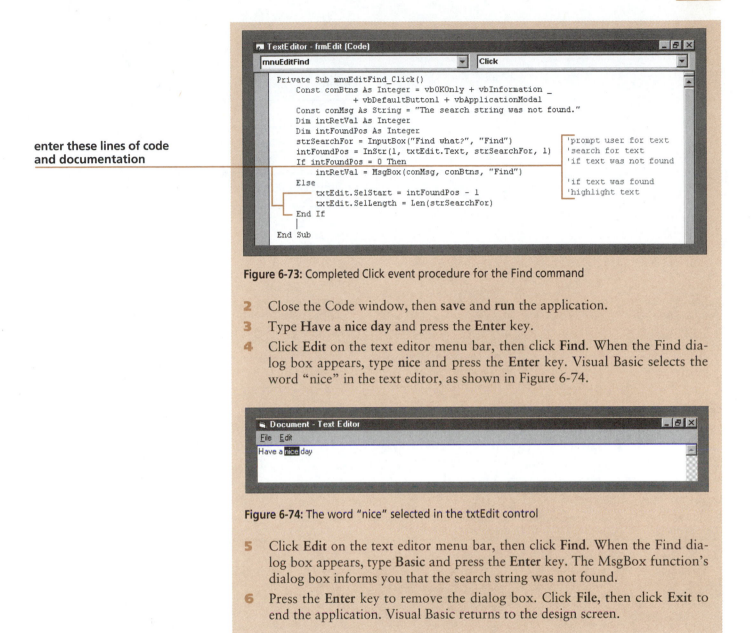

enter these lines of code and documentation

Figure 6-73: Completed Click event procedure for the Find command

2 Close the Code window, then **save** and **run** the application.

3 Type **Have a nice day** and press the **Enter** key.

4 Click **Edit** on the text editor menu bar, then click **Find**. When the Find dialog box appears, type **nice** and press the **Enter** key. Visual Basic selects the word "nice" in the text editor, as shown in Figure 6-74.

Figure 6-74: The word "nice" selected in the txtEdit control

5 Click **Edit** on the text editor menu bar, then click **Find**. When the Find dialog box appears, type **Basic** and press the **Enter** key. The MsgBox function's dialog box informs you that the search string was not found.

6 Press the **Enter** key to remove the dialog box. Click **File**, then click **Exit** to end the application. Visual Basic returns to the design screen.

The Find command will search only for the first occurrence of the search string in the text box. If the user wants to find subsequent occurrences of the search string, he or she will need to use the Edit menu's Find Next command.

Coding the Edit Menu's Find Next Command

The flowchart and pseudocode for the Edit menu's Find Next command are shown in Figure 6-75.

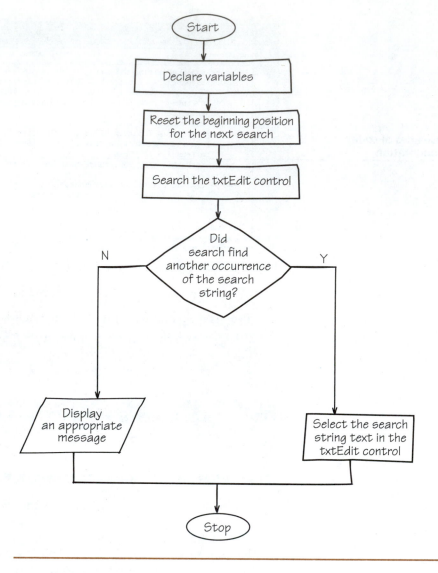

1. Declare variables.

2. Reset the beginning position for the next search.

3. Search the txtEdit control for another occurrence of the search string.

4. If another occurrence of the search string is not found in the txtEdit control, then

    display an appropriate message to the user

    Else

    select the search string text in the txtEdit control

    End If

Figure 6-75: Flowchart and pseudocode for the Edit menu's Find Next command

According to Figure 6-75, you first need to declare the necessary variables. The Find Next command will use three variables: strSearchFor, intFoundPos, and intBegSearch. The strSearchFor variable will store the search string. The intFoundPos variable will store either the number 0, if the search string is not found in the txtEdit control, or it will store the starting position of the search string if the search string is found in the txtEdit control. The intBegSearch variable will store the beginning position for the search. You will need only to declare the intFoundPos and intBegSearch variables in the Find Next command's Click event; the strSearchFor variable is already declared as a form-level string variable in the form's General Declarations section.

To begin coding the Edit menu's Find Next command:

1   Click **Edit** on the form's menu bar, then click **Find Next**. The mnuEditFindNext Click event procedure opens.

2   Press the **Tab** key, then type **dim intFoundPos as integer, intBegSearch as integer** and press the **Enter** key.

According to Figure 6-75, you must reset the beginning position for the next search. The new search should begin with the character that is located to the immediate right of where the search string was last found. For example, if the previous search found the search string at character position 8 in the txtEdit control, then the next search should start at character position 9. At first glance, it may appear that all you need to do is to add 1 to the text box's SelStart property. Recall, however, that when the search string is located in the text box, the Find command's Click event repositions the insertion point to the left of the first character in the search string; it repositions the insertion point in order to highlight the entire search string. In other words, if the search string is found at character position 8 in the txtEdit control, the Find command repositions the insertion point to insertion point position 7. (It may help to refer back to Figure 6-72.) Therefore, to begin the next search with the character to the right of where the search string was last found, you will need to add 2 to the SelStart property. Figure 6-76 illustrates this concept.

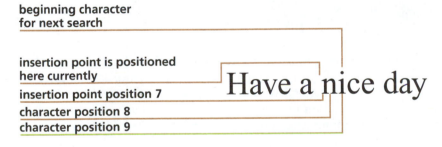

beginning character for next search

insertion point is positioned here currently

insertion point position 7

character position 8

character position 9

Figure 6-76: Illustration of the beginning location for the next search

To continue coding the Search menu's Find Next command, then save and run the application:

1 Type **intbegsearch = txtedit.selstart + 2** and press the **Enter** key.

Now use the Instr function to search the txtEdit control for the search string, which is stored in the form-level strSearchFor variable. If the Instr function does not find the search string, then display an appropriate message; otherwise, position the insertion point appropriately and highlight the search string in the txtEdit control.

2 Maximize the Code window, then enter the additional code shown in Figure 6-77.

the line continuation character (a space followed by the underscore)

enter these 11 lines of code

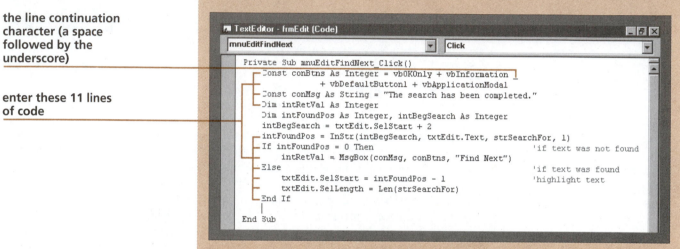

Figure 6-77: Completed Click event procedure for the Find Next command

3 Close the Code window, then **save** and **run** the application.

4 Test the application by entering a few sentences in the text box, then using the Find and Find Next commands to search for one or more words in those sentences.

5 When you are finished testing the application, click **File**, then click **Exit** to end the application.

You have now completed Lesson C. You will finish coding the text editor application in Tutorial 7. For now, you can either take a break, complete the questions and exercises at the end of the lesson, or continue to the Debugging Section. The Debugging Section may contain information that will help you with problems you might encounter when doing the exercises at the end of the lesson.

SUMMARY

To manipulate strings:

- Use the Left, Right, or Mid functions.
- The syntax of the Left function is **Left**(*string*, *length*). The Left function returns the leftmost *length* number of characters from the *string*.
- The syntax of the Right function is **Right**(*string*, *length*). The Right function returns the rightmost *length* number of characters from the *string*.
- The syntax of the Mid function is **Mid**(*string*, *start* [, *length*]). The Mid function returns *length* number of characters of the *string*, beginning at position *start*.

To search a string to determine if it contains another string:

- Use the Instr function. The syntax of the Instr function is **Instr**(*start*, *string1*, *string2*[, *compare*]).
- *Start* is a numeric expression that sets the starting position for the search.
- *String1* is the string expression being searched, and *string2* is the string expression being sought.
- *Compare* is either the number 0 or the number 1. If *compare* is set to its default value of 0, Visual Basic performs a case-sensitive search. If compare is set to 1, Visual Basic performs a case-insensitive search.
- If *string2* is not contained within *string1*, then the Instr function returns the number 0. If *string2* is contained within *string1*, then the Instr function returns the starting position of *string2*.

QUESTIONS

1. Which two functions can you use to manipulate one or more characters from the left side of a string?
   a. IsNumeric
   b. Left
   c. Mid
   d. Right
   e. Xtract

2. Which two functions can you use to manipulate one or more characters from the right side of a string?
   a. IsNumeric
   b. Left
   c. Mid
   d. Right
   e. Xtract

3. The _____ function allows you to extract *length* number of characters from a *string*, beginning with the *start* character.
   a. IsNumeric
   b. Left
   c. Mid
   d. Right
   e. Xtract

4. Assuming that the strMsg variable contains the string "Have a great day", the Left(strMsg, 2) function would return _____ .
   a. a
   b. av
   c. ay
   d. Ha
   e. v

5. Assuming that the strMsg variable contains the string "Have a great day", the Right(strMsg, 2) function would return _____ .
   a. a
   b. av
   c. ay
   d. d
   e. Ha

6. Assuming that the strMsg variable contains the string "Welcome home", the Mid(strMsg, 3, 4) function would return _____ .
   a. com
   b. come
   c. lcom
   d. ome

7. The Left(strName, 3) function is equivalent to which of the following?
   a. Mid(strName, 3, 1)
   b. Mid(strName, 1, 3)
   c. Mid(strName, 3, 0)
   d. Mid(strName, 0, 3)
   e. Mid(strName, 3, 3)

8. Assuming the strName variable contains the name "John Jeffries", the Right(strName, 3) function is equivalent to which of the following?
   a. Mid(strName, 3, 10)
   b. Mid(strName, 10, 3)
   c. Mid(strName, 3, 11)
   d. Mid(strName, 11, 3)

9. Assuming the strMsg variable contains the string "Don't forget to VOTE for your favorite candidate", the Instr(1, strMsg, "vote", 0) function would return _____ .
   a. 0
   b. 16
   c. 17

10. Assuming the strMsg variable contains the string "Don't forget to VOTE for your favorite candidate", the Instr(1, strMsg, "vote", 1) function would return _____ .
    a. 0
    b. 16
    c. 17

11. Assuming the strMsg variable contains the string "Don't forget to VOTE for your favorite candidate", the Instr(10, strMsg, "vote", 1) function would return _____ .
    a. 0
    b. 16
    c. 17

12. Assuming the strMsg variable contains the string "Don't forget to VOTE for your favorite candidate", the Instr(10, strMsg, "vote", 0) function would return _____.

a. 0

b. 16

c. 17

13. You use the _____ property to position the insertion point in a text box.

a. Position

b. SelLength

c. SelPos

d. SelStart

e. SelText

14. In order to highlight a group of characters in a text box, beginning with character 10, you would need to set the SelStart property to _____.

a. 9

b. 10

c. 11

E X E R C I S E S

NOTE: The following list shows the GUI design and programming guidelines you have learned so far. You can use this list to verify that the applications you create in the following exercises adhere to the standards outlined in the book.

- Information should flow either vertically or horizontally, with the most important information always located in the upper-left corner of the screen.
- Maintain a consistent margin of two or three dots from the edge of the window.
- Related controls should be grouped together using either white space or a frame.
- Position related controls on succeeding dots.
- Command buttons should either be centered along the bottom of the screen or stacked in either the upper-right or lower-right corner.
- If the command buttons are centered along the bottom of the screen, then each button should be the same height; their widths, however, may vary.
- If the command buttons are stacked in either the upper-right or lower-right corner of the screen, then each button should be the same height and the same width.
- Use no more than six command buttons on a screen.
- The most commonly used command button should be placed first.
- Command button captions should:
  - be meaningful
  - be from one to three words
  - appear on one line
  - be entered using book title capitalization
- Use labels to identify the controls in the interface.

- Identifying labels should:
  - be from one to three words
  - appear on one line
  - be aligned by their left borders
  - be positioned either above or to the left of the control that they identify
  - end with a colon (:)
  - be entered using sentence capitalization
  - have their BackStyle property set to 0-Transparent
  - have their BorderStyle property set to 0-None
- Labels that display program output (for example, the results of calculations):
  - should have their BorderStyle set to 1-Fixed Single
  - should have their Appearance property set to 0-Flat
  - can have their BackStyle property set to either 0-Transparent or 1-Opaque
- Align labels and controls to minimize the number of different margins.
- If you use a graphic in the interface, use a small one and place it in a location that will not distract the user.
- Use no more than two different font sizes, which should be 8, 10, or 12 points.
- Use only one font type, which should be a sans serif font, in the interface.
- Avoid using italics and underlining.
- Use either white, off-white, light gray, pale blue, or pale yellow for an application's background, and black for the text.
- Use color sparingly and don't use it as the only means of identification for an element in the interface.
- Set each control's TabIndex property to a number that represents the order in which you want that control to receive the focus (begin with 0).
- A text box's TabIndex value should be one more than the TabIndex value of its identifying label.
- Lock the controls in place on the form.
- Assign a unique access key to each essential element of the interface (text boxes, command buttons, list boxes, and so on).
- Document the program internally.
- Enter the Option Explicit statement in the General Declaration section of every form and module.
- Use variables to control the preciseness of numbers in the interface.
- Use the Val function on Text and Caption properties, and when assigning the result of the InputBox function to a numeric variable.
- Set the form's BorderStyle, MinButton, MaxButton, and ControlBox properties appropriately:
  - Splash screens should not have a Minimize, Maximize, or Close button, and their borders should not be sizable.
  - Forms that are acting as dialog boxes should have a BorderStyle property of 3-Fixed Dialog.
  - Forms other than splash screens and dialog boxes should always have a Minimize button and a Close button, but you can choose to disable the Maximize button.
  - Forms other than splash screens and dialog boxes typically have a BorderStyle property setting of either 1-Fixed Single or 2-Sizable.

- Test the application with both valid and invalid data (test the application without entering any data; also test it by entering letters where numbers are expected).

- In the InputBox function, use sentence capitalization for the *prompt*, and book title capitalization for the *title*.

- Center the form on the screen by including the appropriate formulas in the form's Load event.

- Display an hourglass or an arrow and an hourglass if a procedure will take a long period of time.

- Remove excess code from the application.

- Option buttons:
  - Use a minimum of two and a maximum of seven in an interface.
  - Use sentence capitalization for the caption.
  - Use a frame control to create separate groups of option buttons.
  - Select a default button in each group.

- Use sentence capitalization for a frame control's caption.

- Use sentence capitalization for a check box's caption.

- MsgBox function:
  - Use sentence capitalization for the message.
  - Display the application's name in the title bar, using book title capitalization.
  - Display the appropriate icon.
  - Default button should be one that represents the user's most likely action, as long as that action is not destructive.

- Use the SelStart and SelLength properties, as well as the Len function, to highlight (select) the existing text when a text box receives the focus.

- Disable objects that don't apply to the current state of the application.

- List box controls:
  - should contain a minimum of three selections.
  - display a minimum of three selections and a maximum of eight selections at a time.
  - A list box's TabIndex value should be one more than the TabIndex value of its identifying label.
  - Items should be arranged either by use, with the most used entries appearing first in the list, or sorted in ascending order alphabetically, numerically, or chronologically.
  - If the list box allows only one selection, then select a default item when the interface first appears (select either the most used item or the first item in the list).

- Reports should include a report title, column headings, and a "End of report" message. Numbers should be aligned by decimal points on the right of a column.

> ■ Menus:
>> ■ Menu titles should be one word, with the first letter capitalized.
>> ■ Menu items should be from one to three words.
>> ■ Menu items should be entered using book title capitalization.
>> ■ Menu titles and menu items should be assigned unique access keys.
>> ■ Commonly used menu items should be assigned shortcut keys.
>> ■ Place an ellipsis after a menu item's Caption if the item requires additional information.
>> ■ Follow the Windows standards for the placement of menu titles and items.
>> ■ Disable menu items that are not applicable to the current state of the application.
>> ■ Use a separator bar to separate groups of related menu items.

1. Evaluate the following:

Function	Resulting String
Left("Mary Jones", 4)	
Right("Sam Smith", 2)	
Mid("Bobby Day", 1, 1)	
Mid("Jack Li", 3, 2)	

Figure 6-78

2. Assuming that the strStateName variable contains "California", evaluate the following:

Function	Resulting String
Mid(strStateName, 8, 1)	
Left(strStateName, 6)	
Right(strStateName, 5)	
Mid(strStateName, 3, 5)	

Figure 6-79

3. In this exercise you will manipulate strings.

Scenario: Each salesperson at BobCat Motors is assigned an ID number, which consists of four characters. The first character is either the letter F or the letter P. The letter F indicates that the salesperson is a full-time employee; the letter P indicates that he or she is a part-time employee. The middle two characters are the salesperson's initials, and the last character is either a 1 or a 2. A 1 indicates that the salesperson sells new cars, and a 2 indicates that the salesperson sells used cars. The manager wants an application that will allow her to enter the salesperson's number. The application should display the salesperson's employment status (either full-time or part-time), the

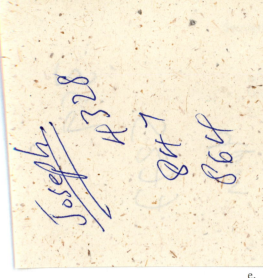

...son's initials, and which type of cars the salesperson sells (either new or used). ...el controls to display the information.

...te an appropriate user interface. (Refer to the list of GUI design and program-...g guidelines at the beginning of the Exercises section.) Be sure to include either a ...t command button or a Print item on a File menu. The Print button or menu ... should print the form.

... the form and the project as lc3Done in the Tut06 folder on your Student Disk.

...e the application according to the information supplied in the scenario. Be sure ...se the MsgBox function to display appropriate messages to the user if he or she ...rs something other than an F or a P as the first character, or if he or she enters ...ething other than a 1 or a 2 as the last character.

... and run the application. Test the application with the following correct ID ...bers: FRJ2, PMM1. Print the interface after entering each employee number.

e. Now test the application with the following incorrect ID numbers: TLL1, FJJ5. On the printouts from step d, write down the error messages that appear after entering each of these incorrect employee numbers.

f. Exit the application, then print the code.

g. Submit the printouts from step d, which contain the error messages recorded in step e, and the code from step f.

4. In this exercise you will manipulate strings.

Scenario: Each employee at Acme Wares is assigned an employee number, which consists of three characters. If the employee is salaried, the second digit in the employee number is a 1—for example, employee number 117 would indicate a salaried employee. If the employee is hourly, the second digit in the number is a 2—for example, employee number 127 would indicate an hourly employee. The manager wants an application that will allow him to enter the employee's number. The application should display the employee's employment status, either salaried or hourly. Use label controls to display the information.

a. Create an appropriate user interface. (Refer to the list of GUI design and programming guidelines at the beginning of the Exercises section.) Be sure to include either a Print command button or a Print item on a File menu. The Print button or menu item should print the form.

b. Save the form and the project as lc4Done in the Tut06 folder on your Student Disk.

c. Code the application according to the information supplied in the scenario. Be sure to use the MsgBox function to display appropriate messages to the user if he or she enters something other than a 1 or a 2 as the second character.

d. Save and run the application. Test the application with the following correct employee numbers: 312, 421. Print the interface after entering each employee number.

e. Now test the application with the following incorrect employee numbers: 1A3, 267. On the printouts from step d, write down the error messages that appear after entering each of these incorrect employee numbers.

f. Exit the application, then print the code.

g. Submit the printouts from step d, which contain the error messages recorded in step e, and the code from step f.

5. In this exercise you will use a sequential access file and a menu control.

Scenario: Computer Warehouse wants an application that will calculate both the total number of items sold and the total number sold by item. The application should allow the user to print the interface.

a. Open the lc5 (lc5.vbp) project, which is located in the Tut06 folder on your Student Disk.

b. Use Windows to copy the lc5.ori sequential access data file, which is located in the Tut06 folder on your Student Disk, to lc5.dat. (Put the lc5.dat file in the Tut06 folder on your Student Disk.) Use WordPad to print the contents of the lc5.dat file.

c. Save the form and the project as lc5Done in the Tut06 folder on your Student Disk.

d. Set the list box's Sorted property to True. Have the application automatically select the first item in the list when the application first appears on the screen.

e. Add a File menu to the application. Include Print and Exit options. Code the Exit option so that it unloads the form. Code the Print option so that it prints the form. Assign the appropriate access keys and the appropriate shortcut key.

f. Add a Statistics menu to the application. Include two options: Calculate Total and Calculate by Item. Assign access and shortcut keys to both options.

g. Code the Calculate Total option so that it calculates the total number sold for all of the items in the lc5.dat file. Display an appropriate message along with the total number sold in the lblTotal control. (For example, display the message "The total number sold is 300." in the lblTotal control.)

h. Code the Calculate by Item option so that it calculates the total sold, from the lc5.dat file, for only the item the user chooses in the list box. (In other words, if the user clicks the ABC11 item in the list box, the Calculate by Item option will calculate and display only the total sold for the ABC11 item.) Display an appropriate message along with the total number sold for that item in the lblTotal control. (For example, display the message "The total number sold for item ABC11 is 50." in the lblTotal control.)

i. Save and run the application.

j. Use the Statistics menu's Calculate Total option to calculate the total number sold. Use the File menu's Print option to print the interface.

k. Click the BDX22 item in the list box. Use the Statistics menu's Calculate by Item option to calculate the number of item BDX22 sold. Use the File menu's Print option to print the interface.

l. Exit the application. Print the code.

m. Submit the printouts from steps b, j, and k, and the code from step l.

6. In this exercise you will use a sequential access file and a menu control to print a report.

Scenario: Computer Warehouse wants an application that can print two different reports. One report will show all of the records contained in the lc6.dat file. The other report will show only the records whose item number matches the item number selected in a list box.

a. Open the lc6 (lc6.vbp) project, which is located in the Tut06 folder on your Student Disk.

b. Use Windows to copy the lc6.ori sequential access data file, which is located in the Tut06 folder on your Student Disk, to lc6.dat. (Put the lc6.dat file in the Tut06 folder on your Student Disk.) Use WordPad to print the contents of the lc6.dat file.

c. Save the form and the project as lc6Done in the Tut06 folder on your Student Disk.

d. Add a File menu to the application. Include Print and Exit options. The Print option should have two submenu options: All Records and Records by Item.

e. Code the Exit option so that it unloads the form.

f. Code the Print menu's All Records option so that it prints a report showing all of the records contained in the lc6.dat file. At the end of the report, display the total number of records printed, as well as an "End of report" message.

g. Code the Print menu's Records by Item option so that it prints a report showing only the lc6.dat records whose item number matches the item number selected in the list box. At the end of the report, display the total number of records printed, as well as an "End of report" message.

h. Save and run the application. First, print all of the records contained in the lc6.dat file, then print only the BDX22 records.

i. Exit the application and print the code. Submit the printouts from step h and the code from step i.

Exercises 7 through 9 are Discovery Exercises, which allow you to both "discover" the solutions to problems on your own and experiment with material that is not covered in the tutorial.

discovery ▶ 7. In this exercise you will use the HideSelection property of a text box.

a. Open the lcEdit application that you created in Lesson C.

b. Save the form and the project as lc7Done in the Tut06 folder on your Student Disk.

c. If you have access to the MSDN Library, then search for information on a text box's HideSelection property.

d. The Find command's Click event uses the InputBox function to ask the user for the search string. Replace the InputBox function with a form that resembles a dialog box. (Recall that you learned about creating dialog boxes in Tutorial 3.) The dialog box that you create should include a text box in which the user enters the search string, a Find Next button, and a Cancel button. You do not need to include a Replace button.

e. Move the code from the Find Next command on the Edit menu to the Find Next button's Click event procedure.

f. Remove the Find Next command from the Edit menu.

g. Modify the Edit menu's Find and Find Next code appropriately.

h. Save and run the application. Type a sentence in the text box, then use the Edit menu's Find command to search for a word in that sentence. When you click the Find Next button, the application should either find the next occurrence of the word, or display a message that the search is complete. The dialog box should remain on the screen when the word is found, and the word should be highlighted in the text box.

i. Exit the application. Print the application's code.

discovery ▶ 8. In this exercise you will manipulate strings.

Scenario: Credit card companies typically assign a special digit, called a check digit, to the end of each customer's credit card number. Many methods for creating the check digit have been developed. One simple method is to multiply every other number in the credit card number by 2, then add the products to the remaining numbers to get the total. You would then take the last digit in the total and append it to the end of the number, as illustrated in Figure 6-80.

```
                         Check Digit Algorithm

Original Number: 1357

Step 1:  Multiply every other number by 2:     1      3      5      7
                                                      *2            *2

         Result  ──────────────────────▶       1      6      5      14

Step 2:  Sum the numbers                        1  +   6  +   5  +  14 = 26

Step 3:  Take the last digit in the sum and                               │
                                                                          ▼
         append it to the original number:      1      3      5      7    6

New Number:      13576
```

Figure 6-80

a. Based on the check digit algorithm shown in Figure 6-80, manually calculate the check digits for the following numbers, then write the new numbers with their check digits. The first example has been completed for you.

Number	Number with Check Digit
1357	13576
4273	_____
3907	_____
4621	_____

b. Open a new project, if necessary. Add a text box, a label control, and a command button to the interface.

c. Save the form and the project as lc8Done in the Tut06 folder on your Student Disk.

d. The application should allow the user to enter the number, including the check digit. When the user clicks the command button, the application should display "Correct" in the label control if the check digit is correct; it should display "Incorrect" in the label control if the check digit is incorrect. In other words, if the user enters 13576 in the text box, the application should display "Correct." However, if the user enters 13579 in the text box, then the application should display "Incorrect."

e. Save and run the application. Use the application to verify the check digits for the numbers shown in Step a.

f. Print the code.

discovery ▶   9.   In this exercise you will manipulate strings and use a sequential access file and a list box.

Scenario: Each salesperson at BobCat Motors is assigned a code that consists of two characters. The first character is either the letter F or the letter P. The letter F indicates that the salesperson is a full-time employee; the letter P indicates that he or she is a part-time employee. The second character is either a 1 or a 2. A 1 indicates that the salesperson sells new cars, and a 2 indicates that the salesperson sells used cars. The manager wants an application that she can use to display one of the following listings in a list box:

1) the names of full-time salespeople
2) the names of part-time salespeople
3) the names of salespeople who sell new cars
4) the names of salespeople who sell used cars
5) the names of full-time salespeople who sell new cars
6) the names of full-time salespeople who sell used cars
7) the names of part-time salespeople who sell new cars
8) the names of part-time salespeople who sell used cars

a. Open the lc9 (lc9.vbp) project, which is located in the Tut06 folder on your Student Disk.

b. Save the form and the project as lc9Done in the Tut06 folder on your Student Disk.

c. Use Windows to copy the lc9.ori sequential access data file, which is located in the Tut06 folder on your Student Disk, to lc9.dat. (Put the lc9.dat file in the Tut06 folder on your Student Disk.) Use WordPad to print the contents of the lc9.dat file.

d. Code the lstChoices control's Click event so that it displays the appropriate listing in the lstNames list box. (*Hint*: Use the Instr function.)

e. Save and run the application. Test the application by displaying each listing. When you display the listing for the full-time salespeople who sell new cars, print the interface.

f. Exit the application, then print the code.

g. Submit the printout from steps c and e, and the code from step f.

DEBUGGING

Technique   Visual Basic's Edit menu provides two commands that you can use to edit the code in an application quickly. These commands are Find and Replace.

Following are two debugging exercises that will allow you to practice this tutorial's debugging technique.

To debug the first application:

1 Start Visual Basic, if necessary, and open the **Debug1** (debug1.vbp) project, which is located in the Tut06 folder on your Student Disk. The user interface contains three label controls, one text box, and three command buttons.

2 **Run** the application. Type **10** in the Old price text box, then click the **5% Increase** button. The "Variable not defined" message appears. Click the **OK** button to remove the message. Visual Basic highlights the error in the cmd5 control's Click event procedure; the application does not recognize the Text1 entry.

3 Click the **Object** list arrow in the Code window to display a list of the object names. The correct name of the text box in the interface is txtOld. You will use Visual Basic's Edit menu to correct the name in the Code windows.

4 Click the **Object** list arrow to close the list of object names. Click **Edit**, then click **Replace**. The Replace dialog box appears as shown in Figure 6-81.

Figure 6-81: Replace dialog box

HELP? You may need to drag the Replace dialog box to another location in order to see the cmd5 control's Click event procedure.

The Replace dialog box contains a Find What text box and a Replace With text box. You enter the search text—the text you want to search for—in the Find What box and you enter the replacement text—the new text—in the Replace With box. In this case, you want to replace Text1 with txtOld.

5 Text1 should already be entered in the Find What box, so you need simply to press the **Tab** key, then type **txtOld** in the Replace With box.

Notice the four option buttons (Current Procedure, Current Module, Current Project, Selected Text) in the Search section of the dialog box. Selecting the Current Procedure option tells Visual Basic to look for the search text in the current procedure only. Selecting the Current Module option tells Visual Basic to perform the search in the current module only; the current module includes all of the procedures in the current form. If you select the Current Project option, every procedure in the entire application is searched. Lastly, if you select the Selected Text option, only the selected text is searched.

In this case, you will select the Current Module option, which will search all of the procedures in the current form.

6 If necessary, click the **Current Module** option button to select it. A black dot should appear inside the option button.

The Replace dialog box also contains three check boxes (Find Whole Word Only, Match Case, Use Pattern Matching). Selecting the Find Whole Word Only check box tells Visual Basic to search for the full word by itself, not as part of another word. In other words, if the search text is "the," Visual Basic should look for "the" as a whole word; it should not find "there," "them," and so on.

tip

If no text is highlighted in the Code window when the Replace dialog box appears, the Selected Text option will be dimmed.

If the Match Case check box is selected, Visual Basic performs a case-sensitive search; otherwise, it performs a case-insensitive search.

If the Use Pattern Matching check box is selected, you can use Visual Basic's pattern matching characters in the Find What text box. For example, you could search for all controls whose name begins with txt by entering txt* in the Find What text box; the asterisk (*) is one of Visual Basic's pattern matching characters. To learn more about the pattern matching characters, use the Help menu to display a Help window on the topic "pattern matching in string comparisons."

In this case you will not need to select any of the three check boxes.

7   Click the **Direction** list arrow. Notice that you can set the direction of the search to either Down, Up, or All. Click **All** in the list.

8   Click the **Replace** button to replace the Text1 entry with txtOld in the cmd5 control's Click event procedure. Visual Basic replaces Text1 with txtOld in the cmd5 control's Click event procedure, then highlights the Text1 entry in the cmd8 control's Click event procedure.

9   Click the **Replace** button to replace the Text1 entry with txtOld in the cmd8 control's Click event procedure. Visual Basic replaces Text1 with txtOld in the cmd8 control's Click event procedure, then displays the "The specified region has been searched" message.

10 Click the **OK** button to remove the message, then click the **Cancel** button to remove the Replace dialog box.

11 Close the Code window, then click the **Continue** button 🔳 on the toolbar. The "Variable not defined" message appears. Click the **OK** button to remove the message. Visual Basic highlights the Label3 entry in the cmd5_Click event.

12 Click the **Object** list arrow. The correct name for the label control is lblNew. Click the Object list arrow to close the list.

13 Click **Edit**, then click **Replace**. Label3 should already be entered in the Find What box, so you need simply to press the **Tab** key, then type **lblNew** in the Replace With box. This time click the **Replace All** button, which will automatically replace all occurrences of Label3 with lblNew. Visual Basic informs you that two replacements were made.

14 Click the **OK** button to remove the message, then click the **Cancel** button to remove the Replace dialog box.

15 Click the **Continue** button 🔳 on the toolbar. The interface appears with 10 in the Old price text box and 10.50 in the New price label control. Click the **8% Increase** button. The New price label control now shows 10.80.

16 Click the **Exit** button to exit the application. You do not need to save the corrected application.

To debug the second application:

1   Open the **Debug2** (debug2.vbp) project, which is located in the Tut06 folder on your Student Disk. The user interface contains three label controls, one text box, and three command buttons.

2   **Run** the application. Use the Edit menu's Replace command to correct the errors. Be sure that the application will work if the user mistakenly enters a letter instead of a number in the text box.

3   When the application is working correctly, print the application's code.

Dialog Boxes and Error Trapping

Completing the Text Editor Application

case ▶ In Tutorial 6 you began creating the Text Editor application for the PAO (Political Awareness Organization). Recall that the PAO sends a questionnaire to the voters in its district. The questionnaire asks the voter to provide his or her political party and age group. The data provided from the returned questionnaires is tabulated by the organization's secretary, who then sends a summary report, along with a cover letter, to the organization's members and to various political offices in the district. In this tutorial, you will finish creating the Text Editor application.

Recall that you coded the Text Editor application's Edit menu, but you did not finish coding its File menu. You will complete the File menu in this tutorial.

Previewing the Completed Application

Begin by opening and previewing the completed Text Editor application for the PAO.

To preview the completed Text Editor application:

1 If necessary, start Windows, then place your Student Disk in the appropriate disk drive.

2 Use the Run command on the Start menu to run the **Edit** (Edit.exe) file, which is located in the Tut07 folder on your Student Disk. The Text Editor application's user interface appears on the screen.

3 Type your first name in the document, then press the **Enter** key.

In Tutorial 6 you previewed the Edit menu; in this tutorial, you will preview the commands on the File menu. Begin with the Save As command.

4 Click **File**, then click **Save As**. When the Save As dialog box appears, open the Tut07 folder on your Student Disk, then type **Preview** in the File name text box. See Figure 7-1.

Figure 7-1: Save As dialog box created by the Common Dialog control

The Save As dialog box shown in Figure 7-1 was created with the Common Dialog control, which you will learn about in Lesson A.

5 Click the **Save** button to save the document.

HELP? If this is the second or subsequent time you are saving the Preview file, a message asking if you want to replace the existing Preview.txt file will appear. Click the Yes button.

6 Type your last name in the document, then press the **Enter** key.

Observe how the New command works.

7 Click **File**, then click **New**. Because the current document was changed since the last time it was saved, a message asking if you want to save the current document appears. Click the **Yes** button. The application saves the current document, then displays a new document.

Next, observe how the Open command works.

8 Click **File**, then click **Open**. Open the Tut07 folder on your Student Disk, then click **Preview.txt** in the File name list box. See Figure 7-2.

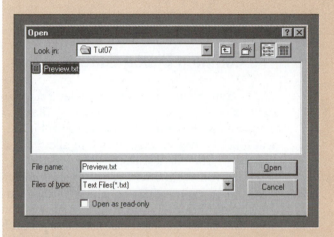

Figure 7-2: Open dialog box created by the Common Dialog control

The Open dialog box, shown in Figure 7-2, also was created with the Common Dialog control.

9 Click the **Open** button to open the file. The application opens the Preview.txt file and displays its contents (your first and last name) in the interface.

Now make a change to the document and use the Save command to save the document under its current name.

10 Delete your last name from the document. Click **File**, then click **Save**. The application saves the document on your Student Disk without asking if you want to replace the existing file.

Lastly, use the File menu's Print command.

11 If your computer is connected to a printer, click **File**, then click **Print**. When the Print dialog box appears, click the **OK** button. The application prints the document. A message box appears on the screen while the document is printing.

12 Click **File**, then click **Exit** to end the application.

In Lesson A you will learn about the Common Dialog control, which will be used in the Text Editor application to display the Save As, Open, and Print dialog boxes. In Lesson B, you will learn how to trap any errors encountered when using the Common Dialog control. You will complete the Text Editor application in Lessons B and C.

LESSON A

objectives

In this lesson you will learn how to:

■ Display standard dialog boxes using the Common Dialog control

■ Set the Common Dialog control's Filter and FileName properties

■ Set the Common Dialog control's Flags property

Dialog Boxes

The Common Dialog Control

The Common Dialog control provides a standard set of dialog boxes for operations such as opening, saving, and printing files, as well as selecting colors and fonts. You will use the Common Dialog control in the Text Editor application, which you will finish coding in this tutorial, to allow the user to open and save the documents that he or she creates. Recall that the PAO's (Political Awareness Organization) secretary will use the text editor to send a cover letter to the organization's members and to various political offices in the district. Before opening the Text Editor application, however, you will open an application that will allow you to practice with each of the standard dialog boxes created by the Common Dialog control.

To open the application that contains examples of the Common Dialog control:

1 Start Visual Basic, if necessary, and open the **Common** (Common.vbp) project, which is located in the Tut07 folder on your Student Disk.

2 Save the form and the project as **laCommon**.

3 Click the **form** to select it. The user interface appears as shown in Figure 7-3.

txtEdit

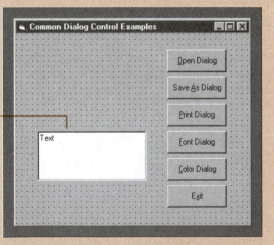

Figure 7-3: frmCommon user interface

This application will allow you to view the Open, Save As, Print, Font, and Color dialog boxes created by the Common Dialog control. First add the CommonDialog tool to the toolbox.

4 Click **Project** on the menu bar, then click **Components** to open the Components dialog box. If necessary, click the **Controls** tab to select it. Scroll the list of controls, if necessary, then click the **Microsoft Common Dialog Control 6.0** check box to select this control. Be sure a checkmark appears in the check box. Click the **OK** button to close the Components dialog box. The CommonDialog tool appears in the toolbox as shown in Figure 7-4.

CommonDialog tool

Figure 7-4: CommonDialog tool in the toolbox

The dlgCommon control is an instance of the CommonDialog class.

5 Double-click the **CommonDialog tool** in the toolbox. The Common Dialog control, which appears as an icon, displays on the form. Set the control's Name property to **dlgCommon**. "dlg" is the three-character ID for the Common Dialog control.

6 Drag the Common Dialog control to the upper-left corner of the form, then lock the controls in place on the form.

7 Click the **Save Project** button 🖫 on the toolbar to save the form and the project.

During design time, the Common Dialog control displays as an icon on the form; you can't size the icon, and it doesn't matter where the icon is positioned on the form. During run time, Visual Basic will display an appropriately sized dialog box, instead of the icon, in a default position in the interface. You tell Visual Basic which type of dialog box to display, as well as when to display the dialog box, by including one of the Common Dialog control's methods in an event procedure. The Common Dialog control's methods, along with an explanation of each, are shown in Figure 7-5.

Method	Purpose
ShowOpen	Displays a standard Open dialog box
ShowSave	Displays a standard Save As dialog box
ShowPrinter	Displays a standard Print dialog box
ShowColor	Displays a standard Color dialog box
ShowFont	Displays a standard Font dialog box

Figure 7-5: Common Dialog control's methods

You need to put only one Common Dialog control on the form. You can then use that one control to display one or more different dialog boxes. In the current application, for example, you will use the dlgCommon control to display the Open, Save As, Print, Font, and Color dialog boxes at different times while the application is running. Begin by coding the Open Dialog command button, which should display an Open dialog box that allows the user to open a file.

Displaying an Open Dialog Box

The Open Dialog command button should display the standard Open dialog box available in Windows applications. First, observe how a standard Open dialog box appears.

To view a standard Open dialog box, then begin coding the Open Dialog command button:

1 Click **File** on the menu bar, then click **Open Project**.

2 Open the Tut07 folder on your Student Disk. See Figure 7-6.

name of the current folder

list of filenames

empty when dialog box appears

type of files displayed in list

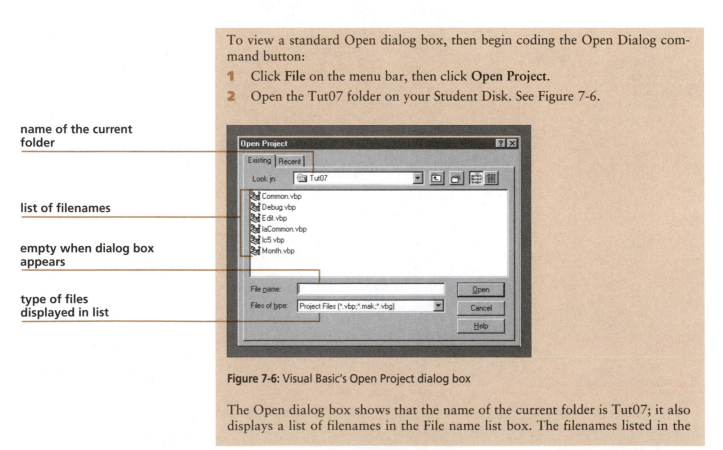

Figure 7-6: Visual Basic's Open Project dialog box

The Open dialog box shows that the name of the current folder is Tut07; it also displays a list of filenames in the File name list box. The filenames listed in the

tip

The asterisk (*) in the filter is known as a wildcard character because, similar to a wild card in a game of poker, you can use it to represent anything you want. In this case, the *.vbp;*.mak;*.vbg filter tells Windows to display all filenames ending in either .vbp, .mak, or .vbg. The * indicates that you are not concerned with the beginning of the filename.

File name list box depend on the entry in the Files of type list box. In the Open dialog box shown in Figure 7-6, for example, the Files of type list box contains Project Files (*.vbp;*.mak;*.vbg), which describe the type of files to display (in this case, project files) and the filter (in this case, *.vbp;*.mak;*.vbg) that determines whether a file is a project file. The filter refers to the extension on the file's name. (Project filenames in Versions 2.0 and 3.0 of Visual Basic end in .mak, rather than the .vbp used in later versions. Project group filenames end in .vbg.) The *.vbp;*.mak;*.vbg filter tells Windows that only files with names ending in either .vbp, .mak, or .vbg are project files, so only files ending in those extensions should be displayed in the File name list box. Notice that the File name text box is empty when the Open dialog box appears.

Many applications allow the user to select from a list of predefined descriptions and filters. For example, Visual Basic's Open Project dialog box allows you to display all of the files contained in the current folder. Observe that now.

3 Click the **Files of type** list arrow.

The standard description and filter for displaying all files in the current folder is All Files(*.*).

4 Click **All Files(*.*)**. Windows displays the names of all files in the current folder.

5 Click the **Cancel** button to close the Open Project dialog box.

Now code the Open Dialog button in the frmCommon form. You will need to use the Common Dialog control's ShowOpen method to display the standard Open dialog box.

6 Open the Open Dialog button's Click event procedure. Press the **Tab** key, then type **dlgcommon.showopen** and press the **Enter** key.

7 Close the Code window, then **save** and **run** the application.

8 Click the **Open Dialog** button. A standard Open dialog box appears.

9 Open the Tut07 folder on your Student Disk. See Figure 7-7.

current folder

list of filenames

this should contain a
description and filter

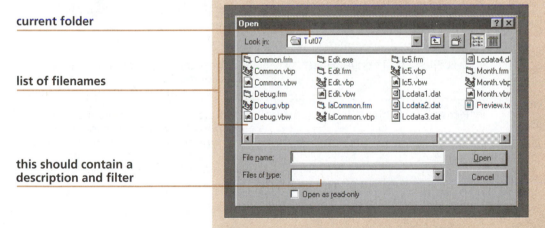

Figure 7-7: Open dialog box created by the Common Dialog control's ShowOpen method

tip

• • • • • • • • • • • • • • • •

The CommonDialog control provides, automatically, context-sensitive Help on the interface of the dialog boxes it creates. You can access this context-sensitive Help either by clicking the What's This ![?] button on the title bar, then clicking the item for which you want more information, or by right-clicking the item for which you want more information, then selecting the What's This command on the popup menu.

The dialog box shows that the Tut07 folder is the current folder; it also displays a list of filenames in the File name list box. Notice that the File name text box is empty when the Open dialog box appears. The Files of type list box is also empty, which is not correct; it should contain the description and filter for the type of files to be displayed in the File name list box. You enter both a description and a filter in the Open dialog box by setting the Common Dialog control's Filter property.

10 Click the **Cancel** button to close the Open dialog box, then click the **Exit** button to end the application. Visual Basic returns to the design screen.

The Filter Property

The **Filter property** stores a string that represents both the description and the filter for the files displayed in the File name list box when either the Open or the Save As dialog box appears. The string, which appears in the Files of type list box during run time, can contain any characters that are valid for a filename, including the * (asterisk).

The syntax of the instruction used to assign the description and filter to the Filter property is *object*.**Filter** = d*escription1|filter1|description2|filter2...*, where both *description* and *filter* are string expressions that specify the type of files to display. As the syntax shows, the Filter property can contain the descriptions and filters for multiple file types. Notice that you use the pipe symbol (|) to separate a *description* from its corresponding *filter*, and to separate one file type's *description* and *filter* from the next file type's *description* and *filter*. When typing the *filter*, be sure you don't include spaces before or after the pipe symbol; if you do, the spaces will be displayed, incorrectly, with the *description* and *filter* values. Figure 7-8 shows examples of Filter property settings.

Filter	Result
"All Files(*.*)|*.*"	Displays the names of all files contained in the current folder.
"Text Files(*.txt)|*.txt|All Files(*.*)|*.*"	Displays the names of either the text files contained in the current folder or all files contained in the current folder.
"Picture Files(*.bmp;*.ico)|*.bmp;*.ico"	Displays the names of picture files contained in the current folder. If a file type has more than one filename extension, notice that you separate the extensions with a semicolon (;).

separate multiple extensions with a semicolon

Figure 7-8: Examples of Filter property settings

In this application, you want the Open dialog box to allow the user either to display the names of only text files in the current folder or to display the names of all files in the current folder.

To set the Filter property in the Open Dialog button's Click event procedure:

1 Open the Open Dialog button's Click event procedure, then maximize the Code window. The Filter property must be set before the Open dialog box is displayed. Enter the Filter property instruction shown in Figure 7-9.

enter this instruction

display text filenames

display all filenames

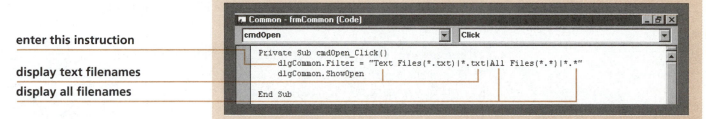

Figure 7-9: Instruction to set the Filter property entered in the Code window

> **HELP?** On most keyboards, the pipe symbol (|) is on the same key as the backslash (\).

2 Close the Code window, then **save** and **run** the application.

3 Click the **Open Dialog** button. The Tut07 folder on your Student Disk should be open. Notice that Visual Basic uses the first filter listed in the Filter property as the default filter in the Files of type list box; in this case the *.txt filter will display only the text files contained in the current folder.

If the user wants to view all of the files in the Tut07 folder, he or she can simply click the Files of type list arrow, then select the All Files(*.*) entry in the list. Display all of the files in the current folder.

4 Click the **Files of type** list arrow.

5 Click **All Files(*.*)** in the list. The names of all the files contained in the Tut07 folder appear in the File name list box.

6 Click a filename in the list. The file's name appears in the File name text box. When the user either selects a file from the File name list box, or enters a name in the File name text box, the file's name is stored in the Common Dialog control's FileName property.

7 Click the **Open** button in the dialog box.

The dialog box closes, but the file does not open. This is because the Open Dialog button's Click event contains only the code to create the Open dialog box; it does not include the code to actually open a file. You will learn how to use the Open dialog box to open a file in Lesson B.

See what happens when you click the Open Dialog button again.

8 Click the **Open Dialog** button. Notice that the File name text box contains the name of the file that you selected earlier. In Windows applications, the File name text box is typically empty when the Open dialog box appears. You can remove the filename from the File name text box by setting the Common Dialog control's FileName property to the zero-length (empty) string.

9 Click the **Cancel** button to close the Open dialog box, then click the **Exit** button to end the application. Visual Basic returns to the design screen.

The FileName Property

The **FileName property** stores the name of the file that appears in the File name text box. To remove the contents of the File name text box, you simply need to assign a zero-length string ("") to the Common Dialog control's FileName property before displaying the Open dialog box. Assigning a zero-length string to the FileName property will clear the contents of the File name text box.

To complete the Open Dialog button's Click event procedure:

1 Open the Open Dialog button's Click event procedure. Maximize the Code window, then enter the additional line of code shown in Figure 7-10.

enter this instruction

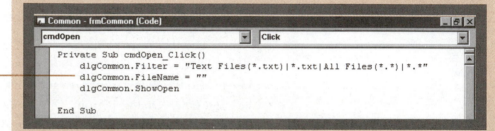

```
Common - frmCommon (Code)
cmdOpen                                          Click
Private Sub cmdOpen_Click()
    dlgCommon.Filter = "Text Files(*.txt)|*.txt|All Files(*.*)|*.*"
    dlgCommon.FileName = ""
    dlgCommon.ShowOpen

End Sub
```

Figure 7-10: Instruction to set the FileName property entered in the Code window

2 Close the Code window, then **save** and **run** the application.

3 Click the **Open Dialog** button.

Now display the names of all the files in the Tut07 folder on your Student Disk.

4 Click the **Files of type** list arrow, then click **All Files(*.*)** in the list.

5 Select a filename, then click the **Open** button. The dialog box closes.

Now see what happens when you click the Open Dialog button again.

6 Click the **Open Dialog** button. Note the File name text box is empty.

7 Click the **Cancel** button to close the Open dialog box, then click the **Exit** button to end the application. Visual Basic returns to the design screen.

Now code the Save As command button to display a standard Save As dialog box.

Displaying a Save As Dialog Box

The Save As command button should display a standard Save As dialog box. Observe what a standard Save As dialog box looks like.

To view a standard Save As dialog box, then begin coding the Save As command button:

1 Click **File** on the menu bar, then click **Save Project As**. If necessary, open the Tut07 folder on your Student Disk. See Figure 7-11.

GUI
Design Tips

Open Dialog Box Guidelines

- The Files of type list box should contain the descriptions and filters that control the display of the filenames in the File name list box.

- The File name text box should be empty when the Open dialog box appears.

current folder

File name list box

current file's name

filter

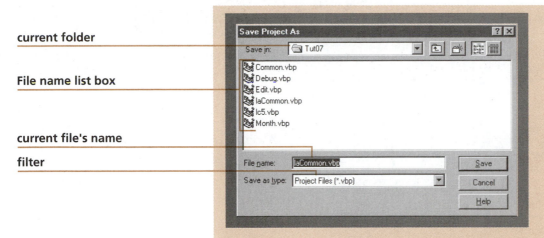

Figure 7-11: Visual Basic's Save Project As dialog box

The dialog box shows that the name of the current folder is Tut07; it also displays a list of files in the File name list box. The filenames listed in the File name list box depend on the entry in the Save as type list box. In the dialog box shown in Figure 7-11, the Save as type list box displays Project Files (*.vbp), which tells Windows to save the file as a project file with a .vbp extension on the filename. Notice that a standard Save As dialog box contains the name of the current file in the File name text box.

2   Click the **Save as type** list arrow, then click **All Files(*.*)** in the list. The File name list box now displays all of the files contained in the current folder.

3   Click the **Cancel** button to close the Save Project As dialog box.

Now use the ShowSave method to code the Save As Dialog command button in the frmCommon form. In this example, you will use the Common Dialog control's Filter property to display only files that end in .txt.

4   Open the Save As Dialog button's Click event procedure. Enter the code shown in Figure 7-12.

enter these two instructions

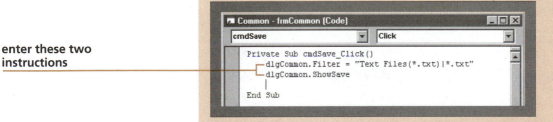

Figure 7-12: Save As command button's Click event procedure

5   Close the Code window, then **save** and **run** the application.

6   Click the **Save As Dialog** button. See Figure 7-13.

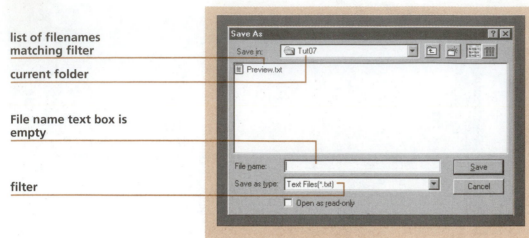

list of filenames matching filter

current folder

File name text box is empty

filter

Figure 7-13: Save As dialog box created by the Common Dialog control's ShowSave method

The Save As dialog box shows that the name of the current folder is Tut07. The File name list box shows a list of filenames matching the filter specified in the Save as type list box. The File name text box is empty.

7 Type **example** in the File name text box.

8 Click the **Save** button. The filename, example, is recorded in the Common Dialog control's FileName property. (Remember, you have not coded the button to actually save the file. At this point, the dialog box merely treats the file as though it has been saved.)

Observe what happens when you click the Save As Dialog button again.

9 Click the **Save As Dialog** button. Notice that the name of the saved file, example.txt, appears in the File name text box when the Save As dialog box appears. Also notice that the Save As dialog box automatically appends the .txt extension to the end of the filename when the file is saved.

10 Click the **Cancel** button in the dialog box, then click the **Exit** button to end the application. Visual Basic returns to the design screen.

GUI
Design Tips

Save As Dialog Box Guidelines

• The Save as type list box should contain the descriptions and filters that control the display of the filenames in the File name list box.

• If the current file is saved, its name should appear in the File name text box when the Save As dialog box appears.

In the next example, you will use the ShowPrinter method to display a standard Print dialog box.

Displaying a Print Dialog Box

The Print Dialog command button should display a standard Print dialog box. In Windows applications, the Print dialog box allows the user to select the printer, as well as the print range, number of copies, paper orientation (portrait or landscape), and so on.

To begin coding the Print Dialog command button:

1 Open the Print Dialog button's Click event procedure.

The method for displaying the Print dialog box is ShowPrinter.

2 Press the **Tab** key, then type **dlgcommon.showprinter** and press the **Enter** key.

3 Close the Code window, then **save** and **run** the application. Click the **Print Dialog** button. See Figure 7-14.

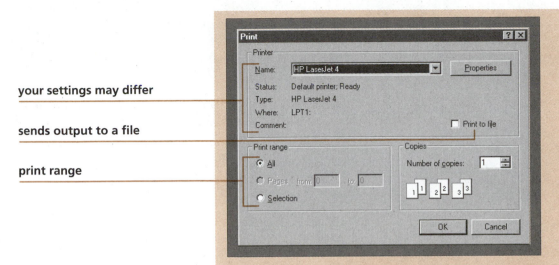

Figure 7-14: Print dialog box created by the Common Dialog control's ShowPrinter method

Notice that the Print dialog box contains options that allow you to select the print range (All, Pages, and Selection), as well as the number of copies to print. You can also choose to print to a file rather than to the printer.

4 Click the **Properties** button. The Properties dialog box appears and displays the option tabs for your printer. On your own, click each of these tabs to view their contents, then click the **Cancel** button twice to return to the application.

5 Click the **Exit** button to end the application. Visual Basic returns to the design screen.

Each of the dialog boxes discussed in this lesson has a Flags property that is used to either return or set the options for the dialog box. For example, in the next section, you will use the Flags property both to disable the Selection option button and to hide the Print to file check box in the Print dialog box. (Refer to Figure 7-14.) When you disable the Selection option button, you prevent the user from printing the selected text in the document. When you hide the Print to file check box, you prevent the user from printing to a file.

The Flags Property

The Common Dialog control's **Flags property** is used to either return or set the options for the dialog box. Each of the different dialog boxes has its own settings for the Flags property. View the Flags property settings for the Print dialog box.

To view the information on the Flags property settings:

1 Click the **dlgCommon** control, then click **Flags** in the Properties list.

2 If you have access to the MSDN Library, then press the **F1** key. The Flags Property (All Common Dialogs) screen appears. Click **Flags Property (Print Dialog)**. The Flags Property (Print Dialog) Help screen appears.

Notice that the syntax to set the Flags property is *object*.**Flags** [= *value*], where *object* is the Common Dialog control, and *value* is one of the constants or values shown in the Help screen's Settings table. A portion of the Settings table is shown in Figure 7-15.

Constant	Value	Description
cdlPDAllPages	&H0	Returns or sets the state of the All Pages <u>option button</u>.
cdlPDCollate	&H10	Returns or sets the state of the Collate <u>check box</u>.
cdlPDDisablePrintToFile	&H80000	Disables the Print To File check box.
cdlPDHelpButton	&H800	Causes the dialog box to display the Help button.
cdlPDHidePrintToFile	&H100000	Hides the Print To File check box.
cdlPDNoPageNums	&H8	Disables the Pages option button and the associated edit control.
cdlPDNoSelection	&H4	Disables the Selection option button.
cdlPDNoWarning	&H80	Prevents a warning message from being displayed when there is no default printer.
cdlPDPageNums	&H2	Returns or sets the state of the Pages option button.
cdlPDPrintSetup	&H40	Causes the system to display the Print Setup dialog box rather than the Print dialog box.
cdlPDPrintToFile	&H20	Returns or sets the state of the Print To File check box.

hides the Print to file check box

disables the Selection option button

Figure 7-15: Flags Property (Print Dialog) Settings table

tip

You can also use the Or operator, rather than the + operator, to set more than one flag for a dialog box. For example, you can use the `dlgCommon.Flags= cdlPDNoSelection Or cdlPDHidePrintToFile` statement to set the Flags property.

Notice that each of the constants listed in the Settings table begins with "cdl"; the cdl stands for Common Dialog control. According to the table, you disable the Selection option button, which will prevent the user from printing the selected text in a document, by setting the Flags property to the constant `cdlPDNoSelection`. You hide the Print to file check box by setting the Flags property to `cdlPDHidePrintToFile`; hiding the Print to file check box prevents the user from printing to a file. To set more than one flag for a dialog box, you simply add the constants together, then assign the sum to the Flags property. In other words, to display the Print dialog box with the Selection option button disabled and the Print to file check box hidden, you would use the instruction `dlgCommon.Flags = cdlPDNoSelection + cdlPDHidePrintToFile`.

To modify the code in the Print Dialog button:

1   Close the MSDN Library window, then open the Print Dialog button's Click event procedure. The Flags property must be set before you display the Print dialog box.

2   Maximize the Code window, then add the instruction to set the Flags property, as shown in Figure 7-16.

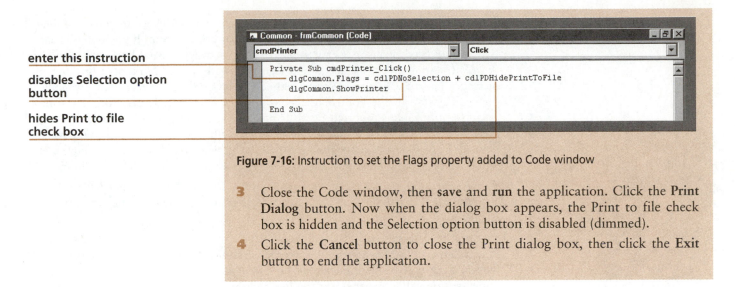

enter this instruction

disables Selection option
button

hides Print to file
check box

Figure 7-16: Instruction to set the Flags property added to Code window

3 Close the Code window, then **save** and **run** the application. Click the **Print Dialog** button. Now when the dialog box appears, the Print to file check box is hidden and the Selection option button is disabled (dimmed).

4 Click the **Cancel** button to close the Print dialog box, then click the **Exit** button to end the application.

In some applications, you may want to allow the user to select the name, type, and size of the font used to display the text in the document; you can use the Font dialog box to do so.

Displaying a Font Dialog Box

The Font dialog box created by the Common Dialog control allows the user to select from a list of fonts, styles, and sizes. You will use the Font dialog box to control the name, style, and size of the font used to display the text in the txtEdit text box on the current form. Most of the code for the Font Dialog button is already entered in its Click event procedure.

To view the code in the Font Dialog command button:

1 Open the Font Dialog command button's Click event procedure. See Figure 7-17.

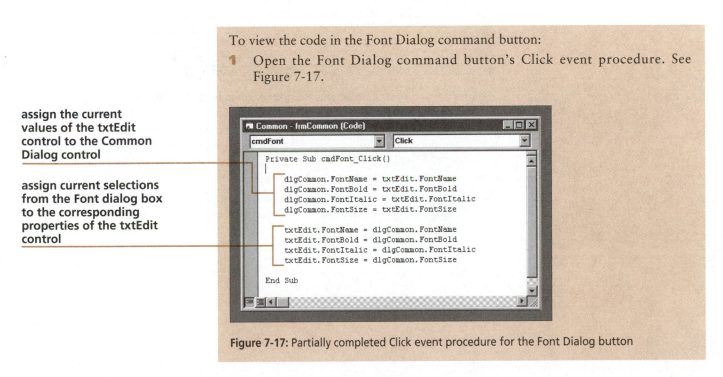

assign the current
values of the txtEdit
control to the Common
Dialog control

assign current selections
from the Font dialog box
to the corresponding
properties of the txtEdit
control

Figure 7-17: Partially completed Click event procedure for the Font Dialog button

Before you can display the Font dialog box, you must set its Flags property to either `cdlCFScreenFonts`, `cdlCFPrinterFonts`, or `cdlCFBoth`. If you don't set the Font dialog box's Flags property to one of these settings, Visual Basic will display the "There are no fonts installed." message, followed by the "No fonts exist." error message. The `cdlCFScreenFonts` setting displays only the screen fonts available on your system in the Font dialog box, and the `cdlCFPrinterFonts` setting displays only fonts supported by your printer. The `cdlCFBoth` setting displays both the available screen and printer fonts. In this example, because you want the user to be able to change the font used in the text box on the screen only, you will have the Font dialog box display only your system's available screen fonts.

2   If necessary, position the insertion point below the P in the Private Sub statement. Press the **Tab** key, then type **dlgcommon.flags = cdlcfscreenfonts**.

The four instructions immediately below the instruction that you just entered assign the current value of the txtEdit control's FontName, FontBold, FontItalic, and FontSize properties to the Common Dialog control. By doing so, these values will be selected in the Font dialog box when the dialog box first appears; this will allow the user to identify how the text is displayed currently.

Now use the ShowFont method to display the Font dialog box.

3   Enter the ShowFont method as shown in Figure 7-18.

enter this instruction

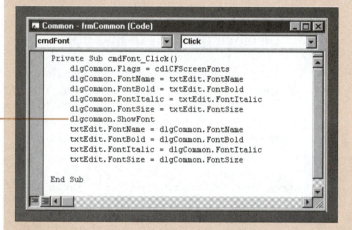

```
Common - frmCommon (Code)
cmdFont                          Click

Private Sub cmdFont_Click()
    dlgCommon.Flags = cdlCFScreenFonts
    dlgCommon.FontName = txtEdit.FontName
    dlgCommon.FontBold = txtEdit.FontBold
    dlgCommon.FontItalic = txtEdit.FontItalic
    dlgCommon.FontSize = txtEdit.FontSize
    dlgcommon.ShowFont
    txtEdit.FontName = dlgCommon.FontName
    txtEdit.FontBold = dlgCommon.FontBold
    txtEdit.FontItalic = dlgCommon.FontItalic
    txtEdit.FontSize = dlgCommon.FontSize

End Sub
```

Figure 7-18: ShowFont method entered in Font Dialog button's Click event

The four instructions below the ShowFont instruction assign the current selections from the Font dialog box to the corresponding properties of the txtEdit control; this will display the txtEdit control's text using the font name, style, and size chosen by the user.

4   Close the Code window, then **save** and **run** the application. Click the **Font Dialog** button. A standard Font dialog box appears as shown in Figure 7-19.

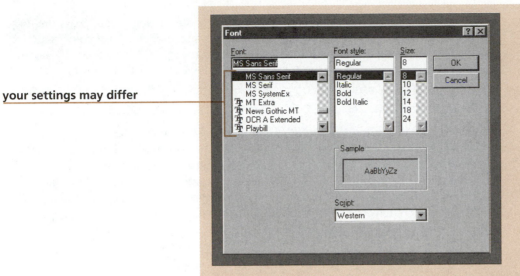

Figure 7-19: Font dialog box created by the Common Dialog control's ShowFont method

your settings may differ

HELP? Your listing of Font names, styles, and sizes may be different from those shown in Figure 7-19, depending on the screen fonts available on your system.

5   On your own, select a different font name, style, and size. Click the **OK** button to close the Font dialog box. The text in the text box displays in the new font.

6   Click the **Exit** button to end the application. Visual Basic returns to the design screen.

As mentioned in Tutorial 2, color is very subjective; what is a pleasing color to you may not be to someone else. In many applications, you may want to allow the user to select the colors used in the interface. You can use a standard Color dialog box to do so.

Displaying a Color Dialog Box

The Color Dialog button in the current form will use the Color dialog box created by the Common Dialog control to allow the user to change the color of the text displayed in the txtEdit text box. The color of the text displayed in a text box is controlled by the text box's ForeColor property.

To code the Color Dialog button:

1   Open the Color Dialog button's Click event procedure.

Before displaying the Color dialog box, you must initialize the dialog box by setting its Flags property to the constant `cdlCCRGBInit`. This setting causes the Color dialog box to select the black color square when the dialog box appears the first time. If the user selects another color square from the Color dialog box, the `cdlCCRGBInit` setting will select the corresponding color square when the Color dialog box appears again.

2   Press the Tab key, then type **dlgcommon.flags = cdlccrgbinit** and press the **Enter** key.

Rather than selecting the black square when the Color dialog box appears the first time, you will have the Color dialog box select the square whose color matches the current setting of the text box's ForeColor property. You can do so by assigning the ForeColor property to the Common Dialog control's Color property.

3   Type **dlgcommon.color=txtedit.forecolor** and press the **Enter** key.

Now use the ShowColor method to display the Color Dialog box.

4   Type **dlgcommon.showcolor** and press the **Enter** key.

All that remains is to assign the color that the user selected from the Color dialog box to the ForeColor property of the txtEdit control. When the user selects a color square from the Color dialog box, the color is stored in the Common Dialog control's Color property. Therefore, in this example, you simply need to assign the dlgCommon control's Color property to the txtEdit control's ForeColor property.

5   Type **txtedit.forecolor = dlgcommon.color** and press the **Enter** key.

6   Compare your code with the code shown in Figure 7-20, and make any needed corrections before continuing.

Figure 7-20: Completed Click event procedure for the Color Dialog button

7   Close the Code window. Use the Properties window to change the txtEdit control's **ForeColor** property to **red**, then **save** and **run** the application. Click the **Color Dialog** button. The Color dialog box appears with the red square selected in the color palette, as shown in Figure 7-21.

red square is selected

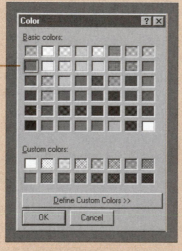

Figure 7-21: Color dialog box created by the Common Dialog control's ShowColor method

8 Select a different color from the Color dialog box, then click the **OK** button. The text in the txtEdit control appears in the new color.

9 On your own, experiment with the Color dialog box. Try using the Define Custom Colors button to create a personalized color. When you are finished experimenting with the Color dialog box, click the **Exit** button to end the application. Visual Basic returns to the design screen.

You have now completed Lesson A. You can either take a break or complete the end-of-lesson questions and exercises. In Lessons B and C, you will finish coding the Text Editor application from Tutorial 6, and learn about error trapping.

S U M M A R Y

To display a standard set of dialog boxes for operations such as opening, saving, and printing files, as well as selecting colors and fonts:

■ Use the Common Dialog control.

■ The ShowOpen method displays a standard Open dialog box. The ShowSave method displays a standard Save As dialog box. The ShowPrinter method displays a standard Print dialog box. The ShowFont method displays a standard Font dialog box. The ShowColor method displays a standard Color dialog box.

To specify both a description and filter for the Open and Save As dialog boxes:

■ Set the Common Dialog control's Filter property. The syntax is *object*.**Filter** = d*escription1\filter1\description2\filter2...*, where both *description* and *filter* are string expressions that specify the type of files to display. The *filter* can contain the asterisk (*) character.

■ Use the pipe (|) symbol to separate a *description* from its corresponding *filter*, and to separate one file type's *description* and *filter* from the next file type's *description* and *filter*. Don't include spaces before or after the pipe symbol. If a file type has more than one filename extension, separate the extensions with a semicolon (;).

To set or return the name of the file in the Common Dialog control's File name text box:

■ Use the Common Dialog control's FileName property.

To set or return the options for a Common Dialog control:

■ Set the Common Dialog control's Flags property. Each of the different dialog boxes has its own settings for the Flags property.

QUESTIONS

1. The _____ control provides a standard set of dialog boxes for operations such as opening, saving, and printing files, as well as selecting colors and fonts.
   a. Box Dialog
   b. Common
   c. Common Dialog
   d. Dialog box
   e. Standard Dialog

2. You use the _____ method to display a standard Open dialog box.
   a. Open
   b. OpenDialog
   c. OpenShowDialog
   d. ShowDialog
   e. ShowOpen

3. You use the _____ method to display a standard Print dialog box.
   a. OpenPrint
   b. PrintDialog
   c. PrintShowDialog
   d. ShowPrint
   e. ShowPrinter

4. The ShowSave method displays a standard _____ dialog box.
   a. Open
   b. Save
   c. Save As
   d. None of the above

5. You use the _____ method to display a standard Color dialog box.
   a. Color
   b. ColorDialog
   c. ColorOpen
   d. ShowColor
   e. ShowColorDialog

6. You use the _____ method to display a standard Font dialog box.
   a. Font
   b. FontDialog
   c. FontOpen
   d. ShowFont
   e. ShowFontDialog

7. The _____ property stores a string that represents both the description and the filter for the files displayed in the File name list box when either the Open or the Save As dialog box appears.
   a. Description
   b. Filename
   c. Filter
   d. Text

8. Which of the following descriptions and filters tells Windows to display only file-names ending in .pic?
   a. `"Picture Files(*.pic)|*.pic"`
   b. `"Picture Files(*.pic"|"*.pic"`
   c. `"Picture Files(*.pic);*.pic"`
   d. `"Picture Files|*.pic|(*.pic)"`

9. Which of the following descriptions and filters tells Windows to display only project filenames—those ending in either .vbp, .mak, or .vbg?
   a. `"Project Files(*.vbp;*.mak;*.vbg)|*.vbp|*.mak|*.vbg"`
   b. `"Project Files(*.vbp;*.mak;*.vbg)|*.vbp;*.mak;*.vbg"`
   c. `"Project Files(*.vbp|*.mak|*.vbg)|*.vbp;*.mak;*.vbg"`
   d. `"Project Files|*.vbp;*.mak;*.vbg|*.vbp;*.mak;*.vbg"`

10. When the user selects a filename from an Open dialog box, the filename is stored in the Common Dialog control's _____ property.
    a. Description
    b. File
    c. FileName
    d. Filter

11. Each of the dialog boxes created by the Common Dialog control has a(n) _____ property that is used to either return or set the options for the dialog box.
    a. Filter
    b. Flag
    c. Flags
    d. Option
    e. Options

12. Before you can display the Font dialog box, you must set the Common Dialog control's _____ property to either cdlCFScreenFonts, cdlCFPrinterFonts, or cdlCFBoth.
    a. Filter
    b. Flag
    c. Flags
    d. Option
    e. Options

E X E R C I S E S

1. a. If you have access to the MSDN Library, then view the Help screen on the Flags Property (Color Dialog). Explain the purpose of the following two settings: `cdlCCFullOpen` and `cdlCCPreventFullOpen`.
   b. Create an application that contains a Common Dialog control and two command buttons. Change the caption for one of the command buttons to Full; change the other's caption to Partial. Code the Full button so that it sets the Common Dialog control's Flags property to `cdlCCFullOpen` before displaying the Color dialog box. Code the Partial button so that it sets the Common Dialog control's Flags property to `cdlCCPreventFullOpen` before displaying the Color dialog box.
   c. Run, but don't save, the application. Observe the difference between the two Flags property settings by clicking each of the command buttons.
   d. Stop the application, then print the code. You do not need to save this application.

2. a. If you have access to the MSDN Library, then view the Help screen on the Flags Property (Open, Save As Dialogs). Explain the purpose of each of the following two settings: `cdlOFNCreatePrompt` and `cdlOFNOverwritePrompt`.
   b. Create an application that contains a Common Dialog control and two command buttons. Change the caption of one of the command buttons to Open. Change the other's caption to Save. Code the Open button so that it sets the Common Dialog control's Filter property to display all of the files in the current folder, and sets the control's Flags property to `cdlOFNCreatePrompt` before displaying the Open

dialog box. Code the Save button so that it sets the Common Dialog control's Filter property to display all of the files in the current folder, and sets the control's Flags property to `cdlOFNOverwritePrompt` before displaying the Save As dialog box.

c. Run, but don't save, the application. Click the Open command button. When the Open dialog box appears, type X in the File name box, then click the Open button. On a piece of paper, write down the message that appears in the message box, then click the No button to remove the message box, and then click the Cancel button to remove the Open dialog box.

d. Click the Save command button. When the Save As dialog box appears, click any filename in the File name list box, then click the Save button. On a piece of paper, write down the message that appears in the message box, then click the No button to remove the message box, and then click the Cancel button to remove the Save As dialog box.

e. Stop the application, then print the code. You do not need to save this application.

3. a. If you have access to the MSDN Library, then view the Help screen on the Flags Property (Font Dialog). Explain the purpose of each of the following three settings: `cdlCFEffects`, `cdlCFTTOnly`, and `cdlCFWYSIWYG`.

b. Create an application that contains a Common Dialog control and three command buttons. Change the caption of one of the command buttons to Effects. Change the second command button's caption to True Type. Change the third command button's caption to WYSIWYG. Code the Effects button so that it sets the Common Dialog control's Flags property to `cdlCFBoth` + `cdlCFEffects` before displaying the Font dialog box. Code the True Type button so that it sets the Common Dialog control's Flags property to `cdlCFBoth` + `cdlCFTTOnly` before displaying the Font dialog box. Code the WYSIWYG button so that it sets the Common Dialog control's Flags property to `cdlCFBoth` + `cdlCFWYSIWYG` before displaying the Font dialog box.

c. Run, but don't save, the application. Click the Effects command button to see the result of setting the Flags property to `cdlCFBoth` + `cdlCFEffects`. Click the Cancel button to remove the Font dialog box.

d. Click the True Type button to see the result of setting the Flags property to `cdlCFBoth` + `cdlCFTTOnly`. Click the Cancel button to remove the Font dialog box.

e. Click the WYSIWYG button to see the result of setting the Flags property to `cdlCFBoth` + `cdlCFWYSIWYG`. Click the Cancel button to remove the Font dialog box.

f. Stop the application, then print the code. You do not need to save this application.

4. a. If you have access to the MSDN Library, then view the Help screen on the Flags Property (Print Dialog). Explain the purpose of each of the following two settings: `cdlPDDisablePrintToFile` and `cdlPDNoPageNums`.

b. Create an application that contains a Common Dialog control and one command button. Change the caption of the command button to Print. Code the Print button so that it sets the Common Dialog control's Flags property to `cdlPDDisablePrintToFile` + `cdlPDNoSelection` + `cdlPDNoPageNums`.

c. Run, but don't save, the application. Click the Print button to see the result of setting the Flags property to `cdlPDDisablePrintToFile` + `cdlPDNoSelection` + `cdlPDNoPageNums`. Click the Cancel button to remove the Print dialog box.

d. Stop the application, then print the code. You do not need to save this application.

In this lesson you will learn how to:
- Save a file using the Save As dialog box
- Write a string of characters to a sequential file using the Print # statement
- Set the Common Dialog control's CancelError property
- Include an error handling routine in code
- Code the File menu's New command

Coding the Text Editor's File Menu

Opening the Text Editor Application

In order to complete the Text Editor application that you created in Tutorial 6, you still need to code the File menu's New, Open, Save, Save As, and Print commands. Begin by opening the Text Editor application.

To open the Text Editor application, then add a Common Dialog control to the form:

1 Start Visual Basic, if necessary, and open the **Edit** (Edit.vbp) project, which is located in the Tut07 folder on your Student Disk.

2 Save the form and the project as **lbEdit**, then click the **form** to select it. See Figure 7-22.

txtEdit

frmEdit

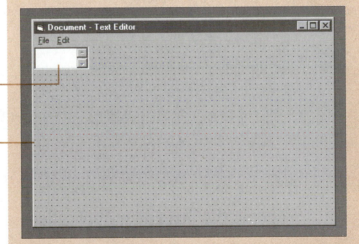

Figure 7-22: Text Editor application's user interface

The application's File menu will use the Common Dialog control, which you learned about in Lesson A, to display the Open, Print, and Save As dialog boxes. Add the Common Dialog control to the interface.

> **3** Click **Project** on the menu bar, then click **Components** to open the Components dialog box. If necessary, click the **Controls** tab to select it. Scroll the list of controls, if necessary, then click the **Microsoft Common Dialog Control 6.0** check box to select it. Be sure a check mark appears in the check box. Click the **OK** button to close the Components dialog box. The CommonDialog tool appears in the toolbox.
>
> **4** Double-click the **CommonDialog tool** in the toolbox. The Common Dialog control, which appears as an icon, displays in the center of the form.
>
> **5** Set the Common Dialog control's Name property to **dlgEdit**.

You can now continue coding the Text Editor application. The TOE chart for the application is shown in Figure 7-23.

Task	Object	Event
Accept and display text entered by the user	txtEdit	None
Open a new document	mnuFileNew	Click
Open an existing document	mnuFileOpen	Click
Save the document using its current name	mnuFileSave	Click
Save the document using a new name	mnuFileSaveAs	Click
Print the document	mnuFilePrint	Click
Exit the application	mnuFileExit	Click
Enable/disable the Cut, Copy, and Paste commands	mnuEdit	Click
Remove selected text from the txtEdit control and place it on the clipboard	mnuEditCut	Click
Copy the text selected in the txtEdit control to the clipboard	mnuEditCopy	Click
Paste the text from the clipboard into the txtEdit control	mnuEditPaste	Click
1. Ask the user for the search string 2. Search the txtEdit control for the first occurrence of the search string	mnuEditFind	Click
Search for subsequent occurrences of the search string	mnuEditFindNext	Click

Figure 7-23: TOE chart for the Text Editor application

Coding the Text Editor Application

The Text Editor application will use two form-level variables. One of the variables will keep track of whether the contents of the document—in this case, the contents of the txtEdit text box—has changed since the last time the document was saved. The other form-level variable will keep track of whether the user selected the Cancel button in the Save As dialog box; if the user selects the Cancel button in the Save As dialog box, the document will not be saved. If the current document is not saved after a change is made to it, then the File menu's Open and New commands, as well as the form's Unload event, will prompt the user to save the document before either a new or an existing document is displayed, or before the application ends.

You also could have declared the form-level variables as String variables, and then assigned, for example, the values "Y" and "N" or "T" and "F" to each. When a variable's values will either be Yes/No or True/False, programmers typically use a Boolean variable rather than a String variable to store those values. When you use a Boolean value, you don't need to place quotation marks around the value, and you don't need to worry about the case you use to type the value.

Both of the form-level variables used in this application will be declared as Boolean variables. As you learned in Tutorial 3, Boolean variables can contain only the Boolean values True and False. You will name one of the variables blnChange and the other blnCancelSave.

To declare the two form-level variables:

1   Open the form's General Declarations section. The `Option Explicit` statement and the `Dim strSearchFor as String` statement appear in the Code window. (Recall that you entered these instructions in Tutorial 6.)

2   Position the insertion point below the Dim statement, then type **dim blnChange as boolean, blnCancelSave as boolean** and press the **Enter** key.

When the Text Editor application is run, the form's Load event will initialize both the blnChange and blnCancelSave variables to False.

3   Open the form's Load event procedure. Press the **Tab** key. Type **blnchange = false** and press the **Enter** key, then type **blncancelsave = false** and press the **Enter** key.

If a change is subsequently made to the text box, the text box's Change event procedure will set the blnChange variable to True.

4   Open the txtEdit control's Change event. Press the **Tab** key, then type **blnchange = true** and press the **Enter** key.

5   Close the Code window, then click the **Save Project** button 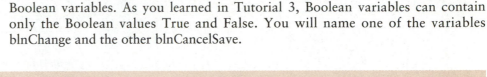 on the toolbar.

The first command you will code is the File menu's Save As command.

Coding the File Menu's Save As Command

As you learned in Tutorial 5, a text box's Change event occurs when either the user or the program code changes the contents of the control.

In Windows applications, the Save As command allows the user either to save a new file or to save an existing file under a new name. In this application, the Save As command will allow the user to save the document—in this case, the contents of the txtEdit control—in a sequential access file. The flowchart for the Save As command is shown in Figure 7-24.

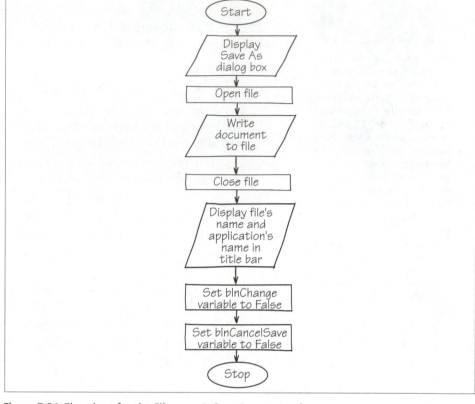

Figure 7-24: Flowchart for the File menu's Save As command

GUI
Design Tips

Save As Command

• In Windows applications, the Save As command allows the user either to save a new file or to save an existing file under a new name.

GUI
Design Tips

Title Bar Information

• When the current document has been saved, the document's name and the application's name appear in the application's title bar. If the current document has not been saved, then the type of document the application creates, along with the application's name, appears in the title bar.

Look briefly at the logic shown in the flowchart. The Save As command's Click event begins by displaying the Save As dialog box on the screen. When the user enters the name of the file to save, the file's name is stored in the Common Dialog control's FileName property. The file is then opened and the document (the text the user entered in the txtEdit control) is written to the file. The file is then closed. Before the procedure ends, the name of the saved file, followed by the name of the application (Text Editor), is displayed in the application's title bar. The blnChange variable is then set to False to indicate that the document has not been changed since the last time it was saved. The blnCancelSave variable is set to False to indicate that the user did not select the Cancel button in the Save As dialog box.

Some of the code for the Save As command has already been entered in its Click event procedure for you.

To view the code in the Save As command's Click event:

1 Click **File** on the frmEdit form's menu bar, then click **Save As**. Maximize the Code window. Notice that the mnuFileSaveAs control's Click event procedure contains the instructions to set the dlgEdit control's Flags and Filter properties.

The `dlgEdit.Flags = cdlOFNOverwritePrompt + cdlOFNPathMustExist` instruction sets the Flags property for the Save As dialog box. The `cdlOFN-OverwritePrompt` setting causes the Save As dialog box to generate a warning message if the user attempts to save a file using an existing name; the user will need to confirm whether he or she wants to overwrite the existing file. The `cdlOFNPathMustExist` setting causes the Save As dialog box to generate a warning message if the user enters a path that does not exist. (The **path** is a string expression that specifies the directory location for the file. The path may or may not include a drive letter specification.) The `dlgEdit.Filter = "Text Files(*.txt)|*.txt"` instruction specifies the description and filter for the files to be displayed in the dialog box's File name list box; in this case, only text files are to be displayed.

Now enter the instruction to display the Save As dialog box.

2 Position the insertion point below the instruction that sets the Filter property, then type **dlgedit.showsave** and press the **Enter** key.

When the user either enters the name of the file to save in the File name text box, or selects an existing name from the File name list box, the file's name is stored in the dlgEdit control's FileName property. Use the Open statement and the FileName property to open a sequential file for Output.

3 Type **open dlgedit.filename for output as #1** and press the **Enter** key.

According to the flowchart, the next step is to write the document (the contents of the txtEdit control) to the sequential file. For that you will need to learn about Visual Basic's Print # statement.

The Print # Statement

In Tutorial 6 you learned how to write records to a sequential file; recall that you use the Write # statement to do so. In the Text Editor application, however, you do not need to write any records to the file; rather, you need to write the contents of a text box, which is simply a string of characters. When writing a string of characters to a sequential file, you use the Print # statement, instead of the Write # statement. The syntax of the Print # statement is **Print #**_filenumber_, [_outputlist_], where _outputlist_ is one or more expressions.

To continue coding the Save As command, then test the Save As command:

1 The Code window for the mnuFileSaveAs control's Click event should be open. With the insertion point positioned below the Open statement, type **print #1, txtedit.text** and press the **Enter** key.

Next, use the Close statement to close the sequential file.

2 Type **close #1** and press the **Enter** key.

Now display the name of the saved file, along with the name of the application, in the form's title bar.

3 Type **frmedit.caption = dlgedit.filename & " - Text Editor"** and press the **Enter** key. (Be sure to enter a space before and after the hyphen.)

Next, set the blnChange variable to False to indicate that no change has occurred in the txtEdit text box since the file was saved. Also set the blnCancelSave variable to False to indicate that the user did not select the Cancel button in the Save As dialog box.

4 Type **blnchange = false** and press the **Enter** key, then type **blncancelsave = false** and press the **Enter** key.

5 Compare your code with the code shown in Figure 7-25.

```
TextEditor - frmEdit (Code)                                    _ □ ×
mnuFileSaveAs                  ▼   Click                        ▼
Private Sub mnuFileSaveAs_Click()
    dlgEdit.Flags = cdlOFNOverwritePrompt + cdlOFNPathMustExist
    dlgEdit.Filter = "Text Files(*.txt)|*.txt"
    dlgEdit.ShowSave
    Open dlgEdit.FileName For Output As #1
    Print #1, txtEdit.Text
    Close #1
    frmEdit.Caption = dlgEdit.FileName & " - Text Editor"
    blnChange = False
    blnCancelSave = False

End Sub
```

Figure 7-25: Click event procedure for the File menu's Save As command

6 Close the Code window, then **save** and **run** the application.

Now test the Save As command.

7 Click **File**, then click **Save As**. If necessary, open the Tut07 folder on your Student Disk. Type **Test** in the File name box, then click the **Save** button. The application saves the Test file as Test.txt in the Tut07 folder on your Student Disk. The form's title bar now shows the path and name of the saved file (either A:\Tut07\Test.txt or B:\Tut07\Test.txt), followed by the name of the application (Text Editor).

Observe the warning message displayed by the `cdlOFNOverwritePrompt` setting in the Flags property.

8 Click **File**, then click **Save As**. Notice that the name of the current file, Test.txt, appears in the File name text box. Click the **Save** button. When the warning message appears asking if you want to replace the existing Test.txt file, click the **No** button.

Observe what happens if the user enters an incorrect path. Recall that the `cdlOFNPathMustExist` setting will display an appropriate message.

9 Type one of the following in the File name text box, depending on the location of your Student Disk.

  a:\tut\test.txt

  b:\tut\test.txt

10 Click the **Save** button. A warning message appears informing you that the path does not exist. Click the **OK** button to remove the warning message.

When you click the Cancel button in the next step, you will notice that the application incorrectly saves the document under its current name. (You can tell that the file is being saved because the light on the drive that contains your Student Disk will flicker momentarily, and you will hear the drive spinning.)

11 The Save As dialog box should still be open. Click the **Cancel** button to remove the dialog box.

  HELP? If the Save As dialog box is not open, click File on the frmEdit form's menu bar, then click Save As.

Although the application should cancel the save, it saves the document under its current name instead. You will correct this problem in the next section.

12 Click **File**, then click **Exit** to end the application. Visual Basic returns to the design screen.

When the user clicks the Cancel button in the Save As dialog box, the application should cancel the save and return the user to the current document. In order to determine if the Cancel button was selected, you need to set the Common Dialog control's CancelError property to True.

Setting the CancelError Property

When the user selects the Cancel button in the Save As dialog box, the save should be canceled and the user should be returned to the current document. You can determine if a Common Dialog control's Cancel button was selected during run-time by telling Visual Basic to treat that selection as an error; you do so by setting the Common Dialog control's CancelError property to True. The **CancelError property**, which can be set to either True or False, specifies whether choosing the Cancel button is treated as an error. The default value of this property is False, which means that no error occurs when the user selects the Cancel button; setting the property to True tells Visual Basic to treat the selection as an error. The CancelError property is usually set at the beginning of the procedure.

To set the Common Dialog control's CancelError property:

1   Click **File** on the frmEdit form's menu bar, then click **Save As**. The mnuFileSaveAs control's Click event procedure appears. Maximize the Code window, then enter the instruction to set the CancelError property as shown in Figure 7-26. Also enter the documentation on that line.

enter this instruction
and documentation

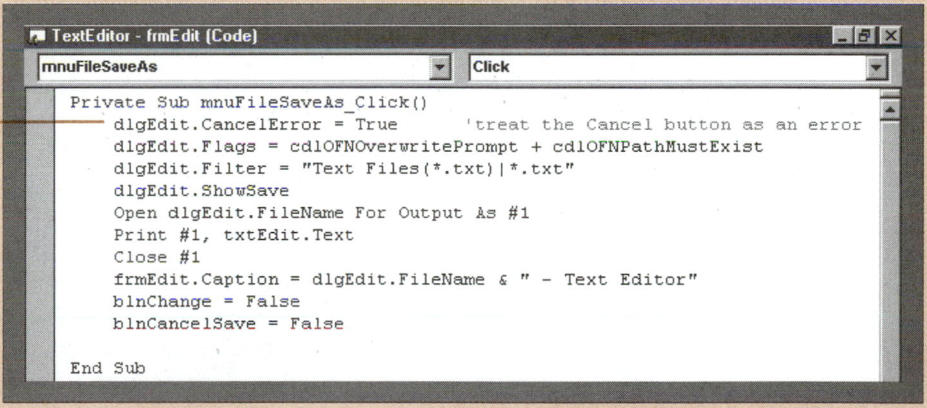

```
TextEditor - frmEdit (Code)
mnuFileSaveAs                                Click

Private Sub mnuFileSaveAs_Click()
    dlgEdit.CancelError = True        'treat the Cancel button as an error
    dlgEdit.Flags = cdlOFNOverwritePrompt + cdlOFNPathMustExist
    dlgEdit.Filter = "Text Files(*.txt)|*.txt"
    dlgEdit.ShowSave
    Open dlgEdit.FileName For Output As #1
    Print #1, txtEdit.Text
    Close #1
    frmEdit.Caption = dlgEdit.FileName & " - Text Editor"
    blnChange = False
    blnCancelSave = False

End Sub
```

Figure 7-26: Instruction to set the CancelError property entered in the Code window

After setting the CancelError property to True, which will generate an error when the user selects the Cancel button during run-time, you then need both to intercept the error and to instruct the application on how to handle the error. The process of intercepting and handling a run-time error is called **error trapping**. The set of instructions that tells the application how to handle the error is called the **error-handling routine**, or **error handler**. In the Text Editor application, the error handling routine will set the blnCancelSave variable to True and then return the user to the current document when an error occurs.

You use Visual Basic's On Error statement to include error trapping in your code.

The On Error Statement and the Error-Handling Routine

The **On Error statement** turns the error trapping process on. The syntax of the On Error statement is **On Error GoTo** *line*, where *line* is either a line label or a line number that identifies the position of the procedure's error handler—the set of instructions that tells the application how to handle the trapped errors. If *line* is 0 (zero), the On Error statement turns the error trapping process off.

For the proper error trapping to occur, the On Error statement must be processed before the error occurs. Therefore, most programmers place the On Error statement at the beginning of the procedure in which the errors they are trying to trap may occur. The On Error statement alerts Visual Basic to watch for any run-time errors in the code listed below the On Error statement. If an error occurs, the On Error statement sends program control to the error-handling routine to determine how to handle the error. How the error is handled depends on the type of error that occurred.

A procedure that includes error trapping will typically follow the structure shown in Figure 7-27.

Private Sub statement

    [Dim statements, etc.]

    On Error GoTo *line*

    [statements]

prevents error handler from being processed when no error has occurred ————— Exit Sub

must end with a colon

error handler ————— *line*:

    [error-handling instructions]

End Sub

Figure 7-27: Structure of a procedure that includes error trapping

Notice the `Exit Sub` statement, which is placed immediately above the error handler in the code. The `Exit Sub` statement does exactly what it implies: it exits the sub procedure immediately. The `Exit Sub` statement prevents the error-handling routine from being processed when no error has occurred. Also notice that *line* located immediately above the error-handling instructions has a colon at the end, but *line* used in the `On Error` statement does not.

In the Text Editor application, you will include the On Error statement in the Save As command's Click event procedure; this will alert Visual Basic to watch for any errors that occur in that procedure. Because the Save As command sets the Common Dialog control's CancelError property to True, Visual Basic will generate an error when the user selects the Cancel button in the Save As dialog box. The On Error statement will trap this error and will send program control to the error handler, which you will name SaveErrHandler. Before discussing the SaveErrHandler routine, enter the appropriate On Error statement in the mnuFileSaveAs control's Click event.

To enter the On Error statement in the mnuFileSaveAs control's Click event:
1   The mnuFileSaveAs control's Click event procedure should be open and maximized. Insert a blank line below the `Private Sub mnuFileSaveAs_Click()` instruction. In the blank line, type **on error goto SaveErrHandler** and press the **Tab** key, then type **'turn error trapping on**.

The error-handling routine, which is named SaveErrHandler, will set the form-level variable named blnCancelSave to True, then simply exit the mnuFileSaveAs Click event without opening the sequential file and writing any information to it. (The form-level blnCancelSave variable, you may recall, keeps track of whether the user selected the Cancel button in the Save As dialog box. The variable will be used by the File menu's New and Open commands, as well as by the form's Unload event.)

To complete the Save As command's Click event procedure:
1   Enter the error-handling routine shown in Figure 7-28. Be sure to enter the `Exit Sub` statement before the error-handling routine.

enter these three lines

```
TextEditor - frmEdit (Code)
mnuFileSaveAs                          Click

Private Sub mnuFileSaveAs_Click()
    On Error GoTo SaveErrHandler     'turn error trapping on
    dlgEdit.CancelError = True       'treat the Cancel button as an error
    dlgEdit.Flags = cdlOFNOverwritePrompt + cdlOFNPathMustExist
    dlgEdit.Filter = "Text Files(*.txt)|*.txt"
    dlgEdit.ShowSave
    Open dlgEdit.FileName For Output As #1
    Print #1, txtEdit.Text
    Close #1
    frmEdit.Caption = dlgEdit.FileName & " - Text Editor"
    blnChange = False
    blnCancelSave = False
    Exit Sub

SaveErrHandler:
    blnCancelSave = True             'save was canceled

End Sub
```

Figure 7-28: Error-handling routine entered in the Save As command's Click event

2   Compare your code with the code shown in Figure 7-28. Make any needed corrections before continuing.
3   Close the Code window, then **save** and **run** the application.
4   Click **File**, then click **Save As**. Click **Test.txt** in the File name list box, then click the **Cancel** button. The Cancel button generates an error that is trapped by the SaveErrHandler routine, which sets the blnCancelSave variable to True and exits the Click event without saving the document.
5   Click **File**, then click **Exit** to end the application. Visual Basic returns to the design screen.

The last procedure you will code in this lesson is the File menu's New command, which should remove the current document, if any, from the screen and from memory, then display a new document.

Coding the File Menu's New Command

In the Text Editor application, the New command on the File menu should remove the current document from both the screen and memory, then display a new document. If the current document has been changed since the last time it was saved, the application should prompt the user to save the current document before it is removed. The flowchart for the File menu's New command is shown in Figure 7-29.

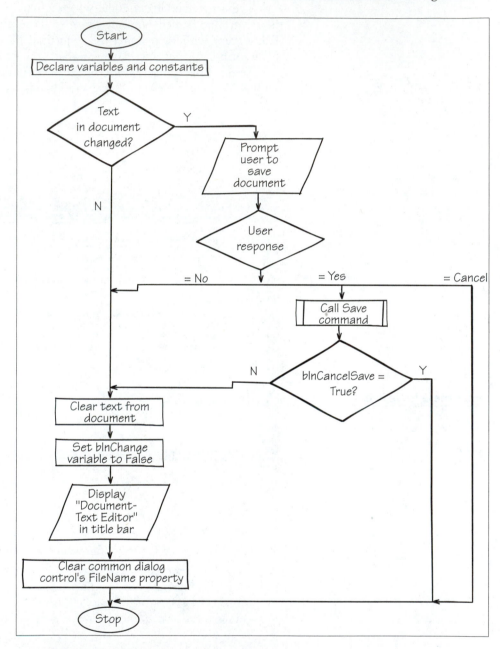

Figure 7-29: Flowchart for the File menu's New command

Briefly study the logic shown in the flowchart. The New command begins by determining if the text in the document was changed since the last time it was saved. If the document has not been changed since the last time it was saved, then a new document is displayed. If, on the other hand, the document has changed since the last time it was saved, the user is asked if he or she wants to save the document. At this point, the user can either choose to display a new document without saving the current document, choose to save the current document before a new document is displayed, or cancel the New command.

If the user chooses to cancel the New command, he or she is simply returned to the current document. If, on the other hand, the user chooses not to save the current file, then a new document is displayed. Lastly, if the user chooses to save the current document before a new document is displayed, then the New command calls the Save command's Click event (which you have not yet coded) to save the document. Notice in the flowchart that when the Save command's Click event procedure ends, the New command's Click event needs to determine if the blnCancelSave variable contains the Boolean value True. If it does, then the document was not saved and the New command should return the user to the current document rather than display a new document.

To begin coding the New command:

1   Click **File** on the frmEdit form's menu bar, then click **New**. Maximize the Code window. The mnuFileNew control's Click event procedure appears as shown in Figure 7-30.

```
TextEditor - frmEdit (Code)                                    _ 8 X

mnuFileNew              ▼        Click                              ▼

Private Sub mnuFileNew_Click()
    Const conBtns As Integer = vbYesNoCancel + vbExclamation _
                    + vbDefaultButton3 + vbApplicationModal
    Const conMsg As String = "Do you want to save the current document?"
    Dim intUserResponse As Integer
    If blnChange = True Then          'text box was changed since last save
        intUserResponse = MsgBox(conMsg, conBtns, "Editor")
        Select Case intUserResponse
            Case vbYes                'user wants to save current file

            Case vbNo                 'user does not want to save current file

            Case vbCancel             'user wants to cancel New command

        End Select
    End If
    txtEdit.Text = ""                 'clear text box
    blnChange = False                 'reset variable
    frmEdit.Caption = "Document - Text Editor"
    dlgEdit.FileName = ""

End Sub
```

Figure 7-30: Code entered in the New command's Click event procedure

tip
••••••••••••••••••
▶ In Windows applications, when the current document has not been saved, the type of document the application creates and the application's name typically appear in the title bar.

The New command's code begins by declaring two constants named conBtns and conMsg and an Integer variable named intUserResponse; the constants and the variable are used by the MsgBox function. As the constants indicate, the MsgBox function's dialog box will display the "Do you want to save the current document?" message, as well as Yes, No, and Cancel buttons.

After declaring and initializing the constants and the variable, a selection structure then compares the contents of the blnChange variable to the Boolean value True. If the blnChange variable does not contain the True value, then no change was made to the document since the last time it was saved; when that is the case, the

tip

• • • • • • • • • • • • • •

Keep in mind that you clear
a text box by assigning a
zero-length string to it.
Assigning a zero-length
string to the text box will
cause the Change event to
occur. Because simply displaying a new document
should not invoke the
prompt to save the file, you
need to set the blnChange
variable to False to indicate
that the document does
not need to be saved at
this point.

New command's Click event clears the contents of the txtEdit control, sets the blnChange variable to False, assigns the string "Document - Text Editor" to the form's Caption property, and sets the Common Dialog control's FileName property to a zero-length (empty) string before ending the procedure.

If, on the other hand, the blnChange variable contains the Boolean value True, then a change was made to the document since the last time it was saved. At this point the New command uses the MsgBox function to display a message asking the user if he or she wants to save the current document. The user can select either the Yes, No, or Cancel button in response to the message. A Case selection structure is used to determine the user's response and take the appropriate action. You will need to complete what the appropriate action is for each of the three responses. Begin with the Cancel button response.

If the user clicks the Cancel button in response to the "Do you want to save the current document?" message, it means that he or she has decided not to open a new document; rather, the user wants to continue working in the current document. In that case, the New command's Click event procedure should simply end. You can use Visual Basic's `Exit Sub` statement to end the procedure when the user selects the Cancel button.

To continue coding the New command's Click event procedure, then save and run the application:

1 Click in the blank line below the `Case vbCancel` statement. If necessary, press the **Tab** key until the insertion point is indented below that statement. Type **exit sub**, which will end the procedure when the user clicks the Cancel button.

Now code the No button response. If the user clicks the No button in response to the "Do you want to save the current document?" message, it means that he or she does not want to save the current document before a new document is displayed. In that case, you simply need to process the instructions found below the `End If` statement. Those instructions display a new document by removing the contents of the txtEdit control, setting the blnChange variable to False, resetting the form's caption, and assigning the empty string to the Common Dialog control's FileName property. For documentation purposes only, you will enter the comment "Process instructions below End If" in the `Case vbNo` clause. That is the only code you will need to enter for that case.

2 Click in the blank line below the `Case vbNo` statement. If necessary, press the **Tab** key until the insertion point is indented below that statement. Type **'process instructions below End If.**

Now code the Yes button response. If the user clicks the Yes button in response to the MsgBox function's message, it means that he or she wants to save the current document before a new document is displayed. In that case the New command will call the Save command's Click event procedure to save the file.

As you learned in Tutorial 4, you use the Call statement to call a user-defined procedure. You can also use the Call statement to call an event procedure. Recall that the syntax of the Call statement is **Call** *name* [(*argumentlist*)]. *Name* can be a user-defined sub procedure, as it was in Tutorial 4, or the name of an event procedure. In this case you will use the instruction `Call mnuFileSave_Click` to call the Save command's Click event procedure. (Recall that you have not yet coded the Save command.)

3 Click in the blank line below the `Case vbYes` statement. If necessary, press the **Tab** key until the insertion point is indented below that statement. Type **call mnufilesave_click** and press the **Enter** key.

When the Save command's Click event is completed, the program will return to the New command's Click event. At that point the New command's Click event must look at the contents of the blnCancelSave variable to determine if the save was canceled. (Recall that the variable will contain the Boolean value True if the save was canceled; otherwise, it will contain the Boolean value False.) If the save was canceled, then the New command's Click event should simply end.

4 Enter the selection structure and documentation shown in Figure 7-31. Also compare your code with the code in the figure and make any needed corrections before continuing.

enter this selection
structure and
documentation

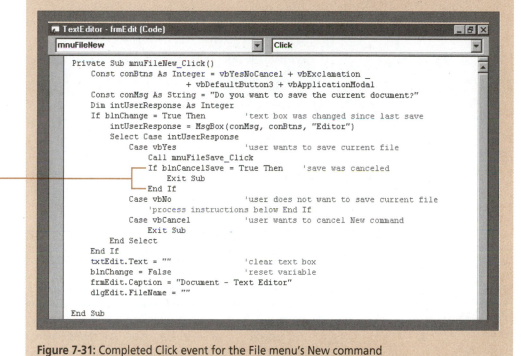

```
TextEditor - frmEdit (Code)
mnuFileNew                              Click

Private Sub mnuFileNew_Click()
    Const conBtns As Integer = vbYesNoCancel + vbExclamation _
                        + vbDefaultButton3 + vbApplicationModal
    Const conMsg As String = "Do you want to save the current document?"
    Dim intUserResponse As Integer
    If blnChange = True Then          'text box was changed since last save
        intUserResponse = MsgBox(conMsg, conBtns, "Editor")
        Select Case intUserResponse
            Case vbYes                'user wants to save current file
                Call mnuFileSave_Click
                If blnCancelSave = True Then    'save was canceled
                    Exit Sub
                End If
            Case vbNo                 'user does not want to save current file
                'process instructions below End If
            Case vbCancel             'user wants to cancel New command
                Exit Sub
        End Select
    End If
    txtEdit.Text = ""                 'clear text box
    blnChange = False                 'reset variable
    frmEdit.Caption = "Document - Text Editor"
    dlgEdit.FileName = ""

End Sub
```

Figure 7-31: Completed Click event for the File menu's New command

You have now finished coding the File menu's Save As and New commands. Before ending Lesson B, you will test both commands.

To test the File menu's Save As and New commands:

1 Close the Code window, then **save** and **run** the application. Recall that the Load event sets both the blnChange variable and the blnCancelSave variable to False.

2 Type your first name in the document, then press the **Enter** key. The txtEdit control's Change event sets the blnChange variable to True to indicate that a change was made to the document.

3 Click **File**, then click **Save As**. Save the file as **Test2** in the Tut07 folder on your Student Disk.

4 Type your last name below your first name in the document, then press the **Enter** key.

Now test the File menu's New command.

5 Click **File**, then click **New**. A message appears asking if you want to save the current document. Notice that the Cancel button is the default button in the dialog box. Recall that the Cancel button should end the New command's Click event procedure and return the user to the current document without saving the document. Click the **Cancel** button. The New command's Click event procedure ends, and you are returned to the current document.

6 Click **File**, then click **New**. Now test the No button, which should display a new document without saving the current one. Click the **No** button. A new document appears on the screen.

You will test the Yes button in Lesson C after you code the mnuFileSave command's Click event. (As you may remember, the Yes button's code contains the Call mnuFileSave_Click instruction.)

7 Click **File**, then click **Exit** to end the application. Visual Basic returns to the design screen.

You have now completed Lesson B. You can either take a break or complete the end-of-lesson questions and exercises. You will complete the Text Editor application in Lesson C.

SUMMARY

To generate a warning message if the user attempts to save a file using an existing name:

■ Set the Common Dialog control's Flags property to `cdlOFNOverwritePrompt`. The user will need to confirm whether he or she wants to overwrite the existing file.

To generate a warning message if the user enters a path that does not exist:

■ Set the Common Dialog control's Flags property to `cdlOFNPathMustExist`.

To determine the name of the file either selected or entered in a Save As or Open dialog box:

■ Use the Common Dialog control's FileName property.

To write a string of characters to a sequential file:

■ Use the Print # statement. Its syntax is **Print #***filenumber*, [*outputlist*], where *outputlist* is one or more expressions.

To treat the selection of the Cancel button in a Common Dialog control's dialog box as an error:

■ Set the Common Dialog control's CancelError property to True.

To turn the error trapping process on:

■ Use the On Error GoTo statement. Its syntax is **On Error GoTo** *line*, where *line* is either a line label or a line number that identifies the position of the procedure's error handler—the set of instructions that tells the application how to handle the trapped errors. If *line* is 0 (zero), the On Error statement turns the error trapping process off.

To include an error-handling routine in your code:

■ Use the structure shown in Figure 7-27.

To invoke (call) an event procedure:

■ Use the Call statement. Its syntax is **Call** *name* [*(argumentlist)*], where *name*, in this case, is the name of the event procedure you want to invoke.

Q U E S T I O N S

1. In Windows applications, the File menu's Save As command allows the user to
   _____ .
   a. save a new file
   b. save an existing file under a new name
   c. both a and b

2. If the current document has been saved, what typically appears in the application's title bar?
   a. the document's name
   b. the application's name
   c. the type of document the application creates
   d. both a and b
   e. both b and c

3. If the current document has not been saved, what typically appears in the application's title bar?
   a. the document's name
   b. the application's name
   c. the type of document the application creates
   d. both a and b
   e. both b and c

4. When the Flags property is set to _____ , the Save As dialog box generates a warning message if the user attempts to save a file using an existing name; the user will need to confirm whether he or she wants to overwrite the existing file.
   a. `cdlOFNOverwritePrompt`
   b. `OverWritePrompt`
   c. `PromptCdlOverWrite`
   d. `WarningOverWrite`

5. When the Flags property is set to _____ , the Save As dialog box generates a warning message if the user enters a path that does not exist.
   a. `cdlOFNPath`
   b. `cdlOFNPathMustExist`
   c. `PathExist`
   d. `PathMustExist`
   e. `WarningPath`

6. Which of the following will display only the names of the Document files (those ending in .doc) in the Common Dialog control's File name list box?
   a. `dlgEdit.Filename = "Document Files(*.doc)|*.doc"`
   b. `dlgEdit.Filename = "Document Files(*.doc)/*.doc"`
   c. `dlgEdit.Filter = "Document Files(*.doc)|*.doc"`
   d. `dlgEdit.Filter = "Document Files(*.doc)/*.doc"`
   e. `dlgEdit.Filter = "Document Files(*.doc);*.doc"`

7. When the user either enters the name of the file to save in the File name text box of a Save As dialog box, or selects an existing name from the File name list box, the file's name is stored in the Common Dialog control's _____ property.
   a. CommonFile
   b. CommonFileName
   c. DialogFilename
   d. File
   e. Filename

8. Use the _____ statement to write records to a sequential file.
   a. Output #
   b. Print #
   c. Record #
   d. Write #

9. Use the _____ statement to write a string of characters to a sequential file.
   a. Output #
   b. Print #
   c. Record #
   d. Write #

10. The _____ property, which can be set to either True or False, specifies whether choosing the Cancel button is treated as an error by Visual Basic.
   a. Button
   b. ButtonCancel
   c. CancelButton
   d. CancelError
   e. ErrorCancel

11. The process of intercepting and handling a run-time error is called _____ .
   a. error interception
   b. error timing
   c. error trapping
   d. run-time interception

12. The set of instructions that tells the application how to handle a trapped run-time error is called a(n) _____ .
   a. event procedure
   b. error processor
   c. error-handling routine or error handler
   d. function
   e. sub procedure

13. In Visual Basic, the _____ statement turns the error trapping process on.
   a. Error
   b. On Error GoTo
   c. On Error Process
   d. Process Error
   e. Trap Error

14. Always enter the _____ statement immediately above the error handler in the code.
   a. End
   b. Exit Error
   c. Exit Handler
   d. Exit Sub

15. The name of the error-handling routine ends with a _____ .
   a. colon (:)
   b. comma (,)
   c. period (.)
   d. semicolon (;)

16. Which of the following will call the mnuFileSaveAs command's Click event procedure?
   a. Call mnuFileSaveAs Click
   b. Call mnuFileSaveAs (Click)
   c. Call (mnuFileSaveAs)
   d. Call mnuFileSaveAs_Click

17. Boolean variables can contain the values _____ only.
   a. True and False
   b. Yes and No
   c. 0 and 1
   d. Boolean variables can contain any values.

E X E R C I S E S

1. In this exercise you will use the Common Dialog control to display the Color and Font dialog boxes.

Scenario: CDA Car Sales wants an application that they can use to calculate the monthly payment on a car loan. The application you will code in this exercise is almost identical to the Month application that you viewed in the Overview section; the only difference is that the application you create in this exercise will include a Format menu instead of a Color menu.

   a. Use Windows to run the Month.Exe file, which is located in the Overview folder on your Student Disk. When the interface appears, notice that the text in the Principal text box is selected. Both the 9.00% rate in the list box and the 5 years option button are also selected when the interface appears. The interest rates in the list box range from 7.00% to 12.00% in increments of .25%. Experiment with this application by calculating the monthly payment using various principals, interest rates, and terms. Also experiment with the File and Color menus. When you feel that you have a good idea of how the application works, exit the application.
   b. Open the Month (Month.vbp) project, which is located in the Tut07 folder on your Student Disk.
   c. Save the form and the project as lb1Done in the Tut07 folder on your Student Disk.
   d. Include the appropriate code to center the form on the screen.
   e. Code the File menu's Exit command so that it unloads the form.
   f. Code the File menu's Print command so that it uses the PrintForm method to print the form.
   g. Code the Format menu's commands appropriately. The Background Color command should allow the user to select a color for the form. The Information Box Color command should allow the user to select a color for the frame control. The Font command should allow the user to control the font name, style, and size of the text appearing in the lblPayment control.

h. Code the Calculate button so that it uses the Pmt function to calculate the monthly payment. (*Hint*: View the Help window on the Pmt function.)

i. Include any additional code as necessary.

j. Save and run the application. Test the application to verify that it is working correctly.

k. Stop the application, then print the code.

2. In this exercise you will use the Common Dialog control to display the Color and Font dialog boxes.

Scenario: In this exercise you will modify the lbEdit project that you created in Lesson B so that it includes a Format menu with Color and Font commands.

a. Open the lbEdit (lbEdit.vbp) project that you created in Lesson B. The file is located in the Tut07 folder on your Student Disk.

b. Save the form and the project as lb2Done in the Tut07 folder on your Student Disk.

c. Include a Format menu in the application. Position the Format menu after the Edit menu.

d. Include two commands on the Format menu: Color and Font. (Remember that both commands will display a dialog box that requires the user to enter additional information. Refer to Tutorial 6 for the GUI design rules for menu commands.)

e. Code the Color command so that it allows the user to select the background color of the txtEdit text box.

f. Code the Font command so that it allows the user to select the font used to display the text in the txtEdit text box.

g. Save and run the application. Test the Format menu's commands to see if they are working correctly.

h. Exit the application, then print the code for only the Format menu's commands.

LESSON C
objectives

In this lesson you will learn how to:

■ Read a string of characters from a sequential file using the Input function

■ Return the number of characters in a sequential file using the LOF function

■ Code the File menu's Save, Print, and Open commands

■ Code the form's Unload event

Completing the Text Editor Application

Coding the File Menu's Save Command

To complete the Text Editor application, you need to code the File menu's Save, Open, and Print commands, as well as the form's Unload event procedure. Begin with the Save command.

In Windows applications, the Save command allows the user to automatically save the current document using its current name. If the current document has not been previously saved, then the Save command displays the Save As dialog box, which allows the user to give the document a name before it is saved. The flowchart for the File menu's Save command is shown in Figure 7-32.

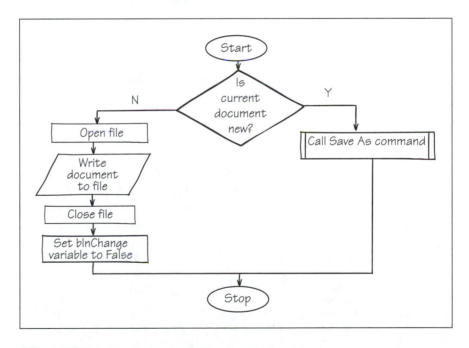

Figure 7-32: Flowchart for the File menu's Save command

According to the flowchart, the Save command first must determine if the current document is a new document—one that doesn't have a name because it hasn't been saved. You can make that determination by looking at the entry in the application's title bar. Recall that if the document hasn't been saved, the application's title bar displays "Document - Text Editor"; otherwise, the title bar displays the name of the saved document along with the name of the application.

If the document is new, then the Save command will call the Save As command's Click event; that event will display the Save As dialog box, which allows the user to enter a name for the document before it is saved. If, on the other hand, the current document is not a new document—it has been saved previously—then the Save command should automatically save the file under its current name.

The code for the Save command is already entered in its Click event procedure.

To view the code in the Save command's Click event procedure:

1 Start Visual Basic, if necessary, and open the **lbEdit** (lbEdit.vbp) project, which is located in the Tut07 folder on your Student Disk.

2 Save the form and the project as **lcEdit**.

3 Click **File** on the form's menu bar, then click **Save**. The Save command's Click event appears as shown in Figure 7-33.

remove this instruction from the Code window

```
TextEditor - frmEdit (Code)
mnuFileSave                    Click

Private Sub mnuFileSave_Click()
    Exit Sub
    If frmEdit.Caption = "Document - Text Editor" Then
        Call mnuFileSaveAs_Click       'new document
    Else                               'existing document
        Open dlgEdit.FileName For Output As #1
        Print #1, txtEdit.Text
        Close #1
        blnChange = False
    End If

End Sub
```

Figure 7-33: Save command's Click event procedure

4 Select the `Exit Sub` statement, which is located below the `Private Sub` statement, then press the **Delete** key to remove the `Exit Sub` statement from the Code window.

The selection structure compares the value in the form's Caption property to the string "Document - Text Editor". If the Caption property contains that string, then the Save command calls the mnuFileSaveAs_Click event to save the document. If, on the other hand, the Caption property contains a value other than "Document - Text Editor", the current sequential file is opened and the txtEdit control's Text property is written to the file. The sequential file is then closed, and the blnChange variable is set to False.

5 Close the Code window, then **run** the application.

6 Type your first name in the document, then press the **Enter** key.

Observe how the Save command works when you use it to save a new document.

7 Click **File**, then click **Save**. Because the current document is new, the Save command calls the Save As command's Click event, which displays the Save As dialog box.

8 Save the file as **Test3** in the Tut07 folder on your Student Disk.

HELP? If this is the second or subsequent time you are practicing this lesson, a prompt asking if you want to replace the existing Test3.txt file appears. Click the Yes button.

9   Type your last name in the document, then press the **Enter** key.

Now observe how the Save command works when you use it to save a document that has already been saved.

10 Click **File**, then click **Save**. Because the current document was saved previously, the Save command automatically saves the file using its current name and location.

11 Click **File**, then click **Exit** to end the application. Visual Basic returns to the design screen.

You will code the File menu's Print command next.

Coding the File Menu's Print Command

In this application, the File menu's Print command will simply print the document on the printer. You will use Visual Basic's PrintForm instruction to code the Print command.

To code the File menu's Print command, then save and run the application:

1   Click **File** on the form's menu bar, then click **Print**. Maximize the Code window. The mnuFilePrint control's Click event procedure appears.

2   Enter the instructions shown in Figure 7-34.

enter these seven
instructions

```
TextEditor - frmEdit (Code)

mnuFilePrint                           Click

    Private Sub mnuFilePrint_Click()
        On Error GoTo PrintErrHandler
        dlgEdit.Flags = cdlPDNoSelection + cdlPDHidePrintToFile + cdlPDNoPageNums
        dlgEdit.CancelError = True
        dlgEdit.ShowPrinter
        PrintForm
        Exit Sub

    PrintErrHandler:
    End Sub
```

Figure 7-34: Code entered in the Print command's Click event procedure

After turning error trapping on, the code sets the Flags property for the Print dialog box. The `cdlPDNoSelection` setting disables the Selection option button. The `cdlPDHidePrintToFile` setting hides the Print to file check box. The `cdlPDNoPageNums` setting disables the Pages option button. The `dlgEdit.CancelError = True` instruction tells Visual Basic to treat the

selection of the Cancel button in the dialog box as an error. The `dlgEdit.`
`ShowPrinter` instruction displays the Print dialog box. The `PrintForm`
instruction prints the form. The `Exit Sub` instruction exits the mnuFilePrint
Click event before the PrintErrHandler code is processed. The PrintErrHandler
code is only processed when an error occurs in the procedure.

3   Close the Code window, then **save** and **run** the application.

4   Type a few words in the document, then press the **Enter** key.

5   Click **File**, then click **Print**. Notice that the Selection and Pages option buttons are disabled; the user can choose to print only the entire document.
Also notice that the Print to file check box does not appear in the dialog
box. If your computer is connected to a printer, click the **OK** button in the
Print dialog box; otherwise, click the **Cancel** button. If you clicked the OK
button, a message box appears, indicating that the document is printing.
Notice that Visual Basic does not include the menu when it prints the form.

6   Click **File**, then click **Exit** to end the application. Visual Basic returns to the
design screen.

The last menu command you will code is the File menu's Open command. The
Open command will allow the user to open an existing document.

Coding the File Menu's Open Command

The File menu's Open command will allow the user to open an existing document
so that he or she can continue working in that document. The Open command
will display the document in the txtEdit control on the form.

The flowchart for the File menu's Open command is shown in Figure 7-35.

After declaring the variables and constants and setting the error trapping, the
Open command's Click event first must determine if the current document was
changed since the last time it was saved. If it wasn't, then the procedure displays
the Open dialog box, which allows the user to select the name of the file to open.
The selected file is then opened, and its contents are displayed in the txtEdit control. The file is then closed, the blnChange variable is set to False to indicate that
no change was made to the document since the last time it was saved, and the
names of both the file and the application are displayed in the application's title bar
before the procedure ends.

tip

When the Open command
displays the contents of
the opened file in the
txtEdit control, it causes
the txtEdit control's
Change event to occur.
Recall that the txtEdit control's Change event con-
tains the `blnChange =`
`True` instruction, which
indicates that the file has
been changed since the
last time it was saved.
Because simply displaying
a newly opened document
should not invoke the
prompt to save the file,
you need to set the
blnChange variable to
False to indicate that the
document does not need
to be saved at this point.

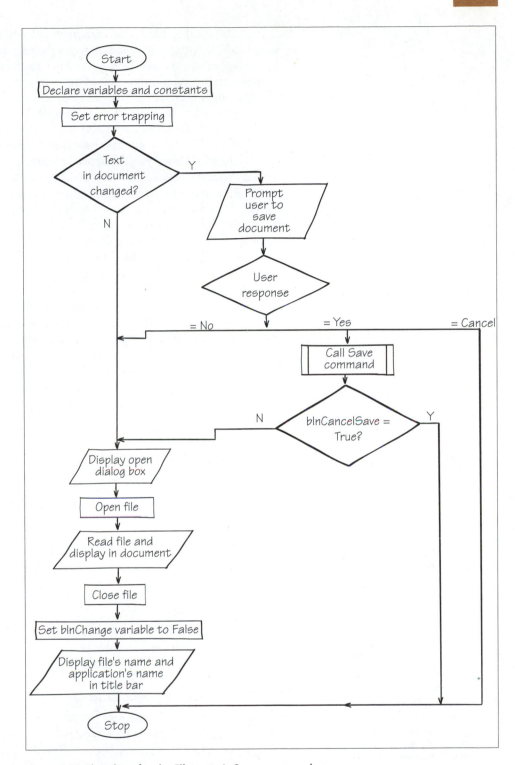

Figure 7-35: Flowchart for the File menu's Open command

If, on the other hand, the current document was changed since the last time it was saved, the Open command prompts the user to save the document. At this point the user can choose either to save the current document before another document is opened, or to open another document without saving the current one, or to cancel the Open operation. If the user chooses to cancel the Open command, he or she is simply returned to the current document. If the user chooses not to save the current document, then the Open command displays the Open dialog box; the selected file is then opened, and its contents displayed in the txtEdit control before the file is closed. The blnChange variable is set to False, and the names of both the file and the application are displayed in the application's title bar before the procedure ends. Lastly, if the user chooses to save the current document before another document is opened, then the Open command calls the Save command's Click event to save the file. As the flowchart shows, when the Save command's Click event procedure ends, the program will return to the Open command's Click event. At that point the Open command's Click event must look at the contents of the blnCancelSave variable in order to determine if the save was canceled. (Recall that the variable will contain the Boolean value True if the save was canceled; otherwise, it will contain the Boolean value False.) If the save was canceled, then the Open command's Click event will simply return the user to the current document. If the save was not canceled, then the Open dialog box is displayed; the selected file is then opened, and its contents displayed in the txtEdit control before the file is closed. The blnChange variable is then set to False, and the names of both the file and the application are displayed in the application's title bar before the procedure ends.

In order to code the Open command, you will need to learn two new functions: Input and LOF.

The Input and LOF Functions

You use the **Input function** to read a string of characters from an open sequential file. The syntax of the Input function is **Input**(*number*, *filenumber*), where *number* specifies the number of characters in the file, and *filenumber* specifies the number used in the Open statement to open the file.

You can use Visual Basic's LOF function to determine the number of characters in the open file. The **LOF function**, which stands for "length of file," returns the number of characters contained in an opened file. The syntax of the LOF function is **LOF**(*filenumber*), where *filenumber* is the number used in the Open statement to open the file.

Most of the code for the Open command is already entered in its Click event procedure. You will need to enter only two additional lines of code.

tip

Unlike the Input # statement, which you used in Tutorial 6 to read the records from a sequential file, the Input function returns all of the characters it reads, including commas, carriage returns, linefeeds, quotation marks, and leading spaces.

tip

You use the FileLen function, instead of the LOF function, to obtain the length of an unopened file. Its syntax is FileLen(*pathname*), where *pathname* is a string expression that specifies the path and name of the unopened file.

To code the Open command's Click event:

1 Click **File** on the form's menu bar, then click **Open**. Maximize the Code window. The Open command's Click event appears.

To complete the Open command's Click event procedure, you will need to enter two additional instructions. The first instruction will use the Open statement to open the file the user selected in the Open dialog box. The second instruction will use the Input and LOF functions to read the contents of the opened file. The Input function will assign the contents of the file to the txtEdit control in the interface.

2 Enter the two additional instructions shown in Figure 7-36.

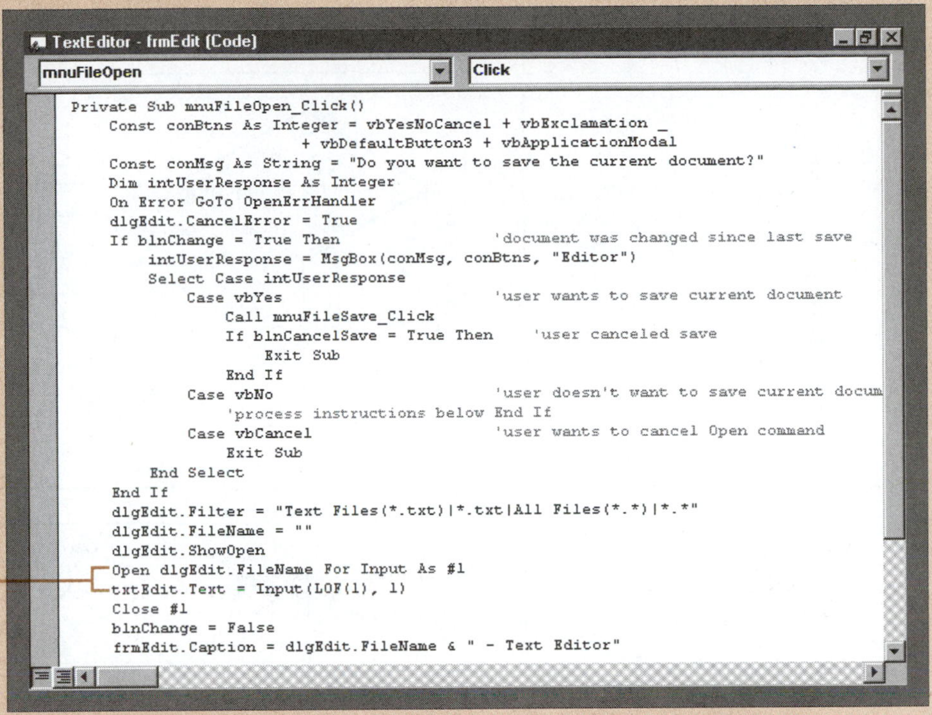

enter these two
instructions

```
TextEditor - frmEdit (Code)

mnuFileOpen                                      Click

Private Sub mnuFileOpen_Click()
    Const conBtns As Integer = vbYesNoCancel + vbExclamation _
                             + vbDefaultButton3 + vbApplicationModal
    Const conMsg As String = "Do you want to save the current document?"
    Dim intUserResponse As Integer
    On Error GoTo OpenErrHandler
    dlgEdit.CancelError = True
    If blnChange = True Then                    'document was changed since last save
        intUserResponse = MsgBox(conMsg, conBtns, "Editor")
        Select Case intUserResponse
            Case vbYes                          'user wants to save current document
                Call mnuFileSave_Click
                If blnCancelSave = True Then    'user canceled save
                    Exit Sub
                End If
            Case vbNo                           'user doesn't want to save current docum
                'process instructions below End If
            Case vbCancel                       'user wants to cancel Open command
                Exit Sub
        End Select
    End If
    dlgEdit.Filter = "Text Files(*.txt)|*.txt|All Files(*.*)|*.*"
    dlgEdit.FileName = ""
    dlgEdit.ShowOpen
    Open dlgEdit.FileName For Input As #1
    txtEdit.Text = Input(LOF(1), 1)
    Close #1
    blnChange = False
    frmEdit.Caption = dlgEdit.FileName & " - Text Editor"
```

Figure 7-36: Instructions to open and read the file entered in the Code window

The `Open dlgEdit.FileName For Input As #1` instruction will open the file that the user selected in the Open dialog box. The `txtEdit.Text = Input (LOF(1), 1)` instruction will read the contents of the file and assign the contents to the txtEdit control.

3 Close the Code window, then **save** and **run** the application.

Use the Open command to open a file.

4 Click **File**, then click **Open**. Use the Open dialog box to open the **Test3.txt** file, which is located in the Tut07 folder on your Student Disk. The Test3.txt file appears in the interface. The application's title bar should display the document's name and the application's name.

5 Click **File**, then click **Exit** to end the application. Visual Basic returns to the design screen.

The last procedure you will view is the form's Unload event. The code for the Unload event has already been entered in its Code window for you; you will need to make only one modification to the existing code.

Coding the Form's Unload Event

The flowchart for the form's Unload event is shown in Figure 7-37.

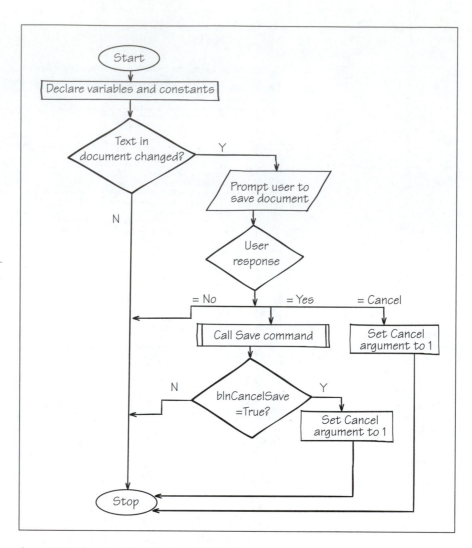

Figure 7-37: Flowchart for the form's Unload event procedure

After declaring the variables and constants, the Unload event first must determine if the current document was changed since the last time it was saved. If it wasn't, the Unload event simply unloads the form and the application ends. If, however, the current document was changed since the last time it was saved, the user is prompted to save the document. At this point the user can choose either to save the document before the application ends, or to end the application without saving the document, or to cancel the Unload event. If the user selects the Cancel button, he or she is returned to the current document; that is accomplished by setting the Unload event's Cancel argument to the number 1. If, however, the user wants to end the application without saving the current document, then the form is unloaded and the application ends. Lastly, if the user wants to save the current document before the application ends, then the Unload event calls the Save command's Click event. As the flowchart shows, when the Save command's Click event procedure ends, the program returns to the form's Unload event. At that point the Unload event must look at the contents of the blnCancelSave variable in order to determine if the save was canceled. (Recall that the variable will contain the Boolean value True if the save was canceled; otherwise, it will contain the Boolean value False.) If the save was canceled, then the Unload event's Cancel argument is set to the number 1, which will prevent the form from being unloaded; otherwise the form is unloaded and the application ends.

tip

Recall from Tutorial 5 that setting the Cancel argument to a nonzero value cancels the Unload event, which prevents the form from being unloaded.

As mentioned earlier, the Unload event's code is already entered in the Code window. You will need to make only one modification to that code.

To modify the code in the form's Unload event, then save and run the application:

1   Open the form's Unload event, then maximize the Code window.

2   Select the End statement located below the `Private Sub` statement, then press the **Backspace** key to remove that line of code. See Figure 7-38.

End statement removed from procedure

```
TextEditor - frmEdit (Code)                                    _ 🗗 ✕
Form                              ▼    Unload                              ▼
Private Sub Form_Unload(Cancel As Integer)                                ▲

     Const conBtns As Integer = vbYesNoCancel + vbExclamation _
                              + vbDefaultButton3 + vbApplicationModal
     Const conMsg As String = "Do you want to save the current document?"
     Dim intUserResponse As Integer
     If blnChange = True Then           'document was changed since last save
         intUserResponse = MsgBox(conMsg, conBtns, "Editor")
         Select Case intUserResponse
             Case vbYes                     'user wants to save current document
                 Call mnuFileSave_Click
                 If blnCancelSave = True Then     'user canceled save
                     Cancel = 1                   'return to document-don't unload form
                 End If
             Case vbNo                      'user does not want to save current docu
                 'unload form and exit
             Case vbCancel
                 Cancel = 1                       'return to document-don't unload form
         End Select
     End If

End Sub
```

Figure 7-38: Form's Unload event procedure

After declaring the necessary variables and constants, the code compares the value in the blnChange variable, which keeps track of whether a change was made to the document, to the Boolean value True. If the blnChange variable does not contain True (in other words, it contains the Boolean value False), the form is unloaded and the application ends. If, however, the blnChange variable contains the True value, then the MsgBox function prompts the user to save the current document. At this point the user can select either the Yes button, the No button, or the Cancel button. If the user selects the Cancel button in response to the "Do you want to save the current document?" message, the Unload event's Cancel argument is set to the number 1 to prevent the form from being unloaded, then the Unload event procedure ends. If, on the other hand, the user selects the No button in response to the "Do you want to save the current document?" message, the form is unloaded and the application ends. Lastly, if the user clicks the Yes button in response to the "Do you want to save the current document?" message, the Unload event calls the Save command's Click event. When the Save command's Click event ends, the Unload event uses the blnCancelSave variable to determine if the user canceled the save. If the user canceled the save, then the Unload event's Cancel argument is set to the number 1 to prevent the form from being unloaded, then the Unload event procedure ends; otherwise, the form is unloaded and the application ends.

3   Close the Code window, then **save** and **run** the application.

Now test the application to see if the Unload event works correctly.

4 Type your first name in the document. Click **File**, then click **Exit**. When the dialog box prompts you to save the current document, click the **Cancel** button. You are returned to the current document.

5 Click **File**, then click **Exit**. When the MsgBox function prompts you to save the current file, click the **No** button. The application ends.

6 **Run** the application. Type your first name in the document. Click **File**, then click **Exit**. When the dialog box prompts you to save the current document, click the **Yes** button. When the Save As dialog box appears, click the **Cancel** button. The application returns to the current document.

7 Click **File**, then click **Exit**. When the dialog box prompts you to save the current document, click the **Yes** button. When the Save As dialog box appears, save the document as **Test3** in the Tut07 folder on your Student Disk. When the message asking if you want to replace the existing Test3 file appears, click the **Yes** button. The application saves the document before the application ends.

Recall that you did not test, completely, the File menu's New command in Lesson B. You will do that now.

To complete the testing of the File menu's New command:

1 **Run** the application. Type your first name in the document. Use the File menu's Save As command to save the file as **Test4** in the Tut07 folder on your Student Disk.

2 Type your last name in the document. Click **File**, then click **New**. A dialog box asking if you want to save the current document appears.

Because the current document already has a name, the Yes button in the dialog box should call the File menu's Save command to automatically save the current document before displaying a new document.

3 Click the **Yes** button. The application automatically saves the current document before displaying a new document.

Now you will open the Test4 file to verify that the document was saved.

4 Use the File menu's Open command to open the **Test4** (Test4.txt) file, which is located in the Tut07 folder on your Student Disk. Notice that the file contains both your first and last name.

5 Click **File**, then click **Exit**. Visual Basic returns to the design screen.

You have now completed Lesson C and the Text Editor application. You can take a break, complete the end-of-lesson questions and exercises, or read and complete the Debugging section. The Debugging section may contain information that will help you when completing the exercises.

S U M M A R Y

To read all of the characters in a sequential file, including commas, carriage returns, linefeeds, quotation marks, and leading spaces:

■ Use the Input function. Its syntax is **Input**(*number*, *filenumber*), where *number* specifies the number of characters in the file, and *filenumber* specifies the number used in the Open statement to open the file.

To determine the number of bytes contained in a file:

■ If the file is opened, use the LOF function. Its syntax is **LOF**(*filenumber*), where *filenumber* specifies the number used in the Open statement to open the file.

■ If the file is closed, use the FileLen function. Its syntax is **FileLen**(*pathname*), where *pathname* is a string expression that specifies the path and name of the unopened file.

Q U E S T I O N S

1. In Windows applications, the Save command allows the user to _____ .
   a. automatically save the current document using its current name
   b. automatically save the current document using a new name
   c. give the file a name if it has not been previously saved
   d. both a and c
   e. both b and c

2. You use the _____ to read a string of characters from an open sequential file.
   a. Get # statement
   b. Get function
   c. Input # statement
   d. Input function
   e. Read function

3. The _____ returns all of the characters it reads from a sequential file, including commas, carriage returns, linefeeds, quotation marks, and leading spaces.
   a. Get # statement
   b. Get function
   c. Input # statement
   d. Input function
   e. Read function

4. The _____ function returns the number of bytes contained in an opened file.
   a. FileLen
   b. Len
   c. LFO
   d. LOF
   e. Num

5. The _____ function returns the number of bytes contained in an unopened file.
   a. FileLen
   b. Len
   c. LFO
   d. LOF
   e. Num

E X E R C I S E S

1. In this exercise you will create a text editor that will allow you to view data files similar to the ones you created in Tutorial 6.

    Scenario: You learned how to create sequential data files in Tutorial 6. Recall that the files you created had a .dat extension. Also recall that you can use either a word processor or a text editor to view the contents of the data files. In this exercise you will create a simple text editor that will allow you to open and view sequential data files. The text editor will also allow you to print the form.

    a. Open a new project, if necessary.
    b. Include one text box on the form.
    c. Save the form and the project as lc1Done in the Tut07 folder on your Student Disk.
    d. Create a simple text editor that contains a File menu with the following commands: Open, Print, and Exit. The Open command should display the Open dialog box and allow the user to view either data files (those whose filenames end in .dat) or all files. The Print command should use the PrintForm method to print the form.
    e. Save and run the application. Test the application by opening and printing the following four files, which are located in the Tut07 folder on your Student Disk: lcdata1.dat, lcdata2.dat, lcdata3.dat, lcdata4.dat.
    f. End the application. Print the application's code.
    g. Submit the printouts from step e and the code from step f.

2. In this exercise you will use the text editor that you created in this tutorial to create a sequential access data file. You will also use a menu control.

    Scenario: Instead of using the Write # statement to create a sequential file that contains records, you can use the text editor that you created in this tutorial.

    a. Open the lcEdit (lcEdit.vbp) project that you finished coding in Lesson C. The project is located in the Tut07 folder on your Student Disk.
    b. Modify the code so that the Common Dialog control will display and save Data Files—those ending in .dat—rather than Text Files.
    c. Save the form and the project as lc2Edit.
    d. Run the application.
    e. Enter the following six records. Each record contains a name, sex, and age. Press the Enter key only when indicated to do so. Be sure to include the quotation marks and commas as shown. Also be sure not to press the Spacebar on your keyboard.

        "Mary","Female",21 <press the Enter key>
        "Terri","Female",18 <press the Enter key>
        "Jim","Male",33   <press the Enter key>
        "George","Male",45 <press the Enter key>
        "Paula","Female",53 <press the Enter key>
        "Fred","Male",25   (DO NOT PRESS THE ENTER KEY)

    f. Use the File menu's Save As option to save the file as lc2.dat in the Tut07 folder on your Student Disk.
    g. Use the File menu's Print command to print the document.
    h. Use the File menu's Exit command to exit the text editor.
    i. Create an application that will read the records in the lc2.dat file. Save the form and the project as lc2Done in the Tut07 folder on your Student Disk.

The application should contain a File menu that includes Print and Exit options. (Be sure to assign the appropriate access keys and shortcut key.) The application should also contain a Display Information button that opens and reads the lc2.dat file that you saved in step f. The button should display the total number of males and the total number of females, as well as the average age of the males and the average age of the females. Display the information in label controls on the form.

j. Code the Print option so that it prints the form. Code the Exit option so that it unloads the form.

k. Save and run the application. Click the Display Information button, then use the File menu's Print command to print the interface.

l. Exit the application, then print the application's code.

m. Submit the printouts from steps g and k, and the code from step l.

Exercises 3 through 6 are Discovery Exercises, which allow you to both "discover" the solutions to problems on your own and to experiment with material that is not covered in the tutorial.

discovery ▶ 3. In this exercise you will learn about the FreeFile function.

a. If you have access to the MSDN Library, then display the Help screen on the FreeFile function. What is the purpose of the FreeFile function?

b. Open the lcEdit (lcEdit.vbp) project that you created in Lesson C. The file is located in the Tut07 folder on your Student Disk.

c. Save the form and the project as lc3Done in the Tut07 folder on your Student Disk.

d. Modify the code so that it uses the FreeFile function appropriately.

e. Save and run the application. Test the application to verify that it is still working correctly.

f. Exit the application.

g. Print the code. Circle the sections of the code you needed to modify in order to include the FreeFile function in the application.

discovery ▶ 4. In this exercise you will learn about the Common Dialog control's FilterIndex property.

a. If you have access to the MSDN Library, then display the Help screen on the Common Dialog control's FilterIndex property. What is the purpose of the FilterIndex property?

b. Open a new project, if necessary. Add the CommonDialog tool to the toolbox. Add a command button and a Common Dialog control to the form.

c. Code the command button's Click event so that it sets the Common Dialog control's Filter property to display all text files (filenames ending in .txt), all picture files (filenames ending in .pic), and all files. After setting the Filter property, the Click event should show the Open dialog box.

d. Save the form and the project as lc4Done in the Tut07 folder on your Student Disk.

e. Run the application, then click the command button. Notice that the first filter listed in the Filter property is the default filter that appears in the dialog box.

f. Stop the application. Open the command button's Click event. Before displaying the Open dialog box, set the Common Dialog control's FilterIndex property to 2.

g. Save and run the application, then click the command button. Notice that the second filter listed in the Filter property is now the default filter in the dialog box.

h. Stop the application. Open the command button's Click event. Modify the code so that the default filter is the third filter listed in the Filter property.

i. Save and run the application, then click the command button to see if the modified code is working correctly.

j. Stop the application. Print the command button's code.

discovery ▶ 5. In this exercise you will learn about the Resume statement.

Scenario: You use the Resume statement to resume program execution after an error-handling routine is finished. Resume, by itself, causes program execution to resume with the statement that caused the error. For example, assume that, when attempting to process a print instruction, an application determines that the printer is not online. When the On Error statement traps this error, it sends program control to the error handler. The error handler instructions can prompt the user to turn the printer on, wait until he or she does, and then use the Resume statement to resume program execution with the print instruction that caused the error.

The Resume Next instruction, on the other hand, causes program execution to resume with the statement immediately following the one that caused the error. If, for example, an instruction causes an "Internal error" (error code 51), the error handler instructions can prompt the user to copy the error message down on paper, wait for the user to do so, and then use the Resume Next statement to resume program execution with the instruction immediately following the one that caused the error.

You use the Resume *line* instruction in cases where the application cannot resume execution either with the instruction that caused the error or with the one immediately below that instruction. Resume *line* allows the error handler to resume program execution at *line*, which is either a line label or a line number that identifies an instruction located somewhere in the procedure.

a. Open the lc5 (lc5.vbp) project, which is located in the Tut07 folder on your Student Disk. Save the form and the project as lc5Done in the Tut07 folder on your Student Disk.

b. Run the application. Click the Calculate button. A dialog box prompts you to enter the sales. Type 900 and press the Enter key. The interface shows that the bonus is $90.00.

c. Click the Calculate button again. This time, type 90000 as the sales and press the Enter key. Visual Basic display the "Overflow" error message. Click the Debug button. The code window shows that the `intSales = Val(InputBox("Enter the sales:", "Entry"))` instruction is causing the "Overflow" error. As you may recall, the maximum number that an Integer variable can store is 32767. Because 90000 is greater than 32767, Visual Basic displays the "Overflow" error message, which indicates that the number you entered is too large for the variable to which it is assigned.

d. Stop the application. Open the Calculate button's Click event procedure. Create the following two constants at the beginning of the procedure: `Const conMsg As String = "The sales amount cannot exceed 32767"` and `Const conBtns As Integer = vbOKOnly + vbInformation + vbDefaultButton1 + vbApplicationModal`.

e. Use the On Error statement to turn the error trapping process on. Send the program to an error handler named CalcErrHandler.

f. Code the CalcErrHandler so that it uses the MsgBox function to display the contents of the conMsg and conBtns constants before exiting the Click event. Assign the MsgBox function's return value to the intTemp variable.

g. Save and run the application. Click the Calculate button. Type 90000 and press the Enter key. A message box informing you that the number cannot exceed 32767 appears. Click the OK button. Notice that the application does not end in an error; rather, it simply returns the user to the interface. Stop the application, then print the code.

h. Open the Calculate button's Click event. Add a blank line below the MsgBox function in the error handler. Type `resume` in the blank line, then press the Enter key. Save and run the application. Click the Calculate button. Type 90000 and press the Enter key. A message box informing you that the number cannot exceed 32767 appears. Click the OK button. Rather than returning the user to the interface, as in step g, the Click event procedure prompts the user to enter the number again. This is because the Resume statement tells Visual Basic to return to the instruction that caused the error and process that instruction again. Stop the application, then print the code.

i. Open the Calculate button's Click event procedure. Change the CalcErrHandler procedure so that it assigns a 0 (zero) to the intSales variable when an error occurs. Put the assignment statement below the MsgBox function statement. Also change the `Resume` statement to `Resume Next`.

j. Save and run the application. Click the Calculate button, then type 75000 and press the Enter key. When the message box informing you that the number cannot exceed 32767 appears, click the OK button. The CalcErrHandler routine sets the intSales variable to 0, and the Resume Next statement tells Visual Basic to return to the line below the one that caused the error. In this case, Visual Basic will return to the `sngBonus = intSales * 0.1` instruction, which calculates the bonus. The `lblBonus.Caption = Format(sngBonus, "currency")` instruction then displays the bonus ($0.00) in the lblBonus control, after which the Click event ends and you are returned to the interface. Stop the application, then print the code.

k. Open the Calculate button's Click event. Click at the beginning of the `lblBonus.Caption = Format(sngBonus, "currency")` instruction, then type Here: and press the Enter key. (Be sure to type the colon after the word Here.) This assigns the name Here to the line that follows it. In this case, Here is the name of the `lblBonus.Caption = Format(sngBonus, "currency")` instruction.

l. Change the `intSales = 0` instruction in the CalcErrHandler routine to `sngBonus = 0`. Then change the Resume Next statement to Resume Here.

m. Save and run the application. Click the Calculate button, then type 75000 and press the Enter key. When the message box informing you that the number cannot exceed 32767 appears, click the OK button. The CalcErrHandler routine sets the sngBonus variable to 0, and the Resume Here statement tells Visual Basic to return to the line named Here (the `lblBonus.Caption = Format(sngBonus, "currency")` instruction), which assigns the contents of the sngBonus variable, formatted to currency, to the lblBonus control. You are then returned to the interface. Stop the application, then print the code.

n. Submit the code from steps g, h, j, and m.

discovery ▶ 6. In this exercise, you will print a report to a file.

a. Open the laPao (laPao.vbp) project, which you created in Tutorial 6. The file is located in the Tut06 folder on your Student Disk.

b. Save the form and the project as lc6Done in the Tut07 folder on your Student Disk.

c. Both the cmdDisplay and cmdEnter buttons' Click events use the Open statement to open a file named pao.dat. Change the "a:\tut06\pao.dat" in both procedures to "a:\tut07\pao.dat". (If your Student Disk is in a different drive, make the appropriate modifications.)

d. Modify the Print Report button so that it prints the report to a sequential access file rather than to the printer. Name the file pao.rpt and save it in the Tut07 folder on your Student Disk.

e. Save and run the application. Add the following five records to the pao.dat file:

Democrat	18-35
Democrat	Over 65
Independent	36-50
Independent	51-65
Republican	Over 65

f. Click the Display Totals button, then click the Print Report button. Click the Exit button to end the application. Print the code.

g. Use a text editor such as WordPad (or Notepad) to open and print the pao.rpt report.

h. Submit the printouts from steps f and g.

D E B U G G I N G

Technique   As you learned in previous tutorials, it is important to test an application with both valid and invalid data. The application should be able to handle the invalid data appropriately; in other words, the application should not "crash"—end unexpectedly—because the user entered invalid data. Once you have determined which types of errors may occur in the application, you can use error trapping, along with the Err object, to instruct the application to take the appropriate action that will prevent the application from "crashing." The Err object is yet another object available in Visual Basic, similar to the Print, Form, and Screen objects that you learned about in previous tutorials.

To practice this tutorial's Debugging technique:

1   Open the **Debug** (debug.vbp) project, which is located in the Tut07 folder on your Student Disk. See Figure 7-39.

Figure 7-39: Debugging example's user interface

2   Save the form and the project as **DebDone** in the Tut07 folder on your Student Disk.

3   Open the Divide button's Code window and view the code in its Click event procedure. The code assigns the contents of the txtNum1 and txtNum2 controls to the sngNum1 and sngNum2 variables, respectively. The code then divides the sngNum1 variable by the sngNum2 variable and displays the quotient in the lblQuotient control.

4   Close the Code window.

Now display a Help screen that shows the types of errors that Visual Basic allows you to trap.

5   If you have access to the MSDN Library, then display the "trappable errors" Help screen. The top portion of the Help screen is shown in Figure 7-40.

	Trappable Errors	

Trappable Errors

<u>See Also</u>   <u>Specifics</u>

Trappable errors can occur while an application is running. Some trappable errors can also occur during development or <u>compile time</u>. You can test and respond to trappable errors using the **On Error** statement and the **Err** object. Unused <u>error numbers</u> in the range 1 – 1000 are reserved for future use by Visual Basic.

Code	Message
3	<u>Return without GoSub</u>
5	<u>Invalid procedure call</u>
6	<u>Overflow</u>
7	<u>Out of memory</u>
9	<u>Subscript out of range</u>
10	<u>This array is fixed or temporarily locked</u>
11	<u>Division by zero</u>
13	<u>Type mismatch</u>
14	<u>Out of string space</u>
16	<u>Expression too complex</u>
17	<u>Can't perform requested operation</u>
18	<u>User interrupt occurred</u>
20	<u>Resume without error</u>
28	<u>Out of stack space</u>

Figure 7-40: Trappable Errors Help screen

Notice that each error is identified by a code and a message. When an error occurs, Visual Basic assigns the error's code to the Err object's Number property; it assigns the error's message to the Err object's Description property. For example, if an application attempts to divide an expression by zero, Visual Basic assigns the number 11 (the error code corresponding to a "Division by zero" error) to the Err object's Number property and it assigns the string "Division by zero" to the Err object's Description property.

6   Scroll the Help screen to view the various trappable errors, then close the MSDN Library window.

Recall that the current application divides the number entered in the Number 1 text box by the number entered in the Number 2 text box, then displays the quotient in the Quotient label control. Although the application is quite simple, it can still "crash" because of errors. You can determine the expected errors in an application by simply running the application and using it improperly—in other words, in a manner that the programmer did not intend. Observe how the application responds when the user clicks the Divide button without entering any numbers in the interface.

7   **Run** the application, then click the **Divide** button. Visual Basic displays error message number 6 ("Overflow") in a dialog box. Click the **End** button in the dialog box to end the application.

Now observe how the application responds when the user enters a string for the second number.

8   **Run** the application again, type **100** in the Number 1 text box, then type **S** in the Number 2 text box. Press the **Enter** key to select the Divide button. Visual Basic displays error message number 11 ("Division by zero") in a dialog box. Click the **End** button in the dialog box to end the application.

You can use error trapping, along with the Err object, to trap both the Overflow and the Division by zero errors, and then take the appropriate action so that the application does not "crash" when these errors occur.

To include error trapping in the Divide button's Click event procedure:

1   Open the Divide button's Click event procedure. Maximize the Code window, then enter the additional code shown in Figure 7-41.

enter these three instructions

enter this instruction

enter these six instructions

```
frmDivide (Code)                                              _ | _ | X

cmdDivide                    ▾     Click                             ▾

Private Sub cmdDivide_Click()
    Const conMsg As String = _
            "Both text boxes must be completed and must contain numbers."
    Const conBtns As Integer = vbOKOnly + vbInformation _
            + vbDefaultButton1 + vbApplicationModal
    Dim intUserResponse As Integer
    Dim sngNum1 As Single, sngNum2 As Single
    On Error GoTo DebugErrHandler
    sngNum1 = Val(txtNum1.Text)
    sngNum2 = Val(txtNum2.Text)
    lblQuotient.Caption = sngNum1 / sngNum2
    Exit Sub

DebugErrHandler:
        Select Case Err.Description
            Case "Overflow", "Division by zero"
                intUserResponse = MsgBox(conMsg, conBtns, "Debug")
        End Select
End Sub
```

Figure 7-41: Error trapping code included in Divide button's Click event procedure

2   Close the Code window, then **save** and **run** the application.

Observe how the application responds when the user clicks the Divide button without entering any numbers in the interface.

3   Click the **Divide** button. The application displays the "Both text boxes must be completed and must contain numbers." message in a dialog box. Click the **OK** button. Instead of crashing, as it did when error trapping was not included, the application returns the user to the interface.

Now observe how the application responds when the user enters a string for the second number.

4   Type **100** in the Number 1 text box, then type **S** in the Number 2 text box. Press the **Enter** key to select the Divide button. The application displays the "Both text boxes must be completed and must contain numbers." message in a dialog box. Click the **OK** button. The application returns the user to the interface.

5   Click the **Exit** button to end the application. Visual Basic returns to the design screen.

Following are two Debugging Exercises for you to try.

Exercises

1. Open the DebDone (DebDone.vbp) project that you created in this Debugging Section. The project is located in the Tut07 folder on your Student Disk.

    a. Save the form and the project as DebDone2 in the Tut07 folder on your Student Disk.

    b. Open the Divide button's Click event procedure. Modify the Case structure so that it uses the Err object's Number property, instead of its Description property, to determine which error occurred.

    c. Save and run the application. Test the application by clicking the Divide button without entering any numbers. Also test the application by entering a string for the second number. Both errors should display the appropriate error message, then return the user to the interface.

    d. End the application, then print the application's code.

2. Open the DebDone (DebDone.vbp) project that you created in this Debugging Section. The project is located in the Tut07 folder on your Student Disk.

    a. Save the form and the project as DebDone3 in the Tut07 folder on your Student Disk.

    b. If you have access to the MSDN Library, then use the Help menu to research the Err object's Raise method. What is the purpose of the Raise method? Close the MSDN Library window.

    c. Open the Divide button's Click event procedure. Modify the code so that it will generate an "Internal error" number 51. The DebugErrHandler code should display the message "Internal error" for this error before returning the user to the application.

    d. Save and run the application. Enter the number 10 in the Number 1 text box, then enter the number 2 in the Number 2 text box. Press the Enter key to select the Divide button. A message box containing the "Internal error" message appears. Click the OK button.

    e. End the application, then print the application's code.

Random Access Files

The Cole's Playhouse Application

case ▶ Every Sunday afternoon, Cole's Playhouse, a small community theater, presents plays featuring local talent. The theater holds only 48 seats, which must be reserved in advance of the performance. No tickets are sold at the door. The manager of the playhouse, Max Phillips, asks you to create an application that will keep track of each patron's name and phone number.

Previewing the Application

As you've done in previous tutorials, you will preview the application before creating it.

To preview the application:

1   If necessary, start Windows, then place your Student Disk in the appropriate disk drive.

2   Use the Run command on the Start menu to run the **Cole** (Cole.exe) file, which is located in the Tut08 folder on your Student Disk. The application's user interface appears on the screen. Mr. Phillips can use this application to record the ticket reservations for each play, but first he needs to open either a new or an existing file.

First open an existing file named Preview.dat.

3   Click **File**, then click **Open**. An Open dialog box appears. Use the Open dialog box to open the **Preview.dat** file, which is located in the Tut08 folder on your Student Disk. Visual Basic displays the interface shown in Figure 8-1.

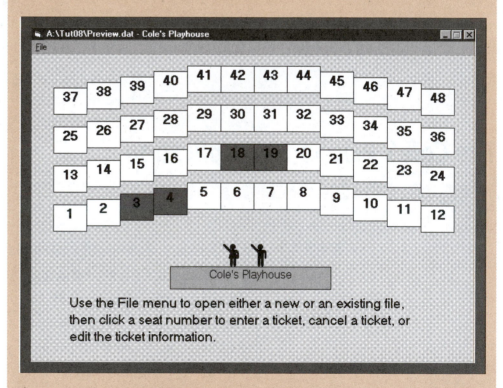

Figure 8-1: User interface for the Cole's Playhouse application

The form uses a label control array to represent the 48 seats in the Cole's Playhouse theater. Notice that some of the label controls are red and some are white. A red label control indicates that the seat is reserved; a white label control indicates that the seat is not reserved. To reserve a seat, you simply click the corresponding label control. Reserve seat number 8.

4   Click seat number 8. The dialog box shown in Figure 8-2 opens.

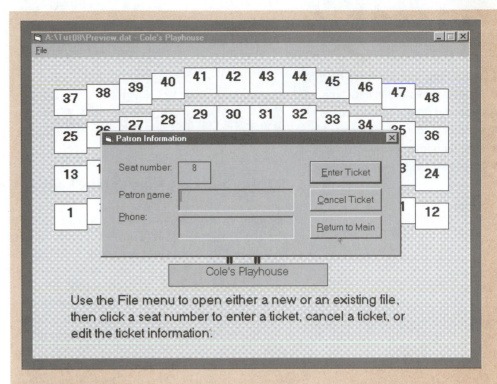

Figure 8-2: Dialog box shown in the user interface

This dialog box is used to enter or cancel a reservation, as well as to return to the screen that displays the theater seats. Reserve seat number 8 for Sue Marlin.

5 Type **Sue Marlin** in the Patron name text box, press the **Tab** key, then type **111–1111** in the Phone text box. Press the **Enter** key to select the Enter Ticket button. The application saves Sue Marlin's name and phone number in a random access file on your Student Disk; it also closes the dialog box and changes the color of seat number 8 to red.

Observe how you cancel a reservation.

6 Click seat number **8**. Sue Marlin's information appears in the form on the screen. Click the **Cancel Ticket** button. The application removes Sue Marlin's name and phone number from the random access file, then closes the dialog box and changes the color of seat number 8 to white.

You can also use the application to create a new file.

7 Click **File**, then click **New**. When the Save As dialog box appears, save the new file as **Prev2** in the Tut08 folder on your Student Disk. The form showing the 48 seats, each colored white to indicate that they are not reserved, appears.

   HELP? If this is the second or subsequent time you are creating the Prev2 data file, the application will display a dialog box asking if you want to replace the existing file. Click the Yes button.

8 Experiment by reserving and canceling seats of your choosing.

9 When you are finished experimenting, click **File**, then click **Exit** to end the application.

In Lesson A you will learn how to use random access files in an application. You will code the Cole's Playhouse application in Lessons B and C as you learn how to refer to a control in another form and also how to use Visual Basic's color constants.

LESSON A
objectives

In this lesson you will learn how to:
- Create a user-defined data type
- Open and close a random access file
- Write data to a random access file
- Read data from a random access file
- Initialize a random access file

Random Access Files

Random Access Files Versus Sequential Access Files

As you learned in Tutorial 6, you can save the data that the user enters, such as the student scores from Tutorial 5 or the questionnaire responses from Tutorial 6, in a data file. A data file, you may remember, is organized into fields and records. A **field** is a single item of information about a person, place, or thing—for example, a Social Security number, a city, or a price. A **record** is a group of related fields that contain all of the necessary data about a specific person, place, or thing. A collection of related records is called a **data file**.

Recall that Visual Basic has three types of data files—sequential access, random access, and binary access. (Although full coverage of binary access files is beyond the scope of this book, you can learn how to open, save to , and read from a binary access file in Appendix C.) A sequential access file is similar to a cassette tape in that each record in the file, like each song on a cassette tape, is both stored and retrieved in consecutive order from the beginning of the file to the end of the file. A **random access file**, on the other hand, is similar to a compact disc (CD) in that each record in the file, like each song on a CD, can be stored and retrieved in any order. That means, for example, that you can read or write the third record in a random access file without first reading or writing the two records that precede it.

As you may know, each song on a CD is associated with a unique number. The number indicates the position of the song on the CD; it allows you to access the song directly. Each record in a random access file also has a unique number, called a **record number**, that indicates its position in the file. The first record in the file is record number 1, the second record is number 2, and so on. You can directly access a record in a random access file by its record number. For this reason, random access files are also referred to as **direct access files**.

The ability to access a record directly allows quick retrieval of information, which accounts for the extensive use of random access files for on-line activities, such as making airline reservations, looking up the prices of items at a store, and approving credit card purchases. In a random access file, you can access record number 500 just as quickly as record number 1. Accessing record number 500 in a sequential access file would take much longer because the program would have to read the previous 499 records first.

You may be wondering why programmers use sequential files at all if random access files are so much faster for retrieving data. Sequential access files are generally used when you are dealing with records that do not all have the same number of fields, or when you want to store text created with a typical text editor, as you did in Tutorial 7.

Before looking at a sample application involving a random access file, you will compare the way records are stored in a sequential access file to the way records are stored in a random access file. This will give you better insight into how the computer accesses the records in each of the two file types, and why the records in a random access file can be processed so much faster than the records in a sequential access file.

Sequential Access Versus Random Access File Storage

Recall that you can use a simple text editor or word processor to view the records in a data file. Figure 8-3, for example, shows a sequential access file, displayed in WordPad, that contains three records. (WordPad is the text editor that is available with Windows 95.)

record

name field

price field

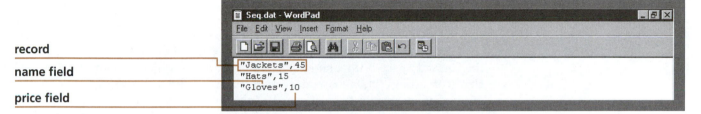

Figure 8-3: Sequential access file displayed in WordPad

Notice that each record appears on a separate line; that is because Visual Basic appends a carriage return character to the end of each record as it writes the record to the file. Each record in the file contains two fields: a name field and a price field. The name field stores strings, as indicated by the quotation marks around the data. The price field stores numbers. The comma, which separates the fields in a sequential access file, indicates where the name field ends and the price field begins.

In a sequential access file, the number of characters contained in a field usually varies from record to record. In Figure 8-3, for example, notice that each of the names stored in the name field is a different length. Because the field lengths are not the same in each record, the length of each record in a sequential access file will vary. That is why records in a sequential access file are referred to as **variable-length records**. Now look at these same three records in a random access file. Figure 8-4 shows a random access file, displayed in WordPad, containing the same three records shown in Figure 8-3.

binary representation of
price field

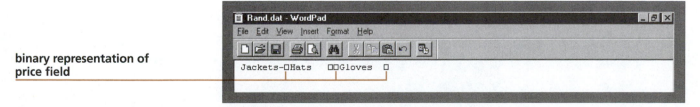

Figure 8-4: Random access file displayed in WordPad

Although the records are the same, notice that the random access file (Figure 8-4) looks different from the sequential access file (Figure 8-3). In the random access file, the three records appear on the same line with no commas separating the fields. The string field in the random access file does not contain quotation marks, and the numbers in the price field display as strange-looking characters. The unusual characters appear because the numeric fields in a random access file are stored in a compressed format, called binary, which allows random access files to use less disk space than sequential access files when storing numbers. Because a text editor interprets all data it reads as text, most of the numbers display as unusual characters because their binary codes are not associated with standard keyboard characters.

Unlike sequential access files, in random access files the number of characters contained in a field must be identical from record to record. When creating a random access file, the programmer first assigns a specific length, in bytes, to each field in the record. A **byte** is the amount of storage needed to hold one character, so you can think of a byte as being equivalent to a character. In the random access file shown in Figure 8-4, the name field has a length of seven bytes (characters) and the price field has a length of two bytes.

If the data in a field is shorter than the length of the field, Visual Basic pads the unused space with blanks (spaces). In Figure 8-4, for example, the four-character string "Hats" is padded with three blanks before being stored in the seven-character name field. If, on the other hand, the data in the field is longer than the length of the field, Visual Basic crops (truncates) the data to fit the field. The eight-character string "Sweaters" would be cropped to a seven-character string ("Sweater") before being stored in the name field. Care must be taken to select the proper field length for string data. You don't want to have a string field so large that it wastes disk space, but you also don't want the field to be so small that it crops most of the strings.

Because the length of the fields in a random access file is identical from record to record, the length of each record in a random access file is also identical. That is why the records in a random access file are referred to as **fixed-length records**.

To summarize, sequential access files store variable-length records, whereas random access files store fixed-length records. The difference in the way the records are stored accounts for the difference in access time. Look at an illustration of this.

Example A in Figure 8-5 on the following page depicts five records stored in a sequential access file on a disk. Example B depicts the same five records in a random access file. The <cr> in the sequential access file stands for carriage return, which Visual Basic appends to the end of each record as the record is written to the sequential access file. To make the random access file illustration easier to understand, numbers are shown in place of the binary characters.

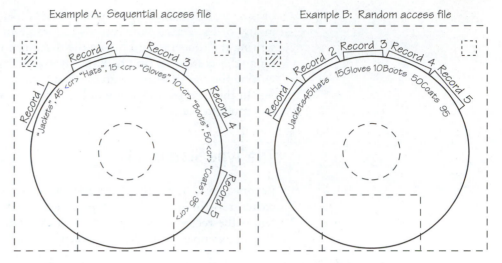

Figure 8-5: Examples of a sequential access and a random access file on disk

Notice that the length of each record in the sequential access file varies. The length of each record in the random access file, however, is nine bytes. Now assume that you want the computer to read the fourth record in the sequential access file. Because the records in a sequential access file are of variable lengths, the fourth record might begin with the sixth character in the file, the 123rd character in the file, or the 179th character in the file; it all depends on the lengths of the first three records. Although the computer does not know the exact location of the fourth record in the file, it does know that the fourth record begins immediately after the third carriage return in the file. (You can verify that by looking at Example A in Figure 8-5.) So, to locate the fourth record, the computer starts at the beginning of the file and reads every character until it finds the third carriage return. The character immediately following the third carriage return is the beginning of the fourth record.

Now assume that you want the computer to read the fourth record in the random access file shown in Figure 8-5's Example B. Recall that each record in the file is nine bytes (characters) long; so the fourth record in the file has to begin with the 28th character. Characters 1 through 9 are record 1, characters 10 through 18 are record 2, and characters 19 through 27 are record 3. To read the fourth record in the file, the computer simply skips over the first 27 bytes (characters) in the file and begins reading with the 28th character.

It may help to picture a file as a book and each record as a chapter in the book. Now assume that you want to find Chapter 4 in a book that does not have a table of contents. If each chapter has a different length, similar to the records in a sequential access file, you would need to start at the beginning of the book and look at each page until you found the heading "Chapter 4." If, however, each chapter contains exactly the same number of pages, similar to the records in a random access file, you would know precisely where Chapter 4 begins and could turn to that page immediately. For example, if each chapter is 20 pages long, Chapter 4 would begin on page 61.

Although this section discussed the difference in reading the records from both file types, the same concepts hold true for writing the records to the file. Because the records in a sequential access file are of variable length, the computer can't write the fourth record before it writes the first three records because it wouldn't know where to start writing. Therefore, the records in a sequential access file must be written to the file in consecutive order from the beginning of the file to the end of the file. The records in a random access file, however, can be written to the file in any order. Because the records in a random access file are all the same length, writing the fourth record before the first three is simple. If each record is 10 bytes long, the computer simply skips over the first 30 bytes in the file and begins writing the fourth record with the 31st byte.

In the next section you will learn how to assign the field lengths to the fields in a random access file.

The Type Statement

Before you can create a random access file, you need to define its **record structure**—the names, data types, and lengths of the fields in the record. You define the record structure with the **Type statement**. Figure 8-6 shows the syntax and an example of the Type statement.

As you learned in Tutorial 6, appending the asterisk and a number to the declaration of a String variable creates a fixed-length string. The number, you may recall, indicates the maximum number of characters the variable can store.

Syntax	Example
Type *structurename*	Type ItemStruc
fieldname1 **As** *datatype*	strName as String * 7
[*fieldname2* **As** *datatype*]	intPrice as Integer
[*fieldnameN* **As** *datatype*]	End Type
End Type	

Figure 8-6: Syntax and an example of the Type statement

The Type statement begins with the keyword **Type** followed by the name of the record structure; the statement ends with the keywords **End Type**. Between the **Type** and the **End Type** keywords, you place the name of each field in the record. The name of the record structure and the names of the fields must follow the same naming rules as for variables. In Figure 8-6's example, the name of the record structure is ItemStruc and the names of the fields are strName and intPrice.

The rules for naming variables are listed in Tutorial 3's Figures 3-4 and 3-5. The standard data types are listed in Tutorial 3's Figure 3-3.

Each field in the record structure must have a *datatype*, which defines the type of data the field will contain. The *datatype* can be any of the standard Visual Basic data types; it can also be another previously defined record structure. For all but the String data type, the length of the field is fixed by the data type you choose. If a field's data type is either Integer or Boolean, for example, Visual Basic automatically assigns a length of two bytes to the field. Visual Basic assigns a length of four bytes to both Long and Single fields; Double, Currency, and Date fields are assigned a length of eight bytes. In the example shown in Figure 8-6, the intPrice field is automatically set to two bytes because its data type is Integer.

If a field's data type is String, as is the strName field in Figure 8-6's example, you must specify the length of the field. You do so by appending both an asterisk (*) and a number, which represents the length of the field, to the data type. The `strName As String * 7` instruction in Figure 8-6, for example, tells Visual Basic to allocate seven bytes (characters) for the strName field.

The Type statement groups several related fields together into one unit—the record structure. The record structure itself actually becomes a data type, called a **user-defined data type**, which is separate and distinct from Visual Basic's standard data types. Figure 8-6's example groups together two fields, strName and intPrice, into a record structure (a user-defined data type) named ItemStruc.

tip

The period between the record variable's name and the field variable's name is called the dot member selection operator. It indicates that the field variable is a member of the record variable.

tip

Not all applications use small integers to identify the items, employees, and so on in a file. For example, a Social Security number, referred to as a key field, is usually used to identify an employee.

Once the user-defined data type (record structure) is created, you can declare a variable of that data type in your code, just as you can with Visual Basic's standard data types. The three-character ID for variables declared as a user-defined data type is "udt". For example, the `Dim udtItemRec as ItemStruc` instruction creates an ItemStruc variable named udtItemRec, similar to the way the `Dim intAge as Integer` instruction creates an Integer variable named intAge. The difference, however, is that the variable declared as a user-defined data type, called a **record variable**, will itself contain one or more variables, called **field variables**. The `Dim udtItemRec as ItemStruc` instruction, for example, creates a record variable named udtItemRec and two field variables, strName and intPrice. When coding, you refer to the entire record variable by its name—in this case, udtItemRec. To refer to the individual field variables, however, you must precede the field variable's name with the name of the record variable in which it is defined. You separate the record variable's name from the field variable's name with a period. The names of the field variables within the udtItemRec record variable, for example, are udtItemRec.strName and udtItemRec.intPrice.

Your Student Disk contains a partially completed application that uses a random access file. To keep the current application simple, the item number used to identify each item will be a small integer that corresponds directly to its record number in the random access file. In other words, item number 1 will be record number 1 in the file, item number 2 will be record number 2, and so on. You will finish coding the application in this lesson.

To open the random access file application:

1 Start Visual Basic, if necessary, then open the **Random** (Random.vbp) project, which is located in the Tut08 folder on your Student Disk. The `Option Explicit` statement has already been entered in the General Declarations section of the form.

2 Save the form and the project as **laRandom**, then click the **form** to select it. See Figure 8-7.

txtNum

txtName

txtPrice

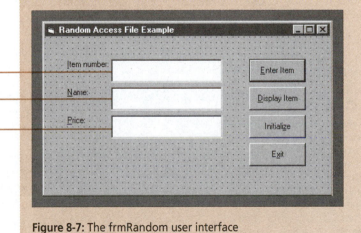

Figure 8-7: The frmRandom user interface

A store owner can use this application to both save and display information about the items he or she sells. To save the item's information, for example, the user simply enters the item's number, name, and price into the appropriate text boxes, then clicks the Enter Item button. The Enter Item button will save the item's name and price in a random access file. The user can display the item's name and price by entering the item's number in the Item number text box, then clicking the Display Item button. Visual Basic will use the item's number to locate the appropriate record in the random access file, and will display the item's name and its price in the Name and Price text boxes, respectively. Now begin coding this application.

Coding the Code Module

The first step in coding this application is to enter the Type statement that defines the record structure for the item records. The record structure indicates the information that you want to save to the random access file. In this case the record structure will contain two fields: the item's name and its price. You will name the record structure, ItemStruc, and the two fields, strName and intPrice.

You enter the Type statement in the General Declarations section of a code module, which you learned about in Tutorial 3. A code module, you may remember, is a separate file, added to your application, that contains only code; it does not contain any forms or controls. When you declare a variable using a data type other than a standard one, Visual Basic searches the code module for a matching Type statement before creating the variable.

> **Keep in mind that the Type statement simply defines the record structure; it does not actually create the record variable or the field variables.**

To add a code module to the current project, then enter the Type statement:

1 Click **Project** on the menu bar, then click **Add Module**. Click **Module** on the New tab of the Add Module dialog box, if necessary, then click the **Open** button. Visual Basic adds the Module1 filename to the Project window, and the General Declarations section of the Module1 module appears on the screen.

2 Enter the instructions shown in Figure 8-8. (Recall that you should enter the `Option Explicit` statement in each module's General Declarations section.)

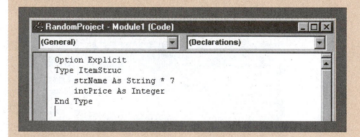

Figure 8-8: Type statement in code module

Each form and module in an application must be saved as a separate file. Because of this, an application can use forms and modules created for another application, often with few or no modifications. Save the current module under a more descriptive name.

3 Click **File**, then click **Save Module1 As**. Save the file as **laModule** in the Tut08 folder on your Student Disk.

4 Close the module's Code window, then click the **Save Project** button on the toolbar.

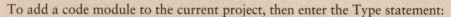

> **By default, items entered in a module are global, which means they are available to every form and module in the entire application. User-defined constants, variables, procedures, and functions can all be global. If you want the item to be available only to the module in which it is defined, you must precede the Type statement with the keyword `Private`—for example, `Private Type ItemStruc`.**

The form's Load event, which is processed when the form is loaded into memory, is the next procedure to code. In the Load event you will include instructions that tell Visual Basic to open the random access file that contains each item's name and price. Before writing this code, however, you will learn how to use the Open statement both to create a new random access file and to open an existing one.

Creating and Opening a Random Access File

tip

Filename should include the drive letter and path, and it must be enclosed in quotation marks. If *filename* is a variable that stores the name of the file, then *filename* should not be enclosed in quotation marks.

As with sequential access files, the **Open statement** either creates a new random access file, if the file doesn't exist, or opens an existing random access file. The syntax of the Open statement used with random access files is **Open** *filename* [**For** *mode*] **As** # *filenumber* **Len** = *reclength*. Notice that the syntax is very similar to the one used for sequential access files. *Filename* is the name of the file you want to open and *filenumber* is the number assigned to the file. Unlike sequential access files, however, where the mode is Input, Output, or Append, the mode for random access files is always Random. Opening a file for Random allows you to both read and write to the file.

The Open statement for a random access file must include the record length (*reclength*) for each record in the file. *Reclength* must be a positive integer between 1 and 32767, inclusive. You calculate the record length by adding together the length of each field in the record variable. Because making that calculation by hand is time-consuming and prone to errors, it is much better to let Visual Basic calculate the record length for you. You do so by including the Len function, which you learned about in Tutorial 4, in the Open instruction. The syntax of the Len function to determine the length of a string, you may remember, is **Len**(*string*). Similarly, the syntax of the Len function to determine the length of a variable is **Len**(*variablename*). When using the Len function in the Open statement, *variablename* refers to the record variable's name. Assuming the record variable's name is udtItemRec and the record length is 9 bytes, the two instructions `Open "a:\Tut08\Item.dat" for Random as #1 Len = 9` and `Open "a:\Tut08\Item.dat" for Random as #1 Len = Len(udtItemRec)` will produce the same result.

tip

Notice that Len is used in two ways in the Open statement. It's easy to confuse them. The Len keyword is a required part of the Open statement and is always to the left of the equal sign. It tells Visual Basic how much space to use on the disk for each record. The Len function, however, measures the length of the record variable as specified in the Type statement. As mentioned earlier, it is optional but its use is recommended. If used, it always appears to the right of the equal sign. In the Open Statement example, the Len function measures the size of the udtItemRec variable; Visual Basic then uses that value as the length required in the syntax of the Open statement.

In the current application, you will place the Open statement in the form's Load event procedure so that the random access file will be opened as soon as the application is run.

Coding the Form's Load Event Procedure

The form's Load event procedure should declare the necessary variables, then open the random access file. In this application the Load event needs one variable—a record variable—that the Len function will use to calculate the record length for the Open statement. You will name the record variable udtItemRec and declare it as a variable of the user-defined type ItemStruc, which is the name of the record structure created with the Type statement. Recall that "udt" is the three-character ID for a variable declared as a user-defined type.

To code the form's Load event procedure:

1 Open the form's Load event procedure. Maximize the Code window, then enter the Dim statement and the Open statement shown in Figure 8-9. If your Student Disk is in the B: drive, be sure to change the a: to b: in the Open statement.

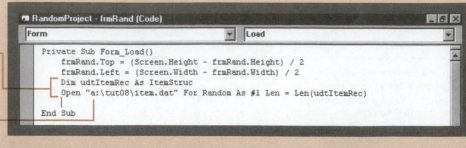

enter these two lines
of code

if your Student Disk is
in drive B:, then change
the drive letter to b:

```
RandomProject - frmRand (Code)
Form                              Load

Private Sub Form_Load()
    frmRand.Top = (Screen.Height - frmRand.Height) / 2
    frmRand.Left = (Screen.Width - frmRand.Width) / 2
    Dim udtItemRec As ItemStruc
    Open "a:\tut08\item.dat" For Random As #1 Len = Len(udtItemRec)

End Sub
```

Figure 8-9: Code entered in the Load event procedure

While the random access file is open, the program can both read records from the file and write records to the file.

2   Close the Code window.

tip

Using the Len function to calculate the record length also has another advantage: if the record length is modified in the Type statement, the Len function adjusts automatically to the new length.

Remember that all open files should be closed before the application ends. Because it's so easy to forget to close the files, you should enter the Close instruction as soon after entering the Open instruction as possible.

Closing a Random Access File

tip

A `Close` statement with no *filenumber* closes all open files.

The **Close statement** closes both sequential access files and random access files. Recall that the syntax of the Close statement is **Close** [#*filenumber*], where *filenumber* is the number used in the Open statement to open the file you now want to close. In the current application you will have the form's Unload event close the Item.dat file before the form is unloaded. You will also enter the `Unload frmRand` instruction in the Exit button's Click event procedure so that it will trigger the form's Unload event.

To continue coding the application:

1   Open the Exit button's Click event procedure. Press the **Tab** key, then type **unload frmrand** and press the **Enter** key.

2   Open the form's Unload event. Press the **Tab** key, then type **close #1** and press the **Enter** key.

3   Close the Code window.

Next you will learn how to write a record (store data) to a random access file on disk.

Writing Records to a Random Access File

tip

Recall that you use the Write # statement to write a record to a sequential access file.

You use the **Put statement** to write a record to a random access file. The syntax of the Put statement is **Put #** *filenumber*, [*recordnumber*], *variablename*. *Filenumber* is the number used in the Open statement to open the file, *recordnumber* is the number of the record to be written, and *variablename* is the name of the record variable. You will use the Put statement in the Enter Item button's Click event procedure to write the item information to the Item.dat file.

Coding the Enter Item Button

The pseudocode for the Enter Item button is shown in Figure 8-10.

---

1. Declare variables and constants

2. Assign the item number to the intItemNum variable

3. If intItemNum > 0 then

    Assign the name and the price to the udtItemRec variable

    Write the udtItemRec variable to the random access file

   Else

    Display "Incorrect item number" message to user

   End If

4. Clear the text boxes

5. Set the focus to the txtNum text box

Figure 8-10: Pseudocode for the Enter Item button

To code the Enter Item button, then save and run the application:

1. Open the Enter Item button's Click event procedure. Notice that the procedure declares two constants and a variable. The constants and the variable will be used by the MsgBox function to display the "Incorrect item number" message to the user.

The Click event procedure requires two additional variables, which you will call intItemNum and udtItemRec. intItemNum, an Integer variable, will store the item's number, which in this application corresponds to the record number. udtItemRec, an ItemStruc variable, will store the record, which consists of an item's name and price. Both variables will be used in the Put statement to write each item's record to the item.dat file.

2. Maximize the Code window. In the blank line below the existing Dim statement, type **dim intItemNum as integer, udtItemRec as itemstruc** and press the **Enter** key.

Now assign the item number, which the user entered in the txtNum text box, to the intItemNum variable.

3. Type **intitemnum = val(txtnum.text)** and press the **Enter** key.

According to the pseudocode, you must now determine if the intItemNum variable contains a number that is greater than zero. The number stored in the intItemNum variable, remember, represents the record number in the file. Because the first record in a random access file is record number 1, any record number that is not greater than zero is invalid.

4. Type **if intitemnum > 0 then** and press the **Enter** key.

If the intItemNum variable contains a number that is greater than zero, then you will assign the values in the other two text boxes (txtName and txtPrice) to the udtItemRec record variable. You do so by assigning the value in the txtName control to the udtItemRec.strName field variable, and assigning the value in the txtPrice control to the udtItemRec.intPrice field variable.

5 Press the **Tab** key, then type **udtitemrec.strname = txtname.text** and press the **Enter** key. Then type **udtitemrec.intprice = val(txtprice.text)** and press the **Enter** key.

Now write the item's record to the random access file. Recall that the syntax of the Put statement is **Put #** *filenumber*, [*recordnumber*], *variablename*. In this case the *filenumber* is 1, the *recordnumber* is the item number stored in the intItemNum variable, and the *variablename* is udtItemRec.

6 Type **put #1, intitemnum, udtitemrec** and press the **Enter** key. When Visual Basic writes the record variable to the file, it writes the information stored in each of the field variables. In this case, for example, Visual Basic will write the information stored in both the udtItemRec.strName and udtItemRec.intPrice field variables to the file.

If the intItemNum variable contains a number that is not greater than zero, then you will use the MsgBox function to display an appropriate message to the user.

7 Press the **Backspace** key, then type **else** and press the **Enter** key. Press the **Tab** key, then type **intanswer = msgbox(conmsg, conbtns, "Random")** and press the **Enter** key. Press the **Backspace** key, then type **end if** and press the **Enter** key.

All that remains is to clear the text boxes and set the focus.

8 Enter the remaining code and documentation shown in Figure 8-11.

Remember to include the record variable's name, not the record structure's name or the names of the field variables, in the Put instruction.

line continuation character

enter these four lines of code

enter this documentation

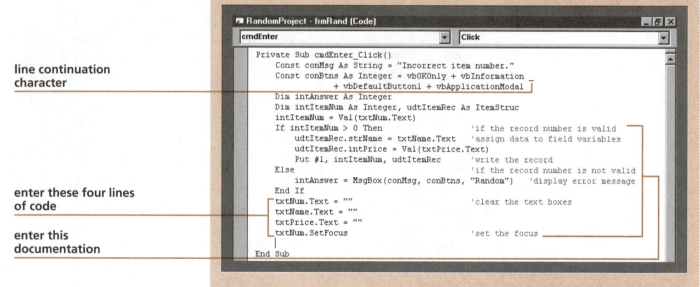

Figure 8-11: Completed Click event procedure for the Enter Item button

9 Compare your code with Figure 8-11 and make any needed corrections before continuing.

Now save and run the application to make sure the code you've entered is working correctly.

tip

It's tempting (and very useful) to test an application with unusual, even absurd values. This example, however, is designed only to help you get the feel of how random access files work. If you enter an unusually large record number, Visual Basic will create a correspondingly large data file that can take up a great deal of space on your disk—and could possibly "crash" the program.

To test the application:

1 Close the Code window. **Save** and **run** the application. Visual Basic executes the instructions in the form's Load event procedure. Because the item.dat file does not yet exist, the Open statement in the Load event first creates and then opens the random access file. The user interface appears on the screen.

In a random access file, you can enter the items in any order. Enter item number 2 first.

2 Type **2** as the item number and press the **Tab** key. Type **Hats** as the item name and press the **Tab** key. Type **15** as the price, then press the **Enter** key to select the Enter Item button. Visual Basic writes the information to the random access file.

Enter the fifth record next.

3 Type **5** as the item number, **Coats** as the item name, and **95** as the price. Press the **Enter** key to select the Enter Item button.

4 Click the **Exit** button to end the application.

If you view the item.dat file in a text editor or word processor, you may find that the data file contains some extra characters, as shown in Figure 8-12. (You can verify this by opening the item.dat file in either a text editor or a word processor. You don't need to be concerned if your data file does not look identical to Figure 8-12, or if your file does not contain any extra characters.)

record 2
garbage
garbage
record 5

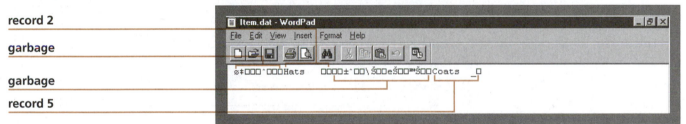

Figure 8-12: item.dat random access file displayed in WordPad

You may find that a random access file contains "garbage"—useless characters in places on the disk where records have not been written. Notice, for example, that the space reserved for record 1 in the item.dat file contains garbage. (Recall that you did not write any information to records 1, 3, and 4—only to records 2 and 5.) This is due to the way your computer's operating system saves and deletes files from a disk. When you save a file to a disk, the sectors that contain the file are marked as "in use." When you delete a file, the regions (sectors) on the disk that contain the file are marked as "available," but the file is not really erased from the disk. Those sectors will contain the remains of old files until you write over that information. When you don't write information to each record in a random access file, the space reserved for the unwritten records can contain anything. The solution to this problem is to initialize—in other words, to clear the disk space for the file.

Initializing a Random Access File

You initialize a random access file by writing spaces to the string fields and a zero to the numeric fields. A random access file should be initialized before any records are written to it. If you initialize the file after records are written to it, the existing records will be overwritten with the spaces and zeros. However, a user may wish to initialize an existing data file so it can be reused for new data. In that case, a confirmation message should appear that lets the user confirm his or her intent.

Before you can initialize a data file, you must estimate the maximum number of records the file will contain. It doesn't hurt to overestimate. Figure 8-13 shows the pseudocode to initialize a data file that will contain a maximum of 10 records.

1. Declare variables and constants
2. Assign 7 spaces to the name field in the udtItemRec variable
3. Assign a zero to the price field in the udtItemRec variable
4. Verify that user wants to initialize the file
5. If the user wants to initialize the file then
    Repeat for intItemNum = 1 to 10
        Write the udtItemRec record to the random access file
    End Repeat For intItemNum
    Display "File was initialized" message to the user
Else
    Display "File was not initialized" message to the user
End If
6. Set the focus to the txtNum text box

Figure 8-13: Pseudocode for the Initialize button

The code to initialize the item.dat file has already been entered in the Initialize button. View that code now.

To view the code in the Initialize button, then save and run the application:
1 Open the Initialize button's Click event procedure, then maximize the Code window. See Figure 8-14.

```
RandomProject - frmRand (Code)                                          _ □ ×
cmdInit                              ▼    Click                              ▼
    Private Sub cmdInit_Click()
        Const conMsg As String = "Do you want to initialize the file?"
        Const conBtns1 As Integer = vbYesNo + vbExclamation _
                        + vbDefaultButton2 + vbApplicationModal
        Const conBtns2 As Integer = vbOKOnly + vbInformation _
                        + vbDefaultButton1 + vbApplicationModal
        Dim intUserResponse As Integer, intItemNum As Integer, udtItemRec As ItemStruc
        udtItemRec.strName = Space(7)
        udtItemRec.intPrice = 0
        intUserResponse = MsgBox(conMsg, conBtns1, "Random")
        If intUserResponse = vbYes Then
            For intItemNum = 1 To 10
                Put #1, intItemNum, udtItemRec
            Next intItemNum
            intUserResponse = MsgBox("File was initialized.", conBtns2, "Random")
        Else
            intUserResponse = MsgBox("File was not initialized.", conBtns2, "Random")
        End If
        txtNum.SetFocus
    End Sub
```

assigns values to field variables in record variable

writes record variable 10 times

Figure 8-14: Code entered in the Initialize button

The code begins by declaring three constants and three variables (intUserResponse, intItemNum, udtItemRec). The intUserResponse variable and the three constants will be used by the MsgBox functions. The intItemNum variable will store the item number, and the udtItemRec variable will store the record—the item's name and price. After the variables and constants are declared, the code uses the Space function to assign seven spaces to the udtItemRec.strName field variable. The syntax of the **Space function** is **Space**(*number*), where *number* is the number of spaces you want. The code also assigns a zero to the udtItemRec.intPrice field variable.

Initializing a data file destroys all data in it; therefore, before initializing a file, you should always present a warning message to the user and give him or her an opportunity to cancel the operation. In this procedure, the MsgBox function verifies that the user wants to initialize the data file. If he or she does, then a For Next loop initializes the file by writing the record variable to the file, 10 times. The record variable, remember, contains seven spaces for the strName field and a zero for the intPrice field. The MsgBox function then displays a message telling the user that the file was initialized, and the SetFocus method sets the focus to the Item number text box.

If, on the other hand, the user does not want to initialize the file, then the MsgBox function displays a message informing the user that the file was not initialized, and the SetFocus method sets the focus to the Item number text box.

2   Close the Code window.

Now initialize the item.dat data file.

3   **Save** and **run** the application. Click the **Initialize** button, then click the **Yes** button to initialize the item.dat file. Click the **OK** button to remove the message informing the user that the file was initialized.

Because the Initialize button destroyed the existing records in the item.dat file, you will need to reenter records 2 and 5.

4   Type **2** as the item number, **Hats** as the item name, and **15** as the price. Press the **Enter** key to select the Enter Item button.

5   Type **5** as the item number, **Coats** as the item name, and **95** as the price. Press the **Enter** key to select the Enter Item button.

6   Click the **Exit** button to end the application.

GUI
Design Tips

Communicating with the User

- If an operation is destructive, prompt the user to verify that he or she wants to proceed with the operation.
- Display messages to inform the user of the status of important events.

If you want to verify that the file no longer contains "garbage," exit the IaRandom application, then open the item.dat file in a text editor or word processor. Any "garbage" that was visible in the file before initialization will now be gone. When you're finished looking at the file, exit the text editor or word processor without saving the file.

Before coding the Display Item button, you will learn how to read a record from a random access file.

Reading Records from a Random Access File

You use the **Get statement** to read a record from a random access file. The syntax of the Get statement is **Get #** *filenumber*, *[recordnumber]*, *variablename*. *Filenumber* is the number used in the Open statement to open the file, *recordnumber* is the number of the record to be read, and *variablename* is the name of the record variable. You will use the Get statement in the Display Item button's Click event procedure to read a record from the item.dat file.

Coding the Display Item Button

To display the name and price of an existing item in the file, the user needs first to enter the item number in the Item number text box, then click the Display Item button. The pseudocode for the Display Item button is shown in Figure 8-15.

---

1. Declare variables and constants
2. Assign the item number to the intItemNum variable
3. If intItemNum > 0 then

   Read the record corresponding to the item number

   Assign the name from the udtItemRec variable to the Name text box

   Assign the price from the udtItemRec variable to the Price text box

   Else

   Display "Incorrect item number" message to the user

   End If
4. Set the focus to the txtNum text box

Figure 8-15: Pseudocode for the Display Item button

Most of the code for this button has already been entered in the Code window for you; only three of the instructions are missing.

To view the code in the Display Item button's Code window, then save and run the application:

1 Open the Display Item button's Click event procedure, then maximize the Code window. Position the insertion point as shown in Figure 8-16.

position insertion point here

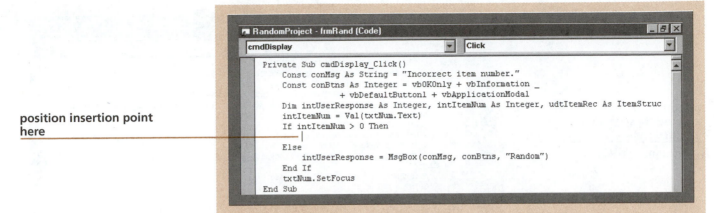

```
RandomProject - frmRand (Code)                                    _ 6 X
cmdDisplay                        ▼      Click                          ▼
    Private Sub cmdDisplay_Click()
        Const conMsg As String = "Incorrect item number."
        Const conBtns As Integer = vbOKOnly + vbInformation _
                    + vbDefaultButton1 + vbApplicationModal
        Dim intUserResponse As Integer, intItemNum As Integer, udtItemRec As ItemStruc
        intItemNum = Val(txtNum.Text)
        If intItemNum > 0 Then
           |
        Else
            intUserResponse = MsgBox(conMsg, conBtns, "Random")
        End If
        txtNum.SetFocus
    End Sub
```

Figure 8-16: Partially completed Code window for the Display Item button

The code begins by declaring two constants and three variables. The intUserResponse variable and both constants will be used by the MsgBox function. The intItemNum variable will store the item number, and the udtItemRec variable will store the record. After the variables and constants are declared, the code assigns the item number, which is entered in the txtNum text box, to the intItemNum variable. If the intItemNum variable contains a number that is greater than 0, then the procedure should read the record from the random access file. Recall that the syntax of the Get statement is **Get #** *filenumber*, *[recordnumber]*, *variablename*. In this case the *filenumber* is 1, the *recordnumber* is the item number stored in the intItemNum variable, and the *variablename* is udtItemRec.

2 In the blank line below the If statement, type **get #1, intitemnum, udtitemrec** and press the **Enter** key. This statement tells Visual Basic to read the record whose record number is stored in the intItemNum variable. As it reads the record, Visual Basic stores the first seven bytes of the record in the udtItemRec.strName field variable and the last two bytes in the udtItemRec.intPrice field variable.

Now display the contents of both field variables, udtItemRec.strName and udtItemRec.intPrice, in the appropriate text boxes.

3 In the blank line below the Get statement, type **txtname.text = udtitemrec.strname** and press the **Enter** key. Then type **txtprice.text = udtitemrec.intprice**.

The Else, MsgBox, End If, and SetFocus instructions are already entered in the Code window for you.

4 Compare your code with the code shown in Figure 8-17. Make any needed corrections before continuing to the next step.

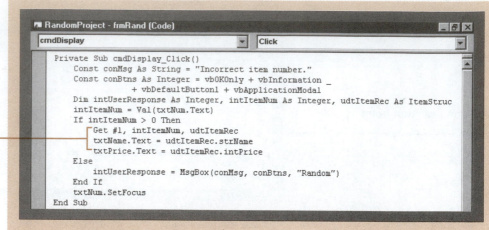

```
RandomProject - frmRand (Code)                                    _ 8 X
cmdDisplay                    ▼      Click                             ▼
    Private Sub cmdDisplay_Click()
        Const conMsg As String = "Incorrect item number."
        Const conBtns As Integer = vbOKOnly + vbInformation _
                    + vbDefaultButton1 + vbApplicationModal
        Dim intUserResponse As Integer, intItemNum As Integer, udtItemRec As ItemStruc
        intItemNum = Val(txtNum.Text)
        If intItemNum > 0 Then
            Get #1, intItemNum, udtItemRec
            txtName.Text = udtItemRec.strName
            txtPrice.Text = udtItemRec.intPrice
        Else
            intUserResponse = MsgBox(conMsg, conBtns, "Random")
        End If
        txtNum.SetFocus
    End Sub
```

be sure that you entered these three instructions

Figure 8-17: Completed Code window for the Display Item button

5   Close the Code window, then **save** and **run** the application.

First display the name and price of an existing item—item 5, for example.

6   Type **5** as the item number, then click the **Display Item** button. Item 5's name (Coats) and price (95) appear in the appropriate text boxes.

Now display the name and price of an item that does not exist—item 1, for example.

7   Type **1** as the item number, then click the **Display Item** button. Nothing appears in the Name text box, and a zero appears in the Price text box; that's because you initialized the name field to spaces and the price field to zero.

8   Click the **Exit** button to end the application. Visual Basic returns to the design screen.

You have now completed Lesson A. You can either take a break or complete the questions and exercises at the end of the lesson.

S U M M A R Y

To determine sequential access versus random access:

■   A sequential access file is similar to a cassette tape. Each song on a cassette tape, like each record in a sequential access file, is both stored and retrieved in consecutive order from beginning to end.

■   A random access file is similar to a CD. Each song on a CD, like each record in a random access file, can be played in any order by accessing its track (record) number.

To create a user-defined data type:

■   Enter the Type statement in the General Declarations section of a code module. Its syntax is:

    Type *structurename*

        fieldname1 **As** *datatype*

        [*fieldname2* **As** *datatype*]

        [*fieldnameN* **As** *datatype*]

    End Type

To add a code module to an application:

- Click Project on the menu bar, then click Add Module. Click Module on the New tab of the Add Module dialog box, if necessary, then click the Open button.

To create or open a random access file:

- Use the Open statement. Its syntax is **Open** *filename* [**For** *mode*] **As #** *filenumber* **Len =** *reclength*.
- *Filename* is the name of the file, including the drive letter and path, and must be enclosed in quotation marks. If the *filename* is stored in a variable or a property, you do not need quotation marks.
- *Mode* is Random. Random mode opens the file for reading and writing.
- *Filenumber* is an integer expression with a value between 1 and 511, inclusive.
- *Reclength* is the length of each record in the file and must be an integer in the range of 1 through 32767, inclusive.

To determine the size of a record:

- Use the Len function. Its syntax is **Len**(*variablename*), where *variablename* refers to the record variable's name.

To close a file:

- Use the Close statement. Its syntax is **Close** [**#** *filenumber*]. *Filenumber* is the number used in the Open statement to open the file. A Close statement with no *filenumber* closes all open files.

To write a record to an open random access file:

- Use the Put statement. Its syntax is **Put #** *filenumber*, [*recordnumber*], *variablename*. *Filenumber* is the number used in the Open statement to open the random access file. *Recordnumber* is the number of the record to write. *Variablename* is the name of the record variable.

To initialize a string to spaces:

- Use the Space function. Its syntax is **Space**(*number*), where *number* represents the number of spaces.

To read a record from an open random access file:

- Use the Get statement. Its syntax is **Get #** *filenumber*, [*recordnumber*], *variablename*. *Filenumber* is the number used in the Open statement to open the random access file. *Recordnumber* is the number of the record to read. *Variablename* is the name of the record variable.

QUESTIONS

1. You use the _____ statement to define the structure of a record.
   a. Declare
   b. Define
   c. Record
   d. Structure
   e. Type

2. Records in a random access file can be accessed _____.
   a. randomly
   b. sequentially
   c. either randomly or sequentially

3. The Type statement must be declared in the _____.
   a. event procedure of an object
   b. General Declarations section of a code module
   c. General Declarations section of a form

4. Which of the following will define a 15-character string field variable named strCity?
   a. `strCity as String`
   b. `strCity as String(15)`
   c. `strCity as String X 15`
   d. `strCity as String by 15`
   e. `strCity as String * 15`

5. If you store the string "Chicago" (without the quotes) in a 15-character field named strCity, what will Visual Basic actually store in the strCity field?
   a. The string "Chicago" (with the quotes).
   b. The string "Chicago".
   c. The string "Chicago" followed by six blank spaces.
   d. The string "Chicago" followed by eight blank spaces.
   e. Eight blank spaces followed by the string "Chicago".

6. A _____ is equivalent to a character.
   a. bit
   b. byte
   c. integer
   d. number
   e. string

7. A field defined as Currency is stored in _____ bytes.
   a. 2
   b. 4
   c. 6
   d. 8
   e. 10

8. You create a random access file with the _____ statement.
   a. Create
   b. Declare
   c. Define
   d. Open
   e. Random

9. You open a random access file with the _____ statement.
   a. Create
   b. Declare
   c. Define
   d. Open
   e. Random

10. You use the _____ statement to write a record to a random access file.
    a. Define
    b. Get
    c. Put
    d. Record
    e. Write

11. You use the _____ statement to read a record from a random access file.
    a. Define
    b. Get
    c. Put
    d. Record
    e. Write

12. Which two of the following `Open` statements are valid? (The name of the record variable is udtEmpRec. Each record is 100 bytes.)
    a. `Open a:\data.dat for random as #1 Len = Len(udtEmpRec)`
    b. `Open a:\data.dat for "random" as #1 Len = Len(udtEmpRec)`
    c. `Open "a:\data.dat" for random as #1 Len = Len(udtEmpRec)`
    d. `Open "a:\data.dat" for random Len = Len(udtEmpRec)`
    e. `Open "a:\data.dat" for random as #1 Len = 100`

13. Which of the following will write the udtEmpRec record, which consists of a last name and a first name, to a random access file?
    a. `Put #1, intRecNum, strLast, strFirst`
    b. `Put strLast, strFirst to #1`
    c. `Put intRecNum, strLast, strFirst to #1`
    d. `Put #1, intRecNum, udtEmpRec`
    e. `Put intRecNum, udtEmpRec to #1`

14. Which of the following will close a random access file opened as file number 3?
    a. `Close filenumber 3`
    b. `Close random #3`
    c. `Close file #3`
    d. `Close #3`
    e. `Close file 3`

15. Which of the following will return the length of the udtStudRec record?
    a. `Len(udtStudRec)`
    b. `Length(udtStudRec)`
    c. `Recordlength(udtStudRec)`
    d. `udtStudRec(Len)`
    e. `udtStudRec(Length)`

16. Unless specified otherwise, an open random access file can be _____.
    a. read from only
    b. written to only
    c. either read from or written to

17. Which of the following will assign 10 spaces to a variable named strFirst?

    a. `strFirst = Blank(10)`
    b. `strFirst = Blank$(10)`
    c. `strFirst = Space&(10)`
    d. `strFirst = Space(10)`
    e. `strFirst = (10)Space`

Use the following information to answer Questions 18 through 26.

```
Type CustStruc
        strName as String * 25
        strPhone as String * 12
        curSalary as Currency
End Type
Dim udtCustRec as CustStruc
```

18. The name of the record structure is _____ .

    a. `strName`
    b. `strPhone`
    c. `udtCustRec`
    d. `curSalary`
    e. `CustStruc`

19. The name of the record variable is _____ .

    a. `strName`
    b. `strPhone`
    c. `udtCustRec`
    d. `curSalary`
    e. `CustStruc`

20. The names of the three field variables are _____ .

    a. `strName`
    b. `strPhone`
    c. `udtCustRec`
    d. `curSalary`
    e. `CustStruc`

21. The length of the strName field variable is _____ .

    a. 8
    b. 12
    c. 25
    d. 45
    e. unknown

22. The length of the curSalary field variable is _____ .

    a. 8
    b. 12
    c. 25
    d. 45
    e. unknown

23. The length of the record variable is _____ .

    a. 8
    b. 12
    c. 25
    d. 45
    e. unknown

24. When coding, you would refer to the strPhone field variable as _____.
    a. `strPhone`
    b. `strPhone.udtCustRec`
    c. `strPhone.CustStruc`
    d. `udtCustRec.strPhone`
    e. `CustStruc.strPhone`

25. When coding, you would refer to the record variable as _____.
    a. strName
    b. strPhone
    c. udtCustRec
    d. curSalary
    e. CustStruc

26. Assume that the intNum variable contains the number 2. Which two of the following will read the second customer record from a file opened as #1?
    a. `Get #1, 2, udtCustRec`
    b. `Get #1, 2, strName, strPhone`
    c. `Get #1, intNum, udtCustRec`
    d. `Get #1, intNum, strName, strPhone`
    e. `Get #1, intNum, udtCustRec.strName, udtCustRec.strPhone`

E X E R C I S E S

1. Write a **Type** statement that defines a record structure named BookStruc. The record structure contains three fields: strTitle, strAuthor, curCost. StrTitle is a 20-character String field, strAuthor is a 20-character String field, and curCost is a Currency field.

2. Write a **Type** statement that defines a record structure named TapeStruc. The record structure contains four fields: strName, strArtist, intSong, and strLength. StrName is a 25-character String field, strArtist is a 20-character String field, intSong is an Integer field, and strLength is a 6-character String field.

3. Write a **Dim** statement that declares a BookStruc variable named udtBookRec.

4. Write a **Dim** statement that declares a TapeStruc variable named udtTapeRec.

5. Write an **Open** statement that opens a random access file named "Books.dat" on your Student Disk. Open the file as #1. The contents of the udtBookRec record variable will be written to the file.

6. Write an **Open** statement that opens a random access file named "Tapes.dat" on your Student Disk. Open the file as #1. The contents of the udtTapeRec record variable will be written to the file.

7. Assume that the intRecNum variable contains the number 5 and the random access file was opened as #1. Write a **Put** statement that will write the contents of the udtBookRec record variable as the fifth record in the file.

8. Assume that the intRecNum variable contains the number 2 and the random access file was opened as #1. Write a **Put** statement that will write the contents of the udtTapeRec record variable as the second record in the file.

9. Assume that the intRecNum variable contains the number 3 and the random access file was opened as #1. Write a **Get** statement that will read the third record in the file. The name of the record variable is udtBookRec.

10. Assume that the intRecNum variable contains the number 5 and the random access file was opened as #1. Write a **Get** statement that will read the fifth record in the file. The name of the record variable is udtTapeRec.

11. Write the statement that will close the file opened as # 1.

Use the following record structure for Exercise 12.

```
Type ComputerStruc
      strName as String * 5
      curCost as Currency
End Type
```

12. a. Write a `Dim` statement that declares a ComputerStruc variable named udtCompRec.
   b. Write an `Open` statement that opens a random access file named "Computer.dat" on your Student Disk. Open the file as #1.
   c. Write the For...Next loop that will initialize the Computer.dat file for 10 records.
   d. Write an assignment statement that will assign the name "IB-50" to the strName field variable.
   e. Write an assignment statement that will assign the number 2400 to the curCost field variable.
   f. Assuming that the intRecNum variable contains the number 5, write the `Put` statement that will write the udtCompRec record as the fifth record in the random access file.
   g. Assuming that the intRecNum variable contains the number 5, write the `Get` statement that will read the fifth record in the random access file.
   h. Write the assignment statements that will assign the value in the strName field variable to the lblName control, and the value in the curCost field variable to the lblCost control.
   i. Write the statement that will close the random access file.

Use the following record structure for Exercise 13.

```
Type FriendStruc
      strLast as String * 10
      strFirst as String * 10
End Type
```

13. a. Write a `Dim` statement that declares a FriendStruc variable named udtFriendRec.
   b. Write an `Open` statement that opens a random access file named "Friends.dat" on your Student Disk. Open the file as #1.
   c. Write the For...Next loop that will initialize the Friends.dat file for five records.
   d. Write an assignment statement that will assign the value in the txtFirst control to the strFirst field variable.
   e. Write an assignment statement that will assign the value in the txtLast control to the strLast field variable.
   f. Assuming that the intRecNum variable contains the number 3, write the `Put` statement that will write the udtFriendRec record as the third record in the random access file.
   g. Assuming that the intRecNum variable contains the number 3, write the `Get` statement that will read the third record in the random access file.
   h. Write the assignment statement that will assign the value in the strFirst field variable and the value in the strLast field variable to the lblName control. (You will need to use string concatenation, which you learned about in Tutorial 3.)
   i. Write the statement that will close the random access file.

14. a. Write a `Type` statement that defines a record structure named CustStruc. The record structure contains three fields: strName, strPhone, curSales. StrName is a 25-character String field, strPhone is an 8-character String field, and curSales is a Currency field.
   b. Write a `Dim` statement that declares a CustStruc variable named udtCustRec.
   c. Write an `Open` statement that opens a random access file named "Customer.dat" on your Student Disk. Open the file as #1.
   d. Write the For...Next loop that will initialize the Customer.dat file for five records.

e. Write an assignment statement that will assign the value in the txtName control to the strName field variable.

f. Write an assignment statement that will assign the value in the txtPhone control to the strPhone field variable.

g. Write an assignment statement that will assign the value in the txtSales control to the curSales field variable.

h. Assuming that the intRecNum variable contains the number 3, write the `Put` statement that will write the udtCustRec record as the third record in the random access file.

i. Assuming that the intRecNum variable contains the number 3, write the `Get` statement that will read the third record in the random access file.

j. Write the assignment statement that will assign the value in the strName field variable to the txtName control.

k. Write the assignment statement that will assign the value in the strPhone field variable to the txtPhone control.

l. Write the assignment statement that will assign the value in the curSales field variable to the txtSales control.

m. Write the statement that will close the random access file.

15. In this exercise you will use a random access file to store data.

Scenario: Over the last several years Martha Martin has purchased a great number of compact discs (CDs). She would like an application that will allow her to keep track of the CDs she owns.

a. Open the la15 (la15.vbp) project, which is located in the Tut08 folder on your Student Disk.

b. Save the form and the project as la15Done in the Tut08 folder on your Student Disk.

c. Add a code module to the project. Define a record structure named CDStruc in the code module. The record structure should contain two fields: strName and strArtist. Define both fields as 20-character String fields.

d. Save the code module as la15Done in the Tut08 folder on your Student Disk.

e. In the form's Load event procedure, define a CDStruc variable named udtCDRec and open a random access file named CDs.dat.

f. Code the Exit button so that it unloads the form. Code the form's Unload event so that it closes the data file.

g. Code the Initialize button so that it initializes the CDs.dat file. To save space on your Student Disk, initialize the file for five records only. Be sure to include a prompt that verifies that the user wants to initialize the file. (You can use the pseudocode shown in Figure 8-13 as a guide.)

h. Code the Enter CD button so that it writes the udtCDRec record variable to the file. Be sure to verify that the CD number is greater than zero. (You can use the pseudocode shown in Figure 8-10 as a guide.)

i. Code the Display CD button so that it displays the CD information (name and artist) that corresponds to the CD number entered by the user. Be sure to verify that the CD number is greater than zero. (You can use the pseudocode shown in Figure 8-15 as a guide.)

j. Save and run the application.

k. To test the application:

1) Initialize the CDs.dat file.

2) Use the Enter CD button to enter the following three records, shown as CD number, CD name, and artist name:

    4, Western Way, Mingo Colfax

    2, Country For All, Barbara Mender

    1, Line Dancing, Helen Starks

3) Type 2 in the Number text box, and then click the Display CD button. The Country For All CD by Barbara Mender should appear in the form.

4) Click the Exit button to end the application.

l. Print the form and the application's code. Also, print the CDs.dat file in WordPad.

LESSON B
objectives

In this lesson you will learn how to:

■ Utilize a control array and a random access file in an application

■ Include Visual Basic's color constants in code

■ Pass information to a sub procedure

The Cole's Playhouse Application

The Cole's Playhouse Application

Recall that Cole's Playhouse presents plays featuring local talent. The theater holds only 48 seats, which must be reserved in advance of the performance. No tickets are sold at the door. The manager, Max Phillips, wants an application that will keep track of the reserved seating for each play. Specifically, Mr. Phillips wants to record each patron's name and phone number.

The Cole's Playhouse application will contain two forms, frmPatron and frmSeat. The sketch of the user interface for both forms is shown in Figure 8-18.

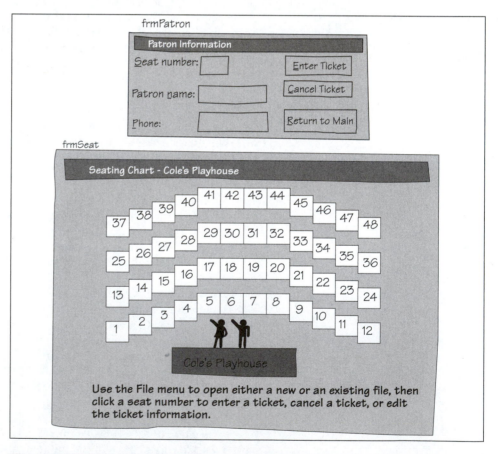

Figure 8-18: Sketches of the forms for the Cole's Playhouse application

Your Student Disk contains a partially completed application for Cole's Playhouse. Open that project now.

To open the partially completed Cole's Playhouse application:

1   Start Visual Basic, if necessary. Open the **Cole** (Cole.vbp) project, which is located in the Tut08 folder on your Student Disk.

The Cole Playhouse project contains two forms, frmPatron and frmSeat. View the frmPatron form first.

2   If neccessary, click **frmPatron (Patron.frm)** in the Project window, then click the Project window's **View Object** 🔳 button. See Figure 8-19.

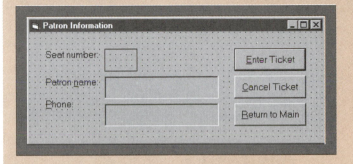

Figure 8-19: frmPatron user interface

The manager can use the frmPatron form to enter the ticket information, cancel the ticket information, or return to the main screen—the frmSeat form.

3   Use Visual Basic's File menu to save the patron form as **lbPatron** in the Tut08 folder on your Student Disk.

4   Click the patron form's **Close** button ❎ to close the patron form.

Now view the frmSeat form.

5   If neccessary, click **frmSeat (Seat.frm)** in the Project window, then click the Project window's **View Object** 🔳 button. The frmSeat form appears on the screen.

6   Use Visual Basic's File menu to save the seat form as **lbSeat** in the Tut08 folder on your Student Disk.

7   Use Visual Basic's File menu to save the Cole project as **lbCole** in the Tut08 folder on your Student Disk.

8   Maximize the seat form. See Figure 8-20.

common dialog control

label control array

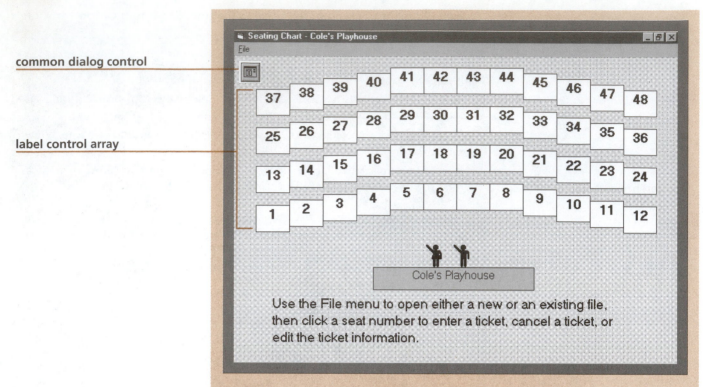

Figure 8-20: frmSeat user interface

As you learned in Tutorial 3, when a project includes more than one form, you must tell Visual Basic which of the forms you want automatically displayed when the application is run. That form, called the **startup form,** can be any one of the forms in the project. In this application, the seat form will be the startup form. When the user wants to enter or cancel a ticket, he or she will need simply to click the appropriate seat number to display the patron form, which contains both the Enter Ticket and the Cancel Ticket buttons. Verify that the seat form is the startup form.

9 Press the **Alt** key to display Visual Basic's main window, which includes the menu bar. Click **Project,** then click **Cole Properties.** The Cole - Project Properties dialog box appears. Verify that frmSeat appears in the Startup Object list box on the General tab, then click the **OK** button to close the dialog box.

The label controls whose captions display the numbers 1 through 48 represent the 48 seats in the theater. Because each of those 48 controls will perform the same function, they were placed in a control array named lblSeat.

tip
. . . .
▶ You can use the F4 key to display the Properties window when the form is maximized. You can also right-click seat number 1 and then select Properties from the popup menu.

To verify that the 48 label controls belong to the lblSeat control array:

1 Click seat number 1. Display the Properties window. Click the **Categorized** tab in the Properties window. If necessary, scroll the Properties window until both the Index and Name properties are visible. (Both properties are listed in the Misc category.) See Figure 8-21.

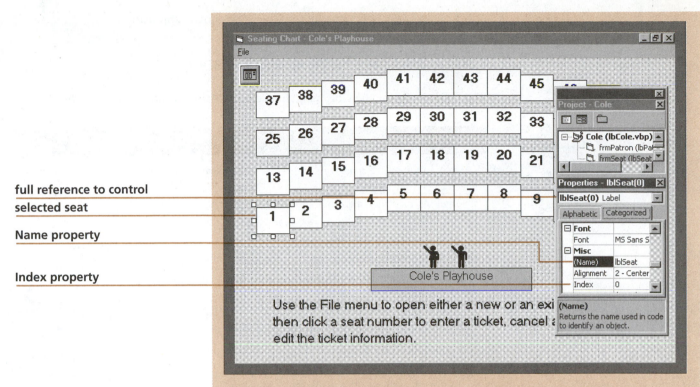

Figure 8-21: Properties window showing Index and Name properties

The full reference to this control—lblSeat(0)—appears in the Object box in the Properties window. Recall that the name of the control array (lblSeat) is stored in the control's Name property, and its index (0) is stored in its Index property. The lblSeat(0) control, which is the first control in the lblSeat control array, corresponds to seat number 1 in the theater.

2   Click seat number **29**. Display the Properties window. If necessary, scroll the Properties window until both the Index and Name properties are visible. The name of the selected control is also lblSeat; its index is 28. Notice that the value stored in the Index property is always one less than the seat number. In other words, the control with index number 28 actually refers to seat number 29.

3   Click the **Alphabetic** tab in the Properties window, then click the **Resize** button to restore the form to its standard size.

The label controls in the lblSeat array have their Visible property set to False, so they will not appear in the interface when the application is run. Verify this by running the application.

4   **Save** and **run** the application. Notice that the lblSeat controls are not visible in the form. If the user wants to record a reservation, he or she will have to use the File menu to open either a new or an existing file. When a new or existing file is opened, the application will display the lblSeat controls in the interface by setting their Visible property to True.

Now use the File menu's Exit command to end the application. (The Exit command already contains the `Unload frmSeat` instruction. The frmSeat form's Unload event contains the `Unload frmPatron` and `Close #1` instructions, which will unload the frmPatron form and close the open data file.

5   Click **File**, then click **Exit** to end the application.

tip

....

▶ Notice that, during run time, the form contains only the Close button and the Minimize button. This is because the form's BorderStyle property is set to 1-Fixed Single, and its MinButton property is set to True.

You can now begin coding the Cole's Playhouse application.

Coding the Cole's Playhouse Application

The TOE chart for the Cole's Playhouse application is shown in Figure 8-22.

Task	Object	Event
Create and initialize a new or existing random access file.	frmSeat.mnuFileNew	Click
1. Open an existing random access file. 2. Change reserved seats to red and available seats to white.	frmSeat.mnuFileOpen	Click
Unload the frmSeat form.	frmSeat.mnuFileExit	Click
Display frmPatron form with patron information showing.	frmSeat.lblSeat control array	Click
1. Unload the frmPatron form. 2. Close the random access file.	frmSeat	Unload
Get patron's name and phone number from the user.	frmPatron.txtName frmPatron.txtPhone	None
1. Write patron's name and phone number to a random access file. 2. Change the reserved seat to red.	frmPatron.cmdEnter	Click
1. Write spaces to the patron's record in the random access file. 2. Change the canceled seat to white.	frmPatron.cmdCancel	Click
Hide the frmPatron form.	frmPatron.cmdReturn	Click

Figure 8-22: TOE chart for the Cole's Playhouse application

For each play, the application will save the reservation information—each patron's name and phone number—in a separate data file. Because the application will need to read and write the patron records in any order, you will store the records for each play in a random access file. Before you can use a random access file, recall that you need to define the record structure for the records; you do so by entering the Type statement in a code module (often just called a module).

To add a module to the project, and then define the record structure:

1 Click **Project** on the menu bar, then click **Add Module**. The Add Module dialog box appears. Click **Module** on the New tab, if necessary, then click the **Open** button. The General Declarations section of the Module1 module appears.

Each record in the data file will contain a patron's name and his or her phone number. You will name the record structure (the user-defined data type), PatronStruc, and the fields, strName and strPhone. strName will be a 20-character String variable and strPhone will be an eight-character String variable.

2 Enter the Option Explicit and Type statements shown in Figure 8-23.

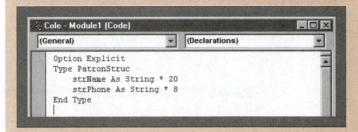

Figure 8-23: Option Explicit and Type statements entered in code module

Now save the code module using a more descriptive name.

3 Use the File menu's Save Module1 As command to save the module as **lbCole**.

4 Close the Code window.

5 Click the **Save Project** button 🖫 on the Standard toolbar to save the project.

Code the File menu's New command first.

Coding the File Menu's New Command

The New command should allow the user to either create a new file or initialize an existing file. The pseudocode for the New command is shown in Figure 8-24.

---

1. Begin error trapping.
2. Set the commmon dialog control's properties.
3. Show the Save As dialog box to get the name of the file from the user.
4. Call the Initialize procedure to initialize the file. Pass the filename to the procedure.

Figure 8-24: Pseudocode for the File menu's New command

Some of the code for the New command has already been entered in its Click event procedure for you.

To view the code in the New command's Click event procedure:

1 Click **File** on the form's menu bar, then click **New**. Maximize the Code window. The New command's Click event procedure appears as shown in Figure 8-25.

tip
••••••••••••••••••
You learned about error trapping and the common dialog control in Tutorial 7.

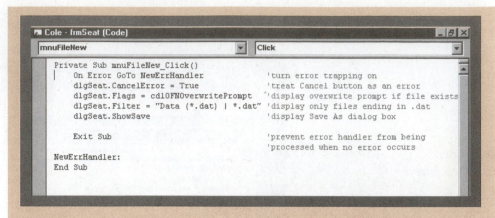

```
Cole - frmSeat (Code)                                      _ | 8 | X
mnuFileNew                    ▼    Click                              ▼
Private Sub mnuFileNew_Click()
    On Error GoTo NewErrHandler              'turn error trapping on
    dlgSeat.CancelError = True               'treat Cancel button as an error
    dlgSeat.Flags = cdlOFNOverwritePrompt    'display overwrite prompt if file exists
    dlgSeat.Filter = "Data (*.dat) | *.dat"  'display only files ending in .dat
    dlgSeat.ShowSave                         'display Save As dialog box

    Exit Sub                                 'prevent error handler from being
                                             'processed when no error occurs
NewErrHandler:
End Sub
```

Figure 8-25: Partially completed Click event procedure for the New command

The procedure turns error trapping on, sets the properties of the dlgSeat common dialog control, and displays the Save As dialog box. The cdlOFNOverwritePrompt flag causes the Save As dialog box to generate a message box if the selected file already exists; the message box contains the "Replace existing file?" prompt. The user will need to confirm whether to overwrite the file. Notice that the error handling routine, which simply exits the Click event when an error occurs, is already entered in the Code window.

After getting the filename from the user, the next step in the pseudocode is to call a user-defined sub procedure, which you will name Initialize, to create the file and initialize it for 48 records. The Initialize procedure will be called only if either the file does not already exist or the user selects the Yes button in response to the "Replace existing file?" prompt generated by the cdlOFNOverwritePrompt flag. If the user selects the No button in response to the "Replace existing file?" prompt, the Initialize procedure will not be called; rather, the user will be returned to the Save As dialog box. In order for the Initialize procedure to know the name of the file to create and initialize, you will need to send (pass) it the contents of the common dialog control's FileName property.

Passing Information to a Sub Procedure

Recall from Tutorial 4 that you use Visual Basic's Call statement, whose syntax is **Call** *name* [(*argumentlist*)], to invoke a user-defined sub procedure. The brackets in the syntax indicate that the *argumentlist* is optional; not all procedures will require information to be passed to it. The RandomNumbers procedure that you created in Tutorial 4, for example, did not need any information to be passed to it. However, in situations where you do have information to send to the sub procedure, you simply include the information in a set of parentheses following the name of the procedure.

The procedure that sends data to another procedure is called the **passing procedure**, and the procedure that receives the data is called the **receiving procedure**. In this case, the New command's Click event (the passing procedure) will pass the contents of the dlgSeat control's FileName property to the Initialize sub procedure (the receiving procedure).

To complete the New command's Click event procedure:

1 Enter the additional instruction and documentation shown in Figure 8-26.

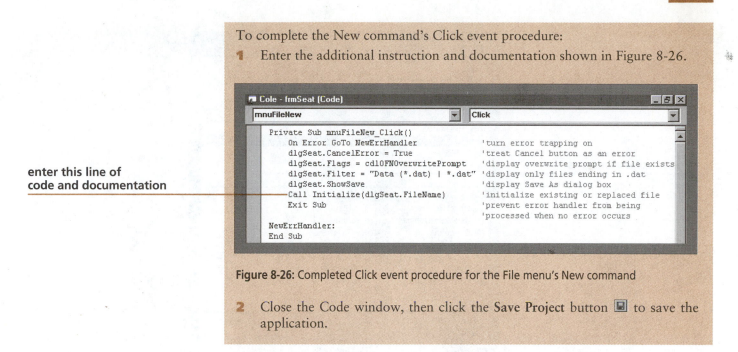

enter this line of
code and documentation

```
Cole - frmSeat (Code)                                                    _ □ ×

mnuFileNew                         ▼   Click                              ▼

Private Sub mnuFileNew_Click()
    On Error GoTo NewErrHandler          'turn error trapping on
    dlgSeat.CancelError = True           'treat Cancel button as an error
    dlgSeat.Flags = cdlOFNOverwritePrompt 'display overwrite prompt if file exists
    dlgSeat.Filter = "Data (*.dat) | *.dat" 'display only files ending in .dat
    dlgSeat.ShowSave                     'display Save As dialog box
    Call Initialize(dlgSeat.FileName)    'initialize existing or replaced file
    Exit Sub                             'prevent error handler from being
                                         'processed when no error occurs

NewErrHandler:
End Sub
```

Figure 8-26: Completed Click event procedure for the File menu's New command

2 Close the Code window, then click the **Save Project** button 🖫 to save the application.

In order to test the New command's code, you first need to create the Initialize procedure. Before doing so, however, you will learn how to use Visual Basic's color constants in your code. You will need to use one of the color constants in the Initialize procedure.

Using Visual Basic's Color Constants

In Tutorial 3 you learned how to create a user-defined symbolic constant. Symbolic constants, you may remember, make your program more self-documenting and, therefore, easier to modify because they allow you to use meaningful words in place of values that are less clear. Because constants play such an important role in creating a well-written program, Visual Basic provides many **intrinsic** (built-in) constants that you can use in your code. Recall from Tutorial 3 that you can view these built-in constants by displaying the Object Browser. Use the Object Browser to view the color constants.

tip

· · · · · · · · · · · · ·

▶ You can also view the
Object Browser by clicking
View, then clicking Object
Browser; or you can use
the F2 key.

To use the Object Browser to view Visual Basic's color constants:

1 Click the **Object Browser** button 🖾 on the Standard toolbar. The Object Browser dialog box appears.

2 Type **colorconstants** in the Search text box, then press the **Enter** key to begin the search.

3 Click the VBRUN library's **ColorConstants** class in the Search Results window. See Figure 8-27.

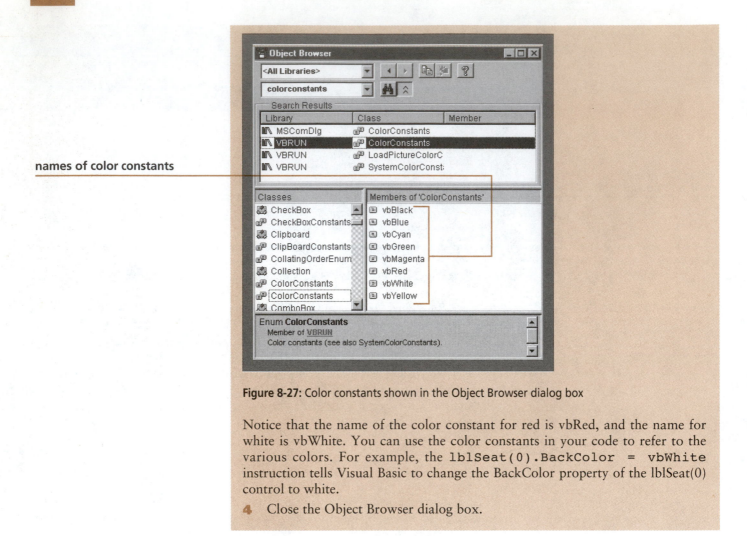

names of color constants

Figure 8-27: Color constants shown in the Object Browser dialog box

Notice that the name of the color constant for red is vbRed, and the name for white is vbWhite. You can use the color constants in your code to refer to the various colors. For example, the `lblSeat(0).BackColor = vbWhite` instruction tells Visual Basic to change the BackColor property of the lblSeat(0) control to white.

4   Close the Object Browser dialog box.

You will use the vbWhite color constant in the Initialize procedure, which you will create in the next section.

Creating a User-Defined Procedure that Receives Data

Recall from Tutorial 4 that a user-defined sub procedure is a collection of code that can be invoked from one or more places in your program. When the code, or a portion of the code, for two or more objects is almost identical, it is more efficient to enter the code once, in a user-defined procedure, instead of duplicating the code in each event procedure. The procedure you will create for the Cole application will open and initialize a random access data file. As you observed in the File menu's New command, the Initialize procedure will be called when the file that the user wants to open doesn't exist; it will also be called in cases where the file exists and the user has chosen to initialize the existing file.

The pseudocode for the Initialize procedure is shown in Figure 8-28.

1. Receive a String variable named strFileName, which will store the name of the file passed to it by the File menu's New command.

2. Declare an Integer variable named intSeat and a PatronStruc variable named udtPatronRec.

3. Assign 20 spaces to the strName field variable in the udtPatronRec variable.

4. Assign eight spaces to the strPhone field variable in the udtPatronRec variable.

5. Close the currently open file, if any.

6. Open the random access file whose name is stored in the strFileName variable.

7. Repeat for each seat in the lblSeat control array

    a. Write the record to the file. The record number should be 1 more than the contents of the intSeat variable.

    b. Change the BackColor property of the corresponding label in the lblSeat control array to white.

    c. Change the Visible property of the corresponding label in the lblSeat control array to True.

    End Repeat for each seat

8. Display the filename and application name in the form's title bar.

Figure 8-28: Pseudocode for the Initialize procedure

Now create the form-level Initialize procedure.

You must open a Code window before you can add a procedure to the application.

To create the Initialize procedure:

1 Open any Code window in the frmSeat form, click **Tools** on the menu bar, and then click **Add Procedure**. The Add Procedure dialog box appears.

2 Type **Initialize** in the Name box.

You want to create a sub procedure, so leave the Sub option button selected in the Type box. The user-defined procedure will be used only by the form in which it is created, so you will make its scope Private.

3 Click the **Private** option button in the Scope box, then click the **OK** button. The Add Procedure dialog box closes and the Code window for the Initialize procedure appears.

As you learned in Tutorial 4, a user-defined procedure can receive variables or constants, called **arguments**, that you send (pass) to it; the arguments, if any, are listed inside the parentheses following the procedure's name. You pass arguments when you want the procedure to process them in some way. For example, you might create a procedure that sorts a list of numbers. The arguments you pass would be the numbers themselves; the procedure would then sort, and perhaps display, those numbers. In this application, the Call statement in the New command's Click event passes the contents of the dlgSeat control's FileName property. The Initialize procedure, which is the receiving procedure, will use that information to create/open and initialize the file.

The names of the receiving procedure's variables do not need to be identical to the names of the variables listed in the `Call` statement. The receiving procedure's variables, however, must be the same type as the passing variables, and they must be listed in the same order as the passing variables. In other words, if the passing procedure sends a String variable first and a Single variable second, then the receiving procedure must receive a String variable first and a Single variable second. In this application the `Call` statement passes a String (the dlgSeat control's FileName property); the Initialize procedure, therefore, will need to list a String variable as its argument.

Variables can be passed either by value or by reference. You control which way they are passed by including the keywords `ByVal` or `ByRef` before the variable's name in the receiving procedure's arguments. When you pass a variable **by value**, Visual Basic creates a copy of the variable in memory, and only the copy is passed to the receiving procedure. Although the receiving procedure can change the contents of the copy, it cannot change the contents of the original variable.

If, on the other hand, you pass a variable **by reference**, Visual Basic passes the variable's actual address in memory. Because the actual address is passed to the receiving procedure, the contents of the variable can be changed permanently by the receiving procedure. Unless specified otherwise, all variables are passed by reference. Figure 8-29 shows some examples of passing information from one procedure to another. The `Call` statements would be entered in the passing procedure; the `Private Sub` statements represent the receiving procedure.

tip

Because passing a variable by value creates another copy of the variable, the application will use more memory than if you pass the variables by reference. Lesson B's Exercise 1 will help clarify the difference between passing by value and passing by reference.

Call statement entered in the passing procedure	Private Sub statement in the receiving procedure
Call DoubleNumber(intNum) Calls the DoubleNumber procedure, passing it the intNum variable.	**Private Sub DoubleNumber(intNum as Integer)** Receives the intNum variable, which was passed by reference. Refers to the intNum variable as intNum.
Call Display(strName, intAge) Calls the Display procedure, passing it the strName and intAge variables.	**Private Sub Display(strStudent as String, intNum as Integer)** Receives the strName and intAge variables, which were passed by reference. Refers to the strName variable as strStudent. Refers to the intAge variable as intNum.
Call Update(intNum) Calls the Update procedure, passing it the intNum variable.	**Private Sub Update(ByVal intNumber as Integer)** Receives the intNum variable, which was passed by value. The copy of the variable is named intNumber.

Figure 8-29: Examples of passing information from one procedure to another

In this application, you will name the receiving variable strFileName and declare it as a String variable. You will pass it by reference, which is the default.

To code the Initialize procedure:

1   Enter the receiving variable as shown in Figure 8-30.

receiving variable's name

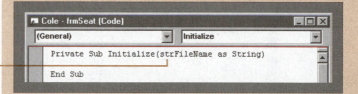

```
Cole - frmSeat (Code)                          _ □ X
(General)                          ▼   Initialize          ▼
    Private Sub Initialize(strFileName as String)       ▲
    End Sub
```

Figure 8-30: Receiving variable shown in Initialize procedure

According to the pseudocode, the Initialize procedure will need to declare an Integer variable named intSeat and a PatronStruc variable named udtPatronRec. Recall that the PatronStruc data type contains two fields, strName and strPhone. To initialize the random access file, the Initialize procedure will assign 20 spaces to the strName field variable and eight spaces to the strPhone field variable. It will then close the currently open file, if any, and open the random access file whose name is stored in the strFileName variable. A For Next loop will write the udtPatronRec record variable to the file, 48 times. It will also change the BackColor property of each of the 48 seats to white, and change each seat's Visible property to True. (Recall that the Visible property of each seat in the lblSeat control array is initially set to False.) Before the procedure ends, it will display the current file's name, along with the name of the application (Cole's Playhouse), in the seat form's title bar.

2   Maximize the Code window, then enter the code and documentation shown in Figure 8-31.

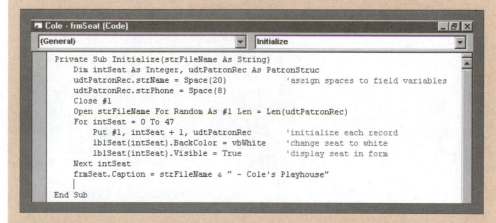

```
Cole - frmSeat (Code)                                      _ 8 X
(General)                              ▼   Initialize              ▼
    Private Sub Initialize(strFileName As String)
        Dim intSeat As Integer, udtPatronRec As PatronStruc
        udtPatronRec.strName = Space(20)          'assign spaces to field variables
        udtPatronRec.strPhone = Space(8)
        Close #1
        Open strFileName For Random As #1 Len = Len(udtPatronRec)
        For intSeat = 0 To 47
            Put #1, intSeat + 1, udtPatronRec       'initialize each record
            lblSeat(intSeat).BackColor = vbWhite    'change seat to white
            lblSeat(intSeat).Visible = True         'display seat in form
        Next intSeat
        frmSeat.Caption = strFileName & " - Cole's Playhouse"

    End Sub
```

Figure 8-31: Completed Initialize procedure

3   Close the Code window, then **save** and **run** the application.

4   Click **File**, then click **New**. When the Save As dialog box appears, save the file as **lbTest** in the Tut08 folder on your Student Disk. Because the file does not exist, the New command creates a new random access file and initializes it for 48 records. The 48 label controls appear in the form with a white background, and the name of the file appears in the form's title bar. See Figure 8-32.

tip

If you omit the Step from the For Next loop, recall that the loop uses a default step of positive 1.

open file's name

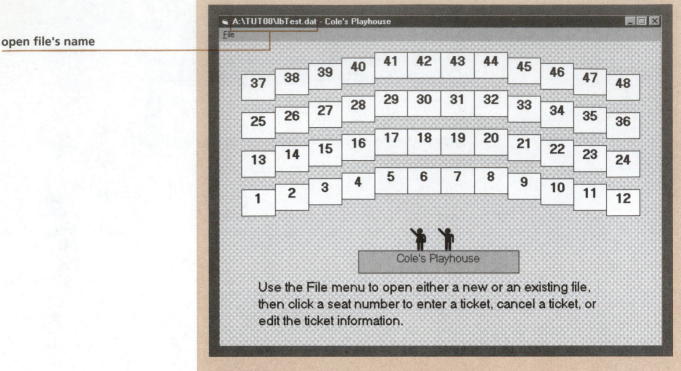

Figure 8-32: frmSeat form showing the filename in the form's title bar

5   Click **File**, then click **New**. When the Save As dialog box appears, click **lbTest.dat** in the filename list box, then click the **Save** button. Because you set the dlgSeat control's Flags property to cdlOFNOverwritePrompt in the New command's Click event procedure, the Save As dialog box displays a message informing you that the lbTest.dat file already exists. The message asks if you want to replace the existing file.

6   Click the **No** button in the message box, then click the **Cancel** button in the Save As dialog box. Visual Basic returns to the frmSeat form. The form's title bar indicates that the lbTest.dat file is still open.

7   Click **File**, then click **Exit** to end the application. Visual Basic unloads the frmSeat and frmPatron forms, then closes the data file before returning to the design screen.

Next, code the File menu's Open command.

Coding the File Menu's Open Command

The Open command should allow the user to open an existing data file so he or she can continue to record reservations for the play. The pseudocode for the Open command is shown in Figure 8-33.

1. Declare the variables.

2. Begin error trapping.

3. Set the common dialog control's properties.

4. Show the Open dialog box to get the name of an existing file from the user.

5. Close the currently open file, if any.

6. Open the file whose name is stored in the dlgSeat control's FileName property.

7. Display the filename and the application name in the frmSeat form's title bar.

8. Repeat for each seat in the lblSeat control array

    a. Change the Visible property of the corresponding label in the lblSeat control array to True.

    b. Read the record that corresponds to the seat in the lblSeat array.

    c. If the record contains a patron's name, then

        change the BackColor property of the corresponding label in the lblSeat

        control array to red to indicate that it is reserved

    Else

        change the BackColor property of the corresponding label in the lblSeat

        control array to white to indicate that it is available

    End If

End Repeat for each seat

Figure 8-33: Pseudocode for the Open command

Most of the code for the Open command has already been entered into its Click event procedure for you.

To view the code in the Open command's Click event procedure:

1 Click **File** on the form's menu bar, then click **Open**. The Open command's Click event procedure appears. Maximize the Code window, then position the insertion point as shown in Figure 8-34.

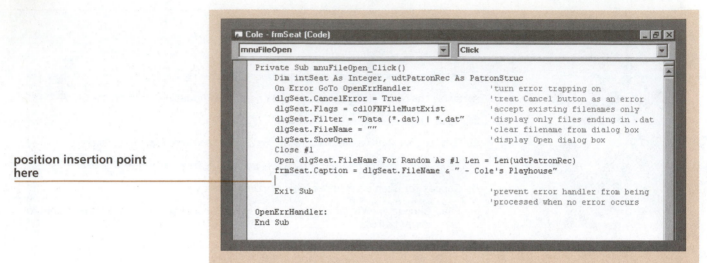

```
Cole - frmSeat (Code)                                              _ 8 X

mnuFileOpen                           ▼      Click                    ▼

Private Sub mnuFileOpen_Click()
    Dim intSeat As Integer, udtPatronRec As PatronStruc
    On Error GoTo OpenErrHandler              'turn error trapping on
    dlgSeat.CancelError = True                'treat Cancel button as an error
    dlgSeat.Flags = cdlOFNFileMustExist       'accept existing filenames only
    dlgSeat.Filter = "Data (*.dat) | *.dat"   'display only files ending in .dat
    dlgSeat.FileName = ""                      'clear filename from dialog box
    dlgSeat.ShowOpen                           'display Open dialog box
    Close #1
    Open dlgSeat.FileName For Random As #1 Len = Len(udtPatronRec)
    frmSeat.Caption = dlgSeat.FileName & " - Cole's Playhouse"
    |
    Exit Sub                                   'prevent error handler from being
                                               'processed when no error occurs
OpenErrHandler:
End Sub
```

position insertion point here

Figure 8-34: Open command's Click event procedure

After declaring the intSeat and udtPatronRec variables, the procedure turns error trapping on, then sets the properties of the common dialog control before displaying the Open dialog box. The dlgSeat control's cdlOFNFileMustExist flag specifies that the user can enter only names of existing files in the Open dialog box's File name text box. If this flag is set and the user enters an invalid filename, the common dialog control will display a warning message.

When the user closes the Open dialog box after selecting the name of an existing file, the currently open file, if any, is closed, and the file whose name is stored in the dlgSeat control's FileName property is opened. The seat form's caption is then changed to reflect the name of the open file. Notice that the error handling routine, which simply exits the Click event when an error occurs, is already entered in the Code window.

According to the pseudocode, you still need to add the code that will display the lblSeat controls in the interface. You also need to add the code to read each record in the open file and, if the record contains a name, set the seat's color to red to indicate that the seat is reserved; otherwise, set it to white to indicate that it is available.

First display the 48 lblSeat controls in the interface by setting each control's Visible property to True. (Recall that the Visible property of the lblSeat controls is initially set to False.) As you learned in Tutorial 5, you use both the Name property and the Index property to refer to a control in a control array. The indexes of the label controls in the lblSeat array are numbered 0 through 47.

2   With the insertion point positioned as shown in Figure 8-34, type **for intseat = 0 to 47** and press the **Enter** key.

3   Press the **Tab** key, then type **lblseat(intseat).visible = true** and press the **Enter** key.

Now read each seat's record from the random access file. If the record contains a name, then change the color of the corresponding seat to red, which indicates that the seat is reserved; otherwise, set the color to white, which indicates that the seat is available. Although the indexes of the controls in the lblSeat array are numbered 0 through 47, the records that store the information about each seat are numbered 1 through 48. In other words, the lblSeat(0) control's information is stored in record 1 in the random access file, the lblSeat(1) control's in record 2, and so on.

Notice that the record number is always one greater than the index number.

4   Enter the code and documentation shown in Figure 8-35.

enter this documentation

enter these seven lines of code and documentation

```
Cole - frmSeat (Code)                                                    _ |□| X
mnuFileOpen                          ▼      Click                              ▼

Private Sub mnuFileOpen_Click()
    Dim intSeat As Integer, udtPatronRec As PatronStruc
    On Error GoTo OpenErrHandler                    'turn error trapping on
    dlgSeat.CancelError = True                      'treat Cancel button as an error
    dlgSeat.Flags = cdlOFNFileMustExist             'accept existing filenames only
    dlgSeat.Filter = "Data (*.dat) | *.dat"         'display only files ending in .dat
    dlgSeat.FileName = ""                           'clear filename from dialog box
    dlgSeat.ShowOpen                                'display Open dialog box
    Close #1
    Open dlgSeat.FileName For Random As #1 Len = Len(udtPatronRec)
    frmSeat.Caption = dlgSeat.FileName & " - Cole's Playhouse"
    For intSeat = 0 To 47
        lblSeat(intSeat).Visible = True             'display seat in form
        Get #1, intSeat + 1, udtPatronRec           'read the record
        If udtPatronRec.strName <> Space(20) Then   'record contains a name
            lblSeat(intSeat).BackColor = vbRed
        Else                                        'record does not contain a name
            lblSeat(intSeat).BackColor = vbWhite
        End If
    Next intSeat
    Exit Sub                                        'prevent error handler from being
                                                    'processed when no error occurs

OpenErrHandler:
End Sub
```

Figure 8-35: Completed Click event procedure for the File menu's Open command

5   Close the Code window, then **save** and **run** the application.

First open an existing file.

6   Click **File**, then click **Open**. When the Open dialog box appears, open the **lbTest.dat** file, which is located in the Tut08 folder on your Student Disk. The form's title bar indicates that the file is open. The seats are white because you have not saved any information for this play.

Now open a data file that contains some records. You will find such a file in the Tut08 folder on your Student Disk.

7   Click **File**, then click **Open**. When the Open dialog box appears, open the **Play.dat** file, which is located in the Tut08 folder on your Student Disk. The form's title bar indicates that the file is open. The reserved seats (seats 2 and 5) are red; the others are white.

Now try opening a file that does not exist.

8   Click **File**, then click **Open**. When the Open dialog box appears, type t8 in the File name box, then click the **Open** button. A message box telling the user that the file cannot be found appears on the screen. Click the **OK** button to remove the message box, then click the **Cancel** button in the Open dialog box. Visual Basic returns to the application.

9   Click **File**, then click **Exit** to end the application. Visual Basic returns to the design screen.

You have now completed Lesson B. You can either take a break or complete the questions and exercises at the end of the lesson. You will complete the Cole's Playhouse application in Lesson C.

SUMMARY

To specify the startup form:

■ Use the *<Project Name>* Properties command on the Project menu. When the *<Project Name>* Project Properties dialog box appears, click the Startup Object list arrow on the General tab, then click the name of the startup form in the list.

To view Visual Basic's built-in constants:

■ Click the Object Browser button 🖫 on the Standard toolbar, or click View, then click Object Browser; you can also press the F2 key.

To pass information to a sub procedure:

■ Use the `Call` statement. Its syntax is **Call** *name* (*argumentlist*), where *argumentlist* is the information you want passed to the procedure.

To create a user-defined sub procedure:

■ If you are creating a form-level sub procedure, open any Code window in the form. If you are creating a global sub procedure, add a module to the project.
■ Click Tools on the menu bar, then click Add Procedure. The Add Procedure dialog box appears.
■ Type the procedure's name in the Name box.
■ If necessary, select the Sub option button in the Type box.
■ If the user-defined procedure will be used only by the form in which it is created, click Private in the Scope box.

To have a sub procedure receive information passed to it with the Call statement:

■ List the variables in a set of parentheses following the procedure's name. The names of the receiving procedure's variables do not need to be identical to the names of the variables listed in the `Call` statement. The receiving procedure's variables, however, must be the same type as the passing variables, and they must be listed in the same order as the passing variables.
■ Variables can be passed either by value or by reference. You control which way they are passed by including the keywords `ByVal` or `ByRef` before the variable's name in the receiving procedure's arguments. When you pass a variable by value, Visual Basic creates a copy of the variable in memory, and only the copy is passed to the receiving procedure. Although the receiving procedure can change the contents of the copy, it cannot change the contents of the original variable. When you pass a variable by reference, Visual Basic passes the variable's actual address in memory. Because the actual address is passed to the receiving procedure, the contents of the variable can be changed permanently by the receiving procedure. Unless specified otherwise, all variables are passed by reference.

Q U E S T I O N S

1. When a multiform project is run, Visual Basic automatically loads and displays the _____ form.
    a. beginning
    b. first
    c. initial
    d. loaded
    e. startup

2. You use Visual Basic's _____ menu to specify the startup form.
    a. File
    b. Options
    c. Project
    d. Startup
    e. Tools

3. Which of the following will invoke the DoubleNumber procedure, passing it the contents of the intNumber variable?
    a. `Call DoubleNumber intNumber`
    b. `Call DoubleNumber (intNumber)`
    c. `Call DoubleNumber(intNumber as Integer)`
    d. `Invoke DoubleNumber (intNumber)`
    e. `Sub DoubleNumber(intNumber as Integer)`

4. The procedure that sends data to another procedure is called the _____ procedure.
    a. invoking
    b. receiving
    c. passing
    d. sub

5. The procedure that receives data from another procedure is called the _____ procedure.
    a. invoking
    b. receiving
    c. passing
    d. sub

6. Which of the following will call a procedure named PrintHeading, passing it no arguments?
    a. `Call PrintHeading`
    b. `Call (PrintHeading)`
    c. `CallSub PrintHeading`
    d. `Invoke PrintHeading`
    e. `Sub PrintHeading`

7. If you invoke the DisplayName procedure, passing it a String variable named strFriend, which of the following is a correct Private Sub statement for the DisplayName procedure?
    a. `Private Sub DisplayName( )`
    b. `Private Sub DisplayName(Call strFriendName)`
    c. `Private Sub DisplayName strFriendName`
    d. `Private Sub DisplayName strFriendName as String`
    e. `Private Sub DisplayName (strFriendName as String)`

8. If you invoke the UpdateAge procedure, passing it a String variable named strFriend and an integer variable named intAge, which of the following is a correct `Private Sub` statement for the UpdateAge procedure?
    a. `Private Sub UpdateAge( )`
    b. `Private Sub UpdateAge(intAge as Integer, strMyFriend as String)`
    c. `Private Sub (UpdateAge) strMyFriend as String, intAge as Integer`
    d. `Private Sub UpdateAge intAge as Integer, strFriendName as String`
    e. `Private Sub UpdateAge (strFriendName as String, intAge as Integer)`

9. You can view Visual Basic's built-in constants by displaying the _____ .
    a. Constant Browser
    b. Constant Viewer
    c. Object Browser
    d. Object Viewer

10. Which of the following is false?
    a. The names of the receiving procedure's variables must be identical to the names of the variables listed in the `Call` statement.
    b. The receiving procedure's variables must be the same type as the passing variables.
    c. The receiving procedure's variables must be listed in the same order as the passing variables.
    d. Variables can be passed either by value or by reference.
    e. You control which way variables are passed by including the keywords `ByVal` or `ByRef` before the variable's name in the receiving procedure's arguments.

11. When you pass a variable _____ , Visual Basic creates a copy of the variable in memory, and only the copy is passed to the receiving procedure.
    a. by copy
    b. by original
    c. by reference
    d. by value

12. When you pass a variable _____ , Visual Basic passes the variable's actual address in memory.
    a. by copy
    b. by original
    c. by reference
    d. by value

13. When you pass a variable _____ , the receiving procedure cannot change the contents of the original variable.
    a. by copy
    b. by original
    c. by reference
    d. by value

14. When you pass a variable _____ , the contents of the variable can be permanently changed by the receiving procedure.
    a. by copy
    b. by original
    c. by reference
    d. by value

15. Unless specified otherwise, all variables are passed _____ .
   a. by copy
   b. by original
   c. by reference
   d. by value

E X E R C I S E S

1. In this exercise you will observe the difference between passing arguments by reference and passing them by value.

   a. Open the lb1 (lb1.vbp) project, which is located in the Tut08 folder on your Student Disk. The interface contains label controls and two command buttons (Display and Exit).

   b. Print the application's code.

   c. Notice that the cmdDisplay control's Click event declares a local Integer variable named intNumber, to which it assigns the number 10. The procedure then calls the DoubleNumber user-defined procedure and passes it the intNumber variable. After processing the instructions in the DoubleNumber procedure, the application returns to the cmdDisplay control's Click event, where the value in the intNumber variable is displayed in the lblNumber control. Notice that the DoubleNumber procedure receives an Integer variable named intNum, which it multiplies by 2. It then displays the product in the lblNum label control. (Recall that the name of the variable in the receiving procedure does not have to match the name of the passing variable.) The DoubleNumber procedure is receiving the variable by reference, which is the default way that variables are passed to procedures. That means that although the receiving variable's name is different from the passing variable's name, they both refer to the same location in the computer's memory. Passing a variable by reference gives the receiving procedure access to the variable in memory.

   d. To see what it means to pass by reference, run (but don't save) the application. Click the Display button. The Display button's Click event calls the DoubleNumber procedure, passing it the intNumber variable, which contains the number 10. The DoubleNumber procedure multiplies the contents of the variable (10) times 2, giving 20, then displays the 20 in the lblNum control. When control returns to the Display button's Click event, the value in the intNumber variable (20) is assigned to the lblNumber control on the form. Notice that the contents of both intNum and intNumber are 20. Click the Exit button to end the application.

   e. To see what it means to pass by value, open the DoubleNumber procedure, which is located in the General Declarations section of the form. Change the `Private Sub` statement to `Private Sub DoubleNumber(ByVal intNum as Integer)`. The `ByVal` keyword tells Visual Basic that the intNumber variable in the passing procedure should be passed by value, and not by reference. That means that Visual Basic will pass a copy of the `intNumber` variable to the DoubleNumber procedure; the name of the copy will be intNum. The DoubleNumber procedure has access to the `intNum` variable, but not to the original intNumber variable in memory. Close the Code window.

   f. Run (but don't save) the application. Click the Display button. On the printout from step b, write down the contents of the intNum and intNumber variables. Also explain why the Display button printed those numbers.

   g. Exit the application. Submit the printout from step b, which includes the information from step f.

2. In this exercise, you will use a random access file.

   Scenario: In Tutorial 5, you created an application that a student in Professor Carver's class could use to calculate his or her grade. Assume that Professor Carver wants to use the application to save each student's name and grade in a random access file. At the beginning of the semester, Professor Carver assigns each student a number from one through 10, so the random access file will need to store a maximum of 10 records. The application should also allow Professor Carver to print the contents of the random access file.

   a. Open the lcGrade (lcGrade.vbp) project, which is located in the Tut05 folder on your Student Disk.

   b. Save the form and the project as lb2Done in the Tut08 folder on your Student Disk.

   c. Modify the application according to the above scenario. For example, you will need to have Professor Carver enter the student's number as well as the student's name and scores. In addition to displaying the grade in the interface, the Display Grade button should write the student's name and grade to the random access file. Name the random access file grades.dat and save it in the Tut08 folder on your Student Disk. Modify the Print button so that it asks Professor Carver if he wants to print the interface or the contents of the random access file.

   d. Save and run the application. Enter the information shown below, displaying the grade and printing the interface after each entry.

Number	Name	Project 1	Project 2	Project 3	Midterm	Final
3	Mark Place	9	10	8	34	45
8	Janice Jones	7	5	0	23	32
2	Paul Penny	8	3	7	40	34

   e. Print the contents of the grades.dat random access file. Show the student's name in the first column of the printout and his or her grade in the second column.

   f. Stop the application, then print the code. Submit the three printouts from step d, the printout from step e, and the code from step f.

   Exercises 3 and 4 are Discovery Exercises, which allow you to "discover" the solutions to problems on your own. Discovery Exercises may include topics that are not covered in the tutorial.

discovery ▶ 3. In this exercise, you will use a random access file.

   Scenario: In Tutorial 6, you created an application that the PAO can use to tabulate the number of Democrats, Republicans, and Independents in each of four age groups. As you may remember, you recorded the information in a sequential access file. In this exercise, you will modify the application so that it records the information in a random access file. The modified application should also allow the PAO secretary to remove a record from the random access file. To keep the PAO file small, you can assume that each questionnaire is numbered from one through 20, so the random access file will need to store a maximum of 20 records only.

   a. Open the laPao (laPao.vbp) project, which is located in the Tut06 folder on your Student Disk.

   b. Save the form and the project as lb3Done in the Tut08 folder on your Student Disk.

   c. Modify the application according to the above scenario. For example, you will need to have the PAO secretary enter the questionnaire's number as well as the respondent's political party and age. You will also need to include a Remove Information button that will allow the user to clear the information from a record in the file. Be sure to modify the code so that it records the information in a random access, rather than a sequential access, file named pao.dat. Save the pao.dat file in the Tut08 folder on your Student Disk.

d. Save and run the application. Enter the information shown below.

Questionnaire number	Political party	Age group
5	Republican	36–50
2	Independent	Over 65
1	Republican	36–50
8	Democrat	18–35
15	Democrat	36–50
10	Republican	36–50

e. Click the Display Totals button, then click the Print Report button.

f. Remove the information in records 8 and 5. Click the Display Totals button, then click the Print Report button.

g. Stop the application, then print the code. Submit the printouts from steps e and f, and the code from step g.

discovery ▶ 4. In this exercise you will create two user-defined functions.

Scenario: In addition to creating a user-defined sub procedure, you can also create a user-defined function procedure. The difference between both procedures is that a function procedure returns a value, whereas a sub procedure does not. In this exercise you will create two function procedures. The first function will increase the number passed to it by 10%. The second function will calculate the cube of the number passed to it.

a. If you have access to the MSDN Library, then display the Help screen on the `Function` statement. Read the information contained in the Help screen, then close the MSDN Library window.

b. Open a new project, if necessary. Save the form and the project as lb4Done in the Tut08 folder on your Student Disk.

c. Double-click the form to open a Code window. Use the Tools menu to add a procedure to the project. Create a Private Function procedure named CalcNewPrice.

d. Change the `Private Function CalcNewPrice( )` statement to `Private Function CalcNewPrice(sngOldPrice as Single) as Single`.

e. This function should increase the sngOldPrice variable by 10%. Enter the `CalcNewPrice = sngOldPrice * 1.1` instruction between the `Private Function` and `End Function` statements. Notice that the name of the function, CalcNewPrice, is used in the equation itself; you return a value from a function by assigning the value to the function's name.

f. Close the Code window. Place a text box, a label control, and a command button on the form. Remove the contents of both the text box's Text property and the label control's Caption property.

g. Open the command button's Click event procedure. You can invoke the CalcNewPrice function simply by using its name in an instruction. In the command button's Click event, enter the following three instructions:

```
Dim sngPrice as Single
sngPrice = Val(Text1.Text)
Label1.Caption = CalcNewPrice(sngPrice)
```

h. Close the Code window. Save and run the project. Enter the number 50 in the text box, then click the Command1 button. The number 55 appears in the label control.

i. Exit the application.

j. Use the Tools menu to add another procedure to the project. Create a Private Function procedure named Cube. The Cube function should receive an Integer variable named intNum. Declare the function as a Single. Code this procedure so that it will find the cube of the number passed to it. (*Hint:* The cube of 2 is 8.)

k. Add another command button to the form. Have this command button's Click event display, in the Label1 control, the cube of the number entered in the text box. (Be sure to invoke the Cube function.)

l. Save and run the application. Enter the number 9 in the text box, then click the Command2 button. The number 729 should appear in the Label1 control.

m. Stop the application. Print the application's code.

LESSON C
objectives

In this lesson you will learn how to:

- Refer to a control in another form
- Clear a record from a random access file
- Use the Trim function

Completing the Cole's Playhouse Application

Coding the lblSeat Control Array

In this lesson you will complete the Cole's Playhouse application. First, open the lbCole project file that you created in Lesson B.

> To open the lbCole project that you created in Lesson B:
>
> **1** Start Visual Basic, if necessary. Open the **lbCole** (lbCole.vbp) project, which is located in the Tut08 folder on your Student Disk.
>
> **2** Save the frmPatron form as **lcPatron** in the Tut08 folder on your Student Disk. Save the frmSeat form as **lcSeat**. Save the Module as **lcCole**.
>
> **3** Save the project as **lcCole** in the Tut08 folder on your Student Disk.
>
> **4** If necessary, click **frmSeat (lcSeat.frm)** in the Project window, then click the Project window's **View Object** button 🔲 to view the seat form. Recall that the 48 label controls, which represent the theater seats, belong to a control array named lblSeat.

The first event procedure you will code is the Click event for the lblSeat control array. The pseudocode for the lblSeat control array's Click event procedure is shown in Figure 8-36.

1. Declare an Integer variable named intSeat and a PatronStruc variable named udtPatronRec.

2. Add 1 to the intSeat variable.

3. Display the contents of the intSeat variable in the lblNum control, which is in the frmPatron form.

4. If the lblSeat control's BackColor property is set to red, then

    a. read the record from the random access file

    b. assign the name to the txtName control, which is in the frmPatron form

    c. assign the phone number to the txtPhone control, which is in the frmPatron form

    Else

        clear the text from the txtName and txtPhone controls, which are in the frmPatron form

    End If

5. Show the frmPatron form.

6. Set the focus in the txtName control, which is in the frmPatron form.

Figure 8-36: Pseudocode for the lblSeat control array

When the user clicks any one of the 48 label controls in the lblSeat control array, the array's Click event should display the frmPatron form on the screen, with the number of the chosen seat displayed in the lblNum control on the frmPatron form. If the seat is reserved, the Click event should also display the patron's name and phone number in the appropriate text boxes in the frmPatron form. If the seat is available, the name and phone number should be blank when the frmPatron form appears. In the next section you will learn how to refer to a control in another form.

Referencing a Control in Another Form

The period between *form* and *control*, as well as the period between *control* and *property*, is called the dot member selection operator. It indicates that the *property* is a member of the *control*, which is a member of the *form*.

When writing Visual Basic code for a form or one of its controls, you can refer to another control in the same form by using the control's name. For example, if the lblNum control was in the same form as the lblSeat control array, you could refer to it as simply lblNum. In this case, however, the lblNum control is not in the same form as the control array—the lblNum control is in the frmPatron form and the control array is in the frmSeat form. To refer to a control in another form, you simply precede the control's name with the name of the form in which it is contained. You separate the form name from the control's name with a period, like this: *form.control*. For example, to refer to the lblNum control in the frmPatron form, you will need to use `frmPatron.lblNum`; otherwise, Visual Basic will not be able to locate the control. To refer to the property of a control contained in another form, you use the following syntax: *form.control.property*.

Now code the lblSeat control array's Click event.

To code the lblSeat control array's Click event:

1 Double-click any one of the label controls in the lblSeat control array. Recall that the controls in a control array use the same Code window, which you can open by double-clicking any of the controls in the array. The Code window for the lblSeat control array appears.

According to the pseudocode, your first step is to declare the intSeat and udtPatronRec variables. intSeat (an Integer variable) will store the seat number, and udtPatronRec (a record variable) will store the patron's record.

2 Maximize the Code window, press the **Tab** key, then type **dim intSeat as integer, udtPatronRec as patronstruc** and press the **Enter** key.

Now assign the appropriate seat number to the intSeat variable. Recall that Visual Basic stores, in the event procedure's Index argument, the Index property of the control that is receiving the event. In this case, for example, if the user clicks seat number 1 (the lblSeat(0) control), Visual Basic records a zero in the Index argument; if the user clicks seat number 45 (the lblSeat(44) control), Visual Basic records the number 44 in the Index argument, and so on. Notice that the Index argument is always one less than the seat number. That means that you will need to add 1 to the Index argument in order to display the proper seat number in the frmPatron form.

3 Type **intseat = index + 1** and press the **Enter** key.

Now assign the seat number to the lblNum control in the frmPatron form.

4 Type **frmpatron.lblnum.caption = intseat** and press the **Enter** key.

According to the pseudocode, the next step is to see if the seat is reserved. In this application, recall that the reserved seats have a BackColor setting of red, whereas the available seats have a BackColor setting of white. If the BackColor setting is red, then you will need to read the patron's name and phone number from the random access file in order to display that information in the frmPatron form. If the BackColor setting is not red, then the name and phone number should be blank when the frmPatron form appears. Use a selection structure to compare the BackColor property to Visual Basic's vbRed symbolic constant.

5 Enter the selection structure shown in Figure 8-37, then position the insertion point as shown in the figure.

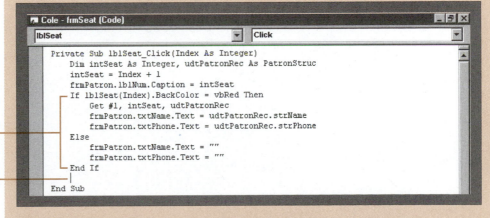

enter this selection structure

position insertion point here

Figure 8-37: Selection structure entered in the lblSeat Click event procedure

According to the pseudocode, you still need to display the frmPatron form on the screen and then set the focus to the txtName control. You can use the Show method, which you learned about in Tutorial 3, to display the form. Recall that the syntax of the Show method is *object*.**Show** [*style*], where *object* is the name of the form you want to display or show. The Show method loads the form into the computer's memory, if necessary, then displays the form on the screen.

6   With the insertion point positioned as shown in Figure 8-37, type **frmpatron.show** and press the **Enter** key.

Now set the focus to the txtName control in the frmPatron form.

7   Type **frmpatron.txtname.setfocus** and press the **Enter** key.

Observe how the application works so far.

8   Close the Code window, then **save** and **run** the application. Click **File**, then click **New**. When the Save As dialog box appears, name the file **lcTest** and save it in the Tut08 folder on your Student Disk. Because the file does not exist, the New command calls the Initialize procedure, which creates and initializes the file. The Initialize procedure also displays the lblSeat control array in the interface, with all of the seats colored white because it is a new file.

HELP? If you are practicing this lesson again, a dialog box asking if you want to replace the file will appear. Click the Yes button.

9   Click seat number 2. The frmPatron form appears on the screen with the number 2 in the lblNum control. The name and phone number text boxes are empty because the ticket for this seat has not yet been purchased. The focus is in the txtName control.

10   Click the frmPatron form's **Close** button ⊠ to close the patron form.

11   Click **File**, then click **Exit** to end the application. Visual Basic returns to the design screen.

tip

....

Notice that the frmPatron form resembles a standard dialog box in that it contains only the Close button; it does not contain the Minimize and Maximize buttons. Recall from Tutorial 3 that you make a form into a standard dialog box by setting the form's BorderStyle property to 3-Fixed Dialog.

You still need to code the frmPatron form, which allows the user to enter the ticket information, cancel the ticket information, and return to the main form—the frmSeat form. Code the Enter Ticket button first.

Coding the Enter Ticket Button

Before you can code the Enter Ticket button, you will need to display the frmPatron form.

To display the frmPatron form:

1   Close the frmSeat form. Click **frmPatron(lcPatron.frm)** in the Project window, then click the Project window's **View Object** button ▣.

The pseudocode for the Enter Ticket button's Click event procedure is shown in Figure 8-38.

1. Declare an Integer variable named intSeat and a PatronStruc variable named udtPatronRec.

2. Assign the Caption property of the lblNum control to the intSeat variable.

3. Assign the Text property of the txtName control to the strName field variable in the udtPatronRec variable.

4. Assign the Text property of the txtPhone control to the strPhone field variable in the udtPatronRec variable.

5. Write the record to the open random access file.

6. Set the BackColor property of the corresponding label control in the lblSeat array, which is located in the frmSeat form, to red.

7. Hide the frmPatron form.

Figure 8-38: Pseudocode for the Enter Ticket button

The first step is to declare the variables. This procedure will need two variables: intSeat and udtPatronRec. intSeat will store the seat number, which will also be the record number in the file. udtPatronRec, a record variable, will store the record—the name and phone number of the patron.

To code the Enter Ticket button:

1 Open the Enter Ticket button's Click event procedure, press the **Tab** key, then type **dim intSeat as integer, udtPatronRec as patronstruc** and press the **Enter** key.

The next step is to assign the appropriate values to the variables. First, assign the seat number to the intSeat variable. The seat number is stored in the Caption property of the lblNum control.

2 Type **intseat = lblnum.caption** and press the **Enter** key.

Now assign the name and phone number to the field variables in the udtPatronRec record variable. The name is in the txtName control, and the phone number is in the txtPhone control.

3 Type **udtpatronrec.strname = txtname.text** and press the **Enter** key, then type **udtpatronrec.strphone = txtphone.text** and press the **Enter** key.

After declaring the variables and assigning the appropriate values to them, you are ready to write the record to the random access file. Recall that you do that with the Put statement, whose syntax is **Put #** *filenumber,* [*recordnumber*], *variablename.*

4 Type **put #1, intseat, udtpatronrec** and press the **Enter** key.

After a seat has been reserved, its BackColor property should be set to red. Recall that the value currently in the intSeat variable is one more than the value in the lblSeat control's Index property. So, to refer to the appropriate seat in the lblSeat array, you will need to subtract 1 from the intSeat variable. For example, if the intSeat variable contains the number 2, you will want to set the BackColor property of the control named lblSeat(1) to red.

5   Type **frmseat.lblseat(intseat – 1).backcolor = vbred** and press the **Enter** key.

The last step in the pseudocode is to hide the frmPatron form, so the user can view the frmSeat form again. You can use the Hide method, which you learned about in Tutorial 3, to do so.

6   Type **frmpatron.hide** and press the **Enter** key.

7   Compare your code with the code shown in Figure 8-39 and make any needed corrections before continuing to the next step.

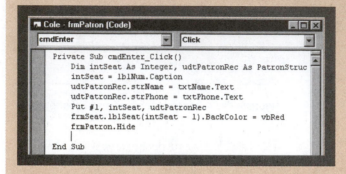

```
Cole - frmPatron (Code)                                    _ □ ✕
cmdEnter                     ▼       Click                          ▼
    Private Sub cmdEnter_Click()
        Dim intSeat As Integer, udtPatronRec As PatronStruc
        intSeat = lblNum.Caption
        udtPatronRec.strName = txtName.Text
        udtPatronRec.strPhone = txtPhone.Text
        Put #1, intSeat, udtPatronRec
        frmSeat.lblSeat(intSeat - 1).BackColor = vbRed
        frmPatron.Hide

    End Sub
```

Figure 8-39: Code entered in the Enter Ticket button's Click event procedure

8   Close the Code window.

Now test the Enter Ticket button to see if its code is working properly.

To test the Enter Ticket button:

1   **Save** and **run** the application. Use the File menu's Open command to open the **lcTest.dat** file, which is located in the Tut08 folder on your Student Disk.

2   Click seat number **2**. The frmPatron form appears on the screen, with seat number 2 in the Seat number label control.

3   Type **Khalid Patel** as the name, then press the **Tab** key, and then type **444-4444** as the phone number. Click the **Enter Ticket** button. Visual Basic writes the name and phone number as the second record in the random access file. The frmSeat form now appears on the screen with seat number 2 colored red.

You can also use the Enter Ticket button to edit an existing record.

4   Click seat number **2**. The patron form, which displays the seat number, as well as the patron's name and phone number, appears on the screen as shown in Figure 8-40.

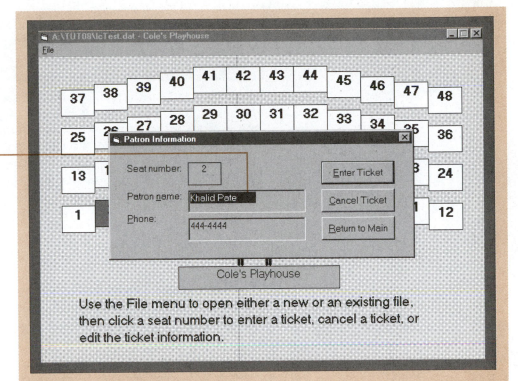

Figure 8-40: Patron form showing patron information for seat 2

notice that the
highlight extends
beyond the name

Notice that the highlight in the Patron name text box extends beyond the 12 characters in the name itself; that's because the patron's name (Khalid Patel) is shorter than the length of the name field in the random access file (20 characters). Recall that when the string data written to a field in a random access file is shorter than the length of the field, Visual Basic pads the field with spaces. In this case, the text box is highlighting the 12 characters in the name, as well as the eight spaces that were added to the name when it was written to the random access file. You can use Visual Basic's Trim function to remove the excess spaces. Before doing so, however, you will change Khalid Patel's phone number to 444-4443.

5   Change the phone number to **444-4443**, then click the **Enter Ticket** button. The new information overwrites the existing record in the file.

6   Click **File**, then click **Exit** to end the application. Visual Basic returns to the design screen.

The Trim Function

You can use Visual Basic's **Trim function** to remove (trim) both the leading and trailing spaces from a string. The syntax of the Trim function is **Trim**(*string*). You will use the Trim function to remove the excess spaces from the patron's name when the name is displayed in the txtName text box.

To include the Trim function in the application's code:

1   Click **frmSeat (lcSeat.frm)** in the Project window, then click the Project window's View Object button .

tip

Visual Basic also has an LTrim function, which removes only the leading spaces from a *string*, and an RTrim function, which removes only the trailing spaces from a *string*. (LTrim stands for "left trim" and RTrim stands for "right trim.") If it's possible that the *string* may contain both leading and trailing spaces, it is safer to use the Trim function in your code; then you are assured of removing all excess spaces.

2 Open the lblSeat control array's Click event procedure. Change the `frmPatron.txtName.Text = udtPatronRec.strName` instruction to **frmPatron.txtName.Text = Trim(udtPatronRec.strName)**.

3 Close the Code window, then close the frmSeat form.

4 **Save** and **run** the application. Use the File menu to open the **lcTest.dat** file, which is located in the Tut08 folder on your Student Disk. When the seat form appears, click seat number **2**. The patron form appears on the screen. Notice that the highlight in the Patron name text box does not extend beyond the name.

5 Close the patron form, then use the File menu to exit the application. Visual Basic returns to the design screen.

Code the Cancel Ticket button next.

Coding the Cancel Ticket Button

The Cancel Ticket button allows the user to remove a patron's name and phone number from the random access file. The pseudocode for the Cancel Ticket button's Click event procedure is shown in Figure 8-41.

---

1. Declare an Integer variable named intSeat and a PatronStruc variable named udtPatronRec.

2. Assign the Caption property of the lblNum control to the intSeat variable.

3. Assign 20 spaces to the strName field variable in the udtPatronRec variable.

4. Assign 8 spaces to the strPhone field variable in the udtPatronRec variable.

5. Write the record to the open random access file.

6. Set the BackColor property of the corresponding label control in the lblSeat array, which is located in the frmSeat form, to white.

7. Hide the frmPatron form.

Figure 8-41: Pseudocode for the Cancel Ticket button

Notice that the pseudocode shown in Figure 8-41 is very similar to the pseudocode shown in Figure 8-38. That means that the code for the Cancel Ticket button will be almost identical to the code for the Enter Ticket button. Therefore, you will copy the code from the Enter Ticket button to the Cancel Ticket button, and then make the necessary changes.

To code the Cancel Ticket button, then test the application:

1 Open the Enter Ticket button's Click event procedure.

2 Select all of the instructions between the `Private Sub` statement and the `End Sub` statement. (However, do not select either the `Private Sub` statement or the `End Sub` statement.) When the appropriate instructions are selected, press **Ctrl + c** to copy the instructions to the clipboard.

tip
• • • • • • • • • • • • • •

▶ To cancel a record having a numeric field, you would write a zero over the existing data in that field.

3 Use the Code window's Object box to open the cmdCancel control's Click event, then press **Ctrl + v** to paste the instructions in the cmdCancel control's Click event procedure.

You will need to make three changes to the code in the Code window. When a ticket is canceled, you will tell Visual Basic to write spaces over the existing name and phone number in the file. You can use the Space function to assign spaces to the strName and strPhone field variables before the udtPatronRec record variable is written to the file. You also need to change the BackColor property of the lblSeat control that corresponds to the canceled seat to white.

4 Enter the changes shown in Figure 8-42.

change these lines of code

change the color in this line of code

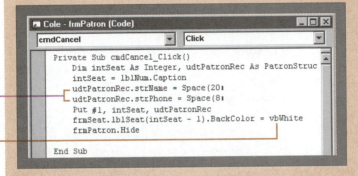

```
Cole - frmPatron (Code)

cmdCancel                              Click

    Private Sub cmdCancel_Click()
        Dim intSeat As Integer, udtPatronRec As PatronStruc
        intSeat = lblNum.Caption
        udtPatronRec.strName = Space(20)
        udtPatronRec.strPhone = Space(8)
        Put #1, intSeat, udtPatronRec
        frmSeat.lblSeat(intSeat - 1).BackColor = vbWhite
        frmPatron.Hide

    End Sub
```

Figure 8-42: Code entered in the Cancel Ticket button's Click event procedure

5 Close the Code window, then **save** and **run** the application. Use the File menu's Open command to open the **lcTest.dat** file. Notice that seat number 2 is colored red, which indicates that it is reserved.

6 Click seat number **2**. Khalid Patel's record appears in the frmPatron form. Click the **Cancel Ticket** button. Visual Basic replaces Khalid Patel's record in the random access file with spaces. When the frmSeat form appears again, seat number 2 is colored white.

7 Click **File**, then click **Exit** to end the application.

The last control you need to code in the frmPatron form is the Return to Main button.

Coding the Return to Main Button

The Return to Main button allows the user to return to the frmSeat form without either entering or canceling a ticket. The user might need to use this button if he or she accidentally clicked the wrong seat, or he or she might simply be interested in the name and phone number of a patron. This button will simply hide the frmPatron form.

To code the Return to Main button, then test the application:

1 Open the Return to Main button's Click event procedure. Press the **Tab** key, then type **frmpatron.hide** and press the **Enter** key.

2 Close the Code window, then **save** and **run** the application. Use the File menu's Open command to open the **lcTest.dat** file. The frmSeat form appears on the screen. All of the seats are colored white because no seat has yet been reserved. (Recall that you canceled seat number 2's reservation in the prior set of steps.)

3 Click seat number 3. The frmPatron form appears. Type **Sue Billings** as the name, press the **Tab** key, then type **111-1111** as the phone number. Press the **Enter** key to select the Enter Ticket button. Visual Basic writes the record to the file, then hides the frmPatron form. When the frmSeat form reappears, seat number 3 is colored red.

Verify that you entered Sue Billings's information correctly.

4 Click seat number 3. The frmPatron form appears with Sue Billings's information showing.

In some applications, it's convenient to be able to move a dialog box to another part of the screen. In the current application, you might want to move the frmPatron form, which is being used as a dialog box, to determine if a seat currently covered by it is reserved.

5 Place the mouse pointer on the Patron Information dialog box's title bar and drag the dialog box to another part of the screen. When the dialog box is where you want it, release the mouse button.

6 Click the **Return to Main** button. The frmSeat form appears once again.

7 Click **File**, then click **Exit**. Visual Basic unloads the forms and closes the data file before returning to the design screen.

You have now completed Lesson C and the Cole's Playhouse application. You can either take a break, complete the end-of-lesson questions and exercises, or continue to the Debugging section. The Debugging section may contain information that will help you complete the end-of-lesson exercises.

S U M M A R Y

To reference the property of a control that is located in another form:

■ Use the syntax *form.control.property*, where *form* is the name of the form in which the *control* is located.

To show a form:

■ Use the Show method. Its syntax is *object*.**Show** [*style*].

To remove a form from the screen, but leave the form in memory:

■ Use the Hide method. Its syntax is *object*.**Hide**.

To remove spaces from a string:

■ Use the Trim, LTrim, or RTrim functions. The syntax of the Trim function is **Trim**(*string*). The Trim function removes both the leading and trailing spaces from the *string*. The syntax of the LTrim ("left trim") function is **LTrim**(*string*). The LTrim function removes the leading spaces from the *string*. The syntax of the RTrim ("right trim") function is **RTrim**(*string*). The RTrim function removes the trailing spaces from the *string*.

QUESTIONS

1. Assume that you are coding an object in the frmFriends form and you want to refer to the Text property of the txtPhone text box, which is also in the frmFriends form. Which of the following could you enter into the Code window?
   a. `frmFriends.Text`
   b. `frmFriends.Text.txtPhone`
   c. `text.TxtPhone`
   d. `txtPhone.Text`
   e. `txtPhone.Text.frmFriends`

2. Assume that you are coding an object in the frmFriends form and you want to refer to the Text property of the txtPhone text box, which is in the frmNumbers form. Which of the following could you enter into the Code window?
   a. `frmFriends.txtPhone.Text`
   b. `frmNumbers.txtPhone.Text`
   c. `text.txtPhone`
   d. `txtPhone.Text`
   e. `txtPhone.Text.frmNumbers`

3. Which of the following methods will display a form?
   a. Access
   b. Display
   c. Form
   d. Show

4. Which of the following methods will remove a form from the screen, but keep it in memory?
   a. Blank
   b. Clear
   c. Erase
   d. Hide
   e. Remove

5. You use the _____ function to remove both the leading and trailing spaces from a string.
   a. Excess
   b. Remove
   c. Trim
   d. Val

EXERCISES

1. In this exercise you will use a control array and a random access file.

   Scenario: Mr. Fletcher, a fourth grade teacher, wants an application that he can use to keep track of the names and grades of his students. In this exercise you will use two forms. One form will use label controls to represent the 20 desks in the classroom. The other form will allow Mr. Fletcher to enter the student's name and grade in a random access file, remove the student from the file, and return to the main form.

   a. Open the lc1 (lc1.vbp) project, which is located in the Tut08 folder on your Student Disk.

   b. Save the frmStudent form as lc1Stud. Save the frmDesk form as lc1Desk. Save the project as lc1Done. (Save the files in the Tut08 folder on your Student Disk.)

   c. Change the frmDesk form's BorderStyle property to 1-Fixed Single. Set its MinButton property to True.

   d. The frmDesk form should be the startup form.

   e. Add a code module to the project. Define a record structure named StudStruc. The StudStruc structure should contain two fields: strName and strGrade. StrName is a 20-character String field structure, and strGrade is a 1-character String field.

   f. Save the code module as lc1Done in the Tut08 folder on your Student Disk.

   g. In the frmDesk form, code the File menu's New command appropriately. (You can use Tutorial 8's Figure 8-24 as a guide.)

   h. Create and code the user-defined Initialize sub procedure. Change the BackColor property of the desks to white. (You can use Tutorial 8's Figure 8-28 as a guide.)

   i. In the frmDesk form, code the File menu's Open command appropriately. (You can use Tutorial 8's Figure 8-33 as a guide.) If a desk is occupied, then change its BackColor property to yellow; otherwise, it should be white.

   j. In the frmDesk form, code the File menu's Exit command and the form's Unload event appropriately. (Use the code for the Cole's Playhouse application as a guide.)

   k. In the frmDesk form, code the lblDesk control array's Click event procedure appropriately. (You can use Tutorial 8's Figure 8-36 as a guide.) If a desk is occupied, then its BackColor property should be yellow; otherwise, it should be white.

   l. Code the Return to Main button in the frmStudent form so that it hides the frmStudent form.

   m. Code the Enter button in the frmStudent form. Make the Enter button the default button (You can use Tutorial 8's Figure 8-38 as a guide.)

   n. Code the Remove button in the frmStudent form. (You can use Tutorial 8's Figure 8-41 as a guide.)

   o. Save and run the application. Create a new file named lc1Test.dat.

   p. Test the application by entering the following records, shown as desk number, student name, and grade. After entering each record its desk in the lblDesk array should be yellow.

      12, Mary Jane, A
      7, Fred Jones, C
      20, Ellen Berry, B

   q. Click desk number 20. Ellen Berry and a grade of B should appear in the frmStudent form.

   r. Ellen Berry has moved to another school. Remove Ellen Berry from the random access file and from the classroom. Her desk in the lblDesk array should be white.

   s. Click desk number 7. Fred Jones and a grade of C should appear in the frmStudent form.

   t. Click the Return to Main button.

u. Use the File menu's Exit command to end the application.

v. Run the application again. Use the File menu's Open command to open the lc1Test.dat file. Add your name and grade to a seat number of your choice, then exit the application.

w. Print the application's code.

2. In this exercise you will use a control array, a random access file, and a list box.

Scenario: Janice and Bob own a restaurant that has a small banquet room. The banquet room, which can accommodate 40 guests, is typically rented out for small weddings. Janice and Bob would like you to create an application that they can use to keep track of each guest's name and meal preference (Steak, Fish, and Vegetarian).

a. Open the lc2 (lc2.vbp) project, which is located in the Tut08 folder on your Student Disk.

b. Save the frmBanquet form as lc2Banq. Save the frmGuest form as lc2Guest. Save the project as lc2Done. (Save the files in the Tut08 folder on your Student Disk.)

c. The frmBanquet form should be the startup form.

d. Add the Steak, Fish, and Vegetarian entries to the lstMeal list box in the frmGuest form. Set the list box's Sorted property to True. The default selection in the lstMeal list box should be Steak.

e. The frmBanquet form contains 40 image controls, which represent the 40 seats in the banquet room. The form also contains an image control, imgSmile. If a seat is occupied, then the smiling face icon should appear in the corresponding imgSeat image control.

f. Add a code module to the project. Define a record structure named GuestStruc. The GuestStruc structure should contain two fields, strName, which is a 20-character String field, and intMeal, an Integer field. The strName variable will store the guest's name, which is entered in the frmGuest form. The intMeal variable will store the index of the list box selection from the frmGuest form.

g. Save the code module as lc2Done in the Tut08 folder on your Student Disk.

h. Add a File menu to the frmBanquet form. The File menu should contain New, Open, and Exit commands. You will need to add the Microsoft Common Dialog control to the application.

i. In the frmBanquet form, code the File menu's New command, Open command, and Exit command. Also code the frmBanquet form's Unload event. You will also need to create a sub procedure that will initialize the random access file and the frmBanquet form.

j. In the frmBanquet form, code the imgSeat control array appropriately. The image controls should display the frmGuest form when clicked. The guest's number and name, as well as his or her meal preference, should display in the frmGuest form.

k. In the frmGuest form, code the Enter, Delete, and Return to Main buttons' Click event procedures appropriately. Occupied seats in the imgSeat array should display the smiling face icon (imgSmile); otherwise, the imgSeat control should be empty.

l. Open a new data file named Banq1.dat. Test the application by entering the following guests anywhere you want:

Sue Shah	select Vegetarian from the list box
Ann Yonkers	select Fish from the list box
Ellen Alders	select Steak from the list box

These seats should display the smiling face icon.

m. Click the seat occupied by Ann Yonkers. Ann's number, name, and meal should appear in the frmBanquet form. Click the Delete button to remove her from the random access file; her seat in the frmBanquet form should now be unoccupied.

n. Use the File menu to exit the application. Rerun the application. Open the Banq1.dat file; the occupied seats should display the smiling face icon. Exit the application.

o. Print the application's code.

3. In this exercise you will modify the application you created in Lesson C's Exercise 1.

Scenario: In Exercise 1, you created an application that Mr. Fletcher could use to keep track of the names and grades of his students. You will now modify the code so that it displays the student's grade in the frmDesk form.

a. Open the lc1Done (lc1Done.vbp) project that you created in Lesson C's Exercise 1.

b. Save the lc1Stud form as lc3Stud. Save the lc1Desk form as lc3Desk. Save the lc1Done code module as lc3Done. Save the project as lc3Done. (Save the files in the Tut08 folder on your Student Disk.)

c. Modify the code so that all occupied seats will display the student's grade in addition to the seat number.

d. Save and run the application. Three grades, which correspond to the three records already in the file, should appear in the frmDesk form. (The seat numbers for these seats should also appear.) The three seats should be yellow, indicating that they are occupied.

e. Enter the following student's information in any of the unoccupied seats: Steven Ivanelli, F. Exit the application.

f. Now change the code so that the color assigned to the BackColor property of a desk depends on the grade. The desks associated with grades of A should be magenta, grades of B should be red, grades of C should be yellow, grades of D should be green, and grades of F should be blue.

g. Save and run the application. Open the lc1Test.dat file. Four grades, which correspond to the four records already in the file, should appear in the frmDesk form. Each different grade should be a different color.

h. Add the following two records in any unoccupied seat in the lblDesk array: Darlene Burnham, D, and Jackie Bunt, B.

i. Exit the application. Print the application's code.

Exercises 4 through 6 are Discovery Exercises, which allow you to "discover" the solutions to problems on your own. Discovery Exercises may include topics that are not covered in the tutorial.

discovery ▶ 4. In this exercise you will modify the Cole's Playhouse application that you created in the tutorial.

Scenario: In this exercise you will modify the code in the lcCole (lcCole.vbp) project so that it allows the user to select the Enter Ticket button only when a name has been entered into the frmPatron form.

a. Theater employees mentioned that if they inadvertently click the Enter Ticket button without entering any seat information, the seat will appear to be reserved when, in fact, the entry is blank. An empty phone field is fine, but a name should be required. If you have access to the MSDN Library, then display the Help screens on the Change event and the Enabled property. Modify the code so that the Enter Ticket button is enabled only when the name entry is completed. (*Hint*: You will need to code the txtName control's Change event.)

b. Save and run the application using the current form, module, and project names. Create a new data file named lc4Test.dat.

c. Click an unreserved seat in the frmSeat form. The Enter Ticket button should be dimmed when the patron form appears. Type your name into the txtName control. As soon as you type the first letter, the Enter Ticket button should darken.

d. Remove your name from the txtName control. When the entire text box is empty, the Enter Ticket button should be dimmed again.

e. Click the Return to Main button. Exit the application. Print the code for the frmPatron form only.

discovery ▶ 5. In this exercise you will create a user's manual for the Cole's Playhouse application.

Scenario: The manager of Cole's Playhouse expressed concerns about training employees to use the application you created. You have agreed to write a user manual to provide a reference for the different functions of your application.

a. Develop a user manual to be used by the employees of Cole's Playhouse. It should include step-by-step instructions for each function of the application. Use the word processor of your choice. Start by creating an outline for the different sections of the manual. Be careful not to skip any of the functions of the program—opening data files, initializing data files, reserving seats, and so on.

b. Next, create the text for each section of your outline. Proofread and edit the text as necessary. To create a truly accurate manual, you must test it. Go through each of the sections while using the program. Keep in mind that the users will not have the working knowledge of the program that you have, so don't make any assumptions.

c. Once the manual is finished, print the final copy. Be sure to have a title page and a table of contents. For more complex applications, an index is important.

discovery ▶ 6. In this exercise you will update records stored in a random access file.

Scenario: Shirts Outlet Store sells a variety of shirts manufactured by three different companies. The specific manufacturer is identified by a letter, which is added to the end of the shirt's item number. For example, the item numbers of shirts manufactured by Cody end in C, the item numbers of shirts manufactured by Adams end in A, and the item numbers of shirts manufactured by Dawn end in D.

Shirts Outlet stores the item number and price of the shirts in a random access file. Periodically a manufacturer will raise the wholesale price, which means that Shirts Outlet Store will need to raise the retail price in order to pass the increase on to the consumer. They want you to create an application that will allow them to update the prices in the random access file. The application should also allow them to print a price list on the printer. The price list should show each item's number, manufacturer (Cody, Adams, Dawn), and price. Print the price list in three columns.

a. First create a simple interface that you can use to enter the following 10 records into a random access file:

Item No.	Price	Item No.	Price
444C	15.75	888A	20.00
111A	16.00	777D	21.50
222A	24.30	555C	45.00
333D	21.56	123C	34.78
666D	34.57	345A	10.0

tip

▶ Use Windows to make a copy of the data file. This way you can use the copy to recreate the data file, if necessary.

b. Next, create a user interface that Shirts Outlet Store can use. Remember that you will need to get the percent increase and the manufacturer from the user. The application should update the random access file by increasing the price of only the items made by that manufacturer. Also recall that the interface should allow the store to print a price list on the printer.

c. Save the form, module, and project as lc6Done in the Tut08 folder on your Student Disk.

d. Run the application. Print the price list with the original prices showing.

e. The Adams company is increasing their prices by 10%. Update the appropriate prices in the random access file.

f. Print the new price list.

g. Exit the application.

h. Print the Shirts Outlet Store's user interface. Also print the lc6Done application's code.

i. Submit the printouts from steps d, f, and h, and the code from step h.

DEBUGGING

Technique In Tutorial 7, you learned how to use the On Error statement to turn on the error trapping process in a procedure. Recall that the syntax of the On Error statement is **On Error GoTo** *line*, where *line* is either a line label or a line number that identifies the position of the procedure's error handler—the set of instructions that tells the application how to handle the trapped errors. Keep in mind that the On Error statement traps all errors that occur in the procedure. While you are testing an application with both valid and invalid data, it helps to include Visual Basic's MsgBox statement in the application's error handlers. The MsgBox statement will allow you to observe the types of errors that can occur in the various procedures; you need to know this information to code the error handlers appropriately.

The MsgBox statement is similar to the MsgBox function, which you learned about in Tutorials 4 and 5; however, unlike the MsgBox function, the MsgBox statement does not return a value. The syntax of the MsgBox statement is **MsgBox** *prompt*, where *prompt* is the message you want displayed in the dialog box. If you use the Err object's Description property as the *prompt*, the MsgBox statement will display a message indicating the error that occurred in the procedure.

Exercises   1. Open the **debug1** (debug1.vbp) project, which is located in the Tut08 folder on your Student Disk. This application allows the user to enter a maximum of 10 records in a random access file, and then displays those records.

   a. Print the code, then study the existing code. **Run** the application. You will notice that the Enter Record and Display Record buttons are disabled. According to the code, the buttons are not enabled until the user opens either a new or an existing file.

   b. Use the application's File menu to open a new file. Name the file **deb1**, and save it in the Tut08 folder on your Student Disk. Notice that the Enter Record and Display Record buttons are still disabled, which means that the code in the File menu's New command is not working correctly.

   c. Use the application's File menu to exit the application.

   d. Open the New command's Click event procedure. When an error occurs in this procedure, the NewErrHandler routine simply exits the procedure. You can use the MsgBox statement, along with the Err object's Description property, to display a message that indicates the error that occurred in the procedure. You will display the message before exiting the procedure.

   e. Insert a blank line below `NewErrHandler:`, then type **msgbox err.description**. Close the Code window, then **save** and **run** the application. Use the application's File menu to open a new file. Name the file **deb1**, and save it in the Tut08 folder on your Student Disk. Visual Basic displays the "Type mismatch" error in the MsgBox statement's dialog box. Click the **OK** button to remove the dialog box, then use the application's File menu to exit the application.

tip

You learned about the Err object's Description property in Tutorial 7's Debugging section.

f. As you may remember from Tutorial 2's Debugging section, a "Type mismatch" error means that Visual Basic has encountered something that it wasn't expecting in an instruction—for example, a string where a number is required or a number where a string is needed. First, search for the error in the New command's Click event procedure, where the error handler is located. You will notice that the instructions in the New command's Click event are correct, so none of them could be causing the error. In addition to searching for the error in the procedure that contains the error handler, you also must search any procedures called by that procedure. In this case, for example, you also must search the Initialize procedure, which is called by the New command's Click event. Because the Initialize procedure does not have its own error handler, it will use the error handler found in the procedure that called it. This means that the New command's error handler (NewErrHandler) will trap the errors that occur in both the New command and the Initialize procedure.

g. Open the Initialize procedure's Code window.

HELP? Open the form's General Declarations section, then use the Procedure box to open the Initialize procedure.

h. Careful study of the Initialize procedure's code shows that the `udtItemRec.sngPrice = Space(5)` is causing the "Type mismatch" error because it is attempting to assign a string—in this case, five spaces—to a numeric variable. Change the `udtItemRec.sngPrice = Space(5)` instruction to **udtItemRec.sngPrice = 0**, then **save** and **run** the application. Use the application's File menu to open a new file. Name the file **deb1** and save it in the Tut08 folder on your Student Disk. After opening the file, the application enables the Enter Record and Display Record buttons, and it displays the name of the opened file (deb1.dat) in the application's title bar.

i. Stop the application, then remove the `MsgBox Err.Description` statement from the New command's Click event. Save the application.

2. Open the **debug2** (debug2.vbp) project, which is located in the Tut08 folder on your Student Disk. This application allows the user to enter a maximum of 10 records in a random access file, and then display those records.

a. Print the code, then study the existing code. Notice that the Initialize procedure has its own error handler named InitErrHander. **Run** the application. You will notice that the Enter Record and Display Record buttons are disabled. According to the code, the buttons are not enabled until the user opens either a new or an existing file.

b. Use the application's File menu to open a new file. Name the file **deb2**, and save it in the Tut08 folder on your Student Disk. Notice that the Enter Record and Display Record buttons are now enabled. The application's title bar, however, does not include the name of the opened file (deb2.dat), as it should.

c. Use this tutorial's debugging technique to debug the application. Indicate the error message on the code printout from step a. Fix the error. When the application is working correctly, print the code.

d. Submit the printouts from steps a and c.

Database Access

Modifying the Cole's Playhouse Application

case ▶ In Tutorial 8, you created an application for Cole's Playhouse, a small community theater that holds 48 seats. As you may remember, the application keeps track of the reserved seats by recording each patron's name and phone number in a random access file. Max Phillips, the manager of the playhouse, has heard that many businesses use databases to keep track of their data. He has asked you to modify the application that you created so that it now uses a Microsoft Access database, rather than a random access file.

Previewing the Modified Cole's Playhouse Application

As in previous tutorials, you will preview the completed application before creating it.

To preview the modified Cole's Playhouse application:

1   If necessary, start Windows, then place your Student Disk in the appropriate disk drive.

2   Use the Run command on the Start menu to run the **cole** (cole.exe) file, which is located in the Tut09 folder on your Student Disk. The application's user interface appears on the screen. See Figure 9-1.

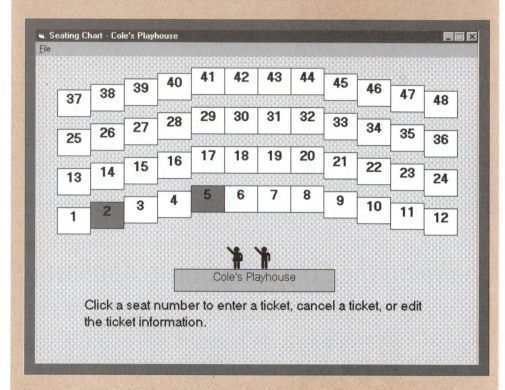

Figure 9-1: User interface for the Cole's Playhouse application

The form uses a label control array to represent the 48 seats in the Cole's Playhouse theater. Notice that two of the label controls are red, while the others are white. A red label control indicates that the seat is reserved, and a white label control indicates that the seat is available. To reserve a seat, you simply click its corresponding label control. Reserve seat number 33.

3   Click seat number 33. The dialog box shown in Figure 9-2 opens.

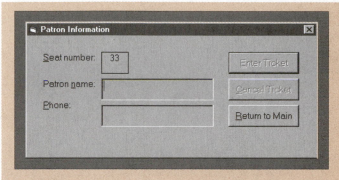

Figure 9-2: Dialog box shown in the user interface

You use this dialog box to enter or cancel a reservation, as well as to return to the screen that displays the theater seats. Reserve seat number 33 for Sue Marlin.

4   Type **Sue Marlin** in the Patron name text box, then press the **Tab** key. Type **111-1111** in the Phone text box, then press the **Enter** key to select the Enter Ticket button, which is the default button in the form. The application saves Sue Marlin's seat number, name, and phone number in a Microsoft Access database on your Student Disk; it also closes the dialog box and changes the color of seat number 33 to red.

Observe how you cancel a reservation.

5   Click seat number **33**. Sue Marlin's information appears in the dialog box on the screen. Click the **Cancel Ticket** button. The application removes Sue Marlin's information from the database, then closes the dialog box and changes the color of seat number 33 to white.

6   Click **File**, then click **Exit** to end the application.

In Lesson A, you will learn how to use Visual Data Manager to create a Microsoft Access database. Then, in Lesson B, you will learn how to use the Microsoft ADO (ActiveX Data Object) data control to access the records stored in a database. In Lesson C, you will create the Cole's Playhouse application that you just previewed.

In this lesson you will learn how to:

- Design a database
- Create a database using Visual Data Manager
- Create an index
- Define data validation rules and data validation text
- Add records to and delete records from a table
- Edit records in a database table
- Search a table for records that match a search criterion

Using Visual Data Manager

Database Concepts and Terminology

In order to maintain accurate records, most businesses store information about their employees, customers, and inventory in files called databases. In general, a **database** is simply an organized collection of related information stored in a file on a disk.

Many software packages exist for creating databases; some of the most popular are dBASE®, FoxPro®, Microsoft Access™, and Paradox®. You can use Visual Basic to access the data stored in these databases. This allows a company to create a standard interface in Visual Basic that employees can use to access database information stored in a variety of formats. Instead of learning each database package's user interface, the employee needs to know only one interface. The actual format the database is in is unimportant and will be transparent to the user.

In addition to allowing you to access the data stored in databases created by other software packages, you can also use Visual Basic to create a Microsoft Access database; that's because Visual Basic contains the same Jet database engine used in Microsoft Access. The **Jet engine** allows databases created in Visual Basic to be read and manipulated by Microsoft Access, and those created in Access to be read and manipulated by Visual Basic.

The databases created by both Visual Basic and Access are relational databases. A **relational database** is one that stores information in tables, which are composed of columns and rows. Each column in a table represents a field, and each row represents a record. As you learned in Tutorial 6, a **field** is a single item of information about a person, place, or thing—such as a name, address, or phone number—and a **record** is a group of related fields that contain all of the necessary data about a specific person, place, or thing. A **table** is a group of related records; each record in the group pertains to the same topic, and each contains the same type of information—in other words, the same fields.

A relational database can contain one or more tables. For example, you would typically store the information regarding the college courses you have taken in a one-table database. The table would consist of a group of related records that each contain a course ID (department and number), course title, number of credit hours, and grade. A database that stores information about a CD (compact disc) collection, on the other hand, would typically use two tables. One table would store the general information about each CD—the CD's name and the artist's name—and the other table would store the information about the songs on each CD—their title and track number. You would use a common field—for example, a CD number—to relate the records contained in both tables. Figure 9-3 shows an example of both a one-table and two-table relational database.

tip

You don't have to be a business to make use of database. Many people use databases to keep track of their medical records, their compact disc collections, and even their golf scores.

tip

The databases are called relational because the information in the tables can be related in different ways.

tip

The column and row format used in a relational database is similar to the column and row format used in a spreadsheet.

One-table college course relational database

ID	Title	Hours	Grade
CIS100	Intro to Computers	5	A
Eng100	English Composition	3	B
Phil105	Philosophy	5	C
CIS203	Intro to Visual Basic	5	A

Two-table CD relational database

the two tables are related
by the CD number

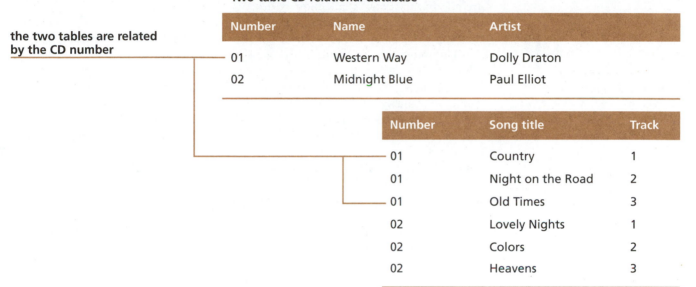

Number	Name	Artist
01	Western Way	Dolly Draton
02	Midnight Blue	Paul Elliot

Number	Song title	Track
01	Country	1
01	Night on the Road	2
01	Old Times	3
02	Lovely Nights	1
02	Colors	2
02	Heavens	3

Figure 9-3: Example of a one-table and a two-table relational database

The advantages of storing data in a relational database are many. Data stored in that format can be retrieved both quickly and easily by the computer. In addition, the data can be displayed in any order. In a CD database, for example, the information can be arranged by artist name, or it can be arranged by song title, and so on. A relational database also allows you to control how much information you want to view at a time. You can view all of the information in the CD database, or you can view only the information pertaining to a certain artist, or only the names of the songs contained on a specific CD.

In this lesson you will learn how to design and create a one-table Microsoft Access database. You will use the one-table database to keep track of the Cole's Playhouse reservations.

Designing the Cole's Playhouse Database

It is important to design a database in such a way as to assure that it meets the user's requirements. When designing a database, you should follow these basic design steps:
1. Identify the information the user will need from the database.
2. Organize the information into one or more tables.
3. Establish relationships between tables (if the database contains more than one table).

4. Create one or more indexes, if necessary.
5. Define data validation rules, if necessary.

You will use these design steps to design the Cole's Playhouse database.

The first step in the design process is to identify the information the user will need from the database; this will help you decide which fields to include in the database. The database that keeps track of the Cole's Playhouse reservations will need to include the seat number, as well as the patron's name and phone number. Each piece of information will become a field in one of the database tables.

Once the information is identified, you then organize the fields into one or more tables. Fields that are logically related should be grouped in the same table. In the Cole database, the seat number, patron name, and patron phone number are all characteristics that uniquely describe each reservation, so the fields should be placed in the same table. Because the Cole database will require only one table, the third design step (establish relationships between tables) is not necessary.

The fourth step in the design process is to create any necessary indexes for the tables in the database. An **index** is a special table, created and maintained by Visual Basic, that allows you to arrange the database records in a specific order, as well as to quickly search the database for information. For each record in a database table, the index stores two fields. The first field, called the **index field**, stores the values contained in the field being indexed. For example, to arrange the reservation records in seat number order, you would create an index for the seat number field. The index field in the index would then contain all of the seat numbers in ascending order. To arrange the records in patron name order, on the other hand, you would create an index for the patron name field. The index field in this index would then contain the patron names.

The second field in the index is called the **pointer field** because it stores a number that represents (points to) the location of the record in the table. For example, if the first seat number in the index field corresponds to record number 6 in the database table, then the pointer field will contain the number 6. The number stored in the pointer field is called the **record number**. Figure 9-4 illustrates the concept of a table and an index using a table named tblPatron, an index named indSeat, and an index named indName. ("tbl" and "ind" are the three-character IDs used to name a table and an index, respectively.) The information in the indSeat index tells Visual Basic how to arrange the records in seat number order. In this case, for example, record number 6 should be first, then record number 2, and so on. The information in the indName index, on the other hand, tells Visual Basic how to arrange the records in order by the patron name. When arranging the records in patron name order, you will notice that record number 2 is first, then record number 5, and so on.

tip

All relational database software packages create and maintain indexes.

tblPatron Table

fldSeat	fldName	fldPhone
38	Smith, Janet	333-3333
15	Hall, Phil	222-2222
43	Williams, Marge	222-3111
44	Williams, Bob	222-3111
24	Jacobs, Jim	211-1111
10	Sprott, Candy	333-7777

indSeat Index

index field	pointer field
10	6
15	2
24	5
38	1
43	3
44	4

indName Index

index field	pointer field
Hall, Phil	2
Jacobs, Jim	5
Smith, Janet	1
Sprott, Candy	6
Williams, Bob	4
Williams, Marge	3

Figure 9-4: Illustration of tblPatron table, indSeat index, and indName index

When new records are added to a table, Visual Basic handles entering the appropriate information in the indexes. If, for example, you enter the information for a new reservation in the tblPatron table, Visual Basic will automatically enter the seat number and corresponding record number in the appropriate position in the indSeat index. Visual Basic will also enter the patron name and corresponding record number in the appropriate position in the indName index.

A table does not have to have an index; if it does, it can have one or more. You may need to create more than one index so that the user can view the table information in different ways. In the tblPatron table, for example, you may want to arrange the records in seat number order so that you can quickly locate the information pertaining to a specific seat in the playhouse. At another time, however, you may want to arrange the records in patron name order so that you can easily find where in the playhouse a patron is sitting.

In addition to allowing the *user* to locate information, an index also allows the *computer* to find information more quickly. Assume, for example, that you want the computer to locate and display the information pertaining to seat number 10. If the data you want to locate is in a field that is indexed, the computer uses the index rather than the database table to locate the information. In Figure 9-4's illustration, the computer would search the indSeat index, rather than the tblPatron table, for seat number 10's record. Because the indSeat index is arranged numerically by seat number, the computer can search the index for the desired record much faster than it can search the database table, which is not arranged in any particular order. When the computer finds the number 10 in the index's index field, it uses the information in the index's pointer field to locate and then display seat number 10's record.

tip

Not every field in a table needs to be indexed. In fact, creating too many indexes can slow down database processing. Only create indexes for fields on which you plan either to order records or to search.

Because the Cole's Playhouse application will require you to locate information by seat number only, you will create an index for only the seat number field in the tblPatron table.

The last step in the design process is to define any necessary data validation rules. **Data validation** refers to the process of ensuring that the data in the database meets certain criteria. A data validation rule places restrictions on the data entered in a field. An hourly wage field in an employee table, for example, would typically contain a validation rule that restricts the field data to only numbers that are greater than or equal to the minimum wage. You will include one data validation rule in the tblPatron table. The validation rule will specify that the seat number must be greater than or equal to 1 and less than or equal to 48. (Recall that Cole's Playhouse has only 48 seats.)

Figure 9-5 shows the final design for the Cole database.

Cole database	
Table name	tblPatron
Field names	fldSeat, fldName, fldPhone
Relationships	None. The Cole database contains only one table.
Index	Create an index named indSeat for the fldSeat field
Validation rule	The fldSeat field must contain a number that is greater than or equal to 1 and less than or equal to 48.

Figure 9-5: Final design for the Cole database

tip

"tbl" and "fld" are the three-character IDs used to name a table and a field, respectively.

Now that you have designed the Cole database, you can begin creating it. You will use Visual Basic's Visual Data Manager to do so.

Using Visual Data Manager to Create the Cole Database

Visual Basic comes with an application named Visual Data Manager that you can use to create a Microsoft Access database, including the indexes and data validation rules. You can also use Visual Data Manager to both add records to and delete records from the database, as well as to search for information in the database.

To use Visual Data Manager to create a Microsoft Access database:

1 Start Visual Basic, if necessary, and then open a Standard EXE project.

2 Click **Add-Ins** on the menu bar, then click **Visual Data Manager**. The VisData window appears.

3 Minimize Visual Basic, then maximize the VisData window.

   HELP? To minimize Visual Basic, click the Project 1 – Microsoft Visual Basic [design] button on the Windows taskbar, then click the Minimize ■ button on the Visual Basic title bar.

The Visual Data Manager's File menu contains the New command, which you use to create a new database.

4   Click **File** on the menu bar. The File menu opens. Notice that the File menu also contains the Open DataBase command, which you use to open an existing database. In this case, you want to create a new database.

5   Point to **New** on the File menu. The New menu opens. Notice that you can use Visual Data Manager to create many different types of database files. In this case you want to create a Microsoft Access database.

6   Point to **Microsoft Access** on the New menu. The Microsoft Access menu appears and displays two commands: Version 2.0 MDB and Version 7.0 MDB. (The MDB stands for "Microsoft Database.")

Create an Access Version 7.0 database.

7   Click **Version 7.0 MDB** on the Microsoft Access menu. The Select Microsoft Access Database to Create dialog box appears.

The Save as type list box in the dialog box contains Microsoft Access MDBs (*.mdb). When you create an Access database, Visual Data Manager appends the .mdb extension to the filename when the file is saved. The .mdb extension indicates that the file is a Microsoft Access database. Use the dialog box to give the database a name (cole) and save it on your Student Disk.

8   Type **cole** in the File name text box. Save the cole database in the Tut09 folder on your Student Disk. The VisData window appears as shown in Figure 9-6.

Database Window

SQL Statement window

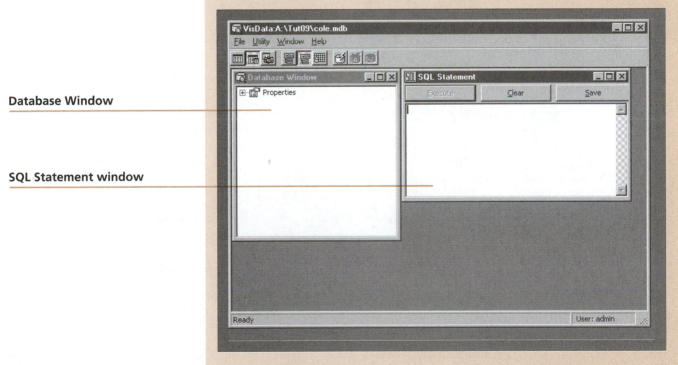

Figure 9-6: VisData window

The VisData application contains two windows: the Database Window and the SQL Statement window. You will use the Database Window to create the tblPatron table for the Cole's Playhouse application. You will not need the SQL Statement window in this application. **SQL**, pronounced like the word "sequel," stands for Structured Query Language and consists of commands that allow you to access the data stored in a database. You will learn about SQL in Lesson B. Use the Database Window to create the tblPatron table.

To create the tblPatron table:

1 Right-click the **Database** window, and then click **New Table** on the popup menu. The Table Structure dialog box appears as shown in Figure 9-7.

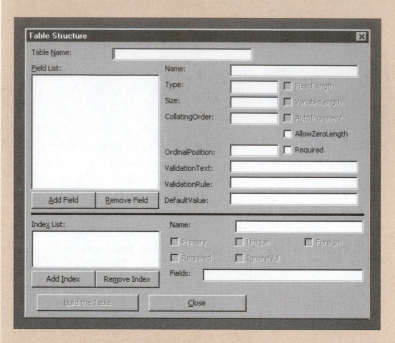

Figure 9-7: Table Structure dialog box

You use the Table Structure dialog box to give the table a name, and also to define information about each field in the table, such as the field's name, data type, and size. You also use it to create an index for the table. You will learn how to create an index later in this tutorial. First give the table a name. Table names typically begin with the three characters "tbl".

2 Type **tblPatron** in the Table Name text box, and then press the **Tab** key to move the focus to the Field List list box.

3 Click the **Add Field** button, which is located below the Field List list box. The Add Field dialog box appears, as shown in Figure 9-8.

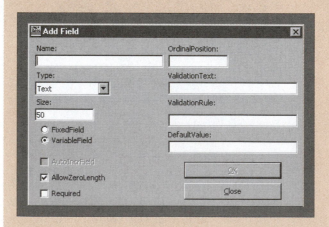

Figure 9-8: Add Field dialog box

You must assign a unique name, as well as a data type and size, to each field in the table. Figure 9-9 shows the 11 valid data types for the table fields.

Data type	Data type
Binary	Integer
Boolean	Long
Byte	Memo
Currency	Single
Date/Time	Text
Double	

Figure 9-9: Eleven data types for table fields

For all but the Text data type, the size of the field is preset by Visual Data Manager and cannot be changed.

Define the seat number field first. Field names typically begin with the three characters "fld".

4   Type **fldSeat** in the Name text box, then press the **Tab** key to move the focus to the Type list box.

The fldSeat field will contain integers only, so you will declare the field's data type as Integer.

5   Click the **Type** list arrow. Scroll the list until Integer appears, then click **Integer** in the list.

You will notice that the size of an Integer field is fixed at 2 bytes. Also notice that the field's Required check box is not selected. The Required check box controls whether a value has to be entered in the field. In this case, because each record should contain a seat number, you will select the Required check box.

6   Click the **Required** check box to select it. Figure 9-10 shows the completed Add Field dialog box for the seat number field.

tip

You can also select a data type by pressing its first letter when the focus is in the Type list box. To select the Integer data type, for example, you could simply press the letter i on your keyboard.

indicates that an entry is required

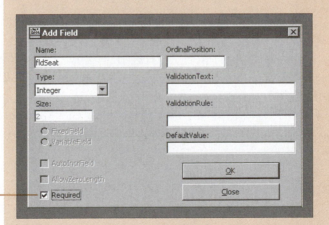

Figure 9-10: Completed Add Field dialog box for the seat number field

7 Click the **OK** button in the Add Field dialog box. Visual Basic removes the field's name from the Name text box and adds it to the Field List list box in the Table Structure dialog box. As you are creating the table, the Field List list box displays the names of all the fields contained in the table.

HELP? You may need to drag the Add Field dialog box out of the way to view the Field List list box in the Table Structure dialog box.

You will now complete the tblPatron table by defining the remaining two fields: patron name and patron phone number.

To complete the tblPatron table definition:

1 Type **fldName** in the Name text box, then press the **Tab** key to move the focus to the Type list box.

The fldName field will contain letters and the comma, so you will declare the field's data type as Text.

2 Verify that the Type list box says **Text**, which is the default field type.

Notice that the Size text box displays 50, which is the default size for a Text field. Recall that you can change the size of a Text field. In this case, the fldName field will need to contain a maximum of 20 characters only, so you will change its size from the default of 50 to 20.

3 Press the **Tab** key to place the insertion point in the Size text box. Change the 50 to **20**.

Notice that the AllowZeroLength check box is selected. When a field's AllowZeroLength check box is selected, Visual Basic allows a zero-length string to be assigned to the field—in other words, it allows the record to be saved without any information entered in the field. In this case, because each record should contain a name, you will deselect the AllowZeroLength check box, which will prevent the user from entering a record that does not contain a name. You will also select the Required check box, which is currently unselected.

4 Click the **AllowZeroLength** check box to remove the check mark, then click the **Required** check box to select it.

5 Click the **OK** button in the Add Field dialog box.

6 On your own, add the remaining field to the tblPatron table.

Name	Type	Size	AllowZeroLength	Required
fldPhone	Text	8	checked	unchecked

7 Click the **OK** button in the Add Field dialog box to add the fldPhone field to the Field List list box, then click the **Close** button in the Add Field dialog box. The Add Field dialog box closes, and the Table Structure dialog box appears as shown in Figure 9-11.

tip

The size of a Text field cannot exceed 255 characters.

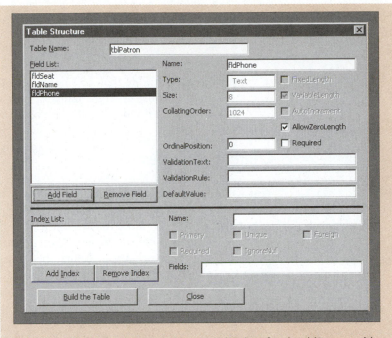

Figure 9-11: Completed Table Structure dialog box for the tblPatron table

HELP? If you inadvertently added an incorrect field, click the field's name in the Field List list box, click the Remove Field button, and then click the Yes button.

When you are finished defining the table, you need to click the Build the Table button to save the table information.

8 Click the **Build the Table** button both to save the table information and to close the Table Structure dialog box.

9 Click the **Plus** box ⊞ that appears next to the tblPatron entry in the Database window, and then click **Fields**. The names of the three fields appear in the Database window, as shown in Figure 9-12.

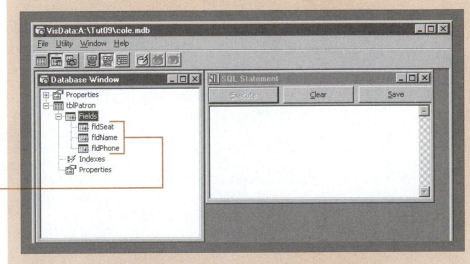

fields you added to the
tblPatron table

Figure 9-12: Three fields contained in the tblPatron table

10 Right-click the **Database** window, and then click **Refresh List** on the popup menu to close both open lists.

After creating a table, you can make changes to it, such as adding new fields, deleting existing fields, creating indexes, and defining any validation rules. First learn how to create an index for the tblPatron table.

Creating an Index

You will create an index for the seat number field in the tblPatron table. This will allow you to view the records in seat number order, and also allow the computer to quickly search the table for a specific seat number. Recall that if the field you want to search is indexed, Visual Basic uses the index, rather than the database table, to find the information. Remember that the computer can search an index much faster than it can search a database table.

To create an index for the tblPatron table:

1 Right-click **tblPatron** in the Database window, then click **Design** on the popup menu. The Table Structure dialog box appears.
You will create an index for the seat number field.

2 Click the **Add Index** button, which is located below the Index List list box. The Add Index to tblPatron dialog box appears, as shown in Figure 9-13.

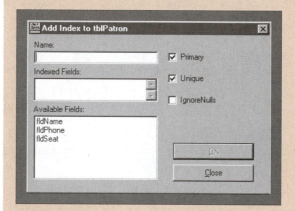

Figure 9-13: Add Index to tblPatron dialog box

You use the Add Index dialog box to add an index to the tblPatron table. First you need to give the index a name. Index names typically begin with the three characters "ind". In this case you want to create an index for the fldSeat field, so you will name the index indSeat. Using a similar name for the index and its corresponding field will help you remember the purpose of the index.

3 Type **indSeat** in the Name text box.

Now select the field you want to index.

4 Click **fldSeat** in the Available Fields list box. fldSeat appears in the Indexed Fields list box.

tip

· · · · · · · · · · · · · · · · · ·

▶ To remove an entry from the Indexed Fields list box, click inside the list box, then use either the Backspace key or the Delete key to delete the entry. To remove an existing index from the Table Structure dialog box, click the index's name in the Index List list box, then click the Remove Index button.

Notice that both the Primary and the Unique check boxes are already selected in the Add Index dialog box. A **primary index** consists of one or more fields that uniquely identify each record in a table. For example, a payroll application's primary index would typically be the Social Security number field. In the tblPatron table, the seat number field uniquely identifies each record.

A table can have only one primary index, and that primary index must contain a unique value for each record in the table. Because the primary index field must be unique, the Unique check box must be selected when creating the primary index. If the primary index consists of more than one field, each field in the index can contain duplicate values, but each combination of values from all the indexed fields must be unique.

When the Primary check box is selected for an index, it tells Visual Basic to arrange the table records in order by that index when the records are first displayed. In this case, for example, the records will be arranged in seat number order when the records are first displayed on the screen.

If the Primary check box is not selected, the index is referred to as a secondary index. A **secondary index** also arranges records in a predefined order, but it is not used to uniquely identify each record in the table. In the case of secondary indexes, the Unique check box may or may not be selected. If the Unique check box is selected, the entries in the secondary index must be unique; otherwise, duplicate entries are allowed. If you were creating a secondary index on the seat number field in the tblPatron table, you would select the Unique check box because each seat number in the table should be unique. If, on the other hand, you were creating a secondary index on the patron name field, you would deselect the Unique check box because a patron could reserve more than one seat.

Because the seat number field should be the primary index, you will leave both the Primary and the Unique check boxes selected.

5 Click the **OK** button to save the index information, then click the **Close** button in the Add Index to tblPatron dialog box. The Table Structure dialog box appears and shows indSeat in the Index List list box.

6 Click the **Close** button in the Table Structure dialog box to return to the Database window.

Next you will define the one data validation rule for the tblPatron table.

Including Data Validation Rules in a Table

Recall that data validation refers to the process of ensuring that the data in the database meets certain criteria. A data validation rule places restrictions on the data that can be entered in a field. When planning the Cole database, recall that you identified the following data validation rule for the tblPatron table:

■ The seat number must be greater than or equal to 1 and less than or equal to 48.

Visual Data Manager stores the validation rules directly in the table itself. By doing so, any application that accesses the table records is forced to uphold the same rules; this provides consistency in the data entered into a database by different applications that have access to the same database information. Visual Data Manager also allows you to specify the message that should appear when a validation rule is broken.

To enter the data validation rule for the tblPatron table:

1 Right-click **tblPatron** in the Database window, then click **Design** on the popup menu. The Table Structure dialog box appears.

2 If necessary, click **fldSeat** in the Field List list box.

You enter the validation rule in the field's ValidationRule text box. You use the ValidationText text box to specify the message your application should display if the value entered by the user doesn't follow the validation rule.

3 Click the **ValidationRule** text box to place the insertion point there.

The validation rule should specify the valid data for that field. When entering a validation rule, you can use mathematical, relational, or logical operators, as well as numbers and strings. In this case, you will use the following validation rule to tell Visual Basic that only seat numbers that are greater than or equal to 1 and less than or equal to 48 are valid: > = 1 and < = 48.

4 Type **> = 1 and < = 48** in the ValidationRule text box.
Now enter an appropriate message in the ValidationText text box.

5 Click the **ValidationText** text box, and then type **Valid seat numbers are 1 through 48.** in the ValidationText text box. See Figure 9-14.

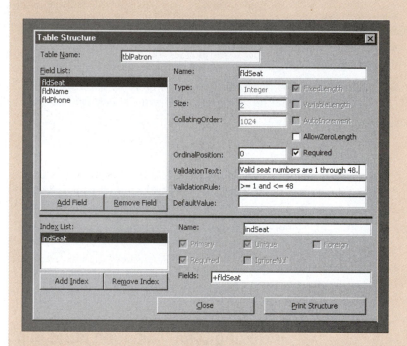

Figure 9-14: ValidationText and ValidationRule entered for fldSeat field

6 Click the **Close** button to save the field information. The Table Structure dialog box closes.

You have now completed creating the Cole database.

7 Click **File** on the VisData menu bar, then click **Close** to close the database.

In addition to creating a database, Visual Data Manager also allows you to open an existing database and view its records, add new records, delete existing records, or search the database for information.

Opening an Existing Database

You can use Visual Data Manager to open an existing database and browse through its existing records, add new records, delete existing records, and search for specific records. Use Visual Data Manager to add some records to the Cole database.

To open the Cole database and add records to it:

1   Click **File** on the VisData menu bar, point to **Open DataBase**, and then click **Microsoft Access**. The Open Microsoft Access Database dialog box appears. Open the **cole** (cole.mdb) database, which is located in the Tut09 folder on your Student Disk.

2   Right-click **tblPatron** in the Database window, and then click **Open** on the popup menu. The Dynaset: tblPatron window appears, as shown in Figure 9-15. A **dynaset** is simply a dynamic set of records that you can use to add, change, or delete records from one or more tables in a database.

number of records in database

record pointer location

scroll bar

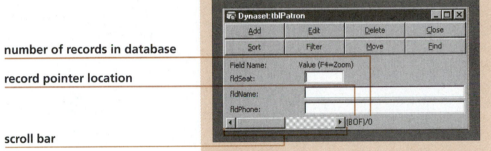

Figure 9-15: Dynaset:tblPatron window

Notice the (BOF)/0 that appears next to the scroll bar at the bottom of the window. (BOF)/0 tells you that the record pointer is located at the beginning of the file (BOF), and the database table contains zero records. When the database table contains some records, you can use the scroll bar to browse through the records.

Also notice the eight buttons that appear below the window's title bar. Figure 9-16 summarizes the purpose of each of the eight buttons.

Button	Use to:
Add	Add a new record
Edit	Edit the current record
Delete	Delete the current record
Close	Close the Dynaset window
Sort	Sort the current records
Filter	Place a filter on the current records
Move	Display the Move dialog box in which you can indicate how many rows you want to move the record pointer either forward or backward
Find	Display the Find dialog box in which you can enter information to perform a search on the records

Figure 9-16: Purpose of the eight buttons that appear in the Dynaset window

Now, add five records to the tblPatron table.

tip

You can also use Alt+A to select the Add button, and Alt+U to select the Update button. Before you can use Alt+U to select the update button, you will need to move the focus out of the fldPhone text box.

To add records to the tblPatron table:

1 Click the **Add** button. Visual Data Manager adds a new, blank record to the end of the table. Now only an Update and a Cancel button appear below the title bar. "Add Record" appears to the right of the scroll bar.

You use the Update button to save the current record's information in the table. If you choose not to enter the current record, you can click the Cancel button to cancel the Add operation.

2 The insertion point is in the fldSeat text box. Type **38** and press the **Tab** key. Type **Smith, Janet** in the fldName text box and press the **Tab** key. Type **333-3333** in the fldPhone text box, and then click the **Update** button to save the current record in the table.

Now add four more records.

3 Use the Add button to add the following four records to the table. Be sure to click the **Update** button after entering each record.

Seat number	Patron name	Patron phone number
15	Hall, Phil	222-2222
43	Williams, Marge	222-3111
44	Williams, Bob	222-3111
24	Jacobs, Jim	211-1111

When you have finished entering the last record, 1/5 should appear next to the scroll bar at the bottom of the window. The 1 indicates that the current record is the first record in the table, and the 5 tells you that the table contains five records.

4 On your own, use the scroll bar buttons to browse through the records. As you browse, notice that the courses display in the order in which they were entered in the table, rather than in seat number order.

Although you specified the indSeat index as the primary index, Visual Data Manager uses that index to arrange the records only when the records are first displayed. Visual Data Manager does not automatically arrange the records in primary index order as new records are added to the table. To arrange the records after new records are added, you need simply to close the table, then reopen it. When you reopen the table, Visual Data Manger will redisplay the records using the primary index.

5 Click the **Close** button. Right-click **tblPatron** in the Database window, then click **Open** on the popup menu. Use the scroll bar to browse through the records. Notice that the records are now arranged in order by the seat number.

Recall that an entry is required in the primary index field. Observe what happens when you try to add a record that does not contain a seat number.

6 Click the **Add** button, and then click the **Update** button. Visual Data Manager displays an error message informing you that the seat number field is required. Click the **No** button to remove the error message.

Now try entering a record with a duplicate seat number.

7 Click the **fldSeat** text box, then enter the following record:

Seat number	Patron name	Patron phone number
44	Sprott, Candy	333-7777

8 Click the **Update** button. Visual Data Manager displays an error message informing you that the changes you requested were not successful because they would create duplicate values in the index, primary key, or relationship. Click the **No** button to remove the error message.

Now replace the 44 in the current record's seat number field with 10.

9 Change 44 in the current record's seat number field to **10**, and then click the **Update** button. Visual Data Manager enters seat number 10's record in the tblPatron table.

Now observe how Visual Data Manager handles an incorrect entry in the seat number field. Recall that the data validation rule in the fldSeat field specifies that the field can contain only numbers that are greater than or equal to 1 and less than or equal to 48.

To see how Visual Data Manager handles an incorrect field entry:

1 Seat number 15's record should be the current record. Click the **Edit** button to edit the current record. Change the 15 in the fldSeat text box to 83, then click the **Update** button. The error message contained in the fldSeat field's ValidationText text box, "Valid seat numbers are 1 through 48.", appears in a message box. Click the **No** button to remove the message box.

2 Change the 83 in the fldSeat text box to **15**, then click the **Update** button.

You can also edit the values in an existing record, as well as sort the records in order by any of the fields in the table.

To edit and sort the table records:

1 Use the scroll bar to display Candy Sprott's record. Assume that Candy's phone number is incorrect; it should be 333-7778.

2 Click the **Edit** button. Change the phone number from 333-7777 to **333-7778**, then click the **Update** button to save the change.

As you may remember, Visual Data Manager does not automatically arrange the records in primary index order as new records are added to the table. Recall that one way to put the records in primary index order is to close the table and then reopen it. In addition to this method, you can also use the Dynaset window's Sort button to sort the records in order by any of the table fields.

3 Click the **Sort** button. A dialog box appears and prompts you to enter the sort column.

To sort the records by the seat number field, you need simply to enter fldSeat in the dialog box.

4 Type **fldseat** in the dialog box, then click the **OK** button. Use the scroll bar to verify that the records are in seat number order.

5 On your own, sort the records in patron name order, then sort the records in seat number order.

In addition to both adding and editing records, you can also delete records from a table and locate one or more records in a table. First you will delete Phil Hall's record, and then you will perform two searches—one to search for seat number 38's record and the other to search for all records whose patron name entry begins with the letter W.

To delete a record from the tblPatron table, then search the table for specific records:

1 Use the scroll bar to make Phil Hall's record the current record, and then click the **Delete** button. When asked if you want to delete the current record, click the **Yes** button. Visual Data Manager removes the record from the table.

Now use the Find button to find and display seat number 38's record.

2 Click the **Find** button. The Find Record dialog box appears.

The Find Record dialog box allows you to enter a search condition that specifies which record or records you want to find. You use the Fields list box to select the field you want to search, and you use the Operators list box to select the appropriate operator. You enter the search string—the value for which you are searching—in the Value or Expression text box. Use the Find Record dialog box to search for seat number 38's record.

3 Click **fldSeat** in the Fields list box, and then click **=** in the Operators list box. Click the **Value or Expression** text box to place the insertion point there. Type **38** in the Value or Expression text box, as shown in Figure 9-17.

be sure this option
button is selected

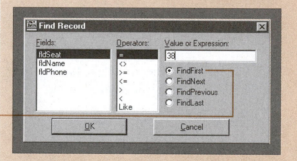

Figure 9-17: Find Record dialog box containing a search condition

4 Click the **OK** button in the Find Record dialog box to begin the search. The Find Record dialog box closes and seat number 38's record appears in the Dynaset window.

Because the entries in the fldSeat field must be unique, this should be the only record for seat number 38 in the table. Use the Find Record dialog box to verify that fact.

5 Click the **Find** button. When the Find Record dialog box appears, click the **FindNext** option button, then click the **OK** button. The Record Not Found message appears. Click the **OK** button to remove the message, then click the **Cancel** button to close the Find Record dialog box.

Now search for the records whose patron name entry begins with the letter W.

6   Click the **Find** button to display the Find Record dialog box. Click **fldName** in the Fields list box, then click the **FindFirst** option button.

Visual Data Manager allows you to use the Like operator and the asterisk (*) wildcard to locate information in any Text field in a table. The * is referred to as a **wildcard** because, similar to a wildcard in a game of poker, you can use the * to represent anything you want. To locate the records whose patron name entry begins with the letter W, you need simply to click fldName in the Fields list box, then click Like in the Operators list box, and then type the string for which you want to search in the Value or Expression text box. In this case, you will enter the letter w followed by the asterisk wildcard in the Value or Expression text box. The w tells Visual Data Manager to find records whose patron name entry begins with the letter w, and the asterisk tells Visual Data Manager that you do not care how many characters follow the w in the string, nor do you care what those characters are. String comparisons made by the Find Record dialog box are not case sensitive; therefore, to find the records whose patron name entry begins with the letter W, you can type the search string (w*) in uppercase or lowercase.

7   Click **Like** in the Operators list box, then change the 38 in the Value or Expression text box to **w***. Verify that the Find Record dialog box looks like the one shown in Figure 9-18.

find all records whose patron name entry begins with w

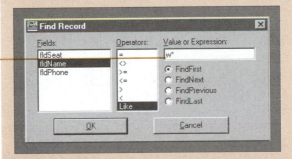

Figure 9-18: Find Record dialog box containing the Like operator and asterisk wildcard

8   Click the **OK** button in the Find Record dialog box to begin the search. The Find Record dialog box closes, and the Marge Williams record—the first record in the table that matches the search condition—appears in the Dynaset window.

9   Click the **Find** button, click the **FindNext** option button, and then click the **OK** button. The Bob Williams record appears.

10 Click the **Find** button, then click the **OK** button. When the "Record Not Found" message appears, click the **OK** button to remove the message, and then click the **Cancel** button to close the Find Record dialog box.

11 Click the **Close** button to close the Dynaset window. Click **File**, then click **Exit** to close Visual Data Manager. Visual Basic returns to the design screen.

Although Visual Data Manager allows you to add, edit, delete, and search the records in a table, its user interface cannot be altered. If you want to give the user a customized interface with which he or she can access the records stored in a database, you will need to create a Visual Basic application. You will create such an application in Lessons B and C.

You have now completed Lesson A. You can either take a break or complete the questions and exercises at the end of the lesson. In Lesson B you will learn how to use the ADO data control to access the records in the Cole database.

S U M M A R Y

To design a database, follow these basic design steps:

- Identify the information the user will need from the database.
- Organize the information into one or more tables.
- Establish relationships between tables (if the database contains more than one table).
- Create one or more indexes, if necessary.
- Define data validation rules, if necessary.

To create a Microsoft Access database in Visual Basic:

- Use Visual Data Manager. You access Visual Data Manager by clicking Add-Ins on Visual Basic's menu bar, then clicking Visual Data Manager.
- You must assign a unique name, as well as a data type and size, to each field in a database table.

Q U E S T I O N S

1. A(n) _____ is an organized collection of related information stored in a file on a disk.
   a. control
   b. database
   c. field
   d. object
   e. record

2. A _____ database is one that stores information in tables, which are composed of columns and rows.
   a. columnar
   b. relational
   c. sorted
   d. tabular

3. A group of related records in a database is referred to as a _____ .
   a. column
   b. field
   c. row
   d. table

4. Which of the following is true about a relational database?
   a. Data stored in a relational database can be retrieved both quickly and easily by the computer.
   b. Data stored in a relational database can be displayed in any order.
   c. A relational database stores data in a column and row format.
   d. All of the above are true.

5. A(n) _____ is a special table, created and maintained by Visual Basic, that allows you to arrange the database records in a specific order, as well as to quickly search the database for information.
   a. control
   b. field
   c. index
   d. order field
   e. sort field

6. The _____ field in an index stores the values contained in the field being indexed.
   a. index
   b. pointer
   c. primary
   d. sort
   e. table

7. The _____ field in an index stores the record number of the corresponding record found in the table.
   a. index
   b. pointer
   c. primary
   d. sort

8. Which of the following is NOT true?
   a. An index allows the user to easily locate information in a database.
   b. An index allows the computer to quickly locate information in a database.
   c. An index allows you to arrange the database records in a particular order.
   d. It takes the computer much more time to search an index than it does to search the database table itself.

9. _____ refers to the process of ensuring that the data in the database meets certain criteria.
   a. Criteria checking
   b. Data validation
   c. Rule enforcing
   d. Standard setting

10. You can use _____ , which is an application that comes with Visual Basic, to create a Microsoft Access database.
    a. Visual Access
    b. Visual Database Creator
    c. Visual Data Creator
    d. Visual Data Manager

11. A table can have _____ primary index(es).
    a. only one
    b. only two
    c. many

12. Which two of the following are true?
    a. A primary index can contain only letters.
    b. A primary index can contain only numbers.
    c. Each record in a table must have an entry in the primary index.
    d. The entries in a primary index must be unique.

13. Which of the following is/are true?
    a. Visual Data Manager stores the validation rules in the table itself.
    b. Visual Data Manager allows you to specify the message that should appear when a validation rule is broken.
    c. When entering a data validation rule, you can use mathematical, relational, or logical operators, as well as numbers and strings.
    d. All of the above are true

14. Assuming that the Like operator is selected in the Find Record dialog box, which of the following Value or Expression text box entries tells Visual Data Manager to search for all records whose fldID entry begins with Eng?
    a. eng
    b. eng*
    c. Find Eng*
    d. Like Eng
    e. Like Eng*

E X E R C I S E S

When designing the databases in these exercises, recall that the basic design steps are:
1. Identify the information the user will need from the database.
2. Organize the information into one or more tables.
3. Establish relationships between tables (if the database contains more than one table).
4. Create one or more indexes, if necessary.
5. Define data validation rules, if necessary.

Also note that the names of tables, fields, and indexes cannot contain spaces.

1. In this exercise you will use Visual Data Manager to create a one-table Access Version 7.0 database. You will also define an index and two validation rules.
   a. Use Visual Data Manager to create a one-table Access Version 7.0 database named la1Done. Save the la1Done database in the Tut09 folder on your Student Disk. The database will allow you to keep track of the college courses you have taken. Figure 9-19 shows the design of the la1Done database. Use this information to define the database.

la1Done database	
Table name	tblCourses
Field names	fldID, fldTitle, fldCredits, fldGrade
Relationships	None. The la1Done database contains only one table.
Index	Create a primary index named indID for the fldID field.
Validation rule	The fldCredits field must contain a number that is greater than or equal to 0 and less than or equal to 6.
	The fldGrade field can contain an A, B, C, D, F, or W only.

Figure 9-19

The fldID field will contain the course IDs, which consist of letters and numbers. The field will need to store a maximum of eight characters. It should require an entry and it should not allow the entry of a zero-length string.

The fldTitle field will contain the course names. The field will need to store a maximum of 30 characters. It should require an entry and it should not allow the entry of a zero-length string.

The fldCredits field will contain the number of credit hours for each course. Define the field as an Integer. The field should require an entry and it should not allow the entry of a zero-length string.

The fldGrade field will contain the grade earned in each course. Define the field as a one-character Text field. The field can accept a zero-length string. An entry in the field is not required.

b. After creating the database, table, and index, use the Print Structure button in the Table Structure window to print the database structure.

c. Use Visual Data Manager to add the following five records to the database:

ID	Title	Credits	Grade
Eng101	English Composition	3	A
Cis141	Intro to Databases	3	B
Cis100	Intro to Computers	5	B
Biol100	Biology	4	C
Cis106	Intro to Windows	3	A

d. Sort the records in order by the ID field.

e. Click the Find button. Use the Find Record dialog box to perform the searches specified in Figure 9-20. Complete the figure's table by entering both the name of the field and the operator you selected, as well as the value or expression you entered in the Value or Expression text box.

How would you locate:	Fields list box	Operators list box	Value or Expression text box
the Eng101 record			
all courses in which you earned an A			
all Intro courses			
the Biology course			
all courses whose ID begins with cis			

Figure 9-20

f. Submit your answers to Figure 9-20, as well as the printout from step b and a disk that contains the la1Done.mdb database.

2. In this exercise you will use Visual Data Manager to create a one-table Access Version 7.0 database. You will also define an index and a validation rule.

a. Use Visual Data Manager to create a one-table Access Version 7.0 database that tracks the basketball scores for your favorite team. Name the database la2Done; name the table tblScores. Save the database in the Tut09 folder on your Student Disk. The tblScores table should contain the name of the opposing team, the date the game was played, your team's score, and the opposing team's score. Use the Text data type for the game date field. Deselect the AllowZeroLength check box for each field, and select the Required check box.

b. Create an index on the opposing team's name field. This index should not be a primary index.

c. Define a data validation rule for the two fields that store the scores; the fields should allow numbers between 0 and 130 only.

d. Use Visual Data Manager to add the following five records to the table:

Opposing team	Game date	Your team's score	Opposing team's score
Jackals	10/04/99	100	96
Hornets	10/06/99	75	90
Jaguars	10/23/99	120	85
Jackals	10/27/99	68	73
Hornets	11/04/99	99	97

e. Sort the records in order by the opposing team's name field.

f. Submit a disk that contains the la2Done.mdb file.

3. In this exercise you will use Visual Data Manager to create a one-table Access Version 7.0 database. You will also define an index and a validation rule.

   a. Use Visual Data Manager to create a one-table Access Version 7.0 database that keeps track of your monthly phone bills. Name the database la3Done; name the table tblPhone. Save the database in the Tut09 folder on your Student Disk. The tblPhone table should contain the month, the year, and the total bill. The year field should be text, the total bill field should be currency, and the month field should be text. Deselect the AllowZeroLength check box for the month and year fields, and select the Required check box for both fields.

   b. Create an index on the month field. This index should be the primary index.

   c. Define a data validation rule for the month field. The field should allow only 01, 02, 03, 04, 05, 06, 07, 08, 09, 10, 11, 12.

   d. Use Visual Data Manager to add the following five records to the table:

Month	Year	Total bill
12	1999	56
02	2000	67
10	1999	45
01	2000	57
11	1999	23

   e. Sort the records in order by the month field.

   f. Submit a disk that contains the la3Done.mdb file.

Exercises 4 and 5 are Discovery Exercises, which allow you to both "discover" the solutions to problems on your own and experiment with material that is not covered in the tutorial.

discovery ▶

4. In this exercise you will use Visual Data Manager to create a one-table Access Version 7.0 database. You will also define a multiple-field index and a validation rule.

   a. Use Visual Data Manager to create a one-table Access Version 7.0 database that contains the names and phone numbers of your friends. Name the database la4Done; name the table tblFriends. Save the database in the Tut09 folder on your Student Disk. The tblFriends table should contain three fields: last name, first name, and phone number.

   b. Because some of your friends may have the same last name, you should arrange the records by first name within last name. In other words, if four of your friends have the last name "Smith," you can tell Visual Data Manager to arrange the Smith records in first name order. Create an index that includes both the last name and first name fields. This index should be the primary index.

   c. Use Visual Data Manager to add 10 records to the table. Be sure that three of the records have the same last name, but different first names.

   d. Close, then reopen, the database table. The records should display in last name order. The records having the same last name should display in first name order.

   e. Submit a disk that contains the la4done.mdb file.

discovery ▶

5. In this exercise you will learn about Visual Data Manager's Data Form Designer.

   Scenario: In this exercise you will create a database to keep track of your CD (compact disc) collection. You will use Visual Data Manager's Data Form Designer to create a form that will allow you to manipulate the records in the CD database.

   a. Use Visual Data Manager to create a one-table Version 7.0 Access database. Name the database la5Done and save it in the Tut09 folder on your Student Disk.

   b. Name the table tblCDs. The table should contain two Text fields: the name of the CD and the artist's name.

   c. The primary index should be the CD name field.

   d. After creating the database table and index, open Visual Data Manager's Utility menu and select Data Form Designer. Use the Data Form Designer to build a form that will allow you to manipulate the records in the CD database. Call the form MyCds.

e. When you are finished building the MyCds form, close the Data Form Designer, then close Visual Data Manager. Notice that the Data Form Designer application places the form (frmMyCds) in the open Visual Basic project.

f. Remove the Form1 form from the open Visual Basic project, then set the startup form to the frmMyCds form.

g. Save the form and the project as la5Done in the Tut09 folder on your Student Disk.

h. Run the project. Click the Add button, then enter a record. Enter five more records.

i. Practice with the Delete, Refresh, and Update buttons that appear in the interface. Also practice with the scroll bar that appears at the bottom of the form.

j. When you are finished practicing with the application, click the Close button.

k. Print the application's code. Submit the code and the la5Done files.

In this lesson you will learn how to:
- Define UDA, OLE DB, and ADO
- Display database records using the ADO data control
- Query a database using the SQL Select command

Using the ADO Data Control

Microsoft's UDA Approach to Accessing Data

Most businesses store data in many different formats (such as spreadsheets, databases, word processing documents, and even e-mail), each format requiring a fundamentally different approach to accessing its data. For years, developers have seen the need for a standard method that could be used to access the data stored in *all* of a company's data sources. Microsoft's approach to solving the data access problem is called Universal Data Access, or simply **UDA**.

The **UDA** approach uses a set of complex interfaces, called **OLE DB** (Object Linking and Embedding Database), that provides uniform access to data stored in a variety of formats. Due to its complex interfaces, OLE DB was not designed to be accessed directly from Visual Basic. Rather, Visual Basic programmers gain access to the OLE DB interfaces through **ADO** (ActiveX Data Objects). You will use OLE DB and ADO to access the data stored in the Cole database that you created in Lesson A.

tip

OLE is pronounced *oh-lay*.

tip

You also can use OLE DB and ADO in Visual C++, Visual J++, Visual FoxPro, VBScript, Jscript, and Visual Basic for Applications (including all of Microsoft Office).

The Cole's Playhouse Application

Recall that Max Phillips, the manager of Cole's Playhouse, has asked you to modify the application that you created in Tutorial 8 so that it uses a Microsoft Access database, rather than a random access file. As you may remember, the Cole's Playhouse application used two forms. The first form—the seat form—contained 48 label controls, each of which represented a seat in the theater. To either reserve or cancel a reservation, the user needed simply to click one of the 48 label controls in the interface, at which time the second form—the patron form—appeared. The patron form allowed the user to record a reservation, cancel a reservation, and return to the seat form.

Your Student Disk contains a partially completed Visual Basic application that you can use to access the records stored in the Cole database created in Lesson A. You will work with the patron form in this lesson; you will add the seat form to the project in Lesson C.

To open the partially completed Cole's Playhouse application:

1   Start Visual Basic, if necessary, and then open the **Cole** (Cole.vbp) project, which is located in the Tut09 folder on your Student Disk.

2   View the frmPatron form. Save the form as **lbPatron**, then save the project as **lbCole**. Click the **form**. Figure 9-21 shows the patron form's user interface.

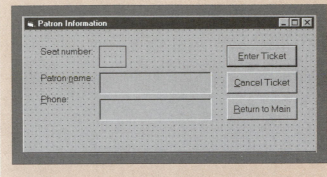

Figure 9-21: Patron form's user interface

The patron form contains a label control named lblNum, and two text boxes named txtName and txtPhone. It also contains three command buttons (cmdEnter, cmdCancel, and cmdReturn) that allow the user to enter a reservation, cancel a reservation, and return to the main form. You will code the three command buttons in Lesson C. In this lesson, you will learn simply how to display the records stored in the Cole database.

Applications that can access and manipulate the data stored in a database are referred to as **data-aware** applications. The simplest way to create a data-aware application in Visual Basic 6.0 is to use Microsoft's ADO (ActiveX Data Object) data control.

Using the ADO Data Control

You can use the **Microsoft ADO data control** to access the data stored in a variety of formats, such as a database, a spreadsheet, or even a text file. In the Cole application, for example, you will use the ADO data control to access the data stored in the Cole database that you created in Lesson A. The ADO data control will establish a link between the database and the other controls in the application's interface.

To add an ADO data control to the Cole application:

1 Click **Project** on the menu bar, then click **Components**. When the Components dialog box appears, click the **Microsoft ADO Data Control 6.0 (OLEDB)** check box on the Controls tab to select the ADO component, then click the **OK** button. Visual Basic places the Adodc tool in the toolbox.

2 Double-click the **Adodc tool** ⬛ in the toolbox. The Adodc1 control appears on the form.

3 Set the Adodc1 control's Name property to **adoCole**. "ado" is the three-character ID used to name an ADO data control.

4 Set the adoCole control's properties as follows:

Height: 345   Top: 2280
Left: 360   Width: 5775

tip

....

▶ The adoCole control is an instance of the ADO data control class.

5 Set the adoCole control's Caption property to **Click the arrow buttons to view the database records.** and press the **Enter** key.

6 Click the **adoCole** control to return to the form. The interface appears as shown in Figure 9-22.

ADO data control

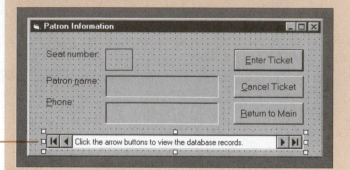

Figure 9-22: ADO data control displayed in the patron form

You use the First Record button and the Last Record button to display the first and last record, respectively. You use the Previous Record button and the Next Record button to display the previous and next record, respectively.

7 Click the **Save Project** button.

After adding the ADO data control to the interface, you then set its ConnectionString property. The ADO data control uses the information in the **ConnectionString property** to establish a connection to the data source. In this case, you want to connect the ADO data control to the Cole database (the data source) that you created in Lesson A.

To set the ADO data control's ConnectionString property:

1 The ADO data control should be selected in the interface. Click **ConnectionString** in the Properties list, then click the ... button in the Settings box. The Property Pages dialog box appears, with the Use Connection String option button selected on the General tab.

   HELP? If the Use Connection String option button is not selected on the General tab, click it to select it.

2 Click the **Build** button on the General tab. The Data Link Properties dialog box appears. The Provider tab, which contains a list of OLE DB providers, should be the current tab.

You use the Provider tab to select the type of OLE DB provider associated with your data source. As you may remember from Lesson A, the Cole database (the data source) is a Microsoft Access database. The OLE DB provider associated with a Microsoft Access database is the Microsoft Jet 3.51 OLE DB Provider.

3   Click **Microsoft Jet 3.51 OLE DB Provider** on the Provider tab. See Figure 9-23.

**allows access to a
Microsoft Access database**

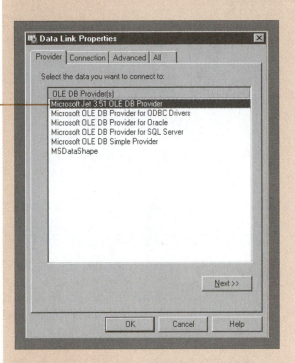

Figure 9-23: Provider tab in the Data Link Properties dialog box

4   Click the **Next >>** button to display the Connection tab in the Data Link Properties dialog box, then click the **...** button next to the Select or enter a database name text box. Click **cole.mdb**, which is located in the Tut09 folder on your Student Disk, then click the **Open** button.

HELP? If you did not create the cole.mdb database in Lesson A, use Windows to copy the cole.ori file, which is located in the Tut09 folder on your Student Disk, to cole.mdb.

The Test Connection button on the Connection tab allows you to test the connection between the ADO data control and your data source—in this case, the Cole database.

5   Click the **Test Connection** button. The Microsoft Data Link message box appears with the "Test connection succeeded" message. See Figure 9-24.

HELP? If the Microsoft Data Link Error dialog box appears with a message telling you that the test connection failed, click the OK button to remove the dialog box. Use Figures 9-23 and 9-24 to verify that you entered the OLE DB provider and the database name correctly, then repeat step 5.

yours may say B:

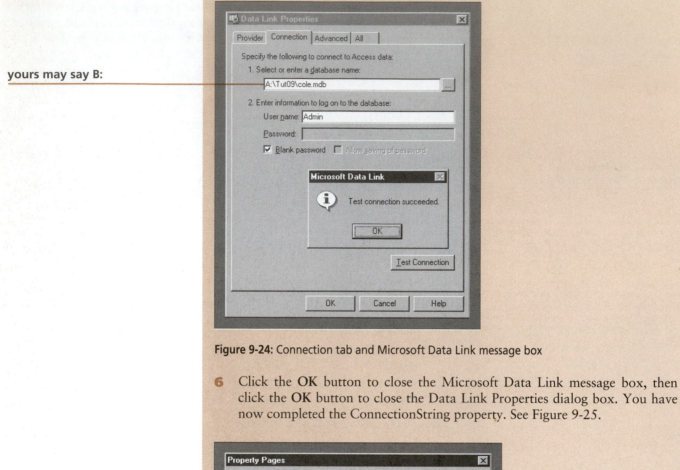

Figure 9-24: Connection tab and Microsoft Data Link message box

6 Click the **OK** button to close the Microsoft Data Link message box, then click the **OK** button to close the Data Link Properties dialog box. You have now completed the ConnectionString property. See Figure 9-25.

the value stored in the
ConnectionString property
includes the provider and
the data source

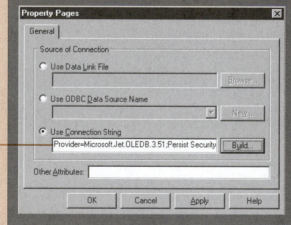

Figure 9-25: General tab showing the value stored in the ConnectionString property

7   To see the entire value stored in the ConnectionString property, click the **Use ConnectionString** text box, then use the right arrow on your keyboard to view the contents of the text box. You will notice that the value stored in the ConnectionString property
`(Provider=Microsoft.Jet.OLEDB.3.51;Persist Security Info=False;Data Source=A:\Tut09\cole.mdb)` includes both the provider and the data source.

8   Click the **OK** button to close the Property Pages dialog box.

In addition to its ConnectionString property, you also must set the ADO data control's **RecordSource property**, which tells the control which database records you want to access. In this case, you want to access all of the records stored in the Cole database's tblPatron table.

To set the ADO data control's RecordSource property:

1   The ADO data control should be selected in the interface. Click **RecordSource** in the Properties list, then click the ... button in the Settings box. The Property Pages dialog box appears. Click the **Command Type** list arrow on the RecordSource tab, then click **2-adCmdTable** in the list. In a few moments, the Table or Stored Procedure Name list box appears in the dialog box.

2   Click the **Table or Stored Procedure Name** list arrow, and then click **tblPatron** in the list. Figure 9-26 shows the completed RecordSource tab in the Property Pages dialog box.

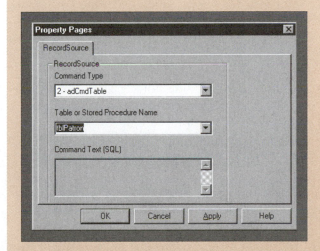

Figure 9-26: RecordSource tab in the Property Pages dialog box

3   Click the **OK** button to close the Property Pages dialog box.

Notice that the method for linking the ADO data control to a database is quite simple. You first add the control to the form, then set its ConnectionString and RecordSource properties.

After placing an ADO data control on the form and setting its properties, you can connect the other controls in the form to it. Connecting a control to an ADO data control is called **binding**, and the connected controls are referred to **as data-aware controls** or **bound controls**. Any control that has a DataSource property can be bound to an ADO data control. In the Cole application, you will bind the lblNum, txtName, and txtPhone controls to the adoCole control. By doing so, the bound controls will display the data from the records specified in the ADO data control's RecordSource property—in this case, the bound controls will display all of the records stored in the tblPatron table.

Binding Controls to an ADO Data Control

You bind a control to an ADO data control by setting the control's DataSource and DataField properties. In the control's **DataSource property** you enter the name of the ADO data control to which the control is to be bound. In the **DataField property** you enter the name of the table field whose contents you want the control to display. You always set the DataSource property first, then you set the DataField property.

> Always set the DataSource property before setting the DataField property. Doing so allows Visual Basic to display a list of field names from which you can select the DataField property value.

To bind the lblNum, txtName, and txtPhone controls to the adoCole control, then save and run the application:

1 Select the lblNum, txtName, and txtPhone controls. Click **DataSource** in the Properties list, then click the list arrow in the Settings box. Click **adoCole** in the list, then press the **Enter** key. Click the **form** to deselect the selected controls.

Now set each bound control's DataField property, which tells the ADO data control the name of the field whose contents you want displayed in the bound control. For example, in the lblNum control, you want to display the contents of the fldSeat field from the tblPatron table. In the txtName text box, you want to display the contents of the fldName field. In the txtPhone text box, you want to display the contents of the fldPhone field. Because each bound control will display a different field from the tblPatron table, you will need to set each control's DataField property separately.

> Recall that the adoCole control's ConnectionString property links the control to the Cole database, and its RecordSource property tells the control to access the records stored in the tblPatron table.

2 Set the lblNum control's DataField property to **fldSeat**. Set the txtName control's DataField property to **fldName**, then set the txtPhone control's DataField property to **fldPhone**.

Now save and run the application to see how it works so far.

3 **Save** and **run** the application. Use the ADO data control's buttons to view the five records. Notice that the five records do not appear in seat number order; rather, they appear in the order in which they were entered in the table. You will learn how to display the records in seat number order in the next section.

The ADO data control allows you to edit the database records. However, after making a change to a record, you need to click one of the ADO data control's arrow buttons to save the change. Clicking an arrow button moves the record pointer to another record, which automatically saves the change made to the current record.

4 Display the Jim Jacobs record, then change the patron's first name to **James**. Click the **Next Record** button ▸ to move the record pointer to the next record. Visual Basic saves the change made to the current record before it displays the next record. You can confirm that the change was saved by moving back to the record for seat number 24.

5 Click the **Previous Record** button ◀ to display seat 24's record again. The patron name is now Jacobs, James.

6 Click the **End** ■ button. Visual Basic returns to the design screen.

Recall that the ADO data control displayed the records in the order in which they were entered in the table. If you want to display the records in a different order, you will need to use the SQL Select command.

Using the SQL Select Command

tip

• • • • • • • • • • • • • • • •

▶ The SQL syntax, which refers to the rules you must follow in order to use the language, was accepted by the American National Standards Institute (ANSI) in 1986. You can use SQL in many database management systems and programming languages.

tip

• • • • • • • • • • • • • • • •

▶ The full syntax of the Select command contains other clauses and options that are beyond the scope of this book. If you have access to the MSDN Library, you can display the Select command's Help screen by searching the entire collection for the Select – SQL topic.

SQL, pronounced like the word *sequel*, stands for **Structured Query Language**. SQL is a set of commands that allow you to access and manipulate the data stored in many database management systems on computers of all sizes, from large mainframes to small microcomputers. You can use SQL commands to store, retrieve, update, and sequence data.

The most commonly used SQL command is the **Select command**, which allows you to select which fields and records you want to view, as well as control the order in which the fields and records appear when displayed. The basic syntax of the Select command is **select** *fields* **from** *table* [**where** *condition*] [**order by** *field*]. In the syntax, *fields* is one or more field names (separated by commas), and *table* is the name of the table containing the fields. The `select fldSeat, fldName, fldPhone from tblPatron` command, for example, will allow you to view all of the fields and records stored in the tblPatron table. The `select fldName from tblPatron` command, on the other hand, will allow you to view only the fldName field for each record.

If you want to view all of the fields in a table, you can enter an asterisk (*) rather than the field names in the *fields* portion of the Select command. The * tells the Select command to display all of the table fields, in the order in which the fields appear in the table. In other words, rather than using the `select fldSeat, fldName, fldPhone from tblPatron` command, you could use the `select * from tblPatron` command. Although both commands will produce the same result, the latter requires less typing.

The **where** *condition* part of the Select command's syntax is referred to as the **where clause**, and it allows you to limit the records that appear when displayed. The **order by** *field* part of the syntax—referred to as the **order by clause**—allows you to control the order in which the records appear when displayed. You will notice that the `where` and `order by` clauses are optional in the Select command.

Use the Select command to view all of the fields and records stored in the Cole database's tblPatron table. You will need to enter the Select command in the adoCole control's RecordSource property.

To view all of the fields and records stored in the Cole database's tblPatron table:

1 Click the **adoCole** control to select it. Click **RecordSource** in the Properties window, then click the **...** button in the Settings box. The RecordSource tab in the Property Pages dialog box appears.

You enter the Select command in the Command Text (SQL) text box. Before you can do so, however, you need to remove the tblPatron entry from the Table or Stored Procedure Name list box, and change the Command Type from 2-adCmdTable to 1-adCmdText.

2 Highlight **tblPatron** in the Table or Stored Procedure Name list box, then press the **Delete** key to remove the entry from the list box. Click the **Command Type** list arrow, then click **1-adCmdText** in the list.

You can now enter the Select command in the Command Text (SQL) text box.

3 Click the **Command Text (SQL)** text box, then type **select * from tblPatron**. See Figure 9-27.

allows access to all
fields in the table

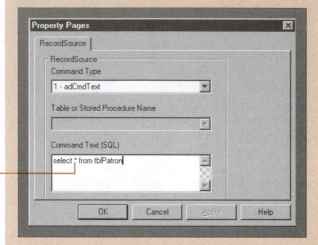

Figure 9-27: Select command that allows you to access all fields and records in the tblPatron table

4 Click the **OK** button to close the Property Pages dialog box, then **save** and **run** the application.

5 Use the ADO data control's buttons to view the five database records.

Notice that the five records do not appear in seat number order; rather, they appear in the order in which they were entered in the table. If you want to display records in a specific order, you need to include the `order by` clause in the Select command.

6 Click the **End** ■ button. Visual Basic returns to the design screen.

7 Click the **adoCole** control. Click **RecordSource** in the Properties list, then click the **...** button in the Settings box. Change the `select * from tblPatron` command to **select * from tblPatron order by fldSeat**. See Figure 9-28.

puts records in
seat number order

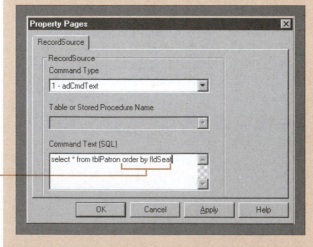

Figure 9-28: Select command that allows you to access all fields and records in the tblPatron table, ordered by seat number

8 Click the **OK** button to close the Property Pages dialog box, then **save** and **run** the application.

9 Use the ADO data control's buttons to view the five database records. Because you used the `order by` clause in the Select statement, the records now appear in seat number order.

10 Click the **End** ■ button. Visual Basic returns to the design screen.

Now assume that you want to display only seat number 24's record. You can do so by including the `where` clause in the Select statement. Recall that the `where` clause allows you to limit the records you want to view. Figure 9-29 shows examples of using the `where` clause in the Select command.

To view	Use this Select command
1. seat 24's record	`select * from tblPatron where fldSeat = 24`
2. all records, in seat number order, whose seat numbers are greater than 20	`select * from tblPatron where fldSeat > 20 order by fldSeat`
3. Candy Sprott's record	`select * from tblPatron where fldName = "sprott, candy"`
4. all records whose phone number begins with 333	`select * from tblPatron where fldPhone like "333%"`

Figure 9-29: Examples of using the `where` clause in the Select command

Study the examples shown in Figure 9-29. Example 1 shows that you use the `select * from tblPatron where fldSeat = 24` command to view only seat number 24's record. Example 2 indicates that you would use the `select * from tblPatron where fldSeat > 20 order by fldSeat` command to view, in seat number order, all records whose seat numbers are greater than 20. Notice that the `where` clause in both examples specifies the search field (fldSeat), a relational operator (=, >), and the search data (24, 20). Because the data type of the search field is Integer, the search data must also be an integer.

As Example 3 in Figure 9-29 shows, you use the `select * from tblPatron where fldName = "sprott, candy"` command to view only Candy Sprott's record. Because the data type of the search field (fldName) is Text, you must enclose the search data (the string literal constant "sprott, candy") in quotation marks. SQL commands are not case sensitive, so you can enter the string literal constant in uppercase, lowercase, or any combination of uppercase and lowercase.

tip

> You also can use the Like operator and the % wildcard in a comparison that involves a numeric field; however, you must enclose the search data in quotation marks to do so. For example, you would need to use the `select * from tblPatron where fldSeat like "2%"` command to display all records whose seat number begins with the number 2.

Figure 9-29's Example 4 shows how you can use the Like operator along with the % (percent sign) wildcard in the where clause. As the example indicates, the `select * from tblPatron where fldPhone like "333%"` command allows you to view all records whose phone number begins with 333. The Select command's Like operator and % wildcard operate similar to Visual Data Manager's Like operator and * wildcard, which you learned about in Lesson A. In both the Select command and Visual Data Manager, the Like operator allows you to compare the contents of a field to a collection of characters. The % wildcard in SQL, like the * wildcard in Visual Data Manager, can be used in place of one or more characters. Try each of the four Select commands shown in Figure 9-29.

To try each of the four Select commands shown in Figure 9-29, then display all of the fields and records:

1 Click the **adoCole** control, then change the Select command in the RecordSource property to **select * from tblPatron where fldSeat = 24**. Close the Property Pages dialog box, if necessary, then **run** the application. Seat number 24's record appears in the interface. Try using the adoCole control's buttons to move the record pointer to another record. You will find that you can view only seat number 24's record. Click the **End** button. Visual Basic returns to the design screen.

2 Change the Select command in the adoCole control's RecordSource property to **select * from tblPatron where fldSeat > 20 order by fldSeat**. Close the Property Pages dialog box, if necessary, then **run** the application. Seat number 24's record appears in the interface. Use the **Next Record** button to view the remaining records. You will find that you can view only the records for seats 24, 38, 43, and 44 because those are the only seats whose seat numbers are greater than the number 20. Click the **End** button. Visual Basic returns to the design screen.

3 Change the Select command in the adoCole control's RecordSource property to **select * from tblPatron where fldName = "sprott, candy"**. Close the Property Pages dialog box, if necessary, then **run** the application. Candy Sprott's record appears in the interface. Try viewing another record. You will find that you can view only Candy Sprott's record. Click the **End** button. Visual Basic returns to the design screen.

   HELP? If Candy Sprott's record does not appear in the interface, stop the application and verify that you entered the Select command correctly. Be sure to enter a space after the comma in the name.

4 Change the Select command in the adoCole control's RecordSource property to **select * from tblPatron where fldPhone like "333%"**. Close the Property Pages dialog box, if necessary, then **run** the application. You will find that you can view only Janet Smith's and Candy Sprott's records because those are the only records whose phone number begins with 333. Click the **End** button. Visual Basic returns to the design screen.

Now change the Select statement so that you can view all of the tblPatron's records in seat number order.

5 Change the Select command in the adoCole control's RecordSource property to **select * from tblPatron order by fldSeat**. Close the Property Pages dialog box, if necessary, then **save** and **run** the application. Use the adoCole control's buttons to view each of the five records. Click the **End** ■ button. Visual Basic returns to the design screen.

You have now completed Lesson B. You can either take a break or complete the questions and exercises at the end of the lesson. You will complete the Cole's Playhouse application in Lesson C.

S U M M A R Y

To use the ADO data control to access the information in a database:

■ Add the Microsoft ADO Data Control 6.0 (OLEDB) tool to the toolbox.

■ Add an ADO control to the interface, then set its ConnectionString and RecordSource properties. The ConnectionString property stores the type of OLE DB provider for your data source, as well as the name of the data source. The RecordSource property stores either the name of a table or an SQL Select command.

■ Bind controls to the ADO data control by setting each control's DataSource and DataField properties. In the DataSource property, enter the name of the ADO data control to which the control is to be bound. In the DataField property, enter the name of the table field you want the control to display. Always set the DataSource property before setting the DataField property.

To select which database fields and records you want to view, as well as control the order in which the fields and records appear when displayed:

■ Enter a Select command in the ADO data control's RecordSource property. The basic syntax of the Select command is **select** *fields* **from** *table* [**where** *condition*] [**order by** *field*], where *fields* is one or more field names (separated by commas), and *table* is the name of the table containing the fields. To select all of the fields in a table, in the same order in which the fields appear in the table, you can use an * in the *fields* portion of the Select command. The `where` clause allows you to select which records you want to view. The `order by` clause allows you to control the order in which the records appear when displayed.

Q U E S T I O N S

1. Applications that can access and manipulate the data stored in databases are referred to as _____ applications.
   a. corresponding
   b. cross data
   c. data-aware
   d. data-corresponding
   e. data-sharing

2. The _____ control allows you to establish a link between a database and the controls in the interface.
   a. ADO data
   b. ADO database
   c. database
   d. linking
   e. table

3. The _____ property stores the name of the OLE DB provider, as well as the name of the database.
   a. Connect
   b. ConnectionString
   c. DatabaseName
   d. RecordSource
   e. Table

4. The _____ property stores either the name of a table or an SQL command.
   a. Connect
   b. ConnectionString
   c. DatabaseName
   d. RecordSource
   e. Table

5. A control that is connected to an ADO data control is called a(n) _____ control.
   a. attached
   b. bound
   c. connected
   d. joined
   e. linked

6. You should always set a bound control's _____ property before setting its _____ property.
   a. Connection, Record
   b. ConnectionString, RecordSource
   c. Data, DataField
   d. DataField, DataSource
   e. DataSource, DataField

7. _____ is a set of commands that allow you to access the data stored in many database management systems on computers of all sizes, from large mainframes to small microcomputers.
   a. ADO
   b. OLE
   c. SQL
   d. UDA

Use the following database table, named tblState, to answer questions 8 through 11.

Field name	Data type
fldState	Text
fldCapital	Text
fldPopulation	Integer

8. Which of the following commands allows you to view all of the records in the tblState table?
   a. select all records from tblState
   b. select * from tblState
   c. select % from tblState
   d. view * from tblState
   e. view % from tblState

9. Which of the following commands allows you to select only the record whose fldState field contains "NY"?
   a. select the "NY" record from tblState
   b. select * from tblState for "NY"
   c. select * from tblState where fldState = "ny"
   d. select * from tblState where "fldState = NY"
   e. select * from tblState where fldState = NY

10. Which of the following commands allows you to select all records whose population exceeds 10,000,000?
    a. select all records where fldPopulation > 10000000
    b. select * from tblState where fldPopulation > 10000000
    c. select * from tblState where "fldPopulation > 10000000"
    d. select * from tblState where fldPopulation > "10000000"
    e. view * from tblState where "fldPopulation" > 10000000

11. Which of the following commands allows you to select only records whose capital begins with the letter S?
    a. select fldCapital = "S" records from tblState
    b. select * from tblState where fldCapital = "S"
    c. select * from tblState where fldCapital = "S*"
    d. select * from tblState where "fldCapital like S%"
    e. select * from tblState where fldCapital like "S%"

E X E R C I S E S

1. In this exercise you will use the ADO data control and the Select command to view the records stored in the la1Done.mdb database that you created in Lesson A's Exercise 1.

   Scenario: In Lesson A's Exercise 1, you created a one-table Access Version 7.0 database that allows you to keep track of the college courses you have taken. The database is named la1Done (la1Done.mdb), and the table is named tblCourses.
   a. Review the database specifications outlined in Lesson A's Exercise 1.
   b. Open the college (college.vbp) project, which is located in the Tut09 folder on your Student Disk. Save the form and the project as lb1Done in the Tut09 folder on your Student Disk.
   c. Add the Microsoft ADO Data Control 6.0 (OLEDB) tool to the toolbox, then add an ADO data control to the form. Cut the ADO data control from the form, then paste it into the Frame1 frame.
   d. Set the ADO data control's Name property to adoCourses. Set its Height, Left, Top, and Width properties appropriately. Set its Caption property to "Click the arrow buttons to display the database records."

e. Set the ADO data control's ConnectionString and RecordSource properties appropriately. Use Microsoft Jet 3.51 OLE DB Provider as the provider for the la1Done.mdb Access database, which is located in the Tut09 folder on your Student Disk. The RecordSource property should allow you to view all of the tblCourses records in course ID order.

f. Bind the three text boxes and one label control to the ADO data control by setting their DataSource and DataField properties.

g. Save and run the application to verify that it displays the five records you added to the database in Lesson A's Exercise 1.

h. Change your grade in the Cis141 class from B to C. Change the credit hours for the Biology class from 4 to 5. (Be sure to use the ADO data control's buttons to move to another record so the change you made will be saved in the recordset.)

i. Stop the application, then print the Form as Text.

j. Use the adoCourses RecordSource property to view the records specified in Figure 9-30. Complete the figure's table by entering the Select command you used in the RecordSource property.

To view all the fields for	Use this Select command
only the Eng101 record	
only courses in which you earned an A; order the records by course ID	
all Intro courses; order the records by course title	
only the Biology course	
all courses whose ID begins with cis; order the records by course ID	

Figure 9-30

2. In this exercise you will complete an application that will allow you to view the records stored in the la2Done.mdb database that you created in Lesson A's Exercise 2. You will use the ADO data control and the Select command to view the records.

Scenario: In Lesson A's Exercise 2, you created a one-table Access Version 7.0 database that allows you to keep track of the basketball scores for your favorite team. The database is named la2Done (la2Done.mdb), and the table is named tblScores.

a. Review the database specifications outlined in Lesson A's Exercise 2.

b. Open the lb2 (lb2.vbp) project, which is located in the Tut09 folder on your Student Disk. Save the form and the project as lb2Done in the Tut09 folder on your Student Disk.

c. Add the Microsoft ADO Data Control 6.0 (OLEDB) tool to the toolbox, then add an ADO data control to the form. You will need to link the ADO data control to the la2Done.mdb database, which is located in the Tut09 folder on your Student Disk. Display all of the fields and records in order by the opposing team's name.

d. Run the application to verify that it displays the five records you added to the database in Lesson A's Exercise 2.

e. Change the opposing team's score for the game played on 10/23/99 from 85 to 95. Also change the 11/4/99 game date to 11/5/99. (Be sure to use the ADO data control's buttons to move to another record so the change you made will be saved in the recordset.)

f. Stop the application, then print the Form as Text.

g. Use the ADO data control's RecordSource property to view the records specified in Figure 9-31. Complete the figure's table by entering the Select command you used in the RecordSource property.

To view all the fields for	Use this Select command
only games in which your team scored more than 80 points; order the records by date	
only games in which your team scored more points than the opposing team; order the records by the opposing team's name	
only games played against the Hornets; order the records by date	
only games played in November; order the records by date	

Figure 9-31

3. In this exercise you will complete an application that will allow you to view the records stored in the la3Done.mdb database that you created in Lesson A's Exercise 3. You will use the ADO data control and the Select command to view the records.

   Scenario: In Lesson A's Exercise 3, you created a one-table Access Version 7.0 database that allows you to keep track of your monthly phone bill. The database is named la3Done (la3Done.mdb), and the table is named tblPhone.

   a. Review the database specifications outlined in Lesson A's Exercise 3.

   b. Open the lb3 (lb3.vbp) project, which is located in the Tut09 folder on your Student Disk. Save the form and the project as lb3Done in the Tut09 folder on your Student Disk.

   c. Add the Microsoft ADO Data Control 6.0 (OLEDB) tool to the toolbox, then add an ADO data control to the form. You will need to link the ADO data control to the la3Done.mdb database, which is located in the Tut09 folder on your Student Disk. Display all of the fields and records in month order.

   d. Run the application to verify that it displays the five records you added to the database in Lesson A's Exercise 3.

e. Change the December bill from 56 to 75. (Be sure to use the ADO data control's buttons to move to another record so the change you made will be saved in the recordset.

f. Stop the application, then print the Form as Text.

g. Use the ADO data control's RecordSource property to view the records specified in Figure 9-32. Complete the figure's table by entering the Select command you used in the RecordSource property.

To view all the fields for	Use this Select command
only phone bills that exceed $50; order the records by the total bill field	
only phone bills for the year 2000; order the records by the month field	

Figure 9-32

discovery ▶ 4. In this exercise you will learn how to change the ADO data control's color and font.

a. Open a new project. Add the Microsoft ADO Data Control 6.0 (OLEDB) tool to the toolbox, then add an ADO data control to the form. Drag the ADO control to the upper-right corner of the form. With the ADO control selected, click Custom in the Properties list. Click the ... button in the Settings box to display the Property Pages dialog box. Practice with the options available on the Color and Font tabs. (*Hint*: Use the Apply button to see your changes without closing the Property Pages dialog box.)

discovery ▶ 5. In this exercise, you will use the And and Or operators in the Select command. To complete this exercise, you must have completed Exercise 1 in both Lessons A and B.

a. Open the lb1Done (lb1Done.vbp) project, which is located in the Tut09 folder on your Student Disk.

b. Use the Select command to display only the Cis100 and Eng101 records, ordered by course ID. After testing the command, record the command on a piece of paper.

c. Use the Select command to display only the records in which you received either an A or a B. After testing the command, record the command on a piece of paper.

d. Use the Select command to display the Cis141 record along with the records for five-credit-hour courses. After testing the command, record the command on a piece of paper.

e. Submit the paper containing the Select commands from steps b, c, and d. You do not need to save the application.

LESSON C

objectives

In this lesson you will learn how to:

■ Use the Recordset and Field objects and the Fields collection

■ Add new records to a recordset with the AddNew method

■ Delete records using the Delete and MoveNext methods

■ Cancel the update of a record using the CancelUpdate method

■ Update the current record using the Update method

■ Test for the end of the recordset using the EOF property

■ Use the ADO data control's Refresh method to recreate the recordset

Writing Code to Add, Delete, and Update Records

The Cole's Playhouse Application

In this lesson, you will complete the multiple-form application for Cole's Playhouse. However, before you can do so, you will need to learn about the Recordset and Field objects. You will also need to learn how to use the ADO data control's Refresh method. First learn about the Recordset and Field objects.

The Recordset and Field Objects

As you learned in Lesson B, you can use the SQL Select command to select one or more records from a database table. Visual Basic treats the collection of selected records as an object, referred to as the **Recordset object**. For example, the `select * from tblPatron` command creates a Recordset object that contains all of the records stored in the tblPatron table. The `select * from tblPatron where fldSeat = 10` command, on the other hand, creates a Recordset object that contains only the record whose seat number field contains the number 10.

Each field contained within the Recordset object is also considered an object, and it is referred to as a **Field object**. The collection of Field objects within a Recordset object makes up what is known as the **Fields collection**. Figure 9-33 illustrates this concept using the Cole database created in Lesson A.

The `select * from tblPatron` command will create the following Recordset object, Field objects, and Fields collection:

Recordset object: All records stored in the tblPatron table

Fields collection: fldSeat   fldName   fldPhone
                       Field object   Field object   Field object

Figure 9-33: Illustration of the Recordset object, Fields collection, and Field objects

As Figure 9-33 illustrates, the Recordset object would contain all of the records stored in the tblPatron table. The Fields collection within the Recordset object would contain three Field objects: fldSeat, fldName, and fldPhone.

Like other objects, the Recordset object has a set of properties that describe its characteristics, as well as a set of methods that allow you to manipulate the records included in the recordset. To code the Cole's Playhouse multiple-form application, you will need to use six of the Recordset object's methods and one of its properties. Figure 9-34 lists the six methods and one property that you will use in the Cole application. The figure also explains the purpose of the methods and property.

Method	Use to
AddNew	Add a new, blank record to the end of the recordset
CancelUpdate	Cancel changes made to the current record
Delete	Delete the current record from the recordset
MoveFirst	Move the record pointer to the first record in the recordset
MoveNext	Move the record pointer to the next record in the recordset
Update	Save the changes made to the current record

Property	Use to
EOF	Test for the end of the recordset. The EOF property contains True if the record pointer is positioned *after* the last record in the recordset; otherwise, the property contains False.

Note: The syntax for invoking a method of the Recordset object is [*form.*]*adocontrol*.**Recordset**.*method*. The syntax for referring to a property of the Recordset object is [*form.*]*adocontrol*.**Recordset**.*property*.

Figure 9-34: Six methods and one property of the Recordset object

The period that appears in the syntax is called the dot member selection operator.

Figure 9-34 lists only the methods and properties that you will need to use in the Cole's Playhouse application. The Recordset object has other methods and properties that are not listed in Figure 9-34.

You can also use the Recordset object's MovePrevious and MoveLast methods to move to the previous and last record in the recordset, respectively.

As Figure 9-34 shows, you use the Recordset object's **AddNew method** to add a new, blank record to the end of the recordset. You use the **Delete method**, on the other hand, to delete the current record from the recordset. After using the Delete method, you must move the record pointer to another record to remove the deleted record from the screen; you can use the MoveFirst or MoveNext methods to do so. The **MoveFirst method** moves the record pointer to the first record in the recordset, and the **MoveNext method** moves the record pointer to the next record.

After making a change to a record, you can use the **Update method** to save the record, or you can use the **CancelUpdate method** to cancel the change so it will not be saved.

In addition to the six methods described in Figure 9-34, you also will need to use the Recordset object's EOF property in the Cole's Playhouse application. Like the EOF( ) function that you learned about in Tutorials 6 and 8, the EOF property also stands for *end of file*. However, unlike the EOF( ) function, which tests for the end of either a sequential or random access file, the **EOF property** tests for the end of the recordset. If the record pointer is positioned after the last record in the recordset, the EOF property contains the Boolean value True. The EOF property contains the Boolean value False, on the other hand, if the record pointer is positioned on or before the last record in the recordset.

Next, learn about the ADO data control's Refresh method.

The ADO Data Control's Refresh Method

As you learned in Lesson B, the ADO data control opens the database whose name is specified in the control's ConnectionString property. It then uses the value stored in its RecordSource property to create the Recordset object. To create a new Recordset object while the application is running, you need first to enter, into a code window, an instruction that resets the ADO data control's RecordSource property. After resetting the RecordSource property, you then need to use the ADO data control's **Refresh method** to reopen the database and recreate the Recordset object. The syntax of the ADO data control's Refresh method is *adocontrol*.**Refresh**.

Now use the six methods and one property of the Recordset object, as well as the ADO data control's Refresh method, to complete the Cole's Playhouse application.

Completing the Cole's Playhouse Application

As you may remember from Tutorial 8, the Cole's Playhouse application uses two forms. The first form—the seat form—contains 48 label controls, each of which represents a seat in the theater. To either reserve or cancel a reservation, the user needs simply to click one of the 48 label controls in the interface, at which time the second form—the patron form—appears. The patron form allows the user to record a reservation, cancel a reservation, and return to the first form. Reserved seats, you may remember, are colored red in the seat form, and available seats are colored white. You will begin completing the Cole's Playhouse application by adding the seat form to the lbCole project that you created in Lesson B.

tip

You also can prevent the user from interacting with the ADO data control by setting the control's Enabled property to False. Whether you hide the data control or disable it depends on the application. If the application never allows the user to interact with the ADO data control, it is best to hide the control to prevent any confusion. However, if the application allows the user to interact with the ADO data control if some condition is met, then you should leave the control visible, but disable it until the condition is met.

To begin completing the Cole's Playhouse application:

1 Open the **lbCole** (lbCole.vbp) project, which is located in the Tut09 folder on your Student Disk. Click **Project** on the menu bar, and then click **Add Form**. Use the Existing tab to open the Seat (Seat.frm) form, which is located in the Tut09 folder on your Student Disk.

The seat form should be the startup form in this application.

2 Click **Project** on the menu bar, and then click **Cole Properties**. Change the Startup Object from frmPatron to **frmSeat**, then click the **OK** button.

3 Save the seat form as **lcSeat**. Save the patron form as **lcPatron**. Save the project as **lcCole**.

In this version of the application, the user will not need to use the ADO data control's buttons to scroll through the records in the recordset. This is because each of the 48 label controls in the seat form will be responsible for displaying the appropriate record in the patron form. Therefore, you will hide the ADO data control by setting its Visible property to False. Setting the Visible property to False does not prevent the ADO data control from accessing the records in the recordset; it merely prevents the user from interacting with the ADO data control.

4 View the patron form, and then set the adoCole control's Visible property to **False**.

5 Close the patron form by clicking its **Close** ☒ button.

6 View and then maximize the seat form. Figure 9-35 shows the seat form's interface.

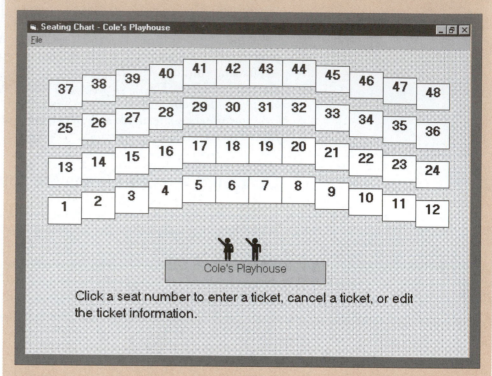

Figure 9-35: Seat form's user interface

The seat form contains a File menu, as well as 48 label controls that belong to an array named lblSeat. The File menu has one command, Exit, which has already been coded for you; it contains the Unload frmSeat instruction. Also coded for you is the seat form's Unload event, which contains the Unload frmPatron instruction.

Recall that the seat form is the startup form in this application. When the seat form appears, the reserved seats should be colored red, and the available seats should be white. Before the seat form can color the seats (label controls) appropriately, its Load event will need to read each record in the adoCole control's recordset; each record in the recordset represents a reserved seat. As you may remember, the seat number is stored in each record's fldSeat field. If the fldSeat field contains the number 1, then the label control whose caption is 1—the lblSeat(0) control—should be colored red. If the fldSeat field contains the number 48, then the label control whose caption is 48—the lblSeat(47) control—should be colored red. Notice that the entry in the fldSeat field is always one more than the value stored in the corresponding label control's Index property. Therefore, to determine the appropriate label control to color red, you will need first to subtract 1 from the fldSeat entry. Figure 9-36 shows the pseudocode for the seat form's Load event.

1. Declare intIndex variable

2. Repeat while it is not the end of the adoCole control's recordset

    a. Subtract 1 from the contents of the current record's fldSeat field, and assign the result to the intIndex variable

    b. Set the BackColor property of the lblSeat(intIndex) control to vbRed

    c. Move the record pointer to the next record in the recordset

  End repeat while

Figure 9-36: Pseudocode for the frmSeat form's Load event procedure

Use the pseudocode shown in Figure 9-36 to code the seat form's Load event.

To code the seat form's Load event, then test the code:

1 Open the seat form's Load event. Press the **Tab** key, then type **dim intIndex as integer** and press the **Enter** key.

Now begin a loop that will repeat its instructions for each record in the record-set. As you learned earlier, you can use the Recordset object's EOF property to determine when you have run out of records—in other words, to determine if the record pointer is positioned at the end of the recordset. Recall that the syntax for using a property of the Recordset object is [*form.*]*adocontrol*.**Recordset**.*property*. In this case, because the adoCole data control is located on the frmPatron form, you will need to precede the control's name with the name of the form on which it resides.

2 Type **do while not frmpatron.adocole.recordset.eof** and press the **Enter** key.

According to the pseudocode, the first instruction in the loop should subtract the number 1 from the current record's fldSeat entry, then assign the result to the intIndex variable. The syntax you use to refer to a field within the Fields collection of a recordset is [*form.*]*adocontrol*.**Recordset**.**Fields**(*field*), where *field* is the name of the field, enclosed in quotation marks. To refer to the fldSeat field, for example, you would use `frmPatron.adoCole.Recordset.Fields("fldSeat")`, which tells Visual Basic that the fldSeat field is located in the Fields collection of the adoCole control's recordset, and that the adoCole control resides on the frmPatron form.

3 Press the **Tab** key to indent the loop instructions. Type **intindex = frmpatron.adocole.recordset.fields("fldSeat") – 1** and press the **Enter** key.

The next instruction in the loop should change, to red, the BackColor property of the label whose index is stored in the intIndex variable.

4 Type **lblseat(intindex).backcolor = vbred** and press the **Enter** key.

The last instruction in the loop should move the record pointer to the next record in the recordset; you can use the Recordset object's MoveNext method to do so.

5 Type **frmpatron.adocole.recordset.movenext** and press the **Enter** key.

Now end the loop.

tip

As you may remember from Tutorial 8, vbRed is one of Visual Basic's intrinsic constants.

6 Press the **Backspace** key, then type **loop**. Figure 9-37 shows the completed Load event for the seat form.

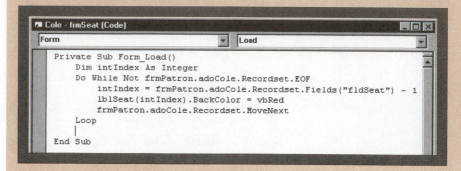

```
Cole - frmSeat (Code)
Form                                          Load
   Private Sub Form_Load()
        Dim intIndex As Integer
        Do While Not frmPatron.adoCole.Recordset.EOF
            intIndex = frmPatron.adoCole.Recordset.Fields("fldSeat") - 1
            lblSeat(intIndex).BackColor = vbRed
            frmPatron.adoCole.Recordset.MoveNext
        Loop
   End Sub
```

Figure 9-37: Completed Load event procedure for the seat form

7 Close the Code window. Press the **Alt** key on your keyboard to display Visual Basic's main window, then **save** and **run** the application. Seats 10, 24, 38, 43, and 44 should be colored red because they are reserved. (Recall that you added these records to the Cole database in Lesson A.)

HELP? If the appropriate seats are not colored red in your application, you may need to recreate the cole.mdb file. You can do so by using Windows to copy the cole.ori file, which is located in the Tut09 folder on your Student Disk, to cole.mdb.

8 Click **File**, then click **Exit**. Visual Basic returns to the design screen.

Next you will code the lblSeat array's Click event.

Coding the lblSeat Array's Click Event

Figure 9-38 shows the pseudocode for the lblSeat array's Click event procedure.

1. If the seat is not reserved then
   a. Add a new record to the recordset
   b. Display the seat number in the patron form's lblNum control
   c. Disable the patron form's Cancel Ticket button
   Else   (the record is reserved)
   d. Display the record in the patron form
   e. Enable the patron form's Cancel Ticket button
   End if
2. Show the patron form
3. Send the focus to the patron form's txtName control

Figure 9-38: Pseudocode for the lblSeat array's Click event

As the pseudocode indicates, when the user clicks an unreserved seat, which is a seat (label control) that is *not* colored red, then the Click event will add a new, blank record to the recordset. It will also display the appropriate seat number in the patron form's lblNum control. In addition, the Click event will disable the patron form's Cancel Ticket button; since this is a new reservation, there is no reservation to cancel, so the Cancel Ticket button is not applicable to the current situation.

If, on the other hand, the user clicks a reserved seat, which is a seat (label control) that *is* colored red, then the Click event should direct the ADO data control to display the record's information in the patron form. In addition, the Click event should enable the Cancel Ticket button so that the user can cancel the reservation if necessary.

The last two tasks the Click event should perform are to show the patron form and to send the focus to that form's txtName control. Use the pseudocode to code the lblSeat array's Click event.

GUI
Design Tips

Disable controls that are not applicable to the current state of the application.

To code the lblSeat array's Click event:

1 Open the lblSeat array's Click event. Press the **Tab** key, then type **if lblseat(index).backcolor <> vbred then** and press the **Enter** key.

Now use the Recordset object's AddNew method to add a new, blank record to the end of the recordset.

2 Press the **Tab** key to indent the selection structure's instructions, then type **frmpatron.adocole.recordset.addnew** and press the **Enter** key.

Now display the appropriate seat number in the patron form's lblNum control. Recall that the seat number is one more than the index of the label control that was clicked. In other words, the seat number that corresponds to the lblSeat(0) control is 1, and the seat number that corresponds to the lblSeat(6) control is 7. Therefore, you will need to add the number 1 to the control array's Index argument before displaying the seat number in the lblNum control.

3 Type **frmpatron.lblnum.caption = index + 1** and press the **Enter** key.

Now disable the patron form's Cancel Ticket button by assigning the Boolean value False to its Enabled property.

4 Type **frmpatron.cmdcancel.enabled = false** and press the **Enter** key.

You have completed the selection structure's True path, so you can now code its False path. Recall that the instructions in the False path will be executed when the user clicks a reserved seat (a red label control) in the seat form.

5 Press the **Backspace** key, then type **else** and press the **Enter** key.

According to the pseudocode, if a seat is reserved, you need to display its corresponding record in the patron form. Here again, recall that the seat number stored in each record's fldSeat field is one more than the index of its corresponding label in the array. To display the appropriate record, you first will reset the ADO data control's RecordSource property by assigning a Select command to it. The instruction you will use is `frmPatron.adoCole.RecordSource = "select * from tblPatron where fldSeat = " & Index + 1`. The `Index + 1` in the instruction represents the number of the seat whose record you want to display. Notice that you can use string concatenation to concatenate the seat number to the Select command.

6 Press the **Tab** key, then type **frmpatron.adocole.recordsource = _** (the underscore) and press the **Enter** key (be sure to enter a space before the underscore in the command). Press the **Tab** key, then type **"select * from tblPatron where fldSeat = " & Index + 1** and press the **Enter** key.

After resetting the RecordSource property, recall that you then must use the ADO data control's Refresh method to open the database and recreate the recordset.

7 Press the **Backspace** key, then type **frmpatron.adocole.refresh** and press the **Enter** key.

The next step in the pseudocode is to enable the patron form's Cancel Ticket button so that the user can cancel the reservation if necessary.

8 Type **frmpatron.cmdcancel.enabled = true** and press the **Enter** key.

You have completed the selection structure, so you can end it.

9 Press the **Backspace** key, then type **end if** and press the **Enter** key.

According to the pseudocode, you still need to show the patron form and set the focus to its txtName control.

10 Enter the two lines of code and the documentation shown in Figure 9-39.

enter this documentation

line continuation character

enter these two instructions

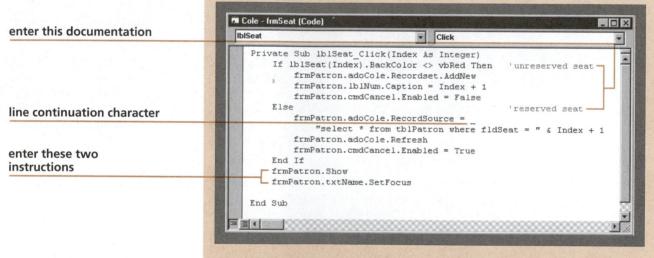

Figure 9-39: Completed Click event for the lblSeat control array

Now that you have completed the Click event for the lblSeat control array, you can test its code.

To test the lblSeat array's Click event procedure:

1 Close the Code window, then **save** and **run** the application.

2 Click seat number **10**, which is reserved. Candy Sprott's record appears in the patron form. Notice that the Enter Ticket, Cancel Ticket, and Return to Main buttons are enabled.

3 Click the patron form's **Close** ☒ button to close the form. (*Important note*: Be careful not to click another seat while the patron form is showing; if you do, Visual Basic will display an error message. In Lesson C's Exercise 1, you will modify the application to prevent this error from occurring.)

Now click an unreserved seat.

4 Click seat number **31**, which is not reserved. A new record appears in the patron form. Notice that the new record's seat number is 31. Also notice that only the Enter Ticket and Return to Main buttons are enabled. The Cancel Ticket button is disabled because the user would have no reason to cancel an unreserved ticket.

5 Click the patron form's **Close** ☒ button to close the form. Click **File** on the seat form's menu bar, and then click **Exit**. Visual Basic returns to the design screen.

You are finished coding the seat form, so you can close it.

6 Close the seat form by clicking its **Close** ☒ button.

Next, code the Return to Main button's Click event. The Return to Main button is on the patron form.

Coding the Return to Main Button

If the user selects the Return to Main button on the patron form, any changes made to the current record should be canceled, and the patron form should be hidden. Figure 9-40 shows the pseudocode for the Return to Main button's Click event.

---

1. Cancel the update of the current record

2. Hide the patron form

Figure 9-40: Pseudocode for the Return to Main button's Click event

tip

Recall that a hidden form is not removed from the computer's memory; it is merely hidden from view.

To code the Return to Main button's Click event, then test the code:

1 View the frmPatron form. Open the Return to Main button's Click event procedure.

As you learned earlier, you can use the Recordset object's CancelUpdate method to cancel the changes made to the current record. You can use the form's Hide method, which you learned about in Tutorial 3, to hide a form.

2 Enter the two instructions shown in Figure 9-41.

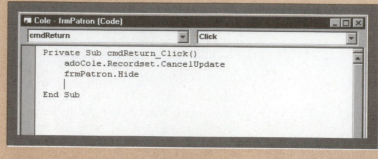

Figure 9-41: Completed Click event for the Return to Main button

3 Close the Code window, then **save** and **run** the application. Click seat number **38**. Janet Smith's record appears in the patron form.

You will make a change to Janet's record, and then click the Return to Main button. The button's Click event should not save the change you made to the record.

4 Change Janet's phone number from 333-3333 to **999-9999**, and then click the **Return to Main** button. The button's Click event returns to the seat form without saving the change you made to Janet's record. You can verify that the change was not saved by displaying Janet's record again.

5 Click seat number **38**. Notice that Janet's phone number is 333-3333. Click the **Return to Main** button to return to the seat form. Click **File**, then click **Exit**. Visual Basic returns to the design screen.

tip
Rather than having the Return to Main button ignore the changes made to the current record, you can code the button so that it asks the user if he or she wants to save the change. You will make this modification in Lesson C's Discovery Exercise 6.

The next event you will code is the Enter Ticket button's Click event. The Enter Ticket button is on the patron form.

Coding the Enter Ticket Button

The pseudocode for the Enter Ticket button's Click event is shown in Figure 9-42.

1. Declare intIndex variable

2. If the user completed the txtName text box then

    a. Subtract 1 from the contents of the lblNum control's Caption property, and assign the result to the intIndex variable

    b. Set the BackColor property of the lblSeat(intIndex) control to vbRed

    c. Update the current record

  Else

    Cancel the update of the current record

  End if

3. Hide the patron form

Figure 9-42: Pseudocode for the Enter Ticket button's Click event

As you may remember from Lesson A, the Cole database requires an entry in the fldName field. Therefore, you shouldn't let the Cole application attempt to enter a record that does not have an entry in the txtName text box. As Figure 9-42's pseudocode indicates, only when the user completes the txtName text box will the Enter Ticket button change the BackColor property of the appropriate lblSeat control to red, and then update the record in the recordset before hiding the patron form. You determine which lblSeat control to color red by subtracting the number 1 from the value stored in the lblNum control's Caption property. Recall that the number in the lblNum control represents the seat number, which is always one more than the lblSeat control's index. For example, if the lblNum control contains the number 1, then you need to change the BackColor property of the lblSeat(0) control, which represents seat number 1, to red.

tip

Recall that you learned about the Trim function in Tutorial 8. The Trim function removes any leading and trailing spaces from a string.

tip

Recall from Tutorial 8 that vbRed is one of Visual Basic's intrinsic constants.

To code the Enter Ticket button's Click event, then test the code:

1 Open the Enter Ticket button's Click event.

First, declare an Integer variable named intIndex.

2 Press the **Tab** key. Type **dim intIndex as integer** and press the **Enter** key.

Now verify that the txtName text box was completed.

3 Type **if trim(txtname.text) <> " " then** and press the **Enter** key.

Next, subtract the number 1 from the lblNum control's Caption property, and assign the result to the intIndex variable.

4 Press the **Tab** key, then type **intindex = val(lblnum.caption) – 1** and press the **Enter** key.

Now use the intIndex variable to change the BackColor property of the appropriate lblSeat control, which is located in the frmSeat form, to vbRed.

5 Type **frmseat.lblseat(intindex).backcolor = vbred** and press the **Enter** key.

As you learned earlier, you use the Recordset object's Update method to save the changes made to the current record.

6 Type **adocole.recordset.update** and press the **Enter** key.

To complete the Enter Ticket button's Click event, you need only to enter the selection structure's False path and then end the selection structure before hiding the patron form.

7 Enter the four additional instructions shown in Figure 9-43, which shows the completed Click event for the Enter Ticket button.

enter these four instructions

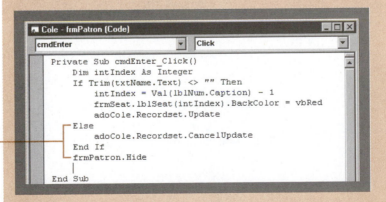

```
Cole - frmPatron (Code)
cmdEnter                          Click

Private Sub cmdEnter_Click()
    Dim intIndex As Integer
    If Trim(txtName.Text) <> "" Then
        intIndex = Val(lblNum.Caption) - 1
        frmSeat.lblSeat(intIndex).BackColor = vbRed
        adoCole.Recordset.Update
    Else
        adoCole.Recordset.CancelUpdate
    End If
    frmPatron.Hide

End Sub
```

Figure 9-43: Completed Click event for the Enter Ticket button

You will now test the Enter Ticket button by making a reservation.

8 Close the Code window, then **save** and **run** the application. Click seat number **48**. The patron form appears with the number 48 entered as the seat number.

9 Type your name and phone number in the appropriate text boxes. Be sure to enter a maximum of 20 characters for your name, and a maximum of eight characters for your phone number. Press the **Enter** key to select the Enter Ticket button, which is the default command button in the patron form. The Enter Ticket button's Click event saves the patron information in the recordset, and the seat form appears with seat number 48 colored red, which indicates that it is reserved.

You can verify that your record was added to the recordset by clicking seat number 48 again.

10 Click seat number **48**. Your record appears in the patron form. Click the **Return to Main** button to hide the patron form.

Now make a change to your phone number.

11 Click seat number **48**. Change your phone number to **999-9999**, then click the **Enter Ticket** button to save the change.

You can verify that the change was saved to the recordset by clicking seat number 48 again.

12 Click seat number **48**. Notice that your phone number is now 999-9999. Click the **Return to Main** button. Click **File**, then click **Exit**. Visual Basic returns to the design screen.

To complete the Cole's Playhouse application, you need only to code the Cancel Ticket button's Click event procedure.

Coding the Cancel Ticket Button

The pseudocode for the Cancel Ticket button's Click event is shown in Figure 9-44.

1. Declare intIndex variable

2. Subtract 1 from the contents of the lblNum control's Caption property, and assign the result to the intIndex variable

3. Set the BackColor property of the lblSeat(intIndex) control to vbWhite

4. Delete the record from the recordset

5. Remove the deleted record from the screen

6. Hide the patron form

Figure 9-44: Pseudocode for the Cancel Ticket button's Click event

The Cancel Ticket button will need simply to change the BackColor property of the appropriate lblSeat control to white, then remove the current record from both the recordset and the screen before hiding the patron form. You determine which lblSeat control to color white by subtracting the number 1 from the value stored in the lblNum control's Caption property. Recall that the number in the lblNum control represents the seat number, which is always one more than the lblSeat control's index.

tip

Although the deleted record will appear on the screen until you move to another record in the recordset, you cannot save the deleted record, nor can you try to delete it again. If you do, Visual Basic will display an error message.

tip

You also can use the Recordset object's MoveNext, MoveLast, and MovePrevious methods to move to the next, last, and previous record in the recordset, respectively.

tip

You should display a message verifying that the user wants to delete the current record before you use the Delete method because the Delete method permanently deletes a record from the recordset. You will make this modification in Lesson C's Exercise 1.

To code the Cancel Ticket button's Click event and then test the code:

1   Open the Cancel Ticket button's Click event.

First, declare an Integer variable named intIndex, and assign to it a number that is one less that the value stored in the lblNum control's Caption property.

2   Press the **Tab** key, then type **dim intIndex as integer** and press the **Enter** key, then type **intindex = val(lblnum.caption) – 1** and press the **Enter** key.

Now use the intIndex variable to change the BackColor property of the appropriate lblSeat control, which is located in the frmSeat form, to vbWhite.

3   Type **frmseat.lblseat(intindex).backcolor = vbwhite** and press the **Enter** key.

The next step is to remove the record from the recordset; you do so by using the Recordset object's Delete method.

4   Type **adocole.recordset.delete** and press the **Enter** key.

The Recordset object's Delete method deletes the current record from the recordset, but it does not remove the record from the screen. To remove the deleted record from the screen, you must move the record pointer to another record in the recordset. You will use the Recordset object's MoveFirst method to do so.

5   Type **adocole.recordset.movefirst** and press the **Enter** key.

The final task for the Cancel Ticket button is to hide the frmPatron form.

6   Type **frmpatron.hide** and press the **Enter** key. Figure 9-45 shows the completed Click event for the Cancel Ticket button.

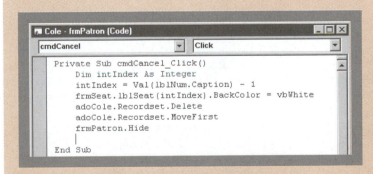

```
Cole - frmPatron (Code)
cmdCancel                          Click

    Private Sub cmdCancel_Click()
        Dim intIndex As Integer
        intIndex = Val(lblNum.Caption) – 1
        frmSeat.lblSeat(intIndex).BackColor = vbWhite
        adoCole.Recordset.Delete
        adoCole.Recordset.MoveFirst
        frmPatron.Hide
    |
    End Sub
```

Figure 9-45: Completed Click event for the Cancel Ticket button

7   Close the Code window, then **save** and **run** the application. Click seat number 48. The patron information for seat number 48 appears in the patron form.

8 Click the **Cancel Ticket** button to cancel seat number 48's reservation. The Cancel Ticket button's Click event removes the record from both the recordset and the screen. The seat form appears with seat number 48 colored white, which indicates that it is not reserved.

You can verify that seat number 48's record was removed from the recordset by clicking seat number 48 again.

9 Click seat number **48**. The patron form appears with the number 48 entered as the seat number. Notice that the patron name and phone number text boxes, however, are empty. Click the **Return to Main** button to hide the patron form.

10 Click **File**, then click **Exit**. Visual Basic returns to the design screen.

You have now completed Lesson C and the multiple-form application for Cole's Playhouse. In this lesson's Exercise 1, you will make four improvements to the application.

S U M M A R Y

To add a new, blank record to a recordset:

■ Use the Recordset object's AddNew method using the following syntax: [*form.*]*adocontrol*.**Recordset.AddNew**.

To delete the current record from a recordset:

■ Use the Recordset object's Delete method using the following syntax: [*form.*]*adocontrol*.**Recordset.Delete**. This method deletes the current record from the recordset; it does not, however, remove the record from the screen. You must move to another record in order to remove the deleted record from the screen.

To move the record pointer to another record in the recordset:

■ Use the Recordset object's MoveFirst, MoveNext, MovePrevious, and MoveLast methods to move the record pointer to the first, next, previous, and last records, respectively. The syntax is [*form.*]*adocontrol*.**Recordset.***movemethod*, where *movemethod* is either MoveFirst, MoveNext, MovePrevious, or MoveLast.

To save the changes made to the current record:

■ Use the Recordset object's Update method using the following syntax: [*form.*]*adocontrol*.**Recordset.Update**.

To cancel the changes made to the current record:

■ Use the Recordset object's CancelUpdate method using the following syntax: [*form.*]*adocontrol*.**Recordset.CancelUpdate**.

To test for the end of the recordset:

■ Use the Recordset object's EOF property using the following syntax: [*form.*]*adocontrol*.**Recordset.EOF** [= *Booleanvalue*]. The EOF property contains the

Boolean value True if the record pointer is positioned after the last record in the recordset; otherwise, it contains the Boolean value False.

To select specific records from an ADO data control's recordset while an application is running:

■ First reset the ADO data control's RecordSource property by assigning a SQL Select command to it. Then use the ADO data control's Refresh method to reopen the database and recreate the recordset.

To open (or reopen) a database and recreate an ADO data control's recordset:

■ Use the ADO data control's Refresh method. The syntax is *adocontrol*.**Refresh**.

Q U E S T I O N S

1. The collection of records from one or more tables in a database is referred to as the
   _____ .
   a. Collection
   b. Database
   c. Recordset
   d. RecordSource
   e. Table

2. You use the _____ method to remove the current record from the recordset.
   a. Delete
   b. Eliminate
   c. Erase
   d. MoveNext
   e. Remove

3. When you delete a record from the recordset, the record is not removed from the screen until you _____ .
   a. click the Delete button again
   b. click the Erase button again
   c. click the Remove button again
   d. move the record pointer to another record
   e. None of the above. The record is automatically removed from the screen when you delete a record.

4. You can use the _____ method to move the record pointer to another record in the recordset.
   a. Continue
   b. Move
   c. MoveNext
   d. Next
   e. NextRecord

5. Which of the following instructions will add a new, blank record to the end of the adoPay control's recordset? The name of the table is tblPerson.
   a. AddNew adoPay.tblPerson.Recordset
   b. adoPay.tblPerson.Recordset.AddNew
   c. adoPay.Recordset.tblPerson.AddNew
   d. adoPay.Recordset.AddNew
   e. Recordset.AddNew

6. Which of the following instructions prevents Visual Basic from saving the changes made to the current record in the adoPay control's recordset? The name of the table is tblPerson.
   a. adoPay.Recordset.CancelSave
   b. adoPay.Recordset.CancelUpdate
   c. adoPay.Recordset.NoChange
   d. tblPerson.Recordset.NoSave
   e. NoUpdate.Recordset.tblPerson

7. Which of the following instructions will remove the current record from the adoPay control's recordset? The name of the table is tblPerson.
   a. adoPay.Recordset.Delete
   b. adoPay.Recordset.Remove
   c. adoPay.tblPerson.Delete
   d. tblPerson.Recordset.Erase
   e. Delete.Recordset.tblPerson

8. Which of the following instructions tells Visual Basic to save the changes made to the current record in the adoPay control's recordset? The name of the table is tblPerson.
   a. adoPay.Recordset.Change
   b. adoPay.Recordset.Save
   c. adoPay.Recordset.Update
   d. adoPay.tblPerson.Update
   e. tblPerson.Recordset.Save

9. Which of the following instructions moves the record pointer to the first record in the adoPay control's recordset? The name of the table is tblPerson.
   a. adoPay.Recordset.LocateFirst
   b. adoPay.Recordset.MoveFirst
   c. LocateFirst.Recordset.tblPerson
   d. Recordset.tblPerson.MoveFirst
   e. tblPerson.Recordset.MoveFirst

10. If the record pointer is positioned after the last record in the recordset, the recordset object's _____ property contains the Boolean value True.
    a. END
    b. EOF( )
    c. EOF
    d. LAST
    e. PTRLOC

11. Which of the following methods opens (or reopens) a database and creates (or recreates) the Recordset object?
    a. RecordNewSet
    b. Recreate
    c. Redo
    d. Refresh
    e. Reopen

E X E R C I S E S

1. In this exercise you will make four modifications to the Cole's Playhouse application that you completed in Lesson C. You will also learn about a form's Activate event.

   a. Open the lcCole (lcCole.vbp) project, which is located in the Tut09 folder on your Student Disk. Save the files as lclPat, lclSeat, and lclDone.

   b. The first modification will prevent the user from entering a reservation that contains more than 20 characters in the Patron name text box or more than eight characters in the Phone text box. (As you may remember from Lesson A, the fldName and fldPhone fields in the Cole database's tblPatron table have a length of 20 and 8, respectively.) Observe what happens if the user enters more than eight characters in the Phone text box. Run the application. Click seat number 6, which is not reserved. When the patron form appears, type nine characters in the Phone text box, then click the Enter Ticket button. Because you entered more characters than are allowed in the fldPhone field, Visual Basic displays a run-time error message in a dialog box. Click the End button in the dialog box to stop the application. The same error would occur if you entered more than 20 characters in the Patron name text box. You can prevent this error from occurring by limiting the number of characters the user can enter into the text boxes. Set the txtName control's MaxLength property to 20, then set the txtPhone control's MaxLength property to 8. Save and run the application. Click seat number 6. When the patron form appears, try typing more than 20 characters into the txtName text box, then try typing more than eight characters in the txtPhone text box. You will find that you will not be able to enter more than the number of characters specified in each text box's MaxLength property. Click the Return to Main button, and then stop the application.

   c. Currently, the Enter Ticket button's Click event verifies that the txtName control contains an entry before allowing a record to be saved in the recordset. Another way to code the Cole's Playhouse application is simply to disable the Enter Ticket button until the user types an entry in the text box. This will be the second modification you will make to the application. First, open the Enter Ticket button's Click event, then delete the `If Trim(txtName.Text) <> "" Then`, `Else`, `adoCole.Recordset.CancelUpdate`, and `End If` instructions. You can prevent the user from inadvertently entering a reservation that does not contain the patron's name by coding the txtName control's Change event. Open the txtName control's Change event. Enter a selection structure that determines if the control's Text property contains a zero-length string. If it does, then disable the Enter Ticket button; otherwise, enable the Enter Ticket button. (*Hint*: Use the Trim function to be sure the user does not save any blank spaces as the name.) Save and run the application. Click seat number 7, which is not reserved. The Enter Ticket and Cancel Ticket buttons should be disabled. Type the letter A in the txtName text box. The text box's Change event should enable the Enter Ticket button. Use the Backspace key to remove the letter A from the text box. The text box's Change event should disable the Enter Ticket button. Click the Return to Main button, and then stop the application.

   d. The third modification will be to the Cancel Ticket button's Click event. Open the Cancel Ticket button's Click event. Modify the code so that it uses the MsgBox function to ask the user if he or she wants to cancel the reservation. Save and run the application. Click seat number 2, which is not reserved. Enter your name and phone number in the patron form, and then click the Enter Ticket button. Seat 2 should be colored red in the seat form. Click seat number 2 again, and then click the Cancel Ticket button. When asked if you want to cancel the reservation, click the No button. Seat 2 should still be colored red in the seat form. Click seat number 2, then click Cancel Ticket. When asked if you want to cancel the reservation, click the Yes button. When the seat form appears, seat 2 should be colored white. Stop the application.

e. The final modification you will make to the application will prevent the user from clicking a seat in the seat form when the patron form is showing. First observe why you should make this change to the Cole application. Run the application, and then click any unreserved seat. Recall that the lblSeat control's Click event adds a new record to the recordset. When the patron form appears, click another unreserved seat. This time Visual Basic display a run-time error message when the lblSeat control's Click event attempts to add another new record to the recordset. Click the Debug button. The `frmPatron.adoCole.Recordset.AddNew` instruction is causing the run-time error because you can't add a second new record without first either updating or canceling the update of the first new record. Stop the application.

f. You can prevent the user from clicking a seat in the seat form when the patron form is showing by making the patron form modal. As you learned in Tutorial 3, a modal form is one that requires the user to take some action in the current form before the focus can switch to another form or dialog box, or before any subsequent code can be executed. You create a modal form by using the number 1 as the *style* in the Show method, whose syntax is *object*.**Show** [*style*]. Open the lblSeat array's Click event. Change the `frmPatron.Show` instruction to `frmPatron.Show 1`. Save and run the application. Click an unreserved seat. When the patron form appears, try clicking another unreserved seat. Because the patron form is modal, you cannot select another seat in the seat form. Click the Return to Main button. Visual Basic displays the "Invalid procedure call or argument" error message. Click the Debug button. Notice that the `frmPatron.txtName.SetFocus` instruction is causing the error. Stop the application.

g. Open the lblSeat array's Click event, if necessary. Because the Show method declares the patron form as modal, the `frmPatron.txtName.SetFocus` instruction will not be executed until the patron form is removed from the screen. The user can remove the form from the screen either by clicking the Close button, which will unload the patron form, or by clicking the Enter Ticket, Cancel Ticket, or Return to Main buttons, which will hide the patron form. (Recall that each command button's Click event contains the `frmPatron.Hide` instruction.) Visual Basic does not allow an application to send the focus to a control that resides in a hidden or unloaded form. The solution to this dilemma is to remove the SetFocus instruction from the lblSeat array's Click event, and include a SetFocus instruction in the patron form's Activate event.

h. If you have access to the MSDN Library, research the form's Activate event. When does the Activate event occur? What is the difference between the form's Load event and its Activate event? Delete the `frmPatron.txtName.SetFocus` instruction from the lblSeat array's Click event. Enter the `txtName.SetFocus` instruction in the patron form's Activate event. Save and run the application. Test the application to verify that the application works correctly.

i. Print the application's code. On the printout, answer the questions posed in step h.

2. In this exercise, you will use a Microsoft Access database. The application you create will allow the user to add and delete records from the database.

Scenario: Mr. Fletcher, a fourth grade teacher, wants an application that he can use to keep track of the seat numbers, names, and grades of his students. Mr. Fletcher's classroom can accommodate a maximum of 20 students.

a. Open the lc2 (lc2.vbp) project, which is located in the Tut09 folder on your Student Disk. Save the frmDesk form as lc2Desk in the Tut09 folder on your Student Disk. Save the frmStudent form as lc2Stud. Save the project as lc2Done.

b. The Access database for this application should contain three fields: fldDesk, fldName, and fldGrade. Use Visual Data Manager to create an appropriate database, then enter the following three records:

Desk number	Name	Grade
12	Janes, Mary	A
7	Jones, Fred	C
20	Berry, Ellen	B

c. Close Visual Data Manager. Add an ADO data control to the frmStudent form. Set its Visible property to False. Set its Name, ConnectionString, and RecordSource properties appropriately.

d. Bind the lblNum, txtName, and txtGrade controls by setting their DataSource and DataField properties.

e. Code the frmDesk form's Load event so that it changes the BackColor property of the occupied desks to vbYellow. The records for the occupied desks are stored in the database you created in step b.

f. Code the lblDesk array's Click event so that it adds a new record to the recordset if the desk is unoccupied. If the desk is occupied, display the appropriate record in the frmStudent form. Disable the frmStudent's Remove button if you are adding a new record; otherwise, enable it.

g. Code the Enter, Remove, and Return to Main buttons in the frmStudent form. The Enter button will allow the user to save the changes made to the current record. It also should change the appropriate desk to yellow. The Remove button will allow the user to remove the current record from both the screen and recordset. It also should change the appropriate desk to white. Be sure to verify that the user wants to delete the record before doing so. The Return to Main button will cancel any changes made to the current record, then hide the frmStudent form.

h. Code the txtName control's Change event so that it does not allow the user to enter a record if the text box is empty. (*Hint*: See step c in Exercise 1.)

i. Set the txtName control's MaxLength property to the size of the fldName field. Set the txtGrade control's MaxLength property to the size of the fldGrade field.

j. Don't allow the user to click a desk in the desk form while the student form is showing. (*Hint*: See steps e through h in Exercise 1.)

k. Save and run the application. The desks corresponding to the records you entered in step b should be yellow; the remaining desks should be white.

l. The student in desk number 12 has moved. Click desk number 12, then use the Remove button to remove the student's record from the recordset and screen. When the frmDesk form appears, desk number 12 should be white.

m. Click an unoccupied desk, then add your name and grade to the recordset. When the frmDesk form appears, your desk should be yellow.

n. Change the grade for Fred Jones, who is sitting in desk number 7, from C to D. Verify that the change was saved by clicking desk number 7, then click the Return to Main button.

o. Stop the application, then print the project's code.

3. In this exercise, you will use a Microsoft Access database. The application you create will allow the user to add and delete records from the database.

Scenario: Janice and Bob own a restaurant that has a small banquet room. The banquet room, which can accommodate 40 guests, is typically rented out for small weddings. Janice and Bob would like you to create an application that they can use to keep track of each guest's name and meal preference (Steak, Fish, or Vegetarian).

a. Open the lc3 (lc3.vbp) project, which is located in the Tut09 folder on your Student Disk. Save the frmBanquet form as lc3Banq in the Tut09 folder on your Student Disk. Save the frmGuest form as lc3Guest. Save the project as lc3Done. View the frmBanquet form. The banquet room contains four tables; each table contains 10 seats. Seats one through 10 are at table 1. Seats 11 through 20 are at table 2.

Seats 21 through 30 are at table 3, and seats 31 through 40 are at table 4. Print the frmBanquet form. On the printout, number the seats appropriately. For example, the imgSeat(0) seat should be numbered 1 on the printout. The imgSeat(39) seat should be numbered 40 on the printout.

b. The Access database for this application should contain four fields: fldTable, fldSeat, fldName, and fldMeal. Use Visual Data Manager to create an appropriate database, then enter the following three records.

Table number	Seat number	Name	Meal
1	9	Jacobs, Mary	Vegetarian
3	25	Patel, Khalid	Fish
3	26	Patel, Sharma	Steak

c. Close Visual Data Manager. Add an ADO data control to the frmGuest form. Set its Visible property to False. Set its Name, ConnectionString, and RecordSource properties appropriately.

d. Bind the lblTable, lblSeatNum, txtName, and txtMeal controls by setting their DataSource and DataField properties.

e. Code the frmBanquet form's Load event so that it displays the smiling face icon in the occupied seats. The smiling face icon is stored in the imgSmile control. The records for the occupied seats are stored in the database you created in step b.

f. Code the imgSeat array's Click event so that it adds a new record to the recordset if the seat is unoccupied. If the seat is occupied, display the appropriate record in the frmGuest form. Disable the frmGuest's Delete button if you are adding a new record; otherwise, enable it.

g. Code the Enter, Delete, and Return to Main buttons in the frmGuest form. The Enter button will allow the user to save the changes made to the current record. It also should assign the smiling face icon to the appropriate seat. The Delete button will allow the user to remove the current record from both the screen and recordset. It also should remove the smiling face icon from the appropriate seat. Be sure to verify that the user wants to delete the record before doing so. The Return to Main button will cancel any changes made to the current record, then hide the frmGuest form.

h. Code the txtName control's Change event so that it does not allow the user to enter a record if the text box is empty. (*Hint*: See step c in Exercise 1.)

i. Set the txtName control's MaxLength property to the size of the fldName field. Set the txtMeal control's MaxLength property to the size of the fldMeal field.

j. Don't allow the user to click a seat in the banquet form while the guest form is showing. (*Hint*: See steps e through h in Exercise 1.)

k. Save and run the application. The smiling face icon should appear only in the seats corresponding to the records you entered in step b.

l. Enter the following guests:

Table number	Seat number	Name	Meal
1	10	Jacobs, Phil	Steak
4	40	Wright, Sam	Fish
4	31	Mendez, Jose	Steak

m. Mary Jacobs, who is sitting at seat number 9, can't make it to the wedding. Cancel her reservation.

n. Jose Mendez, who is sitting at seat number 31, wants to change his meal from steak to vegetarian. Make the appropriate change.

o. Stop the application, then print the project's code.

Exercises 4 through 7 are Discovery Exercises, which allow you to both discover solutions to problems on your own and experiment with material that is not covered in the tutorial.

discovery ▶ 4. In this exercise you will use the ADO data control and the Select command. You will learn how to use the And and Or logical operators in the Select command, as well as how to write a Select command that involves a Date field.

Scenario: Rock International records information about its employees in a Microsoft Access database named lc4.mdb. The database contains one table named tblEmploy. Figure 9-46 lists the contents of the tblEmploy table.

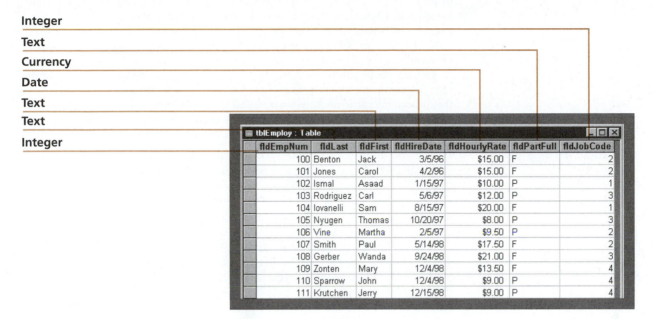

	fldEmpNum	fldLast	fldFirst	fldHireDate	fldHourlyRate	fldPartFull	fldJobCode
Integer							
Text							
Currency							
Date							
Text							
Text							
Integer							
	100	Benton	Jack	3/5/96	$15.00	F	2
	101	Jones	Carol	4/2/96	$15.00	F	2
	102	Ismal	Asaad	1/15/97	$10.00	P	1
	103	Rodriguez	Carl	5/6/97	$12.00	P	3
	104	Iovanelli	Sam	8/15/97	$20.00	F	1
	105	Nyugen	Thomas	10/20/97	$8.00	P	3
	106	Vine	Martha	2/5/97	$9.50	P	2
	107	Smith	Paul	5/14/98	$17.50	F	2
	108	Gerber	Wanda	9/24/98	$21.00	F	3
	109	Zonten	Mary	12/4/98	$13.50	F	4
	110	Sparrow	John	12/4/98	$9.00	P	4
	111	Krutchen	Jerry	12/15/98	$9.00	P	4

Figure 9-46

You will notice that the table contains the employee's number, last name, first name, hire date, and hourly rate of pay. It also contains fields named fldPartFull and fldJobCode. The fldPartFull field indicates whether the employee is full-time (F) or part-time (P). The fldJobCode field indicates whether the employee is an office manager (1), a secretary (2), an accountant (3), or a salesperson (4).

a. Open the lc4 (lc4.vbp) project, which is located in the Tut09 folder on your Student Disk. Save the form and the project as lc4Done in the Tut09 folder on your Student Disk.

b. Add the Microsoft ADO Data Control 6.0 (OLEDB) tool to the toolbox, then add an ADO data control to the form. Set the ADO data control's Name property to adoEmploy. Set its Height, Left, Top, and Width properties appropriately. Set its Caption property to "Click the arrow buttons to display the database records."

c. Set the ADO data control's ConnectionString and RecordSource properties appropriately. Use Microsoft Jet 3.51 OLE DB Provider as the provider for the lc4.mdb Access database, which is located in the Tut09 folder on your Student Disk. The RecordSource property should allow you to view all of the tblEmploy records in employee number order.

d. Bind the appropriate label controls to the ADO data control.

e. Save and run the application to verify that it displays the twelve records listed in Figure 9-46 in employee number order. Stop the application.

f. Open the Select Records button's Click event. You will use this event to enter eight Select commands, one at a time. (The Select commands that you need to enter are listed in the Click event. Recall that you assign the Select command to the ADO data control's RecordSource property. Also recall that you will need to use the ADO data control's Refresh method.) After entering the first Select command, save and run the application to verify that the Select command works, then place an apostrophe (') before the Select command to turn it into a comment. Enter the next Select command, verify that it works, then turn it into a comment. Continue this procedure until you have entered and tested the eight Select commands.

g. Save the application, then print the Select Records button's Click event procedure only.

discovery ▶ 5. In this exercise you will use the ADO data control and the Select command.

a. Open the lc5 (lc5.vbp) project, which is located in the Tut09 folder on your Student Disk. Save the form and the project as lc5Done.

b. Use Visual Data Manager (or Microsoft Access) to open the lc5.mdb database, which is located in the Tut09 folder on your Student Disk. You will notice that the database contains one table (tblPatron) and 10 records. The tblPatron table contains three fields: fldSeat, fldName, and fldPhone. fldSeat is an Integer field, and fldName and fldPhone are Text fields. Close Visual Data Manager (or Microsoft Access).

c. Add an ADO data control to the form. Set the ADO data control's Name property to adoPatron. Also set its other properties appropriately. You will need to link the ADO data control to the lc5.mdb database. The ADO data control should allow you to view all of the tblPatron records in seat number order.

d. Bind only the two label controls to the ADO data control. Do not bind the list box.

e. Study the existing code, then save and run the application to verify that it displays ten records. Stop the application.

f. Set the ADO control's Visible property to False.

g. Open the lstNum control's Click event. Code the Click event so that it displays the record that corresponds to the number selected in the list box. Save and run the application to verify that it works correctly. Stop the application, then print the code for the lstNum control's Click event only.

discovery ▶ 6. In this exercise you will use the Recordset object's EditMode property.

Scenario: Currently, if the user clicks the Return to Main button either after making a change to the current record or after adding a new record, the button's Click event will not save the change. In this exercise you will modify the lcCole application so that it asks the user if he or she wants to save the changes made to the record.

a. Open the lcCole (lcCole.vbp) project, which is located in the Tut09 folder on your Student Disk. Save the patron form as lc6Patron. Save the seat form as lc6Seat. Save the project as lc6Cole.

b. If you have access to the MSDN Library, research the Recordset object's EditMode property. Modify the Return to Main button's Click event so that it uses the EditMode property to determine if the user has added a new record or made any changes to the current record. If the user added a new record, but failed to complete the txtName text box before clicking the Return to Main button, cancel the update; otherwise, ask the user if he or she wants to update the record before returning to the seat form. If the user made a change to an existing record before clicking the Return to Main button, also ask the user if he or she wants to save the change before returning to the seat form.

c. Save and run the application.

d. Click seat number 1, which is not reserved, then click the Return to Main button. The button's Click event should cancel the update before hiding the patron form.

e. Now click seat number 1 again. This time enter your name and phone number in the text boxes, and then click the Return to Main button. The button's Click event should prompt you to save the change. Click the No button. The Return to Main button's Click event should cancel the update before hiding the patron form.

f. Click seat number 1 again. Enter your name and phone number, and then click the Return to Main button. When prompted to save the change, click the Yes button. The Return to Main button's Click event should update the recordset before hiding the patron form.

g. Click seat number 1 again. Change your phone number, then click the Return to Main button. When prompted to save the change, click the No button. The Return to Main button's Click event should cancel the update before hiding the patron form.

h. Click seat number 1 again. Change your phone number, then click the Return to Main button. When prompted to save the change, click the Yes button. The Return to Main button's Click event should update the record before hiding the patron form.

i. Click seat number 1 again, then click the Cancel Ticket button to remove your record from the recordset and the screen.

j. Stop the application, then print the Return to Main button's Click event procedure only.

 **7.** In this exercise, you will modify the lcCole application that you created in Lesson C so that it allows the user to select the database he or she would like to open.

a. Open the lcCole (lcCole.vbp) project, which is located in the Tut09 folder on your Student Disk.

b. Save the frmPatron form as lc7Patron in the Tut09 folder on your Student Disk. Save the frmSeat form as lc7Seat. Save the project as lc7Cole.

c. Select the 48 label controls on the frmSeat form. Change their Visible property to False.

d. Modify the label control that displays the application's instructions so that it tells the user that he or she will need to open a file before entering any reservations. (The label control is on the frmSeat form.)

e. Remove the code from the seat form's Load event.

f. Add the Microsoft Common Dialog Control 6.0 tool to the Visual Basic toolbox.

g. Add a Common Dialog control to the frmSeat form. Name the control dlgCole.

h. Add an Open command on the File menu. Use the pseudocode shown in Figure 9-47 to code the File menu's Open command. (*Hint:* Be sure to treat the Open dialog box's Cancel button as an error.)

1. Declare intIndex variable

2. Set the dlgCole control's Flags property so that the user can open only existing files

3. Set the dlgCole control's Filter property so that the Open dialog box displays only Microsoft Access databases (Recall that Access databases have a .mdb filename extension.)

4. Display the Open dialog box

5. Set the adoCole control's ConnectionString property (*Hint*: Cut the current value of the ConnectionString property from the Properties list, then paste it into the Open command's Code window. Remove the "A:\Tut09\cole.mdb" filename from the command. Use string concatenation to include the dlgCole control's FileName property in the command.)

6. Set the adoCole control's RecordSource property (*Hint*: Cut the current value of the RecordSource property from the Properties list, then paste it into the Open command's Code window.)

7. Invoke the adoCole control's Refresh method

8. Repeat for intIndex = 0 To 47

    a. Assign True to the current lblSeat control's Visible property

    b. Assign vbWhite to the current lblSeat control's BackColor property

End repeat for intIndex

9. Repeat while it is not the end of the recordset

    a. Subtract 1 from the value in the current record's fldSeat field, and assign the result to the intIndex variable

    b. Assign vbRed to the current lblSeat control's BackColor property

    c. Move the record pointer to the next record

End repeat while

Figure 9-47

    i. Save and run the application. Use the File menu's Open command to open the play1.mdb database, which does not contain any reservations. Reserve two seats for this play.

    j. Use the File menu's Open command to open the play2.mdb database, which contains five reservations. Cancel the reservations for seat numbers 4 and 10.

    k. Click File, then click Exit. Print the code for the File menu's Open command.

D E B U G G I N G

Technique

You can use the Debug menu's commands to help debug your code. For example, the Step Into command, which is Tutorial 9's Debugging Technique, allows you to execute the application's code one statement at a time. You can also use the Step Into button on the Debug toolbar to access the Step Into command; or you can press the F8 key on your keyboard.

On your Student Disk are two projects that are not working correctly. You will use the Step Into command to help you debug the projects.

Exercises

1. In this exercise you will use the Debugging Technique to help you debug the debug1 project.

To debug the first project:

1   Start Visual Basic, if necessary, and open the **debug1** (debug1.vbp) project, which is located in the Tut09 folder on your Student Disk. Save the form and the project as **deb1Done** in the Tut09 folder on your Student Disk.

2   Open the Calculate button's Click event procedure.

The code begins by declaring three local variables. The For Next (automatic counter) loop, which starts at 1 and stops at 4, then adds together the numbers 1 through 4. When the For Next loop stops, the value in intSum should be 10 (or 1 + 2 + 3 + 4). The `sngAvg = intSum / intNum` instruction then calculates the average of those four numbers; the answer, which is stored in the sngAvg variable, should be 2.5 (10 / 4). The `lblAnswer.Caption = sngAvg * 2` instruction multiplies the contents of the sngAvg variable (2.5) by 2, giving 5, and displays that amount in the lblAnswer control.

3   Close the Code window. **Run** the application, then click the **Calculate** button. Notice that a 4, instead of a 5 (the correct answer), appears in the Answer label control.

4   Click the **Exit** button to end the application.

Use the Step Into command to execute the code, line by line, until you find the problem.

5   Click **Debug** on the menu bar, then click **Step Into**. Visual Basic highlights the `Private Sub Form_Load()` instruction, which is the first statement Visual Basic executes in this application.

Recall that you can also use the F8 key on your keyboard to access the Debug menu's Step Into command.

6   Press the F8 key on your keyboard. Visual Basic highlights the `frmCalc.Top = (Screen.Height - frmCalc.Height) / 2` instruction—the second instruction executed in this application.

7   Press the F8 key three more times. The frmCalc form appears on the screen.

8   Click the **Calculate** button. Visual Basic highlights the `Private Sub cmdCalc_Click()` instruction.

9   Press the F8 key, repeatedly and slowly, until the `lblAnswer.Caption = sngAvg * 2` instruction is highlighted. As you continue pressing the F8 key, pay close attention to which instructions are being executed.

10   When the `lblAnswer.Caption = sngAvg * 2` instruction is highlighted, position the I-bar I on `sngAvg` in the instruction, as shown in Figure 9-48.

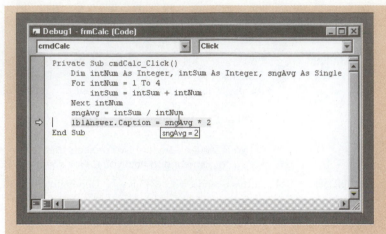

Figure 9-48: Contents of sngAvg variable shown in Code window

Notice that the sngAvg variable contains the value 2 instead of the value 2.5. The sngAvg variable gets its value from the `sngAvg = intSum / intNum` instruction, which is directly above the highlighted instruction. View the values in the intSum and intNum variables.

11 Position the I on `intSum` in the `sngAvg = intSum / intNum` instruction. The value in `intSum`, 10, is correct.

12 Position the I on `intNum` in the `sngAvg = intSum / intNum` instruction. The value in intNum, 5, is incorrect; it should be 4.

Recall that when a For Next loop ends, the value in its *counter* variable is always more than the *endvalue* if the *stepvalue* is positive. In this case, you will need to subtract the number 1 (the *stepvalue*) from intNum before using that variable in the average calculation. Therefore, the instruction to calculate the average of the first four numbers is correctly written as `sngAvg = intSum / (intNum - 1)`. At this point you can either press the F8 key to continue processing the code, line by line, or you can use the Continue button on the toolbar to continue processing the application's code in the usual manner. Just for practice, use the F8 key.

13 Press the **F8** key two more times, then close the cmdCalc control's Code window.

14 When the form appears on the screen, click the **Exit** button, then press the **F8** key until the application ends.

15 Open the Calculate button's Click event procedure. Change the `sngAvg = intSum / intNum` instruction to sngAvg = intSum / (intNum - 1).

16 Close the Code window. **Save** and **run** the application, then click the **Calculate** button. The number 5 should appear in the Answer label control. Click the **Exit** button to end the application.

2. In this exercise you will use the Debugging Technique to help you debug the debug2 project.

To debug the second project:

1   Open the **debug2** (debug2.vbp) project, which is located in the Tut09 folder on your Student Disk. Save the form and the project as **deb2Done** in the Tut09 folder on your Student Disk.

2   View the application's code, then close the Code window.

3 **Run** the application. Type **25000** in the Old salary text box, then click the **Calculate New Salary** button. $25,000.00 appears as the old salary, 6.00% appears as the raise rate, and $26,500.00 appears as the new salary.

4 Click the **Calculate New Salary** button again. Instead of $25,000.00, 6.00%, and $26,500.00, $0.00 appears as the old salary, 5.00% appears as the raise rate, and $0.00 appears as the new salary.

5 Click the **Exit** button to end the application.

6 Press the **F8** key to run the application, line by line. When the frmSalary form appears, type **25000** in the Old salary text box, then click the Calculate New Salary button. (Remember that the problem occurs after you click the Calculate New Salary button the second time.) Find and then correct the problem. When the application is working correctly, print the application's code.

TUTORIAL
10

Variable Arrays

Creating a Payroll Application

case ▶ Colfax Industries has asked you to create an application that the payroll clerk can use to prepare the company's weekly payroll report. The application will need to calculate each employee's gross pay, federal withholding tax (FWT), Social Security and Medicare (FICA) tax, and net pay. Before you can complete this application, you will need to learn how to create and manipulate a variable array, which is simply a collection of variables that are related in some way. You will use a variable array to store the FWT tables, which the application will use to calculate each employee's FWT.

Previewing the Completed Application

As you've done in previous tutorials, you will preview the application before creating it.

To preview the completed application:

1   If necessary, start Windows, then place your Student Disk in the appropriate disk drive. Use the Run command on the Start menu to run the **Payroll** (Payroll.exe) file, which is located in the Tut10 folder on your Student Disk. The Payroll application's user interface appears on the screen. See Figure 10-1.

Ed Siskowski's hours worked

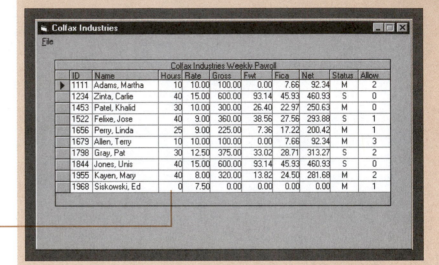

Figure 10-1: Payroll application's user interface

The interface contains a File menu, an ADO data control, and a new control, called the DataGrid control. You will learn about the DataGrid control, which allows you to view the records stored in a database, in Lesson B.

When you run this application, the form's Load event reads the FWT tables from a sequential access file on your Student Disk, and then enters the tables into a variable array in the computer's memory. You will learn about variable arrays in Lesson A.

2   Click the **cell that contains Ed Siskowski's hours worked**.

HELP? A cell is the intersection of a column and row in the grid. The cell that contains Ed Siskowski's hours worked is located in the third column, last row of the grid.

3   Change Ed's hours worked from 0 to **40**, then press the **Enter** key. The DataGrid control calculates and displays Ed's gross pay, FICA tax, FWT, and net pay—the values 300.00, 18.61, 22.97, and 258.42, respectively.

4   Click **File** on the menu bar, and then click **Exit** to end the payroll application.

You will learn about variable arrays in Lesson A. You will begin coding the payroll application in Lesson B, and then complete it in Lesson C.

LESSON A
objectives

In this lesson you will learn how to:
- Create a one-dimensional variable array
- Search a variable array
- Compute the average of an array's contents
- Find the highest entry in an array
- Update the contents of an array
- Create a two-dimensional variable array

Storing Data in a Variable Array

Variable Arrays

In addition to control arrays, which you learned how to create in Tutorial 5, Visual Basic also allows you to create variable arrays. A **variable array** is a group of variables that have the same name and data type and are related in some way. For example, each variable in the array may contain the name of a state, or each may contain an income tax rate, or each may contain an employee record (name, Social Security number, pay rate, and so on).

Unlike control arrays, you can't see variable arrays on the screen. It may help to picture a variable array as a group of tiny boxes inside the computer's memory. You can write information to the boxes and you can read information from the boxes; you just can't see the boxes.

Although variable arrays in Visual Basic can have as many as 60 dimensions, the most commonly used arrays in business applications are one-dimensional and two-dimensional. Figure 10-2 illustrates both a one-dimensional and a two-dimensional array. (Arrays having more than two dimensions, which are used in scientific and engineering applications, are beyond the scope of this book.)

One-dimensional array:				
Nebraska	New Jersey	New Mexico	Tennessee	Texas

Two-dimensional array:		
Adams, Bill 111-11-1111 8.55	Asaf, Nancy 222-22-2222 10.65	Bell, Jack 333-33-3333 7.50
Celt, Carl 444-44-4444 6.35	Dorey, Jill 555-55-5555 7.65	Doty, Jim 666-66-6666 5.25

Figure 10-2: Illustrations of a one-dimensional and a two-dimensional array

As Figure 10-2 shows, a **one-dimensional array** is simply a row of variables. A **two-dimensional array**, on the other hand, resembles a table in that it has rows and columns.

It is not necessary for an array's name to include the word "Array".

Similar to the way Visual Basic assigns a unique number, called an **index**, to each of the controls in a control array, Visual Basic also assigns a unique number, called a **subscript**, to each of the variables in a variable array. You refer to each variable in the array by the array's name and the variable's subscript. The subscript is specified in a set of parentheses immediately following the name. For example, strStateArray(5)—read "strStateArray sub five"—refers to variable number 5 in a one-dimensional array named strStateArray. udtEmpArray(2, 3)—read "udtEmpArray sub two comma three"—refers to the variable located in row 2, column 3, of a two-dimensional array named udtEmpArray. Figure 10-3 illustrates this naming convention.

One-dimensional array named strStateArray:				
strStateArray(1)	strStateArray(2)	strStateArray(3)	strStateArray(4)	strStateArray(5)
Nebraska	New Jersey	New Mexico	Tennessee	Texas

Two-dimensional array named udtEmpArray:		
udtEmpArray(1,1)	udtEmpArray(1,2)	udtEmpArray(1,3)
Adams, Bill 111-11-1111 8.55	Asaf, Nancy 222-22-2222 10.65	Bell, Jack 333-33-3333 7.50
Celt, Carl 444-44-4444 6.35	Dorey, Jill 555-55-5555 7.65	Doty, Jim 666-66-6666 5.25
udtEmpArray(2,1)	udtEmpArray(2,2)	udtEmpArray(2,3)

Figure 10-3: Names of the variables in a one-dimensional and a two-dimensional array

Advantages of Variable Arrays

Programmers use variable arrays to store related data in the internal memory of the computer. By doing so, a programmer can increase the efficiency of an application because data stored inside the computer can be both written and read much faster than data stored in a file on a disk. The following analogy may help illustrate this point. Think of the computer's internal memory as being comparable to the memory cells in your brain. Now assume that someone asks you to name the first U.S. President. Because that information is already stored in your brain, you can respond almost immediately with "George Washington." Similarly, the computer has almost immediate access to the information stored in internal memory—the memory cells in *its* brain.

Now assume that someone asks you to name the eighth U.S. President. If that information is not stored in your brain, you will need to open a history book, find the page containing the listing of presidents, and then read the eighth name—a much more time-consuming process. Similarly, accessing information that is not stored in the computer's internal memory—rather, it is stored in a disk file—takes the computer much longer because it must wait for the disk drive to locate the needed information and then read that information into memory.

In addition to speedier access of information, another advantage of using an array is that data can be entered into an array once, usually at the beginning of the program, and can then be used by the application as many times as desired. For example, assume that you are creating a payroll program. In order to compute the net pay for an employee, his or her federal withholding tax must be calculated. By storing the federal withholding tax table in an array, at the beginning of the program, the application can use that stored information to calculate each employee's federal withholding tax.

Now that you know what variable arrays are and why they are used, you will learn how to create a one-dimensional array.

Creating a One-Dimensional Variable Array

As with simple variables, you must declare a variable array before you can use it. (A **simple variable** is a variable that does not belong to an array.) You declare a variable array with the Dim statement, which is the same statement you use to declare a simple variable. The syntax of the Dim statement to declare a one-dimensional array is **Dim** *arrayname*(*lower subscript* **To** *upper subscript*) **As** *datatype*. *Arrayname* is the name of the variable array; the name must follow the same rules as for simple variables. *Lower subscript* and *upper subscript* are numbers that define the lowest and the highest subscript, respectively, in the array. Although the subscripts can be numbers in the Long data type range, in most business applications, the lower subscript is set to either 0 (zero) or 1. (The applications in this book will use a lower subscript of 1.) *Datatype* is the type of data that the array variables will store; recall that each of the variables in the array has the same data type. The `Dim strStateArray(1 to 5) as String` instruction, for example, declares a one-dimensional array named strStateArray that contains five String variables. The name of the first String variable in the array is strStateArray(1), the name of the second is strStateArray(2), and so on. Figure 10-4 shows other examples of `Dim` statements that create one-dimensional variable arrays.

Dim statement	Result
Dim strMonthArray(1 to 12) as String	Creates an array of 12 String variables
Dim intSquareArray(1 to 5) as Integer	Creates an array of 5 Integer variables
Dim sngNumArray(1 to 10) as Single	Creates an array of 10 Single variables
Dim udtEmpArray(1 to 20) as EmpStruc	Creates an array of 20 EmpStruc variables

Figure 10-4: Examples of Dim statements that create arrays

The `Dim` statement both creates and initializes the array variables in memory. As with simple variables, String and Variant array variables are initialized to a zero-length (empty) string; Integer, Long, Single, Double, and Currency array variables are initialized to 0 (zero). Array variables also can be declared as a user-defined data type, which you learned about in Tutorial 8. In those cases, the field variables that make up the data type are initialized in the same manner as simple variables.

After you declare an array, you can then store data in it.

Storing Data in a One-Dimensional Variable Array

You can enter data into a one-dimensional array in a variety of ways. The examples shown in Figure 10-5, for instance, can be used to enter data into the arrays created by the Dim statements in Figure 10-4.

Example 1:

```
strMonthArray(1) = "January"
strMonthArray(2) = "February"
strMonthArray(3) = "March"
strMonthArray(4) = "April"
strMonthArray(5) = "May"
strMonthArray(6) = "June"
strMonthArray(7) = "July"
strMonthArray(8) = "August"
strMonthArray(9) = "September"
strMonthArray(10) = "October"
strMonthArray(11) = "November"
strMonthArray(12) = "December"
```

Example 2:

```
For intNum = 1 to 5
    intSquareArray(intNum) = intNum * intNum
Next intNum
```

Example 3:

```
For intNum = 1 to 10
    intNumArray(intNum) = Val(InputBox("Enter a number"))
Next intNum
```

Example 4:

```
Do While Not EOF(1)
    intNum = intNum + 1
    Input #1, udtEmpArray(intNum).Name, udtEmpArray(intNum).Salary
Loop
```

Figure 10-5: Examples of entering data into an array

In the first example, the 12 assignment statements will enter the names of the 12 months into the strMonthArray variable array. In the second example, a For Next loop will fill the intSquareArray array with the square of the numbers from 1 through 5. In the third example, the InputBox function within the For Next loop will enter the user's responses into the intNumArray array. In the fourth example, the Input # statement within the Do While loop will read the data from a sequential access file and store it in the udtEmpArray variable array.

Now look at an application that uses a one-dimensional array.

The President Application

On your Student Disk is an application that uses a one-dimensional variable array to store the names of the first 10 U.S. presidents.

To open the President application:

1   Start Visual Basic, if necessary, and open the **Pres** (Pres.vbp) project, which is located in the Tut10 folder on your Student Disk. Save the form and the project as **laPres**, then click the **form** to select it. See Figure 10-6.

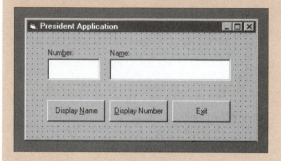

Figure 10-6: The President application's user interface

You can use this application to study for a test on U.S. presidents. When you run the application, it will store the names of the first 10 U.S. presidents in a variable array named strPresArray. The name of the first president will be stored in strPresArray(1), the name of the second president will be stored in strPresArray(2), and so on. You can enter a number between 1 and 10 in the Number text box and then click the Display Name button to display the corresponding president's name. You can also enter the name of a president in the Name text box and then click the Display Number button to display the president's number.

Almost all of the President application is already coded for you; only the instruction to declare the strPresArray variable array is missing. You will enter that instruction next.

Coding the President Application

The Click events of both the Display Name and Display Number buttons will need to access the data stored in the strPresArray array, so you will declare the variable array as a form-level array. As you learned in Tutorial 3, form-level variables are declared in the General Declarations section of the form and are available to all procedures in the form.

To declare a form-level variable array:

1   Open the form's General Declarations section, which already contains the Option Explicit statement.

The strPresArray array will need to store 10 names, so you will declare it as a String array containing 10 variables.

2 In the blank line below the `Option Explicit` statement, type **dim strPresArray(1 to 10) as string** and press the **Enter** key.

Now view the code already entered in the form's Load event.

The Form's Load Event Procedure

The form's Load event procedure will enter the names of the presidents into the strPresArray variable array as soon as the form is loaded into memory. View the code in the Load event procedure.

To view the form's Load event procedure:

1 Open the form's Load event procedure. See Figure 10-7.

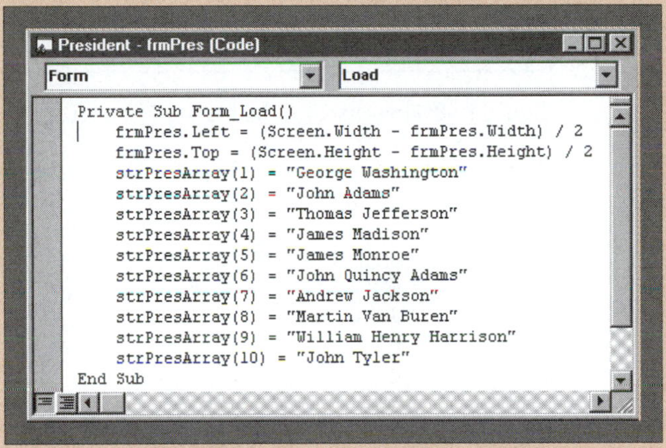

```
President - frmPres (Code)

Form                              Load

Private Sub Form_Load()
    frmPres.Left = (Screen.Width - frmPres.Width) / 2
    frmPres.Top = (Screen.Height - frmPres.Height) / 2
    strPresArray(1) = "George Washington"
    strPresArray(2) = "John Adams"
    strPresArray(3) = "Thomas Jefferson"
    strPresArray(4) = "James Madison"
    strPresArray(5) = "James Monroe"
    strPresArray(6) = "John Quincy Adams"
    strPresArray(7) = "Andrew Jackson"
    strPresArray(8) = "Martin Van Buren"
    strPresArray(9) = "William Henry Harrison"
    strPresArray(10) = "John Tyler"
End Sub
```

Figure 10-7: Load event procedure

When the application is run and the form is loaded into memory, the 10 assignment statements shown in Figure 10-7 will enter the names of the first 10 U.S. presidents into the strPresArray variable array.

Next, view the Display Name button's Click event procedure, which will display the name of the president that corresponds to the number entered in the Number text box.

The Display Name Button

When the user enters a number in the Number text box and then clicks the Display Name button, the name of the president that corresponds to the number should appear in the Name text box. The flowchart for the Display Name button's Click event is shown in Figure 10-8.

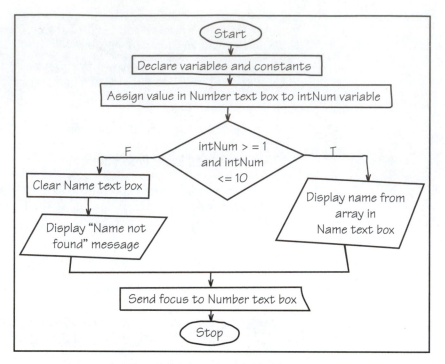

Figure 10-8: Flowchart for the Display Name button's Click event procedure

You will now open the Display Name button's Click event procedure and view its code.

To view the code in the Display Name button's Click event procedure:

1 Open the cmdName control's Click event. Maximize the Code window. See Figure 10-9.

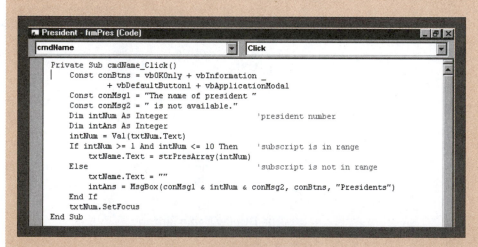

```
President - frmPres [Code]
cmdName                              Click

Private Sub cmdName_Click()
    Const conBtns = vbOKOnly + vbInformation _
            + vbDefaultButton1 + vbApplicationModal
    Const conMsg1 = "The name of president "
    Const conMsg2 = " is not available."
    Dim intNum As Integer                'president number
    Dim intAns As Integer
    intNum = Val(txtNum.Text)
    If intNum >= 1 And intNum <= 10 Then    'subscript is in range
        txtName.Text = strPresArray(intNum)
    Else                                 'subscript is not in range
        txtName.Text = ""
        intAns = MsgBox(conMsg1 & intNum & conMsg2, conBtns, "Presidents")
    End If
    txtNum.SetFocus
End Sub
```

Figure 10-9: Display Name button's Click event procedure

The code first declares three local constants and two local Integer variables named intNum and intAns. The three constants and the intAns variable will be used by the MsgBox function. The code then assigns the numeric equivalent of the txtNum control's Text property to the intNum variable. The selection structure that follows the assignment statement verifies that the intNum variable contains a valid subscript, which is a subscript from 1 through 10. If intNum contains a value that is greater than or equal to 1 and less than or equal to 10, then the txtName.Text = `strPresArray(intNum)` instruction assigns the contents of the strPresArray variable, whose subscript is contained in the intNum variable, to the Text property of the txtName control. If, for example, the intNum variable contains the number 1, the instruction assigns the contents of the strPresArray(1) variable—George Washington—to the txtName control. If, however, the subscript does not fall in the valid range, the selection structure clears the contents of the txtName control and displays a message informing the user that the president's name is not available. The `txtNum.SetFocus` instruction sends the focus to the Number text box.

2   Close the Code window.

See how the Display Name button works.

3   **Save** and **run** the application. The code contained in the form's General Declarations section creates and initializes, to a zero-length string, a variable array named strPresArray. The array contains 10 String variables; each variable is named strPresArray, and each has a unique subscript from 1 to 10. The form's Load event procedure then enters the names of the first 10 U.S. presidents into the array and the user interface appears on the screen. At this point the variable array in memory resembles Figure 10-10.

George Washington
John Adams
Thomas Jefferson
James Madison
James Monroe
John Quincy Adams
Andrew Jackson
Martin Van Buren
William Henry Harrison
John Tyler

Note: You can picture a one-dimensional array as either a row of variables, as shown in Figures 10-2 and 10-3, or as a column of variables, as shown in this figure.

Figure 10-10: Status of strPresArray array in memory

First test the application by entering a valid number—the number 5, for example—in the Number text box.

4   Type **5** in the Number text box and click the **Display Name** button. The Click event assigns the number 5 to the intNum variable. Because you entered a valid subscript, the `txtName.Text = strPresArray(intNum)` statement displays the contents of the strPresArray(5) variable—James Monroe—in the txtName control.

Now see what happens if you enter a number that is not within the lower subscript and the upper subscript of the array; in other words, the number is not within the range of 1 to 10, inclusive.

5   Type **12** in the Number text box and click the **Display Name** button. Visual Basic clears the contents of the txtName control and displays the message "The name of president 12 is not available."

tip

Always test your application with both valid and invalid data. Valid data in this application is any number from 1 through 10, which are the valid subscripts for the array; invalid data is any number that is either less than 1 or greater than 10.

6   Click the **OK** button to remove the message, then click the **Exit** button to end the application. Visual Basic returns to the design screen.

Now view the code in the Display Number button, which displays the number corresponding to the name of the president entered in the Name text box.

The Display Number Button

You can use the Display Number button to display the number of the president whose name is contained in the Name text box. Figure 10-11 shows the flowchart for the Display Number button's Click event procedure.

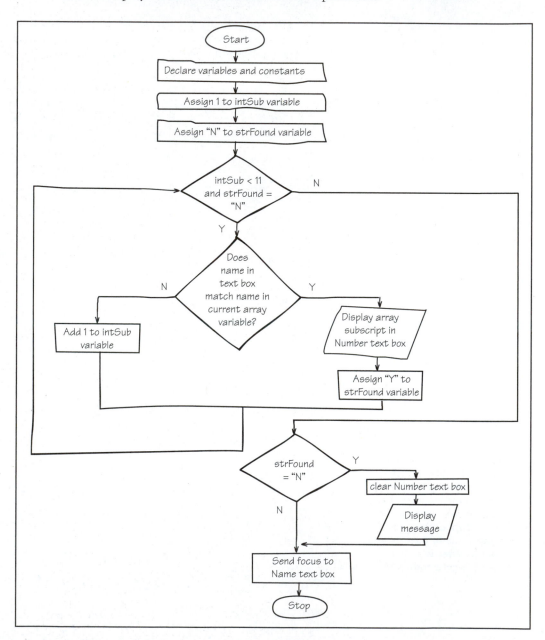

Figure 10-11: Flowchart for Display Number button's Click event procedure

Now view the code that corresponds to the flowchart. The code has already been entered in the Display Number button's Click event procedure.

To view the code in the Display Number button's Click event procedure:

1 Double-click the **Display Number** button, then maximize the Code window. The cmdNum control's Click event procedure appears as shown in Figure 10-12.

tip

You learned about the Trim function in Tutorial 8.

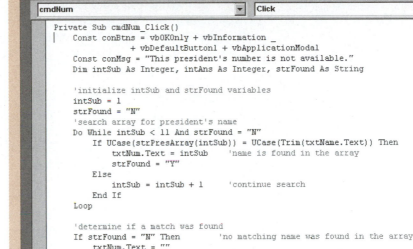

```
President - frmPres (Code)                                          _ | B | X

cmdNum                          ▼     Click                              ▼

Private Sub cmdNum_Click()
    Const conBtns = vbOKOnly + vbInformation _
                    + vbDefaultButton1 + vbApplicationModal
    Const conMsg = "This president's number is not available."
    Dim intSub As Integer, intAns As Integer, strFound As String

    'initialize intSub and strFound variables
    intSub = 1
    strFound = "N"
    'search array for president's name
    Do While intSub < 11 And strFound = "N"
        If UCase(strPresArray(intSub)) = UCase(Trim(txtName.Text)) Then
            txtNum.Text = intSub      'name is found in the array
            strFound = "Y"
        Else
            intSub = intSub + 1       'continue search
        End If
    Loop

    'determine if a match was found
    If strFound = "N" Then          'no matching name was found in the array
        txtNum.Text = ""
        intAns = MsgBox(conMsg, conBtns, "Presidents")
    End If
    txtName.SetFocus
End Sub
```

Figure 10-12: Display Number button's Click event procedure

After declaring the necessary variables and constants, the code initializes the intSub variable to 1 and the strFound variable to "N". Both the intSub and strFound variables are used by the Do While loop to search each of the 10 variables in the array, one at a time, for a name that matches the one entered in the Name text box. If a matching name is found in an array variable, then the array variable's subscript, which is stored in the intSub variable, is assigned to the Number text box on the form, and the strFound variable is set to "Y" to indicate that the search was successful; otherwise, the intSub variable is incremented by one so that the search can continue with the next array variable. Notice that the Do While loop continues searching the array while the intSub variable is less than 11 and the strFound variable equals the letter "N". The Do While loop will stop when either the entire array has been searched (intSub = 11) or when a match is found (strFound = "Y").

After the Do While loop completes its processing, the second selection structure in the procedure is processed. That selection structure compares the contents of the strFound variable with the letter "N". If the strFound variable contains an "N", which means that the Do While loop instructions did not find a matching name in the array, then the MsgBox function displays an appropriate message to the user. The procedure ends by sending the focus to the Name text box. Observe how the Display Number button works.

To observe how the Display Number button works:

1   Close the Code window, then **run** the application.

First enter a name that is in the array.

2   Press the **Tab** key to move the insertion point to the Name text box, then type **John Adams** and click the **Display Number** button. The Display Number button's Click event procedure searches each variable in the array, looking for the name John Adams. Because that name matches the name in the second variable in the array, the number 2 appears in the Number text box. John Adams, therefore, was the second U.S. president.

HELP? If the number 2 does not appear in the Number text box, you may have mistyped the president's name. Type John Adams in the Name text box again and click the Display Number button. Be sure to spell the name correctly and include a space between John and Adams.

Now enter a name that is not in the array.

3   Type **George Bush** in the Name text box and click the **Display Number** button. Because the name George Bush is not in the president array, the MsgBox function displays the message, "This president's number is not available."

4   Click the **OK** button to remove the message, then click the **Exit** button. Visual Basic returns to the design screen.

In the next example you will use an array to store student scores contained in a sequential access file. You will then use the information in the array to calculate the average and highest score. You will also learn how to update the contents of an array.

The Test Score Application

On your Student Disk is an application that uses a one-dimensional array to store the test scores earned by 20 students. The 20 test scores have already been entered into a sequential access file for you. Figure 10-13 shows the test.dat file displayed in WordPad.

tip

You can recreate the test.dat file by using Windows to copy the test.bak file to test.dat. Both files are located in the Tut10 folder on your Student Disk.

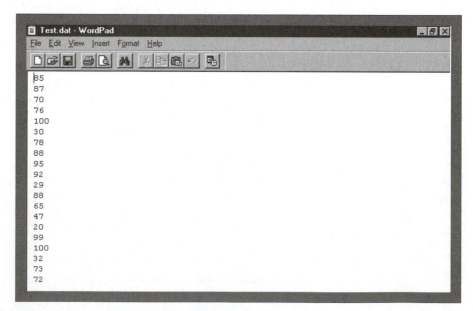

Figure 10-13: test.dat displayed in WordPad

Open the test score application and view its code.

To view the code in the test score application:

1 Open the **Test** (Test.vbp) project, which is located in the Tut10 folder on your Student Disk. Save the form and the project as laTest.

2 Click the **form** to select it. The user interface appears on the screen, as shown in Figure 10-14.

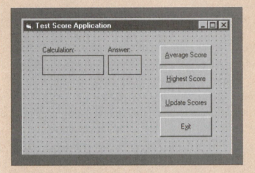

Figure 10-14: Test score application's user interface

An instructor can use this application to calculate and display the average score and the highest score earned by the 20 students. He or she can also use the application to increase each student's test score by a set amount. (Some instructors give additional points to each student to compensate for poorly written test questions.) First, view the code in the form's General Declarations section.

3 Open the form's General Declarations section. See Figure 10-15.

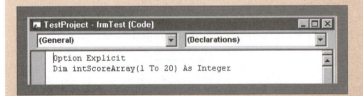

Figure 10-15: Form's General Declarations section

The code begins with the `Option Explicit` statement. The `Dim intScoreArray(1 to 20) As Integer` instruction then declares a form-level array named intScoreArray, which contains 20 Integer variables. Next, look at the code in the form's Load event procedure, where the array is filled with data.

4 Open the form's Load event, then maximize the Code window. See Figure 10-16. If your Student Disk is in the B drive, then change the drive letter in the Open statement to b:.

if your Student Disk is in the B drive, change the drive letter to b:

```
TestProject - frmTest [Code]
Form                              Load

Private Sub Form_Load()
    frmTest.Left = (Screen.Width - frmTest.Width) / 2
    frmTest.Top = (Screen.Height - frmTest.Height) / 2
    Dim intNum As Integer
    Open "a:\Tut10\test.dat" For Input As #1        'open file
    For intNum = 1 To 20                            'fill array with data
        Input #1, intScoreArray(intNum)
    Next intNum
    Close #1
End Sub
```

Figure 10-16: Load event procedure

When the form is loaded into memory, the Open statement will open the test.dat sequential access file for Input. The For Next loop and the Input # statement will then read the 20 test scores from the file, one at a time, and store them in the 20 variables in the intScoreArray array. Notice that the For Next loop's counter variable, intNum, is used as the array subscript. When the For Next loop completes its processing, the sequential access file is closed.

The Average Score button's Click event is the next procedure you will view.

The Average Score Button

The Average Score button will calculate and display the average test score earned by the 20 students. Figure 10-17 shows the flowchart for the Average Score button's Click event procedure.

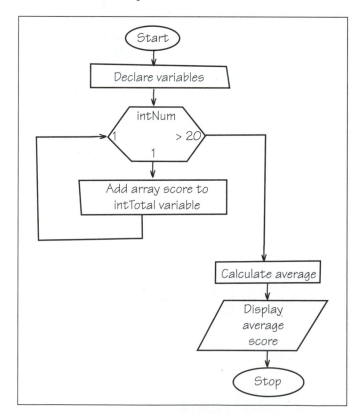

Figure 10-17: Flowchart for Average Score button's Click event procedure

Now view the code entered in the Average Score button's Click event.

To view the code entered in the Average Score button's Click event, then run the application:

1   Open the cmdAvg control's Click event. See Figure 10-18.

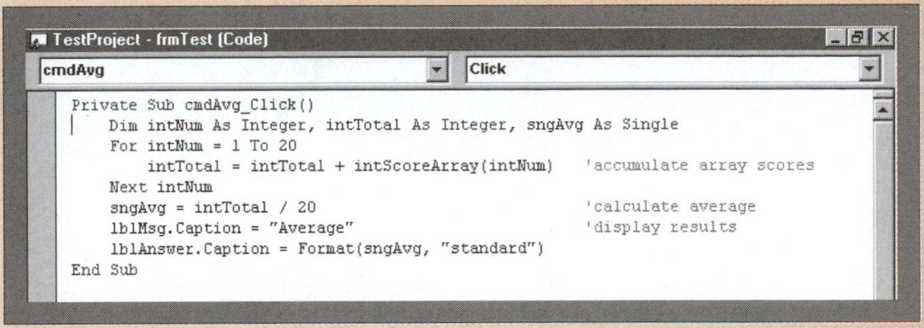

```
TestProject - frmTest (Code)                                    _ |8|X
cmdAvg                              ▼     Click                          ▼

Private Sub cmdAvg_Click()
    Dim intNum As Integer, intTotal As Integer, sngAvg As Single
    For intNum = 1 To 20
        intTotal = intTotal + intScoreArray(intNum)     'accumulate array scores
    Next intNum
    sngAvg = intTotal / 20                               'calculate average
    lblMsg.Caption = "Average"                           'display results
    lblAnswer.Caption = Format(sngAvg, "standard")
End Sub
```

Figure 10-18: Average Score button's Click event procedure

The code declares three local variables: intNum, intTotal, and sngAvg. The For Next loop instructions add the 20 test scores from the array, one at a time, to the intTotal variable. After the test scores are accumulated, the average score is calculated and then displayed in the appropriate label control. Observe how the Average Score button works.

2   Close the Code window, then **run** the application. The form's General Declarations section creates the intScoreArray variable array. The form's Load event procedure then reads the scores from the sequential access file and enters them into the array. The user interface then appears on the screen.

3   Click the **Average Score** button. The button's Click event procedure accumulates the 20 scores. The procedure then calculates and displays the average—71.30.

4   Click the **Exit** button to end the application. Visual Basic returns to the design screen.

Now look at the Highest Score button's Click event procedure, which will display the highest test score.

The Highest Score Button

The Highest Score button will display the highest test score earned by the 20 students. Figure 10-19 shows the flowchart for the Highest Score button's Click event procedure.

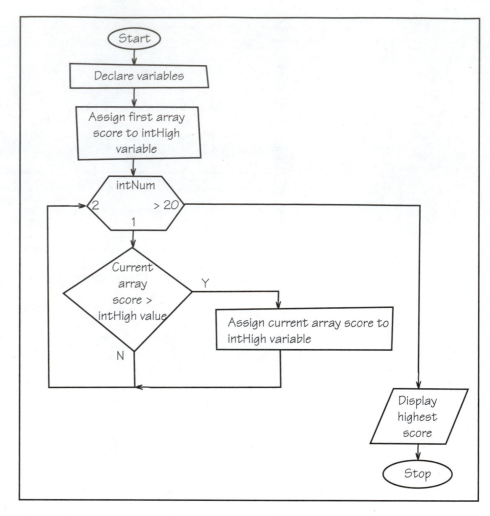

Figure 10-19: Flowchart for the Highest Score button's Click event procedure

Now view the code entered in the Highest Score button's Click event.

To view the code entered in the Highest Score button's Click event, then run the application:

1 Open the Highest Score button's Click event procedure, then maximize the Code window. See Figure 10-20.

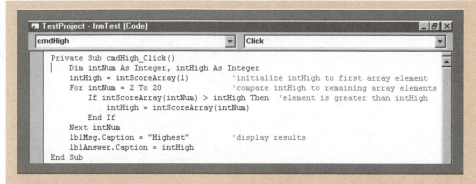

Figure 10-20: Highest Score button's Click event procedure

The code first declares two local Integer variables, intNum and intHigh. It then assigns the contents of the first array variable's test score to the intHigh variable. The For Next loop compares the contents of each of the remaining variables in the array—the variables with subscripts of 2 through 20—to the contents of the intHigh variable. If the test score contained in an array variable is greater than the test score contained in the intHigh variable, then the array variable's test score is assigned to intHigh. For example, if intHigh contains the number 85 and the array variable contains the number 90, then the number 90 is assigned to intHigh. The remaining variables in the array are then compared to the number 90, the current value of intHigh. When the For Next loop completes its processing, the intHigh variable will contain the highest test score stored in the array; that score is then displayed in the appropriate label control on the form. Run the application to see how the Highest Score button works.

2 Close the Code window, then **run** the application. Click the **Highest Score** button. The Click event procedure searches the array for the highest test score and then displays that test score, 100, in the form.

3 Click the **Exit** button. Visual Basic returns to the design screen.

The last procedure you will view in this application is the Click event procedure for the Update Scores button.

The Update Scores Button

The Update Scores button will allow the instructor to update each student's score by a set amount. Figure 10-21 shows the flowchart for the Update Scores button's Click event procedure.

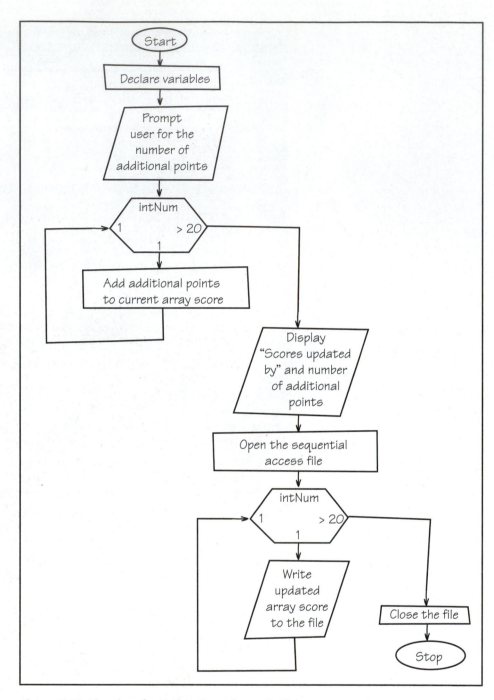

Figure 10-21: Flowchart for Update Scores button's Click event procedure

View the code entered in the Update Scores button's Click event.

To view the code entered in the Update Scores button's Click event, then run the application:

1   Open the Update Scores button's Click event, then maximize the Code window. See Figure 10-22. If your Student Disk is in the B drive, then change the drive letter in the Open statement to b:.

if your Student Disk is in the B drive, change the drive letter to b:

```
TestProject - frmTest (Code)                                      _ □ X

cmdUpdate                            ▼    Click                        ▼

Private Sub cmdUpdate_Click()
    Dim intNum As Integer, intIncrease As Integer
    intIncrease = Val(InputBox("Enter the number of additional points:"))
    For intNum = 1 To 20          'add additional points to each score in the array
        intScoreArray(intNum) = intScoreArray(intNum) + intIncrease
    Next intNum
    lblMsg.Caption = "Scores updated by"        'display message
    lblAnswer.Caption = intIncrease

    Open "a:\Tut10\Test.dat" For Output As #1    'open file
    For intNum = 1 To 20                          'write array contents to file
        Write #1, intScoreArray(intNum)
    Next intNum
    Close #1                                      'close file
End Sub
```

Figure 10-22: Update Scores button's Click event procedure

This procedure declares two local Integer variables, intNum and intIncrease. The InputBox function, which you learned about in Tutorial 3, prompts the user to enter the number of additional points and stores the numeric equivalent of the user's response in the intIncrease variable. The For Next loop then adds the value in the intIncrease variable to each test score in the array. When the For Next loop completes its processing, the message "Scores updated by" and the contents of the intIncrease variable are displayed on the form. The test.dat sequential file is then opened for Output, and the updated scores are written from the array to the file on your Student Disk. The sequential file is then closed. Observe how the Update Scores button works.

2   Close the Code window, then **run** the application.

Add four points to each student's test score.

3   Click the **Update Scores** button. Type **4** in the dialog box, then press the **Enter** key to select the OK button. Visual Basic adds 4 to each score in the array and then writes the updated information to the sequential access file on your Student Disk. "Scores updated by" appears in the Calculation box; the number 4, which is the number of points added to each score, appears in the Answer box.

One way to prove that the Update Scores button increased the test scores by 4 is to click the Highest Score button. Recall that before you updated the test scores, the highest score was 100.

4   Click the **Highest Score** button. Notice that the highest score is now 104 instead of 100.

Now add a negative four points to each test score—in other words, subtract four points from the scores.

5 Click the **Update Scores** button, type – 4 (be sure to type the minus sign) in the dialog box and press the **Enter** key. Visual Basic adds a negative 4 to each score in the array, then displays "Scores updated by" and a −4 in the label controls on the form. Visual Basic then writes the updated information to the sequential access file on your Student Disk.

If you click the Highest Score button, the highest score again should be 100.

6 Click the **Highest Score** button. The highest score is now 100.

7 Click the **Exit** button. Visual Basic returns to the design screen.

In the last example covered in this lesson, you will learn how to create and use a two-dimensional array.

The Classroom Application

On your Student Disk is an application that uses a two-dimensional variable array to store the names of the eight students seated in a classroom. The names of the eight students have already been entered into a sequential access file for you. Figure 10-23 shows the class.dat file displayed in WordPad.

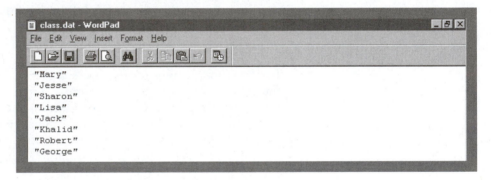

Figure 10-23: class.dat file displayed in WordPad

tip

Recall that an array name does not have to include the word "Array."

Almost all of the classroom application is already coded for you; only the `Dim` statement that declares the strClass two-dimensional String array, which will store the names of the eight students, is missing. The syntax of the `Dim` statement to declare a two-dimensional array is **Dim** *arrayname*(*lower subscript* **To** *upper subscript*, *lower subscript* **To** *upper subscript*) **As** *datatype*. The first set of subscripts represents the number of rows in the array; the second set represents the number of columns in the array. In this case the classroom has four rows and two columns, so the proper `Dim` statement is `Dim strClass(1 to 4, 1 to 2) As String`. First, you will enter the missing `Dim` statement; then you will view the remaining code before running the application.

To open the Classroom application and enter the `Dim` statement that declares the two-dimensional array:

1 Open the **Class** (Class.vbp) project, which is located in the Tut10 folder on your Student Disk. Save the form and the project as **laClass**, then click the **form** to select it. See Figure 10-24.

lblColTwo(3)

lblColOne(3)

lblColOne(2)

lblColOne(1)

lblColOne(0)

lblColTwo(0)

lblColTwo(1)

lblColTwo(2)

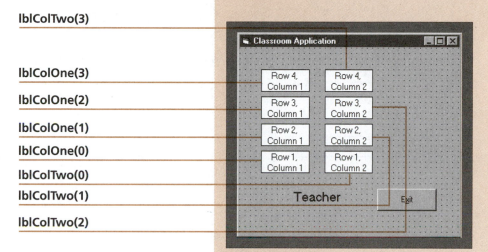

Figure 10-24: Classroom application's user interface

The interface contains eight label controls and one command button. The first column of label controls belongs to a control array named lblColOne; the second column belongs to a control array named lblColTwo. Each seat in the classroom is identified by both a row number and a column number. In order to display the name of the student that sits in a particular seat, the instructor will need simply to click the appropriate label control in the interface.

First enter the `Dim` statement that declares the two-dimensional strClass variable array.

2 Open the form's General Declarations section, which already contains the `Option Explicit` statement. In the blank line below the `Option Explicit` statement, type **dim strClass(1 to 4, 1 to 2) as string** and press the **Enter** key. This instruction will create a two-dimensional variable array named strClass.

The form's Load event procedure will fill the strClass array with the names of the eight students. Figure 10-25 shows the flowchart for the Load event procedure.

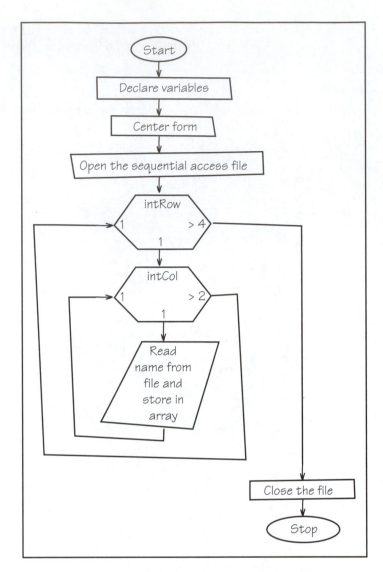

Figure 10-25: Flowchart for the form's Load event procedure

Now view the corresponding code.

To view the code entered in the form's Load event procedure:

1 Open the form's Load event, then maximize the Code window. See Figure 10-26. If your Student Disk is in the B drive, then change the drive letter in the Open statement to b:.

```
ClassProject - frmClass (Code)                                          _ 8 X
Form                              ▼    Load                              ▼
    Private Sub Form_Load()
    |   Dim intRow As Integer, intCol As Integer
        frmClass.Left = (Screen.Width - frmClass.Width) / 2
        frmClass.Top = (Screen.Height - frmClass.Height) / 2
        Open "a:\Tut10\Class.dat" For Input As #1    'open file
        For intRow = 1 To 4                          'fill array with data, row by row
            For intCol = 1 To 2
                Input #1, strClass(intRow, intCol)
            Next intCol
        Next intRow
        Close #1                                     'close file
    End Sub
```

if your Student Disk is in the B drive, change the drive letter to b:

Figure 10-26: Load event procedure

After declaring the necessary variables (intRow and intCol) and centering the form, the code opens, for input, the sequential access file that contains the eight student names. The two For Next loops read the names from the file and enter each name, row by row, into the appropriate variable in the array. The first name in the sequential file (Mary) will be entered into strClass(1, 1) and the second name (Jesse) will be entered into strClass(1, 2). After entering data into the first row, the For Next loops then enter data into the second row of the array; Sharon, the third name in the sequential file, will be entered into strClass(2, 1), and Lisa, the fourth name in the file, will be entered into strClass(2, 2). The For Next loops will then fill the third row with data by entering the fifth name (Jack) into strClass(3, 1) and the sixth name (Khalid) into strClass(3, 2). Lastly, the For Next loops will fill the fourth row with data by entering the seventh name (Robert) into strClass(4, 1) and the eighth name (George) into strClass(4, 2). The sequential file is then closed. Figure 10-27 illustrates the filled array in memory, as well as the seating chart.

tip

You learned about nested selection structures in Tutorial 4. Notice that you also can nest loops, which means that you can place one loop entirely inside another loop. The two For Next loops are referred to as nested loops.

strClass(4,1)	Robert	George	strClass(4,2)
strClass(3,1)	Jack	Khalid	strClass(3,2)
strClass(2,1)	Sharon	Lisa	strClass(2,2)
strClass(1,1)	Mary	Jesse	strClass(1,2)

strClass array in memory

lblColOne(3)	Robert	George	lblColTwo(3)
lblColOne(2)	Jack	Khalid	lblColTwo(2)
lblColOne(1)	Sharon	Lisa	lblColTwo(1)
lblColOne(0)	Mary	Jesse	lblColTwo(0)

Seating chart

Figure 10-27: Status of strClass array in memory and seating chart

Notice that the name of the student sitting in lblColOne(0) is stored in strClass(1, 1). The row number (1), which is the first subscript in the parentheses following strClass, is one more than the index of the label in the control array (0); that's because the array subscripts begin with the number 1, but the indexes of the labels in the control arrays begin with the number 0. Following this logic, notice that the name of the student sitting in lblColTwo(3) is stored in strClass(4, 2). Here again, the row number in the array (4) is one number greater than the index of its corresponding label control (3).

2   Close the Code window.

Next, view the code in the lblColOne and lblColTwo control arrays' Click events, which allow the instructor to display the name of the student sitting in a particular seat. Recall that the four label controls on the left side of the interface belong to the lblColOne control array, and the four label controls on the right side belong to the lblColTwo control array.

To view the code entered in the lblColOne and lblColTwo control arrays' Click events:

1   Double-click any one of the label controls in the first column. The lblColOne control array's Click event procedure appears as shown in Figure 10-28.

stores the index of the label control that is receiving the event

control array name

row number

column number

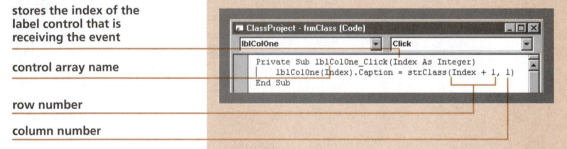

Figure 10-28: The lblColOne control array's Click event procedure

tip

As you learned in Tutorial 5, the Index argument in a control array's event procedure stores a number that represents the index of the control receiving the event.

When the user clicks one of the label controls in the lblColOne control array, you want the corresponding student's name, which is stored in the strClass array, to appear in the label control. The `lblColOne(Index).Caption = strClass(Index + 1, 1)` instruction tells Visual Basic to do just that. The `lblColOne(Index).Caption` part of the instruction tells Visual Basic where to display the name. The `strClass(Index + 1, 1)` part of the instruction tells Visual Basic that the name can be found in the strClass array, in the position whose row number is one number greater than the index of the label control that is receiving the event, and whose column number is 1. If, for example, the user clicks the lblColOne(2) label control, the Click event will display the name found in strClass(3, 1). Now view the code in the lblColTwo array's Click event.

2   Open the lblColTwo control array's Click event. See Figure 10-29.

stores the index of the
label control that is
receiving the event

control array name

row number

column number

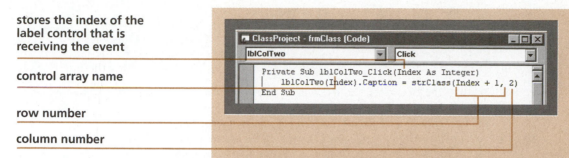

Figure 10-29: The lblColTwo control array's Click event procedure

The only difference between the lblColTwo control array's Click event and the Click event for the lblColOne control array is that the column number in the instruction is now a 2 instead of a 1. Observe how the application works.

3   Close the Code window, then **save** and **run** the application. Click each of the label controls, one at a time. The names of the students should appear as shown in Figure 10-30.

Figure 10-30: Label controls showing student names

4   Click the **Exit** button to exit the application. Visual Basic returns to the design screen.

You have now completed Lesson A. You can either take a break or complete the end-of-lesson questions and exercises.

S U M M A R Y

To declare a one-dimensional variable array:

■ Use the Dim statement. Its syntax is: **Dim** *arrayname(lower subscript* **To** *upper subscript)* **As** *datatype.*

■ *Arrayname* must follow the same rules as for simple variables. *Lower subscript* and *upper subscript* are numbers that define the lowest and the highest subscript, respectively, in the array. *Datatype* is the type of data the array variables will store.

To declare a two-dimensional variable array:

■ Use the Dim statement. Its syntax is: **Dim** *arrayname(lower subscript* **To** *upper subscript, lower subscript* **To** *upper subscript)* **As** *datatype.*

■ *Arrayname* must follow the same rules as for simple variables. *Lower subscript* and *upper subscript* are numbers that define the lowest and the highest subscript, respectively, in the array. *Datatype* is the type of data the array variables will store.

Q U E S T I O N S

1. A variable array is a group of variables that _____ . (Select three.)
   a. are related in some way
   b. belong to a control array
   c. have the same data type
   d. have the same index
   e. have the same name

2. Variables in an array are identified by a unique _____ .
   a. data type
   b. index
   c. name
   d. order
   e. subscript

3. intStock(2) is read _____ .
   a. intStock 2
   b. intStock array 2
   c. intStock parenthesis 2
   d. intStock sub 2
   e. two sub intStock

4. Which of the following is NOT an advantage of a variable array?
   a. Data stored in an array can be accessed faster than data stored in a disk file.
   b. Data stored in an array needs to be entered only once.
   c. Variable arrays use many more variable names.
   d. Variable arrays allow the programmer to store information in internal memory.
   e. When using variable arrays, you will have fewer variable names to remember.

5. Which of the following `Dim` statements declares a one-dimensional variable array named strItem that consists of five variables, each of which can store the name of an item?
   a. `Dim strItem(5 to 1) as String`
   b. `Dim as String strItem(1 to 5)`
   c. `Dim String as strItem(1 to 5)`
   d. `Dim Item as String(1 to 5)`
   e. `Dim strItem(1 to 5) as String`

6. Which of the following is NOT true about the `Dim` statement?
   a. You use the `Dim` statement to fill an array with data.
   b. You use the `Dim` statement to declare a variable array.
   c. The `Dim` statement initializes a String variable array to zero-length strings.
   d. The `Dim` statement initializes a Currency variable array to zero.
   e. The `Dim` statement creates the storage locations in memory.

Use the following array, named strStudent, to answer questions 7 through 9. The array was created with the following `Dim` statement: `Dim strStudent(1 to 5) as String`.

Tom	Mary	Suman	Patrick	Sue

7. The instruction, `Printer.Print strStudent(2)`, will print _____.
   a. Tom
   b. Mary
   c. Suman
   d. Patrick
   e. Sue

8. The instruction, `strStudent(4) = "Jan"`, will _____.
   a. replace the name "Sue" with the name "Jan"
   b. replace the name "Patrick" with the name "Jan"
   c. replace the name "Jan" with the name "Patrick"
   d. concatenate the name "Jan" to the name "Patrick"
   e. have no effect on the array

9. The instruction, `strStudent(1)=strStudent(5)`, will _____.
   a. replace the name "Sue" with the name "Tom"
   b. replace the name "Tom" with the name "Sue"
   c. concatenate the name "Sue" to the name "Tom"
   d. concatenate the name "Tom" to the name "Sue"
   e. have no effect on the array

Use the following array, named curSales, to answer questions 10 through 14. The array was created with the following `Dim` statement: `Dim curSales(1 to 5) as Currency`.

10000	12000	900	500	20000

10. The instruction, `curSales(4) = curSales(4) + 10`, will _____.
   a. replace the 500 amount with 10
   b. replace the 500 amount with False
   c. replace the 500 amount with 510
   d. have no effect on the array
   e. result in an error message

11. The instruction, `curSales(4) = curSales(4-2)`, will _____ .
    a. replace the 500 amount with 12000
    b. replace the 500 amount with 498
    c. replace the 500 amount with False
    d. have no effect on the array
    e. result in an error message

12. The instruction, `Printer.Print curSales(1) + curSales(2)`, will print
    _____ .
    a. 22000
    b. 10000 + 12000
    c. curSales(1) + curSales(2)
    d. curSales(3)
    e. 900

13. Which of the following If clauses can be used to verify that the array subscript, called intX, is valid?
    a. `If curSales(intX) >= 1 and curSales(intX) < 5 then`
    b. `If curSales(intX) >= 1 and curSales(intX) <= 5 then`
    c. `If curSales(intX) <= 1 and curSales(intX) >= 5 then`
    d. `If intX > 1 and intX < 5 then`
    e. `If intX >= 1 and intX <= 5 then`

14. Which of the following will correctly add 100 to each variable in the curSales array?
    a.
    ```
    For intX = 1 to 5 Step 1
        intX = intX + 100
    Next intX
    ```
    b.
    ```
    For intX = 5 to 1 Step 1
        intX = intX + 100
    Next intX
    ```
    c.
    ```
    For curSales(intX) = 1 to 5 Step 1
        curSales(intX) = curSales(intX) + 100
    Next intX
    ```
    d.
    ```
    For intX = 1 to 5 Step 1
        curSales(intX) = curSales(intX) + 100
    Next intX
    ```

Use the following array, named intNum, to answer questions 15 through 21. The array was created with the following `Dim` statement: `Dim intNum(1 to 4) as Integer`.

10	5	7	2

15. The average of the numbers in the intNum array is _____ .
    a. 4
    b. 6
    c. 8
    d. 23.5
    e. 24

16. Which of the following will correctly calculate and print the average of the intNum variables? Assume that intX and intTotal are declared as Integer variables. sngAvg is declared as a Single variable.

a.
```
For intX = 1 to 4 Step 1
    intNum(intX) = intTotal + intTotal
Next intX
sngAvg = intTotal / intX
Print sngAvg
```

b.
```
For intX = 1 to 4 Step 1
    intTotal = intTotal + intNum(intX)
Next intX
sngAvg = intTotal / intX
Print sngAvg
```

c.
```
For intX = 1 to 4 Step 1
    intNum(intX) = intNum(intX) + intTotal
Next intX
sngAvg = intTotal / intX
Print sngAvg
```

d.
```
For intX = 1 to 4 Step 1
    intTotal = intTotal + intNum(intX)
Next intX
sngAvg = intTotal / intX - 1
Print sngAvg
```

e.
```
For intX = 1 to 4 Step 1
    intTotal = intTotal + intNum(intX)
Next intX
sngAvg = intTotal / (intX - 1)
Print sngAvg
```

Only one of the five groups of code shown in Question 16 will print the average of the intNum variables. What will the other groups of code print? Record your answers in questions 17 through 21.

17. The code in question 16's answer "a" will print _____ .
    a. 0
    b. 3.8
    c. 4.8
    d. 5
    e. 6

18. The code in question 16's answer "b" will print _____ .
    a. 0
    b. 3.8
    c. 4.8
    d. 5
    e. 6

19. The code in question 16's answer "c" will print _____ .
    a. 0
    b. 3.8
    c. 4.8
    d. 5
    e. 6

20. The code in question 16's answer "d" will print _____
a. 0
b. 3.8
c. 4.8
d. 5
e. 6

21. The code in question 16's answer "e" will print _____
a. 0
b. 3.8
c. 4.8
d. 5
e. 6

22. Which of the following `Dim` statements declares a two-dimensional String variable array named strItem that consists of three rows and four columns?
```
a. Dim strItem(1 to 3, 1 to 4) as String
b. Dim as String strItem(1 to 4, 1 to 3)
c. Dim String as strItem(1 to 4, 1 to 3)
d. Dim strItem as String(1 to 4, 1 to 3)
e. Dim strItem(1 to 4, 1 to 3) as String
```

Use the following array, named intNum, to answer questions 23 through 28. The array was created with the following `Dim` statement: `Dim intNum(1 to 2, 1 to 3) as Integer`.

10	200	50
300	25	30

23. Which of the following Print statements will print the number 25 from the intNum array?
```
a. Print intNum(1, 2)
b. Print intNum(2, 1)
c. Print intNum(2, 2)
d. Print intNum(1, 3)
```

24. Assume that a sequential access file contains the following numbers, in this order: 10, 200, 50, 300, 25, 30. Which of the following nested For Next loops will fill the intNum as shown above?
```
a. For intCol = 1 to 3 Step 1
      For intRow = 1 to 2 Step 1
          Input #1, intNum(intRow, intCol)
      Next intRow
   Next intCol
b. For intRow = 1 to 2 Step 1
      For intCol = 1 to 3 Step 1
          Input #1, intNum(intRow, intCol)
      Next intCol
   Next intRow
c. For intRow = 1 to 3 Step 1
      For intCol = 1 to 2 Step 1
          Input #1, intNum(intRow, intCol)
      Next intCol
   Next intRow
d. For intCol = 1 to 2 Step 1
      For intRow = 1 to 3 Step 1
          Input #1, intNum(intRow, intCol)
      Next intRow
   Next intCol
```

Only one of the four groups of code shown in question 24 will fill the intNum array as shown. What will the other groups of code do? Record your answers in questions 25 through 28.

25. Show what the intNum array will look like in memory if you use the nested For Next loops shown in question 24's answer "a."

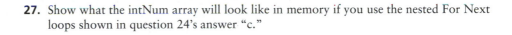

The code shown in question 24's answer "a" will _____ .
a. fill the array incorrectly
b. result in the "Subscript out of range." message
c. fill the array correctly

26. Show what the intNum array will look like in memory if you use the nested For Next loops shown in question 24's answer "b."

The code shown in question 24's answer "b" will _____ .
a. fill the array incorrectly
b. result in the "Subscript out of range." message
c. fill the array correctly

27. Show what the intNum array will look like in memory if you use the nested For Next loops shown in question 24's answer "c."

The code shown in question 24's answer "c" will _____ .
a. fill the array incorrectly
b. result in the "Subscript out of range." message
c. fill the array correctly

28. Show what the intNum array will look like in memory if you use the nested For Next loops shown in question 24's answer "d."

The code shown in question 24's answer "d" will _____ .
a. fill the array incorrectly
b. result in the "Subscript out of range." message
c. fill the array correctly

E X E R C I S E S

NOTE: Unless specified otherwise, write your answers on a piece of paper.

1. a. Write the appropriate `Dim` statement to declare a variable array named strMonth. The array should contain six variables, numbered 1 through 6. Each variable will store a string.
    b. Write the assignment statements that will store the first six months of the year in the array.
    c. Draw the array. Include each variable's name and its contents in the drawing.

2. a. Write the appropriate `Dim` statement to declare a one-dimensional variable array named intScore. The array should contain 10 variables, numbered 1 through 10. Each variable will store an integer.
    b. Write a procedure that will open a sequential access file named scores.dat, which contains 10 scores. The procedure should fill the array with the data contained in the file and then close the file.

3. a. Write the appropriate `Dim` statement to declare a two-dimensional variable array named strEmployee. The array should contain three rows and two columns. (Use a lower subscript of 1.) Each variable will store a string.
    b. Write the code that will open a sequential access file named employ.dat, which contains employee names. The procedure should fill the array with the employee data, row by row, and then close the file.
    c. Now write the code that will open a sequential access file named employ.dat, which contains employee names. This time have the procedure fill the array with the employee data, column by column, and then close the file.

4. In this exercise you will use a sequential access file, a one-dimensional array, and a list box.
    a. Open the la4 (la4.vbp) project, which is located in the Tut10 folder on your Student Disk. Save the form and the project as la4Done in the Tut10 folder on your Student Disk. The interface contains three label controls, a list box, and two command buttons.
    b. In the form's General declarations section, declare a 50-element String array named strCapitals.
    c. In the form's Load event, enter the 50 state names in the list box, and enter the 50 capitals in the String array. The state names and their capitals are stored in a sequential access file named capital.dat, which is located in the Tut10 folder on your Student Disk. The first field in the file is the state name and the second field is the capital. (It may be helpful to use WordPad to print the contents of the capital.dat file.) Also, have the Load event select the first entry in the list box when the interface first appears.
    d. Code the list box's Click event procedure so that it displays the state's capital, which is stored in the array, when you click the state's name. (*Hint*: Review the List box's ListIndex property, which is covered in Tutorial 6.)
    e. Save and run the application. Click Massachusetts in the list box, then click the Print button. Click South Carolina in the list box, then click the Print button. Stop the application and print the code.

5. In this exercise you will use a sequential access file and a two-dimensional array.
    a. Open the la5 (la5.vbp) project, which is located in the Tut10 folder on your Student Disk. Save the form and the project as la5Done in the Tut10 folder on your Student Disk. The interface contains three label controls, a text box, and three command buttons.
    b. In the form's General declarations section, declare a two-dimensional String array named strEmploy. The array should have 20 rows and two columns.

c. In the form's Load event, enter the 20 employee numbers and names in the String array. The employee numbers and names are stored in a sequential access file named employ.dat, which is located in the Tut10 folder on your Student Disk. The first field in the file is the number and the second field is the name. (It may be helpful to use WordPad to print the contents of the employ.dat file.)

d. Code the Find command button's Click event procedure so that it displays the employee's name that corresponds to the number entered in the text box. Display an appropriate message if the employee number is not in the array.

e. Save and run the application. Enter 1019 in the text box, then click the Find button, and then click the Print button. Enter 1031 in the text box, then click the Find button, and then click the Print button. Enter 2000 in the text box. On the first printout, record the error message that appears on the screen. Stop the application and print the code.

6. In this exercise you will use a sequential access file and a one-dimensional array.

a. Open the la6 (la6.vbp) project, which is located in the Tut10 folder on your Student Disk. Save the form and the project as la6Done in the Tut10 folder on your Student Disk. The interface contains four label controls and three command buttons.

b. In the form's General declarations section, declare a 20-element one-dimensional Integer array named intNums.

c. In the form's Load event, enter 20 numbers in the array. The numbers are stored in a sequential access file named points.dat, which is located in the Tut10 folder on your Student Disk. (It may be helpful to use WordPad to print the contents of the points.dat file.)

d. Code the Find command button's Click event procedure so that it displays the lowest number of points stored in the array, and also displays the number of students earning that score (in other words, the number of times that number appears in the array).

e. Save and run the application. Click the Find button, and then click the Print button. Stop the application and print the code.

7. In this exercise you will use two one-dimensional parallel arrays.

a. Open the la7 (la7.vbp) project, which is located in the Tut10 folder on your Student Disk. Save the form and the project as la7Done in the Tut10 folder on your Student Disk. The interface contains three label controls, a text box, and three command buttons. You can use this application to display a student's grade. You simply enter the student's total points in the Total points text box and then click the Display Grade button. The grading scale is shown below.

Minimum Points	Maximum Points	Grade
0	299	F
300	349	D
350	399	C
400	449	B
450	500	A

b. Store the minimum points in a five-element Integer array named intPoints. Store the grades in a five-element String array named strGrades.

c. Code the Display Grade button's click event procedure so that it searches the intPoints array and then displays the corresponding grade from the strGrades array.

d. Save and run the application. Enter 455 in the text box, then click the Display Grade button. The grade should be an A. Click the Print button. Enter 210 in the text box, then click the Display Grade button. The grade should be an F. Click the Print button. Stop the application and print the code.

8. In this exercise you will use two one-dimensional parallel arrays.
   a. Open the la8 (la8.vbp) project, which is located in the Tut10 folder on your Student Disk. Save the form and the project as la8Done in the Tut10 folder on your Student Disk. The interface contains three label controls, a text box, and three command buttons. You can use this application to display a student's grade. You simply enter the student's total points in the Total points text box and then click the Display Grade button. The grading scale is shown below.

Minimum Points	Maximum Points	Grade
0	299	F
300	349	D
350	399	C
400	449	B
450	500	A

   b. Store the maximum points in a five-element Integer array named intPoints. Store the grades in a five-element String array named strGrades.
   c. Code the Display Grade button's click event procedure so that it searches the intPoints array and then displays the corresponding grade from the strGrades array.
   d. Save and run the application. Enter 325 in the text box, then click the Display Grade button. The grade should be a D. Click the Print button. Enter 380 in the text box, then click the Display Grade button. The grade should be a C. Click the Print button. Stop the application and print the code.

9. In this exercise you will modify the application that you created in Lesson A's Exercise 7.
   a. Open the la7Done (la7Done.vbp) project, which is located in the Tut10 folder on your Student Disk. Save the form and the project as la9Done in the Tut10 folder on your Student Disk.
   b. Add an InputBox function to the form's Load event procedure. The InputBox function should prompt the instructor to enter the total number of points that a student can earn in the course.
   c. Currently, the form's Load event procedure contains the assignment statements that enter the data into both arrays. Modify the assignment statements that enter data into the intPoints array according to the grading scale shown below. (For example, if the instructor enters the number 500 in response to the InputBox function, the Load event should enter 450 (90% of 500) as the minimum number of points for an A. If the instructor enters the number 300, the Load event should enter 270 (90% of 300) as the minimum number of points for an A.)

Minimum Points	Grade
Less than 60% of total points	F
60% of total points	D
70% of total points	C
80% of total points	B
90% of total points	A

   d. Save and run the application. Enter 300 as the total number of points possible, then enter 185 in the Total points text box. Click the Display Grade button. The grade should be a D. Click the Print button. Stop the application.

    e. Run the application again. Enter 500 as the total number of points possible, then enter 363 in the total points text box. Click the Display Grade button. The grade should be a C. Click the Print button. Stop the application and print the code.

    f. Submit the printouts and code from steps d and e.

Exercises 10 through 15 are Discovery Exercises, which allow you to both "discover" solutions to problems on your own and experiment with topics that are not covered in the tutorial.

discovery ▶   **10.** In this exercise you will modify the application that you created in Lesson A's Exercise 7.

    a. Open the la7Done (la7Done.vbp) project, which is located in the Tut10 folder on your Student Disk. Save the form and the project as la10Done in the Tut10 folder on your Student Disk.

    b. Modify the application so that it stores the grading table (minimum points and grade) in a one-dimensional array. For example, in the first array variable, store the number 0 and the F grade. (*Hint*: You will need to create a user-defined data type for the points and grade.)

    c. Save and run the application. Enter 425 in the text box, then click the Display Grade button. The grade should be a B. Click the Print button. Enter 375 in the text box, then click the Display Grade button. The grade should be a C. Click the Print button. Stop the application and print the code.

discovery ▶   **11.** In this exercise you will use the `Redim` statement.

Scenario: In Lesson A you completed the Test Score application. Currently the application will work only when the number of records in the data file is 20. Your task in this exercise is to modify the application's code so that it works for any number of records.

    a. Use WordPad to print the contents of the test11.dat file, which is located in the Tut10 folder on your Student Disk. Also print the contents of the test11X.dat file.

    b. Open the laTest (laTest.vbp) project that you created in Lesson A. Save the form and the project as la11Done.

    c. Change the form's Load event procedure so that it uses the Do While loop to read the records from the test11.dat file into the array. Be sure to count how many records are in the file. Call the counter variable intRecCount. (If you need to recreate the test11.dat file, use Windows to copy the test11.bak file to test11.dat.)

    d. Change the Update Scores button's Click event procedure so that it saves the updated records in the test11.dat file, which is located in the Tut10 folder on your Student Disk.

    e. If you have access to the MSDN Library, research the `Redim` statement.

    f. Modify the application's code so that all references to the number 20 are replaced with the intRecCount variable. Be sure that intRecCount is greater than zero before computing the average of the test scores. Use the `Redim` statement to resize the array to accommodate the number of records in the file.

    g. Save and run the application. Test the Average Score and Highest Score buttons to be sure each is working correctly. Test the Update Scores button by increasing each score by five points. Exit the application.

    h. Modify the form's Load event so that it opens the test11X.dat file. Modify the Update Scores button's Click event so that it writes the updated records to the test11X.dat file. (If you need to recreate the test11X.dat file, use Windows to copy the test11X.bak file to test11X.dat.)

    i. Save and run the application. Test the Average Score and Highest Score buttons. Test the Update Scores button by increasing each score by 10 points.

    j. Exit the application, then print the code. Use WordPad to print the contents of the test11.dat and test11X.dat files. Submit the printouts and code from steps a and j.

discovery ▶ 12. In this exercise you will display the average, lowest, and highest sales amount contained in a two-dimensional array, as well as update the sales amounts.

Scenario: JM Sales employs 10 salespeople at each of its two locations. The manager wants an application that she can use to display the average sales amount, the lowest sales amount, and the highest sales amount. The application should also allow the manager to calculate the following year's expected sales by updating the sales figures by a percentage that she enters.

a. Use WordPad to print the contents of the sales12.dat file, which is located in the Tut10 folder on your Student Disk. (If you need to recreate the sales12.dat file, use Windows to copy the sales12.bak file to sales12.dat.)

b. Open the laTest (laTest.vbp) project that you created in Lesson A. Save the form and the project as la12Done. Widen the lblAnswer control.

c. Change the command button captions to Average Sales, Highest Sales, and Update Sales. Add a Lowest Sales command button.

d. Modify the code so that it uses a two-dimensional array named sngSales. Use the `Dim sngSales(1 to 10, 1 to 2) as Single` instruction to create the array. Modify the remaining code appropriately. Read the sales information from the sales12.dat file. Also, save the updated information to the sales12.dat file.

e. Run the application. Test the command buttons. Use 10% as the update percentage. When the application is working correctly, print the application's code. Also use WordPad to print the contents of the sales12.dat file. (Each number in the printout should be 10% greater than the corresponding number shown in step a's printout.)

f. Submit the printouts and code from steps a and e.

discovery ▶ 13. In this exercise you will use a two-dimensional array.

Scenario: M & J Sales employs ten salespeople. The sales for the months of January, February, and March are entered in a file named sales13.dat. The manager wants an application that will print a report showing the bonus percentage, as well as each salesperson's number (1 through 10), total sales, and bonus. The report should also include the total bonus paid.

a. Use WordPad to print the contents of the sales13.dat file, which is located in the Tut10 folder on your Student Disk. (If you need to recreate the sales13.dat file, use Windows to copy the sales13.bak file to sales13.dat.) The first field in each record is the January sales amount, the second field is the February sales amount, and the third field is the March sales amount.

b. Open the la13 (la13.vbp) project, which is located in the Tut10 folder on your Student Disk. Save the form and the project as la13Done in the Tut10 folder on your Student Disk.

c. Code the form's Load event so that it reads the 20 sales amounts from the sales13.dat file and stores them in a two-dimensional array named sngSales. The sngSales array should have 10 rows and three columns.

d. Code the Print Report button so that it prints a report showing the bonus percentage, as well as each salesperson's number (1 through 10), total sales, and bonus. Also print the total bonus paid.

e. Save and run the application. Print the report showing a 10% bonus.

f. Stop the application and print the code. Submit the printouts from steps a and e and the code from step f.

discovery ▶ 14. In this exercise you will update only specific elements in an array.

Scenario: In Lesson A's Test Score example, you learned how to update each of the elements in an array. Mr. Weaver, the instructor using the application, also wants the ability to select which student's score will be updated. In other words, if the third and fifth students should receive an additional number of points, only those students' scores should be updated.

a. Use WordPad to print the contents of the test14.dat file, which is located in the Tut10 folder on your Student Disk. (If you need to recreate the test14.dat file, use Windows to copy the test14.bak file to test14.dat.)

b. Open the laTest (laTest.vbp) project that you created in Lesson A. Save the form and the project as la14Done.

c. Modify the form's Load event so that it opens the test14.dat file. Modify the Update Scores button's Click event so that it writes the updated records to the test14.dat file. Modify the remaining code appropriately.

d. Run the application. Use the Update Scores button to update only the third and fifth scores by five points. Exit the application.

e. Print the code for only the Update Scores button's Click event procedure. Also, use WordPad to print the contents of the test14.dat file. The third and fifth scores in this printout should be five points higher than the corresponding scores in step a's printout.

f. Submit the printouts and code from steps a and e.

discovery ▶ 15. In this exercise you will use a two-dimensional array.

a. In Tutorial 6's Lesson A, you created an application for the PAO (Political Awareness Organization). The files, named laPao, are located in the Tut06 folder on your Student Disk. Copy the laPao files, as well as the pao.dat file, to the Tut10 folder on your Student Disk.

b. Open the laPao (laPao.vbp) project. Save the files as la15Done in the Tut10 folder on your Student Disk.

c. View the PAO project's code. Notice that you used the labels in the control arrays as counters. Recall from Tutorial 3, however, that Visual Basic can process information faster if that information is contained in a variable rather than in the property of a control. Rewrite the PAO application so that it uses a two-dimensional array for the counters.

d. Test the application appropriately, then print the code.

In this lesson you will learn how to:

- Display database records using the DataGrid control
- Update the contents of a database field through code
- Create an object variable and assign an object reference to it
- Round numbers to a specific number of decimal places

The DataGrid Control and Object Variables

The Colfax Industries Payroll Application

As you may remember from the Case outlined at the beginning of this tutorial, Colfax Industries has asked you to create an application that the payroll clerk can use to prepare the company's weekly payroll report. The application will need to calculate each employee's gross pay, federal withholding tax (FWT), Social Security and Medicare (FICA) tax, and net pay.

The payroll information for each of Colfax Industries' 10 employees is stored in a Microsoft Access database named Colfax.mdb, which is located in the Tut10 folder on your Student Disk. The database contains one table named tblEmployees. Figure 10-31 shows the structure of the tblEmployees table, and Figure 10-32 shows the records stored in the tblEmployees table.

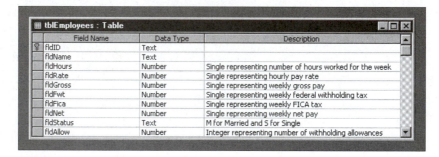

Field Name	Data Type	Description
fldID	Text	
fldName	Text	
fldHours	Number	Single representing number of hours worked for the week
fldRate	Number	Single representing hourly pay rate
fldGross	Number	Single representing weekly gross pay
fldFwt	Number	Single representing weekly federal withholding tax
fldFica	Number	Single representing weekly FICA tax
fldNet	Number	Single representing weekly net pay
fldStatus	Text	M for Married and S for Single
fldAllow	Number	Integer representing number of withholding allowances

Figure 10-31: Structure of the Colfax database's tblEmployees table

fldID	fldName	fldHours	fldRate	fldGross	fldFwt	fldFica	fldNet	fldStatus	fldAllow
1111	Adams, Martha	0	10	0	0	0	0	M	2
1234	Zinta, Carlie	0	15	0	0	0	0	S	0
1453	Patel, Khalid	0	10	0	0	0	0	M	0
1522	Felixe, Jose	0	9	0	0	0	0	S	1
1656	Perry, Linda	0	9	0	0	0	0	M	1
1679	Allen, Terry	0	10	0	0	0	0	M	3
1798	Gray, Pat	0	12.5	0	0	0	0	S	2
1844	Jones, Unis	0	15	0	0	0	0	S	0
1955	Kayen, Mary	0	8	0	0	0	0	M	2
1968	Siskowski, Ed	0	7.5	0	0	0	0	M	1

Figure 10-32: Records stored in the Colfax database's tblEmployees table

As Figure 10-31 indicates, each record contains a field for the employee's ID, name, number of hours worked for the week, hourly pay rate, weekly gross pay, weekly FWT, weekly FICA tax, weekly net pay, marital status, and number of withholding allowances.

Your Student Disk contains a partially completed payroll application that you will use to access the information in the Colfax database. Open that project now.

To view the partially completed payroll application:

1   Start Visual Basic, if necessary, and open the **Pay** (Pay.vbp) project, which is located in the Tut10 folder on your Student Disk. View the form, then save the form and the project as **lbPay**.

The interface contains a File menu that has two options, Print and Exit. Both options have been coded for you: the Exit option contains the `Unload frmColfax` instruction, and the Print option contains the `PrintForm` instruction.

First, include an ADO data control in the interface, and then set its properties appropriately. As you learned in Tutorial 9, the ADO data control allows you to access the records stored in a database. In this case, you will use the ADO data control to access the records stored in the Colfax database.

tip

....

▶ Before making any changes to a database, you should use Windows to make a backup copy of the .mdb file; this will allow you to restore the .mdb file to its original state in case you do not want to save the changes made to the database. Your Student Disk contains a backup copy of the Colfax.mdb database. The name of the backup file is Colfax.bak.

To add an ADO data control to the interface, and then set its properties:

1   Use the Components option on the Project menu to add the **Microsoft ADO Data Control 6.0 (OLEDB)** tool to the toolbox, then double-click the **Adodc tool** 📇 to place an ADO data control in the interface.

2   Set the ADO data control's Name property to **adoPay**, its Height property to **330**, and its Visible property to **False**. Drag the adoPay control to the bottom-left corner of the form.

Now set the ADO data control's ConnectionString and RecordSource properties. Recall that the ConnectionString property identifies the name of your data source, as well as the data source's OLE DB provider. The RecordSource property stores either the name of a table or an SQL Select command that specifies which records you want to access.

3   Click **ConnectionString** in the Properties list, then click the **...** button in the Settings box. The General tab on the Property Pages dialog box appears with the Use Connection String option button selected. Click the **Build** button.

4   When the Data Link Properties dialog box appears, click **Microsoft Jet 3.51 OLE DB Provider** on the Provider tab, then click the **Next >>** button.

5   When the Connection tab appears, click the **...** button to display the Select Access Database dialog box. Click **Colfax.mdb**, which is located in the Tut10 folder on your Student Disk, in the list of filenames, then click the **Open** button.

6   Click the **Test Connection** button on the Connection tab to verify that the connection between the ADO data control and the database succeeded. When the "Test connection succeeded" message appears, click the **OK** button.

7   Click the **OK** button to close the Data Link Properties dialog box; then click the **OK** button to close the Property Pages dialog box.

Next, set the ADO data control's RecordSource property so that it allows you to access all of the records stored in the tblEmployees table. Order the records by employee ID.

8   Click **RecordSource** in the Properties list, then click the **...** button in the Settings box. The Property Pages dialog box appears. Change the command type to **1- adCmdText**, then type **select * from tblEmployees order by fldID** in the Command Text (SQL) text box. Click the **OK** button to close the Property Pages dialog box.

After setting the ADO data control's ConnectionString and RecordSource properties, you then can bind the ADO data control to other controls in the interface. The bound controls will display the information from the Recordset object created by the ADO data control's RecordSource property. In Tutorial 9, you used text boxes and label controls to display the Recordset object's information; in this tutorial, you will use the DataGrid control.

The DataGrid Control

When bound to an ADO data control, the **DataGrid control** displays the information from the recordset created by the ADO data control's RecordSource property. The information displays in a row and column format, similar to a spreadsheet. Each database field appears in a column in the DataGrid control, and each record appears in a row. The intersection of a row and a column in the DataGrid control is called a **cell**. Include the DataGrid control in the payroll application, and then bind it to the adoPay control.

To include the DataGrid control in the payroll application, then bind it to the adoPay control:

1 Use the **Components** option on the Project menu to add the **Microsoft DataGrid Control 6.0 (OLEDB)** tool to the toolbox, then double-click the **DataGrid tool** to place a DataGrid control named DataGrid1 on the form.

2 Set the DataGrid1 control's Name property to **dgdPay** ("dgd" is the three-character ID for the DataGrid control.) Also set its Height property to **3120**, its Left property to **360**, its Top property to **240**, and its Width property to **7215**.

3 Lock the controls in place on the form.

Next, bind the dgdPay control to the adoPay control. You bind a DataGrid control to an ADO data control by setting the DataGrid control's DataSource property.

4 Set the dgdPay control's **DataSource** property to **adoPay.**

During design time, you can display the Recordset object's field names in the DataGrid control by selecting the Retrieve fields option on the DataGrid control's popup menu, which appears when you right-click the control.

5 Right-click the **dgdPay** control. The control's popup menu appears as shown in Figure 10-33.

popup menu

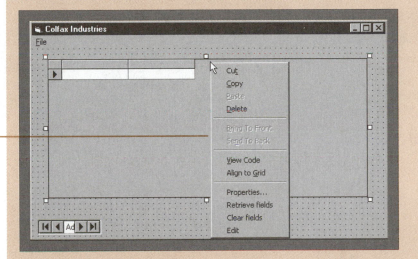

Figure 10-33: DataGrid control's popup menu

6 Click **Retrieve fields** on the popup menu. The Retrieve fields dialog box appears with the "Replace existing grid layout with new field definitions?" message. Click the **Yes** button. The DataGrid control retrieves the 10 field names from the recordset created by the ADO data control and displays each field name in a separate column in the DataGrid control. See Figure 10-34.

column header section

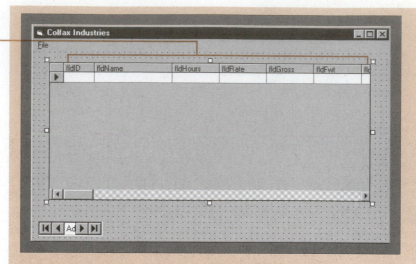

Figure 10-34: Field names displayed in the DataGrid control

You will notice that the DataGrid control enters the field names in its column header section. The field name identifies the information the column will display. In this case, the DataGrid control enters 10 field names in the column header section, but you will notice that you cannot view all of the names at the same time; you will need to scroll the control to view the remaining field names. Although a scroll bar appears at the bottom of the DataGrid control, you can't employ it during design time unless you first put the control in Edit mode.

7 Right-click the **dgdPay** control, and then click **Edit** on the popup menu. Use the scroll bar that is located on the bottom of the control to scroll through the 10 columns.

8 Drag the DataGrid control's scroll box to the left until the fldID field is visible, then click the **form** to cancel the control's Edit mode.

9 Save and run the application. The DataGrid control displays the 10 records stored in the Colfax database's tblEmployees table. Use the control's scroll bar to scroll through the information displayed in the control. The information should agree with that shown earlier in Figure 10-32.

tip

Recall that a cell is the intersection of a column and a row.

In addition to displaying the records, the DataGrid control also allows you to edit the record information while the application is running. To do so, you need simply to click the cell whose contents you want to change, and then type the new entry. For example, change Linda Perry's hourly pay rate from 9 to 11.

To edit the contents of a cell during run time:

1 Click the **cell that contains Linda Perry's pay rate**. The DataGrid control highlights the current contents of the cell—the number 9.

2 Type **11** and then click the **cell immediately below the current one**. The DataGrid control replaces the number 9 with the number 11 in both the cell and the record's fldRate field.

3 On your own, change Linda Perry's hourly rate from 11 to 9.

4 Click **File** on the form's menu bar, and then click **Exit** to end the application.

In the next section, you will learn how to improve the appearance of the data displayed in the DataGrid control.

Improving the Appearance of the DataGrid Control's Data

The DataGrid control provides many properties that allow you to control the appearance of its output. For example, you can change the size of a column, and you can change a column heading to make the heading more descriptive. You also can tell the DataGrid control to align a column's contents either on the right, center, or left of the column, as well as to display numbers with a dollar sign, a percent sign, or a fixed number of decimal places.

The DataGrid control also provides properties that allow you to control how the user can interact with the control while the application is running. For example, you can prevent the user from making changes to the data displayed either in the entire DataGrid control or in one or more of its columns. You also can either allow or prevent the user from adding and deleting records.

To begin making improvements to the appearance of the data displayed in the DataGrid control:

1 Right-click the **dgdPay** control, and then click **Properties** on the popup menu. The Property Pages dialog box appears with the General tab as the frontmost tab. See Figure 10-35.

use to put a title above the column header section

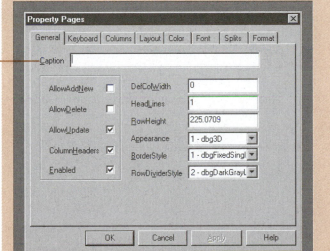

Figure 10-35: General tab in the Property Pages dialog box

tip

You also can set some of the DataGrid control's properties in the Properties window.

You use the DataGrid control's Caption property, whose value you enter in the Caption text box, to assign a title to the DataGrid control. The title will appear above the DataGrid control's header section, and it is used to identify the information that appears in the grid. You will display Colfax Industries Weekly Payroll at the top of the grid.

You also can display the Property Pages dialog box by clicking the DataGrid control's Custom property in the Properties window.

2   Type **Colfax Industries Weekly Payroll** in the Caption text box.

To see the effect of this change without closing the Property Pages dialog box, you need simply to click the Apply button.

3   Click the **Apply** button. Drag the Property Pages dialog box down until you see the title that appears at the top of the grid, and then drag it back up again.

You will notice that the General tab contains five check boxes. Each check box corresponds to a property of the DataGrid control. Figure 10-36 lists the purpose of these check boxes (properties).

Check box (property)	Purpose
AllowAddNew	Allows the user to add records while the application is running
AllowDelete	Allows the user to delete records while the application is running
AllowUpdate	Allows the user to edit existing records while the application is running
ColumnHeaders	Controls whether a header appears above each column
Enabled	Controls whether the control responds to a user-generated event

Figure 10-36: Purpose of the five check boxes (properties) on the General tab

In the Colfax application, you will not allow the payroll clerk to add or delete records while the application is running, so you will leave the AllowAddNew and AllowDelete check boxes unselected. Because the payroll clerk will need to make changes to the data—for example, he or she will need to enter the number of hours worked—you will leave the AllowUpdate check box selected. You also will leave the ColumnHeaders and Enabled check boxes selected, which will display the column headers and allow the user to interact with the DataGrid control, respectively.

As you already observed, the DataGrid control displays in its column header section the actual field names from the recordset. Although a heading such as fldID may be meaningful to the application's creator, it may be confusing to the user. "Employee ID", or simply "ID", would be a better heading for a column that contains the employee IDs. The Columns tab in the Property Pages dialog box allows you to change the column headings.

To change the column headings displayed in the DataGrid control:

1   Click the **Columns** tab on the Property Pages dialog box. See Figure 10-37.

use to select the
column

use to change the
column heading

use to change the field
displayed in the column

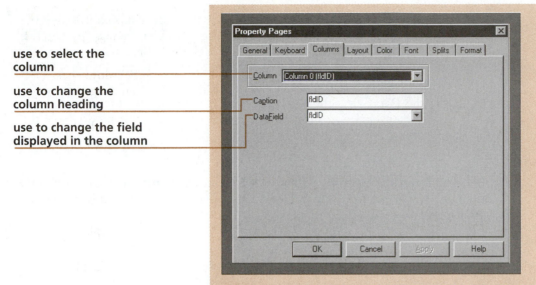

Figure 10-37: Columns tab on the Property Pages dialog box

You use the Column list box to select the column whose heading or data field you want to change. You enter the column heading in the Caption text box, and you select the field you want to display from the DataField list box. In the Colfax application, the fields already display in the correct order, but the headings for each column need to be changed to more descriptive ones. Begin by changing the heading for the first column (Column 0) from fldID to ID.

2   Change fldID in the Caption text box to **ID**.

Now change the heading for the second column, Column 1, from fldName to Name.

3   Click the **Column** list arrow, then click **Column 1 (fldName)** in the list. Change fldName in the Caption text box to **Name**.

4   Use the Column list box and the Caption text box to change the following column headings:

Column	New Heading
Column 2 (fldHours)	Hours
Column 3 (fldRate)	Rate
Column 4 (fldGross)	Gross
Column 5 (fldFwt)	Fwt
Column 6 (fldFica)	Fica
Column 7 (fldNet)	Net
Column 8 (fldStatus)	Status
Column 9 (fldAllow)	Allow

5   Click the **OK** button to close the Property Pages dialog box. Verify that the field headings were changed correctly by right-clicking the **dgdPay** control, then clicking **Edit** on the popup menu. Use the scroll bar to scroll through the 10 field headings. If you find an error, return to the Property Pages dialog box and make the correction.

6   Drag the DataGrid control's scroll box to the left until the ID column is visible, then click the **form** to cancel the control's Edit mode. **Save** the application.

The DataGrid control's output would look more professional if the numbers contained in five of the columns (Rate, Gross, Fwt, Fica, and Net) were formatted to display two decimal places.

To format the numbers displayed in the DataGrid control:

1   Right-click the **DataGrid** control, then click **Properties** on the popup menu. Click the **Format** tab on the Property Pages dialog box.

The Format tab contains a Format Item list box and a Format Type list box. You use the Format Item list box to select the field whose numeric contents you want to format; Column 0 (fldID) is the field currently selected in the Format Item list box. You use the Format Type list box to select the type of format used to display the numbers. The General format, which causes no special formatting to occur, is currently selected in the Format Type list box. Use the list boxes to select the Number format for the fldRate field.

2   Click the **Format Item** list arrow, then click **Column 3 (fldRate)** in the list. Click **Number** in the Format Type list box.

You will notice that when you select the Number format, additional options appear on the Format tab. You use the Decimal places text box to specify the number of decimal places to display, and you use the Use 1000 Separator (,) check box to control whether the comma separator is used in the display. The Negative numbers list box allows you to specify whether negative numbers appear with a leading minus sign or are enclosed in parentheses. In the current application, you will display each employee's hourly rate with two decimal places.

3   Click the **up scroll arrow that appears on the scroll bar to the right of the Decimal places text box** twice. The number 2 appears in the Decimal places text box, as shown in Figure 10-38.

numbers in this column will be displayed with two decimal places

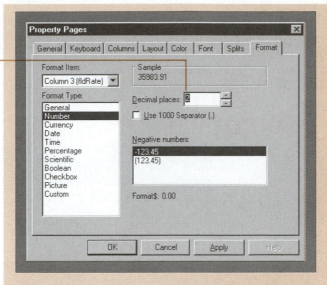

Figure 10-38: Format tab on the Property Pages dialog box

4   Use the Format tab to change the format for the fldGross, fldFwt, fldFica, and fldNet columns to Number with two decimal places.

5   Click the **OK** button to close the Property Pages dialog box. **Save** and **run** the application. Verify that the numbers in the Rate, Gross, Fwt, Fica, and Net columns display with two decimal places. Click **File** on the form's menu bar, and then click **Exit**.

In this application, you will allow the payroll clerk to edit the information in the Name, Hours, Rate, Status, and Allow columns only. However, you will not allow the payroll clerk to change the contents of the ID column because an employee's ID never changes. You also will not allow the clerk to change the contents of the Gross, Fwt, Fica, and Net columns because those values will be calculated by the application. As you learned earlier, you use the AllowUpdate check box on the Property Pages dialog box's General tab to prevent the user from changing any of the data displayed in the DataGrid control. However, you use the Locked check box on the Property Pages dialog box's Layout tab to prevent changes to only specific columns in the DataGrid control.

The Layout tab also contains an Alignment list box that allows you to either right-align, center, or left-align the contents of a column. By default, column values are left-aligned. You will use the Layout tab to right-align the contents of the Hours, Rate, Gross, Fwt, Fica, and Net columns, and to center the contents of the Status and Allow columns.

To prevent changes to specific columns in the DataGrid control, and to right-align and center the entries in a column:

1   Right-click the **DataGrid** control, and then click **Properties** on the popup menu. Click the **Layout** tab on the Property Pages dialog box.

You use the Column list box to select the column whose properties you want to change. You use the Locked check box to specify whether the user can make changes to the data appearing in the column; if the Locked check box is selected, then no editing can occur in the entire column. The Alignment list box allows you to specify the alignment for the entries in the column. Begin by locking the ID column. You can leave the ID column's alignment at its default of 0-dbgLeft.

2   Click the **Locked** check box to select it. See Figure 10-39.

prevents the user from changing the contents of the column

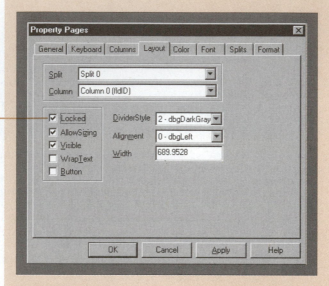

Figure 10-39: Layout tab on the Property Pages dialog box

3   Use the options on the Layout tab to set the Locked and Alignment properties as follows:

Column	Locked	Alignment
Column 1 (fldName)	Unselected	0-dbgLeft
Column 2 (fldHours)	Unselected	1-dbgRight
Column 3 (fldRate)	Unselected	1-dbgRight
Column 4 (fldGross)	Selected	1-dbgRight
Column 5 (fldFwt)	Selected	1-dbgRight
Column 6 (fldFica)	Selected	1-dbgRight
Column 7 (fldNet)	Selected	1-dbgRight
Column 8 (fldStatus)	Unselected	2-dbgCenter
Column 9 (fldAllow)	Unselected	2-dbgCenter

4   Click the **OK** button to close the Property Pages dialog box. **Save** and **run** the application.

5 Scroll the DataGrid control to verify that the entries in the Hours, Rate, Gross, Fwt, Fica, and Net columns are right-aligned, and the entries in the Status and Allow columns are centered.

6 Try clicking a **cell in the ID column.** You will notice that you cannot place the focus in the ID column because the column is locked; the same is true for the Gross, Fwt, Fica, and Net columns.

7 Click the **cell that contains Carlie Zinta's hours worked.** Visual Basic highlights the current contents of the cell, 0. Type **12** and then click **the cell immediately below the current one.** Because the Hours column is not locked, you can make changes to its contents; the same is true for the Name, Rate, Status, and Allow columns.

8 On your own, change Carlie Zinta's hours worked back to 0. Click **File** on the form's menu bar, then click **Exit** to end the application.

You will notice that some of the columns in the DataGrid control are wider than they need to be. For example, the ID column, which will display a maximum of four characters, is slightly wider than needed. To size a column in the DataGrid control during design time, you need first to put the control in Edit mode. You can then drag the column to the desired size.

To size the columns in the DataGrid control:

1 Right-click the **dgdPay** control, and then click **Edit** on the popup menu. Place the mouse pointer on the line that separates the ID and Name headings in the header section. The mouse pointer turns into ✥. Drag the line to the left as shown in Figure 10-40, and then release the mouse button.

appearance of mouse
pointer when sizing

sizing line appears before
mouse button is released

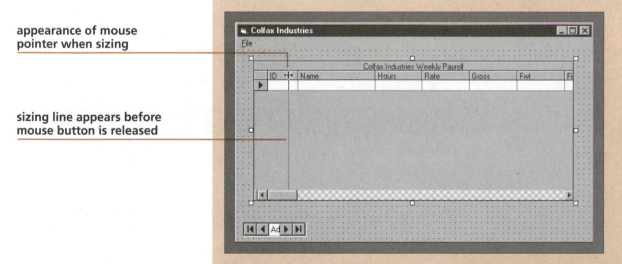

Figure 10-40: DataGrid control showing the correct size of the ID field

2 Size the remaining columns as shown in Figure 10-41.

HELP? To size a column, place the mouse pointer on the line to its immediate right in the column header section.

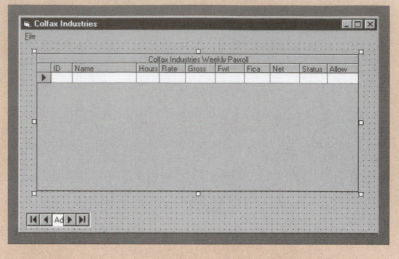

Figure 10-41: Columns sized in grid

3   Click the **form** to leave the DataGrid control's Edit mode, then **save** the application.

The payroll application's interface is now complete, so you can begin coding the application so that it calculates each employee's gross pay, FWT, FICA tax, and net pay. You will have the DataGrid control make these calculations.

Coding the DataGrid Control

When a user completes editing within a DataGrid control cell by moving the focus to either another cell in the control or another control in the interface, or by pressing the Enter key, several of the DataGrid control's events occur. Figure 10-42 lists five of these events and indicates the point at which each takes place. Figure 10-43 shows a graphic illustration of when these five events occur.

Event	Occurs
BeforeColUpdate	after editing is completed in a cell, but before data is moved from the cell to the DataGrid control's copy buffer; can be canceled by setting its Cancel argument to True
AfterColUpdate	after data is moved from a cell in the DataGrid control to the DataGrid control's copy buffer; occurs only if the BeforeColUpdate event is not canceled and a change was made to the cell
AfterColEdit	after editing is completed in a grid cell; occurs even if no changes were made to the cell or the BeforeColUpdate event was canceled
BeforeUpdate	after editing is completed in a record, but before data is moved from the DataGrid control's copy buffer to the ADO data control's copy buffer; can be canceled by setting its Cancel argument to True
AfterUpdate	after changed data has been written to the database; occurs only if the BeforeUpdate event is not canceled

Figure 10-42: Five DataGrid events

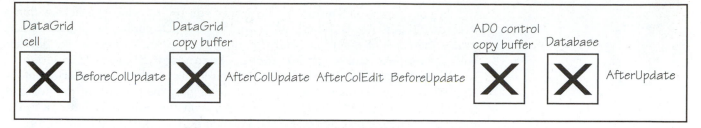

Figure 10-43: Illustration of five DataGrid events

As both figures indicate, the BeforeColUpdate event occurs after editing is completed in a DataGrid cell, but before the data is moved from the cell to the DataGrid control's copy buffer, which is located in the internal memory of the computer. This event gives your application an opportunity to verify the cell's value before the value is committed to the control's copy buffer.

If the BeforeColUpdate event does not contain code that cancels the event, the data is moved to the DataGrid control's copy buffer, at which time the AfterColUpdate event occurs, but only if a change was made to the contents of the cell. The AfterColEdit event is triggered next. Unlike the AfterColUpdate event, the AfterColEdit event occurs even if the BeforeColUpdate event is canceled and even if no change was made to the current cell.

Unlike the BeforeColUpdate, AfterColUpdate, and AfterColEdit events, which occur when the user moves the focus to either another cell in the DataGrid control or another control in the interface, the BeforeUpdate event is triggered only when the user moves the focus to a cell that is located in another row (record) in the DataGrid control. If the BeforeUpdate event is not canceled, the changed data is moved from the DataGrid control's copy buffer to the ADO control's copy buffer, which is also located in the computer's internal memory, and then the data is written to the database. The BeforeUpdate event gives your application an opportunity to validate the cells in the row before the changes are committed to the ADO control's copy buffer. After the data is written to the database, the DataGrid control's AfterUpdate event occurs.

In the Colfax payroll application, you will have the AfterColUpdate event calculate the gross pay, taxes, and net pay. Placing the code in this event instructs the DataGrid control to make the calculations when the user either presses the Enter key or moves the focus to a different cell or control. Figure 10-44 shows the pseudocode for the DataGrid control's AfterColUpdate event.

1. calculate the gross pay

2. calculate the FICA tax

3. call a function to calculate the FWT

4. calculate the net pay

Figure 10-44: Pseudocode for the DataGrid control's AfterColUpdate event

As the pseudocode indicates, the AfterColUpdate event first will calculate the employee's weekly gross pay. To keep the example simple, you can assume that no one at the company works more than 40 hours, so there is no need to worry about overtime pay. (You will include the overtime calculation in Lesson C's Exercise 1.) You calculate gross pay simply by multiplying the number of hours the employee worked (which is stored in the fldHours field) by his or her hourly pay rate (which is stored in the fldRate field). The result of that calculation should be entered in the employee's fldGross field.

As you learned in Tutorial 9, the syntax you use to refer to a field within a Recordset object's Fields collection is [*form.*]*adocontrol*.**Recordset.Fields**(*field*), where *field* is the name of the field, enclosed in quotation marks. To refer to the fldGross field, for example, you would use `adoPay.Recordset.Fields("fldGross")`, which tells Visual Basic that the fldGross field is located in the Fields collection of the adoPay control's recordset. The instruction to multiply the contents of the fldHours field by the contents of the fldRate field and then store the result in the fldGross field is `adoPay.Recordset.Fields("fldGross") = adoPay.Recordset.Fields("fldHours") * adoPay.Recordset.Fields("fldRate")`. As you can see, this instruction is quite cumbersome to write. You can simplify this instruction by creating an object variable and assigning the Fields collection object to it.

Creating an Object Variable

An object variable is similar to any variable, except it holds a reference to an object rather than a value such as a name or a number. You create an object variable using the Dim statement in the following syntax: **Dim** *objectVariableName* **As** *datatype*, where *datatype* can be a specific object type (such as Sheet, Range, or Recordset) or the keyword Object, which can be used to represent a reference to any object. In the Colfax application, you will use the `Dim objFlds As Object` statement to create an object variable that will reference the Fields collection in the adoPay control's Recordset object.

After creating the object variable, you then use Visual Basic's **Set statement**, whose syntax is **Set** *objectVariableName* = *object*, to assign an object reference to the object variable. In the Colfax application, you will use the `Set objFlds = adoPay.Recordset.Fields` statement to assign, to the objFlds object variable, a reference to the Fields collection object, which is a member of the adoPay control's Recordset object. After assigning the reference to the object variable, you can use the shorter object variable's name—in this case, objFlds—in place of the longer adoPay.Recordset.Fields in your code. For example, to calculate the employee's gross pay, you can use the `objFlds("fldGross") = objFlds("fldHours") * objFlds("fldRate")` statement. You now can begin coding the DataGrid control's AfterColUpdate event.

tip

Object variables are stored as 32-bit (4-byte) addresses that refer to objects.

tip

In the Set statement's syntax, *object's* data type must agree with the data type of the object whose name is *objectVariableName*.

To code the DataGrid control's AfterColUpdate event:

1 Open the dgdPay control's AfterColUpdate event, then maximize the Code window.

First, create the object variable and assign an object reference to it.

2 Press the **Tab** key, then type **dim objFlds as object** and press the **Enter** key. Type **set objFlds = adopay.recordset.fields** and press the **Enter** key.

Next, calculate the employee's gross pay.

3 Type **objFlds("fldGross") = objFlds("fldHours") * objFlds("fldRate")** and press the **Enter** key.

The next step in the pseudocode shown in Figure 10-44 is to calculate the FICA tax, which is a combination of Social Security (old age, survivors, and disability insurance) and Medicare (hospital insurance). You calculate the employee's FICA tax by multiplying his or her gross pay, which is stored in the employee's fldGross field, by the FICA tax rate; assume that the FICA tax rate is 7.655%. You will store the result of the calculation in the employee's fldFica field.

4 Type **objFlds("fldFica") = objFlds("fldGross") * .07655** and press the **Enter** key.

According to the pseudocode shown in Figure 10-44, the next step is to call a function to calculate the FWT. You will learn how to create and invoke a function in Lesson C. For now, you can skip this step.

The next step in the pseudocode is to calculate the employee's net pay. You do so by subtracting the employee's FICA and FWT from his or her gross pay. You will assign the result of the calculation to the employee's fldNet field.

5 Enter the net pay calculation and the documentation shown in Figure 10-45.

enter this documentation

enter this documentation

enter this line of code

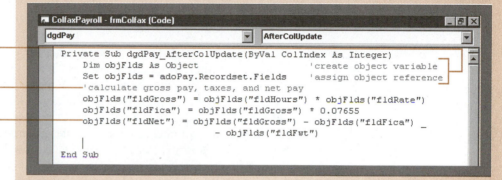

```
Private Sub dgdPay_AfterColUpdate(ByVal ColIndex As Integer)
    Dim objFlds As Object                    'create object variable
    Set objFlds = adoPay.Recordset.Fields    'assign object reference
    'calculate gross pay, taxes, and net pay
    objFlds("fldGross") = objFlds("fldHours") * objFlds("fldRate")
    objFlds("fldFica") = objFlds("fldGross") * 0.07655
    objFlds("fldNet") = objFlds("fldGross") - objFlds("fldFica") _
                      - objFlds("fldFwt")

End Sub
```

Figure 10-45: Completed AfterColUpdate event for the DataGrid control

6 Close the Code window, then **save** and **run** the application.

7 Click the **cell that contains the hours worked for Martha Adams**. Type **30** and press the **Enter** key. The values 300.00, 22.97, and 277.04 appear in the Gross, Fica, and Net columns, respectively. See Figure 10-46.

**the net pay is
off by one cent**

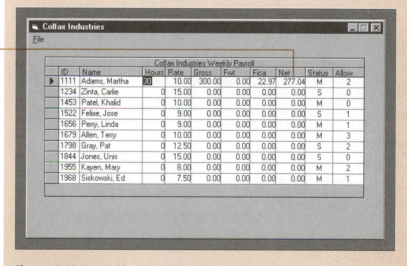

Colfax Industries Weekly Payroll

ID	Name	Hours	Rate	Gross	Fwt	Fica	Net	Status	Allow
1111	Adams, Martha	30	10.00	300.00	0.00	22.97	277.04	M	2
1234	Zinta, Carlie	0	15.00	0.00	0.00	0.00	0.00	S	0
1453	Patel, Khalid	0	10.00	0.00	0.00	0.00	0.00	M	0
1522	Felixe, Jose	0	9.00	0.00	0.00	0.00	0.00	S	1
1656	Perry, Linda	0	9.00	0.00	0.00	0.00	0.00	M	1
1679	Allen, Terry	0	10.00	0.00	0.00	0.00	0.00	M	3
1798	Gray, Pat	0	12.50	0.00	0.00	0.00	0.00	S	2
1844	Jones, Unis	0	15.00	0.00	0.00	0.00	0.00	S	0
1955	Kayen, Mary	0	8.00	0.00	0.00	0.00	0.00	M	2
1968	Siskowski, Ed	0	7.50	0.00	0.00	0.00	0.00	M	1

Figure 10-46: DataGrid control showing computed values for Martha Adams

Notice that the net pay is incorrect; it should be 277.03 (300.00 minus 22.97) rather than 277.04. This slight difference is due to a rounding error that occurs when making the net pay calculation. Although 22.97 appears in the Fica column, the number 22.965 is stored in the fldFica field because the field stores numbers with 5 decimal places. When Visual Basic subtracts 22.965 from 300.00, it results in 277.035, which appears as 277.04 in the cell. You can fix these rounding problems by using Visual Basic's Round function.

8   Type 0 as Martha's hours worked, and then press the **Enter** key. Click **File** on the form's menu bar, and then click **Exit**.

Rounding Numbers

You can use Visual Basic's **Round function** to return a number rounded to a specific number of decimal places. The syntax of the Round function is **Round**(*expression* [,*numdecimalplaces*]), where *expression* is a numeric expression, and *numdecimalplaces* is a number indicating how many places to the right of the decimal are included in the rounding. (If *numdecimalplaces* is omitted, the Round function returns an integer.) For example, `Round(3.235, 2)` will return the number 3.24, but `Round(3.234, 2)` will return the number 3.23. Notice that the Round function rounds the number up only if the number to its right is 5 or greater; otherwise the Round function truncates the excess digits. You will use the Round function to round the results of the gross pay, Fica tax, and net pay calculations to two decimal places. (You also will use the Round function in Lesson C to round the FWT to two decimal places.)

To include the Round function in the payroll calculations:

1   Open the DataGrid control's AfterColUpdate event, then maximize the Code window. Add the Round function to the three calculations as shown in Figure 10-47.

include the Round function in these calculations

```
ColfaxPayroll - frmColfax (Code)

dgdPay                          AfterColUpdate

Private Sub dgdPay_AfterColUpdate(ByVal ColIndex As Integer)
    Dim objFlds As Object                'create object variable
    Set objFlds = adoPay.Recordset.Fields    'assign object reference
    'calculate gross pay, taxes, and net pay
    objFlds("fldGross") = Round(objFlds("fldHours") * objFlds("fldRate"), 2)
    objFlds("fldFica") = Round(objFlds("fldGross") * 0.07655, 2)
    objFlds("fldNet") = Round(objFlds("fldGross") - objFlds("fldFica") _
                        - objFlds("fldFwt"), 2)

End Sub
```

Figure 10-47: Round function included in calculations

2   Close the Code window, then **save** and **run** the application. Type **30** in the cell that contains Martha Adams' hours worked, then press the **Enter** key. The values 300.00, 22.97, and 277.03 appear correctly in the Gross, Fica, and Net columns.

3   Type **0** in the cell that contains Martha Adams' hours worked, then press the **Enter** key. The value 0.00 appears in the Gross, Fica, and Net columns.

4   Click **File** on the form's menu bar, then click **Exit** to stop the application.

You now have completed Lesson B. You can either take a break or complete the questions and exercises at the end of the lesson. You will complete the Colfax payroll application in Lesson C.

S U M M A R Y

To use the DataGrid control:

■   Add the Microsoft ADO Data Control 6.0 (OLEDB) and the Microsoft DataGrid Control 6.0 (OLEDB) tools to the toolbox. Include an ADO data control and a DataGrid control in the interface. Set the ADO data control's ConnectionString and RecordSource properties, then set the DataGrid control's DataSource property. To modify the DataGrid control during design time, right-click the control, then select the appropriate option on its popup menu.

To create an object variable and then assign an object reference to it:

■   Use both the Dim and the Set statements. The syntax of the Dim statement to create an object variable is **Dim** *objectVariableName* **As** *datatype*, where *datatype* can be a specific object type (such as Sheet, Range, or Recordset) or the keyword Object, which can be used to represent a reference to any object. The syntax of the Set statement to assign an object reference to an object variable is **Set** *objectVariableName* = *object*, where *object's* data type must agree with the data type of the object whose name is *objectVariableName*.

To round numbers to a specific number of decimal places:

■   Use the Round function. The syntax of the Round function is **Round**(*expression* [,*numdecimalplaces*]), where *expression* is a numeric expression, and *numdecimalplaces* is a number indicating how many places to the right of the decimal are included in the rounding. If *numdecimalplaces* is omitted, the Round function returns an integer. The function rounds a number up only if the number to its right is 5 or greater; otherwise the function truncates the excess digits.

Q U E S T I O N S

1.   For an ADO data control to access the records stored in a database, you must set the ADO data control's _____ and _____ properties.
   a. ConnectionString
   b. DataBase
   c. DataField
   d. DataSource
   e. RecordSource

2. You bind a DataGrid control to an ADO data control by setting the DataGrid control's _____ property.
    a. ConnectionString
    b. DataBase
    c. DataField
    d. DataSource
    e. RecordSource

3. The intersection of a row and a column in the DataGrid control is called a _____ .
    a. block
    b. cell
    c. field
    d. section
    e. zone

4. To display the database fields in the DataGrid control during design time, you _____ the DataGrid control, then select Retrieve Fields from the popup menu.
    a. click
    b. double-click
    c. right-click

5. You can prevent the user from editing the DataGrid control's data during run time by deselecting the _____ check box, which is located on the Property Pages General tab.
    a. AllowChange
    b. AllowEdit
    c. AllowUpdate
    d. Edit
    e. Update

6. You use the _____ tab on the Property Pages dialog box to change the DataGrid control's column headings to more descriptive ones.
    a. Columns
    b. Edit
    c. Format
    d. General
    e. Layout

7. You use the _____ tab on the Property Pages dialog box to tell the DataGrid control to display a column's numbers with two decimal places.
    a. Columns
    b. Edit
    c. Format
    d. General
    e. Layout

8. You prevent the user from changing the contents of a column in the DataGrid control by selecting the column's _____ check box, which is located on the Layout tab on the Property Pages dialog box.
    a. ColumnLock
    b. ColumnNoEdit
    c. DisallowEdit
    d. Locked
    e. NoEdit

9. You use the _____ tab on the Property Pages dialog box to tell the DataGrid control to align the data displayed in a column.
    a. Columns
    b. Edit
    c. Format
    d. General
    e. Layout

10. To size a column in the DataGrid control during design time, you need first to put the control in _____ mode by right-clicking the control, and then selecting _____ from the popup menu.
    a. Column, Size
    b. ColumnSize, Size
    c. Edit, ColumnSize
    d. Edit, Edit
    e. Size, Edit

11. Which three of the following DataGrid control events occur when the user moves the focus to either another cell in the control or another control in the interface?
    a. AfterColEdit
    b. AfterColUpdate
    c. AfterUpdate
    d. BeforeColUpdate
    e. BeforeUpdate

12. Which two of the following DataGrid control events occur only after the focus moves to another record in the DataGrid control?
    a. AfterColEdit
    b. AfterColUpdate
    c. AfterUpdate
    d. BeforeColUpdate
    e. BeforeUpdate

13. Which of the following statements tells Visual Basic to multiply the contents of the fldNum1 field by the number 3, and then store the result in the fldTot field? The name of the ADO data control is adoNum.
    a. adoNum.Fields(fldTot)= adoNum.Fields(fldNum1) * 3
    b. adoNum.Fields("fldTot")= adoNum.Fields("fldNum1") * 3
    c. adoNum.Recordset("fldTot")= adoNum.Recordset("fldNum1") * 3
    d. adoNum.Recordset.Fields(fldTot)= adoNum.Recordset.Fields(fldNum1) * 3
    e. adoNum.Recordset.Fields("fldTot")= adoNum.Recordset.Fields("fldNum1") * 3

14. Which of the following statements creates an object variable named objFlds that can store a reference to the Fields collection object?
    a. Dim objFlds as FieldsCollection
    b. Dim objFlds as Object
    c. Dim objFlds as ObjectCollection
    d. Set objFlds as Fields
    e. Set objFlds as Object

15. Which of the following statements assigns, to the object variable created in Question 14, a reference to the Fields collection object created by the adoNum control?
    a. Dim objFlds = adoNum.Fields
    b. Dim objFlds = adoNum.FieldsCollection
    c. Set objFlds = adoNum.FieldsCollection
    d. Set objFlds = adoNum.Fields
    e. Set objFlds = adoNum.Recordset.Fields

16. In Questions 14 and 15, you created an object variable named objFlds and assigned a Fields collection reference to it. Which of the following statements will multiply the contents of the fldNum1 field by .15, and then store the result, rounded to three decimal places, in the fldTot field?
   a. objFlds(fldTot)= objFlds(Round(fldNum1) * .15, 3)
   b. objFlds("fldTot")= Round(objFlds("fldNum1") , 3) * .15
   c. objFlds("fldTot")= Round(objFlds("fldNum1") * .15, 3)
   d. objFlds.Fields("fldTot")= Round(objFlds.Fields("fldNum1") * .15, 3)
   e. objFlds.Recordset(fldTot)= Round(objFlds.Recordset(fldNum1) * .15, 3)

E X E R C I S E S

1. In this exercise, you will use an Access database, an ADO data control, and a DataGrid control.

   Scenario: LLM Industries wants an application that the sales manager can use to calculate each salesperson's commission. The salesperson information is stored in an Access database named lb1.mdb, which is located in the Tut10 folder on your Student Disk. The name of the table is tblSales. Figures 10-48 and 10-49 show the database structure and records, respectively.

   ### tblSales : Table

Field Name	Data Type	Description
fldID	Number	Integer representing the salesperson's ID
fldName	Text	Salesperson's name
fldSales	Number	Single representing the monthly sales amount
fldCommission	Number	Single representing the monthly commission

   Figure 10-48

fldID	fldName	fldSales	fldCommission
10	Boone, Janice	0	0
11	Jackson, Bill	0	0
12	Carlisle, John	0	0
13	Baker, Carol	0	0
14	Johnson, Phil	0	0

   Figure 10-49

   a. Open a new Visual Basic project. Save the form and the project as lb1Done in the Tut10 folder on your Student Disk. Include an ADO data control, a DataGrid control, and a File menu in the interface. The File menu should contain two options, Print and Exit.
   b. Set the form's name to frmSales. Set the project's name to LLM. Code the form's Load event so that it centers the form.
   c. Code the File menu's Exit option so that it unloads the form. Code the Print option so that it prints the interface.
   d. Set the ADO data control's properties appropriately. Be sure to link the ADO data control to the lb1.mdb database. Display all of the fields and records in order by the salesperson ID. The ADO data control should not be visible during run time.

e. Set the DataGrid control's properties appropriately. Be sure to bind the DataGrid control to the ADO data control. Display two decimal places in the sales and commission columns, and display the comma separator in the sales column. Right-align the contents of the sales and commission columns. Also, size the columns in the grid, make the column headings more descriptive, and put a title on the grid. Don't allow the user to make any changes to the ID or commission columns.

f. Code the DataGrid control's AfterColUpdate event so that it calculates each salesperson's commission by multiplying his or her sales by 10%. Do not use an object variable. Round the commission amounts to two decimal places.

g. Save and run the application. Enter the following five sale amounts in the sales column: 1000, 5000, 3450, 2165, 4575. Print the interface, then stop the application and print the code.

h. Open the DataGrid control's AfterColUpdate event. Create an object variable and assign the ADO data control's Fields collection object to it. Modify the code appropriately, then save and run the application. Change the first sale amount from 1,000 to 4,590. Print the interface, then stop the application and print the code.

i. Open the DataGrid control's AfterColUpdate event. Create an object variable and assign the ADO data control's Recordset object to it. (*Hint*: Rather than using the `Object` keyword in the Dim statement, use the `Recordset` keyword.) Modify the code appropriately, then save and run the application. Change the last sale amount from 4,575 to 6,900. Print the interface, then stop the application and print the code.

j. Submit the printouts and code from steps g, h, and i.

2. In this exercise, you will use an Access database, an ADO data control, and a DataGrid control.

Scenario: Taft Industries wants an application that the sales manager can use to calculate the new price of each item in inventory. The item information is stored in an Access database named lb2.mdb, which is located in the Tut10 folder on your Student Disk. The name of the table is tblPrices. Figures 10-50 and 10-51 show the database structure and records, respectively.

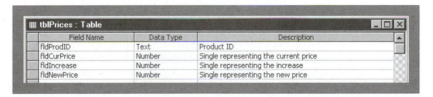

Figure 10-50

fldProdID	fldCurPrice	fldIncrease	fldNewPrice
A9345	0	0	0
A4567	0	0	0
Z5678	0	0	0
B1234	0	0	0
B0133	0	0	0

Figure 10-51

a. Open a new Visual Basic project. Save the form and the project as lb2Done in the Tut10 folder on your Student Disk. Include an ADO data control, a DataGrid control, and a File menu in the interface. The File menu should contain two options, Print and Exit.

b. Set the form's name to frmPrice. Set the project's name to Taft. Code the form's Load event so that it centers the form.

c. Code the File menu's Exit option so that it unloads the form. Code the Print option so that it prints the interface.

d. Set the ADO data control's properties appropriately. Be sure to link the ADO data control to the lb2.mdb database. Display all of the fields and records in order by the product ID. The ADO data control should not be visible during run time.

e. Set the DataGrid control's properties appropriately. Be sure to bind the DataGrid control to the ADO data control. Display two decimal places in the current price and new price columns, and right-align the contents of both columns. Display a percent sign and zero decimal places in the increase column, and center the contents of the column. Also, size the columns in the grid, make the column headings more descriptive, and put a title on the grid. Don't allow the user to make any changes to the product ID or new price columns.

f. Code the DataGrid control's AfterColUpdate event so that it calculates each item's new price by multiplying the current price by the increase percentage. Do not use an object variable. Round the new price to two decimal places.

g. Save and run the application. Enter the following current prices and increase percentages (*Hint*: Enter 10% as .1): 15, 10%, 9.75, 10%, 45.75, 15%, 25, 9%, 10, 25%. Print the interface, then stop the application and print the code.

h. Open the DataGrid control's AfterColUpdate event. Create an object variable and assign the ADO data control's Fields collection object to it. Modify the code appropriately, then save and run the application. Change the first increase amount from 10% to 12%. Print the interface, then stop the application and print the code.

i. Open the DataGrid control's AfterColUpdate event. Create an object variable and assign the ADO data control's Recordset object to it. (*Hint*: Rather than using the `Object` keyword in the Dim statement, use the `Recordset` keyword.) Modify the code appropriately, then save and run the application. Change the last current price from 10.00 to 20.00. Print the interface, then stop the application and print the code.

j. Submit the printouts and code from steps g, h, and i.

3. In this exercise, you will use an Access database, an ADO data control, and a DataGrid control.

   Scenario: Your friend Michael has asked you to create an application that he can use to keep track of the total amount he spends each month on electric, gas, and water. The monthly information is stored in an Access database named lb3.mdb, which is located in the Tut10 folder on your Student Disk. The name of the table is tblUtilities. Figures 10-52 and 10-53 show the database structure and records, respectively.

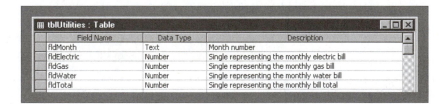

Figure 10-52

fldMonth	fldElectric	fldGas	fldWater	fldTotal
	0	0	0	0

Figure 10-53

a. Open a new Visual Basic project. Save the form and the project as lb3Done in the Tut10 folder on your Student Disk. Include an ADO data control, a DataGrid control, and a File menu in the interface. The File menu should contain two options, Print and Exit.

b. Set the form's name to frmBills. Set the project's name to Bills. Code the form's Load event so that it centers the form.

c. Code the File menu's Exit option so that it unloads the form. Code the Print option so that it prints the interface.

d. Set the ADO data control's properties appropriately. Be sure to link the ADO data control to the lb3.mdb database. Display all of the fields and records in order by the month. The ADO data control should not be visible during run time.

e. Set the DataGrid control's properties appropriately. Be sure to bind the DataGrid control to the ADO data control. Display two decimal places in the electric, gas, water, and total columns, and right-align the contents of these columns. Also display a dollar sign ($) in the total column. Center the contents of the month column. Also, size the columns in the grid, make the column headings more descriptive, and put a title on the grid. Don't allow the user to make any changes to the total column. Allow the user to add records to the grid during run time.

f. Code the DataGrid control's AfterColUpdate event so that it calculates the total of the monthly bills. Use an object variable to refer to the ADO data control's Fields collection.

g. Save and run the application. Enter the following information:

Month	Electric	Gas	Water
01	75.00	125.00	35.00
02	74.35	108.67	30.00
03	67.89	95.45	25.00

h. Print the interface, then stop the application and print the code.

4. In this exercise, you will use an Access database, an ADO data control, a DataGrid control, and a one-dimensional variable array.

Scenario: Jackson Industries wants an application that the clerk can use to keep track of each employee's ID, job code, and job title. After entering the job code, the application should automatically display the employee's job title. The employee information is stored in an Access database named lb4.mdb, which is located in the Tut10 folder on your Student Disk. The name of the table is tblEmp. Figures 10-54 and 10-55 show the database structure and records, respectively.

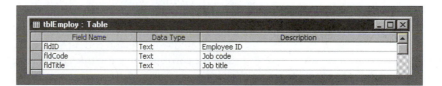

Figure 10-54

fldID	fldCode	fldTitle
111		
222		
333		
345		
456		
567		

Figure 10-55

a. Open a new Visual Basic project. Save the form and the project as lb4Done in the Tut10 folder on your Student Disk. Include an ADO data control, a DataGrid control, and a File menu in the interface. The File menu should contain two options, Print and Exit.

b. Set the form's name to frmEmp. Set the project's name to Jackson. Code the form's Load event so that it centers the form.

c. Code the File menu's Exit option so that it unloads the form. Code the Print option so that it prints the interface.

d. Set the ADO data control's properties appropriately. Be sure to link the ADO data control to the lb4.mdb database. Display all of the fields and records in order by the employee ID. The ADO data control should not be visible during run time.

e. Set the DataGrid control's properties appropriately. Be sure to bind the DataGrid control to the ADO data control. Size the columns in the grid, make the column headings more descriptive, and put a title on the grid. Don't allow the user to make any changes to the employee ID or job title columns.

f. Declare a form-level one-dimensional String array named strTitles. The array should have four elements, numbered 1 through 4.

g. Fill the strTitles array with the following four job titles in the form's Load event: Manager, Secretary, Payroll Clerk, Security Guard.

h. Code the DataGrid control's AfterColUpdate event so that it automatically displays the employee's job title after his or her job code is entered. The job code indicates which job title from the strTitles array to display. For example, if the user enters a job code of 1, the application should display the contents of the strTitles array's first element—in this case, Manager—in the DataGrid control's title field. If the user enters an invalid code (a code that is not 1, 2, 3, or 4), display "Unknown" in the title field. Use an object variable.

i. Save and run the application. Enter the following six codes in the job code column: 1, 3, 2, 4, 1, 7. Print the interface, then stop the application and print the code.

5. In this exercise, you will use an Access database, an ADO data control, a DataGrid control, and a two-dimensional variable array. Before you can complete this exercise, you must have completed Lesson B's Exercise 4.

a. Open the lb4Done (lb4Done.vbp) project that you created in Lesson B's Exericse 4. Save the form and the project as lb5Done in the Tut10 folder on your Student Disk.

b. Link the ADO data control to the lb5.mdb database, rather than the lb4.mdb database. Display all of the fields and records in order by the employee ID.

c. Declare a form-level two-dimensional String array named strTitles. The array should have four rows and two columns.

d. Fill the strTitles array with data in the form's Load event. The first column in the array should store the job codes (A, B, C, and D) and the second column should store the corresponding job titles (Manager, Secretary, Payroll Clerk, Security Guard).

e. Code the DataGrid control's AfterColUpdate event so that it automatically displays the employee's job title after his or her job code is entered. You will need to search the first column of the strTitles array for the job code, and then display the corresponding title from the array's second column. Display the title in the DataGrid control's title field. If the user enters an invalid code (a code that is not A, B, C, or D), display "Unknown" in the title field. Use an object variable.

f. Save and run the application. Enter the following six codes in the job code column: B, D, C, F, A, B. Print the interface, then stop the application and print the code.

Exercises 6 through 8 are Discovery exercises, which allow you to both "discover" solutions to problems on your own and experiment with topics not covered in the tutorial.

discovery ▶ 6. In this exercise, you will learn about Visual Basic's Date, Time, and Now functions.

a. Open the lbPay (lbPay.vbp) project, which is located in the Tut10 folder on your Student Disk. Save the form and the project as lb6Done in the Tut10 folder on your Student Disk.

b. If you have access to the MSDN Library, research Visual Basic's Date, Time, and Now functions.

c. Open the form's Load event. Include an instruction that will display, at the top of the DataGrid control, the control's current title followed by the system date. Save and run the application to verify that it is working correctly, then stop the application and print the code for the form's Load event only.

discovery ▶ 7. In this exercise, you will learn about the DataGrid control's OnAddNew event, as well as Visual Basic's Date function.

Scenario: Mary Jones, the order clerk at Hoyen Inc., needs an application that she can use to enter each order's invoice number, product number, quantity ordered, and invoice date. She would like the application to automatically enter the current date as the invoice date. The invoice information is stored in an Access database named lb7.mdb, which is located in the Tut10 folder on your Student Disk. The name of the table is tblInvoices. Figures 10-56 and 10-57 show the database structure and records, respectively.

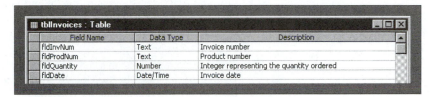

Figure 10-56

fldInvNum	fldProdNum	fldQuantity	fldDate
12345	39AB	10	09/13/1998
12346	87BC	20	09/13/1998

Figure 10-57

a. Open a new Visual Basic project. Save the form and the project as lb7Done in the Tut10 folder on your Student Disk. Include an ADO data control, a DataGrid control, and a File menu in the interface. The File menu should contain two options, Print and Exit.

b. Set the form's name to frmInvoices. Set the project's name to Invoices. Code the form's Load event so that it centers the form.

c. Code the File menu's Exit option so that it unloads the form. Code the Print option so that it prints the interface.

d. Set the ADO data control's properties appropriately. Be sure to link the ADO data control to the lb7.mdb database. Display all of the fields and records in order by the invoice number. The ADO data control should not be visible during run time.

e. Set the DataGrid control's properties appropriately. Be sure to bind the DataGrid control to the ADO data control. Display the date field using the MM/dd/yyyy format. Right-align the quantity column. Also, size the columns in the grid, make the column headings more descriptive, and put a title on the grid. Allow the user to add records to and delete records from the grid during run time.

f. If you have access to the MSDN Library, research Visual Basic's Date function and the DataGrid control's OnAddNew event.

g. Code the DataGrid control's OnAddNew event so that it automatically displays the current date in the fldDate field when a new record is added to the grid. Save and run the application. Enter the following orders:

Invoice number	Product number	Quantity ordered
12347	89CD	30
12348	55AB	10
77777	99AB	20
12350	23CD	10

The current date should appear in the date column.

h. Print the interface. Delete the 77777 record, then print the interface again. Stop the application and print the code.

discovery ▶ 8. In this exercise, you will learn about the Recordset object's RecordCount property. Before you can complete this exercise, you need to complete Lesson B's Exercise 2.

a. Open the lb2Done (lb2Done.vbp) project that you created in Lesson B's Exercise 2. Save the form and the project as lb8Done in the Tut10 folder on your Student Disk.

b. Link the ADO data control to the lb8.mdb database, rather than the lb2.mdb database. Display all of the fields and records in order by the product ID.

c. If you have access to the MSDN Library, research the Recordset object's RecordCount property.

d. As the user enters an item's current price and increase percentage, recall that the DataGrid control's AfterColUpdate event calculates the item's new price. When the user has completed entering the data for all of the items, you will have the application copy the contents of the new price column to the current price column, and then enter zeros in the increase percentage and new price columns. Code the form's Unload event appropriately. (*Hint*: You may want to review the Recordset object's methods listed in Tutorial 9's Figure 9-34.)

e. Save and run the application. Enter the following current prices and increase percentages (*Hint*: Enter 10% as .1): 15, 10%, 9.75, 10%, 45.75, 15%, 25, 9%, 10, 25%. Print the interface, then stop the application.

f. Run the application again. The new prices shown in step e's printout should now appear in the current price column, and the increase percentage and new price columns should contain zeros. Print the interface, then stop the application and print the code.

g. Submit the printouts and code from steps e and f.

LESSON C
objectives

In this lesson you will learn how to:

■ Create a function
■ Pass an array to a function
■ Pass an object to a function

Completing the Colfax Payroll Application

Storing the Federal Withholding Tax Tables in Two Two-dimensional Arrays

As you may remember, the Colfax payroll application needs to calculate each employee's weekly federal withholding tax (FWT), the amount of which is based on the employee's filing status—either single (including head of household) or married—and his or her weekly taxable wages. You calculate the weekly taxable wages first by multiplying the number of withholding allowances by $51.92 (the 1998 value of a withholding allowance), and then subtracting the result from the weekly gross pay. For example, if your weekly gross pay is $400 and you have two withholding allowances, your weekly taxable wages are $296.16 (400 minus 103.84, which is the product of 2 times 51.92). You use the weekly taxable wages, along with the filing status and the weekly Federal Withholding Tax tables, to determine the amount of tax to withhold. Figure 10-58 shows the 1998 weekly FWT tables.

FWT Tables – Weekly Payroll Period

Single person (including head of household)

If the taxable wages are:		The amount of income tax to withhold is		
Over	But not over	Base amount	Percentage	Of excess over
	$ 51	0		
$ 51	$ 517	0	15%	$ 51
$ 517	$1,105	$ 69.90 plus	28%	$ 517
$1,105	$2,493	$ 234.54 plus	31%	$1,105
$2,493	$5,385	$ 664.82 plus	36%	$2,493
$5,385		$1,705.94 plus	39.6%	$5,385

Figure 10-58: Weekly FWT tables for 1998

Married person

If the taxable wages are:		The amount of income tax to withhold is		
Over	But not over	Base amount	Percentage	Of excess over
	$ 124	0		
$ 124	$ 899	0	15%	$ 124
$ 899	$1,855	$ 116.25 plus	28%	$ 899
$1,855	$3,084	$ 383.93 plus	31%	$1,855
$3,084	$5,439	$ 764.92 plus	36%	$3,084
$5,439		$1,612.72 plus	39.6%	$5,439

Figure 10-58: Weekly FWT tables for 1998 (continued)

You will notice that both tables shown in Figure 10-58 contain five columns of information. The first two columns list various ranges, also called brackets, of taxable wage amounts. The first column—the Over column—lists the amount that a taxable wage in that range must be over, and the second column—the But not over column—lists the maximum amount included in the range. The remaining three columns (Base amount, Percentage, and Of excess over) tell you how to calculate the tax for each range. For example, assume that you are married and your weekly taxable wages are $296.16. Before you can calculate the amount of your tax, you need to locate your taxable wages in the first two columns of the Married table; in this case, your taxable wages fall within the $124 through $899 range. After locating the range that contains your taxable wages, you then use the remaining three columns in the table to calculate your tax. According to the table, taxable wages in the $124 through $899 bracket have a tax of 15% of the amount over $124; therefore, your tax would be $25.82, as shown in Figure 10-59.

Taxable wages	$ 296.16
Of excess over	−124.00
	172.16
Percentage	* .15
	25.82
Base amount	+ 0.00
Tax	$ 25.82

Figure 10-59: FWT calculation for a married taxpayer with $296.16 in taxable wages

As Figure 10-59 indicates, you calculate the tax first by subtracting 124 (the amount shown in the Of excess over column) from your taxable wages of 296.16, giving 172.16. You then multiply 172.16 by 15% (the amount shown in the Percentage column), giving 25.82. To that result you add the amount shown in the Base column—in this case, 0—giving $25.82 as your tax.

Now assume that your taxable wages are $600 per week and you are single. Figure 10-60 shows how the correct tax amount of $93.14 is calculated.

Taxable wages	$ 600.00
Of excess over	−517.00
	83.00
Percentage	* .28
	23.24
Base amount	+ 69.90
Tax	93.14

Figure 10-60: FWT calculation for a single taxpayer with $600 in taxable wages

Although the FWT tables use two columns (Over and But not over) to show each range of taxable wages, you need to search only the But not over column to find the range in which your taxable wages reside. To do so, you scan the But not over column, stopping the search when you encounter the first value that is greater than or equal to your taxable wages; your taxable wages will fall in that bracket. Try this using the Single table with taxable wages of $900. The first value in the But not over column is $51, which is not greater than or equal to the $900 for which you are searching, so you must continue the search. The second value in the But not over column is $517, which is also not greater than or equal to $900, so you continue searching. The third value in the But not over column is $1,105, which is greater than the $900 for which you are searching. Therefore, your taxable wages of $900 fall in the $517-$1,105 range, and your tax is $177.14. This amount is calculated by subtracting 517 (the amount shown in the Of excess over column) from the taxable wages of 900, giving 383. The 383 is then multiplied by the amount shown in the Percentage column—in this case, 28%—giving 107.24. To the 107.24 you add the 69.90 shown in the Base amount column, giving a tax of $177.14.

You will store each FWT table in its own two-dimensional array; each array will contain six rows and four columns. So that you do not have to type the table information yourself, the information has been entered in a text file named taxtbls.txt for you. The contents of the taxtbls.txt file, which is located in the Tut10 folder on your Student Disk, are shown in Figure 10-61.

tip

You also can search only the Over column for your taxable wages. You will do so in Lesson C's Exercise 4.

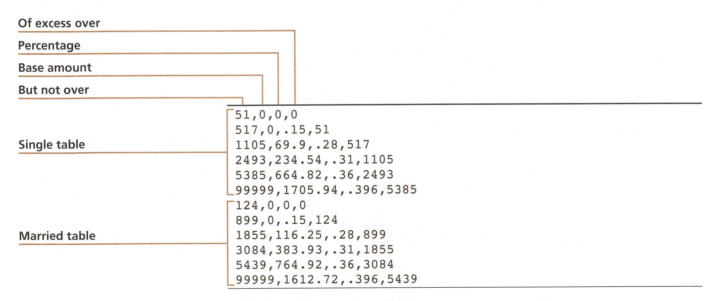

Figure 10-61: FWT tables shown in the taxtbls.txt file

Notice that the file contains 12 records (rows) and four fields (columns). The first six records contain the information from the Single table, and the last six records contain the Married table information. Compare the contents of the file with the contents of the tables shown earlier in Figure 10-58. You will notice that the amounts appearing in the first column of the file correspond to the values listed in Figure 10-58's But not over columns, with two exceptions: the number 99999 is used as the But not over value in both the sixth and twelfth records, which represent the last brackets in each table. You can use any amount as the maximum value for the last bracket, but you must be sure to select a value that you know the taxable wages will never exceed. If you do not use a large enough value, the application will not be able to locate the employee's taxable wage range in the table, and therefore will not be able to calculate the tax. (Recall that the taxable wages are located in the bracket whose But not over amount is greater than or equal to the taxable wages.) In the Colfax company, it is safe to say that no one will be earning more than $99,999 for the week.

As Figure 10-61 indicates, the second field in each record corresponds to the values listed in the Base amount columns of the tax tables, the third corresponds to the values listed in the Percentage columns, and the fourth corresponds to the values listed in the Of excess over columns. To use the tax tables in the current application, you will read the Single table information from the sequential access file into a two-dimensional array named sngSingle, and you will read the Married table information into a two-dimensional array named sngMarried. Before you can read the information into the arrays, you first must declare the arrays. Because more than one procedure will need to use the information stored in the arrays, you will declare each as a form-level array in the form's General declarations section.

To declare the two-dimensional arrays, and then read data into them:

1   Start Visual Basic, if necessary, and open the **lbPay** (lbPay.vbp) project, which is located in the Tut10 folder on your Student Disk. View the form, then save the form and the project as **lcPay**.

2   Open the form's General Declarations section. In the line below the `Option Explicit` statement, type **dim sngSingle(1 to 6, 1 to 4) as single** and press the **Enter** key, then type **dim sngMarried(1 to 6, 1 to 4) as single** and press the **Enter** key.

After declaring the arrays, you then can fill them with the data stored in the taxtbles.txt file, which is located in the Tut10 folder on your Student Disk.

3   Open the form's Load event, then maximize the Code window. Enter the additional code and documentation shown in Figure 10-62. (If the taxtbls.txt file is located on the B drive, change the a: in the Open instruction to b:.)

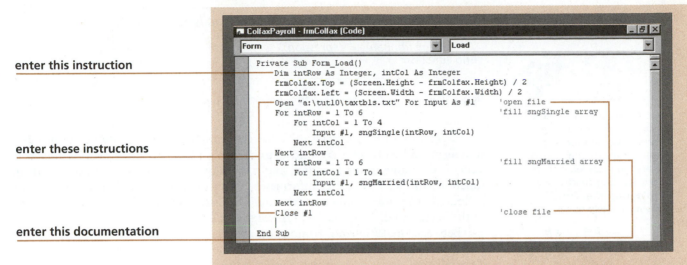

enter this instruction

enter these instructions

enter this documentation

```
ColfaxPayroll - frmColfax [Code]

Form                                              Load

    Private Sub Form_Load()
        Dim intRow As Integer, intCol As Integer
        frmColfax.Top = (Screen.Height - frmColfax.Height) / 2
        frmColfax.Left = (Screen.Width - frmColfax.Width) / 2
        Open "a:\tut10\taxtbls.txt" For Input As #1        'open file
        For intRow = 1 To 6                                'fill sngSingle array
            For intCol = 1 To 4
                Input #1, sngSingle(intRow, intCol)
            Next intCol
        Next intRow
        For intRow = 1 To 6                                'fill sngMarried array
            For intCol = 1 To 4
                Input #1, sngMarried(intRow, intCol)
            Next intCol
        Next intRow
        Close #1                                           'close file

    End Sub
```

Figure 10-62: Completed Load event

The first set of nested For Next loops fills the sngSingle array with the wage and tax information pertaining to the Single tax table. Recall that that information is stored in the first six rows of the taxtbls.txt file. The second set of nested For Next loops fills the sngMarried array with the Married table's wage and tax information, which is stored in the last six rows of the taxtbls.txt file.

4 Close the Code window, then **save** the application.

Now that the arrays are declared and filled with data, you can use them to determine each employee's FWT. You will create a function procedure to calculate the FWT, and then invoke that procedure from the DataGrid control's AfterColUpdate event.

Creating a Function Procedure to Calculate the FWT

Like a sub procedure, which you learned about in Tutorial 1, a **function procedure**, typically referred to simply as a **function**, is a block of code that performs a specific task. However, unlike a sub procedure, a function returns a value. Some functions, such as Val and Round, are intrinsic to Visual Basic. The Val function, you will recall, returns the numeric equivalent of a string, and the Round function returns the result of rounding a value to a specific number of decimal places.

You also can create your own functions, referred to as user-defined functions. After creating a user-defined function, you then can invoke it from one or more places in the program. You invoke a user-defined function in exactly the same way as you invoke a built-in function. As with Visual Basic's built-in functions, you also can pass (send) information to a user-defined function. The basic syntax for creating a user-defined function is shown in Figure 10-63.

Private Function *functionname* [(*arglist*)] **As** *datatype*
    [*statements*]
    functionname = *expression*
End Function

Figure 10-63: Basic syntax for creating a user-defined function

As Figure 10-63 indicates, a function begins with the `Private Function` statement and ends with the `End Function` statement. In the syntax, *function-name* is the name of the function, and it is followed by a set of parentheses. If the function will need to receive information from the procedure that invokes it, you include that information in the function's *arglist*. You use the **As** *datatype* section of the syntax to declare the data type of the value returned by the function.

Between the `Private Function` and `End Function` statements, you can include statements that direct the function on how to perform its assigned task. You tell the function to return a value by assigning the value to the function's name using the following syntax: *functionname* = *expression*. In the syntax, *functionname* is the name of the function and *expression* is the value you want the function to return. *expression* can include numbers, letters, and operators. The statement that assigns a value to the function typically appears immediately above the `End Function` statement. In the next set of steps, you will create a function that can be used in the Colfax application to calculate each employee's FWT.

> **To add a function procedure to the form:**
> 1 Open a Code window, then click **Tools**, and then click **Add Procedure**. The Add Procedure dialog box appears.
>
> Use the Add Procedure dialog box to create a Private function procedure named udfCalcFwt. ("udf" is the three-character ID used for a user-defined function.)
> 2 Type **udfCalcFwt** in the Name text box. Click the **Function** option button, then click the **Private** option button, and then click the **OK** button. Visual Basic displays the udfCalcFwt function template in a Code window.

Figure 10-64 shows the pseudocode for the udfCalcFwt function.

---

1. receive the appropriate array and the object variable from the DataGrid control's AfterColUpdate procedure, and return a Single value
2. declare an Integer variable named intX, a Boolean variable named blnFound, a Single variable named sngTaxable, and a Single variable named sngTax
3. assign 1 to intX
4. assign False to blnFound
5. calculate the taxable wages and assign to sngTaxable
6. repeat while there are array elements to search (intX <= 6) and the taxable wages were not found in the array (blnFound = False)
        if the value stored in column 1 in the current array row is greater than or equal to the taxable wages stored in the sngTaxable variable then
                calculate the FWT and assign to sngTax
                assign True to blnFound to indicate that the taxable wage range was found in the array and to end the loop
        else
                add 1 to intX to move to the next row in the array
        end if
    end repeat while
7. return the FWT by assigning the contents of the sngTax variable to the function

---

Figure 10-64: Pseudocode for the udfCalcFwt function

As indicated in step 1 in the pseudocode, the udfCalcFwt function will receive two items of information from the DataGrid control's AfterColUpdate event procedure; therefore, you will need to list two arguments in the function's *arglist*. The first argument will receive the appropriate array to use to calculate the tax—either the sngSingle or sngMarried array—and the second argument will receive the object variable that contains a reference to the Recordset object's Fields collection—in this case, the objFlds object variable.

The syntax of an argument that allows a procedure to receive an entire array is *arrayName* **( ) As** *datatype*. In the syntax, *arrayName* is the name of the array and it must be followed by an empty set of parentheses; *datatype* is the array's data type. The syntax of an argument that allows a procedure to receive an object variable is *objectVariableName* **As** *datatype*, where *objectVariableName* is the name of the object variable and *datatype* is its data type. You will use `sngArray() As Single` as the udfCalcFwt function's first argument, and `objTemp As Object` as the second argument. As you learned in Tutorial 8, the names of the arguments listed in the receiving procedure (sngArray( ) and objTemp) do not need to be identical to the names of the arguments passed to the procedure (either sngSingle( ) or sngMarried( ) and objFlds).

Also indicated in Figure 10-64's pseudocode, the udfCalcFwt function should return the tax amount as a Single value.

To enter the arguments and the return data type for the udfCalcFwt function, then code the function:

1   Maximize the udfCalcFwt function's Code window, and then enter the two arguments and the return data type shown in Figure 10-65.

enter the arguments and the return data type

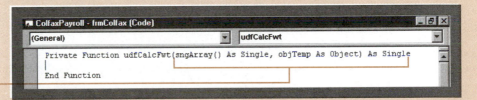

Figure 10-65: Arguments and return data type entered in the udfCalcFwt function

The next step in the pseudocode is to declare four variables: intX, blnFound, sngTaxable, and sngTax. You will use the intX variable to keep track of which row in the array you are currently searching, and you will use the blnFound variable to indicate whether the taxable wages were located in the array. You will use the sngTaxable and sngTax variables to store the taxable wages and tax, respectively.

2   Position the insertion point as shown in Figure 10-65, and then press the **Tab** key. Type **dim intX as integer, blnFound as boolean** and press the **Enter** key, then type **dim sngTaxable as single, sngTax as single** and press the **Enter** key.

According to steps 3 and 4 in the pseudocode, you should assign the number 1, which corresponds to the first row in the array, to the intX variable, and assign the Boolean value False to the blnFound variable.

3   Type **intx = 1** and press the **Enter** key, then type **blnfound = false** and press the **Enter** key.

Now calculate the taxable wages and assign the result to the sngTaxable variable. Recall that you calculate an employee's taxable wages by multiplying the number of his or her withholding allowances by $51.92, and then subtracting that result from his or her gross pay. The number of withholding allowances is stored in the fldAllow field and the gross pay is stored in the fldGross field.

4 Type **'calculate taxable wages** and press the **Enter** key, then type **sngtaxable = objtemp("fldgross") – objtemp("fldallow") * 51.92** and press the **Enter** key.

After calculating the taxable wages, the function should then search the first column of the array, looking for the range in which the taxable wages fall. You will do so by using a loop whose instructions will be repeated as long as there are array elements to search (intX <= 6) and the taxable wage range has not yet been found (blnFound = False). The loop will stop when either the entire array has been searched or the taxable wage range is located.

5 Type **'search array for taxable wage range** and press the **Enter** key, then type **do while intx <= 6 and blnfound = false** and press the **Enter** key.

As step 6 in the pseudocode shows, the loop should contain a selection structure that compares the value stored in the first column of the current array row with the taxable wages stored in the sngTaxable variable. If the value in the array is greater than or equal to the taxable wages, then the function should calculate the FWT and assign it to the sngTax variable. (As you may remember when you earlier used the But not over column of the FWT table to calculate the tax, you stopped the search when you encountered the first value that was greater than or equal to the taxable wages because the taxable wages fell in that bracket.) The function should also assign the Boolean value True to the blnFound variable to indicate that the range containing the taxable wages was found. This will stop the loop from continuing to search the array.

If, on the other hand, the value in the array is less than the taxable wages, then the function should add the number 1 to the value stored in the intX variable, which keeps track of the current array row, so that the search can continue in the next row of the array.

After entering the selection structure, you then can end the loop. The last step in the pseudocode is to return the FWT by assigning the contents of the sngTax variable to the function.

6 Enter the additional code and documentation shown in Figure 10-66.

enter this documentation

enter these instructions

enter this documentation

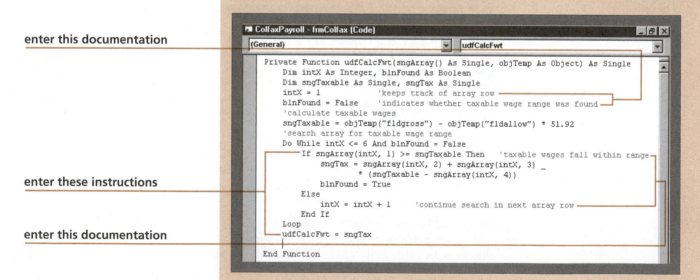

```
ColfaxPayroll - frmColfax (Code)                                    _ 8 X
(General)                              udfCalcFwt

Private Function udfCalcFwt(sngArray() As Single, objTemp As Object) As Single
    Dim intX As Integer, blnFound As Boolean
    Dim sngTaxable As Single, sngTax As Single
    intX = 1                'keeps track of array row
    blnFound = False        'indicates whether taxable wage range was found
    'calculate taxable wages
    sngTaxable = objTemp("fldgross") - objTemp("fldallow") * 51.92
    'search array for taxable wage range
    Do While intX <= 6 And blnFound = False
        If sngArray(intX, 1) >= sngTaxable Then   'taxable wages fall within range
            sngTax = sngArray(intX, 2) + sngArray(intX, 3) _
                    * (sngTaxable - sngArray(intX, 4))
            blnFound = True
        Else
            intX = intX + 1        'continue search in next array row
        End If
    Loop
    udfCalcFwt = sngTax

End Function
```

Figure 10-66: Completed udfCalcFwt function

7 Close the Code window, then save the application.

To complete the Colfax payroll application, you need only to enter the code that invokes the udfCalcFwt function.

Invoking a Function Procedure

Recall that you need to invoke the udfCalcFwt function in the DataGrid control's AfterColUpdate event. As you may remember, the udfCalcFwt function receives two items of information: an array whose data type is Single and an object variable. This means that you will need to pass the function two items of information. The first item will be either the sngSingle or sngMarried array. Which of the two arrays to pass is determined by the entry in the employee's fldStatus field. If the fldStatus field contains the letter S, it indicates that the employee's filing status is Single, so the sngSingle array should be used to calculate the tax. If, on the other hand, the fldStatus field contains the letter M, then the employee's filing status is Married and the sngMarried array should be used. The second item you will need to pass to the function is the objFlds object variable, which contains the reference to the Recordset object's Fields collection. You will assign the function's return value to the employee's fldFwt field.

To complete the payroll application, then test the application:

1 Open the DataGrid control's AfterColUpdate event, then maximize the Code window. Enter the selection structure shown in Figure 10-67.

enter this selection structure

```
ColfaxPayroll - frmColfax (Code)                              _ 回 X

dgdPay                          ▼      AfterColUpdate                   ▼

Private Sub dgdPay_AfterColUpdate(ByVal ColIndex As Integer)
    Dim objFlds As Object                  'create object variable
    Set objFlds = adoPay.Recordset.Fields     'assign object reference
    'calculate gross pay, taxes, and net pay
    objFlds("fldGross") = Round(objFlds("fldHours") * objFlds("fldRate"), 2)
    If UCase(objFlds("fldStatus")) = "S" Then
        objFlds("fldFwt") = Round(udfCalcFwt(sngSingle(), objFlds), 2)
    Else
        objFlds("fldFwt") = Round(udfCalcFwt(sngMarried(), objFlds), 2)
    End If
    objFlds("fldFica") = Round(objFlds("fldGross") * 0.07655, 2)
    objFlds("fldNet") = Round(objFlds("fldGross") - objFlds("fldFica") _
                        - objFlds("fldFwt"), 2)

End Sub
```

Figure 10-67: Completed AfterColUpdate event

Notice that you pass an entire array by using the array name followed by an empty set of parentheses. You pass an object variable simply by using the object variable's name.

2 Close the Code window, then **save** and **run** the application. Enter the hours worked shown in Figure 10-68, then compare your results with those shown in the figure. (Be sure to press the Enter key after making each entry.)

enter these hours

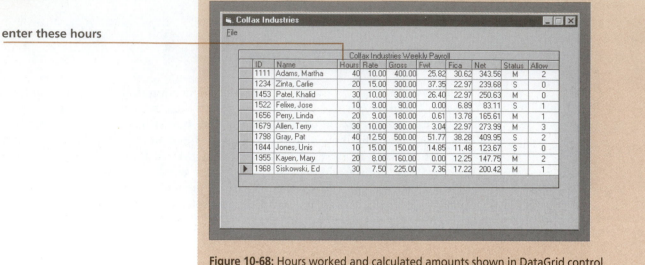

Figure 10-68: Hours worked and calculated amounts shown in DataGrid control

3 Click **File** on the form's menu bar, and then click **Exit** to end the application.

You have now completed Lesson C and the Colfax payroll application. You now can take a break, complete the end-of-lesson questions and exercises, or read and complete the Debugging Section, which may contain material that will help you to complete the exercises.

S U M M A R Y

To create a function procedure:

■ Open a Code window. Click Tools, then click Add Procedure. Type the function name in the Add Procedure dialog box's Name text box. Click the Function option button, then click either the Private or the Public option button, and then click the OK button. You declare the *datatype* of the function's return value by including **As** *datatype* after the parentheses in the function's Private Function statement. You return a value by assigning the value to the function's name using the following syntax: *functionName* = *returnValue*.

To pass an array to a function or sub procedure:

■ Enter the array name and an empty set of parentheses in the procedure's *parameterlist*.

To have a function or sub procedure receive an array:

■ Enter an array name and an empty set of parentheses in the procedure's *arglist*.

Q U E S T I O N S

1. Which of the following statements is false?
   a. A function procedure is a block of code that performs a specific task.
   b. A sub procedure is a block of code that performs a specific task.
   c. A function procedure returns a value.
   d. Val and InputBox are examples of user-defined functions.
   e. You can pass information to a user-defined function.

2. Assume that an application contains a function procedure named udfCalcNewPrice. Which of the following statements tells the function to return the value stored in the sngNew variable?
   a. udfCalcNewPrice = sngNew
   b. udfCalcNewPrice = sngNew as Single
   c. return udfCalcNewPrice = sngNew
   d. return sngNew
   e. sngNew = udfCalcNewPrice

3. Assume that an application contains a function procedure named udfCalcBonus. Which of the following statements invokes the function, passing it the contents of the intSales variable, and assigns the function's return value to the intBonus variable?
   a. Call udfCalcBonus(intSales as Single)
   b. intBonus = udfCalcBonus(intSales)
   c. intSales = udfCalcBonus(intBonus)
   d. return udfCalcBonus(intSales) to intBonus
   e. udfCalcBonus(intSales) = intBonus

4. Assume an application contains a function procedure named udfSearch that receives the contents of an eight-element Single array. Which of the following allows the udfSearch procedure to receive the array?
   a. Private Function udfSearch(sngNums( ) as Single) as Boolean
   b. Private Function udfSearch(sngNums(8) as Single) as Boolean
   c. Private Function udfSearch(sngNums( )) as Boolean
   d. Private Function udfSearch(sngNums(8)) as Boolean
   e. Private Function udfSearch(sngNums) as Boolean

5. Which of the following statements correctly invokes Question 4's udfSearch function? (blnFound is a Boolean variable, and sngData is an eight-element Single array.)
   a. blnFound = udfSearch(sngData( ) as Single)
   b. blnFound = udfSearch(sngData(8) as Single)
   c. blnFound = udfSearch(sngData( ))
   d. blnFound = udfSearch(sngData(8))
   e. blnFound = Call udfSearch(sngData( ))

E X E R C I S E S

1. In this exercise, you will modify the Colfax payroll application that you created in Tutorial 10.
   a. Open the lcPay (lcPay.vbp) project that you completed in Lesson C. Save the form and the project as lc1Done in the Tut10 folder on your Student Disk.

      b. Modify the application so that it pays employees time and one-half for all hours worked over 40.

      c. Save and run the application. Enter 45 hours worked for Martha Adams, 50 for Carlie Zinta, 41 for Khalid Patel, and 52 for Jose Felixe. Enter 5 hours for each of the remaining employees.

      d. Print the interface, then stop the application and print the code.

2. In this exercise, you will modify the Colfax payroll application that you created in Tutorial 10.

      a. Open the lcPay (lcPay.vbp) project that you completed in Lesson C. Save the form and the project as lc2Done in the Tut10 folder on your Student Disk.

      b. Modify the application so that it uses two one-dimensional arrays rather than two two-dimensional arrays to store the FWT tax tables. (*Hint*: You will need to create a user-defined data type to store each table's maximum, base, percentage, and excess over amounts.)

      c. Save and run the application. Enter 40 hours worked for Martha Adams, 35 for Carlie Zinta, 30 for Khalid Patel, and 25 for Jose Felixe. Enter 10 hours for each of the remaining employees.

      d. Print the interface, then stop the application and print the code.

3. In this exercise, you will modify the Colfax payroll application that you created in Tutorial 10.

      a. Open the lcPay (lcPay.vbp) project that you completed in Lesson C. Save the form and the project as lc3Done in the Tut10 folder on your Student Disk.

      b. Modify the application so that it uses one two-dimensional array rather than two two-dimensional arrays to store the FWT tax tables. (*Hint*: Create a user-defined data type to store each table's maximum, base, percentage, and excess over amounts.)

      c. Save and run the application. Enter 20 hours worked for Martha Adams, 15 for Carlie Zinta, 5 for Khalid Patel, and 18 for Jose Felixe. Enter 30 hours for each of the remaining employees.

      d. Print the interface, then stop the application and print the code.

4. In this exercise, you will modify the Colfax payroll application that you created in Tutorial 10.

      a. Open the lcPay (lcPay.vbp) project that you completed in Lesson C. Save the form and the project as lc4Done in the Tut10 folder on your Student Disk.

      b. Modify the application so that it stores, in the first column of the arrays, the amounts listed in the Over column of the tables. You will need to modify the taxtbls.txt file. Save the modified file as taxtbls2.txt.

      c. Save and run the application. Enter 10 hours worked for Martha Adams, 10 for Carlie Zinta, 20 for Khalid Patel, and 10 for Jose Felixe. Enter 20 hours for each of the remaining employees.

      d. Print the interface, then stop the application and print the code and the taxtbls2.txt file.

DEBUGGING

Technique   As you learned in Tutorial 9, you can use the commands on Visual Basic's Debug menu to assist you in debugging your application. You learned about the Step Into command in Tutorial 9. You will learn about the Toggle Breakpoint and Add Watch commands in this tutorial.

Example 1   **The Toggle Breakpoint Command**

On your Student Disk is a project named debug1 that is not working correctly. You will use a breakpoint to help you debug the project.

To test the debug1 project:

1 Start Visual Basic, if necessary. Open the **debug1** (debug1.vbp) project, which is located in the Tut10 folder on your Student Disk.

The two command buttons have already been coded for you. The Exit button will exit the application. The Calculate Average button will calculate and display the average of two numbers that are entered by the user. Run the application and calculate the average of the numbers 5 and 7.

2 **Run** the application. Click the **Calculate Average** button, type 5 in the dialog box and press the **Enter** key, then type 7 in the dialog box and press the **Enter** key. The average of the numbers 5 and 7 should be 6, but it displays incorrectly on the form as 4.

3 Click the **Exit** button. Visual Basic returns to the design screen.

Now open the Calculate Average button's Code window and use a breakpoint to debug its code.

To debug the Calculate Average button's code:

1 Open the Calculate Average button's Click event procedure. See Figure 10-69.

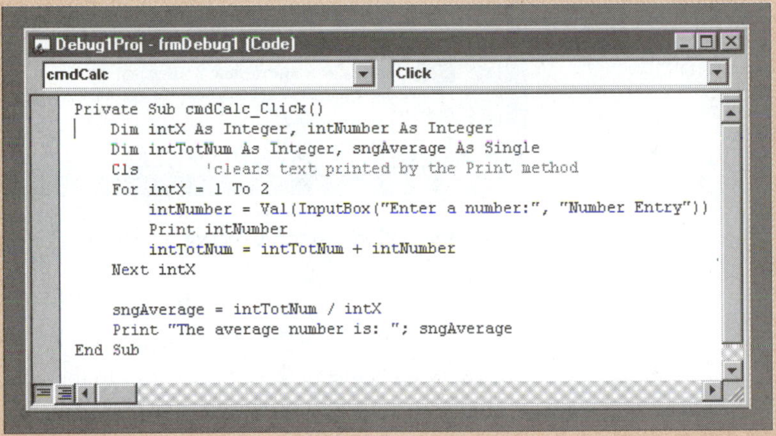

```
Private Sub cmdCalc_Click()
    Dim intX As Integer, intNumber As Integer
    Dim intTotNum As Integer, sngAverage As Single
    Cls        'clears text printed by the Print method
    For intX = 1 To 2
        intNumber = Val(InputBox("Enter a number:", "Number Entry"))
        Print intNumber
        intTotNum = intTotNum + intNumber
    Next intX

    sngAverage = intTotNum / intX
    Print "The average number is: "; sngAverage
End Sub
```

Figure 10-69: Calculate Average button's Click event

The code declares four variables: intX, intNumber, intTotNum, and sngAverage. The intX variable, a counter variable, will be used by the For...Next loop to keep track of the number of items to request from the user—in this case, the application will request two numbers. The intNumber variable will store the user's response to the InputBox function's message. The intTotNum variable will be used to accumulate the numbers entered by the user. The sngAverage variable will store the average of the numbers.

The `sngAverage = intTotNum / intX` instruction is calculating the average incorrectly. That means that either the intTotNum variable or the intX variable contains an incorrect value. To determine which variable—intTotNum or intX—is causing the problem, you will set a breakpoint at the `sngAverage = intTotNum / intX` instruction. When Visual Basic encounters a breakpoint in the code as the application is running, Visual Basic puts the application in break mode, which temporarily halts program execution. When an application is in break mode, you can view the values in the variables.

2 Click anywhere in the `sngAverage = intTotNum / intX` instruction. The insertion point should now be positioned somewhere in that instruction.

3 Click **Debug** on the menu bar, then click **Toggle Breakpoint**. Visual Basic selects the `sngAverage = intTotNum / intX` instruction to indicate that it is a breakpoint.

When you run the application, Visual Basic will put the application in break mode immediately before processing the breakpoint instruction.

4 Close the Code window, then **run** the application. Click the **Calculate Average** button, type 5 and press the **Enter** key, then type 7 and press the **Enter** key. Before processing the `sngAverage = intTotNum / intX` instruction, Visual Basic enters break mode. The cmdCalc Click event appears as shown in Figure 10-70.

breakpoint instruction

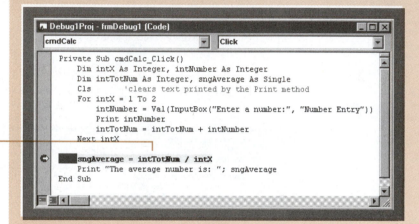

Figure 10-70: Code window showing Visual Basic in break mode

Now that you are in break mode, you can view the values in both the intTotNum and the intX variables to see which one contains an incorrect value.

First view the value in the intTotNum variable. Because you entered the numbers 5 and 7, the value in intTotNum should be 12.

5 Place the I-bar I on `intTotNum` in the `sngAverage = intTotNum / intX` instruction. The number 12, which is the sum of 5 and 7, appears in a box below the variable's name. The intTotNum variable, therefore, contains the correct value.

Now look at the value in the intX variable. Remember that you entered two numbers, so you want the value in intX to be 2.

6 Place I on `intX` in the `sngAverage = intTotNum / intX` instruction. The number 3, instead of the number 2, appears in a box below the variable's name. The intX variable, therefore, is causing the average to be calculated incorrectly. Now that you know which variable is causing the problem, you need to search the code to see how intX gets its value. (It might be helpful to refer to Figure 10-70.)

The intX variable is used as the *counter* variable in the For Next loop. Recall that the For Next loop stops when the value in its *counter* variable is greater than the *endvalue*. In this case, the For Next loop ends when intX reaches 3—one more than the *endvalue* of 2. So although two numbers are requested from the user, the value in intX is 3 when the For Next loop stops. To fix the code, you need simply to change the `sngAverage = intTotNum / intX` instruction to `sngAverage = intTotNum / (intX-1)`. You can now remove the breakpoint and fix the code.

7 Stop the application. Click **Debug** on the menu bar, then click **Clear All Breakpoints**. Visual Basic removes the breakpoint.

8 Change the `sngAverage = intTotNum / intX` instruction to **sngAverage = intTotNum / (intX–1)**. Close the Code window, then **run** the application.

9 Click the **Calculate Average** button, type 5 and press the **Enter** key, then type 7 and press the **Enter** key. The correct average, 6, appears on the form. Click the **Exit** button to end the application. Visual Basic returns to the design screen.

In the next example, you will learn how to use the debug menu's Add Watch command. (You do not need to save the debug1 files.)

Example 2

The Add Watch Command

On your Student Disk is a project named debug2, which is not working correctly. You will use a breakpoint and the Add Watch commmand to help you debug the project.

To test the debug2 project:

1 Open the **debug2** (debug2.vbp) project, which is located in the Tut10 folder on your Student Disk. (You do not need to save the debug1 files.)

View the Display Total button's code.

2 Open the Display Total button's Click event procedure. See Figure 10-71.

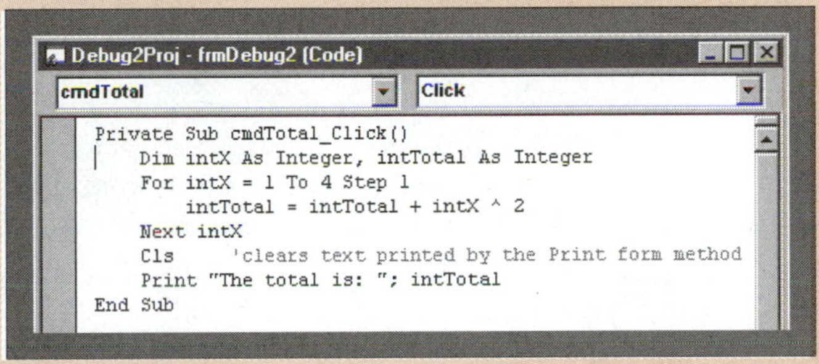

```
Debug2Proj - frmDebug2 (Code)                        _ □ ×
cmdTotal                    ▼    Click                          ▼

Private Sub cmdTotal_Click()
    Dim intX As Integer, intTotal As Integer
    For intX = 1 To 4 Step 1
        intTotal = intTotal + intX ^ 2
    Next intX
    Cls      'clears text printed by the Print form method
    Print "The total is: "; intTotal
End Sub
```

Figure 10-71: Display Total button's Click event

The code adds the squares of the numbers from 1 through 4—in other words, 1 * 1 + 2 * 2 + 3 * 3 + 4 * 4. Run the application to see if it is working correctly.

3 Close the Code window, then **run** the application. Click the **Display Total** button. The application displays the number 30 as the total.

4 Click the **Exit** button to end the application.

Instead of manually computing the sum of the squares to see if the number 30 is correct, you can use Visual Basic's Watches window to view the values in the variables or expressions as the application is running. In this case you will view the values in intX, intX ^ 2, and intTotal. By doing so, you will be able to see how the number 30 was reached, which will allow you to verify that it is the correct answer.

To use the Watches window:

1 Open the Display Total button's Click event procedure. Select **intX** in the `Dim` statement, then click **Debug**, and then click **Add Watch**. The Add Watch dialog box appears as shown in Figure 10-72.

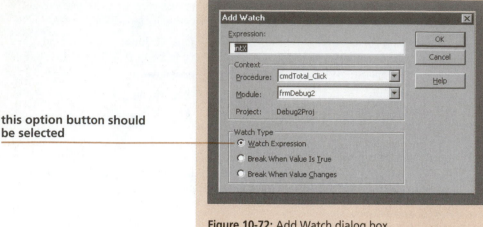

Figure 10-72: Add Watch dialog box

this option button should be selected

The Add Watch dialog box offers three watch types: Watch Expression, Break When Value Is True, and Break When Value Changes. The Watch Expression option button should be selected.

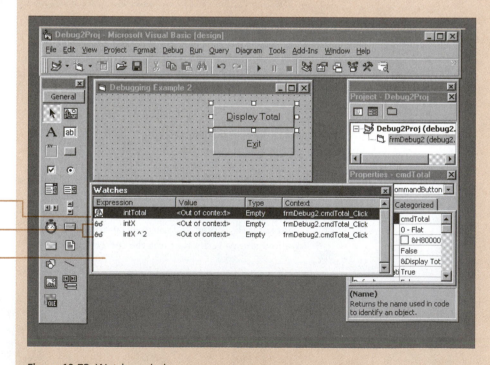

tip

To edit a watch expression, click Debug on the menu bar, then click Edit Watch.

2   Click the **OK** button to tell Visual Basic to watch the current expression—**intX**.

3   Select **intX ^ 2** in the Code window, click **Debug** on the menu bar, then click **Add Watch**, and then click the **OK** button to tell Visual Basic to watch the intX ^ 2 expression.

4   Select **intTotal** in the Dim statement (or in any statement in which it appears). Click **Debug** on the menu bar, then click **Add Watch**. This time, click **Break When Value Changes**, and then click the **OK** button. This tells Visual Basic to put the application in break mode each time the value in the intTotal variable changes.

5   Close the Code window. If necessary, size and position the Watches window as shown in Figure 10-73.

Break When Expression Has Changed icon

Watch Expression icons

Watches window

Figure 10-73: Watches window

Notice the icons to the left of the expressions. The icons tell you which watch type is associated with the expression. The 👓 icon represents the "Watch Expression" type; the ⚓ icon represents the "Break When Expression Has Changed" type.

6 **Run** the application. Click the **Display Total** button. Visual Basic puts the application in break mode after processing the `intTotal = intTotal + intX ^ 2` instruction, which is the instruction that changes the value in the intTotal variable. (You should see the statement selector on the `Next intX` instruction in the Code window, which is the instruction after the `intTotal = intTotal + intX ^ 2` instruction.)

The Watches window shows that the current value of intTotal, intX, and intX ^ 2 is 1. See Figure 10-74.

current value of variables

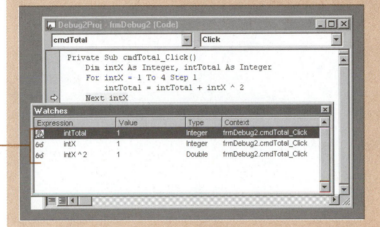

Figure 10-74: Watches window showing current values of variables and expression

7 Click the **Continue** button ▶ on the toolbar to continue processing the application. The Watches window shows that the value in the intTotal variable is now 5 (the prior value of 1 plus 4 more). The value in the intX variable is now 2, and the value of intX ^ 2 is now 4.

8 Click the **Continue** button ▶ to continue processing. The Watches window shows that the value in the intTotal variable is now 14 (the prior value of 5 plus 9 more). The value in intX is now 3, and the value of intX ^ 2 is now 9.

9 Click the **Continue** button ▶ to continue processing. The Watches window shows that the value in the intTotal variable is now 30 (the prior value of 14 plus 16 more). The value in intX is now 4, and the value of intX ^ 2 is now 16.

10 Click the **Continue** button ▶ to continue processing. The correct sum, 30, appears on the form. Click the **Exit** button to end the application. Visual Basic returns to the design screen. Now remove the watch expressions. (In this case you are removing the watch expressions for practice only. Visual Basic automatically removes watch expressions and breakpoints when you either close the current application or exit Visual Basic. Visual Basic does not save watch expressions or breakpoints when you save an application.)

11 The intTotal expression should be selected in the Watches window. Press the **Delete** key. Visual Basic deletes the intTotal watch expression. Press the **Delete** key again to delete the intX watch expression, then press the **Delete** key again to delete the intX ^ 2 watch expression.

12 Close the Watches window, then close the Code window. You do not need to save the debug2 files.

Exercise 1. On your Student Disk is a project named debug3. The project is not working correctly.

a. Open the debug3 project, which is located in the Tut10 folder on your Student Disk.

b. Save the form and the project as deb3Done in the Tut10 folder on your Student Disk.

c. Use this tutorial's debugging technique to debug the application.

d. When the application is working correctly, print the code.

What's New with Visual Basic.NET?

Creating a Visual Basic.NET Windows Forms Calendar Screen Application

case ▶ Pets Online, a small online pet store specializing in supplies for small domestic animals, has just upgraded from Visual Basic 6.0 to Visual Basic.NET, Microsoft's newest Visual Basic software release, and has hired you as a programmer. Your duties include writing applications for the store. Pets Online finds that helping its customers schedule veterinary visits, pet medicine refills, or pet birthday celebrations directly results in increased online sales. Therefore, your first assignment is to create a calendar screen for customers to view while browsing Pets Online's electronic store. The calendar will show the current month and the next month, and the screen should incorporate a picture of Pets Online's logo—an Italian Greyhound—a time display, a calendar, a greeting from Pets Online, and at least one link to another Web site. This first assignment with your new job will give you an opportunity to learn what's new with Visual Basic.NET.

Previewing the Calendar Screen

First, preview the completed calendar application.

To preview the completed calendar application, you must be able to access the Internet and have browser software installed on your computer.

1 If necessary, start Windows, and log onto the Internet. Use the **Run** command on the Start menu to run the Calendar (**calendar.exe**) file, which is located in the Tut11 folder on your computer's hard drive or workstation. A calendar application for Pets Online appears.

2 Review the Calendar application. Click the dates on the calendar. Use the arrows in the upper corners of the calendar to scroll from month to month. Verify that the correct day is showing at the lower-left corner of the calendar. Verify that the displayed time is correct. Click the **Click for a Message** button to see a message from Pets Online to its customers. Click the **Visit our Online Catalog** link to access Pets Online's Web page. See Figure 11-1.

Figure 11-1: Calendar screen

3 Upon finishing your review, click the **Close** button on the Pets Online Calendar title bar to close the application.

Before you create your own Visual Basic.NET Windows Forms Calendar application for Pets Online, you should familiarize yourself with the Visual Studio.NET environment. Tutorial 11 introduces you to some of the new features in the Visual Basic.NET environment. The tutorial also introduces Visual Studio.NET and its new integrated development environment, or IDE. Visual Studio.NET is the latest major release of Microsoft's integrated development environment. All of Microsoft's major programming languages—C++, C#, JScript, Visual Basic, Transact-SQL, and Visual FoxPro—are integrated in Visual Studio.NET and share a single GUI.

Remember to compare your programming tasks and steps in Visual Basic.NET with the tasks and steps you would use to complete the same project using Visual Basic 6.0. In Lesson A, you will be introduced to the Visual Studio.NET environment. In Lesson B, you will begin to create the Pets Online calendar application using Visual Basic.NET Windows Forms. You should complete each lesson and its end-of-lesson questions and exercises before moving on to the next lesson.

In this lesson, you will learn how to:

- Start and exit Visual Studio.NET
- Identify the components of the Visual Studio.NET integrated development environment (IDE)
- Modify your profile in the IDE
- Customize the new Visual Studio.NET IDE
- Become familiar with Solution Explorer
- Work with Dynamic Help
- Use the Task List
- Work with the Command Window

Working with Visual Studio.NET

The Visual Studio.NET Environment

In November 2000, Microsoft unveiled prerelease versions of Visual Studio.NET and Visual Basic.NET. The .NET framework is an exciting new environment for programmers and developers. The Visual Studio.NET IDE consists of a developer's control panel that provides a unified interface for access to project management, source code control, editing, debugging, and documentation features. Developers will no longer have to jump among applications to access a variety of programming tools. Microsoft did not simply add new features to Visual Basic 6.0; instead, Visual Studio.NET and Visual Basic.NET are truly reengineered tools that support Web and enterprise-wide client/server relationships.

The major differences between Visual Basic 6.0 and Visual Basic.NET are the latter's support for true object-oriented programming and Web applications programming. In Tutorial 11, you will learn about developing program interfaces using Visual Basic.NET Windows Forms. Windows Forms in Visual Basic.NET have new form development tools and greater functionality than were available in Visual Basic 6.0. Constructing a Windows Forms application in Visual Basic requires adding a form to the project, dragging a control onto the form, and then double-clicking the control to write code behind the form. This well-known Windows Forms model is used by millions of developers to rapidly construct desktop applications. Visual Basic.NET introduces Web Forms that bring the same design principles and level of productivity to mobile Web applications. In Tutorial 12, you will use new Visual Basic.NET Web Forms to build an application that can be run in a client/server environment such as the Internet. Web Form programming is modeled after the way Microsoft Visual Basic developers write traditional Windows-based applications using Windows Forms.

Tutorials 11 and 12 assume that you have some experience using the Internet and the World Wide Web, or the Web. In a client/server environment, computers share data over a network. On the Web, this data usually is Web pages in the form of HTML, or Hypertext Markup Language, a document layout language that contains tags (code) to instruct a browser program how to display the information on a computer. Clients are the computers that request the data, and servers are the computers that fulfill the data requests.

The new integrated .NET environment simplifies the development of distributed applications. Distributed applications are actually two separate software programs: the back-end (server) software and the front-end (client) software. For example, Web browsers are distributed applications. Browsers require back-end software (found on Web servers) as well as front-end software installed on your workstation (such as Netscape Communicator or Microsoft Internet Explorer).

The .NET environment brings all of Microsoft's programming languages onto a common platform. In Visual Studio.NET, you'll be able to share the same runtime files and use the same data types among different programming languages within the .NET environment.

Before you program an application in Visual Basic.NET, you should experiment with the Visual Studio.NET features.

tip

. . . .

▶ If you have previously opened Visual Studio.NET, your screen might also show features such as the Solution Explorer or Properties window.

To become familiar with the .NET environment and the new IDE:

1   Start Visual Studio.NET by clicking the **Start** button. Select **Programs, Microsoft Visual Studio.NET 7.0, Microsoft Visual Studio.NET 7.0.** Your screen should look like the Visual Studio.NET screen shown in Figure 11-2.

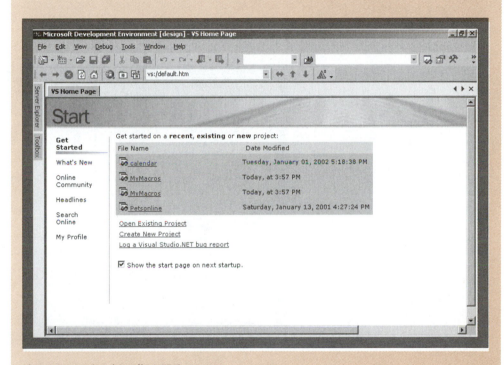

Figure 11-2: Visual Studio.NET Start page

Right away, you will notice that the Visual Studio.NET Start page looks different from the Visual Basic 6.0 interface. The Visual Studio.NET IDE displays links to related documentation on its Start page. Even MSDN Magazine articles can be accessed from the Start page and used as resources for developing applications in Visual Basic.NET. For example, right now you don't have an application or component open. The IDE displays links to information on how to plan an application (the Create New Project link), a selection of common business templates and wizards, and a dynamic list of application templates from various vendors.

As you develop your calendar application in Visual Basic.NET, the IDE keeps track of what part of the application you are working on and displays appropriate content in the Dynamic Help window to aid you in the development process.

Identify the Components of Visual Studio.NET and the new IDE

The Visual Studio.Net IDE has a new, customizable look that integrates Visual Basic and the other Microsoft programming languages. This common IDE also provides better debugging throughout the project. The real strength of the common IDE is in its support for Web applications. This Web support–originally only available in the Visual InterDev Web development system—is a major part of the new functionality of Visual Studio.NET. Web applications can be developed in all of the various Visual Studio.NET languages. This is useful for the programmer, because regardless of what language you are working in, there is now just one IDE to learn, construct, and apply. Better yet, you don't have to switch back and forth between environments to build and debug your code. As a result, programming and development is much easier and faster in this integrated environment than it was in Visual Basic 6.0.

When choosing a new application from the Visual Studio.NET Start page, the common business templates and wizards can be selected from the new common IDE. See Figure 11-3.

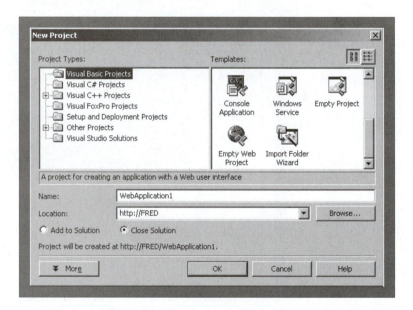

Figure 11-3: Templates and wizards available from the Start page

Modify Your Profile in the Visual Studio.NET IDE

The new Visual Studio.NET IDE allows you to customize various program settings such as keyboard scheme, window layout, and help filter. This collection of customized preferences is called a **profile**.

To modify your profile in your IDE:

1   From the Visual Studio.NET Start page, click the **My Profile** link on the left side of the Start page. The My Profile options appear on the screen. See Figure 11-4.

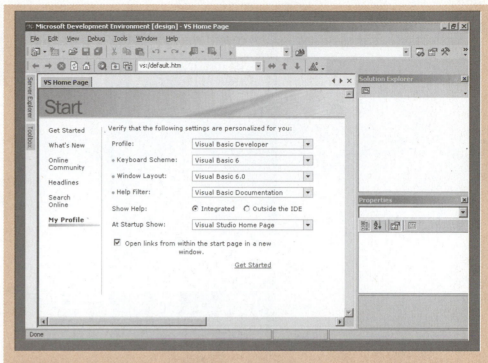

Figure 11-4: Customizing the new Visual Studio.NET IDE

2 Open the Profile drop-down menu and select **Visual Basic Developer**.

3 Verify that the Keyboard Scheme, the Window Layout, and Help Filter are all set to Visual Basic. If necessary, change these settings by opening the drop-down menus and selecting the Visual Basic options.

4 Select the **Integrated** option button for the Show Help choice.

5 In the At Startup Show menu, verify that Visual Studio Home Page is the selected setting.

6 Verify that the check box for Open links from within the start page in a new window is checked.

7 Click the **Get Started** link to return to the project home page.

Like Visual Basic 6.0, the new IDE provides a Toolbox where various programming elements are stored. You can hide or dock the Toolbox using the Auto Hide feature.

To toggle the Auto Hide feature of the Toolbox:

1 Click the **Toolbox** title bar on the far left side of the IDE.

2 Click the **Push Pin** 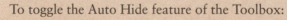 to activate the Auto Hide feature. See Figure 11-5. If the Auto Hide feature is turned on, the Toolbox will disappear. If not, it will remain visible on the Start page. If necessary, click the **Push Pin** again to ensure that the Auto Hide feature is on.

tip

The Visual Basic.NET Help filter lists the possible default filters for documentation in the Microsoft Developer Network (MSDN). The Help filter that you select applies to the Start page and MSDN documentation, but does not apply to the content displayed in the Dynamic Help window.

tip

Docking is a method of securing an object so that it doesn't move on the form.

Push Pin

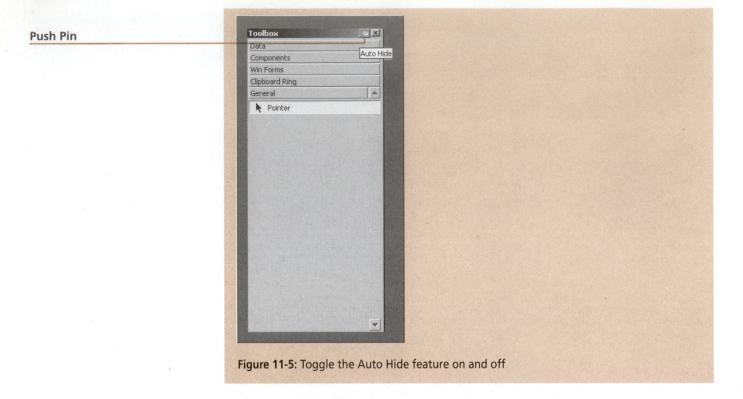

Figure 11-5: Toggle the Auto Hide feature on and off

Customizing the New Visual Studio.NET IDE

You can customize many of the IDE's menu features. Customization of the IDE allows you, as a developer, to set the IDE to your particular needs, making you both more efficient and effective in your application development, since you will not need to reset the IDE each time you enter the environment. The settings specified in the following steps let you set your IDE to Visual Basic Developer mode, with Visual Basic keyboard scheme and window layout. You will also set your help documentation to filter for Visual Basic information.

To customize your IDE:

1   Click the **Tools** menu on the IDE toolbar. Select **Options**. See Figure 11-6.

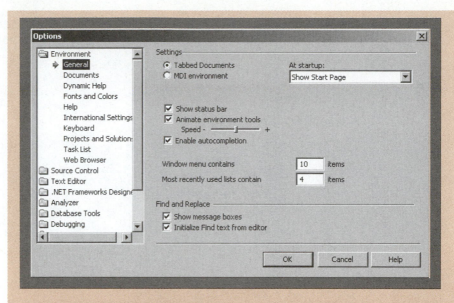

Figure 11-6: Customizing the IDE with the Tools Options menu

2   On the left side of the Options window, open the **Environment** folder at the top of the selection list, if necessary. Choose **General**.

Under Settings, you will see a check box called Animate Environment tools. When it is on, this feature lets you change the speed at which the tools work in the IDE. You can experiment with the various tool speeds until you find the settings that are right for you. At the bottom of the Options window, notice the Find and Replace feature, which is new to the Visual Studio.NET environment. It adds functionality to your coding.

3   Select **Documents**, also in the Environment folder. Change the settings so that the IDE detects when there is a change outside the Visual Studio.NET environment. However, do not have the IDE automatically load the changes.

4   Again, in Environment, select **Web Browser** and set the default search page to http://msdn.microsoft.com, as shown in Figure 11-7. Notice that now you can view your source code many different ways to enable you to move quickly from different environments as you create distributed applications. Your source code can be viewed in the Source editor, an HTML editor, or an external editor such as Notepad.

**type this URL as the
default setting**

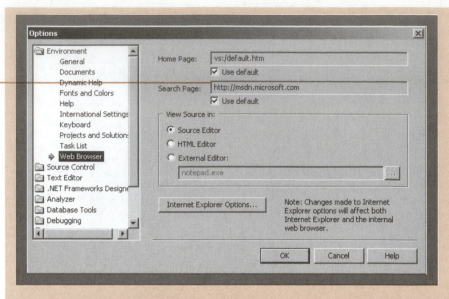

Figure 11-7: Customizing the Web browser environment

5 Go back to the left side of the Options window and scroll down until you see the Projects folder (second from the bottom). Select **Projects**. Under Projects select **Web Settings**.

6 Change the radio button from FrontPage to **File share** as your preferred file access method, if necessary.

7 Click **OK** to close the Options window.

> **Solution files can be easily recognized by their .sln extension.**

> **Visual Basic.NET automatically creates the calendar\ bin and calendar \ obj folders in your Tut11 folder.**

> **In Visual Basic 6.0, project files were created with the extension .vbp. In Visual Basic.NET, projects are created with the extension .vbproj. You will see this extension when you view your Visual Basic.NET files in Windows Explorer.**

Using Solution Explorer

Earlier in this tutorial, you learned that the Visual Studio.NET IDE allows you to create distributed application solutions. New to the IDE are **solutions**, which are containers for specific project types at each of the logical application tiers. The IDE shows these project types in the Solution Explorer, which displays a list of all the projects that are part of the current solution along with their corresponding files and directories. A solution can include several projects, even if they are written in different programming languages. The Solution Explorer is a powerful tool for programmers. It saves time when editing multiple-file projects and provides an intuitive view of all files in a given project.

To familiarize yourself with the Solution Explorer:

1 Click **File** on the IDE menu bar, then select **Open Solution**.

2 From your Tut11 folder, open the **Example** folder. Double-click the file named **Example.sln** to open it. Notice that the .sln file extension designates solution files.

3 The Solution Explorer appears as a window on the right side of your screen.

If you are creating a distributed application that includes Web pages as part of its solution, you can use the Show All Files button to view the Web pages and the code behind them.

4   At the top of the Solution Explorer window, click the **Show All Files** button . See Figure 11-8.

the Show All Files button

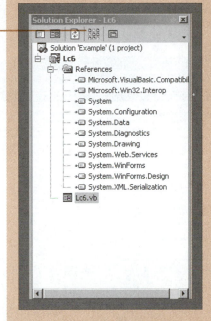

Figure 11-8: The Solution Explorer window

tip

You can also open the Solution Explorer from the menu bar. Choose View, Solution Explorer. The shortcut key combination to perform the same task is Ctrl + R.

5   Close the Solution Explorer window.

6   From the File menu, select **Close Solution**.

Working with Dynamic Help

The development environment in the Visual Studio.NET IDE has an improved Help feature that is more comprehensive and dynamic than Help in Visual Basic 6.0. No matter where you are in the IDE—the Start page, Visual Basic.NET, or C++—the Dynamic Help window allows you to access context-sensitive help with one click. The Dynamic Help feature tracks the actions you have made while in the IDE —for example, it is aware of the placement of the cursor, as well as the items that have the focus in the IDE. Dynamic Help can sort through MSDN topics and provide pointers to information specific to your current task.

tip

You can also activate Dynamic Help from the menu bar by choosing Help.

To use Dynamic Help:

1   Click **Dynamic Help** at the lower-right portion of the IDE screen. It is located just under the Properties window and has a blue circle with a question mark in it for easy visibility.

2   Click the **Search** button on the Dynamic Help title bar.

3   Under the Search title bar, you will see two text boxes. In the Look for text box, type **Web Form**. In the Filtered by text box, select **Visual Basic Documentation** from the drop-down list. Click the **Search** button.

4   Your search should return many items that provide information for Web Forms, as shown in Figure 11-9. The returned items will be related to the keywords "Web Form". Select the first item returned and read the information.

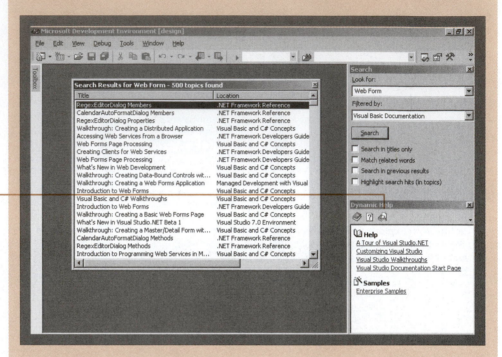

Figure 11-9: Dynamic Help titles returned

5   Close the Dynamic Help window, then close the Search Results window.

Using the Task List

Another new feature in the Visual Studio.NET IDE is the Task List. The Task List feature was formerly available only to developers working in Visual InterDev and Visual J++. It allows you to mark code with comments related to tasks that need to be done. For example, you might want to add a note to your code to remind yourself to create a separate module to link to your current project. The Task List feature then parses and displays these comments so that you can view them and even annotate them, if necessary.

To use the Task List feature:
1   Click **View** on the IDE menu. Select **Other Windows** and then select **Task List**.
2   Click the words **Click here to add a new task**.

the Search icon

tip
• • • • • • • • • • • • • •
You will work with Visual Basic.NET Web Forms in Tutorial 12.

3 Type **To Do: Add Timer Control to Calendar application.**

4 Click the **Done** column to add a check. Notice that the text you entered in Step 3 appears with a line through it, to indicate that the task has been completed. Your window should look like Figure 11-10.

5 Close the Task List window.

click the Done column

type the task here

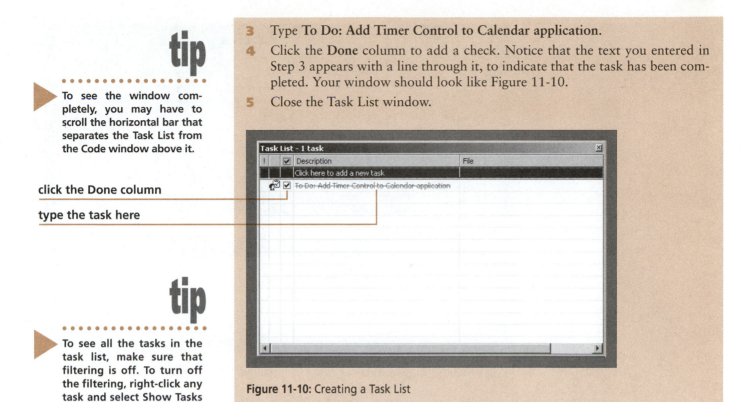

Figure 11-10: Creating a Task List

The Command Window

In the new Visual Studio.NET IDE Command Window, you can perform search and replace operations across the Visual Studio.NET environment using the find, navigate, and execute features—all in a single input line. These new Command Window features add more functionality for the programmer than was available in the Visual Basic 6.0 IDE. One of the new features of the Visual Studio.NET environment's Command Window is extended IntelliSense. The IntelliSense feature automates routine and complex tasks. It automatically suggests actions based on steps you have made previously in the IDE. Such entries could include projects you opened, help searches you have executed, any text you have typed, or any click you have made.

To use the Command Window feature:

1 Click **View** from the IDE menu. Select **Other Windows** and **Command Window**.

2 The Command Window should be visible at the bottom of your screen. See Figure 11-11. Notice how the window looks like a DOS prompt.

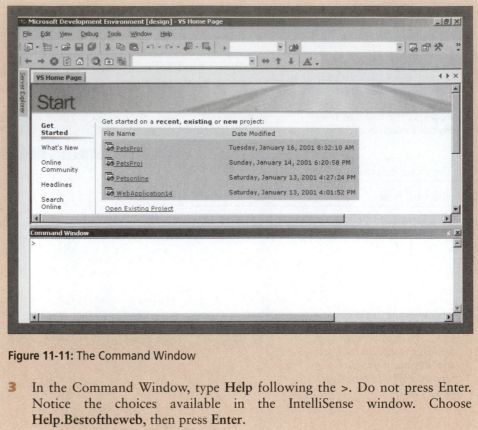

Figure 11-11: The Command Window

3   In the Command Window, type **Help** following the >. Do not press Enter. Notice the choices available in the IntelliSense window. Choose **Help.Bestoftheweb**, then press **Enter**.

4   After reviewing the items that are returned, close the Command Window.

5   Close Visual Studio.NET.

You have now completed Lesson A. You can either take a break or complete the end-of-lesson questions and exercises.

S U M M A R Y

To start Visual Studio.NET:

■   Click the Start button.

■   Choose Programs, Microsoft Visual Studio.NET 7.0, Microsoft Visual Studio.NET 7.0.

To modify your profile in the IDE:

■   From the Start page, click the My Profile link.

■   Choose Visual Basic Developer from the Profile menu and make the necessary changes to the various settings.

To toggle the Auto Hide feature of the Toolbox:

■   Click the Toolbox title bar and then click the Push Pin.

To customize the new Visual Studio.NET IDE:

- Select Options from the Tools menu.
- Open the Environment folder and select General.
- Choose Documents, also under the Environment selection. Change the settings so that the IDE will detect when it is changed outside the environment. Do not have the IDE automatically load the changes.
- Choose Web Browser and set the default search page to http://msdn.microsoft.com.
- Open the Projects folder (second from the bottom) and select Web Settings.
- Change the radio button from FrontPage to File share as your preferred file access method.

To use Solution Explorer:

- Click File from the IDE menu bar, then Open Solution.
- Navigate to your Tut11 folder, select the Calendar folder, and click Open.
- Click the Show All Files button.

To use Dynamic Help:

- Click Dynamic Help, then click the Search button on the Dynamic Help title bar.
- Enter a topic in the search box and filter by Visual Basic Documentation.

To use the Task List:

- From the menu bar, click View, Other Windows, Task List.
- Click the words, "Click here to add a new task", then type a task description.
- Click the Done column to indicate that the task has been completed.

To access the Command Window:

- From the menu bar, click View. Select Other Windows and Command Window.

QUESTIONS

1. Visual Basic.NET is a part of the new _____.
   a. Integrated Development Environment (IDE)
   b. Visual InterDev Web development system
   c. Visual Studio.NET
   d. all of the above

2. The IDE of Visual Studio.NET provides _____.
   a. end-to-end debugging
   b. a common environment for the Microsoft programming languages
   c. a common environment to build and deploy code
   d. all of the above

3. The new IDE can display links to related documentation based on the features or technologies currently in use from _____.
   a. the Web
   b. the MSDN library
   c. Dynamic Help
   d. all of the above

4. If you're in the IDE, but don't have an application or component open, the IDE displays links to information on _____.
   a. how to plan an application
   b. a selection of common business templates and wizards
   c. a dynamic list of application templates from third-party vendors
   d. all of the above

5. The _____ feature of the Toolbox allows it to be toggled from visible to hidden.
   a. Auto Hide
   b. Auto Run
   c. Auto Toggle
   d. Push Pin

6. To set the preferred access connection mode to File Share, you must choose _____.
   a. Tools menu, Options
   b. View, Other Windows
   c. File, Open Solution
   d. none of the above

7. The _____ displays an organized list of all of your Visual Basic.NET projects and their corresponding files and directories that are part of the current solution.
   a. Dynamic Help
   b. Command Window
   c. Solution Explorer
   d. Solution Editor

8. The _____ tracks your query selections and provides pointers to relevant information specific to the current development task.
   a. Dynamic Help
   b. Command Window
   c. Solution Explorer
   d. Solution Editor

9. The Task List feature was formerly only available to programmers and developers in _____.
   a. Visual InterDev and C++
   b. Visual InterDev and Visual J++
   c. C++ and Visual J++
   d. none of the above

10. Programmers who prefer to use the keyboard can use the _____ as a method to perform searches, navigate to windows and items in a solution, and execute commands.
    a. Dynamic Help
    b. Command Window
    c. Solution Explorer
    d. Solution Editor

EXERCISES

1. In this exercise, you will use Dynamic Help to search for information on some of the Visual Basic.NET features you will use in Lesson B.
   a. Start Visual Studio.NET, if necessary.
   b. Activate Dynamic Help from the menu bar. Choose Help, Dynamic Help.

    c. Choose Index on the Help bar and look for Inheritance in Visual Basic. Be sure to filter by Visual Basic Documentation.

    d. Under Inheritance, select in Visual Basic. In the Index Results window, choose Inheritance Basics.

    e. You should now see some basic information about Visual Basic.NET inheritance.

After reviewing the information, answer the following questions about Visual Basic.NET inheritance:

    f. What new keyword sequence can be used to create a new class based on an existing class?

    g. Derived classes can inherit, but can also do what?

    h. Visual Basic.NET introduces what statements and modifiers to support inheritance?

    i. Derived classes can override inherited methods with new implementations. Visual Basic.NET introduces what modifiers for controlling property and method overriding?

    j. List two rules that apply to Visual Basic.NET inheritance.

    k. Close the Help and Index Results windows.

2. Visual Studio.NET lets you access an online community of Microsoft public developer newsgroups from the Start page. Accessing the resources of the Visual Studio.NET and Visual Basic.NET communities can aid you in programming and developing applications.

    a. From the Start page, click the Online Community link.

    b. Choose the link to the Microsoft.public.dotnet.languages.Visual Basic community. This newsgroup may also be accessed from the URL news://msnews.microsoft.com/microsoft.public.dotnet.languages.Visual Basic. If this group is not available, choose another Visual Basic newsgroup.

    c. Use the Microsoft Outlook Newsreader or another newsreader software to join in (or at least observe) the online discussion.

    d. Explore the discussion and write a 200-300 word essay about the current conversations of the newsgroup concerning Visual Basic. Make sure your essay answers the question: What's new with Visual Basic.NET?

3. As you learned in the lesson, the Auto Hide feature of the Toolbox turns the Toolbox on and off with the click of the Push Pin. Set your Toolbox so that the Auto Hide feature is Off.

    a. Make sure that the Visual Studio.NET IDE is set up so that you see the Visual Basic.NET Start page.

    b. Click the Get Started link to return to the project home page. Click the Toolbox title bar on the far left side of the IDE.

    c. Click the Push Pin.

    d. Verify that the Auto Hide feature is off. The Toolbox should not disappear when you move the mouse pointer off it. The Toolbox should remain visible on the Start page.

    e. Follow the same process to turn off the Auto Hide feature of the Help menu.

discovery ▶ **4.** Earlier in this tutorial, you looked at many ways that the new Visual Studio.NET has increased greater customization of its IDE. Another new feature that the new Visual Studio.NET IDE supports is macro recording and programming using Visual Studio Macro (VSM). VSM simplifies integration of other tools or applications, such as Microsoft Project or Outlook, into the Visual Basic.NET application development cycle. This exercise allows you to explore VSM and create a directory structure you can use as you work in Visual Basic.NET.

    a. To view the Macro Explorer, from the IDE menu, select View, Other Windows, and Macro Explorer.

    b. Close Visual Studio.NET.

    c. From Windows Explorer, locate the MyMacros.vsmacros file. Copy MyMacros.vsmacros from the location where this file exists (from your Visual Studio.NET installation to your Tut11 folder). For example, if you installed Visual Studio.NET on the C: drive and are logged on as Administrator, the file path would be C:\Documents and Settings\Administrator\My documents\Visual Studio Projects\VSMacros\MyMacros.

d. If necessary, click Yes to overwrite the file.

e. Start Visual Studio.NET.

f. From the IDE menu, select File and Open Solution. In the Open Solution dialog box, change the Files of type to All Project Files.

g. Navigate to your Tut11 folder and open the MyMacros.vsmacros file. If you see a message box asking if you want to unload MyMacros and load the new project, click Yes.

h. In the Macro Explorer window, navigate the tree of MyMacros. You should see the VSMacros in your module.

i. Close the Macro Explorer window.

discovery ▶   5.   In this exercise, you will learn how to upgrade Visual Basic 6.0 applications to Visual Basic.NET. To do this, you will use the upgrade tool that is included as part of Visual Basic.NET. The upgrade tool runs automatically once you open Visual Basic 6.0 projects in Visual Basic.NET.

Note: If you have a project written in Visual Basic versions 1 through 5, you should load it into Visual Basic 6.0 before upgrading it to Visual Basic.NET. Be sure when you are upgrading your Visual Basic version 1 through 5 projects to Visual Basic 6.0 that you also upgrade your Microsoft ActiveX controls and compile and save them in Visual Basic 6.0 before upgrading to Visual Basic.NET.

Both Visual Basic 6.0 and Visual Basic.NET can be installed and executed on the same computer. You may even discover that components written in Visual Basic.NET can interoperate with Microsoft Component Object Model (COM) components written in earlier versions of Visual Basic and other languages. The COM is a software architecture that allows applications to be built from binary software components. COM is the underlying architecture that forms the foundation for higher-level software functions, like those provided by Visual Basic.NET. For example, you can drop an ActiveX control written in Visual Basic 6.0 onto a Visual Basic.NET Windows Form, use a Visual Basic 6.0 COM object from a Visual Basic.NET class library, or even add a reference to a Visual Basic.NET library to a Visual Basic 6.0 executable file. To upgrade a Visual Basic 6.0 project to a Visual Basic.NET project:

a. From the IDE menu, choose File, Open, File and navigate to your Tut11 folder.

b. In Windows Explorer, open the vb6.vbp project from your Tut11 folder. This is an application created in Visual Basic 6.0.

c. The upgrade tool will automatically open and you will see the upgrade tool wizard screen. Click Next. This upgrade tool wizard will create a new Visual Basic.NET project. Upgrade your Visual Basic 6.0 project to this new Visual Basic.NET project. You will be asked to specify the type of project to create. Select the option to upgrade your current project to an .exe file, then click Next.

d. Verify that the project will be created in your Tut11 folder (change the code to indicate the path to your Tut11 folder, if necessary). If you receive an error message, accept the default directory. Click OK when you are asked if you want to create the directory.

e. During Step 4 of the wizard upgrade process, you will be asked to wait a few minutes while the tool automatically upgrades your Visual Basic 6.0 project to Visual Basic.NET.

f. At Step 5 of the wizard upgrade process, your project has been upgraded to Visual Basic.NET. Click Finish to complete the process.

g. Now run the new program in Visual Basic.NET to verify that the upgrade was successful.

h. Close Visual Studio.NET.

In this lesson, you will learn how to:

- Start Visual Basic.NET
- Create a Windows Forms application
- Add a label control to a Windows Forms application
- Add picture, text, frame, and button controls to a Windows Forms application
- Add ActiveX calendar, date, and time controls to a Windows Forms application
- Add code to the Windows Forms application
- Add a Link Label to a Windows Forms application
- Add a menu and menu items to a Windows Forms application
- Print the underlying code of a Windows Forms application
- Save and exit a Windows Forms application

Creating a Windows Forms Application Using Visual Basic.NET

Starting Visual Basic.NET

Now you will begin creating the Pets Online application that you learned about in this tutorial's case introduction. The first step of building any Visual Basic.NET application is to start Visual Basic. When you select a Windows Application from the New Project dialog box, you will notice a few differences from the same process in Visual Basic 6.0. In Visual Basic.NET, as soon as you click OK in the New Project dialog box, Visual Basic.NET creates a solution with a Visual Basic project in it. This project contains references and one class. A **class** is a Visual Basic packaged object. The class has behaviors and properties that describe members of the class. Objects that you created in your Visual Basic 6.0 applications were objects of a particular class. For example, a radio button defines properties, events, and methods that all members of the radio button class support. A command button can never be a member of this class since its properties, events, and methods differ from those of a radio button. Visual Basic.NET will name the class you will create in this project Form1.vb. Begin your project by starting Visual Basic.NET.

To start Visual Basic.NET:

1 Click the **Start** button, select **Programs, Microsoft Visual Studio.NET 7.0, Microsoft Visual Studio 7.0.** (If Microsoft Visual Studio.NET 7.0 does not appear on the Programs menu, then point to Microsoft Visual Basic.NET 7.0 on the Programs menu.) The Visual Studio.NET 7.0 copyright screen appears momentarily, and then the Start page dialog box appears.

2 Click the **Create New Project** link.

3 If necessary, select **Visual Basic Projects** from the Project Types frame and **Windows Application** from the Templates frame, as shown in Figure 11-12.

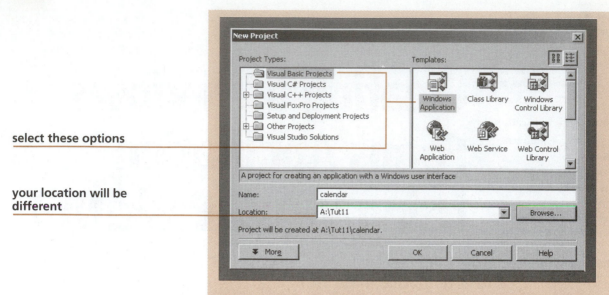

Figure 11-12: The Visual Basic.NET New Project dialog box

select these options

your location will be
different

4 In the Name text box, type **calendar** to create a new project named "calendar".

5 Click **Browse** and navigate to your **Tut11** folder. Click **OK**.

6 Now you should see a new Windows Forms application in the Visual Basic.NET window, as shown in Figure 11-13.

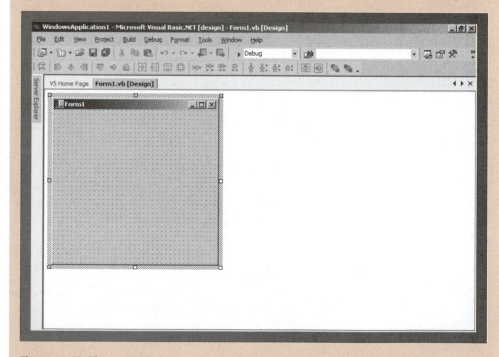

Figure 11-13: The new Windows Forms application window

Using Windows Forms

Windows Forms, or Win Forms, is the new forms tool in Visual Basic.NET. It replaces the Visual Basic Form that you used to create program interfaces in Visual Basic 6.0. Windows Forms provides improved features that make it easier for you to create interfaces for your Visual Basic programs. Like the Visual Studio.NET IDE, Windows Forms provides a standard development platform across the different languages supported by Visual Studio.NET. New features include the Menu Designer—an in-place menu editor—Control Anchoring, Control Docking, and the Component Tray. With Control Anchoring and Control Docking, you can remove most of your old Visual Basic 6.0 Form resize code, which is no longer necessary in Visual Basic.NET. The new Visual Basic.NET Component Tray monitors the addition and removal of Visual Basic design elements, or components. Menu elements and date/time elements are examples of components. The Component Tray stores components.

Viewing Code in Windows Forms

At first glance, you will see that Visual Basic.NET Windows Forms looks similar to the Visual Basic 6.0 Form. However, unlike Visual Basic 6.0, the new form module contains all of the code to instantiate the form and the runtime instance of the controls created on the form. In Visual Basic 6.0, this code was hidden from the programmer. Now, in Visual Basic.NET, it is automatically generated and made available to you in the Windows Forms application.

Practice using Windows Forms by viewing the form code for the calendar application.

To view the code:

1 Double-click the calendar form displayed in your window. This form was automatically created when you created the new project.

2 View the code automatically generated by Windows Forms. See Figure 11-14.

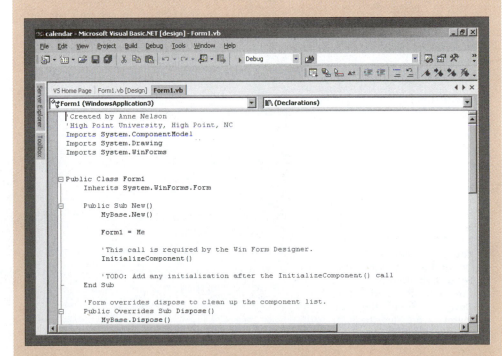

Figure 11-14: The new Windows Forms Code View

The Imports statements that you see at the beginning of the project code make available to your project various code libraries within the Visual Studio.NET framework. The default library settings for Windows Forms are Imports System, System.Collections, System.Core, System.ComponentModel, System.Drawing, System.Data, and System.WinForms libraries.

Differences Between Visual Basic.NET Windows Forms and Visual Basic 6.0 Forms

Windows Forms is, for the most part, compatible with the forms package in Visual Basic 6.0, which means that most of the time, forms created in Visual Basic 6.0 will work in Visual Basic.NET. The key differences are as follows:

- There is no shape control in Windows Forms. You will find that square and rectangular shapes in Visual Basic 6.0 will be upgraded to Visual Basic.NET labels. Unfortunately, ovals and circles cannot be upgraded at all. You will have to re-create them in Visual Basic.NET.
- There is no line control in Windows Forms. Again, Visual Basic 6.0 lines will be upgraded to Visual Basic.NET. Diagonal lines are not upgraded and will have to be re-created.
- As you learned in Tutorial 6, Lesson B, in Visual Basic 6.0, there was one menu control, called Menu. Menu could be opened as a MainMenu or ContextMenu. In Visual Basic.NET, Visual Basic 6.0 menu controls can be upgraded to MainMenu controls, but you will not be able to use them as ContextMenus. You will have to re-create your ContextMenus.
- Visual Basic.NET Windows Forms does not support the Form.PrintForm method.

Notice in your calendar code the statement `InitializeComponent`. This component is used by the development environment to maintain the property values you set in Design View.

Recall that in Visual Basic 6.0, you place initialization code for a form in the Form_Load event procedure. You should include initialization code for the form in the class constructor for the Windows Forms, `Public Sub New()`. The `Public Sub New()` constructor replaces the Form_Load event. `Public Sub New()` loads and initializes all of the controls on the form prior to execution.

Setting Appearance Properties

Next, you will work in the Visual Basic.NET Design View and experiment with properties of controls.

tip

You can also switch to Design View by clicking the Form 1.vb [Design] tab in the IDE, choosing View, Designer from the IDE menu, or pressing the Shift + F7 key combination.

To add methods and properties to your empty form for the Pets Online application:

1 Open the Solution Explorer, if necessary. Switch to Design View by clicking the **View Designer** [⊞] icon in the Solution Explorer.

2 In the Properties window, scroll to the Size property. Size the form so that it is 504 × 400 pixels. The default size of a form is 300 × 300.

3 Set the text property to **Pets Online Calendar**. This sets the title for your form.

4 Set the start position property to **CenterScreen**. This sets the screen location where the form appears at start up.

If your Properties window is not showing, you can click the Properties icon at the upper-right corner of your window, choose View Properties from the menu bar, or press the F4 key.

5   To set the background color of the form to a pale yellow, select the **BackColor** property, select the **System** tab, and choose **Info**.

Now that you have set the general appearance of the form, you will add some controls.

Adding a Label Control to the Windows Forms Calendar Application

The first control you will work with in Visual Basic.NET is the label control. What was the Caption property of a label control in Visual Basic 6.0 is now called Text. If you upgrade a project from Visual Basic 6.0 to Visual Basic.NET, all instances of the Caption property are automatically changed to Text. Select the label tool from the Toolbox to create a label.

To add a label control to your calendar application:

1   If necessary, turn on the Toolbox Auto Hide feature.

2   Move your pointer over the **Toolbox** tab, located on the left edge of the screen. The Toolbox now appears on the screen.

3   From the Toolbox, select **Win Forms,** if necessary, to display the tools available in the Windows Forms application.

4   Select the **Label** control from the Win Forms Toolbox to activate the Label control. It is the second control from the top, as shown in Figure 11-15.

the Label control

Figure 11-15: Using a Windows Forms Label control

5   Drag the Label tool and drop it on the Windows Forms application.

6   In the Properties window, set the Location property to **32 × 16** pixels.

7   Set the Label Size to 240 × 80 pixels.

8   So that the user can tab from control to control on the form, set the Tab Index to 1.

9   Still in the Properties window, select the Text property and change the label's text to **Pets Online**.

10 Choose the Font property and change the font to **36 points, bold italic, Monotype Corsiva** typeface.

11 Set the label text to be center aligned by changing the TextAlign property to **Center**.

12 The label won't have a border, so set its BorderStyle property to **none**.

13 Verify that the label's BackColor property color is the same as that of the form.

14 Set the **Anchor** property to **All** so that the label is docked.

The form with its label should look like Figure 11-16. Next, you will add more controls to your calendar application.

Figure 11-16: A Label control on the form

Adding Picture, Text, and Frame Controls

There are minor differences among the common controls used in Visual Basic 6.0 and their Visual Basic.NET counterparts. In the Windows Forms application, the functionality of Visual Basic 6.0 controls still exists; however, the names, various properties, and methods have been changed. For example, what was a Command Button in Visual Basic 6.0 is now a Button in Visual Basic.NET. The ListBox in Visual Basic.NET uses InsertItem instead of AddItem, as it did in Visual Basic 6.0. The Windows Forms controls are much more powerful and flexible in Visual Basic.NET than in Visual Basic 6.0. They can be used by means of inheritance to created even more powerful applications.

Windowless controls, such as the Label and Image controls, provided low-level functionality at a very low cost of resources in Visual Basic 6.0. In Visual Basic.NET, however, there are no windowless controls. The Visual Basic 6.0 label has been replaced by a label control that has a **window handle**. A handle is a 32-bit positive integer that Windows uses to identify a window or another object, such as a font or bitmap. Windows assigns a handle to a window when it is created. The handle is freed when the window is destroyed. Although the handle remains the same for the lifetime of the window, there is no guarantee that a window will have the same handle if it is destroyed and recreated. Therefore, if you store a handle in a variable, keep in mind that the handle will no longer be valid if the window is destroyed.

Image controls are not used in Visual Basic.NET; instead, a PictureBox provides similar functionality.

To create these controls in your calendar application:

1. Point to the **Toolbox** to activate it. Select **PictureBox**.

2. Insert a **PictureBox** control to the right of the label. On the Properties window, set the PictureBox's Location to **312 × 8**, Size to **112 × 104**, and, if necessary, change the BackColor to **Info on the System tab**.

3. To insert the image file **Issy.jgp** from your Tut11 folder, select the **Image** property in the Properties window. Click the **ellipsis** (three dots), navigate to the file, and select it.

4. Set the SizeMode property to **StretchImage**.

5. Set the Tab Index to **2**.

6. Lock the image and anchor it in its location at the upper-right corner of the form by changing the Anchor property to **TopRight**.

7. Press the F5 key to run your Windows Forms application. Your application will look like Figure 11-17.

Figure 11-17: The Label and PictureBox controls in a Windows Forms application

8. Close the form and the Output Box.

Next, you will add Windows Forms time-based controls to your application.

Adding ActiveX Calendar, Date, and Time Controls

Visual Basic.NET provides simplified methods of adding time-based controls to an application. In Visual Basic 6.0, to add a clock program to the IDE, you must load an ActiveX Control that comes with Visual Basic. You do this by selecting Windows Common Controls 2-6.0 in the Components dialog box to add the calendar control to the Toolbox. An alternate method is to use a label control to display the time once you configure the Timer control.

In Visual Basic.NET, the process is much easier. The DateTimePicker and MonthCalendar are ActiveX intrinsic controls included in Visual Basic.NET—they are built right into the core Visual Basic.NET code. You never have to add them to the Toolbox.

To add the time to your calendar application:

1 Verify that you are in Design View.

2 Activate the Toolbox. Select the **DateTimePicker**. Drag your pointer to the Design View of your Windows Forms application.

3 In the Properties window, set the Size property of the DateTimePicker to 112 × 20 and the Location to 312 × 136.

4 Set the ValueSet to **False**.

5 Set the Tab Index to **4**.

6 Set ShowUpDown to **True** and Format to **Time**.

7 Format the font as **Microsoft Sans Serif, bold, 10 point**.

Although you have added time features that can be set to display a calendar, there may be cases where you want to add a separate calendar to your application.

To add the calendar to your calendar application:

1 Select the **MonthCalendar** control from the Toolbox (it is located directly below the DateTimePicker control).

2 Draw a control of size **192 × 153**. Set the control's location at **56 × 112**.

3 Set the Tab Index to **3**. View the form in Design View. With a label, picture, time, and calendar loaded onto your form, it should look like Figure 11-18.

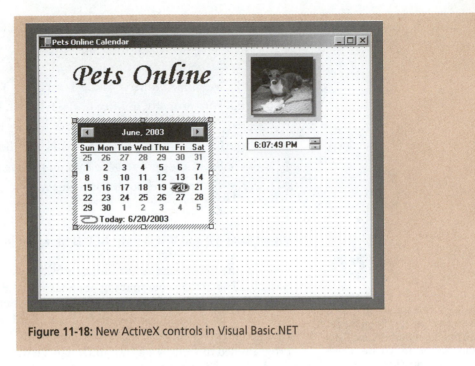

Figure 11-18: New ActiveX controls in Visual Basic.NET

Next, you will add some features to truly customize your application.

Adding a Button Control and Code

Recall that Pets Online wants its customers to be able to click a button to see a message reminding them to schedule an appointment for their pet with a veterinarian. You will use the Visual Basic.NET Button control to handle this task.

To add a Button control to your calendar application:

1   Select the **Button** control from the Toolbox. On the form, draw a button with these properties: Location 312 × 224 and Size 112 × 40.

2   Set the BackColor property to **Info**, if necessary.

3   Change the button's Text property to **Click for a Message!**. Set its Font property to **10 point, bold, Microsoft Sans Serif** typeface. Set its TextAlign property to **MiddleCenter**.

4   Set the Tab Index to **5**.

Now that you have added the button to the form, you must program it with the appropriate message.

To add a text box that is launched by a button:

1 Select the **TextBox** control from the Toolbox. On the form, draw a TextBox across the bottom of the form.

2 Set the Multiline property of the TextBox to **True**.

3 Set the Font property to **Microsoft Sans Serif, Bold, 10 point**.

4 Set the TextAlign property to **Center**.

5 Set the Location property to **56 × 288**. Set the Size to **384 × 56**.

6 Set the BackColor property to **Info on the System tab** with no visible border.

7 Set the Text property so that it is empty.

Visual Basic 6.0 and Visual Basic.NET: Differences in Coding

One of the most significant differences between Visual Basic 6.0 and Visual Basic.NET is in the programming of code. Visual Basic.NET is now truly an object-oriented programming language with true object class inheritance.

You will programatically add functionality to the Button control you just created. In other words, the Windows Forms application button must now be programmed in Code View, not in Design View.

In Visual Basic 6.0, the programmer did not see the code for many controls. Visual Basic 6.0 automatically added to the program the references to the control instances created on the form. In Visual Basic.NET, when you are in Design View, you will notice that all of the code is visible. The Visual Basic.NET programmer can view what was the "hidden" code used to create objects from their underlying classes in Visual Basic 6.0. For example, the code for the button you just created was automatically created by Visual Basic.NET and it instantiated the button.

tip

> As you learned in the overview at the beginning of this book, inheritance is the ability to create one class from another.

tip

> To view code, you can also click the F7 key, click the Code view button at the top of the Solution Explorer window, or right-click the Windows Forms application and choose View Code.

To view your Windows Forms application code:

1 Click the **Form 1.vb*** tab at the top of the Windows Forms window so that you can view the code. See Figure 11-19.

click this tab

the Imports statement

code that determines the application's inheritance

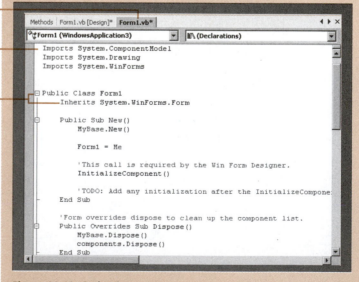

```
Methods  Form1.vb [Design]*  Form1.vb*

Form1 (WindowsApplication3)            (Declarations)

    Imports System.ComponentModel
    Imports System.Drawing
    Imports System.WinForms


Public Class Form1
    Inherits System.WinForms.Form

    Public Sub New()
        MyBase.New()

        Form1 = Me

        'This call is required by the Win Form Designer.
        InitializeComponent()

        'TODO: Add any initialization after the InitializeCompone
    End Sub

    'Form overrides dispose to clean up the component list.
    Public Overrides Sub Dispose()
        MyBase.Dispose()
        components.Dispose()
    End Sub
```

Figure 11-19: Code View

Look at the code that has been generated as you created your Pets Online application. The first code you see is the `Imports` statement. The word `Imports` indicates that Visual Basic.NET has built namespace classes around a common system entity. This `Imports` statement is the programmer's interface for a class. It reveals the properties, methods, and even events of the class.

The Imports statement created a namespace available to the calendar application that you are creating for Pets Online. Following the Imports statement is code denoting the inheritance of the application.

Polymorphic programming, now supported in Visual Basic.NET, can eliminate the need for using Select Case logic. Polymorphism means "taking on many forms." In Visual Basic 6.0 you used the keyword **implements** to mimic polymorphism. With it, a class or classes could exhibit many behaviors (or *implement* many interfaces or even the same interface). In Visual Basic 6.0, the result of calling a method or changing a property depended on the context in which it was used (the class from which it was called). In Visual Basic.NET, any class can serve as an interface for another class. The interface class is created in the same manner as any other class. A derived class has the ability to redefine properties or methods of a parent class.

Completing the Code for the Button

Now you will add the code that displays the text box and the message that appears when the button is clicked.

tip
....
Visual Basic.NET normally generates the code for control event handlers. If you do not see the appropriate code, switch back to the form and double-click the control.

To make the button on your Pets Online application functional, you will need enter code in your calendar application:

1 If necessary, switch to Code View by pressing the **F7** key.

2 Scroll to the code that was created by Visual Basic.NET when you added the Button control. The code reads:

```
Protected Sub Button1_Click(ByVal sender As Object,
    ByVal e As System.EventArgs)
```

Press the **Enter** key and type the following code for the button Click event:

```
Dim strMsg As String
strMsg = WeekdayName (2, False, Microsoft.VisualBasic.
    FirstDayOfWeek.System)
strMsg = strMsg & " is a great day to schedule your
    pet with a check up at your local Veterinarian's
    office. Pets Online reminds you that a healthy pet
    is a happy pet!"
TextBox1.Text = strMsg
```

3 Save your Windows Forms application by choosing **File**, **Save All** from the menu.

Variable Declarations in Visual Basic.NET

In Visual Basic.6.0, every variable declared in a Dim statement had to be explicitly given a type. In Visual Basic.NET, however, all variables in a single Dim statement must have the same type and that type need only be declared after the last variable is declared. In Visual Basic 6.0, Dim statements were executed in the order in which they appeared in the source code, and were then in effect for the rest of the procedure. In Visual Basic.NET, however, the scope of a variable is restricted to the smallest area possible. Variables are declared only when they are first used. This allows variables to be limited to parts of procedures.

Review your code. Notice the code below the Button's Click event. It should read as below. Make any changes necessary.

```
Protected Sub Form1_Click(ByVal sender As Object, ByVal e
As System.EventArgs)
End Sub
```

Passing Parameters in Visual Basic.NET

When you passed parameters to a subroutine or function in Visual Basic 6.0, you did so in one of two ways: either by value (`ByVal`) or by reference (`ByRef`). `ByVal` means that the value of the variable used in the parameter list of the call is passed to the called procedure. The contents of the variable will be unchanged by anything you do to the destination variable in the called procedure.

In Visual Basic.NET, the parameters are passed `ByVal` by default, with the exception of references to classes, interfaces, and arrays, which are still passed `ByRef` by default. In Visual Basic 6.0, recall that if a procedure definition did not specify either `ByRef` or `ByVal` on an argument, then Visual Basic assumed it to be `ByRef` and the value of the parameter could be changed.

Before continuing, confirm that the message button works as intended.

To test the button:

1 Press the F5 key to run your Pets Online application. Your application should look like Figure 11-20 once it executes the button's Click event (your dates and time will differ).

Figure 11-20: Button Click event displays result

2 End the application by clicking the **Close** button on the window's title bar. Close the Output window, if necessary.

Notice that in your program, the clock is updated by your system. Click the calendar and move from month to month. Verify that your message is centered, spelled correctly, and appears in bold type.

Adding a Link Label to the Windows Forms Calendar Application

Pets Online wants its customers to be able to click a link to its online catalog. You can use the new Visual Basic.NET LinkLabel control to do this. This control, like other new controls—such as Tray Icon and Print Preview—are new to Visual Basic.NET and provide additional common functionality for developers. The LinkLabel control allows you to create and add Web-style links on your Windows Forms application. You can use the LinkLabel control much like you use the Label control. The LinkLabel control has properties for hyperlinks and link colors. When you use this control, the link text appears underlined and the cursor changes to a hand as the mouse pointer moves over it. When the link is clicked, an actionable event occurs. You can change the link's color to indicate that it has been visited. The LinkClicked event determines what happens when the link text is selected. Upon clicking the link, the user's browser "jumps" to the URL set by the programmer.

Next, you will add a LinkLabel to your calendar application. When a customer clicks the link, his or her browser will display Pets Online's catalog.

To add a LinkLabel to your calendar application:

1 Switch to Design View, if necessary. Select the **LinkLabel** control from the Toolbox. On the form, draw a LinkLabel control under the DateTimePicker. In the Properties window, set the Location property to **320 × 176**. Set the size to **104 × 24**.

2 Set the Text property to **Visit Our Online Catalog**.

3 To determine which part of the caption will be indicated as a link, click the **LinkArea** property and select **Online Catalog**.

4 Set the TextAlign property to **Center**.

5 Set the LinkBehavior property to **HoverUnderline**.

6 Set the Font property to **Microsoft Sans Serif, 8 point, bold**.

7 Change the ForeColor to **Blue on the Web tab**.

8 Change your view to Code View and in the LinkClick event handler, set the LinkVisited property to **True** by typing the word True at the LinkLabel control, as follows:

```
LinkLabel1.LinkVisited = True
```

9 Use the Process.Start method to start the default browser with a URL. To use the Process.Start method you need to add a reference to the System.Diagnostics namespace. To do this, type the following code beneath the LinkLabel control:

```
System.Diagnostics.Process.Start
("http://italiangreyhound.org/items.html")
```

tip

To link to a different form with a LinkLabel control, change the code in the event handler to invoke the Show method. This opens another form in the project. Be sure to set the LinkVisited property to True as you did when you used the LinkLabel control to link to a Web page.

10 To verify that your LinkLabel has been properly coded, click the link to activate the link event. Your browser will be automatically launched from your application. From your Windows Forms application, press the F5 key to run your application. Move your pointer over the LinkLabel control. Click the control to activate it. You should be redirected to a Web page with the URL http://italiangreyhound.org/items.html. The page should look like the one shown in Figure 11-21.

Figure 11-21: Using the LinkLabel control to link your form to a Web page

Adding a Menu and Menu Items

For increased application functionality, you may want to add menus to your Windows Forms. With the new Visual Basic.NET Menu Designer control, you can quickly and easily add menus to Windows Forms application, modify them, and view them without having to run the application. A menu on Windows Forms application is created with a MainMenu object, which is a collection of MenuItem objects. You can add menus to Windows Forms at design time by adding a MainMenu control to the form and then appending menu item objects to it using the Menu Designer. Menus can also be added in the code by adding one or more MainMenu controls to the form and adding MenuItem objects to the class collection. The methods in this tutorial show how to create a simple menu named File, using both the Menu Designer and code.

To add a menu and menu items to your calendar application in Design View:

1   In the Toolbox, double-click the **MainMenu** control. You will see the MainMenu item on the form. The MainMenu control will be added to your Component Tray. In Design View, your calendar application should look like the application shown in Figure 11-22.

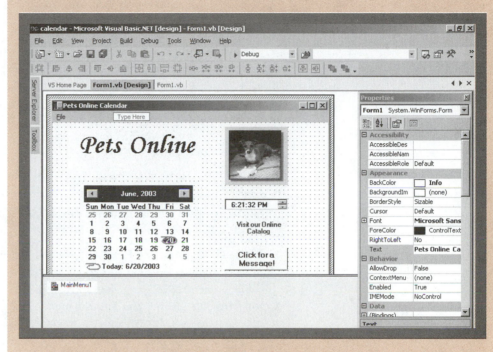

Figure 11-22: Adding a MainMenu control to the Component Tray

2   Click the **MainMenu control** on the form. The text "Type Here" is displayed.

3   Click the displayed text, and type **File** to add the File choice to your menu.

4   In the Properties window, change the Text property to **&File**. You can add another menu item by clicking another Type Here area within the Menu Designer. You can click the area below the current menu item to add another entry to the same menu or you can click the area to the right of the current menu item to add a submenu.

5   To continue creating your menu, click directly under the File menu item you just created. Now add a submenu item named New to the new File menu by typing **&New** in the Type Here text box. Continue to follow this same procedure to add two new submenu items to File. Again, click directly under the menu item you just created. In the Type Here text box, type **Save &As**. Click again. In the Type Here text box, type **E&xit**. Your form should now display a File menu from the Windows Forms application menu bar with three levels of submenus. In the Exit menu item's Property window, change the Name property to **itmExit**.

tip

Depending on how your system settings are configured, you might not need to click to see the words Type Here appear on the menu.

6   To create a separator bar above New on your menu, right-click the word **New**. Choose **Insert Separator** from the menu selection. Repeat to insert a separator bar under the words Save As.

7   Select each menu item, and in the Properties Window, select the corresponding shortcut combination. For example, for File choose Ctrl + F, for New choose Ctrl + N, for Save choose Ctrl + A, and for Exit choose Ctrl + X.

As in Visual Basic 6.0, you can code your menus programmatically. You should also experiment with the code-based method of adding a menu to your application.

To add a menu and menu items in Code View to your calendar application:

1   Double-click the **MainMenu1** control in the Component Tray. This will take you to Code View.

2   In Code View, add to the Controls collection of the form a MainMenu control within a public subroutine. Verify that the following code has been generated:

```
Public Sub AddMenuAndItems()
End Sub
```

Position the insertion point between these two lines.

Now that you have added a MainMenu control to your calendar application, you will want to add menu items to it. When adding menu items in code, the Menu Designer allows you to add menu items to your MainMenu control at design time, as you did with the form method. Menu contents are kept within a collection, so you can add menu items to a menu at run time by adding MenuItem objects to this collection.

3   To complete the menu that you are creating programmatically, add the following code:

```
Dim mnuFileMenu as New MainMenu
Me.Menu = mnuFileMenu
```

4   Within the subroutine, create MenuItem objects to add to the MainMenu object's collection by entering the following code beneath the code you typed in Step 3:

```
Dim myMenuItemFile as New MenuItem()
Dim myMenuItemNew as New MenuItem()
```

5   Within the subroutine, set the Text property for each of these menu items by entering the following code beneath the code you typed in Step 4:

```
myMenuItemFile.Text = "&File"
myMenuItemNew.Text = "&New"
```

tip

A MainMenu object contains no default menu items. The first menu item added becomes the menu heading. This is why you need to set the Text property of myMenuItemFile to &File.

6   Within the subroutine, create the top-level menu item and add subsequent menu items to it by entering the following code beneath the code you typed in Step 5:

```
mnuFileMenu.MenuItems.Add(myMenuItemFile)
myMenuItemFile.MenuItems.Add(myMenuItemNew)
```

tip

▶ You can also add menu items dynamically when they are created. When you do this, the properties are set at the time of their creation and addition. To do this within the calendar application, use the following code in your subroutine: `mnuFileMenu.MenuItems .Add("Save &As")`.

You can add MenuItem objects to the MenuItems collection of the parent MenuItem to create submenus. If you want to add a third menu item to the calendar application as a submenu of the second menu item, you include the following code in your subroutine: `myMenuItemNew.MenuItems.Add(myMenuItemFolder)`.

You will need to also add the code for the Click event for the Exit option. When the user clicks this option on the menu, the application should use the Close statement to Close the form. The Close statement is new to Visual Basic.NET. In Visual Basic 6.0, you used the Unload statement to perform the same task.

To code the Exit option:

1   Switch to Designer View for your form. Click **File** on the form's menu bar to open the File menu. (Be sure to open the form's File menu, not Visual Basic's File menu.)

2   Double-click **Exit** to open the itmExit control's Code window. The Code window opens and displays the Click event procedure, which is the only event procedure a menu control recognizes.

3   Press the **Tab** key, type **Me.Close**() and press the **Enter** key. The Close statement triggers the form's Close event, which removes the form from the memory and from the screen.

4   Test your calendar application. Run the application by pressing the **F5** key. Check to make sure that the menu appears on your form. Test the Exit item. Your calendar application should look like the one shown in Figure 11-23.

Figure 11-23: A menu with menu items displayed

To print, you can also choose the Printer icon on your toolbar or press Ctrl + P.

Printing Windows Forms Application Code

To archive your code for later use, you may want to print your application code. This can be done easily.

To print the code:

1 Verify that you are in Code View.

2 From the IDE menu bar, select **File, Page Setup**. Select the **Line numbers** check box to number the code lines for reference.

3 Click **OK**.

4 From the menu bar, select **File, Print** and click **OK**.

Saving and Exiting a Windows Forms Application

You have now completed the development of the Pets Online Windows Forms application. You should save all the components of this application before you exit Visual Basic.NET. If you are distributing your application to a user, you will need to give the user a copy of the calendar.exe file and a copy of the Visual Basic runtime file (msvbvm60.dll), just as you do with Visual Basic 6.0. The msvbvm60.dll file is located in the Windows\System folder. It comes with Visual Basic.NET; however, Microsoft allows you to distribute the file with your applications without violating any licensing agreement. In Visual Basic.NET the executable file is made when you save all files. You can retrieve the executable file from your calendar\bin folder and copy it to a disk for sharing.

You can also click Ctrl + Shift + S to save all components of your application.

To save your calendar application:

1 From the IDE menu, click **File, Save All**.

Retrieve the executable (.exe) file and then run it from Windows.

2 Right-click the **Start** button on the Windows taskbar. Select **Explore**.

3 Using Windows Explorer, select the executable file from your Tut11\calendar\bin folder and move it to a floppy disk. Rename the moved file **calendar.exe**.

Test the executable file to make sure it works correctly. First exit Visual Basic.NET.

4 Exit Visual Basic.NET.

5 To run the file from Windows, click **Start**, then click **Run**. Select the **Browse** button and navigate to the floppy disk where you moved the executable file. Click **calendar.exe**, then click the **Open** button.

6 When the Run dialog box appears again, click the **OK** button. The application will run in Windows and will appear on your screen. Verify that all of the events are running properly in the application.

7 Click the Close button on the title bar to end the application.

You have now completed Lesson B. You can either take a break or complete the end-of-lesson questions and exercises.

SUMMARY

Windows Forms is the new forms tool in Visual Basic.NET. Windows Forms provides added control when designing the look and feel of an application. Like Visual Studio.NET, Windows Forms provides a standard development platform across the different languages supported by Microsoft. There are minor differences between the common controls used in Visual Basic 6.0 and Visual Basic.NET. In the Windows Forms application, you have the same functionality as with the Visual Basic 6.0 controls; however, the names and various properties and methods have been changed.

Visual Basic.NET includes several changes to the core Visual Basic language that make it a true object-oriented language (Visual Basic 6.0 was only object-based or component-oriented). Visual Basic.NET supports polymorphic programming and true inheritance—this support is often considered the differentiator that defines a language's true object-oriented nature. Polymorphism is the ability to use two different objects and two different types that both implement the same method, allowing programmers to write code that calls the method, regardless of the type of object in use at the moment. In Visual Basic.NET, you can use polymorphism with inherited interfaces.

To start Visual Basic.NET:

■ Click Start from the Windows taskbar, choose Programs, and Visual Studio.NET. Select Create New Project.

To add controls to Windows Forms:

■ Select the desired control from the Toolbox on the left side of the screen. Change the control's properties either in Code View or the Properties window. To change from Design View to Code View, press the F7 key.

To add a menu and menu items to a Windows Forms application:

■ In the Toolbox, double-click the MainMenu control. A menu is added to the form displaying the text "Type Here". Continue designing your form in either Design View or Code View.

To save, print, and exit a Windows Forms application:

■ To save, select File, Save All from the menu bar. The executable file that you can share with others is located in the bin folder of your application folder—in this case, the Calendar folder in your Tut11 folder.
■ To print your code, select File, Print from the menu bar. If you want to number the code lines, select Page Setup prior to printing, and click the Lines Numbered check box.
■ To exit Visual Basic.NET, click the close button on the title bar.

QUESTIONS

1. The Visual Basic.NET new forms package is called _____.
   a. Win Forms
   b. Windows Forms
   c. Form
   d. Visual Forms

2. _____ is new in Visual Basic.NET.
   a. An in-place menu editor
   b. Project Explorer
   c. Solutions Manager
   d. The Label control

3. The Visual Basic 6.0 square and rectangular shapes are now _____ controls in Visual Basic.NET.
   a. text
   b. shape
   c. design
   d. label

4. One way to switch to Design View is to press _____.
   a. F7
   b. F5
   c. Shift + F7
   d. Ctrl + F5

5. To view the Properties window, you can select View, Properties from the menu bar or press the _____ key.
   a. F1
   b. F4
   c. F5
   d. F7

6. The Visual Basic 6.0 Caption property of a label is now called _____ in Visual Basic.NET.
   a. Text
   b. Cap
   c. Label
   d. Tally

7. Visual Basic.NET no longer supports windowless controls such as the image and _____ controls.
   a. Text
   b. Cap
   c. Label
   d. Tally

8. The ability to inherit the Public interface, but not the implementation of a class, is called _____.
   a. polymorphism
   b. inheritance
   c. interface inheritance
   d. superclass inheritance

9. The default parameters are passed as _____ by default in Visual Basic.NET.
   a. `ByVal`
   b. `ByRef`
   c. both a and b
   d. neither a nor b

10. As you did in Visual Basic 6.0, if you are distributing your application to a user, you will need to give the user a copy of the _____ and a copy of the Visual Basic runtime file (msvbvm60.dll) located in the Windows\System folder.
    a. application
    b. Windows Forms file
    c. Solution files
    d. executable file

EXERCISES

1. In this exercise, you will explore more form changes in Visual Basic.NET.
   a. Open Visual Basic.NET, if necessary. From the menu bar, select Help, Search.
   b. Type "Form Changes in Visual Basic.NET" in the Look for text box.
   c. Select and read several of the articles.
   d. In a table, list the task to be performed in Visual Basic.NET Windows Forms, how it is accomplished in Visual Basic 6.0, and how it is accomplished in Visual Basic.NET. Your table should have a minimum of five records of tasks. Do not list tasks that you have developed in this lesson.

2. Within Windows Forms Design View, you can view your project's forms and view their controls. Open your calendar application to practice using the Solution Explorer.
   a. To view forms in the Windows Forms Designer in the Solution Explorer window, double-click the form.
   b. To view the code in a form in the Solution Explorer window, select the form and then click the View Code button.

3. As you saw when you created the calendar application, most forms are designed by adding controls to the form to define a user interface. You used several types of controls in the calendar application. All of the controls were used to display information or accept user input. In this exercise, you will create a new Windows Forms application and add controls to it. Practice drawing a control on a form:
   a. Start a new Visual Basic.NET project by selecting File, New, Project from the menu bar. Save the new project as Ex 3 in your Tut11 folder.
   b. In the Toolbox, click the control you want to add to your form.

   Each control has a default size defined. You can add a default-sized control to your form by dragging it from the Toolbox to the form.

   c. On the form, click the location where you want the upper-left corner of the control to be, and drag to where you want the lower-right corner of the control to be located. The control is added to the form with the specified location and size.
   d. In the Toolbox, click a different type of control and drag it to your form. The control is added to the form at its default size.

   You can also double-click a control in the Toolbox to add it to the upper-left corner of the form in its default size. Try this technique with another type of control.

   e. From the Toolbox, double-click the Button control to add it to your Windows Forms application.

   You can also add controls dynamically to a form at run time. Add a Text box control that appears when a Button control on your form is clicked.

   f. Switch to the Code window.

g. Create a Private member variable for the button within your class using the following code:

```
'Visual Basic
Private Button1 As Button
```

h. In the method that handles the Click event for a Button control within your form's class, insert the following code to add a reference to your control variable. Also, set the control's Size and Location, and add the control:

```
Protected Sub Button1_click (ByVal sender As Object, ByVal e
 As System.EventArgs)
     Dim StrMsg as New String
     StrMsg = "Testing my Click Event!"
     TextBox1.Text = strMsg
     End Sub
Protected Sub Form1 Click (ByVal sender As
object, ByVal e As System.EventArgs)
End Sub
```

i. Save and close your calendar application.

4. Create an access key for Windows Forms controls. Recall that you learned about access keys in Tutorials 2 and 6. An access key allows the user to use a shortcut to activate, or "click" a control, by pressing the Alt key simultaneously with a predefined access key. You may also want to set your application so that the user can click a preset button that will cause the application to print without pressing Alt + the predefined access key. Create an access key for a control at design time.

a. On a new form, create a button control. In the Properties window, set the button's Text property to a string that includes an ampersand before the letter that will be the shortcut. For example, to set the letter "P" as the access key, type "&Print" into the button's Text property label.

Create an access key for a button control at run time:

b. In the Code window, set the Text property to a string that includes an ampersand. The subroutine should read:

```
Private Sub CreateShortCut()
Button1.Text = "&Print"
End Sub
```

discovery ▶ 5. In Visual Basic 6.0, you used the Ctrl + Alt + C shortcut key combination to open the Call Stack window, which displayed a list of all active procedures or stack frames for the current thread of execution (available only in run mode). You will be happy to know that Visual Basic.NET handles this task using the same shortcut key combination. In break mode, the shortcut key combination for both Visual Basic 6.0 and Visual Basic.NET that resumes execution of code from the current statement to the selected statement is Ctrl + F10. However, many default shortcut keys differ in Visual Basic.NET from their Visual Basic 6.0 versions. In this exercise, you will explore the differences between Visual Basic 6.0 and Visual Basic.NET default shortcut keys.

a. Open Visual Basic 6.0 in a separate window.

b. Click the following default shortcut keys in both versions of Visual Basic and write down the description of the action. Set up two columns for your answers. Label one column Visual Basic 6.0 and the other Visual Basic.NET.

　a. ALT + *
　b. Alt + Backspace (also Ctrl + Z)
　c. Alt + F3 + B
　d. Alt + F3 + C
　e. Alt + F3 + N
　f. Ctrl + R
　g. Alt + F10
　h. Ctrl + Shift + F5

discovery ▶   6. In Visual Basic.NET, the easiest way to inherit a Windows Form or other object is to use the Inheritance Picker. With it, you can take advantage of code or user interfaces that you have already created in other solutions. The first step is to ensure that the project containing the form to be inherited has been built into a .dll executable file. To verify that the calendar.vbproj file has been built into a .dll executable file:

a. Verify that calendar.vbproj is open. If necessary, in Visual Basic.NET, select File, Open, Project, and open calendar.vbproj from your Tut11/calendar folder.

b. From the menu bar, choose Build. You will see the solution builder output displayed in your Output window. The final display should read Done. Build: 1 succeeded, 0 failed, 0 skipped.

To create a Visual Basic.Net Windows form inherited from an existing form using the Inheritance Picker:

c. From the Project menu, select Add Inherited Form. The Add New Item dialog box opens.

d. Select Local Project Items from the Categories pane on the left side of the window. Select Inherited Form from the Templates pane on the right, and name it in the Name box. Click the Open button to proceed. The Inheritance Picker dialog box opens.

e. Click the Browse button. Within the Select a file which contains a component to inherit from dialog box, navigate to the project containing the form or module you desire. Click the name of the appropriate .exe or .dll file to select it and click the Open button. This returns you to the Inheritance Picker dialog box, where the component is now listed, along with the project where it is located. Select the component and click the OK button.

f. In the Solution Explorer, the component is added to your project. If it has a user interface, the controls that are part of the inherited form will be colored differently and, when selected, have a border indicating the level of security that the control has on the superclassed form. The border characteristics that correspond to the different security levels are listed in Figure 11-24.

Security level of control	Border of control on inherited form
Public	Standard sizing handles. Control may be sized and moved. The control can be accessed internally by the class that declares it and externally by other classes.
Protected	Blue and white sizing handles. Control's user interface may not be resized or moved. Can be accessed internally by the class that declares it and any class that inherits from the parent class, but cannot be accessed by external classes.
Private	Shown on the form, properties visible in Properties window. However, all aspects of the control are considered read-only. You cannot move or size the control, or change its properties. If the control is a container of other controls, such as a group box, new controls cannot be added and existing controls cannot be removed, even if those controls are public. The class that declared it can only access control.

Figure 11-24: A control's security levels on the superclassed form

More on Visual Basic.NET and the Internet

Creating a Visual Basic.NET Web Forms Application

case ▶ Pets Online, the small online pet store that hired you as a Visual Basic.NET programmer, wants you to create several forms for its Web site. Your duties include creating several Web pages for Pets Online using Visual Basic.NET, the newest version of Microsoft's Visual Basic programming software. The Web form you create will give visitors an interface to the Pets Online Web pages. Building on the skills you learned in your first assignment—the calendar application you created in Tutorial 11—you now must create a programmable Web page that includes data and event handling code. Your application will incorporate both HTML and Web Forms controls.

Previewing the Web Forms Application

Using Visual Basic.NET, you can build Web interfaces, called Web Forms, similar to the Windows Forms application you created in Tutorial 11. New to Visual Basic.NET, Web Forms are the perfect tools for building interactive Web applications since they allow interaction between the client and the server.

Web Forms let you use drag and drop operations to create user interfaces for Web pages. Web Forms provide a variety of custom-generated tools that support HTML, the design language of the Web. You can also write the server-based code for each Visual Basic object just as you wrote code for your Windows-based forms in Tutorial 11. Web Forms code resides on the Web server and the HTML code is generated for you by Visual Basic.NET.

Before starting the lesson, you should preview a Web form that was created using Visual Basic.NET.

To preview the completed screen:

1   If necessary, start Windows. Use the **Run** command on the Start menu to run the **Petsonline** (Petsonline.exe) file, which is located in your Tut12 folder. (Depending on which version of Windows you are running and how Windows is set up on your computer, you may see the .exe extension on the filename. If you do, click the Petsonline.exe filename.)

2   Click the **Open** button. Click the **Browse** button to locate your file. The Browse dialog box closes and the Run dialog box appears again, displaying the path for the Petsonline.exe file. Click the **OK** button. The completed Pets Online application appears on your screen.

3   Preview the Pets Online application, which is a welcoming message to visitors. Click the **Show!** button. Verify that the words displayed read "Welcome to Pets Online!", as shown in Figure 12-1. Upon finishing your preview, close the application.

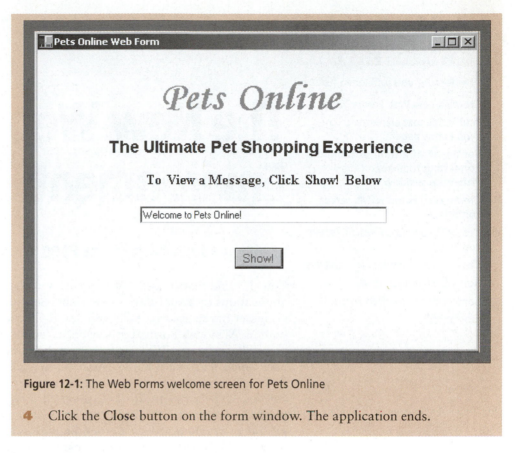

Figure 12-1: The Web Forms welcome screen for Pets Online

4 Click the **Close** button on the form window. The application ends.

Before you create your own Visual Basic.NET Web Forms application for Pets Online, you will learn about the new Web features in the Visual Basic.NET environment. Remember to compare your programming tasks and steps in Visual Basic.NET with the tasks and steps you would use to complete the same project using Visual Basic 6.0.

In this lesson, you will learn how to:

■ Create a new Web Forms page

■ Add HTML text elements to the Web Forms page

■ Set the HTML attributes using the Formatting toolbar and the Properties window

■ Create Web Forms HTML server controls

■ Create Web Forms ASP.NET server controls

■ Create event handlers for controls

■ Run Web Forms controls

■ Save and exit the Web Forms application

The New Web Forms Environment

Creating a New Web Forms Page

You will find that creating Web Forms is similar to creating traditional Windows applications in Visual Basic. The Visual Studio.NET environment gives the programmer the ability to create both desktop applications, as you did in Tutorial 11 with the Windows Forms application, as well as Web applications. In this tutorial, you will create two Web Forms applications for Pets Online: a welcoming Web page and a data page. With Visual Studio.NET and Web Forms, you can rapidly develop Web applications that can be used across computing platforms and with various Web browsers. In Web programming, as in all programming, keep in mind that an application is only a software program. It can be as simple as a single line of programmed code or as complex as a program comprising hundreds of pages. A Web application, in turn, can be as simple as a single Web page or Web Form, or it can be a complex Web site containing hundreds of lines of code.

As you program Web Forms, you will use the same techniques that you learned for building Windows Forms.

Even if you do not know anything about Hypertext Markup Language (HTML), you can create Web Forms using Visual Basic.NET. Every Web page is stored as an HTML document. A standard Web Forms page consists of a Web Form "markup" file. This file contains the HTML code that can be translated into a Web-ready visual representation of the page. This visual representation is coded in HTML. HTML is composed of a set of elements, called tags, that define a document and instruct Web browser software how to display it. The markup file also has a source file that contains event handling code. Compared to standard programming runtimes, the Web Forms page has a very fast run-time performance based, in part, on its source code. Both the markup file and the source file of the Web Forms page reside and run on a Web server, where they generate Web pages in response to requests from clients. The Web page is sent from the server over the Web to the client. The client computer displays the page in a browser program. Visual Basic.NET Web Forms can even be used with wireless devices such as the new mobile phone and hand-held computer technologies.

Another new feature of Visual Studio.NET is ASP.NET, formerly referred to as ASP+. The user interface for Web Forms pages consists of a file containing the HTML markup code and special Web Forms components, such as HTML controls. This file, with the markup and Web Forms-specific components, is referred to as the page. The page works as a container for the text and controls you want to display. The page is a file with the extension .aspx. Active Server Pages, or ASPs, are the pages in your Web Forms application with the file extension .aspx. You will access the PETS database from an .aspx page. Accessing databases using ASP.NET is a common technique used by developers for displaying data to Web site visitors.

The basic process of creating a Web application using Web Forms is to create a Web Forms page in a new Visual Basic.NET project, drag a control to a page (form), and then double-click the control to add code in Code View. The process is identical to the one you used in Tutorial 11, when you created the calendar application. You will begin creating a Web Forms application by creating a Web Forms page for the Pets Online application.

> Important note: Your Web server must have Microsoft Internet Information Server (IIS), Version 4 or later, and the .NET Framework installed on it. Be sure to check with your instructor to make sure the appropriate software is installed.

> Important note: Be sure to verify that the default Web access mode for the project is set to FrontPage and that the project folder at the URL that you specified when you created the project can be opened with FrontPage. From the Windows taskbar, select Start, Settings, Control Panel, Administrative Tools, and Internet Services Manager. Select the Default Web Site and run the Check Server Extensions task.

To create a new Web Forms page:

1 If necessary, start Visual Basic.NET by clicking the **Start** button on your Windows taskbar. Choose **Programs, Microsoft Visual Studio.NET 7.0, Microsoft Visual Studio.NET 7.0**. The Start page opens.

2 From the IDE menu bar, select **File, New, Project** to open the New Project window.

3 In the Project Types pane on the left side of the New Projects window, select **Visual Basic Projects**, if necessary. In the Templates pane on the right side of the window, select **Web Application**. Your screen should look like the screen shown in Figure 12-2.

your server name will
be different

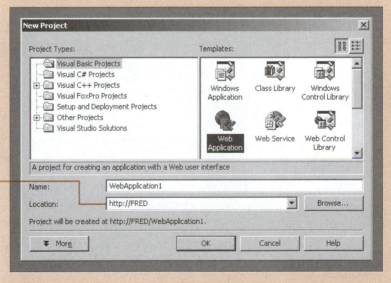

Figure 12-2: Selecting a new Web Forms application

4 In the Name text box, delete the default name and type **Petsonline** to name your project.

5 In the Location box, type the URL of the Web server where you want to create your project, if necessary. Be sure to include the http:// portion of the URL. Click **OK**.

A new Web Forms page called Petsonline has now been created and should appear similar to Figure 12-3. At this point, you have created a Web page, but it is not yet "live," that is, it will not be accessible to site visitors until Pets Online publishes the page on the Web.

Notice that by default, Visual Basic.NET has named the page WebForm1. The WebForm1.aspx page is displayed in Web Forms Design View, and by default the page is displayed as shown in Figure 12-3. The text shown in the page instructs you to change layout modes if you wish.

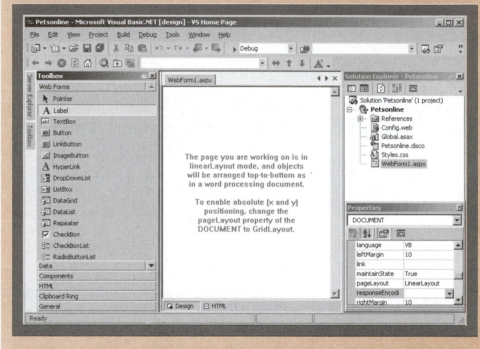

Figure 12-3: WebForm1.aspx page in Design View

HELP? Web access can fail even if the FrontPage server extensions are installed. In this case, ask your instructor or IS manager for help. He or she might need to run the Internet Service Manager and check the server extensions.

Now that you have set up a Web page, you will begin to add text to it. You will learn how to do this in the next section.

Adding HTML Text to the Web Forms Page

Every Web page is stored as an HTML document. HTML tags format Web Forms so they can be accurately created and displayed by Web browser programs. HTML tags are enclosed in angled brackets (< >). These tags are divided into two broad categories: those that define how the body of the document is to be displayed by the browser; and those that define information about the document, such as the title or relationships to other documents.

You have used controls, or objects placed on forms, in every tutorial of this book. In Web Forms, the controls are HTML objects. Figure 12-4 shows common Web Forms HTML controls and their corresponding HTML tags.

Control	Corresponding tag	Description
HtmlAnchor	`<a>`	Creates an anchor
HtmlButton	`<button>`	Uses Click events to allow connectivity between client and server
HtmlSelect	`<select>`	Allows a client to select content on Web Forms page
HtmlTextArea	`<textarea>`	Designates a text area of a Web Forms page
HtmlInputButton	`<input type="button">`	Creates a button control
HtmlInputRadioButton	`<input type="radio">`	Creates an input radio button control
HtmlInputText	`<input type="text">` and `<input type="password">`	Creates an input text control
HtmlInputImage	`<input type="image">`	Creates an input image
HtmlInputFile	`<input type="file">`	Creates an input file
HtmlForm	`<form>`	Creates a client form
HtmlImage	`<img>`	Creates a Web Forms image
HtmlTable	`<table>`	Creates a Web Forms table
HtmlTableRow	`<tr>`	Creates a Web Forms table row
HtmlTableCell	`<td>`	Creates a Web Forms table cell
HtmlGenericControl	Any other unmapped tag, such as `<div>` or `<span>`	Creates a generic Web Forms control such as divide or span

Figure 12-4: HTML controls and their corresponding HTML tags

You will begin customizing your Web Forms page by adding text to it using the Visual Basic.NET HTML editing features.

To add text to your Web Forms page:

1 Switch to Design View, if necessary.

2 At the top of the page, type **Pets Online**. Press **Enter**. On the second line, type **The Ultimate Pet Shopping Experience.**

Next, you will format the text to give it a pleasing appearance.

Setting HTML Text Attributes

Just as you formatted and set attributes for text in Windows Forms, you will use the Formatting toolbar to set the HTML text attributes for your Web Forms application.

To use the Formatting toolbar to set HTML text attributes:

1   Verify that your Formatting toolbar is displayed by selecting **View**, **Toolbars**, and **Formatting** from the IDE menu. Do not clear the Formatting check box.

2   You will change the text attributes using the Formatting toolbar. To change the HTML text style, place the pointer in the first line of HTML text that reads, "Pets Online". On the Formatting toolbar, locate the Block Format drop-down list arrow. Click the **arrow** and select **Heading 1**.

3   To set text characteristics, select the text by triple-clicking the words "Pets Online". Click the **Foreground Color** button of the Formatting toolbar, choose **dark green #009900**, and click **OK**. Next, select the **Italic** and **Center** formatting icons. Change the font to **Monotype Corsiva**, size 7.

4   Highlight the second line of text. Select the **Foreground Color** button and choose **dark blue #000099**. Change the font to **Arial**, size **4**, and select the **bold** and **centered** attributes.

5   In the Properties window, select **DOCUMENT** from the drop-down list. Scroll and select **bgColor**, then click the **ellipsis** (three dots). Click the **System Colors** tab and choose **InfoBackground** (#ffffe1) for a light yellow for the Web Forms background color. Click **OK**. Your Web Forms page should look like Figure 12-5.

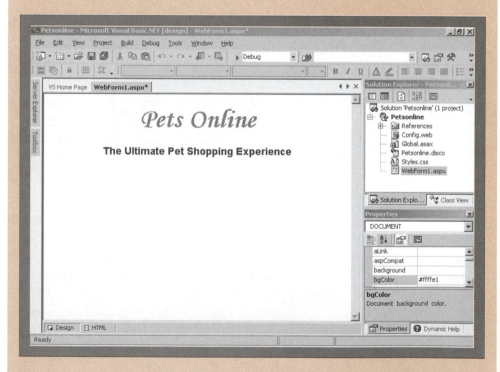

Figure 12-5: Adding text and text attributes to the Web Forms page

Creating Web Forms HTML Server Controls

A server control is a type of control that acts as a communications link between client applications and the server. Server controls have properties, events, and methods that are specifically tailored to perform the tasks associated with the server. Server controls in Visual Basic.NET can be Web or HTML controls.

Web controls work specifically with a Web Forms page, allowing you to add, modify, or delete Web Forms content. Both of these control types create HTML code that can be used on various hardware platforms and software browsers. This is important when building a Web Forms application, because a programmer can never be sure what type of hardware or software clients will be using when they access a Web page.

The Web Forms HTML controls exist within the System.Web.UI.HtmlControls namespace. They are part of the HtmlControl base class. These controls are associated with any tag containing the runat="server" attribute. The only way for an ASP.NET page to recognize that you are using a Web Forms server control is to have the runat="server" attribute included in the control tag. If it is omitted, Visual Basic.NET will only recognize the control as HTML. The runat="server" indicates that the server will validate the code. For example, the following HTML code creates an instance of a Web Forms HTML input control in which the input source is a text box:

```
<input type="text" runat="server" id="PetstextBox1"
value="">
```

Next, you will add an HTML server control called a TextField to your Web Forms application. Once the Pets Online application is published on the Web, this server control will be used to add connectivity between your Pets Online Web page and the visitor to the page.

tip

You may need to toggle the Auto Hide feature of the Toolbox to make it visible. To do so, click the Toolbox title bar on the far left side of the IDE and click the Push Pin. If the Auto Hide feature is turned on, the Toolbox will disappear. If not, the Toolbox will remain visible on the Start page. If necessary, click the Push Pin again to ensure that the Auto Hide feature is on.

To add an HTML server control:

1   Verify that you are in Design View and that the insertion point is at the end of the second line of text. Press **Enter** once to move the insertion point down one line in your form.

2   Type **To View a Message, Click Show! Below.** Change the various text properties so that the text is Times New Roman, Heading 1, size 2, black, and center aligned.

3   From the HTML tab of the Toolbox, select the **Text Field** control and drag it onto the page to the right of the text you just entered. This creates in the page an HTML <FORM> element that adds an <INPUT TYPE="Text"> element to your page. Click the **HTML** tab at the bottom of the window. Scroll to the bottom of the form to verify that the <FORM> element has been added.

4   Switch to Design View. Add two spaces between the text and the HTML control by placing the insertion point after the text and pressing **Enter**.

5   Convert the HTML text element to a Web Server TextField control by right-clicking it and then selecting **Run As Server Control** from the shortcut menu. The Web Server control is now identified as an HtmlInputText control. Two attributes are added to the element when you do this. The first, an ID attribute, is how you identify the control in code. Notice that the ID attribute is set by default to Text1. The second attribute, RUNAT=SERVER, marks the element as a control. It makes the element visible to the Web Forms server code as a programmable element.

6 In the Properties window, change the Size to 40.

7 Right-click the **Text Field** control and choose **View in Browser**. This may take several seconds. If you have not saved your project, Visual Basic.NET will prompt you to do so before previewing it in the browser. Notice that there is now a new tab at the top of the IDE that lets you preview your project in the browser within the IDE. Your project should look similar to Figure 12-6.

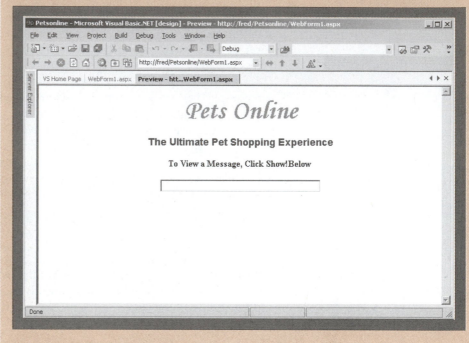

Figure 12-6: Previewing the Web Forms page in the browser

8 At the top of the IDE, click the **WebForm1.aspx** tab to leave the browser preview and return to the form.

Creating Web Forms Server Controls

As you learned in this lesson, there are two types of controls on a Web Forms page: HTML server controls and Web Forms server controls. The Web Forms controls exist within the System.Web.UI.WebControls namespace and are part of the WebControl base class. They include traditional form controls such as TextBox and Button controls, which you used in Tutorial 11. Web Forms server controls also include higher-level controls, such as Calendar and DataGrid controls.

Visual Basic.NET Web Forms server controls have several new features that simplify development efforts. Web Forms server controls automatically detect the capabilities of the client browser and can customize the form properties and appearance to make the best use of that browser's capabilities. This feature is called Automatic Browser Detection. The WebControl base class gives Web Forms server controls properties that are common to all types of controls. Some of the common controls that you have worked with include ForeColor, BackColor, and Font.

In Tutorial 9, you created forms that were data bound to an Access database. As you will see in Lesson B of this tutorial, in Web Forms pages any property of a control can be data bound. This feature allows Web Forms controls to be used to call the contents of a data source.

Web controls appear in the HTML markup as namespace tags. They have a prefix that is used to map the tag to the namespace of the run-time component. The rest of the tag is the name of the run-time class itself. Web Forms controls, unlike HTML controls, must also contain a runat="server" attribute. For example:

```
<asp:TextBox id="PetstextBox1" runat="server"
Text=""></asp:Textbox>
```

Web Forms Controls

This section gives you a brief outline of the most common Web Forms server controls. You will use several of them as you create your Web Forms application. The Visual Basic.NET code used to include the Web Forms server control in your application follows each control's description. Notice that each control's code is enclosed in the < and > brackets used to enclose HTML tags.

The Label Control The Label control is used to display either read-only unchanging (static) text or data-bound dynamic text in the page. Sample Visual Basic.NET code for a Web Forms label control is displayed in Code View as:

```
<asp:Label runat="server" Text"Label1" Font-
Bold="true"></asp:Label>
```

The TextBox Control Similar to the Label control, the TextBox control is used to allow editing of text on a form and can be data bound. The TextBox control supports single-line, multiline, and password text input. Sample code for a Web Forms TextBox single line control is displayed as:

```
<asp:TextBox runat="server" Text"TextBox1" Font-
Bold="true"></asp:TextBox >
```

Sample code for a Web Forms TextBox multiline control is displayed as:

```
<asp:TextBox runat="server" Mode="Multiline" Rows="4"
Text"TextBox1"></asp:TextBox >
```

Sample code for a Web Forms TextBox password control is displayed as:

```
<asp:TextBox runat="server" Mode="Password"></asp:TextBox >
```

The CheckBox Control The CheckBox control is used to create a check box on a Web Forms application. Sample code for a Web Forms CheckBox control is displayed as:

```
<asp:CheckBox runat="server" Text="CheckBox1"
Checked="true"></asp:CheckBox>
```

The RadioButton Control The RadioButton control, also called an Option Button, is similar to the CheckBox control. However, it is used when you want to display a group of choices of which only one can be selected at a given time. Sample code for a Web Forms RadioButton control with four buttons is displayed as:

```
<asp:RadioButton runat="server" Text="RadioButton1"
GroupName="Group1" Checked="true"></asp:RadioButton>
<asp:RadioButton runat="server" Text="RadioButton2"
GroupName="Group1" Checked="false"></asp:RadioButton>
<asp:RadioButton runat="server" Text="RadioButton3"
GroupName="Group1" Checked="false"></asp:RadioButton>
<asp:RadioButton runat="server" Text="RadioButton4"
GroupName="Group1" Checked="false"></asp:RadioButton>
```

The DropDownList Control The DropDownList control is used to create selections for a series of choices. The user clicks a down-pointing arrow to display the drop-down list, then makes a choice from one of several options. The choices can be unchanging and read-only, as shown below, or populated from a data source. Sample code for a Web Forms DropDownList with three selections is displayed as:

```
<asp:dropdownlist runat="server">
<asp:ListItem Text="Choice1" Value="1" selected="true">
<asp:ListItem Text="Choice2" Value="2">
<asp:ListItem Text="Choice3" Value="3">
</asp:dropdownlist>
```

The Button Control The Button control generates a button icon used to submit a Web Forms page to the server for processing. Sample code for a Web Forms Button control is displayed as:

```
<asp:Button runat="server" Text="Click"></asp:Button>
```

The LinkButton Control The LinkButton control is used to create a link that, once clicked, displays a hyperlinked page. Sample code for a Web Forms LinkButton control is displayed as:

```
<asp:LinkButton runat="server" Text="Click"></asp:Button>
```

The ImageButton Control The Image Button control is used to submit pages from the Web client to the server and back. It returns the page as an image rather than text and can provide the x- and y-coordinates of the position on the page where the user clicked for proper positioning of the image. Sample code for a Web Forms ImageButton control is displayed as:

```
<asp:ImageButton runat="server"
ImageUrl="Issy.bmp"></asp:Button>
```

The Calendar Control The Calendar control allows navigating between dates on the calendar. It can also be used to make date selections and date ranges. It looks just like the Calendar control you created in Tutorial 11, except this control supports connectivity between the client and the server. Sample code for a Web Forms Calendar control is displayed as:

```
<asp:Calendar runat="server" DayNameFormat="FirstLetter">
<property name=SelectedDayStyle>
<asp:TableItemStyle Font-Bold="True" BackColor="">
</property>
...
</asp:Calendar>
```

Adding Web Forms Server Controls to Your Project

You will now add a Web Forms server control to your Pets Online Web Forms application. This new control will add functionality to the Web page. You will add a Button control that will automatically detect the capabilities of the client browser and customize the page's properties and appearance to make the best use of that browser's capabilities.

When Pets Online publishes the Web Forms page as part of its Web site, the Button control generates a button icon that can be used by a Pets Online visitor to submit the page from his or her computer (the client) back to the server on the button's Click event.

To add a Button control to your Web Forms page:

1   From the menu bar, select **View**, **Designer** to switch to Design View, if necessary.

2   Place the insertion point at the end of the TextField control that you created earlier in this tutorial. Recall that after you created the TextField control, you converted it to a server control using the shortcut menu. With the insertion point positioned at the end of the TextField control, press **Enter** once to move down one line in your Web Forms page. The insertion point should now be under the TextField control you created earlier.

3   From the Web Forms tab on the Toolbox, click the **Button** control. Drag and drop the **Button** control onto the page under the HTML TextField control.

4   Switch to HTML view by clicking the HTML tab at the bottom of the IDE. Scroll to the bottom of the page. Notice that the element you just created is named <asp:Button...>.

5   Switch back to Design View. Select the **Button** control. In the Properties window, change the button's Text property to **Show!**.

6   Press the F5 key to run your Web Forms application. Your application should look like Figure 12-7.

tip

The Web Forms tab of the Toolbox is only available when you are in Design View of the Web Forms designer.

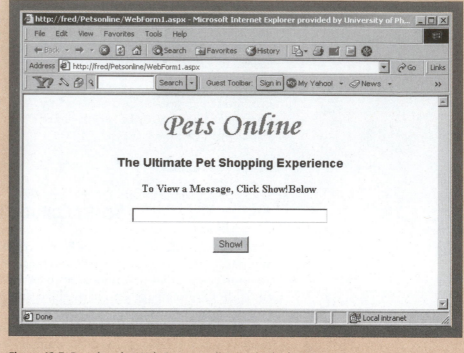

Figure 12-7: Running the Web Forms application in the browser

HELP? If your application doesn't run correctly, check to make certain that Microsoft.NET Framework SDK is installed on your computer. Ask your instructor for further assistance, if needed.

Now you will work with the TextBox server control, which is one of the Web controls that allows the end user to submit data on the Web page that is processed by the server. In the Pets Online Web application, a visitor to the Web page will be able to use the TextBox control to submit information from his or her computer to the Pets Online computer.

To experiment with the server controls:

1   Type the name of your pet into the TextBox you created earlier in this tutorial. If you don't have a pet, you can type any name into the TextBox.

2   Press the form's **Show!** Button to verify that you can click it.

3   Choose **File**, **Save All** from the IDE menu bar. Close the application and return to the Web Forms page.

tip

If you watch the status line of the IDE while your program is compiling, you will see a message that indicates that the update succeeded.

tip

If you press F5 in Visual Studio.NET, all of the pages in the project are saved, the project is built, and the project's Start page is launched in debug mode.

Creating an Event Handler

Your project's Start page is the WebForm1.aspx by default, since it is the only Web page you have created so far. However, if you add pages and want to set a Start page, select the page in Solution Explorer, right-click, and choose Set As Start Page.

In the last section, you learned how to create Web Forms server controls. Server controls on Web Forms can handle many different types of events, such as Click or Load. The code to handle a Web Forms event is executed as server code, which means that the code is executed on the server rather than on the client. For example, when the user clicks a server Button control, the Web Forms page is sent to the server and the server examines the event information to determine what action is needed. If your form includes event handler code, then that code will be executed. When the code is finished running, the page is sent back to the client's browser.

To create an event handler for the Web server Button control you created in the previous set of steps:

1. If necessary, switch to Design View. Click the **WebForm1.aspx** form, if necessary, to activate it.
2. Double-click the **Show!** button on the form. The Web Forms Designer opens the Visual Basic.NET code class file for the current form and creates an event handler for the Button control's Click event. Your Web Forms Designer-generated code should appear as follows:

```
Public Sub Button1_Click(ByVal sender As Object, ByVal
  e As System.EventArgs)



    End Sub
```

Position the insertion point between these two lines of code, if necessary.

Next, modify the event handler to display a message in the HtmlInputText control. To do so, you enter code as a subroutine.

3. Type the following code:

```
Text1.Value = "Welcome to Pets Online!"
```

4. Select **File, Save All** from the IDE menu.

Running the Web Forms Application

You can also preview your Web Forms page in the browser by choosing View in Browser when you are in Design View.

You cannot run the Web Forms application until the class file has been compiled. However, you can view the page in your browser by clicking the PreviewWebForm1.aspx tab at the top of your IDE.

To compile the page's class file and run the page:

1. Press the **F5** key to compile the page's class file and run it in debug mode by launching the default browser.
2. Press **Show!** to execute the Click event. Your run application should look like Figure 12-8.

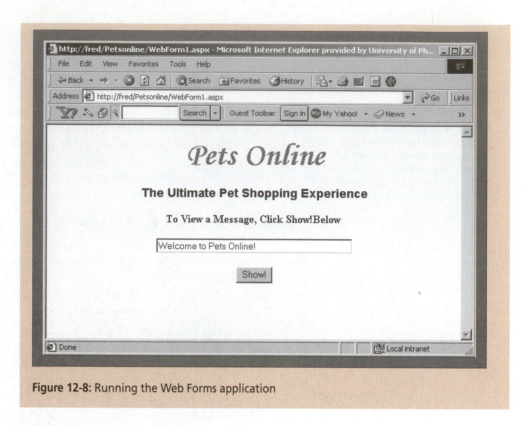

Figure 12-8: Running the Web Forms application

Saving and Exiting the Web Forms Application

Before exiting Visual Basic.NET, you should save all the components of your Web Forms application. As you learned in Tutorial 11, in Visual Basic.NET an application's executable file is created automatically when you save all files.

To save the Petsonline Web Forms application:

1 Close the browser and return to the Web Forms page.

2 Press **Ctrl + Shift + S**. All components of your project will be saved in your Petsonline folder. This folder is located in the wwwroot folder in the inetpub folder on your hard drive. These folders are automatically created when you create your Web Forms application.

3 Exit the Pets Online application.

4 Close Visual Basic.NET.

You have now completed Lesson A. You can either take a break or complete the questions and exercises at the end of the lesson.

SUMMARY

Visual Basic.NET Web Forms are used to create applications in which the primary user interface is a Web browser. Web Forms are useful in creating Web sites and applications intended to be available publicly through an intranet or the World Wide Web.

Like Visual Studio.NET, Visual Basic.NET Web Forms are platform-independent. Users can interact with your Web Forms application regardless of what type of browser they have or what type of computer they are using. Because of their reliance on HTML, Web Forms are also suitable for text-intensive applications and non-Web contexts. Programs—such as the cash registers you created earlier in this text—that do not rely heavily on graphics are well suited to Web Forms.

To create a new Web Forms page:

- Click the Start button.
- Choose Programs, Visual Studio.NET 7.0, Microsoft Visual Studio.NET 7.0.
- Choose Web Applications from the right pane.

To add HTML text and attributes to the Web Forms page:

- In Design View, type the text into your form.
- To change the type, use the formatting toolbar.

To create Web Forms HTML server controls:

> For Web Forms to allow interactivity between the client and the server, server controls must be used.

- From the HTML tab of the Toolbox, choose the control you want and drag it onto the Web Forms application. This will create an HTML <FORM> element in the page. It also adds an <INPUT TYPE=""> element to the page.
- To convert an HTML element to a control, right-click it. Select the Select Run as Server Control option from the shortcut menu. The element will be converted to an HtmlInputText control. At this time, Visual Basic.NET adds two attributes to the element: ID and RUNAT=SERVER.

To create Web Forms ASP server controls:

- While in Design View of the Web Forms page, choose a control from the Web Forms tab on the toolbar. Drag and drop the control onto your page. This creates an ASP.NET server control element.
- The control is named <asp:"controltype">.

To create an event handler:

- In the WebForm1.aspx page, double-click the ASP.NET server control to open the Visual Basic.NET code class file for the current form. Double-clicking automatically generates an event handler for the control's event in Visual Basic.NET code.
- Add the System-generated code as necessary for the event.

To run the Web Forms application:

■ Press F5 to compile the page's class file and run the application in debug mode.

To save and exit the Web Forms application:

■ To save, depress Ctrl + Shift + S.
■ To exit, depress Alt + Q.

QUESTIONS

1. The Active Server Pages.NET (ASP.NET) is also known as _____.
   a. Integrated Development Environment (IDE)
   b. Visual InterDev Web development system
   c. Visual Studio.NET
   d. Web Forms

2. Web Forms simplifies the development of Web applications by _____.
   a. providing an event-based programming model on the server similar to the forms-based development model used by the Microsoft Visual Basic development system
   b. allowing complete separation of HTML markup from application logic
   c. providing a rich design-time and rapid application development experience
   d. all of the above

3. Server controls are used to create the _____ for your Web application.
   a. user interface
   b. client-side scripts
   c. .NET SDK
   d. none of the above

4. HTML controls exist within the _____ namespace and derive from the HtmlControl base class.
   a. System.Web.Controls
   b. System.Web.UI.HtmlControls
   c. Namespace.Controls
   d. System.Object

5. HTML controls are instantiated for any tag containing the _____ attribute.
   a. Web Forms
   b. HtmlInputText
   c. runat="server"
   d. server messaging tag

6. A feature provided by Web controls that simplifies development efforts is _____.
   a. rich and consistent object model
   b. data binding
   c. both a and b
   d. neither a nor b

7. An example of a Web control that has been implemented for Visual Basic.NET is _____.
   a. Label
   b. CheckBox
   c. RadioButtonList
   d. all of the above

8. The _____ Web Forms control is used to allow navigating between dates and make date selections.
   a. Panel
   b. Table
   c. Calendar
   d. HyperDate

9. A run-time advantage to Web Forms is that they _____
   a. deliver a programming and executing framework that enables developers to implement server-generated HTML pages
   b. compile an executable file upon clicking File, Make executable from the menu
   c. create a second file for back-up purposes
   d. both a and b

10. You cannot run the Web Forms page until the _____ file has been compiled.
    a. class
    b. run-time
    c. server at
    d. runat=server

E X E R C I S E S

1. When designing an application in Visual Basic.NET that involves a user interface, you have two development tool choices: Windows Forms and Web Forms. Both have full design-time support within the development environment. Both can provide a rich user interface and advanced application functionality to solve business problems. How, then, do you decide which Visual Basic.NET technology is appropriate for your situation? Use dynamic help and search MSN articles to help you write a 100- to 200-word essay that supports your choice. To use the Visual Basic.NET dynamic help:
   a. Start Visual Studio.NET, if necessary. Click Dynamic Help at the lower-right of the IDE screen.
   b. Click the Search button on the Dynamic Help title bar.
   c. Enter keywords in the search box and filter by Visual Basic Documentation.

2. The local utility company, Power Services, wants you to create Web Forms for its online presence. Create a page that has both an HTML control and an ASP.NET control.
   a. In your Tut12 folder, create a subfolder named Power. Start a new application, name it Ex2A, and set its location to the Tut12/Power folder.
   b. In Design View, drag and drop a text box control and change it to reflect the company's name.
   c. Choose Web Forms from the Toolbox and drag and drop a Web Forms button control onto your page. Use the event handler as necessary to make your program appropriate to the button's task. (*Hint*: The button uses an on-click event.)
   d. Change the background color of your Web Forms page to blue. Add other formatting as you like.
   e. Choose File, Save All to save your project.

3. When you are ready to test the Web Forms page you designed in Exercise 2, you should compile and run it by building the Web Forms page. To build a Web Forms page:
   a. Open the project you created in Exercise 2.
   b. In Solution Explorer, right-click the Web Forms page and choose Set As Start Page.
   c. From the Build menu, choose Build.
   d. Save the page as Ex3A in your Tut12/Power folder.
   e. Open your browser and point it to your server, project, and page.

4. Add a new HTML label server control to the Web Forms page created in Exercise 2. This is like adding any HTML element. However, you must convert the element to a control so that you can work with it in server code. Adding HTML server controls to a Web page is a two-step process.

   a. Open the Web Forms page you created in Exercise 2. From the HTML tab of the Toolbox, drag an HTML Label control onto the page.

   b. Set the control's ID attribute to a unique value for the page.

   c. Set the RUNAT=SERVER attribute to convert the element to a control.

   d. Save the page as Ex4A in your Tut12/Power folder.

   e. Preview your page in browser view or run the application.

discovery ▶ 5. There are times when you'll find it more practical to create a control at run-time rather than at design time. For example, it would be more practical to dynamically generate rows for a table as results are displayed. This is appropriate since you don't know before your search results are returned just how many rows you will need. For this exercise, add another control to the Web Forms page you created in Exercise 2. Add this control to your Web Forms page programmatically. In order to programmatically add a control to a page, the form must include a container application for the new control. An application that creates a data object is called a source application or server application and the application to which the object is copied is called the container application or client application (see Appendix C). To add a control to your Web Forms page:

   a. Open the Ex2A Web Forms page. Create a Label control on the form and set its properties in Code View. Have the label display the words "Sample Label".

   b. Add the new Label control to the Controls collection. Use a complete Page_Load method that creates as many label controls as the user has selected from a drop-down list called DropDown1. The label should display the word "Label" plus a counter. The container for the controls is a Panel ASP.NET control called "Panel1."

   c. Save the page as Ex5A in your Tut12/Power folder.

discovery ▶ 6. At times, you will want to store HTML elements in the IDE Toolbox. After you have placed text and objects on your page, you can drag them from the page and store them in the Toolbox. This is useful if you have customized an object or text and want to keep it for use in other projects. To store an element in the Toolbox:

   a. Open the Web Forms page that you created in Exercise 2.

   b. Select one or more of the elements on the page.

   c. Drag the selected element(s) to the General tab in the Toolbox.

   d. Right-click the element in the Toolbox to bring up the shortcut menu.

   e. Select Rename Item from the shortcut menu.

   f. Type a descriptive name of your choosing for this item.

   g. Close Visual Basic.NET

Elements that you drag to the Toolbox are attached to the Visual Studio.NET IDE rather than to the document. Whatever you drag to the Toolbox from one document will be available to you while you work on other documents.

In this lesson, you will learn how to:

- Create a Data-Access Component
- Bind the DataGrid
- Add a Details Panel to Web Forms
- Deploy the Web Forms application project

Completing Your Web Forms Application Project

The Pets Online Web Application Data Project

Pets Online, like most businesses, stores data in many different places. These may include spreadsheets, databases, word processing documents, and even HTML Web pages. Accessing the information in each of these data stores requires different methods. As you learned in Tutorial 9, the Microsoft approach to a standard method for accessing a company's data is called Universal Data Access, or simply UDA.

As you may remember, the UDA approach uses many complex interfaces, called Object Linking and Embedding Database (OLE DB), and cannot be accessed directly from Visual Basic. Instead, Visual Basic programmers access the OLE DB through data control components called ActiveX Data Objects, or ADO. In this lesson, you will use OLE DB and ADO data control components to access the data stored in Pets Online's database file using the Pets Online Web application you will create with Web Forms.

Learning More About Web Application Projects

In Lesson A, you learned that to create a Web Forms page, you first need to create a Web Forms application project. This type of project is used for creating an application with a Web-user interface. As with the projects you created in Visual Basic 6.0, the Web application project serves as a container. It stores information about what files, components, and references belong with your application. It also stores information about what actions should occur in order to build and deploy your application.

Technical Requirements for Your Web Applications Project

Web applications in Visual Basic.NET require that you run Microsoft Internet Information Server (IIS) on your computer. IIS is the Microsoft Web server software program. Programming Web applications that are more complex than the ones in this text requires other technical features that are beyond the scope of this book. Refer to a Web development text for more information.

The Visual Studio.NET Cache

When you create a Web application project, the files in your Web application will be stored in two different places. The primary location is the Web server, where the application is stored; however, Visual Studio.NET also keeps files in a local cache on the programmer's computer. The cache is a temporary directory used by Visual Studio.NET for storing your Web application project files. You will see references to the cache when you are creating a deployment project later in this lesson. There are two reasons for the creation of this cache. First, as a designer, you may require file-level access to your project files. Second, keeping files in a cache allows you to work in offline mode. You are in offline mode when you are not connected to the Internet.

When connected to the Internet and working online, the cache is always synchronous with the actual project files on the server. When in offline mode, you will not be able to access live content over the Internet. If you are working in offline mode, the files will be synchronized when you reconnect to the server project. When you update files in your project, the updates are written to both the server and the cache.

Files Created with Web Applications

When you create a Web application project in Visual Basic.NET, a project structure is automatically set up in the file system on your computer. Visual Basic.NET also sets up a Web application on the target Web server. On the server machine you designate, a physical folder will automatically be created by Visual Basic.NET under Inetpub\wwwroot. The folder is marked as an IIS application, though Visual Basic.NET does not create a virtual IIS directory.

On your computer, Visual Basic.NET creates a solution file with information about the project and some global information about the solution. In the Pets Online project in Tutorial 11, you worked with the Solution Explorer and viewed these types of files in the Solution Explorer window (see Figure 11-8).

Creating the PetProj Web Application Project

In Lesson A, you created a Web Forms page for Pets Online. In this lesson, you will create a Web database application for the company. As you learned in Tutorial 9, you can use data control components to access data stored in a database. Before you begin to create your Web application project, check with your instructor to verify that the computer on which you are working is running IIS with FrontPage Server Extensions installed. If your operating system is Microsoft Windows 2000 Professional, you will find the IIS and FrontPage Server Extension components on your installation disk. Your computer must also be running Microsoft Access 2000 to run the PETS database.

The first step in creating your Web application project with data access control components is to create the Pets Online Web Forms project. This project will be a new Web application that will allow connection to an Access database named PETS.

To create the Web Form:

1   Start Visual Studio.NET.

2   Press **Ctrl + N**. Choose **Visual Basic Projects** in the left pane of the New Project window and **Web Application** in the left, if necessary. In the Name text box, delete the default name and type **PetProj**. Notice the default location name. You should see something similar to http://MyServerName. Choose **OK**.

The application wizard will build the necessary files, including the WebForm1.aspx, which will contain the visual representation of the Pets Online Web Form and the WebForm1.vp file. As you learned in Lesson A, this file contains the code for event handling and other programmatic tasks.

> **HELP?** During this file building process, if your Web access fails, you may see a Web Access Failure dialog box. Visual Basic.NET will ask if you would like to open the project with a shared file path. (Recall that you specified your directory path earlier in the tutorial.) If this dialog box appears, either accept the location A:\Pages\PetProj or click Browse, change the directory to a location of your choice, and press Enter. You should inform your instructor that you received this error.

Next, add text to the page.

3   Make sure your WebForm1.aspx page is active.

4   Type **This Pets Online .NET Project Creates an Application with a Web-User Interface.**

Next, you will add a data control component to your project that will allow you to connect to the PETS Access database.

5   Open the Solution Explorer window, if necessary. In the Solution Explorer, right-click the Web application project name, **PetProj**.

6   Point to **Add** and click **Add New Item**.

Your window should look like Figure 12-9.

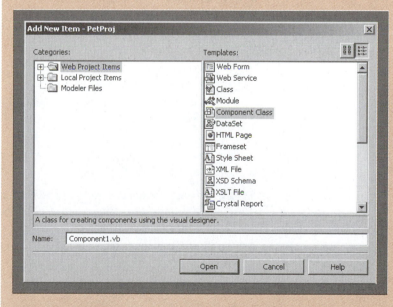

Figure 12-9: Adding a component to the new Web Forms application project

7   In the Add New Item dialog box, double-click Component Class in the right pane. This will create a new .vb file in your project. Do not choose a name for the file. Let it default to Component1.vb.

Creating a Data-Access Component

In Tutorial 9 you learned how to use the Visual Basic 6.0 Visual Data Manager to create a Microsoft Access database and how to use the data-access component, the Microsoft ActiveX Data Object (ADO) data control, to access the records stored in the database. Client-server applications that utilize either the Web or a LAN can use data-access components like the ADO data control component you created in Tutorial 9 to integrate information stored in a variety of databases. In addition to Microsoft ActiveX Data Objects (ADO), other examples of these components include OLE DB and Open Database Connectivity (ODBC).

Recall that you can use a data control component, sometimes called a data component, to access the data stored in a variety of formats, such as a database, a spreadsheet, or even a text file. Data control components can also be used to bind data values into HTML code transmitted to the client as Web pages. In this lesson you will create the component in Visual Basic.NET and also write the necessary code to fill the data control component with data from your PETS database found in your Tut12 folder.

To add and configure a data source, follow the steps below:

1   Click the **Component1.vb[Design]** tab to activate it, if necessary.

2   From the Toolbox, choose the **Data** tab and drag and drop the **ADODataSetCommand** onto the Component1.vb[Design] page. This will start the DataSetCommand Configuration Wizard. Choose **Next** to continue to the second page of the wizard.

3   In the Choose Your Data Connection page, click the **New Connection** button.

4   In the Provider tab of the Data Link Properties dialog box, choose **Microsoft Jet 4.0 OLE DB Provider**. Click **Next**.

As you learned in Tutorial 9, Visual Basic contains the same Jet database engine used in Microsoft Access. The Jet engine allows databases created in Access to be read and manipulated by Visual Basic.

5   In the Connection tab of the Data Link Properties dialog box, type the path to the PETS database file in your Tut12 folder (or click the three dots to navigate to the file location). Leave the user name and password text boxes empty. Clear the Blank password and Allow saving password check boxes, if necessary.

6   Test the connection to the database by pressing the **Test Connection** button at the bottom of the dialog box. A dialog box with the message "Test Connection Succeeded" should appear. Click **OK**.

HELP? If your connection fails, use Windows Explorer to verify that your database exists where you have specified in the DataSetCommand Configuration Wizard. Repeat Steps 1 through 5 until your connection is successful so you can proceed.

7   Once you have established a connection, click **OK** and then click **Next** to advance to the Choose a Query Type page.

You may remember that in Tutorial 9 you learned that SQL is a set of commands that allow you to access and manipulate the data stored in many database management systems. You used the SQL Select command to control the order of the data stored in the database to which you had bound controls from your Visual Basic application. Now you will use the Visual Basic.NET DataSetCommand Configuration Wizard to choose a SQL query type to access the PETS database.

8   Select the **Use SQL statement** option button, if necessary. Click **Next**.

By choosing to use SQL statements, you will be able to specify a Select statement to load data and the wizard will generate the Insert, Update, and Delete statements to save data changes to your PETS database. You may remember that in Tutorial 9 you had to enter the Select command in your ADO control component's RecordSource property. Here, in Visual Basic.NET, the wizard will do the work for you.

9 Click the **SQL Builder...** button to select the data that the DataSetCommand should load into the DataSet, which is a cache of data retrieved from a data source. In this case, the data source is your PETS database.

10 In the Tables tab of the Add Table dialog box, select **Main** if necessary. Click the **Add** button, and then click the **Close** button to add the Main table from the PETS database.

11 Individually select the **vacc_id**, **name**, **species**, **birthdate**, and **notes** check boxes, and then click **OK**. The Generate the SQL statements page displays the SQL statement that has been created for the Main table. Verify that your SQL statement reads `SELECT vacc_id, name, species, birthdate, notes FROM Main`. These are the fields from the Main table of the PETS database to which the Web-user interface of your Pets Online Web application will connect. Adding the SQL statements in Visual Basic.NET with the DataSetCommand Component Wizard requires fewer steps and less knowledge of SQL than is needed to perform the same task using Visual Basic 6.0.

12 Click **Next** to advance to the last page of the wizard and click **Finish**.

Upon clicking Finish, your Web application project will now be connected to the Main table of the PETS database. The adoDataSetCommand1 and adoConnection1 objects also have been created and added to your Component Tray. Your screen should look like Figure 12-10.

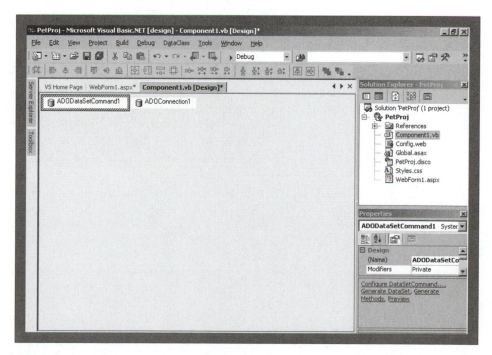

Figure 12-10: Creating the data access component

Now you will generate and fill the DataSet for the data control component.

To generate the DataSet:

1 Click the **Component.vb [Design]** page to make it the active page of your application project, if necessary. From the menu bar at the top of your screen, select the **DataClass** menu. Select **Generate DataSet...** from the DataClass menu. The Generate DataSet Class dialog box appears.

2 Type **myDataSet** in the text box and click **OK**. The myDataSet object appears in the Solution Explorer, as shown in Figure 12-11.

the new **myDataSet** object

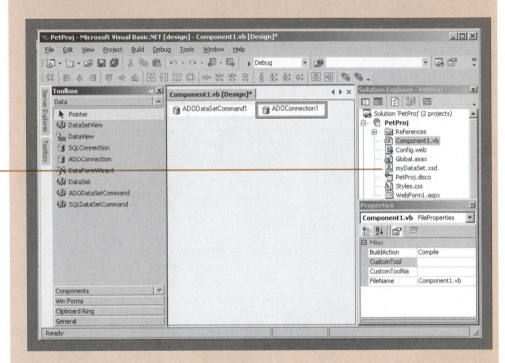

Figure 12-11: Generating and filling the DataSet

3 From the DataClass menu select **Generate DataSetCommand Methods** (see Figure 12-12). This will conveniently add subroutines to your Visual Basic.NET code to fill and update the DataSet that you have just selected—the Main table of the PETS database.

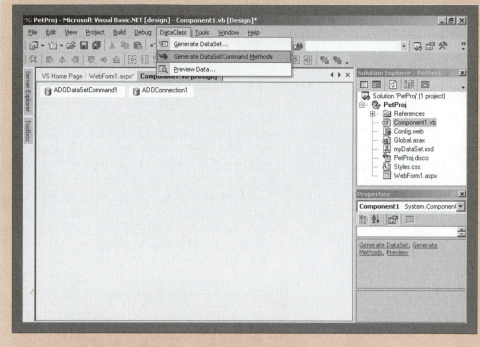

Figure 12-12: Selecting the Generate DataSetCommand Methods option

Binding the DataGrid

In Tutorial 9 you learned how to bind Visual Basic 6.0 controls to an ADO data control component. In Visual Basic.NET, the Web Forms application project provides an easy and flexible way of binding your controls to information in a data store. Recall that connecting a control to an ADO control is called binding and that the connected control components are referred to as bound controls. The way Visual Basic.NET handles data binding in Web Forms differs from how previous versions of Visual Basic handled the task. Visual Basic.NET data binding even differs from the methods used in Windows applications.

In Visual Basic.NET Web Forms, the page accesses data in the form of classes. These data classes expose the raw data as properties for updating the Main table in the PETS database. In the steps below, you will use your PetProj Web Forms page to create a new data class. This new class will incorporate a new component called a **data adapter** that can interact with the PETS database and PetProj Visual Basic.NET code. The data adapter writes the data from the PetProj Web application back to the PETS database.

The strength of Web Forms is that they can take advantage of almost any publicly available information, such as information accessible on the Web. Even simple controls, like those you learned to create in Lesson A, can bind to public property on a Web Forms page.

Now you will add a DataView object to the Pets Online Web Forms page and use it to link the DataGrid to the DataSet. In Tutorial 10, you learned that when you bound to a data control component, the DataGrid control displayed the information from the recordset. The DataGrid control provides many properties that allow you to control the appearance of the DataGrid output. It also provides properties that allow you to control how the user interacts with the control while the application is running. In this lesson, you will also use the DataView object to view and display data from the Main table in your PETS database. After you add and configure a DataView object, you can select the Main table in your PETS database. In other projects you might have many tables in a DataSet from which to choose. Here, your DataSet is defined as the PETS database and in the PETS database, there is only one table—the Main table.

To begin the binding process, add the PETS database DataSet to the form:

1 Select the **WebForm1.aspx** tab so it is the active page.

2 From your Toolbox, select the **Data** tab. Drag and drop the **DataSet** component onto the WebForm1.aspx page. The Choose a DataSet dialog box appears.

3 Select the **Typed DataSet** option, if necessary. Click **OK**.

4 From the drop-down list, select **PetProj.myDataSet**, which is the name of the DataSet that you created, preceded by the project name. This adds the DataSet component to your Web Forms page.

5 Click **OK**.

Next, fill the DataSet with data.

6 On the Toolbox, choose the Data tab. Drag and drop the **DataView** control onto the WebForm1.aspx page. You should see a new object, dataView1, added to the Component Tray.

7 Select the **DataView1** object in the Component Tray at the bottom of the WebForm1.aspx page and press **F4** to display the object's Properties window.

8 Click the Table property drop-down list arrow and select **myDataSet1, Main** from the list. You may need to click the plus sign (+) to the left of myDataSet1 to expand the selection, enabling you to view the Main table to select it. The Table property indicates the table from which this DataView retrieves data. You have selected the Main table from the PETS database.

Your IDE should look like Figure 12-13.

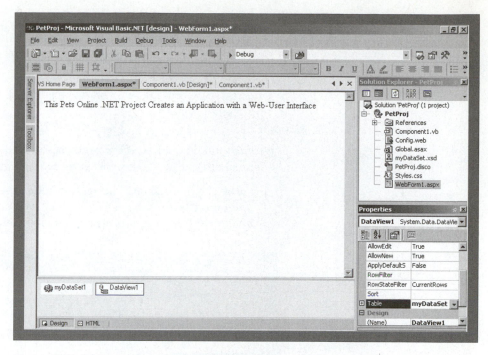

Figure 12-13: Adding and configuring the DataView

Finally, to complete the binding process, you will add and configure the DataGrid.

To add and configure the DataGrid:

1 Verify that the WebForm1.aspx page is active.

2 From the Toolbox, select the **Web Forms** tab. Drag and drop a **DataGrid** onto the WebForm1.aspx page. If necessary, reposition the DataGrid on the WebForm1.aspx page. To do so, click the DataGrid and drag and drop it below the line of text. If necessary, position the insertion point at the end of the line of text and press **Enter** to reposition the DataGrid.

3 Right-click the **DataGrid** and select **Property Builder** from the shortcut menu.

4 Select **General** if necessary, from the left side of the Property Builder dialog box. Click the list arrow to display the choices and set the DataSource to **DataView1**. To set the Data Key Field to **vacc_id**, which is the primary key (identifying element) of the Main table in the PETS database, click the **list arrow** in the Data Key Field box and select **vacc_id**. Check the **Show Header** check box only. Visual Basic.NET will automatically generate the DataGrid fields for you from the selected data source, PETS.mdb Main table.

5 Complete the Properties Builder dialog box. Click **Columns** from the pane. Clear the **Create columns automatically at runtime** check box. Scroll down in the Available Columns list until you can expand the Button Column node. Expand the Button Column node and add a Select button by choosing the word **Select** and clicking the **right arrow** between the two lists.

6 To create the additional column in your DataGrid, type the word **Species** in the Header Text textbox. Click the Sort Expression **list arrow** and choose **species**. Click the Text Field **list arrow** and choose **species**.

7 Select the **name** field from the Available Columns list and click the **right arrow** between the two lists so that the Name field appears in the Selected Columns window.

8 In the Header Text box, type **Pet's Name**.

9 Click **OK**. Your DataGrid now displays only these two fields from the Main table of the PETS database, as shown in Figure 12-14.

HELP? If your DataGrid does not appear below the text, place the insertion point directly after the "e" in "Online" and press the Enter key. This will add an additional line to your project and make it easier to position the DataGrid.

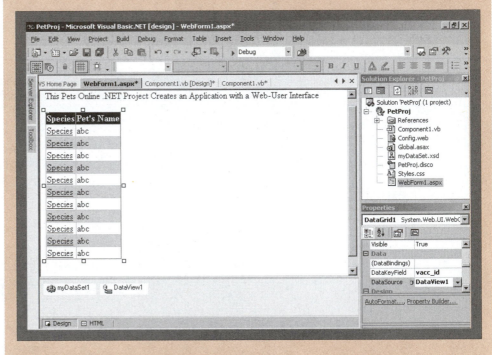

Figure 12-14: Adding and configuring the DataGrid

As you learned in Tutorial 10, the DataGrid control component, when bound to an ADO data control component, displays the data to which it is bound. In this lesson, you are binding the Main table of the PETS database to your Web Forms page. The information is displayed in the DataGrid in a row and column format, similar to a spreadsheet. Each database field you have chosen from the Main table of the PETS database appears in a column in the DataGrid, and each record appears in a row. Though the DataGrid is now visible, you must bind the data in your table to the columns of the DataGrid. To continue the binding process, in the code, you will declare the component object at the top level of the WebForm1.vb page and bind the data to the DataGrid.

To bind the data to the DataGrid:

1   Right-click the **WebForm1.aspx** page and choose **View Code** from the short-cut menu. This adds a WebForm1.vb page to the project.

2   In the WebForm1.vb page, you must declare a component object at the top level of the WebForm1 class and bind the data to the columns of the DataGrid by adding the DataBind() to the WebForm_Load sub. To accomplish this task, the subroutine must be modified. Change your code so that it looks like Figure 12-15.

add these three lines of code

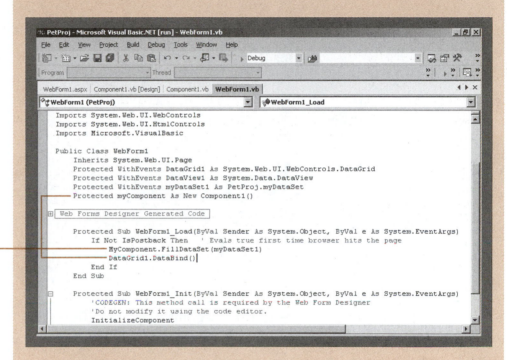

Figure 12-15: Code to declare a component object and bind the data

The last step in the binding process is to test the project.

To bind and test the project:

1   Select **Build** from the IDE menu bar.

2   Choose **Build PetProj1** from the Build menu.

3   After your project successfully builds, close the output window if it is visible and choose **File, Save All** from the menu to save your project.

4   Press **F5** to run your project in a browser window and display data from the PETS database on the Pets Online Web Forms page. Your application should look like Figure 12-16, although your URL and browser window title will be different.

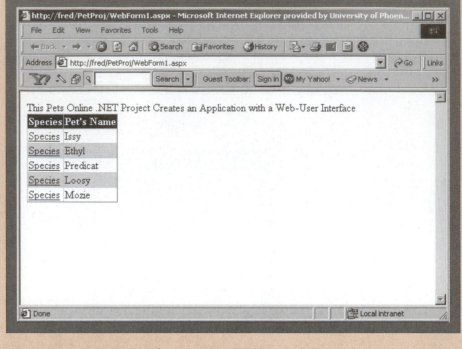

Figure 12-16: Displaying data from the PETS database on the Pets Online Web Forms page

tip

If you do not have a browser window open, Visual Basic.NET will automatically open one when it runs the Pets Online application project. The Web Forms page will appear in the browser, as shown in Figure 12-16.

5   Close the browser window and return to Visual Basic.NET. Close the Output and Task List windows if they are visible.

Adding a Details Panel to Your Web Forms Application

You can access additional information about the animals in the Pets Online database without cluttering the DataGrid with unwanted information from your database. The Details Panel allows you to view this additional information by filtering the Main table in the PETS database so that only the currently selected row is displayed. Before you add the Details Panel, you will add a second Data View with which the Details Panel will interact.

tip

If the selection you want is not visible on the Toolbox, right-click the Toolbox when it is displayed and choose Show All Tabs. This Show All Tabs is a toggle button. When checked, it will display all available Toolbox tabs. If you think the appearance of the Toolbox is too cluttered when viewing all tabs, you may reverse the process by right-clicking the Toolbox when open, and choosing Show All Tabs again.

To add a second DataView:

1   Verify that the WebForm1.aspx page is active.

2   Add a second DataView to the WebForm1.aspx page by selecting **Data** in the Toolbox. Drag and drop the **DataView** control onto the WebForm1.aspx page. A new object named DataView2 is created.

3   Select the **DataView2** component. Press **F4** to display the Properties window.

4   Under the Data category, select the **Table** property, as you did with the DataView1 component, to link it to myDataSet1.main. You may have to expand the myDataSet component by clicking the plus sign (+) to expose the Main table.

You will now continue to add controls to your WebForm1.aspx page. Add Label controls that correspond to data columns and bind each label to the second DataView.

To add Label controls:

1. Verify that you are in the WebForm1.aspx page. Drag and drop a **Label** control from the Web Forms tab of the Toolbox onto the WebForm1.aspx page. Add four labels to your WebForm1.aspx page, one each for the name, species, birthdate, and notes detail fields of your Main table.

2. Select each label and bind it to the appropriate field by selecting a **label** and pressing **F4**. This displays the Properties window. If necessary, expand the Data category in the Properties window by clicking the **plus sign** (+).

3. In the Properties window, select the **DataBindings** property page by clicking the **ellipsis** button (three dots) next to DataBindings.

4. In the DataBindings dialog box, select the **Text** property from Bindable Properties in the left pane. Bind the first label control to the name field of the Main table in the PETS database. Click the **Simple Binding** radio button. Expand the DataView2 component until the name column appears. Select **name**.

5. Select the **General {0}** format from the Format drop-down list.

6. Click **OK**.

7. In the Label properties window, add text to describe the label. For the first label, type **name**.

8. Continue the process for the remaining three labels: species, birthdate, and notes. Set the data binding for each of the three to **text** and use a simple binding to bind each to the appropriate column under the DataView2 component, just as you did with the first label. Again, format each as **General {0}** and click **OK** when you complete the process for each label.

9. Click each label and move the label directly under the DataGrid. You may need to place the insertion point directly after the DataGrid and press the **Enter** key to move the first label below the DataGrid.

10. Press **F5** to run the application. Click **Close** to end the application. Return to the Visual Basic.NET window.

The last step in adding the Details Panel to the Web Forms page is to add the necessary code to show only the information you filtered from your database. Activating the Details Panel is similar to performing a query that returns only a single row from the Main table. The DataKeys property, which you will specify when you create the DataGrid programmatically, is a means for uniquely identifying each row of the table. You will determine the value of the identifier, or key, for the selected row by mapping the item index to a matching key. This key, which is a valid vacc_id from the Main table, can now be used to uniquely select the row you want to use. This works because the vacc_id is the primary key, or unique identifying element, for each record of the database.

To activate the Details Panel:

1 Verify that you are in the WebForm1.aspx page.

2 Double-click the **DataGrid1** object. This will add a SelectedIndexChanged event handler to your code and switch you to WebForm1.vb.

3 Scroll until you see the DataGrid1_SelectedIndexChanged method of the code, and set the dataView2.RowFilter so that it will select only the row you want to display. Bind each label that you are using by calling DataBind on that label in the DataGrid1_SelectedIndexChanged subroutine. Place these calls *after* the row filter change has been set. Modify your code so that it looks like Figure 12-17.

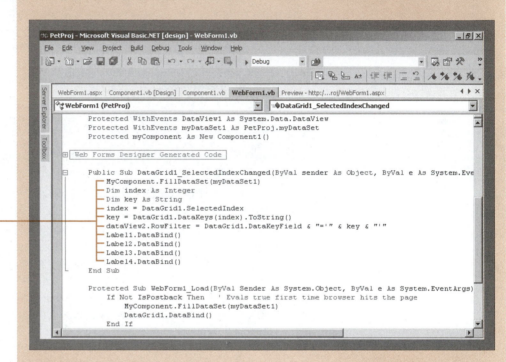

add these ten lines of code

Figure 12-17: Code to filter information from the database

4 Build and start the project. Test your project. Your Web Forms application project will run in a browser window. You should now be able to click a species and review the details with the new species information. Your application should look like Figure 12-18. After you have tested the project, close the browser window and return to the Visual Basic.NET window.

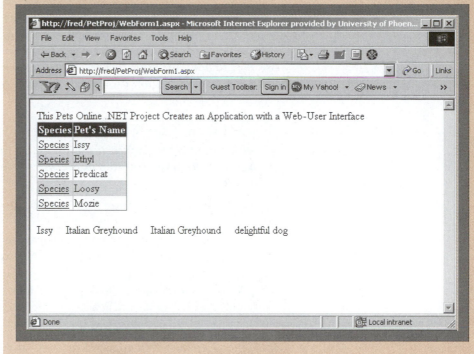

Figure 12-18: Running the Pets Online Web Forms application with two DataView objects and a Details Panel

Deploying the Web Forms Application Project

The last step needed to complete your Web Forms application project is to deploy the project. The term deploy literally means "to spread out." You will spread the Pets Online application project to the Internet. Deployment involves uploading all the individual pages, graphics, and programmatic elements of your Web Forms application project to the Internet and fully testing the Web Forms page for functionality. It is also possible to deploy applications to an intranet site, allowing a company's employees to access the project to retrieve information.

In this step, you deploy your Pets Online project, PetProj. To do that, you will first switch from **debug build**—the mode you have been using to test your project—to **release build**, and rebuild the project so that it will be ready to deploy. A Visual Basic.NET solution and its individual projects are usually built and tested in a debug build. Debugging is a two-step process. During the first step, the compile-time errors are corrected. These errors include incorrect syntax, misspelled keywords, and type mismatches. During the second step, the debugger is used to detect and correct programming logic errors and errors in sequencing, branching, and interaction among the program components.

When a project or solution is fully developed and sufficiently debugged, its components are compiled in a release build. By default, a release build uses what Visual Basic.NET calls **optimizations**. Optimized builds are smaller and run faster than builds of the same project or solution that have not been optimized. You will use release build for your finished Web application project so that the project has the advantages of optimization when it is deployed.

To deploy the project:

1 Verify that your PetProj application is open and running and that the Solution Explorer is visible. If necessary, press Ctrl + R to make the Solution Explorer visible.

2 Right-click the **PetProj(1Project)** solution in Solution Explorer. From the shortcut menu, point to **Add**. Select **New Project**.

3 Select the **Setup and Deployment Projects** folder from the Project Types pane and select **Deploy Wizard** from the Templates pane.

4 Visual Studio.NET requires that you give your project a new name before it can be deployed. In the Project Name text box, type **MyWebApp** to rename your deployed project. Click **OK** to launch the Deployment Project Wizard.

5 In the Deployment Project Wizard, click **Next** on the first wizard screen.

6 Select **Deploy a Web application** and click **Next**.

7 Select **Primary output from PetProj** and **Content Files from PetProj**, then click **Next**. At the next page, add no additional content files, just click **Next**.

8 Type the name of your server in the text box. Select **No, create the project and I will deploy it later**. Click **Next**.

9 On the summary sheet, click **Finish**.

10 In the File System Editor, right-click the **Web Application Folder** in the left pane. In the shortcut that appears, point to **Add** and select **Web Folder**.

11 Rename the new folder **Bin**.

12 Select the Web Application folder in the left pane. In the Web Application folder, select all the .dll files that show in the right pane. These files are necessary for the project to be deployed to the Internet and accessed publicly. Drag and drop all of the .dll files into the Bin folder.

13 Deploy the solution by clicking **Deploy Solution** on the Build menu.

14 Run your deployed solution. In a new browser window, type the URL for your server: *http://ServerName/PetProj/WebForm1.aspx*, substituting your project's Web application name and server name in the appropriate area of the path.

tip

If the File System Editor is not the current window, right-click the deployment project folder in the Solution Explorer. Choose View, and select File System.

Notice that the correct versions of all the DLL files used by your application were automatically deployed to the server. This ensures that installation of other applications on this server will not damage your application through the use of incompatible file versions.

Finally, you must save and exit the Web Forms application project.

To save the Web Forms application:

1 Select **File, Save All** from the menu bar.

2 Click the **Close** button on the title bar to exit the application.

3 Close Visual Basic.NET.

S U M M A R Y

Visual Basic.NET Web Forms and server controls speed up application development of Web pages and applications. The Web application project serves as a container for all of the associated files and components. It stores information about what files, components, and references belong with your application, and what should happen with these files in order to build and deploy your application.

Web application projects require:

- Access to a development computer running Microsoft IIS.
- Administrative privileges (create privileges) on the IIS server.
- The Visual Basic.NET framework installed on the server.

To create a Web application project:

- Create a Web Forms page.
- Add the Component class.

To create the Data-Access Component:

- Add and configure a data source.
- Generate and fill the DataSet.

To bind the DataGrid:

- Add a DataSet to the form.
- Fill the DataSet with data.
- Add and configure the DataView.
- Add and configure the DataGrid.
- Test the project.

To add a Details Panel to the Web Forms page:

- Add a second DataView.
- Add Label controls.
- Activate the details.

To deploy the Web Forms application project:

- Add a new project to the Solution Explorer.
- Set up and deploy the project.
- Move the appropriate files to the Bin folder.
- Build and run the project.

To save and exit the Web Forms application project:

- Choose File, Save All from the menu bar.
- Click the Close button on the IDE title bar.

QUESTIONS

1. The Web Forms project represents the _____ application.
   a. main
   b. first
   c. deployment
   d. trial

2. Web Forms pages access data in the form of _____.
   a. tables
   b. collections
   c. objects
   d. classes

3. Visual Studio.NET keeps files in a local _____ to allow you to work in offline mode.
   a. cache
   b. file
   c. folder
   d. method

4. When you create a Web application in Visual Basic.NET, the system establishes a Web application on _____ and sets up a project structure on _____.
   a. your computer, the Web server
   b. the Web server, your computer
   c. the Web server, the Web server
   d. your computer, your computer

5. To hold your Web applications project, a physical folder is created on your computer in what folder?
   a. www.root
   b. Inetpub
   c. both a and b
   d. neither a nor b

6. How many types of Web application projects can be created with Visual Basic.NET?
   a. 1
   b. 2
   c. 3
   d. 6

7. Web application projects are _____-based; they reflect the actual content of the Web page directly in which you are working.
   a. file
   b. folder
   c. directory
   d. platform

8. A _____ is used to access the data stored in a variety of formats and to bind data values.
   a. DataView
   b. DataGrid
   c. DataSet
   d. data control component

9. _____ is used to access the data stored in a variety of formats and to bind data values.
   a. DataView
   b. Build
   c. Data Link Properties
   d. A DataSet

10. The _____ allows you to view additional information about the selected items in your database without cluttering the DataGrid with extraneous material.
a. DataView
b. Label
c. DataGrid
d. WebForm_Load

EXERCISES

Prior to completing the Exercises, you should create a new folder within your Tut12 folder named ExercisesB. Copy the PetProj folder and all of its contents to the new Tut12/ExercisesB folder. Open the Tut12/ExercisesB folder to confirm that it contains the PetProj folder. These exercises are sequential. You must complete them in order.

1. In this exercise, you will modify your Web Forms page to make it more visually appealing. In Lesson B, you created a generic Web Forms page in your Web Forms application project. Modify the page to make it more attractive to the end user: the customer.
a. If necessary, launch Visual Basic.NET. From the Tut12/ExercisesB folder, open the PetProj Web Forms application project that you created in this lesson.
b. Activate your WebForm1.aspx page.
c. In the Properties window, change the background color of the form to light yellow.
d. Add both an HTML control and a Web Forms control to your page.
e. Move your DataGrid and labels so that they are easier for a customer to read after the project is deployed.
f. Save the project in your Tut12/ExercisesB folder. Run the project, then close it.

2. In this exercise, you will change the data-access component to which your project is set. Create a second database in Access 2000 named DOG with fields similar to those found in the PETS database. In the DOGS database, create only one table and name it Main_Dogs. Include at least three records in the Main_Dogs table. Create a data-access component that sets the new DOGS database to your PetProj Web Forms application project. To add and configure the data source:
a. Open the PetProj.vbproj file from your Tut12/ExercisesB folder.
b. From the Data tab of the Toolbox, drag ADODataSetCommand onto the Component Designer.
c. Click New Connection in the Choose Your Data Connection menu.
d. In the Provider tab of the DataLinkProperties dialog box, choose Microsoft Jet 4.0 OLE. In the Connection tab of the DataLinkProperties, type the path to the server and the logon information. Test the connection.
e. Select the DOGS database from the database list. Click OK and return to the wizard.
f. Click Next to advance to the Choose a Query Type page and set up a query that is appropriate to the fields and data in your Main_Dogs table.
g. Click Finish to connect your data source to the Main_Dogs table in the DOGS database and to create the objects: adoDataSetCommand and adoConnection.
h. Choose File, Save from the menu and close the project.

3. Generate and fill the DataSet you created in Exercise 2.
a. Open the PetProj.vbproj file from your Tut12/ExercisesB folder.
b. Activate the Component1.vb[Design] and then select Generate DataSet from the DataClass menu.
c. In the Generate DataSetClass dialog box, enter an appropriate name for your DataSet. You may want to choose a name that clearly distinguishes this DataSet from others by referencing part or all of the database—for example, DogsDataSet. Click OK.
d. Select Generate DataSetCommand Methods from the DataClass menu. This will conveniently add the subroutines to your code that will fill and update the DataSet.
e. Save the ExB.vbproj project.

4. Bind the DataGrid to the DataSet you just created. To do so, you will need to add a DataView object to your Web Forms page and use it to link the DataGrid to the DataSet.
   a. Open the ExB.vbproj file.
   b. To add a DataSet to the form, drag DataSet from the Toolbox Data tab onto the form.
   c. Select the name of the DataSet from the drop-down list.
   d. To fill the DataSet with data, declare programmatically a component object at the top level in the WebForm1 class.
   e. Add and configure the DataView.
   f. Add and configure the DataGrid.
   g. Test your project, then save it.

5. Add a Details Panel to your Web Forms page. This will allow you to view additional information about the selected items from your Main_Dogs table without cluttering the DataGrid you just created with extraneous material.
   a. Open the ExB.vbproj file.
   b. Add another DataView item to the form.
   c. Add a Label control for the Dataview. The Label control should correspond to the data columns of your Main_Dogs table. Be sure to bind each label to the DataView you created in Step E of Exercise 4.
   d. Activate the details by adding the appropriate code to the DataGrid#_SelectedIndexChanged method.
   e. Set the DataView row filter so that it will select only the row you want.
   f. Bind each label that you are using by calling DataBind on that label in the DataGrid#_SelectedIndexChanged subroutine. Be sure to place the calls *after* the row filter change has been set.
   g. Save, build, and start the project. Verify that you can click your data and update the details with the new information.

discovery ▶

6. You can bind any property or properties of a Web Forms server control to a source of data. The procedure to data bind a control is slightly different for ASP.NET server controls and for HTML server controls than for Web Forms. In this exercise, you will bind data to an ASP.NET server control in your Web Forms page:
   a. Open the ExB.vbproj file.
   b. Verify that either the PETS or DOGS database is available as a data source on your page.
   c. Switch to Design View and select a Label control.
   d. In the Properties window, click the ellipsis button next to Databindings to open the Databindings dialog box.
   e. In the Bindable list, select the property to bind.
   f. To create your own data binding expression, choose Customer binding expression and then Enter.
   You can also bind data to an ASP.NET server control using a Properties builder.
   g. Verify that you are still in Design View. Select the ASP.NET server control and then open the Properties window.
   h. At the bottom of the window, choose Property Builder and choose the General tab.
   i. Select a data source from the DataSource list.
   j. Select a field name from the DataKeyField list. This will not be displayed in the control, but it is useful to maintain for each item in the control.
   k. Save, build and, run your program.
   l. Debug the program if necessary.

Creating a Web Page with Visual Basic

Important note: To complete this appendix, you must have access to Internet Explorer 4.0 or later.

Visual Basic allows you to create two types of Internet applications: IIS applications and DHTML applications. All processing for an IIS application happens on the Web server, whereas most of a DHTML application's processing happens on the browser computer. DHTML applications require the end user to have Microsoft Internet Explorer 4.0 or later, while IIS applications are browser and operating system independent. In this appendix, you will use DHTML to create a Web page.

Creating Your First Web Page

As you probably already know, the **Internet** is the world's largest computer network, providing connections for millions of computers all around the world. The most popular service provided by the Internet is the **World Wide Web**, which consists of documents called **Web pages** that contain information pertaining to a particular topic. A Web page can include text, graphics, animation, sound, and video, as well as one or more **hyperlinks** that allow the user to "jump" to related information either on the same or a different Web page. You view a Web page using a program called a **Web browser**; Internet Explorer and Netscape Navigator are two popular Web browsers. In this appendix, you will learn how to use Visual Basic to create a Web page.

Every Web page is stored as an HTML document. **HTML** stands for **Hypertext Markup Language**, which is the language used to create Web pages. The HTML document contains the information pertaining to a topic, as well as instructions that tell the Web browser how that information should appear on the screen. For example, the instructions may tell the browser to display certain text in boldface or italics. Even if you do not know anything about HTML, you still can create a simple Web page in Visual Basic. For example, in this Appendix you will create the Web page shown in Figure A-1, which contains text, an image control, and a hyperlink.

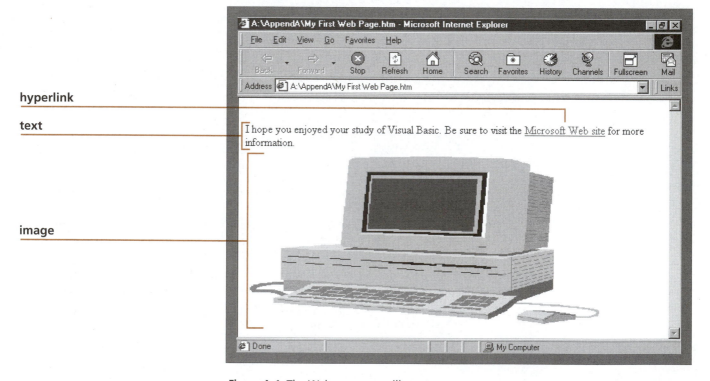

Figure A-1: The Web page you will create

Visual Basic is not designed to be an advanced HTML editor and it does not contain some of the features you will find in many HTML editors. However, Visual Basic allows you to create relatively simple Web pages without having to know how to write HTML.

To create the Web page shown in Figure A-1:

1   Start Visual Basic. When the New Project dialog box appears, scroll the New tab's list box, if necessary, and then click **DHTML Application**. (DHTML stands for Dynamic Hypertext Markup Language.) Click the **Open** button. Visual Basic opens a new DHTML project. See Figure A-2.

> **HELP?** If Visual Basic is already running, click File, then click New Project to open the New Project dialog box. Then click DHTML Application on the New tab.

main window

Project window

Toolbox window

Properties window

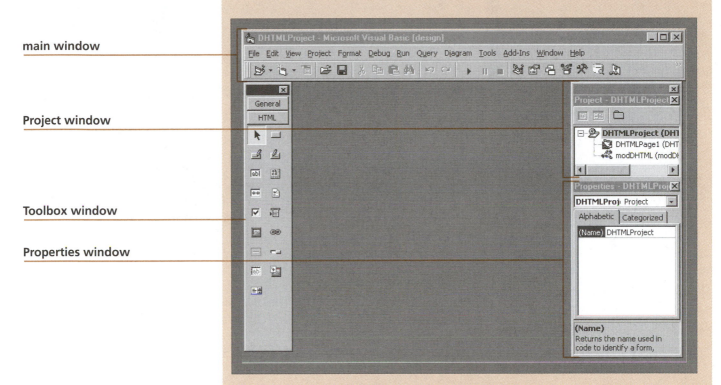

Figure A-2: DHTML project interface

As Figure A-2 indicates, the DHTML project interface includes Visual Basic's main window, Project window, and Properties window, as well as a Toolbox window that contains the set of DHTML tools you use when designing your Web pages.

Notice that three entries appear in the Project window: the name of the DHTML project (DHTMLProject), the name of the first Web page (DHTMLPage1), and the name of a module (modDHTML). You won't have use for the module file in this project, so you can remove it.

2   Right-click **modDHTML (modDHTML)** in the Project window, then click **Remove modDHTML**.

Now give the DHTML project a more meaningful name.

3   Change the project's Name property to **FirstWebProject**.

Next, display the DHTMLPage1 object.

4   Click **DHTMLPage1 (DHTMLPage1)** in the Project window, and then click the Project window's **View Object** button. Visual Basic displays the DHTML page designer window for page 1 of the DHTML project. See Figure A-3.

title bar

toolbars

treeview pane

detail pane

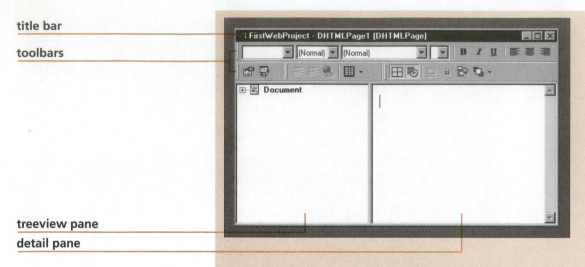

Figure A-3: DHTML page designer window for page 1

You use the DHTML page designer window to design your Web page. If you want to include more than one Web page in a project, you can use the Add DHTML Page option on the Project menu to add another page to the project. Visual Basic will provide a separate page designer window for each page included in the project.

As Figure A-3 indicates, the page designer window contains a title bar, toolbars, and two panes: the treeview pane and the detail pane. The **detail pane** presents a drawing surface on which you can create a new page or edit an existing page, and the **treeview pane** displays a list of all of the elements included in the detail pane. For now, you will use only the detail pane. You will learn more about the treeview pane later in this appendix.

First, you will make the detail pane larger so that you can use more of its drawing surface. Then you will add some text to the detail pane.

5 Maximize the page designer window, then drag the bar that separates the designer window's panes until the detail pane is the size shown in Figure A-4, and then release the mouse button. Click in the detail pane, if necessary, and type the two sentences shown in the figure, then press the **Enter** key. (Don't be concerned if the information in the treeview pane changes. You will view that information later in this appendix.)

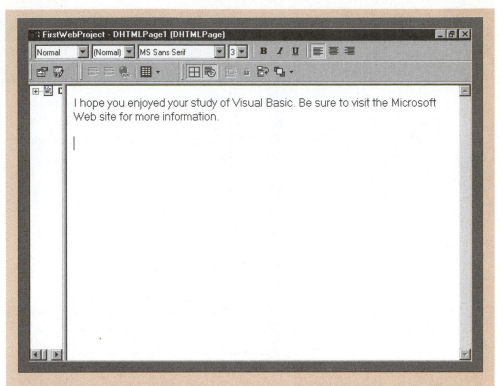

Figure A-4: Current status of page designer window

Notice that you can add text to a Web page simply by typing the text in the page designer window's detail pane. Now observe how easy it is to add an image to your Web page.

6 Restore the page designer window, then double-click the **Image tool** in the toolbox to place an image control in the detail pane. Maximize the page designer window, then drag and size the image control as shown in Figure A-5.

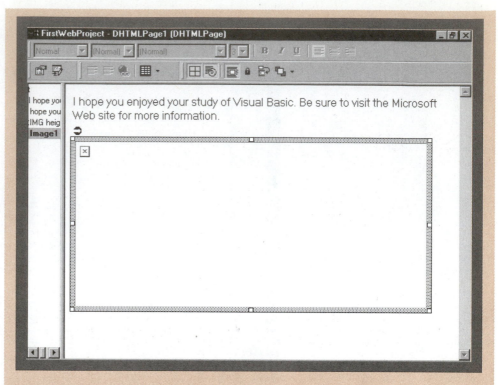

Figure A-5: Correct placement and size of image control in the detail pane

The Image tool in the DHTML project's toolbox is not the same as the Image tool found in a standard project's toolbox; rather, it is a special Image tool for use on Web pages.

You use the image control's Custom property to display the control's Property Pages dialog box, which contains options that allow you to set the control's various properties. You will use the Property Pages dialog box to select the file whose picture you want displayed in the image control.

7 Press **Alt** to display Visual Basic's main window, then click **View**, and then click **Properties Window**. Click **(Custom)** in the Properties window, then click the **...** button in the Settings box to open the image control's Property Pages dialog box. Click the **...** button that appears to the right of the Image source text box. The Open dialog box appears. Use the Open dialog box to locate the Computer.wmf file, which is typically located in the Program Files\Microsoft Visual Studio\Common\Graphics\Metafile\Business folder on either the local hard drive or the network drive. Click **Computer.wmf**, then click the **Open** button, and then click the **OK** button. A picture of a computer appears in the image control.

Next, you will make the phrase, Microsoft Web site, into a hyperlink that will connect the Web page to Microsoft's home page at http://www.microsoft.com.

8 Select the phrase Microsoft Web site, then click the **Make selection into link** button on the page designer window's toolbar. The phrase appears as yellow lettering on a black background. You will notice that the phrase is underlined, which indicates that it is a hyperlink.

Now you need to provide the hyperlink with the address of Microsoft's home page.

9 Press **Alt** to display Visual Basic's main window, then click **View**, and then click **Properties Window**. Use the Object box in the Properties window to select the **Hyperlink1 (DispIHTMLAnchorElement)** element. Click (**Custom**), and then click the ... button in the Settings box. The hyperlink's Property Pages dialog box appears. Click the **Link type** list arrow on the General tab. Scroll the list, then click **http:**. You will notice that this places http:// in the Link text box. Click **after the second slash in the Link text box**, then type **www.microsoft.com** as shown in Figure A-6.

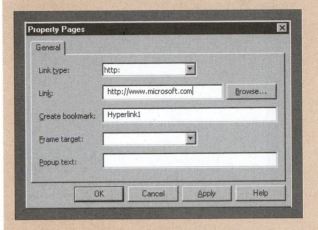

Figure A-6: Completed Property Pages dialog box for the hyperlink

10 Click the **OK** button to close the Property Pages dialog box. Click **after the period in the second sentence** to cancel the selection of the hyperlink phrase. Now save the Web page and project.

11 Press **Alt** to display Visual Basic's main window, then click **File**, and then click **Save DHTMLPage1 As**. When the Save File As dialog box appears, open the AppendA folder on your Student Disk, then type **ApCPage** in the File name text box. Notice that the file will be saved as a Designer File with a .Dsr extension. Click the **Save** button.

12 Press the **Alt** key again, then click **File**, and then click **Save Project As**. Save the project as **ApCProject** in the AppendA folder on your Student Disk. As with all project files, the file will be saved with a .vbp extension.

Now view the contents of the treeview pane, which shows a hierarchical listing of the elements included in the detail pane.

To view the contents of the treeview pane:

1 Drag the bar that separates both designer window panes to the right as shown in Figure A-7, then click Document in the treeview pane.

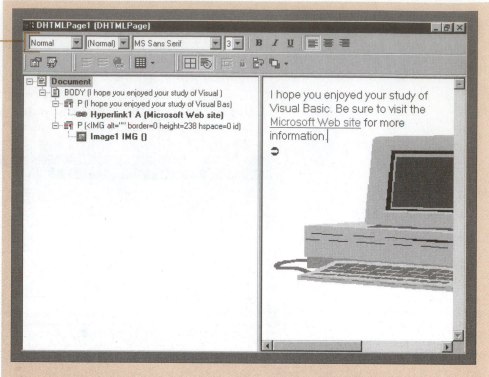

Figure A-7: Contents of treeview pane shown in the designer window

HELP? If a plus box appears in the treeview pane, click the plus box.

All of the elements included in the Web page belong to the Document object.

2   Click **Body (I hope you enjoyed your study of Visual)**. Visual Basic selects all of the elements that make up the body of the document—in this case, it selects two paragraphs, denoted by the letter P.

The paragraphs in a Web page, as well as the objects within the paragraphs, can be selected individually. Try this now.

3   Click **P (I hope you enjoyed your study of Visual Bas)**. Visual Basic selects the first paragraph, which contains two sentences and a hyperlink.

4   Click **Hyperlink1 A (Microsoft Web site)**. Visual Basic selects only the hyperlink defined in the first paragraph.

5   Click **P (<IMG alt='"' border=0 height=238 hspace=0 id)**. (Your height value may differ.) Visual Basic selects the second paragraph, which contains only the image control.

6   Click **Image1 IMG ()**. Visual Basic selects only the image control included in the second paragraph.

tip

You can delete a para-graph, as well as an object within the paragraph, by right-clicking the object in the treeview pane, and then selecting Delete on the popup menu. You also can delete an object by right-clicking it in the detail pane, and then selecting Cut on the popup menu.

After creating the Web page, you then instruct Visual Basic to create the appropriate HTML code for you.

To tell Visual Basic to create the HTML code for your Web page, then view the HTML code:

1   Click the **DHTML Page Designer Properties** button ⚿ on the page designer's toolbar. The DHTMLPage1 Properties dialog box appears. Click the **Save**

HTML in an external file option button, then click the **New** button. The Create HTML file dialog box appears. Notice that the file will be saved as an HTML file.

2   Open the AppendA folder on your Student Disk, then type **My First Web Page** in the File name text box, and then click the **Save** button. A:\AppendA\My First Web Page.htm appears in the text box above the New button. (Your text box may say B:\AppendA\My First Web Page.htm.) Click the **OK** button.

3   When the Save internal HTML dialog box appears, click the **Yes** button. The AppendA folder on your Student Disk should be open. Type **My First Web Page** in the File name text box and press the **Save** button.

4   Click the **Launch Editor** button 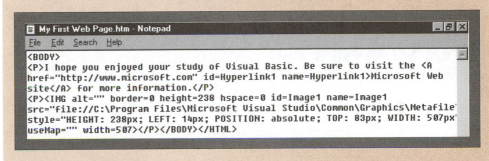 on the page designer's toolbar. Maximize the editor window. Figure A-8 shows the HTML code generated by Visual Basic.

```
My First Web Page.htm - Notepad
File  Edit  Search  Help
<BODY>
<P>I hope you enjoyed your study of Visual Basic. Be sure to visit the <A
href="http://www.microsoft.com" id=Hyperlink1 name=Hyperlink1>Microsoft Web
site</A> for more information.</P>
<P><IMG alt="" border=0 height=238 hspace=0 id=Image1 name=Image1
src="File://C:\Program Files\Microsoft Visual Studio\Common\Graphics\Metafile"
style="HEIGHT: 238px; LEFT: 14px; POSITION: absolute; TOP: 83px; WIDTH: 507px"
useMap="" width=507></P></BODY></HTML>
```

Figure A-8: HTML code generated by Visual Basic

If you are familiar with HTML, you will recognize the code shown in Figure A-8.

5   Close the editor window.

All that remains is to view your Web page using a browser. You can either run the project while you are in Visual Basic, or you can start Internet Explorer and use the Open option on its File menu to open the .htm file. You will use the latter method.

To view your Web page:

1   Exit Visual Basic. When you are asked if you want to save the file, click the **Yes** button.

2   Start Internet Explorer. Click **File**, then click **Open**. Open the **My First Web Page.htm** file, which is located in the AppendA folder on your Student Disk. Your Web page appears in the Internet Explorer browser as shown earlier in Figure A-1. (You may need to maximize the browser window.)

3   Click **Microsoft Web site**. In a little while, you should be brought to Microsoft's home page. Close Internet Explorer.

You now have completed Appendix A.

Visual Basic's Drag-and-Drop Feature

The Flags Application

As you already know, when you are creating a user interface during design time, you can drag controls on the form and drop them in the desired location. Visual Basic's **drag-and-drop feature** extends this ability to the user during run time by allowing the user to drag objects on the form and then drop them in either the same or a different form. The term **drag** refers to the process of holding down the left mouse button as you move the mouse; the term **drop** refers to releasing the mouse button in order to end a drag operation. You will use the drag-and-drop feature in the Flags application, which you will complete in this appendix.

To complete the Flags application:

1   Open the **Flags** (Flags.vbp) project, which is located in the AppendB folder on your Student Disk. Save the form and the project as **ApBFlags**. The user interface is shown in Figure B-1.

imgFlag control array

imgCountry control array

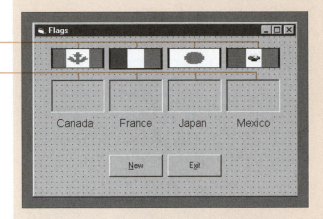

Figure B-1: User interface for the Flags application

When the user drags a flag from the imgFlag array to the corresponding country in the imgCountry array, the flag should disappear from the imgFlag array and appear in the imgCountry array. For example, if you drag Japan's flag to the imgCountry control located above the Japan label, the flag should disappear from the imgFlag(2) control and appear in the imgCountry(2) control. To use Visual Basic's drag-and-drop feature, you need to learn two properties (DragMode and DragIcon) and one event (DragDrop).

The DragMode Property

The ability to drag a control during run time is determined by the value in the control's **DragMode property**. When the DragMode property is set to 1-Automatic, you can drag the control by positioning the mouse pointer on the control and then pressing the left mouse button down as you move the mouse.

To enable dragging of the imgFlag controls:

1   Click the **imgFlag(0)** control to select it, then press the **Ctrl** key as you click the **imgFlag(1)**, **imgFlag(2)**, and **imgFlag(3)** controls. The four controls should be selected.

2   Change the DragMode property for the four controls to **1-Automatic**.

3   **Save** and **run** the application. Practice dragging and dropping the flag icons anywhere on the form. Notice that the mouse pointer drags a rectangle when you drag the object. When you drop the icon, it will still be in its original location because you have not coded the application to do otherwise.

4   Click the **Exit** button. Visual Basic returns to the design screen.

The mouse pointer would look more meaningful to the user if, during the drag-and-drop operation, the pointer were the same shape as the icon you are dragging. You can control the icon that Visual Basic displays when an object is dragged by setting the control's DragIcon property.

The DragIcon Property

The **DragIcon property** determines the icon to be displayed when you are dragging a control. In this application, you will set each imgFlag control's DragIcon property to the same setting as its Picture property. You can do so in either the Properties window or a Code window. In this application, you will code the form's Load event to set each imgFlag control's DragIcon property.

To set the DragIcon property of the imgFlag controls:

1   Open the form's Load event, then enter the code shown in Figure B-2.

```
Project1 - frmFlags (Code)
Form                                          Load

Private Sub Form_Load()
    Dim intX As Integer
    frmFlags.Top = (Screen.Height - frmFlags.Height) / 2
    frmFlags.Left = (Screen.Width - frmFlags.Width) / 2
    For intX = 0 To 3
        imgFlag(intX).DragIcon = imgFlag(intX).Picture
    Next intX

End Sub
```

Figure B-2: Form's Load event procedure

2   Close the Code window. **Save** and **run** the application. Practice dragging and dropping the flags on the form. Notice that the mouse pointer turns into the appropriate icon during the drag operation.

3   Click the **Exit** button. Visual Basic returns to the design screen.

Now that the icons can be dragged, the next step is to tell the imgCountry array how to respond when the user drops an icon into one of the controls in the array. You will do so by coding the imgCountry array's DragDrop event.

The DragDrop Event

When you drag a control over an object and release the mouse button, the object's **DragDrop event** occurs. The control being dragged is referred to as the **source**, and the object on which it is dropped is referred to as the **target**.

To code the imgCountry array's DragDrop event:

1 Double-click one of the controls in the imgCountry array. Use the Procedure box to open the control array's DragDrop event, then maximize the Code window.

The DragDrop event displays four arguments within the set of parentheses: Index As Integer, Source As Control, X As Single, and Y As Single. The Index argument, you may remember from Tutorial 5, keeps track of which control is receiving the event. The Source argument refers to the control being dragged. You can use this argument to refer to the properties and methods of that control—for example, Source.Visible would refer to the Visible property of the control that is being dragged. The X and Y arguments in the DragDrop event procedure refer to the horizontal and vertical position of the mouse pointer within the target object.

In this case, if the index of the imgFlag control being dragged matches the index of the imgCountry control on which it is being dropped, then you want to remove the flag from the imgFlag control and place it in the imgCountry control.

2 Press the **Tab** key, then type **if index = source.index then** and press the **Enter** key.

3 Press the **Tab** key, then type **imgcountry(index).picture = source.picture** and press the **Enter** key. This will assign the icon in the imgFlag control to the image control in the imgCountry array.

4 Type **source.picture = loadpicture( )** and press the **Enter** key. This instruction will remove the flag from the imgFlag control.

5 Press the **Backspace** key, then type **end if** and press the **Enter** key.

6 Close the Code window, then **save** and **run** the application. Practice dragging and dropping the flags into the imgCountry controls. Be sure to try to drop a flag in an incorrect country. When you drop a flag into its matching country, the flag disappears from the imgFlag control and appears in the imgCountry control.

7 Click the **Exit** button. Visual Basic returns to the design screen.

Next you will code the New button.

Coding the New Button

When the user clicks the New button, its Click event should remove the flags from the imgCountry control array and place them back into the imgFlag control array.

To code the New button:

1 Double-click the **New** button to open its Click event procedure.

2 Press the **Tab** key, then type **dim intX as integer** and press the **Enter** key.

3 Type **for intx = 0 to 3** and press the **Enter** key.

4 Press the **Tab** key, then type **if imgflag(intx).picture = 0 then** and press the **Enter** key.

5 Press the **Tab** key, then type **imgflag(intx).picture = imgcountry(intx).picture** and press the **Enter** key.

6 Type **imgcountry(intx).picture = loadpicture( )** and press the **Enter** key. This instruction will remove the flag from the imgCountry control.

7 Press the **Backspace** key, then type **end if** and press the **Enter** key.

8 Press the **Backspace** key, then type **next intx** and press the **Enter** key.

9 Close the Code window. **Save** and **run** the application. Practice dragging and dropping the flag icons, then click the **New** button. The New button's Click event removes the flags from the imgCountry controls and places them in the imgFlag controls.

10 Click the **Exit** button. Visual Basic returns to the design screen.

Currently, the flag icons are located immediately above their corresponding countries. To make the application more challenging, you will arrange the imgCountry controls, along with their corresponding label controls, so that they are not immediately below their respective flags.

11 Unlock the controls, then drag the imgCountry controls and their corresponding label controls so that the controls are not immediately below their respective flags. Lock the controls.

12 **Save** and **run** the application. Practice dragging and dropping the flag icons.

13 Click the **Exit** button. Visual Basic returns to the design screen.

You have now completed the Flags application and Appendix B.

EXERCISE

1. Use the drag-and-drop feature to create a tic-tac-toe game. Print the form and the code.

Using the Clipboard, DDE, and OLE

Important Note: You must have access to Microsoft Excel 97 or higher to complete Appendix C using the computer.

One advantage of using Windows applications is that they can share data with each other; because of this, a Windows application can include data created by other Windows applications. For example, you can create a Visual Basic application that contains records from a Microsoft Access database, data from a Microsoft Excel worksheet, and a paragraph from a Microsoft Word document. In addition to using the ADO data control, which you learned about in Tutorial 9, three other methods are available for sharing data among applications: the clipboard, DDE, and OLE. You will learn to use these three methods in this Appendix.

In this appendix you will learn how to:

- Define the terms DDE, OLE, embed, link, source application, server application, destination application, and client application
- Use the clipboard to copy data from one Windows application to another
- Use DDE to copy data from one Windows application to another
- Add an OLE container control to a form
- Embed data in an application using OLE
- Use the Open statement and the SaveToFile and ReadFromFile methods to save and retrieve embedded data
- Link data in an application using OLE
- Update the contents of an OLE control using the Update method

Using the Clipboard, DDE, and OLE

Using the Clipboard to Share Data Among Windows Applications

The simplest method of exchanging data between applications is to use the clipboard. The data in one application is either cut or copied to the clipboard, then pasted into another application. Although the clipboard provides an easy way to copy data, it does have one drawback: the copied data has no link to the application that created it. In order to update the copied data, you would need to open the application that created the data, edit the data, copy the data to the clipboard, then paste it into the other application again. Observe this now by using the clipboard to copy information from a Microsoft Excel worksheet to a Visual Basic application.

To use the clipboard to copy data from Microsoft Excel to Visual Basic:

1   Start Visual Basic, if necessary. Open the **Clipbd** (Clipbd.vbp) project, which is located in the AppendC folder on your Student Disk.

2   Save the form and the project as **ApCClipbd** in the AppendC folder on your Student Disk.

The form contains an Exit command button, a label control, and an image control. See Figure C-1.

imgSales

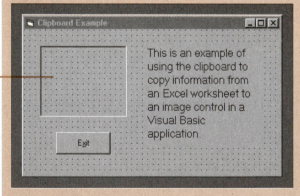

Figure C-1: The Clipboard example's interface

You will now copy data from an Excel worksheet to the clipboard, then paste the data in the image control on the Visual Basic form. First copy the data to the clipboard.

3   Start Microsoft Excel, and then maximize the Excel window, if necessary.

4   Click **File** on the menu bar, then click **Open**. Open the **Sales** (Sales.xls) file, which is located in the AppendC folder on your Student Disk.

5   Select cells **A1 through B6**, as shown in Figure C-2.

> **HELP?** To select cells A1 through B6, first click cell A1 to select it. Then, hold down the left mouse button and drag the mouse pointer to cell B6. When cells A1 through B6 are selected, release the mouse button.

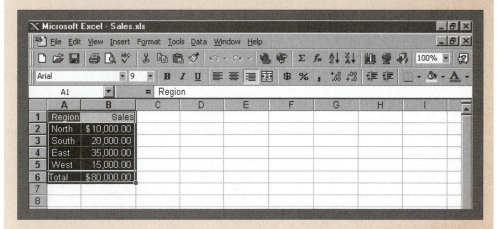

Figure C-2: Cells A1 through B6 selected in the Sales worksheet

6   Click **Edit** on the Excel menu bar, and then click **Copy**. Windows copies the information in the selected area to the clipboard. A moving border appears around the selected area in the worksheet. Now paste the copied information into the image control in the Visual Basic application.

7   Make Microsoft Visual Basic the active application.

> **HELP?** You can make an application the active application by clicking its application button on the taskbar.

8   Click the **imgSales** control to select it. Click **Edit** on the menu bar, then click **Paste**. (Be sure you do not click Paste Link.) Windows pastes the contents of the clipboard into the imgSales control as shown in Figure C-3.

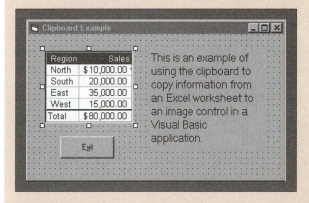

Figure C-3: Worksheet data pasted into the imgSales control

Observe what happens when you make a change to the data in the Excel worksheet.

GUI
Design Tips

Using the Clipboard to Copy Data to a Visual Basic Application

- Start the application that contains the data. Also start Visual Basic.

- Activate the application that contains the data.

- Select the data you want to copy to the Visual Basic application.

- Either copy or cut the selected data to the clipboard.

- Make the Visual Basic application the active application.

- Use the Paste command on Visual Basic's Edit menu to paste the data from the clipboard into the Visual Basic application.

9 Make Microsoft Excel the active application. Press the **Esc** key to remove the moving border around the selected cells, then click cell **B2**, which contains the sales for the North region. Type **20000** and press the **Enter** key. $20,000.00 appears in cell B2, and the total sales amount in cell B6 changes to $90,000.00.

10 Make Microsoft Visual Basic the active application. Notice that the image control shows that the sales for the North region are still $10,000.00.

Recall that using the clipboard to exchange information has one drawback: the only way to update the copied data is to open the application that created the data, edit the data, copy the data to the clipboard, then paste it into the other application again. Do that now.

11 Make Microsoft Excel the active application. Select cells **A1 through B6**. Click **Edit** on the menu bar, and then click **Copy**. Windows copies the information in the selected cells to the clipboard. A moving border appears around the selected area in the worksheet.

12 Make Microsoft Visual Basic the active application. Click the **imgSales** control to select it. Click **Edit** on the menu bar, and then click **Paste**. The North region's sales are now $20,000.00, and the total sales are $90,000.00. Save the ApCClipbd project.

Now that you have observed how to use the clipboard to copy data from one Windows application to another, you can open a new project in Visual Basic and also close the Sales.xls file in Excel.

13 Visual Basic is currently the active application. Click **File** on the menu bar and then click **New Project**. Open a Standard EXE project.

14 Make Microsoft Excel the active application. Click **File** on the menu bar, and then click **Close**. When you are asked if you want to save the changes to the Sales.xls file, click the **No** button.

15 Make Visual Basic the active application.

DDE is the second method of sharing data between Windows applications.

Using DDE to Share Data with Other Applications

DDE, which stands for **Dynamic Data Exchange**, is another method of copying data from one Windows application to another. When using DDE, both the application that supplies the data, called the **source application**, and the application that receives the data, called the **destination application**, must be running at the same time in order for the exchange of data to occur. To update the data in the destination application, you first open the source application, then edit and save the data in the source application. The changes you make in the source application will appear automatically in the destination application. Try this by using DDE to copy data from an Excel worksheet to a Visual Basic application.

tip

. . . .

Not all applications support DDE.

To use DDE to copy data from Microsoft Excel to Visual Basic:

1 Visual Basic should be the active application. Open the **Dde** (Dde.vbp) project, which is located in the AppendC folder on your Student Disk.

2 Save the form and the project as **ApCDde** in the AppendC folder on your Student Disk.

In Visual Basic, only the text box, picture box, and label controls support DDE; those are the only controls that you can copy data into using DDE. In the frmDDE form, you will copy information from an Excel worksheet to a picture box control. A **picture box control** is similar to an image control; both can be used to display a graphic.

3 Click the **form**, and then double-click the **PictureBox** tool in the toolbox. A picture box control appears in the interface. Change the picture box control's properties as follows:

AutoSize: **True**

Left: **360**

Top: **360**

You will now copy the information from an Excel worksheet to the clipboard, then use DDE to paste the information into the picture box. First copy the information to the clipboard.

4 Make Microsoft Excel the active application. Open the **Bonus** (Bonus.xls) file, which is located in the AppendC folder on your Student Disk.

5 Select cells **A1 through B6,** as shown in Figure C-4.

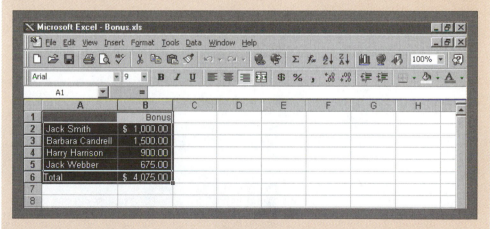

Figure C-4: Cells A1 through B6 selected in Bonus worksheet

6 Click **Edit** on the menu bar, and then click **Copy**. Windows copies the selected information to the clipboard.

Now use DDE to paste the information into the picture box in the Visual Basic application.

7 Make Visual Basic the active application. Click the **picture box control** to select it. Sizing handles appear around the control, and the form's title bar is highlighted. Click **Edit** on the menu bar to open the Edit menu. See Figure C-5.

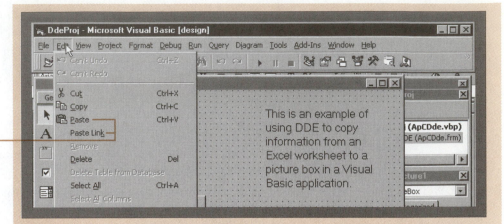

Paste and Paste Link commands

Figure C-5: Open Visual Basic Edit menu

HELP? If the Cut, Copy, and Paste commands on the Edit menu are dimmed, click Edit to close the Edit menu. Click the picture box control on the form, then click Edit to open the Edit menu again.

Notice that the Edit menu has a Paste command and a Paste Link command. As you observed when you copied the Sales worksheet information to the image control in the previous section, the Paste command merely copies the contents of the clipboard to the selected control; it does not maintain any connection between the original data and the copied data. The Paste Link command, however, not only copies the contents of the clipboard to the selected control, it also maintains a link between the original data and the copied data so that a change made to the original data affects the copied data.

8 Click **Paste Link** on the Edit menu. Windows copies the data from the clipboard into the picture box control. The Paste Link command tells Windows to maintain a link between the original data and the copied data. See Figure C-6.

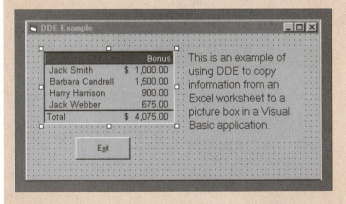

Figure C-6: Bonus worksheet pasted in picture box control

Observe what happens when you use Excel to make a change to the Bonus worksheet.

9 Make Excel the active application. Press the **Esc** key to remove the moving border around the selected cells. Click cell **B2**, which contains Jack Smith's $1,000.00 bonus. Type **800** and press the **Enter** key. Jack Smith's bonus changes to $800.00, and the total bonus amount changes to $3,875.00.

10 Click **File** on Excel's menu bar, and then click **Save**.

11 Make Visual Basic the active application. See Figure C-7.

new data

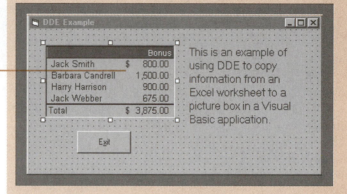

Figure C-7: frmDDE form showing new data in the Bonus worksheet

Notice that the picture box control now shows Jack Smith's bonus is $800.00, and the total bonus amount is $3,875.00.

Now save and run the ApCDde project to confirm that Windows maintains the connection between the original data and the copied data when the project is running.

12 **Save** and **run** the ApCDde project.

Now change Jack Smith's bonus back to $1,000.00.

13 Make Excel the active application. Click cell **B2**, which contains Jack Smith's $800.00 bonus. Type **1000** and press the **Enter** key. Jack Smith's bonus changes to $1,000.00, and the total bonus amount changes to $4,075.00.

14 Click **File** on Excel's menu bar, and then click **Save**.

15 Make DDE Example the active application. $1,000.00 displays as Jack Smith's bonus, and $4,075.00 displays as the total bonus amount. See Figure C-8.

picture box reflects changes in data

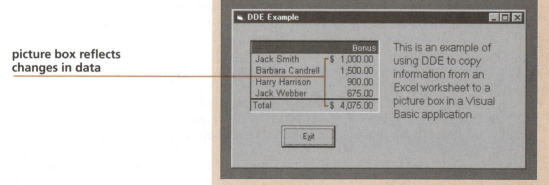

Figure C-8: frmDDE form showing changes made in the Bonus worksheet

GUI
Design Tips

Using DDE to Copy Data to a Visual Basic Application

- Start the source application, then open the document that contains the data. Also start Visual Basic, and open the application to which you want to copy the data.

- Make the source application the active application.

- Select the data you want to copy to the Visual Basic application.

- Either copy or cut the selected data to the clipboard.

- Make the Visual Basic application the active application.

- Select either a picture box, text box, or label control.

- Use the Paste Link command on Visual Basic's Edit menu to paste the data from the clipboard into the selected control.

▶ Not all applications support OLE, and some OLE applications do not support all of the features of OLE.

▶ An application that contains an embedded object will require more disk space when saved than an application that contains a linked object. That's because an application that contains an embedded object must store the entire object, whereas an application that contains a linked object needs to store only a pointer to the object.

16 Click the **Exit** button in the DDE Example form. Visual Basic returns to the design screen. Click the **Save Project** button. Click **File** on the menu bar, then click **New Project**. Open a Standard EXE project.

17 Make Microsoft Excel the active application. Click **File** on the menu bar, and then click **Exit** to close the Excel application.

18 Make Visual Basic the active application, if necessary.

When using DDE, remember to open the source document (in this case, the Bonus worksheet) before opening the destination document (in this case, the ApCDde project). If you open the destination document before opening the source document, Visual Basic will display the "No foreign application responded to a DDE initiate" message.

The third method of exchanging data between Windows applications is OLE.

Using OLE to Exchange Data

OLE, which stands for **Object Linking and Embedding** and is pronounced oh-lay, is yet another mechanism for sharing data between Windows applications. The data that is copied from one application to another is referred to as an object. An object can be, for example, a Microsoft Excel worksheet or a Microsoft Word document. The application that created the data (object) is called the **source application** or **server application**, and the application to which the object is copied is called the **container application** or **client application**.

Like the clipboard and DDE, OLE allows you to create an application that displays data from many different applications. Unlike the clipboard and DDE, however, OLE allows you to start a Windows application from inside another Windows application. For example, OLE enables you to start Excel from a Visual Basic application that contains an Excel worksheet. The user can then edit the data from within the application in which it was created or, in many cases, from within the Visual Basic application.

When using OLE to copy an object from a server application to a client application, you can choose to either embed the object or link the object. The difference between embedding and linking is where the object is stored. When you embed an object, the object is stored in the client application, where it exists as a separate entity; changes made to the object in the server application do not affect the object embedded in the client application, and vice versa. For example, if you embed the data from an Excel worksheet into a Visual Basic application, a copy of the worksheet data is stored in the Visual Basic application. Any changes you make to the data in the Visual Basic application affect only the copy of the data; the changes do not affect the original data. Also, any changes you make to the original data in Excel do not affect the copy of the data in the Visual Basic application.

When you link an object to a client application, on the other hand, only a pointer to the original object is stored in the client application. Changes made to the object in the server application affect the object in the client application, and vice versa.

You would embed an object, rather than link it, if you didn't want changes to the original object to affect the object in the client application, and vice versa. You would link an object, rather than embed it, if you did want changes made to the original object to be reflected in the client application, and vice versa. Assume, for example, that at work you are required to use a specific form letter that was created in Microsoft Word. You would like to include the Word document in a Visual Basic application; however, the document is used by a number of people in your office, and those co-workers sometimes make changes to it. If you do not want the changes that others make to the Word document to be reflected in your Visual Basic application, then you would need to embed the Word document in the application. If, on the other hand, you do want the changes to be reflected in your Visual Basic application, then you would need to link the document to the application. This concept is illustrated in Figure C-9.

Embedding:

copy of Word
document is
stored in Visual
Basic destination
application

Linking:

pointer to Word
document is stored in
Visual Basic destination
application

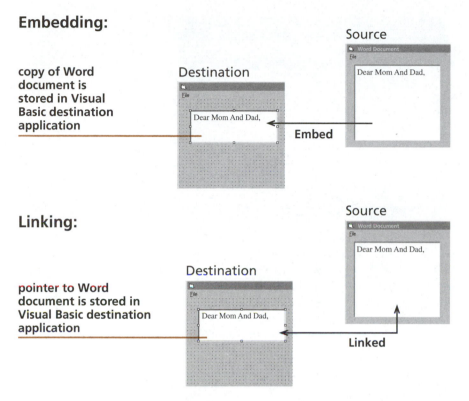

Figure C-9: Illustration of embedding and linking

You link and embed objects in Visual Basic by including the **OLE container control** in a Visual Basic application. First you will learn how to use Visual Basic's OLE control to embed an Excel worksheet in a Visual Basic application, then you will learn how to link an Excel worksheet to a Visual Basic application.

Embedding an Excel Worksheet in a Visual Basic Application

You use Visual Basic's OLE container control to embed an object in a Visual Basic application. In this case, the object will be a Microsoft Excel worksheet. Recall that when you embed an object in a client application, the object is stored in the client application.

To embed an Excel worksheet in a Visual Basic application:

1 Visual Basic should be the active application. Open the **Embed** (Embed.vbp) project, which is located in the AppendC folder on your Student Disk.

2 Save the form and the project as **ApCEmbed** in the AppendC folder on your Student Disk.

The File menu in the frmEmbed form contains three commands: Save Worksheet, Print, and Exit. The Print and Exit commands have already been coded for you. You will code the Save Worksheet command later in this lesson.

3 Click the **form**, then double-click the **OLE tool** 🖾 in the toolbox. An OLE container control appears momentarily, then the Insert Object dialog box appears as shown in Figure C-10.

your Object Type list may be different

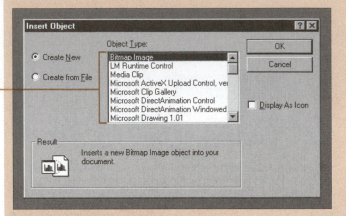

Figure C-10: Insert Object dialog box

The Insert Object dialog box allows you to embed a new or existing file; it also allows you to link an existing file. The Object Type list box lists the type of objects that your system can either link or embed. (Your list may be different from the one shown in Figure C-10.) The Excel worksheet that you will embed in the current application is an existing file, so you will need to select the Create from File option button.

4 Click the **Create from File** option button to select it.

The file that you will embed is named Region (Region.xls) and is located in the AppendC folder on your Student Disk.

5 Click the **Browse** button. The Browse dialog box appears. Open the AppendC folder on your Student Disk. Click **Region** (Region.xls) in the Browse dialog box, then click the **Insert** button. The Browse dialog box closes, and the Insert Object dialog box appears.

Because you want to embed the Excel file in the Visual Basic application, be sure that the Link check box in the Insert Object dialog box is not selected. The completed Insert Object dialog box is shown in Figure C-11.

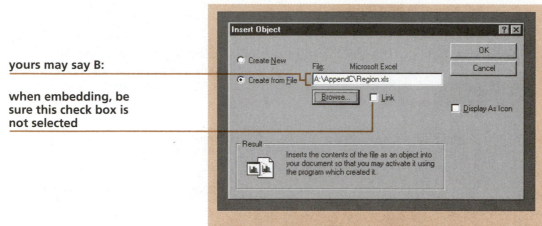

Figure C-11: Completed Insert Object dialog box

yours may say B:

when embedding, be sure this check box is not selected

6 Click the **OK** button. In a few moments the Region.xls worksheet appears inside the OLE container control. Set the OLE container control's Left property to **360** and its Top property to **360**. Also set its Name property to **oleSales** and its **SizeMode property**, which contains a value that specifies how Visual Basic resizes the OLE control and its object, to **2-AutoSize**. When set to 2-AutoSize, Visual Basic resizes the OLE control to display the entire object contained within the control. Click the **OLE** control in the form. See Figure C-12.

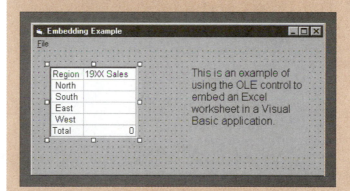

Figure C-12: Region.xls worksheet embedded in OLE container control

> ## GUI
> ### *Design Tips*
>
> **Using the OLE Control to Embed Data in a Visual Basic Application**
>
> - Start Visual Basic, which is the client (container) application. You do not need to start the server (source) application.
>
> - Add an OLE container control to the Visual Basic form.
>
> - Select either the Create New option button or the Create from File option button in the Insert Object dialog box.
>
> - If you are embedding an existing file, select the filename in the Browse dialog box. Be sure the Link check box in the Insert Object dialog box is not selected.

The OLE control allows you to edit the Excel worksheet from within the Visual Basic application.

Editing Embedded Data

Visual Basic's OLE control allows you to use the source application's menus and/or tools to edit the embedded data in the client application. In the ApCEmbed application, for example, the OLE control enables you to use Excel's menus to edit the worksheet data while you are in the Visual Basic application. Observe how this works.

To use the Visual Basic application to edit the worksheet data:

1   **Save** and **run** the ApCEmbed application.

You can edit the worksheet data simply by double-clicking the OLE control in the form.

2   Double-click the **OLE control**, which contains the embedded Excel worksheet. In a few moments the interface appears as shown in Figure C-13.

Excel menus

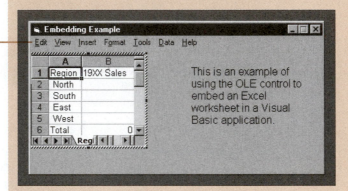

Figure C-13: Excel menus shown in the ApCEmbed Visual Basic application

The OLE control replaces the ApCEmbed application's File menu with Excel's menus.

Now enter the 1999 sales for the four regions.

3   Click cell **B1** in the worksheet, type **1999 Sales**, and then press the **Enter** key.

4   Type **500** in cell B2 and press the **Enter** key.

5   Type **300** in cell B3 and press the **Enter** key.

6   Type **400** in cell B4 and press the **Enter** key.

7   Type **200** in cell B5 and press the **Enter** key.

Notice that the total sales, 1400, appears in cell B6. Now use Excel's Format menu to change the appearance of the worksheet.

8   Select cells **A1 through B6**. Click **Format** on the form's menu bar, and then click **AutoFormat**. When the AutoFormat dialog box appears, click **Accounting 3**, and then click the **OK** button. The worksheet is formatted with the Accounting 3 format.

9   Press the **Esc** key to remove Excel's menus from the form's menu bar. The ApCEmbed application's File menu reappears in the menu bar, as shown in Figure C-14.

tip

In Discovery Exercise 4 you will learn how to display both the application's menu and Excel's menus at the same time.

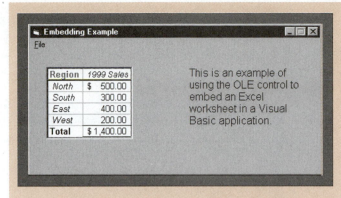

Figure C-14: Current status of OLE control and menu bar

10 If your computer is connected to a printer, click **File** on the form's menu bar, and then click **Print**.

11 Click **File** on the form's menu bar, and then click **Exit**. Visual Basic returns to the design screen.

The changes you made to the worksheet are not saved in the OLE control. You can verify this by running the application again.

12 **Run** the ApCEmbed application. Notice that the OLE container control does not reflect the changes you made to the embedded worksheet. Click **File** on the form's menu bar, and then click **Exit**.

In the next section, you will learn how to both save and retrieve the changes made to an embedded object.

Saving and Retrieving the Changes Made to an Embedded Object

Most times you will want to save the changes made to an object embedded in a Visual Basic application so that the changes will appear the next time you run the application. To do so, you need simply to save the object in a separate file that has been opened for binary access, and then read the file each time the application is run.

As you learned in Tutorials 6 and 8, before you can save information to or read information from a file, you first must use the Open statement to open the file. The syntax of the Open statement that opens a binary access file is **Open** *pathname* **For Binary As** *filenumber*, where *pathname* is the name of the file you want to open and *filenumber* is an integer between 1 and 511, inclusive.

After opening the binary access file, you can use the OLE container control's **SaveToFile method** to save the object to the file. The syntax of the SaveToFile method is *object*.**SaveToFile** *filenumber*, where *object* is the name of the OLE control and *filenumber* is the number used in the Open statement to open the binary access file.

In the current application, you will code the File menu's Save Worksheet command so that it saves the changes made to the embedded Region worksheet. You will do so by using the Open statement to open a binary access file named ApCRegion.ole. You will then use the SaveToFile method to save the contents of the OLE container control in the ApCRegion.ole file.

To code the File menu's Save Worksheet command and then test the command:

1   Open the Click event procedure for the File menu's Save Worksheet command, then enter the code shown in Figure C-15. (If necessary, change the a: in the Open statement to the letter of the drive that contains your Student Disk.)

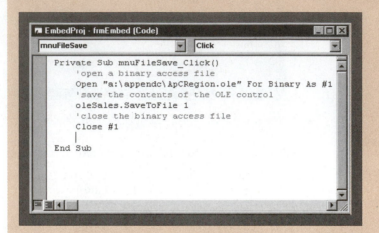

```
EmbedProj - frmEmbed (Code)

mnuFileSave                    Click

Private Sub mnuFileSave_Click()
    'open a binary access file
    Open "a:\appendc\ApCRegion.ole" For Binary As #1
    'save the contents of the OLE control
    oleSales.SaveToFile 1
    'close the binary access file
    Close #1
    |
End Sub
```

Figure C-15: Code entered in the Click event procedure for the File menu's Save Worksheet command

2   Close the Code window, then **save** and **run** the application.

Enter the 1999 sales for the four regions, and then format the worksheet.

3   Double-click the **OLE control.** Click cell **B1**, type **1999 Sales** and press the **Enter** key. Type **500** in cell B2 and press the **Enter** key. Type **300** in cell B3 and press the **Enter** key. Type **400** in cell B4 and press the **Enter** key. Type **200** in cell B5 and press the **Enter** key. Select cells **A1 through B6**. Click **Format** on the form's menu bar, and then click **AutoFormat**. When the AutoFormat dialog box appears, click **Accounting 3**, and then click the **OK** button.

4   Press the **Esc** key to remove Excel's menus from the form's menu bar.

Now save the embedded worksheet to the ApCRegion.ole file.

5   Click **File** on the form's menu bar, then click **Save Worksheet**. Visual Basic saves the contents of the OLE container control in the ApCRegion.ole file on your Student Disk. Click **File** on the form's menu bar, and then click **Exit**.

After saving an object in a binary access file, you can use the OLE container control's **ReadFromFile method** to read the file each time the application is run. The syntax of the ReadFromFile method is *object*.**ReadFromFile** *filenumber*, where *object* is the name of the OLE control and *filenumber* is the number used in the Open statement to open the binary access file.

In the current application, you will code the form's Load event procedure so that it first opens and then reads the information stored in the ApCRegion.ole file.

To code the form's Load event procedure:

1   Open the form's Load event procedure, then enter the code shown in Figure C-16. (If necessary, change the a: in the Open statement to the letter of the drive that contains your Student Disk.)

enter these six lines ────────────────

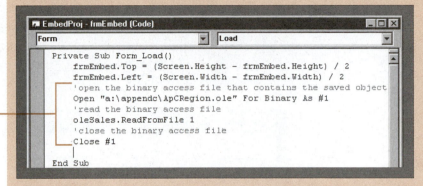

```
EmbedProj - frmEmbed (Code)                                    _ □ X
Form                            ▼    Load                           ▼
  Private Sub Form_Load()
      frmEmbed.Top = (Screen.Height - frmEmbed.Height) / 2
      frmEmbed.Left = (Screen.Width - frmEmbed.Width) / 2
      'open the binary access file that contains the saved object
      Open "a:\appendc\ApCRegion.ole" For Binary As #1
      'read the binary access file
      oleSales.ReadFromFile 1
      'close the binary access file
      Close #1

  End Sub
```

Figure C-16: Code entered in the form's Load event procedure

2   Close the Code window, then **save** and **run** the application. Notice that the OLE container control now shows the changes made to the embedded Excel worksheet.

3   Click **File** on the form's menu bar, then click **Exit**.

Recall that the SaveToFile method merely saves the contents of the OLE container control in a binary access file; it does not change the contents of the Region.xls Excel file. If you want the Region.xls file to reflect changes made to the worksheet displayed in the ApCRegion application, you should link the Region.xls file to the ApCRegion application, rather than embed it. In the next section, you will learn how to link an Excel worksheet to a Visual Basic application.

Linking an Excel Worksheet to a Visual Basic Application

You also use Visual Basic's OLE container control to link an object to a Visual Basic application. In this case, you will link a Microsoft Excel worksheet.

To link an Excel worksheet to a Visual Basic application:

1   Open the **Link** (Link.vbp) project, which is located in the AppendC folder on your Student Disk.

2   Save the form and the project as **ApCLink** in the AppendC folder on your Student Disk. The File menu contains two commands, Print and Exit, which have already been coded for you.

3   Click the **form**, then double-click the OLE tool 🖼 in the toolbox. The OLE control appears momentarily, and then the Insert Object dialog box appears.

You will link an existing Excel worksheet file named Items.

4 Click the **Create from File** option button to select it. Click the **Browse** button. The Browse dialog box appears. Open the AppendC folder on your Student Disk. Click **Items** (Items.xls) in the Browse dialog box, and then click the **Insert** button. The Browse dialog box closes and the Insert Object dialog box appears.

If you want to link an object, rather than embed it, you must select the Link check box.

5 Click the **Link** check box. A check mark appears in the Link check box, as shown in Figure C-17.

yours may say B:

when linking, be sure this check box is selected

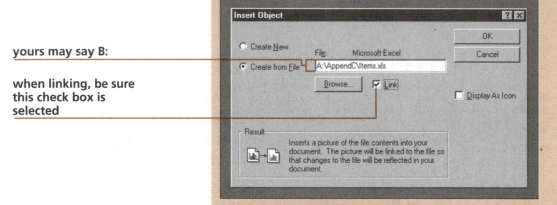

Figure C-17: Insert Object dialog box showing link to an Excel worksheet

6 Click the **OK** button. In a few moments the Excel worksheet appears inside the OLE container control.

7 Set the OLE container control's Left property to **360** and its Top property to **360**. Set its SizeMode property to **2-AutoSize**, and its Name property to **oleInventory**.

8 Click the **form's title bar** to return to the form. Figure C-18 shows the Excel worksheet displayed in the OLE container control.

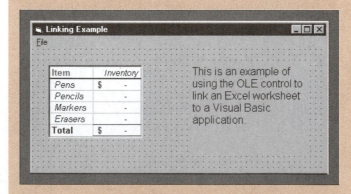

Figure C-18: Items.xls worksheet linked in OLE container control

Each time you run the current application, you want Visual Basic to use the Items.xls file on your Student Disk to update the contents of the OLE container control. In other words, if you use the Excel application to make a change to the

Items.xls file, you want the current application to reflect that change. You tell Visual Basic to update the OLE container control each time the current application is run by including the OLE container control's Update method in the form's Load event.

Update Method

When an object is linked to a client application, you can use the OLE control's **Update method** to retrieve the current data from the server application before the data is displayed in the client application's OLE control. The syntax of the Update method is *object*.**Update**, where *object* is the name of the OLE container control.

To include the Update method in the form's Load event:

1 Double-click the **form** to open its Code window. The form's Load event, which contains the instructions for centering the form, appears. Position the insertion point in the line below the centering instructions. Press the **Tab** key, if necessary, type **oleinventory.update** and then press the **Enter** key.

2 Close the Code window, then **save** and **run** the application. In a few moments the user interface appears with the Items.xls worksheet displayed in the OLE container control.

You can edit a linked object in the same manner as you edit an embedded object—simply by double-clicking the OLE control. Use the OLE control to change the Pens inventory dollar amount to $200 and the Markers inventory dollar amount to $400.00.

3 Double-click the **OLE control**. The OLE control starts Excel and displays the Items.xls worksheet as shown in Figure C-19.

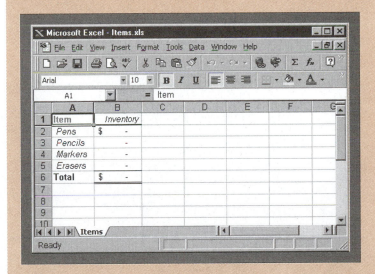

Figure C-19: Items.xls worksheet displayed in Excel

HELP? If the Excel application window is maximized, click its Restore button.

4 Click cell **B2**. Type **200** and press the **Enter** key. Click cell **B4**. Type **400** and press the **Enter** key. The total inventory amount changes to $600.00.

5 Click **File** on the Excel menu bar, and then click **Save** to save the changes to the Items.xls file.

GUI
Design Tips

Using the OLE Control to Link Data to a Visual Basic Application

- Start Visual Basic. You do not need to start the application that contains the data to be copied.
- Add an OLE container control to the form.
- Select the Create from File option button in the Insert Object dialog box.
- Select the filename in the Browse dialog box.
- Be sure the Link check box in the Insert Object dialog box is selected.

6   Click **File** on the Excel menu bar, and then click **Exit** to close Excel. Notice that the OLE control also shows that the inventory dollar amounts for the Pens and Markers are 200.00 and 400.00, respectively.

7   Click **File** on the form's menu bar, and then click **Exit** to end the application. Visual Basic returns to the design screen. Don't be concerned that the changes made to the worksheet do not appear in the OLE control. When you run the ApCLink application, the Update method in the form's Load event will retrieve the most current information from the Items.xls file and display it in the OLE control. Confirm that now.

8   **Run** the application. Notice that the OLE control shows the correct dollar amounts for the Pens and Markers.

9   Click **File** on the form's menu bar, and then click **Exit**. Visual Basic returns to the design screen.

You have now completed Appendix C. You can take a break or complete the questions and exercises at the end of the appendix. (If you are asked if you want to save the ApCLink files, click the No button.)

S U M M A R Y

To copy data from one Windows application to another:

■   Use one of the following: the clipboard, DDE, or OLE.

To embed or link objects to a Visual Basic application:

■   Use the OLE container control.

To resize the OLE control to display the entire object contained within the control:

■   Set the OLE control's SizeMode property to 2-AutoSize.

To open a binary access file:

■   Use the Open statement. Its syntax is **Open** *pathname* **For Binary As** *filenumber*, where *pathname* is the name of the file you want to open and *filenumber* is an integer between 1 and 511, inclusive.

To save the contents of the OLE container control to a file:

■   Open a binary access file, then use the **SaveToFile method** to save the object to the file. The syntax of the SaveToFile method is *object*.**SaveToFile** *filenumber*, where *object* is the name of the OLE control and *filenumber* is the number used in the Open statement to open the binary access file.

To display the contents of a binary access file in the OLE container control:

◼ Open the binary access file, then use the **ReadFromFile method** to read the file each time the application is run. The syntax of the ReadFromFile method is *object*.**ReadFromFile** *filenumber*, where *object* is the name of the OLE control and *filenumber* is the number used in the Open statement to open the binary access file.

To tell Visual Basic to retrieve the current data from a server application before the data is displayed in an OLE control in the client application:

◼ Use the Update method in the client application form's Load event procedure. The syntax of the Update method is *object*.**Update**, where *object* is the name of the OLE container control.

Q U E S T I O N S

1. Which of the following can be used to copy data from one Windows application to another?
    a. clipboard
    b. DDE
    c. OLE
    d. all of the above

2. Which of the following is true?
    a. The drawback to using the clipboard to copy data is that you can't copy text.
    b. The drawback to using the clipboard to copy data is that the copied data has no link to the application that created it.
    c. In order to use the clipboard to copy data into a Visual Basic application, the Visual Basic form must include a data control.
    d. In order to use the clipboard to copy data into a Visual Basic application, the Visual Basic form must include a DDE control.
    e. In order to use the clipboard to copy data into a Visual Basic application, the Visual Basic form must include an OLE control.

3. When using DDE, the application that supplies the data is called the _____ application.
    a. active
    b. client
    c. destination
    d. source

4. When using DDE, the application that receives the data is called the _____ application.
    a. active
    b. client
    c. destination
    d. source

5. Which of the following is true?
   a. When using DDE, both the source application and the destination application must be running at the same time in order for the exchange of data to occur.
   b. When using DDE, only the source application needs to be running in order for the exchange of data to occur.
   c. When using DDE, only the destination application needs to be running in order for the exchange of data to occur.
   d. When using DDE, neither the source application nor the destination application needs to be running in order for the exchange of data to occur.

6. The Edit menu's _____ command maintains a link between the original data and the copied data.
   a. Copy
   b. Cut
   c. Paste
   d. Paste Link

7. Which of the following is false?
   a. When using OLE, you can either link or embed an existing file.
   b. When using OLE, you can either link or embed a new file.
   c. When using OLE, the application that contains the original data is called the server application.
   d. When using OLE, the application that contains the copied data is called the client application.

8. If you don't want changes to the original object to be reflected in the application that contains the copied object, and vice versa, you should _____ the object.
   a. embed
   b. link

9. If you want changes to the original object to be reflected in the application that contains the copied object, and vice versa, you should _____ the object.
   a. embed
   b. link

10. You use the _____ control both to embed and to link an object in a Visual Basic application.
    a. data
    b. frame
    c. image
    d. OLE

11. When set to 2-AutoSize, an OLE control's _____ property resizes the OLE control to display the entire object contained within the control.
    a. AutoAdjust
    b. AutoSize
    c. Fill
    d. Size
    e. SizeMode

12. To tell Visual Basic to retrieve the current data from the server application before the data is displayed in the client application's OLE control, enter the OLE control's _____ method in the form's Load event procedure.
    a. AutoDisplay
    b. AutoSize
    c. AutoUpdate
    d. Retrieve
    e. Update

13. You save the contents of an OLE control to a(n) _____ access file.
 a. binary
 b. OLE
 c. random
 d. sequential

14. You use the _____ method to save the contents of an OLE control to a file.
 a. Save
 b. SaveFile
 c. SaveOLE
 d. SaveOleFile
 e. SaveToFile

15. You use the _____ method to retrieve the information from a file and display it in an OLE control.
 a. Read
 b. ReadFromFile
 c. ReadFromOle
 d. ReadToFile
 e. ReadToOLE

16. Assume that data in an Excel worksheet was copied to the clipboard, then pasted into a Visual Basic application. Explain how to edit the copied data.

17. Assume that you used DDE to copy the data in an Excel worksheet to a Visual Basic application. Explain how to edit the copied data.

18. Assume that you used OLE to embed an Excel worksheet object in a Visual Basic application. Explain how to edit the data in the embedded object. Does the edit have any affect on the original object?

19. Assume that you used OLE to link an Excel worksheet object to a Visual Basic application. Explain how to edit the data in the linked object. Does the edit have any affect on the original object?

E X E R C I S E S

1. In this exercise you will link an Excel worksheet to a Visual Basic application. In order to complete this exercise, you will need access to Microsoft Excel 97 or higher.
 a. Use Microsoft Excel to create a worksheet that keeps track of your yearly income and expenses for the previous two years. Enter the data into the worksheet, then save the worksheet as lc1Done.xls in the AppendC folder on your Student Disk.
 b. Use Excel to print the lc1Done.xls worksheet.
 c. Create a Visual Basic application that links the lc1Done.xls file in an OLE control. The application should allow the user to print the interface.
 d. Save the form and the project as lc1Done in the AppendC folder on your Student Disk.
 e. Save and run the application. Test the application by changing two of the expense amounts. Print the interface, then exit the Visual Basic application.
 f. Print the code.
 g. Use Excel to print the lc1Done.xls worksheet. On the printout, circle the two expense amounts that you changed.
 h. Submit the printouts from steps b, e, and g, and the code from step f.

Exercises 2 through 5 are Discovery Exercises, which allow you to both discover the solutions to problems on your own and experiment with material that is not covered in the tutorial.

discovery ▶ 2. In this exercise you will embed an existing Word document in a Visual Basic application. In order to complete this exercise, you will need access to Microsoft Word 97.

   a. Use Microsoft Word to create a two-paragraph letter of your choice. Type [Enter date here] at the top of the letter. Type [Enter name and address here] in the appropriate place in the letter. Save the letter as lc2Done.doc in the AppendC folder on your Student Disk.

   b. Use Word to print the letter.

   c. Create a Visual Basic application that embeds the lc2Done.doc file in an OLE control. The application should allow the user to print the interface.

   d. Save the form and the project as lc2Done in the AppendC folder on your Student Disk.

   e. Save and run the application. Test the application by entering the date, as well as the name and address of one of your friends or relatives. Print the interface, then exit the Visual Basic application.

   f. Submit the printouts from steps b and e.

discovery ▶ 3. In this exercise you will link a graphic created in Microsoft Paint to a Visual Basic application. In order to complete this exercise, you will need access to Microsoft Paint.

   a. Use Microsoft Paint to create a graphic. Save the graphic as lc3Done in the AppendC folder on your Student Disk.

   b. Use Paint to print the lc3Done graphic.

   c. Create a Visual Basic application that links the graphic file to an OLE control. The application should allow the user to print the interface.

   d. Save the form and the project as lc3Done in the AppendC folder on your Student Disk.

   e. Save and run the application. Test the application by changing the color and size of the graphic. Print the interface, then exit the Visual Basic application.

   f. Submit the printouts from steps b and e.

discovery ▶ 4. In this exercise you will learn about a form's NegotiateMenus property and a menu control's NegotiatePosition property.

   Scenario: Recall that when you double-clicked the Excel worksheet in the ApCEmbed application, Excel's menu replaced the application's menu. In this exercise you will learn how to display both Excel's menus and the application's menu at the same time.

   a. Open the ApCEmbed (ApCEmbed.vbp) project, which is located in the AppendC folder on your Student Disk. You created the project in Lesson C. Save the form and the project as lc4Done in the AppendC folder on your Student Disk.

   b. If you have access to the MSDN Library, then display the Help screens on a form's NegotiateMenus property and a menu control's NegotiatePosition property.

   c. Assume that you want to add Excel's menus to the end of the application's menu. What is the appropriate setting for the NegotiateMenus property and for the NegotiatePosition property?

   d. Set the NegotiateMenus property and the NegotiatePosition property in the ApCEmbed application so that Excel's menus will be displayed after the application's menu.

   e. Save and run the application. Double-click the Excel worksheet. Excel's menus should appear after the application's File menu on the menu bar.

   f. Exit the application.

   g. Submit your answers to step c.

discovery ▶

5. In this exercise, you will link a Microsoft Excel worksheet to a Visual Basic application. You will also embed a Microsoft Word document in the application. To complete this exercise, you must have access to both Microsoft Excel 97 and Microsoft Word 97.

   Scenario: Each semester you seem to run out of money quickly and have to write home for more. To make your plea to your parents more convincing, you decide to create an application that includes a Microsoft Excel worksheet and a Microsoft Word document. In the Excel worksheet you will list your expenses. You will use the Word document to write the note to your parents asking them to send you more money.

   a. Use Visual Basic to open the Money (Money.vbp) project, which is located in the AppendC folder on your Student Disk.

   b. Save the form and the project as lc5Done in the AppendC folder on your Student Disk. The File menu's Print and Exit commands have already been coded for you.

   c. The AppendC folder on your Student Disk contains an Excel worksheet named Expenses.xls that lists your expenses for the Fall semester. The worksheet also contains a chart that displays the expenses in a 3-D pie graph. Use the OLE control to link the Excel worksheet to the lc5Done application. Set the OLE control's Name property to oleExpenses. Set its Left property to 360, its Top property to 360, and its SizeMode property to 2-AutoSize.

   d. Each time you run the lc5Done application, you want Visual Basic to use the Expenses.xls file to update the contents of the OLE control. Include the appropriate Update method instruction in the form's Load event.

   e. Use the OLE control to embed a new Microsoft Word document in the lc5Done application. When the new Word document appears in the OLE control, press the Esc key to both remove the Word menu and return to the form, then click the OLE control that contains the empty Word document. Set the OLE control's Name property to oleNote. Set its Height property to 2055, its Left property to 360, its SizeMode property to 1-Stretch, its Top property to 3000, and its Width property to 7695.

   f. Code the File menu's Save Note command so that it saves the contents of the oleNote control to a binary access file named lc5Note.ole.

   g. Save and run the application. Double-click the OLE control that contains the empty Word document. The OLE control starts Microsoft Word, and the Word menus appear in the form's title bar. Type a note asking your parents for more money.

   h. When you are finished typing the note, use the Spelling and Grammar command on the Word Tools menu to verify the spelling in the document. If the document contains any misspelled words or any grammatical errors, the Spelling and Grammar checker will alert you and make suggestions. Either ignore the error (assuming it is not an error) or accept one of the checker's suggestions. When the message "The spelling and grammar check is complete." appears, click the OK button.

   i. Press the Esc key to remove the Word menus. Click File on the form's menu bar, and then click Save Note. If your computer is connected to a printer, click File on the form's menu bar, and then click Print. Click File on the form's menu bar, and then click Exit. Visual Basic returns to the design screen.

   j. Save and run the application again. Add another sentence to the note you typed in the oleNote control. Save the contents of the oleNote control. If your computer is connected to a printer, print the form. Exit the application.

   k. Print the application's code.

   l. Submit the printouts from steps i and j, and the code from step k.

Creating Your Own ActiveX Control

Before Visual Basic 5.0, the controls utilized in Visual Basic applications had to be created in programming languages such as C or C++. You can now use Visual Basic to create custom controls, called ActiveX controls, that can be included not only in a Visual Basic application, but on a Web page on either the Internet or a corporate intranet as well. The controls you create are called ActiveX controls because they are based on Microsoft's **ActiveX technology**—a technology that allows you to create cross-platform, language-independent controls. In this appendix you will learn how to create an ActiveX control and how to include the control in a Visual Basic application.

Creating Your First ActiveX Control

Assume that in many of your applications you have need of a control that allows the user to enter a number in the range of 0 through 10. Visual Basic already has a variety of controls that can be used to accomplish this task—a text box, list box, option buttons, and so on. Although any of these controls could be used, you decide to create a custom control instead.

You can create a custom control from scratch, on your own, or you can use one or more of Visual Basic's standard controls to create a custom control. In this case, you will use two of Visual Basic's standard controls, the label control and the horizontal scroll bar control, to create a custom control called EnterNumbers.

Begin by opening an ActiveX control project.

1 Start Visual Basic. On the New Project dialog box's New tab, click **ActiveX Control**, and then click the **Open** button. The Project1-UserControl1 (UserControl) interface appears.

You design your custom control, referred to as a **user control**, in the gray area of the interface. Before doing so, give the user control a more meaningful name.

2 Set the UserControl1 control's Name property to **EnterNumbers**.

Now put a label control on the interface, then set its properties.

3 Double-click the **Label** tool ▣ in the toolbox. Set the label control's properties as follows:

Name:	**lblNum**	Caption:	0
Alignment:	**2 – Center**	Font size:	12
Appearance:	**0-Flat**	Left:	0
BackStyle:	**0-Transparent**	Top:	0
BorderStyle:	**1-Fixed Single**	Width:	600

Now add a horizontal scroll bar to the interface.

4 Double-click the **HScrollBar** tool ▣ in the toolbox. Set the horizontal scroll bar's properties as follows:

Name:	**hsbNum**	Top:	500
Left:	0	Width:	600

The scroll bar should allow you to scroll through a range of numbers beginning with 0 and ending with 10. Therefore, you will set the scroll bar's Min property to 0 and its Max property to 10. Because you want to scroll through these numbers in increments of 1, you will set the scroll bar's SmallChange property to 1.

5 Set the hsbNum control's Max property to **10**. Also verify that the scroll bar's Min property is set to 0 and its SmallChange property is set to **1**.

Now size the gray area of the user control's interface so that it is the same size as the label control and the scroll bar control.

6 Click the gray area in the interface. Sizing handles appear around the gray area. Size the gray area as shown in Figure D-1.

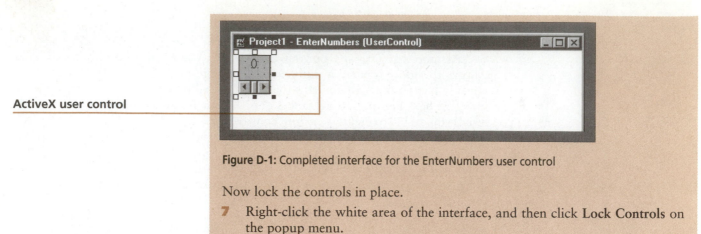

ActiveX user control

Figure D-1: Completed interface for the EnterNumbers user control

Now lock the controls in place.

7 Right-click the white area of the interface, and then click **Lock Controls** on the popup menu.

The interface for the EnterNumbers user control is now complete, so you can begin coding it. The only events you will need to code are the horizontal scroll bar control's Change event, which occurs when the user clicks one of the scroll arrows, and its Scroll event, which occurs when the user drags the scroll box. During run time, the current location of the scroll box in the scroll bar is stored in the scroll bar control's Value property. You will assign the Value property to the lblNum control's Caption property, which will display the number in the interface.

To code the EnterNumbers user control, then place the control in the toolbox:

1 Open the hsbNum control's Change event. Press the **Tab** key, type **lblnum.caption = hsbnum.value** and then press the **Enter** key.

2 Copy the `lblNum.Caption = hsbNum.Value` instruction to the clipboard, and then paste the instruction in the hsbNum control's Scroll event.

3 Close the Code window.

When you have finished creating the user control, you need simply to save it, then click its Close button to place it in the toolbox.

4 Click **File** on the menu bar, and then click **Save EnterNumbers As**. Save the file as **EnterNumbers.ctl** in the AppendD folder on your Student Disk.

5 Click the **Close** button on the Project1 – EnterNumbers (UserControl) window. The EnterNumbers user control appears in the toolbox. Position the mouse pointer as shown in Figure D-2.

tip

The "ctl" in the filename stands for "control."

position mouse pointer here

Figure D-2: The EnterNumbers user control shown in the toolbox

You have now created your first user control. To test your control to see if it works properly, you will need to include it in a standard EXE project. Do that now.

To test the EnterNumbers user control:

1   Click **File** on the menu bar, and then click **Add Project**. Click **Standard EXE** on the Add Project dialog box's New tab, then click the **Open** button to add a Standard EXE project to the current application. Visual Basic adds the Project2 project, which contains the Form1 form, to the current application.

2   Click the **form**, then double-click the **EnterNumbers** tool in the toolbox to place an EnterNumbers control on the form.

3   Right-click **Project2** (Project2) in the Project window, then click **Set as Start Up. Run** the application. Click the **EnterNumbers control's right scroll arrow** several times. Each time you click the right scroll arrow, the number in the label control increases by a value of 1.

4   Continue clicking the **right scroll arrow** until the number 10 appears, then click the **right scroll arrow** again. Notice that the right scroll arrow does not allow you to enter numbers greater than 10. (Recall that you set the Max property of the user control's horizontal scroll bar component to 10.)

5   On your own, verify that the left scroll arrow will not allow you to enter numbers less than 0. (Recall that the Min property of the user control's horizontal scroll bar component is set to 0.)

6   Click the **End** button ■ on the Standard toolbar to stop the application.

Now that you know that your user control is working correctly, you can include it in a Visual Basic application. First close the current application.

7   Click **File** on the menu bar, and then click **New Project**. When you are asked if you want to save the changes to the files, click the **No** button. Open a Standard EXE file.

In the next section you will learn how to include your custom user control in a Visual Basic application.

Including a Custom User Control in a Visual Basic Application

Skater's Ice House hosts many skating competitions. The manager would like a record of the scores, from 0 to 10, given to each of the five competitors. Your Student Disk contains a Visual Basic application that Skater's Ice House can use to record and print the five scores earned in each competition. You will use the EnterNumbers user control in this application to allow the manager to enter the five scores.

To include the EnterNumbers user control in a Visual Basic application:

1 Open the **IceHouse** (IceHouse.vbp) project, which is located in the AppendD folder on your Student Disk. Save the form and the project as **ApDIceHouse** in the AppendD folder on your Student Disk.

Now add the EnterNumbers user control to the toolbox. Recall that the control is saved in the EnterNumbers.ctl file.

2 Click **Project** on the menu bar, and then click **Add User Control**. Click the **Existing** tab. If necessary, open the AppendD folder on your Student Disk. Click **EnterNumbers** (EnterNumbers.ctl), then click the **Open** button. When the message appears informing you that the EnterNumbers control was changed by Visual Basic from public to private, click the **OK** button. Visual Basic adds the EnterNumbers tool to the toolbox.

3 Double-click the **EnterNumbers** tool in the toolbox. Visual Basic adds the EnterNumbers control to the form. Drag the EnterNumbers control to a location immediately above the Skater 1 label control.

4 Place four more EnterNumbers controls on the form and position them as shown in Figure D-3.

position five user controls as shown

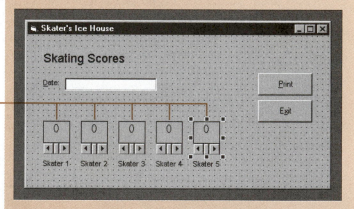

Figure D-3: Five EnterNumbers controls shown in the interface

5 **Save** and **run** the application. Enter **March 21, 2000** in the Date text box, then use the five user controls to enter the following five scores: **9, 8, 5, 10, 6**.

6 If your computer is connected to a printer, click the **Print** button.

7 Click the **Exit** button to end the application.

You have now completed Appendix D. You can either exit Visual Basic or practice creating your own custom controls.

Index

Special Characters

\ (backslash), VB 138, VB 139
> (greater than operator), VB 245
< (less than operator), VB 245
% (percent sign), VB 682
& (ampersand), VB 120, VB 122, VB 198
' (apostrophe), VB 134
* (asterisk), VB 138, VB 523, VB 584
+ (plus sign), VB 138, VB 199
- (minus sign), VB 138
/ (slash), VB 138
= (equal sign), VB 245
>= (greater than or equal to operator), VB 245
<= (less than or equal to operator), VB 245
<> (not equal to operator), VB 245
^ (caret), VB 138
| (pipe symbol), VB 524
... (ellipsis), VB 470
. (period), VB 132

A

abstraction, VB 6
access keys, menus, VB 470
accumulators, VB 354–362
    flowchart, VB 355
Active Server Pages (ASPs), VB 846
ActiveX controls, VB 73, VB 826–827, VB 920–924
    creating, VB 921–923
    in general, VB 826–827
    including in applications, VB 924
ActiveX Data Objects (ADO), VB 672, 863, VB 866. See also ADO data control
ActiveX technology, VB 920
Add button, Dynaset window, VB 661
Add Field dialog box, VB 654–656
Add Form command, VB 221–222
AddItem method, VB 420–421
addition operator (+), VB 138
Addition option button, coding, VB 298–299

AddNew method, VB 690
Add User Control dialog box, VB 74
ADO See ActiveX Data Object
ADO data control, VB 673–678
    preventing user interaction, VB 691
    Refresh method, VB 691
AfterColEdit event, VB 768–769
AfterColUpdate event, VB 768–769
    coding, VB 770–772
AfterUpdate event, VB 768
aligning numbers in columns, VB 445–448
ampersand (&)
    access keys, VB 120, VB 122
    concatenation operator, VB 198
And operator, VB 250, VB 251, VB 252–253
apostrophe ('), comments, VB 134
appearance, mouse pointer, VB 224–225
appearance properties. See Windows Forms
Appearance property, user interfaces, VB 114–115
Append mode, sequential access files, VB 426, VB 427, VB 428
application(s). See also specific applications
    adding existing forms, VB 215–216
    container (client), VB 822
    debugging, VB 148
    destination, VB 819
    ending, VB 49
    exiting, VB 64
    OOED. See planning OOED applications
    printing, VB 77–78
    sharing data among. See sharing data among applications
    source (server), VB 819, VB 822
    starting, VB 49
    testing. See testing applications

application modal dialog boxes, VB 316
arguments, VB 380–381, VB 613
arrays. See control arrays; one-dimensional variable arrays; two-dimensional variable arrays; variable arrays
arrow keys, scrolling Properties window, VB 25
ASP.NET, VB 846
ASPs. See Active Server Pages
assemblers, VB 3
assembling documentation, VB 149
assembly languages, VB 2–3
assignment statements, VB 131–132
    dot member selection operator, VB 132
asterisk (*)
    field length, VB 584
    wildcard, VB 523
attributes, VB 6–7
Automatic Browser Detection, VB 852
automatic counter loop, VB 340–344
Average Score button, VB 732–733

B

BackColor property, VB 28
background, user interfaces, VB 113–114
BackStyle property, user interfaces, VB 113–114
backup copies, files, VB 757
base class, VB 6–7
BASIC, VB 3–4
BeforeColUpdate event, VB 768–769
BeforeUpdate event, VB 768
binding controls, VB 678–679
blnChange variable, VB 558, VB 560
book title capitalization, VB 103
Boolean data type, VB 166–167
BorderStyle property, VB 64, VB 146–147, VB 607
    user interfaces, VB 114–115

bound controls, VB 678
bugs, VB 96. *See also* debugging
button control, code and, VB 827–828
buttons. *See* command buttons; *specific buttons*
buttons argument, VB 316
    settings, VB 400

C

Calculate Order button
    coding, VB 139–142
    modifying code, VB 192–198
Calendar control, VB 855
Calendar Screen, previewing, VB 802–803
Call statement, VB 296–297, VB 610
Cancel argument, Unload event, VB 564
CancelError property, VB 545–547
    On Error statement, VB 546–547
Cancel Ticket button, coding, VB 634–635, VB 700–702
CancelUpdate method, VB 690
capitalization
    Dim statement, VB 195
    InputBox function prompt, VB 202
    sentence and book title, VB 103
    UCase function, VB 256–257
Caption property, VB 25–26, VB 45–46
Case form, selection structure, VB 261–262
case sensitivity, UCase function, VB 256–257
centering contents of label controls, VB 399
Change events, VB 395–398
    txtEdit control, VB 560
check boxes, VB 287–288. *See also specific check boxes*
    adding to forms, VB 287–288
    selecting and deselecting, VB 323
    standards, VB 287
classes
    base, VB 6, VB 7
    behaviors and, VB 819, VB 829
    derived, VB 6
CheckBox control, VB 853
classroom application, VB 738–743
clearing text boxes, VB 550
Clear method, VB 477
Clear Screen button, coding, VB 135–138

Click event, triggering, VB 299
Click event procedure, Verify Answer button, VB 309, VB 311–312
client application, VB 904
Clipboard
    copying to, VB 133
    sending and retrieving graphics, VB 479
    sharing data among applications, VB 898–900
Clipboard object, VB 477–478
Close button, VB 49, VB 147, VB 401
    Dynaset window, VB 661
Close statement, VB 430–431, VB 588
closing. *See also* exiting
    random access files, VB 588
    sequential access files, VB 430–431
code, VB 60, VB 129
    for button control, VB 827–828
    compressing, VB 141
    hidden, VB 828
    printing, VB 836
    removing from Code window, VB 194
    viewing in Windows Forms VB 821–822
    writing, VB 60–64
coded controls, removing from forms, VB 223–224
code library, VB 822
code modules
    adding to projects, VB 180–181, VB 218–221
    coding, VB 586–587
code templates, VB 62
Code window, VB 60–64
    adding procedures to applications, VB 613
    changing display, VB 76–77
    control arrays, VB 380–381, VB 629
    removing code, VB 194
coding, VB 129–146
    assembling documentation, VB 149
    assignment statements, VB 131–132
    BorderStyle property, VB 146–147
    Click event procedure, VB 195–197
    ControlBox property, VB 146–147
    Format function, VB 144–146

internal documentation, VB 134–135
    MaxButton property, VB 146–147
    methods, VB 133–134
    MinButton property, VB 146–147
    testing and debugging applications, VB 148
    Val function, VB 143–144
    Visual Basic 6.0 compared to Visual Basic.NET, VB 828–829
    writing equations, VB 138–139
Cole's Playhouse application, VB 577–579, VB 645–647
Colfax Industries payroll application, VB 756–758
color
    user interface backgrounds, VB 113–114
    user interfaces, VB 112–113
color constants, VB 611–612
Color dialog box, displaying, VB 533–535
column(s), DataGrid control. *See* DataGrid control
column headings, VB 449
    DataGrid control, VB 762–764
command buttons, VB 8
    adding to forms, VB 59
    compared to radio buttons, VB 819
    default, VB 207
    sizing, VB 111
comma separator, Print method outputlist, VB 438, VB 439
Command Window, using, VB 813–814
Common Dialog control, VB 520–522
    context-sensitive Help, VB 524
    FileName property, VB 526
    Filter property, VB 524–525
    Flags property, VB 529–531
    methods, VB 521–522
compilers, VB 3
    making executable files, VB 79
Component Tray, VB 821
compressing code, VB 141
concatenating strings, VB 198–201
ConnectionString property, VB 674–677
constants
    intrinsic, VB 204
    literal, VB 169

symbolic, VB 169, VB 183–185
Const statement, VB 184
container application, VB 904
control(s). *See also specific controls*
    adding to forms, VB 43–44
    binding, VB 678–679
    canceling selection, VB 48
    coded, removing from forms, VB 223–224
    cutting from forms, VB 66, VB 284
    data-aware (bound), VB 678
    default property, VB 137
    deleting, VB 44
    disabling, VB 379, VB 695
    displaying, VB 68–72
    drawing in frames, VB 289–290
    enabling, VB 379
    hiding, VB 68–72
    label controls, VB 43
    locking. *See* locking controls
    moving, VB 44
    multiple, changing properties, VB 47–48
    properties. *See also specific properties*
    sizing. *See* sizing controls
    speed of processing, VB 436
Control Anchoring, VB 821
control arrays, VB 374–386
    Code window, VB 629
    coding, VB 382–384, VB 627–630
    coding GotFocus event, VB 384–385
    creating while adding controls to form, VB 374–377
    Enabled property, VB 379–380
    indexes, VB 374
    referencing controls in other forms, VB 628–630
    using existing controls, VB 377–379
    viewing Code window, VB 380–381
ControlBox property, VB 146–147
Control Docking, VB 821
Copy command, coding, VB 480
copying
    to Clipboard, VB 133
    forms to projects, VB 221–225
counters, VB 354–362
    flowchart, VB 355
Critical Message icon, VB 315
Currency data type, VB 166–167

Currency format, VB 145
Cut command, coding, VB 481

D

data. *See also* attributes
    sharing among applications. *See* sharing data among applications
    storing in variables, VB 169–170
    testing applications, VB 148
data adapter, VB 869
data-aware controls, VB 678
database(s), VB 648–666
    concepts and terminology, VB 648–649
    creating, VB 652–658
    data validation rules in tables, VB 659–660
    definition, VB 648
    designing, VB 649–652
    existing, opening, VB 661–665
    indexes. *See* index(es), databases
    OLE DB, VB 672
    relational, VB 648
    software packages, VB 648
database fields, VB 648, VB 652
    index, VB 650
    pointer, VB 650
    Text field size, VB 656
database records, VB 648, VB 652
    deleting, VB 664–665
    editing and sorting, VB 663
data elements, VB 424
data entry, one-dimensional variable arrays, VB 723
DataField property, VB 678
data files, VB 423–431
    direct access, VB 580
    random access. *See* random access files
    sequential access. *See* sequential access files
DataGrid, binding, VB 869–874
DataGrid control, VB 758–773
    changing appearance of data, VB 761–768
    coding, VB 768–773
    object variables, VB 770–772
    rounding numbers, VB 772–773
DataSource property, VB 678
data types
    guidelines for assigning, VB 166–167
    selecting, VB 655

    user-defined, VB 584–585
    variables, VB 164–165
data validation, VB 652
data validation rules, tables, VB 659–660
Date data type, VB 167
DateTimePicker, VB 826
DDE (Dynamic Data Exchange), sharing data with other applications, VB 900–904
debugging, VB 11, VB 148
decimal point
    aligning whole numbers, VB 445
    fixed, VB 166
    floating, VB 165–166
decision structure. *See* selection structure
declaring variables, VB 168–169
default
    command buttons, VB 207
    selection in list boxes, VB 423
default option button, VB 299–301
Default property, VB 207
Delete button, Dynaset window, VB 661
deleted records, VB 701
Delete method, VB 690, VB 701
deleting. *See also* removing
    controls, VB 44
    paragraphs and objects in Web pages, VB 808
    records in tables, VB 664–665
derived class, VB 6
design time, VB 19
destination application, VB 900
detail lines, VB 449
detail pane, DHTML page designer window, VB 886, VB 888
Details Panel, VB 874–877
DHTML Application, VB 883, VB 885–891
dialog boxes, VB 214, VB 520–535. *See also specific dialog boxes*
    application modal, VB 316
    Common Dialog control. *See* Common Dialog control
    displaying. *See* displaying dialog boxes
    standards, VB 221
    system modal, VB 316
    Windows, making forms resemble, VB 219–221
Dim statement, VB 168, VB 170, VB 171, VB 195

direct access files, VB 580
disabling controls, VB 379
disk space, embedding data, VB 904
Display Grade command button,
    coding, VB 391–395
displaying
    code in Code window, VB 76–77
    Code window for control
      arrays, VB 380–381
    color constants, VB 611–612
    controls, VB 68–72
    forms, VB 216–218
    HTML code, VB 890–891
    menu options, VB 9–10
    Properties window, VB 113
    scroll bars, VB 467
    Web pages, VB 891
displaying dialog boxes, VB 522–529
    Color dialog box, VB 533–535
    Font dialog box, VB 531–533
    Open dialog box, VB 522–526
    Print dialog box, VB 528–529
    Save As dialog box, VB 526–528
Display Item button, coding,
    VB 594–596
Display Name button, VB 725–728
Display Number button, VB 728–730
Display summary information check
    box, VB 321–323
Display Totals button
    coding, VB 431–434
    EOF function, VB 434
distributed applications, VB 804
division operator (/), VB 138
documentation, VB 77–78
    assembling, VB 149
    internal, VB 134–135
Do Loop...Until statement, VB 344
dot member selection operator (.),
    VB 132
Double data type, VB 167
Double type variables, VB 165–166
Do Until loop, VB 344–348,
    VB 356, VB 360–362
    example, VB 349–352
    flowchart and pseudocode,
      VB 346–348
Do While loop, VB 344–349,
    VB 356–360
    example, VB 348–349,
      VB 352–354
    flowchart and pseudocode,
      VB 346–348
Do While...Loop statement, VB 344

drag-and-drop feature, VB 892–896
    coding buttons, VB 896
    DragDrop event, VB 895
    DragIcon property, VB 894
    DragMode property, VB 893–894
DragDrop event, VB 895
dragging, definition, VB 892
DragIcon property, VB 894
DragMode property, VB 893–894
DropDownList control, VB 854
dropping, definition, VB 892
Dynamic Data Exchange (DDE),
    sharing data with other applica-
    tions, VB 901–904
Dynaset window, VB 661

E

Edit button, Dynaset window, VB 661
editing
    embedded data, VB 908–909
    table records, VB 663
Edit menu, VB 223
    coding, VB 478–480
    coding commands, VB 480–482
    coding Find command,
      VB 497–501
    coding Find Next command,
      VB 501–504
    creating, VB 474–475
Editor tab, Options dialog box,
    VB 72–73
ellipsis (...), VB 470
embedding data, VB 905–911
    disk space, VB 904
    editing embedded data,
      VB 908–909
    saving and retrieving changes
      to embedded objects,
      VB 909–911
empty strings, VB 136
Enabled property, control arrays,
    VB 379–380
enabling controls, VB 379
encapsulation, VB 6
End command, VB 31
ending applications, VB 49
End statements, VB 62
End Sub keyword, VB 62
Enter Information command button,
    coding, VB 426
Enter Item button, coding,
    VB 589–591
EnterNumbers user control, coding,
    VB 840–841
Enter Ticket button, coding,
    VB 630–634, VB 698–700

EOF function, VB 434
EOF property, VB 690
equal to operator (=), VB 245
equations, VB 138–139
error handling routine, VB 545,
    VB 546–547
error trapping, VB 545
event(s), VB 60, VB 133. *See also*
    specific events
    identifying, VB 100–101
Event Handler, creating, VB 857
event procedures, VB 60
Excel
    copying data to Visual Basic,
      VB 901–904
    embedding worksheets in Visual
      Basic. *See* embedding data
    linking data to Visual Basic
      applications, VB 911–914
executable files, VB 423
    making, VB 78–79
Exit button
    entering Unload statement in
      Click procedure, VB 403
    moving code to Unload event,
      VB 402
exiting. *See also* closing
    applications, VB 64
    Visual Basic, VB 32
exponentiation operator (^), VB 138
exposed attributes/behaviors, VB 6
expressionlists
    To and Is keywords, VB 266–270
    Select Case statement,
      VB 263–266
extended selection structure,
    VB 261–262

F

field(s)
    databases. *See* database fields
    data files, VB 424, VB 580
Field object, VB 689
Fields collection, VB 689
field variables, VB 585
file(s). *See also* projects
    backup copies, VB 757
    data. *See* data files; sequential
      access files
    determining length, VB 562
    executable. *See* executable files
    removing from projects,
      VB 181, VB 182–183
FileLen function, VB 562

File menu
    New command, VB 548–552,
        VB 609–610
    Open command, VB 616–619
filename(s), saving files under different
    names, VB 48–49
FileName property, VB 526
filename variable, VB 587
Filter button, Dynaset window,
    VB 661
Filter property, VB 524–525
Find button, Dynaset window,
    VB 661
Find command, Edit menu, coding,
    VB 497–501
Find Next command, Edit menu,
    coding, VB 501–504
Fixed format, VB 145, VB 446
fixed-point numbers, VB 166
fixed-space fonts, VB 441–442,
    VB 444
F1 key, accessing Help, VB 42
F4 key, displaying Properties win-
    dow, VB 606
F5 key, running applications, VB 49
Flags application, VB 892–893
Flags property, VB 529–531
flickering, user interface, preventing,
    VB 217
floating-point numbers, VB 165–166
flowcharts, VB 90
    selection structure, VB 243–244
flowlines, VB 244
focus, user interfaces, controlling,
    VB 118–119
font(s), VB 47
    printers, VB 441–445
    user interfaces, VB 111–112
Font dialog box, displaying,
    VB 531–533
Font property, VB 47–48
form(s)
    adding command buttons, VB 59
    adding controls, VB 43–44
    adding image controls, VB 57–58
    copying to projects, VB 221–225
    displaying, VB 216–218
    existing, adding to forms,
        VB 215–216
    hidden, VB 697
    loading, VB 216–217
    making nonresizable,
        VB 219–221
    making to resemble standard
        Windows dialog boxes,
        VB 219–221

modal, VB 216
modeless, VB 216
format(s), VB 144–146
    predefined, VB 145
Format function, VB 144–146,
    VB 446–448
form-level variables, VB 171,
    VB 176–178, VB 190–192
Form.PrintForm method, VB 822
Form window, VB 18, VB 19–20
For Next loop, VB 340–344
For...Next statement, VB 340
frame(s), drawing controls in,
    VB 289–290
frame controls, VB 824–825
    adding to forms, VB 65–67,
        VB 283–284
    standards, VB 283
function(s), VB 143. *See also specific*
    functions
function keys
    accessing Help, VB 42
    displaying Properties window,
        VB 606
    running applications, VB 49
function procedures, VB 787–791
    creating, VB 787–790
    invoking, VB 790–791

G

Get statement, VB 594
GetText method, VB 477
global variables, VB 171, VB 179–181
GotFocus event, VB 321
    control arrays, VB 384–385
grade calculation application,
    VB 337–338
grand totals, VB 449
graphical user interfaces (GUIs), VB 4
graphics
    sending and retrieving to and
        from Clipboard, VB 479
    user interfaces, VB 111
greater than operator (>), VB 245
greater than or equal to operator
    (>=), VB 245
GUIs (graphical user interfaces), VB 4

H

headings, columns. *See* column
    headings
Help menu, VB 39–42
Help system, VB 39–42
    context-sensitive Help, VB 524

using dynamic Help, VB 811–812
hidden attributes/behaviors, VB 6
hidden forms, VB 697
Hide method, VB 216–217
hiding
    controls, VB 68–72
    Windows 95 taskbar, VB 18
Highest Score button, VB 733–735
high-level languages, VB 3
highlighting existing text, VB 321
HTML. *See* Hypertext Markup
    Language (HTML)
HTML editors, VB 884
Hypertext Markup Language
    (HTML), VB 804, VB 846, VB 884
    adding to Web Forms, in general,
        VB 848–849
    displaying code, VB 890–891
    server controls, VB 851–852
    tags, VB 849
    text attributes, VB 850

I

icons, VB 282
If...Then...Else statement, VB 245–250
    relational operators, VB 245–247
IIS. *See* Microsoft Internet
    Information Server
image controls, adding to forms,
    VB 57–58
Imports statement, VB 822, VB 829
incrementing, VB 354
indentation, instructions within
    loops, VB 435
index(es), control arrays, VB 374
index(es), databases, VB 650–652
    creating, VB 658–659
Indexed Fields list box, removing
    entries, VB 659
index field, VB 650
Index property, VB 374
    Index argument versus, VB 381
Information Message icon, VB 315
inheritance, VB 6
Initialize procedure, VB 612–616
initializing, VB 354
    random access files, VB 592–593
    variables, VB 169
In keyword, expressionlists,
    VB 266–270
InputBox function, VB 201–203
Input function, VB 562–563
Input mode, sequential access files,
    VB 426, VB 427

input/output symbol, VB 244
Input statement, VB 435
instances, VB 6
Instr function, VB 496–497
instructions, indenting within loops,
        VB 435
intCounter variable, VB 308
integer(s), VB 165
        small, VB 585
Integer data type, VB 166
integer operator (\), VB 138, VB 139
interface, class and, VB 829
internal documentation, VB 134–135
interpreters, VB 3
        making executable files,
        VB 78–79
intrinsic constants, VB 204
invalid data, VB 148
iteration. *See* repetition structure

J

Jet engine, VB 648
justifying numbers in columns,
        VB 445–448

K

key(s)
        access, menus, VB 470
        shortcut, VB 470
keyboard
        accessing Help, VB 42
        displaying Properties window,
        VB 606
        running applications, VB 49
        scrolling Properties window,
        VB 25
keywords, VB 62. *See also specific
        keywords*

L

label controls, VB 8, VB 43,
        VB 823–824, VB 825, VB 853
        centering contents, VB 399
        setting properties, VB 45–48
        updating, VB 435–438
Label tool, VB 43
lblSeat array, coding Click event,
        VB 694–697
LCase function, VB 256–257
Left property, VB 46–47
Left string function, VB 491–494

Len function, VB 588
        Verify Answer button,
        VB 320–321
Len keyword, VB 587
less than operator (<), VB 245
less than or equal to operator (<=),
        VB 245
Like operator, VB 682
line control, VB 822
LinkButton control, VB 854
linking data, VB 911–914
        Update method, VB 913–914
LinkLabel control, VB 831
list boxes, VB 8, VB 418–423
        adding items during run time,
        VB 422
        adding to form, VB 418–420
        AddItem method, VB 420–421
        default item selection, VB 423
        ListIndex property, VB 422–423
        order of items, VB 422
        Sorted property, VB 422
        standards, VB 419
ListIndex property, VB 422–423
literal constants, VB 169
Load event procedure, VB 220–221,
        VB 725
        coding, VB 828–829
        random access files, coding,
        VB 586–588
loading forms, VB 216, VB 217
LoadPicture function, Verify Answer
        button, VB 312–313
Load statement, VB 216–217
local variables, VB 171, VB 173–176,
        VB 190–192
Lock Controls command, VB 120
locking controls, VB 119–120, VB 290
        moving locked controls, VB 119
LOF function, VB 562–563
logical operators, VB 250–256
        truth tables, VB 250–251
Long data type, VB 166
Long type variables, VB 165
loop condition, VB 339
looping. *See* repetition structure
LTrim function, VB 633

M

machine languages (code), VB 2
main window
        DHTML Application, VB 803
        Visual Basic startup screen,
        VB 18–19
Make command, VB 79

Math application, VB 237–240
mathematical operators, VB 138
MaxButton property, VB 146–147
menu(s), VB 8, VB 468–484. *See
        also specific menus*
        access keys, VB 470
        adding in Windows Forms,
        VB 832–835
        adding to forms, VB 468–474
        coding, VB 478–480
        coding commands, VB 480–482
        coding items, VB 476–477
        creating, VB 474–475
        designing, VB 471
        item captions, VB 470
        separator bars, VB 473–474
        shortcut keys, VB 470
        title captions, VB 470
        viewing options, VB 9–10
menu bar, VB 19
menu control, VB 822
Menu Designer, VB 821
Menu Editor, VB 468–474
methods, VB 133–134. *See also
        specific methods*
        Common Dialog control,
        VB 521–522
Microsoft ADO data control. *See*
        ADO data control
Microsoft Development Network
        (MSDN), VB 39, VB 787
Microsoft Internet Information
        Server (IIS), VB 863
Mid function, VB 494–496
milliseconds, VB 223
MinButton property, VB 146–147,
        VB 607
Minimize button, removing,
        VB 219–221
Minus box, VB 23
mnemonics, VB 3
Mod (modulus arithmetic operator),
        VB 138–139
modal forms, VB 216
modeless forms, VB 216
modes, sequential access files,
        VB 426–427
modulus arithmetic operator (Mod),
        VB 138–139
monospaced fonts, VB 441–442,
        VB 444
MonthCalendar, VB 826
mouse pointer, appearance,
        VB 224–225
Move button, Dynaset window,
        VB 661

MoveFirst method, VB 690
MoveLast method, VB 690, VB 701
MoveNext method, VB 690, VB 701
MovePrevious method, VB 690, VB 701
moving
    controls, VB 44
    locked controls, VB 119
MSDN (Microsoft Development Network), VB 39, VB 787
MsgBox function
    communicating with users, VB 399–401
    standards, VB 316
    Verify Answer button, VB 313–319
MultiLine property, VB 467
multiplication operator (*), VB 138

N

name(s)
    files, saving files under different names, VB 48–49
    variables, VB 167–168
Name property
    objects, VB 26–27, VB 45
    projects, VB 28
namespace tag, VB 853
negation operator (-), VB 138
nested selection structures, VB 257–261
New command
    coding, VB 609–610
    File menu, VB 548–552
newline character, VB 204
New Project dialog box, VB 17
New tab, New Project dialog box, VB 17
not equal to operator (<>), VB 245
Not operator, VB 250–251
numbers
    DataGrid control, VB 764–765
    justifying and aligning in columns, VB 445–448
    positive, VB 439
    rounding, VB 772–773

O

object(s), VB 6, VB 7, VB 819. *See also* control(s); *specific controls*
    deleting from Web pages, VB 808
    embedded. *See* embedding data
    identifying, VB 99–100
Name property, VB 26–27, VB 45
Object box
    Code window, VB 60, VB 61
    Properties window, VB 24
Object Browser dialog box, VB 204–206
    viewing color constants, VB 611–612
Object data type, VB 167
Object Linking and Embedding (OLE)
    exchanging data, VB 904–911
    linking data, VB 911–914
Object Linking and Embedding Database (OLE DB), VB 672, VB 863
object-oriented design (OOD), VB 5
object-oriented/event-driven (OOED)
    high-level languages, VB 5. *See also* planning OOED applications
        problem solving approach with, VB 93–95
object-oriented programming (OOP), terminology, VB 5–7
object variables, creating, VB 770–772
OLE. *See* Object Linking and Embedding (OLE)
OLE container control, VB 905–908
exchanging data, VB 904–911
    linking data, VB 905–914
OLE DB. *See* Object Linking and Embedding Database
one-dimensional variable arrays, VB 720, VB 722–738
    creating, VB 722
    president application, VB 724–730
    storing data, VB 723
    test score application, VB 730–738
On Error statement, VB 546–547
OOD (object-oriented design), VB 5
OOED. *See* object-oriented/event-driven high-level languages; planning OOED applications
OOP (object-oriented programming), terminology, VB 5–7
Open command
    coding, VB 560–563, VB 616–619
    Input function, VB 562–563
    LOF function, VB 562–563
Open dialog box, VB 519
    displaying, VB 522–526
    guidelines, VB 526
opening. *See also* starting
    existing databases, VB 661–665
    existing projects, VB 31–32
    new projects, VB 31
    random access files, VB 587
    sequential access files, VB 426–428
Open statement, VB 426–427, VB 587, VB 909
optimizations, VB 878
option buttons, VB 8, VB 282–286
    adding to forms, VB 283
    coding, VB 292–294, VB 298–299
    default, VB 299–301
    grouping, VB 283–286
    standards, VB 283
    Value property, VB 322
Option Explicit statement, VB 171–173, VB 192
Options dialog box, VB 72–73, VB 141
order
    list box items, VB 422
    order of precedence for calculations, VB 139
order by clause, Select command, VB 679, VB 680
Or operator, VB 250–253
    setting flags for dialog boxes, VB 530
outputlist, Print method
    calculations, VB 439
    separators, VB 438–439
Output mode, sequential access files, VB 426–427

P

Package and Deployment Wizard, VB 79
PAO (Political Awareness Organization) application, VB 413–416
paragraphs, deleting from Web pages, VB 890
parameter passing, VB 830–831
passing procedure, VB 610–611
passing variables, VB 614
Paste command, VB 205, VB 902
    coding, VB 481–482
Paste Link command, VB 902
payroll application, VB 717–719
percentages, VB 139
Percent format, VB 145
percent sign (%), wildcard, VB 682

period (.), dot member selection operator, VB 132
PetProj project
  creating, VB 864–865
    debug build mode, VB 877
    release build mode, VB 877
Pets Online Web Application Data Project, VB 863
picture box control, VB 901
picture control, VB 824–825
pipe symbol (|), filters, VB 524
planning OOED applications, VB 96–105
  identifying events, VB 100–101
  identifying objects, VB 99–100
  identifying tasks, VB 97–98
  sketching user interface, VB 102–104
Plus box, VB 23
plus sign (+), concatenating strings, VB 199
pointer field, VB 650
Political Awareness Organization (PAO) application, VB 413–416
positive numbers, VB 439
posttest loop, VB 345
precedence order, VB 139
predefined formats, VB 145
president application, VB 724–730
pretest loop, VB 345
Print command, coding, VB 559–560
Print dialog box, displaying, VB 528–529
Printer keyword, VB 438
PrintForm method, VB 133
printing applications, VB 77–78
Print method, VB 381, VB 438–448
  font type and size, VB 441–445
  justifying and aligning numbers in columns, VB 445–448
Print Order button, coding, VB 131–135
Print Report button, modifying Click event procedure, VB 450–451
Print statement, VB 543–545
Private keyword, VB 62
Private statement, VB 171
Procedure box, Code window, VB 60, VB 61–62
procedure-oriented high-level languages, VB 3–4
  problem solving approach with, VB 90–92

profile, modifying, in general, VB 806–807
program(s), VB 1
program files. See executable files
programmers, VB 1
programming, object-oriented, terminology, VB 5–7
programming languages, VB 1
  assembly languages, VB 2–3
  high-level languages, VB 3
  history, VB 2–5
  machine languages (code), VB 2
  object-oriented/event-driven high-level languages, VB 5
  procedure-oriented high-level languages, VB 3–4
  Windows GUI, VB 4
Project Explorer window, VB 18, VB 30
projects. See also file(s)
  adding code modules, VB 180–181, VB 218–221
  copying forms to, VB 221–225
  existing, opening, VB 31–32
  Name property, VB 28
  new, opening, VB 31
  relation to solution, VB 810, VB 819
  removing files, VB 181, VB 182–183
  saving. See saving projects
Project window (Project Explorer window)
  DHTML Application, VB 885
  Visual Basic startup screen, VB 21–23
prompts, InputBox function, capitalization, VB 202
properties. See also attributes
  assigning during run time, VB 131–132
Properties list, Properties window, VB 24–25
Properties window, VB 18, VB 23–28. See also specific properties
  deleting highlighted text, VB 116
  DHTML Application, VB 885
  displaying, VB 113, VB 606
Property Pages dialog box, VB 762, VB 889
proportionally-spaced fonts, VB 441–442
pseudocode, VB 90, VB 131–135
  selection structure, VB 242–243

Public statement, VB 168, VB 171
Put statement, VB 588

R

RadioButton control, VB 854
random access files, VB 580–597
  closing, VB 588
  coding Load event procedure, VB 587–588
  creating, VB 587
  initializing, VB 592–593
  opening, VB 587
  reading records, VB 594–596
  record structure, VB 584–587
  sequential access files versus, VB 580–584
  writing records to, VB 588–591
Randomize statement, VB 292
ReadFromFile method, VB 910
reading records
  from random access files, VB 594–596
  from sequential access files, VB 435
receiving procedure, VB 610
record(s)
  canceling, VB 635
  databases. See database records
  data files, VB 424, VB 580
  deleted, VB 701
  reading. See reading records
  variable-length, VB 581
  writing. See writing records
record numbers, VB 580, VB 650
record pointers, VB 427–428
Recordset object, VB 689–690
RecordSource property, VB 677
record structure, random access files, VB 584–587
reference, passing variables by, VB 614
Refresh method, VB 691
relational databases, VB 648
relational operators, VB 245–247
Remove command, VB 181
removing. See also deleting
  coded controls from forms, VB 223–224
  files from projects, VB 181, VB 182–183
  Maximize and Minimize buttons, VB 219–221

repetition structure, VB 339–363
  counters and accumulators,
    VB 354–362
  Do While and Do Until loops,
    VB 344–354
  For Next loop, VB 340–344
report titles, VB 449
Resize event, VB 468
Resume statement, VB 546
Return to Main button, coding,
  VB 635–636, VB 697–698
Right string function, VB 491–494
Rnd function, VB 292
Round function, VB 772–773
rounding numbers, VB 772–773
RSet statement, VB 446–448
RTrim function, VB 633

S

Save As command, VB 29
  coding, VB 541–545
  Print statement, VB 543–545
Save As dialog box, VB 518
  CancelError property,
    VB 545–547
  displaying, VB 526–528
  guidelines, VB 528
  warning messages, VB 543
Save command, coding, VB 557–559
Save Project As command, VB 29
Save Project button, VB 117
SaveToFile method, VB 909
saving projects, VB 29–30
  current name, VB 117
  different name, VB 48–49
Screen keyword, VB 220
Screen object, VB 220
scroll bars, displaying, VB 467
ScrollBars property, VB 467
Scroller control, adding to form,
  VB 73–76
Select Case statement, VB 262–266
Select command, VB 679–683, VB 689
selecting data types, VB 655
selection/repetition symbol, VB 244
selection structure, VB 241–270
  Case form, VB 261–262
  flowcharts, VB 243–244
  If...Then...Else statement. See
    If...Then...Else statement
  To and Is keywords in expres-
    sionlists, VB 266–270
  logical operators, VB 250–256
  nested, VB 257–261
  pseudocode, VB 242–243

Select Case statement,
  VB 262–266
  UCase function, VB 256–257
SelLength property, VB 479
  Verify Answer button, VB 319
SelStart property, Verify Answer
  button, VB 319
SelText property, VB 478
semicolon separator, Print method
  outputlist, VB 438, VB 439–440
sentence capitalization, VB 103
separator(s), Print method outputlist, VB 438
separator bar, menus, VB 473–474
sequence structure, VB 63
sequential access files, VB 425–426
  closing, VB 430–431
  opening, VB 426–428
  random access files versus,
    VB 580–584
  writing to, VB 429–430
sequential processing, VB 63
serifs, VB 112
server application, VB 904
server control, HTML server controls,
  VB 851–852
SetFocus method, VB 134
Set statement, VB 770
SetText method, VB 477
Settings box, Properties window,
  VB 24
shape control, VB 822
sharing data among applications,
  VB 898–914
  Clipboard, VB 898–900
  DDE, VB 900–904
  OLE, VB 904–914
shortcut keys, VB 470
Show method, VB 216–217
simple variables, VB 722
Single data type, VB 167
Single type variables, VB 165–166
size, Text fields, VB 656
sizing
  command buttons, VB 111
  by users, VB 147
sizing controls, VB 44
  along with forms, VB 467–468
Skate-Away Sales application,
  VB 89–95, VB 161–163
small integers, VB 585
software packages, VB 648
Solution Explorer, using, VB 810–811
solution, relation to project, VB 810,
  VB 819
Sort button, Dynaset window, VB 661

Sorted property, VB 422
sorting, VB 422
  table records, VB 663
source application, VB 901, VB 904
Spc function, VB 440
splash screens, VB 15, VB 59, VB 64,
  VB 147
SQL. See Structured Query
  Language (SQL)
Standard format, VB 145
Standard toolbar, VB 19
Start command, VB 31
  running applications, VB 49
starting. See also opening
  applications, VB 49
  Visual Basic, VB 17–19
start/stop symbol, VB 244
startup form, specifying, VB 215–216
startup screen, VB 18, VB 19–28
  Form window, VB 18, VB 19–20
  main window, VB 18–19
  Project Explorer window,
    VB 18, VB 21–23
  Properties window. See
    Properties window
  Toolbox window, VB 18,
    VB 20–21
Static statement, VB 171
static variables, VB 307–308
storing data in variables, VB 169–170
string(s), VB 136, VB 491–505
  coding Edit menu's Find com-
    mand, VB 497–501
  coding Edit menu's Find Next
    command, VB 501–504
  concatenating, VB 198–201
  empty, VB 136
  Instr function, VB 496–497
  Left and Right functions,
    VB 491–494
  Mid function, VB 494–496
  trimming spaces, VB 633
  zero-length, VB 136
String data type, VB 166–167
Structured Query Language (SQL),
  VB 653
  Select command, VB 679–683,
    VB 689
Sub keyword, VB 62
sub procedures, VB 62
  passing information to,
    VB 610–611
subscripts, variable arrays, VB 721
subtraction operator (-), VB 138
Subtraction option button, coding,
  VB 298–299

symbolic constants, VB 169,
VB 183–185
syntax, VB 62
system modal dialog boxes, VB 316

T

Tab function, VB 440–441
TabIndex property, VB 118–119,
VB 122–123, VB 290
table(s)
databases, VB 648
data validation rules, VB 659–660
deleting records, VB 664–665
indexes. *See* index(es), databases
Table Structure dialog box, VB 654
Task List, VB 812–813
tasks, identifying, VB 97–98
testing applications, VB 148, VB 727
unusual values, VB 591
test score application, VB 730–738
text, existing, highlighting, VB 321
text boxes, VB 8, VB 93–94
clearing, VB 550
user interfaces, VB 115–117
TextBox control, VB 853
text control, VB 824–825
Text Editor application, VB 466–467,
VB 517–519
Text fields, size, VB 656
Text property, user interfaces, VB 115
time-based controls. *See* Windows
Forms
Timer controls, VB 223
title(s), reports, VB 449
title bar, VB 542
DHTML page designer window,
VB 886
TOE charts, VB 97–101
Toggle Folders window, VB 23
To keyword, expressionlists,
VB 266–270
toolbars, DHTML page designer
window, VB 886
Toolbox window, VB 18, VB 20–21
DHTML Application, VB 885
Top property, VB 46–47
totals, VB 449
treeview pane, DHTML page designer
window, VB 886, VB 889–890
Trim function, VB 633–634
truth tables, VB 250–251

tutorials, using effectively, VB 10–11
two-dimensional variable arrays,
VB 720, VB 783–787
classroom application,
VB 738–743
txtEdit control, Change event, VB 560
Type statement, VB 584–587

U

UCase function, VB 256–257
UDA. *See* Universal Data Access
undeclared variables, avoiding,
VB 171–173
Universal Data Access (UDA),
VB 672, 863
Unload event, VB 401–403
Cancel argument, VB 564
coding, VB 563–566
Unload statement, VB 62, VB 216,
VB 217
Update method, VB 690, VB 913–914
Update Scores button, VB 735–738
updating, VB 354
label controls, VB 435–438
user(s)
communicating with, VB 593
preventing interaction with
ADO data control, VB 691
sizing by, VB 147
user-defined data type, VB 584–585
user-defined functions, VB 787
user-defined procedures, receiving
data, VB 612–616
user-defined sub procedures,
VB 294–296
modifying, VB 300–301
user interfaces, VB 20, VB 109–125.
See also graphical user interfaces
(GUIs)
access keys, VB 120–123
Appearance property,
VB 114–115
background color, VB 113–114
BorderStyle property,
VB 114–115
color, VB 112–113
controlling focus, VB 118–119
fonts, VB 111–112
graphics, VB 111
locking controls, VB 119–120
preparing to create, VB 110–115
preventing flickering, VB 217

sketching, VB 102–104
text box controls, VB 115–117
Text property, VB 115

V

Val function, VB 143–144
valid data, VB 148
value, passing variables by, VB 614
Value property, option buttons,
VB 322
variable(s), VB 164–181
data types, VB 164–165
declarations, VB 829–830
declaring, VB 168–169
form-level, VB 171, VB
176–178, VB 190–192
global, VB 171, VB 179–181
initializing, VB 169
local, VB 171, VB 173–176,
VB 190–192
naming, VB 167–168
object, creating, VB 770–772
passing, VB 614
scope, VB 170–171
simple, VB 722
speed of processing, VB 436
static, VB 307–308
storing data in, VB 169–170
undeclared, avoiding,
VB 171–173
variable arrays, VB 720–792
advantages, VB 721–722
definition, VB 720
one-dimensional. *See* one-
dimensional variable arrays
two-dimensional. *See* two-
dimensional variable arrays
variable-length records, VB 581
Variant data type, VB 166–167
vbCritical setting, MsgBox function,
VB 315
vbExclamation setting, MsgBox
function, VB 315
vbInformation setting, MsgBox
function, VB 315
vbQuestion setting, MsgBox function, VB 315
vbRed constant, VB 693
vbYesNoCancel setting, MsgBox
function, VB 315

Verify Answer button, VB 308–321
    Click event procedure, VB 309,
      VB 311–312
    flowchart, VB 310
    Len function, VB 320–321
    LoadPicture function,
      VB 312–313
    MsgBox function, VB 313–319
    SelStart and SelLength properties,
      VB 319
View Code button, VB 23
viewing. *See* displaying
View Object window, VB 23
Visible property, VB 68–72
Visual Basic
    coding differences, VB 828–829
    compared to Visual Basic.NET
      VB 804–805, VB 822
    copying data from Excel,
      VB 901–904
    embedding Excel worksheets in.
      See embedding data
    exiting, VB 32
    linking Excel worksheets,
      VB 911–914
    running, VB 7–8
    starting, VB 17–19
Visual Basic.NET
    optimizations, VB 878
    parameter passing, VB 830–831
    starting, VB 819–820
    variable declarations,
      VB 829–830
Visual Data Manager. *See* database(s)
Visual InterDev, VB 812
Visual J++, VB 812
Visual Studio.NET cache, VB 864
Visual Studio.NET environment
    ASP.NET, VB 846
    components, VB 806
    in general, VB 804–805
    IDE, VB 806
Visual Studio.NET IDE
    Command Window, VB 813–814
    customizing, VB 808
    dynamic Help, VB 811–812
    modify your profile, in general,
      VB 806–807
    Solution Explorer, VB 810–811
    Task List, VB 812–813

W

Warning Message icon, VB 315
Warning Query icon, VB 315
Web application projects
    Data–Access component,
      VB 866–868
    file creation, VB 864
    PetProj project, VB 864–865
    technical requirements, VB 863
    Visual Studio.NET cache, VB 864
Web browser, VB 884
Web Forms
    See also Web Forms page; Web
      Forms server controls;
      Windows Forms
    binding the DataGrid,
      VB 869–874
    deploying, VB 877–879
    Details Panel, VB 874–877
    Event Handler creation, VB 857
    Pets Online Web Application
      Data Project, VB 863
    previewing, VB 844–845
    running, VB 857–858
    saving and exiting, VB 858–859
    Web application projects, VB 863
Web Forms page
    adding HTML
      in general, VB 848–849
      HTML text attributes,
        VB 850
    creating, VB 846–848
    HTML server controls,
      VB 851–852
Web Forms server controls
    adding to project, VB 855–856
    creating, in general, VB 852–853
    discussed, VB 853
      Calendar control, VB 855
      CheckBox control, VB 853
      DropDownList control,
        VB 854
      ImageButton control, VB 854
      Label control, VB 853
      LinkButton control, VB 854
      RadioButton control, VB 854
      TextBox control, VB 853
Web pages
    creating, VB 883–891
    definition, VB 884
    displaying, VB 891

What's This button, VB 524
where clause, Select command,
    VB 679, VB 680–682
Windows
    GUI, VB 4
    Windows 95 taskbar, hiding,
      VB 18
Windows Forms
    See also Web Forms
    appearance properties
      in general, VB 822–823
      label control, VB 823–824
      picture, text, frame controls,
        VB 824–825
    calendar application
      adding links, VB 831–832
      label control, VB 822–823
    code viewing in, VB 821–822
    differences between Visual
      Basic.NET Windows Forms
      and Visual Basic 6.0 Forms,
      VB 822
    menu and menu items,
      VB 832–835
    printing code, VB 836
    saving and exiting, VB 836
    starting Visual Basic.NET,
      VB 819–820
    time-based controls
      button code, VB 829
      button control, VB 827–828
      Calendar Forms application
        links, VB 831–832
      in general, VB 826–827
      parameter passing,
        VB 830–831
      variable declarations,
        VB 829–830
    using, in general, VB 821
World Wide Web, VB 884
Write statement, VB 429–430
writing code, VB 60–64
writing records
    to random access files,
      VB 588–591
    to sequential access files,
      VB 429–430

Z

    zero-length strings, VB 136

END-USER LICENSE AGREEMENT FOR MICROSOFT SOFTWARE

IMPORTANT-READ CAREFULLY: This Microsoft End-User License Agreement ("EULA") is a legal agreement between you (either an individual or a single entity) and Microsoft Corporation for the Microsoft software product identified above, which includes computer software and may include associated media, printed materials, and "online" or electronic documentation ("SOFTWARE PRODUCT"). The SOFTWARE PRODUCT also includes any updates and supplements to the original SOFTWARE PRODUCT provided to you by Microsoft. By installing, copying, downloading, accessing or otherwise using the SOFTWARE PRODUCT, you agree to be bound by the terms of this EULA. If you do not agree to the terms of this EULA, do not install, copy, or otherwise use the SOFTWARE PRODUCT.

SOFTWARE PRODUCT LICENSE

The SOFTWARE PRODUCT is protected by copyright laws and international copyright treaties, as well as other intellectual property laws and treaties. The SOFTWARE PRODUCT is licensed, not sold.

1. **GRANT OF LICENSE.** This EULA grants you the following rights:

   1.1 **License Grant.** Microsoft grants to you as an individual, a personal nonexclusive license to make and use copies of the SOFTWARE PRODUCT for the sole purposes of evaluating and learning how to use the SOFTWARE PRODUCT, as may be instructed in accompanying publications or documentation. You may install the software on an unlimited number of computers provided that you are the only individual using the SOFTWARE PRODUCT.

   1.2 **Academic Use.** You must be a "Qualified Educational User" to use the SOFTWARE PRODUCT in the manner described in this section. To determine whether you are a Qualified Educational User, please contact the Microsoft Sales Information Center/One Microsoft Way/Redmond, WA 98052-6399 or the Microsoft subsidiary serving your country. If you are a Qualified Educational User, you may either:

   (i) exercise the rights granted in Section 1.1, OR

   (ii) if you intend to use the SOFTWARE PRODUCT solely for instructional purposes in connection with a class or other educational program, this EULA grants you the following alternative license models:

   (A) **Per Computer Model.** For every valid license you have acquired for the SOFTWARE PRODUCT, you may install a single copy of the SOFTWARE PRODUCT on a single computer for access and use by an unlimited number of student end users at your educational institution, provided that all such end users comply with all other terms of this EULA, OR

   (B) **Per License Model.** If you have multiple licenses for the SOFTWARE PRODUCT, then at any time you may have as many copies of the SOFTWARE PRODUCT in use as you have licenses, provided that such use is limited to student or faculty end users at your educational institution and provided that all such end users comply with all other terms of this EULA. For purposes of this subsection, the SOFTWARE PRODUCT is "in use" on a computer when it is loaded into the temporary memory (i.e., RAM) or installed into the permanent memory (e.g., hard disk, CD ROM, or other storage device) of that computer, except that a copy installed on a network server for the sole purpose of distribution to other computers is not "in use". If the anticipated number of users of the SOFTWARE PRODUCT will exceed the number of applicable licenses, then you must have a reasonable mechanism or process in place to ensure that the number of persons using the SOFTWARE PRODUCT concurrently does not exceed the number of licenses.

2. **DESCRIPTION OF OTHER RIGHTS AND LIMITATIONS.**

   a. **Limitations on Reverse Engineering, Decompilation, and Disassembly.** You may not reverse engineer, decompile, or disassemble the SOFTWARE PRODUCT, except and only to the extent that such activity is expressly permitted by applicable law notwithstanding this limitation.

   b. **Separation of Components.** The SOFTWARE PRODUCT is licensed as a single product. Its component parts may not be separated for use on more than one computer.

   c. **Rental.** You may not rent, lease or lend the SOFTWARE PRODUCT.

   * **Trademarks.** This EULA does not grant you any rights in connection with any trademarks or service marks of Microsoft.

   d. **Software Transfer.** The initial user of the SOFTWARE PRODUCT may make a one-time permanent transfer of this EULA and SOFTWARE PRODUCT only directly to an end user. This transfer must include all of the SOFTWARE PRODUCT (including all component parts, the media and printed materials, any upgrades, this EULA, and, if applicable, the Certificate of Authenticity). Such transfer may not be by way of consignment or any other indirect transfer. The transferee of such one-time transfer must agree to comply with the terms of this EULA, including the obligation not to further transfer this EULA and SOFTWARE PRODUCT.

   e. **No Support.** Microsoft shall have no obligation to provide any product support for the SOFTWARE PRODUCT.

   f. **Termination.** Without prejudice to any other rights, Microsoft may terminate this EULA if you fail to comply with the terms and conditions of this EULA. In such event, you must destroy all copies of the SOFTWARE PRODUCT and all of its component parts.

3. **COPYRIGHT.** All title and intellectual property rights in and to the SOFTWARE PRODUCT (including but not limited to any images, photographs, animations, video, audio, music, text, and "applets" incorporated into the SOFTWARE PRODUCT), the accompanying printed materials, and any copies of the SOFTWARE PRODUCT are owned by Microsoft or its suppliers. All title and intellectual property rights in and to the content which may be accessed through use of the SOFTWARE PRODUCT is the property of the respective content owner and may be protected by applicable copyright or other intellectual property laws and treaties. This EULA grants you no rights to use such content. All rights not expressly granted are reserved by Microsoft.

4. **BACKUP COPY.** After installation of one copy of the SOFTWARE PRODUCT pursuant to this EULA, you may keep the original media on which the SOFTWARE PRODUCT was provided by Microsoft solely for backup or archival purposes. If the original media is required to use the SOFTWARE PRODUCT on the COMPUTER, you may make one copy of the SOFTWARE PRODUCT solely for backup or archival purposes. Except as expressly provided in this EULA, you may not otherwise make copies of the SOFTWARE PRODUCT or the printed materials accompanying the SOFTWARE PRODUCT.

5. **U.S. GOVERNMENT RESTRICTED RIGHTS.** The SOFTWARE PRODUCT and documentation are provided with RESTRICTED RIGHTS. Use, duplication, or disclosure by the Government is subject to restrictions as set forth in subparagraph (c)(1)(ii) of the Rights in Technical Data and Computer Software clause at DFARS 252.227-7013 or subparagraphs (c)(1) and (2) of the Commercial Computer Software-Restricted Rights at 48 CFR 52.227-19, as applicable. Manufacturer is Microsoft Corporation/One Microsoft Way/Redmond, WA 98052-6399.

6. **EXPORT RESTRICTIONS.** You agree that you will not export or re-export the SOFTWARE PRODUCT, any part thereof, or any process or service that is the direct product of the SOFTWARE PRODUCT (the foregoing collectively referred to as the "Restricted Components"), to any country, person, entity or end user subject to U.S. export restrictions. You specifically agree not to export or re-export any of the Restricted Components (i) to any country to which the U.S. has embargoed or restricted the export of goods or services, which currently include, but are not necessarily limited to Cuba, Iran, Iraq, Libya, North Korea, Sudan and Syria, or to any national of any such country, wherever located, who intends to transmit or transport the Restricted Components back to such country; (ii) to any end-user who you know or have reason to know will utilize the Restricted Components in the design, development or production of nuclear, chemical or biological weapons; or (iii) to any end-user who has been prohibited from participating in U.S. export transactions by any federal agency of the U.S. government. You warrant and represent that neither the BXA nor any other U.S. federal agency has suspended, revoked, or denied your export privileges.

7. NOTE ON JAVA SUPPORT. THE SOFTWARE PRODUCT MAY CONTAIN SUPPORT FOR PROGRAMS WRITTEN IN JAVA. JAVA TECHNOLOGY IS NOT FAULT TOLERANT AND IS NOT DESIGNED, MANUFACTURED, OR INTENDED FOR USE OR RESALE AS ON-LINE CONTROL EQUIPMENT IN HAZARDOUS ENVIRONMENTS REQUIRING FAIL-SAFE PERFORMANCE, SUCH AS IN THE OPERATION OF NUCLEAR FACILITIES, AIRCRAFT NAVIGATION OR COMMUNICATION SYSTEMS, AIR TRAFFIC CONTROL, DIRECT LIFE SUPPORT MACHINES, OR WEAPONS SYSTEMS, IN WHICH THE FAILURE OF JAVA TECHNOLOGY COULD LEAD DIRECTLY TO DEATH, PERSONAL INJURY, OR SEVERE PHYSICAL OR ENVIRONMENTAL DAMAGE.

MISCELLANEOUS

If you acquired this product in the United States, this EULA is governed by the laws of the State of Washington.

If you acquired this product in Canada, this EULA is governed by the laws of the Province of Ontario, Canada. Each of the parties hereto irrevocably attorns to the jurisdiction of the courts of the Province of Ontario and further agrees to commence any litigation which may arise hereunder in the courts located in the Judicial District of York, Province of Ontario.

If this product was acquired outside the United States, then local law may apply.

Should you have any questions concerning this EULA, or if you desire to contact Microsoft for any reason, please contact Microsoft, or write: Microsoft Sales Information Center/One Microsoft Way/Redmond, WA 98052-6399.

LIMITED WARRANTY

LIMITED WARRANTY. Microsoft warrants that (a) the SOFTWARE PRODUCT will perform substantially in accordance with the accompanying written materials for a period of ninety (90) days from the date of receipt, and (b) any Support Services provided by Microsoft shall be substantially as described in applicable written materials provided to you by Microsoft, and Microsoft support engineers will make commercially reasonable efforts to solve any problem. To the extent allowed by applicable law, implied warranties on the SOFTWARE PRODUCT, if any, are limited to ninety (90) days. Some states/jurisdictions do not allow limitations on duration of an implied warranty, so the above limitation may not apply to you.

CUSTOMER REMEDIES. Microsoft's and its suppliers' entire liability and your exclusive remedy shall be, at Microsoft's option, either (a) return of the price paid, if any, or (b) repair or replacement of the SOFTWARE PRODUCT that does not meet Microsoft's Limited Warranty and that is returned to Microsoft with a copy of your receipt. This Limited Warranty is void if failure of the SOFTWARE PRODUCT has resulted from accident, abuse, or misapplication. Any replacement SOFTWARE PRODUCT will be warranted for the remainder of the original warranty period or thirty (30) days, whichever is longer. **Outside the United States, neither these remedies nor any product support services offered by Microsoft are available without proof of purchase from an authorized international source.**

NO OTHER WARRANTIES. TO THE MAXIMUM EXTENT PERMITTED BY APPLICABLE LAW, MICROSOFT AND ITS SUPPLIERS DISCLAIM ALL OTHER WARRANTIES AND CONDITIONS, EITHER EXPRESS OR IMPLIED, INCLUDING, BUT NOT LIMITED TO, IMPLIED WARRANTIES OR CONDITIONS OF MERCHANTABILITY, FITNESS FOR A PARTICULAR PURPOSE, TITLE AND NON-INFRINGEMENT, WITH REGARD TO THE SOFTWARE PRODUCT, AND THE PROVISION OF OR FAILURE TO PROVIDE SUPPORT SERVICES. THIS LIMITED WARRANTY GIVES YOU SPECIFIC LEGAL RIGHTS. YOU MAY HAVE OTHERS, WHICH VARY FROM STATE/JURISDICTION TO STATE/JURISDICTION.

LIMITATION OF LIABILITY. TO THE MAXIMUM EXTENT PERMITTED BY APPLICABLE LAW, IN NO EVENT SHALL MICROSOFT OR ITS SUPPLIERS BE LIABLE FOR ANY SPECIAL, INCIDENTAL, INDIRECT, OR CONSEQUENTIAL DAMAGES WHATSOEVER (INCLUDING, WITHOUT LIMITATION, DAMAGES FOR LOSS OF BUSINESS PROFITS, BUSINESS INTERRUPTION, LOSS OF BUSINESS INFORMATION, OR ANY OTHER PECUNIARY LOSS) ARISING OUT OF THE USE OF OR INABILITY TO USE THE SOFTWARE PRODUCT OR THE FAILURE TO PROVIDE SUPPORT SERVICES, EVEN IF MICROSOFT HAS BEEN ADVISED OF THE POSSIBILITY OF SUCH DAMAGES. IN ANY CASE, MICROSOFT'S ENTIRE LIABILITY UNDER ANY PROVISION OF THIS EULA SHALL BE LIMITED TO THE GREATER OF THE AMOUNT ACTUALLY PAID BY YOU FOR THE SOFTWARE PRODUCT OR U.S.$5.00; PROVIDED, HOWEVER, IF YOU HAVE ENTERED INTO A MICROSOFT SUPPORT SERVICES AGREEMENT, MICROSOFT'S ENTIRE LIABILITY REGARDING SUPPORT SERVICES SHALL BE GOVERNED BY THE TERMS OF THAT AGREEMENT. BECAUSE SOME STATES/JURISDICTIONS DO NOT ALLOW THE EXCLUSION OR LIMITATION OF LIABILITY, THE ABOVE LIMITATION MAY NOT APPLY TO YOU.